THE FOUNDING OF THE SECOND
BRITISH EMPIRE 1763-1793

VOLUME II

THE FOUNDING OF THE SECOND BRITISH EMPIRE
1763–1793

VOLUME II

NEW CONTINENTS AND CHANGING VALUES

by

VINCENT T. HARLOW
C.M.G., M.A., D.LITT.

*Late Beit Professor of the History of the British Empire
and late Fellow of Balliol College, Oxford*

LONGMANS

LONGMANS, GREEN AND CO LTD
48 Grosvenor Street, London W1
*Associated companies, branches and representatives
throughout the world*

© *Longmans, Green & Co Ltd 1964*
First published 1964

*Printed in Great Britain by
Northumberland Press Limited
Gateshead on Tyne*

CONTENTS

MAPS

FOREWORD

Vincent Harlow had been working on this his second volume even
before the first was published. The whole work had been planned and
many of the transcripts of records made over twenty years ago. The
first volume had been completely rewritten when after the war he had
looked at it critically once more and found it did not satisfy his exacting standards. Of this present volume he had rewritten the chapters
on India during sabbatical leave over two years ago. He spent some
period of most days in term and vacation writing at home in Old
Marston. When he died suddenly in the early evening of 6 December,
1961, he had been working that morning and afternoon on the second
section of Chapter IX, and had remarked that he felt that it was going
particularly well. Already his narrative had progressed well beyond his
terminal date of 1793. But his method was far ranging and, though the
merest scraps survived to indicate his intention, it is clear that he would
have carried the story of British interest in Spanish American Colonies
to the achievement of their independence.

In what I have done to complete Professor Harlow's work I have
permitted myself the minimum of intervention. The bulk of this
volume remains substantially as he left it in what he regarded as its
finished form. I have limited myself to minor corrections of fact and to
some hesitant pruning of the more obvious repetitions. The work as it
stands falls inevitably short of his plan of contents. Though he seems
to have contemplated no chapter reviewing the events of the period in
the old West Indies or the Maritime Colonies of North America, there
was provision for a discussion of the issues involved in the foundation
of Sierra Leone and of New South Wales in a chapter significantly
entitled 'Plantations in place of Colonies'. This I have made no
attempt to write. There are scattered references in his files of transcripts,
but no indication of the way in which he proposed to treat them. Nor
am I sure where he stood in what he called the 'O'Brien-Manning Clark
controversy' on the origins of Australian settlement. Again, a third
section of Chapter IX would have dealt with the Free Port System and
a quantity of raw material in his files was at hand to make this an
important discussion; but since, a pupil of his, Frances Armytage, has
written a monograph on this subject, of which he spoke with warm
approval, it seemed unnecessary here to interleave his material with her
narrative. But readers of this volume should be aware of the importance
he attached to that development and of the way he would have fitted
it so neatly into his main thesis.

What was necessary, of course, was some conclusion to bring together
the themes of the two volumes and to characterise the pattern of this
formative period. This task I have tried, if inadequately, to fulfil.
The only clue which we had was its title; and by dint of collecting
hints throughout his work and by digesting the conclusions of his
many chapters, I have tried to piece together the sort of brooding

A*

epilogue he would have so enjoyed writing. Those who knew him well
can picture the relish with which he would have conjured with his
major themes and the dedication with which he would have woven a
final, compelling and majestic tapestry of his chosen period. It is sad,
indeed, that this should have been attempted by another pen.

Throughout the two volumes it was Gretta Harlow who typed the
chapters from draft to final copy. In a special sense this work is also hers.

May 1963

F. McC. Madden

CHAPTER I

PERSPECTIVE

THE men who founded the second British Empire during the reign of George III revived a policy which had animated their predecessors in the age of the Tudors. The concept of an 'empire' of ocean trade routes, protected by naval bases and nourished by commercial depots or factories, received a new impetus with the growth of British sea power and industrial productivity and changed the character of overseas expansion. The influence of this concept was persistent and in some directions totally unexpected. In pursuing it the British found themselves impelled into a modification and then into a gradual abandonment of mercantilist principles in favour of free trade: a revolution in method which induced diverse consequences. For a nation which had won first place as a manufacturer, unrestricted trade greatly widened and deepened the range of non-territorial imperial expansion. Moreover, a metropolitan Power which placed its own colonies on the same commercial footing as foreign countries was committed to a course which stimulated the growth of colonial nationalism and of a type of relationship basically different from that obtaining in any other modern empire. Lastly, and paradoxically, the pursuit of markets in preference to 'dominion' led the British in India to acquire sovereign control over a larger and more densely populated area than had any other Europeans since the days of Cortez and Pizarro. And in due course that circumstance greatly influenced their policy concerning other territories bordering the Indian Ocean.

At an early stage the merchant adventurers who initiated this incalculable enterprise began to assail the sea and land monopolies which had been long established by other European Powers. The Elizabethans in their day had challenged the exclusive claims of Spain in the New World with piratical pinpricks, but their Georgian successors were far more powerfully equipped. Moreover, they employed devices which indicated a new empiricism in commercial method.

They compelled the Spaniards to accept the free navigation of the Pacific and the Dutch to accept the same principle and practice in the Malacca Strait and the Eastern Seas. Pioneers such as Dalrymple, Light, and Raffles pursued the idea of a free entrepôt, where the products of Britain, India, Indonesia, and China could be exchanged, until the project materialised in the founding of

1

Penang and then of Singapore. Similarly, when Captain Cook finally disproved the legend of a great Austral continent southward of the Horn or the Cape of Good Hope, that unpromising waste of waters was utilised by Charles Jenkinson (Lord Hawkesbury) for developing a flourishing whale fishery, which in his estimation became more profitable and convenient for national needs than the acquisition of a great territory.[1]

Nor was the conception of 'informal' empire confined to the Orient and the Pacific. As the United States of America (which was an empire or commonwealth of settlement) drove steadily westward, the British expectation that the Mississippi Basin would accrue to them as an expanding market for their manufactures was fulfilled. A similar incentive with regard to the vast potential market of the American empire of Spain gave rise to the establishment of Free Ports in the British West Indies, the function of which was to puncture the walls of Spanish trade monopoly and to insinuate a stream of British manufactures; and as Spanish imperial authority began to weaken, the British vigorously renewed their ancient policy of 'liberation' in order to secure open doors into the independent Latin American republics.[2]

While busily engaged in undermining the exclusiveness of other nations, they strove, as far as changing circumstances would permit, to retain their own – as witness the long struggle to exclude American shipping from the British West Indies. But in demanding free entry into every ocean and unrestricted access to all markets overseas while refusing to concede (except in a few special cases) the principle of reciprocity, they were in effect reducing the mercantilist theory of trade *ad absurdum*. Growing confidence in the competitive power of their industrial products, together with the need for an ever increasing supply of cheap raw materials, then induced the British under the leadership of Huskisson and his successors to lower the shield of tariff preference and eventually to discard it altogether.

The adoption of this confident policy still further extended the invisible frontiers. In the later 19th century the 'informal' empire of British commerce and capital investment penetrated deeply into the Latin American republics and into China. The entrepôt of Hong Kong and the international Treaty Ports along the coasts of China were not dissimilar in purpose from the earlier Free Ports facing the gateways of Central America.

The wherewithal for this global enterprise was supplied by means of drastic (and unregulated) industrialisation. Britain, in fact, was leading the way into a new age of technology which was to convulse human society. Rapidly changing conditions within her

---

[1] See Chap. V, pp. 293-328, below.
[2] See Chap. IX, pp. 615-661, below.

own borders produced an abounding urban population among whom there was much hardship and dislocation; and so took place the second great wave of migration from the British Isles. The State which had lost interest in colonies and had concentrated its efforts in another direction found itself once more the centre of a large and growing colonial Empire – in British North America, Australasia, and southern Africa. The development was viewed in Whitehall and Westminster without enthusiasm, and the more so when land hunger, wars with native tribes, and international boundary disputes, the old familiar faces, reappeared.

As an adjunct to an informal empire of trade relationships, colonies were an embarrassment. They expected the Mother Country as a matter of course to give their produce high preferential treatment as a return for the privileged position enjoyed in the Colonies by British goods and ships. But Britain herself was operating in a different dimension. Having out-distanced her industrial rivals, she could (for the nonce) command the colonial markets without artificial protection, and yet for the sake of these unnecessary aids she was, in effect, imposing a hardship upon her own export trade by tariff discrimination against many foreign raw materials which enhanced the cost for the British consumer. The old defensive argument that this was a price worth paying, since you could be sure of a colonial supply in time of war, whereas your foreign supplier might become your enemy, made less and less appeal to a nation whose navy controlled all the ocean routes which linked the primary producers overseas and the European recipients. When Britain finally abolished all discriminating duties and repealed the Navigation Acts, she seceded, in a commercial sense, from her own Colonial Empire.[3]

While thus renouncing the traditional basis of empire for herself, Britain maintained that she was not deserting the Colonies but, on the contrary, was emancipating them. They must accordingly stand on their own feet in every respect and as quickly as might be, taking their proper place as independent units in a free (and safe) global system. Political *laissez aller* was the inevitable concomitant of economic *laissez faire*.

For a metropolitan power whose economy was geared to an expanding empire of world trade the gradual dissolution of a privileged and burdensome empire of colonial dependencies was a neat theoretical solution. Neat, but based upon unreal assumptions.

---

[3] Cf. J. G. Gallagher and R. E. Robinson, ' The many-sided expansion of British industrial society can be viewed as a whole of which both the formal and informal empires are only parts. Both of them then appear as variable political functions of the extending pattern of oversea trade, investment, migration and culture. If this is accepted, it follows that formal and informal empire are essentially inter-connected and to some extent interchangeable.' (' The Imperialism of Free Trade ', *Econ. Hist. Rev.*, 2nd series, vol. VI, no. 1 (1953), p. 6.)

When Britain's long industrial lead began to shorten, when the dream of international security and unrestricted trade receded, and the European world reverted to its customary condition of dangerous disequilibrium, there was a quick revulsion in Britain, dictated by sentiment and self-interest. It was a revolt against the cold-shouldering of kinsmen overseas who, though on occasion troublesome and expensive, were also reliable friends in time of need. Yet, even in this warmer 'family' atmosphere, all proposals for reintegration, whether as an imperial federation or a *zollverein,* were rejected both at home and overseas. The concept of 'Greater Britain' was too confined. Instead, an association evolved of like-minded but self-managing nation-states, the outward and visible links of which have become increasingly informal. Thus the altered course followed by Britain in founding the second Empire created a dichotomy between a system of oceanic trade and an empire of settler-colonies, which was resolved (with the potent aid of colonial nationalism) in the emergence of a Commonwealth.

While this system helped to dissolve a centralised empire, it also operated by a seeming paradox to lead Britain step by step into becoming a great Asian territorial Power. The Indian adventure was neither foreseen nor planned. How was it then that the British in their far-ranging search for markets and exotic commodities were led in this instance and some others to contradict their own principle of trade-without-dominion?

There are, or have been, two types of non-territorial 'empire'. The original form was confined to the business of providing a channel of commodity exchange between two or more productive states; and the people who linked them together in this way were essentially entrepreneurs, producing little or nothing themselves, but rendering a valuable and profitable service by means of trading depots, transport facilities (usually by sea), and their own commercial and financial expertise. From time immemorial small seafaring peoples had interested themselves for this purpose in coastlines and islands, where they established 'factories' and sometimes settlements to tap the produce of powerful and wealthy inland principalities. The Greeks of the Ionian coast, for example, grew to opulence as middlemen to the successive conquerors who gained control over the inland trade routes of Asia Minor. In different circumstances and on a larger scale the Phoenicians developed a carrying trade; the sea-girt Republic of Venice developed a great empire of trade between the Orient and mediaeval Christendom, and in northern waters a similar function was exercised by the Hansa League of maritime city-states. These, and others, developed non-territorial empires of trade; but if their clients fell into anarchy or, alternatively, grew stronger and became ambitious to manage their own maritime commerce, the entrepreneurs lost their markets and were put out of business. Their 'empires' collapsed.

The later type of non-territorial empire, as developed by Europeans in the 18th and 19th centuries, and particularly by the British, was based on ancient practice, but the circumstances were different. European merchants in Asia were not merely entrepreneurs. Most of them were citizens of powerful nation-states, producing substantial exportable surpluses, either in the form of manufactured articles or bullion or both; and at the same time their own native Europe afforded a vast market for the products of Asia which they acquired. In short, they were more than agents selling their services: they were principals in the business.

As in ancient times the successful operation of a non-territorial empire of trade depended upon the existence of a strong, stable, native administration in the territories concerned. Unless law and order were locally guaranteed, alien merchants could not profitably function, being politically defenceless. But the British, and their rivals the French and Dutch, representing as they did an economic invasion of the Orient, were more formidable, more tenacious, and less disposed to retreat if the local situation deteriorated. When the native government was strong but corrupt and extortionate, they usually followed the practice of their ancient and mediaeval predecessors and endured oppressive exactions so long as a reasonable margin of profit still remained, endeavouring to protect their interests by the use of appropriate forms of influence at the potentate's court. But if the ground became more treacherous still, if the indigenous government fell into decay and chronic disorder began to supervene, the Europeans (having command of the sea, more effective weapons, and better discipline) began to break away from the customary practice in such circumstances, and refused to cut their losses and leave the country. Instead, they decided to preserve the trade, which had become almost essential to their own national economy, by providing the requisite political stability themselves. They became rulers of alien races – and so stumbled unawares into a new world of political and psychological experience.

In their global search for markets it was not to be expected that the British would always be able to deal with strongly established governments. Inevitably in some regions the political ground would be, or would become, treacherous. If in such a case the profits were substantial, the temptation to intervene and impose law and order frequently proved irresistible, particularly when the alternative was to abandon the field to a European competitor. There were always powerful sections of opinion at home which violently opposed intervention, but in fact 'trade without dominion' and ' trade preserved by dominion' were alternative methods of serving the same commercial end. The British remained first and foremost a nation of shopkeepers. Or so they thought.

It seems probable that in ages to come they will be remembered in India, if at all, not as the prosperous sellers of Lancashire textiles nor even as the builders of railways and irrigation dams, but as administrators, and later as the (reluctant) introducers of their own form of political philosophy and institutions. In the later 18th century the British as a society came very near to being rotted by the getting and spending of Indian loot. But once they began to rule, the basis of their self-interest changed. They became a government, and as such it was to their interest to ensure a healthy revenue; and that, they discovered, involved the suppression of predatory adventurers (British and Indian) and the provision of reasonable security for the wealth-producer, the Indian peasant. This, together with a surviving sense of decency and a dawning sense of moral obligation, impelled them to grope their way uncertainly among the complexities of Indian land tenure and of Muslim and Hindu law and legal process.

Soon the task of building and extending a great system of government began to absorb their interest: not the nation at large, but sons of the manse and the manor and of the new 'men of property'. The commercial motive remained, of course, and indeed increased in importance as the products of British machines began to acquire a vast market in India at the expense of the village looms; but the maintenance of the Pax Britannica and its attendant prestige afforded a deep psychological satisfaction and became almost an end in itself.

The merchant adventurers who were chiefly responsible for the founding of the second Empire unwittingly led their countrymen into strange and exacting experiences. Economic emancipation, imposed by the Metropolis upon the Colonies, powerfully contributed to the dissolving of a centralised Empire into a loosely associated Commonwealth: but a Commonwealth of Europeans.

Clive's assumption of political control in Bengal brought his own country and part of Asia into a close association, the ultimate effects of which are not yet calculable. Moreover, the need to safeguard their position and interests in India was a prime factor in drawing the British up the Nile Valley from Cairo to Kampala and into East Africa, and from the Cape of Good Hope, 'the Gibraltar of the Indian Ocean', through southern Africa and across the Zambesi. Accordingly, large parts of Asia and Africa have been brought within the penetrative influence not only of a European nation-state but of a fellowship of Western democracies. The Commonwealth is in process of becoming multi-racial. As such it is supremely challenged.

CHAPTER II

INDIA: THE PROBLEM OF GOVERNANCE[1]

1. TRADERS INTO RULERS

In the early 17th century Asia presented to European eyes a massive front of ancient and highly organised civilisations: autocratic princes ruled over vast regions of dense population. Englishmen, such as Sir Thomas Roe, assumed that as traders they would be no more concerned with the politics of great empires than were the merchants of the Muscovy Company with the internal affairs of the Russias or the merchants of the Levant Company with those of the Ottoman Turks. The essential requirement for a profitable trade was security, and this could be provided by the prince of a disciplined state. Automatically the 'Company of Merchants of London trading into the East Indies' adopted the traditional technique and secured official permits allowing them to establish factories and to enjoy specific trading privileges under the patronage of the ruling sovereign – in this case the Moghul Emperor. They were foreign merchants, admitted on sufferance because they were useful, just as the Hansa merchants of the Baltic had been given special privileges and royal protection in London and Hull.

If the Moghuls had been able to establish their Empire in Hindustan as securely as did the Tartar Manchus, the European factories dotted along the Indian coasts would presumably have continued as commercial enclaves analogous to the subsequent Treaty Ports in China. But even under the great Akbar, who consolidated his conquests by efficient and just administration and careful conciliation of his Hindu subjects, defeated dynasties reasserted themselves from time to time and were not easily suppressed. In the time of Shah Jahan (1627-1658) Muslims became the ruling class to a much greater extent than before, and the magnificence of the court was sustained by merciless exploitation of the peasant cultivator. But it was under Shah Jahan's successor, Aurangzeb (1658-1707), that Muslim domination began to weaken and the foundations of the Moghul system were undermined. Unlike his predecessors, Aurangzeb was a fanatical champion of Islam. His sustained attacks upon Hinduism and the exclusion of Hindus from high office in the Empire began to destroy the basis of Akbar's success. Loyalty was weakened at a time when the régime was subjected by Aurangzeb to excessive strain. For twenty

---

[1] W. H. Moreland and Sir Atul Chandra Chatterjee, *A Short History of India* (Lond., 2nd edn., 1944), pp. 240-2.

7

five years he was engaged in incessant fighting in the south, and his absence encouraged many Hindu chiefs in northern India to become rebellious. And in other areas Moghul officials gathered power into their own hands. The central administration began to run down. When Aurangzeb died, the Rajputs (Akbar's great supporters) had been rendered hostile, and the marauding Marathas, soon to become the terror of India, were unsubdued. Even after 1707 a statesman might have retrieved the situation, if only in the northern regions; but a succession of palace revolutions and short-lived rulers enabled the great feudatories, and in some cases ambitious adventurers, to defy imperial authority and indulge in internecine war. During the fifty years which followed the death of Aurangzeb, the Empire disintegrated.

In view of what happened after that collapse it is perhaps well to recall that the English had then been on the fringes of India for a century and a half and during that long period had remained isolated and ignorant of Indian affairs. Originally they had hoped to do business by direct and comprehensive contacts with the 'interior', but that expectation did not materialise. Although the London merchants trading to the East Indies received their second charter of incorporation in 1609, it was not until three years later and after many setbacks that they secured their first footing on the coasts of India. In 1612 Thomas Aldworth obtained a grant from Akbar's successor, the Emperor Jahangir, to establish a factory or trading station at Surat. Determined to establish, if possible, a broader and more secure basis for their trade, they obtained the sanction of James I to send an ambassador with a royal commission (but at the Company's expense) to the court of the Moghul Emperor to negotiate a comprehensive commercial treaty.

Sir Thomas Roe, who was selected for the task, was actively interested in overseas commercial expansion, and his mission to India started a long and distinguished diplomatic career.[2] The purpose of the embassy was to negotiate a treaty which would have opened all the territories of the Moghul Empire to English trade under agreed conditions and to provide security by establishing a diplomatic channel for adjusting any disputes which might subse-

---

[2] In 1610-11 he carried out an extensive exploration of the lower Amazon and certain of the rivers of Guiana, with the support of Prince Henry, Sir Walter Ralegh and others, in search of Manoa, the legendary kingdom of El Dorado. On his return he dispatched two more expeditions to Guiana and established a trading station at the mouth of the Amazon. Roe's purpose seems to have been the economic penetration of the region between the Amazon and the Orinoco with the connivance and aid of discontented Spanish colonists. (See J. A. Williamson, *The English in Guiana*, Oxford, 1923, pp. 52-60, and my *Ralegh's Last Voyage*, Lond., 1932, pp. 13-21, 42, etc.) On his return journey from India he visited Persia with an eye to developing trade relations, and as ambassador to the Ottoman Porte (1621-8) he secured privileges for English merchants and improved relations between England and Algiers.

quently arise between the merchants and local officials. A precisely similar purpose, as we shall see, animated the British Government and Company in 1792 in sending Lord Macartney to the Manchu Court at Peking.[3] But the regulation of trade between nation-states by means of diplomatic negotiation was a typically Western concept. Great emperors did not so demean themselves. Moreover the English had very little to offer in return for the extensive privileges that they were seeking, and Jahangir was not prepared to deviate from normal usage by taking English merchants under his direct protection, as was desired, and so exempt them from control by the local governors. Roe remained at court for almost three years and by his demeanour won respect for himself and his nation in spite of Portuguese hostility. But in the end he had to be content with a gracious letter from Jahangir to King James and a *farman* providing favourable conditions of trade at Surat and certain inland towns in that vicinity.[4]

As Roe observed the Eastern scene, his conviction deepened that the English should avoid the policy of the Portuguese and Dutch in acquiring and fortifying territorial possessions and should confine themselves strictly to trade. The Portuguese, he wrote, were beggared by the expense of their troops. Portugal ceased to profit by the Indies when she began to defend them. 'It hath been also the error of the Dutch, who seek plantation here by the sword . . . Let this be received as a rule, that if you will profit, seek it at sea, and in quiet trade; for without controversy, it is an error to affect garrisons and land wars in India.'[5]

The Company was in full agreement. During the middle years of the century their trade was vigorously extended (in spite of fierce opposition from the Portuguese and Dutch) by establishing new factories on the Coromandel coast and in Orissa and Bengal; and in 1668 Charles II thankfully handed over Bombay to the Company at a nominal rent. Some of these developments, however, took them outside the effective orbit of Moghul power. In 1640, for example, Dutch hostility made the commerce of the English factory at Masulipatam so precarious that the Council there decided to remove and make a fresh start under more secure conditions. A strip of land some 230 miles to the south was acquired from the local Hindu rajah with permission to build thereon a fortified factory, which was named Fort St. George. The protection of its guns quickly attracted European traders and Indian middlemen, and the town of Madras came into existence. A fortified commercial centre on the Dutch model had been established. Its founder,

---

[3] See Chap. VIII below.

[4] Sir W. Foster, *England's Quest of Eastern Trade* (Lond., 1933), pp. 280-7.

[5] *The Embassy of Sir Thomas Roe* . . . , ed. by (Sir) W. Foster, Hakluyt Soc., vol. II, p. 344.

Francis Day, received a signal mark of the Company's displeasure, for they disliked intensely the new form of expense to which he had committed them.

The establishment of Fort St. George was a portent rather than a change of policy. But in the course of the later decades of the 17th century foreign traders encountered a rising tide of disorder, induced by a progressive weakening of imperial power in the north and the failure of Aurangzeb to establish his own authority in place of the southern kingdoms of Golconda and Bijapur which he had destroyed. The changing situation and its implications for the English were pointed out in 1677 by Gerald Aungier, President of the Surat factory and Governor of Bombay. The state of India, he wrote, was much altered: the justice and respect previously accorded to foreigners were quite laid aside, and the English, who had patiently endured many wrongs, were become slighted. 'Our complaints, remonstrances, paper protests, and threatenings are laughed at, . . . in violent distempers violent cures are only successful . . . the times now require you to manage your general commerce with your sword in Your hands.'[6]

The pursuit of trade, sword in hand, was a curious combination of activities; but the old security afforded by imperial protection was going. Resolute and ambitious men like Sir Josiah Child, the virtual dictator of the Company's affairs in London, and Sir John Child of Bombay, decided that the English must provide their own, as others were doing. Coastal trading depots, hitherto existing on sufferance, must become self-reliant enclaves with a recognised status, capable of defending themselves against neighbouring war lords, and vested with a local revenue to support the military charges. Bombay, Madras and, later, Calcutta were to serve the sort of purpose of mediaeval Calais under the Merchants of the Staple. Not less than that, and not more.

Their first effort in this direction produced humiliating results. An attempt to force the hand of the Emperor Aurangzeb brought them near to total expulsion. In 1690 they received an imperial pardon and a new licence to trade on payment of a fine and a promise to behave themselves in future. Twenty-five years later an embassy under Surman and Stephenson made the journey from Calcutta to Delhi and, after long delay, secured the grant of certain privileges and formal recognition of status in the Empire. These had a certain legalistic significance, but in a deteriorating situation the throne of the Moghuls had been occupied in quick and bloody succession by the creatures of palace revolutions. The future security of the English traders would depend upon their ability to defend their maritime bases of Calcutta, Madras and Bombay, and

---

[6] India Office Records, O.C.4258, quoted by P. E. Roberts, *History of British India* (Oxford, 3rd edn., 1952), p. 43.

to establish stable relationships with the regional rulers who had wrested *de facto* independence from Delhi.

For a while it seemed possible that this might happen, and that the English Company would remain indefinitely as merchant princes on the coasts, fulfilling a function in relation to the Indian principalities not unlike that of Venice in mediaeval Europe. By virtue of sea power the three bases could reinforce each other (when the monsoons permitted) and could draw upon a reservoir in England of ships, men and equipment. For some thirty years after the embassy of 1715 the Company's servants quietly consolidated their coastal positions, achieved reasonable working relations with neighbouring princes, and accordingly saw the volume of their trade steadily increase. Each of the three principal centres grew into a large and prosperous commercial settlement. Strongly fortified and garrisoned, and providing order and freedom from capricious exactions, they attracted Armenian, Indian and European traders, financiers and middlemen in large numbers. Calcutta was in general on good terms with a succession of able Subadars of Bengal, and Madras at this time was fortunate in that the Carnatic, along the Coromandel coast, and the great principality of Hyderabad, had both become areas of strong stable government. Nizam-ul-Mulk, the ruler of Hyderabad, was able to hold his own against the incursions of the Marathas and so incidentally provided a protective barrier.

Bombay, on the other hand, which had never been within the orbit of effective Moghul authority, had to face the full force of Maratha onslaughts by sea as well as by land. Fighting for survival, the Bombay Presidency began to develop strong military and naval forces, despite alarmed protests from the Directors at home. Until about 1718 Bombay was in great peril, but from then onwards the contest was more equal. In 1739 the Governor and Council concluded the first British treaty with the Marathas by which the Peishwa of the Confederacy granted the Company freedom to trade throughout his territories.

The Marathas were a formidable fighting force, but they were essentially marauders. Had they possessed the necessary internal cohesion and administrative ability, they might well have become the successors of the Moghuls and founded a great Hindu empire. In that event the English Company, alongside the French, Dutch and Portuguese, would presumably have remained on the coasts, having extra-territorial rights in their enclaves and profiting by an expanding commerce until modern times, as they did in China. But the Maratha clans were incapable either of founding an all-India *raj* of their own or, on the other hand, of leaving their northern and southern neighbours in peace. In the early 1740s they burst into the Carnatic and in the north defeated the

Subahdar of Bengal in battle. For a while Madras was in peril, and Calcutta hastily strengthened its defences.

Yet in spite of Maratha turbulence the attainment of a reasonable degree of indigenous stability in India, based on Bengal in the north and Hyderabad and the Carnatic in the south, does not appear to have been inherently impossible. During the troubled period after the death of Aurangzeb in 1707 the English Company had every reason to be satisfied with the growth of their trade in India and their increasing capacity to defend it. The directorate in London were by tradition and conviction extremely hostile to any involvement in dynastic wars, and it is clear that until the 1740s the Company servants in India had little acquaintance with the shifting relations between the various Indian principalities and the complicated intrigues of their courts.

The situation changed when France decided to strike at the Indian trade of her British rival. The ancient competition between these two thrusting peoples had spread out from the home Continent across the Atlantic and into the Indian Ocean, moving with the general expansion of the Europeans overseas. France was at once a great (agricultural) land power in Europe and also a maritime state with ports fronting the North Sea, the Atlantic and the Mediterranean. In this dual situation she tended to alternate between territorial ambitions in Europe and the development of an empire overseas. On their side the British, as a small island people evolving from feudalism towards middle-class industrialism, concentrated upon maritime affairs.

With the shift of power from Madrid to Versailles the British at frequent intervals endeavoured to 'contain' French ambitions in Europe (whether under Bourbon, Jacobin or Napoleonic leadership) and to protect the island base by calling the profits and ships of a 'new world' of oceanic commerce to redress the balance. As British weightage in Europe increased with the growth of their maritime resources, the French became increasingly concerned to cut the commercial tentacles of their rivals by naval, military and diplomatic action overseas; and this in turn provoked the British to respond in kind – in North America, the Caribbean, and in Eastern waters. In the later 19th century, when the rise of Germany threw France on the defensive in Europe, the focus of Anglo-French competition moved to the valley of the Nile and the basin of the Niger.

When, therefore, Britain aligned herself in 1741 with hard-pressed Austria against the preponderant and predatory combination of France, Spain and Prussia, the very substantial trade which the English Company had built up on the coasts of India invited French attack. The original plan, as agreed between the French

Ministry of Marine and La Bourdonnais, involved no more than a heavy raid on English commerce, but Joseph François Dupleix, the new Governor-General of the French possessions in the East, strove to enlarge it into a war for the expulsion of the rival Company from India. The military operations were a minor affair, and although the British were greatly alarmed by the French capture of Madras in 1746, their position as a whole remained unshaken. But the political consequences were immense.

The servants of the two European trading companies had dared to wage war against each other on Indian soil, an act of contumacy which in earlier days would have evoked swift imperial retribution. Their private war drew them from their coastal strongholds into the hinterland. For the first time they became acquainted with 'the geography of the country a hundred miles round their settlements'[7] and they learned many other things as well. Behind the façade of dynastic authority which they had hitherto accepted at its face value they found that the states in southern India were rife with internal faction and intrigue, and each was engaged in complicated manoeuvres against its neighbours. Rulers and would-be rulers were participating in a scramble, the prizes of which were thrones and territorial revenues, and the hazards palace murders and local wars.

The Europeans were no longer suppliants for trading privileges and protection. Already the English at Madras had been awarded the management of an additional port in return for supporting a successful claimant to the throne of Tanjore. And more significant still, Dupleix, having quarrelled with the Nawab of the Carnatic over the future possession of Madras after its capture, had challenged him with a small but efficient force and had put the Nawab's unwieldy army to rout. It was becoming clear that the disciplined garrisons of Europeans and Indian sepoys, which had been formed to defend the coastal enclaves, were greatly superior in the field to the ill-trained and usually ill-paid levies of Indian princes.

Pondering on these matters, Dupleix decided to intervene. The humdrum routine of the counting-house disgusted him; and in any case he saw no future for the French East India Company, which was entirely dependent on Government support and control and was making no headway as compared with the broadly-based and expanding commerce of the English. For Dupleix the weakness of the French Company, the confused situation in south India, and his own predilections, all pointed to the political weapon as the only one with which he could effectively oppose the nation of shopkeepers. In a general scramble for power an outside broker should be able to exact a high price from chosen clients for skilled military

---

[7] Roberts, *op. cit.*, p. 105.

and political support which could be decisive. Dupleix had good grounds for rating his services so highly, for he had a *flair* for diplomatic finesse and intrigue, and he soon acquired a mastery of the intricacies of interstate politics and dynastic feuds in south India.

The weakness of the design lay in its incapacity to carry the weight of its own success, and Dupleix's success was spectacular. By 1751 he was at the height of his prestige and influence in south India with Chanda Sahib, Nawab of the Carnatic, and Mozaffar Jang, Subadar of the Deccan, as winning candidates and grateful clients. Continued French domination inland threatened to ruin the trade of the English at the ports. Yet when the latter after feeble and clumsy beginnings took up the challenge in earnest under the leadership of Clive and Stringer Laurence, their strong commercial position, especially in Bengal, furnished resources far exceeding those available to Dupleix. He gambled – brilliantly – ' on margins ', but by 1754 he was at the end of his tether with an empty treasury and with allies disillusioned by his defeats in the field. He was superseded, and the Governments of Britain and France agreed to terminate this unofficial war in India on a basis of non-interference in the internal affairs of Indian states. In reality such a reversion to the *status quo ante* was scarcely practicable. The decisive stage of the Anglo-French contest in India began four years later as part of the world-wide struggle known as the Seven Years War. Under the terms of the Treaty of Paris in 1763 French political power in India was eliminated; and that verdict was not subsequently reversed, despite the high hopes of Vergennes to the contrary in 1781-2[8] and the later designs of Napoleon.

In the course of a war which had spread to almost every state in south India the outlook of the servants of the English Company had completely changed. Commercial profit (their own and secondarily that of their employers) was still the prime consideration; but they had become a participating element in Indian polity and were no longer external to it. They became practised in oriental diplomacy and well versed in the deployment of military support as a diplomatic instrument. As such they not only secured the enlargement of their trading privileges but also won political profits in the form of lavish personal gifts and the allocation of territorial revenues from specified districts. Their growing assurance, rapacity, and influence within the Indian feudal system alarmed the Indian nawabs, hitherto their patrons, and also their own masters, the Court of Directors in faraway Leadenhall Street, who from early days had been dogged by the fear of losing control.

---

[8] See vol. I., Chap. VII, of this work.

When, therefore, the English Company was suddenly threatened with expulsion from Bengal (by far the most important region for their commerce), the Company's servants were no longer isolated suppliants but Indian politicians, conscious of their military strength and cynically familiar with the lusts which the anarchy of a dissolving empire had released. In the northern and central regions, where martial and predatory races were involved, the competition for thrones was even more fierce than in the south and was rendered the more so because one of the prizes was control over the helpless occupant of the imperial throne itself.

While the Marathas 'tore away from the Empire most of central India', the Nawab of Oudh (a Persian) achieved virtual independence, and to the north-west of that State the Afghan Rohillas conquered and held a region beyond the Ganges. As always in India, internal disintegration incited invasion from the north. The scene has been well summarised by a recent historian: 'In 1739 Nadir Shah of Khorasan, having made himself King of Persia, overran Afghanistan and swept on to Delhi, where he looted and massacred at will, carrying away untold treasure and the peacock throne made for Shah Jehan. On his assassination one of his Afghan officers, Ahmad Shah Abdali, advanced from Herat to seize the Punjab, which he achieved by 1748, and left a Rohilla to command the Moghul armies. In 1741 Aliverdi Khan, a Tartar adventurer, having slain the heir of his benefactor, established himself as Nawab of Bengal with his Pathan troopers.'[9] In many regions the Hindu population (nobles, merchants and peasants) had exchanged one alien rule for the greater misery of another.

Under the harsh but shrewd government of Aliverdi Khan the English at Calcutta grumbled but increased in wealth and influence, while Hindu resentment smouldered. The death of this able ruler in 1756 thrust Bengal into the general anarchy. When Aliverdi's strong hand was removed and he was succeeded by his weakling grandson, Siraj-ud-Daulah, the Hindu zemindars, merchants, and bankers perceived that their opportunity of getting rid of Muslim domination had come at last. Vicious, irresolute, and frightened, the new Nawab began to persecute some of his most influential subjects and then decided to destroy the British, who had offended him on several counts. Rash and ill-considered though his plan was, he was right in regarding the Europeans as potential allies of the Indian and Armenian merchant groups, for the need to defend their commercial interests tended to draw them together. If the English Company, which was too strongly established for comfort, were eliminated, the French at Chandernagore and the Dutch at Chinsura would cease to be of consequence, and the

---

[9] Sir Keith Feiling, *Warren Hastings* (Lond., 1954), p. 14.

Nawab's Indian opponents would be greatly weakened. The sequel is well known and may be briefly summarised.

In June, 1756, an army of 50,000 attacked Calcutta. Disgracefully abandoned by the Governor and the military commander, and defending fortifications which had fallen into decay, the garrison held out for four days and surrendered when their strength had been reduced to 170 men. Then followed the deaths in the Black Hole and the devastation of the settlement. In December Clive arrived by sea from Madras with a force of 900 Europeans and 1,500 sepoys and supported by a fleet under Admiral Watson. On 2 January, 1757, Calcutta was recaptured and a second attack by the Nawab's army was beaten off.

Neither Clive nor Siraj-ud-Daulah was in a position to force conclusions. For Clive the outbreak of a world war with France made it imperative to seize Chandernagore before Lally and de Bussy could intervene from the south. And the Nawab also found himself in a dangerous situation. In this same month of January, 1757, the ruthless Afghan ruler of the Punjab, Ahmad Abdali, swept down upon imperial Delhi and sacked it. Alarmed by this new peril at his back, Siraj-ud-Daulah agreed to reinstate the English with enhanced privileges. But French promises of support sounded fairer in his ears than British grievances (which were genuine), and after reluctantly permitting Clive to take possession of Chandernagore, he swung back to the French side. Thereupon the British joined in the conspiracy to dethrone him. In doing so they became involved in and themselves adopted the trickery characteristic of such dynastic upheavals. The decisive factors throughout the proceedings were Clive's masterful personality and his small, efficient army of about 3,200 men. After the chosen pretender, Mir Jaffir, had bound himself in close alliance with the British, matters were brought to a head. At the rout (rather than the battle) of Plassey Siraj-ud-Daulah's army of 50,000 was defeated and scattered, while Mir Jaffir with his own force remained an inactive observer, waiting to betray the loser. Siraj-ud-Daulah was murdered within a week by Mir Jaffir's son, and the new Nawab was enthroned at Murshidabad by Clive himself, who received gifts from his client amounting to about £240,000, while lesser but substantial sums were handed out to members of the Calcutta Council.

Siraj-ud-Daulah's attempt to expel the British merchants thus converted a Hindu plot against a Muslim ruler into a revolution which established a foreign trading Company as the dominant force throughout Bengal and the adjacent provinces of Bihar and Orissa. The new régime afforded a classic example of the evils inherent in the exercise of power without responsibility. Clive's initiative in response to a dangerous situation had thrust the English Company into a political position which was too anomalous to endure and from which it was impracticable to withdraw.

Technically the foreign traders still remained outside the political system in Bengal, except that they held the *zemendari* of Calcutta. The new Nawab, like his predecessor, was the imperial subahdar, responsible for the administration of the country through his officials and local magnates. Outside Calcutta and certain adjacent revenue-producing districts, the British had no share in or responsibility for the government of the people, and yet they were committed to maintaining the Nawab on his throne. Whether they liked it or not, their material interests were bound up with the stability and solvency of the régime for which they had become the sponsors. The implications of that fact although ultimately inescapable were not readily appreciated. The process of realisation and the consequent grappling with problems unprecedented in their political experience constitute one of the most critical phases in the history of British rule over alien peoples.

The new situation quickly induced a clash of interest between the Company's servants in Bengal and the Company itself. For their part many of the men on the spot, suddenly armed with supreme power, treated the Nawab's treasury and the general resources of the country as objects of lawless plunder. On the other hand the Company was now required (if it was to survive in northern India) to underwrite 'the law' of the State and maintain its viability. The dangers of the situation were not immediately apparent to the Court of Directors in London. The Company remained a commercial concern, and it was assumed that the chief result of Clive's assertion of power, apart from assured security, would be a flow of substantial contributions from the Nawab in return for military support. Such contributions would swell the Company's 'investment' in Indian goods for sale in Europe. Otherwise, little change.

The true position gradually revealed itself. Three times within five years the puppet ruler of Bengal, having been fleeced and rendered viciously desperate, was deposed by the Calcutta Council and replaced by another, who in turn was forced to hand over huge sums as the price of his elevation. Upright men on the Council (including Warren Hastings) protested strongly and frequently but without avail. And while the servants of the Company cheated their employers, they amassed large fortunes for themselves in private trade by compelling the nawab of the day to exempt them from the normal internal dues. They were thus able to put the native merchant out of business, while they and their agents (or *gamstahs*) used their mastery to exploit and impoverish the native producers from whom they made their purchases. Repeated orders from London forbidding the receiving of presents and the pursuit of private trade were defied and regulations for reform were ignored. Moreover the consequences of this behaviour extended beyond the frontiers of Bengal. The maltreatment of Mir Kasim, the successor of Mir Jaffir, involved the British in an entirely unnecessary war with the ruler of Oudh and the Emperor, Shah Alam. The decisive victory of Baxar greatly enhanced British military prestige, but the Company had been drawn into the very centre of the Indian maelstrom and stood exposed to the danger of a general combination against them. By 1764 it had become evident to frightened and angry Directors and Proprietors in London that their employees, as the lords and oppressors of Bengal, were completely out of hand and were a menace to the Company. Drastic disciplinary action was urgently needed. But beyond that particular operation lay the far more difficult problem of how far and by what means an association of foreign traders from the other side of the world could or should attempt to supervise the internal administration of an Indian State, ignorant as they were of its complex of Hindu and Muslim law and social custom.

It was not enough to reduce the Company's Servants to obedience: they must also be transformed into quasi-civil servants. The alternative was to abandon a dominant position and clear out of northern India altogether. As the most powerful of the British trading corporations the Company occupied too important a place in the national economy to be allowed to ruin itself through the folly of its servants. Step by step the Government of the day intervened; but it did so with hesitation and distaste, for the very power of the Company, entrenched behind chartered rights, rendered such intervention politically dangerous. Moreover the imposition of the Government's authority involved the creation and management of a new administrative machine, and this was a task which an 18th-century Government was very ill-equipped to undertake, particularly in the case of strange communities in a distant continent.

The practical issues were these, in ministerial order of priority. How could a commercial corporation with greatly increased resources and (temporarily) disordered finances be enabled and compelled to assist the State by providing a direct and regular contribution to the national revenue? On the face of it that object appeared to involve no more than a negotiated bargain with the Treasury and a short Act of Parliament; but in the event it proved as disappointing as the parallel efforts to obtain contributions towards imperial defence from North American settlements or from an autonomous Ireland. Secondly, the corporation in question was no longer a normal trading organisation to be mulcted in respect of 'excess profits', but had acquired a form of territorial jurisdiction in a foreign country and was making a dangerous mess of it. It had become a distinct political personality, owing theoretical allegiance to a foreign Emperor, and it was also an incorporated society of British subjects, exercising extensive privileges under the authority of a charter from the British Crown. The interests and the good name of the nation required that the State, as such, should intervene and impose effective supervision. The obligation itself was sufficiently difficult and unpalatable, but politicians quickly discovered that much more was involved than reaching a *modus vivendi* with obstinate Directors and truculent Proprietors in Leadenhall Street. Unless the Government was prepared to resume the Charter and undertake direct administrative responsibility in Bengal – an impossible proposition – there was no alternative but to devise some method of working continuously through the executive instruments of the Company in order to reassert and maintain control over the British personnel in India, who in their own way were as recalcitrant and as powerful as the merchants of New England. But that, of course, was not the limit of the commitment. By the acquisition in February, 1765, of the *nizamat* (the judicial and general administration) in Bengal from the Nawab, and of the *diwani* (the revenue administration) a few months later from the Emperor, the Company became inescapably responsible for the government and welfare of a complex Asian society representing many layers of diverse tradition. And since the Company was the delegate of the British Crown by royal charter, the State was drawn into the business in the wake of the Company. Moreover Clive's belief that, when the Company's employees had been disciplined, British authority could be restricted to general supervision and the receipt of revenue balances, while the native administration was left to manage the business in its own way, was quickly disproved by the event.

A problem arose which was as novel then as it has since become familiar. How far was it desirable or practicable to penetrate the outer and inner layers of an alien community with British ideas of law and administrative method? Was the maximum or minimum of interference the *desideratum*? From now on these difficult questions were to exercise the minds of British politicians and administrators with regard to many non-European areas of the world. The parallel problem has been that of Britain's changing role as a Mother Country when confronted by the developing nationalism of her settler Colonies. In our own time these lines have ceased to be parallel: they have converged and become intertwined. Politicians of the late 18th century had little to guide them in dealing with either; and it is one of the ironies of the situation that a colonial revolt in British North America and a no less challenging revolution in northern India were thrust simultaneously upon the

attention of a weak Administration at the head of which stood a
distracted and benevolent Lord North.

2. BRITISH DEFIANCE IN BENGAL AND
CLIVE'S DUAL SYSTEM

The contumacy of British-Indian 'nabobs' was as troublesome to
British administration, and in some respects as dangerous, as that
of John Adams and Franklin, and of Flood and Grattan. In so far
as the struggle lay between the metropolitan Government and a
delegated authority operating overseas, the issue was characteristically colonial. The constitutions of colonies and of chartered trading
companies stemmed from the same root. They did so because both
these types of overseas organisation were alternative instruments
designed for the same purpose. In mediaeval times merchants
engaged in exporting cloth and other commodities to Europe
formed themselves into organised groups known as Merchant
Adventurers. Of these the London Adventurers, later known as
the Merchant Adventurers of England, had become predominant
by the beginning of the 16th century with a monopoly-area extending from the Somme to the Skaw. As 'regulated' groups, of which
each member shipped his own goods as a private adventurer, they
were guilds for foreign trade. But when the English economy was
strong enough to launch out into more distant and hazardous
markets, the principle of a joint stock, also of mediaeval origin,
was adopted to attract capital and spread the risks. The first English
Chartered Company trading on a joint stock, the Muscovy Company, which had essayed the dangerous voyage to the White Sea in
1553, was so arranged as a matter of convenience and safety.[10]
Similarly in 1581 the Levant Company, seeking the products of
the Middle East and Asia, started with a joint stock; but in later
years the comparative safety of the voyage to Smyrna encouraged
its members to undertake separate ventures on a 'regulated' basis.
It was these Turkey Merchants who, with their eyes on Asia, obtained a charter in 1600 to trade direct to the East Indies by the
ocean route. The new (East India) Company developed by stages
towards a joint stock on modern lines. From 1661 an annual dividend was declared from the profits and a buyer of shares automatically became a freeman of the Company.

Chartered Companies of both varieties were incorporated
societies, enjoying exclusive privileges and organised on a standard
model, deriving from that of the mediaeval guilds. The Freemen
elected a body of Directors or Assistants to hold office for a term
of years and managed much of their business through elected committees. As self-governing corporations the more successful of them

---

[10] Sir John Clapham, *A Concise Economic History of Britain . . . to 1750* (Cambridge, 1949), p. 262.

became powerful in national affairs. Though frequently under attack from opponents of monopoly, they were generally regarded as indispensable for sustaining important branches of overseas trade. Governments looked to them for financial support and were susceptible to pressure from their spokesmen in Parliament. With their privileges guaranteed by royal charter they acquired a status comparable with that of the City of London and other municipal corporations whose chartered rights were by tradition an inviolable part of the 'liberties' of England.

The founding of colonies in North America and the islands of the Caribbean was also regarded as a commercial venture. By this means it was hoped to acquire independent supplies of precious metals and naval stores, and other primary products would be grown by English emigrants instead of being purchased from foreigners. New sources of raw materials and new markets would be *created*. In foreign trade the invested capital was laid out in bullion or in goods for barter: in colonisation it would be expended in transporting and equipping settlers whose toil would produce the dividends. As seen from the City of London it was a difference of technique, not of object. It was natural, therefore, that the traditional device of the privileged chartered company should be applied to this new branch of overseas commerce. The Charter which was granted in 1609 to 'The Treasurer and Company of the Adventurers and Planters of the City of London for the First Colony in Virginia' was modelled on that accorded to the East India Company nine years earlier.[11] The Great and General Court of the Company, which was to meet four times each year on prescribed dates, was given authority (in 1612) to appoint and remove the Governor and other officers as well as the members of the Council in Virginia, and to determine all matters of government, trade, and the granting of land.[12]

Unable and unwilling to undertake direct responsibility for such enterprises itself, the Crown followed the time-honoured device of delegating extensive powers to those who were prepared to do so. By the same token a single proprietor who offered to risk his capital in establishing a settlement was vested with vice-regal authority. The first Earl of Carlisle, for example (backed by a group of London capitalists), received Letters Patent in 1627 creating him absolute lord proprietor of a number of West Indian islands, to be held of the Crown by knight service with as ample royalties and jurisdiction as had ever been possessed by any Bishop of Durham within his bishopric or county palatine.[13] The Earl was

---

[11] Sir A. B. Keith, *The First British Empire* (Oxford, 1930), p. 23.

[12] Under the original provisions of 1609 wide powers had been conferred upon the Council in Virginia.

[13] J. A. Williamson, *The Caribbee Islands under the Proprietary Patents* (Oxford, 1926), p. 40.

to make laws with the assent of the majority of the freeholders, and was authorised to erect courts, appoint judges, and enforce obedience by corporal punishment or sentence of death.

The weakness inherent in such wide delegations of power was obvious enough. Companies and proprietors alike failed to exercise control over their nominal servants in remote regions, who quickly and decisively asserted themselves. The extreme example of what could happen was afforded by the proceedings of the Massachusetts Bay Company. The intention of the Charter granted in 1628 was to 'constitute a corporation in England like that of the East Indian and other great Companies', but the usual stipulation that the government of the Company must be located in England was omitted. The circumstances of this remarkable omission have long been the subject of controversy, but the consequent decision of the General Court in 1629 to remove themselves to New England and to transfer thither 'the whole government together with the Patent' was momentous. The normal company structure (Governor, Deputy-Governor, and eighteen Assistants elected by the Freemen), with all the customary rights and privileges, ceased to be the controlling agency in England and became the settlers' own instrument of local government. 'It made the charter of a trading company the written constitution of a colony.'[14] In order to put an end to a situation which had produced a virtually independent republic, the Crown at last succeeded in vacating the Charter in 1684 by a writ of *scire facias*, and under a revised Charter in 1691 established direct 'royal' government. Sixty years earlier James I had revoked the Charter of the Virginia Company and had promulgated a new constitution by which the affairs of Virginia were to be managed by a Council in England, consisting of a Governor and twelve Assistants, which was to appoint a governor and a council of twelve to act in the Colony, and was itself to be subject to the authority of the Privy Council. These and similar measures taken elsewhere were symptomatic of the long and partially successful struggle of the Stuart sovereigns to establish royal government throughout the American and West Indian Colonies on a basis of uniformity and central control.

In the struggle to subordinate the Chartered East India Company to state direction, which continued for some fifteen years, successive Governments encountered resistance which was grounded on ancient precedents. The tradition of delegated authority in the management of maritime trade and settlement was all the more formidable in this case because the dimensions of power and responsibility were so greatly enlarged. Never before in clashes between Government and 'chartered rights' had the national

---

[14] Keith, *op. cit.*, p. 19.

economy been so deeply involved; and never before had the prospects of the national exchequer receiving a substantial territorial
revenue from overseas appeared so promising, or the problem of
controlling a chartered corporation in the administration of territory been so difficult and dangerous. It is the potency of tradition,
operating in a new order of magnitude, which explains so much of
the weakness of the compromise embodied in the Regulating Act
of 1773, the reckless attempt of Fox in 1784 to cut through the web
of constitutional precedent, and the clever compromise subsequently devised by Dundas and Pitt which, in effect, made Dundas
the first Secretary of State for British India.

The parallel problem of how to secure an obedient and yet
strong executive instrument in India was likewise influenced by
commercial-colonial precedent. The original method of administering both trading depots and colonial settlements had been to concentrate local authority in the hands of the Governor and a
nominated Council, appointed by the corporation or proprietor
in England, and exercising executive, legislative and judicial
functions. While the home authority was alive to the need for
vesting its Governor with powers adequate for maintaining control
in the territory or factory, it was no less aware that a too-powerful
Governor might defy, or at any rate circumvent, instructions.
Hence the tradition that a Governor's discretionary powers must
be limited through the medium of a Council appointed at home:
a tradition which the State inherited and continued. As the Crown
in the 17th century assumed direct control in one colony after
another, the policy was followed by checking the power of the
(royal) Governor by naming the Councillors in the Governor's
Commission and by filling subsequent vacancies on the formal
recommendation of the Board of Trade. The Governor's nominations were, it is true, usually accepted, but all members of Council
owed their appointment to the Crown.[15] On assuming control the
State usually inherited from the colonising Company or the proprietor a situation in which the executive functions of the
Governor in relation to his Council were not closely defined. 'The
early governor was not the executive of a settled political community. In addition to his political functions he was often
the manager or superintendent of an essentially commercial
enterprise.'[16]

Yet even when colonies in the Western Hemisphere developed
as political communities and a governor had to do with aggressive
elected assemblies, the home Government still tended to vacillate
about his executive powers and tried to regulate his functions as

[15] Keith, *op. cit.*, p. 191.
[16] H. B. Greene, *The Provincial Governor in the English Colonies of North America* (Harvard Historical Studies, VII). Harvard, 1906 edn., p. 31.

the Crown's representative on principles that were not easily
reconcilable. On the one hand, Ministers were insistent that, in
giving effect to directions from home, he must not evade or dilute
his responsibility by trying to share it with his Council. On the
other hand, they took care to use the Council as a check upon his
executive functions. Many of the powers granted to him by his
Commission and Instructions could be executed only with the
advice and consent of his Council.

His power to suspend members of Council came to be regarded
as liable to misuse and was restricted in 1698 in Instructions issued
to Francis Nicholson as Governor of Virginia. In order to render
the councillors 'less liable to arbitrary and ill-grounded recalls',
Nicholson was required to send home a full report of his reasons
for any suspension. This provision became common form and so
continued until 1715, when a further restriction was considered
desirable. In future the suspension of a member could only take
effect if approved by a majority of the Council. This, however, was
found to be too severe a limitation, being apt to render the
Governor helpless in cases where the Council was dominated by a
powerful family clique. The Board of Trade accordingly veered
round and decided to allow the Governor to suspend by his own
authority if and when his reasons for doing so were 'not fit to be
communicated to the Council'. But he must report his reasons
forthwith, and it sometimes happened that in such cases the
Governor was over-ruled and the Councillor in question was
reinstated.[17]

The relationship between Governor and Council in Calcutta,
Madras and Bombay was similarly regarded by the East India Company and for like reasons. From early days the Company directorate, fearing insubordination, had set narrow limits to the powers
of their Governors. At the Council Board he was little more than
primus inter pares: the extent of his actual authority was proportionate to his personality. When, therefore, the Company's acquisition of territorial jurisdiction was accompanied by defiance on the
part of their own officers in Bengal and the North Administration
was obliged to intervene, there was a strong tradition against
entrusting a Governor with wide discretionary powers. Under the
Regulating Act the desire to secure the subordination of the overseas executive caused the traditional policy of checking and curbing a Governor through his council to be sharply emphasised; and
ten years of confused experimentation took place before the alternative and revolutionary principle of a strong executive head in the

---

[17] L. W. Labaree, *Royal Government in America: a study of the British Colonial
System before 1783* (New Haven and London, 1930), pp. 153-55. Cf. the same author's
Royal Instructions to British Colonial Governors, 1679-1766 (New York and London,
1935), vol. I, Pt. I, pp. 3-86, and Greene (*op. cit.*), chaps. II, V, and VI.

territory, strongly controlled from the metropolis, was at last adopted.

As politicians and government servants grappled uncertainly with the ancient problem in a new form of how to assert the authority of the State over a chartered (and faction-ridden) corporation and over its subordinate (and mutinous) governments overseas, colonial precedents were recalled. During the debates in the Commons on the India Judicature Bill in 1772 Governor Johnstone rose in his place to cite the authority of Thomas Pownall, a former Governor of Massachusetts and author of the famous work, *The Administration of the Colonies.*

My mind [said Johnstone] is come to this determination, that the Crown, under certain conditions, should grant the lands to the East India Company, as was done in the cases of New England and several other of our chartered Colonies. The mode is easy, as the words empowering conquest, and promising all future reasonable grants, in each of the charters, are literally the same. For this information, as cases in point to settle the minds of men who wish to act by precedent, I am obliged to a worthy member in my eye, who has made the constitution of the Colonies his particular study. The situation in Philadelphia, the most perfect government under the King, fully illustrates and vindicates my view. The East India Company should appoint, and the King approve of the Governor. The distribution of justice should flow from the throne. . . . The Commander-in-Chief of the troops should be named by the Company, and appointed by the King: all the lesser offices should be in the Company. A legislative authority should be established on the spot: without this, we are like a ship deprived of a rudder.[18]

The idea of establishing a (nominated) legislative council in Bengal was to be seriously considered. But the Atlantic seaboard of North America, peopled for the most part by migrants whose political thinking was saturated by the traditions of Westminster and English local government, was a different world from that of the ryots and zemindars of Bengal. Colonial precedents were not as directly or as easily applicable as Johnstone thought; but no others were available. In the great period of argument and experiment which laid the foundations of British rule in India, Ministers of the Crown struggled to adjust the powerful traditions of commercial and colonial administration to a new situation. In the face of strenuous resistance both at East India House and from the 'colonial' governments in India they gradually and by devious

---

[18] *Parl. Hist.,* vol. XVII, 377-8. Thomas Pownall was at this time M.P. for Tregony. Governor Johnstone was a strong 'Company' man and much involved in manœuvres designed to protect his brother, John Johntsone, from the consequences of his nefarious activities in Bengal.

methods evolved a new system of metropolitan control. At the same time circumstances compelled them to embark upon the strange and difficult business of adapting British law and procedure to the complexities of ancient and alien custom. It is only by relating the consequent trials and errors to the background of contemporary experience and prejudice that they can be adequately appraised.

In tracing the process it will be necessary to alternate between Calcutta and London, since 'the problem of governance' involved central and local issues which were interlocked. The situation required the creation of an executive instrument in India capable of converting the Company's servants into an honest civil service and of establishing through them efficient and humane supervision of a native feudal system which was corrupt and chaotic. A study of the successive attempts to devise such an executive instrument will take us to East India House and Westminster and then at intervals to Bengal in order to observe the repercussions. Similarly, the long struggle of the King's Administration to establish some form of effective control over a commercial company which was becoming a territorial power occasioned a series of administrative experiments at home which, because they gradually drew the Government into undertaking direct responsibilities in India, must be examined as an imperial metropolitan issue as well as a formative stage in the first establishment of a British *raj* in Asia. In attempting this constitutional and administrative analysis, the history of the British in India at the time and the internal history of the East India Company will be described very summarily and only in so far as the analysis itself requires.[19]

After the victory of Plassey and Clive's enthronement of a Nawab who in practice was no more than the Company's executive agent, it is conceivable that the administration of Bengal could have been continued as that of a 'Protected State'. On that basis the Company's representatives would have supported the Nawab's domestic authority with as little interference as possible, confining their own activities to the maintenance of security, the 'investment' of surplus revenue received from the Nawab's Treasury, and external trade. But a complex and delicate relationship of that sort would have required a trained civil service (which had not yet emerged in Britain itself), guided by specialised experience and a high tradition of public service. The Company's employees had gone out to India to make their fortunes by private trade, and the political power which Clive's revolution placed in their hands

---

[19] With reference to the internal history of the Company I have drawn freely upon the two standard works: Lucy S. Sutherland, *The East India Company in Eighteenth-Century Politics* (Oxford, 1952), and C. H. Philips, *The East India Company 1784-1834* (Manchester, 1940).

afforded a wonderful opportunity for doing so on the grand scale. The nawabship was wrecked by extortion when it should have been established as an instrument of government, and the economy of the country was undermined by the enforcement of exclusive privileges in internal trade. Moreover, the arrogant contempt for the distant authority of the Company, induced by the possession of political and military power on the spot, was progressively enhanced as employees infiltrated into the governing body. Returning home with their wealth in increasing numbers, they secured votes for themselves and their friends by the purchase of East India stock, and lined up with the opposition in General Courts in order to thwart inconvenient investigation and disciplinary action.

The authority of the Directors was thus weakened from within at a time when its effective exercise in Bengal was becoming desperately urgent. In the election of April, 1763, Laurence Sulivan, the tough and resilient Chairman, had won a clear victory (with Government assistance) over an opposition led by Clive, who had plunged into Company politics to ensure the retention of his cherished *jagir* of £10,000 a year. But it was evident that Clive and his supporters were re-organising their forces and biding their time. Meanwhile Sulivan was striving to assert control over a situation in Bengal which was fast slipping into anarchy. His ideas about administrative reform were sensible, and he followed the sound principle of relying on the judgement and authority of the Governor on the spot. But Vansittart was a sick man about to retire, and the majority of his Council were themselves leading the campaign of plunder.

When it became known that Vansittart's efforts to obey instructions were being met by open defiance on the part of his Council, the Directors decided to dismiss four senior and influential servants and to nominate John Spencer of Bombay to succeed Vansittart. It was a courageous decision, for the dispossessed would certainly swell the ranks of the opposition among the Proprietors. But before these orders could be dispatched, news arrived in February that the Nawab, Mir Kasim, had revolted and was waging war against the Company in alliance with the Nawab of Oudh. A deplorable experiment in 'paramountcy' had crumbled into confusion, bringing the very existence of the Company to hazard.

Thoroughly alarmed, the bulk of the Proprietors turned to Clive as the strong man who alone could save the régime which he had created. The opportunity had come: the opportunity to vindicate his achievements, guarantee his rewards, and discomfit his foes.

After a preliminary round of attacks upon the Direction for its alleged mishandling of Bengal affairs, a carefully prepared plan of campaign was put into operation. At a General Court on March 12 it was moved and carried with acclamation that Clive be sent out to Bengal with supreme civil and military authority. But he and his supporters had decided to exact certain conditions, and these were only allowed to emerge *seriatim*. When Sulivan and his fellow Directors accepted the situation and declared their readiness to give full co-operation to Clive while he was in Bengal, the latter announced that he could not accept the appointment while the Sulivan group remained in office. The issue was decided at a fiercely contested election on 12 April which the Clive party only won with the aid of powerful intervention by the Grenville Administration and by a very narrow majority. Half the Directors returned were of the Sulivan party, but in the subsequent election to the chair Sulivan himself was replaced by Clive's supporter, Thomas Rous. Thereafter a further condition was advanced, which at an earlier stage would have had little chance of acceptance – that Clive's *jagir* should be continued to him for a further ten years. The requirement was now accepted after a long and bitter wrangle.[20] This determination to consolidate his position at East India House before setting forth was understandable enough, for Sulivan was his bitter opponent and the purge and reassertion of discipline which he was about to undertake could not fail to raise up powerful and revengeful enemies.

In insisting that Clive must be invested with supreme civil and military powers, the alarmed Proprietors had adopted a course of action which broke away from the long-established tradition that the discretionary power of governors overseas, whether colonial or in trading factories, must be strictly confined by instructions from home and by the necessary concurrence of executive colleagues on the spot. That principle had always been strongly held with regard to the settlements of the Company, and the Governor of Fort William, Calcutta, as President of the Council, was normally little more than *primus inter pares*: an arrangement which had been reduced to absurdity when the majority of the Bengal Council defied the Company's authority and prevented Vansittart from carrying out the Company's orders for reform. The theoretical danger of an over-powerful governor had been replaced by the actual menace of an executive body in revolt and rushing down a very steep place. It was evident that the system of Governor-in-Council could not work in such circumstances, and yet Clive could scarcely purge and reconstitute the Company's organisation in Bengal single-handed. In the event a curious expedient was adopted, evidently at Clive's own suggestion, which is of considerable signifi-

---

[20] For a full account of these proceedings within the Company during 1763 and 1764 see L. S. Sutherland (*op. cit.*), Chap. V. The feud between Clive and Sulivan, which now became chronic, does not appear to have arisen from any major cause of quarrel but by a kind of geometric progression of friction, induced by the clash of two strong and ambitious personalities. The feud greatly injured both of them and exacerbated dissensions in the Company at a critical period.

cance in relation to subsequent administrative developments in India. Clive's extraordinary powers were, so to say, put into commission. Four selected persons were associated with him as a 'Select Committee', which was authorised to assume control over the heads of the Council if the situation in Bengal was found to require it.

We have thought proper [the Directors stated] to appoint a Committee on this Occasion, consisting of his Lordship, Mr. William Brightwell Sumner, Brigadier-General Carnac, also Messrs. Harry Verelst, and Francis Sykes, to whom we do hereby give full Powers to pursue whatever means they shall judge most proper to attain these desirable Ends; but, however, in all Cases where it can be done conveniently, the Council, at large, is to be consulted by the said Committee, though the power of determining is to be in that Committee alone. We further direct, that as soon as Peace and Tranquillity are restored and established in the Subahship of Bengal, then the said extraordinary Powers are immediately to cease, and the said Committee be dissolved.[21]

It also provided that, if Bengal were invaded, the Committee was to be in sole control of defence with the addition *ad hoc* of the artillery Commandant. The device of concentrating authority in Bengal in the hands of five specially selected individuals was subsequently adopted in the Regulating Act, but with the important difference that a majority could veto any action proposed from the Chair. On this earlier occasion the gravity of the situation enabled Clive to ensure his own undisputed mastery. He was allowed to choose the members himself: nothing was said about decisions requiring the sanction of a majority vote; and there was no stipulation about a quorum.[22] In the circumstances opposition to Clive by members of the Committee would have been a hazardous undertaking, but nothing of the sort emerged. All four were men of integrity and wide experience in Indian affairs, and they worked unitedly under his leadership – even the obstreperous soldier, John Carnac.

The creation of a high-powered executive with almost plenipotentiary powers was accepted by the Directors with reluctance.

---

[21] Directors to President and Council, Bengal, 1 June, 1764. Printed in *Fourth Report from the Committee of Secrecy on the State of the East India Company* (Reports from Committees of House of Commons, reprinted 1804, vol. IV, pp. 147-8). Subsequent references to documents reproduced by the Secret or Select Committee will be briefly cited in the following form: *Nth (Secret)* or *(Select) Rept.*, vol. —, pp. —.

[22] See Sir John Malcolm, *Life of Clive* (Lond., 1836), vol. II, p. 236. In April, 1764, Clive had laid before the Court of Directors a general indication of his plans for Bengal, had insisted that John Spencer be sent back to Bombay, and had repeated his previous demand for an extended recognition of his *jagir*. These conditions had been accepted by the Directors, although opposed by Sulivan and his supporters. When they were considered at a General Court on 2 May, the opposition had concentrated upon the question of the *jagir*. (See Sutherland, *op. cit.*, pp. 130-1.) Until the election of 1765 Clive's supporters in the Direction had a very narrow majority.

They clung to the improbable hope that Clive might after all be able to work with the Council and avoid establishing the new *Junta*; and in any case the Committee with its special powers was to be dissolved as soon as order had been restored and the normal form of conciliar government was to be at once resumed. Clive, however, thought differently. A few months after his arrival in Bengal he set out a plan of government in a letter to the Directors. The previous system under which an unwieldy Council of sixteen members had dictated to the Governor was impossible. 'The Office of Governor,' he wrote, 'has been in a Manner hunted down, stripped of its Dignity, and then Divided into Sixteen Shares.' Of late years the gentlemen in Council had been actuated by a very obstinate and mischievous spirit. It was the duty of the Council on all occasions to support the dignity of the Governor's office and to make his authority appear 'as extensive as possible in the Eyes of the People'. But he must not, Clive was careful to add, be allowed to become an autocrat. 'This should be the outward Appearance of Administration, though in Reality the Council must be allowed a Freedom of Judgment; and when they perceive in the Governor a Tendency to absolute or unjustifiable Measures, it then becomes their Duty to check him. . . . The best Governor should not, except in Cases of Necessity, be suffered to conclude any Points of Importance without the Sanction of the Board.'

How was this *desideratum* to be secured? The answer, said Clive, was a (standing) Select Committee, consisting of five gentlemen of ability and resolution, men well versed in the Company's affairs and of unquestioned integrity. They would be no less capable than a Council of preventing ill conduct on the part of the Governor, and the system afforded additional advantages which could rarely be expected from the whole body of Councillors.

A Select Committee, composed of such Men, will transact more Business in a Week, than the Council can in a Month. The Opinions and Judgment of Five Men are as securely to be relied on, even in Affairs of the utmost Consequence, as Sixteen: They are less liable to Dissention, and it may be said beyond a Contradiction, that their Administration is more distant from democratic Anarchy.

The Council would not, however, be a useless body. While the Committee was chiefly engaged 'in watching and repairing the main Springs of Government', the Council would attend to many other 'Movements of the Grand Machine'; and in order that the Committee should not be able to carry their powers to dangerous lengths, it could be provided that they must submit their proceedings to annual review by the Council, who could transmit their opinions to the Court of Directors. This should not, however, apply to political matters of secrecy, when prudence might require that knowledge of resolutions taken should be confined to a few. The present Committee, he added, had laid most of their proceedings before the Council from time to time, and they intended to continue the practice.[23]

In May, 1766, the Directors responded to these proposals by formally confirming the Committee in its full powers, 'to do every Act and Deed which may contribute to preserve Peace, Tranquillity, Discipline, Harmony, good Order and Subordination in the Settlement'.[24] But while they agreed that these powers should remain in force as long as Clive was in Bengal, they gave instructions that the Committee was not to continue after his departure 'unless he shall judge it for the Interest and Benefit of the Company'. He did so judge it. In January, 1767, at his last meeting with the Committee before taking ship for England, he announced: 'I do not hesitate to pronounce that the Select Committee must be continued . . . without Recess or Prorogation.' Harry Verelst, his successor as Governor, was nominated President, to serve with four other designated members. 'This Committee,' he added, (is) 'justly considered as the Cabinet Council, wherein the most material political Affairs are proposed, digested, and determined upon.' Membership conferred 'the sanction of ministerial importance'.[25]

From being an *ad hoc* commission, appointed to supersede the normal government in Bengal only for so long as the situation required, it had become under Clive's direction an inner executive, framing policy and operating in a manner not unlike the Secret Committee of the Court of Directors at home. Clive remained convinced that this 'Cabinet' system must continue as a permanent feature of government: otherwise control would slip again and the old indiscipline and confusion return.

But the Directors at home would have none of it. Such a body could become altogether too powerful, and in any case the Select Committee was anathema to influential persons (now sitting and voting in the Court of Proprietors) who had been disciplined by it. To Clive's disgust and anger unity of control was destroyed by handing back many of the Committee's powers to the Council. Five years later in the House of Commons he made this one of his principal charges against the Directors.

Their next step was to destroy the powers of that Committee whose conduct they had with reason so happily approved of. They divided the powers; they gave half to the Council, and left the other half with the

---

[23] Clive to the Directors, Calcutta, 30 Sept. 1765. *3rd (Select) Rept.*, vol. III, pp. 391-8.
[24] Directors' General Letter to Bengal, 17 May, 1766. *4th (Secret) Rept.*, vol. IV, p. 192.
[25] Clive to Verelst and Members of the Committee, recorded in Minutes of the Select Committee, 16 Jan., 1767. *Ibid.*, vol. IV, pp. 153-4.

B*

Committee. The consequence was, the Council and Committee became distracted by altercations and disputes for power, and have ever since been at variance, to the great detriment of the service.[26]

On 10 April, 1765, Clive and his party landed at Madras to be greeted with startling news. Mir Kasim, the Nawab of Bengal, with the Emperor, Shah Alam, and the ruler of Oudh had been defeated at the hard-fought battle of Baxar. The Emperor had at once submitted, and thereafter the resistance of Oudh had been completely broken. From being in danger of expulsion from Bengal the English Company had suddenly become the most powerful military and political force in Hindustan. Intoxicated by the turn of events, the Bengal Council had crowned their long defiance of Company orders by exacting presents amounting to almost £140,000 from the new ruler whom they had installed in Bengal and requiring him to continue all the privileges of private trade which had been repeatedly forbidden. Moreover, they had followed this up, in February, 1765, by placing the effective administration of Bengal in the hands of a deputy Nawab, whose appointment and dismissal were to be subject to their approval. They had taken this step in order to strengthen their own control over the country; but their action had involved the Company in internal Indian administration, rendering it in effect responsible for the *nizamat*, the management of all matters relating to criminal justice and defence. The resultant problem was urgent as well as difficult since the Bengal Council, as the controlling body, was itself rotten with corruption and devoid of any sense of responsibility either to London or to the Bengalis.

Clive had expected that his primary task would be to retrieve the situation at Calcutta by repeating the achievement of Plassey. But the peril of military disaster had been exchanged for the dangers of victory. Apart from cleansing the Augean stable (to use his own favourite allusion) and establishing an honest regime in Bengal, he found that the victory of the previous year was still being exploited at a distance of 700 miles from base and that he had to do with Company employees, intoxicated with power, 'who thought of nothing but a march with the King to Delhi'. Military men and civilians alike were obsessed with the idea that their mastery of Bengal could now be extended to the Moghul Empire as a whole. Whatever the pettifogging Directors in London might say (too late), there was nothing to prevent the Company from reinstating the suppliant Emperor on the peacock throne and then presiding as a Varangian Guard over the destiny and resources of

---

[26] Debate on the East India Judicature Bill, 30 March, 1772. *Parl. Hist.*, vol. XVII, 365. By 1770 the Select Committee had become chiefly occupied as a committee of investigation into revenue collection. See Minutes, *4th (Secret) Rept.*, vol. IV, pp. 213-15, 249-51.

a reintegrated Empire. In the apparent circumstances the idea was understandable: but in the conditions then prevailing, it was frenzy.

When Clive stepped ashore at Fort William on 5 May, the situation required that he should do three things before he concluded his mission and returned home. He was required to suppress abuses and restore discipline, and secondly to define and regulate the relationship between the Company, as overlord, and the indigenous administration in Bengal. But the third posed a problem of a different order. The conquest of Oudh and the subsequent advance of the troops towards Delhi were about to precipitate the Company into a ruinous adventure from which it would be difficult, if not impossible, to withdraw.

His handling of this issue shows Clive at his best. The Company, he observed, had at last reached the critical period which he himself had long foreseen. 'I mean that Period which renders it necessary to determine whether we can or shall take the Whole to ourselves.' Bengal was under control again, and Siraj-ud-Daulah, ruler of Oudh and imperial *Vizier*, had been driven from his dominions. 'It is scarcely Hyperbole to say, Tomorrow the whole Mogul Empire is in our Power.' As a military force the Company was becoming irresistible; but in Clive's judgement the political implications presented a different prospect. If the Company chose to become the power behind the imperial throne, France and Holland would be provoked to a challenge, and the very princes selected for British countenance and support would be hostile and envious. 'Ambition, Fear, Avarice, would be daily watching to destroy us.'

He announced his policy in clear terms. The march on Delhi would be stopped and the Company's conquests and possessions bounded 'absolutely' to Bengal. At the same time he was emphatic that the Company must recognise that they were no longer a purely commercial undertaking.

I could have wished that our Operations had been carried out upon a Plan of more Moderation, and that we had not been obliged to maintain any other Military Force, than what might be sufficient to preserve and pursue our Commercial Advantages; but since our Views are extended, and since Commerce alone is not the Whole of the Company's Support, we must go forward; to retract is impossible.[27]

In the following July and August Clive and Carnac negotiated agreements with Siraj-ud-Daulah and with the Emperor. Under the Oudh treaty the Nawab agreed to pay an indemnity of fifty lakhs of rupees and entered into a defensive alliance with the Company, who on their side were to provide troops for the defence of

---

[27] Clive to Thos. Rous, Chairman of the Court of Directors, Madras, 17 April, 1765. *3rd (Secret) Rept.*, vol. III, pp. 404-5.

his frontiers when he needed them. All his dominions, with the exception of two small districts, were restored. This had been done, as Clive explained to the Directors, not so much with a view to binding a new ally with ties of gratitude, but primarily in pursuance of his policy of not extending the Company's territorial possessions. Retention of the conquered country would have proved impracticable. Oudh would have been exposed to acts of oppression and 'innumerable abuses' which distant authority in Calcutta would have been unable to prevent or remedy. Grievances would have fomented unrest, leading inevitably to another war. The draining away of resources in the attempt to maintain control over the new acquisition would have endangered the Company's position in Bengal itself, and ultimately the Company would have sunk under its inability to sustain the weight of its own ambition.[28] When the Directors received Clive's reports, they fervently agreed. They were determined 'to make the Provinces of Bengal, Bihar, and Orissa, the utmost Bounds of our political Views or Possessions'.[29]

The agreement with the Emperor involved a momentous change in the Company's status in India. While rejecting out of hand all schemes of conquest under imperial auspices, Clive had already decided to define and consolidate the Company's position in Bengal by securing the *diwani,* or right to collect and administer revenues by grant from the Emperor. A dangerously fluid situation would thus be exchanged for recognised powers and status as a Moghul feudatory within a specified region. As a fugitive and suppliant Shah Alam readily acceded to Clive's proposals. The *diwani* was granted as well as the reversion to the Company of Clive's *jagir* with its revenues upon the termination of Clive's own tenure. In return the Emperor received a fixed annual tribute of 26 lakhs and for the further support of his imperial dignity the districts of Korah and Allahabad which had been withheld from Oudh. It was also arranged that the Nawab of Bengal should receive an annual subsidy of 53 lakhs of rupees.[30]

Clive did not fail to emphasise in his letters to the Directors that, when all charges on the revenue had been met, a very substantial surplus would accrue to the Company: nor did he fail to profit personally from the improved prospects of East India stock. At the same time the acquisition of the *diwani* was regarded by him as

---

[28] Clive to Directors, 30 Sept., 1765 (*loc. cit.*). Clive's caution was well justified by the event. In the stormy years ahead the Company was hard put to it to defend the existing frontiers against the onslaughts of the Marathas and other external enemies. Cf. Roberts (*op. cit.*), p. 162.

[29] Directors to President and Select Committee in Bengal, 17 May, 1766. *3rd (Select) Rept.*, vol. III, pp. 398-400.

[30] For the English versions of Shah Alam's four *Firmans* to the Company, dated 12 Aug., 1765, see *ibid.*, pp. 447-9.

the essential basis of a reformed and stable system of government in Bengal. Internal revolutions were a thing of the past. 'Ambitious Mussulmen' would lack the means of effecting them since the revenues now belonged to the Company; and the Company's Servants would lack inducement. There would be no object in elevating a new nawab who was unable to pay for the honour by depleting the till.

Clive's purpose in assuming the *diwani* (apart from the financial advantage) was not to increase British intervention, but, on the contrary, to confine it within the narrowest possible limits. The removal of treasury control to Fort William was intended to prevent the revenue from flowing into channels where it could be tapped by Company Servants. Moreover, the latter were to be excluded from the duties and responsibilities of revenue collection. 'The Power of supervising the Provinces, though lodged in us, should not, however, in my Opinion, be exerted.' To do so was neither practicable nor desirable. 'Three times the present Number of Civil Servants would be insufficient for that Purpose.' If, on the other hand, the management were left in the hands of Bengali officials, the Company would be under no additional expense. Admittedly the revenues would suffer loss through peculation, but gross offenders could always be detected and punished, and there would also be 'some satisfaction in knowing that the Corruption is not among ourselves'. Clive's determination to keep out of the internal administration of the country as far as possible was dictated by the conviction that the Company was totally unfitted for the task. By adhering to this policy the abuses which inevitably sprang from the exercise of territorial authority would, he declared, be effectually obviated.

There will still be a Nabob, with an Allowance suitable to his Dignity, and the territorial Jurisdiction will still be in the Chiefs of the Country, acting under him and the Presidency in Conjunction.

Clive relied on firm control at the top. The affairs of the new Nawab, a worthless young man, were put under the joint management of three trusted Indian Ministers whom Clive appointed; and Francis Sykes, a member of the Select Committee and a man of 'inflexible integrity', was established at the Durbar as Resident with authority to inspect the treasury accounts from time to time as directed by the Governor and Council. 'But,' reiterated Clive, 'we are never to interfere in the Appointment or Complaint of any Officer under the Government,' or in any measure of revenue administration unless some extraordinary conduct of the Ministers rendered alteration essential.[31]

---

[31] Clive to the Directors, 30 Sept., 1765 (*ibid.*), pp. 394-5.

Such were the outlines of Clive's famous 'Dual System' – the first British experiment in 'indirect rule'. It resembled the Roman technique rather than that of modern Britain, but the common factor was expediency. The English Company was not equipped for the task of direct administration: both the personnel and the specialised knowledge were lacking. Clive's avoidance of it was almost universally approved in England.[32] The Directors were emphatic in their support of non-intervention. The office of *diwan*, as exercised by the Company, must extend no further than the superintendence of revenue collection. 'And this,' they announced in ignorant cheerfulness, 'we conceive to be neither difficult nor complicated.' They noted that the Nawab's officials made an annual bargain with each zemindar or land-holder, and they opined that the Company's only concern would be to ensure that the agreed payments of land-tax were strictly enforced. If necessary the Company's assent to the annual assessments might be stipulated; but that must be the limit of interference.

This we conceive to be the whole Office of the Dewanny. The Administration of Justice, the Appointment of Officers or Zemindarries, in short, whatever comes under the Denomination of Civil Administration, we understand is to remain in the Hands of the Nabob or his Ministers.[33]

They could not be expected to foresee that the receipt and disbursement of a revenue which chiefly derived from the land must inevitably involve them and their employees in the appalling complexities of Indian land tenure, and that the conditions under which land was held constituted the nerve-centre of the economic, social, and administrative life of the country. If Warren Hastings or Cornwallis ever found time to read the official correspondence of 1765-6, his occasional smile must have been sardonic. Moreover a truncated *diwani* would be all the more difficult to operate since *de facto* supervision of the complementary branch of administration, the *nizamat,* had already been assumed.[34] In the prevailing circumstances Clive's compromise was the only sort of arrangement that could be contemplated, but when he wrote that the Company must go forward and that to retract was not possible, he was stating a truth the implications of which were beyond the horizon. His system represented a most significant stage in the hesitant evolution of a British *raj.*

Meanwhile Clive had been strenuously engaged in that part of his task which he described as cleansing the Augean stable. Within four days of his arrival in Calcutta on 3 May he exercised his

---

[32] Cf. H. Verelst, *Rise, Progress and Present State of the English Government in Bengal* (Lond., 1772).

[33] Directors to President and Select Committee, 17 May, 1766.

[34] Cf. *supra*, p. 32.

discretionary power and established the Select Committee as the supreme authority in Bengal, thus virtually superseding the Council, with which, as then constituted, it was obviously impossible to work.[35] Two members of the Committee, Sykes and Sumner, had accompanied Clive on the voyage out: the other two, Verelst and Carnac, were senior Servants, already in Bengal. The Committee began its inquisition without delay, and the frauds and abuses which were revealed lost nothing in Clive's telling of them. The investigation was thorough and fearless. The worst offenders were dismissed or suspended from their posts, and their punishment by way of prosecution in the courts was left to the Company at home.[36]

Company Servants were obliged to sign a penal covenant, previously prepared by the Directors, against receiving presents; they were forbidden henceforth to take part in the inland trade; and all Free Merchants and other Europeans residing and trading up-country were to withdraw to the Presidency by 21 October. The last provision, which had been ordered by the Directors, was particularly drastic. While agreeing with its necessity, the Select Committee observed that its effect would be to deprive many persons 'of real merit' of their means of subsistence.

In the execution of their invidious task Clive and his colleagues naturally aroused widespread resentment which took the form of defiance and social boycott from the civilians and an organised mutiny on the part of the army officers. The 'Young Gentlemen of the Settlement' – mere boys, arrogant with sudden riches and premature power – organised themselves into non-co-operative associations. 'Each,' runs the wrathful report, 'would seem to think himself qualified to transact your mighty affairs in Council at an age when the Laws of his Country adjudge him unfit to manage his own concerns to the Extent of Forty Shillings: . . . it becomes a fair Struggle whether we or the Young Gentlemen shall in future guide the Helm of Government.'[37]

They met their match in Clive; but far more dangerous was the smaller group of older covenanted Servants, men of wide experience in Indian intrigue, commercial and political, and of great influence at home. These were typified by John Johnstone, a member of Council. Hard pressed by the Committee's enquiries, he

---

[35] ' Of a board then sitting at the Presidency, consisting of the President and Eight Members, Five of those Members were themselves the accused, who, by having a Majority of Voices would of consequence become the Judges of their own Conduct.' Report of the Select Committee to the Directors, 30 Sept., 1765. *3rd (Select) Rept.*, vol. III, p. 439.

[36] The Minutes of the Select Committee from 7 May to 7 July, 1765, are printed *verbatim* in *3rd (Select) Rept.*, vol. III, pp. 405-27. See also pp. 428-46.

[37] Report of the Select Committee to the Directors, 31 Jan., 1766. *4th (Select) Rept.*, vol. III, p. 519.

denounced it as an unlawful body which had trampled upon his rights as a Briton. Having penned an impudent defence of his actions,[38] he hastily took ship for England, where he headed a powerful group of malcontents in the Court of Proprietors – and waited for Clive to come home.

The Directors were wont to describe the problem of governance in Bengal in terms of a metaphor. They spoke of the 'barriers of the Country Government' having been broken down. These, they declared, must be repaired and all future penetration by Europeans be prevented. In fact the old positions could not be re-established. Clive advanced the Company's administrative frontiers and then erected a new wall of partition which he expected to endure. But the barriers, both political and commercial, were, in reality, very fragile, and they would only hold if the British personnel exercised discipline and self-restraint in respecting them. In that regard the outlook was unpromising. For some years a stream of senior men had been going home to enjoy their fortunes, and youngsters, who would normally have served a lengthy apprenticeship as Writers, were promoted too quickly to positions of power and influence where they promptly imitated their elders. The shortage of reliable and experienced men was so acute that Clive imported four senior Servants from Madras, and he urged the Directors to supply the Settlement with young men, 'more moderate and less eager in their Pursuit of Wealth'. The Company needed men who would give twelve to fifteen years of faithful service and be content to retire with a fortune of reasonable size and 'honourably acquired'.

In order to attract such men and establish a tradition of public service Clive proposed the complete abolition of licensed private trading and a substantial increase in official salaries. But that was to expect a corrupted trading corporation to behave with a sense of public duty. Failing to carry the Directors with him, he devised an alternative method of increasing the regular emoluments. The monopoly of the wholesale trade in salt was vested by him in an official 'Society', the profits of which (amounting to not less than £120,000 a year) were distributed among the Company's Servants according to a graduated scale. When the Directors expressed their strong dislike of the scheme as oppressive and restrictive,[39] Clive protested hotly that it had been misrepresented: it was not oppres-

---

[38] See Johnstone to the Governor and Council, Fort William, 1 Oct., 1765. *Ibid.*, pp. 536-42.

[39] 'With respect to the Company, it is neither consistent with their Honour, nor their Dignity, to promote such an exclusive Trade. As it is now more immediately our Interest and Duty to protect and cherish the Inhabitants, and to give them no Occasion to look on every Englishman as their national [? natural] Enemy, a Sentiment we think such a Monopoly would necessarily suggest; we cannot therefore approve the Plan you have sent us for trading in Salt, Beetle Nut, Tobacco . . . and do hereby confirm our former Orders for its entire Abolition.' Directors to Select Committee, 17 May, 1766 (extract). *4th (Secret) Rept.*, vol. IV, pp. 192-3.

sive, since the selling price to the Indian retailer was strictly regulated at reasonable levels; nor had the trade been previously free for the Nawab had always kept the salt trade as a monopoly, farming it out to favourites who had forced the price up for the peasant consumer by squeezing the middlemen. Something of the evil odour of previous abuses in the field of internal trade clung to the scheme; but strictly regulated as it was, and in the absence of other resources, there seems to have been little valid objection to it.[40] After running for two years, it was abolished; but the motivating principle was conceded. Henceforth the emoluments of senior Servants were to be very substantially increased by a percentage charge on the revenues.[41]

By strong-arm methods Clive halted oppression and corruption and reduced a rebellious personnel to obedience; but he failed, almost inevitably, in his further object of laying the foundations for a civil service. The difference between the alternative of a moderate fortune after twelve or fifteen years' honest service and an enormous one gained by disreputable means in less than half that time was too great, and particularly so when the Directors, in 1770, rescinded the prohibition of their predecessors against private trade. It was not to be expected that the harder course would be generally adopted and become traditional until a strong man of unquestioned integrity had remained in command for a considerable period. Clive's tenure of the governorship lasted for a year and eight months; but even if the changing political situation at home and his own health had permitted a longer tenure, he was himself too vulnerable to attack to have been able to anticipate the work of Cornwallis. His lofty condemnation of oppression and corruption, which was perfectly sincere, tended to lose its cutting edge in view of his own immense accumulation of wealth. He always

---

[40] Cf. Sumner's explanation of the scheme (which he himself had organised) before the Select Committee of the House of Commons. ' The Plan,' he stated, ' was thus calculated to bring Salt at a more reasonable Price to the Hands of the Consumer; to increase the Revenues to the Company £120,000 *per annum*; and to hold out such Rewards of Fidelity to their Servants, as might engage them, by Ties of Interest and Gratitude, to a cordial discharge of their Duty.' *4th (Select) Rept.*, vol. III, p. 466.

[41] Under this arrangement the Governor's salary of £4,800 was increased to a total of about £24,000, and in some years considerably more; the Second in Council received £368 plus £2,687; and other Councillors £342 plus £1,194. But junior grades, who came ' below the line ' and did not receive this form of augmentation, continued to fare badly. A Senior Merchant received £81 p.a., a Junior Merchant £75, a Factor £60 and a Writer £50. And although there was free board and lodging, numerous allowances for special duties and perquisites not shown in the Returns, there was little inducement to ignore trading opportunities and to concentrate on being a civil servant. See ' An Account of the Stated Salaries and Allowances . . .' *9th (Secret) Rept.*, vol. IV, p.460. For the commissions paid to each named individual between 1767 and 1771, see *ibid.*, pp. 162-75. The compiler of ' General View of the Stated Salary, Allowances . . . from 1762 to 1772 ' (*ibid.*, pp. 461-502) seems to have confused sterling with current rupees.

denied with scorn (and truth) that he had ever sunk to the practices of a poacher in Bengal; but the guilty men were none the less enabled to challenge his credentials as gamekeeper. In thus protecting themselves they largely stultified the effect of his reforms. Under the régime of his honest but irresolute successor, Harry Verelst, the old abuses gathered strength again and flooded in over the barriers.

Clive made two contributions of enduring importance for the future. After suppressing rebellious movements among the civilians and the army officers[42] who were dreaming of reconquering the Empire in the name of Shah Alam, he stabilised the external situation by devising an intermediate status for the Company as an imperial feudatory. It is not too much to say that this adjustment of relations saved the Company in Bengal from being overwhelmed and greatly influenced the form of later British expansion in India. Secondly, at a time of grave crisis, he demonstrated the necessity for a powerful governorship, supported by a small compact executive body; and although Warren Hastings was to be confronted with a travesty of what Clive had intended, the principle was adopted and effectually implemented under the India Act of 1784 and so became in the 19th century a basic feature of the administrative edifice.

---

[42] The dangerous character of the mutiny of the army officers is shown in the fully documented account, entitled ' Narrative of the Defection of the Officers of the Army in Bengal in the Year 1766 ', *9th (Secret) Rept.*, vol. IV, pp. 671-715. The ostensible cause of the trouble was Clive's order that the double field allowance (*batta*), which had been granted as a special concession during military operations in 1757, must cease from 1 Jan., 1766. On several previous occasions specific orders to that effect had been issued by the Directors and had been successfully defied. Clive's order, following upon his extremely unpopular action in stopping ' the march to Delhi ' and reversing the policy of territorial conquest, brought the prevailing anger and disappointment to a head and inspired a revolt which was evidently intended to break the authority of Clive and the Select Committee. Secret ' Committees of Correspondence ' were organised in each brigade under the guise of Free Mason lodges, and a fund for the support of the mutineers was organised, to which many of the civilians contributed. Efforts were made to induce the officers at Madras to support them by refusing to move if ordered by Clive to come to Bengal. It had been intended that a mutiny of the whole army of 20,000 men should take place on 1 June; but evidence of the conspiracy was discovered, and the leaders were obliged to take action (towards the end of April) before they were fully prepared. Their object was to overthrow the existing government and put the army in control. According to the ' Narrative ' the demand for the continuance of the double field allowance (in time of peace) was to have been followed by three more: (i) the abolition of the new penal covenants against receiving presents from Indian princes; (ii) the abolition of the Select Committee; (iii) a standing order from the Directors guaranteeing that none of the Bengal officers would be replaced. Clive's commanding personality and the loyalty of some of the senior officers saved a situation which revealed only too clearly the need for drastic administrative reforms.

3. THE COMING OF STATE INTERVENTION

So far, we have been observing the Company from the outside, that is to say, as a governing body faced with a revolution in its affairs overseas and a revolt among its Servants. Clive's attempt to hold the situation by stabilising relations with the Emperor and the ruler of Oudh, devising a dual system of administration inside Bengal, and reasserting the authority of the Directors as the supreme executive, was necessarily based on the assumption that the management in London would function as before. The constitution of the Company was overwhelmed by a combined invasion of its own employees and speculators in East India stock. An assault of this sort was theoretically possible because the executive of a joint-stock company is controlled by an electorate of purchasable votes, that is to say, by the holders of stock which can be bought on the open market. In this case it actually happened, because the fortunes acquired in Bengal enabled employees to qualify as Proprietors on a large scale (at the rate of £500 per vote) and so protect themselves and their plunder by transferring from the dock to the bench. The malcontents who by this method shifted their resistance from Calcutta to London were later reinforced from Madras, notably in the persons of Paul Benfield and other predatory creditors of the Nawab of Arcot. The process continued until it became possible for Burke to declare in a rhetorical flourish but with a considerable measure of truth: 'The servants in India are not appointed by the Directors, but the Directors are chosen by them . . . The seat of the supreme power is in Calcutta.'[43]

Clive's acquisition of the *diwani* exposed the Company management to further assault from a different quarter. As soon as the exciting news reached London (on 20 April, 1766), the price of East India stock began to soar, moving quickly from 164 to 200 and within twelve months to 273. Clive himself had anticipated this reaction by sending urgent instructions to his attorneys, while he was still at Madras, to buy up all the stock that his capital and credit could afford, thus using official foreknowledge for his private profit. Other wealthy men in London followed suit and bought heavily. Powerful groups of speculators began to 'bull' the stock; and since a substantial increase in the dividend was the best means of maintaining the rise, they began to invade the Court of Proprietors in order to compel the Directors to acquiesce. By splitting about £150,000 of stock they temporarily created 300 votes, and at a General Court on 26 September they used this voting power to force an increase in the annual dividend from six to ten per cent.[44]

Among the Proprietors was a body of sober men, well versed in

---

[43] Burke's speech on Fox's India Bill, 1 Dec., 1783. *Parl. Hist.*, vol. XXIII, 1371-2.
[44] This is a brief summary of Dr. Lucy Sutherland's analysis (*op. cit.*), pp. 140-6.

the Company's business, who knew better than to countenance such folly; but their support of the Directors in resisting it was weakened by the abstention of the Clive group, and the formidable coalition of speculators and Bengal malcontents had their way. In other words, the new wealth-getting opportunities brought about a subversion of the Company's Constitution at the very time when the governing body was required to rise to the responsibilities of statecraft. Some of the leading men, such as Sulivan, were capable of doing so. Prominent Directors of other chartered companies, before and since, have been efficient territorial administrators. But in these other cases their territorial resources were not so great as to incite invasion and subversion. By contrast, the East India Company was wrecked as an instrument of government because its wealth-producing acquisitions in India generated a pressure too great to be withstood.

The 'revolt of the nabobs', which had overborne the restraining barriers in India and then invaded the governing body in London, developed into a protracted conflict with the State itself. As a problem in the exercise of metropolitan control over territories and interests overseas the struggle with the General Court of the East India Company,[45] which continued for some twenty years, was almost as intractable as that with the American colonists or with Grattan's Irish Parliament. Whereas the Americans and then the Anglo-Irish based their resistance to Westminster on the rights of distinctive communities, the English rulers of territories acquired in India fought against the claims of the State in the formidable name of chartered liberties.

One of the major preoccupations of British Ministers after 1763 was the problem of how to spread the overhead expenses of an expanding Empire. In terms of national indebtedness the cost of victory had been exceptionally heavy. To the country squire who paid land tax it seemed that the benefits of expansion accrued to others, while the burden was unduly concentrated upon himself. The obvious and logical method of spreading the load, it seemed, was to raise revenue on the other side of the Atlantic where contributions to the general war effort had been unimpressive. There was, in addition, a specific financial problem. Successive Ministers were required to devise a workable system for the administration and defence of an expanding American frontier, now released from French restraint, and were confounded by lack of funds. In March, 1766, Rockingham's Administration repealed the Stamp Act: some

---

[45] The only chartered company to acquire great resources in the modern history of the British Empire has been the British South Africa Company; but in this case wealth came from gold and diamond mining and not in consequence of territorial status. In the forceful hands of Cecil Rhodes the Company's constitution was a virtual dictatorship which at the time of the Jameson Raid and on other occasions exerted considerable influence over Government policy.

three weeks later Clive's despatches reached London, announcing (with great exaggeration) that in future the East India Company could expect a clear surplus of over £1,650,000 per annum from the territorial revenues of Bengal, Bihar and Orissa. Providentially, it seemed, a new Empire in India had been brought into being just in time to redress the financial balance of the old.

That, quite naturally, was the reaction of the Chatham-Grafton Ministry which took office at the end of July and also of the King himself. The latter declared that 'the only adequate means' of restoring the nation's finances was for Parliament to take 'such part that shall be judged expedient out of the Territorial Revenues now received contrary to their Charter by the Company';[46] and Chatham described the Bengal revenues as 'a kind of gift from heaven'. A month after taking office the Administration formally notified the Company that its affairs were to be brought under consideration in Parliament. Chatham saw no difficulty. A trading company had acquired certain territorial rights in a foreign land. The accruing political revenues, as distinct from trading profits, were accordingly the rightful property of the State which furnished indispensable military and naval support. As its agent in this non-commercial sphere the Company would be required to render an account of its receipts, and Parliament apparently was to investigate and then determine the annual amount to be handed over to the Exchequer. There was to be no argument; and, quite naturally at this early stage, there was no thought that the Government should assume responsibility. At this same time Clive was assuring the Directors that they could be the recipients of taxes without becoming involved in obligations towards the taxpayers. No less plausible, therefore, was the proposition that the British Government could tap the flow of surplus revenue at the London end without interfering with the Company in the management of its business.

The claim to take part in the political profits established a direct Government interest in the viability of its agent; and this agency as an instrument of government was being subverted by nabobs and speculators. Infiltration from that quarter impelled the Government to intervene from their side in order to safeguard the new national interest which had been created.

As was to be expected, the initial intervention was negative and preventive. The sole concern was to strike a bargain and to obviate

<hr />

[46] The King to Grafton, 24 Feb., 1767. *Correspondence of Geo. III,* vol. I, p. 452. Three months earlier (on 9 Dec., 1766) when action was pending in the House of Commons, he wrote to Grafton: 'On the issue of this Day, I think the real glory of this Nation depends.' He was convinced that, if the Ministry were resolute, 'there will be the greatest Majority ever known in that House, and . . . that it will be from conviction that this is the only safe method of extracting this Country out of its lamentable situation owing to the load of Debt it labours under.' *Ibid.,* pp. 423-4.

the risk of default by preventing the Company from jeopardising its solvency. To proceed further would lead on to difficult and dangerous ground. Hard-pressed Directors, thwarted by subversive opposition, accordingly received scant assistance from Ministers as they struggled to exercise 'imperial' functions. When the Company's executive proved unable to do so it became evident that the Government must. Moreover the force of administrative necessity began to be reinforced by the pressure of public indignation as Indian abuses were revealed by parliamentary investigations. A simple demand for a contribution to the Exchequer thus drew the Ministry and its successors step by step into a long scrambling contest with defiant nabobs who with their allies had stormed the Company's closet. It was in certain aspects a 'colonial' revolt in caricature. Caricature, because the rebels were defending stolen plunder and the facilities afforded by anarchy. But the revolt was also formidable and its consequences were profound. By rallying resistance in the name of chartered liberties the rebels were able for almost twenty years to obstruct the Government of the day in its uncertain efforts to provide decent government for an exploited native population. Yet the revolt of the nabobs forced an issue, and the cumulative result of the struggle which they precipitated was a revolutionary extension of state regulation and state responsibility.

The process by which an 18th-century State was impelled into interfering and gradually assuming control over a 'private' enterprise of national importance was chequered by false starts and cumbersome compromises. The complicated negotiations between Government and Company from 1766 to 1773 need not concern us here except to note the various pressures upon the Administration which conditioned the form and extent of their intervention.[47] In the first phase, which lasted from August, 1766, to June, 1767, the Chatham-Grafton Ministry was engaged in a wrangle with the Company over the revenue question. When Chatham's idea of a simple parliamentary *diktat* proved impracticable and his own nervous breakdown left a two-group Administration leaderless, Parliament lost much of its proper authority in dealing with an influential but subordinate organisation. The Chathamites, now led by Shelburne, and the Townshend group, drifting apart on American issues, also disagreed about the handling of the East India Company. While Townshend was all for avoiding trouble in order to secure as large a revenue contribution as possible, the former hoped to combine a financial settlement with some reform of the Company's constitution. In consequence the two groups frequently worked against each other in Company politics: if one backed the Directors and their following at a given juncture, the

---

[47] They have been analysed in detail by Dr. Lucy Sutherland (*op. cit.*), Chaps. VI-VIII.

other tended to support the Sulivan opposition. The split on the Government side was naturally exploited by the Rockingham and Grenville parties of the parliamentary Opposition. Defence of the Company was a profitable method of embarrassing the Administration, and each of the Opposition parties added to the confusion by backing different sides in the General Court.

In such circumstances it is not surprising that the Government's handling of the business in the Commons was 'pitiable'. A general enquiry into the affairs of the Company was launched without any terms of reference having been agreed in Cabinet; and when the matter came to issue in the House, Ministers (in the face of a united Opposition) openly contradicted each other on the extent and purpose of the enquiry. No planned enquiry was, in fact, possible at that time since Charles Townshend's eagerness to secure an Indian revenue made him hostile to any form of investigation which might jeopardise the business. The enquiry achieved nothing, but it started the long process of probing into Indian abuses which gradually enlightened and aroused public opinion.

Townshend's attitude needs to be related to the general background of imperial affairs. While the Chathamites advocated restraint in dealing with the recalcitrant Americans, Townshend made up his mind to ease his budget difficulties and to make political capital for himself by reviving the policy of colonial taxation. On 26 January, 1767, he astonished the House and his own colleagues by announcing his confident determination to raise a revenue in North America almost sufficient to defray the defence charges. A month later the Opposition groups made their own bid for popularity by carrying a motion for the reduction of the land-tax from 4/- to 3/- in the pound, thus reducing income by £500,000. Townshend thereupon threatened to withhold the budget unless Shelburne produced an American frontier scheme which would effect immediate and drastic economies. Since this was impracticable, ministerial anxiety to balance American expenditure with an Indian income became acute.[48]

Meanwhile the Directors of the Company and Sulivan on the opposition side of the General Court were putting forward a series of rival proposals, designed for the dual purpose of satisfying the Government with an allocation and the powerful group of speculators with a rising dividend. When in early May the dividend prospect began to look less promising, the speculators and their allies, the returned Company Servants, demonstrated their power and the extent to which they had subverted the Company's constitution by defying the Directors and carrying a resolution to raise the dividend to $12\frac{1}{2}$ per cent – the second rise within eight months.

---

[48] Cf. vol. I of this work, pp. 184-9.

The Johnstone group received their cut off the joint by a resolution which put a stop to the impending prosecutions of returned
Servants. The reaction of the Government to this piece of contumacy was swift and sharp. A Bill was introduced, despite all
protests and the open dissent of Townshend and Conway, preventing the Company from making any increase of dividend within the
next year without consent of Parliament.[49] The imposed restraint
was no more than a short-term emergency measure and was far
removed from any idea of equipping the Company with a constitution adequate for the discharge of its new territorial functions;
but the first step in State intervention had been taken.

In an attempt to escape the dividend restraint the Company had
committed itself (on 20 May) to an improved offer of a fixed annual
payment to the State of £400,000. The offer was accepted, but the
dividend Bill became law nonetheless. In consideration of the
stipulated payments the Company's right to its territorial acquisitions and revenues was confirmed but for two years only.[50] The
Directors suffered a further disappointment. In the petition to the
Commons conveying the offer a request had been made that Parliament should 'provide effectual methods' for recruiting the forces
needed to defend the Indian territories and for 'regulating the
Company's civil and military servants there'.[51] But a disintegrating Ministry was not interested. All such matters could be brought
into consideration in two years' time, perhaps by someone else. It
was assumed – wrongly, in fact – that the national exchequer could
now rely on an assured contribution of £400,000 a year. Alongside
that figure should be placed another. The Supplies granted by
Parliament in 1767 on account of American and other colonial
charges amounted to approximately £428,000.

From the Government point of view the Agreement of 1767
represented an adequate adjustment of relations between State and
Company; and there appeared to be no obvious reason why, with
suitable modifications from time to time, the arrangement should
not continue indefinitely. The principle of a general supervision
of the Company's financial policy had been established. Beyond
that point lay political dangers. The business of ruling Indian

---

[49] 7 *Geo. III, cap. 49.* Shortly afterwards another Act was passed which was
intended to check disorder in the General Court by requiring that stock-holders must
be in possession of the qualifying amount of stock for six months before becoming
eligible to vote. The intention was to prevent the abuse of splitting large holdings of
stock in order to create a *bloc* of temporary votes. Unfortunately the measure had
the effect of making matters worse. When the question at issue was thought to be
sufficiently important, large holders were prepared to risk splitting their stock for as
long as six months (instead of a few days or weeks as before), thus increasing the
ferocity of party strife and jeopardising the Company's financial stability and their
own. (See Sutherland, *op. cit.*, p. 182.)

[50] 7 *Geo. III, cap. 57.*

[51] See the Company's Petition, *Parl. Hist.*, vol. XVI, 344-6.

provinces was generally regarded as being too onerous a burden to be borne by the slender administrative framework of the State, and in any case the undertaking would involve a very substantial increase in Government patronage and so expose Administration to damaging attack at a vulnerable point. A watchful Opposition would jump at the chance of combining championship of chartered rights with denunciation of Crown influence. The alternative was to vest the Company's executive with the administrative and judicial authority which the new circumstances in India required. But here again the difficulties were formidable. Effective disciplinary powers in the hands of a strongly established Directorate was the last thing that corrupt Servants would accept, and any Administration which sponsored such reforms would encounter organised resistance in the General Court and in Parliament. A Chatham might have carried it with a high hand and compelling oratory: but not a Grafton or a North, and especially at a time when the American quarrel was moving steadily towards the catastrophe of war.

In January, 1769, after protracted negotiations, the Grafton Ministry renewed the Agreement with certain concessions to the Company for a further five years.[52] And then within a few months reality forced its way to the surface. The perilous situation of the Company as a political Power, induced by its internal weakness and instability, became increasingly apparent. In Bengal relations with neighbouring rulers became uneasy and Clive's dual system quickly collapsed under the well-intentioned but ineffective Verelst and his successor Cartier. Exhortations from the Directors were naturally unavailing when Servants in Calcutta understood that previous offenders were not only safe from prosecution but had also gained a compelling influence in the General Court; and when the Company's Service ignored the bounds set by Clive, the native administration under the nominal authority of the Nawab was helpless. When, therefore, the great famine of 1769-70 began, the anarchy in the administration immensely increased its horrors. The sufferings of the peasants were exploited by Company servants who made a corner in rice, selling it at high prices, and enforced the continued exaction of land-tax with cruel severity. It has been estimated that ten millions died, about a third of the total population.

At the same time other perils were accumulating in the South. Inside the Carnatic the Madras Presidency was dominant; but

---

[52] 9 Geo. III, cap. 24. The annual payment (in two half-yearly instalments) remained at £400,000, but with the proviso that this sum would be reduced pro rata with a reduction of dividend. If the latter fell to 6 per cent or below, all payment to the State was to lapse. As a further concession the Company was permitted to raise the dividend to a maximum of $12\frac{1}{2}$ per cent on condition that the increase did not exceed 1 per cent in any one year.

since there was no question of acquiring the *diwani*, exploitation by Company Servants was concentrated upon the treasury of the dependent ruler, as it had been in Bengal after Plassey. In Madras it was assuming a form which proved peculiarly injurious to the Company's authority. Muhammad Ali of Arcot, the titular ruler of the Carnatic, owed everything to the Company in more senses than one. Having been assessed in huge sums for the cost of the campaigns against the French which had placed him on the throne as the British nominee, he had begun to borrow from junior members of the Presidency, who found this method of investing their trading profits extremely lucrative. It also provided the Nawab with an increasingly valuable form of insurance against his own removal. The process continued in a geometrical progression until the Nawab and his creditors became indispensable to each other. It has been well said that Muhammad Ali corrupted the whole administration of the Presidency by his collusive financial dealings with Paul Benfield and his associates. The Arcot Creditors became a great vested interest, pressing the priority of their claims over those of the Company itself through a powerful organised group among the Proprietors. The Bengal rebels within the governing body began to receive a notable reinforcement. So much so that even Pitt in 1784 thought it wiser to compound the scandal rather than give the money-lenders their deserts.

The immediate danger from Madras, however, arose from its external relations. Across the frontiers of the Carnatic the Presidency was faced by three formidable Powers – Haidar Ali, who had usurped the throne of Mysore, the Nizam of Hyderabad, and the predatory Marathas. Instead of standing neutral and leaving these rivals to their private wars, as the Directors commanded, Madras persisted in taking sides and did so with such a combination of rashness and inconsistency that they incurred the enmity of all three. In 1768 they were obliged to sign a humiliating peace treaty with the Nizam, and in 1769 Haidar Ali dictated his own terms within sight of Madras itself. Their folly continued until it provoked the desperate crisis of 1780-1, when the Presidency was only saved from annihilation by the brilliant intervention of Warren Hastings from Bengal.

The Company's position in India was in jeopardy, undermined from within by gross abuses and from without by the hostility of Indian rulers needlessly incurred. Deterioration was moving steadily towards dissolution. Accordingly the march of events exerted unremitting and increasing pressure upon Ministers and Directors in London to take remedial action before it was too late.

The news that Haidar Ali was devastating the Carnatic, which reached London late in May, 1769, came at a time when reports were being received of a concentration of French forces in Mauritius. The prospect of a renewal of French intervention in India and at such a juncture was alarming. The first reaction was a panic flight from the Company's stock. Many were ruined, including the Chairman of the Court of Directors, Sir George Colebrook; and many others, like Laurence Sulivan, now Deputy-Chairman, were financially crippled. Leading men who were responsible for dealing with critical problems in India were distracted by personal misfortunes and the needs of distressed friends; the shock to public confidence sharpened the prevailing resentment against the Company in general. On the Government side the prospect of its agent becoming embroiled with a coalition of Indian Powers, perhaps aided and organised by the French, was so alarming that the Ministry made an abortive attempt, as will be seen, to establish its own separate direction of foreign affairs in India. Meanwhile the new Directorate (including Sulivan, who had at last fought his way back to office in the April election) was planning drastic action against the underlying menace of internal disorder in the Presidencies. Instructively they turned to the old device of a special commission to be sent out to India with plenipotentiary powers.

The terms of reference of the 'Superintending Commission' were as comprehensive as those previously issued for Clive and his colleagues. The three Commissioners were given authority to manage 'all the Business and Affairs' of the Company in India. All matters touching war and peace and all negotiations with Indian rulers were to be under their direction. They were to reorganise the revenue administration along such lines as they might deem to be 'just and necessary'. They were also given full power 'for correcting all Abuses and obtaining the necessary Reformation in the State of the Company's Affairs, as well Civil and Military, throughout India'; and to that end they were empowered to suspend or dismiss any President, member of Council, or military officer. The votes of two Commissioners were to prevail; and if one of the three died and there was disagreement between the other two, the decision of the senior was to be conclusive.[53]

Difficulties with the Government and dissensions over rival candidates delayed matters for almost three months, but they were finally resolved in September, and early in October Scrafton, Vansittart, and Forde set out on a mission which was intended to revolutionise the Company's management of its Indian affairs. After touching at the Cape of Good Hope, their ship, the frigate *Aurora,* was never heard of again. Yet, even if the Commissioners had survived to reach India, it is extremely doubtful whether they

---

[53] The text of the Commission, with comments thereon by Charles Yorke and Sir William de Grey, the Attorney-General (dated 10 and 17 Sept. respectively), are printed in *1st (Secret) Rept.*, vol. IV, pp. 12-14.

could have solved the problem. Draconian measures might have imposed a temporary discipline; but, as before, dismissed recalcitrants would have hastened home to become Proprietors. The Government had indeed promised Colebrooke and Sulivan to support legislation to arm the Company with judicial powers, but only a very resolute Government would have been prepared to run the political risks involved in provoking organised resistance in the General Court and in Parliament. And in any case the Directorate, under constant pressure, would have been a very uncertain instrument of justice.

The inability of the Grafton Ministry to sustain such a challenge had already been demonstrated. During the summer of 1769 the Administration had become less and less enamoured of the plan to send out a Company's Commission whose wide powers included the direction of policy in issues of war and peace. They disliked the fact that the Rockingham Opposition was using the selection of commissioners to consolidate the rival factions in the Company against ministerial influence; and they disliked still more the prospect of this uncontrolled 'Company' Commission handling a situation in South India which might well precipitate a major war. This aspect of the matter was underlined when the Directors asked for naval assistance. In his dealings with the Company, Lord Weymouth, Secretary of State, always insisted that in their *political* activities they must follow the directions of the Government which afforded them protection. Already in October, 1768, he had sharply reprimanded the Directors for contravening that rule by authorising a settlement off the Borneo coast without previous consultation.[54] In August, 1769, he attempted a drastic extension of this principle by threatening to withhold naval assistance unless the Commodore of the squadron, Sir John Lindsay, was included in the Commission.[55] A little later he went still further and declared that the Crown must have direct diplomatic relations with the Nawab of Arcot because his accession to the throne of the Carnatic had been formally recognised by Britain in the Treaty of Paris. In effect this amounted to a claim (which had the King's approval) that the Crown, and not the Company, should in future manage relations with 'Crowned Heads' in India. In Burke's phrase the General Court 'took fire' at this attempted invasion of their preserve: the ranks closed – to the great happiness of the parliamentary Opposition – and the Government was forced to retreat. A compromise was reached. Administration accepted the Company's choice of commissioners and approved the terms of their Commission. Lindsay was not included. While in India he was to

---

[54] See vol. I, pp. 86-8.
[55] Burke to Rockingham, 13 Aug., 1769. *Burke Correspondence* (Lond., 1844), vol. I, pp. 184-5.

act as the Crown's representative, but he must do no more than 'assist' the Company's Commissioners in matters affecting war and peace.[56]

The upshot could have been predicted. When Lindsay reached Madras, the Governor, Josias Du Pré, and the Council refused his request for assistance in delivering the King's letters to the Nawab of Arcot. Lindsay explained that 'the great object' of his mission was 'to maintain Peace in India agreeable to the express stipulation of the 11th Article of the Treaty of Paris', and he followed this up with a letter requesting in the King's name an account of all the transactions of the Company's servants with the Nawab since 1763. The request was refused. Governor and Council, however, admitted that the Carnatic was in a precarious situation and that they were very apprehensive of a war with the Marathas. Thereupon Lindsay besought them 'in the politest terms' for an account of the political state of the Country and offered 'the assistance of His Majesty's name and the sanction of his authority if they thought it could be of use in negotiating Treaties, or could contribute in effecting a permanent peace'. 'But,' reported Lindsay, 'they have totally refused to co-operate with me.' He then had recourse to the Nawab and assured him that if it should appear that the distresssed condition of his Country was due to 'the intrigues of any of His Majesty's Subjects', he could depend on the King's protection. He asked the Nawab for a full account of all his transactions with the Company's Servants, 'that His Majesty might be enabled to redress past evils as much as possible, and that measures may be taken to prevent the like for the future'. After some hesitation (for the Presidency did not fail to point out the ambiguity of Lindsay's status) astute Muhammad Ali disclosed enough to give the Ministry a pretty clear impression of what had been happening.[57] With that Lindsay had to be content. Weymouth's attempt to assume control over relations with Indian States had been defeated by resistance in London; and when a royal envoy in less ambitious terms had offered the services of the Crown as mediator, he (and the Crown) had been humiliated by the local 'settlers'.

The failure of Lindsay's mission, which became known to Ministers in March, 1771, did nothing to relieve the Government's uneasiness. They were becoming increasingly aware that the Com-

---

[56] A copy of Weymouth's secret instructions to Lindsay, dated 13 Sept., 1769, is in *Home Misc. Series*, vol. 101, ff. 1-11.

[57] Memorandum by Sir John Lindsay (copy in the King's handwriting), dated Madras, 13 October, 1770, and received 21 March, 1771. *Correspondence of Geo. III*, vol. III, pp. 236-9. Cf. 'Abstract of a letter from Sir John Lindsay at Madras' of the same date and also in the King's handwriting. (*Ibid.*, pp. 161-4.) In asking the Nawab to state his grievance against Company Servants, a step which went far beyond what had been agreed with the Directors, Lindsay was obeying private instructions (Weymouth to Lindsay, 13 Sept., 1769). (*Home Misc. Series*, vol. 101, f. 128, cited by Sutherland (*op. cit.*), p. 200.)

pany was dangerously entangled in Indian affairs and furthermore that its defences were inadequate to meet a major attack. This was a situation which threatened national security more obviously than did internal abuses in Bengal or the Carnatic, and yet effective supervision of the Company's external affairs also required a curtailment of the Company's functions by legislation. The new Administration under North, which had been constructed (in January, 1770) from the fragmentation of Grafton's Ministry, lacked the requisite quality and cohesion. Even so, drastic intervention of that order was not yet politically feasible. Against the entrenched forces of resistance in the General Court and Parliament an 18th-century Administration needed the propulsion of a major crisis and a roused public opinion. Although both of these were, in fact, taking shape by August, 1771, they were not yet manifest, and North clung to the hope that a collision could be avoided and that the Company would be capable of producing its own agreed scheme of reform which Parliament could accept as a basis for legislation.

In normal circumstances the prospect that the organised groups of returned nabobs in the Court of Proprietors would agree to measures subjecting them and their clients in India to discipline and judicial process would have been slight indeed. But in 1771-2 they had good reason for avoiding internal dissension and proceeding warily. The knowledge that the Company was heading for grave financial trouble was becoming public property, and a number of books and pamphlets were exposing the scandals of Bengal and Madras in lurid terms. Moreover the appointment of Warren Hastings as Governor of Bengal had been followed by the return to office of Laurence Sulivan as Deputy-Chairman. The close alliance between a great administrator on the spot, who was remodelling the revenue system and all that went with it,[58] and the plotter-statesman Sulivan, who was co-operating with the Ministry, offered an opportunity of reformation through joint Government-Company action which was unlikely to recur.

Sulivan's first efforts in this direction were inauspicious. In his view there were two priorities: strengthened military power in India and adequate judicial authority to discipline Company Servants. In 1770 and again in 1771 he promoted a Recruiting Bill in the Commons which was to give the Company wider powers in raising European troops for the defence of its territories. But on each occasion the Bill was lost through lack of the promised support from Government. The need was sufficiently evident and had been urged by Clive and others ever since the acquisition of the Bengal *diwani*; but the measure aroused little interest save that

---

[58] See pp. 73-86 below.

of jealousy, and the Ministry preferred to avoid possible trouble among its supporters by remaining passive.[59]

By January, 1772, however, public anger against the Company and its Servants was rising strongly, and North was impelled to hold out some expectation of remedial action. He did so by including a general assurance of intention in the Speech from the Throne at the opening of the new session. The concerns of the Country in remote places, it was stated, were so peculiarly liable to abuses and so exposed to dangers 'that the interposition of the legislature for their protection may become necessary'.[60] The words were misleading since they implied that the Government was about to take the initiative, whereas, in fact, North was leaving it to Sulivan to resolve all difficulties by producing and securing the Company's assent to a measure which Administration would then support in Parliament. The concentration of emphasis upon parliamentary 'interposition' in East Indian affairs in the King's speech and in the speeches supporting the Address of Thanks naturally conveyed the impression that the Ministry intended to introduce a far-reaching plan of its own, perhaps after a parliamentary enquiry.[61]

---

[59] The Bill of 1771 was lost in a thin House by 51 to 50. One of the arguments used against it was that the Company's higher rates of pay would injure recruitment for the regular army. Others argued that German and Irish Catholic recruits would be apt to desert and join the armies of Indian Princes; and when these two categories were excluded at the Committee stage, the opponents then argued that the Bill was worse than before since the whole of the annual recruitment (1,600 men) would now be drawn from England. The passage of the Bill seems to have been very desirable on humanitarian grounds alone. According to General Smith previous recruits had been 'the riff-raff of the people, chiefly boys under 17, or old men above 40 or 50 years old, and fitter at their arrival in India to fill the hospital than the ranks'; and the Speaker described the Company's methods of decoying these unfortunates as 'most infamous'. (Parl. Hist., vol. XVII, 169-173.)

[60] The point that the interests of the nation in the Far East might need 'protection' by the interposition of the Legislature reflected George III's attitude more closely than that of North. He had complimented North on the draft speech (6 Jan., 1772. Correspondence of Geo. III, vol. II, p. 309), and there may be a hint of the King's desire (explicitly stated in 1773) that North should take the bull by the horns and produce his own plan, when he remarked that the session looked like being an easy one and so would 'enable Administration to propose right measures, and not to postpone any from apprehension of difficulties'. (The King to North, ? Feb., 1772. Ibid., p. 310.) No other legislation had been foreshadowed in the King's Speech.

[61] In moving the Address Lord Hinchinbrooke said that 'whenever it shall be found that . . . such abuses prevail as expose them [the Indian settlements] to danger, we shall think it our duty to endeavour, by every regulation in our power, to remedy those evils . . .'. Mr. Vane, the Seconder, was rather more explicit, declaring 'that the malversation of the East India Company's servants called loudly for their interposition and that he trusted they would have an opportunity of displaying their legislative wisdom in adjusting these matters'. After citing a number of the accusations being levelled at the Company and its Servants, 'he hinted that at present the Company had not that power over their Servants, to compel their orders to be obeyed, nor to prevent them from enriching themselves in an arbitrary manner at the expence of the Company, ruin to the nation, and perhaps . . . the entire loss of those dominions to Great Britain'. (Parl. Hist., vol. XVII, 232-7.) Dr.

When there was no sign of a grand inquest, and when at the tail end of the session Sulivan's Judicature Bill made its appearance, angry members fell upon the measure, treating it, quite unfairly, as a ridiculous mouse not even produced by His Majesty's mountain. The collision which North had hoped to avoid was thrust upon him.

Sulivan's reforms were substantial, and many of them formed the basis for subsequent legislation. His Bill prohibited Governors and members of Councils under heavy penalties from engaging in any form of trade. They were to be administrative officers in receipt of large fixed salaries. All Servants were barred from the inland trade, and the Company's disciplinary powers were to be strengthened and given statutory force. The central feature of the scheme was a new judicial system in Bengal. The Mayor's Court in Calcutta, the personnel of which was notoriously ignorant and arbitrary, was to be replaced by a Court of Judicature, consisting of four judges, appointed by the Directors, sitting without a jury, and exercising jurisdiction throughout Bengal. In this Court Indian complainants could sue Europeans, although the latter could only sue Indians in the courts of the Nawab. The exclusion of the Presidency Governments from personal trading activities was, of course, essential, and the establishment of an independent judiciary in Bengal would be a valuable safeguard against oppression; but the determining factor was the governing body in London which was incapable of taking its own medicine. Dominated by a variety of subversive pressures, it could not of its mere motion transform itself into an impartial instrument of the rule of law. Until that was done, and it could only be done by some form of State intervention, institutional reforms in India would continue to be *verba et praeterea nihil*.

The behaviour of the North Administration at this juncture was very revealing. Since they did not intend to implement the promise in the King's Speech by promoting their own legislation, it was obviously important that reforms emanating from the Company should have been agreed beforehand with the Ministers of the Crown. When Sulivan in the Commons moved for leave to bring in his Bill (on 30 March), North indeed supported the motion but made the astonishing admission that he had not seen a copy

---

Sutherland has pointed out (*op. cit.*, p. 230) that Mr. Vane's speech ' made it clear that all the Government was recommending was the legislation designed to strengthen the control of the East India Company over its servants which Sulivan was working within the Company to procure '. But the House had been led to expect something very different. The marked contrast between the portentous pronouncements at the opening of the session and the limited action at second-hand which North intended probably reflects the divergence between his cautious attitude and that of his more fire-eating colleagues which emerged later.

of the measure, 'but only a sketch of it'.[62] In a later debate he maintained that it was 'much more proper' that a Bill should have been initiated by the Company than by Administration, and he gave the Sulivan Bill his general support; but he refused to accept responsibility for it, saying that a measure of such importance could not be expected to pass 'without many material alterations'. In short, the House was left to make its own decisions and with no evidence before it upon which to form a judgement. The real reason for this chaotic procedure was disagreement in the Cabinet, which Wedderburn, the Solicitor-General, was at no pains to conceal. At the Committee stage (on 18 May) Thurlow, the Attorney-General, and Wedderburn challenged the clause which provided that the judges in the new Court of Judicature were to be nominated by the Company. This, they insisted, was an inalienable prerogative of the Crown. A fundamental question of that sort should, of course, have been resolved in previous negotiation, and Sulivan, as the Company's spokesman, had no option but to declare that he must abandon the Bill altogether if it were so amended.

Thereupon Wedderburn lost, or made show of losing, his temper. To whom did 'the dictator of Leadenhall' think he was talking, and where? The Directors might be monarchs of an empire, but this was the House of Commons and not the Secret Committee at East India House. Sulivan, he continued, had apparently forgotten the terms upon which this Bill had been allowed to make 'so great a progress' in the House. No one in Administration had agreed to all its provisions, 'and it was tolerated on the footing only of its being capable of amendment'. Thurlow and he, as the Law Officers of the Crown, had been called, 'not to the birth, but to the christening of this foundling'. They had met and discussed it with the Directors at a tavern, and a jolly meeting it had been; but when with some difficulty he had subsequently seen a copy of the Bill, he had decided that he could not give his approval to the substance of it, and Sulivan was therefore not justified in associating his name with the measure. The hapless North was in a dilemma. He could not, he said, agree with the Solicitor-General in rejecting the Bill as a whole: even if they could not agree about

---

[62] While the Company was to formulate its own recommendations for internal reform, North seems to have hoped, like Grafton and Weymouth, that the Crown would be able to check abuses in India by assuming a controlling influence in defence and external affairs. On 29 Jan., 1772, a week after the opening of the session, he declared that the dispatch of a naval squadron to the East Indies had been necessary, 'not only to cope with the French, but to be a check upon the present officers of the Company, who for want of proper laws, disobeyed their masters, and and thereby as suddenly as exorbitantly, increased their own finances; a conduct which might hazard the loss of those dominions to this kingdom . . . and make the English hated by the people over whom they tyrannised'. (*Parl. Hist.*, vol. XVII, 241.)

this clause, there were many others 'which ought to pass'. On the other hand, he could not agree with Mr. Sulivan: it was essential that the nomination of the judges should be by the Crown. Having thus committed himself, he was at once accused of seeking to increase Crown patronage, 'already too powerful'. The nomination of a few judges would start a process which would grow, 'till it swallowed up all Bengal'. The Bill lingered on for a few more weeks and then died quietly with the close of the session in early June.

North's ambiguity in this business was only partly due to his chronic habit of postponing decisions. The Indian question had become politically dangerous. At the beginning of the session North was confronted by the awkward fact that public indignation had become too deeply roused to be ignored and yet this indignation lacked coherence for it covered widely different intentions. Many were genuinely moved by the lurid revelation of abuses in recent publications and looked to the Administration to initiate strong remedial action; others, like Alderman Beckford, represented the traditional dislike of the Company's restrictive monopoly, now reinforced by resentment against the ostentatious luxury of returned Company's Servants; and again others, while alert to defend the privileges of the Company and the influence of their friends within it, were determined to exploit the general anger in pursuing their personal vendetta against Clive on the floor of the House. Within the Ministry the Bedford group were pressing for a drastic assertion of governmental control in Indian affairs which would have split the Administration and alienated the 'nabobs'; and on the Opposition side the Rockinghams, under Burke's direction, were waiting to pounce as soon as it became possible to accuse North and his colleagues of seeking to increase the influence of the Crown at the expense of chartered rights.[63]

North had tried to extricate himself by getting the Indian problem dealt with in the Commons as a non-party issue. A reforming measure, produced by the Company itself, would take the wind out of the Opposition's sails and avoid the danger of a mutiny within the Cabinet. Introduced as a 'private member's bill' it could be debated and amended clause by clause on a free vote of the House. North's tactics were a fumbling attempt to evade ministerial responsibility. The idea of leaving a divided and inexpert House to hammer out its own policy could have no other result but irrita-

---

[63] Cf. John Macpherson to Warren Hastings, Madras, 12 Oct., 1772. 'The Cabinet are not unanimous as to India Measures. Lord North is afraid to meddle, without doing so effectually. The Bedford people and Grafton wish him to interfere – that he might stand the danger of breaking the Ice and they reap the Advantage, and then tumble him from his seat . . . Opposition were watching Administration on Indian Affairs. If the Company is attacked, they support her.' *Hastings Papers, Addit. MSS.*, 29, 133, f. 261.

tion and confusion. Instead of the expected Government measure, which would have afforded the opportunity (eagerly awaited) for a grand inquest into Indian affairs, came Sulivan's Bill, ill-supported, suspect, and introduced towards the tail-end of the session. On 13 April (three days before the Bill had its First Reading) General Burgoyne captured the mood of the House by moving for a Select Committee of thirty-one to engage in a comprehensive enquiry into the condition of the Company and of British affairs in India. The members were to be chosen by ballot and should continue to sit during the summer recess. The intention, he declared, was not to throw all the Company's affairs into the hands of the Crown. 'I only contend, that if by some means sovereignty and law are not separated from trade . . . India and Great Britain will be sunk and overwhelmed, never to rise again '.[64] The motion was carried without a division.

So began the long series of investigations which provided Parliament with a vast accumulation of printed evidence. In the process, men such as Jenkinson, Robinson and later Dundas acquired expert knowledge which enabled them to become the principal architects of British rule in India. Burgoyne's Select Committee worked hard (or, at least, some of them did) in this unfamiliar field; but they lost their way in a wilderness of paper, and no vestige of a constructive plan emerged. It was easy enough for Burgoyne to state the necessity of separating the exercise of sovereignty from the pursuit of trade, and indeed the problem of 'an empire within an empire' could no longer be evaded. But any movement in the direction of aggrandising the Crown at the expense of chartered privilege would be fraught with political hazards. In the circumstances of the time only a strong and united Ministry, skilfully led, could so enlarge the power and patronage of the State; and even they would probably find it expedient to placate the 'Indian' rebels and their allies with unpalatable concessions. Charles Fox was to learn that lesson too late and to his lasting cost and the younger Pitt in time and to his profit. Ironically enough, English politicians of the late 18th century were called upon to establish centralised control in Indian affairs while accepting an unprecedented devolution regarding the affairs of North America. It is not surprising that many of them condemned the dichotomy as illogical.

In Indian affairs economic necessity provided the compulsion. The imminent threat of financial collapse on the part of the Company finally compelled the North Administration to intervene,

---

[64] *Parl. Hist.*, XVII, 435-9. North supported the motion for a Select Committee, saying that he would have been for it ' the first day of the session, as he always thought it the most proper mode ', an observation which drew the following retort from Col. Barré: ' The noble lord told us that, in the beginning of the session, he was in confusion: confusion, in the middle too we are in, and in confusion we shall end . . .' (*Ibid.*, 461).

and, having intervened, to establish some form of state control in order to prevent the recurrence of a menace to the national economy. That the Company would have difficulty in meeting its monetary obligations had been fairly widely known since the summer of 1771. Fearing a catastrophic fall in the stock price, the Directors decided to run the risk of maintaining the dividend at the permitted maximum of $12\frac{1}{2}$ per cent, while trying to weather the period of stringency by means of short-term loans. But the Company was no longer a purely commercial concern, facing a temporary unbalance between trading receipts and expenditure. Until the crisis was upon them, even the Directors were unaware of the magnitude of the commitments with which the Company was being saddled on the security of the territorial revenues. Economic depression in Bengal, followed by a terrible famine, had diminished the revenue at a time when undisciplined Company Servants were putting increasingly insupportable burdens upon it.[65] The mounting obligations could only be met by a correspond-ing (and impracticable) increase in the sale of Indian goods in London. Early in June, 1772, London was hit by a severe financial crisis, which temporarily paralysed credit and brought the impend-ing collapse of the East India Company into immediate prospect. As Treasury officials examined the Company's accounts during August and September, it gradually became apparent that the trouble was too deep-seated to be rectified by a loan and other short-term expedients which the Directors urged. On 22 September the latter could no longer conceal the true situation and recom-mended the postponement of the half-yearly dividend. At once the price of the Company's stock tumbled and angry panic reigned. Early in October North agreed that the intervention of the legis-lature had become necessary: the recess was curtailed; and Parlia-ment reassembled on 26 November to deal with the situation.

To what extent and by what means should the State intervene? In the debates North asserted the principle that all territorial rights acquired by British subjects automatically vested in the Crown, but he also made it clear that there was no immediate intention of assuming direct administrative control.[66] He at once moved for the appointment of a Secret Committee to examine and

---

[65] These may be grouped under three heads: (i) exorbitant expenditure on for-tifications, frequently used to conceal malversation; (ii) excessive buying of goods for the 'investment' by swelling the Bonded Debt in India; (iii) even more excessive remission at home of private fortunes by Bills of Exchange which had to be met in London by the Company from the proceeds of its sales. When these bills mounted while sales slowed down, the situation became dangerous. For the year 1771 alone the Company was made liable for Bills of Exchange amounting to £1,063,067 (while the permitted maximum was £200,000) and the total for the years 1771-73 was £1,578,000. *Parl. Hist.*, vol. XVII, 677, and Sutherland (*op. cit.*), p. 226 and Chap. VIII *passim*.

[66] *Parl. Hist.*, vol. XVII, 803 and 832.

report on the Company's financial situation and the management of its affairs. An enquiry of this sort by a strong team could be expected to furnish the essential data which the Government needed in order to determine the nature and extent of the assistance required from the Exchequer and to frame safeguarding regulations against a repetition of the crisis. It could also extract from the Company's ledgers and correspondence detailed information to elucidate the complicated problems connected with revenue collection, defence and political relations in Bengal. But it was not competent to work out a constitutional and administrative plan for the future, involving as it would the issue of state control. As before, North hoped that the Company could be induced to produce its own scheme of reform, this time under the pressure of financial need; but the Directors were themselves divided and had lost control over the angry and recalcitrant Proprietors. No effective help was forthcoming from that quarter. Moreover he had to reckon with George III who was highly incensed by the contumacy as well as the 'rapine' of his subjects in Leadenhall Street and Bengal and was all for drastic action.

The King had been impatient over the cautious reference to the Company in the Speech from the Throne,[67] and he had warned North on the day before Parliament met that 'any wavering now' would be 'disgraceful' to North personally and destructive to the public good. On the following day he wrote again, urging North to be prepared with a plan of his own in case the Company failed to produce acceptable terms. ' If you are open to their ideas nothing will be done, for everyone will have schemes incompatible with those of the others you may consult.'[68] The King was, of course, right, but he over-simplified the problem and does not appear to have realised, as North did, how ignorant and inadequate the Government was in approaching the complexities of Indian affairs.

The First Minister relied on the Secret Committee to produce the required information; and when it became obvious that the Government must itself devise a constitutional plan, he turned to the shrewd and reliable Jenkinson. As a Treasury expert the latter had already secured useful statistics from the Directors when they had applied for a loan during the summer, and these furnished a basis for the investigation. The formal chairman of the Committee was Alderman Harley, but Jenkinson was the directing member

---

[67] In its final form the passage read: ' When, therefore, I received information of the difficulties in which that Company appear to be involved, I determined to give you an early opportunity of informing Yourselves fully of the true state of their affairs, and of making such provisions for the common benefit and security of all the various interests concerned, as you shall find best adapted to the exigencies of the case.' *Parl. Hist.*, vol. XVII, 517-18.

[68] The King to North, 25 and 26 Nov., 1772. *Corr. of Geo. III*, vol. II, pp. 407 and 408.

and prepared the famous nine reports which were successively presented to Parliament between 7 December, 1772, and 30 June of the following year.[69] The production within about seven months of these documentary collections with comment was a very considerable feat of skilful selection and intensive labour. To some extent they overlap with the reports of Burgoyne's Select Committee, which continued its own omnibus enquiries in the new session; but they are better planned and more closely related to administrative problems. They afford a very valuable exposé of the Company's economic structure and the cumulative abuses which had brought on the crisis. On the basis of this information Jenkinson, with the aid of John Robinson and other Treasury officials, planned the Loan Act which provided the Company with an Exchequer grant of £1,400,000 on stringent though not unreasonable conditions.[70] From the same source Jenkinson derived a working knowledge of the Company's administrative system at home and overseas.

The Bill which gradually took shape during the winter months of 1772-3 was compiled from a number of different sources, but the editor-in-chief, so to speak, was Charles Jenkinson. In a letter to him some years later Burke wrote: 'I know you to be remarkably conversant in India affairs and that you had taken a leading part in the Act for altering the constitution of the Company and establishing the Interference of the King's Government in their affairs by enacting that the most capital part of their affairs shall be regularly laid before the Ministers.'[71] The basic questions about the extent and method of state supervision were, of course, for Cabinet decision; but in this, as in so many other matters, North leaned heavily on Jenkinson's knowledge, judgement and enormous capacity for hard work. During the next nine years the latter acted as an informal Minister for India Affairs with John Robinson in the role of Under-Secretary. Indeed without the wide-ranging labours of these two men it is difficult to see how the machinery of government under the North Administration could have avoided collapse.

By early March the outline of the Bill had been agreed in Cabinet, for on 15 March General Caillaud wrote to the anxious Hastings to tell him that he had seen a draft and giving him an accurate summary of its main provisions.[72] On 3 May North introduced Resolutions in the Commons indicating the lines of the

---

[69] Drafts of parts of the Reports, some in Jenkinson's own handwriting, are to be found scattered among the Liverpool Papers.

[70] *13 Geo. III, cap. 64.*

[71] Burke to Jenkinson, undated copy but probably Aug. or Sept., 1780. *Addit. MSS.*, 38,404, f. 202.

[72] John Caillaud to Warren Hastings, 15 March, 1773, London. *Addit. MSS.*, 29,133, f. 443.

intended legislation, and on 18 May presented the Bill itself. The King grudgingly acquiesced in the plan as a minimum first instalment of Government control.

Before considering the contents of the Bill, it will be worth while to examine the process of compilation, noting particularly what Jenkinson and North rejected from the medley of proposals submitted. Suggestions began to come in as soon as the session opened. 'A variety of plans were brought forward and submitted to the consideration of Government,' some by Company Servants and others by men of political experience at home; but most of the proposals, we are told, were concerned with particular points rather than with 'a general system'.[73] As Jenkinson sifted this miscellany and gradually constructed a Bill in consultation with North, a course had to be steered between contrary currents. On the one hand, public indignation against the Company and its arrogant Servants reinforced the views of the King and the more aggressive members of the Ministry who favoured strong-arm methods. But against that was the administrative weakness of Whitehall and the political danger of playing into the hands of Opposition by proposing a further increase in the influence of the Crown at the expense of a chartered corporation. The outcome was a carefully balanced compromise.

Under the mistaken impression that the extremists in the Government were about to triumph, Sulivan approached North himself through a friendly intermediary with a scheme of his own which included substantial concessions. But North refused to advance so far along the path of intervention, and the proposals were rejected. Sulivan reported his efforts and their failure to his ally, Warren Hastings.

From a Conviction that the Bedford Party . . . wish'd to act with great violence, I very early convey'd my ideas to the Fountain head – they were these – a permanent Direction – the right of voting [as a Proprietor] extended from 6 to 12 Mo^s. – no Judges – the Mayor's Court, if practicable, to be made more independent – the Crown to have one person in our Council at Bengall – another in the Direction at home, privileg'd as Inspectors: to sit in all Committees without a voice – the Gov^t and Council to be made amenable to Parliam^t, and this I consider'd as giving the Legislature complete constitutional control.[74]

---

[73] John Bruce, *Historical Views of Plans for the Government of British India* . . . (Lond., 1793), p. 55. This work, which was published anonymously in 1793, was compiled from official sources on the instructions of Henry Dundas as a digest of the various proposals which had been previously put forward for regulating Indian affairs. Bruce had been Professor of Moral Philosophy at Edinburgh and tutor to Dundas's son (C. H. Philips, *The East India Company, 1784-1834*, Manchester, 1940, p. 72).

[74] Sulivan to Hastings, 13 Oct., 1773. *Addit. MSS.*, 29,134 (Hastings Papers), f. 69.

Subject to this last condition, he added a revolutionary suggestion – one which Hastings himself had been urging in private
letters. Immersed in the enormous task of constructing a decent
and orderly system for Bengal, Hastings had become convinced that
he could only ensure lasting stability if he were given a lengthy
term of office and a 'discretionary power' to over-rule his Council
in 'urgent and extraordinary cases'. He should also be authorised
to veto nominations and to dismiss in civil appointments. Only by
such a concentration of authority, he argued, would it be possible
to maintain vigour and efficiency.[75] Taking his cue, Sulivan proposed that the man on the spot should be made directly responsible
to Parliament – and then be trusted.

Knowing that the creation of a Governor-Generalship was
already 'a fix'd, favourite point with Government', he urged that
Hastings in that office should be given emergency powers similar
to those vested in the Dutch Governor-General in Batavia and so
be able to assert an over-riding authority in any of the Presidencies
in the event of a crisis. 'I borrowed my ideas,' wrote Sulivan, 'not
only from reading, but [from] an instance which will never leave
my memory – it was this: The Dutch deposit all power with their
Governor-General to be exercised as he thinks fit. When he assumes
the Dictator a certain habit [i.e. uniform] with a Truncheon pro-
claims his office . . . but alas your new System must have no less
than 5 Truncheons . . . I contended to give absolute power *to you*
alone – I failed.'[76] The Dutch precedent was apt enough and was also
cited by Sir John Dalrymple in a scheme which he submitted
directly to the King. The Governor, he proposed, should have 'the
executive power' and his Council should be consultative.[77]

At no stage, however, can there have been any prospect that the
Government would be prepared to entrust the chief executive
officer in India with such discretionary powers. The colonial
tradition, as we have seen, was to curb the Governor by requiring
him to function by and with the assent of his Executive Council,
and that principle was maintained even under the Quebec Act of
1774, which in other respects represented a drastic break with
tradition.[78] The contrary principle of trusting the man on the spot
with authority commensurate with his responsibilities was eventually adopted in the time of Cornwallis, but only after some
thirteen years of further trial and error. Furthermore, Hastings as

[75] Sir Keith Feiling, *Warren Hastings* (Lond., 1934), pp. 103-4.

[76] Sulivan to Hastings, 20 Dec., 1774. *Addit. MSS.*, 29,135, f. 401.

[77] 'Such a Scheme for Bengal as the Proprietors would probably consent to.'
Endorsed: 'R. 21 Decr 1772 from Sir John Dalrymple.' *Corr. of Geo. III*, vol. II,
pp. 418-22.

[78] See Instructions to Governor Carleton, 3 Jan., 1775, para. 2. (*Documents
relating to the Constitutional History of Canada, 1759-1791*, ed. Short and Doughty,
Ottawa, 1918 edn., p. 595.)

the holder of the new post of Governor-General was a Company man, responsible in the first instance to the Directors, although formally nominated by the King in Parliament.[79] It must have seemed obvious, therefore, that the management of Indian affairs should be controlled by a majority of Government nominees in his Council.[80] The psychological inferno which developed in the Bengal Council Chamber as the result of the protracted duel between Hastings and Francis was not, of course, foreseen.

While North and Jenkinson planned to exercise a powerful influence in India, they shrank from involving the Government in any form of dual control in London. Clive proposed that they should. In a useful but discursive memorandum which he sent in just before Parliament assembled he suggested that two Directors should be nominated by the Crown, who would be members *ex officio* of all standing committees, 'but precluded from filling any of the chairs'. A connexion between 'the executive Government' and the Company, argued Clive, had become necessary, for the latter was not competent to deal with political measures, while the former was not qualified to manage commercial matters. A joint authority was needed because trade and revenue administration were too closely interwoven to be handled separately, and it would be 'more constitutional than the appointment of a controuling power on the part of the State'. [81] It will be noted that this

---

[79] Numerous candidates were pushed for the Governor-Generalship, but Jenkinson afterwards admitted that he had been 'very much prejudiced in favour of Mr. Hastings and by my influence in the Secret Committee on Indian Affairs I contributed greatly to spread his Reputation'. Jenkinson to General Clavering, 13 Dec., 1776. *Addit. MSS.*, 38,306, f. 102.

[80] Cf. Sulivan's comment: 'Yet even with harmony in your Council (so much to be desired), your task is extremely arduous. Scripture says its impossible to serve two Masters, unhappily the Legislative [*sic*] and the Company are in direct opposition – you are responsible to both – we know the safest side and who must conquer.' (Sulivan to Hastings, 8 Dec., 1773, *ut supra*.)

[81] A detailed summary of Clive's memorial (which was dated 24 Nov., 1772) is printed in *Historical View of Plans . . . (ut supra)*, pp. 55-69. Between May and November, 1771, a number of tentative approaches had been made to Clive through his friend Wedderburn, the Attorney-General, with a view to obtaining his advice on a plan for Indian affairs. On 29 Oct., 1771, Wedderburn reported that North had expressed 'the strongest wish' to receive instruction from Clive upon the subject; but no meeting with North or other Ministers seems to have taken place. When in the following year Clive came under heavy fire in Parliament for his conduct in India, he ceased to be a possible consultant, even though he was now a political supporter. At an interview with North early in November, 1772, the Minister, Clive reported, 'seemed industriously to avoid entering upon the subject of India affairs'. 'I do verily believe,' he added, 'from sheer indolence of temper, he wishes to leave everything to Providence and the Directors.' He had, however, submitted a 'political paper' to North, and this together with 'a sketch of my ideas' was the basis of the memorial of 24 November which his friend, Strachey, drafted for him. (See letters printed in Malcolm, *Life of Clive*, Lond., 1836, vol. III, pp. 265-72, 303-5.) Apart from one or two general principles and the establishment of the Governor-Generalship, very few of Clive's proposals are reflected in the Regulating Act.

proposal is very similar to that of Sulivan, Clive's arch-enemy. Sir John Dalrymple went further still and proposed that half the Directors should be appointed by the Crown to hold office 'during pleasure'. Theoretically there was much to be said for the idea of a joint authority: it would have been less cumbersome than the subsequent device of a Board of Control. But in the prevailing circumstances the Crown representatives would have been either passive observers or, if masterful, the focus of violent dissensions. North and Jenkinson were firm believers in the efficacy of rule through influence.

Such then were some of the numerous suggestions submitted to Government and the nature of the response which they evoked. It now remains to take note of the positive decisions incorporated in the Act.[82] The general line was to avoid a collision with the Company at the centre, while imposing a form of 'royal' government in India. Even so, the provision in the Bill that the Governor and Council in Bengal were to be nominated by the Crown instead of the Company was hotly contested at the Committee stage in a 'seven hours' altercation.[83] This was rightly regarded as crucial since the Bengal executive was to become the central instrument of policy in India, exercising authority over the other Presidencies in matters of defence and external relations. The ostensible compromise by which the Governor-General and Council of four was to comprise three 'royal' and two 'Company' representatives must have appeared at the time to be a substantial victory for the Government, affording a reliable means of maintaining control, for, as already noted, the Governor-General could not over-ride a majority decision in Council; and if Hastings resigned or died during the five-year period, his successor was to be one of the royal nominees.[84]

The authority of the Crown was also imposed in the field of 'colonial' legislation by extending the royal prerogative of disallowance to all ordinances passed by the Governor-General and Council for the regulation of the Bengal factories. All such ordinances were to be transmitted to a Secretary of State for submission to the King, who was authorised to signify disapprobation within two years of their issuance under the Sign Manual: a form of exercising the prerogative which did not pass without criticism.[85]

---

[82] 13 Geo. III, cap. 63.

[83] Parl. Hist., vol. XVII, 891.

[84] 'The Crown,' noted Sulivan, 'has carefully preserv'd a Majority. The Comp^y having (the) Govr Genl and Mr Barwell, and the other line Genl Clavering, Monson, and Mr Francis. The Succession also well secur'd, Genl Clavering following you, and Monson next.' Sulivan to Hastings, 13 Oct., 1773. Addit. MSS., 29134, f. 69.

[85] Parl. Hist., XVII, 914. The normal procedure for colonial laws was to submit them to the Board of Trade, who, after consulting their own legal advisers and the Law Officers (and where necessary the Departments concerned), reported to the Privy Council. The final decision was promulgated in an Order by the King in Council.

An appeal might be made by any individual to the Privy Council against an ordinance within sixty days of its publication either in India or London.

The intervention of the State in Indian affairs was further marked by the establishment of a Supreme Court of Judicature in Bengal, the Chief Justice and the three other members of which were to be appointed by the Crown. The purpose of this tribunal, which superseded the corrupt and inefficient Mayor's Court in Calcutta, was to put 'teeth' into the elaborate provisions of the Act (largely borrowed from Sulivan's Bill) against abuses by Company Servants.[86] Analogous in purpose to the Tudor Court of Requests, it was to hear and determine complaints of crimes or oppressions against any British subjects resident in Bengal, Bihar or Orissa, as well as any civil actions brought against them or against any other person who at the time was 'directly or indirectly' in the service of the Company. The unforeseen effect of this last provision was to bring within the jurisdiction of the Court, with its alien law and procedure, a wide range of Hindus and Muslims, including important officials and landlords, who, because they collected revenue, could be said to be indirectly in the Company's service.[87] Unaware of the complexities, the British Government and people were becoming involved for the first time in the problem which arises when their own *corpus* of law impinges upon the customary law of a different culture.[88]

The primary purpose in establishing a Supreme Court on the spot was to provide effective protection for the native population against oppression, but when British subjects were brought within the discipline of a royal court permanently established in Calcutta, a large breach was made in the Company's *imperium*. Moreover the Court of King's Bench in London was empowered to call by

---

[86] They may be summarised as follows: (i) no person employed in any office in India to be eligible for election as a Director until after two years' residence in England; (ii) the Governor-General, the members of his Council, the judges of the Supreme Court, forbidden to engage in any form of private trade; (iii) all Company Servants concerned in revenue collection or the administration of justice, and their agents, debarred from private trade outside Calcutta; (iv) no person holding civil or military office under the Crown or the Company to receive any gift or gratuity; (v) any British subject in India convicted of receiving more than 12 per cent on a loan to forfeit treble the value of the capital and to be liable to imprisonment at the discretion of the Supreme Court; (vi) no one dismissed or having resigned from the Company's service to engage thenceforth in any form of trade in India without special licence.

[87] Hastings had, however, expressed his alarm to the Directors and to Lord Mansfield about persistent reports of 'an unadvised system' of law for Bengal being compiled at home and had urged that the way to rule Indians 'with ease and moderation' was through their own law and customs. (Feiling, *op. cit.*, p. 103.) He had advocated the retention on a reformed basis of the Mayor's Court in Calcutta instead of a new Court of Judicature with extensive jurisdiction. But his proposals, in this as in other respects, had been ignored.

[88] Cf. Sir C. Ilbert, *The Government of India* (Oxford, 1907 edn.), pp. 41-55.

writ of *mandamus* for the examination of witnesses and the transmission of their sworn proceedings under seal; and in case of parliamentary proceedings regarding offences in India the Lord Chancellor and the Speaker of the House of Commons were similarly authorised to call for evidence by warrant. A broad foundation was laid even though certain parts of it were shaky and uncertain. The consequential task of establishing an uncorrupt professional administration in the Indian Presidencies preceded, and may perhaps have stimulated, a similar process at home.

The assertion of a controlling influence in London was more difficult and was, of course, the crux of the problem, for unless it was achieved a defiant Court of Proprietors would remain the ultimate masters of the situation. The King and the Bedford group would, no doubt, have welcomed the imposition of direct ministerial control on the confident assumption that a parliamentary majority was assured and that an insolvent Company would be unable to resist; but North and his trusted advisers, Jenkinson and John Robinson, were more cautious. The governing body was not overtly subordinated to Government but rendered amenable to its influence. The Court of Proprietors, as the elective assembly, was tamed by being reconstituted, and the new method of electing Directors went far towards ensuring a compliant executive.

The qualification for a Proprietor's vote was raised from £500 to £1,000 of stock which was to be held for twelve, instead of six, months before the shareholder was enfranchised. The primary purpose of this long-advocated reform was to check the artificial creation of voting support before an election by temporary stock-splitting, but it had the further effect of disenfranchising 1,600 Proprietors and thus reducing the General Court to an oligarchy. And this trend was greatly accentuated by a proposal, moved by Rose Fuller at the Committee stage and incorporated in the Bill, for a system of plural voting. A Proprietor with £3,000 of stock was given two votes at any election or ballot: a holder of £6,000 of stock three votes, and of £10,000 four votes.[89] The combined effect was to render stock-splitting no longer worth while, but the voting power was now so concentrated that the 'managers' for the Government were able to exercise a powerful influence. Yet it was

---

[89] It is surprising that so fundamental an alteration in the Company's constitution should have been adopted by Government at the instance of a private member and almost as an afterthought. It is stated in the *Parliamentary History* (XVII, 891) that Rose Fuller's proposal was ' over-ruled ', but it was, in fact, included in the statute. The explanation may be that North had second thoughts and adopted the amendment later in the Committee stage. Although the comment of Sir Francis Sykes, that the Bill was so undigested and inconsistent that it was ' cut and hacked all to pieces ' in the Commons, was prejudiced and inaccurate, there was a fierce struggle in Committee. ' Almost each sentence of the Bill afforded a topic for censure; clause by clause was disputed ' (see Sykes to Warren Hastings, 8 Nov., 1773, *Addit. MSS.*, 29,134, f. 121, and *Parl. Hist.*, vol. XVII, 890).

not a consistently commanding influence. As in the case of the Parliament of Ireland the organised ranks of Government supporters in the General Court were apt to disintegrate in a crisis when the wishes of Adminstration became too unpopular and too much in conflict with self-interest. ' Management ', whether at Westminster, Dublin, or East India House, was an irritating and exhausting business and of limited reliability.

The power of the General Court was further weakened by rendering its control of the Directors, the Company's ' Cabinet ', more remote and indirect. Before the Company became a territorial Power the choice of Directors had been largely determined by seniority and specialised experience: an agreed ' House List ' was frequently elected *en bloc*. But when the Court of Proprietors was transformed by an invasion of nabobs and their nominees, the annual election of the whole Directorate afforded full play to faction and feud. It clearly tended, states the Preamble to the Act, ' to weaken the Authority of the Court of Directors and to produce Instability in the Councils and Measures of the said Company '. It was now provided that the twenty-four Directors should hold office for four years, six retiring (and not being immediately re-eligible) each year. The election of only a quarter of the whole at any one time could not greatly influence policy and in fact aroused little interest. Under this arrangement the Chairman and Deputy-Chairman would be in a position to develop long-term plans, and the Ministry could be reasonably confident of securing the election of men who would be co-operative.

The Directors were required by the Act to transmit to Government all correspondence from India within fourteen days of its arrival. Authenticated copies of such parts as related to the management of the revenues were to go to the Treasury, while those relating in any way to ' the Civil or Military Affairs and Government of the said Company ' were to be sent to a Secretary of State. On the face of it this provision amounted to no more than that the Ministry was to see the incoming reports but was not even to be informed about the outgoing decisions. In practice, however, it proved to be of considerable importance. The Government was no longer in the dark. There are indications that the hard-working Treasury official, John Robinson, discussed the letters from India with North and Jenkinson and acquired as the Government spokesman some influence with the Directors in drafting the replies.[90]

Because the Regulating Act was quickly followed by the American Revolution and a desperate war, it stood as an instrument of government for eleven years, which was neither the intention nor the expectation of its authors. North regarded it as no more than a

---

[90] See, for example, Robinson to Jenkinson, 23 Oct., 1777. *Addit. MSS.*, 38,209, f. 180.

first tentative step in a progression of experiment. It is accordingly unfair to judge the measure, as is frequently done, as though it represented the whole and the best that North and his advisers were capable of contriving. In moving on 9 March the Resolutions which indicated the terms of the proposed loan to the Company, North remarked that, if they were accepted, 'we shall then have an opportunity, session after session, of making ourselves . . . thorough masters of East India affairs'.[91] By so educating themselves they would be enabled to select only such plans as would alleviate past and prevent future misfortunes. In his final speech on the Regulating Bill (10 June) he declared that, if its provisions did not afford a thorough remedy for existing evils, 'the House might still go on to correct and amend by future regulations'.[92] George III likewise assumed that the Act was a first instalment which would be elaborated by supplementary legislation based upon an annual parliamentary scrutiny.[93] In sum, the subordination of the other Presidencies in their external affairs to a Governor-General in Calcutta, who was himself to be controlled by a Crown-appointed majority in his Council, the establishment of a Crown-appointed Supreme Court to discipline the European population in the Bengal Presidency, the reduction of the General Court of the Company to a 'manageable' oligarchy, and the strengthening of the Company's executive while subjecting it to the scrutiny of Administration, represented a substantial degree of state intervention. Many unforeseen defects became apparent in the operation of the Act; but in view of the prevailing prejudices and governmental inexperience in Indian affairs, it seems improbable that any Administration at that time could have moved further into this novel and difficult field.

4. WARREN HASTINGS AND PHILIP FRANCIS

At noon on 19 October, 1774, General Sir John Clavering, Colonel George Monson, and Mr. Philip Francis came ashore at Fort William and walked (with offended dignity) the short distance to Government House where Warren Hastings and a company of senior officials awaited them. The atmosphere of suspicion and

---

[91] *Parl. Hist.*, vol. XVII, 805.

[92] *Ibid.*, 903.

[93] ' I trust that with a constant inspection of those Affairs Parliament may yet avert the ruin to which the Company has nearly been plunged into . . .' Later he wrote: ' I received the draught of the Bill which seems to me to be as perfect as the first attempt of redressing the dreadful evils that the rapacity of individuals have [sic] occasioned, and by annual additions may in the end in some degree curb if not eradicate what otherwise must render that trade the ruin . . . of this Country.' (The King to North, 9 March and 3 May, 1773. *Corr. of George III*, vol. II, pp. 458-9, 479-80.) The implication seems to be that total eradication of abuses was impossible until the State assumed complete control.

hostility which pervaded the gathering must have turned the subsequent banquet into a stiff and uncomfortable occasion. Next day the three newcomers met Hastings and Richard Barwell in Council, and the ensuing wrangle indicated clearly enough that a majority opposition was already consolidated.

It was not that the North Administration had planned to overthrow Hastings.[94] On the contrary Jenkinson had been instrumental in securing his nomination as Governor-General. But that office had been created for the purpose of curbing the dangerous irresponsibility of Madras and Bombay and establishing centralised control over the Company's external relations in India. This was a field of national interest in which the Crown, as we have seen, had striven to impose its authority and without success. Since, therefore, the President and Council of Bengal were now to wield the additional powers of a Governor-General in Council, it was all the more needful in the eyes of the Home Government that theirs should be the prevailing influence at the Council Board.

The method by which the three members of Council who were to operate this delicate function were selected was symptomatic of the political and social structure of 18th-century England. Clavering was a brave and experienced soldier, closely associated with political supporters of the Court and highly regarded by George III who had already bestowed upon him marks of the royal favour.[95] He was also choleric, prickly on matters of status, and rather stupid. The King pressed his claims insistently, even against strong parliamentary support for another military man, General Monckton. Clavering was nominated second in Council, the designated successor to the Governor-Generalship during the five-year period of the Act, and (at his own insistence) Commander-in-Chief of all the Company's troops in India. An honest soldier, thus equipped, could surely be relied on to stand no nonsense from rapacious officials or insubordinate officers. But more was now required in Bengal than the hand of a disciplinarian. Such a man in the intricate problems involved in governing an alien and heterogeneous society was out of his depth. Monson was in many ways a smaller edition of Clavering. A good soldier with the 'right' sort of social and political connexion, he was viewed by the King with an apprais-

---

[94] On 8 June, 1773, the King had written to North: 'If any of the Council at Bengal have acted in conjunction with Mr. Hastings, the naming one of them will be right; but if otherways, I can see no reason for putting he who has done his duty, and those who have not on a foot.' In other words, Hastings, who was recognised as having done his duty, should be supported by one member of the old Council if an honest one could be found. North replied: 'It is thought also to be right not to discourage the Gentlemen at present there too much, by totally excluding any of them from the Council. The Senior Counsellor whose abilities are spoken of as considerable is one Mr. Richd Barwell. His name, therefore, will be proposed.' (*Corr. of Geo. III*, vol. II, pp. 496-7.)

[95] The King to North, and North to the King, 8 June, 1773 (*ut supra*).

ing but indulgent eye. 'I have ever found him desirous of Service, and though not a shewy Man, has excellent Sense.' A useful Number Two.

There had been difficulty in finding a suitable candidate for the fourth place in Council although several names had been canvassed. At a late stage that of Philip Francis was brought forward and strongly pressed by his patrons, including the perennial Secretary at War, Lord Barrington, under whom he had served for ten years as first clerk at the War Office. At the time he had been out of employment, having resigned his clerkship in 1772, and had been thinking of trying his fortune in North America. It is evident that neither George III nor Lord North knew much about him. The former had been told that he was 'a Man of tallents', and the latter referred to him as 'a Mr. Francis who was lately in the War Office'; an able man, so it was said, but his being 'so lately a Clerk in an Office' was an objection.[96] Time, however, was running out, and in default of a stronger candidate the name of Francis was inserted in the draft Bill as a junior and almost as a stop-gap.

Francis was the son of a schoolmaster-parson who had been private chaplain to Lady Caroline and tutor to Charles Fox. An environment well calculated to stimulate a love of learning and also a sense of exclusion. Philip developed a deep interest in the classics and in political theory; but instead of going on to a university from St. Paul's School he became a junior clerk in the Secretary of State's office. There he used his quick intelligence to establish a network of useful contacts, notably with Robert Wood, Secretary to the Treasury, through whose influence he became private secretary to Lord Kinnoul in Portugal and then to Chatham. In the 20th century he would have climbed to the top of the ladder in the civil service – respected but disliked by his subordinates, who would have suffered from the results of his sense of frustration that he was not the Secretary of State.

His appoinment to the Bengal Council suddenly opened a door to great opportunities. Clavering and Monson were connected with the Clive group in Parliament, and with them Francis became a

---

[96] The story that George III had Francis posted to India because he believed him to be the author of *The Letters of Junius* and that as an exile in Calcutta he would 'write no more' in that capacity, is of course a myth. It is clear from the cited letter to North that the King knew nothing about him except that he was said to be an able official. Moreover it seems (to the present writer) most improbable that Francis was, in fact, Junius. (Cf. Sir Charles Dilke, *Papers of a Critic*, London, 1875, vol. II.) The correspondence between Junius and his publisher, H. S. Woodfall, indicates that the former was a political magnate of wealth and position. On the other hand, a more recent identification of Junius with Lord Shelburne (C. W. Everett, ed. *The Letters of Junius*, Lond., 1927) seems equally wide of the mark. Apart from the fact that Junius referred to Shelburne in a letter addressed to Chatham in damaging and contemptuous terms (Everett's edition, p. 361), the terse and pointed style of Francis is in strong contrast with the diffuse and sometimes obscure style of writing which was characteristic of Shelburne.

frequent and intimate visitor at Clive's home. Clive himself no doubt welcomed the chance of becoming patron and adviser to the 'Court' party in the new Bengal Government as a further means of preserving his influence in Indian affairs. His outlook was frequently reflected in the views subsequently expressed by Francis; but whether he encouraged the plot to overthrow Hastings is not proven. There is, however, no doubt that the three Councillors, led by Francis, matured their plans to that end during the ten months which elapsed between the passing of the Regulating Act and their departure for India. Soon after their arrival Francis wrote: 'I am now, I think, on the road to be Governor of Bengal, which I believe is the first situation in the world obtainable by a subject.' That ambition obsessed and tormented him for the rest of his life. In later years the wish to rule in India was reinforced by a consuming passion to reverse the national verdict in respect of Hastings and himself. The culminating bitterness came in 1806, when, upon the death of Cornwallis, his 'right or claim' to the office, as he put it, was finally rejected by Fox.

The inauguration of a new régime in Bengal would in normal circumstances have coincided with a change in policy. Such, of course, had been the Home Government's intention. The majority in the reconstituted Council, who had been selected by the Crown, were expected to impose the authority of the State over the Company's Servants and put an end to their extortion. Hastings and Barwell, both honourable men in North's estimation, were expected to co-operate in the good work. Francis accordingly assumed that he and his two colleagues upon arrival would establish a new dispensation which he himself would direct.

Instead of that the newcomers found that the old dispensation under Hastings was in the middle of a comprehensive programme of reform. The whole administrative system was in process of reconstruction – a field of policy barely within the consciousness of the Government at home. Hastings's aim, as he explained, was to create a strong and prosperous Province and by a vigorous external policy to exert a stabilising influence beyond its borders. Oudh was to be the principal buttress, and he had just participated in the Nawab-Vizier's conquest of the predatory Rohillas by way of reinforcing it against Maratha expansion. Clearly the new members of the Bengal Council could not inaugurate a new régime if they endorsed existing policy.

In external affairs it was easy to be different. The Rohilla war had been a calculated stroke of *realpolitik* on Hastings's part, and Francis was quick to recognise it as a promising object of accusation. The underpinning of Oudh was replaced by an attitude of non-involvement which would be popular in London; but the ruler was so weakened by financial exactions as to be incapable of resisting attack unaided. On the personal side, Hastings's trusted sub-ordinates were removed, and a pressure campaign was waged to make his position intolerable. At the Council table Francis strove to break through his opponent's guard with rapier thrusts of innuendo and calculated insult. At the head of the table sat the spare and apparently impassive figure of the outvoted President, as tenacious and as intellectually agile as Francis himself.

For two years Hastings had been immersed in the task of reviv-ing a prostrate Bengal, increasingly conscious that he alone was of the stature to achieve it. It is evident from his letters and despatches that the prospect possessed him with a fierce resolve to do a great work of reconstruction and to see it through, if need be, *contra mundum*. This driving force made him ruthless when opposed, and often cynical in financial transactions. It also armoured him with an almost superhuman capacity for self-control. The patience with which he endured derived not so much from a negative stoicism as from a volcanic determination that he, and his work with him, should survive and be vindicated.

The new Councillors were confronted by 'work in progress' in the field of judicial and administrative reform which involved a fundamental issue. How far (if at all) and by what methods should the British manage the internal government of the country? This was not provided for in the Regulating Act nor was it ground which a newcomer would choose for asserting his ascendancy over a rival well versed in Moghul and Hindu procedure; but the initiative in refashioning Bengal could only be wrested from Hastings by producing an alternative policy, and Francis did so with alacrity, for the situation challenged his intellectual pride.

When Francis entered the lists, Hastings had already gone far in internal reconstruction. On becoming Governor of Bengal in 1772 he had been instructed by the Directors to replace the Nawab's Naib or deputy, Mohammed Reza Khan, who, as such, was the regent for the British in their capacity of *diwan*. The Directors also gave orders that in future the Company was itself to collect the revenue, but characteristically they had omitted to indicate how it was to be done. Hastings was thus committed to a policy of administrative intervention which would involve an unprescribed but fundamental adjustment between British and native authority.

The assortment of undigested information was in Hastings's own phrase 'as wild as the chaos itself'.[97] The British were caught in a dilemma. They had become entangled in spite of themselves in the business of governing a complex and disordered society while they yet lacked the technical knowledge required for devising a workable compromise between British supervision and the

---

[97] See Feiling (*op. cit.*), pp. 96-7.

indigenous operation of local institutions. Clive's confident expectation that his countrymen could wield the power and receive the revenue while evading responsibility for internal management had been falsified. Normally the *diwan* was in charge of all matters relating to revenue administration, which involved land tenure, and civil justice; but in the case of Bengal these functions had been artificially divided between the supreme executive of the English Company and the Indian Treasury at Murshidabad. The former had been ignorant as well as rapacious, while the Indian authority had deteriorated as the result of its subordination, and also because it had to rely on a system of local administrators and civil courts which had lapsed into confusion and corruption. The collection of land-tax was in the hands, not only of (virtually) hereditary zemindars, but also zemindars self-created, and a host of lesser men who had inserted themselves into the system, 'until at last, below layer upon layer of sub-sub-infeudation, lay naked and despoiled the tiller of the soil'.[98] The judicial side was no less chaotic. With the collapse of Moghul authority a mass of minor jurisdictions had grown up, some Muslim and some Hindu. As in the time of Stephen and Matilda in England every little local magnate seized as much judicial power as he dared, using it as an instrument of oppression and extortion.

Faced with this welter which was almost beyond comprehension, the English Company had established their own Supervisors in each district by way of regulating the competing authorities. Agents were set to oversee the agents. It was as though the proprietor of a large business, having concluded that the managing director had lost control, established his own personal representative in each branch office to keep an eye on the staff who were suspected of robbing the till and mishandling the customers. Most of the Supervisors were mere youths, but since they represented 'the boss', they quickly became masters of the district. They were also masterless, for in the circumstances of the time they were not under effective discipline from Calcutta. The old evil of trade monopolies reappeared, and they dominated, not only the *diwani* courts, but also the criminal courts of the *nizamat*, which were responsible to the Nawab – himself a pensioner of the English Company but still a Moghul viceroy.

Hastings approached the problem with a practical knowledge of Indian institutions and custom and with a sensitive understanding of the Bengali temperament. The policy which he adopted was highly significant. British authority should be confined to the centre, but there it must be made absolute. In the districts the British Supervisors ought to be withdrawn altogether and local

---

[98] P. Woodruff (*pseud.*), *The Men who Ruled India* (Lond., 1953), vol. I, p. 136.

government should be reconstructed in accordance with Indian tradition and manned by Indian officials. In adopting the principle of indirect rule, he rejected the policy of his predecessor, Harry Verelst, who had held that with time the Supervisors could be turned into honest administrators, easing the lot of the villager by an intimate and knowledgeable paternalism. Hastings, on the other hand, considered that the 'fierceness' in European manners and the wideness of the gulf between British and Indian institutional ideas required that the Company should be content to reform the State in accord with native tradition and thereafter to confine themselves to the role of supreme umpire. The competing merits of these alternative methods of administration have exercised the minds of British statesmen and officials from that day to this.

In rejecting a policy of direct rule Hastings was influenced by his conviction that the Company's position in Bengal, which had arisen from an exceptional combination of circumstances, could not be expected to endure. He worked, therefore, to resuscitate Bengal as an Asian society and to revive its ancient trade routes through the Himalayas and westward to Jeddah and Egypt, so making Calcutta one of the great *emporia* of the East and the principal centre of British influence.[99] His belief that influence offered greater advantages than direct territorial 'dominion' reflected the prevailing trend in British expansion overseas, but it was no longer practicable in Bengal. British control at the centre operating through a reformed Indian administration in the districts represented an untenable half-in half-out position. In the Indian States which at a later stage accepted a treaty relationship with the Paramount Power, Britain avoided responsibility and left domestic affairs to the princely ruler. Bengal might well have furnished the first example of this aloof and negative policy, had not Clive accepted the profits of the *diwani* and so rendered thorough-going intervention unavoidable. Cornwallis and his successors were in no doubt that direct rule from the top to the bottom was the best for all concerned. Nonetheless, Hastings's policy of blending British principles of justice with the traditional institutions of the people has exerted an enduring influence among his countrymen.

It was not possible to abolish the office of Supervisor as he wished to do, for the Proprietors in London would not have tolerated such a curtailment of patronage. Hastings therefore surrounded them with a barrier of restrictions and transferred many of their functions to an Indian deputy. They were renamed Collectors and the number of districts was reduced. At the same time British control at the centre was tightened. The office of Naib or Nawab's deputy

---

[99] See Chap. VI below.

was abolished, and the Treasury was moved from Murshidabad to Calcutta, where its operations were directly controlled by a newly established Board of Revenue. And through this body (which became visitatorial) the Collectors were brought to heel and a beginning was made in the task of training them into being responsible administrators. In 1773-4 the actual collection of tax was transferred to Indian agents (*aumils*) under the superintendence of six Provincial Councils, each composed of the Company's European Servants in the area.

On the judicial side Hastings and his Committee of Circuit constructed a system of courts on the Moghul basis of the *Nizamat* and the *Diwani*. At district level the Collector presided over a local *diwani* court with the assistance of Indian officials, while the corresponding criminal (*foudjari*) court was managed by the Khazi and the Mufti of the district, aided by professional expositors of Hindu and Muslim law. But the Collector was required to review the proceedings of the criminal court and ensure that 'the Decision passed was fair and impartial'. In Calcutta two *Sadr* or appeal courts were established. The superior civil court (*Sadr Diwani Adalat*) which received appeals from the Collectors' courts (in cases involving more than 500 rupees) was presided over by the President and two other members of Council: and the corresponding court of criminal appeal (*Sadr Nizamat Adalat*) was in the charge of an Indian judge assisted by assessors.

Criminal process was the concern of the Nawab in the exercise of the *Nizamat* and was outside the province of the *Diwan*. But Hastings resolved to have done with a dualism which put a premium on murder and other felonies. The President in Council was empowered to review proceedings in criminal appeals as was the Collector in his district. Many traditional but oppressive fees were abolished, and it was laid down that in all suits respecting marriage, inheritance, caste, and other religious usages, Hindu and Muslim law must invariably be adhered to.[100] Not the least of the difficulties was to know what 'the law', a palimpsest of precept and custom, might be, and Hastings initiated the formidable task of research and codification.

There was, however, a still deeper morass to be traversed. Land tax provided the bulk of the country's revenue, and the Company's demands upon it were excessive and insistent. Assessment and collection had fallen into chaos. These factors in combination vitiated any effort to establish economic security or just administration. Ostensibly the system was straightforward and its operation ascertainable. The local magnate or zemindar collected tax from the peasant cultivators in accordance with a set of *pottahs*

---

[100] *A Plan for the Administration of Justice . . . 15th August, 1772.* Printed in *7th (Secret) Report* (Repts. from Commons Committees, vol. IV, pp. 348-51).

or agreements, while he himself was required to pay to the Treasury the annual sum at which he had been assessed. In theory he retained approximately ten per cent of what he collected from the ryots. With the passage of time Akhbar's fiscal structure had fragmented, and, as imperial control weakened, local tyranny had subverted intricacy with confusion. The zemindars (originating in several different ways) had gradually acquired by use or had seized by force territorial authority which varied widely from district to district. Peasant holdings, too, showed bewildering ramifications of tenure, and it was often extremely difficult to distinguish between peasant-tenants and the numerous grades of minor zemindars.[101]

When the foreign trading Company who had so eagerly accepted the office and emoluments of *diwan* decided to operate the system themselves, their Servants in Calcutta were painfully aware that nothing less than the compilation of a Domesday Book could lighten their darkness. The rights and obligations of those who claimed to be zemindars could perhaps be ascertained by laborious documentary research; but who could or would say what the ryot was under contract to pay, what he could reasonably be expected to pay under prevailing conditions, and what he actually paid? He would be too frightened of the local lord to reveal extortion; and the zemindar and the *kanongoe* (the hereditary keeper of local land records and originally an imperial officer set to watch the zemindar) conspired to conceal the true rates from the inquisitive foreigner.

When Hastings inherited this situation in 1772 the country was still prostrated by the effects of the terrible famine of two years before. He and his advisers decided rightly to institute a five-year,

---

[101] See the standard work on this complicated subject, B. H. Baden-Powell, *The Land-Systems of British India* (3 vols., Oxford, 1892) and particularly (for Bengal) Vol. I, Book I, Chap. V, Sect. I-V, and Book II, Chap. III, Sect. II. The author of *The Men who Ruled India* summarises the land-holding situation. ' Some [zemindars] were the descendants of assignees, officials to whom in lieu of salary the Emperor had given the right to collect and keep the King's share of the harvest. With the decay of the Empire, it cannot have been difficult for an unscrupulous assignee to rivet his hold so firmly that it would descend to his son. There were others to whom the assignment had been made not as salary but as pension: these rewards, known as *jagirs,* would still more easily become hereditary . . . Then there were mere farmers of taxes, contractors who had bought from the Emperor permission to collect the King's share, or who had contracted to collect it in return for a commission. Some of these too had acquired a right of their own and their origin had been forgotten. One class only really resembled English landlords. They were the descendants of chieftains who before the Moghuls came had either been independent or had paid a shadowy allegiance to some greater chief. They had submitted and paid the Emperor a tribute, perhaps half the share they were computed by the revenue office to collect. Below the zemindars was an elaborate gradation of subordinate holders of sub-infeudated rights, while the rights of a tenant's holding came in process of time to be shared by a swarm of relatives and other associates.' (Vol. I, pp. 136-7.)

instead of an annual, settlement of the revenue to induce stability and so encourage cultivation. Unfortunately his determination to break through the conspiracy of concealment and discover the real revenue potential led him into the error of putting the rights of collection up to auction. Many zemindars were ousted in the ensuing competition and others crippled themselves in outbidding the new speculators. The inducement to squeeze the ryots was proportionately enhanced. Afterwards Hastings admitted that the rates had been too high, although adjustments had been made in cases of hardship. The experience confirmed his opinion that it was not practicable to establish a just and efficient system until a mass of detailed and reliable information had been assembled. The essential thing was to get at the facts on the ground; and this in 1774 he was planning to do.

In his determination to establish the rule of declared law, to stabilise revenue assessment at a realistic level, and to protect the peasant from extortion by clearly defined contracts, Hastings had been led inevitably to restrict the powers and reduce the status of the zemindars. With the reform and re-institution of the ancient criminal and civil courts their usurped judicial functions virtually disappeared and they were left with nothing more than the handling of petty offences. Again, the introduction of a simplified system of excise removed the basis of the old vicious practice by which the zemindars paid a lump sum to Government in respect of internal duties and then fleeced traders in transit. And in the all-important field of land revenue direct contact between the Treasury at Calcutta and the peasant holders was increasing, and many zemindars, for one reason or another, found themselves virtually pensioned off with a subsistence allowance. A reduction of their swollen powers was inevitable if the cultivator of the soil was to be delivered from the manifold oppressions which he endured; but the corollary was a steady widening of British responsibility for the management of local affairs.

Philip Francis observed all these developments with a hostile eye. If they were allowed to mature, Hastings would become a self-appointed Satrap, and the British in Bengal would become inextricably involved in a political association with 'Moormen' and 'Gentoos'. That must not happen. As Francis well knew, the Home Government had appointed Clavering, Monson and himself as 'Crown Agents' to protect the State from being involved in Indian wars and to discipline the Company overseas. If the Company's Servants became the effective rulers of the country, controlling all the local instruments of administration, they would establish a territorial *imperium* against which even a Government-controlled Directorate would find it increasingly difficult to prevail. Clive's conversation had always been full of insistence that the activities of Company Servants must be confined to the utmost possible extent within the 'Ditch' at Calcutta.

From every angle, therefore, it was most desirable that Hastings's administrative reforms should be denigrated and destroyed. More than that, they must be replaced by a totally different system, bearing the name of Francis. The Rohilla war was proving a useful ground for censure and the campaign to blacken Hastings's character promised well; but the intellectual pride no less than the ambition of Francis demanded that he should challenge Hastings as a statesman and prove him fundamentally wrong. The conduct of the personal vendetta has often been described, but the theoretical ideas which Francis propounded call for greater attention than is usually given to them since they exerted a considerable influence on Charles Fox and afterwards to some extent on Dundas, and through him on Pitt.

Francis was an intellectual, widely read in constitutional law and soaked in the ideas of the political economists of the age. It was accordingly as a political theorist of 18th-century Europe that he approached the problem of the British position in Bengal. Once the relevant principle had been discovered, a logical system could be deduced which would inevitably fit into the universal pattern: the Great Chain of Being. Between this and the empirical approach of Hastings, the practical administrator, there was a great gulf. As Francis saw it, the ambiguity of the British position must be replaced by precise definition. The existing situation under which the Company exercised important sovereign functions while the sovereignty of the country still vested in the Nawab as a feudatory of the Emperor was, of course, illogical, and Francis concluded that the 'Undivided Sovereignty' of Bengal, as a Province of the British Empire, must be assumed by the British Crown. 'This I consider as a fundamental Principle, without which no Measures taken here can be regular, systematical, or secure.' But this was not to be a sanction for meddling in the internal management. Quite the contrary. If the controlling Power had been free to ignore the previous measures of its agent, the Company, and make a fresh start, he would have had no doubts about what the ideal arrangement would be.

Conforming to the Simplicity of Eastern Manners, and to the summary and simple Principles of Asiatic Policy, I should not hesitate to affirm, that the internal Administration should be committed to one or more considerable Moormen [i.e. Muslims]; that Moormen chiefly should be employed in the Offices of Government; that the Cultivation of the Soil should be left with the Gentoos, whose Property it is, and the Revenue fixed for ever. . . .[102]

---

[102] 'Plan and Letter of Mr. Francis, 22 January, 1776.' (See n. 104, p. 81 below.)

In fact the system which he actually propounded was not very
different from this description of his ideal. The proper course, he
declared, was to get back as closely as possible to 'the Model', the
ancient constitution of the country. The key person had been the
zemindar, and he must be rehabilitated, for in the mind of Francis
he was comparable with an English lord of the manor and justice of
the peace. He should be reinstated as the Government's executive
agent in all local affairs, collecting 'rent' from his 'tenants' and
paying land-tax out of the proceeds, while exercising once more
his (alleged) right to preside over the criminal court of his district,
pronouncing and executing sentence for all except capital offences.
'The zemindars,' proclaimed Francis, 'are, or ought to be, the
Instrument of Government in almost every Branch of Civil
Administration.'

This picture of the zemindarship distorted the facts by over-
simplification. The title, as we have seen, had come to comprise a
bewildering variety of functions and status, variously derived and
frequently usurped. To have committed the business of government into the hands of this miscellany of local land-holders would
have perpetuated confusion and oppression. Moreover he ignored
the fact that Akhbar had relied on a hierarchy of imperial officials
in each province to act as watchdogs. The British, on the other
hand, were to be withdrawn entirely as soon as the native administration was in working order. An important step in that direction
was enforced by Francis on the strength of a despatch from the
Court of Directors which reached Calcutta in June, 1775. This
despatch (dated 3 March) was a hesitant and ignorant effort and
included an instruction to reinstate Mohammed Reza Khan as Naib
or Deputy, but without extensive powers and rather by way of
compliment. Francis seized the opportunity and with the aid of
his two supporters in Council restored both the office of Naib with
full powers and the jurisdiction of the Nawab himself and abolished
Hastings's criminal courts. Thus the system which Francis devised
from his theoretical reasoning and fought so bitterly to establish
would have substituted George III for the Emperor Shah Alam as
sovereign of Bengal while the internal government of the country
would have been delegated to a self-contained Indian executive,
operating through the comprehensive agency of the zemindars.

Why did Francis champion a policy of non-involvement? Apart
from the need to be different from Hastings his declared reasons
have a significance beyond the immediate occasion. If Crown control in Bengal was to be effective (as the Home Government
intended) it must operate within a strictly limited sphere. The
Company must therefore be disentangled from territorial administration; and the way to do that was to stop their vicious practice
of squeezing out the greatest possible revenue which impelled

their Servants to become tax assessors and collectors. Accordingly they must cease to manage the revenue themselves and be content, like any normal Government, to balance income against estimated charges. With revenue needs reduced to reasonable proportions it would be possible to establish a simple and automatic system of assessment which the Bengalis could run themselves. Invoking once more ancient Moghul precedent[103] and using the ideas of John Shore, he proposed that a flat rate of land tax should be worked out for the zemindars, based on an average of the receipts for the three preceding years, and that this rate should be guaranteed as a Perpetual Settlement.

In advocating this simple method of resolving all difficulties Francis took high ground. The device of farming the district revenue to the highest bidder was wrong in principle and had brought many zemindars to ruin. Furthermore the policy which Hastings in his alleged solicitude for the ryot was advocating would thrust British authority between 'landlord' and 'tenant' in order to dictate the terms of every 'lease'. This was an invasion of the zemindars' rights of property: 'a Business of detail, which in no way belongs to Government, which we are in no Sense equal to.' If left to themselves zemindar and ryot would soon come to an agreement in which each party would find his advantage. The interference which Hastings was contemplating would subvert the natural order, extinguishing 'those successive Ranks of Subordination in Society through which the Operations of Government descend'. The zemindars were the country gentlemen, the true proprietors of the land; and the ryots should be left to their paternal care. 'The Scheme of every regular Government,' declared Francis in a characteristic flourish, 'requires that the Mass of the People should labour, and that the Few should be supported by the Labours of the Many; who receive their Retribution in the Peace, Protection, and Security which accompanies just Authority and regular Subordination.'

The consolidation of aristocracy in Bengal was well calculated to appeal to the Home Government as the proper method of rendering Company interference unnecessary. Furthermore, Francis maintained, this plan would establish the only feasible relationship between Britain and a distant non-European dependency. The

---

[103] Francis cited his precedent thus. After the conquest of Bengal Akhbar had established a standard *jummah* or valuation, the annual contribution due from each zemindar had been known and fixed, the tax had been light and the collection easy. In reply Hastings pointed out that Francis had misinterpreted the statistics, overlooking the fact that the value of money in the time of Akhbar had been five times higher than it was then, that there was documentary evidence to show that under the Moghuls defaulting zemindars had been flogged, tortured and dismissed; and that the acccumulated burden falling on the ryot had become so great and so obscured that a just scale of tax was impossible until there had been a thorough investigation of the facts in every district.

cultivators of the soil would be barely conscious of the paramount
Power and would look to their traditional lord, the rehabilitated
zemindar, who for them would in all respects be 'the Government'.
On these terms the people of Bengal would be left 'in the full
enjoyment of their own Laws, Customs, Prejudices, and Religion';
and on these terms they would as readily submit to British rule as
to any other, 'nor would it ever be lost but by foreign conquest'.
Indeed, added Francis, it was a question whether a great acquired
dominion, situated at an immense distance from the seat of Empire,
could be retained by any other principle.[104]

If the scheme propounded by Francis had been adopted as official
policy, there would have been no British *raj* in India. Bengal
would have become a Protected State in which George III of Britain
would have replaced the Moghul Emperor in external relations,
defence, and overseas trade; but outside Calcutta the daily life of
the people would have remained virtually untouched. Presumably
a similar aloofness and detachment would have been adopted in
other territories which became part of 'British India'. Whatever
the outcome of such a relationship, the face of 20th-century India
would certainly have worn a different aspect.

Francis's notions were doctrinaire and motivated by personal
considerations, but they were not evolved *in vacuo*. They derived
initially from Clive, and they reflected the general attitude of his
countrymen who were eager to win profits in Asia while shunning
the burdens and hazards of government. Their rivals, the French,
were of the same mind. Dupleix had striven to establish, not a
French *raj*, but the paramountcy of French influence; and in 1782
a French observer sourly condemned the establishment of British
rule in Bengal as a cardinal error. Europeans in India should

---

[104] The above summary of Francis's scheme is drawn from two sources: (i) *Plan and
Letter of Mr. Francis, Respecting the Collection of the Revenues, the Administration
of Justice and the Rights of the Zemindars or landlords*, Fort William, 22 January,
1776. Printed in *6th (Select) Committee Report on the Administration of Justice
in India*, App. 14 Repts. from Committees of the House of Commons, vol. V, pp.
913-24; (ii) numerous Minutes on the subject by Francis, printed with Hastings's
replies. (*Ibid.*, App. 15, pp. 939-85.) Francis's chief mentor in these matters seems to
have been John Shore, but while the latter advocated the consolidation of the
position of the zemindar as land-holder, he strongly opposed the 'perpetual'
character of Lord Cornwallis's land settlement of 1789, and in that year he minuted:
'Much time will, I fear, elapse before we can establish a system perfectly consistent
in all its parts, and before we can reduce the compound relation of Zemindar to
Government, and of a raiyat to a Zemindar, to the simple principles of landlord and
tenant.' (See Baden-Powell, *op. cit.*, vol. I, p. 520.) The Francis plan of vesting
all local administration in the zemindars naturally appealed to the Home Government. In 1781 Jenkinson wrote: 'A great deal has been written by Mr. Hastings,
Mr. Francis and others on the Management of the Revenue, but particularly the
Landed Revenue of Bengal: I agree almost entirely with Mr. Francis in every point
that has reference to this Object, vizt., That the Landed Revenue should be again
put under the Management of the ancient Zemindars, as far as is consistent with
the Circumstances of the Country, and the present State of that Body of Men.'
(*Addit. MSS.*, 38,398, f. 75.)

confine themselves to fortified trading posts with just enough
adjoining territory to cover overhead expenses and no more.
Dominion would be self-destructive, for in the end India, having
learned European methods of warfare, would free herself from
foreign servitude.

*Tout système d'ambition échouera avec le temps à une si grande
distance et dans la partie du monde la plus peuplée: il ne servira à la
longue qu'à faire perdre aux nations Européennes qui n'auront pas été
modérées, et leur territoire et peutêtre jusqu'à leurs relations de
négoce. . . .*[105]

During the years 1775 and 1776 Hastings's revenue policy – like
all else – was under constant attack in Council. Both sides were
preparing the ground for the decision about a new settlement
which would have to be taken before June, 1777, when the five-
year leases were due to expire. In a series of formal Minutes, Francis,
supported by Clavering and Monson, ventilated his Moghul
nostrums, and it was evident that when the time came the majority
would (Directors permitting) enforce their scheme. For his part
Hastings fought a rearguard action in the hope that time would
prove to be on his side. In March, 1775, he dispatched his own
'Plan', supported only by Barwell, to the Directors. It came close
to the principle of a Perpetual Settlement.[106] Indeed as he subsequently observed, he had no quarrel with that as the ultimate
objective and was working towards it. 'I lengthened the Period of
the Leases, which before was Annual to Five Years. This was considered by many as a bold Innovation. If a Perpetual Assessment
should ever be allowed to take place, I should hope to be remem-

---

[105] *Mémoire sur la paix prochaine.* Endorsed: '*Par M. Bruny, 2 juillet, 1782.*'
Enclosed in Bruny to Vergennes, 4 July. *A.A.E., Angleterre,* vol. 537, ff. 285 and
291. Cf. *Observations sur les Indes orientales* . . . Endorsed: *9bre, 1782. Ibid.,* vol.
539, f. 81.

[106] 'Plan of Messrs. Hastings and Barwell for letting the lands in Bengal after the
Expiration of the Five Years Leases', enclosed in their letter to the Directors, 28 March,
1775. Printed in *6th (Select) Rept. on Justice,* App. 12, vol. V, pp. 903-7. The
principal proposals were: (i) that all new taxes imposed upon the ryots since the
Company obtained the *Diwani* in 1764-5 be abolished; (ii) that the rights pertaining
to each zemindari be sold by public auction; (iii) that the revenue to be paid by
the purchaser be fixed at the average of what had actually been collected in the
three preceding years, with an allowance of 5 per cent for the charges of collection
and 10 per cent for his own remuneration; (iv) that the revenue remain fixed at that
rate for the life of the purchaser; (v) that the Government be free to re-sell in the
event of default; (vi) that on the death of any purchaser the zemindari to devolve
to his heir, with whom a new lease was to be arranged (under a specified procedure which must not in any case carry an increase of more than 10 per cent
over the preceding lease; (vii) that if the zemindar refused the lease on the terms
proposed he was to receive an allowance of 10 per cent on the preceding settlement
and the Government would be at liberty to farm out the zemindari on the best
possible terms procurable.

bered as at least one of the first Projectors of it.'[107] In January, 1776, Francis sent to the Directors his own proposals in the long and elaborate memorandum which has already been described. Then in the following June Monson died and by means of the casting vote Hastings resumed control. That did not mean, of course, that peace reigned once more in the Council Chamber. Francis and Clavering fought every inch of the ground, maintaining a barrage of insult and innuendo at the Board and a stream of accusation in letters to Ministers in London.

Previous experience had convinced Hastings that a just and reliable revenue settlement was impossible until the real value of the lands had been ascertained by detailed enquiries in every district. On 1 November, 1776, he formally proposed the appointment of a special Board, working under his own immediate control, to carry out this formidable investigation. The purpose, of course, was to furnish materials from which accurate assessments could be made, but Hastings intended that this enquiry should go to the root of the fiscal system. The welfare of the peasant cultivator ' ought to be the immediate and primary care of Government '. He must be secured in the perpetual and undisturbed possession of his land and protected against arbitrary exactions. In that regard edicts and proclamations were useless. The zemindar's interest was to extract the greatest rent he could from the ryot, and it was equally against his interest to have the rents and the limits of his authority over the ryot precisely stated in a registered contract. The proposed investigation must, therefore, include the collection of copies of the existing *pottahs* or agreements and the schedules of land rates. ' The Foundation of such a Work must be laid by Government itself.'[108]

Hastings thus contradicted in the flattest terms the policy which Francis had been striving to establish. In the latter's contention it was not the business of Government to interfere between the zemindar and his ryots, nor was it competent to do so. The Governor-General's challenge was taken up at once, and although Francis no longer commanded a majority in Council, he fought the ' Battle of the Minutes' with a tenacity equalled only by that of Hastings himself. The struggle on this issue continued from November until the following April: a five months' dialectical duel with no holds barred. It was an astonishing performance. Minute followed answering Minute and was answered again until the total filled some sixty-four closely printed foolscap pages. As a delaying action designed by Francis to hold up the proposed

[107] Governor-General's Minute, dated 31 March, 1777. Printed in *6th (Select) Rept.* (*ut supra*), pp. 998-1001.
[108] Governor-General's Minute in *Fort William Revenue Consultations*, 1 Nov., 1776. Extract printed, *ibid.*, p. 940.

enquiry until it was too late for the purpose of the new settlement it succeeded. But for him the struggle meant much more than that. The recorded debate, when it reached London, *must* demonstrate that the clear light of his intelligence had exposed a rival's misconceptions and had revealed the true solution to the Bengal problem by deduction from first principles. If he failed in this, Hastings would remain the acknowledged expert (even though he were proved a miscreant) and himself as no more than an interesting theorist. The answering tenacity of Hastings was sustained by an emotion no less potent: Bengal was his child. Moreover Francis fought at a disadvantage. His lack of administrative experience outside Calcutta gave full rein to the doctrinaire quality of his mind which prevented him from adjusting theory to unfamiliar reality.

Again and again during the contest Hastings, with great patience, showed that Francis's picture of the ancient system was historically unsound and that he had failed to take account of subsequent accretions which had become embedded in its texture. When cornered by hard fact, Francis would switch the attack and call to his aid some principle for which he claimed a universal validity; and to that Hastings would coldly reply that he was more used to the practice of business than to speculation and begged to be excused from discussing abstract principles except in the strict context of the revenue problems of Bengal. He indicated incisively that the *dicta* of Montesquieu, Adam Smith, and others about the incidence of land-tax were irrelevant because the circumstances in Bengal were totally different. To be accused by implication of being misinformed and guilty of muddled thinking was for Francis (who despised the intelligence of his fellows and relied on the pre-eminence of his own) very much worse than being charged with crimes. Injured pride and frustration festered into a consuming hate.

In the event neither Hastings nor Francis persuaded the Directors. Harassed by financial pressure and almost as out of depth as the Ministers, they gave orders for a return to annual assessments, thus opting for immediate profits in preference to investing in long-term stability. The argument continued until Cornwallis made his decision and persuaded the home authorities to adopt the draconian solution of a Perpetual Settlement.

Hastings himself was no advocate of direct rule. In fact, the difference in administrative method between the Clive-Francis policy and that of Hastings was not nearly so wide as Francis tried to make out; but the objects of the two policies were fundamentally different. The former stood for the *status quo ante* on grounds of expediency, as the only available method of avoiding British involvement: the latter sought to remodel native institutions and then to operate through them in rebuilding a contented Province. A policy of remote control was no longer practicable in Bengal, but it found expression in Britain's subsequent relationship with the Princely States. On the other hand, Hastings initiated a form of constructive indirect rule and in doing so committed his country-men more deeply than he had intended. The continuing process of reform in Bengal impelled his successors into undertaking direct local administration. Ironically enough, Philip Francis himself contributed powerfully to the intervention which he had denounced. In the prosecution of his long vendetta (through the medium of Burke) he probably did more than any other person to compel Government and Company to grasp the nettle of incurred responsibility.

The opposed attitudes of Hastings and Clive-Francis were both symptomatic of the contemporary eagerness to establish and extend spheres of trading privilege, while avoiding as far as possible the burdens of territorial rule. Hastings himself envisaged Bengal as a great productive centre of a British commercial nexus, command-ing the ancient trade routes to China, the Persian Gulf and the Red Sea; but, being by nature a pro-consul, he became absorbed in the exhilarating task of reconstructing Bengal as a state and in under-pinning its security by skilful diplomacy. He, and a growing pro-portion of those who followed him in the Company's service (from Governors-General to Collectors), found in this the most satisfying of human enterprises.

In Bengal the progression into territorial rule, hesitant though it was, became inevitable as soon as the *diwani* was accepted. Easy profit in the form of unearned income stimulated an appetite which caused the Company to undertake the business of collecting the revenue themselves, and that in turn drew them inexorably into the complexities of full magistracy. A chain of causation resulted. Honest and efficient administration, to be achieved, would require a Governor-General vested with supreme power. Yet such a con-centration of authority would be permitted only to a trusted (and obedient) servant of the King's Government, and that was imposs-ible until the Ministers of the Crown had secured effective control over the Company's political activities. Hastings pleaded for the necessary powers in vain: they were accorded to Cornwallis, but he was virtually a King's Minister.

It is possible for an alien authority to impose taxes, maintain order, and defend frontiers without knowing much about the social and religious *ethos* of the subject community; but that is not the case in the administration of justice. The aliens encounter judicial processes, formal and customary law which are permeated with the communal and religious sanctions of the people. Here again the English Company had no option but to intervene once they had assumed the functions of *diwan,* which included the determination of all types of civil litigation. Hastings, as we have seen, reconstructed the entire edifice of both civil and criminal courts, providing European supervision, but retaining traditional forms and relying on Hindu and Muslim experts as exponents of the law.

Unhappily the anomalous position of the British in Bengal caused this sensible working arrangement to be overthrown. According to Indian constitutional theory these foreign officials were deputies of the Moghul Emperor, exercising the privileges and duties of imperial *diwan* on his behalf. In the eyes of Westminster they were a bunch of contumacious British subjects who were gravely injuring the national economy and bringing their country's name into disrepute; and since previous efforts to bring them to book in the law courts of London had failed, it was becoming apparent that an engine of the King's justice must be established to deal with them in Calcutta.

The intention was limited and specific; but the Company's Servants and the free merchants were no longer an isolated enclave. They had penetrated the administrative and commercial texture of Bengal, and in pursuing these frontiersmen British justice, as expressed in Statute and Common Law, invaded the sphere of the Koran and the sacred precepts of Hinduism. Once more the Government of George III stumbled into a new field of experience which was to be of cardinal importance in determining the character of British rule in India and the nature of the legacy of law which it was to leave behind it.

In May, 1773, a year after the failure of Sulivan's Judicature Bill, the Commons Secret Committee on Indian affairs, led by Charles Jenkinson, produced a report on the administration of justice in Bengal, 'considering it as one of the most important Objects of their Appointment'.[109] The report claimed no more than that it provided 'the necessary Groundwork' for devising proper regulations for the future, but it affords valuable evidence of the extent to which Jenkinson grasped the situation and of his reactions to it. Evidence was taken from a number of expert witnesses, including Harry Verelst and Francis Sykes, and the Committee relied greatly on Hastings's plan of judicial reform which is summarised in the Body of the Report and reproduced *in extenso* as an appendix.

They were at pains to understand and expound the constitution of the 'Country Judicature' under the Moghuls and the corruption and oppression which had subverted it as the Empire crumbled. They drew attention to the powerful interference exercised by the

---

[109] *7th (Secret) Report,* 6 May, 1773. (Vol. IV, pp. 321-51.)

Company's Servants even in criminal cases, which appeared to the Committee 'to be the strongest evidence of the absolute Sway and Controul to which the whole Administration of Government, and particularly the Courts of Justice, have submitted, since the Company's Accession to the Dewanee'. They took note but were not convinced by Verelst's assurance of the effectiveness of the Company's policy in maintaining the ancient courts while gradually correcting the abuses which had crept in. 'It does not appear to your Committee,' they reported, 'what Effects may have thence resulted towards the better Administration of Justice.'

They then turned to the more familiar subject of the Mayor's Court in Calcutta, which (under the appellate authority of the President and Council) exercised civil and criminal jurisdiction over British subjects within the confines of the Town and Fort and the dependent Factories by virtue of a royal Charter of Justice issued in 1753.[110] They condemned it on the grounds that it was partial and arbitrary, ignorant of the law, and of inadequate authority. Indian complainants could not expect redress when the Company was judge in its own cause. It was ignorant: the so-called judges were mere junior Servants. 'Although these Courts, at least with respect to Europeans, are bound to judge according to the Laws of England, yet the Judges of these Courts are not required to be, and in fact have never been, Persons educated in the Knowledge of those Laws by which they must decide.' It was inadequate, because under the terms of the Charter its jurisdiction as a Court of Oyer and Terminer and Gaol Delivery was confined to offences committed in Calcutta and its subordinate Factories. 'The Consequence of this, in the present Situation of Bengal, is, that there are many of His Majesty's subjects residing in Bengal, neither under the Protection or Controul of the Laws of England, nor amenable to the Criminal Judicatures of the Country.'[111] They also understood that, while the Mayor's Court was bound to judge according to the laws of England, 'at least with respect to Europeans', the rule of judgement in the Zemindari Courts of Calcutta which dealt with native Indian cases, 'is supposed to be the Customs and Usage of the Country', and that the criminal (or *foudjari*) branch of this

---

[110] Under Letters Patent, dated 1661, the Company had been empowered to appoint Governors and other officers who were to exercise civil and criminal jurisdiction in the several factories according to the laws of England. The situation was so vague and unsatisfactory that, on petition from the Court of Directors, further Letters Patent were issued in 1726 extending and defining the functions of the Court of the Mayor and Aldermen of Madras and establishing similar Courts in Calcutta and Bombay. As the authority and activities of the Company expanded, the malpractices and inadequacy of these courts became increasingly serious and efforts to improve them were made in new Letters Patent in 1740 and again in 1753. (Cf. J. W. Kaye, *The Administration of the East India Company*, 2nd edn., Lond., 1853, pp. 318-26.)

[111] *7th (Secret) Report (ut supra)*, p. 333.

Court had concurrent jurisdiction with the Mayor's Court in the field of Oyer and Terminer, and Gaol Delivery.[112]

Such, in the view of Jenkinson and his fellow members of the Committee, was 'the necessary groundwork' for judicial reform in Bengal. On this basis the Crown was empowered to establish by Letters Patent a Supreme Court of Judicature, consisting of a Chief Justice and three other judges, which was to have authority over all British subjects throughout Bengal, Bihar and Orissa – to determine complaints for crimes and oppressions and all civil actions brought against them. And then came the fatal addition: 'and against any Person who shall . . . have been employed by, or shall then have been, directly or indirectly, in the Service of the said United Company, or of any other of His Majesty's Subjects.' The intention was plain. In establishing a royal court of justice to bring the British in Bengal under discipline and to afford effective protection and redress to the Bengalis, Jenkinson and his advisers clearly added this clause in order to prevent the delinquents from sheltering behind their *banyans* and their Indian commercial partners. It seems unjust to blame the drafters for ambiguity. They could not be expected to anticipate that the judges of the new court would interpret the clause as covering every Bengali who was even remotely connected with administration, including all zemindars on the ground that they collected land revenue. The result was a wholesale invasion of the jurisdiction of the 'country' courts, whereas the intention of the Act was to leave them alone, while establishing a special tribunal for bringing British subjects and immediate native agents within the King's justice. In the reverse type of case – where a European entertained a grievance against an Indian – the Act provided that the Supreme Court could only take cognisance of it if the sum involved exceeded 500 rupees and if the Indian concerned had previously agreed in the contract that any dispute arising could be taken to that court.

The Act tacitly assumed that the rule of judgement would be the law of England, and naturally so since the purpose was to subject the British in Bengal to the rigour of their own law. The inclusion of the Indian agents was part of that purpose. To have stated in the Act that the whole *corpus* of English Statute and Common Law was to apply was impracticable, for no clear ruling as to how far English law extended even to British settlements in North America and the Caribbean had ever been achieved. The judges were expected to use their common sense.

---

[112] *Ibid.*, p. 331. The Committee also noted that it had been ruled by the Court of Revenue in Calcutta 'that the Jurisdiction of the Zemindari Court of Calcutta might extend over all Persons, as Agents or Gomastahs, in the Service of any English Merchants, or of any native residing in Calcutta; and that as (and when) the Persons in question appear to stand in that Predicament, they should be sent to Calcutta, to answer the Suit of their Principals'.

It is sometimes said that the Charter of Justice, issued in the form of Letters Patent on 26 March, 1774, which established the Supreme Court of Judicature, was inconsistent with the Act; but that is not strictly accurate. The Charter faithfully implemented the relevant provisions of the Act, but in defining the powers of the new Court it incorporated, quite legitimately, the jurisdiction of the Mayor's Court of Calcutta as set out in the previous Charter of 1753. Accordingly, as a Court of Oyer and Terminer and Gaol Delivery, Elijah Impey and his three colleagues were empowered to adjudicate in all cases of murder and other felonies, forgeries, perjuries and other crimes committed within the confines of the town of Calcutta and its subordinate factories, that is to say, committed by any inhabitant, European or Indian. But unhappily the judges afterwards ignored the traditional *caveat* which followed: ' and [are] in all Respects to administer Criminal Justice, in such or like Manner and Form, *or as nearly as the Condition and Circumstances of the Place and the Persons will admit of,* as our Courts of Oyer and Terminer, and Gaol Delivery do . . . in . . . England.' Outside Calcutta and the other Factories criminal jurisdiction was limited to British subjects and to Indians directly or indirectly in the service of a British subject or of the Company.[113]

In short, the intention of the Act was to provide for a powerful Court, capable of enforcing the King's justice upon the Company in Bengal and upon all British subjects there, together with their hangers-on. The Charter constituted such a Court on the model of the Court of King's Bench – an august judiciary which had a large civil jurisdiction, had acquired a general superintendence over criminal justice, and had been wont to entertain complaints against all royal officials ' and bid them do their duties '.[114] Vested with such powers and with such a tradition behind them, it would be perilously easy for zealous judges, fresh from England and filled with self-importance and a sense of mission, to encroach upon other jurisdictions as their mediaeval predecessors had done with such effect.

Elijah Impey, the Chief Justice, with his three colleagues, Robert Chambers, Stephen Le Maistre, and John Hyde, reached Calcutta some ten days before Francis, Clavering and Monson. While the three Councillors intended to assert their administrative supremacy as the emissaries of the Crown, the judges were no less ambitious to establish their authority as the dispensers of the King's justice. It would be their pleasurable duty to bring British subjects in

---

[113] The Letters Patent of 26 March, 1774, are printed *in extenso* in *Report from the Committee on Petitions relative to the Administration of Justice in India,* 8 May, 1781 (vol. V, *ut supra,* App. I, pp. 59-69).

[114] F. W. Maitland, *The Constitutional History of England* (Cambridge, 1909 edn.), pp. 134-5.

Bengal within the rule of law; and since it was evident from the Report of the Commons Secret Committee that the native courts were both corrupt and also dominated by the Company's Servants, the 'Supreme Court of Judicature' must live up to its name and extend the blessings of impartial British justice to the unfortunate Bengalis as widely as possible.

The sequel is well known. Interpreting their jurisdiction over Indians resident in the town of Calcutta and those 'indirectly' in the service of a British subject in the widest sense, they arrested the persons and distrained upon the property of zemindars and other Indians of substance all over Bengal. In this process social and religious customs were outraged, and the Company's exercise of the *diwani* was disrupted. Even worse, the Bengalis were subjected to the ferocity of the unreformed penal code of 18th-century Britain. There was little excuse for that, since the application of British law even to British Colonies in the Western Hemisphere had been empirical and cautious; and there was no excuse at all for the execution of the notorious Nandkomar for forgery under an English statute. Indeed none of the parties involved in that case emerged scatheless. Nandkomar received a technically fair trial, but the judges did not exercise, as they should have done, the power granted to them by the Charter of suspending the execution of a capital sentence until the King's pleasure was known.

A precedent lay to their hand. In 1765 the President and Council had repieved another Indian, named Radachurn Mettre, who had been condemned to death for forgery. On that occasion an Indian petition had been presented, stressing the general consternation which this application of English law had caused. They had no means of knowing, the petitioners observed, when they transgressed, 'many things being, it seems, capital by the English laws, which are only fineable by the laws of your petitioners'. For their part, Francis, Clavering and Monson, who had tried to use Nandkomar and his villainous past to ruin Hastings, did not lift a finger to save a man who had become an embarrassment; and Hastings himself, seeing a deadly enemy caught in the toils, refrained from exercising the prerogative of mercy and coldly left him to die.

The alarming activities of the Supreme Court drew Hastings and his opponents in the Council into an unwonted accord. Reports of what was happening were prepared and dispatched to the Court of Directors, who on 2 May, 1776, gathered them up in a comprehensive review which they submitted to Lords North and Weymouth. The Supreme Court was accused of extending its authority to *persons* whom Parliament had not intended to subject to its jurisdiction, and secondly of taking cognisance of *matters* which Parliament had intended to leave 'to other Courts'. A formidable array of such encroachments was presented, and the Directors (fortified by a full brief) then proceeded to put a number of test questions, designed to illustrate the logical absurdity of the judges' position.

If the latter persisted in applying the whole of the criminal law of England – 'and they must so proceed if they mean to be consistent with themselves' – would they be able to sentence Bengalis to transportation to His Majesty's Colonies in North America or to work in the hulks on the River Thames? The statute of James I against bigamy provided that a convicted person should 'be burnt in the Hand if he can read and hanged if he cannot read'. Was the Court authorised to apply this statute to the natives of Bengal, where polygamy was recognised and protected? If so, the English judges would be able to try, convict, and impose the punishments prescribed for bigamy in respect of 'the Subahadar of Bengal and all his Court'. Perhaps even more important in the eyes of the Directors was their point that, if the judges were not restrained from interfering with the *diwani* courts, the difficulties in collecting the revenue would become insuperable, 'and the Loss to the Company immense'.[115]

Meanwhile the situation in Bengal had reached deadlock. The Governor-General in Council forbade zemindars to recognise the jurisdiction of the British judges, and the latter retorted by declaring the executive guilty of contempt of court. Yet, although Hastings and Francis inevitably stood together in this quarrel, their attitudes towards the introduction of the British judicial system were widely different. The Francis faction, as the advocates of a strictly limited protectorate system, denounced the imposition of an alien judiciary as destined to make the British position in Bengal untenable. Hastings, on the other hand, adhered to his general conception of an all-pervading British authority, operating through Indian *media*, and accordingly came to the conclusion that the judicial dualism, established by the Regulating Act, must go. Since (against his advice) a 'Supreme Court' of British judges had been created, it must cease to act as an external arbiter between the Company and the people of Bengal and be incorporated as part of a unified system of courts, applying an amalgam of English and Indian law.

Hastings knew that Impey was a moderate man (unlike some of his colleagues), although stiff and pompous, and that his Court had prevented many grave oppressions. He approached him and persuaded him to co-operate in working out a 'Plan' which was

---

[115] Directors to North/Weymouth, with enclosures, 2 May, 1776. Printed in *Report from the Committee of Petitions (ut supra)*, pp. 82-88. Feiling (*op. cit.*), p. 218, summarises the situation thus: 'Justice almost ceased. Impey complained that, outside Calcutta, his Court suffered an absolute boycott. The Company courts dared not act for fear of prosecution and fine. Hastings actually suggested a move of the government elsewhere, to escape " the devil of the law ".'

sent home in January, 1776. Two months later Impey and Robert
Chambers produced a draft statute which was dispatched for the
consideration of the Ministry.[116] The scheme was characteristically
bold and logical. The sovereignty of Bengal, Bihar, and Orissa was
to be vested in George III, 'saving the just rights and claims of
Nazims and Princes and the rights the Company enjoy'. The
distinction between *Diwani* and *Nizamat*, which had given rise to
many abuses, was to be abolished, and the jurisdiction of the
Supreme Court was to be united with that of the Company.

Impey agreed to become President of the Company's civil
court, the *Sadr Diwani Adalat*, the appellate court for Provincial
Councils and the subordinate *diwani* courts, which would consist
of members of Council and the judges sitting together. A similar
conjunction was arranged on the criminal side, where Governor-
General and Chief Justice would act together in reviewing the
sentences of the Nazim. Such a unification of judicial functions
involved a conception of British sovereignty over Bengal that was
far in advance of what was then practicable at the London end, and
it was not adopted. The Supreme Court must be retained as an
instrument of British justice in an alien land and be strictly confined to its proper purpose of imposing the Rule of Law upon the
Company's Servants.[117]

When to the stream of invective against Hastings was added a
flood of recrimination from warring councillors and judges, Jenkinson and Robinson at the receiving end were appalled. As we shall
shortly see, these two indefatigable officials were labouring to bring
about a comprehensive reconstruction of government in India; but
the recalcitrance of the Company and the distraction of North,
submerged in a revolution and then in a world war, frustrated
them. Sadly they came to recognise that no more could be achieved
in the circumstances than a limited patching of the existing system,
which had itself been intended only as a stop-gap. For that reason
Hastings's scheme of judicial unification, which would have involved
the formal establishment of British sovereignty over Bengal, was

---

[116] A copy of the scheme, entitled 'Plan for better Administration in Bengal, by
Mr. Hastings', is in Jenkinson's papers, *Addit. MSS.*, 38,398, ff. 268-78. For observations on the Plan with additional proposals by Robt. Chambers see *ibid.*, ff.
288-303. Cf. 'A Bill for the better government of kingdoms or provinces under the
government and control of the Governor-General and Council at Bengal and for
the administration of justice therein.' *Addit. MSS.*, 29,207, ff. 72-117.

[117] The tone of satisfaction with which (Sir) J. W. Kaye, writing as late as 1853
(*Administration of the East India Company*, p. 332), observed that the Crown
judicature thereafter kept quiet and refrained from interference in the Company's
courts is very noticeable. 'From this time,' he writes, 'to the present, the Crown
Courts have maintained themselves in a state of comparative quiescence, and
though, ever and anon, they have come into collision with the Company's servants,
there have been none of those open scandals and insolent outrages which in the
first years of the Regulating Act convulsed society, and well-nigh overturned the
administration.'

far beyond the horizon.[118] Indeed, it became a question whether the British judicature in Bengal was to survive at all. Company Proprietors raised a clamour for the abolition of a court which they had detested from the outset, and some in official circles were inclined to agree that it must go. Despite the urgency of the situation the Government did nothing about it for six years. The frank apology which Jenkinson made to Clavering in 1776 provides a striking illustration of the strains and divisions which increasingly afflicted the North Administration.

I have done all I can to bring Government to some regulation with respect to the Supreme Court; for till that is done, I don't see how Your Business can properly go on . . . I own I am against proceeding at once to the Destruction of it; I do not yet see reason sufficient for that. I think it ought to be restrained and regulated, and this I imagine may without any great difficulty be done; but for this purpose it is necessary to have the Sanction of some Law Authority, and of these some are unable and some unwilling to give any Assistance. The Papers have been the greatest part of the summer before the Attorney (Thurlow); he declines giving any positive advice, but inclines to think, as I am told, that the Court should be destroyed, or at least wholly refounded.

The papers, added Jenkinson, were now to be sent to the Privy Council, and Sir Eardley Wilmot and Sir Thomas Parker were to be asked to attend as consultants. This, he thought, was the most likely way of bringing the matter to a decision, 'but it ought to have been put into this Channel six months ago'.[119] Yet no action emerged. When the Government at last (in 1781) decided to retain the Court, while restricting it to the original purpose, he conveyed to Sir Robert Chambers the opinion which he had so long held but had been unable to induce the Ministry to implement.

I am sorry . . . to confess, that I cannot, in general, approve of Your conduct. It is sufficient for me to say, that you appear to have been too much attached to Professional Ideas, proper indeed for this country, but not proper for that to which you were sent. You have not paid an attention sufficiently liberal to the Manners and Prejudices of the Natives and to the Privileges of those who are of a higher rank among

---

[118] Hastings was well aware of the far-reaching implications of his proposed remodelling of the Bengal judicature and took the opportunity to enlist the aid of Impey and Chambers in drafting provisions for the reconstruction of the central executive. In commenting on the draft Bill which they were preparing, Chambers added: 'but as the Administration of Justice and the making of Laws are the only subjects of that Bill, the enlargement of the Governor-General's authority and other alterations which I have ventured to propose in the executive powers of the Governor-General and Council must, if thought necessary, be separately enacted.' Note to Hastings's Plan by (Sir) Robt. Chambers, 25 March, 1776. *Addit MSS.*, 38,398, f. 317.

[119] Jenkinson to Clavering, 13 Dec., 1776. *Addit. MSS.*, 38,306 (Letter Book), ff. 102 *et seq.*

them . . . You have so constituted Your Court, that the charge of it to the Company affords them a just ground of complaint, and in Your Process you have adopted all the English forms which are tedious and in no respect fitted for the Government of Bengal. . . .

This subject, added Jenkinson, would be very much agitated during the ensuing session of Parliament. He himself had done what he could to prevent the intended abolition of the Court, and he was hopeful that 'the great abilities of the Chancellor' would enable him 'to propose something' that would remedy the evils and also satisfy public opinion at home.[120] On that the comment might perhaps be made that if Thurlow had applied his mind to the business at the time of the drafting of the original Judicature Act (when he was Attorney-General), much confusion could have been obviated.

The amending Judicature Act of 1781 (which was largely the work of Edmund Burke) not only closed the breach through which the judges had invaded the jurisdiction of the 'Country' courts but also established a number of important principles. The Governor-General and Council were not to be subject to the jurisdiction of the Supreme Court but were to remain liable to any complaint before a competent court at home. The Supreme Court was not to have any jurisdiction in matters concerning the revenue or its collection; and no person was to be subject to it on account of being a land-holder or a farmer of land-rents. Indians employed by the Company or by a British subject were not to come within the jurisdiction in any matter of inheritance or contract, except in actions for wrongs or trespasses; and in order that this category should be precisely defined and known, all such agents were to be registered, and no British subject was thenceforth to employ any Indian agent who was not so registered. The function of the court as a tribunal for the protection of the Indian population was thus preserved and defined.

The vexed problem of the kind of law to be applied was now faced. The authority of the Court to determine actions and suits against all persons resident in Calcutta was confirmed, but with the proviso that matters of inheritance or contract must be dealt with according to Hindu or Muslim law and usage; and it was further provided that the customary rights and authority of heads of families, Hindu or Muslim, over their families were to be pre-served. 'Nor shall any Acts done in consequence of the Rule and

---

[120] Jenkinson to Chambers, 1 October, 178[0]. *Addit. MSS.*, 38,308, ff. 179-80. The date of this letter as given in Jenkinson's letter-book (1 October, 1781) is clearly a mistake for 1 October, 1780. The 'ensuing session' began on 31 October, 1780, and petitions (from Hastings and others) against the proceedings of the Court were received by the Commons on 1 Feb., 1781. After a debate on 12 Feb., the petitions were referred to a Select Committee, and the resulting amending Act received the royal assent early in July, 1781.

Law of Cast[e], respecting the Members of the said Families only, be held and adjudged a Crime, although the same may not be held justifiable by the Laws of England.' Furthermore, the Court was authorised to frame new forms of legal process for use in civil and criminal suits against Indians which could be 'accommodated' to their religion and manners.

At the same time the authority of the British Crown, as the Fount of Justice, was reaffirmed and extended. All new forms of process must be transmitted as soon as issued to a Secretary of State to receive the royal 'approbation, correction, or refusal'. Secondly, the Governor-General and Council were empowered to frame regulations from time to time for the provincial courts – 'which Regulations his Majesty in Council may disallow or amend'.[121]

Ostensibly the situation remained much the same. The dualism between Company and native authority and between Company and Crown continued. In reality the British position in Bengal had changed profoundly. The necessity of extending the discipline of royal justice to British subjects who had swollen to the proportions of overseas 'palatine earls' had brought about the establishment of a Court of King's Bench in the chief city of a foreign realm. The penetration of these British subjects into the administrative structure of Bengal had then induced the Crown judges to attempt to impose British law and process upon the entire country. The crisis was resolved by forcing them back within the frontiers of a strictly limited jurisdiction; but in the course of doing so the British Crown assumed responsibility for directing the shaping of a new

---

[121] *21 Geo. III, cap. LXX.* The jurisdiction of the Governor-General and Council as a civil court of appeal from the Provincial Courts was confirmed, and they were further empowered, as a court, to try charges of abuse and extortion committed in the collection of revenue, provided that the punishment did not extend to death, maiming or perpetual imprisonment. The Bill was based on recommendations made by the 'Committee on Petitions', but two years later the chairman of the Committee, General Richard Smith, stated in the House that, although the measure had taken its rise in the committee and had been called 'General Smith's Bill', Burke was its real author, 'for, except some legal knowledge which he (Smith) had imparted to him, the whole of it belonged of right to that right hon. member' (*Parl. Hist.*, XXIII, 1238). In supporting the Bill at the Report Stage (27 June, 1781) Burke observed that 'we had suffered enough in attempting to enervate the system of a country, and we must now be guided, as we ought to have been with respect to America, by studying the genius, the temper, and the manners of the people, and adapting them to the laws that we establish'. (*Ibid.*, XXII, 555.) It is indicative of the paralysis which was afflicting the North Administration that this important measure did not emanate, as Jenkinson had hoped, from the Government, but from a member of a Select Committee who was a leading figure on the Opposition benches. In the Spring of 1781 Jenkinson wrote: 'I might safely leave this Business (i.e. the regulation of the Court of Judicature) with the Committee of the House of Commons, who are now enquiring into it, and with his Majesty's Law Servants, who will, I make no doubt, advise what it may be proper to do therein: but I will take the Liberty of offering a few observations on this subject . . .' (*Addit. MSS.*, 38,398, f. 76).

D*

judicial system on the basis of an amalgam of British legal principles and indigenous law and custom. Whatever the theoretical
status of the Nawab of Bengal and the chartered rights of the
Company, the British Government had become involved in an
essential function of imperial rule. On the other side of the world
and in different circumstances the same policy of adopting and
adapting indigenous law and procedure to British principles (as
far as appeared practicable) were being applied under the Quebec
Act in the case of the French Canadians.[122] In Bengal economic
profit and an emergent sense of humane obligation were pushing
a bewildered Government of Europeans further and further away
from the practice of 'informal' empire into the exacting task of
formal *raj* in the midst of an Asian world.

5. JENKINSON AND ROBINSON, 1776-1781

From the compilation of the Regulating Act until the fall of the
North Administration ten years later the 'management' of Indian
affairs on behalf of the Government was in the hands of the capable
John Robinson, supervised by Charles Jenkinson and fitfully
directed by Lord North. The Act of 1773 had been intended as a
holding operation to subsist for five years only; and in any case the
Company's charter was due to run out in 1780. During this interim
period the two 'Men of Business' intended to acquire the knowledge and experience which they needed to devise an acceptable
and durable system of state control over the affairs of the new
empire in Asia. Meantime they relied on governmental influence
in guiding the Company directorate at home and the reconstituted
executive in India.

From the start everything that could go wrong with these plans
and expectations did. The new majority in the Bengal Council
declared war on the Governor-General; and before long the judges
of the Supreme Court (the trusted instrument of royal discipline)
came near to bringing the administration of the country to standstill. Government officials and Directors became the recipients of a
cascade of charge and counter-charge. Hastings's arrangement with
Impey indeed brought the judicial conflict to an end; but, as we
have seen, Jenkinson had to wait until 1781 before he could induce
the Government to come to a decision and apply the solution which
he had so long proposed.

---

[122] The analogy was not overlooked at the time. A marginal note on the rough
draft of the Jenkinson-Robinson memorandum of 1781 is as follows: 'Why should
not there be a Clause similar to that inserted in the 14th Geo. 3rd C. 83. s. 8
respecting the inhabitants of Canada, declaring that the Laws, Usages and Customs
of Bengal, etc., should continue to be the Law of those Countries in all Cases
where the Civil Rights or property of the ancient Inhabitants are concerned?'
Addit. MSS., 38,398, ff. 77.

On the parallel issue of restoring harmony in the Bengal Council the obvious course in the view of the Administration was to recall Hastings. Yet here again they were frustrated. When Robinson in May, 1776, tried to secure recall, the parliamentary Opposition intervened at East India House and joined forces with the various groups of Proprietors who regarded an attack on Hastings as a threat to their own interests, and the proposal was defeated by a substantial majority in a General Court. After this initial failure the organised influence of Administration over the government of the Company in routine matters became more effective, but the personal self-interest of the troops always set a limit to their amenability.

The position of the Imperial Government *vis-à-vis* the assembly of a chartered corporation which had acquired political power over wide territories was not so very different from its relationship with the Anglo-Irish Parliament. In both cases control-by-influence proved a brittle instrument, apt to break when it was most needed; in both cases the uncommitted members tended to form a factious alliance with the Opposition at Westminster; and in Indian as in Irish affairs the Imperial Government, by weakening its agent, itself incurred responsibilities without adequate power to discharge them. Pitt, as we have already seen, became progressively disillusioned with this unreliable and ultimately dangerous method of managing Ireland;[123] and after five years' experience of trying to get things done by a similar management of the Company Robinson confessed to Jenkinson that he despaired of the system.[124]

By the summer of 1778 the time available for planning a new arrangement was running short. Matters would come to a head during the ensuing session when legislation would be needed to replace the Regulating Act, due to lapse in 1779, and when the Company would be obliged to apply for a renewal of their charter. Robinson naturally appreciated the advantage of combining these two operations. A renewal of the Company's privileges could, he hoped, be used as a bargaining weapon to secure once more a substantial annual contribution to the Treasury and to enforce acceptance of increased state control over the Company's political affairs. He underestimated the Company's capacity for resistance and overestimated the bargaining power of the Government.

During the summer recess Robinson prepared a memorandum for the consideration of North and Jenkinson which became the basic document on the subject. At the outset he decisively rejected the proposition that the State should itself assume the administration of the Indian territories, while confining the Company to its original business of trade. None of the plans put forward, he wrote,

---

[123] See vol. I, Chap. XI.
[124] Cf. Sutherland (*op. cit.*), pp. 305-10, 336.

offered any prospect that these territories would be better managed by the Government than they would be by the Company, provided that the Company's constitution was 'amended and made subject to the Superintendence and frequent control of the Legislature'. Moreover, trade and administration in India were so intimately connected that it would be impolitic to attempt to separate them. Such considerations apart, the establishment of 'imperial' authority in Indian affairs was out of the question, and for two compelling reasons. In the first place, it was wrong in principle, and secondly in the prevailing circumstances it was utterly impracticable.

I am violently against Pledging the Revenues and substance of this Country for the security of these acquisitions, in return for any advantage by way of Revenue, that might be derived from them; and yet this must be the case, if the Government take the management of them into their own hands.

Let the State derive financial strength from the overseas enterprise of its subjects; but the substance of England must not be pledged to maintain the security of a distant territorial empire. Then followed a frank confession that the Government of the day was too weak, too hard pressed, to be capable of undertaking such a burden, even if it had been sound policy. The American Colonies were in revolt, France had declared war, and the Ministry were so beset at home that it was scarcely able to retain due respect and authority. In the midst of difficulties and calumnies, 'I think that the Errors which must be committed in the management of such Acquisitions, at so great a distance from the seat of Government, had better fall upon the Directors of the Company than fall directly upon the Ministers of the King'.

Even so, Robinson clung to the hope that his masters could be persuaded and the Company compelled to adopt direct and effective Government supervision. Indeed, his ideas were bolder and more optimistic than those which Pitt and Dundas formulated six years later in far more favourable circumstances. Robinson regarded the constitution of the Company as essentially a *Colonial* Constitution, and as such it presented in his view the same sort of caricature of the parent constitution as did the governments of the rebellious Colonies in America. 'I consider,' he wrote, 'the Court of Directors as the Executive Government, and I would have them continue so.' But this executive should be effectively controlled by the Metropolitan Government, and to that end he proposed that the Crown should nominate half the Directors. In another version of the Memorandum he went further still and tentatively suggested that perhaps the Crown might be authorised to appoint a 'Governor' who would preside over the Court of Directors as the elected Chairman had done hitherto.

It would be easy to show that many of the Charter Governments in the Colonies who had originally Charters similar to that which the East India Company possess at present, and were considered merely as Commercial Companys, upon their obtaining Territorial Acquisitions, were formed into Governments upon the Model just described.

By way of rendering this drastic proposition less unpalatable, he suggested that it could be qualified, ' tho' in my opinion the principle does not require it ', by providing that the Crown-appointed Directors should be inhibited from serving on all committees concerned with ' the Business of Buying and Selling '. A similar plan, as we have seen, had been previously suggested by Clive, and Robinson's ideas (by way of Dundas) greatly influenced Fox and Burke when they came to devise their ill-fated India Bill.[125]

Regarding the Court of Proprietors as analogous to a colonial Assembly, Robinson would have contracted its swollen powers to put an end to a similar recalcitrance. Nothing, he declared, could be more absurd and preposterous than the existing system. The government of several Asiatic provinces at a distance of six thousand miles was ultimately in the hands of the Proprietors, ' the most Democratic Body that ever existed ', which not only made laws for these provinces but interfered in their execution whenever they thought fit.

If every inferior part of the British Government is to resemble the British Constitution, let us at least so alter the Government of the Company as to reduce it, as near as circumstances will admit, to the model of that Constitution, as it stands at present. . . .

Thus did Robinson adumbrate the doctrine of ' assimilation ' to the parent constitution as the sovereign remedy for disobedience to metropolitan authority. The same prescription was applied by William Grenville after American independence to provide a workable form of representative government in Canada.[126] Robinson accordingly proposed that the powers of the General Court of the Company should be confined to declaring dividends (within a prescribed scale), electing Directors, and ordering the prosecution at law of misbehaving Servants. They should continue to legislate for the future government of the Company's concerns, but the Court of Directors – like an Executive Council – should have the power of veto, and all such measures should be subject to the final approval of the King in Council. Similarly in India: the appointment of the Governor-General, members of the Bengal Council, Commanders-in-chief and the Presidents of all settlements should be given ' entirely to the Crown '.

---

[125] See pp. 124-140 below.
[126] See Chap. X below.

This was strong meat to expect the distressed Administration to present and a politically powerful corporation to digest, and Robinson was aware of the fact. As a minimal alternative he suggested that the provision in the Regulating Act which required the Directors to transmit to the King's Ministers all incoming despatches relating to government and revenue should be supplemented by a requirement that no orders touching these matters were to be sent out to India until the King's Ministers had seen and approved them. And if the appointment to senior posts in India must remain with the Directors, the Crown should be authorised to make its own nomination if the Directors failed to secure royal approval for a nominee of their own within fourteen days of the vacancy being known. Furthermore, in order to prevent the Directors from continuing 'improper persons' in their service, the Crown should be given the power of dismissal. 'These last ideas,' declared Robinson, 'are wretched expedients to supply the place of real authority in the Crown which it ought to have, but which in these times Parliament may not be disposed to give it.'

This exposition of what was needed to put the relations of State and Company on a satisfactory basis well illustrates the general ministerial attitude in this period towards the problem of managing an overseas empire. As they saw it, two issues were involved – one administrative and the other financial. With the extension of imperial interests both in North America and in India the long-standing need to assert adequate control in matters of general imperial concern assumed increasing importance. At the same time the rising costs of maintenance and defence (in the West and in the East) caused them to associate the objective of central control with the need to induce the overseas units to make a direct contribution to the expense account. The expanding frontier in North America had fused and sharpened this dual issue and a revolution had been precipitated. The principle of central direction was vitiated when used as an instrument of coercion; but the double objective remained. Pitt pursued it in 1785 with an autonomous Ireland, on the basis of a negotiated bargain; and between 1778 and 1781 Jenkinson and Robinson wrestled with the East India Company with similar ends in view. But their determination on behalf of the Government to secure a 'contribution' undermined their already weak position in trying to impose effective political control.

The need for financial assistance was acute, and in this case the prospect of getting it appeared to be exceptionally favourable.[127] Here was an imperial corporation which had now recovered its

---

[127] Robinson assured the King that the moment had come when by prudence and attention to East Indian affairs 'a fund of wealth and power' would accrue to the public, 'which will surprise almost the warmest imagination'. Robinson to the King, 7 June, 1778. *Addit. MSS.*, 37,833, f. 228.

prosperity, was in receipt of a large territorial revenue, and was also a suppliant for the renewal of its chartered privileges. Robinson accordingly proposed that annual payments into the national exchequer as provided for in 1773 should now be resumed, and he calculated that this would amount to £400,000 per annum. On their side the Company shareholders would receive a dividend of 12½ per cent. In addition the Company should be required to provide the State with a loan of £2 million, to be raised by issuing bonds and to continue for the period of the renewed charter, which should be limited to five or seven years. As a further contribution he proposed that the cost of any naval or military force sent by Government to the Indian Ocean should, after passing the Cape of Good Hope, be defrayed out of the Company's Indian revenues. This, he pointed out, would be a great saving to Government, freeing it from the payment of ' Enormous Bills ' which it could not control.

Robinson's ambitious scheme was considered at a meeting of North, Jenkinson and himself early in November, 1778, and was evidently approved in general terms;[128] but the other Ministers showed no sign of applying their minds to the question. Robinson was not able to open conversations with the Chairman and Deputy-Chairman of the Company until the following February, and the weakness of his bargaining position was all too evident. Lacking solid Cabinet support, he was asking the Company to bind themselves in future to making substantial contributions to the State out of their profits and at the same time to surrender their autonomy in political and military affairs. Even on the part of a strong Government in time of peace it would have been a hazardous exercise.

After several discussions with the ' Chairs ', Robinson gave them a written summary of the proposals and asked them to submit propositions to Lord North on that basis. The paper recited the financial requirements and then outlined the proposed new model of the Company's constitution. Indeed Robinson was confident enough to add to his scheme a further instrument of control: ' A Secret Committee of Directors to be nominated by the Crown to manage the Political, Civil and Military Affairs of the Company.'[129]

The Directors sent in their propositions on 5 March. They accepted in principle the demand for a loan and that the State should participate each year in any surplus profits after the sum required to distribute a dividend of 8 per cent to the shareholders had been deducted. But they stipulated, *inter alia*, that the renewed Charter should run for 14 years, instead of seven, with three years' notice; and the constitutional reforms were countered with the

---

[128] See Robinson to Jenkinson, 9 Nov., 1778. *Addit. MSS.*, 38,567, f. 4.
[129] ' No. 1 Sketch for Propositions. 20 Feb., 1779.' *Addit. MSS.*, 38,403, f. 2.

observation that they could 'form no Opinion upon these Ideas without further Information from Lord North'.[130]

Several weeks of stiff bargaining ensued. The struggle centred on the financial provisions, for North had given optimistic assurances in Parliament on this score in his budget speech. The demands for state control began to fade into the background.[131] At the end of April a desperate effort was made to reach, at any rate, a limited agreement. Robinson was deputed to consult Wedderburn, the Solicitor-General, in spite of the fact that the unfortunate North was being plagued at that time by his factiousness and evil temper.[132] Robinson sent him an amended set of financial propositions and suggested that everything else should be temporarily abandoned.

The regulations proposed in this respect to . . . the power and regulation of the General Courts of Proprietors, the Election and nomination of Directors, and a secret Committee of Directors with proper powers for enabling them to direct and govern the Territorial Acquisitions in India and their Settlements, and such other regulations for the better management of the Company's affairs, as on further consideration shall be found necessary, may be a subject proper for Parliament in the next Session when they can be fully discussed.[133]

Wedderburn and he met and went through the paper together, agreeing to delete a number of other unpalatable proposals. North approved and on 3 May Robinson sent the papers to the King. In his covering letter Robinson explained that the controversial

---

[130] A copy of them is in *ibid.*, f. 5.

[131] See 'Abstract and Comparative State of the several Propositions for the Renewal of the East India Company's Charter.' The successive exchanges between Government and Company are tabulated under the following heads: 'Propositions received from the Directors on 5 March, 1779': 'Ideas on the Propositions received . . . 5 March, 1779': 'Queries from Secret Committee of Directors on Ideas delivered': 'Answers to Queries from Secret Committee': 'Answers from Secret Committee to Lord North's Ideas': 'Propositions received from Directors on 29 Jan., 1780': 'Propositions received from Directors on 6 Nov., 1780'. *Addit. MSS.*, 38,404, ff. 374-81.

[132] Wedderburn was at this time intriguing for a peerage and a Secretaryship, or alternatively the office of Lord Chief Justice, and was threatening to overthrow the Administration if left unsatisfied. In his agitation North unburdened himself to the King, who in a very kind reply advised North to place his chief political confidence in Chancellor Thurlow, 'who is a very firm and fair Man'. This was cold comfort, since Thurlow (in East India as in other matters) was following his usual practice of ignoring state papers sent to him for comment and advice. The King also suggested that Henry Dundas, the Lord Advocate, should be taken into confidence concerning measures in Parliament. (See the King to North, 21 April, 1779; Jenkinson to the King, 28 April; Robinson to the King, 6 June. *Corr. of Geo. III*, vol. IV, pp. 327, 329, 349.) The situation of North, as First Minister, engaged in a major struggle with the East India Company, and looking round in desperation for the legal advice which he needed, affords a sufficient commentary on the condition of the Administration.

[133] 'No. 3. Ideas on the Indian Propositions received from the Court of Directors of the East India Company.' *Addit. MSS.*, 38,403, f. 13.

matters had been dropped solely in order to expedite the business and avoid long discussion in Parliament. The plan now, he added, was to continue things as they were until the expiry of the Charter in April, 1780, to 'get the money' by settling with the Company, and to leave the rest for the time being – ' because at this late period of the Session the whole can't be properly discussed, and because also Mr. Robinson fears that if the whole was now brought on, proper attention would not be had to that corrective Power in his Ideas most essential and necessary to be given to the Crown over the Company '.[134]

Yet even the money was denied them. On the morning of 8 May North again saw the Chairman and Deputy-Chairman. They submitted a paper, and when North had read it, he 'apprehended that the business was at an end '. Failing prior agreement with the Company, he was faced with the dangerous prospect of trying to impose a settlement by legislation in the face of attack from the Opposition and probably also from the ministerial side. Yet some action was imperative, for the five-year tenure of the Governor-General and Council in Bengal, as provided in the Regulating Act, was due to run out in September. Robinson was instructed to send all the relevant papers to Jenkinson and to prepare forthwith a short bill for Jenkinson's inspection. North himself would introduce it in the Commons, and, as he informed Robinson, he would 'take some other method about his Money '.[135]

Eleven days later he surprised a thinly-attended House by moving for leave to bring in a Bill for continuing the Regulating Act and the appointment of officers named therein for a further twelve months. When Colonel Barré wished to know what had become of the Company's negotiable securities on which £1,200,000 were to have been raised, North was obliged to admit that 'the mode alluded to for raising the £1,200,000 had not been approved by the Company '. He, therefore, intended to raise that sum on the credit of the Exchequer. Although the Bill was a mere stop-gap, Barré was not deterred from seizing the opportunity to assert that the Minister was interfering in the Company's affairs and had 'filched away the patronage of that great and opulent body '.[136]

---

[134] Robinson to the King, 3 May, 1779 (draft). *Addit. MSS.*, 37,834, f. 68.

[135] Robinson to Jenkinson, 8 May, 1779. *Addit. MSS.*, 38,403, f. 92. See also Jenkinson to Robinson, 12 May. *Addit. MSS.*, 38,306, f. 143.

[136] *19 Geo. III, cap. LXI*, and *Parl. Hist.*, vol. XX, 637-61. Apart from the Proprietors' resistance to constitutional reform North would have found it extremely difficult at that juncture to give the Governor-General power to over-ride his Council, as he with Jenkinson and Robinson wished, when that office was held by Warren Hastings. Philip Francis had been doing his utmost to prevent an extension of Hastings's term (see Sutherland, *op. cit.*, p. 342, n. 5), and on 11 May – at the very time when the Bill for continuing the existing officers in Bengal was drafted – the King wrote North to say, acknowledging two letters from Francis which North had sent him: ' The Company is ruined and Parliament turned into ridicule

The line of counter-attack which Fox was to ignore so rashly was even now ready for use. First round to the Company, and decisively.

The ordeal through which England was passing afforded a singularly unpromising occasion for carrying out an act of bold unpalatable statesmanship. The unflagging persistence of John Robinson in trying to achieve it was as admirable as it was unavailing. In the West, French sea-power and colonial anger in arms were destroying an empire. Ireland had caught the revolutionary infection. At home, a kindly country gentleman, pitchforked into the seat of power by caprice of fortune, was pleading with his resolute Sovereign that he felt himself 'perfectly unequal to the present circumstances of the country'.[137] While his colleagues ignored his leadership and intrigued against each other, he sought in vain to bring together a broader coalition under a new leader – Earl Gower or another. Then in 1780 an outburst of religious fanaticism enabled mob brutality to break through the thin crust which protected organised society and to terrorise a helpless London in the so-called Gordon riots.

These were the circumstances in which Lord North was called upon to break the autonomy of a powerful corporation which had developed a novel form of empire in the East. He was not the man, nor was this the occasion, urgently needful though the assumption of metropolitan control had become. The spasmodic negotiations which took place from 1779 to 1781 reveal a number of significant features.[138] In the first place, the Cabinet as such scarcely functioned on this issue. North himself, over-burdened and distracted, could not be induced to apply his mind to it for more than brief intervals, and on constitutional questions Robinson received virtually no guidance from the Lord Chancellor and the other Law Officers.[139] Secondly, the system of controlling the Proprietors by governmental influence, which Robinson had been operating with some success, broke down. The Proprietors revolted and compelled the Directors to stand out for more favourable financial terms. The struggle accordingly centred on the monetary bargain, and

---

unless Mr. Hastings is instantly removed from his situation. I hope you will therefore direct Mr. Robinson without the loss of a minute to see the Chairman and Deputy-Chairman and have the legal steps taken for removing Hastings and Barwell, and that two men of "integrity and firmness" must be sent to fill up the Commission.' (*Corr. of Geo. III*, vol. IV, p. 339.)

[137] North to the King, 4 June (1779). *Ibid.*, pp. 368-9.

[138] They are traced in detail by Dr. Sutherland (*op. cit.*), Chap. XII.

[139] See Robinson to Jenkinson: " I can't ever get even Attention paid to anything of the kind from our Friend [North], which is really discouraging to have them only considered as Waste Paper . . .' (30 Sept., 1779). 'The Chancellor has had the Papers from the Direction a Week this Day and nothing done . . .' (11 Dec., 1779). ' Indeed and indeed if some System is not fixed and established and steadily pursued, I fear we shall lose that most valuable Country, for which we might be the Manufacturers in many things as we were for America . . .' (7 Feb., 1781). *Addit. MSS.*, 38,212, ff. 126, 281, and *Addit. MSS.*, 38,214, f. 188.

Ministers were faced with the situation that if they adopted the fundamental reforms which Robinson so earnestly desired and sponsored them in Parliament without the prior agreement of East India House, they would expose a vulnerable flank to the Opposition.[140]

In April, 1780, governmental influence in the General Court was so diminished that there was imminent danger of a hostile Court of Directors being chosen at the forthcoming election. To avert it North and his two advisers at last decided to accept the offer of an alliance with the redoubtable Laurence Sulivan and his heterogeneous (and in some cases disreputable) supporters. A pro-Government directorate was the result with Sulivan as Deputy-Chairman and later Chairman. The ambition which he had long cherished seemed almost within his grasp. His aim was to establish himself in supreme and lasting control of the Company's affairs, working in close co-operation with his ally, Warren Hastings, who was to be similarly supreme in India. For that reason he had urged, in 1772, the creation of Crown-appointed Directors and a Governor-General who would be master of his Council and of the other Presidencies.[141] In their need the Government had aligned themselves with him and with Hastings. All that was needed to consolidate the system, wrote Sulivan to Hastings, was that North should insert the necessary constitutional changes in the new Charter Act.[142] North had agreed, he added, that he must be retained in the directorate, and he relied on the Minister to carry it through.

The creation of a supreme Company executive, as the Government's instrument, and a supreme executive officer in India were also Robinson's objectives. In spite of repeated delays and disappointments he still thought (in August, 1780) that 'to regulate a constitution', although a business of great magnitude, was not insurmountably difficult. Yet the autumn and winter months saw no break in the deadlock over the financial terms in spite of Sulivan's interest in reaching an accommodation, and North, who had been ill, made no move. In his original memorandum of 1778 Robinson had expressed the doubt whether Parliament 'in these times' would be prepared to entrust the Crown with 'the real

---

[140] The only reference to constitutional change in the Propositions submitted by the Company on 29 Jan. and on 6 Nov., 1780, was the negative statement (in January): 'The Powers of Nominating and Removing the Gov.-Genl. and Council of Bengal to be vested in the Court of Directors.' *Abstract and Comparative State of the Several Propositions . . . Addit. MSS.*, 38,404, ff. 374-81.

[141] See pp. 62-3 above.

[142] Sulivan afterwards described them in the following terms: ' *clearly* extending the authority of the Governor-General and Council over all India; and making you [i.e. Hastings] Dictator; arming the Directors with greater powers; and preventing those who have passed the Chairs [i.e. himself] from being excluded by rotation.' Sulivan to Hastings, 8 June, 1781. *Addit. MSS.*, 29,149, f. 243. (Quoted by Sutherland, *op. cit.*, pp. 360-1.)

authority which it ought to have ', and that doubt began to harden into certainty. On 12 January, 1781, he had a significant interview with Edmund Burke. At this meeting Burke put forward a number of suggestions regarding the affairs of the Rajah of Tanjore, and the conversation then turned to the wider issue of the Company and its future constitution. The discussion, reported Robinson, produced three 'agreed ideas'. They were, in fact, very similar to the alternative proposals which he himself had put forward in 1778 as essential *minima* if a fundamental reform of the Company's constitution proved impracticable. Burke, as an influential member of the Opposition with a special interest in India, had indicated how far he was prepared to go, and Robinson had assented. The agreed propositions were as follows:

1st That a Power be given to the Governors abroad to Negative the Introduction of new Business in the Council and to stop the Proceedings.

2d That the Court of Directors should Communicate their correspondence and orders to India in like manner as they are directed to transmit those from India.

3dly That the Governors abroad in all their Conduct and Transactions with the Country Powers should be governed and bound by Instructions from His Majesty.[143]

These were accepted by Jenkinson and on his advice were adopted by the Government. They were the only administrative reforms to be introduced in Parliament. Opposition was to be minimised by not attempting to go beyond the understanding reached with Burke.[144] At last in February, when legislative action could be delayed no longer,[145] a meeting of Ministers took place, and after a full discussion Jenkinson was requested to formulate a plan, 'on which Parliament might properly proceed to settle . . . this great concern', if possible with the Company's assent but if

---

[143] 'Minutes taken of Ideas on East Indian affairs suggested by Mr. Burke for Consideration, 12 Jan., 1781.' At the end of the paper a note is added: 'Another meeting to be held.' *Addit. MSS.*, 38,405, f. 10. Cf. Robinson to Jenkinson, 18 Jan., 1781. 'I send you also . . . Burke's paper of Ideas taken down at our meeting . . . but I am sorry that I must send you the rough draft.' *Ibid.*, f. 8. I have preferred to quote the three Propositions set out as a marginal note in the draft of Jenkinson's subsequent memorandum (*Addit. MSS.*, 38,398, f. 82) rather than the 'shorthand' version in the Minutes.

[144] Burke was as good as his word. When North made his general motion relative to the Company's affairs on 9 April, 1781, Burke warned him against beginning the business by 'an act of violence' in employing parliamentary action to extort monetary contributions from the Company, but he concluded 'by pledging himself, and those in opposition with whom he had conversed on the subject, to support the noble lord in everything that should appear to them conducive to the joint interest of the Company and the kingdom'. *Parl. Hist.*, vol. XXII, 113-14.

[145] In May 1780 a short Bill had been passed continuing the existing legislation for still another year. By Feb. 1781 a decision had thus become urgent if a new Charter Act was to be got through before the end of the session.

necessary without it. Jenkinson thereupon produced a memorandum which provided a plan of proceeding in Parliament and a
policy directive. North subsequently followed both in detail.

On the policy side Jenkinson incorporated almost *verbatim* large
parts of Robinson's memorandum of 1778, quoting his major proposals as the ideal arrangement and then coming down decisively
in favour of the Robinson-Burke compromise.[146] As to the constitutional set-up in India he took his stand on the Regulating Act
– of which he himself had been the principal architect. 'I continue
of Opinion that the Principles are right, and that we ought still to
support them', but in several respects he wished to see them reinforced. Much the most important of his proposals in this connexion
related to the powers of the Governors. Burke (whom he cited) had
proposed that they should be given a negative in all matters before
their respective Councils. Jenkinson agreed but wished to go
further. A veto, he wrote, would suffice in the inferior settlements,
but the Governor-General ought in addition to be given the
positive power to over-ride. 'The Governor-General of Bengal,
tho' bound in every Measure to advise with his Council, should be
at liberty to act contrary to their advice if He will take the Measure
upon Himself.' In that eventuality he and every Councillor should
be obliged to state their opinion with their reasons, and their signed
statements should be sent home to the Directors. This provision
was to be a familiar feature of 'Crown Colony' government in later
years, but it was clean contrary to the prevailing colonial tradition.
When North in the Commons afterwards advanced in a tentative
way the idea of strengthening the Governor-General's powers,
General Richard Smith retorted that if the noble Lord knew as
much of the abuse of power in India as he did he would rather
think it wise to lessen than to increase the power of any person in
high office there.[147] The proposal was dropped: neither the veto
nor the positive discretionary power was conferred.

As to the Supreme Court of Judicature in Bengal Jenkinson
recommended that it should certainly be continued in spite of the
Proprietors' efforts to get rid of it, for it embodied one of the basic
principles of the Regulating Act, but its jurisdiction should be
confined within the limits originally intended; and he expressed the
hope that its disciplinary value might be increased by extending

---

[146] There is a fair copy of the whole of this composite document in *Addit. MSS.*,
38,400, ff. 64-97, but in summarising Jenkinson's conclusion I have used the
annotated draft in *Addit. MSS.*, 38,398, ff. 70-83 because of the informative marginal
comments which it contains. There is a draft of Jenkinson's preamble to the 'Plan'
in *Addit. MSS.*, 38,398, ff. 57-63. For Dr. Sutherland's identification and dating of
this (unsigned and undated) memorandum see *op. cit.*, p. 354, n. 3. It seems probable
that Jenkinson and Robinson collaborated in producing it, particularly in view of
the reliance which the former placed, in formulating his conclusions, on the terms
of the agreement reached in the Robinson-Burke conversations.

[147] *Parl. Hist.*, vol. XXII, 330.

its authority to British subjects resident in Madras and Bombay. The nomination of the Governor-General and his Councillors should remain with the Directors, but the negative given to the Minister should also continue. 'He will seldom have it in his Power to appoint the Person that he wishes, but He will always have it in his Power to prevent the appointment of any Person Manifestly improper.' Similarly, in order to safeguard the superintending authority of the Governor-General and Council, the Court of Directors (who were jealous of it) should be required to send copies of all comumnications between themselves and the subordinate Presidencies to Calcutta.

Turning then to the constitution at the centre, Jenkinson set out Robinson's original proposals as being the *desiderata,* that is to say, that the powers of the Court of Proprietors should be drastically reduced and that the Crown should appoint half the Directors and a 'Governor' to preside. He even added a further argument from colonial analogy in support of the proposition.[148] But it was not, he concluded, politically feasible.

However proper this may be in Theory, I am fearful that it would be impossible in the present state of things to go so far, and it might be dangerous perhaps to attempt it; We must revert therefore to Expedients less effectual, and which will prove in the end less Advantageous, perhaps, to the Company as well as to the Publick.

The 'expedients' which he advocated were those which Robinson had agreed wih Burke. He was entirely of Burke's opinion, he wrote, that the Directors should be required to communicate their outward correspondence to the King's Ministers in like manner as they were already directed to transmit those from India. 'The very Communication of these Orders implies that the King's Ministers have a Right to interfere in the Orders sent to India with their Advice at least, and this makes them in some degree responsible.' He also approved Burke's suggestion that the Governments abroad should be governed and bound by instructions from the King in all transactions with the Country Powers. He ventured, however, to suggest an amended procedure.[149] Let the Directors

---

[148] 'It would be easy to show that many of the Charter Governments in the Colonies who had originally Charters similar to that which the East India Company possess at present, and were considered merely as Commercial Companys, upon their obtaining Territorial Acquisitions, were formed into Governments upon the Model just described.' This may be Jenkinson's own comment: it does not appear in Robinson's memorandum of 1778. It may, however, derive (together with some other points) from a memorandum which Robinson is known to have produced in Oct. 1779.

[149] Jenkinson's desire not to go beyond what Burke would support is evident. 'I agree with Mr. Burke . . . if he will allow me to make one alteration which appears to me to be unexceptionable.'

continue to be the sole channel of communication in these matters, but obeying such instructions as they might receive from Ministers. If the Crown as well as the Court of Directors communicated with the Presidencies, the Company's Servants would 'frequently receive contradictory Orders'. By these proposals, Jenkinson concluded, 'the whole *Political* Power over the Company's Settlements in India would devolve on the Crown', while the civil government and the management of their trade and revenues would remain with the Company – 'subject however to Advice and Admonition from the Ministers of the Crown, as implied in . . . Mr. Burke's Propositions'. These seemed wise and salutary regulations, and they were perhaps 'as much as it would be prudent to aim at in the present State of Things'.

Having made reasonably sure of a safe passage in the Commons on the issue of state control, the Government proceeded to apply parliamentary coercion to the refractory Proprietors on the financial side. Having successfully stalled on this for almost three years, they were confidently defiant. In Jenkinson's opinion they would never come to any reasonable agreement with Government, 'unless they are by some means or other compelled to it'. Even under the pressure of parliamentary resolutions, and despite Sulivan's efforts in the directorate, they put up a fierce and prolonged resistance. It was not until 26 June that the Company presented their formal petition to Parliament, seeking renewal of the Charter and setting out agreed financial conditions.[150] The long battle was over: the

---

[150] On 9 April North moved that on the 25th of the month the House should consider the proper method of managing the territorial acquisitions and revenues of the Company and of securing to the public 'a just proportion' of the profits. In his speech he outlined all the proposals in Jenkinson's memorandum. This move was intended (as Jenkinson had suggested) to compel the Company to offer terms before Parliament took action. On the 27th, however, he was obliged to admit that he was not in a position to present specific propositions, for he had failed to reach agreement with the Directors; and he asked for an adjournment. On 9 May, this performance was repeated. On 29 May, North had to report that the Proprietors had assumed the offensive: they were about to ballot in a General Court on a proposition to lend to the Exchequer a sum not exceeding £600,000, in return for Exchequer bills which the Company was to be free, if the need arose, to cash in payment of their customs duties. This, said North, was a totally unacceptable form of loan, and it would, moreover, 'virtually put an end to the claim of the public to the Company's territorial possessions by assuming that no money was due to the public from the Company'. In order to anticipate the ballot North moved a resolution that in the opinion of the House three-quarters of the net profits of the Company after the payment of a dividend of 8 per cent ought to be paid into the Exchequer. (This was the arrangement which he had consistently pressed from the outset.) The resolution was agreed to after an amendment had been defeated by 151 to 52. On 28 May North proceeded with his other Resolutions. On 1 June further pressure was applied by introducing a Bill for securing to the public the payment of three-quarters of the net surplus for the years 1778 to 1781. Then came the final struggle and a settlement on 25 June. (See *Parl. Hist.*, vol. XXII, 108-19, 200-4, 303-36, 531-8, 574-85.)

approved propositions were cast into legislative form, and the Bill was quickly passed at the tail end of the session.[151]

Sulivan viewed the outcome with anger and dismay. North lacked nerve, he informed Hastings, and the result was 'a paltry performance'. His disappointment was very understandable: the hope of a Sulivan-Hastings hegemony in Indian affairs, which he had laboured so long to attain, was gone. The fact that the North Administration was at this time securing majorities in the Commons of 70 and upwards was insufficient ground for assuming that only courage was required to carry a measure reducing the Company's automony to the status of a colonial dependency. There is little doubt that Jenkinson's judgement was sound in rejecting the enterprise as unjustifiably hazardous, even though the King and several Ministers were in favour of it. The establishment of direct control by the State would have involved in practice a very great extension of Crown patronage. A unitary executive for Indian affairs, comprising Crown as well as Company representatives and directed by a Crown-appointed President, was theoretically the best solution; but it was never effected. Patronage was the stumbling block.

The 'State' was too narrowly based to be readily trusted with responsibilities which changing conditions increasingly demanded that it should assume. Even though the reaction after the Gordon riots and the snap general election which followed had temporarily strengthened the North Administration, Dunning's famous Resolution was on the record. During the debates on the Company's affairs in 1781 there were clear indications that Opposition elements were eagerly waiting for the Government to provide them with a wonderful opportunity. Consequently the Charter Act of 1781 left the mob of factious Proprietors as masters of the Company's central executive. Even the system of control-by-influence had broken down.[152] On the other hand the gains had not been negligible. The King's Ministers could now dictate the Company's 'foreign' policy and could also bring pressure to bear regarding the management of the internal affairs of the Presidencies by means of 'advice and admonition'. Again, the Proprietors' campaign to get rid of the Supreme Court of Judicature in Bengal as an unwarrantable interference had been successfully resisted, even though Jenkinson had been unable to get its jurisdiction extended to Madras and Bombay.

In retrospect the emphasis placed upon the financial bargain

---

[151] *21 Geo. III, cap. 65.* Robinson's strenuous part in this contest is indicated in his numerous letters to Jenkinson. (See *Addit. MSS.*, 38,405 and 38,214 *passim*.)

[152] See Jenkinson's disgusted comment: 'I grow every day to have a worse opinion of these Gentlemen [the Directors] and wish therefore to have as little Connection or intercourse with them as possible; I am sure I can have none to any good purpose.' Jenkinson to Dundas, 10 Sept., 1781. *Addit. MSS.*, 38,308, f. 168.

seems inordinate, but the wartime strain upon the national finances was compulsive. Moreover North's unusual pertinacity in seeking to tap this revenue from the Orient was dictated not only by financial need but also by the fact that the payment of an annual quota was considered to involve acknowledgement of the territorial soverignty of the Crown *vis-à-vis* the Company, which was being disputed. The deteriorating position of the Company in India deprived North of most of his expectation.[153] On the other hand, the Company was induced to accept responsibility for the future of a substantial part of the cost of Crown troops and naval vessels sent to India at the Company's request. A valuable (and unique) contribution to imperial defence had been secured. Perhaps the chief significance of this struggle between the metropolitan Government and a powerful imperial corporation is to be found in the growing recognition by Ministers that the occasion could not be postponed much longer when the State would be compelled by its material interests as well as by considerations of honour to assume responsibility, unwelcome and hazardous as the operation would be.

---

[153] He was obliged to abandon the claim for a loan of £1 million or more as well as the payment of a fine in return for renewal of the charter, and the stipulation in the new Act for annual payments from the net surplus proved almost as illusory as the previous arrangement of 1769.

CHAPTER III

THE FRONTIERS OF STATE CONTROL

1. THE ADVENT OF HENRY DUNDAS

THE struggle over the Charter Act of 1781 provided Henry Dundas with a political opportunity which he was quick to seize and exploit. When Jenkinson's recommendations were adopted by the Cabinet in the Spring of 1781 and the drafting of a bill became urgent, Dundas was brought in to assist as Thurlow's representative. Robinson and Dundas, both shrewd politicians, were already well acquainted,[1] and they worked long hours together on the basis of the Robinson-Jenkinson plan. As the clauses were drawn, Dundas took them along to Thurlow for approval.[2]

Dundas came of an old Scottish family which had bred many lawyers, and he had continued the tradition in a distinguished career at the Scottish bar and then as Lord Advocate. Elected as member for Midlothian at the general election of October, 1774, he had won increasing esteem and influence in the Commons by his courage and administrative capacity until he had become one of North's most valued supporters. Enjoying the further advantage of the Lord Chancellor's confidence, he was just the man whom North needed to take the lead for Administration in this difficult subject. His legal experience and political adroitness made him particularly well fitted to deal with technical and controversial evidence. Moreover, the rising importance of India in public estimation as a compensatory field for the probable loss of the American Colonies was being strongly reinforced by anxiety lest misbehaviour and contumacy would force the British out of the Orient, leaving a clear field for her rivals in both hemispheres. 'The East,' it was said, 'was now almost our last stake.'[3] In short, Indian affairs offered a hazardous but promising road to political

---

[1] For numerous letters between Robinson and Dundas see *Hist. MSS. Comm. Abergavenny MSS.*, 10th Rept. (1887), App. VI.

[2] See Robinson to Jenkinson, 23 April, 1781: 'The Advocate came here yesterday and staid all Night. He has collected all the Ld. Chancellor's Ideas about the India Business, who thinks perfectly in it and is warm in it – We last night went thro' the Bill I had prepared a long while ago, great part of which will adapt itself to the Present Plan, and the Advocate took it with him to Town, to show the Chancellor who said he wished to see something put on paper of a Bill.' *Addit. MSS.*, 38,405, f. 109. On the following day Robinson wrote again: 'Having this Moment finished some remarks on the Company propositions delivered this Day, I send both to you for your perusal . . . I expect the Advocate to breakfast with me, probably it may suit you to see him while he is here.' *Ibid.*, f. 114. Cf. Same to same, 26 April, 1781. *Addit. MSS.*, 38,216, f. 76.

[3] *Annual Register* for 1781 (2nd edn., Lond., 1791), p. 192.

eminence: a challenging opportunity which the long-sighted Dundas seized and held with sustained tenacity.

As a specialist on India Jenkinson had almost ten years' start of him and was his equal in shrewdness and efficiency; but he lacked Dundas's easy geniality and resilience. Jenkinson found his *métier*, as we shall see, in a more impersonal sphere, as 'managing director' of British overseas trade. For the next twenty years the dominating interest of Dundas was British policy in India and the Far East, and his original mentors were Robinson and Jenkinson. As he worked on the Bill with its two authors, he quickly mastered his brief and made their ideas for a progressive assertion of state control his own.

North also accepted the view, circumstances permitting, that this process ought to be continued and he indicated as much in Parliament.[4] For his part Robinson remained convinced that something more than 'wretched expedients' could be effected. 'Indeed and indeed,' he declared to Jenkinson, 'if some System is not soon fixed and established and steadily pursued, I fear we shall lose that most valuable Country, for which we might be the Manufacturers in many things as we were for America.'[5] Hence his anger and disgust when North passively allowed the Opposition to seize the initiative in investigating abuses. On 24 January, 1781, the two petitions from Bengal protesting against the activities of the Supreme Court had been presented to the House, and on 12 February General Richard Smith moved for a Select Committee to consider them.[6] When the ballot for the fifteen members took place a few days later, the Government was caught unprepared and all but a few of the places were filled by their opponents. Thus was established the Committee which under the dedicated leadership of Burke (and with the vengeful Francis at his elbow) prepared the famous series of Reports which stung the national conscience and began to inculcate a sense of responsibility which deeply influenced subsequent relations with non-European peoples, and not only in India.

---

[4] On 25 May, 1781, he propounded the idea that the Governor-General might be empowered under certain conditions to act independently of his Council and that the Presidents of Councils in the other Presidencies might be given a negative. He then added that these propositions were only put forward for the information of the House, 'that they might turn their minds towards them against another Year, when . . . the House might have the opportunity of considering them with all the attention which their consequence and their novelty required.' *Parl. Hist.*, vol. XXII, 326.

[5] Robinson to Jenkinson, 7 Feb., 1781. *Addit. MSS.*, 38,215, f. 188.

[6] *Parl. Hist.*, vol. XXI, 1175-1207. Cf. *Annual Register* for 1781, pp. 175*-9*. In commenting on the appointment of the Select Committee in a letter to Jenkinson (14 Feb., 1781) Robinson wrote: 'I told Lord North what it would be, which he treated as indifferent, and which I wish he may find so, but it is entirely in the hands of Opposition. What a figure will this make in India. What will be the effect of it there?' (*Addit. MSS.*, 38,215, f. 203.)

This, however, was action promoted by the Opposition, who found that exposure of Indian abuses was an effective method of harassing a Government already hard pressed. When the news arrived of Hyder Ali's invasion of the Carnatic and the imminent peril of Madras, an opportunity occurred of regaining something of the initiative for the Ministry, and North was induced to move (on 30 April) for a Secret Committee to investigate the causes of the new menace and the present condition of British possessions in that region. This time the ballot was carefully organised and the chosen members were almost entirely pro-Government.[7] The core of the new Committee, which was empowered to sit in India House, examine the Company's papers, and make recommendations, con-sisted of Dundas (the chairman), Jenkinson and Robinson. Thus the architects of the India Act of 1781, with Dundas as their leader, were enabled to prepare the way for the sort of 'system' in Indian affairs which Robinson had advocated for so long.

During the years 1781 and 1782, while the North Administration disintegrated and political groups fell into a state of flux and con-fusion, the formidable labours of these two Committees, in effect, gave direction to Britain's future policy in India. 'It was Dundas, building on the experience of Robinson, Jenkinson, and their friends, who laid down the nature of the reforms; it was Burke and his associates who made some sweeping reforms inevitable.'[8]

It may be true that the Secret Committee went further than North had intended,[9] but there seems little doubt that he had already decided that he had found in Dundas a strong and capable supporter to whom he could hand over – with a sigh of relief – the supervision of Indian affairs. As early as June, 1781, there were

---

[7] In the debate on North's motion (*Parl. Hist.*, vol. XXII, 119-38) the Opposition put up a strong but unsuccessful resistance to the appointment of a 'Secret' Committee.

[8] Sutherland (*op. cit.*), p. 369.

[9] In moving for a Secret Committee North resisted pressure to widen its terms of reference to include the situation in Bengal, remarking that, while he recognised that the situation in every part of the British possessions in India called for investi-gation, ' he meant to take them up one by one for the sake of greater ease and accuracy' (*Parl. Hist.*, vol. XXII, 135). On 4 Dec., 1781, the Secret Committee's terms of reference were enlarged to include the origins and present state of the Maratha War and all other hostilities in which the Presidency of Bengal had been or was then engaged. On the same day the Select Committee, which had been initially concerned with the administration of justice in Bengal, was further in-structed to ' consider how the British Possessions in the East Indies may be held and governed with the greatest security and advantage to this Country and by what means the happiness of the native inhabitants may be best promoted '. (Sutherland, *op. cit.*, p. 367 n. 2 and p. 368 n. 1.) Thomas Orde, who afterwards became one of Pitt's chief ' men of business ', brought himself to notice by his industry as a member of the Secret Committee. In April, 1782, Dundas in the Commons singled him out for special compliment: ' such were the talents of Mr. Orde in this business of investi-gation, that no minister who meant to act honestly, could possibly overlook him, or neglect to employ his great abilities in the service of his country.' (*Parl. Hist.*, vol. XXII, 1276.)

rumours that Dundas was to be appointed to a new Secretaryship of State for India, and in a letter to his son he did not deny that something of the sort was in contemplation.[10] About a month later he reported to his brother that North had offered him a seat at the Treasury Board. The ground upon which the offer had been made, he explained, was Lord North's desire 'that I should be in a situation which placed me constantly near himself . . . meaning that in that situation with the assistance of a secretary or two under me, I might take the management of the affairs of India into my hands'.[11] He added that he had been told as an inducement that this step would lead as a matter of course to his appointment as Chancellor of the Exchequer, Paymaster, Treasurer of the Navy, or Secretary of State for India. The offer was, however, declined – possibly because the Ministry, as then constituted, had too precarious a look or because North had not been sufficiently specific about the creation of an Indian Secretaryship. Nonetheless North clung to Dundas both for general support and as his right-hand man in Indian affairs. On the eve of a new session of Parliament in November North sent him an urgent request to leave Scotland in time to be in his place for the opening debates.

The result of our first day's debate will be of infinite consequence. On the second day, we must reappoint the Secret Committee and we hope to see you again at the head of it. At the meeting after Christmas we shall probably take some steps in India business, if any step appears necessary or expedient. In all these matters Your presence is absolutely and indispensably requisite. . . .[12]

By the beginning of March, 1782, it was evident that the North Administration was on the point of dissolution, and in order to save the situation Dundas suggested (through Robinson) that Pitt and some of his young friends might be brought in. Pitt was to be Treasurer of the Navy, and for himself Dundas suggested a new office which he styled 'Secretary for India and Plantations'.[13] The proposed alliance was, in fact, an impossible combination. On 15 March the Ministry only survived a motion of no confidence

---

[10] ' Your news of my being Secretary of State for India has not yet been communicated to me. Whatever temptations may come in my way, I don't think I shall be induced to quit the King's Advocateship . . .' Dundas to his son, Robert, 16 June, 1781. Quoted by H. Furber, *Henry Dundas, First Viscount Melville* (Oxford, 1931), pp. 11-12.

[11] Dundas to his brother, Robert, 12 July, 1781. Quoted by C. Matheson, *The Life of Henry Dundas, First Viscount Melville* (London, 1933), pp. 69-70.

[12] North to Dundas, 18 Nov., 1781. *Melville MSS. North Corresp.*, Nat. Library of Scotland. Quoted by Furber (*op. cit.*), p. 13.

[13] Dundas further suggested that, if North's own resignation proved unavoidable, an attempt should be made to form a coalition with either the Rockingham or the Shelburne Whigs, but he himself would go out with North. See Furber (*op. cit.*), p. 15. For a further account of Dundas's part in attempts to reconstruct the Ministry, see Matheson (*op. cit.*), pp. 74-9.

by a margin of nine votes: it was clearly impossible for it to go on and five days later North thankfully resigned.

In the political wilderness Dundas remained cheerful and confident. The mutual jealousies of the Whig groups would in his opinion render them incapable of maintaining a stable Administration for long, and an alliance between one of these groups and the followers of North (and the King) would prove to be the solution. Meanwhile he himself was in a strong independent position. Because of his outstanding ability, courage, and calculating ambition he was regarded on all sides as a valuable and potentially attainable asset: both Shelburne and Fox went out of their way to pay him compliments. Furthermore by prodigious labour he had used his opportunities as chairman of the Secret Committee to master a mass of documents at East India House so that on Indian questions he was now widely regarded as the authoritative parliamentary leader. With a general clamour that 'something must be done about India' (provided, of course, that remedial action did not bear too hardly on vested interests), no Administration in the 1780s could expect to get along without the aid of such a man; and Dundas was not unaware of the fact. Burke, who was working just as hard on the Indian data, was a prophet, whose emotional denunciations tended to weary the House: Dundas, no less expert, was an experienced 'man of business'.

When the Rockingham Ministry took office, Dundas lost no time in asserting his position as the director of Indian policy. On 9 April he 'called the attention of the House to the long meditated and important consideration of the East-India affairs'. In a speech of about three hours' length he surveyed the conduct of the three Presidencies in their relations with Indian states from the time of Clive. Happy had it been for Britain, he declared, if Clive's policy of avoiding territorial commitments had been continued instead of embarking upon offensive military operations with a view to conquest. A flourishing trade was imperilled; the Presidencies were burdened with debt; and the British had incurred the distrust and enmity of dangerous neighbours. He called upon the present Ministry to support him in carrying the business through: if they had other plans, he would readily adapt or abandon his own. But it was essential that something material be done and that quickly.

On all sides his analysis was acknowledged as a 'masterly' performance, and his theme that interference in the wars and intrigues of Indian Princes had produced nothing but disgrace and financial embarrassment exactly expressed the prevailing mood. Fox urbanely informed him that there could be no better way of supporting the Rockingham Administration than by bringing forward measures to eradicate corruption and peculation, whether at home or abroad; but he was quick to condemn his tentative suggestion of sending out a special commission, armed with plenipotentiary powers, to restore peace and carry out reforms. Was he not aware that the device of sending Supervisors had been tried before and had repeatedly failed?

Fox then went on in a strain which is of interest in the light of his own proposals of the following year. It behoved Dundas and the House in general to be on their guard to prevent any system of reform in India, or elsewhere, from increasing 'the undue influence of the Crown'. The intervention of the Crown was the worst possible sort of intervention. He was not prepared to give an opinion on the best means of carrying out the necessary reforms, but on a first view of the business he would advise the House 'to stick to its constitutional province, to abstain as much as possible from interfering with the Government, but to let those who were responsible, and ought to be responsible, direct the executive branch'. The true function of Parliament was to control: when necessary it should be resorted to; but it should never be 'too ready to interfere in the first instance'.[14]

This was standard 'Rockingham' doctrine; but on this occasion Fox was giving Dundas a clear warning that his favourite idea of a Secretary of State for India, responsible to the Crown for the administration of the Indian territories – and all the patronage therein involved – would be opposed by the Government. In 1783, when called upon to frame his own system, Fox again refused to consider the establishment of so dangerous a Crown Minister, and in consequence he was driven into the fatal alternative of vesting the power and influence in Parliament as distinct and separate from the King-in-Parliament.

On 15 April Dundas followed up his oration by proposing a set of forty-five Resolutions, based on the first two Reports of the Secret Committee. They comprised a forthright condemnation of 'all schemes of conquest and enlargement of dominion' and a critical survey of the external policy of the three Presidencies. Bombay (and to a lesser extent the Governor-General) were criticised for becoming involved in an impolitic and dangerous war with the Marathas, and Madras for inflaming the resentment of the Nizam of Hyderabad so that the British were threatened by a general confederacy against them. It was the duty of the Court of Directors, ran the 44th Resolution, to recall such senior officers in the Presidencies as appeared to have been chiefly responsible for wilfully pursuing a policy tending to inspire distrust in the moderation, justice and good faith of the British nation.

Two days later Dundas moved another set of twenty-two Resolutions relating to the conduct of the Government of Madras: their

---

[14] For Dundas's speech and the ensuing debate see *Parl. Hist.*, vol. XXII, 1275-90.

criminal lethargy which had left Madras unprepared for Hyder Ali's invasion of the Carnatic and the huge and complicated scandal of the Nawab of Arcot's debts. Out of this second series arose a third, comprising twenty-four Resolutions, relating to the enormous peculations of Sir Thomas Rumbold, now a member of Parliament. The upshot of these last was a bill of pains and penalties against Rumbold; but in spite of Dundas's dogged pertinacity in this ungrateful task, the bill was eventually dropped because of continued failure to muster a quorum. It is significant of the situation that, while men viewed wealth-getting in India by force and fraud with distaste and fear and were genuinely behind Burke and Dundas for a reform of the system, the prosecution of individual delinquents was not popular: they were usually influential and one prosecution might lead to another – nearer home.

No one was disposed to deny that Dundas had done an extremely thorough job with a lawyer's clarity and objectivity. When challenged as to whether he had any 'specific measures' to put forward on the basis of his Resolutions, he was cautious. They would at any rate, he answered, be on record in the *Journals* of the House: they would be 'a kind of law, both to His Majesty's Ministers and the Court of Directors'. He did not know what measures the Ministry might have in contemplation: if they had any which differed from his, he would not press his own. But he admitted that he had proposals to put forward, 'that would appear to arise out of the Resolutions themselves'.[15]

Dundas knew well enough that the Rockingham Administration had neither the time nor the mind to frame a new system of Indian management, and so become involved in a struggle with the Company. Committed to 'economical' reform, at odds among themselves, and pledged to rescue the nation from a now unpopular war, they had other matters to absorb their attention. Yet most people, whether in Parliament, East India House, or the coffee houses, were uneasily aware that the position of the British in India was hanging in the balance. According to the news Hastings was doing prodigious things in saving the military situation; and yet Burke and his associates (and they were all honourable men) were denouncing him as a monster. A month later (on 30 May) the Commons resolved on Dundas's motion that Warren Hastings ought to be recalled. The Court of Directors complied, but the Proprietors saw this as a first step in a general purge, mustered their forces, and in a General Court carried a vote rescinding the order. The Proprietors were still the masters.

If Dundas had brought in his India Bill at this juncture he

---

[15] For the text of the three sets of Resolutions and a summary of the debates thereon (15 to 29 April) see *Parl. Hist.*, vol. XXII, 1291-1331. Debates on the Reports of the Select Committee alternated with these.

might have split the Ministry, for its terms would certainly have been rejected by Fox and the Rockingham Whigs, whereas Shelburne and the Chathamites (whose ideas about the position of the Crown in the constitution were very different) would have been disposed to favour it, as presumably would many followers of North and the Court. But Dundas perceived a better road to his goal. Through the good offices of his friend and ally, Thurlow, he was introduced to Shelburne, who paid him court in a number of conversations which centred on India and Scotland.[16] On 1 July (1782) Rockingham died: the King immediately called upon Shelburne to form an Administration: Fox and his friends refused to serve under Shelburne; and Dundas became Treasurer of the Navy and controller of Scottish patronage. Had the Ministry survived the debates on the peace treaties in the following February, there is little doubt that Shelburne and Dundas would have introduced a Bill under which the latter would have exercised increased governmental control as Secretary of State for India in effect if not in name, while the office of Governor-General, to be held by Cornwallis, would have been strengthened.[17]

When the efforts of Dundas to save the Government by an alliance with North were defeated by Pitt's resistance and when Fox rejected the terms offered by Pitt, the formation of the Fox-North Coalition, incongruous as it was, became almost inevitable. Pitt and Dundas went into opposition, and on 14 April, 1783, the latter as a private member introduced his India Bill. It had, of course, no chance of survival, for its principles were anathema to Fox and his friends; but Dundas, sitting alongside Pitt, was determined to chalk out his own position on India for future reference. He was also quite sincere in his anxiety to see the conduct of Indian affairs put on a sound basis before it was too late.

The Bill derived directly from the ideas and experience of Robinson and Jenkinson. It went further with regard to state control than Jenkinson had thought 'prudent' two years before and not so far as Robinson had originally proposed. Its central feature was the vesting of supreme power in India in the Governor-General, who was to be authorised, if need arose, to over-ride his Council and act independently. The procedure laid down to cover this eventuality was elaborate. If the Governor-General disagreed with the majority of his Council on a given proposal, he was to adjourn the discussion, 'if the case would admit of delay', for at least twenty-four hours. When the Council had reassembled he was to read out the proposal at issue and take the opinion of each member, beginning with the youngest. If a majority was still against him and he himself remained of the opinion 'that the measure

---

[16] Matheson, *Life of Dundas*, p. 85.
[17] Cf. vol. I, p. 419, n. 29 of this work.

would be for the safety of the State and for the interest of the Company', he was to order the opinion of each member to be entered on the record and was then to take an oath, declaring that he, in his conscience, regarded the measure as expedient and in the public interest. Thereupon the motion would become valid, and he might order it to be put into immediate execution. In that event four copies of all the relevant proceedings were to be sent at once to England by different routes for the consideration of the Court of Directors and the approval or disallowance of a Secretary of State.[18]

Since the Governor-General in such a case, declared Dundas, should have the sole power, 'so he should have the whole responsibility on himself'.[19] It was a revolutionary proposal, representing a clear break with colonial tradition. Only the extreme necessity of imposing discipline and establishing effective control over the 'foreign policy' of the Company's Servants in India induced Ministers and Parliament, slowly and with great reluctance, to arm the man on the spot with supreme power and thereafter to trust him. When at last in 1786 Dundas had his way and Cornwallis was made master of his Council, a precedent had been established which was followed after 1793 when conquered French, Dutch and Spanish dependencies were brought within the British Empire. Thus Robinson and Dundas may be numbered among the progenitors of British Crown Colony government.

The functions of the Governor-General, particularly with regard to external affairs, were listed and defined, and in order to give precision to his authority over the subordinate Presidencies he was authorised to visit them with such members of his Council as he might think fit to take with him, enquire into any troubles, suspend and imprison the trouble-makers, and appoint others in their place pending the decision of the Directors. Furthermore the Governor-General was also to be Commander-in-Chief. Aware that the establishment of a dictatorship in Calcutta would be extremely unpalatable both in Parliament and with the Company, and especially when Burke and the Select Committee were pouring out denunciations against Warren Hastings, Dundas repeated his previous opinion that the recall of Hastings was a necessity. But the Shelburne Administration, he hastened to add, had found in

---

[18] This was based on one of Robinson's proposals, but it is noteworthy that the detailed procedure as set out in the Bill follows almost word for word the plan suggested about the year 1779 by the barrister, John Lind, who had been employed at the Treasury to 'collect and methodise' the various proposals sent in by Warren Hastings, Philip Francis, Sir Elijah Impey and others. See Bruce, *Historical Views of Plans for the Government of British India . . . , (ut supra)*, pp. 77-81. Lind stated that he had modelled this procedure on that of the Dutch in relation to the Governor-General of Batavia. Laurence Sulivan had made a similar proposal, based on the same precedent. See p. 62 above.

[19] *Parl. Hist.*, vol. XXIII, 758.

Lord Cornwallis a most proper person to assume the supreme government in India. On this man with his unsullied integrity, ample fortune, and military experience, the late Ministry had 'justly built all their hopes of the salvation of our dying interests in Asia'.

If one man was to wield supreme authority in the conduct of British affairs in India, it was clearly necessary that he himself should be made effectively responsible; and responsible, not to a weak Court of Directors liable to be over-ruled by the Proprietors but to the metropolitan Government. On the other hand, it was equally evident that Fox and his supporters in the Coalition Ministry, no less than the Company, would resist the corollary of increased Crown influence. Dundas accordingly limited his proposals in this connexion to securing effective Crown control over the selection and removal of the chief executive officers in India, that is to say, the Governor-General and his Council and the Governors and Councillors in the subordinate Presidencies. In all these cases the initial appointment was to vest in the Crown, and all were to be removable by an order from the King under his sign manual and counter-signed by a Secretary of State.[20] In the event of a vacancy arising in any of these offices, including that of the Governor-General, the Court of Directors were to retain the right of appointment, but subject to the King's approval; and if the Directors refused to comply the Crown was to appoint the person of its choice. In view of the recent action of the Proprietors in preventing the Directors from recalling Hastings at the behest of Parliament, the future position with regard to the recall of senior officers was to be strongly safeguarded. If the Court of Directors became dissatisfied with any Governor or Councillor, they were to be empowered to make representations to the King, and thereupon they were to follow 'such measures as, in his royal wisdom, he should think fit to prescribe to them'. But such representations were not to be amended or rescinded by the Court of Proprietors.

Under this Bill no attempt was made to establish an overt form of control over the Company's executive in London, and the bulk of the patronage was left at the Company's disposal. There was nothing, for example, corresponding to Robinson's original suggestion of a new Board of Direction with half of its members appointed by the Crown. Dundas intended to rely on a Governor-General who had been selected by Government, had been given ample and defined powers, and held office during the pleasure of the Crown

---

[20] As in the Regulating Act, a new Governor-General and Council were to be named in the proposed Bill. The recall of Governors and Councillors in the other Presidencies were to be by royal order, and a copy of all such Orders was to be sent to the Chairman and Deputy Chairman of the Court of Directors within fourteen days of being signed.

and not of the Company. In all matters of major policy in India he could be expected, therefore, to follow, and could be relied on to execute the wishes of a Secretary of State on pain of recall.

The other provisions of the Bill were concerned with remedial measures in India. Following suggestions by Hastings, Chambers and others, Dundas would have established a 'subordinate legislature' in Calcutta, comprising the Governor-General and Council, the Chief Justice and the other judges of the Supreme Court. Its ordinances were to provide for the good government of the British Possessions: they were not to operate upon His Majesty's natural-born subjects in any way repugnant to the laws of England, and they were not to conflict with the religions, laws, and customs of India. All proposed ordinances were to receive three readings and were to pass by a majority of votes and be approved by the Governor-General. Copies were to be sent home to the Directors, and the Chairman was to submit them to the King for approval within fourteen days of receipt. Appeals against any ordinance might be submitted to the Crown within sixty days of promulgation and with the consent of the Privy Council could be declared void. Two years before, Jenkinson had considered this idea and had rightly turned it down as being unnecessary.[21]

On the vexed question of land tenure in Bengal the Bill followed the policy advocated by Philip Francis in seeking to restore the zemindars on a footing 'as secure, as permanent, and as stable as any freehold in England'.[22] On the other hand, Dundas was not

---

[21] 'Much has been said,' wrote Jenkinson in 1781, 'by Mr. Hastings and others who have acted as Councillors or Judges in Bengal on the Appointment of a subordinate Legislature in that Country. In all Countries governed as Bengal is and always must be, the Legislative Authority is lodged in the same hands with the Executive. There is, however, an excellent Regulation on this Subject in the 13th Geo. 3ᵈ C. 63, Sec. 36 and 37 (i.e. empowering the Governor-General and Council to make regulations subject to disallowance by the Crown), and in my opinion nothing need be added on this head.' (*Addit. MSS.*, 38,398, f. 76.)

[22] The obsession of Francis with his vendetta against Hastings and his part in directing the reforming wrath of Burke and the Select Committee in that direction have tended to obscure the very considerable influence which Francis exerted at this time over the general formulation of policy with regard to India. His doctrine of non-involvement in the politics and wars of Indian States and that the internal administration of Bengal could and should be handed back to the zemindars was eagerly accepted by many in preference to the hazardous and expensive ' imperialism ' of Hastings. Cf. Jenkinson's remark: ' I agree almost entirely in Opinion with Mr. Francis in every point that had reference to this object, vizt, That the Landed Revenue should again be put under the Management of the ancient Zemindars, as far as is consistent with the Circumstances of the Country and the present state of that Body of Men.' *Addit. MSS.*, 38,398, f. 76. Cf. Burke's speech on 1 Dec., 1783: ' This man [Francis], whose deep reach of thought, whose large legislative conceptions, and whose grand plans of policy made the most part of our reports, from whence we have all learned our lessons, if we have learned any good ones; this man, from whose materials those gentlemen who have least acknowledged it [i.e. Dundas and Jenkinson among others] have yet spoken as from a brief.' *Parl. Hist.*, vol. XXIII, 1368-9.

prepared to leave the zemindars to make their own terms with the
ryots, as Francis had proposed. After a comprehensive investigation
the ryots were to be given *pottahs* or contracts 'at reasonable and
fixed rates'. Finally, in accordance with the recommendations of
the Secret Committee, the Governor-General and Council were
to sort out the financial transactions of the Company Servants of
Madras with the Nawab of Arcot and the Rajah of Tanjore and to
make recommendations for 'adjusting and liquidating' the enormous accumulation of debt. In his opinion, declared Dundas, most
of them were 'the debts of corruption'. In the event he was obliged
to eat his words about that formidable scandal which was not finally
liquidated until 1830.

Such was the Bill which Dundas introduced in April, 1783.[23] If
the Shelburne Administration had survived (with the support of
North), this would have been the framework of a Government of
India Act, with Cornwallis as Governor-General and Dundas as
Secretary of State for India.[24] The Bill, as we have seen, derived
from ideas and experience of Robinson and Jenkinson, supplemented by the findings of the Secret Committee. Ten years later
John Bruce, a protégé of Dundas, claimed that 'out of this plan
arose the system, which has since that time been adopted, in which
the controul of the state over Indian affairs has been established'.

The Bill had, of course, no chance of acceptance by the Fox-
North Ministry. Burke opposed it on several grounds and hinted
that, instead of a noble personage as Governor-General, 'a man of
middling rank' might be more suitable. The name of Philip
Francis was probably in his mind. Fox followed with a speech in
which, we are told, he 'combated the Lord Advocate's arguments
in a most masterly style'. Fox and Burke had other ideas, and
they were put into legislative shape during the summer recess.
Dundas's measure was still-born, but his immediate object had
been achieved. He was now publicly identified with a plan and a
policy for India. Afterwards Fox was repeatedly obliged to defend
his own India Bills against the criticism that the Dundas proposals
were a sounder alternative.[25]

---

[23] As already noted (p. 120, n. 18 above), John Bruce in his *Historical View of
Plans for the Government of British India* . . . , which was published in 1793 when
the renewal of the Company's Charter was again under consideration, based his
account on 'office' memoranda and other official documents to which as personal
assistant to Dundas he would be given access. In the above summary of Dundas's
India Bill I have drawn upon this compiler's very full description of it (pp. 120-132).
See also Dundas's speech in introducing the Bill and the ensuing debate (*Parl. Hist.*,
vol. XXIII, 757-62).

[24] This is, I think, evident, even though Dundas afterwards declared that 'the last
Administration had no hand in forming it: that it was drawn only by a few
members of the Secret Committee'. *Parl. Hist.*, vol. XXIII, 1402.

[25] See, for example, *Parl. Hist.*, vol. XXIII, 1202, 1276-77, 1377 (Burke), 1410-12,
1415; vol. XXIV, 27-51.

2. CHARLES FOX AND THE GORDIAN KNOT

On 18 November, 1783, Charles Fox rose in his place to move for leave to bring in two India Bills. One was 'for vesting the affairs of the East India Company in the hands of certain Commissioners', and the other 'for the better government of the Territorial Possessions and Dependencies in India'. The problem of Britain in India had come to a head and decisive action by the Government of the day was no longer escapable. Public opinion was disturbed and angry. Recent events had shown how a false step in diplomacy by any one of the Company's Governments could expose British interests in India to the danger of extinction by inducing a combination of hostile forces, headed by the Marathas and instigated by the French. Furthermore, the great volume of evidence produced by the Select and Secret Committees of peculation and extortion in India, and the impassioned crusade of Burke, were at last arousing genuine indignation and a dawning sense of responsibility. The claims of humanity and national self-interest were combining in a demand for decisive remedies: mere palliatives, it was repeatedly asserted, were no longer acceptable. And yet any 'decisive remedy' would involve an extension of State authority and patronage which could be represented as a threat to the uncertain balance of the 18th-century constitution.

Nevertheless, immediate action was required, for the Company was again in financial difficulties resulting from the stress of war, and Treasury aid was out of the question without 'redress of grievances'. The same Company which was calling for assistance had recently defied the Commons Resolution requiring the recall of Warren Hastings. A man had been shielded who in the eyes of Burke and the Select Committee was the mainspring of all the tyranny and corruption which they had exposed.

The Fox-North Coalition had thus no option but to act – with speed and over quaggy ground. The Speech from the Throne at the close of the previous session on 16 July had stated that consideration of East Indian affairs would have to be resumed as early as possible;[26] and during the summer recess Fox and Burke with the aid of others set to work to provide a new system. Evidence of the authorship of the plan, which caused Fox to be relegated to the political wilderness for twenty-three years, is slight. On the strength of an urgent request to Burke to furnish his draft of 'the bill', it is sometimes assumed that Burke was the only begetter of the scheme.[27] It seems more probable, however, that this letter

---

[26] *Parl. Hist.*, vol. XXIII, 1121-2.
[27] See Arthur Pigot to Burke (undated, but probably September or October, 1783): 'I shall be particularly obliged to you to send me, as soon as ever you come in, so much of the bill, or instructions for the bill, as you have in the state in which it

refers to the *second* Bill (for the better government of the territories in India) and not to the first Bill establishing a Board of
Commissioners at home.

The Bill to remedy abuses in India accurately reflects the attitude
of mind which possessed Burke in consequence of his investigations.
His indignation over Hastings's strong-arm methods is apparent in
many of the prohibitory clauses; and so too is the powerful influence upon him of Philip Francis as the protagonist of non-involvement in Indian affairs and of administrative withdrawal in
Bengal.[28] The first object of the Bill was to prevent the Presidency
Governments from conducting external policies on their own:
in all relations with Indian States they were to be subjected to rigid
control by the new Board of Commissioners.[29] As a further precaution Governors were to remain in subjection to their Councils.
They were permitted to postpone discussion of an issue in Council
for a stated number of times and for a stated overall period, but
no more. The second object was to safeguard the interests of
Indians. Zemindars were to be reinstated, as in the Dundas Bill,
and were to be protected for the future by means of a perpetual
settlement of their 'rent'. Malpractices by Company Servants
were cited and their continuance was strictly forbidden, as on many
previous occasions; and there were numerous clauses to safeguard
the position of protected native princes. Finally the Nawab of
Arcot and all other protected princes were forbidden thenceforth
to mortgage or pledge land or revenue to any British subject, and
the tangle of Arcot and Tanjore debts was to be thoroughly
investigated and a report submitted to the Commissioners forthwith.

This, said Burke, was to be 'the Magna Charta of Hindustan'.
It was a high-minded effort to establish principles and extinguish
abuses, but it failed to provide an operable system of administration to give effect to the principles. In his view the first essential

---

is; as it will very much forward my work. Indeed, I cannot begin till I get it; and,
therefore, shall expect it impatiently. I would leave my servant to bring it, if I had
one with me.' Endorsed in Burke's hand: ' From Mr. Pigot who finished the India
Bill from my drafts.' *Burke Correspce*: ed. Earl Fitzwilliam and Sir Richard Bourke
(Lond., 1844), vol. III, p. 22. Cf. Sutherland (*op. cit.*), p. 397. (Sir) Arthur Pigot
was afterwards Attorney-General in Lord Grenville's Ministry of 1806.

[28] For example, the Presidency Governments were forbidden, except on express
order from the Commissioners, to make any acquisition of territory, to enter into
any offensive alliance ' for the purpose of dividing or sharing any country or territory whatsoever ', or to hire out British or native troops to any Indian State or
to enter into any agreement for the maintenance of such troops in the territory of
any independent prince. The text of the Bill is printed in *Parl. Hist.*, vol. XXIV,
72-89.

[29] This, in principle, was one of the ideas which Burke had suggested to Robinson
in 1780. The last of his three Propositions on that occasion had run: ' That the
Governors abroad in all their Conduct and Transactions with the Country Powers
should be governed and bound by Instructions from His Majesty.' (See p. 106 above.)

was to reduce the problem of India to manageable proportions by restricting British interference to the barest minimum. That done, the Company's employees were to be held within these narrow limits and kept under discipline by means of direct detailed control by an executive body in London – at 6,000 miles' remove. The project was impracticable; but this determination to halt the process of *imperium* in India before it was too late reflected a general sentiment. The legislative effort represented the mind of Burke at its best and at its weakest.

On the other hand, there is evidence to show that the first Bill, which provided a system of State control over the Company's affairs (upon which all else hung), was substantially the work of Fox himself.[30] His approach to the problem (and from the outset he showed his awareness of its critical importance for the new Administration) was conditioned to a considerable degree by the trials and errors of his predecessors. The time had come when the dangerous nettle had to be grasped: effective control over the Company's activities must be established. But where and how? Previous attempts at direct intervention in India had not been happy. The device of sending out a 'select committee' or royal commission with plenipotentiary powers offered no continuing solution. Order and discipline had been temporarily restored by this means when it was Clive's own chosen instrument, but in weaker hands it had proved ineffective. When Dundas had suggested its revival as an emergency measure Fox had promptly reminded the House of its record of failure.

The system of 'indirect rule' over the Company's political and administrative affairs, laboriously constructed under the North Ministry, had also broken down. A Secretary of State could now scrutinise outgoing as well as incoming correspondence, but the executive instrument upon which he must rely, that is to say, the Directors, was ineffective both at home and abroad. In trying to direct developments in India they were hopelessly feeble, for they

---

[30] See *Memorials and Correspondence of Charles Fox* (Lond., 1853-57), vol. II, pp. 216-18. Burke would, of course, be consulted, and he must have assented to the scheme, for the second Bill hinged upon it; but in the subsequent debates he concentrated upon the woes of India and the guilt of Hastings. He was, indeed, in an embarrassing position, for the proposed extinction of the Company's political and administrative functions was in flat contradiction to his own repeated contention, when in opposition, that chartered rights were inviolable. Hitherto he had insisted that the proper way to remedy abuses in India was to strengthen the Company's authority over its own servants. In his long and eloquent speech in the House on 1 December (afterwards published in pamphlet form) he again defended the commercial privileges of the Company, but laboured to justify the proposed elimination of their *political* authority on the ground that they had notoriously betrayed their 'trust'. In this speech he referred to 'the scheme of the mover of this Bill, the scheme of his learned friend', and he concluded with a glowing tribute to Fox, which began' 'And now, having done my duty to the Bill, let me say a word to the author' (*Parl. Hist.*, vol. XXIII, 1312-86).

lacked sanctions and their exhortations were usually many months behind events; and at home they were subject to the caprice of the Proprietors. Reliance on the exercise of Government influence to keep the Proprietors in step with the policy of the Administration had proved illusory. Only the iron endurance and sometimes ruthless methods of Warren Hastings had saved the situation in India during a series of menacing crises; and yet this was the man whom Burke was execrating as the prime example of the tyranny which supervenes when a subject arrogates to himself the powers of a proconsul.

Last in the sequence of constitutional experiments and proposals had come the Bill devised by Henry Dundas with the advice of Jenkinson and Robinson. As we have seen, it relied on two related principles: the Governor-General was to be established as master of his own Council and of the subordinate Governments of Madras and Bombay, and secondly all senior officials in India were to be selected and subjected to recall by a Secretary of State on behalf of the Crown. Neither of these ideas was acceptable to the Portland (or Foxite) Whigs. The notion of an all-powerful Governor-General who might become a defiant *conquistador* was particularly repugnant to a Burke or a Francis. When Dundas became its advocate, Fox had been quick in his denunciation; and during the subsequent debates he repeatedly rejected the plan as dangerous and unsound.

If it was thought to be too hazardous to entrust the man on the spot with wide powers, the creation of a strong organ of state control at the centre became even more needful. A Secretary of State for India with a department of his own? Yet here again the political situation dictated a negative. Having allied with North and his Crown-supported friends, Fox and his Whig colleagues as the declared opponents of Crown influence would be vulnerable above all others if a charge of increasing that influence could be brought home to them with any plausibility; and it was precisely the accusation which the Opposition was confidently waiting to employ if the new Ministry ventured to establish a Department of State which directly or indirectly would have at its command the resources of Indian patronage. North himself, as First Minister, had recognised the danger and had dodged it by means of cautious compromise; and now Fox in his turn rejected the proposition, mocking Dundas for his known ambition to be the first holder of such an office. In avoiding one bog Charles Fox fell into another of a like sort, but greater in depth.

The idea of thrusting the East India Company to one side and vesting the entire direction of British Indian affairs in a parliamentary commission was certainly startling in its boldness and novelty. Whether the plan was conceived in the quick impetuous mind of Fox himself, or was suggested to him by John Lee, the

E*

Attorney-General (who helped in the drafting) or by another, is of minor importance; but the plan itself is significant as an attempt to resolve an unprecedented imperial problem by breaking away from established convention. A state whose own institutions were formed on the principle of representation was required to redeem its good name by establishing a system of controlled bureaucracy which would afford just and humane government in respect of some 30 million people who were diversely alien in race, religion and culture. With the exception perhaps of Henry Dundas, every British statesman of the late 18th century approached this problem with reluctance and distaste and with a determination to confine a hazardous commitment within the narrowest possible limits.

Fox proposed that the entire management of the territorial possessions, revenues and commerce should be withdrawn from the Directors and Proprietors and vested in a commission or supreme council, consisting of seven named Members of Parliament with Earl Fitzwilliam as Chairman. These seven were to be appointed Directors of the Company. As in the case of Hastings and his Council under the Regulating Act, their appointment would derive from the statute, but any vacancies occurring by death, resignation or removal were to be filled by the Crown under the Sign Manual. Fox described the plan in his opening speech as the creation of a Board, 'who should be invested with full power to appoint and displace officers in India, and under whose control the whole government of that Country should be placed'.[31] The Board would operate under the very eye of Parliament; and all their proceedings, which were to be recorded, would be subject to the constant scrutiny of both Houses. Any disputes between the Governor-General and his Council or between the Government in Calcutta and the other Presidencies, and any charges of peculation or extortion or of breach of treaty or other injury done to a native prince must be referred to the Board with all the relevant evidence, and the Board must give a speedy verdict. If it was decided not to recall the accused or order a prosecution at law, the individual members of the Board must record their reasons in the journal of their proceedings. Thus disciplinary action as well as policy decisions would come under regular parliamentary review. In order, as Fox asserted, that the Board should have adequate continuity for establishing its authority and effecting reforms, the original members were to hold office for a period of three to five years. (Burke preferred a full five-year tenure but Fox eventually decided on four.) At the same time it was provided that the King might remove any of them 'upon an address of either House of Parliament'.[32]

---

[31] *Parl. Hist.*, vol. XXIII, 1200.
[32] The text of the first Bill is printed in *Parl. Hist.*, vol. XXIV, 62-72.

The Company's trade was to be kept as distinct as possible from the affairs of government and was to be managed by a subordinate body of eight 'Assistant Directors'. All of those nominated were Proprietors, owning not less than £2,000 of stock. They were to function under the orders of the Board, which was empowered to remove any of them if found guilty of neglect or misdemeanour. Any vacancy by death, resignation or removal was to be filled by a majority vote of the Proprietors.[33]

It was a well-integrated administrative scheme, providing a powerful central executive which was also a tribunal. The Proprietors, stripped of political power, were left to get on with their business as merchants, but they – like the Servants in India – were placed under the discipline of the Board acting as a Watch Committee. Yet, armed as it would have been with direct and comprehensive authority, it may be doubted whether this Board could have exerted effective control at so great a remove over the shifting issues of Indian administration and diplomacy. Twelve months was the usual interval between the dispatch of a communication to India and the arrival of the reply in London. The central authority needed a proconsul to ensure the implementation of its policy. But Fox and his advisers were adamantly against it. Power, declared Fox again and again, must be concentrated at home 'under the eye of this House' and must not be committed 'to an individual at the distance of half the globe'. Even so, the central machine, as planned by Fox, was superior to the heat-engendering compromise afterwards devised by Pitt and Dundas.

The flaw in Fox's system is notorious. He would have established a powerful executive instrument separate from and independent of the Cabinet. In theory, at least, its existence would have retarded the evolution of collective ministerial responsibility. Fox's adoption of such a plan is a measure of the disrepute into which the ministerial system had fallen. Significantly it resembled the practice of Colonial Assemblies in North America in appointing Committees from their own members as a means of capturing executive functions which properly belonged to the Governor. But the danger of Fox's constitutional unorthodoxy can be greatly exaggerated. Pitt was theoretically correct when (in 1784) he declared:

Earl Fitzwilliam, Sir, by that Bill, had power to involve this Country

---

[33] Fox said that he agreed with the view 'that it was absurd that a body of merchants should be supposed capable of managing and governing great territories, and entering into all the mazes and refinements of modern politics'. He also agreed with the Company's contention 'that it was equally absurd to suppose that mere statesmen were qualified to enter into and conduct the complicated branches of a remote and difficult trade'. His idea, therefore, 'was to form a mixed system of government, adapted, as well as the nature of the case would admit, to the mixed complexion of our interests in India'. *Ibid.*, vol. XXIII, 1200.

in war with France or with Holland, not only without the direction, but without the privity of the government of this country.[34]

It is not, however, credible that Earl Fitzwilliam, as Fox's nominee, would have attempted to pursue an Indian policy which was not in accord with the views of the Administration. If only for party reasons he could be expected to proceed in close consultation with his political chief; and if he and his successors had been unwise enough to take a divergent line the last word would lie with the majority in the Commons, that is to say, with the Government of the day. In practice the system would probably have worked with reasonable efficiency, but in the prevailing political climate its acceptance was beyond 'the art of the possible'. Indian affairs had become too important to be delegated in this way, and public alarm could too easily be roused against it.

The constitutional defect could have been remedied if the chairman of the Board of Commissioners had been appointed a Minister (like the heads of the Treasury and Admiralty Boards), but that was exactly what Fox was determined not to do. Indian patronage would have been formally vested in the Crown, and the Fox-North Coalition could have been represented as having advanced a further stage in their subversion of the constitution by reinforcing North's 'phalanx' with a cohort of Nabobs' dummies.

I submit [said Fox], to every man who hears me, what would be the probable comments of the other side of the House, had I proposed either the erection of an Indian Secretary [of State], or the annexation of the Indian business to the office which I hold.[35]

The Pitt-Grenville Opposition was confident that Fox would have no option but to do so: indeed so confident that a prepared attack on this front was delivered as soon as Fox had made his introductory speech and before there had been an opportunity to read and digest the Bill. Pitt opened with the familiar gambit that the measure was 'an entire abrogation of all the ancient charters and privileges by which the Company had been first established and had since existed'. As for the influence of the Crown – 'had it ever been in its zenith,' he asked, 'equal to what it would be, when it should find itself strengthened by the whole patronage of the East, which the right hon. secretary was going to throw into the hands of the Crown?'[36] Two days later William Grenville followed the line of his young leader but even more extravagantly.[37]

When the text of the Bill had been scrutinised, the attack was

---

34 *Parl. Hist.*, vol. XXIV, 409.

35 *Ibid.*, vol. XXIII, 1414.

36 *Parl. Hist.*, vol. XXIII, 1209-10.

37 'A thousand and ten thousand times greater strength would be added to the Crown, than which by all our reformers had been taken from it.' *Ibid.*, 1230.

quickly switched to much more promising ground. Jenkinson (who had now abandoned North) declared that the plan was a dangerous innovation in the Constitution, for it would set up 'a species of executive government, independent of the check or controul of the crown'.[38] Pitt went further. The present Ministers – as distinct from the Crown – would be armed with an influence to be dreaded. 'Their privileges would be so extensive as to give them a party that no power could resist, whether they were in power or out of power.' It was a plot, laid at the very beginning of the session, in order that Fox 'might obtain the noble end of settling the ministers in unbounded and absolute power'.[39] As the debates proceeded the violence of the language increased until it was freely stated that the intention was to transfer the royal diadem from the brow of His Majesty to that of Charles Fox.

Such an imputation could hardly have been sustained against any normal Ministry, but in the circumstances of the alliance between the Foxite Whigs and the followers of North it was deadly. It would have been difficult for Lord Temple to have canvassed the Lords for the King on the ground that the Bill would enlarge the sinister influence of the Crown; but this new argument had the desired effect, for it played on the prevalent alarm that the wealth of the Nabobs might be able to outbid all competitors and establish a group in the Commons sufficiently numerous to dominate the contending factions.

Fox had asked for trouble and got it; but it does not necessarily follow that the accusation which destroyed him was true. The picture which Pitt and his adherents painted was of a Foxite *junto* using the nominations to posts in India as a means of buying placemen in the House, who would thereafter continue to support their party indefinitely whether in office or out of it. The argument does not bear examination. British Ministers had striven to control both the Irish Parliament and the General Court of the East India Company by the use of influence, and it had been repeatedly demonstrated that the clients deserted their paymasters as soon as self-interest indicated that they should. As Fox pointed out, there was nothing to prevent a new Ministry (commanding a majority in the Commons) from dismissing the appointed Commissioners and replacing them with their own nominees; and he might have added that in such circumstances the recipients of Foxite bounty would have everything to gain by transferring their allegiance. The argument, in fact, only held on the extreme hypothesis that the Fox-North Administration while in office would be able by this means to buy up so many seats that they could never be turned out; a proposition which not only presupposed the unswerving loyalty

---

[38] *Ibid.*, 1238.
[39] *Ibid.*, 1244.

of the *vendus* on every issue but also involved a gross exaggeration
of the proportion of seats in the House that could be secured by
such means.[40]

Fox rejected the imputation with angry contempt. Again and
again he insisted that the Board of Commissioners must be assured
of a reasonable length of tenure if they were to achieve order and
discipline and establish a sound and humane policy in India. With
a large majority at his back and unaware of the plot which Jenkinson and Robinson were hatching with Dundas and the Grenville
group, it seemed reasonable to assume that the Commissioners
would be left undisturbed to get on with the job for the statutory
four-year period. The continuity which he sought was afterwards
achieved (owing to Pitt's long tenure of office) through the Board
of Control. When the Opposition went on repeating that a Foxite
Board could retain their posts and continue to dispense Indian
patronage after a Foxite administration had left office, he made the
valid retort that his Commissioners could in that event be replaced.
But with characteristic vehemence and indiscretion he also declared
that his purpose was to establish 'a permanent system' as the sole
effective method of extinguishing abuses. He was right, of course;
but permanence and removability were incompatible arguments.
A reasonable prospect of continuity might have been attained if
the Board of Commissioners had been drawn from both sides of the
House, but that possibility was ruled out by the unpopularity of
the Coalition, even if it had been contemplated.[41]

In 1784 when it was all over and Fox had been successfully dismissed and discredited, Pitt admitted by implication that all the

---

[40] The existing East India interest in the House of Commons consisted of two
groups: the Nabobs and their relatives, popularly known as the Bengal Squad,
which was concerned to defend their profits and their friends in India and included
the Arcot interest and the Hastings interest, and secondly the City-and-Shipping
interest, consisting chiefly of merchants and bankers who had become influential in
the Company's affairs at home and were concerned to defend its commercial and
other privileges. In November, 1783, the former group comprised 31 Members in
Parliament, of whom 20 supported Fox, and the latter group comprised some 27
members, of whom 21 were supporters of Fox. As the result of his India Bill 6 of the
former and 6 of the latter group deserted him and joined the Opposition (C. H.
Philips, *The East India Company, 1784-1874*, Manchester, 1940, p. 24). Unless Fox's
Commissioners had been prepared to ignore their statutory duties as inquisitors (in
full view of the Commons), they would inevitably have incurred the hostility of the
Bengal Squad.

[41] The leading experts on India – Jenkinson, Robinson and Dundas – had deserted
and all those who were drifting in the same direction were obviously unavailable.
Burke defended Fox with the query: 'Whom should he name? Should he name his
adversaries? . . . Should he name those to execute his plans who are the declared
enemies to the principles of his reform?' The true answer was that this of all plans
needed to be 'bi-partisan' and that the political situation created by the alliance
of North and Fox made it impossible. Care was taken to select men of known
integrity and in 1784 Pitt admitted it: 'That Board undoubtedly was composed of
men of great integrity and fair honour.' (*Parl. Hist.*, vol. XXIV, 325.) But that of
course was after the battle.

rodomontade about a sinister and uncontrollable *junto* had been baseless. Mr. Fox, he then said, had repeatedly asserted that the seven Commissioners could not but be dependent upon the majority in the House, that is to say upon the Government of the day. 'Why, Sir,' Pitt continued, 'if they will turn round with every new minister, how is the system said to be permanent amidst all the changes of administration?'[42] It was a good debating point, and Fox had exposed himself to the thrust; but by denying permanence Pitt had tacitly accepted the truth of removability. The legend of Fox commanding for the rest of his career, whether in or out of office, a Board of his own nominees, 'by whom India was to be converted into one vast political engine' threatening the independence of Parliament had worn thin to the point of transparency; but it had served its purpose.

The merits and demerits of Fox's unfortunate measure are, indeed, of less importance than the ideas which gave it shape, for these made a significant contribution to the evolution of an effective system of state control in Indian affairs. In 1783 everyone in Parliament was uncomfortably (or indignantly) aware that 'something must be done' and that the time when a Ministry could get by with half measures had passed. The initiative taken by Dundas, with the authority of the Secret Committee behind him, had compelled the Portland Administration to promise a measure of their own for the ensuing session, and Pitt had not failed to warn them that mere 'palliatives' would not do.

When Parliament was prorogued in mid-July, Fox was thus left with the task of producing a comprehensive system by the end of the recess. It must be drastic and therefore unpopular with the Company and its powerful supporters; and it must be designed at speed and without the help of the chief specialists in Indian administration, for Jenkinson and Dundas had already joined themselves to Pitt, and Robinson was moving (without undue ostentation) in the same direction. The only person available with extensive knowledge of Indian affairs was Burke, a retributive prophet, but a man 'with no administrative sense'.[43] It was the sort of challenging situation that was well calculated to incite Fox's innate propensity, as at the faro table, to hazard all at a throw. His opponents had demanded decisive action, and, by God, they should have it.[44] All British officials (and peculators) were to be brought under the direct discipline of the State, operating through an omnipotent

---

[42] *Parl. Hist.*, vol. XXIV, 409.

[43] Dr. Sutherland's apt description (*op. cit.*, p. 400).

[44] In introducing his scheme he acknowledged that some would think it 'abundantly too harsh', but he reminded the House that Pitt had admonished them during the previous session to 'look their real situation with regard to India in the face', and he taunted his opponents about their assumption that he would be unable to devise a scheme adequate to the situation. *Parl. Hist.*, vol. XXIII, 1199.

instrument. By that means territorial expansion would be permanently halted; corruption would be stamped out; and the business of territorial administration would be handed back to the rehabilitated zemindars.

A powerful instrument of control was necessary, but where was this dangerous source of power to reside? Not in a supreme Governor-General, as Dundas had urged. The anger of Burke and the Select Committee over the open defiance practised in India (and with particular reference to Hastings) ruled that right out. The supreme authority, said Fox, must be 'at home' and yet not in the hands of a Secretary of State. The alternative was a Commission, and the idea that it should consist of private members of Parliament, not formally associated with the Administration, seems to have been suggested by the impressive operations of the Select and Secret Committees.[45] Their predecessors in the days of Clive had done useful work, but these later committees had proved to be something of an administrative phenomenon, and particularly the Secret Committee under Dundas. The latter, as we have seen, had become, in effect, a policy-making body producing a great *corpus* of principles for the future conduct of Indian affairs which the House had debated and adopted. Some similar body, established by statute with ample and specific executive authority, was what Fox required.

A sufficiency of power was one requisite; and no less important in the opinion of Fox and Burke was that it should be exercised on an independent basis similar to that enjoyed by the judiciary. Their declared purpose was to establish a supreme authority for Indian affairs which would function as undisturbed as possible by the fluctuating pressures of domestic politics. The reasons which they gave for this unprecedented step are revealing.

Make these Commissioners [said Fox] removeable at will, and You set all the little passions of human nature afloat . . . This Bill invests them with the power for the time specified upon the same tenure that British judges hold their station, removeable upon delinquency, punishable upon guilt; but fearless of power if they discharge their trust. . . .[46]

The same concept was expounded by Burke. They were to hold office for the stated period during good behaviour.

That good behaviour is as long as they are true to the principles of the Bill; and the judgement is in either House of Parliament. This is

---

[45] Fox paid a handsome tribute to ' the very great ability and precision ' which had distinguished the Reports of both Committees. Persons with different political affiliations had worked together with a prudence that was ' perfectly astonishing ', and the Secret Committee had formulated principles in the shape of Resolutions which had been ratified by the House. *Ibid.*, 1188-89.

[46] *Parl. Hist.*, vol. XXIII, 1415.

the tenure of your judges; and the valuable principle of the Bill is to make a judicial administration in India.[47]

The concept was that of a tribunal or public service commission enjoying the independence proper to the judiciary. As such it must have continuity and so be able to resist political pressure on the part of the nabobs and their allies in the task of disciplining officers in India. The Commissioners in office could always be turned out by a new Ministry; but Fox evidently hoped that there would not be a clean sweep upon a change of administration and that the power of dismissal by parliamentary resolution would be employed only in case of misbehaviour, as with a judge. As vacancies occurred by death or retirement, the Government of the day would be able to make its own recommendations to the Crown. When the struggle was over and Pitt was in office, Fox declared in the House, 'that he would suffer his India Bill to be new modelled, reserving only, that it was made a permanent system, and that the seat of government was established at home, not in India'.[48]

The idea of a standing Commission may have emanated from Burke who, as the author of the Judicature Amending Act and the famous Seventh Report of the Select Committee, was obsessed with the notion of saving the situation in India by means of an omnipotent and invulnerable tribunal. The laudable object was to prevent thirty million Indians from being plundered; but he tried to ignore the (now) inescapable corollary that they must be justly ruled. Hating the imperialism of Hastings, he took refuge in the comfortable doctrine of Francis: 'leave it to the zemindar, who knows his business.'

From the outset Fox realised that his India Bills were a gamble which might bring about his downfall. In introducing the measure he said that he knew 'that it had considerable risk in it'; and nine days later during the Second Reading debate he declared: 'I

---

[47] Cf. an earlier passage in the same speech: 'The Bill before you cuts off this source of [ministerial] influence. Its design and main scope is to regulate the administration of India upon the principles of a court of judicature; and to exclude, as far as human prudence can exclude, all possibility of a corrupt partiality, in appointing to office, and supporting in office, or covering from injury or punishment, any person who has abused, or shall abuse his authority. At the Board, as appointed and regulated by this Bill, reward and punishment cannot be shifted and reversed by a whisper.' (Ibid., vol. XXIII, 1378-9, 1382.)

[48] Parl. Hist., vol. XXIV, 378. On 20 Feb., 1784, Mr. Marsham reported to the House that he had waited on Mr. Fox to learn his intention with regard to Mr. Pitt's impending (first) India Bill. Fox had replied that, 'provided Mr. Pitt would consent that the government of India should be in this Country, and be permanent at least for a given number of years, he would leave it entirely to that right hon. Gentleman to settle the article of patronage as he pleased'. Ibid., 633. Later he said: 'Could the Commissioners have continued in office one moment after an Address? . . . They must have retired. . . . My board had not complete permanency, but it had a chance for permanency by its constitution.' The source of all the weakness in managing Indian affairs, he added, had arisen from 'the variations which happened in our Government at home.' Ibid., 1132-33.

know that in doing so, I put my own situation, as a minister, to the hazard.' If he fell on account of this, he would fall in a great and glorious cause.[49] As on other occasions he was not only rash but politically insensitive, miscalculating the nature of the risk and the ground of the attack. From his speeches it is evident that he anticipated a hostile combination in the Commons of the East India groups with the King's friends. In the event his first Bill passed the House with a comfortable majority of 208 to 102, while the accusations about unconstitutional and nefarious designs which did so much to blast his career roused in him, not merely violent anger, but astonishment. He had been similarly stung – and surprised – by the revulsion which had greeted his alliance with North.

There is evidence to show that the plan for India was worked out in haste and without sufficient time to consider its implications. Lord Loughborough, who was receiving draft clauses from various sources and forwarding them to Fox with comments, was still raising queries of substance three days after the Bill had received its first reading; and he did not receive the draft of the second Bill until four days before its introduction in the Commons.[50] The decision to cut the Gordian Knot of relations between

---

[49] *Parl. Hist.*, vol. XXIII, 1206, 1278. The same awareness and acceptance of risk is expressed in his private correspondence. ' I am not at all ignorant,' he wrote, ' of the political danger which I run by this bold measure but, whether I succeed or no, I shall always be glad I attempted because I have done no more than I was bound to do.' Fox to a friend, 1783. (*Memorials of Fox*, vol. II, p. 219.)

[50] In a letter to Fox (undated, but docketed ' 23 November, 1783 ') Loughborough wrote: ' Upon reading the Bill, I think it is fairly implied in the second enacting clause, that the Commissioners are to communicate all correspondence to and from India to the Secretary of State, in the same manner that the Directors were bound to do . . .' (The clause in question vested in the Commissioners all the powers previously exercised by the Directors and Proprietors, ' subject to such limitations and restrictions as in this Act, or in any other Act, the provisions whereof are not hereby altered or repealed, are contained for the government and management of the said territorial possessions . . .'.) Although not strictly necessary, he saw no reason why explicit provision should not be made for the submission of correspondence. Some handle might be taken to asperse the intention of the Bill, as aiming to withdraw the Commissioners from any dependence on Government, if the authors of the Bill allowed that such an omission existed. (*Memorials and Correspondence of Charles Fox*, vol. II, pp. 217-18.) His hint was not, however, taken. In an earlier letter (also undated) he pointed out other dangers: ' I have sent you the two additional clauses; the second, I think, is a very ticklish point. Though it is clearly necessary that the Directors should be members of Parliament, as much as the Lords of the Treasury and Admiralty, . . . You will be teezed with declamations on the Act of Settlement, and all the lawyers against you will maintain that it is clear upon that Act, that the office disqualifies, and that you mean to undermine the principles of the Act by creating a shoal of officers by Parliament.' *Ibid.*, vol. II, pp. 216-17. This point was met by a declaratory clause that the office of Commissioner, when filled by the King under the Sign Manual, was not to be deemed to be within the purview of the Act of Settlement, and that any person, so appointed, would not be disqualified as a member of Parliament.

Governor Johnstone during the First Reading debate on 20 November declared: ' The Bill had come suddenly upon gentlemen, even the chairman of the Company had not heard of it till it had been opened by the right hon. Secretary.' Sir Henry

Government and Company relieved Fox of the necessity of entering into the sort of interminable negotiation with the Directors and Proprietors which had plagued Lord North; but the price for that relief was high. Inevitably the plan was matured in secrecy, and the Company was kept in the dark until the moment when Fox announced the terms of the Bill in the Commons.

The announcement was the signal which Fox's opponents had been waiting for. Wary negotiations had been going on for many months between Pitt and the King with a view to establishing a mutually acceptable basis for a new Administration. At the same time John Robinson had been working with Jenkinson and Richard Atkinson, an agent of Paul Benfield, to establish an alliance between the Pitt Opposition and the panic-stricken India interest. The link was Dundas, who had long been acquainted with Robinson and Jenkinson and was now employing Atkinson, a close associate of Robinson, as his go-between.

As soon as the terms of the India Bill were known these three were encouraged to make arrangements for its defeat in the Lords. During the first week in December a canvass was made which ensured that there would be a majority against it in the Upper House if the King clearly indicated his wishes. Everything stood prepared for the blow, Atkinson reported to Robinson, 'if a certain person has courage to strike it'. On 11 December Temple left the royal presence with the famous slip of paper. Four days later Pitt, Dundas, Robinson and Jenkinson met secretly at Dundas's house, and Robinson produced a list to show that, upon the rejection of the Bill, a majority in the Commons hostile to the Coalition could be expected. The Lords duly rejected the measure, and before the end of the month Pitt accepted appointment as First Minister. In due course he and Dundas were called upon to pay the price which the India group exacted for services rendered.[51]

For some sixteen years the Government of Britain had been challenged in India by a revolt of its own subjects. These by means of their Indian wealth had subverted the constitution of the East India Company and so assumed virtual control over a jurisdiction which in its own way was as autonomous as that of the Massachusetts Bay Company had been. From that vantage point they had infiltrated into the precincts of Westminster itself; and in

---

Fletcher, the Chairman, then rose to say that he had been asked in the Court of Directors ' if he knew in what manner the Company was to be attacked by Government ', and he had answered that the Ministers had not acquainted him with their intentions. (*Parl. Hist.*, vol. XXIII, 1235-36.)

[51] C. H. Phillips, ' The East India Company " Interest " and the English Government, 1783-4.' (*Trans. Roy. Hist. Soc.*, 4th Series, vol. XX, pp. 83-101); W. T. Laprade (ed.), *Parliamentary Papers of John Robinson* (Lond., 1922), p. 105 *et seq.*; D. G. Barnes, *George III and William Pitt, 1783-1806* (Stanford and Oxford, 1939), Chap. II.

India their involvement in the wars and intrigues of princes threatened the interests of Britain with extinction. Slowly and cautiously and against formidable resistance the metropolitan authority had striven to assert a modicum of control. Fox came on the scene when a combination of circumstances had brought the long struggle to a head. To liquidate the Company as a political institution, while leaving it to manage (under supervision) its commercial monopoly, was the logical solution which all his pre-decessors had judged to be politically impossible. The method which he proposed was rash and wrong-headed; but the assumption of direct responsibility by the State, which he tried to achieve by a single unorthodox stroke, had to come. Eventually the control of Indian affairs was concentrated in the hands of a Minister and an advisory Council in London, almost completely insulated from domestic politics, operating through a Governor-General and a highly concentrated bureaucracy.

By 'reforms' Fox and Burke meant the prevention of future injuries. Their two Bills were exclusively concerned with the enforcement of prohibitions and penalties. The humanitarianism of Burke in relation to India was preventive and negative. Moved by passionate anger against the Company's employees as masterless men, a source of disgrace to the British name and a menace to the British constitution, his purpose was to punish delinquents and to reduce their opportunities of doing further mischief to a minimum. British penetration must be halted and the native population pro-tected by insulation. The notion that Warren Hastings, or any successor of his, should be given more and not less power and that the corps of Company officials could be reformed and then used in a new system of good government was foreign to his thought: indeed dangerous nonsense. The only decent course in his view was to confine British interference to a narrowly limited form of 'protectorate' and to rely on local indigenous institutions. The zemindars ('the gentry of the country', as Fox called them) must resume their proper status and functions. If reinstated and secured in the possession of their lands under the guarantee of a fixed and perpetual 'land tax', they could be relied on to maintain order and dispense justice in the districts, extracting no more than was reasonable from the ryots. It was a policy derived from Clive, per-colating to Burke and Fox through Philip Francis, and it left a lasting mark; but it wrongly assumed the survival of a firm structure of local government in the Presidencies. Limited administrative responsibility was no longer a practicable proposition.

The same determination to call a halt is manifest in the insist-ence that there must be no further involvement in the rivalries of warring Indian princes. External relations in India were to be strictly controlled by the Board of Commissioners, and elaborate restrictions were imposed upon the Presidency Governments in order to effect the maximum degree of isolation. They were forbidden, unless expressly authorised, to 'make or accept any acquisition whatsoever, whereby the territory of the said united Company shall be increased or extended'. These were not merely the sentiments of Fox and Burke. They derived directly from the Dundas Resolutions of April, 1782, which had embodied the conclusions of the Secret Committee and had been adopted by the Commons with general assent. Resolution 44 had declared 'that it is the opinion of this Committee [of the whole House] that . . . to pursue schemes of conquest and extent of dominion are measures repugnant to the wish, the honour, and policy of this nation'.[52] The frequent repetition of this affirmation of policy in later years illustrates the long rearguard action at home against the expense and hazards of *imperium*.

The various 'systems' put forward between 1782 and 1784 for the purpose of establishing control in Indian affairs differed widely; but throughout these envenomed debates there was a general consensus of opinion that political intervention in India had increased, was still increasing, and must be diminished – to the absolute minimum. On more than one occasion Lord John Cavendish declared that 'he wished to God every European could be extirpated from India and the country resorted to merely on the principles of commerce'. And by that he meant that 'the trade between Great Britain and Industan might be carried on in like manner as we now carry on our trade with China'. He admitted that this was not possible, but the British connexion with India should be approximated to that subsisting with regard to China as closely as the different political circumstances would permit.

George Dempster (another Rockingham Whig) regretted that territory had been acquired in India; these acquisitions had proved 'a serious and solid incumbrance to the Company'. And on another occasion he lamented that the navigation to India had ever been discovered and urged the Ministry 'to abandon all idea of sovereignty in that quarter of the globe'. It would be much wiser for them to establish one of the princes as Emperor of Delhi, 'and to leave India to itself'. Thereupon Sir Henry Fletcher, who had just resigned from being Chairman of the Company and was to have been one of the senior Commissioners, rose up to say that,

---

[52] The proposition was also stated in the First Resolution and formed the keynote of the whole: ' That the orders of the court of directors of the East India Company, which have conveyed to their servants abroad a prohibitory condemnation of all schemes of conquest and enlargement of dominion, . . . were founded no less in wisdom and policy, than in justice and moderation.' Every infringement of these orders had tended ' in a chief degree to weaken the force and influence, and to diminish the resources of the Company in those parts '. *Parl. Hist.*, vol. XXII, 1292 and 1302.

while he agreed with Dempster, he could not agree that it would be right to give up the Indian territories, for if they were evacuated some other European nation, probably France, would seize them: 'and then this nation, once so glorious, having lost her western and eastern empires, would become insignificant in the eyes of Europe and the world'.[53] There it all was: the steady determination of that generation to pursue 'trade without dominion', a concept which greatly influenced the character of British enterprise overseas during the next hundred years – and underneath an uneasiness lest renunciation of dominion, if carried too far, might result in abdication to the French rival and so reduce a commercial island to 'insignificance'.

3. THE PITT-DUNDAS COMPROMISE

On 2 December at two o'clock in the morning the youthful Pitt announced in the Commons: 'If the House should think it right to throw out this Bill, which I trust they will, I pledge myself to bring forward a bill for the regulation of India, not subject to these objections, not charged with this violence. It is not matured in my mind; but the idea is formed.'[54] The scorn and derision with which this declaration was received by Fox and his supporters appeared to be well warranted, for two and a half hours later the Coalition mustered 217 against 103 of the Opposition. Yet Pitt had good reason for his confidence: the preparations for the 'stroke' in another place were almost complete, and when called upon to produce an alternative system for India he would have Henry Dundas, the ablest of the Indian specialists, at his side.

Perhaps the most significant feature of the fierce debates on Fox's measure was the attention which Government speakers paid to the plan which Dundas had introduced eight months before. Underneath the diatribes about 'influence' and about Warren Hastings, the basic argument had centred upon the relative merits of Fox's scheme of an omnipotent Commission in Westminster and the Dundas plan of a supreme Governor-General, guided by a Secretary of State in the Cabinet. As if sensing the probability that Pitt would identify himself with the latter, Fox immediately followed up Pitt's declaration with an elaborate attack upon the Dundas proposals.[55]

---

[53] These quotations are taken from a number of debates in 1783. (*Ibid.*, vol. XXIII, 801, 1231, 1301-2.)

[54] *Parl. Hist.*, vol. XXIII, 1405-6.

[55] *Ibid.*, 1406-34. Fox said: 'I will leave the House and the kingdom to judge which is best calculated to accomplish those salutary ends; the Bill of the learned gentleman (Dundas), which leaves all to the discretion of one man, or the Bill before you, which depends upon the duty of several men, who are in a state of daily account to this House, or hourly account to the ministers of the Crown, of occasional

The new Ministry took office on 19 December, 1783, and on 14 January Pitt moved for leave to bring in his own India Bill. There had been little time for thinking out a new system, and in the circumstances the adoption of the ready-made views of his lieutenant might have seemed the easiest course. In fact, at that particular juncture they were politically impossible. As the leader of a minority administration Pitt could afford even less than Fox to expose himself to the charge of inflating royal influence by putting the authority and patronage of the Company in the hands of a Minister of the Crown, and it was necessary to implement the alliance with the India groups which Robinson and Atkinson had arranged. In the event the Bill which he introduced in January, 1784, was closer to the system of Fox than to that of Dundas; but the ultimate object of all three, whether overt or concealed, was the elimination of the Company except as a commercial house.

In attacking Fox's 'violence', Pitt had become the defender of chartered rights and the ally of the India interests. Accordingly his own plan had to be such that the Proprietors would think it unwise to reject. Fortunately for Pitt they had been so shattered by Fox's scheme and their last-minute escape from it that they were willing to make substantial concessions to their deliverer. Afterwards, when they had recovered their breath and had also laid Pitt under an obligation during the general election, they were to prove much less amenable. Now, however, they accepted his apparent compromise without difficulty so that he was able to announce in the Commons that his proposals – in contrast to those of Fox – had been discussed and agreed beforehand with the Court of Proprietors.

Pitt, like Fox, discovered that there was little room left for manœuvre. The revelations of the Select and Secret Committees, the acceptance of the Dundas Resolutions embodying the Secret Committee's conclusions, the marked impression made by the forthright terms of Dundas's Bill, and finally the shock tactics of Fox, represented a growing recognition that the State must – by one device or another – assume control of external administration in India. To proceed as though these matters could be neatly severed from the Company's trade was still a useful political gambit; but trade was interlocked with revenue and so with politics.

State control would involve a leap in the dark; and the prospect was as distasteful to the politicians (Henry Dundas excepted) as it was to the Company itself. Politicians feared that Indian influence, when brought directly into Westminster, would overwhelm the

---

account to the proprietors of East India stock. . . . But the learned Gentleman wishes the appointment of an Indian Secretary of State in preference to the Commissioners: in all the learned gentleman's ideas on the government of India, the notion of a new secretary of state for the Indian Department springs up. . . .'

traditional methods of manipulation and thus destroy the balance of the Constitution. Burke, Francis, and many others fiercely rejected the argument that the establishment of dominion over remote and strange races in India had become the unavoidable means of securing the profits; and those who came to accept it as inevitable did so with reluctance, regarding it as a hazardous business for Britain and an unnatural relationship for the peoples involved.

> Nature and fate [observed Pitt] had ordained, in unalterable degrees, that Governments to be maintained at such a distance, must be inadequate to their end. In the philosophy of politics, such a government must be declared irrational . . . inconvenient to the mother and supreme power, oppressive and inadequate to the necessities of the governed. In such a scene . . . there could be imagined no theoretical perfection – it must be a choice of inconveniencies.[56]

Pitt went on to state that his plan was based on three principles: that the civil and military government and the collection of revenue could no longer remain with a company of merchants but must be placed under the 'effectual control' of Government; that the Company's commerce should be left 'as much as possible' to their own superintendence; and that the Servants in India, while compelled to obey and prevented from indulging in rapacity and 'inordinate ambition', must be given sufficient discretionary power to ensure security and good government. This last principle represented a compromise between the views of Dundas and those of Fox and Burke. The latter (with Warren Hastings never far from their thoughts) regarded discretionary power on the spot as the root cause of every evil.

The authority of the State was to be exercised by a Commission as powerful as that proposed by Fox; but it was to be a standing committee of the Privy Council, of which the Home and Colonial Secretary and the Chancellor of the Exchequer were always to be members. The Commission or Board was thus integrated with the Cabinet of the day. The record of all Company proceedings, together with all incoming despatches and all draft instructions proposed to be sent out to India, must be submitted to the Board; and if a draft related to civil, military or revenue matters, the Court of Directors must adopt any alterations which the Board might require. There would be very few subjects which could not plausibly be interpreted as falling within one or other of these three categories;[57] and by way of providing an ostensible safeguard

---

[56] *Parl. Hist.*, vol. XXIV, 321 (14 Jan., 1784).

[57] The terms of the general directive were widely expressed: 'Be it further enacted, that the said Board shall be fully authorised and empowered . . . to check, superintend, and control, all acts, operations, and concerns, which *in any wise relate to* the civil or military government or revenues of the territories . . .' The text of Pitt's (first) India Bill is printed in *Parl. Hist.*, vol. XXIV, 413-20.

for the Company it was stipulated that the Directors might appeal
to the Privy Council against any instruction which they considered
to be beyond the Board's terms of reference. Not surprisingly this
provision was greeted by the Fox-North Opposition with 'smiles
and sneers', and Burke afterwards castigated it as a piece of
hypocrisy, being in effect no more than an appeal 'from the
Minister to the Minister'.

With regard to the burning issue of patronage it was intended
that the State should control the senior appointments in India.
Henceforth the Crown was to appoint the Commanders-in-Chief
in the three Presidencies, thus securing direct overall authority in
military affairs. The nomination of the Governor-General, the
Presidents in Madras and Bombay, and the members of the three
Councils was to remain with the Directors but subject to the
approval of the King. If the Directors failed to produce an approved
nominee within a specified time, the Crown itself was to fill the
vacancy, and in respect of all these posts the Crown was to have
the power of recall. The Directors would retain the formal *congé
d'élire,* but under these arrangements Governments in India were
persons in whom they had confidence.

At that point direct state control over the personnel in India was
to halt. Fox would have gone the whole way: his Commissioners
were to have brought the entire service under a central discipline.
Pitt was too astute to be so logical; but, by leaving the bulk of the
patronage with the Company, he left disciplinary authority in the
hands of a body notoriously incapable of enforcing it. The better
alternative, as Dundas had urged, was to move the seat of discipline
from London to Calcutta: to reinforce the powers of the Governor-
General, to render him accountable, and then to trust him. In the
debates Pitt paid lip service to that principle, but he did nothing
at this stage to implement it. The Governor-General's authority in
'internal regulation' was left as it was and Pitt even suggested that
he should continue to have a council of four. Had that been done
another trio could have repeated the tactics of Francis, Monson and
Clavering. In the later Bill Dundas persuaded him to reduce the
number of councillors to three in every Presidency; but the stronger
proposal, which Dundas had included in his own Bill, that the
Governor-General be given authority to over-ride his Council was
not adopted until Cornwallis insisted upon having it. No Government welcomes the problem of an over-powerful subject; and
Warren Hastings, notwithstanding the limitations upon his
authority, had proved a formidable prince palatine.

In the absence of a punitive control operating from London and
of a supreme Governor-General, it was clearly desirable to invent
some other disciplinary device. Otherwise the Opposition would be
able to assert that Pitt's plan was deficient in 'teeth' as compared

with that of his predecessor. Pitt was constrained to fall back
on the unhopeful expedient of arranging for the trial of cases of
extortion and peculation by a special tribunal in London. Ten
years before, provision had been made for the Court of King's Bench
to take cognisance of such cases, but the practical difficulty of
securing adequate and reliable evidence from India had rendered
the plan inoperative. Then had come the establishment of a
Supreme Court of Judicature in Calcutta, wielding the authority
of King's Bench and with the unfortunate results already described.

Pitt's judicial scheme was so elaborate and cumbersome that one
might be led to suspect that it was not seriously intended and was
no more than a diversionary move to keep Burke and his fellows
talking, which they certainly did at great length; but the plan which
he outlined in January,[58] when leading a minority Ministry, was
in fact included in the subsequent Act in full detail. The prescribed procedure was as follows. Upon an information being laid
against any person returning from India for alleged extortion or
other misdemeanour, the Court of King's Bench was empowered
to apprehend the accused until he had entered into a sufficient
recognisance. Having examined him, the Court could then in its
discretion deliver the record of the information and the defendant's
plea to the Lord Chancellor, who must thereupon issue a commission under the Great Seal.

The procedure for constituting the Commission was very curious
and resembled the Fox-Burke idea of using Parliament as a special
tribunal. Within thirty days of the beginning of every future
session of Parliament the doors of the House of Lords and of the
House of Commons were to be locked on some occasion when not
less than fifty Lords and in the case of the Commons not less than
two hundred were present. The Upper House was thereupon to
choose twenty-six of its members and the Lower House forty by
ballot. These lists were to be submitted to three judges, representing respectively the Courts of King's Bench, Common Pleas, and
Exchequer. Within twenty days of receiving the lists the judges
were to convene a meeting of those selected. Their names were to
be placed in a box; and as they were drawn out the defendants could
exercise the right of challenging up to thirteen of the peers and
twenty of the commoners, while the Attorney-General for the
prosecution could challenge any of them.

The names of the first four peers and the first six commoners
to be drawn out which were not so challenged were to be inserted,
together with those of the three judges, in a special Commission
by the Lord Chancellor, and the tribunal so constituted must open
proceedings against the accused within ten days. If, however, less

---

[58] *Parl. Hist.*, vol. XXIV, 328.

than four peers or six commoners survived the process of challenge, fresh lists must be selected by the two Houses of Parliament and the whole process be repeated. If the accused were convicted and fined, he must submit himself to examination by the Court of Exchequer in respect of his assets, and upon refusal he was to forfeit his entire estate and be committed to prison.

The intention was to establish an *ad hoc* court, comprising three of His Majesty's judges and an elective panel of parliamentary assessors. Apart from the difficulty of relying upon written depositions from India, the procedure for constituting the tribunal was an administrative nightmare. It seems odd that two such clear-headed persons as Pitt and Dundas should have seriously thought that it would work. Yet they seem to have done so.[59] After being incorporated in the Act of 1784 much further labour was devoted to it and in 1786 the scheme was re-enacted in an amended form.[60] Although it soon passed into the limbo of forgotten legislation, it was significant as the last of a series of attempts to fashion a weapon of judicial process which could operate as an instrument of overseas discipline. These experiments were part of a long process of British trial and error. When the scheme became known in India, it evoked furious indignation and threats of organised resistance among the Company Servants.[61] Discipline was eventually imposed, not by means of judicial process, but by strong executive action in India strongly supported by Government at home.

If the Commons had accepted his first Bill, Pitt would have followed it up, as he explained, with a supplementary measure establishing his special tribunal and incorporating most of Fox's second Bill for the prevention of abuses. But it was obvious enough that the Coalition majority would lose no time in throwing out the rival measure, and they did on the Second Reading (23 January) by 222 votes to 214. Fox immediately rose and successfully moved for leave to bring in another India Bill of his own. He would insist, he said, on two principles only and these were fundamental: that the Government of India should be 'permanent', rendered so by the authority of Parliament, and that it must be established 'at

---

[59] The idea seems to have emanated from Dundas. During one of the debates on his second India Bill (19 July, 1784) Pitt admitted that he had not originally been 'particularly tenacious' about it, but he went on to say that the more he thought about it and heard it discussed, the more convinced he became of its necessity. 'The new judicature was a necessary part of the whole system', and without it the other provisions in the Bill 'would appear extremely defective'. *Parl. Hist.*, vol. XXIV, 1149-50. The Opposition did not fail to draw comparisons with the Court of Star Chamber and to inveigh at great length against the omission of trial by jury. The relevant sections in the Act of 1784 are numbers LXIV-LXXXII (*24 Geo. III, sect. 2, cap. XXV*).

[60] *26 Geo. III, cap. LVII.* The amended system was almost as elaborate as the original, but the requirement that Company Servants must deliver inventories of their estates and effects were repealed.

[61] See pp. 211-14 below.

Home'. Everything else in his system was secondary and could be adapted to meet the inclinations of the Country.[62] But Fox's system for India had ruined him. The Opposition's majority was shrinking daily. The future of British India lay with Pitt.

The young Prime Minister's Bill had served its purpose: an alternative system had been proclaimed. Yet paradoxically the preliminary exercise, planned at a time of political weakness, was more uncompromising than the later Bill which was drafted and carried after an overwhelming victory at the polls. During that contest Pitt received powerful support from the Bengal Squad and the price extracted proved to be substantial.

The resounding failure of Fox's attempt to establish an integrated control left Pitt no option but to accept some form of 'double' government in Indian affairs. However determined he and Dundas might be that the Administration should be the masters, the process of adjusting the frontiers of authority would inevitably expose the Government to bargaining pressures, for the India interests with money to burn were politically powerful. The emerging relationship between the Ministers of the Crown, as superintendents, and the Court of Directors, as agents, was therefore bound to be imprecise and difficult. The arrangement could work with reasonable efficiency only if the agents could be induced to behave as the compliant instrument of governmental policy.

Richard ('Rum') Atkinson at once perceived the importance of ensuring that this should become established practice. Under Lord North, when Jenkinson and Robinson had striven with inadequate authority to guide the Directors, Atkinson had acted as a go-between; and now that the State was about to assume wide powers, it was clear to him that friction could easily bring the new machine to a standstill. In that event the surviving elements of the Company's authority might well suffer final extinction. This could be avoided if he himself were adopted by the Government as their manager or 'Undertaker' (as in the Irish system) at East India House. As the associate of Paul Benfield and the powerful group which represented the interests of the Arcot creditors and as the political ally of Pitt and Dundas, Atkinson was well placed to fill such a role. When, therefore, the April elections to the Court of Directors were impending, he suggested that he and Francis

---

[62] In a later debate (on 2 July, 1784), Fox urged Pitt 'to take away the powers of mismanagement from the courts of directors and proprietors, and from the servants abroad. The Company was at present a sink of corruption and iniquity; and, let the right hon. Gentleman do what he would with the patronage, he would be satisfied, if it was taken from the Company.' For his part he would rather neither the Directors nor the Crown had it, but of the two evils he would choose, if he must, that the patronage should be 'at the whole disposal of the Crown' (*Parl. Hist.*, vol. XXIV, 1082). But that was just what the 'Country Gentlemen' were terrified of.

Baring, leader of the City interest, should gain control over the Court by joining forces with Laurence Sulivan, who was ready to co-operate in promoting the kind of reforms which the Government required. But Dundas feared and disliked the Hastings-Sulivan group, and Pitt forbade the alliance. 'Your decided negative', Atkinson afterwards wrote to Dundas, 'upon him [Sulivan] for chairman blew up the whole Plan.'[63]

Pitt achieved his prime object in keeping the Foxites out of the Direction, but Sulivan's exclusion from the chair alienated him from the Ministry; and he and his supporters were formidable. 'United with Hastings, the Power *here* will be in their hands', warned Atkinson, 'even if Government should recall Mr. Hastings from Bengal.'[64] Eventually Sulivan demonstrated his power and gave effect to his resentment by exposing Dundas to a public humiliation.

During the summer of 1784 while the India Bill was in preparation, Atkinson pressed the two Ministers to adopt the bold course of establishing direct control inside the Court of Directors by altering its constitution. In a paper submitted to Dundas he proposed that the Chairman of the Court should be nominated by the Crown. This, he maintained, would win the trick, even if the personnel of the Direction remained otherwise unaltered. But the Ministers would have none of it: indeed, they could not. Dundas may have had private thoughts about it,[65] but Pitt could not expose himself to the charge of imitating Fox by grabbing patronage and doing 'violence' to the Company.

On 21 July, when the India Bill was at an advanced stage in the Commons, Atkinson made a last-minute attempt to gain his point. At an interview with Dundas and in a letter to him on the following day he tried to get round the patronage difficulty by suggesting that all appointments by Directors should be made by ballot so that the Crown-appointed chairman would have no 'peculiar' patronage of his own. He also suggested that the term of office of Directors should be extended and their numbers reduced. 'To do this,' he wrote, 'by parliamentary nomination of sixteen or any other number out of the present twenty-four would do the business very effectively without the nomination of the Chairman.'[66] If Pitt would do neither of these things, he and his ally, Baring, saw no chance of 'doing any good' but by retracing their steps with Sulivan

---

[63] Atkinson to Dundas, 22 July, 1784. 'Private.' Printed by Holden Furber (from the original in his possession) in his article, 'The East India Directors in 1784', *Journal of Modern History*, vol. V (1933), pp. 478-95.

[64] *Ibid.*, p. 483.

[65] A Chairman of the Court, appointed by Pitt and himself and drawing all wavering Directors to the side of the Crown's Ministers, would have been a god-send to Dundas at the Board of Control.

[66] Atkinson to Dundas, 22 July, 1784, ed. Furber (*loc. cit.*), p. 484.

and attempting a coalition with his dominant faction. The idea of constituting an executive body on which Crown and Company representatives sat together offered clear advantages. Variants of it had been previously mooted, as we have seen, both by Sulivan himself and by John Robinson, but Pitt was not in a position to entertain it.

Six months later when the Board of Control had been established under the Act, Atkinson made a final effort to achieve some degree of integration between the Board and the Court. In a private letter to Dundas of 31 January, 1785, he urged once more the necessity of reforming the Court of Directors. Otherwise there would be only two choices. Either the preservation of India would be left 'at critical moments' to the discretion of the Governor-General on the spot, or 'the Board of Control must assume the Character and Functions of Mr. Fox's Commissioners'.[67] Neither, asserted Atkinson, were 'admissable propositions'. Perhaps not, if the Act were respected, but Dundas with Pitt's support was determined that the latter proposition should be turned into reality; and not merely from personal ambition to become Secretary of State for India. For the rest of his career his central interest was the development of a national policy in the Far East which, beginning with a thorough reformation of the administration in British India, was to transform the economic connexion with India into a reservoir of power for the expansion of 'informal' empire into the wide markets of Further Asia.[68]

Meanwhile, from April to July, 1784, the fateful general election had been in progress. Pitt was assured of a large majority beforehand. In the second week of December, 1783, the King had instructed John Robinson, expert in these matters, to work out estimates of the various groups in the Commons under the Fox-North Ministry and the probable composition of a new House in the event of a general election. Robinson calculated that if those who were known to be 'pro' and those who were 'hopeful' ran true to expected form, Pitt would be returned with 369 supporters as against an Opposition of 189, that is to say, with a majority of 180. His majority turned out to be 168. In two subsequent memoranda Robinson broke down the English boroughs and the prospective candidates into six groups, which included 39 assured friends, 65 who were open to persuasion on one count or another, 51 to be had 'for money', and 17 open boroughs which could probably be gained at some expense.[69] He also suggested the appropriate tactics to be adopted in each case.

---

[67] Atkinson to Dundas, 31 Jan., 1785, ed. Furber, p. 489.
[68] See Chapter VIII below.
[69] W. T. Laprade (ed.), 'Parliamentary Papers of John Robinson, 1774-1784' (*Trans. Royal Hist. Soc.*, 3rd Series, vol. XXIII (1922), pp. 65-118).

Upon the dissolution of Parliament on 25 March, Robinson set to work with his customary efficiency, and Pitt actively participated, as the Windsor archives show, suggesting here a sheriff's place and there a baronetcy.[70] The King's chosen Minister was assured of a substantial majority, for George III had never lost an election and the Fox-North alliance was unpopular. In these circumstances it may seem odd that Pitt should have thought it necessary to court such dangerous allies as the India interests and particularly when an unpalatable settlement of the India problem was impending.

Part of the reason may have been his determination to avoid too great dependence upon royal support. For this purpose he had held off a dissolution for three months, using the interval to strengthen his personal position in the House and in persistent efforts to negotiate an alliance with the Portland Whigs.[71] If Fox and Portland had been less stiff in demanding his resignation as a prior condition, a Whig coalition could have imposed its will upon the monarch.

In looking for support in an extraordinary situation, Pitt turned naturally enough to the India interests who had cause to be grateful to him as their deliverer. The support which they gave him was substantial in its results, but it placed him under an awkward obligation, and one which, as it turned out, need not have been incurred. Pitt sought and obtained subscriptions from nabobs for campaign purposes; and Richard Atkinson, the associate of Dundas and Robinson in the plot against the Coalition, was very active during the Spring of 1784 in electioneering on Pitt's behalf. So much so indeed that Robinson expressed his dislike of the lavish way in which he was spending nabobs' money to buy seats[72]: Atkinson was spoiling the market and reinforcing a phalanx which proved recalcitrant.

The choice of Atkinson was perhaps unavoidable in the circumstances, but in view of his unsavoury reputation as a fraudulent contractor and as attorney for Paul Benfield, the disreputable leader of the Arcot creditors, it was unfortunate. Afterwards, when the Government's action about the Arcot debts had been dragged into public view, Burke accused Pitt and Dundas of making a corrupt bargain in return for services rendered. 'You all remem-

---

[70] The King applied to the banker, Henry Drummond, for a loan of £24,000 for election purposes, but the latter replied that he could manage only £10,000, and he ventured to remind the King that either he or Lord North still owed him £38,000 (capital and interest). Greatly shocked, the King sent Robinson to enquire of North, who admitted Drummond's accuracy, but declared his total inability to pay. Thereupon the King with characteristic integrity shouldered the burden and began to repay in annual instalments of £5,000. Geo. III to Drummond, *Royal Archives, Windsor.*

[71] On this see D. G. Barnes, *George III and William Pitt, 1783-1806* (Stanford and Oxford, 1939), chap. II and particularly pp. 103-4.

[72] Laprade (*op. cit.*), *intro.* p. xii *et seq.*

ber,' he flung out, 'that in the same virtuous cause he [Atkinson] submitted to keep a sort of public house or counting-house, where the whole business of the last general election was managed. It was openly managed by the direct agent and attorney of Benfield.'[73] There was exaggeration here, for Atkinson did not manage 'the whole business', nor was he the determining factor in the election; but the fact remains that the new Administration was supported by at least thirty-six members of the India interests of whom fifteen were sitting in Parliament for the first time. Fourteen members of the Arcot interest were returned and of these eleven were supporters of Pitt. Fox had fourteen East Indian adherents in all, and only two of them were new members.[74]

There was a double sequel. The enlarged ranks of the Bengal Squad, sitting behind Pitt, compelled him to modify the terms of his India Bill, and a few months later the Arcot creditors against all public expectation had their enormous and largely bogus claims accepted as valid without enquiry and with a fund of repayment (with interest) charged on the depleted revenues of the Carnatic.

Pitt's intentions with regard to the future management of Indian affairs had been indicated clearly enough when he introduced and expounded the earlier outline Bill. The Government of the day, operating through a committee or board of the Privy Council, would, in effect, supersede the Directors of the Company in all civil, military and financial administration in India. The Company as a commercial corporation would continue with certain limitations to appoint its Servants overseas and to manage its trade monopoly, but subject, even in this sphere, to an important condition, that Government control was to apply in any commercial matters which in any way affected the Indian revenues. Since the Company carried on scarcely any genuine 'trade' in India itself and was concerned with exporting surplus *revenue* in the form of Indian goods, the Government would be in a position to impose its will in every branch of the Company's administration apart from the technical business of shipping and selling. In fact, nothing less than this would suffice to rescue the British position in India. Pitt and Dundas were fully aware that they must assume as much authority as Fox would have done, but it had to be achieved by more circumspect and devious methods.

[73] *Parl. Hist.*, vol. XXV, 250. This impassioned and devastating speech was documented by Burke and printed in pamphlet form. It is included in his *Works* (Lond., 1862 edn.), vol. IV, pp. 195-444. Burke described Atkinson as ' the grand contractor ', a man whose name ' will be well remembered as long as the records of this House, as long as the records of the British treasury, as long as the debt of England shall endure '.

[74] These are the calculations of Professor C. H. Philips, *The East India Company, 1784-1834* (Manchester, 1940), pp. 29-30 and App. I. Cf. the same author's ' The East India Company "Interest " and the English Government, 1873-4 ' (*Trans. Roy. Hist. Soc.*, 4th Series, vol. XX, 1937).

Their plan, as outlined in January and elaborated by Dundas[75] during the summer, was not, as it turned out, sufficiently discreet or devious. Although it was clear enough that the Company could no longer avoid surrendering substantial powers to the State, the India interests were now ready for a stiff rearguard action: they had recovered from their previous panic and were conscious of their new parliamentary strength. When the Directors were shown the draft Bill in June they resisted vigorously. The clause providing that the new Board of Commissioners was to 'direct' (as well as 'superintend' and 'control') all acts relating to civil, military and revenue matters would give them a power to originate orders and instructions which 'would annihilate the Executive power of the Company'; and in objecting to other clauses they tried to retain the right to initiate despatches. But almost all their objections were rejected as 'inadmissable'.[76]

On 14 July, when the Bill had reached the committee stage in the Commons, the Directors returned to the charge. A detailed *critique* was prepared and sent to Pitt. The offending word 'direct' was again resisted, and they pressed for a modification of the clause which required them to submit *all* their transactions to the inspection of the Board. 'It has been the firm Resolution of the Company to reserve to themselves the intire controul of their Trade and only to give a Controul to Government respecting the civil and military Government and Revenues.' It would be 'wholly useless' to Government to have copies of their transactions 'respecting the ordinary Detail of their Affairs'. In the sphere where Government control was to be accepted there was no objection to copies of all documents being submitted. 'But further than this it is conceived is unnecessary and would go beyond the Objects of the Bill.'[77] They little knew, or if they suspected, they preferred not to recognise, what was coming to them.

On 20 July so much of the Bill as had gone through the Com-

---

[75] It was widely recognised in the Commons during the debates that Dundas had been the architect of the Bill, and there seems to be no doubt that that was so.

[76] Professor Philips (*East India Company*, p. 31) prints a summary of a document in the *Pitt Papers* (P.R.O. 8/358) which sets out in three columns the draft clauses, the Directors' criticisms, and Dundas's comments.

[77] On certain points they offered to compromise. While maintaining their objections to 'the general Powers of Secret orders' to be given to the Board of Control, they expressed their readiness to consent 'if passed through the medium of the Secret Committee [of the Directors] in matters of War or peace . . . and so that orders to Commanders-in-Chief pass through the medium of the Council Boards of the respective Presidencies'. The device of operating through the Secret Committee (consisting of the Chairman, Deputy Chairman and one other Director) was subsequently put to effective use by Dundas. With regard to the clause empowering the Crown to recall Company Servants the Directors suggested that this power 'be reciprocal in the Crown and the Company', and the proposal was adopted. Also, the clauses requiring the reinstatement of zemindars and polyars (copied from Fox's Bill) were omitted at their suggestion and replaced by provision for an enquiry into the claims of dispossessed landholders. ('Directors' Minutes, 1784' in *Pitt Papers*, P.R.O. 8/355.)

mons in committee was read at the Court of Directors, with the agreed amendments, 'but no comments made'; and on the following day the whole Bill was read, 'but no Remark entered'.[78] The reason for this cessation was that the battle had been transferred to the floor of the House of Commons, and a strange scene was there enacted. In moving for leave to bring in the Bill (on the 6th) Pitt had frankly stated the substantial powers which the Government proposed to assume, but at the same time he attempted the impossible task of convincing the suspicious that he did not intend to establish a new system. Indeed he was doing no more, he protested, than adapt the old constitution of the Company in the national interest. The Board of Control was not really an innovation, 'because the same powers of controul had been given to the secretaries of state by various acts of parliament, but unfortunately they had never been exercised'.[79]

The phalanx of almost forty East India supporters of Government was not deceived, and when the House went into committee on the Bill the exiguous Opposition watched with unconcealed enjoyment while these supporters of Administration forced Pitt into retreat. The Bill as presented to Parliament would have armed the State with a number of novel powers. The Commanders-in-Chief in each of the Presidencies would have been appointed by the Crown, and the Board of Control was to have been empowered to send out orders to them separately and independently of the civil government. This plan reflected one of Dundas's prime objects: to integrate the armed forces of the Crown and the Company under a Command directly controlled by the Home Government in order that the latter should be able to put an end to military adventures. The consequent separation of the civil from the military power in India could have been disastrous. Secondly, the Crown was to be given the decisive voice in the election of the Governor-General and the members of his Council and of the Presidents and Councillors in Madras and Bombay by a provision that the Company's nominations would be 'subject to His Majesty's approbation'.[80]

---

[78] *Ibid.*, pp. 27-8.

[79] For Fox's speech on 6 July see *Parl. Hist.*, vol. XXIV, 1085-1100. Party politics had divided Government and Opposition as to method, but there was unanimity on the proper object of British policy in India. In referring to the clause abjuring schemes of territorial expansion (which had also appeared in the Dundas Bill of 1783 and in that of Fox) Pitt declared: 'The first and principal object would be to take care to prevent the government (in India) from being ambitious and bent on conquest. . . . Commerce was our object, and with a view to its extension, a pacific system should prevail and a system of defence and concilation.' *Ibid.*, vol. XXIV, 1095; cf. also 1090.

[80] Professor Philips (*East India Company*, p. 41, n. 2) states that the *Cambridge History of India*, vol. VI, p. 12, 'mistakenly suggests that the "Crown Approval" first appeared in the Act of 1833', and (at p. 33, n. 2) he states that 'the qualifying clause, "subject to His Majesty's approbation", was removed in 1786, and not restored until 1813'. The power of the Crown to veto these appointments was

Thirdly, the Board was to have had discretionary authority to send orders to the Presidency Governments without the knowledge of the Directors. This last was the most significant of all, for in effect it would have given the Government direct administrative control in India.[81]

All these forthright measures were removed from the Bill at the insistence of the India interests. Numerous alterations were also made in the procedure of the parliamentary tribunal and the punitive provisions against peculation. According to Lord North 102 clauses were amended in committee.

The Opposition naturally made the most of the situation. Sheridan scornfully declared that the Bill 'had been so altered, so mangled, and so transformed, that it did not appear like the same Bill'.[82] In a later debate Burke painted a colourful picture of what had occurred. The public, he said, had been an indignant witness to the ostentation with which Richard Atkinson and his India colleagues had made the measure 'their own'.

As fast as the clauses were brought up to the table they were accepted. No hesitation; no discussion. They were received by the new minister, not with approbation, but with implicit submission.[83]

That was going much too far, but there is independent evidence that the generality of Pitt's supporters were angry at the dictatorial

---

introduced *for the first time* in 1813 (*53 Geo. III cap. 155, sect. LXXX*). The provision does not appear in the Act of 1784, and Pitt's withdrawal of it is specifically described in the record of the Commons debate at the committee stage: ' Mr. Dempster said, he would state his objections to the principle of the Bill, but without arguing about them. The negative of the Crown upon the Company's appointment – (Mr. Pitt said in a low voice across the House, " I will give up that ") – the appointment of the three commanders-in-chief – (" I will give that up also ") . . .' (*Parl. Hist.*, vol. XXIV, 1146). It had, however, been overlooked that in the Charter Act of 1781 (*21 Geo. III cap. LXV, sect. XXXVI*) the Company had been empowered upon the death or resignation of the Governor-General to appoint a member of the Bengal Council as his successor ' by and with the consent of his Majesty ', signified under the Sign Manual. In order to remove any ambiguity a short Act was passed in 1786 (*26 Geo. III cap. XXV*) which enacted that, ' for removing all Doubts . . . be it enacted . . . That his Majesty's Approbation of the Nomination and Appointment of the Governor-General, and of the several other Members of the Council of the Presidency of Fort William in Bengal is not, nor shall be necessary to render such Appointments respectively good and effectual in Law.'

[81] Lord Loughborough reminded the Ministry of this attempt on their part during the debates in 1788 on the Declaratory Bill. ' At this,' he said, ' the Directors took an alarm, and, considering it as a total assumption of their rights, contested against it; the clause was in consequence given up and omitted in the Committee.' (*Parl. Hist.*, vol. XXVII, 235).

[82] He also pointed out (not very consistently) that ' the Indian phalanx, those Swiss guards of Eastern peculation ' had secured little more than a nominal concession from Pitt in the arrangement that secret orders from the Board must go out through the medium of the Secret Committee of the Directors: ' To please them, the right hon. Gentleman had suffered them to have a secret committee of three directors; but the Company were not a bit nearer, for those three directors were sworn not to divulge any thing done in council ' (*Parl. Hist.*, vol. XXIV, 1200-1).

[83] *Ibid.*, vol. XXV, 249-50.

attitude of the Bengal Squad.[84] Philip Francis in his turn made a detailed comparison between the Bill in its original shape and as it had emerged. He concluded:

The crown and the commissioners surrender almost everything they had taken, and the directors are re-invested with a power which evidently supposes them fit to be highly trusted. But the trust, as it stands, is incomparable with the control. The first Bill, placing no confidence in the directors, divests them of all power: the amended Bill continues a check, in which the same want of confidence is implied, yet restores them to a power which ought never to be given to men who are distrusted.[85]

The comment which came perhaps nearest to the mark was made by Fox. The Bill, he said, worked upon the Company's rights 'by slow and gradual sap'. If it was right to vest the powers of the Court of Directors in a board of Privy Councillors (which he denied), it should at any rate be done openly. 'A great nation ought never to descend to gradual and insidious encroachment.'[86]

It was easy to say that from the Opposition benches. The alternative was to force the Bill through in its original shape without concessions. In spite of his huge (and heterogeneous) majority Pitt was not prepared to do this and so defy a group to whom he was under an obligation and also incur the charge of being only a little less 'violent' than Fox himself. Instead, he and Dundas paid the demanded price by handing back certain powers to the Directors, but they retained the powerful engine of control which they had devised. They themselves, as the managers of the Board, would be in a position to invade the intermediate zone between trade and government by means of executive action which could not be effectively resisted. Encroachment on the part of the State 'by slow and gradual sap' was bound to prevail. In the first place, the right of the Directors to appeal to the Privy Council against a Commission of Privy Councillors was valueless. Secondly, the device whereby the Court of Directors could operate at will through a Secret Committee, comprising the Chairs and one other Director, could exclude the Court of Directors as such from the ordering of any major issue. Finally, the appeal to Parliament, which Pitt had represented as a further safeguard for the Company, was naturally used by the Government itself in order to consolidate its executive gains by means of declaratory legislation.

---

[84] See Daniel Pulteney, M.P., to the Duke of Rutland, 13 August, 1784. 'It is the language very much at present among some of Pitt's country supporters in the House, that he is too full of *concession*, and there is a sort of jealousy against his East India friends, which I think may possibly break out next year.' (*Hist. MSS. Comm., 14 Rept. App. Pt. I*, vol. III, p. 131.)

[85] *Parl. Hist.*, vol. XXIV, 1175.

[86] *Ibid.*, 1128.

Accordingly the Bill has been described with some justification as 'dishonest'.[87] Pitt and Dundas responded to blackmail by being disingenuous. The arrangement by which one executive authority drafted despatches for India and another was empowered to dictate drastic and sometimes fundamental alterations was, in itself, a clumsy if unavoidable compromise, well calculated to engender frictional heat; but the pretence that the Directors remained masters of their house, subject only to supervision in certain specified concerns, necessitated an acrimonious struggle in which the spirit and sometimes the letter of the statute were progressively violated.

The India Act of 1784 marked the culmination of a protracted struggle between a hesitant State and a mutinous corporation. In 1764 Clive had confidently promised the nation that his intervention in Bengal would provide them with a large territorial revenue without involving them in internal administration. The reality, as we have seen, proved to be quite different. In the pursuit of private gain British subjects became deeply involved in the anarchic politics of Bengal and Madras and in relations with other Indian Powers and at the same time subverted the constitution of their nominal masters in London. Across the Atlantic British Ministers were faced with the parallel problem of trying to delimit, administer and defend a frontier which recalcitrant settlers were steadily pushing outward. In India the frontiers of power were not only expanding territorially, but within the regions already under supervision they were invading the administrative tissues of alien and complex societies. This latter aspect was completely novel. It became increasingly clear that defiant British subjects must be brought to heel, and the profits which they were appropriating to themselves must be preserved for Britain as a State. But how far was it necessary to accept and assume control over internal administrative penetration in the Indian Presidencies in order to satisfy these two requirements?

For twenty years bewildered Ministers, handicapped by the political power of an almost autonomous chartered corporation and by the very limited administrative capacity of the governmental machine, resorted to palliatives which proved inadequate. Meanwhile abuses in India were becoming increasingly injurious to British interests. Enquiry leading to effective remedial action was imperative, and a weak Administration relied on the succession of Select and Secret Committees of the Commons to provide guidance and incidentally to inform and mobilise parliamentary opinion. And so the significant spectacle developed of country squires and merchants with the aid of a few specialists being set to wrestle with a vast Indian documentation, replete with strange nomenclature

---

[87] See Philips (*op. cit.*), p. 34.

representing the intricacies of Hindu and Muslim law, social custom and administrative practice. Seldom, if ever, has an external problem of the British State received so thorough and protracted an examination. The voluminous Reports provided a great quarry of information, although the compilers were more concerned to indict individuals than to provide policy recommendations.

The turning point came with the Resolutions which emanated from the Secret Committee led by Dundas, upon which his own abortive India Bill was based. In spite of the cross-currents of political faction and the East India pressure groups, parliamentary opinion had slowly come to accept the necessity of state control in some decisive form; but it had taken twenty years of ineffectual compromise and much washing of dirty Anglo-Indian linen to bring them to it.

It was significant for the future course of British policy in Asia and Africa that (political animosities apart) two schools of thought should have developed. That led by Fox, Burke and Philip Francis advocated total and direct state control in order to confine the participation of British officials in local Indian administration to the narrowest possible limits; and their proposal to vest this new source of power and influence in the legislature arose from their distrust of the executive as then constituted. Pitt and Dundas, on the other hand, regarded the Cabinet as the proper authority to superintend all imperial affairs; and they, unlike their opponents, accepted the principle of direct administration by a reformed and disciplined British Service as the only reliable method of establishing justice and prosperity.

Nonetheless Pitt and Fox both represented the general attitude in their determination to put a stop to wars and territorial expansion which piled up debts and made dangerous enemies. They differed as to method, but for each the purpose of state intervention was to provide an instrument of restraint: to clamp down on would-be *conquistadores,* prevent entangling alliances, and put an end to injurious peculation. It was symptomatic that the Pitt-Dundas Act should have laid it down that the first step under the new régime was to be a drastic reduction in the civil and military personnel in India: the Directors were prohibited from making any fresh appointments until the total reductions had been approved by the Board of Control as sufficient.

The idea of limitation, although appearing to be common sense at the time, proved to be an illusion. Having intervened to save a wealth-producing agency from self-destruction and to enforce a halt in political commitment, the State became thereby involved in a process by which the power vacuum left by the fallen Moghuls was gradually filled by Britain. A metropolitan state cannot halt a moving frontier: it can only disengage by abdication.

Neither Pitt nor Dundas invented the system of 'double government'. It was an extended application of the old device which had been embodied in the Regulating Act of 1773. The desultory supervision of a Secretary of State was replaced under the compulsive pressure of events by close control through a body which in effect was a standing committee of the Cabinet; but the diarchical concept remained. The system continued in operation until the dissolution of the Company in 1858, for the compromise reflected the national outlook. Successive ministries, preoccupied with domestic affairs and European diplomacy, continued to put up with the irritating handicaps of the system rather than incur the obligations and potential risks of direct sovereignty. Like the chartered corporations in North America and the Caribbean of the 17th century and their successors in Africa, 'John Company' was retained as long as possible as a useful *locum tenens*. Yet masterful administrators in the course of the 19th century, recognising the logic of events, forced the Company, and therefore the State, into an expanding *imperium,* as men like Fox, Burke and Philip Francis had feared they would. It was a passing phase which lasted for the brief span of little more than a century and then reverted to 'informality'; but the interlude left a deep mark on the political and economic structure of India and exerted a profound influence on the evolution of a Commonwealth.

Twenty years of investigation into abuses and of ineffectual efforts to impose discipline upon the British rebels in India had given rise to a mounting anger at home. The arrogance and ostentation of returned 'nabobs' had aroused jealousy as well as anger, and it was realised that the prevailing misconduct was a disgrace which was injuring the national interest. Pitt undoubtedly expressed a widely accepted, if utilitarian, view when he declared that Britain's future expectations of commercial profit from India 'must chiefly depend' on preventing extortion and establishing the happiness and tranquillity of the inhabitants. Whether public opinion at that stage followed Burke to the higher level of recognising a moral responsibility and a positive 'trust' may perhaps be doubted. Not unnaturally his protracted and embittered indictment of Hastings defeated its object by inducing a mood of bored exasperation.[88] But before that, in 1785, he had sadly confessed : 'I wish that some more feeling than I have yet observed for the sufferings of our fellow creatures and fellow subjects in that oppressed part of the world had manifested itself in any one quarter of the kingdom, or in any one large description of men.'[89]

As with the slave trade, slavery, and conditions at home in mines

---

[88] *Parl. Hist.*, vol. XXIV, 1090.
[89] *Works* (Lond., 1862 edn.), vol. IV, p. 316. (' Speech on the Nabob of Arcot's Debts.')

and factories the practical application of humane principles involved a widening of the horizons of public responsibility at the expense of sectional interests; and that in the nature of things could not be easy. Nevertheless the stringent provisions of the Act of 1784, an enactment at last backed by adequate executive power, enabled the upright Cornwallis to set a new standard; and it was remarkable how quickly the great majority of the Company Servants, particularly the youngsters, became absorbed in the business of learning to understand the needs and promoting the well-being of a peasantry which had been cruelly oppressed for centuries.

4. STATE CONTROL AND REFORM

The Letters Patent appointing the 'Commissioners for the Affairs of India' passed the Great Seal on 31 August, 1784. Those named of the Commission were – the two *ex officio* members, Lord Sydney (as Secretary of State) and Pitt (as Chancellor of the Exchequer), with Henry Dundas, Lord Walsingham, W. W. Grenville, and Lord Mulgrave. These were the six unpaid Privy Councillors as provided in the Act. The Secretary of State was to preside when present, or, failing him, the Chancellor of the Exchequer; and in the absence of both of these the senior Commissioner present was to take the chair.[90] A preliminary meeting took place on 3 September and as soon as it was over Dundas wrote to the 'Chairs' to say that there were 'several particulars' which he would be glad to talk over with them by way of facilitating a business of such material interest to the Company and the public, and that he proposed to visit India House for the purpose on a stated day and hour.[91] Five days later the first formal meeting of the Board took place when the six officials, who were to comprise the office staff, were sworn in.[92] A new era had begun in the history of British relations with India.

---

[90] A copy of the Letters Patent is in *Pitt Papers*, P.R.O. 8/355.

[91] Dundas to the Chairs, 3 Sept., 1784. *Letters from the Board of Control to the Court of Directors*, vol. I, p. 1. (Hereinafter cited as *B-C Letters*.)

[92] The original staff, most of whom were to serve the Board for many years, consisted of the following: C. W. Boughton Rouse, Secretary, at a salary of £1,500 p.a.; the Hon. William Brodrick, under-secretary, at £600 p.a.; Francis Russell, Solicitor to the Board, at £600 p.a.; James Bradley, Chief Clerk, at £400 p.a.; William Cabell, Second Clerk, at £300 p.a.; and John Meheux, Third Clerk, at £150 p.a. In addition there was an Accountant at £130 p.a., three messengers at £50 each, an Office Keeper at £48 p.a., and a House Keeper at £48 p.a. In response to a request for a clerk who was well versed in the Company's organisation the Directors recommended that William Cabell be transferred to the service of the Board, where his unique knowledge of the Company's archives proved invaluable. John Meheux rose to be Chief Clerk in 1804. By the Charter Act of 1793 (*33 Geo. III, cap. 52*) it was provided that the Commissioner named first in the Letters Patent should be President and receive a salary of £2,000 p.a. and that there should be two additional Commissioners who would be paid at the rate of £1,500 p.a. and would not be Privy Councillors. At the same time the office staff was considerably increased in order to cope with the volume of work. (See *Home Misc. Series*, vol. 341. This large volume is entirely devoted to matters of office organisation, routine and personnel.)

The only member of the Commission with any detailed knowledge of Indian affairs was Henry Dundas, and it became immediately evident that it was he whom Pitt intended to be the manager
– under his own direct supervision. As for Dundas himself this
was a disappointing substitute for the earlier expectation of becoming the first Secretary of State for India, and he viewed the ambiguity of his situation with glum distaste. It would be necessary on the
one hand to assert his ascendancy at the Board, and on the other to
tame a recalcitrant Court of Directors. He set about the dual task
with his customary resolution and abounding energy.

The nominal President of the Board was Lord Sydney: a decent,
honest sort of man, but totally lacking in constructive ideas and
very dilatory in handling official business. On one occasion Grenville's brother, the Marquis of Buckingham, wrote tartly from
Dublin Castle: 'Lord Sydney does not seem inclined to extend his
correspondence beyond his usual line of answering my letters five
weeks after they arrive.'[93] Overwhelmed with responsibility for
Home, Irish and Colonial affairs and with no special knowledge of
India, he was easily thrust to one side. In 1789 he willingly relinquished his office in favour of William Grenville and retired from
political life.[94] Of the other members of the Board Lord Mulgrave
had probably been chosen because Pitt relied on him for military
advice, but Dundas had his own very definite ideas about military
policy and reorganisation in India. Lord Walsingham came into
collision with Dundas almost at once: after 1787 he attended
rarely and was dropped in 1790.

William Wyndham Grenville, a cousin of Pitt and representing
with his brother, Buckingham, the powerful Grenville clan, was in
a different category. He and Dundas quickly became Pitt's closest
associates, constituting with him the celebrated 'Triumvirate',
which virtually ran the Government as an informal inner executive.
In the first months of the Board's existence Dundas and Grenville
wrote to each other as though they were joint managers of it, and
on one occasion Grenville reported that he was 'chin deep in
Indian despatches'; but as the latter became immersed in other
affairs of state, the detailed management of Indian business was
left increasingly to Dundas. Yet Grenville was far from becoming
a cypher in this field of policy. He continued to be a regular
attender at the meetings, becoming titular President in 1789 as

---

[93] Buckingham to Grenville, 8 April, 1788. *Grenville Papers (Dropmore)*, (*Hist.
MSS. Comm.* 13th Rept., App. Pt. III) vol. I, p. 315.

[94] By way of consolation he received the 'quiet' and not unremunerative post
of Chief Justice in Eyre. In reporting this to his cousin, Lord Cornwallis, he wrote:
'I can assure you that I am perfectly satisfied and grateful to the King, as well as
sensible of the friendship of Mr. Pitt. My appetite is not so keen, nor my digestion
so quick, as those of some of my neighbours.' Sydney to Cornwallis, 27 Jan., 1790.
Cornwallis Correspondence, ed. Chas. Ross (Lond., 1859), vol. II, p. 32.

F*

Sydney's successor, and he took an active part in the proceedings of the 'Secret' Board.[95] Sometimes when matters of exceptional importance arose, secret letters were sent direct to the Bengal Government, signed by Pitt, Dundas and Grenville.[96] The procedure affords a typical example of how the Triumvirate functioned.

It must have been obvious enough to the other members of the Board that Dundas had been designated, in effect, as the Prime Minister's deputy for Indian affairs. Within a few months of the Board's inception Dundas rebuked the Company's secretary, Morton. He had found that in the past few days several paragraphs of draft despatches had been sent to the Board, but that a private copy had not been sent to himself. 'This creates great inconvenience which Mr. Dundas hopes Mr. Morton will endeavour to prevent in time to come.'[97] Some weeks later he called for a personal copy of the Company's home establishments which had been sent to the Board a few days before, and he added a request 'that the Papers for his use may in future be directed to *him* at the Office of the India Board'.[98]

For the first twelve months Pitt kept away from the Board. During that time he was heavily engaged in his unsuccessful struggle to adjust commercial and defence relations with Ireland. He may have stayed away, too, in order to leave Dundas more free to establish his authority. But from the outset Pitt's superintendence of Indian business was close and continuous. Every projected measure in the great task of reorganisation and reform was referred to him for advice and approval. And two years later Dundas reported: 'Mr. Pitt is a real active member of the Board and makes himself thoroughly master of the business.' In another letter he wrote: 'on this or any other subject of importance Mr. Pitt is privy to everything I write.'[99] And on his side Pitt informed Cornwallis: 'Mr. Dundas, I know, writes fully on every point, and his letters convey my sentiments as well as his own.'[100]

From September, 1785, onwards Pitt was a very frequent attender at the Board,[101] and it is noticeable that, when he presided, the letter which was prepared and signed at the end of the meeting, embodying the agreed amendments to the Directors' draft despatches, was in Pitt's style and was not couched in the hectoring terms usually adopted by Dundas. On these occasions the letter, while firmly insistent, took higher ground and was more conciliatory

---

[95] For this administrative development see pp. 176-9 below.
[96] For examples of such letters see *Home Misc. Series*, vol. 289 (10), pp. 511-530.
[97] Dundas to Morton, 21 March, 1785. *B-C Letters*, vol. I, p. 57.
[98] Cabell to Morton, 3 May, 1785. *Ibid.*, p. 86.
[99] Dundas to Cornwallis, 'Private', 29 July, 1787 and, 'Secret and Confidential', 22 July, 1787. *Cornwallis Correspce.*, vol. I, p. 33 and App. XVII, p. 536.
[100] Pitt to Cornwallis, 'Secret', 2 August, 1787. *Ibid.*, p. 337.
[101] For some statistics of attendance see p. 244 below.

in tone; and Pitt took these opportunities of stressing a favourite theme of his: that the Directors must break the habit of using threats and abuse against their Servants. In one despatch the word 'shameful' was altered to 'unwarrantable' and with this comment: 'We are sure it must be your disposition as much as ours to treat the members of your Supreme Government in India with every possible respect, for in preserving their Dignity, you in truth are preserving your own.'[102] At another meeting when Pitt was in the chair the same point was made more elaborately with reference to a despatch for Madras:

If we have in some instances softened the expressions of your intended Orders to your Presidency of Madras, we have not done so from any desire to prevent you from censuring these Acts of your Servants which there is solid reason to disapprove, but because we would have even censure conveyed in terms suited to your own dignity, as representing the executive Authority of Great Britain in its Indian Possessions, and to the elevated situation of those you address, so that the minds of persons exercising high national trusts may not be hurt by a language of asperity applied to the less important acts of their administration, whilst Justice calls upon you to ratify and applaud many others of a more delicate and consequential nature, in which your highest interests have been honourably consulted.[103]

The object of such admonitions was to impel a body of merchants to behave with the dignity and sense of responsibility required of imperial administrators. Hitherto they had threatened and abused out of frustration: now they were to become the (obedient) instrument of the metropolitan State in transforming a corps of *franc-tireurs* into a loyal and disciplined service.

Such was the *milieu* in which Dundas was called upon to re-fashion and control the conduct of British affairs in India: a docile Board of Commissioners, a restive and sometimes hostile Court of Directors, a deeply interested Prime Minister as senior partner, and (before long) a powerful Governor-General who co-operated with the home Government almost as closely as the Lord Lieutenant of Ireland. These three men – Dundas, Pitt and Cornwallis – worked together with a rare singleness of purpose. 'We never before,' declared Dundas to Cornwallis in a burst of sincere, if somewhat complacent, enthusiasm, 'had a Government of India, both at home and abroad, acting in perfect unison together, upon principles of perfect purity and integrity; these

---

[102] *B-C Letters*, 27 Jan., 1787, vol. I, pp. 162-3.

[103] *Ibid.*, 28 June, 1787, vol. I, pp. 189-94. Earlier in this letter the following pointed observation was made: 'We have very frequently observed that menace in your former Correspondence with your Servants, but have not met with any instance of its being carried into effect.'

ingredients cannot fail to produce their consequent effects.'[104]

It was frequently said at the time (and has been since) that Dundas concentrated on India as the most promising opening by which to establish himself at Pitt's right hand and climb into the Cabinet as Secretary of State. These considerations were certainly an incentive, for Dundas was an ambitious ' career ' politician; but he was more than that. He saw the re-organisation of the economic and administrative system in India as the creation of a source of power, which, conjoined with the industrial potential of Britain itself, would provide the means for building a great empire of trade throughout the Far East. He was one of those exceptional politicians who on being appointed Secretary of State for India or the Colonies have become so absorbed in the task that they have preferred it to all others. In 1794 he resigned the office of Home Secretary, which included Irish, Colonial and Indian affairs, in order to relieve Pitt of an awkward dilemma in reconstructing the Ministry.[105] In arguing against Pitt's insistent plea that he should become Secretary of State for War, Dundas indicated how much the resignation from his previous office had meant to him.

It would be gross affectation and adverse to the truth was I to state to you that in the Present State of the Dependencies of the British Empire, to have been the colonial Minister of this Country was not the object of my Predilection in every View I could take of it.[106]

And in the course of ' a ten years administration of India ' the general run of events, many of them critical, had left him, he continued, ' without reproach '. Four years later he begged Pitt to make a new arrangement which would relieve him of some of his war-time burden ' and allow me to attend solely to my Indian Department '.[107]

The task for which Dundas had been made primarily responsible involved a complete overhaul and reconstruction of the system of management. Retrenchment and reform, to be effective, would require a drastic rationalisation involving the elimination of all posts in the Service found to be not essential. A considerable number of the Company's Servants might therefore expect to find

---

[104] Dundas to Cornwallis, 21 March, 1787. ' Private and Confidential '. *Cornwallis Correspce.*, vol. I, p. 292.

[105] Pitt's intention had been to leave in Dundas's charge ' all the colonies of Great Britain added to the East India Department, with the conduct of the war while it lasted ' and to bring in the Duke of Portland as Secretary of State for Home and Irish affairs. Unfortunately Pitt had not made himself sufficiently clear and Portland had understood that he was to have the whole Department. Dundas thereupon resigned in order to ensure the adhesion to the Government of the Portland Whigs. (See Matheson, *Life of Henry Dundas*, Lond., 1933, pp. 201-3.)

[106] Dundas to Pitt, 9 July, 1794. *Pitt Papers*, P.R.O. 38/8/157.

[107] Dundas to Pitt, 10 Feb., 1798. *Ibid.*

themselves retired on pension as the scrutiny proceeded. At the root of the problem was the confused state of land revenue assessment and collection in Bengal which provided the financial basis of the British position in India. Warren Hastings, as we have seen, had initiated a comprehensive inquisition into this intricate complex of obligation, but the incidence of war had interrupted it. The Act of 1784 required a full investigation and the establishment of a just and coherent system: a most formidable task.[108] Provision was also made for another investigation, the difficulties of which were of a different order. This related to the chaotic finances of Madras, where the Nawab of Arcot, nominal ruler of the Carnatic, was immersed full fathom five in debt to a crowd of Company Servants and was enjoying the situation to the discomfiture of the Company and the misery of the peasants. On the military side there was great need to create an integrated and disciplined command out of the Company's European contingents (which were notoriously bad), their native troops, and the 'King's regiments in India'.

Much of this re-organisation would be impossible without the co-operation of a strong Governor-General on the spot, armed with controlling authority, and that had not yet been secured when the India Board came into operation. But in spite of anticipated trouble with the Directors Dundas threw himself into his complicated and onerous task with all his energy and capacity for business. Unlike most of his contemporaries he was in no doubt about the British position being essentially imperial. He had no patience with the idea of an ambiguous protectorate and frequently referred to 'the British Empire in India' and British 'sovereignty'. But, like everyone else, he assumed that the frontiers of territorial rule could be strictly confined. His attitude towards the problem of Bombay, for example, illustrates this point of view. While recognising its importance as a refuge for shipping during the North-East Monsoon and its great strategic value for land operations, he was concerned that it was a financial drain upon the Bengal revenues. He was against enlarging its territory by war, he informed the Governor-General, but if a negotiated bargain could be made so as to secure 'a revenue nearly adequate' for maintaining a sufficient garrison there, it would be very desirable.[109]

---

[108] The purpose of the enquiry, as stated in Sect. XXXIX of the Act, was to redress all injuries that might have been suffered by native landholders, 'and for settling and establishing, upon Principles of Moderation and Justice, according to the Laws and Constitution of India, the permanent Rules by which their respective Tributes, Rents, and Services, shall be in future rendered and paid to the said United Company, by the said Rajahs, Zemindars, Polygars, Talookdars, and other Native Landholders'.

[109] See Dundas to Cornwallis, 3 April, 1789. *Cornwallis Correspce.*, vol. I, App. XXVI, p. 557.

The first and essential task in his view was to convert British India into a viable business concern. That done, a few years of honest and efficient administration would bring prosperity back to the land and to peasant industries. The drain of specie from India through the remittance of private fortunes to Europe would be stopped, and with intelligent management an increasing output of Indian manufactured goods and primary products could provide a source of economic power for Britain in a complex of world trade. Always sanguine, Dundas saw no reason why improving conditions should not enable the investment in the form of Indian textiles for sale in Europe to be substantially increased, thus promoting the development of London as an oriental emporium. Looking eastward, he hoped that enhanced Indian productivity would help the British Company to diversify its stock-in-trade for the China market so that tea might be bought in Canton with British and Indian goods instead of with British and Indian bullion.

I am satisfied [he wrote] that by the export of British manufactures and Bengal commodities to China, a sufficient fund will at last be found in China for answering the purposes of that valuable trade. . . .[110]

This idea of converting the cash purchase of China tea into a triangular exchange of commodities led Dundas into the wider enterprise of securing a vent for British and Indian goods throughout the Chinese Empire. By the summer of 1787 he was planning the official embassy to Peking which was eventually led by Lord Macartney. Its purpose was to circumvent the Hong monopoly at Canton and by establishing diplomatic relations with the Emperor to open that vast region (and more particularly the northern provinces) to the woollen and other manufactures of Britain and the products of India. In explaining the project to Cornwallis, he wrote that the isolation of the Company's representatives at Canton had long been an object of regret.

I have learnt from various quarters, that a mission directly from the King to the Emperor of China would probably have the desired effect of obtaining to us a commercial establishment; and if that be obtained it would answer very valuable purposes, both in respect of providing China investments, and in respect of the aid it would afford to the vent both of British and Indian manufactures and produce, in the Empire

---

[110] *Ibid.*, p. 558. Apart from the possibility of selling opium to China, Cornwallis was not optimistic about the Indian aspect of this proposition, and Dundas chided him for it. In this same letter he wrote: 'I always thought your despatches too desponding upon the object of supplying, or at least aiding the China investment, by means of the trade and other resources of Bengal, but I think you have of late made considerable exertions towards that object, and I am positive that the idea, perseveringly followed up, will work its own way at length. . . .'

of China and its dependencies. I know not whether it will succeed or not, but I am sure it is worth the attempt. . . .[111]

The plan represented a significant blending of the techniques of 'formal' and 'informal' empire. A similar manifestation was the active interest which Dundas took, like Warren Hastings before him, in a project to re-open a direct trade between India and Cairo and through that centre to the countries of the Middle East.[112]

In pursuing his eastern policy Dundas always treated the strategic position of the Dutch in the Indian Ocean and the Indonesian Archipelago as a factor of prime importance. In contrast to the narrowly traditional view of the Company he insisted that British and Dutch interests in these regions were essentially complementary. The spice trade of the East Indies was a reservoir for Dutch oceanic trade in the same sort of way that home industries and Indian products could be for the British. He accordingly worked for an Anglo-Dutch partnership in eastern waters which would secure the Dutch in their own commercial sphere while affording the British joint access to vital strategic bases. When diplomacy failed and the United Provinces veered into the orbit of revolutionary France, Dundas insisted that Britain must have possession of the Cape of Good Hope and the invaluable harbour of Trincomali in Ceylon with assured security of passage through the Strait of Malacca.[113]

Linked with this policy was the protection of British interests in India against French sea-power by the acquisition of potential and actual naval bases in the Bay of Bengal and the Indian Ocean. From the same point of view he compelled the Company – at the expense of a head-on collision with the Directors and their parliamentary supporters – to acquiesce in a substantial reinforcement of 'King's' troops in India, so that if war broke out an immediate offensive could be launched in the Indian Ocean or the East Indies against a European enemy.

The idea of penetrating the great markets of Asia and creating a network of commercial and naval depots along the routes of ocean trade was not new. It had been vigorously pursued by enterprising groups, as we have already seen, for some twenty years. But Dundas was the first statesman to give shape to this national trend in a coherent and massive policy. In promoting, utilising and safeguarding the resources of India for the extension of British

---

[111] Dundas to Cornwallis, 21 July, 1787. *Ibid.*, vol. I, p. 327. Dundas added that he had every reason to believe that the French were very anxious to acquire such a situation in that part of the world. For an account of the Macartney embassy to Peking see Chap. IX below.

[112] See Chap. VIII below.

[113] See vol. I, Chap. IV of this work and Chap. VI below.

economic power he was (in that sphere of national affairs) the fore-runner of Palmerston.[114]

With such far-reaching plans in mind Dundas needed as free a hand as possible in the conduct of Indian affairs. Had it been practicable, something on the lines of Fox's scheme for total state control would have suited him well; but when the difficult alternative of 'double government' was made even more difficult by the reduction of the over-riding powers of the State during the passage of Pitt's Bill, Dundas evidently decided that he must recover the ground lost to the Court of Directors by applying executive pressure. The task promised to be particularly troublesome since Pitt's flat refusal to countenance a working alliance with Sulivan and his group left Dundas in the awkward position of dealing with a Directorate in which a resentful man held a commanding position. Sulivan supported Warren Hastings, whom Dundas feared and disliked, and Hastings was regarded with favour by several members of the Government, including Lord Thurlow.

Dundas approached the task of reconstructing the conduct of British affairs in India in a mood of gloom and despondency. When a collision with the Directors occurred almost immediately, he wrote to Grenville in terms almost of despair. The difficulties need not be formidable, he wrote, provided that the Board was given fair play, but that he saw plainly they were not to have.

We are appointed to control the civil and military affairs of India; at the head of the first *will remain Mr Hastings*. That you may depend upon. . . . Joined to this a determined faction in the India House operating against us; and to conclude, all the most obstinate part of His Majesty's Ministers respectively countenancing the heads of faction both at home and in India. Under all those circumstances it is Don Quixotism with a witness to attempt what we are attempting. . . .[115]

Dundas need not have been so troubled. Sulivan was not entirely unco-operative and in any case had only two more years to live, and Hastings had no intention of continuing as Governor-General under the new Act. But the Ministers on the Board were evidently determined to begin as they intended to continue, and when the

---

[114] For an illuminating study of Palmerston's ' imperial ' policy in the basin of the Indian Ocean and beyond see R. J. Gavin, ' Palmerston's Policy towards the East and West Coasts of Africa, 1830-65 ' (unpublished Ph.D. thesis, Cambridge, 1958).

[115] Dundas to Grenville, 27 October, 1784. *Grenville Papers (Dropmore) Hist. MSS. Comm.*) vol. I, pp. 240-1. (The words printed in italics were underlined in the letter.) Dundas added that he wished Grenville's talents and integrity could be employed in some other situation where he could do some good to the public. As for himself, he wished that he was back at the Bar, ' where, if I can do no good to the public, I will at least escape the disgrace which, if I remain where I now am, I am positive awaits me '. Grenville replied on the same day that the circumstances were certainly in many respects unfavourable. ' But with a good cause, with upright intentions . . . *nil desperandum.' Ibid.*, p. 241.

first batch of draft despatches for India arrived from Leadenhall Street they subjected them to drastic treatment.

The business covered by the despatches included the customary mass of detail as well as a number of major policy issues. Determined to establish its authority, the Board reviewed everything and altered much. Long series of 'paragraphs' were expunged and new ones (drafted by Dundas) were substituted, reversing and modifying the Directors' decisions. The chief issue which arose in this initial encounter involved the entire financial structure of the Madras Presidency and its future relations with the local princes.

The Board, however, was unwise enough to attempt at the same time to interfere with the Company's appointments, which were not its concern. Since Pitt had withdrawn the provision in his Bill to make senior appointments subject to Crown approval, the Board had no standing in the matter except the power of recall. Nevertheless they struck out a paragraph in which the Directors had confirmed the promotion of Colonel Ross Lang by the Madras Government to be Commander-in-Chief of the Company's forces in that Presidency and substituted another, which made the Directors refuse to confirm the appointment as being inexpedient and improper. There was a turbulent background to this particular case which illustrated the friction which often arose between the military command of the Company and that of the Crown as well as the general tendency of the soldiers to flout the authority of the civil power;[116] and Dundas was determined to stamp this out by a thorough re-organisation of the system. But in attempting to veto an appointment the Board had over-reached itself.

The Court of Directors promptly referred the case to George Rous, the Company's counsel; and when the latter stated that he was 'clearly of the opinion that the board of Commissioners had exceeded their power' and that the Madras Government and the Directors had acted in strict conformity with the Act, the latter joined battle with grim satisfaction.[117] If, they replied, the Board thought the appointment improper, there was a power of removal vested in the Crown, but with all respect they must submit 'that the exercise of the power exclusively vested in this Court to appoint

---

[116] On 17 Sept., 1783, Major-General Stuart had been dismissed the Company's service by the Madras Government for disobedience, and Major-General Burgoyne, the senior officer in His Majesty's service in Madras, was ordered to take command of the King's forces. Stuart thereupon declared that he would continue to give orders to the King's troops and Burgoyne said that he would obey. Burgoyne refused to accept the command himself, 'because I think it militates against my Duty to the King and my obedience as an Officer'. Stuart was then arrested, and the next senior officer, Colonel Ross Lang, was sent for the same day and was offered the command. He accepted and was gazetted as 'Lieut-General in the Honble Company's Service and Commander-in-Chief of their Forces on this Coast' until the pleasure of the Court of Directors was known. See *Home Misc. Series*, vol. 342, p. 109 *et seq.*

[117] Opinion of Counsel – George Rous, 25 Oct., 1784. *Ibid.*, pp. 105-7.

all the Company's servants, Civil and Military, would be rendered nugatory if a negative could be put thereupon by an alteration made by your Board of the paragraph notifying the Act of Appointment'. In their opinion the action of Madras in making this appointment at a critical and alarming juncture was 'wise, temperate and decisive for the support of good order and legal Government'.[118] The Board climbed down.

Although the Directors had vindicated their right in this instance, the Commissioners continued to apply heavy pressure whenever a nomination came up which seemed to them unsuitable. Often they had good reason: reformation of the administrative system could be vitiated by promoting men who were incompetent or corrupt. When, for example, they attempted to stop the provisional appointment of John Hollond of the Madras Council as a successor to the governorship there on the ground that he was an Arcot creditor, their misgivings were justified by the event. In 1790 Hollond was suspended from being acting-Governor and charged with corruption and peculation.[119] On this occasion the Directors were admonished to avoid not only 'blameable appointments but such as may be open to plausible misrepresentation', and the Board concluded with a homily:

We are convinced nothing can give proper Dignity and Energy to the Governments in India but a scrupulous attention in every appointment to chuse such Persons as may not only be above the Commission of any Crime but exempted from the smallest suspicion of being exposed to any interested or improper Bias in the execution of the trusts reposed in them.

The rejoinder of the Directors was tart to the point of acidity.[120] They probably appreciated that there was a certain irony in the situation when Dundas and his colleagues applied these unimpeachable sentiments to the case of an Arcot creditor.

The Commissioners were struggling to enforce a sense of public responsibility in the management of the Company's patronage, and their persistence is shown by numerous examples in their correspondence with the Directors. Sometimes, however, their intervention descended to a pettifogging level which only induced irritation and a disposition to be recalcitrant on important issues. While

---

[118] Court to Board, 2 Nov., 1784. *C-B Letters*, vol. I, p. 24 *et seq.*

[119] See Government Notification in *Madras Courier*, 10 Nov., 1790. Printed in H. D. Love, *Vestiges of Old Madras, 1640-1800* (Indian Records Series), Lond., 1913, vol. III, p. 402.

[120] After countering the Board's arguments, they proposed to deliver themselves as follows: 'For these reasons we humbly conceive that the System of Patronage which you profess to combat is wholly foreign to our Conduct in these particulars.' Discretion, however, prevailed and the offensive words 'profess to' were crossed out in the draft, and the erasure was confirmed in the margin. See *Home Misc. Series*, vol. 342, p. 89.

conceding that the Directors had the right of appointment and recall, the Board insisted that they could not censure their Servants without official sanction. The absurd situation thus arose that notifications of dismissal were allowed to pass, but the Directors' reasons were deleted; and as the latter very sensibly observed, inability to censure would reduce their authority to contempt and might force them to dismiss in order to 'protect themselves from insult'.[121]

Meanwhile Dundas and his colleagues were grappling with the financial anarchy prevailing in the Presidency of Madras. The situation was endangering the existence of the British position in southern India and immediate action was required. The Nawab of Arcot was a dependent of Madras, and his situation was not unlike that of the puppet nawabs of Bengal in the days of Clive. But in Arcot's case he himself had controlled the revenues while the Company (for its own security) had been obliged to supplement the Nawab's defence contributions in time of war with large sums from other sources – mostly from Bengal. In 1767 the Nawab had borrowed some £450,000 from private lenders, most of whom were Company Servants. A rot set in, for it was easy money, eagerly provided and quickly spent. An enormous debt accumulated, and the security was the land revenue which was assigned in parcels to the creditors who made the most of their opportunities, 'acting', as the Directors put it, 'in the capacity of Native Bankers'. Moreover many of these 'debts' were either fraudulent or grossly inflated.

The Nawab owed the Company some £3 million for defence and administrative expenses; and in order to create a conflict of interest between the Company and his creditors he had formally admitted the validity of all the private debts. Thus Nawab and creditors had joined in a conspiracy which, while defrauding the Company and plundering the landholders, had reduced the Carnatic to bankruptcy and administrative confusion. In an effort to retrieve the situation Lord Macartney, the Governor of Madras, had in 1781 taken over the management of the revenue – to the wrath of the creditors. But even so the deterioration had continued. On 31 October, 1783, the arrears due in the Civil and Military Departments amounted to over £371,000 and by the end of January, 1784, had risen to about £509,000.[122]

---

[121] See, for example, Board to Court, 7 July, 1785 (B-C Letters, vol. I, pp. 212-15); Minutes of the Court of Directors, 8 July; Court to Board, 11 July (C-B Letters, vol. I, pp. 330-9). There was also intermittent warfare between the Board and the Court over the allowances claimed by individual officers which the Board persisted in controlling as being a 'revenue' matter. See, for example, the cases of Major Geils (1787) and of Major Hart (1809) (Home Misc. Series, vol. 342, pp. 457-63, 711-801).

[122] 'Carnatick Revenue and Debts.' A memorandum 'Approved in Committee, 2 Novr., 1784' (Home Misc. Series, 342, pp. 95-101). A copy was sent as an annexure to the Court's letter to the Board of the same day (C-B Letters, vol. I, pp. 37-42).

Wider issues were involved. Until the financial mess had been cleared up, it was impossible to establish an orderly administration or to regularise arrangements for mutual defence with the Nawab against the threat of aggression from outside, particularly from Tipu Sultan, the ambitious ruler of Mysore. The grave internal weakness of the Carnatic in the face of Haidar Ali's invasions had been revealed by the Secret Committee under the leadership of Dundas; and the latter in April, 1782, had carried a set of resolutions in the Commons which stated that the declared inability of Arcot to provide either troops or funds during the crisis of 1780 because of his load of debt had rendered it essential that 'new and effective regulations' should be made with regard to the Nawab's revenues, debts and military establishment. It was further resolved that in ascertaining the debts of Arcot and Tanjore with a view to their liquidation and discharge 'all just distinctions ought to be made between the claims of the different creditors', and a principal object in the investigation must be the discovery and punishment of peculation.[123]

A year later (April, 1783) Dundas incorporated this provision in his own unsuccessful India Bill, and in moving for leave to bring in the measure he stated that the claims of the creditors ought to be minutely enquired into, 'because though he doubted not but some of them might be just debts, still he was of opinion that the greatest part were the debts of corruption'.[124] The proposition was adopted by Fox and Burke and was followed in the Act of 1784.[125] Thus it was Dundas who was chiefly responsible for establishing the principle that the debt scandal must be sorted out before it would be possible to cleanse the Madras Administration and strengthen the dangerously exposed position of that Presidency by means of dependable treaty relations for joint defence with Arcot and Tanjore.

The Board of Control took the problem into consideration at their second meeting (on 22 September, 1784), and six days later they requested the Directors to furnish a complete statement, 'drawn from the best materials in their possession', of the revenues of Arcot and Tanjore, with such explanations as might tend 'to elucidate the state and produce of those Countries'.[126] The policy which they adopted affords an apt illustration of the official attitude with regard to the British position in India. Direct administration

---

[123] 'Resolutions respecting the Government of the Presidency of Fort St. George.' *Parl. Hist.*, vol. XXII, 1318-21.

[124] *Ibid.*, vol. XXIII, 758.

[125] Fox's (second) Bill, which was almost certainly compiled by Burke, had included the further enactment that neither Arcot nor Tanjore nor any other protected native prince in India was to assign or pledge any territory or the revenue thereof to any British subject and that it was to be unlawful for any British subject to accept such assignments or pledges. Unhappily for the future this prohibition was not repeated in the Pitt-Dundas Act of 1784.

[126] Minutes of the Board, 29 Sept., 1784.

of the Arcot and Tanjore territories was avoided. Instead of being eliminated as in Bengal, the two rulers were to be rehabilitated, but subject to safeguards to ensure that there would be a common front, under British control, whenever the Carnatic might be invaded. Accordingly the assignment of the revenues which Maccartney had taken over was to be handed back, but in times of emergency financial control was to revert to the Madras Government. Yet the status and dignity of the princes must be preserved; and so, instead of imposing this arrangement 'in the harsh Form of a Condition connected with the surrender of the Assignments', it was to be inserted in 'a solemn and permanent Treaty'.

The principle upon which we have proceeded is that of ascertaining precise and fixed boundaries between our own Interests and those of the Powers connected with us in the Carnatick, in so far as they were capable of being separated, and ought in expediency to be so separated; and on the other hand we have adopted a Line of mutual Interest and inseparable Connexion in time of War. . . .[127]

As to the debts, the Board had before them a draft despatch in which the Directors had followed the requirement of the Act, distinguishing three categories of loans and ordering the Madras Government to carry out an enquiry into their legality and justice as the basis for a scheme of liquidation. The claims fell into three clearly defined classes: the 'Old' loan of 1767, the 'Cavalry' loan of 1781, and the 'New' Consolidated loan of 1777. Of the estimated total of £2,560,000 the first two together amounted to approximately £760,000. It was generally agreed that there were genuine debts, contracted by the Nawab in times of emergency and with the knowledge and assent of the Company; but the bulk of the claims, as consolidated in 1777 and amounting to almost £2 million, were suspect as being, in Dundas's earlier phrase, 'debts of corruption.' After examining a mass of records ordered up from East India House, including the relevant correspondence between Bengal and Madras, the Board on 8 October came to the astonishing decision to admit the whole of the creditors' claims without further investigation. Dundas was requested to rewrite the draft despatch in that sense and to circulate the amended version 'for the Revisal of the

[127] Board to Court, 15 Oct., 1784. B-C Letters, vol. I, pp. 9-19. On the same day another letter was sent to the Directors returning their draft letter to Arcot, which had been remodelled to avoid any possibility of misconstruction. Now that there was peace in the Carnatic and a new form of administration was being established, Arcot must be told respectfully but firmly 'that such an Arrangement should now take place, as might insure to you a permanent and beneficial Interest resulting from your connexion with him upon the Coast'. If such arrangements were adopted, the Board was hopeful that 'solid advantages' would accrue to the British possessions in the Carnatic and would 'render them collaterally a substantial Barrier of Defence to the other British Possessions in India' in the event of a major threat. (Ibid., pp. 21-3.)

Members of the Board, who will thereupon assemble to perfect the same '.[128] A week later the Directors were apprised of the scheme which they were to accept. The Nawab would be required to set aside an annual sum of £480,000 from his revenues. The first charge on this fund was to be the annual interest on the Cavalry and the New Consolidated loans, and the balance was to be used in equal proportions for the redemption of the debt due to the Company (without interest) and the principal and accumulated interest of the three classes of private debt *seriatim*. The liquidation of all debts was calculated to reach completion in the eleventh year.[129]

Dundas and his colleagues defended their action on grounds of expediency. The first two classes of private debt were demonstrably valid, but they frankly admitted that the debts of 1777 stood in a different light: 'they were contracted without any Authority from the Company, were consolidated in no respect under their sanction, and have never been recognised by them.' Nevertheless they insisted that further investigation on the spot would be futile and the consequent delay would postpone the re-establishment of 'credit and circulation in a Commercial Settlement'. Repeated enquiries in the past had failed to elicit the information required, and time made it increasingly unlikely that the facts could be ascertained; 'and [they added] we think that the proof of the origin of these Debts, as originally contracted, cannot with propriety be thrown on the present Holders of Bonds issued in 1777'. What they did not say, though they implied it, was that an inquisition conducted by the Governor of Madras and members of his Council would have set the Madras administration by the ears, and would

---

[128] See Minutes of the Board, 5, 6, 7, and 8 October, 1784. Grenville seems to have done a good deal of detailed work in preparing the scheme. On 1 Nov. Dundas wrote to him: ' As you have had so much consideration on that subject, I have sent the paper [an advance copy of the Directors' protests against the decision about the Arcot debts, dated 2 Nov.] to you, and if you think it proper to enter into any further explanation upon it, something founded upon the paper of account prepared by you, showing the operation practically of our arrangement, will be the best return to make' (*Grenville Papers (Dropmore)*, vol. I, p. 242). An exposition along these lines was incorporated in the Board's reply to the Court of 3 Nov.

[129] It was not in fact completed until 1804. When the long period of intermittent warfare began with the outbreak of the third Mysore war in 1790, the Governor-General authorised the resumption of control over the Arcot revenues for defence purposes, and payments to the creditors were suspended. Later, payments were started again but at a reduced rate – with the creditors' consent. When in 1794 the Directors proposed to take unilateral action in suspending payments altogether, Dundas protested vigorously. ' I have uniformly been of opinion,' he wrote, ' that the Agreement entered into, in 1785, between Your Presidency at Madras, the Nawab of Arcot, and the private creditors of the Nawab . . . did establish Rights which could not be altered without the consent of all the contracting Parties in that Agreement.' He was not prepared, he added, to acquiesce in transactions ' which I consider perfectly unjust '. Dundas to the Court, 21 Dec., 1795, *B-C Letters*, vol. I, pp. 399-403. Cf. the previous opinion of Cornwallis – Gov.-General in Council to the Court of Directors, 5 June, 1788. *Cornwallis Corr.*, vol. I, pp. 353-5.

have held up the economic and military reconstruction of the Presidency for a dangerously long time.[130] These were plausible reasons and there was some substance in them; but the fact remains that this action of Dundas (for the responsibility was primarily his) was unjust and disgraceful.

There is some evidence to give colour to the view that Dundas and Pitt did come to an understanding with Colonel John Call and the Arcot group during the summer of 1784 that there would be a settlement of the debts without investigation as a return for support at the general election.[131] On the other hand, it is to be remembered that they had paid a considerable price at the behest of the India interest by weakening the terms of their Bill, and it seems improbable that Pitt's pride, combined with his constant determination to win the respect of the nation as a Minister of integrity, would have allowed him to go further and pay a second time by assenting to a corrupt and unjust bargain. Out of his overwhelming majority in the Commons only eleven were representatives of the Arcot creditors.[132] Eighteen years later Dundas referred to the debts which they had found themselves 'under the necessity of confirming'; but it does not necessarily follow that the compulsion was that of blackmail.

There was nothing defensive or conspiratorial in Dundas's references to the matter in his private letters to colleagues at the time. On 2 November, a few hours before the arrival of the official copy of the Directors' 'Representation', he wrote to a member of the Cabinet, who may have been Lord Thurlow, that he understood the Directors were 'very much dissatisfied' with some parts of the amended despatches. 'That I naturally expected, but I have a perfect satisfaction in the recollection of all we have done.'[133]

---

[130] An enquiry was actually held into the various claims of other alleged creditors who did not come within the three recognised categories, known collectively as the Registered Debt. These other claims were examined between 1785 and 1791 by a committee at Madras which left the task uncompleted. In 1805 a commission in London was set up, assisted by investigators in Madras. Out of £30,400,000 claimed only £2,687,000 was allowed. This commission did not complete its labours until 1880! (Cornwallis Corr., vol. I, p. 224, n. 5.)

[131] This interpretation is favoured by C. H. Philips (op. cit., pp. 36-41) and H. Furber, Journal of Modern History (loc. cit.).

[132] Ibid., p. 41.

[133] Dundas to Lord ——, 2 Nov., 1784. Pitt Papers, P.R.O. 30/8/157. Dundas continued: ' We endeavoured (and I trust succeeded) to get to the bottom of every subject by a laborious search into the Records of the Company, and the result has been to enable us to decide upon those various Objects of Party and Intrigue which have distracted the Settlement of Madras for these twenty years past, and we have thoroughly discussed and put in train of arrangement every point connected with the affairs of the Carnatick . . .' The Board now intended to do the same with regard to the Bengal Provinces. ' This is the best contradiction we can give to the charge of our India Bill being frivolous and inefficient.' I infer that the recipient of this letter was a Cabinet Minister because Dundas concluded with a precise statement of the classes of document which the Board had arranged to send to the King in order that he might be kept fully apprised of what they were doing.

When Cornwallis in Bengal heard of the decision, he wrote to Dundas that, although they had never discussed the subject together, 'yet I can have no doubt that we must think alike about them, and that you only consented that their fraudulent and infamous claims should be put into any course of payment because you could not help it'.[134] To that Dundas replied:

My prejudices were once as strong against the claims of the Nabob's private creditors as any that you can entertain, and the feelings of all my colleagues at the Board were the same. Against many of them the prejudice still remains, but from the time we examined the whole subject to the bottom, which we did in the most laborious manner, we became perfectly satisfied that every consideration of wisdom and policy suggested the propriety of the arrangement of the 9th of December, 1784. We remain of the same opinion still. . . .[135]

Having examined the complications involved, Dundas and Grenville evidently decided that the anarchic conditions prevailing in Madras called for a quick settlement to clear this corrosive business out of the way in the interests of internal stability and military security. Apart, however, from the moral issue, they committed a political blunder. The news that there was to be no enquiry into creditors' claims could not fail to 'leak', since so many bondholders in London as well as Madras would be affected; and the information would provide the Foxite Opposition with a wonderful chance to proclaim that it was the Government and not they who entertained corrupt designs in conducting Indian affairs. The man who exploited, if he did not actually create, this opportunity was Laurence Sulivan, who had resented the failure of Atkinson and Dundas to form an alliance with him and procure his election to the chair.[136]

In September he, with the rest of the Hastings group in the Directorate, deserted Atkinson (a leader of the Arcot interest) and enabled Nathaniel Smith, the Chairman, to carry a draft despatch which challenged the legality of many of the private debts and required the Madras Government to carry out a detailed examination of the claims. When the Board on 15 October returned the despatch rewritten with a long letter explaining and defending the debt settlement which they intended to impose, a committee of Directors prepared and delivered (on 2 November) a formidable *riposte,* covering the debt question and all the other matters at issue with the Board. They also forwarded an elaborate memorandum on the financial situation of the Carnatic under the pro-

---

[134] Cornwallis to Dundas, 4 Nov., 1788. *Cornwallis Corr.,* vol. I, p. 388.
[135] Dundas to Cornwallis, 3 April, 1789. *Ibid.,* App. XXVI, p. 558. He added: 'I perfectly approve of every step you have taken to check the petulance of the creditors, and to support the authority of the Madras Government.'
[136] See pp. 146-8 above.

posed arrangements.[137] On the following day the Board countered the allegations and ordered the Directors to send off the amended despatches and the letter to the Nawab forthwith. Later, copies of these (confidential) documents were given secretly by a Director, who may have been Sulivan, to Debrett, who published them.

On 28 February, 1785, Fox in the Commons moved for papers on the Arcot debts and Burke rose and made a passionate and eloquent assault on Dundas and the Board. The general election, he asserted, had been won by Atkinson and nabobs' gold, and this surrender to the Arcot creditors was the price exacted, representing 'collusion and participation in a common fraud'. But the speech went into complicated detail and was over-charged. The House grew bored, and Pitt after a whispered consultation with Grenville decided (thankfully no doubt) that there was no need for him to intervene. At one o'clock in the morning the motion was rejected by 164 to 69. Burke published his speech in pamphlet form, and some of the Board-Court documents were included in an appendix of 121 pages.[138]

It was a sorry business and an unfortunate start to a sincere and determined campaign to reform and restore the British position in India. The true charge against Dundas, it seems, is not that he engineered a corrupt bargain, but that in his impatience to establish stability in southern India he burdened the reduced population of a devastated region for many years with what Cornwallis described as 'a load of iniquity'. The noxious story of the Arcot debts has been examined in some detail because it illustrates many of the facets of the contemporary situation in British-Indian affairs: the determination of Dundas to coerce the Directors into becoming an obedient instrument of state action; the interplay of factions among the Directors which made co-operation so difficult; the first reaction of the new controlling agency to financial banditry on the part of British subjects overseas; and the Government's compromise policy of preserving the status and functions of dependent princes

---

[137] Board to Court, 15 Oct, (B-C Letters, vol. I, pp. 9-19, 21-23); Court to Board, 2 Nov. (C-B Letters, vol. I, pp. 24-36) with the annexure, 'Carnatick Revenues and Debts' (Ibid., pp. 37-42); Board to Court, 3 Nov. (B-C Letters, vol. I, pp. 29-36). On 21 October the Directors ordered all relevant documents to be supplied to the Company's Counsel, George Rous, and he was asked to state an opinion as to whether the Board had not exceeded its statutory powers in the case of the Arcot debts and the appointment of Colonel Ross Lang. With regard to the former Rous replied (on 25 October) that, although the Act clearly intended that there should be an enquiry in India, the Legislature had given the Commissioners the power of deciding 'in what manner and to what extent this enquiry shall be made, and I think the Court of Directors will not be justified in refusing obedience' (Home Misc. Series, 342, pp. 105-7). It is perhaps significant that a majority of the Court, led by Smith and Sulivan, ignored this legal Opinion and went ahead with their plans to challenge the Board.

[138] For the debate see Parl. Hist., vol. XXV, 162-259. Burke's speech with the appendix was reprinted in Works (Lond., 1826 edn.), vol. IV, p. 185 et seq.

while trying to ensure that they and their resources would be at command in times of peril.

The counter-attack delivered on all fronts by a majority of the Directors, and followed up by their attempt to 'expose' Dundas in Parliament over the Arcot business, confirmed his worst apprehensions and stiffened his determination to gain the mastery. A weapon lay to his hand. Under the Act of 1784 it was provided that if the Board should be of opinion that the subject matter of any of their deliberations 'concerning the levying of War or making of Peace, or treating or negociating with any of the Native Princes or States of India' required secrecy, they were empowered to send secret orders to the Secret Committee of the Court, who, 'without disclosing the same', were to transmit them to India together with their own signed instructions requiring obedience thereto. The answers of the Presidency Governments were to be sent to the Secret Committee under sealed cover and the latter must transmit them forthwith to the Board. Thus the old-established Secret Committee of the Court, consisting of the Chairs and one other (elected) Director, was reduced to a passive instrument of the Board.[139]

In the ordinary course of business the Board could do no more (at any rate in theory) than amend draft despatches initiated by the Court; but when the secret channel was used the Board prepared its own orders and the Secret Committee acted as a post office. In the plain sense of the Act the use of the latter procedure was limited to external relations, but Dundas stretched its application. By insisting that the Arcot debt arrangements and the surrender of the revenue assignment must be included in a 'treaty' with the Nawab (who was no more an independent Prince than Mir Jafar of Bengal had been), he could bring the affairs of Madras under direct control of the Board at will. In view of the embittered struggle over the debt settlement a few months before, this choice of battleground was exceptionally provocative, but the Presidency Government was mutinous and corrupt and Madras occupied a critical position in relation to Mysore, Hyderabad and the Marathas.

On 7 April, 1785, the Board (for the first time) went into secret session.[140] In their first 'secret' minute it was recorded that they

---

[139] During the debates on the Bill Sheridan had mocked the 'Indian phalanx' of the Government side on this account. The three Directors would cut a ridiculous figure, being forbidden to divulge anything that passed through the Secret Committee. They might therefore hear measures being propounded at a Court of Directors which were directly contrary to decisions which had been secretly determined and yet be debarred from giving more than 'a nod or a wink across the table, or a grave shake of the head, to intimate they knew something which they dare not divulge' (cf. p. 153 above).

[140] A separate book of Secret Minutes was kept from then on. A careful perusal of these minutes from April, 1785, until 1800 shows that it was only on rare occasions that the Board employed the secret procedure in matters other than external relations. From 1793 all matters relating to the conduct of the war in and around India were dealt with in this way.

had considered 'the situation and probable Resources of the Carnatic' as represented in the latest despatches from Madras and that in view of the change of Governor it was thought advisable to transmit secret instructions to the Governor-General.[141] The secretary was therefore ordered to write to the Chairman of the Court of Directors that the Board desired his attendance at noon on the following day 'with the other members of the Secret Committee'.[142] The three gentlemen – Nathaniel Smith, William Devaynes, and Laurence Sulivan – duly attended.[143] Since it was these three who had led the counter-attack against the Board, the situation was not devoid of piquancy.

In the following year control over the Secret Committee was tightened. Under the Act of 1784 its members had been forbidden to divulge any information which they might receive in that capacity, but the amending Bill which Dundas introduced in the Commons in March, 1786, included clauses which required them to take an oath of secrecy.[144] In matters of defence and diplomacy the secret procedure was clearly justified, but it was provocative to extend its use to cover the financial arrangements with Arcot; and on this issue a storm broke. When the Directors submitted a despatch for Madras in April, 1786, the Board deleted the paragraphs which dealt with the revenue assignment. 'We think it more proper,' they explained, 'that such Instructions as it is now necessary to transmit upon that subject, should go through the Channel of your Secret Committee, and we shall send a Draft to them for that purpose.'[145] The Board thereupon went into secret session, drafted a letter of their own and sent orders to the Secret Committee for its immediate despatch.[146] Two days later the Directors referred the relevant documents to George Rous, the Company's Counsel, requesting him to state an opinion whether the Board of

---

[141] Lord Macartney had retired from the Governorship of Madras and had been offered, but eventually declined, the post of Governor-General. Sir Archibald Campbell had been appointed to Madras.

[142] Secret Minutes of the Board, vol. I, No. I.

[143] At the meeting the Board, 'after conferring for some time with the members of the Secret Committee upon the affairs of the Carnatic and the Madras Presidency ', decided to suspend the debt arrangements and the surrender of the revenue assignment until Campbell had arrived in Madras. Letters in this sense were drafted on the spot and were 'sent to the Secret Committee, with the Board's directions, that the Letters be severally dispatched.' *Ibid.*, No. 2 (8 April, 1785). On the following day the Board wrote to Campbell that they intended ' previous to his departure for India, to form their resolutions upon the Civil and Military Establishments of Madras, and wish to have frequent opportunities of Communication with him on the Affairs of the Carnatic '. (Ordinary) Minutes of the Board, 9 April.

[144] *26 Geo. III, cap. 16, sect. XVI and XVII.* This was a miscellaneous amending Act, representing a general tidying-up of the Act of 1784. Its most important provision was to empower the Governor-General and the Presidents of Madras and Bombay to over-ride their Councils (see p. 179 ff. below).

[145] Board to Court, 26 April, 1784 *B-C Letters*, vol. I, pp. 144-6.

[146] Secret Minutes of the Board, 26 April, 1786, vol. I, No. 11.

Control was authorised 'to correspond with and give Directions to the Presidency of Fort St. George through the Secret Committee'. On 2 May Rous's Opinion was delivered and was considered on the 10th. The Nawab of Arcot, wrote Rous, whatever he might be in form, was 'in effect the Administrator of the Civil Government of Countries conquered and defended by the British Arms', holding those territories on the well-understood condition that he supplied the means of defence out of his revenues. The whole effect of the Act of 1784 would be lost in respect of Madras if the intercourse with the Nawab were confined to the Secret Committee, 'because this intercourse involves directly the Arrangements respecting the Military force, and indirectly every Interest of that Settlement'. If the subject should appear equally important to the Court of Directors as it did to him, 'I should rather advise an application to Parliament to explain this Clause in the Act and confine it to its true object'.[147]

Having digested this challenging interpretation, the Court decided to seek the opinion of the Law Officers of the Crown which was delivered on 13 June. As perhaps some of the Directors anticipated, the answer was unfavourable to the Company, taking a strictly legalistic line.[148] The first reaction of the majority was to submit, but one of them, Samuel Smith, immediately retorted with a fiery letter of resignation. If the Board, he wrote, by a forced construction of the phrase, 'negociations with Native Princes', could deal with Princes and States on matters *not* involving peace or war, 'the whole Political Correspondence is taken from the Court and given to the Board exclusively as a Secret Correspondence. . . . Thus almost the whole transactions of India may be concealed from the Knowledge of the Court of Directors'.

I am sensible [he added] the object of Mr Pitt's Bill was to superintend and controul, with a view to prevent the abuses in India and not to wrest from the Company the Political Management of its Affairs, nor was it then urged that the proper Government for India was a Government of Secrecy.[149]

Two days later an amended resolution was moved declaring that it was expedient to apply to Parliament 'for a further explanation and more correct limitation' of the power claimed by the Board;[150] and on the 16th a General Court of Proprietors resolved to investi-

---

[147] Rous's Opinion, 2 May, 1786, in *Home Misc. Series*, vol. 342, p. 394 *et seq.*

[148] It was obvious enough. Since the debt settlement and the terms of the surrender of the revenue assignment had been included in a 'treaty' with the Nawab, the business arising fell within the definition of the Act (i.e. 'treating or negociating with any of the Native Princes'), and it was therefore within the Board's discretion to deal with it as a matter of secrecy. *Ibid.*

[149] Samuel Smith to the Court, 13 June, 1786. *Ibid.*, pp. 375-84.

[150] Minutes of the Court, 13, 14 and 15 June.

gate the situation of the Company under the operation and effect of the India Act in a fortnight's time. When they reassembled on the 30th a strongly worded resolution was carried which adopted the line taken by Samuel Smith.[151] But Sulivan was dead, and without the experienced leadership of that doughty fighter, the majority which he had held together in the Direction began to disintegrate. The motion of 15 June in favour of an appeal to Parliament was postponed on five successive occasions; and when it was at last debated on 29 November, caution prevailed. A unanimous resolution called upon the Chairs to wait upon Mr. Pitt. If Parliament were invoked would he assist them? On the morning of 13 December the Chairs were received by the Prime Minister, who gave them the cold answer that was to be expected. He said, they reported to their fellow Directors, 'he cannot agree in the Sentiments expressed in the resolution concerning the Conduct of the Rt. Honble. the Board of Commissioners for the Affairs of India and does not see any ground for an Application to Parliament on the Subject'.[152] The Company had received a significant rebuff: a presage of the decisive defeat which they suffered two years later when the Government itself used the weapon of an appeal to Parliament. It seems odd, even when taking into account the long tradition of Company influence in Parliament, that so many of them should have assumed that the India Act did not intend what it said, and that they should have imagined that Pitt and Dundas in the plenitude of political power would abandon their original (and declared) intention to assume effective control over 'the affairs of India'.[153]

In fact an integrated system for that purpose was rapidly constructed both at home and in India. At the London end the Board's power to modify and even reverse the Directors' decisions was, as we have seen, freely used from the outset, while the device of the Secret Committee enabled the Government to take direct action in managing foreign relations and military operations as well as the financial arrangements of Madras. Even more important perhaps

[151] It was resolved that the powers claimed by the Commissioners under the Act were subversive of the authority of the Court of Directors and the chartered rights of the Company and tended to establish 'a Secret System of Government highly dangerous to the Interests of the Public and the Company' (Minutes of the (General) Court, 30 June, 1786).

[152] Minutes of the Court, 13 December. The Proprietors in General Court kept it up for a while longer, but on 15 Feb., 1787, when a ballot was called on a motion to appoint a committee to consider appropriate action for the preservation of Company rights, the motion was lost by 145 to 97. (*Ibid.*, 20 Dec., 1786, and 15 Feb., 1787.)

[153] In Sect. VI of the Act it was explicitly stated that the Commissioners were empowered 'to superintend, direct and controul all Acts . . . *which in any wise relate to* the Civil or Military Governments or Revenues of the British Territorial Possessions in the East Indies'. Efforts to secure the deletion of the word 'direct' had been defeated. (See p. 151 above.)

was the change in the situation of the Governor-General. Warren Hastings, like Clive before him, had dealt with a Court of Directors who could usually be relied on to do what his own group of organised supporters told them to do. Now the focus of power had shifted to a Minister of the Crown with wide statutory powers who was closely supported by the Premier. Although appointed and paid by the Directors like his predecessor, Cornwallis became to all intents a member of His Majesty's Administration. As soon as he arrived in Calcutta he started a private correspondence with Dundas, and the latter eagerly responded, always consulting Pitt before propounding the project in mind. Decisions were often reached in this way without prior reference to the Chairs or even to members of the Cabinet with the exception of Grenville. Indeed the private letters which passed between Dundas and Cornwallis increasingly resemble policy-making consultation between a secretary of state and a viceroy.

This integration of control in Indian affairs came only just in time, for there was much basic reconstruction to be done and there were not many years of peace ahead in which to do it. The first of these tasks was urgent and burdened with detail. By the Act of 1784 the Directors had been required to undertake an immediate scrutiny of all the civil and military establishments in India and the Presidency Governments had been ordered to furnish lists of all posts with their emoluments. The Directors were then to apply 'every practicable Retrenchment and Reduction' in compiling a uniform establishment. Until this 'perfect list' had been completed and put into operation they were forbidden to send any new Servants out to India below the rank of Councillor or Commander-in-Chief.

It was clear enough that the Directors would be in no hurry to obey this unpalatable injunction. The swollen ranks of the sinecurists would be revealed; many of their friends and dependants would be thrown out of employment; and their own patronage would be permanently reduced. In face of their tardiness Dundas began to chafe. Apart from the need to cut expenditure this was the very root of administrative reform. It was also politically important. If nothing materialised before Parliament re-assembled, the Opposition would not fail to exploit the situation, asserting that the system of divided authority had demonstrably broken down.[154]

---

[154] The early aggressiveness of Dundas towards the Court of Directors derived from his conviction that he was not to be given 'fair play' and that, unless their resistance was speedily overcome, the parliamentary Opposition would be able to ridicule the Board of Control as a weak and ineffective substitute for the comprehensive authority of Fox's parliamentary Commission. In November, 1784, he wrote: 'I am sanguine enough upon the subject to believe that before the Expiration of next Winter, we shall have done more than was expected from us in the course of several Years. This is the best Contradiction we can give to the charge of our India Bill being frivolous and inefficient.' (*Pitt Papers*, P.R.O. 8/157.)

In December, 1784, he wrote to Grenville from Edinburgh, begging him either directly or through Pitt 'to urge the Chairman, in the most earnest manner, to bring forward their ideas, particularly upon the intended reduction of their establishment; for, upon this point, we will be particularly pressed'. He would, he assured Grenville, return to Town in plenty of time to complete everything before Parliament met, 'if the Directors will only let the business out of their hands'.[155]

It irked him extremely (for his political career was at stake) that he must sit with folded hands, as he put it, 'till the Court of Directors shall send us materials to operate upon'; but the business of constructing a streamlined administrative service with proper salary scales was so fundamental that he decided to take the initiative himself. In January, 1785, Francis Russell, the Board's Solicitor, wrote in some perturbation to Thomas Morton, secretary to the Court, to say that he was being pressed by the Board for a survey of the civil establishments in India which he could not even begin to consider until he had received the various lists for which he had asked the Company's Auditor some time before. Would Morton please comply with his request 'with all possible expedition?' Evidently Russell was alive to the complexity of the task which he had been set. An exploratory comparison of the list of Covenanted Servants in Bengal with the proceedings of the Bengal Council had revealed 'very considerable and numerous salaries paid to native and European officials who are not Covenanted Servants'. The lists which he needed must 'exhibit the whole of the expence incurred in every branch of the Civil Service', and it would save delay if Morton would send him each list as soon as it was ready. In view of the great bulk of documentary material involved he asked that at least one experienced archivist might be assigned for the purpose to William Cabell and himself and the services of at least twenty writers.[156]

That was in January. Three months later the Directors submitted a draft despatch which would have slashed the civil establishment of Bengal right and left.[157] The Board replied that they were happy to observe that the Directors had brought retrenchment under their serious deliberation, but 'a cursory Inspection' really would not do. 'The whole extent of your Establishments,

---

[155] Dundas to Grenville, 9 Dec., 1784. *Grenville Papers (Dropmore)*, vol. I, p. 243.

[156] Russell to Morton, 11 Jan., 1785. *B-C Letters*, vol. I, pp. 45-8. The irritated Court took umbrage over this requisition as not coming directly from the Board. Russell was obliged to apologise, and a formal letter from the Board was substituted for Russell's missive. (*Ibid.*, pp. 51-2.)

[157] Boughton Rouse, Secretary to the Board, said that the despatch in question, 'by Retrenchments in some, and the total abolition of other Offices, goes to reduce the Establishment in Bengal nearly to the State in which it stood in 1776'. Salaries and emoluments would be cut by more than £500,000 p.a. (Boughton Rouse to Thos. Morton, 24 March, 1785. *B-C Letters*, vol. I, pp. 68-71.)

the proper functions of the several Officers, the very form and arrangement of your Territorial Administration are involved in it.' Unhappily, the reply went on, the Board were not yet in a position to discharge their duty in this regard since the materials available to them were considerably deficient, 'notwithstanding the laborious researches made by our Officers under our own direction'. The despatch must be held up. The consequent delay was regrettable, but they were sorry to have to observe that their requisitions on this subject were not being obeyed with the punctuality which in other respects they had had the satisfaction to experience. It was essential that members of the Board should have before them all the relevant information to enable them to satisfy the expectations of the Legislature and the public on this important subject.[158] Behind this stately reprimand lay four months of frustrated effort by the officials of the Board.[159]

Dundas had set them and the twenty toiling writers in East India House an almost impossible task. He was asking for a historical record of every appointment in every department of the Governments of Bengal, Madras, Bombay and Bencoolen, together with a complete survey of the costs of collecting the revenues and administering justice from 1775 up to 1783. He was demanding the compilation of an administrative encyclopaedia covering a period during which there had been many shifts and improvisations in all the departments. Moreover these were not tidily self-contained units but merged almost imperceptibly into local indigenous systems. Dundas was not dealing with something analogous to a government department at home where extravagance and redundancy could be quickly ascertained by statistical analysis.

The Directors pointed out some of these difficulties. Although they were not legally bound to do more than afford access to their archives, nevertheless the team of writers would continue to copy papers under the direction of the Board's officials; but the prepara-

---

[158] Board to Court, 24 March, 1785. *B-C Letters*, vol. I, pp. 64-8.

[159] On the same day (24 March) the Board instructed its Secretary, Charles Boughton Rouse, to write to his opposite number, Thomas Morton, to bring pressure to bear in less diplomatic and more detailed terms. This he did with a will. One of the first acts of the Board, he wrote, had been to instruct their Solicitor, Russell, to prepare 'the most minute and distinct Statement he could obtain from the Company's Records' of the origin, duties, salary and so forth of every office held by Company Servants in the East Indies. From December onwards Russell had made repeated applications under the Board's authority for the establishment lists, and finally on 21 January an express order of the Board had been issued for the required lists and papers. But Russell had had no luck. 'To this Hour,' he informed the Board, 'he has not been able to procure any part of them.' Moreover Rouse himself had never had the list of unemployed Civil Servants for which he had asked on 28 January last. Without such data the Board could not possibly decide on the sweeping reductions enumerated in the draft despatch for Bengal. He ended with a flourish: the public weal, the good government of India, and the interests of the individuals involved, alike demanded a full examination of the retrenchments proposed. In short, get on with the job. (Rouse to Morton, *ut supra*.)

tion of such complicated returns must take a long time. Meanwhile substantial reductions in expenditure were urgently necessary, and if the Board persisted in holding up their orders for immediate economies the Directors must disclaim responsibility for the consequences.[160]

After the Chairman had sought a personal interview with Dundas to represent the extreme urgency of certain economies in Bengal, the latter relented and amended versions of the despatches in question were allowed to be sent off as a temporary expedient.[161] But the comprehensive survey continued, and the minutes and correspondence of the Board indicate how hard they worked on it. Two months later they sent to the Directors for their consideration 'the following general outlines of the Plan which we have already formed'.[162] In each Presidency the work of the various subdivisions of departments was to be concentrated in three Boards – Military, Revenue, and Trade – operating under the direction of the President in Council. To the Military Board would belong 'the whole detail' of military business, and it would consist exclusively of senior military officers. The Board of Revenue would be responsible for the collection and administration of every branch of the revenues and would control the officers concerned therewith. It would consist of one of the two junior members of Council 'and four other of the most intelligent of the Senior Servants of the Company'. It was to have no power to issue money except by warrant from the Council.

The Board of Trade was to comprise the other junior member of Council with four of the most able of the senior Servants. Since commerce was the Company's concern, the Court was requested to prepare as quickly as possible a detailed plan of commercial establishments under the respective Boards of Trade. These were to be 'sufficient' for the commercial purposes of the Company, and no more, 'considering it as essential that the different branches of your Trade should be conducted on the strictest Commercial Principles, by which alone those great National objects of advantage can be obtained, for which such considerable exclusive

---

[160] Court to Board, 30 March, 1785. *B-C Letters*, vol. I, pp. 81-9.
[161] Minutes of the Board, 5 April.
[162] 'Our attention,' they wrote, 'has been for a considerable time almost unremittingly directed to this object, which we every day feel more to be of absolute and indispensable necessity.' Their scheme owed much to Laurence Sulivan who, although a sick man, had submitted his own plan of reorganisation, both at home and in India, which derived from his unique experience in Company affairs. When Dundas saw it, he had immediately commended it to the serious consideration of the Court. (Board to Court, 4 April, 1785, *B-C Letters*, vol. I, pp. 73-5, and Minutes of the Board of the same date.) Sulivan's plan on the home side for simplifying and concentrating the work of the standing committees of the Court of Directors unfortunately foundered because of the consequential disturbance of patronage. (See Philips, *op. cit.*, pp. 44-5.)

Privileges have been granted and continued to the Company'. It was essential that the personnel of the Boards of Trade should be of high quality: in the past the reverse had been the case as numerous complaints in the Company's records showed. And then came a suggestion based on a principle often stressed by Hastings and later repeated by Cornwallis, that the most effective way of discouraging peculation and securing honest and efficient service was to pay good salaries. Since the Bengal Board of Trade was to be reduced to five, their emoluments 'ought to be at least double of what they now are'.[163] While the Directors were urged to expedite their 'purge' of the commercial establishments, the Board would continue their work of overhauling the rest of the departments.

Other features of the Board's scheme were the abolition of all minor posts below the salary level of £400 and the employment of native writers 'in the inferior detail of the Company's business'. The heaviest cuts were to fall on the military side of the Company's expenditure, but in one salutary respect – the provision of more and better doctors for the troops serving in an unhealthy climate – Dundas intended that considerably higher salaries should be paid 'to induce the first Medical Talents to court Your Service'. In the 18th century even the 'first' rank of medical skill was not high, but the Directors were short-sighted enough to demur and the proposed increases were reduced. The upshot, however, was an addition of 87 'surgeons' (mostly for Madras) in the hospitals and for service with the battalions.

The Directors received the Board's ideas with a sour reserve which was not sweetened by the acrimonious dispute then in progress over the Madras appointment of Colonel Ross Lang.[164] As soon as the Board had produced its plans in detail they would give them the full consideration which a scheme of such magnitude required. They took immediate exception, however, to the proposal that the Military Boards should consist exclusively of military men. One or two *Civil* Servants should be members, particularly since the Board apparently intended that the heaviest cuts were to fall on the military side.

During the subsequent discussions (in August and September) the Directors raised a number of specific objections, but the scheme as a whole met with little opposition: the need for drastic economies was too evident.[165] On one important issue, however, they had their way. Armed with a supporting despatch from Warren Hastings, they urged that the proposed reduction of the European

---

[163] The existing rate was £1,500 p.a.

[164] See p. 167 above.

[165] For the exchanges on the retrenchment scheme see Board to Court, 24 March, 7 April, 16 June, 18 August, 5 Sept., 1785 (*B-C Letters*, vol. I, pp. 64-8, 76-80, 97-102, 109-17, 120-22), and Court to Board, 30 March, 29 June, 26 August (*C-B Letters*, vol. I, pp. 81-9, 114-15, 134-43).

infantry in Bengal to less than 4,500 was dangerous, and the Board evidently agreed to a force of rather more than 5,000.[166] As will be seen, Dundas was working towards a 'royal' in place of a Company's army in India.

The proposal to employ Indian clerks was strongly opposed. This was the only way, the Directors declared, that the Company's Servants could acquire the necessary detailed knowledge of official business to qualify them for superior posts. But the Board refused to budge on this. The great object, wrote Dundas, was the formation of a standard establishment, not to be altered without positive orders. 'If therefore in forming such an Establishment any of your business can be cheaper and as well done by Native Servants than Europeans, it would be the reverse of economy to send out Europeans to discharge those duties.'

It was a task of immense labour and took more than two years to complete. As soon as Cornwallis arrived in Calcutta (in September, 1786) he began a systematic overhaul of arrangements in Bengal, Bihar and Orissa, and also in Oudh; and Dundas quickly learned to rely on his judgement in this as in many other matters. In June, 1787, the Board observed: 'The general Policy has been to give your several Presidencies a liberal degree of discretion in fixing the Salary they might think suitable to the importance or labour of the Offices.'[167] The retrenchment, which threw many Company Servants out of employment and incidentally reduced the Directors' patronage, was an indispensable factor in enabling the Governor-General to impose discipline and inculcate reforms.[168]

It was estimated that the reductions in the civil and military establishments would effect an annual saving of some £500,000: an economy which mitigated but could not, of course, resolve the pecuniary embarrassments of the Company. Its economic position was anomalous. As a commercial concern, enjoying a national monopoly, it normally earned substantial profits in buying tea in

---

[166] Dundas, who had been consulting Sir Archibald Campbell prior to his departure to take up the post of Governor of Madras, had argued that the security of Bengal primarily depended upon the maintenance of adequate forces in Madras and Bombay.

[167] Board to Court, 28 June, 1787 (*B-C Letters*, vol. I, pp. 189-94). They went on to state (in somewhat pompous terms) that 'as on the one hand you are under the necessity of reducing the number of Your Offices, and are determined to deprive those you leave of the means of all secret unavowed Emoluments, so on the other hand You ought to adopt it as a Principle to make the allowances to Offices such as ought to exclude all temptation to your Servants to act contrary to their duty as chalked out to them by your Orders'.

[168] 'Many Civil servants,' Cornwallis reported, 'are at present unemployed, and the operation of the new revenue arrangements will soon make a great addition to the number of those already in that disagreeable predicament: I hope that few of those at home will think of returning, and I see no probability of our having occasion for a supply of writers in less than two years at the soonest.' (Cornwallis to the Court, 4 March, 1787. *Cornwallis Corr.*, vol. I, App. XV, p. 530.)

China and selling it in an expanding market. As a territorial Power
in India it compensated for its weakness as a seller of British goods
by making a profit out of its political position, buying textiles and
other Indian products out of 'surplus' revenue and selling them
in Europe and elsewhere. But the territories which produced the
revenue had to be defended even when the devastation of war had
diminished or extinguished the income. During the contest with
France and her Indian allies from 1775 onwards Hastings had
saved the situation by daring (and expensive) military measures
and high-handed methods of extracting monetary contributions.
When the last stage in the peace settlement was reached by an
agreement with Tipu of Mysore in March, 1784, the Company's
debts in India had risen to about £8 million, while it was calculated that demands on the Company's treasury at home, due to be
met between March, 1786, and 1790, would amount to almost £6
million. In addition there was the normal servicing of the bonded
debt and the cash required for the current supply of their trade.[169]

This shortage of available reserves to meet short calls was endemic
and had given rise, as we have seen, to frequent appeals to Parliament for financial assistance; but the war debts incurred in India
gave the situation a new urgency. On the face of it the position
appeared to be grave, and yet the Company's earning potential
on the long term was fully adequate to meet its obligations.[170]
The Company was under-capitalised, and in that respect the situation was relieved by the issue of £800,000 of new stock in 1786 and
a further £1 million in 1789.[171]

The attention of the Board of Control was drawn to the urgency
of the debt question in April, 1785, when they received a communication from the Bombay bondholders, making strong representations about their loans and pointing out that the good faith
and credit of the Company were at stake. The Directors had, in fact,
just drafted a despatch requesting the Bombay Government to

---

[169] See Board to Court, 10 Sept., 1785. *B-C Letters*, vol. I, p. 125.

[170] It was thus always possible for partisans in and out of Parliament to draw a
gloomy picture of impending ruin or on the other hand to make cheerful statements
about viewing purely temporary embarrassments against a background of expanding
profits. This was particularly marked in the debate of 5 May, 1785, on expenses
in India. Philip Francis, supported by Fox and Burke, gave a horrific account and
demanded a committee to discover the true financial situation, whereas Nathaniel
Smith and Francis Baring (Directors) with Major Scott (defending Hastings's administration) maintained that the latest accounts from India showed that Bengal was perfectly capable of paying off its own debts as well as those incurred in Bombay
(*Parl. Hist.*, vol. XXV, 517 *et seq.*).

[171] In Jan., 1787, Dundas sent a memorandum to Cornwallis which showed that
India stock, which had fallen to 120 in Dec., 1783, at the time of Fox's Bill, was
standing at 163 in Jan., 1787, although the capital had been increased by £800,000;
and 5 per cent India Bonds, which had been at a discount of 80/- in 1783, were in
1787 at a premium of 63/- in spite of the fact that the interest was to be reduced to
4 per cent in March of that year. (*Cornwallis Corr.*, vol. I, p. 277.)

compile a statement of debts incurred in that Presidency, but the Board urged them to tackle the question comprehensively. 'We think it is highly incumbent upon you to form a complete account of all your Debts in India, with a state of their rise and progress, which may enable you to form an Arrangement for securing the regular payment of Interest to your Creditors in every part of India without distinction, and may lead to an entire liquidation of your Debt, as speedily as the state of the Company's affairs will permit.'[172]

The Directors were fully alive to the need for liquidating these debts, but when Dundas in July began to press upon them a plan of his own there were doubts and divisions. Prolonged discussions took place with the Secret Committee, and alternative plans were presented to the Board on 16 August by a group of Directors led by Sulivan. But Dundas was determined to carry his own scheme, and evidently Pitt was persuaded to intervene, for he attended and presided at meetings of the Board for the first time while this issue was being decided. On 2 September Pitt was in the chair when Devaynes, Smith and Sulivan, the three members of the Secret Committee, attended the Board. After a 'full discussion' the latter gave way and agreed that the Dundas plan should be tried and formally requested the Board to send them 'their opinion upon the Measures they think expedient to be adopted in the present situation of the Company's Affairs'.[173]

Eight days later Pitt again presided when the Board finally approved a long and elaborate memorandum. Arguments were adduced to show that the Company was not in a position to pay off its debts in India while at the same time using the profits of the Investment to meet its obligations in England. 'The amount which the Company can safely undertake to pay to their Creditors abroad, is limited by the same circumstances which confine the means of realising their Indian Resources in England.' All debts repaid to European creditors in India would speedily be remitted to Europe 'by such Channels as may be open for the purpose', and would thus, in effect, swell the total amount of revenue drawn from India; and the larger the payments so made the greater would be the danger of exhausting the resources of the Company's Territories and lowering (by competition) the Company's profits on the sale of Investment goods. This was the essential principle: 'that no more can be drawn from India with safety to that Country by the Company's Servants than by the Company itself, and that payments made to them in India and brought home through the medium of Foreign Trade must, by prejudicing the Sale of the Company's Investment, diminish their Resources at home.'

It was accordingly proposed that the Company's annual Invest-

---

[172] Board to Court, 9 April, 1785. *B-C Letters*, vol. I, pp. 81-2.
[173] See Minutes of the Board, 16 August, 2, 5, 8, 9, and 10 Sept., 1785.

ment should be raised from its usual total of about £1,000,000 to
£1,500,000, and it was reckoned that on a conservative estimate the
goods so purchased would sell in London for £2,400,000, that is
to say, an additional income of approximately £800,000 would be
obtained.[174] The debts in India should be funded and the creditors
induced to agree to their transference to England by bills of
exchange on the Company at a declared rate of exchange, and these
would have to be met out of the increased income. The operation
would, however, have been gradual. Up to 1790 there would be
home commitments to be met amounting to about £6 million, and
a sales income of £2,400,000 'would be little more than sufficient
(in addition to the other Funds raised at home) to discharge those
debts at the periods when they fell due'.

How then was the additional burden of transferred Indian debt
to be borne? Dundas was convinced that he had found the answer.
Various circumstances indicated that the annual amount remitted
by Company Servants 'through other Channels' was almost as large
in toto as the Company's Investment. 'We are convinced that the
operation of the proposed plan will for several years to come provide a Channel of remittance for the Fortunes of Individuals,
diminishing thereby the drain occasioned by Foreigners trading
on their Capitals.' Thus by attracting the flow of 'private' profit
into the Company's channel the burden of debt would be lifted
and the economy of the nation as well as of the Company would be
enormously strengthened.

In the final peroration of their memorandum the Board drew
attention to what they considered to be both the commercial and
and the political advantages of the scheme. On the commercial side
they repeated that the effect of the operation would manifestly
tend to destroy the competition of foreigners trading with the
fortunes of the Company's Servants in India. 'It is undoubtedly a
great advantage to the Company, that by keeping, as it were, the
purse of these Individuals, they are left the Masters to carry on
their Commerce in the mode most consistent with the prosperity
of their Provinces or their general Interests at home.' It was also
claimed that the political benefits would be immense. As long as

---

[174] This agrees pretty closely with an estimate by Cornwallis some four years later.
'The income of Bengal exceeds its expenditure by above two millions, and although
the other Presidencies are a great drain upon us, yet, on the general state of the
finances throughout India, we can, without increasing our debts, send home an
investment from the different settlements, which costs us £1,300,000, and which
will sell in Europe for £2,400,000, which, besides at least a million of profit which
the Company receives from the China trade, must I think enable them to pay off
at least a million of their debt annually in England.' (Cornwallis to the Bishop of
Lichfield and Coventry, 23 Feb., 1789. *Cornwallis Corr.*, vol. I, pp. 409-10.) This,
of course, was a peacetime estimate. In the following year (1790) the renewed
aggression of Tipu initiated another prolonged period of war which caused a fresh
accumulation of debt.

the Company was heavily in debt to its own Servants in India it would remain dangerously vulnerable to intrigue and mischief-making.[175]

The hesitant Directors acquiesced and the Board went so far as to initiate the draft despatches on the subject.[176] But Dundas's high expectations did not materialise. After an initial response the transference of debt to England diminished to inconsiderable proportions. Most of the creditors preferred to leave their money where it was, and the individual speculator was not induced to use this channel of remittance, for he could do far better for himself by investing his profits with French or Dutch traders in India who were hungry for capital. In September, 1786, Dundas tried to retrieve the situation by sending Cornwallis an extract from a private letter which he had received from Francis Baring. This, he wrote, 'will furnish you with some arguments to convince the creditors in India of the wisdom of accepting the propositions which have been made to them'.[177] A year later he returned to the charge. The Directors were informed that subsequent events had confirmed the Board in their view that the best course was to get the debts in India transferred to Britain and they had therefore prepared draft despatches for Bengal, Madras and Bombay which answered in detail the points which had been raised by Cornwallis and cleared away as far as possible the obstacles which had impeded the success of the original plan.[178] But this time the Directors were more resistant to the idea of increasing the load of debt-redemption in London. They were prepared to adopt the draft despatches provided that the Board would guarantee support if financial assistance became necessary to fulfil the engagement. The answer to that was an anticipated negative.[179]

Cornwallis, however, was co-operative. 'I approve very much,' wrote Dundas in 1789, 'of the settlement you have made of the exchange for the purpose of bringing home the debts; the measure

---

[175] This memorandum of 22 folio pages (*B-C Letters,* vol. I, p. 125[1-22]) includes a very useful analysis of the Company's trade-structure at the time, which was no doubt compiled by officials of the Board. On the theoretical side it affords an interesting combination of the exuberant confidence of Dundas about the plan itself and Pitt's more cautious exposition of the general principles underlying Anglo-Indian economic relations.

[176] This was technically illegal; but the Board justified itself in that the Secret Committee of the Directors (at the meeting on 2 Sept.) had formally requested the Board to send them their ' ideas of directions to be sent to Bengal '. At the conclusion of their memorandum the Board frankly admitted that they had gone 'far beyond' their terms of reference. What they had stated should be taken ' by no means as any intention on our part to prescribe to you in cases which the Legislature has left to your discretion '. Nevertheless the Board had brought very strong pressure to bear.

[177] Dundas to Cornwallis, 21 Sept., 1786. ' Private.' (*Cornwallis Corr.,* vol. I, pp. 264-5.)

[178] Board to Court, 17 July, 1787. (*B-C Letters,* vol. I, p. 211.)

[179] Board to Court, 30 July. (*Ibid.,* p. 219.)

is a very favourite one with me . . .' It was perhaps not a bad thing, he added, that the debts should come home gradually, provided that the prospect of a period of peace held good. 'But if that was interrupted, it would be very inconvenient for you to have such a load of debt upon your revenues in India.' And so it proved. Within a year Tipu Sultan attacked Travancore and a third war between the British and the ruler of Mysore began.

The plan was not popular with the Company because in effect they preferred that the Governments in India should (somehow) cope with deficits on the spot while, of course, maintaining the flow of the Investment. A parallel flow of debts to London, swelling the volume of direct obligation, might be sound finance; but it could give rise to short-term stringency and reduced dividends. Understandably enough the Servant-Creditors in India preferred high-interest rates on the spot.[180] Although abortive the scheme represented a well-intentioned effort by Dundas, supported by Pitt, to consolidate the Company's finances and to strengthen Britain's commerce by stopping the leaks through foreign trade.[181] He had every intention of extruding the Company as soon as might be from all participation in political, diplomatic and military affairs in India; but as long as it retained its restrictive commercial monopoly (which he disliked) he was determined that the Company should function as an instrument of *national* expansion, and that would involve adaptations which the Directors might not like.

Since his policy was to develop the British position in India as a source of economic power, reinforcing a general penetration of the Far East by British trade, he employed a particular technique in planning its defence. It must be organised as a dual-purpose strategic base, capable, on the one hand, of quick co-ordinated action in protecting Bengal, the central reservoir, with its essential outposts to the south and west against attacks by other Indian Powers and, on the other, of providing a striking force at short notice to capture oceanic bases held by France, Spain or Holland upon the outbreak of a European war. Since commercial power in eastern waters was a national enterprise of supreme importance, it

---

[180] On 13 Nov., 1786, Cornwallis wrote to his friend Shelburne (now Marquis of Lansdowne): ' If You have any regard for the interests of the Company, you must not oppose any good plan for relieving us from a debt, which bears so heavy and ruinous an interest. My situation would have been easy if the plan of last year had succeeded.' (*Cornwallis Corr.*, vol. I, pp. 236-7.) In the Charter Act of 1793 the scheme was repeated with the further provision that if the amount of debt so transferred in any one year fell below a total of £500,000, the Presidency Governments could fund the difference by means of local loans. This (permissive) process was to continue until the existing debts, totalling about £7 million, had been reduced to £2 million. (*33 Geo. III, cap. 52, sect. CVIII to CX.*)

[181] There seems to be little, if any, warrant for the view that Dundas deliberately devised the scheme in order to embarrass the Company and force it to become a suppliant for Government assistance.

followed that the military weapon ought to have unity of command and discipline and as an instrument of policy ought to be exclusively in the hands of the State.

When Pitt and Dundas took charge of Indian affairs this was far from being the case. The military establishment comprised some regiments of the British Army which were maintained in India at the Company's expense, a European force recruited by the Company in Britain and led by officers holding the Company's commission, and (thirdly) sepoy regiments led by British officers in the Company's service.[182] All officers in the Company's service from Commanders-in-Chief downwards were appointed and controlled by the Court of Directors. In the sepoy regiments (then as later) there was usually a strong bond of attachment between officers and men, and they constituted a formidable fighting force which neither the French nor Dutch in India had been able to rival. But when funds ran low during an expensive campaign, these regiments were apt to receive scurvy treatment with regard to arrears of pay, which was dangerous as well as inhumane.[183] As for the Company's European force it was a notorious scandal, largely because of the wretched system of recruiting at home. It was therefore not surprising that Dundas decided from the outset that all military forces in India must be amalgamated under the Crown and that there must be a permanent and greatly increased establishment of King's troops.

Shortly after the Board of Control had been established Dundas wrote to Lord Sydney pointing out that the Board must soon undertake a scrutiny of the military establishments in India and that it would be very necessary that they should be told in confidence what the views of Government were on the subject, at any rate in outline, so that they might keep them in mind when making new arrangements. His own personal opinion could be expressed in one sentence: 'I cannot conceive any thing more preposterous, than that the East India Company should be holding in their hands a large European Army exclusive of the Crown.' As long as the Company was permitted to hold the Indian revenue it must of course meet military expenses on the spot; but beyond that – 'I cannot see any good reason why the British Empire in India is to be protected

---

[182] The King's troops at that time consisted of six regiments (one cavalry and five infantry), which could only muster about 5,000 effectives. The Company's European troops were nominally 6,000, and the sepoy regiments (exclusive of those at Bombay) numbered about 60,000. *Cornwallis Corr.*, vol. I, p. 341.

[183] In an 'Extract of a Letter from Madras, dated 14 October 1784', which was forwarded to George III, the unnamed author (evidently a senior officer in a King's Regiment) wrote: 'At Trichinopoly, among the Black Troops, something still more cruel has happen'd. They discharg'd above 1000 Men who have serv'd the whole War, and had 18 Months Arrears due, without paying them a Shilling: a scrap of Paper, worth little, and in their minds nothing, was all they got to say so much was due to them – the wretches were starving . . .' (*Royal Archives, Windsor*).

by any other troops than those employed for the protection of the rest of the Empire. I see many reasons against it.'

He proceeded to state them. Jealousy and friction were excited between the two Services – which was true. It was an embarrassment to have the Company's recruiting system competing with that of the regular Army. Moreover, when under the existing arrangement an emergency arose, King's troops were sent out East in a hurry with unfortunate results, whereas if King's regiments did a regular spell of duty in India as they did in the West Indies and other territories overseas, they would become familiarised with the service and the climate, 'and an Order to go to India would not be considered, as I believe it generally is, by His Majesty's troops, as an order of Banishment'. Again, amalgamation would greatly contribute to extirpate 'that pernicious Idea of Plunder and Corruption which exists in the Indian Army as now Constituted'.[184]

Our force now, and hereafter, must be regulated by the intelligence we have of the force kept up by our European rivals, at the Mauritius, Pondichery, Ceylon, or other places in India. Taking it for granted that India is the quarter to be first attacked, we must never lose sight of keeping such a force there as will be sufficient to baffle all surprize. In that shape, I believe, the attack will first be made.

It would be very necessary that Sydney should bring the matter to the attention of the King at an early stage, and he himself would speak to Pitt about it at the first opportunity. He was aware that the plan could not be carried out immediately, but he did not regard the difficulties as insuperable. 'All communication upon it must be very confidential, for if prematurely known, the supposed loss of power and patronage might create disgust in the East India Company, and it will require some management and address to carry it smoothly into execution.'[185] It would indeed: in fact more management and address in handling angry Proprietors than Dundas had yet acquired.

His hope that the plan would be considered and approved in principle by the Cabinet was not fulfilled, and for a long time it lay, in his own phrase, 'perfectly dormant'. But he eventually succeeded in convincing Pitt that it should be accepted as Government policy at any rate on a long-term basis. Ministers discussed the problem with Cornwallis before he left for India at the end of April, 1786, and he was given a long memorandum by Sir George Yonge, the

---

[184] On this point he added: ' Every Cadet who goes out to India, goes there with his mind previously corrupted by the Idea that he is going to make a fortune, without any of those honourable motives which actuate a Soldier . . .' This was true of many of the youngsters who had gone out, but the observation does less than justice to many who gave long and faithful service and in the end found themselves (without a fortune) on the half-pay list.

[185] Dundas to Sydney, 2 Nov., 1784. *Pitt Papers*, P.R.O. 8/157.

Secretary at War, in which the consolidation of the two armies was treated as almost settled unless unforeseen difficulties arose but leaving Cornwallis to recommend a detailed plan.[186]

The difficulties were formidable, but Dundas was nothing if not tenacious. With Pitt's approval he submitted his ideas to the King. The latter lent a ready ear, for the existence of a private army of his own subjects offended his sense of military decency. On being informed by Pitt in 1784 that the Court of Directors intended to appoint General Sir Archibald Campbell to be Governor and Commanding Officer at Madras, he had replied: 'Whilst the Army in India remains in such unfit hands as those of a Company of Merchants, I cannot expect any good can be done and therefore do not interest myself much as to the Officer that shall be appointed.'[187] He now instructed Sir George Yonge and General Sir William Fawcett to discuss the scheme with Dundas in person. Yonge submitted a lengthy report to the King who eventually gave his approval and directed that the plan be referred to the Cabinet.

Yet even on the King's side there were difficulties, for he was adamant against abandoning the rule that an officer holding the King's Commission took seniority over all Company officers of the same rank and he demurred at the idea that a lieut.-colonel from the Company's service should be eligible to take command of a regiment in the new consolidated army. Much more serious were the political obstacles, and Dundas endeavoured to overcome them by argument. In a memorandum to Pitt, which seems to have been intended for the Cabinet, he contended that much as the Directors might dislike the loss of their military patronage, they could not avow it as a ground of public opposition; and as a secret motive for resistance it would be so unpopular and corrupt that there could be no difficulty in counteracting its effects. It was objected that there might be a general clamour against the danger of giving the Crown this great additional patronage. Admit the fact, wrote Dundas, but deny the conclusion.

It is true there will be more military promotion in the distribution

---

[186] Ross, *Cornwallis Corr.*, vol. I, pp. 341-2.

[187] The King to Pitt, 23 Sept., 1784 (*Royal Archives, Windsor*). George III would have much liked to see the Company's army 'nationalised' by the India Act of 1784. When Pitt reported during the debates on that measure that Colonel Cathcart had made a very sensible maiden speech, the King replied that he was not surprised: Cathcart was 'a Sensible Young Man'. He then seized the opportunity to air his opinion. 'I am certain He cannot have said any thing in favour of the Troops in India remaining in the hands of the Company, but must have enforced that they ought to be those of the Nation, though paid by the Company.' If that were done, 'a total stop would be put to the shameful mode of increasing the number of Officers every hour to answer the Views of particular persons . . . besides putting the Military in that Country on a respectable foot which Officers belonging to a Company cannot pretend to'. Geo. III to Pitt, 3 July, 1784. *Pitt Papers*, P.R.O. 8/103. The original draft is in *Windsor Archives*.

of the King, but if those Indian possessions are at all to be retained, it can only be by a large European force . . . to be regulated in its operations by the Government of the Country, and to act in concert with the general strength of the Empire. Under these circumstances it is a solecism to suppose it can be with propriety placed anywhere but in the hands of the first executive magistrate of the State.

The danger attending the transfer of patronage was not, he continued, very formidable in view of the unattractive nature of the service in a hot climate and a distant country. His plan would operate by easy stages until the whole European army in India became the army of the King; 'and if the Directors of the East India Company should entertain a disposition to resist it, the unpopularity of the resistance in their own army would deter them from the attempt'.[188]

Dundas had many gifts, but political sensitivity was not one of them. His enthusiasm for a given project and his buoyant self-confidence so often led him into wishful thinking. Nonetheless his plan with minor modifications was adopted. It was based on the proposition that the security of the British territories in India urgently required a permanent reinforcement of some 15,000 disciplined European troops. The Ministers concerned agreed with this, especially in view of the disturbing reports being received from Cornwallis, who, while reporting favourably on the quality of the King's troops and the sepoy regiments, was scathing about the Company's European corps as being a rabble.[189] Since it was agreed that the European establishments must in any case be increased by three King's regiments to remedy this weakness, Dundas proposed that new regiments should be raised on a new principle. They were to be officered partly from supernumeraries on the Army List and partly from Company officials in India who would receive King's commissions and brevet rank. The embodiment of regiments on this basis would start a process which would bring about 'the consolidation of the two armies into one'.

On 22 July, 1787, Dundas wrote a 'secret and confidential' letter to Cornwallis, expounding the plan and calling for his co-operation. The Directors knew nothing about the plan which was 'altogether

---

[188] Printed in Ross (*loc. cit.*), vol. I, pp. 342-4.

[189] Cf. Cornwallis's warning to the Directors. The abuse in recruiting Europeans at home was scandalous, 'and if not corrected, may endanger the safety of your possessions in this quarter of the globe. The best men were drafted to the artillery, but the Company's infantry regiments were in a deplorable state, seriously under strength, and consisting mainly of foreigners, sailors, invalids and vagrants. The most shameful abuse was the nominal recruiting of men 'who never meant to serve, and indeed, are unfit for the duties of private soldiers, but who procured themselves to be enrolled as recruits, merely to get a passage on board the chartered ships to India'. (Cornwallis to the Court of Directors, 16 Nov., 1786. *Ibid.*, pp. 241-2.)

a secret as yet', and the intention was to keep it so 'for some months'. He still hoped to persuade the King to give at least some lieut.-colonel's commissions to Company officers: unless that was done the plan would not do complete justice to the Indian Army. The King's officers would be appointed immediately to the new regiments, and he assumed that it would be left to Cornwallis to select names of meritorious Company officers who were to be offered King's commissions in them.

As in his letter to Sydney three years before he stressed the strategic reasons for a strong European army unified under the Crown. Bombay was so important (in relation to the Marathas) and so weak in point of European force that he had obtained the approval of the King and Pitt to the immediate transfer of a King's regiment thither from Madras, and one of the new regiments would also be sent to Bombay. So much by way of ensuring internal security. 'Besides this I have made up my mind to it as a principle of Indian administration, that we ought at all times to keep a force there not only for defence, but active operations.' If war broke out in Europe it would be too late to start raising the European army in India to a war establishment. It must in his opinion be kept at all times on such a scale that a Governor-General on receiving notification from London would be 'instantly ready to begin offensive operations against Pondicherry, Trincomale, the Dutch possessions in the Eastern Isles, or, in short, anywhere that appears best calculated to add to our own strength or annoy the enemy'.[190] The Court of Directors had not yet been told. In the following October they were and with explosive consequences.

The talk about being instantly ready for offensive operations was not mere sabre-rattling. During the previous year reports had been coming in from Paris about the activities of an influential group at the French Court which was co-operating with the Patriot party in Holland to gain control in the East Indies and Ceylon and to over-throw British power in India; and in the summer and autumn of 1787 the British Cabinet watched with anxiety the growing ascendancy of France in Dutch affairs; to that was added, in September, the possibility of France joining Russia and Austria in dismembering the Turkish Empire. A general European war appeared to be imminent in which France would strike in India and Egypt. The crisis passed when the French Government backed down and on 27 October formally abandoned intervention in Dutch affairs.[191]

---

[190] Dundas to Cornwallis, 22 July, 1787. *Ibid.*, pp. 533-6. Pitt was of the same mind. Some days later he himself wrote to Cornwallis that if a rupture with the Estates of Holland were to take place, he must at once send an expedition to capture the Dutch naval base at Trincomali in Ceylon, while a force would be sent from England to seize the Cape. Pitt to Cornwallis, 2 Aug., 1787. *Pitt Papers*, P.R.O. 8/102. Cf. J. H. Rose, *Life of William Pitt*, Pt. I, p. 370.
[191] See J. H. Rose (*op. cit.*), Chaps. XV and XVI.

A fortnight earlier the British Government had decided to send four King's regiments to India,[192] and on the 17th the Court of Directors (at a hastily convened meeting and by a majority of one) agreed to accept and pay for them.

The reversal of that vote and the prolonged conflict which ensued between Company and Government have been described elsewhere.[193] The Company contended that they were not obliged under the Act of 1781 to pay for the transport and upkeep of King's troops unless they had formally asked for them. That was the ostensible point in dispute, but the real grounds for their resistance were much more fundamental. The Board of Control, backed by the Cabinet, insisted on giving effect to the Dundas plan, and it was quickly evident that this would involve a material diminution of the Company's status and functions. The Directors were informed that it was for His Majesty's Government to determine at any time the number of King's troops to be stationed in India, nor was it likely that Ministers would alter their opinion that the four new regiments must remain as a permanent addition to the strength. The Directors also learned that the regiments in question were to be constituted on a new principle of amalgamation: approximately half of the officers were to be drawn from the regular army and the rest were to be Company officers. Obviously this was intended to be the first stage in the elimination of the Company's European army – and the Company's military patronage. If they were to consent, the Directors protested, the consequence would be that 86 additional officers in the British Army would go to India, ' while 600 Officers in the Company's service, inured to the Climate, are out of employment, and upwards of 1,800 Officers will be superseded in their respective Ranks '.[194]

For four months the exchange went on until there was complete deadlock. On 23 February, 1788, the Directors were informed that

---

[192] Geo. III to Pitt, 12 Oct., 1787. *Pitt Papers*, P.R.O. 8/103.

[193] Philips (*op. cit.*), pp. 54-60.

[194] From the outset Pitt and Dundas had been anxious to settle this thorny question as equitably as possible, but, as we have seen, the King had created difficulties. On 21 Nov., 1787, the Directors had proposed sending an application to the King to grant equal ranks to Company officers serving with the King's forces in India or else to withdraw the four regiments. The large number of Company officers on half-pay at home held a meeting and appointed a committee to represent their interests. ' With them,' wrote Dundas, ' we had meetings, and . . . we soon discovered that nothing would be satisfactory but a communication of brevet rank to the Company's officers by King's Commissions . . .' (*Cornwallis Corr.*, vol. I, p. 376). Pitt went into the matter in detail with Lord Sydney and Sir George Yonge and wrote on 27 March, 1788, to the King recommending that this should be done; and on the following day the King agreed. Dundas followed this up with a soothing letter to the effect that ' as it is only *local* Brevet ', the effect of it would ' die away ' immediately the recipient ceased to serve in India. (Pitt to the King, 27 March; the King to Pitt, 28 March; and Dundas to the King, 2 April. *Windsor Archives.*) A grievance accordingly remained. But during the clash in the Commons (from 25 Feb. to 14 March) the Government had had no answer ready to the charge of injustice to the Company's officers.

the Government had decided that in two days' time they would move for leave to bring in a Bill 'for removing any doubts respecting the Power of the Commissioners for the Affairs of India to direct that the expence of raising, transporting and maintaining such troops as may be judged necessary for the security of the British Territories and Possessions in the East Indies should be defrayed out of the Revenues arising from the said Territories'.[195]

The Ministry had, in fact, been forced on to the defensive. The position had been reversed. In 1786-7 it was the Company which had sought to appeal to Parliament against the Board on their use of the Committee of Secrecy; on that occasion the Proprietors had agreed to abandon the contest out of deference to Pitt. It seemed that Dundas was right in his cheerful assurance that ministerial influence in the General Court was paramount and to be relied on. North and Jenkinson with memories of East India House, and indeed anyone with experience of the Irish parliamentary oligarchy, could have warned him of the illusion. The *parlement* at East India House had been browbeaten, not nursed; and in the case of the India Interest the general alarm and suspicion over the Board's encroachments had been sharpened by the Pitt-Dundas attitude towards the proposed impeachment of their favourite Hastings. The atmosphere was congenial to revolt, and when the long wrangle over the four regiments revealed the far-reaching implications of the plan, many of those who normally supported Government decided that the opportunity had come to fight for the preservation of the compromise of 1784 and that they had a case well calculated to excite popular sympathy.[196] On previous occasions Directors and Proprietors had protested in vain against initiatives taken by the Board, but on this issue they were able to adopt an attitude of masterly inactivity by simply refusing to transport the regiments on the Board's terms.

Thus it was the Government and not the Company which was forced to appeal to Parliament and on very disadvantageous ground. Having taken its stand, the Ministry could not possibly retreat. India had become the fulcrum of British overseas expansion and therefore a major factor in British diplomacy. Pitt and Dundas were both convinced that the effective defence of Britain's position in India was in jeopardy and could be sustained only by

---

[195] Of the considerable documentation relating to this controversy see especially *Minutes of the Board*, 29 Nov., 7 and 8 Dec., 1787; 12, 14, and 23 Feb., 1788 (Pitt was present at all these meetings); and Sydney to Chairs, 14 Feb., Court to Board, 20 Feb., and Board to Court, 23 Feb. (*B-C Letters*, vol. I, pp. 230-33, 236-9, *C-B Letters*, vol. I, pp. 391-3).

[196] As Dundas afterwards admitted, the outcry on behalf of the Company's army officers had considerable effect in the General Court of Proprietors, 'and detached from us many of the very steady adherents of Government on other occasions'. Dundas to Cornwallis, 26 March, 1788. *Cornwallis Corr.*, vol. I, p. 367.

integration with that of the Empire as a whole. Yet the tide of
international emergency which could have floated them over the
bar of popular opposition had receded, and the Ministry was left
in the position of having to bring in a Declaratory Bill which pur-
ported to do no more than 'remove all doubts' about the Board's
statutory authority, but which in effect would authorise the transference of the power of the sword in India from the Company to
the Crown.

When, therefore, Pitt moved for leave to bring in the Bill he
was treading difficult and possibly dangerous ground. The stiff-
necked young man who still persisted in scarifying Fox for the
violence of his India Bill was requesting Parliament to declare that
his own measure had in fact empowered a Pittite Board of Commissioners to do what it liked with the Company's army and the
Company's revenues. For the Opposition the situation was a gift
from on high.

For their part the Administration had hoped to postpone the
reference to Parliament until Cornwallis's despatches on the subject had arrived. Much of the rodomontade about Crown patronage
and hardship to Company officers could have been obviated had
they been able to cite his authoritative approval of the scheme and
his detailed recommendations on relative rank and seniority. But
the East Indiaman *Ravensworth* was badly delayed on her voyage
home and the clamour among the Proprietors and the public
generally rose to such a pitch that it became impossible to wait any
longer.[197] 'Will the President of the Board of Control,' asked Philip
Francis in the House, 'take upon him to affirm that Lord Cornwallis has advised and recommended it to Government to send out
a reinforcement of four regiments?' A report to that effect had
been 'industriously circulated'. Was it true? Thus challenged,
Dundas could do no other than remain seated and silent, and
Francis made the most of the Ministry's embarrassment.[198]

From the outset the proceedings in Parliament went badly for
the Government. In his introductory speech Pitt asserted the right

---

[197] See Dundas to Cornwallis, 6 March, 1788. 'The real fact is, that we have
waited impatiently for Your Report on the subject, because we think it will be
favourable to the Indian officers; and backed by your authority, who are yourself
high in the King's service, it would add a great strength to our opinions' (*Cornwallis Corr.*, vol. I, p. 362). It would not have helped them much, however, for
when it did arrive it was found to emphasise the practical difficulties of amalgamation. As part of its offensive the Company had drawn the Government into a
pamphlet war. See for example the forthright statement of the Company's case in
*A Hasty Sketch of the Conduct of the Commissioners for the Affairs of India, with
a concise State of the Case relative to the Four Regiments* . . . (London, 1788), and
on the other side: *Review of the Contest concerning Four New Regiments,
graciously offered by His Majesty to be sent to India* . . . *Gratefully accepted by
the Court of Directors of the East India Company, Who, on the Change of circumstances, have Rescinded their Resolution* . . . (Lond., 1788).
[198] *Parl. Hist.*, vol. XXVII, 211-12.

of the Board to send out any reinforcements to India that might be
thought necessary and insisted that the Company could not refuse
to meet the cost out of the revenues which were being thus protected. The general reaction was unfavourable. Francis Baring,
then Chairman of the Court of Directors, who normally supported
the Government and the Board, declared that the proposed Bill
would put an end to the Company and all its property, and Fox
made the debating point that on this basis the whole of the Indian
revenues could be swallowed up, leaving the Company with no
investment and therefore no commerce. Thereupon Dundas in his
blustering way said the wrong thing. If, he declared, it were found
necessary to employ the whole in preserving the Territories, he
would not leave a single rupee to the Company for its Investment.
The debate ended with Pitt being directly challenged to say exactly
what his purpose was in bringing in such a Bill.

On 3 March, when the debate was resumed, Pitt did his best to
repair the damage.[199] His right honourable friend had 'put an
extreme case'. He had only meant that in case of urgent necessity
commercial considerations must give way to security demands. 'The
power vested in him by the Act was not to be wantonly and rashly
employed, but to the best of his judgment for the general advantage of the Empire.' Having said that, Pitt at last came out into the
open. The consolidation of the royal and the Company forces in
India as one army under the Crown was highly desirable and must,
sooner or later, be attempted. Ministers had devised the new
arrangement in the case of the four regiments with that object in
view. Moreover this policy was in accord with his 'avowed objects'
in framing the India Act.

He then proceeded to make a declaration which confirmed the
worst fears of the India group. The Act had left commercial matters
alone, but its principal object had been 'to take from the Company the entire management of the territorial possessions and the
political government of the country'. Since this was the responsibility of the Board, it was common sense to suppose that they must
have 'the management of the revenue' by which alone they could
provide for security and defence.

The House in general was clearly startled and disturbed. Members might indeed have recalled that Pitt had held similar language
when introducing his original India proposals, but the House
recalled the soothing assurances which had been given during the
debates on the later Bill which became law. The marked contrast

---

[199] The first reading took place on 27 Feb., and the Company's petition against
the Bill was presented two days later. The subsequent debates in the Commons
took place between 3 March and 14 March. (*Ibid.*, 71-153, 177-219.) It was debated
in the Lords on 17, 18 and 19 March, where it was violently opposed by Shelburne
(Lansdowne). *Ibid.*, 219-63.

between these and the new pronouncement provided debaters of the calibre of Fox, Burke, Sheridan and Francis with a wonderful opportunity for counter-attack. On numerous occasions they had asserted – to the point of tedium – that Parliament and nation had been deceived in November, 1783, and that Pitt's India Act was dishonest; but now the Government itself was providing the ammunition. The new military plan for India and Pitt's open declaration of unlimited political and financial authority enabled the Opposition leaders to proclaim that it was the present Ministers (and not they) who were the guilty men, who stood self-confessed despite their previous protestations in their determination to seize dangerous executive powers and still more dangerous patronage. If the Government controlled revenue it was nonsense to claim that the Company had been left in effective control of their trade.

As the attack developed Fox and his close associates began to receive support from many who were not normally their friends. Although Pitt and Dundas had made great efforts to protect the interests of the Company's military officers under the proposed amalgamation, strong feeling had been worked up on their behalf in the House and outside; and the respected Colonel Fullarton expressed a widespread opinion when he warned the House against any plan which failed to do them full justice. 'As we owe an empire to their exertions,' he said, 'so we may lose it by their discontents.' Another cross-current which weakened the Government's position was the very evident jealousy and dislike of Dundas as the Indian dictator.[200] But most significant of all perhaps were the speakers who usually supported Pitt and who now stated in moderate terms that they had understood in 1784 that the Government was not assuming more than a general superintendence, whereas this Declaratory Act asserted a positive and detailed direction.

In the small hours of the morning of 6 March Dundas himself made matters worse by addressing a weary and exasperated House for more than three hours in a tedious speech on the scandalous condition of the Company's recruiting service. The situation was indeed dangerous, as Cornwallis had repeatedly warned him; but that was not the point which interested Parliament. The tide was running against the Government. When the House at last divided at about eight o'clock that morning the Ministry's strength dropped from the usual 240 or more to 182, while that of the Opposition rose to 125. Four days later Pitt rallied his followers by introducing

---

[200] As, for example, the challenge of Philip Francis to Pitt: 'When You passed the Act of 1784, did You, or did You not, mean and resolve to give to Mr. Dundas (You know very well that the words " Board of Control " are nothing but a periphrase) to apply the whole revenue of India to the expense of . . . whatever military force he thought proper? ' (*Ibid.*, 206).

some placating amendments;[201] but it was generally held that without this gesture he and his Bill would have been defeated.[202]

Pitt's very large majority in the House was not a political party but a loose association of groups which had little in common save personal regard for their leader and a canny appreciation that Fox and North were 'out' (provided that George III remained of sound mind) for an indefinite period. Different groups on different occasions accordingly indulged in the luxury of resisting Pitt, often with the support of individual Ministers, when a particular prejudice or vested interest appeared to be threatened. His Anglo-Irish proposals, his support for the abolition of the slave trade and for parliamentary reform, are cases in point. In practice this 'unreformed' Parliament after the election of 1783 was much more volatile and independent than the disciplined majorities of modern times, obedient to the Whip. The fact that Pitt ran into trouble in the Commons when he finally decided to take the East India bull by the horns was symptomatic and indicated a widespread reluctance, deriving from a variety of reasons, to allow the Government, as such, to become too deeply or directly involved in Indian affairs.

This parliamentary battle was the culmination of a tortuous struggle between State and Corporation which had gone on for almost twenty years. The subversion of the Company's constitution by its employees in India and their defiance of successive Ministries represented a revolt against Westminster which in its own way was almost as difficult to handle as the parallel revolt of the American colonists. The British-Indian revolt was a prolonged and scrambling affair because the circumstances were peculiar. The rebels, as we have seen, had entrenched themselves within the metropolitan citadel by securing substantial representation in the imperial Parliament. Secondly, public opinion outside the India groups was divided and confused. On the one hand, the cascade of reports

---

[201] The Board was restricted to a total establishment of 20,245 officers and men (8,045 King's troops and 12,200 Company troops) which could be charged to the Indian revenues: but Pitt made it clear that this limitation could not be held to apply in an emergency. The Board was also forbidden to order any increase of salary or the giving of a gratuity to any Company Servant unless the proposal had originated with the Directors and been approved by Parliament. Itemised annual accounts of revenue and expenditure in the Presidencies and of all classes of debt were to be laid before Parliament. The practical importance of these provisos was slight. (*28 Geo. III, cap. XVII.*)

[202] See for example General Grant to Cornwallis, London, 6 April, 1788. ' In course of the debates . . . a number of members appeared to be wheeling, and I believe Opposition were sanguine in their expectations of oversetting the Ministry. . . . Upon the whole, Mr. Pitt never has had such a push made against him; it was thought necessary to call in the outposts, and the auxiliary troops were brought from Scotland ' (*Cornwallis Corr.*, vol. II, p. 374). The alarm in Government circles vented itself in an outburst of hostility (and jealousy) against Dundas. See Lord Sheffield to William Eden, 21 March, 1788: ' Pitt's friends are vociferous against Dundas. Some say they will ruin him, but I cannot flatter myself ' (*Addit. MSS.*, 34,428, f. 11).

from Select and Secret Committees had revealed administrative abuses and irresponsible and dangerous interventions in Indian politics which the Directors were incapable of preventing. On the other hand, if the State took charge, there would be an increase in the power and influence of the King's Ministers: a distasteful proposition. Accordingly the establishment of State control was gradual, marked at each stage by hesitation and compromise.

Ostensibly the Declaratory Act of 1788 did no more than affirm that the Board of Control had, in fact, been empowered in 1784 to charge the India revenues with the costs of such forces as they might deem necessary to be sent out, but in practical effect it validated the detailed direction of affairs which the Board had assumed. Thenceforward the Ministry were masters, but only, so to speak, at one remove. The Company was still the administrative agent.

This in the opinion of Dundas was to be considered no more than the penultimate stage. The final objective was the administration of the British-Indian territories by the India Board, operating directly through the Governor-General and the Presidency Governments, while the Company would revert to the trading role which they had filled before Clive had turned them into controllers of revenue. That the management of a national asset of such magnitude should be in the hands of a company of merchants was a 'preposterous' arrangement. When propounding his scheme for a unified 'royal' army in India he had reminded Cornwallis that the Company's Charter was due to expire in a few years' time. 'In whosoever hands the Government of this country may then be,' he added, 'I do not believe the Executive Government in India will be left on the footing it now is, and in all our arrangements we must have a view to that consideration.'[203]

The Company's Charter was due for renewal in April, 1794, and Dundas hoped and expected that the State would then take over the political, financial and military administration of the Territories, opening the trade in India to private merchants, and leaving the Company with its exclusive privileges in the China trade. On 1 October, 1791, he sent private and elaborate instructions to Francis Russell, the Board's solicitor, for a new Charter Act along these lines.[204] Lengthy consultations ensued. The Company's monopoly and its large importation of Indian piece goods into the home market were unpopular with the manufacturing interests; but after the unfavourable reception given to the Declaratory Act it was evident that State intervention had been pushed under prevailing conditions to the limit of public acquiescence. To have attempted to convert the Company's employees in India into 'civil

---

[203] Dundas to Cornwallis, 29 July, 1787. 'Private.' *Cornwallis Corr.*, vol. I, p. 332.
[204] For the text of these instructions see *Home Misc. Series*, vol. 413(6), pp. 241-99.

servants' would have roused a hornet's nest on the old issue of Crown patronage.

The contrast between Dundas's original expectations and the modest plan which was eventually adopted by Government can be clearly seen in Bruce's book which was prepared from official documents under Dundas's direction and published in 1793.[205] The decision to leave the previous arrangement as it was except for a few minor modifications was probably taken before the declaration of war against the French Jacobins, but that momentous event and the huge majority in Parliament which was now united in support of the Government's war policy would have rendered a major controversy at home and an administrative revolution in India highly inexpedient.[206]

The Charter Bill which Dundas introduced in the Commons on 23 April, 1793, accordingly left the existing relationship between State and Company virtually unchanged.[207] The primacy of Dundas at the Board was further reinforced by providing that the President should have an original and a casting vote, that there should be two additional (and salaried) Commissioners who would not be Privy Councillors, and that three should constitute a quorum. The overriding authority of the Governor-General in his Council and over the other Presidency Governments was confirmed.

On the commercial side a number of new provisions indicated the trends of Dundas's policy of trade expansion in Asian waters. Just at this time Lord Macartney was on his way to Peking at the head of a special embassy to the Emperor, the purpose of which was to open the huge market of China to British manufactures.[208] The new Bill provided that if any cession of territory were obtained,

---

[205] J. Bruce, *Historical View of Plans for the Government of British India . . . and outlines of a Plan . . . for the Asiatic Interests of Great Britain*. See Preface and p. 191 *et seq.* Bruce had recently resigned from his professorship at Edinburgh University to become an official of the India Board, ' as his whole time is occupied by Indian compilations and other business under Mr. Dundas' (Dundas to the King, 25 Sept., 1792. *Royal Archives, Windsor*). In expounding the ' plan ', Bruce stated some of its general principles: British rule in India could not follow the tradition of representative government; but it must be maintained by an administration, ' local, discretionary and prompt ', derived from a grafting of ' the mild maxims of British Government and laws ' on Asiatic institutions. The native population must be further conciliated by a declaration of general tolerance in religion and a guarantee of protection under their own laws.

[206] The powerful influence of Cornwallis had been exerted against making any substantial change. Having been asked by Dundas for his private opinion, he had replied: ' I am not surprised that after the interested and vexatious contradictions which you have experienced from the Court of Directors, you should be desirous of taking as much of the business as possible entirely out of their hands.' But he proceeded to advance cogent political and economic reasons against doing so. Cornwallis to Dundas, 4 April, 1790. ' Private and Confidential.' *Selections from the State Papers of the Governors-General of India: Lord Cornwallis*, ed. Sir G. Forrest (Oxford, 1926), vol. II, pp. 185-93.

[207] *33 Geo. III, cap. LII.*

[208] See Chap. VII below.

'distinct and separate from the Continent of China and wholly free from any Jurisdiction or Authority of the Chinese Government', and a commercial depot were established there, it would be lawful for any British subject to export British (and Irish) manufactures thither in the Company's ships and to reside there under restrictions approved by the Board. Similarly the current efforts to open a trade in furs from the North-West Coast of America to China and Japan were encouraged by a clause which required the Directors to admit such traders into their area of monopoly under regulations to be approved by the Commissioners.[209] Again, the new State-aided Southern Whale Fishery was assisted by a requirement that Directors must permit the whalers to sail into the Pacific round Cape Horn under certain restrictions.[210] Finally, by way of stimulating the export of British manufactures to India the Company was put under an obligation to provide at least 3,000 tons of shipping each season at reasonable rates for the use of private merchants wishing to participate in the Indian trade. Ostensibly this last provision broke the Company's monopoly in the interests of the manufacturers, but its practical effect was negligible. Apart from other difficulties the Indian demand for British goods during this period was almost non-existent.

While the Company thus remained the administrative agent of the Government in Indian affairs, Dundas had secured one of his objects in establishing some degree of control over its commercial policy and so to that extent preventing its exclusive privileges from being used as a barrier against British commercial penetration into the markets of the Pacific. Nonetheless he was in an uncomfortable and ironical situation when he rose in the Commons to introduce the new Charter Bill, for he was obliged to advance arguments in defence of the Company's political and commercial status which were notoriously in flat contradiction to his convictions. He even went so far in defending the official policy as to declare his disagreement with Cornwallis, who had proposed that the appointment of Governors and Councillors in the Presidencies should be vested in the Crown. This loyal but embarrassing performance evoked a brilliantly derisive attack from Philip Francis. Otherwise the measure was languidly debated in a thinly attended House. Few, if any, at that juncture expected or desired 'innovation'. The Bill passed its third reading with 132 votes to 26.[211]

The dual system continued. Since 1788 it had worked more smoothly, for the Company had been cowed and Dundas began to improve his technique in practising the art of governing by influence. But it was at best a cumbersome machine in which

---

[209] See Chap. V below.
[210] See Chap. VII below.
[211] See *Parl. Hist.*, vol. XXX, 660-701, 935-48.

friction was always latent. Acrimonious disputes flared up in 1809, 1814, and again in 1819,[212] and the close association which sub-sisted between Dundas and Cornwallis was not always maintained by their respective successors. As late as 1847 the then President of the India Board, John Hobhouse (afterwards Lord Broughton) complained bitterly of his difficulties to Palmerston:

Indeed with the present head of the Indian Government [Sir Henry Hardinge] and such a Secret Committee as I have now to deal with, all cordial co-operation from these quarters would be quite out of the question.[213]

Nevertheless the system of authoritative superintendence which Dundas and Pitt established between 1784 and 1788 as the alterna-tive to a declaration of sovereignty and direct State management continued for seventy years. In India, as subsequently in Africa, an arrangement by which a commercial corporation managed the business and acted in some degree as a political buffer, while the Government held the necessary powers to prevent them from get-ting into mischief, suited the interests and temperament of a nation of shopkeepers: which is a contemptuous, though not inaccurate, way of describing a people who have normally preferred profitable cargoes to the precarious splendours of peacock thrones.

5. THE GOVERNOR-GENERAL

From the time of Clive and his acquisition of the *diwani* British subjects in India had successfully defied the authority of West-minster. The creation of a superintending Board of Privy Coun-cillors did not solve the problem. Dundas and his colleagues worked extremely hard at the London end, curbing extravagance in the establishment and remodelling many unwise despatches; but they could not of their mere motion enforce obedience in a distant land. The home Government needed a responsive and powerful instrument in the form of a Governor-General who could dictate, if need arose, to his Council and to the other Presidencies. In his own India Bill Dundas had proposed that the Governor-General should be entrusted with these necessary powers, but the Act of 1784 had fallen short of what was required.

No one had had such painful experience of the need for supreme executive authority as Warren Hastings, and he had watched with anxiety the appearance of Fox's India scheme. Worn and beset with many difficulties, his passionate pride in achievement still

---

[212] For details of these disputes see *Home Misc. Series*, vol. 342, pp. 711-842.
[213] Hobhouse to Palmerston, 3 April, 1847. *Palmsterston Papers* (Broadlands). Quoted by R. J. Gavin, ' Palmerston's Policy towards the East and West Coasts of Africa, 1830-65 '. (Unpublished Ph.D. thesis, Cambridge, 1958.)

made him ready to stay on in India to consolidate his work and fame, provided that he was given the necessary authority. In Pitt he recognised a man who refreshingly put the national interest first, and under whom he was ready to give devoted service. He wrote and said so – and afterwards bitterly regretted it. Pitt's India Act with its punitive clauses, its compulsory inventory on oath for returning Servants, and the standing judicial inquisition horrified him. It was more injurious, he declared, to his fellow Servants, to his own authority and character, and to the national honour, than anything which even Burke, Fox and Francis could have invented. 'I would not, for any honours that the King could bestow, stay to be the instrument of the vengeance that hangs over the service.'[214] Yet the very fact that he interpreted the Government's measure as a vendetta, an act of vengeance, shows how completely he misunderstood the prevailing climate of public opinion.

His stature as *imperator* in war, diplomacy, and in understanding the needs and outlook of the Indian peoples was magnificent; but his careless indifference in all matters relating to finance was indicative of his order of priorities and left his subordinates free to plunder if they had a mind to. From the politicians' point of view he was an over-powerful subject who was on the wrong side of the fence. What was needed now was a Government servant, in effect though not in name, who would work with the Cabinet as closely as the Lord Lieutenant of Ireland and who would preserve what Hastings himself had rescued by establishing a loyal and disciplined bureaucracy.

The Court of Directors decided to offer the Governor-Generalship to Lord Macartney, the retiring Governor of Madras, who had long been manœuvring for the post.[215] A man of wide political and diplomatic experience, he had dealt resolutely with the appalling mess in which the Arcot revenues and debts were submerged, but his assumption of superior knowledge, combined with ineptitude in handling the external relations of Madras, had brought him into frequent collision with Hastings. Before accepting the offer he decided to wait until his return to England when he could state in person his conditions of acceptance. In an interview with William Devaynes and Nathaniel Smith, Chairman and Deputy-Chairman, in January, 1786, he warned them of 'the new spirit of Combination and opposition' which had spread in both the civil and military departments. Even the most decisive support from home would be insufficient to cope with it unless the powers of the Governor-General were increased.

---

[214] Quoted by Sir K. Feiling, *Warren Hastings*, p. 325.
[215] For Macartney's activities in Madras see the very useful collection, *Private Correspondence of Lord Macartney, Governor-General of Madras, 1781-85*, ed. C. Colin Davies (Royal Hist. Soc., 1950. Camden Third Series, vol. LXXVII).

He made three points. In the first place he insisted that the Commander-in-Chief must be brought under control of the civil power, as was the case in all colonial dependencies and had been so in India until 1774. Under the present system there were two independent powers in the same government. 'The troops look up to the Military Chief alone, and are totally withdrawn from all obedience or attention to the regular Government of the Country.' With unpleasant memories of violent conflicts with Sir Eyre Coote, Macartney proposed that a new Commander-in-Chief should be sent out with Instructions which would explicitly make him subordinate to the civil government.

Secondly, he criticised the provision in the Act of 1784 which required that promotion among the civilian Servants was to be determined according to seniority. This had been done to prevent favouritism and jobbery, but Macartney argued that the civilians could not be brought back to obedience unless the Governments in India were empowered to pay due regard to merit and qualifications.

At present it would seem that some of the Company's Servants acted in India as if they conceived they had an irremovable tenure of their respective Stations, having formed a band, and adopted principles, which nothing appears likely to break or correct, but the possibility of a preference being given to new Servants in their room. Persons holding considerable Offices there are from the idea of Independence among the most forward to oppose the Act of the Legislature of this Country.

Finally, and most important of all, the Governor-General must be given authority to act independently of his Council. If he were, he could be an instrument of happiness to India and of substantial permanent advantage to Britain; but if not, he might well became 'a shadow without substance, and might undertake responsibility for an Object without the means of attaining it'.[216]

For all this Hastings himself had long contended, but Macartney's conditions could only be met by means of legislation and they were referred to Pitt and Dundas. Macartney, however, was only a second string: Ministers and Directors alike wanted Lord Cornwallis for the post. The general consensus of opinion that the integrity and personality of Cornwallis made him the one man to set the India house in order constitutes a remarkable tribute to his

---

[216] ' Heads or Minutes of a Conversation between Lord Macartney and the Chairman and Deputy-Chairman of the East India Company, 13 January 1786.' (*Pitt Papers*, P.R.O. 30/8/355.) The King, who received Macartney in audience on the same day, does not appear to have been favourably impressed. To Lord Sydney he observed: ' I think the Resignation of Lord Macartney (from Madras) *not an unfavourable event.*' (The words in italics are underlined by the King.) And to Pitt he wrote: ' I yesterday saw Lord Macartney, nothing dropped from him that marked any desire of accepting the offer of the East India Company have made him . . . it certainly was no object to Me to dive into his future intentions . . .' (The King to Sydney, 10 Jan., and to Pitt, 14 Jan., 1786. *Royal Archives, Windsor*.)

quality. As long ago as May, 1782, his friend Shelburne had singled him out for the task, offering him the combined posts of Governor-General and Commander-in-Chief, which Cornwallis had accepted, but with considerable reluctance. Apart from a desire to remain a soldier and in Europe, he had always considered that the powers of the Governor-General under the Regulating Act of 1773 were much too limited, and he had informed Shelburne that his acceptance must be subject to the proviso that 'the affairs of India were so arranged that I could go with a prospect of being useful to my Country'.[217] When Fox and North came in they had sent him 'some civil messages', and he had agreed to stand by his engagement to go out to India.[218] Then came Dundas's India Bill of 1783 with its reliance on the supreme authority of the Governor-General to effect reforms; and in the Commons he had made it clear that Cornwallis was the person designated.

In April, 1784, and again some six weeks later Lord Sydney approached him on Pitt's behalf with the suggestion that he should go to India as Commander-in-Chief; and on the second occasion Sydney said that he was sure that Mr. Pitt would wish him to hold the civil as well as the military command, and he added that the Company was also anxious that he should be the man. But Cornwallis refused to commit himself until he knew what the powers of the Governor-General were to be.

I told him that . . . as soon as their plan was digested and put into an intelligible form (which by his conversation I should think was not in much forwardness), I would consider whether I could undertake it with any degree of safety for myself or appearance of utility to the public.[219]

During the summer months while the India Bill was having its difficult passage through Parliament, the ministerial pressure continued. But by the beginning of August when the Bill reached the Committee stage it had become evident that Pitt was not prepared to invite further opposition by vesting the Governor-Generalship with the decisive authority which Cornwallis considered essential. In a courteous letter to Sydney, Cornwallis withdrew from the

---

[217] Cornwallis to Pitt, 8 Nov., 1784. *Cornwallis Corr.*, vol. I, p. 186. Cf. Shelburne (Lansdowne) to Cornwallis, 27 April, 1791. *Ibid.*, vol. II, p. 123.

[218] Although he opposed the Coalition, Cornwallis afterwards wrote to his friend, Colonel Ross (21 Dec., 1784): 'You know I was partial to a great part of Fox's Bill.' *Ibid.*, I, p. 190. This measure would not, however, have given the Governor-General the powers which Cornwallis demanded.

[219] Cornwallis to Ross, 9 and 25 May, 1784. *Ibid.*, I, pp. 174-5. Cf. Sydney to the King, 19 April (draft), reporting the indecisive result of his first approach to Cornwallis. No further step could be taken, he added, until after the following day when the Directors were to choose the new 'Chairs'. (C.O.77/25. *Secy. of State's Corr. – East Indies.*)

field.[220] For six months he was left in peace, and then in February, 1785, Pitt sent for him urgently and after some conversation about the possibility of his going to India asked him to talk to Dundas. The latter was explicit on the essential point, as Pitt had not been. ' He told me that if I would say I would go, many things which I objected to in the Bill should be altered.' But Cornwallis detected that there was disagreement among the Ministers : the ground was not firm. After taking twenty-four hours to think it over, he returned 'a very civil negative'.[221]

Ministers and Directors decided to offer the post to Macartney, but he insisted on coming home first; and when he arrived (in January, 1786) he made, as we have seen, the same sort of stipulations as Cornwallis. Matters were at a standstill. Hastings had returned to England in the previous June : the equivocal John Macpherson was in charge in Bengal; and Dundas's plans for remodelling the Indian system (and vindicating the India Act) required that a strong and trusted colleague should be installed as Governor-General without any further delay. At last Dundas had his way and Pitt agreed that Cornwallis must be secured even at the price of confronting Parliament with an amending Act.

The proposal of going to India [wrote Cornwallis] has been pressed upon me so strongly, with the circumstance of the Governor-General's being independent of his Council, as intended in Dundas's former bill, and having the supreme command of the military, that, much against my will and with grief of heart, I have been obliged to say Yes.[222]

Having done so, he had a series of lengthy consultations with Dundas who expounded the Government's policy of reform, retrenchment and consolidation in its various implications. Hitherto Cornwallis had shared the popular criticism of Dundas in his management of affairs at the Board;[223] but when the new Governor-General set out for India in the beginning of May, 1786, the two men thoroughly understood each other. Their co-operation was close and intimate, even when they disagreed.

The introduction of a Bill empowering Governors in India to over-rule their Councils came at a particularly awkward juncture

---

[220] Cornwallis to Sydney, 4 August. *Cornwallis Corr.*, vol. I, p. 180. Nine days later Sydney asked General Sir Guy Carleton whether he would consider going as Commander-in-Chief to Bengal – ' but I have not authority from the Company to offer it to you '. Carleton promptly replied with a disdainful refusal to serve under the Company. ' Should they add the supreme civil authority, with the most ample emoluments avarice could demand, all these could not tempt me in the smallest degree.' (Sydney to Carleton, 13 August, 1784, and Carleton's reply on the following day. *C.O.* 77/25.)

[221] Cornwallis to Ross, 23 Feb., 1785. *Cornwallis Corr.*, vol. I, p. 191.

[222] Cornwallis to Ross, 23 Feb., 1786. *Ibid.*, p. 215.

[223] On 21 Dec., 1784, he had written to Ross: ' Our friend Dundas, although a very clever fellow, is, I fear, but a short-sighted politician.' *Ibid.*, p. 190.

for the Ministry, for Burke and Francis were busily preparing their charges of tyrannical conduct on the part of Cornwallis's predecessor. It was obvious that the Opposition would use the alleged misconduct of Hastings as a damning reason for withholding arbitrary power from any Governor-General; and they did so with violence.

The Bill which Dundas brought in on 16 March provided that the Governor of an Indian Presidency could at his discretion overrule, positively or negatively, the majority opinion in Council. In that event the views and reasons of each member present must be recorded in full in the Secret Consultations. The Governor's order, which would have the force of law, must also be signed by the Councillors, but the Governor would be solely responsible. There were safeguards: the discretionary power would not apply in the case of an acting-governor, nor could it be used in respect of judicial matters or general regulations for order and civil government. Another clause made it permissible for the Governor-General to be also Commander-in-Chief.[224]

Burke, Fox and Francis all inveighed against the Bill as imposing arbitrary and despotic government in India. It was a libel on the British constitution and the liberties of the people of England, Burke declared. Why, asked Francis, have a Council at all? To such sallies Pitt and Dundas both gave the answer that the person entrusted with the administration of the country was indeed invested with more power, 'but he had therefore the greater responsibility'.[225]

It was a novel principle in overseas administration, necessary for the Indian occasion, but contrary to the tradition that executive power, whether at home or abroad, ought to be circumscribed. Its adoption in British India had accordingly been long delayed, though frequently advocated. Indeed, it is almost certain that the compromise of 1784 (which had reduced the Council from four to three) would have been maintained, had it not been for the steady refusal of Cornwallis to attempt the task unless his conditions were accepted. As modern experience has shown, the very fact that a Governor overseas is formally vested with 'reserve'

---

[224] 26 Geo. III, cap. 16. As previously noted, Dundas took the opportunity of giving legislative force to the requirement that all members of the Secret Committee of the Court of Directors must take an oath of secrecy and in a prescribed form. In the original draft the Bill had included clauses which relaxed the requirement of the India Act that promotion must be determined by seniority and permitted the sworn statement of profits, which every Servant was required to make on returning to England, to be kept secret unless and until it was decided to prosecute. But these relaxations were postponed at the instance of the Opposition and no action was taken about them until the new Charter Act of 1793.

[225] For the debates on the Bill see Parl. Hist., vol. XXV, 1266,1293 (Commons) and 1338-48 (Lords). The Bill passed the Commons on 27 March and the Lords on the 31st.

powers is usually sufficient of itself to render their employment very rarely necessary.

Macartney had not spoken without his book when he warned the Chairman and Deputy-Chairman that a 'new spirit of Combination and opposition' had spread through both the civil and military departments in India, and that men in senior positions were, 'from the idea of Independence', among the most forward in organising resistance to the terms of the India Act. Pitt's measure had faithfully copied many of the punitive clauses in Fox's second India Bill, which Burke had drafted, and others had been added. When reports of the Act of 1784 reached India, the Company Servants were astonished and enraged to find that the whips of Fox and Burke had been replaced by the scorpions of Pitt and Dundas. The tacit defiance which had gone on so long and so lucratively became vocal and organised. It was no wonder that Cornwallis and Macartney had both insisted that a concentration of supreme power was necessary to re-establish discipline.

Hastings himself remained aloof from the movement, but about a month after his departure the officers of the Third Brigade, stationed at Cawnpore, elected a committee to formulate grievances and established contact with similar committees at other stations.[226] Then in July of that year (1785) the civilians of Calcutta began to organise. Significantly the leading spirit was a person of the seniority of Harry Vansittart. On 25 July the 'Inhabitants of Calcutta' at a public meeting passed a set of resolutions which condemned the India Act of 1784 in terms which recalled American denunciations of the Intolerable Acts. His Majesty's subjects in the East Indies were entitled to the protection of the laws of England in common with other subjects of the realm: the obligation of Servants upon their return to Britain to deliver upon oath an inventory of their whole property under penalties of excessive severity was grievous and oppressive, as was their liability to be sent forcibly to England to stand trial for offences alleged to have been committed in India: the new Court of Judicature established for trying such charges was 'a tribunal unrestrained by the settled rules of Law, and subject to no appeal, depriving them of their undoubted Birth right, the trial by Jury'. All these were 'Violations of the Great Charter of our Liberties and infringements of the most sacred Principles of the British Constitution'. The dichotomy between the demands of British subjects overseas for 'liberty' and the British Government's sense of obligation on behalf of indigenous peoples had made its appearance.

Dundas himself was directly attacked in a further Resolution, that it was a grievous injury that Company Servants were now

---

[226] 'Resolutions framed on 13 and agreed to on 17 March, 1785, by the Officers of the Third Brigade stationed at Cawnpore.' (C.O. 77/25.)

liable to be dismissed and recalled at the pleasure of the Crown – 'which is in other words at the will of the Minister'. It was agreed that an organised campaign must be undertaken to compel the Government to repeal the obnoxious clauses of the Act. A committee of fifteen from among the more senior officials was chosen, which was to prepare petitions to the King and both Houses of Parliament and to organise a network of correspondents in the up-country stations of the Bengal Presidency and with the other Presidencies. Subscriptions were paid to meet necessary expenses and the committee was given a free hand.

On 13 August Vansittart sent a copy of the Calcutta Resolutions to Madras. In a covering letter he explained that his committee had been authorised to correspond with the other Presidencies in order to secure a united resistance.

We are satisfied that you, Gentlemen, think of the Act as we do, and that you will not hesitate, therefore, to adopt similar measures with ourselves. To the success of these measures Union, Consistency and Vigour are alike indispensable. The first we are assured will prevail, since by the late Act of Parliament all have been equally aggrieved, and no doubt, therefore, all are equally disposed and determined to seek a Redress of their Grievances.[227]

Madras responded promptly. During September a number of public meetings were held in the Town Hall of Fort St. George: a committee, with William Wynch as chairman, was constituted and prepared a draft addressed to the Crown and petitions to both Houses of Parliament. After considerable discussion and amendment they were publicly exhibited for the addition of signatures, and on 2 October, 1785, they were duly dispatched by Wynch to Lord Sydney.[228]

The malcontents clearly expected to receive strong support in Parliament as they had done in 1781. At a meeting in Madras on 29 September it was resolved that the petitions must be sent home forthwith, because it was 'very important' that they should arrive in time for consideration during the 1786 session.[229] On 7 March and before the petitions had arrived Philip Francis rose in the Commons to move for leave to bring in a Bill to amend the India Act of 1784. It was, he declared, a matter of public notoriety that this Act had been received in India with great discontent, 'and that

---

[227] A copy of the Calcutta Resolutions, together with an account of the meetings and (curiously enough) of Vansittart's letter to Wynch of Madras, is in *C.O.* 77/25.
[228] For the text of the Madras petitions and Wynch's letter to Sydney see *ibid.* Wynch was an 'old hand' who had served for eighteen years in the Madras Presidency and was at this time a Commissioner of the Board of Accounts. The Wynch family provided a succession of men who served in the southern Presidency for some 200 years. (See H. D. Love, *Vestiges of Old Madras*, vol. II, pp. 318-19.)
[229] *Ibid.*

petitions against it were preparing to be sent over to be laid before Parliament'. He might, he said, be accused of acting precipitately and unfairly to the petitioners themselves in not waiting for their petitions to arrive, but he denied that he was trying to make mischief out of 'the present temper of the discontented parties'.

He proposed to remodel the India Act in three major particulars. In the first place, there must be one central authority instead of the present dualism of Board and Court, which placed 'all the nominal power of the Company in one set of men and all the real power in another . . . A more plausible pretence for disobedience cannot easily be imagined.' Secondly, the tendency to make the Governor-General a dictator must be stopped. He would go back to the Regulating Act of 1773 and put him under a Council of four. 'In a plan of general reform, an united Governor and Council may do much – a single person can do nothing.' Thirdly, the system of inquisition and arbitrary judicial procedure, as provided in the Act, was a general menace to the whole kingdom. 'My intention is to tear it out of the statute-book.' After a short debate 'the previous question' was put and carried.[230] Nine days later Dundas introduced the Government's own amending Bill giving Governors in India over-riding powers.

That there was a widespread spirit of resistance among the Company's Servants in India was well known in London. Whether Francis had been in correspondence with the malcontents does not appear, but he knew that petitions asking for the repeal of many parts of the India Act were on the way; and it is evident enough that he had planned to anticipate Dundas by delivering a full-scale attack on the Act, backed by the resentment of the civil and military services in India. But the petitions, which might conceivably have won over the support of the India interests in Parliament, were not lying on the table. The plan misfired.[231]

At the beginning of September, 1786, Lord Cornwallis arrived

---

[230] *Parl. Hist.*, vol. XXV, 1202-1244.

[231] The organised protests from India were not, however, in vain: indeed, the malcontents secured a major concession. When introducing the Government's Amending Act on 16 March, Dundas said that he had taken 'considerable pains' to ascertain what it was that the Company Servants chiefly complained of in the 1784 Act and that since their chief objection appeared to be against the requirement to submit on oath a detailed inventory of their assets on returning home, he had decided in the amending Bill to limit the scope of the inventory and to allow the statement of the fortune brought home to be kept secret unless and until it was decided that legal proceedings must be instituted. He would also propose some modifications in the prescribed procedure for choosing the parliamentary members of the new Court of Judicature. (*Parl. Hist.*, vol. XXV, 1267-8.) The Government, however, accepted Sheridan's suggestion that these matters should be left over and dealt with separately in a subsequent measure. This was done later in the session and the result was a considerable victory for the Company Servants, for the key clause about the hated inventory was repealed outright. (See 'An Act for the further Regulation of the Trial of Persons accused of certain Offences committed in the East Indies . . .' *26 Geo. III, cap. LVII, Sect. XXXI.*)

in Calcutta as Governor-General with supreme power. He brought to his formidable task an honesty of purpose which was not only absolute, but – and this was almost as important – universally known to be such. He was, however, entering a world of Asian subtleties and complexities which was completely strange to him, and he was faced by a body of his fellow-countrymen who knew that world (or, at any rate, its outward and seamier aspects) well, and they were in an ugly and resentful mood. There was a strong *esprit de corps* among them which was potentially valuable, even though the *corps* tended to resemble soldiers of fortune in a mediaeval 'Free Company'. Their habit of treating any form of metropolitan authority with contemptuous defiance had a long history and was all the more insidious and difficult to crush because it took the form of evasion instead of open rebellion. The disobedience of this powerful and influential British community overseas against successive Governments at home had been brought to a head by the Acts of 1784 and 1786, and it had to be broken once and for all if the British position in India was to be saved by being reconstructed on a decent and stable basis.

If Cornwallis had been faced with total corruption and non-co-operation, his task would have been almost impossible notwithstanding his unlimited authority. As it was he found very great difficulty in selecting reliable advisers. But some of those holding senior posts in Bengal or as Residents at Indian Courts – such as James Anderson, Charles Warre Malet, John Shore and Jonathan Duncan – were men of integrity and wide knowledge of Indian affairs and were ready to give loyal service. Such men were indispensable and Cornwallis trusted them, even if he did not always accept their advice. Moreover even those whose primary object was plunder and a quick get-away to England (or Scotland) were beginning to realise that the age of freebooters was coming to an end and that the only alternative, if they were to remain in India, was the career of a normal civilian or military officer with a reasonable competence at the end of it. Perhaps the most remarkable aspect of the Cornwallis régime was the response which he was able to evoke in establishing a genuine 'Service', so laying foundations for the admirable work of their successors.

The investigation, and still more the effective suppression, of what has been accurately described as 'the gross jobs and corrupt practices which had disgraced former governments'[232] was slow and uphill work. For the first few months he was hard at work in the field of diplomacy, getting clear of the dangerous engagements into which Macpherson had entered with the Marathas and other Powers then at war with Tipu of Mysore. He then began a thorough

---

[232] Ross (*loc. cit.*), vol. I, p. 224.

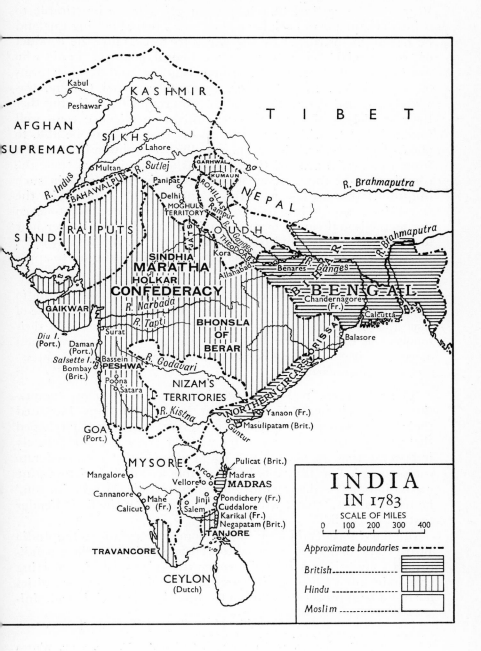

KASHMIR

AFGHAN
SUPREMACY

T I B E T

Kabul

Peshawar

SIKHS

Lahore

Multan

R. Indus

BAHAWALPUR

R. Sutlej

GARHWAL

KUMAUN

NEPAL

R. Brahmaputra

Panipat

Delhi

MOGHUL
TERRITORY

ROHILLAS

Rampur

SIND

RAJPUTS

JATS

R. Ganges

OUDH

THEODORE

Kora

Allahabad

R. Brahmaputra

SINDHIA

MARATHA

HOLKAR

CONFEDERACY

Benares

R. Ganges

B E N G A L

GAIKWAR

R. Narbada

BHONSLA
OF
BERAR

Chandernagore
(Fr.)

Calcutta

R. Tapti

Diu I.
(Port.)

Daman
(Port.)

Surat

R. Godavari

O
R
I
S
S
A

Balasore

Salsette I.

Bombay
(Brit.)

Bassein

PESHWA

Poona

Satara

NIZAM'S
TERRITORIES

NORTHERN CIRCARS

GOA
(Port.)

R. Kistna

Guntur

Yanaon (Fr.)

Masulipatam (Brit.)

MYSORE

Arcot

Pulicat (Brit.)

Mangalore

Vellore

Madras

MADRAS

Cannanore

Mahé
(Fr.)

Jinji

Salem

Pondichery (Fr.)

Cuddalore

Calicut

Karikal (Fr.)

Negapatam (Brit.)

TANJORE

TRAVANCORE

CEYLON
(Dutch)

INDIA
IN 1783

SCALE OF MILES

0   100   200   300   400

Approximate boundaries ‒ · ‒ · ‒ ·

British ‒‒‒‒‒‒‒

Hindu ‒‒‒‒‒‒‒

Moslim ‒‒‒‒‒‒‒

investigation of every administrative department in the Presidency. Very soon he realised that it was not going to be practicable to bring delinquents to book for past offences. Before leaving England he had been instructed by the Directors to examine the conduct of 'commercial' Servants under the Bengal Board of Trade who were suspected of making fraudulent contracts and of other forms of malversation. In November, 1786, he reported that he was already persuaded that there was much ground for believing that their suspicions of corruption or culpable negligence were well founded, but 'I will not venture to say that we shall be able to obtain legal proofs of either'. It was difficult to obtain information from Indians because of their customs and prejudices, 'and the combination of these servants that have been concerned in such iniquitous transactions may throw insuperable obstacles in the way of investigation into past abuses'.[233] The real need was to learn the methods and causes of misbehaviour in order to discover how to stop the loopholes and remove the incentives. By August, 1787, he had taken the measure of the problem and had begun to apply remedies.

> I am sorry to say [he informed Dundas] that I have every reason to believe that at present almost all the collectors are, under the name of some relation or friend, deeply engaged in Commerce, and, by their influence as collectors and Judges of Adaulet, they become the most dangerous enemies to the Company's interest and the greatest oppressors of the manufacturers.

The reason was inadequate salaries alongside enormous temptations. Appreciating this, Cornwallis had substantially increased their allowances and commission on revenue collection. He hoped that Dundas would approve, 'for without them it was absolutely impossible that an honest man could acquire the most moderate competency'. This liberality had been followed up by strict revenue regulations and orders against engaging in trade. 'I promise you,' he told Dundas, 'that I will make an example of the first offender that I can catch.'[234]

Dundas in the midst of his economy campaign at the India Board could hardly be expected to welcome an increase in expenditure. Cornwallis was indeed co-operating vigorously in effecting economies by abolishing sinecures and eliminating opportunities for fraud or extravagance, but on the question of providing admini-

---

[233] Cornwallis to the Secret Committee of the Court of Directors, 16 Nov., 1786. *Cornwallis Corr.*, vol. I, pp. 243-4.

[234] Cornwallis to Dundas, 14 August, 1787. 'Private.' *Ibid.*, pp. 281-7. Warren Hastings had urged the need for better salaries long before, and some increases had been made, chiefly in the more senior posts; but war conditions and the short-sighted niggardliness of the Directors had prevented the process from being carried nearly far enough.

strative officers with proper salaries he remained immovable. A few years later he made his point in a letter to Pitt in blunt terms:

> No reduction can be made in the civil establishment of Bengal that would in reality promote economy – those persons who hold offices of great labour and great responsibility must be well paid, or they will for the most part betray their trust.[235]

The prime example of the need for paying generous salaries was the post of British Resident in the dependent buffer State of Oudh. Until Cornwallis cleansed what he described as ' the Augean stables of Benares and Lucknow', the Resident had received an official salary of £1,350 while his actual annual income was in the region of £40,000 – 'exclusive of the complete monopoly of the whole commerce of the country'. It was generally supposed that in return for 'all these good things' the Residents at Benares had not been ungrateful to the friends of the Governor-General. Even under a reformed system the temptations in Oudh would remain abnormally great: 'the Rajah is a fool, his servants rogues, every native of Hindostan (I really believe) corrupt, and Benares 600 miles from Calcutta.' Yet Oudh was in a key situation, and good management there would ' raise our character and reputation in the remotest parts of Hindostan'. With great reluctance he appointed as Resident one of the most valuable men in the Bengal Service whom he could ill spare, Jonathan Duncan, the secretary of the Public and Revenue Department.[236]

To establish standards of upright administration in a morass of Indian extortion and at a time when venality was very prevalent in Britain was a most formidable undertaking. Cornwallis summarised his own achievement with warrantable pride.

> I have been a most rigid economist in all cases where I thought rigid economy was true economy, I abolished sinecure places, put a stop to jobbing agencies and contracts, prevented large sums from being voted away in council for trumped-up charges [i.e. expenses]; and have been unwearied in hunting out fraud and abuse in every department.

In consequence the Bengal expenses had for the first time fallen

---

[235] Cornwallis to Pitt, 6 Nov., 1788. *Ibid.*, p. 391.

[236] Cornwallis to Dundas, 14 Aug., 1787 (*loc. cit.*). Duncan was Governor of Bombay from 1795 until his death in 1811. The new system which Cornwallis introduced in relation to Oudh represented an attempt to confine British control within specified limits – a policy of limited liability which, as we have seen, had been repeatedly and unsuccessfully pursued in Bengal in earlier times. ' The basis for an agreement appeared to me to be, that we should disclaim all manner of interference in the revenues, collections, commerce, and internal management of the country, and that on the other hand we should have the entire direction of political [i.e. diplomatic] matters, and . . . that it should be clearly admitted that they looked to us solely for defence. . . .' Cornwallis to Dundas, 16 Feb., 1787. ' Private.' *Ibid.*, vol. I, p. 257.

short of the estimates. He then adverted to his central principle. He could never think it a wise measure in India to place men in great and responsible situations without giving them the means over a period of years of acquiring 'honestly and openly' a moderate fortune out of their regular emoluments. He then added a comment which was significant of the future. 'The Company has many valuable servants; the temper of the times is changing. Men are beginning to contract their present expenses and future views.'[237]

Cornwallis had a stiff struggle to persuade the home authorities that generous salaries were an essential economy. More difficult still was his stand against the use of British India as a tom-tiddler's ground for adventurers. From the Prince of Wales downwards he was harassed by requests to find a lucrative post for some indigent friend, and there were others who smuggled themselves out to India, often in the guise of recruits for the Company's army. To the former he was politely unaccommodating,[238] and the latter sort were ordered back to England.[239] 'I am still persecuted every day,' he protested to Sydney in 1788, 'by people coming out with letters to me, who either get into jail, or starve in the foreign settlements. For God's sake do all in your power to stop this madness.'[240]

It was possible, though not easy, to keep the door barred against private scallawags, but a Governor-General could not, of course, prevent the employment of influence in high places in the annual recruitment of new writers and cadets. The age of competitive examinations was not yet. The biographers of Dundas have shown well enough that the general belief that he flooded the Services in India with his own Scottish clients was very greatly exaggerated; and in any case many men who gave long and distinguished service in India were so chosen. Nevertheless the strenuous efforts of Cornwallis to create an administrative Service based on merit and devotion to duty was not assisted by episodes such as the one about to be described.

---

[237] Cornwallis to John Motteux, Chairman of the Court of Directors, 16 Dec., 1787. 'Private.' *Ibid.*, p. 318. Cf. Cornwallis to Dundas, 26 Aug., 1787. 'I am doing everything I can to reform the Company's servants, to teach them to be more economical in their mode of living and to look forward to a moderate competency. . . . But if all chance of saving any money and returning to England, without acting dishonestly, is removed, there will be an end of my reformation.' *Ibid.*, p. 290.

[238] See, for example, his letter to Lord Southampton, 7 Nov., 1789. *State Papers: Cornwallis*, ed. Forrest, vol. II, pp. 80-1.

[239] To one of these Cornwallis wrote a stinging note. He was extremely surprised to learn that he had come out to India. Having refused the earnest entreaties of some of his nearest relations and best friends, it was improbable that he would make an exception in his case. 'If I was inclined to serve you, it is wholly out of my power to do it without a breach of my duty. I most earnestly advise you to think of returning to England as soon as possible. After the 1st January next, I shall be under the necessity of sending you thither.' This letter was written on 23 Aug., 1787. *Ibid.*, p. 289.

[240] Cornwallis to Sydney, 7 Jan., 1788. 'Private.' *Ibid.*, p. 322.

In August, 1792, Dundas wrote to the King to remind him that some weeks previously he had mentioned that the Queen and Princess Augusta had 'some Commands' to convey to Mr. Dundas connected with the Indian Department.

This is the Season at which Mr Dundas arranges everything of that Nature, and He trusts it is unnecessary for him to express the satisfaction He will at all times derive from being enabled to execute any Commands coming from the Quarters to which His Majesty referred.[241]

Yet despite such impediments Cornwallis was able to effect a remarkable transformation in the Bengal Presidency.[242] When Charles Jenkinson (now Lord Hawkesbury) recommended a Mr. Beachcroft for an important commercial post, Cornwallis replied that he knew Beachcroft's father and thought well of the son, 'who is a young man of good character'. He doubted whether he was sufficiently experienced for the post which Hawkesbury had indicated, but he would look out for a suitable opening for him. He then delivered a thrust which might well constitute Cornwallis's epitaph as the founder of an Indian Civil Service:

But here, my Lord, we are in the habit of looking for the man for the place, and not the place for the man.[243]

It was a new criterion; and without its firm application on the spot the work of the India Board at home would have been of little avail.

There was, however, one administrative function (and it was central to all else) which could not be reformed by internal discipline alone, and that was the management of the land revenue. Gross peculation in the Revenue Department was almost traditional, but nothing effective could be done about it until the system itself had been overhauled. The task was daunting in the extreme, but it was fundamental. From the point of view of the East India Company the amount and the reliability of the flow of revenue in Bengal determined their profits in the sale of India goods in London and their capacity to meet the cost of defending the three Presidencies; and what was perhaps rather more important the character of revenue assessment and collection dictated the prosperity or otherwise of the country and conditioned the daily lives

---

[241] Dundas to the King, 3 August, 1792. *Royal Archives, Windsor.*

[242] The Governor-General's zeal for reform could not, however, penetrate as far as Madras. When he went there in 1790 to conduct the war against Tipu of Mysore he made the following comment: 'The whole system of this Presidency is founded on the good old principles of Leadenhall-street economy – small salaries and immense perquisites, and if the Directors alone could be ruined by it, everybody would say they deserved it, but unfortunately it is not the Court of Directors, but the British nation who must be the sufferers' (Cornwallis to Dundas, 31 Dec., 1790. 'Private.' *Cornwallis Corr.*, vol. II, p.. 67-8).

[243] Cornwallis to Hawkesbury, 10 Aug., 1789. *Ibid.*, vol. I, p. 435.

of all but a small fraction of the population. The productivity of
the land and consequently the revenue had declined alarmingly: it
was estimated that about one-third of all the Company's territory
in India was uncultivated and desolate because harassed zemindars,
precariously situated, avoided the risks of development and forced
extortionate terms upon the unfortunate ryots.

The gradual collapse of the Moghul system, which had been
superimposed upon a mosaic of Hindu tenures and obligations, had
resulted in a chaotic situation which the improvisations of British
officials in Calcutta and local peculation had done nothing to
remedy. The intricacy of the problem derived from the infinite
variation in the relationship of Government to zemindar and
the zemindar to the local ryots. In each locality (and sometimes in
one village) there were differences of tenure, differences in the
quality of the soil and in methods of land and crop valuation. To
understand and assess was a task, said John Shore with his profound
knowledge of the subject, 'beyond the investigation, or almost
comprehension, not merely of a collector, but of any man who has
not made it the business of his life'.[244]

By an Act passed in 1784 the Governor-General had been
required to investigate the alleged grievances of land-holders and
'to establish permanent rules for the settlement and collection of
the revenue'. Cornwallis's advisers quickly enlightened him about
the impossibility of making any such attempt until a detailed
enquiry had been made into ancient usage and existing practice,
district by district. For three years Shore, with the assistance of
Jonathan Duncan, James Grant and other specialists, laboured
on this task and collected an enormous mass of information. Meanwhile Cornwallis held his hand and continued the system of annual
assessments with the continual dislocations and evasions which
they inevitably caused.

Warren Hastings had been aware of the need for a Domesday
Book and had made a start; but in fact the task required a very
large team of experts working continuously for a long period and
neither the trained personnel nor the requisite time were available.
On the other hand a decision of some sort was urgent, for until
it had been taken there could be no security for anyone on the
land, no effective reform of the Revenue Department, and no prospect of reviving the country's prosperity. And so arose the famous
argument between Shore, the expert, and Cornwallis, the practical
administrator. Both agreed that the assessment of each *Zemindari*
must be moderate and, once determined, must stand for a long
period: only so could the holder be encouraged to sink capital in

---

[244] See 'Minute of the Governor-General', 10 Feb., 1790. *Ibid.*, vol II, App.
XXXII, pp. 463-78. Also printed in *State Papers: Cornwallis*, ed. Forrest, vol. II,
pp. 84-116.

improvements, foster productivity, and (it was intended) be compelled to abide by equitable agreements with the ryots. But Shore argued for security and revision after ten years. By that time much fuller information would be available and the whole system could be improved by adjustments made in the light of further experience.

Cornwallis, on the other hand, insisted that the settlement between Government and land-holders must be permanent and irrevocable. Ten years might seem a long time, but the conduct of the zemindar towards talukdars and ryots would be constantly influenced by the thought that when the time came his assessment would be reviewed and might be considerably increased if the value of the land had been raised. As an administrator responsible for a country which had been heavily drained of its wealth, while its chief wealth-producing agency, agriculture, had been driven into decay by maladministration, Cornwallis was determined to bring about a great revival by giving the man in charge of the land a security that would be absolute. The zemindars, as a class, were notoriously spendthrift, short-sighted, and oppressive, but Cornwallis was convinced that by this means he could both ensure their loyalty and turn them into good agriculturists.

The stubborn argument was referred home for decision; and, as is well known, Pitt and Dundas closeted themselves at Wimbledon for ten days in order to study the issue undisturbed. It may be doubted whether they fully understood all the implications even then; but in any case their decision in favour of Cornwallis and against Shore was a foregone conclusion. From Dundas's own Resolutions of 1783 onwards every measure brought before Parliament relative to India had advocated 'permanency' as the great *desideratum*, which was natural enough in a parliament of landowners who thought in terms of freehold, land tax, and rent.

The case for and against the Perpetual Settlement has been a subject of long controversy among historians of India and need not detain us here. The arrangement achieved its principal purpose in reviving the prosperity of Bengal, turning it into the most flourishing region in the sub-continent. The price paid for that great achievement was heavy. The freezing of the land revenue deprived future Governments in Bengal of the main resource for meeting growing community needs and necessitated heavier taxation elsewhere to fill the gap, while the Bengal land-holders 'sat pretty' and reaped an ever increasing harvest of dues.[245] Perhaps the chief defect was the failure to give adequate recognition and protection to the status of the ryot. In his regulations Cornwallis made some

---

[245] The total annual sum to be paid by the zemindars amounted to £3,750,000, while by the early years of the 20th century they were receiving in 'rents' more than £13 million. P. E. Roberts, *History of British India*, 3rd edn., Oxford, 1952, p. 230.

provision for the safeguarding of their interests, but he relied on the Courts, which became choked with litigation and ineffective for the purpose. The settlement was between Government and zemin-dars alone: the inclusion in it of the ryot's *pottahs* (specifying monetary obligations and customary rights) would have given them a similar permanent security. As it was, they had to fight their own battles with the zemindars and frequently with unhappy results for themselves. Yet the inclusion of this host of complicated local contracts in one comprehensive settlement was beyond the capacity of the administration, apart from the extremely long delay that would have ensued. The verdict of the historian, P. E. Roberts, seems incontrovertible:

Had the Permanent Settlement but been postponed for another ten or twenty years, the capacities of the land would have been better ascertained. Many mistakes and anomalies would have been avoided, and the reforms brought about by Cornwallis himself in the civil service would have trained up a class of officials far more competent to deal with so vast and intricate a subject.[246]

To that Cornwallis would undoubtedly have replied that the postponement of a permanent arrangement would have involved postponing the revival of Bengal's prosperity, and this he could not contemplate, for the wellbeing of the people, the loyalty of the zemindar class, and the finances of the East India Company all depended upon it.

The Governor-General had also been required to establish permanent rules for the administration of justice, 'founded on the ancient laws and local usages of the country'. To establish courts which would apply customary law and be beyond the influence of bribery or intimidation was, of course, no less fundamental than the formation of an honest civil service and an orderly revenue system. Fortunately in this highly technical field Cornwallis had little more to do than put the finishing touches to the work already done by Hastings.[247] Two pyramids of courts, civil and criminal, were constructed, with village tribunals at the base, and ascending through district and provincial courts to the civil court of appeal (*Sadr Diwani Adalat*) and to the court of appeal in criminal causes (*Sadr Nizamat Adalat*). And the first fruits of a further project which Hastings had initiated was produced in the form of a detailed Code of Regulations, compiled by George Barlow, for the guidance of officials in the new judical system: a forerunner of the great Penal Code, which may perhaps prove to be one of the more durable monuments to the short-lived British *raj* in India.

---

[246] This author provides an excellent summary of the pros and cons. *Ibid.*, pp. 228-31.

[247] See pp. 74-75 above.

A comparison between the situation after 1786 when a supreme Governor-General managed affairs in intimate consultation with a *de facto* secretary of state for Indian affairs and the Prime Minister, while the Court of Directors – no longer subservient to the Proprietors – acted on the whole as obedient agents, and the situation of twenty years before indicates the magnitude of the revolution which had been gradually effected. Clive's acquisition of revenue management in Bengal and neighbouring areas and the establishment of a similar, though less formal, financial control in the Carnatic had enabled the Company's employees to establish a lawless *imperium* of their own, the resources of which were employed to 'storm the closet' at East India House and to establish a body of 'Nabobs' Friends' at Westminster, who were not only a serious nuisance, but whose operations induced something akin to obsession over the danger of Indian wealth and patronage being used to over-set the balance of the constitution.

And so began the long, confused and hesitant attempts of the State to suppress an overseas revolt which had penetrated the precincts of Parliament and frequently thwarted the efforts of the State by playing the Opposition groups against the Government. During these twenty years much more than a problem of discipline was involved, and the experience gained exerted a deeply formative influence upon later policy in this and other parts of the world.

The swing of commercial interest to the markets of the East, already described in the present work,[248] received a tremendous reinforcement when India, hitherto a disappointing market, became through the medium of Indian textiles a financial reservoir. The realisation that, as such, the British territories were in imminent danger of being ruined forced the issue and brought the Commons to accept even the drastic and unorthodox scheme of Fox and Burke and afterwards a House very differently composed acquiesced, though without enthusiasm, in Pitt's Board of Control.

That the imposition of just and orderly government in India had become a necessity in the national interest and that jobbery had become insufferably injurious to it afforded a salutary lesson which held far-reaching consequences for the future. Alongside economic self-interest was a genuine indignation which slowly rose to the level of a sense of moral responsibility.

These two motives, so often interwoven, compelled Ministers, administrators in India, and to some extent Parliament at home, to grapple with the intricate problems involved in grafting British ideas of law and government upon alien institutions which only a few specialists understood. The question thus forced upon public attention was how far British administrative penetration should

---

[248] See vol. I, Chaps. II, III, and IV.

proceed. All without exception agreed with the official abjuration of wars of conquest: they ate up revenue and were apt to set up a dangerous chain reaction. But how far should the British stand forth as rulers in their own right, discarding the fiction of being mere feudatories on sufferance, and how deeply should 'direct' rule be injected in the Presidencies? At once a cleavage of opinion arose. Hastings, Dundas, and Cornwallis, each in his own way was an 'imperialist' who viewed the future of British influence and power in India in the grand manner, although they differed as to methods. Dundas, for example, would have declared British sovereignty and relegated the Company to the position of a non-monopolistic trading corporation, while Cornwallis (and the majority of his generation) thought it wiser that the Company should continue to manage Indian affairs on an agency basis while the State exercised a discreet supervision in the background. But the 'imperialists' were in no doubt that the protection of Britain's interests and of native welfare alike required the exercise of direct British rule.

On the other hand, there were those, such as Burke and Francis (a man with a strain of idealism in the welter of his venom), who saw British intervention as a plague of locusts, inevitably and always, and fought to restrict it within the narrowest possible limits. Leave the zemindars and talukdars, benign country gentlemen, in peace: trust them to manage and care for their local ryots as in the golden prime of Akbar, and all would be well. These violently divergent reactions were to appear again and again in the 19th century in different forms, circumstances, and places, for they were symptomatic of the make-up of the British people. Historians have tended too long to regard British administrative experience in India as operating in a closed circuit.

Clive had riveted attention upon India. The financial prospects which he had held out appeared to fit so well into the developing pattern of trade expansion in the vast markets beyond the Indian Ocean and to be dazzling compensation for the loss of a colonial empire in North America. Indeed if anything like the amount of parliamentary time and committee work had been devoted to the Western problem as was given to Indian questions during these years, it is just conceivable that a *modus vivendi* with an independent America might have been reached.

Henry Dundas had little in common with Warren Hastings, but they were at one in regarding a revived and effectively defended Bengal as a source of wealth and power, strategically situated between the industries of Britain and the markets of the North and South Pacific.

CHAPTER IV
PITT'S ADMINISTRATIVE METHODS AND OVERSEAS AFFAIRS

GOVERNANCE in India was one of a group of problems, including those of Ireland, the American Colonies and Canada, which simultaneously confronted politicians at Westminster. Between the American and the Irish demands for political and economic self-determination there was a significant interaction; and both of these challenges were very much in the minds of statesmen when they found themselves obliged to review the problem of governance in Canada.

The demand by an enclave in Ireland, British in origin, to supersede the metropolitan authority as the rulers of an alien people and the British reactions to that challenge have been considered in the previous volume of this work.[1] Parallel with that and coincidental with it, though set in very different conditions, was the problem, which we have now examined, of a defiant British trading community in India which had acquired territorial jurisdiction within the 'Pale' of the three Presidencies. The resolution of this dilemma not only involved the imposition of a system of State control over a chartered company and the formation of a disciplined civil service, but it also impelled Ministers to formulate basic principles relating to customary law, religious toleration, land tenure, taxation, and local government, under which all Indians resident in British-controlled territories would in future be ruled. The esoteric conditions prevailing in the Asian subcontinent, which remained a closed book at home to all but a few initiates, has induced a tendency to treat the British position in India as *sui generis*. Yet the principles worked out in British India in later years exerted a profound though unobtrusive influence over administrative policy in South-East Asia and Africa.

In our own time the emergence of a Commonwealth in which many races have equal status has forced us out of the 19th-century habit of thinking in terms of geographical compartments and has

---

[1] The habit of treating the history of Ireland as part of the domestic history of Britain by reason of geographical proximity and because Irish representatives temporarily sat at Westminster and agitated British politics by their demands, dies hard. Perhaps the emergence of a Republic of Ireland outside the membership of the Commonwealth and a Government of Northern Ireland which, while being part of the United Kingdom, enjoys a form of internal responsible government not dissimilar to that proposed by Lord Durham for Canada, may induce us Anglo-Saxons (the Scots and Welsh are not so complaisant) to see the history of Anglo-Irish relations in a more realistic perspective.

compelled us to recognise the wide interpenetration of ideas which has occurred. For the statesmen of the late 18th century who did so much to shape the Second Empire, such ideas were either non-existent or still in embryo, but they too looked at the Empire comprehensively although from a different standpoint. In that period the executive machine was so small, and executive authority under Pitt's leadership was so highly concentrated, that the same few minds were occupied simultaneously with the entire range of overseas affairs. In consequence there was close co-ordination of effort.

The rehabilitation of the national economy and the release of Britain's great industrial potential, long thwarted by political confusion, corruption, and the drain of war, was Pitt's prime objective; and his success in this depended in large measure upon the expansion of British exports. Accordingly he and his close associates worked to produce conditions overseas that would be best calculated to promote that end. The chief requisites were: an efficient, soundly financed, system of oceanic defence, the provision of reliable and acceptable forms of government where territorial jurisdiction was necessary and unavoidable, and above all the development of new markets and sources of primary materials in distant continents. In all this there was a strong element of central planning and direction.

Pitt's conception of imperial defence was that of a common pool to which all the territorial units contributed, but centrally directed from London in accordance with overall strategic and diplomatic requirements. An Irish contribution to the general defence of the Empire, it will be recalled, was the essential *quid pro quo* which Pitt tried so hard to secure in return for reciprocal commercial concessions. In the same period Pitt and Dundas asserted metropolitan control over diplomatic relations and the use of the armed forces in India (paid for out of Indian revenues), although they failed in the secondary object of merging King's and Company's regiments into a unified army under the Crown. And Dundas as Secretary of State for Home, Colonial, Irish, and Indian affairs, did his best to elicit contributions to their own defence from West Indian legislatures.

In matters of overseas government Pitt's team aimed at reliability as a metropolitan requisite, and acceptability on the part of the governed. For British India the instrument was a bureaucracy, operating under a supreme but responsible executive officer and giving full recognition to local institutions and custom. For 'Western' Communities the dual requirement was met by 'assimilation' to the parent constitution, that is to say, the reproduction of its equipoise between executive power, aristocratic restraint, and the representation of the commonalty, thus avoiding the unbalance which had enabled American extremists to gain the mastery.

From this point of view Dundas, under Pitt's supervision, strove to persuade the Anglo-Irish aristocracy to save themselves from the menace of Jacobinism by taking the Catholic aristocracy into partnership; and when that idea was furiously rejected Pitt decided to carry 'assimilation' to its logical extreme by bringing the Irish to Westminster. In his turn William Grenville (himself prominent at the India Board and formerly Vice-President of the Board of Trade) similarly sought to reproduce the true image of the British constitution in Canada as the only means of preventing a repetition of the American catastrophe.

Finally, and comprehending all else in their estimation, was the great task of repairing and developing the national economy by promoting trade expansion in new Continents. On the first and urgent question as to what was to be done about trade relations with the Americans, there was a difference of approach. Pitt and Grenville, following the ideas of Shelburne, were disposed to continue most of their colonial privileges on a reciprocal basis, for they were good customers as well as kinsmen, even though they were becoming serious competitors in the Indian and Pacific Oceans. Charles Jenkinson at the Board of Trade, on the other hand, was more attached to the traditional policy in respect of aliens, and steadily opposed reciprocity whenever it was mooted, whether with the Irish, the French, Dutch, or Americans. These last were formidable, and he wished to keep them out of the West Indies and the carrying trade as much as possible: they would buy British manufactures anyway – or so Sheffield and others assured him. In negotiating the Anglo-American settlement of 1793, known as Jay's Treaty, Grenville, as Foreign Secretary, made considerable concessions, though not enough to satisfy American demands. But on the general issue of extending the empire of trade Pitt and his three associates – Dundas, Grenville and Jenkinson – were at one. While Dundas as controller of the East India Company's regional monopoly was behind every important commercial enterprise in Far Eastern waters, Jenkinson was managing director of the rest.

These and related enterprises will be recounted in the chapters that follow; but before doing so it will be worth while to take a look at the administrative machine which Pitt established. Even without such direction the penetration of distant seas would, of course, have continued, for the work of the Georgian navigators had revealed the potentialities of the Pacific and the routes thereto, and there was the growing impulsion of new industrial energy and inventiveness. But it was unusual for a British Administration to take the lead in such matters: normally Ministers were content to wait until they were pushed. When, therefore, initiative and selective support were afforded by governmental agencies, it is clearly important to appreciate how they functioned.

When Pitt at last agreed to accept office in December, 1783, the personnel of the Cabinet which he was able to assemble was exceptionally weak. This was due to the deep political confusion attending the break-up of the North régime which had been accentuated by the subsequent split in the Rockingham Administration and the fall of Shelburne. When the first offer to Pitt had been promptly and wisely declined, the King tried to avert a Fox-North alliance by reconstituting a North Administration with Dundas, Jenkinson and Thurlow as the principal Ministers, and when that proved impracticable he reluctantly approached the Portland-Fox Whigs. His misgivings were confirmed when Portland stiffly insisted that the Sovereign must first accept a party policy and that Ministers, being collectively responsible, would resign in a body if and when confidence was withdrawn. This was a concept of the constitution which George III always denounced as subversive and indecent, and the negotiation terminated abruptly.

Pitt was again approached and again declined, but this time after considerable hesitation. Upon his refusal the King angrily surrendered and the Fox-North coalition was admitted to office. It seems that Pitt had hoped for a Whig reunion which would have put him, theoretically at any rate, in an unassailable position; but he was not prepared to be too dependent on royal support with its consequential limitation of policy. His fixed intention was to stand forth as the inaugurator of a new and more wholesome era in national affairs. He was now working in close consultation with his cousins, Lord Temple and William Grenville, and they had privately assured the King of their readiness to rescue him from the Coalition as soon as a suitable opportunity offered.[2]

The manœuvres which took place during the summer and autumn months of 1783 reveal what in Pitt's estimation was at stake. When the Coalition had been broken, as was intended, what sort of political system would be substituted? A united Whig Ministry pledged to moderate reform and a continued limitation of Court influence, or a return to the system of which North had been the unhappy instrument?

In May Pitt demonstrated his position for the edification of the King, on the one side, and the Foxites on the other by moving Resolutions in the Commons for a very moderate reform of Parliament, and he took the opportunity of delivering a forthright attack on the secret influence which, he said, was 'sapping the very foundations of liberty by corruption'. In July Thurlow invited

---

[2] J. Fortescue (ed.), *Correspondence of George III*, vol. VI, pp. 306-7.

him to dinner and made cautious soundings, particularly with reference to Crown influence. Afterwards Pitt informed Temple that he had responded by saying that he was personally pledged to support a measure of parliamentary reform 'on every seasonable occasion' and that any idea of extending the influence of the Crown 'on the foundation of the old politics of the Court' was out of the question, although such means as were fairly in the hands of Ministers could undoubtedly be exerted.

The Grenvilles as representing one of the great Whig houses had no particular enthusiasm for reform as such, but they recognised that the young leader's views, which had a political value, should be conciliated: they were also aware that the gesture could be cheaply made since 'seasonable occasions' for making any alterations of importance in parliamentary representation were unlikely to occur. Commenting on the reported interview with Thurlow, Temple agreed that Pitt was pledged to parliamentary reform, but he added (and underlined the words): *whenever there is a reasonable prospect of success*. As to Thurlow's soundings about the use of Crown influence Temple was categoric: 'we cannot be too explicit in our refusal to engage in government upon the avowed or implied system of replacing in the hands of the Crown that influence which has been already taken from it.' He concluded with the observation that the King now realised that he could not replace the Coalition by patching up the old system under North, Thurlow and Gower and that the Pitt-Grenville group was in fact 'his only resource', but that the King and Thurlow were trying to bring them round as nearly as possible to their own ideas. If Pitt stood firm, said Temple, the game could not succeed. To the King himself Temple advised delay in order to give time for the unpopularity of the Fox-North combination to take effect.

From Pitt's point of view the ideal solution would have been a union of Whig groups under his own leadership. Failing that he was ready to take office as the political heir of Chatham and Shelburne, a moderate reformer who would not press his views unseasonably. As such he could hope to attract deserters from the Foxites without forfeiting the necessary support of the King's friends. But he would not be a King's man dependent upon Court favour.

When the Coalition was dismissed and Pitt took office in December with the support of a minority, George III pressed for a quick dissolution on the strength of Robinson's calculation that the return of the Ministry with a majority of about 180 could be confidently expected. But Pitt very sensibly held off. The King had never lost a general election; and North had enjoyed (if that is the right word) a similar majority. In any case, given time, a considerable thinning of the shaken ranks of Fox and North could be expected, and Pitt proceeded to use the interval in making one more effort to induce Portland and Fox to join him in establishing a comprehensive Whig administration.

The King could not well prohibit his chosen Minister from seeking to attract additional support, but the prospect of Egyptian bondage if Pitt succeeded was a nightmare. The tact and shrewdness which George III displayed during this ordeal has been admirably portrayed elsewhere.[3] His handling of the situation was exactly right because he understood politicians. He rightly gauged Pitt's haughty reaction when Portland and Fox insisted that a Minister in a minority must first become respectable by resigning and curtly rejected Pitt's demand that the partnership should be negotiated on 'equal' terms. The experienced monarch salved the wounded pride of this son who exhibited all of his father's unquestioning sense of destiny by setting alongside Portland's arrogance (which he himself had tasted), royal courtesy and patience.

The Foxites had missed a wonderful opportunity, though whether a Ministry of all the Whig talents would have cohered for long may perhaps be doubted. The general election of 1784 took place and George III was very busy and spent money which he could ill afford. The anticipated victory was achieved, but the result was substantially a vote of censure upon North and Fox and of support for an injured monarch. There was admiration for the courage and brilliance of Chatham's son; but he had not, of course, been returned at the head of a coherent – and still less of a reforming – party. A succession of political humiliations was to teach him that. The measure of his disappointment is perhaps indicated by the relentless rancour with which he pursued Fox over the Westminster Scrutiny, which was not in character, and by his hypersensitivity when accused of being the creature of secret influence. 'I know of no secret influence,' he once burst out. 'I hope that my own integrity would be my guardian against that danger. This is the only answer I shall ever deign to make to such a charge.'[4]

On the other hand, he was aware that circumstances had made him indispensable to the Sovereign. A weapon was at hand although it could not be too frequently used. Furthermore he was supremely confident that his gifts and complete self-dedication would establish and sustain him as the nation's leader. When experience taught

---

[3] D. G. Barnes, *George III and William Pitt*, 1783-1806, Chap. III.

[4] Earl Stanhope, *Life of William Pitt* (Lond., 1861), vol. I, p. 171. This emotional overtone was very noticeable, for example, when he was reproached in Jan., 1784, for not taking a more prominent part in supporting a petition for parliamentary reform. If he had done so, he retorted, he would have given an opportunity to the Opposition to cry out that he had presumed to pollute with defiled hands the fair petition of the people, 'that he, the creature of secret influence, had dared to interfere when there was a question of a measure which was to root influence out of that House'. (*Parl. Hist.*, vol. XXIV, 350.)

him that there were strict limits in certain directions beyond which
he would not be followed, he accepted the fact philosophically (to
the grief of friends like Wilberforce), not because he had grown
cynical, but because his predestined guardianship of the nation's
welfare was so much more important.

As for George III he had good reason to be well satisfied with
his bargain. He had escaped the yoke of a Whig dictatorship, and
he had secured the services of one who gave every promise of being
able to maintain political stability (which he longed for) and to
promote economic recovery. The young man's leanings towards
reform were perhaps a little disquieting, and on one occasion the
King took the precaution of letting his sentiments on the subject
be known among Pitt's colleagues by means of a private letter to
Lord Sydney.[5] Thurlow as Lord Chancellor was a useful curb in
Cabinet and in the Lords: the second line of Crown defence if the
dykes broke in the Commons. The King had not been able to
bring Pitt and the Grenvilles as close to his own ideas of a 'system'
as he would have liked, but he was shrewd enough to appreciate
that the heterogeneous character of the Ministry and of its body of
supporters in Parliament had provided the coach with a very
efficient brake. Pitt would learn.

He did so learn, and sacrificed a number of cherished hopes in
the process; but he also achieved an unforeseen degree of authority
as the head of the Administration. In the changed political circumstances this was almost bound to have happened, but the King's
health was a supplementary factor. In February, 1789, after
recovering from his first mental attack he wrote to Pitt:

I must decline entering into a pressure of business, and indeed for
the rest of my life shall expect others to fulfill the Duties of their
Employments, and only keep that superintending Eye which can be
effected without labour or fatigue.[6]

As the years went by the mutual respect of these two men, so
utterly different in background and temperament, deepened. Each
recognised in the other a fellow professional. For them politics
was the breath of life and not just an exciting or lucrative hobby,
and the management of the State's affairs was their reason for
existence. Pitt was as miserable when Addington temporarily took
over as George himself would have been if he had ever carried
out his threats to retire to Hanover.

It is against this background that Pitt's ministerial arrangements,
which greatly influenced the direction of overseas affairs, should
be considered. The Ministry which took office in December, 1783,
and resumed with very few changes after the general election, was

---

[5] The King to Sydney, 19 March, 1785. 8 a.m., *Royal Archives, Windsor.*
[6] The King to Pitt, 23 Feb., 1789. *Pitt Papers*, P.R.O. 8/30/103.

very similar to the Shelburne Administration – but without Shelburne.[7] It included some elderly Chathamites, a few of Pitt's personal friends of his own generation, and some of the old guard who normally looked to the throne for guidance. Of the seven members of Cabinet only Pitt himself was in the Commons. Thurlow was in again as Lord Chancellor almost as of right. The Foreign Secretary was Lord Carmarthen, 'elegant Carmarthen' as Wilberforce dubbed him, modest and well liked by the foreign envoys, but sadly ignorant of European affairs. 'Not an enterprising Minister' was the verdict of John Adams, the American representative. 'Tommy' Townshend, Lord Sydney, returned to the Home and Imperial Secretaryship which he had held under Shelburne, but his limited capacity proved unequal to the immense volume and diversity of business of that overcharged office. Charles Pratt, Earl Camden, a follower of Chatham, who as President of the Council had given Shelburne somewhat wavering support, also resumed his former office. He had never been a decisive character, and he was now seventy years of age and frail. These, with Earl Gower as Privy Seal and Earl Howe at the Admiralty, made up a very mediocre Cabinet team. Apart from Pitt himself, the only member with a forceful personality and ability as a debater was Lord Thurlow, and he soon became a source of dissension. Pitt was allergic alike to his rudeness, his open contempt for any sort of reform, and to his position in the Cabinet as the royal watchdog. He seems to have consulted the Lord Chancellor as little as possible, and the latter retaliated with gibes at Government measures and men which finally became insufferable. Not a very hopeful team for the inauguration of a new era in national affairs.[8]

There was administrative talent on the Government side in the Commons, but for various reasons the persons concerned could not immediately be raised to Cabinet rank. Henry Dundas, Lord Advocate for Scotland, had hoped to become the first Secretary of State for India, but he had to be content for the nonce with the

---

[7] For various reasons Pitt was right to drop Shelburne, and the latter was content to retire to Bowood; but there was no excuse for Pitt's shabby behaviour towards his former chief who had pressed Pitt's claim upon the King to be his successor. It was not until the Duke of Rutland, a personal friend of Pitt, had made a vigorous protest against the omission to provide any mark of recognition of Shelburne's great achievements in negotiating the peace treaties that Pitt proposed that he be raised to the rank of marquis, and even then his dilatoriness was markedly discourteous. (See Fitzmaurice, Life of Shelburne, vol. III, pp. 417-26.)

[8] Cf. William Eden to Morton Eden, 29 July, 1785. 'The course and conduct of this Business [Ireland] has shewn that Mr. Pitt possesses infinite Talents and much political Courage; but it has also shewn that his Ministry has no efficient men belonging to it in any of the efficient Offices except Himself and the Chancellor . . . it is very unpleasant to any man of spirit to stand at the Head of such a system, and I do not suppose that He can long bear it with much Patience.' (Auckland Papers, Addit. MSS., 34,420, f. 57.) The method which he adopted to meet this situation will be considered in the present chapter.

Treasurership of the Navy and with being unofficial head of the India Board. Seven years later he became Home and Imperial Secretary, but Sydney had had the prior claim.

There was also Charles Jenkinson, a first-rate 'man of business'. In 1784 there was evidently strong pressure from Thurlow and others to bring him into the Cabinet.[9] But the Opposition was already making a great play with the argument that Pitt was a creature of the Court, and Jenkinson was notorious as having been the managing director of Court influence. A compromise was reached (which profoundly affected the character of British overseas commercial policy) by appointing him in March, 1784, as the leading member of the new Committee of the Privy Council for Trade and Plantations.

The third person of whom Pitt was to make great use in the future was his cousin, William Wyndham Grenville. Yet here again there were good reasons why his advance had to be gradual. He was twenty-four years old, the same age as Pitt, and his only experience of office had been as Chief Secretary for Ireland in 1782-3 under his brother, Lord Temple; and it was perhaps not irrelevant to the situation that the latter had withdrawn from the Government, after holding the seals as Secretary of State for three days, under threat of impeachment for his intervention in the Lords.[10] William Grenville was appointed joint Paymaster-General and was brought in as a member of the India Board and of the Committee for Trade, becoming Vice-President of the latter body two years later.

Pitt inherited an administrative system which had fallen into serious confusion under the combined stress of war and political upheaval. Lord North had frequently complained in his distressful way that the Departments had developed the habit of taking their several courses with scant reference to himself or to each other and that he had neither the time nor the aptitude to remedy the situation. Then drastic and necessary cuts had been applied during the Rockingham and Shelburne Ministries, but neither had survived long enough to follow up administrative reductions with rationalisation.

As soon as Pitt was firmly in the saddle he was faced with issues which had lost none of their difficulty from being fended off. The national economy had been strained and its latent power needed release and encouragement. The future relations of Britain with self-governing Ireland and independent America involved the

---

[9] ' I take it for granted the struggle is to get Jenkinson into the Cabinet.' Shelburne to Barré, Nov., 1784. Printed in Fitzmaurice, *Shelburne*, vol. III, p. 424. The pressure was eventually successful. See below, p. 240, n. 27.

[10] The evidence in the *Dropmore* papers makes it clear that Temple resigned to save the Administration from embarrassment, and not of resentment.

settlement of unprecedented problems. The British position in India demanded detailed and expert administrative control. And in foreign affairs Britain stood isolated while Anglo-French rivalry had not abated.

To deal efficiently with such a concatenation required an integrated team of able administrators and the Cabinet of 1784 did not contain the material. Gradually the men whom Pitt needed were promoted to the key positions, but the process took time. It was not until June, 1789, that Sydney was given the hint and thankfully resigned in favour of Grenville, receiving a viscountcy and a pension of £2,500 a year. In 1791 Grenville handed over to Dundas,[11] while he himself replaced Carmarthen at the Foreign Office where he remained for ten years. An attempt to get rid of Thurlow in 1789 failed in face of the King's stubborn and pathetic resistance, but an ultimatum from Pitt in 1792 finally secured his removal. Thereafter Grenville, who had been raised to the peerage in the previous year, led for the Government in the Lords.

Meanwhile Pitt himself had been virtually directing foreign policy and at the Treasury was remodelling the national finances and the fiscal system. And in order to rebuild the strength of the navy under his personal direction he replaced Lord Howe at the Admiralty in 1788 with his own brother, Chatham. 'This circumstance,' wrote Dundas, 'gives a wonderful cement of strength and power to Mr. Pitt's Government by connecting the Treasury and Admiralty so closely together.'[12] Thus within about six years an inner Cabinet had been formed, consisting of three men who between them controlled every important aspect of government and who worked – indeed almost lived – together. No such centralised direction of affairs had been achieved since the early days of the elder Pitt.

Yet the 'Triumvirate' had been in effective operation before the entry of Grenville and Dundas into the Cabinet. Their co-operation with Pitt began with his assumption of office. The methods employed (outside the formal Cabinet) are of particular relevance to the conduct of British policy overseas during the formative period between the wars. In fact the lines of emphasis in that policy and the manner of its implementation cannot otherwise be accurately appreciated.

The circumstances in which a new executive instrument was created for the management of commercial and colonial affairs

---

[11] Pitt had hoped to include Lord Cornwallis (Sydney's cousin) in his select group of Ministers on completing his term as Governor-General, and in 1791 he suggested to Cornwallis that he might succeed Dundas in the Home Department; but he decided that he lacked the gifts of a politician and courteously declined. (See Sydney to Cornwallis, 16 June, 1791, and Cornwallis to Pitt. 23 Jan., 1792. *Cornwallis Corr.*, vol. II, pp. 143-5.)

[12] Dundas to Cornwallis, 13 July, 1788. *Ibid.*, vol. I, p. 406.

were exceptional. In addition to the problem of India Pitt had inherited from Fox the vexed question of future relations with America. Were the ships and cargoes of the former Colonies to be treated as alien or be given special status privilege? The American Intercourse Bill, planned by Shelburne and introduced in March, 1783, by Pitt, had been shelved by the Coalition; but Fox had sent David Hartley to Paris and had supported his efforts to meet the wishes of the American Commissioners for an Anglo-American commercial treaty on a basis of reciprocity. Then organised pressure at home had obliged the Coalition to reverse its policy with the Order in Council of 2 July.

In November Pitt had called upon the Government to produce 'a complete commercial system suited to the novelty of our situation'. That was easily said, but after he had taken office the new Ministry was warned that any attempt to readmit American shipping into the West Indian carrying trade would be met with formidable resistance. Pitt decided to fall back on the procedure which Fox had contemplated, that is to say, an official enquiry at which the various interests involved could state their case.[13]

There was, however, the practical difficulty that no machinery appropriate for the purpose was in being. In 1782 Burke's Act had abolished the Colonial Secretaryship and the Board of Trade and Plantations which had existed in varying forms since 1668. Responsibility for the remaining Colonies had been transferred to the Home Department and the work of the Board had been distributed among committees of the Privy Council.[14] The adjustment of trade relations between the Empire and the United States was urgent in itself and the decisions taken would determine to a considerable degree the future character of the shrunken colonial system. Moreover the state of the national economy required a planned direction of external trade as a whole.

Burke's Act had included a provision that the work of the old Board of Trade and Plantations might be undertaken by a special committee of the Privy Council and in March, 1784, Pitt acted upon it. For various reasons he moved cautiously, making it clear that the institution of the new committee was tentative and provisional.[15] The previous body, consisting of eight salaried members of parliament and some *ex officio* members, had been more interested (according to Burke) in patronage than the national interest. Certainly its proceedings had been leisurely and mechanical, con-

---

[13] For an account of Anglo-American commercial affairs in 1783 see vol. I, Chap. IX of this work.

[14] See C. M. Andrews, *Guide to the Materials for American History to 1783 in the P.R.O.* (Washington, 1912), vol. I, pp. 100-3.

[15] Cf. A. L. Lingelbach, ' The Inception of the British Board of Trade ' (*Am. Hist. Rev.*, vol. XXX, July, 1925, p. 708).

cerned with the application of established regulations. A changed
and changing situation called for a policy-forming instrument of
high quality, but unfortunately good and eligible material was
scanty.

Even so, the personnel of this pilot Committee was odd. Most of
the Privy Councillors who were summoned to it were distinguished
only in their titles and many who attended the inaugural meeting
on 5 March were rarely seen there again.[16] Pitt himself for obvious
reasons kept out of it (until 1786): Dundas and Grenville were
included, and so was Charles Jenkinson. Dundas had consistently
advocated a policy of sensible generosity towards the Americans,
and Grenville was of similar mind. On the other hand, Jenkinson
from the beginning of the American disputes had been implacable
and vindictive. In matters of trade regulation (as in all else) he was
a strict traditionalist. No formal chairman of the committee was
nominated, but Jenkinson at once took the lead, as was probably
intended and as Dundas was to do at the India Board six months
later. The outcome of an investigation into the American question
under the direction of Jenkinson was almost a foregone conclusion.
Why was he selected?

His past reputation as the manager of Court influence made him
a political liability and he had not been included in the Ministry.
The influence of his ally, Thurlow, who pushed him strongly and
successfully at a later stage, may have helped to secure this foothold for him; but the principal reason seems to have been that Pitt
recognised his value as a first-rate administrator with an exceptional knowledge of commercial affairs.

The decision was highly significant. Pitt must have known well
enough that he was introducing an awkward element into what
would probably become a key situation, but he was clearly prepared
to pay the price in order to obtain efficient service. The stiffening
of public opinion over America was unmistakable, and when the
Committee after a thorough and well-conducted investigation lasting three months reported in favour of maintaining the principles

---

[16] The members were: the Earls of Aylesford, Effingham, and Clarendon, Lord
Frederick Campbell, Viscount Howe (added 8 March), the Bishop of London, Lord
de Ferrars, Lords Grantham, Walsingham, Grantley, Sydney, the Honble. Thos.
Harley, Sir Joseph Yorke, Charles Jenkinson, Sir John Goodricke (added 8 March),
Henry Dundas, James Grenville, W. W. Grenville. The following were added later:
Lord Mulgrave (11 June), William Eden (9 Dec., 1785), William Pitt (1 Jan., 1786)
and Lord Carmarthen (13 Jan., 1786). The original Committee had no staff of its
own, but the services of two Privy Council clerks, Stephen Cottrell and William
Fawkener, and of Grey Elliott, Under-Secretary at the Plantation Bureau (a one-man
sub-department established by Shelburne and attached to the Home Department)
were made available. (*B.T.* 5/1, p. 1; cf. correspondence by these three officials
in *B.T.* 3/1.) Grey Elliott's letters cease in the summer of 1787 and he evidently died
within a few months (see H. T. Manning, *British Colonial Government after the
American Revolution, 1732-1820* (Yale and Oxford, 1933), p. 76). Cottrell and
Fawkener served the Committee for Trade for many years.

of the Navigation Acts without modification, Pitt acquiesced,[17] and when approached by John Adams, the American Minister, he declined to re-open the question. David Hartley was recalled from Paris, and when that inveterate optimist disobeyed and hung on there during the summer months in a last effort to salvage something of his hopes of a commercial treaty, he was curtly dismissed.

It may well be that Pitt underestimated the tenacity of Jenkinson and the power that gradually accrued to him as the recognised spokesman for British merchants and industrialists. Nor could he have foreseen that Jenkinson would be able to thwart his wishes in certain aspects of the Anglo-French commercial treaty and even more so in the subsequent negotiations about maritime relations with Holland. Nonetheless one gets the clear impression that Pitt did not rue his bargain. It was characteristic of him that he was prepared to consolidate his selected team by modifying or even abandoning lines of policy to which he was personally attached.

Having submitted their report on Anglo-American trade in June, the Committee settled down to the wide range of commercial and colonial business previously undertaken by the old Board. It included diverse subjects: the review of colonial legislation, the constitution of New Brunswick upon its separation from Nova Scotia, the establishment of Anglican bishoprics in Canada, quit rents in Jamaica, a tussle with the Barbados Assembly over fees, the Newfoundland fishery and its trade connexions with the United States. The relevant documents were dealt with under reference from the Home Department, and the fact that the Home and Imperial Secretary was a member of the Committee must have done much to obviate the rivalry between the two authorities in colonial affairs which had sometimes arisen in the past.[18] Indeed the prompt dispatch of so much of the colonial business by the Committee must have been a great relief to Sydney and Grey Elliott, his sole assistant on the colonial side.

Having adjudicated on Britain's future trade relations with the United States, this Committee was directed by Pitt to undertake two further investigations. The first related to Ireland and the second to France. It is significant that Pitt took them in that order

---

[17] His acquiescence was not, however, passive. In the Pitt Papers there is an undated memorandum in his handwriting, headed ' Precis – Committee of Trade ' and endorsed ' Observations &c – Mr. Pitt No. 243 '. The document includes a long list of searching questions with page references to relevant passages in the Committee's report concerning the availability and cost of possible Canadian supplies for the West Indian Islands, comparative British and American freight charges, etc. (*Pitt Papers*, P.R.O. 8/30/195).

[18] At a meeting on 11 July, 1787 (when the Board consisted of Hawkesbury, Pitt and Grenville) it was decided that documents relating to colonial government or colonial defence ' should always be transmitted to one of His Majesty's principal Secretaries of State to whose Department it belongs. . . . It may not, however, be improper at the same time to send Copies to this Committee for information of their Lordships.' *B.T.* 5/4, p. 318.

in spite of the fact that the latter had become an urgent issue. In the peace treaty with France, Shelburne and Vergennes had agreed to a stipulation that a further treaty providing for a reciprocal lowering of tariffs must be negotiated within a specified period; but Pitt and Carmarthen had been dragging their feet and Vergennes was now bringing vigorous pressure to bear. Pitt's negative attitude seems to have been partly due to the prevailing mistrust on the British side over France's aggressive moves with regard to Holland, Egypt, and the Indian Ocean.[19] But after the general election was over he became intent on his great plan for bringing Britain and Ireland together in close association. Early in October, 1784, he informed Rutland, the Lord-Lieutenant, of his design 'to give Ireland an almost unlimited communication of commercial advantages' in return for a progressive contribution to imperial defence and what would have amounted to a unified direction in all external affairs. Pitt was ardent for this, and it seems clear that he intended to achieve Anglo-Irish commercial solidarity before making a bargain with France.

The thorough investigation of the Irish question which Jenkinson and the Committee carried out between 29 January and 8 March, 1785, and the sequel, have already been narrated.[20] Jenkinson was all for binding Ireland by specific pledges and limitations; and when Pitt's original Resolutions were met by organised uproar, Jenkinson obligingly prepared a more elaborate set of resolutions which mollified the British manufacturing and shipping interests but were rejected out of hand by the Irish Legislature. After the wreck of his Irish scheme in August Pitt showed himself in no haste to try another fall with the industrialists over France. An immediate difficulty was the need to find an able negotiator to replace Crauford in Paris. At last in the beginning of December William Eden, clever but untrustworthy was induced to leave the ranks of the Opposition and undertake the task. On the 9th he was made a member of the Committee for Trade and four days later the name of Carmarthen, the Foreign Secretary, was added; but it was not until late in January, 1786, that the Committee, with Eden and Carmarthen present, began daily consultations with the merchants and manufacturers. They continued for some two months in an amicable atmosphere and Eden finally departed for Paris at the beginning of April.[21]

---

[19] For the negotiations leading up to the Anglo-French commercial treaty see J. H. Rose, *William Pitt*, Pt. I, Chap. XIV.

[20] In vol. I, Chap. XI, of this work.

[21] See William Eden to Morton Eden, 27 Jan., 1786. 'I write this from the Council Board, where I am at present passing *every* morning, and all the morning, in examinations of merchants and manufacturers upon various branches of commerce.' He did not think it possible to proceed to Paris before early March at the soonest. 'It is some satisfaction, however, that our inquiries go forward pleasantly,

Having carried out three major investigations in the field of international trade, and having taken a firm hold in colonial administration and imperial commerce, the Committee had proved its value. Indeed it had become indispensable as an instrument of government in overseas affairs. In the following July Pitt decided to establish it on a permanent footing. This step formed part of a comprehensive re-organisation of the administrative machine. 'I am just now,' he wrote to his mother, 'in the beginning of some very necessary arrangements to put the business of Government into a form that will admit of more regularity and despatch than has prevailed in some branches of it. The first step is the appointment of a new Committee of Trade, which becomes every day more and more important.'[22]

On 23 August the Committee of 1784 was dissolved and a new Committee of the Privy Council for Trade and Plantations was commissioned. In structure and functions it closely resembled the pre-1782 Board of that name except that its members in that capacity received no salary. Most, though not all, of the members of the previous committee were appointed to the new one, together with Sir Lloyd Kenyon, Master of the Rolls, and Thomas Orde, Chief Secretary for Ireland. In addition many of the chief officers of state were nominated *ex officio*.[23] These were not expected to attend in the normal way, but an individual request for attendance was sent when some particular question was at issue. The Archbishop of Canterbury, for example, was present by request on several occasions when ecclesiastical arrangements in the Canadian Provinces were under consideration. Also included were the Speaker of the Irish House of Commons and any Privy Councillors holding office in Ireland.[24] As an indication of the intended permanence of the

---

and with much liberality and singular good temper among the trading interests.' A constant attender at the Board, he added, was Sir Joseph Yorke. (He continued to be so for several years, although his career as a professional soldier, followed by twenty years at the Hague (1760-1780) as the British representative, were not very strong qualifications.) 'The others,' wrote Eden, 'are Mr. Jenkinson, Mr. Grenville, Lord Mulgrave, Lord Carmarthen, Lord Walsingham, &c., and we sit every day in the week.' (*Auckland Journal and Corr.*, Lond., 1861, vol. I, p. 94.)

[22] Dated 13 July, 1786. Printed in Stanhope, *Life*, vol. I, p. 306. Cf. Pitt to Wilberforce, 23 Sept., 1786. 'I am very glad you like our new Board of Trade, which I have long felt to be one of the most necessary and will be now one of the most efficient departments of Government.' *Private Papers of William Wilberforce*, ed. A. M. Wilberforce, Lond., 1897, pp. 15-17.

[23] These were: The Archbishop of Canterbury, First Lord of the Treasury, First Lord of the Admiralty, the Principal Secretaries of State, the Chancellor, the Under-Treasurer of the Exchequer, the Speaker of the House of Commons, and any Privy Councillor who held the office of Chancellor of the Duchy of Lancaster, Paymaster-General, Treasurer of the Navy, or Master of the Mint.

[24] The purpose of this last provision, as Pitt explained to the Lord-Lieutenant, was to 'establish a regular and easy Communication, which might be of material use on all questions of foreign treaties and other commercial points which extend to both Countries'. Pitt to Rutland, 19 August, 1786. *Pitt-Rutland Corr.* (Lond., 1890), pp. 158-61.

new Board of Trade and Plantations (for such in effect it was) it was provided with its own staff and premises.[25]

The management of this body, which was to take a commanding part in the direction and development of British maritime enterprise, was entrusted to Jenkinson as its first President with William Grenville as his deputy. Shortly before this appointment he had been given the office of Chancellor of the Duchy of Lancaster and had been raised to the peerage as Lord Hawkesbury. The former right-hand man of the King and Lord North had established himself in the camp of the young reformer. Evidently anticipating raised eyebrows on the part of Hester, Dowager Countess of Chatham, her son reported his decision somewhat defensively:

Mr Jenkinson is to preside, with the honour of a peerage. This, I think, will sound a little strange at a distance, and with reference to former ideas; but he has really fairly earned it and attained it at my hands.[26]

Attained *at my hands* and not by way of the royal closet. True enough, but Pitt was sensitive on the point.[27] Sixteen years before, Jenkinson had told Tommy Townshend that he had made his way ' by industry, by attention to duty and by every honourable means I could devise '.[28] For the next fifteen years he applied the same efficient concentration of effort to the wide ramifications of the Board's business and became the acknowledged expert.

The activities of the Board with regard to colonial administration have been described elsewhere.[29] They corresponded closely to those of its predecessor before 1782, although more caution was now shown in dealing with colonial governments, and business was transacted with greater dispatch. The great difference lay in the constructive and aggressive policy which the new Board applied in exploring distant markets and fostering fresh sources of primary products.

---

[25] In addition to Cottrell, Fawkener and Grey Elliott, who were to continue to serve as before, there was an establishment of six clerks – one chief clerk (George Chalmers) at £500 p.a., one clerk at £200, and one at £150, and one at £120, and three at £100; an office keeper at £50, ' one necessary woman ' at £50, and three messengers at £50 each. *B.T.* 5/4, p. 11.

[26] Letter of 13 July, 1786 (*ut supra*).

[27] At the same time it is evident that Thurlow had been pestering Pitt about bringing Jenkinson into the Administration. There had been talk of a push in that direction in 1784 (see p. 233, n. 9 above), and in August, 1785, Loughborough had written to William Eden (both of them being at that time hostile to Pitt): ' It is said that Mr. Jenkinson is to be made a Peer at the desire of the Chancellor who complains that he was so ill supported [in the Lords] . . . if office is added to the Peerage, I think it will hurt Pitt materially . . .' (*Auckland Papers, Addit. MSS.,* 34,420, ff. 87-8). In 1787 there had been further gossip on similar lines.

[28] Quoted, (Sir) L. B. Namier, *The Structure of Politics*, p. 15.

[29] H. T. Manning, *British Colonial Government after the American Revolution,* particularly Chap. III.

Pitt's immediate concern, however, was to use the enhanced authority of the new Board to guide the negotiations with France, now at an advanced stage, and to prepare the way for new trade arrangements with Spain and Russia, and he himself took an active and continuous part in the proceedings. Between 24 August and 14 November, 1786, the Board concentrated on these subjects and held twenty meetings. Hawkesbury and Grenville attended all of them, and Pitt fourteen. On five occasions Irish representatives attended.[30] From the outset it was a small concentrated body. Usually there were only four members present: three with Carmarthen or Sir Joseph Yorke. During the first twelve months of its existence the Board held 99 meetings. Of these Hawkesbury attended all, Grenville 94, and Pitt 58.[31]

For a Prime Minister who was himself handling a mass of administrative detail and by personal intervention co-ordinating the work of many Departments, while the weakness in debating power on the Government side compelled his constant attendance in the Commons, this was a very considerable performance. Nor was his attendance at the Board confined to periods when topics of major importance were under consideration. When circumstances allowed he attended regularly even when only routine business was being transacted. By this means he was able to keep his finger on the immense range of the Board's activities.

The record of attendance during the month of March, 1787, when the business was almost entirely of a routine nature, provides a typical example during these early years.[32]

3	March	– Hawkesbury, Pitt, Grenville.
8		– Hawkesbury, Grenville, Yorke.
9		– Hawkesbury, Pitt, Grenville, Carmarthen.
10		– Hawkesbury, Pitt, Grenville.
17		– ditto.

---

[30] Compiled from the Minutes in *B.T.* 5/4.

[31] These figures are produced by Miss A. L. Lingelbach in *Am. Hist. Rev.* (*ut supra*), p. 711.

[32] Minutes in *B.T.* 5/4. An example of a rather different kind is afforded by the attendances during the months of June and July, 1788, when the meetings were fewer than usual and the only non-routine business was the consideration of protests from delegates of the manufacturers against the increasing importation of piece goods by the East India Company. There were nine meetings, of which Pitt attended seven and Dundas two (because the E.I. Coy. was concerned) (*B.T.* 5/5). Pitt's attendance at the Board was by no means passive or perfunctory. See, for example, a note from from Stephen Cottrell, one of the senior clerks, to Hawkesbury, dated 14 Feb., 1787, in which he informs him ' by direction of Mr. Pitt, that Mr. [Josiah] Wedgwood, Mr. Craushay and Mr. Hilton have been written to desiring their attendance upon the Committee to-morrow at 12 o'clock. Mr. Walker of Rotheram is also to attend, but Mr. Pitt himself sends to him for that Purpose '. Pitt had also said that he would see Hawkesbury and explain why these witnesses had been summoned. (*Liverpool Papers, Addit. MSS.*, 38,221, f. 191.)

19 March – Hawkesbury, Grenville, the Speaker, Arch-
                bishop of Canterbury.
21   – Hawkesbury, Pitt, Grenville.
24   –   ditto.
26   –   ditto.
27   –   ditto.
28   –   ditto.
29   – Hawkesbury, Grenville, Yorke.

It was not possible for Pitt to maintain so close a supervision indefinitely, and from 1789 his attendance, although still frequent, particularly in times of crisis, became more irregular. More and more Hawkesbury became the managing director until to all intents he became the Board in his own person, but wielding far more extensive authority than a modern President of the Board of Trade. Technically the Board in Hawkesbury's time was no more than an advisory committee which made recommendations under reference, but in practice it wielded increasing executive authority. Evidence would be heard, a policy decision taken, and a draft Order in Council prepared which went through the formalities almost automatically. Moreover the Board initiated legislation. A succession of important measures relating to commerce were drafted (under Pitt's supervision) and introduced in Parliament with apparently little, if any, reference to the Cabinet as such. Other Departments increasingly referred questions with commercial implications to the Board and the advice given was almost invariably taken. Such a concentration of power was almost inevitable with a chairman who was an expert, who devoted his entire energies to the job and scarcely missed a meeting year in and year out. Without the Prime Minister's vigorous supervision this strong executive instrument might well have promoted that habit of departmental self-determination which Pitt had set himself to eliminate.

Because of his technical knowledge Hawkesbury's requested attendances at Cabinet meetings became frequent, and the fact that he was not a member of the Cabinet became increasingly awkward. He had been elevated to the peerage largely because Thurlow had insisted that he must have assistance in bringing forward Government measures because of the incapacity of his ministerial colleagues in the Upper House; and when Hawkesbury explained and defended the Anglo-French commercial treaty in the Lords he did not fail to emphasise the point that he was no Minister and therefore not responsible for the measure. Thereupon the Duke of Norfolk retorted that he ought to be.[33] Unfortunately he was disliked almost as widely as he was respected. Rumour had it that his name had been mentioned as a possible successor to

---

[33] Wraxall, *Memoirs* (Lond., 1884), vol. IV, p. 420.

Carmarthen as Foreign Secretary and that Camden had promptly threatened to resign if he was brought into the Cabinet in any office.[34]

In January, 1791, Pitt decided that he must be included and offered him a seat in his capacity as President of the Board of Trade but on condition that he exchanged the Duchy of Lancaster for the Mint. After delaying his answer he astonished Pitt and Grenville by refusing the exchange. The terms in which Grenville reported this unexpected *contretemps* to his brother, Buckingham, indicate his dislike of the colleague at the Board with whom for five years he had been in daily contact:

Whether he is playing any game in this we are unable to discover. . . . It was not until two days ago that this great man gave his answer, and therefore it is still, I think, by no means impossible that his stomach may come down when he sees Pitt determined to abide by this as a condition. On the whole it may only be a piece of magnificance, in order to give his admission to the Cabinet the appearance of a favour done by him, instead of one received.[35]

In his letter to the King proposing this and other ministerial changes Pitt had clearly explained his reasons for wishing to bring Hawkesbury into the Cabinet. It would gratify him and would be 'liable to no Inconvenience, but might on the contrary, be of considerable advantage from the great Variety of Commercial Points which are continually blended with other Transactions'.[36] Hawkesbury, however, was a seasoned politician, coolly aware of his value. Three months later he entered the Cabinet – and without vacating the chancellorship of the Duchy.[37] The episode throws a sidelight on temperament and outlook: Pitt's impersonal recognition of Hawkesbury's usefulness and importance, Grenville's irritation and his close identification with Pitt, and Hawkesbury's own formidable tenacity. All these were factors in the shaping of national policy overseas. In this way Pitt established – cautiously at first – an administrative instrument which he himself closely supervised; and then as it grew in power and prestige he regularised

---

[34] See General James Grant to Lord Cornwallis, 10 Jan., 1787. *Cornwallis Corr.*, vol. I, p. 274.

[35] He went on to say 'how much this unexpected difficulty has hurt both Pitt and myself'. Grenville to Buckingham, 4 Feb., 1791. *Courts and Cabinets of Geo. III* (Lond., 2nd edn., 1853), vol. II, p. 187. Pitt had wanted to be able to offer the post of Chancellor of the Duchy with a seat in the Cabinet to the Duke of Grafton. It was not the Duke's presence which Pitt desired but the support of his group in the Commons. 'Although much active Assistance is not to be expected from the Duke's Habit of Life, Mr. Pitt does not see any other Arrangement by which as considerable an Accession of strength could be procured to Government.' Pitt to the King, 29 Jan., 1791. *Royal Archives, Windsor*. Grafton, however was not responsive, and the plan fell through. Pitt to the King, 22 Feb. *Ibid.*

[36] Pitt to the King, 29 Jan. *Ibid.*

[37] See Pitt to the King, 29 April. *Ibid.*

the position by bringing its President into the Cabinet Council.

The India Board, which first met on 8 September, 1784, was complementary to the Board of Trade and Plantations. Both were standing committees of the Privy Council, and both were concerned with the administration of dependent territories overseas and with the promotion of an empire of trade in their respective hemispheres. The consistent support and guidance which Hawkesbury gave to the system of Free Ports in the Caribbean as a means of insinuating British wares into the markets of Spanish America ran parallel with the efforts of Dundas with regard to South-East Asia, China and Japan. Each in the hands of a capable and absorbed managing director became a powerful instrument of commercial strategy, and Pitt with Grenville constituted the co-ordinating link.

The following table of attendances at the India Board provides some indication of the degree of attention which each of the senior members devoted to its business.

Year and Number of Meetings	Pitt	Dundas	Grenville	Sydney
(8 Sept.-31 Dec.) 1784 20	nil	15	20	9
1785 57	8	50	53	8
1786 39	8	37	22	2
1787 43	36	41	19	3
1788 32	19	26	32	4
1789 25	18	16	24	nil
1790 32	12	26	13	
1791 25	18	25	7	
1792 21	7	21	nil	

(Sydney resigned as Secretary of State in June, 1789, and was replaced by Grenville, who in that capacity became titular President of the Board. Pitt usually took the chair when he was present, but not always.)

As already noted, Pitt rarely attended the India Board during the first two years of its existence and the operative combination was Dundas and Grenville.[38] Even then, however, the private letters between Dundas, Pitt, and Cornwallis show how closely the Prime Minister was supervising Indian affairs. From 1793 onwards Pitt's attendance was frequent though more irregular and Grenville resumed active membership. More and more the regular business was left to Dundas, and under his influence the Indian Ocean with its strategic outliers was recognised as a major factor in the military-commercial contest with France upon which the political and ideological outcome in Europe so much depended. Whenever an important war operation in Eastern waters was pending the Triumvirate took action as the Board of Control in secret session. The following secret Minute of 9 February, 1795, signed by the three, illustrates the usual procedure.

The Board, having taken into consideration the present State of Holland in consequence of the recent conquests of the French in that Country and the probability of their endeavors to secure the distant Possessions of that Republic, agreed upon the Draft of a Letter to the Governments of India, informing them that the Stadsholder had given orders to the Governors of the different Dutch Settlements to admit His Majesty's Ships and Troops to the possession of them until a General Peace . . . ; and the said Draft having been signed, was transmitted to the Secret Committee [of the Court of Directors], with directions to dispatch the same in the usual form.[39]

In the early days of the Administration the inception and development of these two Boards, under Hawkesbury and Dundas respectively, provided Pitt with flexible and powerful executive instruments for the conduct of all external affairs except that of

---

[38] The normal attendance was three or four. During the first two years it usually comprised – Dundas, Grenville, Walsingham and/or Musgrave, with occasional visits from Pitt or Sydney. From time to time fresh Commissioners were appointed, as for example, Lord Frederick Campbell and Dudley Ryder (afterwards Earl of Harrowby) in March, 1790, and the Duke of Montrose and Thomas Steele (Secretary to the Treasury) in May, 1791. But such recruits tended to drop out after a year or so, presumably bored with being passive spectators. There was, however, a certain amount of interchange between Boards. For example, Dudley Ryder of the India Board succeeded Grenville in 1791 as Vice-President of the Board of Trade. The above table is compiled from *Minutes of the Board of Control*, vol. I.

[39] *Secret Minutes of the Board of Control*, vol. I (Secret, No. 65), 9 Feb., 1795. A fortnight later Pitt, Dundas and Grenville signed a draft for the Governments of India, directing them to give positive instructions to the commanders of the Company's armed vessels to obey all orders received from the commanders of His Majesty's Ships on that station (*ibid.*, Secret, No. 76, 24 Feb.). Between April, 1785, and June, 1798, eighty-seven secret letters were sent to the Secret Committee of the Court of Directors for transmission (without amendment) to the Governments in India, and these were all signed by Dundas and most of them by Pitt and Grenville. Sometimes another member of the Board who was present also signed.

diplomacy. As the supervisor, with Grenville's assistance, of both Boards, while being Chancellor of the Exchequer, virtually Foreign Secretary, and in effective control of the Admiralty through his brother, Pitt improvised a personal system at a time when the Cabinet was mediocre and disunited; but it placed an almost intolerable burden upon his own shoulders. When Grenville, Dundas, and then Hawkesbury were brought into the Cabinet this system became incorporated in the normal organ of executive responsibility. Then the Prime Minister (himself in control of several Departments), working in the closest association with Grenville and Dundas as the two Secretaries of State, operated an informal inner Cabinet;[40] and by this means the conduct of Home, Imperial and Foreign affairs, and later of war, reached an exceptional degree of integration. This development was of particular importance during the formative years of peace between 1784 and 1793, for it provided planned direction and encouragement to maritime enterprise at a critical stage. In the chapters that follow an attempt will be made to portray the nature and the immense range of that directed enterprise.

The system of an inner Cabinet operating through the Boards of Treasury, Admiralty, Trade and Plantations, and of India, did not, of course, become a permanent feature of the constitution. It did not outlive Pitt's first Administration, but it did mark a break with the inter-departmental disintegration which had been progressively evident during the preceding decades. Moreover this concentration of authority did not rest on a slavish subordination to the views of the leader. Dundas was closer to Hawkesbury than to Pitt and Grenville in his views about the slave trade, and Hawkesbury was persistently more rigid than the other three in questions of commercial regulation. Pitt preserved this consolidation by modifying and suspending action on aspects of his policy where there was important disagreement.

Nor did the system, involving as it did constant attendance at executive boards, mean that the Ministers concerned became, so to speak, their own civil servants. On the contrary the corps of officials which was built up at these Boards – men such as George Chalmers and John Reeves, William Brodrick and William Cabell – became encyclopaedic in their specialised knowledge, spent the rest of their careers in the same office, and were a notable addition to the professional, as distinct from the semi-political, group of officials. The

---

[40] One of many examples of its operation in practice is afforded in a letter from Grenville to Pitt in October, 1794. Pitt and Dundas had taken a certain line with regard to Prussia with which Grenville, as Foreign Secretary, disagreed. He wrote: ' The worst thing that can happen is that you and Dundas should be *acting* on one line and I on another, for this must defeat both chances. It would be very desirable that before we have another Cabinet on the Subject, we should have discussed this point a little among ourselves.' (*Pitt Papers*, P.R.O. 8/30/140.)

temporary device of putting so much Government business into ministerial commission probably accelerated instead of retarding the growth of a professional civil service.

With a small closely-knit team of Ministers the interplay of personalities was of particular importance in relation to policy. William Pitt was a Grenville on his mother's side and inherited a large share of that family's aloof reserve and pride. On the other hand he was the descendant of a line of Pitts, forceful and impetuous characters who had been restrained by no inhibitions. The personality which emerged from the confluence of these two strains was further complicated by the profound influence exercised by the father.

Recognising the intellectual brilliance of his second son, Chatham deliberately groomed him for national leadership, teaching him the arts of oratory and guiding his studies. Chatham's conviction that he was the only one of that generation capable of leading the nation to the heights of greatness was transmitted to the son as an inherited trust and obligation. At the same time the mental affliction of the father during his latter darkened years could not fail to have an unhappy impact upon a young and sensitive mind. The aloof detachment of a Grenville must have seemed a necessary safeguard against the latent emotionalism of a Pitt. And that defensive mechanism became taut when, at the age of twenty-three, he stood forth as the King's First Minister to face the jeers of massed opponents grown mature in political sin.

It is not surprising, therefore, that as a public man he held a demeanour of haughty reserve, while in private among intimate friends he was witty and warm-hearted. Wilberforce, that lifelong friend whose affection became tinged with sadness for a lapsed reformer, admitted that there was an element of pride in him, but asserted that it was mostly excessive shyness. 'He was one of the shyest men I ever knew.'[41] On the other hand, when Colonel Barré offered to go and see Pitt about his ostentatious neglect of Shelburne, the latter replied: 'I know the coldness of the climate you go into, and that it requires all your animation to produce a momentary thaw.'[42]

He was, it seems, both proud and shy. As a companion he could be delightful: he was kind to subordinates; but an intuitive understanding of men was outside his range.[43] His pride, often mistaken for conceit, was curiously impersonal for he identified himself

---

[41] 'Sketch of Mr. Pitt', by William Wilberforce, reprinted in *Private Papers (ut supra)*, p. 66.

[42] Fitzmaurice, *Life of Shelburne*, vol. III, p. 422.

[43] 'He appeared to me to be defective in his knowledge of human nature, or that from some cause or another he was less sagacious than might have been expected from his superior talents, in his estimate of future events, and sometimes in his judgement of character . . .' Wilberforce, 'Sketch' *(ut supra)*, p. 71.

completely with the task of national revival which was his life and his birthright. The great ultimate object must always be served. Hence his tolerance when colleagues disagreed with him, his readiness to abandon or compromise on a project if opposition grew strong, his lofty contempt for the arts of 'influence', and his calm acceptance of its benefits when Dundas (like Newcastle in Chatham's time) managed the business for him. The true test of his service to Britain, in overseas affairs as at home, is to attempt to visualise the course of events after 1783 if he had never entered politics.

William Wyndham Grenville was a solid man in every sense. Young as he was, his build and gait were ponderous, his manner cold and formal.[44] Deeply versed, like his cousin, in classical litera- ture, he had a disciplined mind. Although no orator, his speeches in Parliament were cogently expressed and well-informed. He was at his best with a pen in his hand. In the course of a long career he wrote a very large number of letters on public and family affairs. They were shrewd, lively, and sometimes pungent. He is seen at his most attractive in his regular correspondence with the Marquis of Buckingham (Lord Temple). In dealing with the grievances of this touchy and petulant elder brother he showed unwearying patience and affection.

When allotted the task of finding a solution for the constitutional dilemma which had arisen in Canada, he went to the root of the matter, examining the problem against the background of the American revolt, and devised a system of government which was intended to obviate the institutional defects which had subverted the Old Colonial System. His plan, which was accepted by Pitt without demur, created problems of its own, but it constituted a landmark in the history of Canada and in the constitutional evolu- tion of the second Empire.[45] He was a strong and consistent sup- porter of the movement to abolish the slave trade, held enlightened views about commercial relations with other Powers, and shared Dundas's insistence on the importance of establishing a chain of strategic bases between Britain and the Far East. It was on the application of this last principle in the proposed terms of the impending Treaty of Amiens that Grenville broke with Pitt in October, 1801. As Foreign Secretary during ten increasingly difficult years (1791-1801) he was resolute but not always tactful. On the other hand, he negotiated the Anglo-American commercial treaty of 1794 with outstanding skill. He was by no means a satellite of Pitt; he was too intelligent and strong a man for that, and he had the powerful political influence of the Grenville clan behind him. But he was devoid of the arts of the politician. Throughout the

---

[44] Wraxall (*Memoirs*, vol. IV, p. 101) described him as 'destitute of suavity'.
[45] See Chap. X below.

long life of the Administration Grenville remained a key man, working in the closest association with the Prime Minister. The Grenville brothers had helped to steer him into office during the tricky winter months of 1783, and the two cousins understood each other, sharing the same social and cultural background.[46] And yet after the first few years Grenville began to yield first place at Pitt's side to a gifted politician – Henry Dundas.

We have already encountered 'Harry the VIIIth of Scotland' on various occasions, and it only remains to take a look at his personal relations with Pitt and Grenville. Dundas came to Westminster to make his way by proving his worth in much the same spirit as so many of his fellow Scots went out to India. The same shrewd weighing of the odds which caused him to choose India as the most promising field for specialisation also dictated the transfer of his service from North to Shelburne and then took him at the critical juncture to the side of Pitt. This last move was an act of calculated courage, for in the winter of 1783 the possibility that the inexperienced Pitt, with all his youthful brilliance, would become the winner appeared to most observers as an outside chance.

In 1784 Pitt was in urgent need of an Indian expert; and by the time that Pitt's measure was through, Dundas had become the obvious choice as manager of the India Board. From then on he was in almost daily contact with his chief on Indian affairs, and in that sphere Pitt gave him his entire confidence. India, originally singled out as a useful means of political advance, absorbed him as no other task ever did; and to the political leader, whom he had selected out of self-interest, he gave unswerving devotion. When Pitt died Dundas wrote to Lady Ann Barnard: 'I have no resources in store by which I can meet such a Calamity.'

Yet Pitt did not gratify his ambition to be admitted to the Cabinet as a Secretary of State for some time. It was Grenville who was consulted about ministerial changes and who received the Seals of the Home Department in 1789. Two years later when Grenville was about to be transferred to the Foreign Department, Pitt proposed to the King that Cornwallis should become Home Secretary on his return from India and that Dundas should act as a stop-gap, knowing (wrote Pitt) that he could be fully relied on 'for the most cordial and efficient Co-operation in Business in the Interval, and that He would with entire satisfaction quit to make Room for Lord Cornwallis, retaining only the Conduct of the Business of India, as President of the Board of Controll, which situation, when the Charter is renewed, might naturally be separ-

---

[46] The appraisal of Grenville in J. H. Rose, *Pitt*, Pt. I, pp. 280-1, seems to do him less than justice.

ated from the Office of Secretary of State'.[47] When, however, Corn-wallis declined, Dundas received the coveted post.

In that capacity the range of his influence broadened out extensively. The accumulation of postponed decisions left behind by Sydney was tackled with vigour – the constitutional problem in Ireland, colonial matters in the Canadian Provinces and the West Indies, relations with the Dutch in the Indian Ocean, and political management at home. With regard to this last he worked exceedingly hard, particularly in Scotland, where his influence in selecting and marshalling the fifty-four members as a Government phalanx became supreme. In all such matters he worked in daily consultation with Pitt whose visits to Wimbledon became increasingly frequent. As confidence and friendship grew, he did not hesitate to chide his chief when he was dilatory. The latter had to be prodded in matters of patronage, and this irked Dundas, who claimed and with much justification that he himself had become 'a cement of political strength to the present Administration'.[48] In 1791, for example, he addressed Pitt in forthright terms: 'You have done very wrong in postponing the King's signature to the Scotch Pensions Warrants to so late a Period. If those of a political tendency are not in my hands before the end of this week, I shall feel exceedingly awkward: all explanations why Promises are not performed are very unpleasant and most particularly so when I cannot exculpate myself except by shifting the Blame upon You.'[49] Yet for more than twenty years Dundas invariably addressed him as 'My dear Sir', and Pitt responded with 'Dear Dundas'.

Gossips and satirists made great play with the charge that Dundas insinuated himself into Pitt's confidence by exploiting his liking for alcohol. 'In the hours of private conversation,' wrote Wraxall, 'moistened and exhilarated by wine, when the Minister gladly unbent his mind, Dundas won his way and obtained a pre-eminence in his regard.' Such remarks were indicative of the widespread jealousy excited by the Scottish lawyer's success with the great man. 'Always at command,' added Wraxall, – 'unencumbered with modesty or fastidious delicacy.'[50] True, but the malice obscures the point that Dundas, though sometimes defective in judgement, was a statesman in his own right and a tower of strength in most aspects of national policy. The working partnership of the day often extended hilariously far into the night because the jovial, fearless,

---

[47] Pitt to the King, 29 April, 1791. *Royal Archives, Windsor.* This seems to be a clear indication that Pitt had no intention of doing anything drastic (as Dundas hoped) when the Company's charter ran out.

[48] In a letter to Grenville in 1789, quoted in Rose, *Pitt*, Pt. I, p. 278.

[49] Dundas to Pitt, 20 June, 1791. *Pitt Papers*, P.R.O. 30/8/157.

[50] *Memoirs*, vol. IV, p. 101. Cf. Lord Bulkeley to Buckingham, 26 March, 1788. 'Dundas sticks to Pitt as a barnacle to an oyster-shell.' *Courts and Cabinets of Geo. III*, vol. I, p. 364.

down-to-earth Scotsman, who was manly enough to retain his
northern pronunciation and to refuse to anglicise his manners, was
just the man to attract and relax the English aristocrat who had
been caught up too soon in affairs of state, for which he had been
trained from childhood almost as for the priesthood.

For Grenville the charms of conviviality offered, one suspects, a
more limited appeal. In a letter to Pitt he once described his
cousin's favourite tipple as 'that infernal beverage called Port'.[51]
Nor could he be expected to relish the growing ascendancy of
Dundas. The two Secretaries of State, however, worked closely and
amicably together under the unifying supervision of Pitt. Later
under the strain of war there was occasional friction. In 1796
Grenville sent Pitt an extremely stiff protest about the behaviour
of Dundas in sending him an instruction (through an under-
secretary) to provide equipment for French royalists. That, said
Grenville, was not the business of the Foreign Office: the responsibility lay with Dundas himself as Secretary for War, and nothing
less than a direct order from the King would induce Grenville to
undertake it. 'I had hoped, on the footing on which I have lived
with Mr. Dundas, that it could never have been necessary for me
to come to an official and formal explanation with him on the
duties annexed to our different stations in the King's service.'[52] In
1800 Dundas gave vent to an outburst against Grenville: 'I wish
he would exercise his genius for two Months in executing as well
as planning, and then he would learn that, however desirable the
end might be, it is necessary there should be the *means*.'[53] These
were passing irritations, but the Triumvirate was less closely knit
than before, and the Cabinet team had been broadened and reinforced by newcomers.

Finally, there was Charles Jenkinson, Lord Hawkesbury. He
was the indispensable odd man out. In a curious way he had always
been that.[54] We have already seen him as the hard-working 'civil

---

[51] Grenville to Pitt, May, 1797. *Pitt Papers*, P.R.O. 30/8/140.
[52] Grenville to Pitt, 25 Jan., 1796. *Grenville Papers (Dropmore)*, vol. III, pp. 167-8.
[53] Dundas to Pitt, 11 April, 1800. *Pitt Papers*, P.R.O. 30/8/157.
[54] He was very much aware that he was widely regarded as having been a sinister
backstairs influence in politics. In response to a request that he might use his
influence with the King he replied to the applicant: 'I never have had any such
Access since I was myself in His Majesty's Service as Secretary at War, except in
two or three particular occasions of great Importance when He had no Minister
and when I attended His Majesty at his express Commands, so totally without
Foundation are all the foolish reports that are circulated for Party Ends on this
subject in the Newspapers, and should not deny an intercourse of this sort if it
existed, for instead of being asham'd of it, I should think it an Honour, unless I
was conscious of having made an improper use of it.' (Jenkinson to William de
Lorne, 3 Nov., 1785, *Liverpool Papers, Letter Book*, vol. 120; *Addit. MSS.*, 38,309,
ff. 104^v-5.) For some time he was suspicious of the Pitt Administration. In Nov.,
1784, he wrote: 'To a discreet Friend it is always right to tell the truth. I support
the present Government because it is what my Sovereign has chosen, and it Deliver'd

servant' who, with John Robinson, laboured over the problem of India and generally kept a ramshackle executive machine in some sort of movement. He was also an economist. After making his mark as a student at University College, Oxford, he had taken a special interest in the structure of commerce, with particular reference to commercial treaties and neutral rights in time of war. In 1758 he published his *Discourse on the Conduct of Government respecting Neutral Nations*. His subsequent work *Coins of the Realm* was reprinted by the Bank of England in 1880. And afterwards during the time of the Fox-North Coalition, while in discreet retirement, he compiled his *Collection of Treaties between Great Britain and the Powers from 1648 to 1783*. Its publication in 1785 was exceedingly well-timed.

During this long span of years he acquired an almost unrivalled knowledge of the mechanics of trade, shipping, tariffs and currency, and established wide contacts with commercial and industrial interests. His equipment, therefore, as the first President of the new Board of Trade was formidable; and the Department, as Pitt had prophesied, quickly became one of the most efficient of the organs of government. An economist of the old school, he regarded theorists such as Adam Smith and Richard Price as dangerous heretics who, if allowed to have their way, could irremediably weaken the nation in relation to rival Powers. He had a sincere admiration for Pitt, but unhappily the young Prime Minister and his two chosen henchmen were all too evidently infected with these new-fangled doctrines; and Hawkesbury in his persistent laconic way applied the curb whenever possible.

Although Pitt's personal supervision of the Board's work, followed by Hawkesbury's inclusion in the Cabinet, ensured administrative cohesion, this difference of emphasis in policy produced awkward situations from time to time, and these were not eased through the medium of social intimacy. Although he belonged to an old-established Oxfordshire family which descended from the Elizabethan merchant-traveller, Anthony Jenkinson, he had entered

---

Him from the hands of Men whom He did not like, and who I believe had used Him ill, but I cannot so far forget the former conduct of some of the present Ministers as to place implicit Confidence in them till I have seen more of their Behaviour.' He concluded by indicating (without actually mentioning the name) that he considered Dundas to be an unscrupulous political adventurer, a type which he had always hated (to J. Home, 16 Nov., 1784. *Ibid.*, f. 98ᵛ). Almost a year later he refused to try to obtain a post in India for the son of one Robert Adair. 'I have never yet ask'd a Favor from the present Government' (to R. Adair, 22 Sept., 1785. *Ibid.*, f. 101ᵛ). Shortly afterwards he did approach Pitt on behalf of an old friend, Dr. Lloyd, Dean of Norwich, but with great reluctance. 'There are circumstances between Mr. Pitt and me (such as I cannot explain by Letter) which have obliged me to urge the Request not quite in the way I could wish.' (Letters to Dr. Lloyd and to Pitt, 27 Sept., 1785. *Ibid.*, ff. 103 and 104.) From 1786 he worked closely and on the whole amicably with Pitt at the Board of Trade, but he and his ally Thurlow looked sourly on the new men and on many of their ideas.

politics without the advantage of influential family connexions. From his first step as private secretary to Lord Bute he had advanced himself, politically and financially, with wary caution, trusting no one and giving nothing away. 'Supple, patient, mild, laborious, persevering, attentive to improve the favourable occasions which presented themselves, he never lost the ground he had once gained.'[55] He was (in every sense) a plain man, more at home with books and in talk with merchants than in fashionable society: flights of wit and fancy and the flourishes of oratory left him at his normal temperature – cold.

His appearance and manner were heavy handicaps. Long, lean and ugly, he would converse pleasantly and without affectation, but his eyes were usually cast downward with a fluttering motion of the eyelids. Inscrutable and furtive was the common impression. Few men can have been more clear-sighted in assessing their own limitations: he had no wish for the responsibilities and publicity of high office. But he loved the role of *éminence grise*; he knew that he could always make himself necessary and could in consequence exact his price. The Triumvirate dined and wined with him on occasion, but one receives the impression that their relations with this awkward, formidable man were no more than correct.[56]

---

[55] Wraxall, *Memoirs*, vol. I, p. 419.

[56] If this chapter seems somewhat incomplete, it may be that Vincent Harlow intended to make certain additions. Draft notes entitled *Pitt and his cabinet colleagues* were found among his papers and formed the basis for a talk to undergraduate history societies in 1959. I have incorporated some part of these notes into this chapter, and have also written on similar lines a contribution on the *Imperial machinery of the younger Pitt* in a forthcoming *festschrift* for Sir Keith Feiling. For this essay I made use not only of my own materials, but of Harlow's transcripts now deposited in Rhodes House Library. [F. Madden.]

CHAPTER V

NEO-MERCANTILISM UNDER
LORD HAWKESBURY

1. THE NAVIGATION ACTS AFTER AMERICAN INDEPENDENCE

WHEN Pitt took office in December, 1783, he inherited in addition to domestic issues two problems of the first importance in overseas affairs. One was the future position of the British in India and the other involved a decision about the place of the thirteen American States in the economy of a reconstituted and changing Empire. The successive efforts of Shelburne and Fox to meet the American wish for a close commercial alliance an reciprocal terms, the initial British reaction in favour of the idea, and the propaganda campaign against the consequential relaxation of the Navigation laws, have been described in the previous volume of this work.[1]

The Americans wanted and (at that stage) badly needed an economic partnership; but an *equal* association in trade presented difficulties almost as great as the political concept of ' federal union '. In direct trade across the Atlantic and with British territories in India they were given a privileged status not accorded to any other foreign Power. These arrangements were mutually beneficial. But the Americans wanted something more and their demand arose from the fact that, although politically independent, they were still to a considerable extent economic dependencies. As primary producers in a world of closed colonial systems they still needed the colonial privilege of being allowed to exchange their lumber and foodstuffs for sugar and other products of the British West Indies, and to sell these in British ports buying manufactured goods with the proceeds.

If this had been granted, the Americans would have continued to operate the triangular traffic between North America, the West Indies, and Britain which they had previously captured from British shipowners. It was not difficult for the latter, led by the redoubtable Lord Sheffield, to rouse public opinion in favour of regaining a lost traffic which should be employed to fortify the nation's mercantile marine and thus the sea-power upon which national survival depended. In response to public clamour the Order in Council of July, 1783, had barred American ships from the Islands while continuing to allow the entry of American pro-

---

[1] Vol. I, Chap. IX.

duce. The traffic between the United States and the British West Indies was reserved for British-owned and British-built vessels with British crews. As William Knox, who had drafted the Order, proudly claimed, he had cut the essential ' link ' in the chain of the American circuitous voyage.

The reaction of the West Indian planters was not long in coming. In January, 1784, the West India Committee in London instructed their chairman, Lord Penrhyn, to make vigorous representations to the new Administration. They met again on 6 February, when Penrhyn reported that he had 'repeatedly attended Mr. Pitt', who had assured him that the King's Ministers were ready to do all in their power to assist the Sugar Islands, 'consistent with the Interests of the Mother Country'. Pitt had also suggested that the West India Committee should report exactly what kind of adjustments they desired. A petition was promptly prepared and sent to the Privy Council, setting forth the distressed state of His Majesty's Sugar Colonies and urging an immediate resumption of a free trade with the United States. Unless that was done the plantations would be crippled by seasonal scarcities, and therefore ruinously high prices, in respect of timber and essential provisions. Indeed the distress was already so great that 'not a Moment should be lost in giving such relief '.[2]

Clearly a policy decision could no longer be postponed, and Pitt fell back on the device of an official enquiry which Fox had had in in mind; and since no official body appropriate for the purpose then existed, Pitt took the opportunity to establish the preliminary committee of Privy Council for trade and overseas plantations. Two days after its inception (on 8 March) the Committee began the enquiry which continued without intermission for almost three months.

Two questions had to be decided. Was the British carrying trade to be sacrificed to the interests of the West Indian sugar industry? If on the contrary American shipping was to be excluded, was it practicable to carry the principle of imperial self-sufficiency further still by excluding American products as well, filling up the gap with supplies from the Canadian Colonies? For a committee which was dominated by Jenkinson, the friend and ally of Lord Sheffield, the answer to the first question was almost a foregone conclusion, as Pitt must have been well aware. At an early stage in the proceedings the Committee decided that in considering the shipping question the criterion must be whether American supplies could not be brought to the Islands by British (and Canadian) ships ' at such a Price as may enable the West India Planters to cultivate *to sufficient Profit,* though not with so great Advantage as if the

---

[2] Minutes of the Board, *B.T. 5/1,* pp. 2-4. Cf. Minutes of the West India Committee, especially on 27 February, 5 and 30 March, 1784. P.R.O. 80/8/352.

ships belonging to the subjects of the United States were allowed to be employed therein '.[3]

In other words, the Committee gave notice that they would be satisfied if British shippers were able to show that they could provide a reasonably adequate service, even though a consequential rise in the prices of timber and provisions reduced the planters' profits. The West Indians were thrown on the defensive. They brought a considerable weight of evidence to demonstrate existing hardship and that certain commodities at certain seasons would be virtually unobtainable; but they could not, of course, prove that the theoretical proposition was impossible.

The Committee showed itself much more interested in the possibility that the Americans might retaliate by putting an embargo on British manufactures. William Knox, a leading witness, was emphatic in repudiating the danger. No such prohibition could be enforced. Despite the existing exclusion of American ships from the West Indian trade 'the Orders from thence for our Manufactures are at this Time greater than at any period of the former Peace '.[4] When the other possibility was put to him, that American merchants might refuse to sell lumber and provisions to British ships, he was equally positive. The southern States, he declared, had lost all their shipping during the Revolution, and it was not to be supposed that they would refuse to do business just because the ships of New England were excluded. And if 'from any sudden resentment' they did combine and refuse exportation, there was a remedy: 'The Owners of the British ships in the American Seas were much in the habit of having double Registers, and would probably qualify themselves as Ships belonging to Americans by having Owners resident in those States.'[5] Jenkinson made a note of that and afterwards took action, for it was obvious that the same game could equally well be played on the American side.

Similar questions about possible retaliation were put to Brook Watson, who had been Commissary-General of the Forces in North America, and his answers evinced a like confidence. He admitted that an embargo on British ships in the ports of the southern States would have an injurious effect upon Britain's position as the *entrepôt* for American produce in respect of tobacco and rice and to some extent of indigo; but he added that it would certainly be of more material and immediate prejudice to themselves.

Being asked whether in such case the Commerce of this Country would not materially suffer by being no longer the place where the Subjects of the said States would make up their assortments of Goods

---

[3] *B.T.* 5/1 (Evidence and Report), p. 21. (The italics are inserted.)
[4] *Ibid.*, p. 43.
[5] *Ibid.*, p. 37.

for the American Markets? Replied – the American States can make them up no where else.[6]

Although there seems to have been lingering apprehension about American retaliation,[7] the Committee had no difficulty in deciding that the risk, such as it was, was worth taking for the sake of regaining the carrying trade. That was the real point at issue. As for the West Indian planters there was no doubt at all that they must take the rough with the smooth.

The Committee cannot conclude what they have to Report to Your Majesty on this Head without observing of how great importance it will be to the security of Your Majesty's Islands in the West Indies, and to the property of those planters who have offered this Representation to Your Majesty, in any future War, that the Vessels of Your Majesty's Subjects and the Sailors that Navigate them should be increased in those Seas, to the Diminuation of the Naval Strength of other Countries, so that the planters seem not to be aware that the consequence of success in their present application must eventually be not beneficial, but on the contrary even dangerous to themselves, by diminishing those resources of Naval Strength on which the safety of the British Islands particularly depends.[8]

This declaration is the keynote of the Report: an expanding imperial commerce must be guaranteed by the development of seapower to which all concerned must in one form or another make their contribution. The price required of the West Indian planters was to put up with 'some small inconvenience' in receiving their American supplies by British transport.

The Committee was clearly less interested in the future proposition that Canada and the Maritime Provinces could replace the United States as the West Indian suppliers, thus establishing between Britain, British North America, and the British West Indies a completely closed circuit. The Canadian team, led by Governor Sir Guy Carleton, made a strong plea that this could and should be done. They painted a picture of the wilderness blossoming as the rose and in remarkably quick time. Ainslie, Collector of Customs at Quebec, held out great hopes of a large grain produc-

---

[6] *Ibid.*, p. 59.

[7] For example, Knox was asked whether he did not think that if British vessels were prevented by an American embargo from trading between the Islands and United States ports it would become necessary to obtain supplies from the foreign Islands, and whether in that case 'We should not suffer nearly as much in our Navigation as if We opened our West Indian Ports to the Ships of the United States'. In reply, he admitted that such a course would in that eventuality become necessary for the time being, but he fell back on the argument that 'the consequences would not be ultimately so prejudicial' because the Canadian Colonies would in due course be able to supply all that was needed. (*Ibid.*, pp. 41-2.)

[8] *Ibid.*, p. 233.

tion in Canada if sufficient encouragement were given, and Quebec
was the natural vent for all the American timber cut in the region
about Lake Champlain. Brook Watson asserted his complete confidence that Canada 'in the course of three years from this time
will be able to furnish every article which can be wanted for the
West Indian Islands from North America at moderate Prices'.

Carleton himself frankly used the occasion for a political purpose.
He informed the Committee that he had received applications for
land from all parts of the American States, and if the intended land
grants to Loyalists in Nova Scotia were speeded up so that cultivation could begin that Spring, 'Nova Scotia with Canada might be
able to furnish a supply to the whole extent both of Lumber and
provisions before the end of 1785.' When asked about prices, he
was more guarded: they might furnish supplies at as cheap a rate
as the Americans, 'but cannot answer with precision'. In Carleton's mind that was a secondary consideration. The 'taint of the
Republican Spirit', he declared, was not confined to the Revolted
Provinces, but had spread in some degree to other parts of North
America and even to the West Indies. Those planters who had
petitioned for a free trade with the Americans were not looking
beyond the objects of immediate profit and appeared to be unaware
that by fostering the resources of a foreign Power they were
endangering themselves by diminishing the naval strength of
Britain. Let Nova Scotia be developed as a great Loyalist stronghold by providing the settlers with this ready-made market in the
West Indies. 'If the Loyalists prevail, they will contribute pro-
portionably to their Own and to the National Strength and
Prosperity.'[9]

There was much sympathy for the Loyalists, and the provision
of new homes for them north of the American border was a convenient means of discharging an obligation; but there was little
enthusiasm for re-entering the business of colonisation and none
at all for the possibility that a New England might arise in Nova
Scotia.[10] Moreover it was evident that the Canadian case was hypothetical and unreal. In years to come the northern territories might
become a granary; but in the meantime Americans must be able
to sell their produce to pay for British manufacturers, the Sugar
Islands must have supplies, and it was to Britain's advantage to
continue to be the European *entrepôt* for American rice and
tobacco. In short, the Americans must hand over the West Indian
carrying trade, but the old triangular exchange of *goods* must continue. Apart from that one exception, the necessity of maintaining

---

[9] *Ibid*. Carleton's evidence, pp. 26-31.

[10] Cf. Chap. X below. Among other inducements Carleton held out the prospect
that New England shipwrights might be induced to transfer their skills to Nova
Scotia.

the former economic partnership was tacitly, but effectually, recognised.

In recommending that the Order in Council of 2 July, 1783, be confirmed as standing national policy, the Report concluded on a high note.

The United States of America are now become, at their own option, an independent State . . . They have no right to say that they will be Independent of Great Britain and yet Enjoy all those Advantages, to which, by virtue of their former Dependence and Connection they were before entitled.[11]

The permission granted to them by the Council Order to sell their produce in the British West Indies was a favour and indulgence extended to no other foreign Power, and they could not with justice complain because they were not to enjoy that commerce as fully as in former times, especially in view of the fact that they had voluntarily agreed by treaties with France and Holland not to grant any commercial preference to the subjects of Great Britain. If, however, the American States, 'through Resentment or mistaken policy', imposed restrictions upon British trade to their ports, the outcome could be awaited with equanimity.

The Excellency of the Manufactures of Great Britain, aided by the credit at which they can be sold, will force a Vent through every Obstacle which can be opposed to them.

This supreme industrial self-confidence (which emerged at an earlier stage than is sometimes assumed) had become the driving force behind British overseas policy in every ocean.

There were other sources of friction between Britain and the United States, such as the retention of the frontier posts and debts owing to Loyalists, but it is true to say that Britain's persistent effort to exclude the United States from the West Indian carrying trade was the operative factor in preventing Anglo-American amity at a formative stage. And ironically enough, in spite of the price paid in loss of goodwill, the attempt failed. As professor G. S. Graham has shown,[12] the triangular traffic between Britain, the United States, and the Islands did not develop, because large ocean-going vessels were unsuited for the transport of the staples involved, their working costs were high, and they could not time their arrival in the Islands with sufficient precision to catch the seasonal market. On the other hand the Americans before the war had supplied the British (and foreign) Islands by means of a shuttle

---

[11] *B.T.* 5/1, pp. 247-9.

[12] *Sea Power and British North America, 1783-1820* (Cambridge, Mass., and Oxford, 1941), Chap. IV. Cf. the same author's *British Policy and Canada, 1774-1791* (Lond., etc.), pp. 81-3.

service, operated by single-deck sloops or schooners of 60 to 100 tons which made two and sometimes three voyages a year. If these vessels, arriving at the right time and offering timber, fish, biscuit and flour at lower prices, could not smuggle their cargoes into a British island (as they frequently did), there were always the foreign islands and particularly such useful international depots as Dutch St. Eustatius.

In December, 1785, Governor Lincoln of St. Vincent's reported to Lord Sydney that it was common practice for ships from the foreign islands, 'especially from St. Eustatia', to bring goods of American origin into the British islands, and he added that, as the law stood, there was 'no means of checking this barter'. This communication was considered by the Board of Trade in the following February[13] and a scrutiny was ordered of the naval officers' lists of vessels entering and clearing British West Indian ports during the previous six months. The result of the investigation apparently startled their Lordships, for they recorded that 'great Quantities of Goods and Merchandizes' had been imported which were not the growth or production of the foreign territories from which they came,[14] and orders were given to the Attorney- and the Solicitor-General to examine the legal position. In consequence a special clause was added in 1787 to the Continuing Act (27 Geo. III, cap. VII) for the regulation of Anglo-American trade which enacted that henceforth no supplies were to be imported 'from any Foreign West Indian Island into any British Island'.

The reaction of the West India Committee was vigorous, and the arguments used were significant. A deputation waited upon the Board on 21 May, 1787, and urged that the merchants and shippers 'may not be prepared for this measure nor have provided Vessels sufficient for carrying on the Trade directly to the United States

---

[13] At the same meeting (14 Feb., 1786) the Board flatly rejected a memorial from John Braithwaite, Agent for the Assembly of Barbados, requesting 'some further intercourse' with the U.S.A., and proposing that a clear-cut discretionary power be given to the West Indian Governors to admit American vessels in specified circumstances. The Board recorded that they saw no reason to alter their decision in their Report of 31 May, 1784, 'especially as the experience of Two Years has shewn that the Commerce and Supply of His Majesty's Islands have not suffered from the Regulations subsisting under His Majesty's Orders in Council. . . .' (Minutes of the Board, B.T. 5/3, pp. 149-52).

[14] Grey Elliott conducted the investigations and was aghast at what he found. During the three months ended March, 1786, the following vessels had arrived in Antigua: from Britain 17, from U.S. 19, from St. Eustatius and other foreign islands 50. He had then had returns prepared of vessels arriving and their cargoes in each of the Leeward Islands for the six months, 1 October, 1785, to 1 April, 1786, and the same pattern had emerged. Moreover this practice of buying provisions (chiefly in exchange for rum) from St. Eustatius and other foreign islands was spreading to Jamaica. It was being carried on 'to an extent which I could not have conceived. . . . In short, my Lord, unless this vile practice is put an end to, all Your Lordship has done is in vain'. G. Elliott to Hawkesbury, 17 and 23 July, 1786. Liverpool Papers, Addit. MSS., 38,219, ff. 245-6, 281-2.

of America', and they asked that it be recommended to Lord Sydney that he should send out instructions to all West India Governors to pay the greatest attention to any distress that might arise from this new provision and to avail themselves of their discretionary power 'for Granting Relief'. The Board (consisting on this occasion of Hawkesbury, Pitt and Grenville) were not, however, disposed to give way. A state of emergency, they decided, could not be recognised after 1 October of that year, and thereafter the new prohibition must be strictly enforced. It was ordered that a letter be written to Lord Sydney accordingly.[15]

Brave words; but a harassed Governor, faced by an angry Council and Assembly of planters who claimed that their rum and sugar were in jeopardy from lack of casks and their Negro labour in danger of going hungry, found it easier to declare an emergency and open the island's ports than to obey orders from distant London. In fact the erection of a legal barrier between Americans with goods to sell and planters eager to receive them was not likely to be much more effective than the Spanish barrier against British manufactures in Central America. New England merchants were not noticeably slower in pushing their wares than the British.

The extent to which American supplies were smuggled in, either directly by American ships or indirectly from the foreign islands, is not, of course, ascertainable. In 1785 while on the West Indies station Captain Horatio Nelson was astonished at the open way in which American ships were given entry and took vigorous (and very unpopular) action against them.[16] But that was at an early stage and before naval and other forms of pressure had made the illicit traffic more difficult. The frequent complaints from the British Islands that supplies were scarce and dear seem to indicate, on the one hand, that the foreign traffic, while not suppressed, was severely restricted, and, on the other, that British vessels did not adequately fill the gap by a regular service. Then the strain of war broke the tenuous monopoly.

With the opening of the long struggle with France in February, 1793, the demands upon British shipping were enormously extended, while the United States as a neutral acquired greatly increased opportunities in trading with European belligerents in the Caribbean and elsewhere. The British peace-time device of acquiescing in the opening of ports by West Indian Governors in an emergency was given a general sanction in April, 1794, by an

---

[15] Minutes of 26 July, 1786 (*B.T. 5/3*, p. 417), 8 March, 1787 (*B.T. 5/4*, p. 202), and 21 May, 1787 (*ibid.*, pp. 282-3). Cf. Minutes of the West India Committee 8 May, 1787 (P.R.O. 30/8/352).

[16] See Nelson's letters of 20 March and 28 June, 1785, and 21 March, 1790, printed in *British Colonial Developments, 1774-1834: Select Documents*, ed. Harlow and Madden (Oxford, 1953), pp. 265-7 and 269. Extracts from a number of other documents cited in the present chapter are printed in § IIIA of this collection.

act which enabled such actions to be legalised by Orders in Council. For all practical purposes the Navigation Acts in this regard were suspended for the duration of the war. Indeed, the pressure of changing economic conditions – much more than any theory – was steadily undermining the traditional system.[17]

In a war which was bound to involve the western hemisphere and the Indian Ocean as well as Europe it was obviously important for Britain to regularise relations with France's previous associate, the United States. The fact that retaliatory action against British shipping had been taken by certain of the American States and that Congress in 1789 had enacted an American Navigation Act had caused the Board of Trade to undertake a full-scale enquiry into all branches of Anglo-American trade, which was presented to the Privy Council and printed for official use in January, 1791.[18] As an analysis of a mass of statistical and other data it was one of Jenkinson's most impressive productions. The gist of the Report was to the effect that the export of British manufactures to the United States enjoyed a highly satisfactory predominance, that every effort should be made to secure guarantees against possible discrimination, that in return Britain might agree never to tax American imports more heavily than those of the most favoured nation, and that the British freight monopoly in the West Indies should be left alone.

The Report was intended both as a brief and as a directive for the Minister whom it was intended to accredit to Washington. On the outbreak of war with France the need to come to terms with the American Government became urgent, and at last an Anglo-American Treaty was negotiated. William Grenville, as Foreign Secretary, and Alexander Hamilton, his opposite number, were both desirous of adjusting differences and restoring cordiality, but the task would have been easier if the negotiations had taken place in time of peace. War conditions, and particularly the problem of Neutral Rights, restricted the field of manœuvre. The special position of the direct trade between Britain and the United States and of American traders in the ports of India was confirmed, but the Americans, as always, had their eye on the triangular trade – in spite of the fact that this concession, as they well knew, would have entailed Britain's abandonment of the traditional system of navigation.

---

[17] See Graham, *British Sea-Power . . . (ut supra)*, pp. 65-9. Cf. H. T. Manning (*op. cit.*), pp. 280-2.

[18] *Report . . . on the Commerce and Navigation between His Majesty's Dominions, and the Territories belonging to the U.S.A.* Manuscript copies are in *B.T. 6/20* and *Addit. MSS.*, 38,349, pp. 255-302. It was reprinted in *Collection of Interesting and Important Reports and Papers on Navigation and Trade, 45*. Jefferson's summary of the Report was printed by the Dept. of State, Washington, in 1888. Jefferson described it as a ' document of authority '. (See Graham, *op. cit.*, p. 59.)

On that, as on other commercial matters, Grenville was less rigid than Jenkinson, who was adamant against a surrender of the principle. The Treaty which was signed by Grenville and John Jay, the American envoy, on 19 November, 1794, included the notorious Article XII which would have opened the ports of the British West Indies to small American vessels of not more than 70 tons on level terms with British shipping. Although American ships (of all sizes) were already doing business in the British Islands under the *ad hoc* arrangements permitted by the Act of April, 1794, this provision amounted to a major concession. It would have recognised and established an American shuttle service with the Islands by formal treaty. But this was not the triangular trade which the New England merchants wanted. The Article went on to stipulate that the West Indian produce thus transported must go to the United States – and stay there. The American Government must declare that it would 'prohibit and restrain' the carrying of any molasses, sugar, coffee, cocoa or cotton in American vessels either from the British Islands or the United States to any part of the world. As is well known, the United States Senate rejected this Article of the Treaty. Not only was it an affront to require the American Government to impose a rigorous restraint upon its own nationals, but the effect would have been to prevent the re-exportation to Europe of foreign as well as British West Indian products.[19] From the British point of view, on the other hand, it was precisely that which must be prevented. Under pressure of circumstances they were to accept the Americans as West Indian suppliers; but Britain in common with other European Powers must preserve for its own benefit the transportation of colonial products to the home market. Still more important was it to prevent the neutral Americans in time of war from pouring a stream of French and other foreign Caribbean commodities into the ports of Britain and Europe.

Long before the actual Revolution American merchants had secured the major share of the West Indian carrying trade and had defied the rules by trading with foreign dependencies and by buying directly from European markets. When they became the nationals of a foreign State, Britain after a short period of hesitation decided that in the interests of maritime security the anomalies could be removed and should be. But the pressure of economic circumstance was operating in the other direction. The United States were impelled by their situation to penetrate more and more deeply into the British economy, and Great Britain was likewise

---

[19] Professor S. F. Bemis makes this point at pp. 258-9 in his standard work, *Jay's Treaty: A Study in Commerce and Diplomacy* (New York, 1924). Other aspects of the Treaty relating to British hopes of a commercial penetration of the Mississippi by way of Canada and the Old North-West will be considered in the following chapter (pp. 595-615 below).

impelled to accept the fact, ancient laws of trade notwithstanding: which is another way of saying that they became progressively interdependent in spite of political separation.

The pattern was changing. On the one side, the Americans (as agriculturists) were pushing westward, taking possession, and developing the greater part of a rich continent, while the merchants and shipmasters of the Atlantic seaboard sent ships far afield in search of profitable cargoes. On the other side, the British (as industrial pioneers) were seeking markets for their wares and supplies of raw materials in every continent. American shipping resumed its former dominance in furnishing the British Islands with supplies.[20] Alongside that, however, the direct traffic between Britain and the West Indies rose steeply. The custom house value of the exports from England to the Islands increased from about £1½ million in 1787 to almost £6 million in 1799.[21] This was partly due to the war-time seizure of foreign islands by which Britain gained temporary control over the disposal of all Caribbean production: it was also due to the growing success of the Free Port system in attracting buyers of British manufactures from Spanish America. Again, while 90 per cent of the imports into the United States were British and included an ever-increasing flow of manufactured commodities into the new Middle West, the transport of these goods across the Atlantic became virtually an American monopoly. In 1790 about 43 per cent of the tonnage engaged in this traffic was American, but from that year onwards (i.e. before war conditions supervened) the proportion began to rise until by 1800 it had reached 95 per cent.[22] Yet on the British side this represented a switch and not an over-all diminution. Shipping registered in British territories rose from 16,079 vessels (1,540,146 tons) in 1792 to 24,418 vessels (2,616,965 tons) in 1814.[23]

Anglo-American economic interpenetration was thus deep and wide. Lord Sheffield had prophesied that, unless the orthodox rules were enforced, the United States would disrupt the imperial system – which in the traditional sense it did – and that in consequence British registered shipping employed in trade would suffer a decline – which it did not. Although a vigorous competitor in many fields the independent American Republic became a very important component of Britain's 'informal' empire of trade, and so she remained until she herself became a great industrial Power and developed an informal commercial empire of her own.

---

[20] For the three years, 1789-92, the total average tonnage of American ships entering the United States from the British West Indies was 4,461 tons. For the year 1793-4 it amounted to 58,989 tons. (See Graham, *op. cit.*, p. 69, n. 28.)

[21] See returns of Inspector-General of Imports and Exports, P.R.O. (Customs 5).

[22] See statistical table in Bemis (*op. cit.*), p. 40, n. 4.

[23] Geo. Chalmers, *The State of the United Kingdom at the Peace of Paris, Nov. 20, 1815* (Lond., 1816 edn.), p. 12; cited in Graham, p. 181, n. 7.

Informality, however, was never Jenkinson's mode. He preferred to stick to the rules, especially in cases where in his view their enforcement was a condition of national security. When the merchant marine of the Empire was abruptly divided by a political act into two separate parts, the rules required that each must operate to the greatest possible extent as a self-contined national organisation. But it was obviously futile to make regulations for the exclusion of 'American' shipping in certain areas of trade if in fact the ships themselves were not sorted out from the previous common pool and effectively labelled according to the new national categories. Before 1783 slightly more than one-third of the total merchant marine had been American-built.[24] A ship built and registered in New England was often sold in a British port, and it was common practice for ships to be jointly owned by British and British-Colonial commercial houses working in partnership. William Knox in 1784 had mentioned as a well-known fact that British vessels engaged in trans-Atlantic trade were in the habit of carrying double registers, that is to say, two sets of ship's papers, so that entry could be made into a North American or a Caribbean port under the flag of Britain or of the United States as convenience might dictate. For the Americans, legally barred from the British Islands, the incentive to do likewise was clearly much stronger. And there were plenty of old British (and Irish) registers to be had.

Captain Nelson and Captain Collingwood both produced evidence of what was going on from their own experience on the West Indies station. For example, the latter described how he had detected an American ship trading under British colours in Basseterre Roads at St. Kitts. On being questioned the captain had produced a register, dated 12 December, 1779, at Cork, a Mediterranean Pass for the same year, and a set of seamen's Articles. But it was noticed that the ship's name in these Articles had originally been *Polly,* but had been altered to *The Friends* in order to agree with the register and the pass. Further investigation had revealed that the ship was, in fact, new, having been built at Boston and launched in November, 1784. Thereupon Collingwood gave orders for the vessel to be seized.[25]

During the year 1785 the Committee for Trade[26] was immersed in business arising from Pitt's proposed Anglo-Irish commercial treaty and in preparing a report for the remodelling of the New-

---

[24] See vol. I, p. 475, n. 37.

[25] Report of the Customs Commissioners (see p. 266 below).

[26] In order to differentiate the Committee for Trade established experimentally in 1784 from the Committee for Trade established as a permanent department in 1786, I refer to the former as the 'Committee' and to the latter as the 'Board of Trade'. The second body was frequently described as a Board at the time, and as such it has had a continuous existence (under the authority of an Order in Council of 1786) until the present day.

foundland fishery. As soon as these matters were out of the way the Committee was formally requested by a Privy Council Order of 1 March, 1786, to consider the advisability of framing legislation for enforcing the Navigation Acts, 'and for preventing the Frauds practised respecting Registers and providing other Securities for ascertaining the Build and property of British Ships'. Jenkinson (not yet raised to the peerage) went to work at once. Evidence was taken from underwriters about the relative merits of British, French and American ships and the respective insurance rates, and a nine-point questionnaire was prepared for transmission to the Commissioners of Customs, who were requested to furnish a detailed report under these heads.[27] Jenkinson also wrote asking for assistance to his old acquaintance, John Pownall, a specialist in these matters and a member of the Customs Board; and the latter promptly framed proposals.[28]

Probably owing to Pownall's initiative the Customs Board worked at speed and within a month produced a long detailed report with a number of documentary appendixes.[29] Jenkinson and the Customs Commissioners worked closely together over these recommendations which (with one or two important exceptions) constituted the raw material for the subsequent statute. On 25 April Jenkinson sent a copy of the Bill 'for the Increase and Encouragement of Shipping and Navigation' to Camden, Lord President of the Council, who had promised to look it over. 'The Commissioners of the Customs and myself,' wrote Jenkinson, 'have taken great Pains to make the Bill as perfect as we were able.'[30]

In its final shape it was a formidable instrument of policy. As from 1 August, 1786, no foreign-built vessel (except those seized and condemned as lawful prize), although owned by British subjects and navigated according to law, 'shall be any longer entitled to any of the Privileges or Advantages of a British Built ship'. Foreign vessels, however, which had been in the possession of

---

[27] Minutes of the Committee for Trade, *B.T.* 5/3, pp. 185-92.

[28] Pownall to Jenkinson, 14 and 19 March, 1786. *Addit. MSS.*, 38,219, ff. 46 and 48. On 14 March the Committee acknowledged the receipt from the Customs Board of a ' very able and clear account of tonnage and ships cleared' and asked for it to be continued down to Christmas, 1785. *B.T.* 5/3, p. 233.

[29] The report is in *B.T.* 5/3, pp. 287-313, and the Appendixes at pp. 323-33. App. I consists of cases of fraud and evasion supplied by the Admiralty from naval officers' reports, and the last is ' An Account of the Total Number of Ships and Vessels, their Tonnage and number of men, belonging to each respective Port in Great Britain, that traded to and from Foreign Ports, Coastwise, or were employed as Fishing Vessels etc. in the year 1875'. The totals are given as follows: ' Oversea ' – 3,061 ships of 464,438 tons with 36,925 men; 'Coasting Vessels ' – 3,445 ships of 256,648 tons with 17,107 men; ' Fishing Vessels ' – 1,420 ships of 30,540 tons with 6,737 men. Grand total: 7,926 ships, 751,626 tons, and 60,769 men.

[30] He added that copies of ' the amended Bill ' (i.e. as already amended at the Committee stage in Parliament) had been sent to the Attorney-General and the Solicitor-General for their comments. *Addit. MSS.*, 38,309, f. 107.

British subjects at home or in British territories overseas before the 1 May of that year were not to lose their trading privileges. The coastal traffic of the British Isles and of the Colonies was made henceforth a British reserve by requiring that all vessels down to 15 tons must have British registration.

No vessel built in the American Colonies or owned by an American colonist during the periods when a British Act prohibiting trade with those Colonies was in force could be entitled to British registration; and furthermore no British subject usually resident in a foreign country could be the owner, in whole or in part, of a British-registered vessel unless he was a member of a British factory or of a commercial house 'actually carrying on trade in Great Britain or Ireland'. As will be noted, this latter restriction aroused strong opposition in an unexpected quarter.

Then followed a series of provisions for the prevention of future evasions and fraud. Before a certificate was issued the ship in question must be strictly examined, measured, and its tonnage ascertained. Its original name must not be altered and must be conspicuously displayed at the stern. Bonds on a graduated scale up to £1,000 for a ship exceeding 300 tons were to be given and would be forfeit if the certificate of registration was 'sold, lent, or otherwise disposed of'. And, 'whereas many foreign-built Ships and Vessels belonging to, or pretending to belong to, his Majesty's Subjects, have, by fraudulent Contrivances, and under false Pretences, obtained Registers', enabling them to trade with British Colonies, it was enacted that the registers of all ships purporting to be British were to be called in and cancelled and new certificates issued to such of them as, after a strict examination of their history, were found to satisfy the conditions of the Act. Since this was bound to be an enormous and exacting operation, time was allowed for its completion: twelve months for ships registered in Britain and the adjacent islands, eighteen months for ships registered in Colonial ports, and thirty months for ships engaged in trade or fishing beyond the Cape of Good Hope or Cape Horn. At each stage in these adjustments heavy penalties were prescribed for neglect or disobedience. Finally, all the laws of trade and navigation not expressly altered or repealed by the new Act were to continue in full force and effect.[31]

The entire merchant marine of the Empire down to little coasting vessels of 15 tons was thus to be brought under scrutiny in order that all concealed aliens might be extruded and trading privileges effectively confined to ships built as well as owned by British subjects. The measure was not concerned with regulating the trade itself: that was being done by short Acts on specific issues and

---

[31] 26 Geo. III, cap. 60. I have not attempted to summarise the numerous technical details in this Act which runs to forty-four Sections.

by Orders in Council. 'It is a Bill,' Jenkinson explained, 'for the increase of Naval Power.' In moving for leave to bring in the Bill he elaborated this theme. Under the protection of navigation laws from the Middle Ages onwards British shipping had steadily increased, but now under changed conditions the old regulations must be amended to prevent abuses and to secure for Britain the full advantages of her navigation trade. Above all care must be taken 'to preserve to ourselves the ship-building trade', and that could only be done by altering the law so that no ship in future could be deemed British-built that was not actually built in Britain or the British Dominions. In recent years the total tonnage had been increasing rapidly and by proper encouragement its growth could be immense.

If proper means could be devised to secure the navigation trade to Great Britain, though we had lost a dominion, we might almost be said to have gained an empire.

An empire of ships and ocean-routes. The House listened to his solid discourse with respectful, if unexcited, attention. Pitt supported and proposed supplementary regulations to prevent frauds in making out bills of lading, and the Bill was brought in.[32] It seems to have passed through all its stages with little discussion.[33] There was no question that the purpose of the measure commanded general support, but Jenkinson had not satisfied everyone. Indeed the clause which prohibited British citizens resident in foreign countries from being whole or part owners of a British-registered ship evoked strong, though ineffectual, protests. While the Bill was awaiting its third reading (in June) a merchant, named Mark Gregory, offered Jenkinson some trenchant criticisms. He had branches of his business, he explained, in Barcelona and Stockholm which were managed by his partners. Why make 'so many unnecessary provisions, as this Bill does, against foreigners being concerned in British ships'? The exclusion of British subjects established abroad, whether they had become citizens of a foreign State or not, was 'unpolitick and unjust'. It would merely injure British navigation. If the clause was directed against the American States, then he would mention that American participation was 'no evil', and he proceeded to make a prophecy which was justified by the event. 'There is more reason to fear that British subjects will be concerned in building Ships in those States for carrying on the Trade

---

[32] *Parl. Hist.*, vol. XXV, 1372-6.

[33] Unfortunately there is no record in the *Parliamentary History* of the subsequent debates, but Jenkinson claimed that it was the only important measure in the course of fifty years which had not met with a dissenting voice. In 1792 in the House of Lords he looked back with satisfaction to the successful operation of his Navigation Act of 1786, to which he partly attributed the increase in British shipping from 7,926 ships of 751,626 tons in 1785 to 16,079 of 1,540,145 tons in 1792. *Ibid.*, vol. XXXI, 139-41.

betwixt this Country and that, and I believe it is at present practised, than there is that Americans will take share in British-built
ships.' He concluded with a forthright thrust. ' I will only beg leave
to repeat that as the Bill extends the Registry of British shipping
ten times further than ever yet practised, it should not inflict
formalities that are not known to be of real utility.'[34]

A few days later an agent, named George Crawford, sent Jenkinson a memorandum which had been hastily compiled by a group
of British merchants in Rotterdam, setting out the injury which
the Bill would inflict upon them. As the Bill was about to have its
third reading, he sent the memorandum in its rough state to save
time and begged for an immediate interview. But the offending
clause went through unaltered. Such was Jenkinson's rigid determination to prevent Americans or any other foreigners from gaining a share in the profits of the British carrying trade – even at the
price of depriving certain British subjects of theirs.

Power at sea – the prerequisite of ' opulence ' – must be expanded
even to the detriment of immediate profit. The clause in question
had carried the doctrine to its logical extreme. At the same time
Jenkinson was consistent in resisting pressure from sectional interests. He had declared that one of the prime objects of the Bill was
to stimulate the building of British ships, and the shipowning and
shipbuilding interests were naturally agog. Meetings took place at
Sheffield House, and Jenkinson's friend and ally, Lord Sheffield,
was brought into consultation, as he usually was on such occasions.
From their point of view the re-modelling of the navigation laws
offered a wonderful opportunity for ensuring that the remaining
Colonies in North America did not replace New England as competitors in building and operating ' British ' vessels within the
imperial system. During the enquiry into the West Indian trade
Sir Guy Carleton had urged that if Canada and the Maritimes were

---

[34] Gregory to Jenkinson, 8 June, 1786. *Addit. MSS.*, 38,219, f. 170. When the U.S.
Congress in 1789 established preferential rates for American ships entering and
clearing American ports some British shipbuilders at any rate contemplated taking
the action which Gregory had anticipated. In 1790 Jenkinson wrote: ' I am very
sorry to be informed . . . of what I had already heard from other Quarters, that
some of the Merchants of this country are going to employ their Capitals in building
American Ships and thereby to encourage the Navigation of the United States and to
discourage our own. I wish that any Measure could be taken to prevent this mischief
and to punish severely those who have so little sense of the Duty they owe to their
country, but as this is a private transaction and may be so conducted as to be
incapable of legal proof, I think it will be very difficult to apply any adequate
Remedy to it.' (Jenkinson to Hy. Wilchen, 25 Jan., 1790. *Addit. MSS.*, 38,310,
f. 47ᵛ.) A week later the same observations (in almost the same words) were recorded
in the Minutes of the Board of Trade. ' Their object,' the Minute continued,
' is to obtain all the priviledges and advantages granted to American Ships, but for
this purpose it is necessary that these Ships should be navigated by Three fourths
American Mariners. This conduct is clearly detrimental in a high Degree to the
Interests of this Country. . . .' The Law Officers were asked whether any legal
action against such offenders was possible. (*B.T.* 5/6, pp. 38-40.)

developed as a substitute for the American States New England would be encouraged to establish shipyards in Nova Scotia. That was not the idea of the shipping interests in Britain. Their aims were reflected in the recommendations of the Customs Board. It had been suggested by the Commissioners that a duty of £5 for every £100 of the value should be imposed on every ship built and registered in a colonial port on its first arrival in Britain. In justification of this proposed tax it had been argued that it would 'not more than compensate' for the revenue that would have been received on the foreign materials, subject to duty, which would have been 'necessarily used' if the ship had been built in Britain. Furthermore an impost of this sort 'might also be the means of encouraging the building Ships in Great Britain by putting the Builders here and those in the Colonies on a more equal footing'.[35]

Although almost all of the proposals submitted by the Customs Board were adopted, the Committee for Trade decided that this one 'should be postponed for further consideration', and it was in fact ignored when the Bill was drafted.[36] Sheffield and his associates were not, however, disposed to accept defeat. On 6 May Sheffield reported to Jenkinson that he had again seen 'some of those who so eagerly, and I think reasonably, wish that some advantage should be given' to ships built in Britain, and he had informed them that he understood there was no intention of taking any steps for that end at present. They had agreed not to press the matter further by presenting a memorial to the Treasury. But, added Sheffield, if Administration would countenance the proposition, he would encourage the shipbuilders to organise a nation-wide campaign.

He then proceeded to launch an even more ambitious proposal to the same end. He reminded Jenkinson that they had discussed these matters together and that Jenkinson had asked him to report on what was being said about the Bill. He would now do so. The considered view was that 'the only compleat method' of preventing frauds was to put an end to the registration of ships in colonial ports. Governors in the remaining Colonies should be instructed to issue licences to plantation-built ships 'to pass directly to Britain there to be registered'. The only exception to this rule should be in the case of small coasting vessels carrying provisions to the West

---

[35] B.T. 5/3, p. 312.

[36] It was belatedly considered on 8 June, when the Bill was about to receive its third reading. Evidence was taken from James Anderson, who had resided in Boston from 1753 to 1775. Asked whether he knew of any orders recently given by British merchants for ships to be built in British North America, he replied that he had been informed that a number of ship's carpenters had recently gone to Canada to build several ships there. He was then asked: 'What was the motive of those persons in going out to build ships in Canada?' and he replied: 'I did not enquire particularly, but suppose it was an idea that they could build cheaper in Canada than in Great Britain.' Ibid., pp. 407-8.

Indies. In other words Canada and the Maritimes might (in theory) be allowed to build ships but the profits which they would earn were to be centred in Britain.

Sheffield stated the case with his usual polemical vehemence. 'They say the Bill will be almost nothing unless it goes further than it now does, . . . that it would now be no injury to the remaining Colonies, but hereafter when they are established in the business of building large ships, they would have reason to complain of any innovation or check.' The proposed regulation would pass, he thought, without opposition, and he was so convinced of its importance that he hoped Jenkinson would see some of the leading shipbuilders and owners before making a final decision. 'I shall only add that it may prove much better to do the business now than that Government should be forced into it hereafter at an improper time, and when it may be very difficult, and that the advantage now to be attained is not merely the wish of Shipbuilders, Masters and owners but of many of the best Politicians of the Country.'[37]

Jenkinson's response to this onslaught was prompt and decisive:

I have had the Honour of your Letter. I cannot alter my Opinion on the Subject to which it relates. I shall have no Objection to hear the Question agitated in the House of Commons, and shall in such Case pay due Attention to the Arguments that may be urged on both sides; but it is a Business which I cannot take upon myself to bring forward, and if those concerned in Shipping think I have done nothing unless this Point is obtained, I am sorry to find that I have laboured so much in vain. If they say this with a view to drive me to do that which I disapprove, though they think otherwise, they are ungrateful.[38]

The episode is significant on two counts. It shows, if demonstration were needed, into what extremes of policy a powerful sectional interest was ready to push an Administration for the sake of its own selfish advantage. It also affords a significant illustration of Jenkinson's own position. He had no compunction in obstructing the efforts of a colony to engage in an enterprise in competition with the Mother Country (as, for example, a fishery); but when the maritime security of the Empire was involved, he fostered the resources of all for the benefit of the whole.

The construction of a strict imperial navigation system obviously required that the autonomous State of Ireland should be an integral part of it, especially in view of the débâcle over the proposed Anglo-Irish commercial union of the previous year. If the Irish Parliament elected to define and regulate 'British' shipping in terms different from those of Westminster, a large hole would be torn in the comprehensive system which Jenkinson was planning. When sending

[37] Sheffield to Jenkinson, 6 May, 1786. *Addit. MSS.*, 38,219, f. 122.
[38] Jenkinson to Sheffield, 7 May, 1786, *Addit. MSS.*, 38,309, ff. 108ᵛ-9.

the draft Bill to Earl Camden in April he had taken the opportunity of giving him a reminder: 'I hope that Care will be taken that a Bill properly drawn to the same purpose passes in Ireland, which is absolutely necessary.'[39] Two days later he wrote to Lord Earlsfort, Chief Justice of Ireland, in considerable perturbation. The 'ideas' for an Irish Navigation Act which Earlsfort had kindly sent him showed that the Government in Dublin 'have not the least Knowledge of the Contents of the [British] Bill'. It was not his fault if the responsible Minister (Sydney) had failed to keep the Irish Government informed of what was taking place. He hastened to disabuse the Chief Justice of the notion that the Bill was concerned with adjusting duties on hides or any other commodity. Its purpose was the increase of naval power, 'and Ireland is as much interested in the Advantages to be derived from it as Great Britain'.[40]

Eventually (in March, 1787) after much consultation and exchange of drafts between London and Dublin an Irish Navigation Bill, similar in all important particulars to the British Act, was passed by both Houses 'with general concurrence'.[41] In complimenting John FitzGibbon (afterwards Earl of Clare) on his part in piloting the measure through the Irish Commons, Jenkinson observed: 'When the Measure is compleated, I shall from that Moment consider the two Kingdoms as once more united, so far as relates to Maritime Policy and Naval Power; the Point of all others in which it is most important that they should be united, as most conducive to their Prosperity and common defence.'[42]

---

[39] Jenkinson to the Lord President of the Council, 25 April, 1786. *Ibid.*, f. 107.

[40] Jenkinson to Lord Earlsfort, 27 April, 1786. *Ibid.*, ff. 107v-108v.

[41] The drafting of the Irish Bill was a lengthy process. In June, 1786, John Foster (Speaker of the Irish Commons) forwarded amendments, stating – 'You will observe that the Alteration in the latter end is to obviate any Doubts about the Act intending to give Privileges in any Port of *Ireland* and also to get rid of the Expression of British Subjects, which, as used here, would insinuate that Irish residents were not so, and about which we need not give room to speculative Politicians to frame a Question.' (Foster to Sackville Hamilton (who forwarded the documents to Thos. Orde) 8 June, 1786. *Addit. MSS.*, 38,219, f. 166.) In January, 1787, Jenkinson returned the original Irish draft which FitzGibbon had left with him and also enclosed an amended version. He apologised for the delay but explained that this draft had passed through many hands and had received many revisions – a process which he hoped would have the advantage of 'saving our Friends in Ireland some Trouble'. A copy was being sent 'in form' by Lord Sydney to Orde 'to be laid before His Majesty's Servants in Ireland'. Further amendments of detail were then made in Dublin. 'The Alterations you have made in it,' wrote Jenkinson, 'appear to me to be judicious and well calculated to remove Objections on your side of the Water and cannot, I am sure, be in the least Degree disapproved of here.' (Jenkinson to FitzGibbon, 13 Jan. and 19 March, 1787. *Addit. MSS.*, 38,309, ff. 135 and 144v. See also Jenkinson to Hely Hutchinson, 21 March, and to FitzGibbon, 27 March. *Ibid.*, ff. 145 and 146v.) When the Bill was at last through the Irish Lords FitzGibbon wrote to Jenkinson on 2 April that the completion of this measure 'has I trust removed every difficulty from a Final Settlement between this Country and Great Britain' (*Addit. MSS.*, 38,221, f. 321). The 'final settlement' which FitzGibbon desired and finally achieved was the Act of Union.

[42] Jenkinson to FitzGibbon, 19 March, 1787 (*ut supra*).

The emphasis throughout is upon the promotion of naval power as the indispensable weapon in pursuing a policy of maritime expansion. In his own view and that of most of his countrymen this Act was the most important achievement of his career. For us with retrospective wisdom it is easy to conclude that he was, in fact, refurbishing a weapon which was becoming increasingly inappropriate in a changing situation. It proved ineffective against the Americans who remained interlocked with the economy of the Empire from which they had seceded. Jenkinson watched the proliferation of British tonnage with pride and satisfaction, and yet the oceanic discoveries of James Cook and the dynamic force of British industrialisation were the true begetters. In a situation where an empire had at a stroke lost a third of its merchant marine by American secession and had only just scraped home in a contest with the combined sea-power of France, Spain and Holland, nothing was more understandable than the determination to nurse depleted resources by traditional methods.

The chief significance of the Navigation Act of 1786 is not in its appropriateness or otherwise to the occasion, but as a manifestation of the national conviction that ocean trade was a superior substitute for a lost dominion, just as a strictly limited 'dominion' in India was to be organised as a source of economic power in relation to the seas beyond.

One more region must be considered to complete the pattern of trans-Atlantic commerce as it emerged after the shock of American secession, and that is Newfoundland. The prolific cod fishery of the Banks, with the off-shore fishery and the salmon of its creeks, had been regarded since the early 16th century as an ideal source of maritime strength.[43] It answered all the requirements of mercantilist doctrine. The great demand for salted fish in the Roman Catholic countries of Europe and on the plantations of the Sugar Islands afforded ready and profitable markets, and the necessity of transportation stimulated the building of ocean-going ships and the training of crews who came home at the end of the fishing season and were conveniently available for naval conscription as and when required. In 1761 the then Board of Trade had expressed the general attitude in Britain when it declared Newfoundland 'as a means of wealth and power' to be worth more than Louisiana and Canada put together.[44]

The problem which faced Jenkinson and Pitt was whether the

---

[43] For the history of the Newfoundland fishery and its various ramifications see the following works: R. G. Lounsbury, *The British Fishery at Newfoundland, 1634-1763* (New Haven, 1934); H. A. Innis, *The Cod Fisheries* (New Haven and Toronto, 1940); G. S. Graham, *Sea Power and British North America (ut supra)*, Chap. VI; and *Newfoundland: Economic, Diplomatic and Strategic Studies*, ed. R. A. MacKay (Toronto, 1946).

[44] *Addit. MSS.*, 35,913, f. 73. Cited by Graham (*op. cit.*), p. 75.

ancient value of this national asset could be preserved and developed under the new dispensation, for Newfoundland was even more closely interlocked with the American economy than the Sugar Islands to the south. New Englanders took part in the fishery which furnished them with an important commodity for the mixed cargoes which they shipped to the Caribbean. Indeed the British fisheries off Newfoundland, Nova Scotia, Labrador and the estuary of the St. Lawrence were necessary to their livelihood, and continued access thereto had been granted to citizens of the United States by the Peace Treaty – much to the chagrin of their French allies.[45] On their side the British fishermen were dependent upon the New Englanders who supplied them with most of their provisions and that indispensable comfort in a bleak climate, West Indian rum.

There was a further problem and one of old standing. The interior of Newfoundland was a forbidding wilderness which had not attracted agricultural settlers. The Island was accordingly regarded as 'a great English ship', moored off a rich source of supply. The fishing grounds were as effectively British as if they had been located off the Scilly Isles. Until the late 17th century the 'fishing' ships, coming out from Poole and Dartmouth and other West Country ports with their consignments of fishermen and small boats to do the actual off-shore fishing, had returned home at the end of the summer season with their cargoes, equipment and (most important) their fishermen. Then the methods began to change. Along the coast the venturers staked out claims which they used as 'rooms' for beaching their ships during the season, and where they erected permanent buildings such as drying sheds and store houses. They also began to encourage their fishermen to stay behind for the winter to build boats and prepare for the following season. Increasingly time-expired indentured servants of the venturers elected to become settlers, and 'by-boat keepers' became boat-owners. By 1785 there were between ten and twelve thousand of them. In consequence the organisation of the fishery changed. The resident boatmen became the producers (like small-holders raising a cash crop), and St. John's became the mart where the West Country merchants acquired the fish for export in exchange for equipment and provisions. The boatmen were entirely in the hands of the merchants, who kept them in economic servitude and themselves collected handsome profits.

The changed circumstances caused disquiet in official circles. The unwanted colony was providing a valuable stimulus to the economy of New England and making wealth for Dorset and Devon, but every man who became domiciled in Newfoundland passed out of reach and so diminished the resources of British man-

---

[45] See vol. I, pp. 297, 300-2. The Americans were not, however, granted the right to dry and cure their fish ashore.

power at sea. A trained seaman was more valuable to the State than even a skilled craftsman; and in the later 18th century public sentiment was strongly opposed to losing either.

After 1783 the immediate problem was the adjustment of trade relations between Newfoundland and the American States; and the necessary action in that regard revived the old question of whether it was possible to put a stop to the process of settlement, for the more a colony developed the greater the dependence upon New England for food. The West Country venturers with their associates in St. John's organised themselves as 'The Committee of Merchants of Great Britain interested in the Trade and Fisheries of Newfoundland', and as such they proved as pertinacious in battling for their own advantage as the West India Committee or the Shipping Interest.[46] In dealing with them and the issues involved Jenkinson as always maintained a rigid adherence to the principle of the navigation laws and a resolute resistance to a pressure group representing sectional interest.

The merchants concerned made the initial mistake of demanding two incompatible things: the total exclusion of American trade from Newfoundland and the formal recognition of rights of settlement. A colony (as they were soon made to realise) could not continue to exist without American supplies. On 10 December, 1784, the Privy Council ordered the Committee for Trade to consider and report on memorials which had been received from Poole and Dartmouth 'against the permitting any Intercourse of Trade' between the United States and Newfoundland, and the Committee took evidence during the following January. The merchants drew a horrific picture of what would happen if the Americans were allowed in on any terms. They would smuggle in every kind of commodity including the products of France through the neighbouring Island of St. Pierre where they had 'a great trade'. 'Any intercourse with America,' declared Mr. Lister of Poole, 'may hinder the British Merchant carrying out supplies and the whole trade will fall into the hands of France and America.' Another merchant, named Jeffry, went further still and insisted that if American produce was allowed to be imported, even in British bottoms, Britain would lose the entire trade. But Jenkinson and his colleagues had heard that kind of special pleading before. When Mr. Ougier of Dartmouth had been driven to admit that the fishery had been carried on with great success from British ports before the war when two-thirds of the supplies came from American sources, he had this question put to him:

Can you assign the reason why the Fishery was carried on with so

---

[46] The assault party of this group consisted of the two M.P.s for Poole, and a number of representative merchants from Poole and Dartmouth. One of the M.P.s was distinguished from his fellows by the name of Michael Angelo Tylor.

much vigor and advantage from this Country when there was such
large supplies of Bread and Flour from America, though you now
say, that any supply even in British ships from thence would destroy
that trade?

Forthright common sense was provided by Vice-Admiral John
Campbell, Governor of Newfoundland. The whole evidence of the
merchants, he attested, was founded on misrepresentation. They
were already better off than before the war because American shipping was now automatically excluded; but if the merchants were
to have a monopoly in supplying food, clothing and equipment, the
purchaser could not hope for reasonable prices. 'The Fishermen
are in debt to the Merchants carrying on the Trade from this
Country and entirely at their Mercy.' As for the Americans,
although allowed by the Peace Treaty to fish, 'they have never yet
been troublesome', but 'the whole Fleet of England' could not
prevent them from using their opportunities of selling flour and
bread to the fishermen.[47]

The Committee was convinced. To restrict the supply of bread
and flour to Britain and the remaining British Colonies in North
America would raise prices and cause distress to the inhabitants
of Newfoundland, 'and to prevent this it is necessary to open the
market and introduce competition' by allowing these commodities
to be imported from the United States. The merchants, being
called in and informed of the decision, 'acquiesced'. Soon they
were to swing round and become the champions of American
supply, particularly when licences to export British corn became
difficult to obtain. The Committee recommended that a Bill be
immediately drafted, permitting the importation of American
bread, flour and livestock (and no other commodities) if conveyed
in British ships sailing under special licence from some port in the
British Isles. This regulation, it was explained in the Report, was
intended as 'an experiment' and the proposed Act should therefore be in force for the current year only. A Bill in this sense was
rapidly passed through Parliament and thereafter received annual
renewal until 1788.[48] In that year the position was again reviewed

---

[47] Evidence taken on 17 and 24 Jan., 1785. *B.T.* 5/2, p. 94 *et seq.* and p. 120
et seq.

[48] 25 *Geo. III, cap. 1.* The form of the special licence (in stringent terms) was
included in the Act which provided that the issue of licences must cease on 30 June.
1785. The Act itself was to determine on 26 March, 1786. Fresh evidence was taken
and the situation reviewed by the Committee for Trade on 14 Jan., 1786. They
reported that they saw no reason for altering the opinions which they had expressed
the year before. Bread, flour and oatmeal had been kept at a reasonable price, and
the system of special licences had worked well. According to the Customs returns
for 1785 the British Isles had provided 59,997 cwts. of foodstuffs, the United States
10,648 cwts., and the British North American Colonies 50 cwts. These last, however,
were beginning to export considerable quantities of lumber to Newfoundland.

and a standing arrangement was provided by statute prohibiting the importation of American provisions, but vesting a discretionary power in the local authorities to permit entry as and when necessary.[49]

The report also noted that the practice of American vessels coming into Newfoundland under false register had grown to such an extent that 'some new regulation is necessary to prevent the continuance of this abuse and to secure to this country the benefits arising from the Act of Navigation'.[50] Thus the principle – American goods when necessary but not American ships – was being applied with varying methods to both Newfoundland and the Sugar Islands.

It remained for the Committee for Trade to overhaul the organisation of the Newfoundland Fishery as such, and this was done a year later. Much evidence was taken and statistical data collected; and with the aid of his expert officials, George Chalmers and John Reeves, Jenkinson produced his usual thorough and substantial report which was at once put into legislative form.[51] The prime object of the Act,[52] as its title indicated, was 'to amend and render more effectual the several Laws now in force for encouraging the Fisheries carried on at Newfoundland . . . from Great Britain, Ireland, and the British Dominions in Europe'. It formed part of Jenkinson's great drive to increase the naval man-power of Britain. To that end the scale of bounties payable in respect of ships engaging in the Banks (as distinct from the off-shore) fishery was

---

There was also reason to expect that in future these Colonies would also supply livestock, but – ' as this sort of provision is principally calculated for the Inhabitants of Newfoundland, *whose residence there it has always been the policy of the Government of this country to discourage,* and as it has little to do with the subsistence of the Fishermen and of those who go from Europe . . . We think that less attention need on that account be paid to this Object.' *B.T. 5/3,* pp. 26-8.

[49] On 9 Feb., 1788, evidence was given before the Board of Trade which drew an optimistic picture of the agricultural development achieved in Canada by Loyalist settlers. The Board decided in consequence of this information to propose a Bill prohibiting American importation, ' but [it was added] as the Crops in Canada may in some years be Deficient, or the want of Grain in Europe may be so great as considerably to enhance the price of Corn ', it would likewise be proposed to Parliament that the local authorities should be empowered ' occasionally to grant Licences ' for the importation of American produce in British ships (*B.T. 5/5,* pp. 32-9). This was done by the miscellaneous statute, *28 Geo. III, cap. 6.* Adam Lymburner and other Canadian spokesmen took this opportunity to press their case for a new constitution on British lines. Under the existing French system of tenure the opening of new land to agriculture by Loyalists would be ' a tedious and expensive Operation, and can only be undertaken when the Subject has acquired a due respect for, and confidence in, the Governing powers '. (See Chap. X pp. 748 below.)

[50] Report dated Feb., 1785. *B.T. 5/2,* pp. 155-9.

[51] The Report, dated 17 March, 1786, was afterwards included with the three reports of a select committee of the Commons dated 26 March, 24 April, and 17 June, 1793, in *Report on the Trade of Newfoundland* (2 vols., Lond., 1793). The three select committee reports were reprinted in *Reports from Committees of the House of Commons, 1715-1801* (Lond., 1803), vol. X, p. 392 *et seq.*

[52] *26 Geo. III, cap. 26.*

substantially increased, and elaborate provisions were enacted for keeping out foreign competitors.

When Jenkinson and his colleagues encountered the awkward fact that a small colonial settlement had taken root in Newfoundland, showed every sign of increasing, and was supported by the Dorset and Devon merchants who were making a good thing out of the off-shore fishing which the settlers operated, they naturally refused to give it encouragement. The merchants' plea that Palliser's Act of 1775 ought to be amended so as to enable them to have a valid title as 'property' to the land and buildings erected thereon along the coast was rejected out of hand, and increased penalties were imposed for seamen who deserted their service.[53] In introducing the Bill in the Commons Jenkinson stated that the fishery could be preserved as British only by confining it to British ships navigated from Britain and by preventing 'any permanent settlement' being made on the Island.

The obvious consequence of such a settlement would be, as it happened in New England, that the colony would take the fishery into its own hands, and they would thereby be ultimately and perpetually lost to this Country.[54]

For that reason the merchants' demand to be allowed to hold land and property in the Island was inadmissible. Jenkinson was stating a doctrine to which he was strongly attached; and yet, apart from the penalties for desertion, his Act ignored the colony problem. Indeed he had already defended the cause of the coastal settlers against merchant rapacity in the matter of their food supplies. But he was resolved that Newfoundland should not grow from this nucleus of poverty-stricken boatmen into another competitive New England.

For the same reason no other British Territory in the Western Hemisphere was to be allowed to convert Newfoundland into a colonial fishery. In October, 1788, Rear-Admiral Elliott, Governor of Newfoundland, reported to Lord Sydney that during the fishing season just ended no less than 19 ships from Bermuda had participated, 'and with such prospect of success as to create an alarm'. He had therefore issued strict orders to the Customs Officers not to admit any vessel in future to land and dry fish upon the Island except those arriving from the British Isles, and he had written to the Governor of Bermuda requesting him to warn off Bermudans from coming the following year. Hearing of this, John Brickwood, Agent for Bermuda, sent in a letter of protest. The question was

[53] See *B.T.* 5/3, p. 128.
[54] Summarised in Adam Anderson, *Origin of Commerce* (Lond., 1801 edn.), vol. IV, p. 612. There is no record of the debates on this Bill in the *Parliamentary History*.

referred to the Board of Trade who (within three weeks) investigated and came to a decision.

In his evidence Admiral Elliott, who seems to have been well briefed by the British merchants, declared that he understood that 120 vessels from Bermuda might be expected to come next season, and if this were permitted enough ships would arrive in the course of years from the various British Colonies to occupy the whole of the Trade to the exclusion of His Majesty's European subjects, 'for the Inhabitants of the Island of Bermuda and of His Majesty's Dominions in North America can navigate their vessels much cheaper than we can by means of their Slaves'. There was also every reason, he added, to apprehend that they might employ in the fishery citizens of the United States.

Whereupon their Lordships were pleased to Order, that John Reeves Esquire, Law Clerk to the Committee, do prepare a clause to be inserted in some Bill to be offered to Parliament next Session, for prohibiting any Fish from being landed and dried on the Shores of the Island of Newfoundland which have not been taken and caught by persons [from the British Isles] who have a right to land and dry the same there.[55]

The protest of the Agent for Bermuda was in vain. In the following January he returned to the charge, supported by a memorial from the inhabitants of Bermuda, praying that the law might be altered so that they might have such privileges and protection as the Board might think proper. But the answer was a flat negative; 'it would not be advisable to depart from the principle on which the Trade to Newfoundland had hitherto been carried on'.[56]

As a measure for stimulating the British fishery on the Banks the Act of 1786 achieved some degree of success, for the ships engaged in it increased from 141 in 1785 to 187 in 1792. At the same time, however, the off-shore fishery also expanded and more substantially. The number of 'sack' ships, which obtained cargoes of fish at St. John's on the 'truck system' rose from 85 (9,202 tons) in 1785 to 173 (16,838 tons) in 1786, while the total tonnage so employed in 1792 was 21,275. In fact new venturers from many ports in England, Ireland and Scotland were putting ships and

---

[55] Evidence taken on 18 Nov., 1788. *B.T.* 5/5, pp. 163-6. The Board took its stand on Palliser's Act of 1775 (*15 Geo. III, cap. 31*) which enacted (*Sect. IV*) that the privilege of drying and curing fish on the Newfoundland coast was not to be enjoyed by British subjects coming from any territories other than His Majesty's dominions in Europe.

[56] Minute of 29 Jan., 1789. *B.T.* 5/5, p. 186. In the following March Sir Hugh Palliser wrote to Jenkinson on the subject, and the latter replied that he was fully apprised of 'all the Ill Consequences' that would attend any such indulgence to the Bermudans and had therefore 'in direct Terms' refused the request and had 'taken measures to prevent a Repetition of this Evil in future'. Jenkinson to Palliser, 22 March, 1789, *Addit. MSS.*, 38,310, f. 33v.

capital into this latter business[57]: competition sharpened and many of the West Country merchants who had so long preserved a monopoly were forced into bankruptcy.[58] The structure of the fishery was changing, and if profit margins were narrower, they were much more widely distributed; and the growth of the fishery as a national industry was impressive. Because the chief interest was directed to 'sack' or trading ships which bought fish as they might buy sugar, traditionalists like Jenkinson shook their heads over a new commercial trend which appeared to diminish the number of 'green' men trained to the sea; but, even so, it cannot be maintained that the official stimulus to the fishery did not, in fact, augment the nation's resources in maritime man-power.

With great labour Jenkinson and his assistants had produced a massive *corpus* of legislation which reconstructed the 'navigation trade' of Britain after American independence. The concessions reluctantly made in the case of American produce and then of American shipping were regarded as temporary expedients to be abrogated as soon as might be. That was according to the rules; but experience showed that Britain and the nascent United States could not treat each other like normal foreign Powers. The British, as they fully expected, continued to dominate the American market with their manufactures; but it came as a shock when the Americans from 1789 gave preferential rates to their own shipping and began to oust them from the trans-Atlantic traffic. Other adjustments took place, but Britain, the United States, British North America, and the British West Indies remained commercially interlocked. The new focus bent and finally broke the old Navigation system; but when war broke out in 1793 there were few in England who would not have agreed that Pitt and Jenkinson between them had provided the nation with the essential means for survival.

2. THE SEARCH FOR COTTON

Before sugar became the great staple in the West Indies the first British settlers in the early 17th century had earned a livelihood by growing cotton and tobacco.[59] The latter crop disappeared before the superior cultivation of Virginia, but in some of the British Islands cotton-growing continued on a minor scale. In England the demand was small, for the carding and spinning of the cotton and

---

[57] Returns of naval officers commanding on the Newfoundland station made for the Board of Trade. Printed in D. Macpherson, *Annals of Commerce* (Lond., 1805 edn.), vol. IV, pp. 257-8. The number of local boats (which did the actual off-shore fishing) remained relatively stable during these years at about 1,900. The number of persons who wintered in Newfoundland in 1785 is given at 10,244, in 1789 at 19,106, and in 1791 at 16,097.

[58] See Graham (*op. cit.*), pp. 110-11.

[59] See Harlow, *History of Barbados*, 1625-85 (Oxford, 1926), pp. 16 and 21, and C. S. S. Higham, *Development of the Leeward Islands . . . 1660-88* (Cambridge, 1921), p. 185.

weaving the linen and cotton yarn were handicrafts practised at home by the various members of the family. The total value of all cotton goods manufactured in Britain was estimated in 1760 to amount to no more than £200,000 a year.[60] Then in 1767 Hargreaves initiated the brilliant series of mechanical inventions, culminating in Arkwright's spinning frame and Cartwright's power loom, which transformed Britain's economic position in the world. Writing in 1832 Professor J. R. McCulloch observed: 'Little more than half a century has elapsed since the British cotton manufacture was in its infancy: and it now forms the principal business carried on in the country . . . The skill and genius by which these astonishing results have been achieved have been one of the main sources of our power.' It was primarily this resource, he added, which had borne the nation through 'the late dreadful contest' with Napoleon and was now giving it strength 'to sustain burdens that would have crushed our fathers'.[61]

In 1785 Arkwright's patent ran out and further improvements followed in quick succession. The machines and the capital were available for the production of cotton cloth at cheap rates and in increasingly large quantities. But the multiplying machines had to be fed; and this posed a new problem for under the laws of trade the importation of foreign produce was strictly regulated. In the British Empire of the 18th century the production of raw cotton was negligible. The best kinds of 'yellow' cotton were grown, first (in order of quality) in Siam, India and parts about Malacca, secondly in Portuguese Brazil and Dutch Guiana, and thirdly in some of the French Islands of the Caribbean. An inferior species, known as 'white' cotton, was grown in European Turkey and the Eastern Mediterranean.

As early as 1765 the manufacturers complained that direct importation from the country of origin, as allowed under the Navigation Acts, was insufficient for their needs, and they succeeded in getting a notable exception being made in their favour. By an Act in 1766 it was provided that henceforward anyone might import foreign cotton into any Island of the British West Indies duty free; that no duty should be payable on its re-exportation therefrom; and that anyone might import cotton into the British Isles (in British ships) from any place whatever free of duty.[62] This opening of the doors, which was afterwards described as 'permitted

---

[60] J. R. McCulloch, *A Dictionary of Commerce and Commercial Navigation* (Lond., 1844 edn.), pp. 430-1.

[61] McCulloch (*op. cit.*), p. 430.

[62] 6 Geo. III, cap. 52. Entitled ' An Act for repealing certain Duties in the British Colonies . . . and for further encouraging . . . several Branches of the Trade of this Kingdom and the British Dominions in America ', it was an omnibus measure which made adjustments in the duties on a variety of imported commodities, including foreign coffee and indigo. Cf. the Free Port Act of the same year.

evasions or rather legal violations ', had the desired effect of increasing the importation particularly of Turkey cotton by way of Flanders, Holland and Denmark, and lowering the price.[63] But it was not until after 1783 under peace conditions and with improved machines that the output of cotton piece goods began to rise steeply and with it the demand for the raw material.[64]

The industry was flourishing, but officials and others began to look askance at this growing dependence upon foreign sources of supply. The prime consideration of the manufacturers, of course, was cheap cotton wool and plenty of it, but even they became aggrieved against Portugal, one of the leading suppliers. As the demand mounted, the Portuguese supply of Brazilian cotton rose from a mere 1,000 bags a year to 11,663 in 1788 and then steadily upward to 46,628 bags, valued at £582,850, in 1792. But while Portugal drove this thriving trade, she continued to prohibit the importation of British cotton fabrics, reserving her home market for Indian muslins and other piece goods imported from Portuguese Goa. In the opinion of Manchester and Glasgow this was all wrong. The Anglo-Portuguese balance of trade had turned against Britain: Portugal paid for her Goan imports in specie since she had nothing to offer in return except a little wine; and since Brazilian cotton was allowed into Britain duty free, the Portuguese ought to respond by admitting British cotton fabrics either free or under a very small duty 'as a matter of reciprocity'. In other words a new industry in Britain had forced a breach in the national system of trade, and now its operators with whetted appetites for markets were urging the Government to persuade the Portuguese to revolutionise their own. 'I need not mention to you,' wrote one Glasgow merchant to another, 'the Advantages which such a field of Consumption as Portugal and her South American Settlements would give to the Cotton Manufacturers of this Country: They are abundantly evident.'[65] The line of attack was very significant for

---

[63] See ' Brief Statement of Facts relative to the Growth of Cotton and its importation into this Country' (1790). *Addit. MSS.*, 38,350, ff. 6-18.

[64] The total import of cotton wool into Britain from all countries rose from 11,380,338 lbs. in 1784 to 22,600,000 lbs. in 1787. Custom House returns printed in Bryan Edwards, *History of the British West Indies* (Lond., 1819 edn.), vol. II, p. 323.

[65] Robert Findlay of Glasgow to William McDowall, 12 July, 1793 (MS. in my possession). Findlay enclosed a detailed ' State of Trade between the British Dominions and the Port of Lisbon for the year 1791 '. The values of the commodities exported from Lisbon are given in Portuguese currency. McDowall was about to set out for London and Findlay concluded his letter: ' I will follow such directions as you may think proper to point out for procuring such Memorials to the Ministry from our Publick Bodies here as you may judge necessary.' In an ' office ' memorandum (undated but probably 1790 or 1791) it was stated that ' within a few years ' the importation from Portugal of Brazilian cotton had risen to 25,000 bags (of 200 lbs. weight) annually, ' and likely to go on increasing to the prejudice of our Colonies owing to the Brazills being so peculiarly adapted for the production of this Article '. Portugal, it was added, was drawing £220,000 p.a. from England for raw cotton while inhibiting the importation of British cotton goods

the future. When Spain and Portugal saw no reason for lowering their walls of imperial monopoly, British industrialists (actively supported by their Government) began to drive holes through them.

Since dependence upon foreign Powers for an important raw material was regarded with apprehension, it behoved the Government to try to rectify the situation without injuring a spectacular new industry. Two possible methods were available. One was to stimulate cotton production in sub-tropical regions within the Empire, and the other was to induce foreign colonies to bring their own cotton to neighbouring British Territories: colonial production, so to speak, at one remove. Hawkesbury[66] applied himself to both methods with his customary vigour and tenacity. In 1785 Sydney had sent a despatch to all West Indian Governors requesting them to encourage the production of cotton. But such admonitions were usually regarded as common form and could not be expected of themselves to have much practical effect, especially in the case of West Indian planters who knew from past experience the vulnerability of cotton to pests and bad weather, and whose capitals were heavily committed to sugar and rum.

Bryan Edwards, Jamaican planter and West Indian historian, was in favour of the project, not only because of the benefits that would accrue to Britain, but also because the cultivation of cotton, requiring much less capital than sugar, could attract the small man and so increase the depleted European population: 'It is to such men chiefly that the West Indies are to look for safety in the hour of danger.' At the same time he pointed out that the quality and price of Jamaican cotton was almost 30 per cent lower than that grown in Dutch Guiana. 'The most bigoted planter of the British West Indies' must realise that the introduction of a better species of cotton plant was 'indispensably necessary'.[67]

It was to this that Hawkesbury turned his attention. On 23 February, 1787, the Board of Trade (consisting on this occasion of

---

(*Addit. MSS.*, 38,226, f. 12). A similar account of the situation was given in an official despatch from Lisbon by the Honble. Robt. Walpole. It was calculated, he wrote, that not less than 50,000 bags of Brazilian cotton (at £10 per bag) would be exported from Portugal to Britain in 1791. The Brazil merchants always insisted on ready money, and since Britain was 'greatly in debt' to Portugal, few or no bills of exchange could be procured in London or Lisbon, and the British buyers were obliged to obtain specie at about 8½ per cent above the regular rate of exchange. This 'enormous Exchange' together with the exorbitant price of the cotton was a heavy burden on the British manufacturer. (Walpole to Grenville, 12 Oct. and 2 Nov., 1791.) Grenville on 24 October ordered extracts from these despatches to be sent to the Board of Trade *B.T. 1/1 (In-Letters)*.

[66] Since Jenkinson's activities in this and subsequent parts of the volume took place after he had been raised to the peerage in 1786, he is described henceforward by his title.

[67] Bryan Edwards (*op. cit.*), vol. II, p. 317. Edwards had been in England in 1784 and had given evidence before the Committee for Trade.

Hawkesbury, Pitt and Grenville) decided to summon a number of cotton specialists to attend in order that the Board might consider 'the most effectual mode of promoting the cultivation of the finer sorts of Cotton in the British West Indian Islands'. Three days later they arrived with specimens of the various kinds of cotton and explained the differences in quality and price. The cheapest came from Salonika and Smyrna and some of the British West Indies, while the best and most expensive came from Brazil and Guiana. A quantity of the inferior kind, it was stated, was imported by the East India Company; and in response to further questions at a later meeting John Hilton declared: 'Cotton imported from the East Indies to Europe has never been in such Quantities as to deserve even the name of a Trade, but the greatest part has always been imported by the French and that generally of the finest quality.'

The Board concentrated on India. 'Is it your Opinion,' they asked, 'that the superiority which the Manufacturers in the East Indies have in their cotton manufacture depends on the nature of the Cotton Wool, or the manner of spinning or weaving it?' The self-confident answer was characteristic of the men and their time. The Indians did not weave better than the British, but they did spin a finer and more even yarn. 'But,' it was added, 'we are coming near them very fast.'[68] It was a presage of the future when the mills of Lancashire would replace the product of the Indian village and convert India (for a few generations only) into a market for textiles and a supplier of the raw material. But the immediate concern of the Board was to discover, either in India or elsewhere, the best and most suitable kind of cotton seed for the British West Indies and then to induce the planters to grow it.

Hawkesbury turned to Sir Joseph Banks, President of the Royal Society, for advice and help; and it was given with alacrity. Banks has been described and without exaggeration as 'one of the very great Englishmen of the second half of the eighteenth century'.[69] His quality was not that of genius but derived from the wide range of his interests which he pursued throughout a long life with tremendous energy and a sound judgement. His mind was absorbed in discovery: geographical discovery in remote seas and little-known continents and botanical investigation arising out of travel in such regions. His influence on the history of his country was many-sided and important because he constantly sought to promote

---

[68] Minutes of 23 and 26 Feb. and 1 May, 1787. *B.T.* 5/4, pp. 192, 196-200, and 262.

[69] Review article, 'Joseph Banks in His Letters' in *The Times* of 20 Dec., 1958, written on the occasion of the publication of *The Banks Letters. A Calendar of the manuscript correspondence of Sir Joseph Banks preserved in the British Museum . . . and other Collections in Great Britain*, ed. Warren B. Dawson (Lond., Brit. Mus., 1958).

national expansion by giving practical application to new knowledge about the earth and its natural resources.

As a young and wealthy landowner he had accompanied Captain Cook on his voyage round the world in 1768-71, taking with him at his own expense a party of six scientists and three artists. During the voyage he collected specimens of plants in South America, Australia and South Africa. The influence of that experience was great and lasting and made him a pioneer in the development of new resources in the Pacific, an advocate of plantation development in Australia, and a vigorous promoter of exploration in northern and western Africa. He combined the persistent curiosity of the scientist with a merchant's practical exploitation of new opportunities. He was, so to speak, the 'backroom boy' to whom many of those responsible for the founding of the Second Empire turned for specialist advice. The correspondence between Banks and Hawkesbury extended over many years, and their common interest in overseas development established mutual esteem.

In August, 1787, Banks sent in a specimen of cotton wool grown from Persian seed, which, he suggested, might be examined as one of the superior varieties which might be suitable for the West Indies.[70] Hawkesbury took prompt action. The specimen was forwarded to William Frodsham, agent for the cotton manufacturers of Manchester. A copy of the letter from Banks was enclosed, and it was explained that the Board of Trade were extremely desirous by all possible means to promote the cultivation of fine cotton in British territories 'in order to prevent the present great Importations from other foreign Powers'.[71]

Frodsham duly consulted seventeen manufacturing firms in and around Manchester and sent in a report representing their opinions. The specimen had been found to be of very fine quality and 'if cultivated in our Colonies so as to retain its native quality' would be a very valuable acquisition and would be worth the high price of three shillings per pound or even more.[72] When pressed on the point, however, he made it clear in a further report that his constituents in view of past experience considered that good quality seed, when transplanted to the British West Indies, tended to deteriorate. The finest cottons were grown in Continental regions between 15° north and 15° south latitude, and he himself had never

[70] He had already supplied some seeds of Nankin cotton which the Board had ordered to be sent to the Agent for Barbados 'with a recommendation that they may be transmitted to the Island for Cultivation'. Minute of 23 May, 1787 (B.T. 5/4, p. 287).

[71] Minute of 29 Aug. (ibid., p. 340). Cf. Hawkesbury to Banks, 31 Aug. 'I will not fail to inform you of the Result of my enquiries . . . I return you many thanks for the Trouble you are so obliging as to take in this and other Business of the like Nature, from which I have no doubt that the Public will derive great benefit.' (Addit. MSS., 38,310, f. 5.)

[72] Minute of 8 Oct., 1787. (B.T. 5/4, p. 362.)

seen cotton of high quality from the West Indies except from Cayenne and Tobago, which were adjacent to South America.

Therefore, if I might be permitted to give my single Opinion where to plant the finest Cottons in our own Dominions, and where it is most natural to expect they would retain their native Qualities, I should suppose near the River Gambia, Cape Coast Castle and down to Accra upon the African Continent the most likely place to try the Experiment, and more particularly so as it grows there spontaneously. . . .[73]

But Hawkesbury and the Board were evidently not disposed to become involved in costly and doubtful enterprises in association with that unreliable body, 'the Committee of Merchants Trading to Africa', and the suggestion was ignored. Their interest was concentrated upon reviving and improving cotton cultivation in established British settlements in the West Indies. They referred once more to Sir Joseph Banks. Was it his opinion that this Persian cotton 'could be cultivated to advantage in our West India Islands', and what steps would he suggest the Board might properly take to encourage the growth of it? Banks replied with cheerful optimism: 'I have no doubt that the Privy Council for Trade will be able by their Patronage to introduce the Culture of this Species of Cotton into our Colonies in the West Indies without incurring any Expence whatever to Government.'[74]

It was evident that Hawkesbury and Pitt, while determined to stimulate the production of British-grown cotton, were not prepared to resort to the time-honoured method of subsidising it by granting bounties. When it was discovered that the specimen of Persian cotton provided by Banks had been grown, not in Persia, but in Barbados, the Board summoned John Hilton from Manchester and enquired 'what beneficial offers' the manufacturers might be inclined to make to the owner of this cotton in order to induce him to part with a quantity of his seed.[75] But Manchester was not responsive. Clearly they preferred the assured high quality of the Brazilian product and did not wish to become involved in expense in connexion with the British Islands. Inferior grades could be freely obtained from Flemish, Dutch and Danish enterpreneurs.

---

[73] Frodsham to the Board of Trade, 30 Nov., 1787. (Copy in *Banks MSS*. I was permitted by the courtesy of Mr. Bernard Halliday, Bookseller, of London, to make transcripts of this small group of Banks's Papers while they were in his possession.) Frodsham added that experimental plantings of this seed might be made in some of the Islands which most nearly resembled West Africa in latitude, soil and situation; but he added the warning that the planters should always use fresh seed of the highest quality from other countries, 'for by planting the same Seeds again on the same Soils the Quality will certainly deteriorate'. He had previously (on 20 October) written to Banks in similar terms. (*Ibid.*)

[74] Banks to William Fawkener (Privy Council clerk seconded to the Board of Trade), 14 Oct., 1787. *Ibid.*

[75] Minute of 21 Nov., 1787. *B.T. 5/4*, p. 386.

In December the enterprising Barbadian planter (one Langford Millington) who had grown the Persian cotton and was then in London, was invited to attend the Board together with Sir Joseph Banks. On two successive meetings he was subjected to lengthy examination about his experiment. His information seemed encouraging. Persian seed had been introduced into Barbados some twelve years before. Little had been done about it, but in 1785 he himself had responded to Lord Sydney's despatch on cotton cultivation and had planted some of the seed with good results. The plants were taller and stronger than other varieties and more resistant to disease. He presented two more samples of his cotton, eighteen ounces of picked and half a pound of unpicked, and these too were sent to Manchester for testing.

But the Board of Trade was in a difficulty both on financial and technical grounds. Again they enquired whether the manufacturers would meet the cost of promoting the cultivation of this promising variety and if they could suggest improved methods of hand-picking and cleaning to lessen production costs, 'so that the Cotton may be brought to market for the benefit of the manufacturer and yield a profit to the planter'.[76] But that was not Manchester's business. The Government needed the technical advice of experienced and efficient growers, a station for agricultural research in the Islands – and a Colonial Development Corporation.

A more promising proposition was to take advantage of the British position in India and draw supplies from that country where fine cotton had long been grown and on a great scale. Brooding on the need to promote the prosperity of Bengal, Cornwallis had written several despatches, advocating in the first place the encouragement of foodstuffs such as sago and date palms to obviate famine in Bengal in times of drought, and secondly the establishment in Calcutta of a botanical garden for fostering new crops of commercial value. Greatly interested, Dundas sent copies of these despatches to Banks (in June, 1787) and asked for his advice. The latter responded with enthusiasm.

If we consider but for a moment that the greatest part of the merchandises imported from India have hitherto been manufactured Goods, of a nature which interfere with our manufactories at home; that our cotton manufactories are increasing with a rapidity which renders it politic to give them effectual encouragement, and that a profit of Cent per Cent is to be got with certainty upon the importation of the raw material of Cotton . . . how is it possible to encourage even sufficiently every thing which tends to the cultivation of raw materials in India?

In that country labour was abundant and very cheap, and

---

[76] Minutes of 8 and 15 Dec. *Ibid.*, pp. 406 and 409.

primary products of many sorts, such as medicinal drugs, dyeing materials and spices, could be cultivated, which would find a ready market in Britain. He went on to make a point that was characteristic of the growing commercial interest in the East.

Why then should not raw materials of every kind, furnished by the intertropical climates, except perhaps sugar, be sent to us from the East Indies, cheaper than they can be from the West, where the immense price of labour performed by Slaves, purchased at extravagant rates, more than compensates for the difference of distance, and consequent enhancement of freight and charges in bringing the produce home?[77]

In the distant background of these rhetorical questions lay many revolutionary changes – the abolition of the slave trade, slave emancipation, the abolition of the East India Company's monopoly, and the gradual withdrawal of tariff protection for West Indian sugar. The notion that Lancashire and Glasgow should draw large supplies of cotton from India was prophetic, but in 1787 the economy of the East India Company was based on selling the cotton manufactures of India in Britain itself and in Europe. The machines of the West were not yet sufficiently developed to overwhelm the hand looms of the Indian village.

Since a large importation of Indian cotton was impracticable, Banks supported Hawkesbury's drive for British-grown cotton by promoting the transplantation of Indian cotton seed to the West Indies. At his suggestion the Board commissioned a certain Anthony Hove to go on a special trip to India for the purpose of collecting plants and seeds of the finest types of cotton grown in the Gujarat region for distribution in the West Indies.[78] The scheme chimed with Banks's other plan of providing the Islands with a new source of food by furnishing them with bread-fruit plants from Tahiti. Captain Bligh began his unfortunate voyage to the Pacific for that purpose in the same year.

On arrival in Bombay Hove applied himself to his task with energy and success. In February, 1788, he forwarded to Banks his first consignment of cotton seed and then proceeded to collect a wide range both of seeds and plants. Unfortunately the amenities of European life in Bombay seem to have gone to his head. Instead of keeping within the £300 allowed him for expenses while in India, he drew bills of exchange on Hawkesbury to the tune of £2,125, and the latter suspended payment until Hove had returned

---

[77] Banks to Dundas, 15 June, 1787. (Copy.) *Royal Archives, Windsor.*
[78] Hove set out in the East Indiaman, *Hastings*, early in April, 1787. At Hawkesbury's request he was supplied with technical information by John Hilton of Manchester, and he was ordered to conform in all respects to instructions prepared by Sir Joseph Banks. (See Chalmers to Hilton, 30 March, and Fawkener to Banks, 2 April, *B.T. 3/1 (Out-Letters)*, pp. 76-7.)

and given an account of himself – which he was peremptorily ordered to do.[79] On the arrival of his first consignment (in October, 1788) the Board gave orders 'that Letters be written to the Governors of His Majesty's Islands in the West Indies, transmitting to each of them a parcel of the said cotton seeds of the finest quality which their Lordships, from their desire to promote the growth of Cotton and with it the Interests of His Majesty's West Indian Islands, have procured from India, and desiring them to distribute the said Seeds among the Planters under their Governments in such a manner as will best insure the salutary ends for which they were obtained'.[80]

When Hove arrived with the main collection, those of the plants which had survived the voyage were examined by Banks and samples of the various types of seed were sent to Manchester for testing. At Hawkesbury's request Banks edited Hove's very diffuse report, retaining only those parts which provided practical guidance on cotton cultivation. He was also asked to write a letter under his own signature recommending that trials be made of the different kinds of Indian seed. Hawkesbury added that he would send this letter to the various Island Governments, 'and the weight of Sir Joseph Bankes' authority as well as of his arguments might prove the means of inducing the Planters to avail themselves of the Advantages which are on this occasion held out to them and which from Indolence or Prejudice they might perhaps be otherwise too apt to neglect'.[81] Finally in April, 1790, copies of the letter, the edited report, and parcels of the more suitable varieties of seed were dispatched to the Island Governments.

The response, though limited, was encouraging. The Superin-

---

[79] Minute of 29 Nov., 1788. *B.T.* 5/5, pp. 170-1. The incident aroused considerable annoyance in official circles. Hawkesbury informed Banks that he had discussed the matter with Pitt who agreed with him 'that Hove had better have abandoned the Object of his Commission than have put the Publick to so great an Expence'. (Hawkesbury to Banks, 9 and 27 Sept., 1788. *Addit. MSS.*, 38,310, ff. 23 and 26.) The manner of the recall throws an interesting sidelight on ministerial relations. Hawkesbury asked Banks to write the letter since it was he who had conducted the previous correspondence with Hove; and on receiving this letter Hawkesbury sent it to Grenville with the observation: 'As You have opportunities of seeing Mr. Pitt, I wish You would shew it to him and obtain his Opinion upon it, so that it may be sent (if he approves of it) by the Packet over land' (Hawkesbury to Grenville, 2 Oct., 1788. *Ibid.*, f. 26). The procedure also furnishes a further illustration of the tight control over departmental detail which Pitt exercised during this period.

[80] Minute of 31 Oct., 1788. *B.T.* 5/5, pp. 155-6. Hawkesbury's determination to acquire information about the technique of cotton cultivation was shown at this meeting of the Board. A volume of treatises on cotton culture, published in Amsterdam, was submitted on request, and it was ordered that a translation be made for the Board's use.

[81] Hawkesbury to Banks, 3 Oct., 1789. (*Addit. MSS.*, 38,310, f. 43.) Cf. Minutes of 30 Sept., 1789, and 20 April, 1790. *B.T.* 5/6, pp. 12 and 189-94. Banks also secured an independent supply of seeds from Dacca, 'universally allowed . . . to be the only sort from whence the Natives of Bengal can manufacture their superfine Muslims'. Banks to Hawkesbury, 5 May, 1789. (*Addit. MSS.*, 38,224, f. 117.)

tendent of the botanical garden in St. Vincent reported that the first consignment of Gujarat seed had been planted, and was in a thriving condition and likely to be found in time a valuable acquisition to the Islands. A similar report was received from the Earl of Dunmore, Governor of the Bahamas. He forwarded a sample of cotton raised from this seed, which, he said, was 'thought to be of the finest quality ever produced in these Islands'.[82]

It remains to consider the extent to which cotton production in the West Indies was actually increased. The number of mills in Britain driven by steam or water-power was multiplying with great rapidity and the demand for the raw material was insatiable. Good cotton was accordingly demanding high prices, and in some of the Islands (notably Barbados, Jamaica and the Bahamas) there was a marked shift to cotton cultivation even before the stimulus of Hawkesbury's campaign. In 1788 Governor Parry of Barbados reported that the price of slaves in that Island had more than doubled within a few years, 'owing chiefly to the accidental Circumstance of the increased Cultivation of Cotton in consequence of its increased price'.[83]

The increase in the importation into Britain of raw cotton from the British West Indies was spectacular, as the following Custom House returns indicate: [84]

$$
\begin{array}{lll}
\text{1761-1765 (annual average)} - & 3,338,346 \text{ lbs.} \\
\text{1771-1775 (} \quad ,, \quad ,, \quad) - & 2,587,204 \;,, \\
\text{1781-1785 (} \quad ,, \quad ,, \quad) - & 6,130,951 \;,, \\
\text{1791-1795 (} \quad ,, \quad ,, \quad) - & 11,602,659 \;,, \\
\text{1801-1806 (} \quad ,, \quad ,, \quad) - & 16,292,088 \;,,
\end{array}
$$

In 1787 the total importation of cotton from all parts of the world amounted to 22,600,000 lbs., of which 9,396,921 lbs. came from the British Islands.[85] At first glance, therefore, it would seem that they achieved the surprising feat of producing some 40 per cent of Britain's total cotton consumption. That, of course, was not the case. Their own production increased considerably, but the very great flow of cotton from the British West Indies to British mills was attained by diverting foreign-grown cotton into this

---

[82] Minutes of Aug., 1790. *B.T.* 5/6, pp. 288-9.
[83] 'Further Answers to Heads of Enquiry transmitted by Governor Parry' (in connexion with the Board of Trade's enquiry of 1788 into the Slave Trade). Copy in P.R.O. 30/8/384. Parry added that it was difficult to estimate the proportion of acres under sugar and under cotton, but that the latter was 'encreasing every year for several years together, and the former in consequence decreasing'. For the same occasion John Braithwaite, Agent for Barbados, submitted an 'Account of Slaves and Produce in Barbadoes' which put cotton production in the Island for 1753 at 650 bags, for 1784 at 8,253 bags, and for 1786 at 9,420 bags. (*Ibid.*)
[84] Printed in Bryan Edwards (*op. cit.*), vol. V, App. No. XXV, pp. 28-9.
[85] *Ibid.*, vol. II, pp. 322-3.

channel; and that in itself was a new development of which Hawkesbury was the chief promoter.

The primary purpose of the chain of Free Ports which was
established in the British Islands was to provide depots for the sale
of British manufactures to foreign, and especially Spanish settlers,
who would be induced to go there (in defiance of their own laws)
because the goods were so much cheaper than when bought at home
after being imported indirectly through the parent state in Europe.
A secondary but complementary purpose was to receive in exchange
sub-tropical products, such as cotton, cocoa and indigo, which
Britain needed and which her own Caribbean colonies could not
supply in sufficient quantities.[86] With regard to cotton the arrangement was particularly attractive, for British piece goods and other
manufactured articles secured direct access to a potentially vast
market, while an essential raw material was obtained at much
lower rates than when purchased indirectly in Europe. The mercantilist barriers of rival Powers were circumvented in both directions.

Statistics of the Free Port trade are necessarily imperfect, for
much was left unrecorded in order to protect the clandestine customer from the inquisitiveness of his own officials. But fairly reliable
records were kept of the quantities of foreign importations, and
they indicate the very useful diversion of foreign cotton which was
achieved.

Importation of Foreign Cotton into British 'Free Port' Islands[87]

Year	Jamaica	Dominica	Grenada
1788	1,811,668 lbs.	414,000 lbs.	325,850 lbs.
1789	*2,425,885	*835,000	*675,150
1790	2,408,950	420,250	542,500
1791	2,864,390	930,300	708,970
1792	3,221,321	87,270	1,017,732
1793	982,700	142,500	1,530,776
1794	2,078,080	13,820	455,780
1795	737,320	37,150	782,429
1789	*Comprising— 1,925,885 French 446,250 Spanish 53,750 Dutch	*Comprising— 603,000 French 226,500 Spanish 5,500 Dutch	*Comprising— 328,750 Spanish 320,400 Dutch 26,000 Danish

[86] On the working of the Free Port system Harlow had planned to include an
additional section of Chapter IX.

[87] This table is compiled from – 'An account of the Goods, Wares and
Merchandize imported into and exported from the British West India Islands in
Foreign Bottoms in Conformity to the several Acts of Parliament called the Free
Port Acts . . .', prepared each year by Thos. Irving, Inspector-General of Customs
(*Customs 17/10* in the P.R.O.). The figures quoted do not include importations into
British Islands of cotton from foreign entrepôts (such as Dutch St. Eustatius) in
British ships.

In 1793 the total importation of cotton into the British Islands from all sources amounted to 3,692,926 lbs., while the British planters themselves produced approximately 7,000,000 lbs. Thus foreign supplies increased the output of the British Colonies by about 50 per cent.

With the onset of war in 1793 and the resumption of the traditional game of beggar-my-neighbour by seizing the 'sugar' islands of European rivals the cotton situation changed dramatically. The French Islands grew finer cotton than the British and more of it. With the capture of Martinique and St. Lucia in 1794 a process began which gradually diverted a great flow of French and then Dutch cotton directly to Britain. The surrender of Dutch Guiana (Demerara, Berbice and Surinam) in 1803 brought within the British commercial system a cotton-growing region which was second only to Brazil in the Western Hemisphere.[88] In some respects the monopoly of Caribbean cotton production acquired by the use of British sea-power was even more important than the war-time monopoly in sugar.

The position as it had developed in the later stages of the war is indicated by the figures for the year 1812. Out of a total production of 15,728,000 lbs. of cotton in the Caribbean area controlled by Britain the conquered territories supplied 11,414,000 lbs.[89] Meanwhile, however, two new phenomena were beginning to appear: one was the invasion of the Indian market by British piece goods and the revolutionary change which transformed India from an exporter of cotton manufactures into a supplier of the raw material, and the other was the emergence of the United States under the stimulus of British demand as a grower of cotton on a gigantic scale. Britain's importation of Indian cotton, which was no more than 760,000 lbs. in 1793, had risen six years later to almost 7,000,000. By 1835 it had reached $41\frac{1}{2}$ million, and in 1841 it stood at 97 million. Yet even this was a small affair compared with the rise in American production. While Britain's purchase of United States cotton in 1793 was a mere 152,000 lbs., the amount rose to almost 7 million lbs. in 1799. In 1835 it was 284 million, and in 1841 it had reached the enormous total of 358 million lbs.[90] The British West Indies could not stand up to such competition, and during this period their cotton production sank to a mere $1\frac{1}{2}$ million lbs. and thereafter virtually disappeared. It was unfortunate that during the years of severe social and economic dislocation after

---

[88] The output of Demerara cotton (which was of fine quality) rose from 3,593,000 lbs. in 1799 to 4,012,000 lbs. in 1809 and then to 7,331,000 lbs. in 1810. (*Ibid.*, and B. Edwards, vol. V, App. No. XXXI, p. 40).

[89] B. Edwards, vol. V, App. No. XXX, p. 37.

[90] *Customs 17/10* and statistical tables in McCulloch (*op. cit.*), pp. 432-3.

slave emancipation most of the Islands had reverted to a precarious dependence on sugar.

A revolution had happened in the economic relations of Britain and India, and in the course of building up a world-wide primacy in cotton manufacture Britain had still further increased Anglo-American interdependence. In attempting to put the early stages of British cotton development in perspective I have gone far beyond the chronological limits of the present volume. The sustained efforts of Hawkesbury and Sir Joseph Banks to stimulate and improve the cultivation of cotton within the Empire were indicative of the new vigour and purposefulness which industrialisation at home was imparting to British policy overseas; and the eagerness of government and of industry to tap new sources of supply in any part of the world betokened a global outlook that would find the practical limits of territorial empire too confined.

3. THE SEARCH FOR OIL

There is no better or more comprehensive manifestation of British overseas commercial policy during this period than the sustained and highly successful effort of the Government of the day to seek out and establish an all-British supply of animal oil in the Arctic seas and in the southern regions of the Atlantic and Pacific Oceans. Just as industry and locomotion in the mid-20th century need petroleum oil from the lower layers of the earth's crust (while awaiting the mass production of nuclear power) so in this earlier period the oil obtained from whales and seals was required to lubricate the new machines and light the streets of London and the new industrial towns. The competitive search for it was a source of friction with the United States, contributed to a crisis with Spain which came near to precipitating a European war, and was a prime incentive in forcing open the *mare clausum* of the Pacific, thus introducing into new continents and islands the goods, institutions and vices of a revolutionary Western world.

The story may be taken as beginning in the Island of Nantucket near the coast of Massachusetts, where a Quaker community of some 5,000 people made a living by hunting whales and seals in the northern waters between Greenland and Labrador and southward along the coast of Brazil. In every sense they were a close community, bound together by a peculiarly distinctive religious way of life, by inter-marriage, and by a common interest in a single industry. The coopers, boat-builders, and other craftsmen who prepared the 'outfit' for a whaling ship charged their neighbour at economical rates, both because he was a neighbour and a 'Friend', and also because the financial success of a whaling expedition was of vital concern to all. On this basis the Nantucketers more than held their own with competitors from Boston, New Bedford and other New England ports; and as British colonists they enjoyed an assured market for oil and whale-bone in the metropolitan market.[91]

For such a community, with its complete dependence upon the British buyer, the American Revolution was a calamity. In 1775 Nantucket responded to a call to join the war against Britain by sending a deputation to the Massachusetts Assembly with a memorial declaring their intention to take no part in the conflict. That, of course, did not endear them to their fellow Americans, nor did it save them from the attentions of British cruisers and privateers, who (the Nantucketers claimed) captured about 200 of their vessels and seized property in their warehouses to the value of almost £200,000.[92]

The exclusion of the Americans during the war years gave the whalers from Britain a free field. Enjoying the further advantage of a substantial bounty, calculated on the tonnage employed, the British fishery in northern waters entered on a period of great expansion in which London and Liverpool participated as well as the original whaling ports of Whitby and Hull. This was the culmination of a long uphill struggle. In the late 16th century the British had been the pioneers, but the Dutch had subsequently ousted them. In spite of Government support the British whalers had not succeeded in re-establishing themselves until the mid-18th century and then only with the assistance of expensive bounties.[93]

---

[91] For the history of this island community written by one of their number see Obed Macy, *History of Nantucket* (Boston, 1835).

[92] See 'Paper Received from Mr. Roach' (1785). *B.T.* 6/95 (Misc.). The name of this leading Nantucketer was sometimes spelt Rotch. The estimate of losses in ships and property seems to have been exaggerated. In 1774 Nantucket had a whaling fleet of 150 vessels, averaging 100 tons a vessel (G. S. Graham, 'The Migrations of the Nantucket Whale Fishery', *New England Quarterly*, vol. VIII, p. 181, n. 6).

[93] In 1613 James I granted the exclusive right to engage in the Greenland Fishery to the Muscovy Company, and with disastrous results. From about 1618 the British were entirely superseded by the Dutch. Under Charles II an unsuccessful effort was made to regain a footing by an Act (25 *Car. II, cap.* 7) which allowed the importation of oil and whale-bone by English ships free of duty, allowed foreign owners resident in England to take part, and enacted that one half of the harpooners and mariners might be foreigners. In 1694 a charter was granted to an exclusive Company which was permitted to employ foreigners in their crews up to a proportion of two-thirds. This Company struggled on for some years with little success and finally went bankrupt. The South Sea Company which succeeded to its rights was no more successful and the Fishery was abandoned. In 1733 Parliament made a fresh effort by granting a bounty of 20/- per ton on all British vessels taking part in it, and seven years later the bounty was increased to 30/- and the crews were exempted from conscription in the Navy. In 1749 the bounty was raised to 40/- and remained at that level until 1771. In that year the Board of Trade decided that the whaling industry was so well established that the bounty might be gradually reduced: after five years to 30/- and after a further five years (i.e. in 1781) to 20/-. Even the merchants concerned admitted that after 1750 and particularly from 1775 the trade had 'flourished greatly', but when the time came in 1781 to lower the

After so long a struggle the nation in general and the whalers in particular were not disposed to throw away the advantage which the American rebellion had afforded.[94] By an Order in Council in 1783 the continued exclusion of American oil was assured by the imposition of an aliens duty of £18. 3. 0. per tun, which being approximately equal to the current selling price amounted to a prohibition. John Adams in 1785 pressed Pitt to re-open the British market to American whale-oil and some years later Jefferson wrote bitterly of Britain's policy of 'founding their navigation on the ruins of ours', but all the efforts of Adams and Jefferson were of no avail.[95] Oil extracted from certain parts of the sperm whale was greatly superior to that of the 'black' whale, and the former branch of the industry had been very largely in American hands.[96] The steep rise in demand and the new situation created by American independence convinced the Government that the building-up of a British sperm-oil industry was an object of great national importance.[97]

Meanwhile the chief specialists in that business, the Quakers of Nantucket, were in a desperate plight. Since the indispensable British market was for practical purposes closed to them, they decided to explore the possibilities of transferring themselves with their ships and equipment to the inner side of the British tariff wall, by migrating either to Nova Scotia or to Britain itself. Some opted for the former and some for the latter. In the early summer one group sent a memorial to Governor Parr of Nova Scotia asking that they and their families might be permitted to come there in order to establish a whaling settlement. For a struggling Colony, burdened with an influx of refugee Loyalists, the prospect of becoming Britain's chief supplier of a lucrative and essential commodity was as attractive to Parr as the settlement of Flemish weavers in East Anglia had been to Edward III.

---

bounty to 20/- they persuaded a willing Government to raise the bounty once more to the top level of 40/-. See evidence of the merchants and the Mayor and Burgesses of Kingston-upon-Hull (B.T. 5/3, pp. 335-40). Cf. 'A List of the Statutes relative to the Whale fishery, and also a Statement of the general purport of each Act' (B.T. 6/93), and William Scoresby, History and Description of the Northern Whale Fisheries (Edinburgh, 1820), vol. II, Chap. I.

[94] In 1776 British vessels imported 2,024 tuns of oil from the Greenland Fishery: in 1781 the total amounted to 1,899 tuns and 1785 to 4,033 tuns (B.T. 6/93). A tun = 252 imperial gallons.

[95] See Graham (loc. cit.), pp. 184 and 187.

[96] It was stated in 1786 that 'the Quantity of Oil imported from America in one year was 5,000 Tuns which sold for £200,000, and your Memorialists have the greatest Reason to believe that two thirds came from Nantucket' (Memorial of the London whalers, Enderby, Champion and St. Barbe. B.T. 6/93).

[97] A contractor for the servicing of street lamps in London, Westminster and other towns reported in 1791 that of the different types of oil for lighting purposes spermaceti oil was the best and most carefully prepared (B.T. 5/7, pp. 312-17). London alone spent some £300,000 p.a. on maintaining street lamps and had by this means made its streets reasonably safe.

Possibly under pressure from the merchants of Halifax the Governor decided to take a risk. The Nantucketers were told that, provided they took the oath of allegiance, they would be received with all their property and ships for carrying on the whale fishery from Nova Scotia. He went further and promised that oil taken by vessels 'now upon their voyages' belonging to those who moved into the Province would be shipped to England accompanied by his personal recommendation that the consignment should be treated as exempt from foreign duty. Thus encouraged, four vessels with full crews arrived in September, 1785, to be followed by four more conveying their families. A site for the new settlement was surveyed at Dartmouth (across the harbour from Halifax) and the Legislative Council spent £1,500 in building houses and meeting other costs of the new settlement. Parr wrote glowing accounts to Lord Sydney of the era of prosperity which this acquisition would bring to Nova Scotia – and hoped for the best.

Sydney did not reply for some six months: a delay which enabled a small whaling settlement at Dartmouth to become established. It was usual for Sydney to take a long time in dealing with a problem, but Governor Parr's *démarche* represented only one aspect of the Nantucket issue as seen by the Government, and this formed part of a wider question of national policy which involved a re-modelling of the whole system of maritime trade. In developing a British industry there were many precedents for employing foreign experts. Dutch harpooners, boat-steerers and even mariners had been used extensively in British whaling ships, and American specialists in the spermaceti oil business would be particularly valuable. But to allow them to be used for the establishment of a *colonial* oil factory would create a potential competitor. Furthermore (and this consideration carried even greater weight) the Americans of Boston, New Bedford and Martha's Vineyard would be provided with a convenient avenue through which their own oil could be smuggled into Britain as a British product.[98]

The Government's verdict was finally given in a despatch from Sydney in April, 1786. Parr was rebuked for having acted without

---

[98] Before the migration to Nova Scotia had taken place the Agent for Nova Scotia, Richard Cumberland, in July, 1785, submitted (somewhat unfortunately) a memorial to the Committee for Trade, representing that the oil merchants of Nantucket and other New England ports were establishing resident agents in Halifax 'under pretence of Emigration' who obtained clearance from thence of American-caught oil, thus avoiding the aliens duty. The Committee decided that there was insufficient evidence on which to take action but ordered that instructions be sent to the Lieut.-Governors of Nova Scotia and New Brunswick 'to be vigilant' (*B.T.* 5/2, p. 317). Parr investigated and reported that he had found no evidence of any extensive importation of American oil (Graham, *loc. cit.*, p. 187). But that did not prevent the London whalers from constantly urging the danger. 'If the Nantucket men have privileges granted to them to settle in Nova Scotia . . . [they] will carry it on under many collusive and clandestine practices with the people of Boston'. (Memorial by Sam Enderby and others, 1786, *B.T.* 6/93.)

authority: it was improper that American citizens should be given the privileged assistance accorded to Loyalists; and American whalers who wished to migrate must in future come to Britain and operate from there. He was, however, permitted to admit Nantucketers as settlers and provide them with land, and no action was taken against the whalers who had already arrived.[99] Parr was disappointed, but he had not been entirely defeated. From a small beginning the whale settlement of Dartmouth, backed by the Halifax merchants, gradually became a valuable asset for Nova Scotia.

Meanwhile another group of Nantucketers had been exploring the possibility of taking their families, ships and gear to Britain: colonisation in reverse, so to say. Their leader, Mr. Roach, sailed for London with his sons in July, 1785. On arrival he toured the West Country looking for a suitable port where he and his following might settle, and he was interviewed by Pitt, who passed him on to Hawkesbury and the Committee for Trade. Hawkesbury and Roach seem to have disliked each other at sight. The former had no love for New Englanders – haughty rebels and Britain's keenest competitors; and one can well understand the attitude of the trans-Atlantic Quaker, a disapproving stranger in the middle of London worldliness and ill at ease in the chilly presence of the English politician with the flickering eyes. He afterwards described Hawkesbury as one of the greatest enemies of America to be found in the British nation.[100]

Roach, however, saw only one side of the question, and, being a New Englander, he did not underestimate the value of what he had to offer. His terms were not light: free entry for twenty whaling ships with equipment and personal effects, equal participation in British bounties, compensation for losses incurred by moving, and assistance in fitting out new cooperages, forges, and so forth. The bill would amount to some £20,000. On his side Hawkesbury appreciated the importance of attracting this specialised experience to Britain and offered financial assistance for the migration; but he was not prepared to allow Nantucket owners to be eligible for British bounties as Roach required.[101]

---

[99] Graham (*loc. cit.*), p. 193.

[100] In an unsigned ' office ' memorandum of 1786 he is referred to in the following terms: ' A Mr. Roach, a Quaker of Nantucket, is a person of the greatest property of that Island and has the greatest Influence amongst the fishermen, and wherever he goes it's supposed the greatest number of their fishermen will go also. This Gentleman with his sons is now in London waiting to know the determinations of Government '. (*B.T. 6/93.*)

[101] The Customs Commissioner were strongly opposed to this concession (see p. 299 below). It was this refusal which ' frustrated the scheme ' (Jas. Philipps to Pitt, 5 March, 1788. P.R.O. 30/8/43). In the Board of Trade papers there is an ' office ' memorandum (with marginal comments) setting out the proposals to be made to Roach. It begins – ' The people from Nantucket must come directly from

Having received assurances of a welcome in France, Roach decided that he could do better there and departed for Dunkirk. The French Government was keen to outbid the British and Louis XVI took a personal interest in the proposition. Roach accepted the terms offered, which included a substantial bounty. Thirty-three Nantucket families went to Dunkirk and established a successful whale fishery, although the French themselves were not thereby induced, as their Government had hoped, to emulate the immigrants' example.[102]

In considering their policy the British Government was thus confronted with two new oil-producing centres, one in Nova Scotia and the other in France. In February, 1786, the Privy Council in response to petitions from the British whalers ordered the Committee for Trade to investigate the whole position and embody their recommendations in a Bill for Parliament. There were three issues to be determined. To what extent should the State continue to subsidise the industry in the Greenland seas? What support should be given to the new enterprise in the southern regions of the Atlantic and Pacific? Since the latter was operated almost entirely by ex-Nantucketers, employed by British owners, what

---

thence to Great Britain.' Their ships, which were not to exceed 100 tons, might come in free, each transporting 25 persons and their personal effects. On arrival £10 for passage money was to be paid to 'every Master of a Family, Owner Whaler or Mechanic, connected with the Fishery and becoming a British Subject'. For every boy between 15 and 18 years £7.10.0, for every boy under 15 and for every female £5. Grants of £70 to £100 were to be made for erecting houses, and any such houses were to revert to the public if and when the first possessor ceased to reside in Britain. In fitting out their vessels three-fourths of the crew must be of their own number or British subjects resident in the British Isles, and one-fourth might be foreigners. Mr. Roach was to receive a 'gratification' of £3 for each person coming in and taking the oath of allegiance. 'If these terms are complied [with], a Treaty to be entered into with the Pool and Dartmouth merchants to provide a Settlement and a Capital.' (*B.T.* 6/93.) The details of this plan were proposed in a memorandum, endorsed 'Observations on Mr. Rotch's Proposals' N.D. (*B.T.* 6/95.) The estimated expenditure was: £3,375 for passenger fares, £8,500 for houses, and £1,125 for contingencies, making a total of £13,000. 'An Act,' it was added, 'would be necessary to free the ships and naturalise the Emigrants'. For a more hostile reaction see 'Mr. Rotch's Proposals with . . . Observations', Jan. 24, 1786 (*B.T.* 6/95). It may be, however, that the above terms were those which Hawkesbury offered to Roach on a later occasion during the summer of 1786 (see p. 306 below).

[102] The bounty was at the rate of 50 livres (about 42/-) per ton on the tonnage of each vessel undertaking a whaling voyage. When no more Nantucketers arrived the French Government lowered their import duty on American oil by way of discouraging further migrations to British territories. (Jefferson, *Report on the Cod and Whale Fisheries* . . . p. 7. Cited in Graham, *loc. cit.*, p. 190.) In response to official enquiries Lord Gower reported from Paris in 1792 that, in spite of the success of the Nantucket men, there was a single instance of a whaling ship being commanded by a French captain. The Nantucketers were obliged to include a proportion of French sailors in their crews, but they were considered a useless burden. 15 ships (total tonnage – 3,720) had left Dunkirk for Greenland and Brazil in 1789, 18 ships in 1790, and 24 in 1791. 8,067 hogsheads (i.e. 2,017 tuns) of oil had been brought to Dunkirk in 1790. (Lord Gower to Lord Grenville, 10 Feb., 1792. Paris. Forwarded to the Board of Trade, 4 April. *B.T.* 1/3 – In-Letters.)

should be done to encourage more American whalers to transfer themselves and their skills?

The Greenland group went into action in defence of their high bounty of 40/- per ton which was due to lapse that year. They acknowledged that the exclusion of American oil (by the imposition of an aliens duty of £18.3.0) had enabled the British fishery to flourish as never before: the price of oil, it was true, had risen from the low level of £17 per ton since the cessation of American supplies, but it now stood at the 'reasonable' figure of £21 and was gradually diminishing; they were beginning to establish an export trade in oil and whale-bone to Europe. But if the bounty were reduced all this would be lost. Furthermore, it was right that the industry should be strongly supported by the State for it was 'a source of naval power' employing 6,000 hardy and experienced seamen.

The counterblast from the Customs Commissioners was significant and trenchant. They examined the position from the point of view of the national revenue, and they found it indefensible. In the course of the previous year, they reported, the bounties paid to ships fitted out in the ports of England alone had amounted to no less a sum than £84,122, which worked out at an average of £600 per ship – 'and is an Expence of such Magnitude, that in their Judgment the Public ought to be relieved from it and the Trade left to stand upon its own Bottom'. The double privilege of American exclusion and the forty-shilling bounty was attracting more and more ships into the trade. During the current season the number fitting out had risen from 153 to 190 so that the public burden was likely to increase to about £113,000.

The scale of the subsidisation was extravagant and unnecessary. A ship of 300 tons, receiving a bounty of £600, brought home a cargo to an average value of £997, 'so that to encourage the Adventurer to embark in this Trade the Public pays out of its Revenue a Premium of three-fifths of the value of the Produce, uncompensated by any Duty'. The consumer paid £21 per tun for his oil, but the real price which the Adventurer received from the consumer and the general public combined was £34. Furthermore the public was subsidising the export of this produce to foreign nations to the tune of 60 per cent of its value. If Adam Smith ever read this report he must have smiled, albeit a little wryly.

As Hawkesbury afterwards remarked in Parliament, he found himself in the position of an umpire between the Greenland merchants and the Customs Commissioners. Like a good politician he compromised, but the Report which he had drafted for the Committee of Trade leaned heavily towards the view of the Commissioners. 'No wise Nation,' he wrote, 'ever attempted to carry on any Branch of Trade on a like footing for a length of time.' It was recommended that a reduced bounty of 30/- be granted for five years, and this was intended to be the first stage in a graduated elimination. The merchants moaned – and survived.

The Report also expressed agreement with the counter-charge that the Greenland Fishery was not, as the merchants contended, a great 'nursery' for British seamen, since only one-third of the crews were required to be British and the remainder were in fact Dutch and German. Hawkesbury did his best to rectify this by recommending that the new Bill should require that three-fourths of the crews must be British, but he frankly recognised that this provision would be of little avail since the skilled personnel (line managers, harpooners, etc.) were totally exempt from pressing for the Navy, as were the crews from 1 February each year until their return. 'As the period for this Exemption is exactly that when in Time of war Your Majesty's Fleets are fitting out, it deprives Your Majesty of the advantage of availing Yourself of their Service just in the Moment when the Publick has most Occasion for them.'[103] The propaganda line, so long and so successfully maintained, that whaling was 'a source of naval power' was being challenged and exposed.[104] Hawkesbury fostered its development from 1786 on other and more valid grounds: that it could become an important pioneer of commerce in unfrequented seas.

The whaling grounds in the vicinity of Greenland and Davis Strait were providing the British market with the products but on expensive terms. On the other hand it was known that the prized sperm-whale was abundant beyond the Capes of Good Hope and Horn; and these were the gateways into regions with a vast trading potential. If a whaling industry in these areas could be established, Britain could supply herself and Europe at cheap rates independently of the Americans. In the wake of the whalers other British traders would follow. The furtherance of this plan became one of the central objects of Hawkesbury's commercial policy. Once more the discoveries of Captain Cook were influencing the direction of British overseas expansion.

While the Greenland situation was being investigated (during March, 1786) the possibilities of development to the south were also being considered. A petition for Government support had been

---

[103] 'Draft Report of the Lords of the Committee for Trade upon the Memorials of the Merchants and others concerned in the Whale Fishery, 7 April, 1786.' (*B.T.* 5/3 pp. 334-9. Another copy in *B.T.* 6/93.)

[104] In a Commons debate on 12 April Pitt made the same point. 'The Greenland Fishery was by no means to be regarded as a source for increasing the number of seamen for the navy'. Some of the men were exempt from impressment for the whole of the year 'and all of them for a considerable part of it'. Was it sound policy to subsidise 6,000 seamen at the rate of £13 a man, 'when at no time we were able to obtain more than 500 of that number to serve on board our ships of war?' (*Parl. Hist.*, vol. XXV, 1381-4).

presented by a group of owners who had already made a start in this direction.[105] By far the most important of these were the two Samuel Enderbys, father and son. They were the leading pioneers in an enterprise which was to make the family name famous in the South Seas. Before 1775 the father had owned whaling ships, based on Boston, which operated in the south Atlantic, and from that port he had been a large importer of American oil into Britain. When revolution became imminent his whaling ships avoided Boston and brought their cargoes direct to London. The official response was prompt. In 1775 a clause was inserted in an Act (chiefly relating to Newfoundland) which offered premiums to the five British-built and British-owned ships which returned with the largest cargoes from a whaling expedition to the southward, and in the following year the Enderbys and others fitted out twelve ships from London, so inaugurating the British Southern Whale Fishery.[106]

Enderby and his associates presented their case before the Committee for Trade with considerable skill. Enderby explained that many of his crews were American (mostly Nantucketers) who had been in his service for the past ten years, that his son had visited Boston since the Peace 'expressly to get information about this fishery and to engage Nantucket men to come over to England', and that by preserving and retaining the New England men throughout the difficult years of the War it had been possible for a number of Englishmen to become experienced in this new branch of whale fishing. Some of Enderby's earliest apprentices were now expert harpooners. All the other adventurers, it was stated, had followed the same method, and all worked on the 'incentive'

---

[105] A memorial from Samuel Enderby, John St. Barbe (also prominent in the Greenland Fishery) and Alexander Champion on behalf of themselves and others, praying for the granting of certain bounties, was received by the Committee for Trade on 4 Feb., 1786, and referred to the Customs Commissioners. On 13 March the merchants were informed that the Committee for Trade was now ready to take their memorial into immediate consideration, and they were invited to name a day on which they could attend, bringing with them detailed statistics of oil prices, fitting-out expenses, etc. Their examination began five days later. (*B.T. 5/3*, pp. 111, 231, and 263-5.)

[106] The premiums for the five ships were: £500 for the largest cargo of oil, £400 for the next largest, and then £300, £200, and £100. The premiums were to be available each season for eleven years. (*15 Geo. III, cap. 31, Sect. III.*) These arrangements were confirmed and elaborated in a special Act in the following year (*16 Geo. III, cap. 47*). No ships sailed in 1775: the twelve fitted out in 1776 were small (total tonnage 1,977), but as the range of the voyages increased larger ships were used. In 1785 there were 18 ships with a total tonnage of 4,105. From 1779 to 1783 inclusive only about six ships were fitted out each season. ('An Account of the Number of Ships and their Tonage fitted out in Great Britain for the Southern Whale Fishery . . . 13 March, 1786.' *B.T. 6/93*.) The merchants stated that in 1785 about 650 tuns of oil had been brought home from the South and had sold for £27,300. ('Paper delivered in by the Petitioners, St. Barbe, Enderby and Son, 22 March, 1786.' *Ibid.*)

system of distributing among the crew seven-sixteenths of the value of the cargo instead of wages.

They asked for a bounty of 40/- on the tonnage of their ships for three years, and they justified the request on the following grounds:

It will be an inducement to the Americans to settle in England, and it will be the means of establishing the Fishery here in preference to Nova Scotia, where it will be out of the Power of the Government to prevent American oil from coming here free of duty, and from its near situation to the Massachusetts will be a cover to a great deal of American property and whaling Vessels. . . .[107]

Enderby, Champion and St. Barbe followed this up with what was then a novel request, that they might have permission to go round the Cape of Good Hope, 'where they are credibly informed there are great Numbers of Whales'. So many whales had been killed or wounded off Brazil that the hunting there was becoming precarious. If permission could be obtained for going beyond the Cape, 'they have no doubt of success'. This proposition, involving as it did an invasion of the monopoly area of the East India Company, aroused Hawkesbury's keen interest and they were questioned closely.

The Government, however, was not prepared to be committed to a system of high bounties as in the Greenland Fishery. A bounty on tonnage was refused, and Hawkesbury advised then 'to think of some other mode' whereby Parliament might be induced to grant them some aid 'towards carrying on this fishery with Spirit'. They then came back with a proposal for a graduated bounty on the amount of oil imported, provided that it was taken southward of seven degrees of north latitude 'and as far to the Eastward and Westward as the Owners shall think proper to Send their ships, even round the Cape of Good Hope as far to the Eastward as the East end of the Island of Madagascar'.

Pitt was consulted and Admiral Sir Hugh Palliser, the Newfoundland expert, was brought in to advise.[108] The official attitude was summed up by Palliser: 'I think the Fishery may be much increased and extended by encouraging the most adventurous to extend their searches after Whales, which I understand many of them are disposed to do, to Cape Horn and the Cape of Good Hope. By this means many fresh places of resort for Whales may be discovered and certain distant Seas and Coasts, now very little

---

[107] The memorial of Enderby, Champion and St. Barbe, which was referred to the Committee of Trade by the Treasury on 21 Jan., 1786. The original is in *B.T. 6/93*.

[108] Palliser, who approved and supported the whalers' project, had been in touch with them for some months. (See Palliser to Hawkesbury, 23 Nov. 1785. *B.T. 6/93*.)

known, may be explored and be better known, which may here-after be of use in other respects.'[109]

It was decided that a bounty system was inappropriate and objectionable, but that the Southern whalers should be given substantial financial incentives in the form of premiums, that the East India Company (and the South Sea Company) must be induced to allow them to make voyages within their monopoly areas, and that statutory encouragement under strict regulations should be given to the migration of whalers from New England. On 3 May, 1786, the Committee for Trade approved the report and recom-mendations which Hawkesbury had prepared. The policy objectives are clearly indicated: the trade must be secured for Britain and it must be pushed in the South Seas.

This Trade . . . is of great Importance in the present Moment, when the American Fishery is declining and it is doubtful to what Countries the People heretofore employed in it may resort, and whether Great Britain, or any other Foreign Country, may get possession of it, that a proper effort should now be made to secure to this Country the advantages of a Fishery which was once so lucrative to the Americans.

The emphasis on the South Seas is shown in the scale of premiums to be offered. In addition to an increase in the number of old premiums from five to twenty for vessels sailing south of 7° N. latitude, a special set of premiums, ranging from £700 to £300, was to be provided for the five vessels bringing home the largest cargoes of oil which had been on the voyage for not less than eighteen months and had made their catch beyond the line of 36° S. latitude. The Report was signed while the battle with the East India Company was still in progress, so that it was not possible to do more on that count than point out the advantages that would accrue if 'these Corporations' claiming an exclusive right of navigation in the South Seas would give the desired permission.

This may tend to encourage the Spirit of Adventure, to promote Navigation, and to render this Fishery still more extensive and bene-ficial to this Country . . . , and it is with this view principally that the Committee have recommended the larger sett of the premiums before mentioned.[110]

The mere suggestion of such an irruption into their preserves caused a rush of blood to the heads of many East India Directors.

---

[109] The above account of the negotiations with the Southern whalers is based on the relevant Minutes of the Committee for Trade in *B.T.* 5 and on a large collection of memoranda and correspondence in *B.T.* 6/93 and 95.

[110] ' Report of the Lords of the Committee for Trade proposing certain Premiums, etc., for the Encouragement of the Southern Whale Fishery, May 3, 1786 ' (*B.T.* 5/3, pp. 457-69. Another copy in *B.T.* 6/93).

When the proposal was referred by the Court to the Committee of Correspondence, the latter (on 25 April) resolved that, while they were not sufficiently informed of the details of the plan to form any opinion, they were led to fear that it might be 'exceedingly injurious' to the Company and for the following reasons. Whaling ships might carry goods for the Indian market to the Cape of Good Hope and other ports, selling them there to Company's ships in exchange for the products of India which they could bring home. Secondly, Company ships on the voyage from India to China might rendezvous with the whalers and supply them with trade goods 'for their homeward Voyages or to be carried to America'. Furthermore the confining of these whalers to particular latitudes would in practice be ineffective, for under pretence of accidents or stress of weather they would go 'to other Places'; and covenants to protect the Company's privileges, however strictly worded, would be exceedingly difficult to enforce from lack of proof.

Besides these Reasons the Committee also suspect that the fishing Trade proposed will not be found to answer to the Projectors for want of Fish, the danger of those Seas, etc., which induces a Suspicion that there must be some other Object in view.

If on further consideration it was thought that the Company should not entirely oppose the project, it ought to go no further than licensing 'a very few ships' for one voyage only. The Chairman and Deputy-Chairman were requested to confer with Mr. Pitt and Mr. Dundas, using these and any other arguments that might occur to them and requesting the fullest details. The dog in the manger was barking furiously.

A series of bilateral discussions took place in which the participants were: Pitt and Dundas, the 'Chairs' representing the Court of Directors, the Committee for Trade, and the Southern Whalers. On 1 May the Committee for Trade summoned the Enderbys, Champion and St. Barbe and asked them whether they would be prepared to apply for licences to the East India Company to pass beyond Cape Horn and the Cape of Good Hope and would give security not to engage in any illicit trade, to which they replied that they had 'no sort of objection'. On 3 May the Committee wrestled with the Chairman and Deputy, who offered objections and desired to refer the proposals to the Court of Directors. On the following day the whalers appeared before the Court and were presented with a set of regulations. They were to be permitted entry into the South Seas under licence, but within strict geographical limits and subject to very elaborate prohibitions and penalties. These the whalers accepted; but it was not until 26 May that the Directors finally wrote to the Committee for Trade agreeing to the detailed regulations which were to be incorporated in the Act.[111]

The Company had given way under Government pressure. Their apprehensions were understandable enough. For them the Pacific was the back door to the Indian Ocean and the China Seas and Cook had undone the lock. Moreover the Enderby group were intelligent and aggressive men who were not slow to appreciate that they enjoyed Government favour and that the Company was on the defensive. Their ambition was to range the Pacific without hindrance. During the next sixteen years or so they pressed periodically to have their fishing limits extended, and stage by stage the Company was obliged to retreat.

A touch of fantasy was added to this battle against exclusive privilege by the claims of the South Sea Company. George Chalmers was put on to investigate this, and he did so with a thoroughness worthy of an historian. In a memorandum for Hawkesbury he traced the history of the Company from its inception and noted its failure to trade in the Pacific, its heavy losses in the Greenland Fishery, and that since 1753 it had been 'merely a money corporation'. Its claim to an exclusive trade was, he contended, 'baseless' and could be set aside if it were thought necessary to include a clause in the forthcoming statute explicitly permitting the whalers to double Cape Horn.[112] Yet chartered rights, even dubious ones, were a touchy political issue. Instead of the permissive clause suggested by Chalmers it was enacted that every vessel intending to frequent any part of the seas comprised in the boundaries of the exclusive trade of the South Sea Company must obtain a licence from the Company before proceeding on the voyage. The licences were not, of course, issued free of charge.

The Act of 1786 'for the Encouragement of the Southern Whale Fishery'[113] proved to be the foundation of an important industry and a stimulus to exploration and maritime expansion. It was a characteristic example of the overseas policy of the Pitt Administration. It is also significant in that it reflects the pressures with which Ministers had to contend and the extent to which they were prepared to break with tradition in promoting a new development under novel conditions. In what form should State assistance be afforded for the new industry? The Customs Commissioners (watchdogs of the revenue and the laws of trade) were strongly opposed, as in the case of the Greenland Fishery, to a comprehensive bounty system, and Hawkesbury reverted to premiums; but he achieved his

---

[111] Minutes of 1 and 3 May, 1786 (*B.T. 5/3*, pp. 379 *et seq.* and 397); Resolutions of the Court of Directors, 4, 10 and 11 May. (Copies in *B.T. 6/93*.)

[112] 'Collection as to the South Sea Company, 26 May, 1786, by Mr. Chalmers.' (*Ibid.*) Cf. Minutes of the Court of Directors of the South Sea Company, vol. 28. (*Addit. MSS.*, 25,522).

[113] 26 Geo. III, cap. 50.

object by quadrupling their number and adding special 'prizes' for vessels bringing oil from the South Seas.

Since the project involved the substitution of a British organisation for an American one, exceptional measures were needed to acquire the requisite expertise from the rival. The Nantucket crews of Enderby and his colleagues were the essential nucleus, and the Act accordingly recognised the *de facto* position by providing that the ships could be manned by Protestant aliens who were already established in Britain. But for the sake of furthering a special object the Act went even further than this in deviating from tradition. The London whalers wanted more Nantucketers, especially those who were setting up a rival business in Nova Scotia. Hawkesbury agreed, and a special clause was included to attract more Protestant aliens who were experienced in the industry. Up to forty of their ships would be accepted in Britain with their families and crews. Provision was made for such ships to be licensed by Order in Council to operate from Britain as though they were British and to import their oil duty-free. And this was done in spite of a vigorous protest from the Customs Commissioners. To encourage the citizens of a foreign Power to come over and to give their ships the privileges of British bottoms was, they declared, directly contrary to the (Hawkesbury) Act of Navigation which at that very time was before Parliament. It was a shrewd thrust, but it did not prevail.

On the other hand the Commissioners had their way on another point which proved to be crucial. In a memorandum they wrote: 'We cannot possibly recommend an extension of those bounties to subjects of the United States, even upon the conditions proposed in the Clause.' Apart from other considerations the concession would 'open a wider door for the practice of Frauds': foreigners were already attempting to claim oil bounties and exemption from Duties to which they were not entitled.[114] The offending clause was amended accordingly – and the Nantucketers stayed at home.[115]

Again the tussle with the East India Company resulted in a

---

[114] 'Remarks by the Commissioners of Customs.' 10 May, 1786. *B.T. 6/93.*

[115] Hawkesbury afterwards stated that immediately after he had been appointed President of the new Board of Trade (August, 1786) he had a further interview with Mr. Roach of Nantucket who was re-visiting England from Dunkirk. 'He [Hawkesbury] took up this Business, and having provisionally settled with Mr. Pitt what it might be proper to offer to induce the people of Nantucket to come and settle in this Kingdom, etc., saw Mr. Rotch [*sic*] and opened the propositions to him. Mr. Rotch was so far from finding fault with the Terms offered that he acknowledged that they were handsome, but he declined accepting them, and from his Conversation Ld. H. had then Reason to conclude that He had already entered into some Engagement with the Government of France.' (This quotation is from a memorandum which he sent to Charles Greville on 29 Sept., 1792. *Addit. MSS.*, 38,310, f. 81ᵛ *et seq.* Another copy is in *Addit. MSS.*, 38,351, ff. 261-4.)

modification of traditional usage which had important consequences. The Government had intended that the whalers should
have free entry into the South Seas, and in spite of resistance the
Company was obliged to concede the principle. Nevertheless they
successfully insisted on geographical limits which excluded the
whalers from the Indian Ocean and a large part of the Pacific.
Whaling ships which reached the region of the Cape of Good Hope
were not permitted to go to the east of it or to sail further north
than 30° S.; and those which rounded the Horn might not go
further north than the Equator or more than 500 leagues west of
the American coast. But the penetration had begun, and it was
manifestly impossible to hold it back. The establishment of a
convict settlement at Botany Bay in 1787 (Enderby himself providing transport for some of the first contingents) and the conquest of
Dutch Cape Colony in 1795 were from the Company's point of
view even more ominous intrusions.

The action of the State in promoting a new branch of maritime
industry, centred in Britain, which was to lead a commercial
invasion of the Pacific, thus brought into play a variety of conflicting views and interests, represented by Ministers, ' John Company ',
fishery merchants, and North American settlers. Among these and
with its own contribution to the contending elements was the
strenuous campaign of the Honble. Charles Fulke Greville to
secure a share in the new enterprise for Milford on the coast of
Wales.

Milford Haven was, and is, one of the finest harbours in the
British Isles and until recent times was also one of the most
neglected. About the year 1784 Sir William Hamilton, owner of
the Pembrokeshire estate which included Milford, paid a visit there
with his nephew, Charles Greville.[116] The latter (who had been
Treasurer of the Household during the Fox-North Administration)
was in financial straits, and his uncle encouraged him to ' chalk
out some improvements ' to enable the natural advantages of
Milford to be utilised. In 1785 Hamilton and Greville encountered
the Nantucketer, Roach, during his tour of the West Country in
search of a suitable place for a settlement. A number of conversations ensued which convinced Greville (and apparently Roach)
that Milford was the ideal place and Greville sent a memorial to
the Privy Council to that effect.

Roach's subsequent refusal to accept Hawkesbury's terms because
they did not include Government bounties or premiums dashed
Greville's hopes. He blamed the influence of the Enderby group for

---

[116] In Wraxall's *Historical Memoirs* (vol. III, p. 206) Dr. Doran inserted the
following note: ' Sir William is said to have paid his nephew's debts on condition
that he surrendered the lady who lived under his protection, and whom Sir William
afterwards married – the erring yet ill-used Emma, Lady Hamilton.'

the withholding of this inducement and the Government for its short-sightedness in allowing France to outbid them. The London whalers were, however, as anxious as he was to secure further recruits from Nantucket, and their influence caused Hawkesbury to include the general invitation in the Act of 1786 which was repeated two years later. But none of the Nantucket men responded. Most of them were poor men who expected compensation for property left behind and a considerable outlay to set them on their feet in a new abode.

Greville insisted that the only way to secure their skill and experience was to do this and attach the offer to a particular place, that is to say, Milford Haven. Meanwhile his attention had been caught by the migration from Nantucket to Dartmouth, Nova Scotia. In his view a colonial whaling settlement was almost as deplorable as a French one; but since Parr had been forbidden to admit any more American whalers it was not too late, he thought, to recover the lost ground. In June, 1790, he wrote to Grenville, the Home and Colonial Secretary of State, setting out his plans for Milford and proposing that an agent, one Charles Stokes, should be sent to the American States and Nova Scotia on a tour of investigation and propaganda. The letter was referred to the Board of Trade, who invited Stokes himself to attend. At the meeting the Board decided that it might be desirable to renew the encouragement given in the Acts of 1786 and 1788 for foreign Protestant whalers to come to Britain and it was agreed to furnish Stokes with letters of introduction to British Consuls and the appropriate colonial Governors.[117] He sailed a few days later, worked his way from the southern States northward and so to Nantucket and then to Nova Scotia. From Boston (in November, 1790) he sent preliminary reports and on his return home some months later he gave full accounts to both Hawkesbury and Greville. At Nantucket he found that there was still a community of some 4,500 people, who were continuing the whaling business. Many were disposed to consider migration, but he frankly admitted that others, and particularly those owing pre-Revolution debts to British merchants, were disposed, if they moved at all, to join their brethren at Dunkirk. Their appeal for assistance to Congress, they told him, had been ignored. Get in quickly, urged Stokes, before the French offer better terms. If left to themselves, 'these valuable people will be in the course of a few years entirely lost to every country'. Nantucket, however, struggled through, and in the mid-19th century was second only to New Bedford in renewed expansion which was out-rivalling the British.

Stokes was also received in friendly fashion by the Nantucket

---

[117] Minutes of 3 July, 1790. *B.T.* 5/6, p. 261.

immigrants at Dartmouth, Nova Scotia, and much against his will Lieut.-Governor Parr gave his official support. Stokes exhibited a copy of the Board of Trade's invitation, and some who were disgruntled at being cut off from their relatives by the official refusal to admit any more American whalers signed a memorial to Sir William Hamilton asking to be informed what his terms might be on removal to Milford. On the other hand most of the Nantucketers were now financed by the Halifax merchants who were extremely sore with the British Government (and said so) for trying to filch settlers whose loss would weaken the Colony's economy and cause the £1,500 of public money spent on accommodating them to be wasted. Stokes, however, returned full of optimism, and Greville put further proposals to the Government for a scheme of 'assisted' immigration. The latter wrote in jubilation that 40 sail with a total complement of 600 men might be expected from Nantucket and a further 19 sail from Dartmouth – 'which I flatter myself I shall see within three years if Government shall patronise a Colony in Milford by acceding to the proposals before them'.

When Greville presented a migration scheme which he had agreed with Timothy Folger and Samuel Starbuck of Dartmouth, Nova Scotia, the Board of Trade decided to recommend financial support. 'It would be right,' they recorded in April, 1791, 'by reasonable encouragements to induce any of the Inhabitants of His Majesty's Colonies in America concerned in this Fishery to remove to Great Britain.' The Treasury was to be asked to determine the sums to be allowed for defraying the costs of removal from Nova Scotia and 'any other pecuniary inducements to be offered to them for that purpose'. The terms worked out by the Treasury (in effect by Pitt) were not ungenerous although on a limited scale.[118] The response, however, proved to be meagre.[119]

Meanwhile under the authority of an Act of Parliament authorising Hamilton to improve the communications at Milford, Greville was at work preparing for the reception of the settlers.[120] Milford was made a market town, a daily postal service was extended thither

---

[118] Minute of April, 1791. *B.T.* 5/7, p. 131. The terms were as follows: a sum of up to £50 for the transport of each family of five or more to be paid upon arrival; £2,000 to be dispensed as compensation for loss incurred in removal, subject to producing a certificate from the Lieut.-Governor of Nova Scotia and giving security to settle in Britain; and a first cargoe of oil to be admitted duty-free if brought from a colonial port. Being British citizens the immigrants would, on becoming residents, automatically qualify for whaling premiums and the privilege of duty-free importation. The Government refused the somewhat impudent request that they should buy the whalers' property in Nova Scotia, which was valued at £5,985: they were told that they must sell it themselves. Pensions of £150 p.a. were to be paid to Folger and Starbuck for their lives and the lives of their wives on the ground that they were Loyalists.

[119] See pp. 313, 315 below.

[120] *30 Geo. III, cap. 55.* This was one of many Acts passed during this period for the improvement of roads, bridges, canals, etc., in specified localities.

from Haverfordwest, quays and roads were built, and plans were drawn up for rows of new houses to accommodate the newcomers, an inn for passengers and a customs house. With a further £6,000, wrote Greville, he could convert the two 'pills' or inlets into magnificent deep-water docks (there was a 25-35 ft. tide) which could take first-rate ships of the line. In short, Milford Haven was to become New Nantucket, where the scattered remnants from Dartmouth and possibly Dunkirk would be re-united with their brethren.[121]

In 1792 Greville's hopes were high. The Privy Council in the previous year had confirmed the recommendation of the Board of Trade that a further Act be passed to encourage foreign whalers to settle in Britain, and Greville claimed that firm arrangements had been made with sixteen or seventeen families to come to Milford from Dartmouth with their ships during the autumn of 1792 and in the following spring. But delays were taking place and Greville scented opposition from that now powerful body, 'The Committee of South Whalers from London', that is to say, Enderby (father and son), Champion (father and son) and John St. Barbe. In July, 1792, he wrote to them describing all his plans for Milford. Would they prefer that he pressed on for a renewal of the general invitation by another Act of Parliament or that he should apply for an Order in Council authorising the admission (to Milford) under specified conditions of 40 families and 20 vessels? He then went on to advertise – somewhat ingenuously – the advantages which the whaling settlement at Milford was going to enjoy. He intended to organise the industry with 'small Capitals in the Hands of intelligent Persons' and to establish a more economical method of providing 'outfits' for the voyage. He did not propose to bring *all* the Nantucketers to Milford, for that would overstock the market and seriously lower the price of oil; yet competition and lowered prices were for the benefit of the nation at large.[122] No doubt the London whalers smiled.

St. Barbe responded by saying that his committee were very strongly opposed to any further invitations to Nantucketers. 'The

---

[121] Stokes to Hawkesbury, and Stokes to Greville, Boston, 25 Nov., 1790. (*Addit. MSS.*, 38,225, ff. 339-41): Memorandum by Chas. Greville (N.D., but from internal evidence written early in 1791. *Royal Archives, Windsor*): Lt.-Gov. Wentworth of Nova Scotia to Greville, 24 Oct., 1792 (*Addit. MSS.*, 33,228, ff. 92-7), and the official correspondence of Parr and Wentworth on the subject (*C.O. 217/56*). Cf. G. S. Graham (*loc. cit.*), pp. 195-8.

[122] 'Letter to the Committee of South Whalers from London, sent to Mr. St. Barbe, 7 July, 1792' (Endorst. of copy enclosed in Greville to Hawkesbury, 14 Aug., 1792. *Addit. MSS.*, 38,228, f. 7 *et seq.*). Greville's opening passage was scarcely tactful: 'Although in 1785 the influence of your Committee with Lord Hawkesbury tended to limit the liberality and Justice of this Country to the Nantucketers, and in fact deprived me of the chance of settling Mr. Rotch and his Family at Milford, the Event has confirmed my Prediction to the Privy Council in 1784, that France would gain a Whale Fishery by our folly.'

Fishery being now perfectly established in Great Britain, we are under no apprehension of its being injured by the trade carried on out of America.' They agreed, however, about the desirability of getting rid of the Dunkirk rivalry. The French Government was in confusion, and as soon as they defaulted on their obligations, ' which we think at no distant date ', the Dunkirkers would readily accept an invitation to transfer themselves to Britain, and the Committee were ready to co-operate with Greville to secure legislation for that purpose. They were sorry that they could not agree about the Nantucketers, but it would be folly to invite foreigners to participate in a business which had been built up with very great toil, risk and expense. ' We import now as much as all Europe can consume. What must be the consequence should double the quantity be imported? '[123] The answer, of course, was ' cheap oil and increased consumption '; but the social structure of 18th-century Europe excluded the masses as a potential market for most commodities.

St. Barbe concluded his letter with an oblique retort to Greville's mention of small capitals and cheap outfits. The Southern Whale Fishery, he explained, were encouraged to use large and therefore expensive ships. ' I believe one principal motive of our Privy Council in the encouragement they give Ships going round the Capes was the grand object of Discovery, which in our opinion will tend to great utility to this Kingdom.'

Greville seized on the prospect of support with regard to the Dunkirkers. He wrote to Pitt asking that the proposed Bill renewing the general invitation to foreign whalers should be held up and that if a group of not more than forty families should offer to settle ' in any one British port ' (i.e. Milford) for carrying on the fishery, Pitt would then introduce a special measure, granting them all the privileges of British citizens upon their arrival, the admission of their personal property duty-free, and that their ships not exceeding twenty in number should be given British registration. The effect would have been that the Dunkirk settlement, having moved *en bloc* to Milford, would have competed strongly with the London group, and while their smaller vessels would probably not have ventured on the long voyage beyond Horn and Good Hope, the increased supplies of oil would have reduced and perhaps eliminated the profit margin.[124]

Pitt promised to consult Hawkesbury, and a fortnight later Greville had his answer. It was not possible, wrote Hawkesbury, to respond to his proposals without consulting the merchants concerned in the South Whale Fishery, whose ' spirited endeavours '

---

[123] John St. Barbe to Greville, 2 Aug., 1792. *Ibid.*, f. 19.
[124] ' My requisition submitted to Mr. Pitt, 14 Aug., 1792 ' (endorst.) (*Addit. MSS.,* 38,228, f. 21).

L

had effected an importation of oil now greater than Britain's total consumption. Great care must be taken to avoid doing them material injury 'by introducing Foreigners into the Kingdom as Rivals to them'. Nothing could be done until Parliament reassembled about Christmas time and in the meanwhile no Minister could take action that would 'pledge Parliament to the Measure', especially when it was contrary to the declared opinion of those already concerned in the trade.[125]

Greville was not given to accepting a negative. He retorted: 'You alarm Mr. Pitt's caution without adducing any grounds to direct his Judgment to the Merit of the Case.' Hawkesbury, he wrote, would not believe him in 1786 when he gave warning that Roach would not accept the limited offer then made by Government and would make a settlement in France. In consequence Britain had lost the foreign market in oil. A (small) group of Nantucketers had now reached Milford from Nova Scotia: they were experienced whalers and men of good character. He himself was completely committed to the Milford project, and expected further official support to bring it to fruition.[126]

Hawkesbury looked into the matter again and then sent him a memorandum containing his 'honest and deliberate Sentiments upon the Subject'. It was an even more decisive affirmation of the Government's policy. The number of ships, he wrote, which had fitted out for the southern fishery in the previous year had been 'exceedingly great', almost double the number in previous years; and it was impossible to foresee the effect upon the market price of oil when these returned.

It is certainly not for the Interests of the Public that the present Adventurers should have a Monopoly so as to raise the Price of Oil extravagantly to the Detriment of the Consumer. But it is the duty of Government not to afford Encouragement to rivals, who may so over-stock the Market as to bring Ruin on the present Adventurers, who in promoting their own Interests, have with great Spirit established and extended this Fishery in Great Britain.

It would, therefore, be highly imprudent without further investigation and without hearing all parties to adopt any new plan either by way of general invitation or of special assistance in respect of a particular port; but any engagements already entered into by Government would be honourably fulfilled.[127]

In their determination to sustain the Southern whalers as the pioneers of commercial penetration in the South Seas Hawkesbury

---

[125] Hawkesbury to Greville, 29 Aug., 1792 (draft). *Ibid.*, ff. 34-5.

[126] Greville to Hawkesbury, 11 Sept., 1792. *Ibid.*, f. 51.

[127] Hawkesbury to Greville, with enclosure, 29 Sept., 1792. (*Addit. MSS.*, 38,310, f. 81 *et seq.*)

and Pitt were not prepared to weaken or antagonise them. Schemes for inducing Nantucketers to migrate either from Dunkirk or Nova Scotia must be strictly limited by that consideration. In fact the Board of Trade was aware that the capital and ships of Halifax merchants, reinforced by American technicians, had established a thriving whale fishery in Nova Scotia. They did not like it, but their action in imposing a differential tariff on colonial-produced whale oil amounted to a tacit acceptance of a *fait accompli*.[128]

Greville, however, persisted, and under stress of bombardment Hawkesbury requested his right-hand man, George Chalmers, to review all the relevant documents and report. He did so (on 30 April, 1793) in an incisive memorandum. It was right to offer some encouragement to colonial whalers to come to Britain but not to Milford Haven only: the merchants of other ports would justly complain. Out of the £2,000 allowed by the Treasury for removal expenses, £1,342 17. 6 had been paid to the six Nova Scotia whalers who had actually arrived in Milford. The Government had met its commitment, but they had not intended that this limited project should be merely a preliminary step to a much wider scheme of providing financial assistance to immigrants from Nantucket – 'an entire new description of men, namely, the Citizens of the United States of America'.[129]

When Greville, undaunted, put forward fresh proposals in the following September, Hawkesbury once more referred the issue to Chalmers, who was less polite and even more forthright than on the previous occasion. He repeated the argument that the market in oil was overstocked and added that ships were being withdrawn from the fishery. 'Yet this is the moment when Mr. Greville proposes that twenty Ships should be admitted to Registry for the purpose of introducing twenty families into the fishery.' Under Hawkesbury's fostering care the trade had developed as far as it could well go unless new markets could be found. In 1792 fifty-nine ships had returned, bringing oil, whale-bone, seal skins, and ambergris to the total value of more than £189,000. This was Hawkesbury's achievement and 'ought not to be distressed or

---

[128] In 1788 the Board had learned from a London merchant recently returned from Halifax that 14 vessels (total tonnage 1,674) regularly sailed from Nova Scotia to hunt black and sperm whale off the coast of Brazil. Of these ships four belonged to Nantucket men, settled at Dartmouth, but, being poor, they had sold the majority of the shares in them to Halifax merchants, who were the owners of the other 10 vessels. Almost the whole of the crews were Nantucketers, who consisted of 15 to 20 families. The oil produced was all exported to Britain. (Evidence of John Turner, 10 Jan., 1788. *B.T.* 5/5, pp. 6-15.) An import duty of 15/5d. per tun was imposed on British colonial oil. This impost, although slight compared with the foreign duty of £18.3.0, amounted to a considerable preference in favour of whalers resident in Britain when considered in conjunction with the substantial premiums for which the latter were eligible.

[129] Memo. by Geo. Chalmers, 30 April, 1793, forwarded to Hawkesbury on the same day. (*Addit. MSS.*, 38,229, ff. 13 and 16-22.)

disturbed in order to promote individual projects which have no claim upon the Government'. To that he added a significant comment. When the Fishery was first established there was 'an implied trust created between the Government and the Adventurers': if the latter carried on they would continue to receive protection. 'Upon the whole,' concluded Chalmers, 'the pointed answer to Mr. Greville is: what you propose is not a good to be desired, but an evil to be avoided. The Government do not want to have more ships, at present, in this fishery, but more Markets for the produce of it.'[130] Chalmers was a good civil servant.

Most men after such repeated rebuffs would have given up; but Greville battled on and in 1795 he at last had his way. In that year a new General Act 'for further encouraging and regulating the Southern Whale Fisheries' was passed.[131] Two earlier statutes had provided inducements to foreign whalers to come and reside in Britain in general terms, but the Act of 1795 specified Milford Haven as the destined place of settlement. Foreigners, not exceeding forty, who had been previously engaged for at least three years in whale fishing were permitted to come to Milford Haven any time before 1 January, 1799, with their families and not more than twenty of their vessels, each of which must be manned by at least twelve seamen experienced in whaling. The immigrants might bring their furniture and stock duty-free; they must give security to reside in Britain for at least three years; and on taking the oaths of allegiance their ships would be given British registry (as whalers) and they would then be eligible for the premiums and in general to all the rights and privileges of natural-born subjects.

The invitation was clearly directed to the American whalers of Dunkirk. When Greville had put the proposition to Pitt in 1792 the Prime Minister had been 'cautious'; but in 1795 when the French Directory were attacking Britain through her overseas territories and commerce the prospect of eliminating a branch of French oceanic trade was not irrelevant to the general issue. Greville had secured his Act of Parliament, but he did not get the whalers either from Dunkirk or elsewhere. In any case a large capital investment would have been required, which was not forthcoming. Moreover Milford was a long way from the urban centres of oil consumption. For ten years Greville had laid siege to an embarrassed Government and against powerful opposition from a whaling organisation in London which was the Government's protégé. He had won the day, but only on paper. Whaling ships

---

[130] Chalmers to Hawkesbury, 28 Sept., 1793. (*Ibid.*, f. 79.) It seems clear from this and other statements about over-supply that British oil, which was not cheap, had not secured much of a market in Europe.

[131] 35 *Geo. III, cap. 92.* Cf. D. Macpherson, *Annals of Commerce* (Lond., 1805), vol. IV, pp. 346-7.

bringing cargoes from the South Seas did not tie up at the quays which he had built, nor did the rows of busy streets with inns and all the accessories of a sea industry materialise. In our own time Milford Haven is indeed becoming a great port and refinery, but for oil of another kind.[132]

Meanwhile the invasion of the Pacific was proceeding. While the whalers were thrusting into the seas beyond the Horn and the Cape of Good Hope, other traders and explorers (British, American and Russian) were following up the pioneer work of Cook's third voyage along the north-west coast of America. A brisk trade in seal and other furs developed, attempts were made to establish a trans-Pacific fur trade with China, and the search for a sea passage between the Pacific and the North Atlantic was renewed. From all quarters the vast claims of exclusive right which Spain had tried to insist upon so long were being thrust aside. Effective patrol of the wastes of the Pacific was, of course, impracticable; but the Spanish Government disposed its *guarda costas* to protect the coasts of South America from intruders and the Pacific side of the northern Continent. Clashes between the invaders and the defenders were inevitable.

The rising tension was indicated by a new form of intrusion. Whalers found that the skins and blubber of seals were a valuable subsidiary to their main quest; and these animals were to be obtained in great quantities on the beaches of islands and along mainland coasts claimed as Spanish territory. When enquiries were made about the legality of such visits the official answer was in accordance with British tradition: there was no reason why British vessels should not visit 'desert' coasts not occupied by a European Power, but on entering a port permission must be sought from His Catholic Majesty's subjects if any such were found to be there.[133] The following episode illustrates the situation which developed. In April, 1789, two whaling vessels from London, the *Sappho* and the *Elizabeth and Margaret,* put in at Port Desire (Puerto Deseado) on the Patagonian coast for water and repairs, and while this was going forward some of the crews were occupied in catching seals

---

[132] In addition to the documents already cited I have made use of the numerous letters from Greville to Hawkesbury (with enclosures) in the latter's collected papers, particularly *Addit. MSS.*, 38,225 to 38,229.

[133] For example, in 1788 a certain J. N. Leard, who had been a Master in the Royal Navy, on returning from a seal-hunting voyage along the coast of Patagonia, proposed that an organised sea fishery should be established in that region but wished to know what the legal position was, 'as it is not my wish to carry on the Fishery or visit any place that would give Offense to the Spaniards – which would also hurt myself and connexions. I therefore most humbly request to be informed of the Propriety of carrying on the Fishery at the aforementioned Coasts'. At the suggestion of Lord Stanhope he prepared a memorandum on the subject and sent copies to Pitt, Carmarthen, Hawkesbury, Chatham and Hood. (See Leard to Hawkesbury, 16 July, 1788, and 'Observations on the Seal Fishery. signed J. N. Leard'. *B.T. 6/95*.)

on Penguin Island about four leagues away. A Spanish frigate and two other armed vessels then appeared on the scene, and the Commodore sent to each of the English captains (Hopper and Middleton) a list of questions to be answered respecting their port of origin, business, destination, whether they carried a Spanish passport and had made contact with the native Indians. The information was given and each added the stock reply that he did not know that this coast belonged to the King of Spain but looked on it as a desert coast which no country claimed and that if he had encountered any of His Catholic Majesty's subjects he would have asked permission before entering the Port. The Spanish Commodore was polite but uncompromising.

All foreign Nations [he wrote] must abstain from frequenting the Seas, Coasts and ports of all these Provinces and their districts as the pretext fishing whales is invalid . . . because it is upon the King of Spain's Seas, who orders that, as under this motive several vessels have come and are coming on the Smuggling trade and others prejudicial to the State, the greatest care be used to hinder these Excesses. . . .

Spanish warships, he added, were stationed in the Rio de la Plata and had strict orders to cruise along the Patagonian coast and the Falkland Islands and to prevent by force all whaling and sealing operations by any nation, 'though in the Public Seas'. The English ships must complete their repairs within six days and depart, and the crews must stop hunting seals at once. Hopper and Middleton were studiously civil and complied, for access to a harbour for repairs and refreshment was essential on a long whaling voyage.[134] The Spanish officer supplied Middleton with some provisions to expedite his departure, but he was obliged to leave 7,000 seal skins behind.

When the *Sappho* and the *Elizabeth and Margaret* returned to London and the story was told, the Committee of Southern Whalers went into action. A memorial was presented (in October, 1789) to the Board of Trade complaining of the Spanish action, and the Board promptly held an enquiry which was attended by Joseph Lucas (one of the owners) with Enderby and Champion.[135] Ministerial consultations evidently followed, for in December Hawkesbury on behalf of the Board of Trade sent an elaborate memorandum to the Foreign Secretary, the Duke of Leeds, which was in effect the draft of a formal representation from the British

---

[134] The two captains had evidently been carefully instructed before setting out. They kept copies of all their letters to the Spaniard (' Jamon de Clairace ') and the two sets are in almost identical terms. The Spanish officer did his best with a queer mixture of English and Spanish, and his letters were ' translated ' on being brought to London. They are all in the bundle, *B.T.* 6/95.

[135] Minutes of 16 and 20 Oct., 1789. *B.T.* 5/5, pp. 386, 388-9.

Government to the Court of Madrid.[136] After describing the action taken against the *Sappho* and the *Elizabeth and Margaret* at Port Desire, the document recited articles in Anglo-Spanish treaties from 1667 onwards. None of these justified the 'preposterous' action which had now been taken.

The Board then stated a case. If the Spanish Court should support its officer in his claim to exclude British vessels from fishing in any part of the seas of South America, 'such a Claim ought to be denied and resisted as not founded either in the Law of Nations or in any subsisting Treaty'. It was the more important to do so now since the preservation of the Southern Whale Fishery depended on it: 'a Fishery which has of late years employed great numbers of ships fitted out by His Majesty's Subjects at a very considerable Expence and which is every year increasing and thereby improving and extending the Trade and Navigation of His Majesty's Dominions.'

In order to remove every just ground of suspicion on the part of the Spanish Government that the King's Ministers entertained any design of encouraging British subjects to carry on a contraband trade with the Spanish Colonies under pretence of this whale fishery, 'it may be proper to assure the Court of Madrid that it is by no means the Intention of the British Government that the Masters of British Ships concerned in this Fishery should remain at Anchor or be found hovering near the Coast of the Spanish Dominions in America'. Indeed the merchants concerned had stated in evidence that the spermaceti whale was usually caught ten leagues out and the black whale at about five leagues.

The tender point, of course, was the growing practice of actually landing on territory claimed by Spain in order to hunt seals, and this was dealt with in a forthright style. When British subjects landed on uninhabited islands for this purpose, 'and even on the desert Shores of those parts of the Continent where as yet no Settlements have been made', it was impossible to pretend that their real reason for doing so was to engage in illicit commerce with Spanish colonists.

It may be proper to insist that the Crews of British Fishing Ships shall be suffered to land or go on shore at such Places for the purpose before mentioned, but with an express Assurance that the Government of this Country has no Intention to form any Settlement thereon.

The memory of the Foreign Secretary was then refreshed with a *résumé* of the Falkland Islands crisis of 1770.[137] Although the British

---

[136] The formula used was: 'I am now directed by the Lords of the Committee to transmit to Your Grace, in obedience to His Majesty's Commands (i.e. the King in Council), their Opinions on this important Subject, so far as it has any reference to Trade and Navigation.'

[137] See vol. I, pp. 22-32.

had withdrawn, they had never acknowledged the Spanish claim to sovereignty over those Islands. Other claims with regard to unoccupied regions of the American mainland were dubious, but it was 'not necessary to discuss this Point at present'. Nevertheless it could not be inferred that the crews of British ships employed in these fisheries 'may not occasionally land thereon, either for the purpose of killing seals or for making necessary Repairs to their Vessels, or for supplying themselves with Water'.[138]

When some four months later news reached London that a Spanish naval force had seized British vessels in Nootka Sound, near Vancouver Island, for doing precisely these things, the stage was already set. Pitt at once took up the challenge and prepared, if need was, to go to war on the issue; and war would have broken out if Spain could have secured the active support of France or some other maritime Power.[139]

Apart from the wider issues involved the Anglo-Spanish Convention of 1790 conceded exactly what the Southern whalers had asked for in the previous year. It was agreed by the contracting Powers that their respective subjects 'shall not be disturbed or molested, either in navigating or carrying on their fisheries in the Pacific Ocean, or in the South Seas, or in landing on the coasts of those seas, in places not already occupied, for the purpose of carrying on their commerce with the natives of the country. . . .' This sweeping concession was qualified by certain provisos which were no hindrance to the whalers. The fishery was not to be made a pretext for illicit trade with Spanish settlements; and with regard to the east and west coasts of South America and the adjacent islands no settlements were to be established south of the regions already occupied by Spain, but there would be liberty to land for the purposes of the fishery and to erect huts and temporary building 'serving only for those purposes'.[140] This latter proviso was in itself a concession. In five years Samuel Enderby and his associates by their initiative and tenacity and with Hawkesbury's steady support had come a long way.

The gates into the Pacific were open, and there seemed to be no good reason why the whale and seal traders should not be the means of establishing a general commerce in that Ocean, thus providing Britain with fresh lines of trade communication with China and possibly Japan; and if Captain Vancouver could discover, as was hoped, a short sea passage between the west coast of North America and the Atlantic, the British oceanic network would become global. The link between the established chain of trade, Britain – India – Far East, and the new potential, Britain – Pacific – western

---

[138] *B.T.* 5/5, pp. 408-24. (4 Dec., 1789.)
[139] For the history of the Nootka Sound crisis see Chap. VII below.
[140] The text of the Convention is printed in *Parl. Hist.*, vol. XXVIII, 916-18.

'Canada', was Canton. Thus the actual and the potential could
not be integrated without inducing (or compelling) the East India
Company to relax its monopoly. Having successfully eliminated
the Spanish claim to exclusive privilege, the Pitt Administration
were strongly disposed to overcome the resistance of the English
Company.

Previous experience indicated that this would not be easy. When
the Government had first decided to promote a southern whale
fishery, the Directors' opposition had caused the permitted entry
into the South Seas under the Act of 1786 to be confined within
the narrowest possible limits. Within a year the battle had been
renewed. The whalers' Committee applied to the Board for an
amendment to the Act so that their ships on doubling the Cape
of Good Hope might go as far north as the equator and as far to
the eastward as 54° E. longitude. These limits, they explained,
would exclude them from interfering with the French settlements
in the Islands of Mauritius and Bourbon.[141] In full agreement
Hawkesbury referred the proposal, not in the first instance to the
Company, but to the India Board, who replied that there could not
be 'any reasonable objection' on the part of the Company to the
whalers' request.[142]

Dundas and the India Board had – not for the first time –
spoken without the book. When after further discussions with the
whalers the Board of Trade decided in March, 1788, to promote
a new statute 'for the further encouragement' of the Fishery, the
Directors renewed their opposition. John Motteux and Nathaniel
Smith (Chairman and Deputy-Chairman) attended the Board and
argued against the proposed extensions. They were thereupon
requested to lay the draft clause before the Court of Directors,
acquainting them with the reasons why the Board 'wish to grant
such extension of Limits' and their desire to receive the Company's assent thereto 'with all convenient speed'.[143]

The Company gave way to the extent of opening the South
Pacific as far west as 180° (which excluded Australia and New
Zealand) but under increased penalties and safeguards against
engaging in trade, and they successfully insisted on drawing the
eastward limit in the Indian Ocean at 51° longitude 'and no
farther'.[144] Although the new Act had granted the southern

---

[141] Minute of 31 October, 1787. *B.T. 5/4*, p. 377.
[142] W. Brodrick (India Board) to W. Fawkner (Board of Trade), 2 Nov., 1787.
B.T. 6/95.
[143] Minute of 26 March, 1788 (*B.T. 5/5*, p. 63). Cf. Minute of 7 March (*Ibid.*,
pp. 53-5).
[144] 'Resolution of the Court of Directors respecting an intended Clause in the
New South Whale Fishery Bill, 27 March, 1788,' and 'Proposed Clause as amended
by the East India Company. Received 7 April, 1788' (*B.T. 6/95*). The Act is –
28 Geo. III, cap. 20.

whalers wider limits as well as premiums for the longer voyage beyond the Capes, they were not content. In less than a year Enderby submitted a petition on behalf of his Committee, praying, among other things, for a further extension of latitude west of Cape Horn and relief from the expense of licences. They were an aggressive body and evidently thought that by continuous pressure they could get rid of the East India Company's restrictions altogether; but on this occasion they had unwisely made the pace too hot. They were peremptorily informed (on 29 April, 1789) that it would not be proper to recommend a measure to Parliament at that time to comply with their petition.[145]

When six months later the *Sappho* and the *Elizabeth and Margaret* returned to London with their story of expulsion from Port Desire, the southern whalers became the representatives of a national grievance, and when the way was cleared by the Convention of 1790 the British Government prepared to use them as an instrument of a more ambitious national policy. In January, 1791, the familiar trio, Enderby, Champion and St. Barbe, attended the Board of Trade and put a series of pertinent questions about the interpretation of the Convention. Where were the farthest settlements of Spain on the east and west sides of South America and on the west coast of North America? Had they the right in case of distress to enter any Spanish port for relief? And so on. Then, unabashed by their previous rebuff, they asked for special legislation to enable them to take full advantage of the Convention 'without being under the necessity of applying for any Licences'. They also asked for an additional duty on imported foreign seal skins and the granting of more premiums, 'as the number of ships in this Fishery is so much increased'. The merchants, declared Enderby, intended to order their captains 'to go wherever they find the prospect of greatest advantage'.[146]

The Board listened and then put a question of their own: 'Do

---

[145] Minutes of 27 and 29 April, 1789 (*B.T. 5/5*, pp. 261 and 267). Although the development of a whale fishery in the Pacific was a favourite project with Hawkesbury, he was careful, as with other enterprises, to protect the public against unjustified subsidisation. On 1 Nov., 1787, he had written to Sir Hugh Palliser: ' I have received some new Propositions from the Persons concerned in the Southern Whale Fishery, and as I rely much on Your judgement in this Business, I send enclosed a Copy of them and I shall be much obliged to You if You will favour me with Your Opinion upon them. This fishery has been wonderfully successful and the Profits that are derived from it are very great. It wants therefore no encouragement but such as it may be wise to grant. If you are acquainted enough with this Order of Men, [you will] not . . . be surprised if in their Demands they are sometimes a little unreasonable.' (Hawkesbury's Letter Books. *Addit. MSS.*, 38,310, f. 9.)

[146] On 8 January, 1791, Mr. Sydenham Teast, ' a principal merchant of Bristol engaged in the Southern Whale Fishery', had written to the Board putting similar questions, ' so that he may know how to carry on the Trade and Fishery in the Southern Seas and pacifick Ocean with benefit to himself, but without infringing any part of the said Convention'. (Minute of 12 Jan., 1791. *B.T. 5/7*, p. 6.)

you conceive that it will be ever for the Interest of the merchants concerned in the Southern Whale Fishery to send a Ship across the Line in the Pacific Ocean upon a Fishing Adventure and to go to the Western Coast of North America?' The query evidently took the merchants by surprise. It was noted that they did not agree in their answers: the question was put to them severally in writing for their consideration, and they withdrew. Thereupon some quick thinking took place, for on the following day the Board had before them a letter signed by Enderby and the other members of the Committee stating that the signatories *were* of opinion that the southern whalers should be given permission to sail north of the Equator in the Pacific 'for the joint purpose of Fishing and of trading with the Natives on the North-West Coast of America'. On the strength of that reply the Board referred the merchants' queries about the interpretation of the Convention and their request for unrestricted action to the Duke of Leeds. No action, it was intimated, would be taken in the matter until the Foreign Secretary had been able to inform them of the sentiments of His Majesty's Government.[147]

It is evident from what followed that the purpose of the Board was to encourage the southern whalers to become the principal instrument of the Government's policy of trade expansion in the north Pacific. Their London Committee represented a powerful group which could be more effective in developing a trans-Pacific commerce than the smaller fry – Dixon, Meares, Portlock and Etches – who had initiated it. Moreover the whalers were already well established within the East India Company's areas of exclusive privilege; and if the opportunities arising from the Anglo-Spanish Convention were to be adequately exploited, that part of the Company's monopoly must receive drastic modification. From the official point of view a strong commercial organisation operating in the South Seas might well extend its range further north and broaden the base of its enterprise. In practice, however, the acquisition of whale-oil and seal furs south of the Equator was a completely different business from obtaining furs from North American Indians and using them as the basis for trade in the ports of Asia.

On 10 February the Board of Trade instructed the Attorney- and the Solicitor-General to scrutinise the charters of the East India, South Sea, and Hudson's Bay Companies and to report their opinion whether any of these Companies by reason of exclusive privileges granted to them 'have such an Interest as entitles them to exclude the rest of His Majesty's subjects from carrying on their Commerce and Fisheries in those parts where such privileges have

---

[147] Minutes of 20 and 21 January, *Ibid.*, p. 16 *et seq.*

never been exercised . . . or have not been exercised for a great number of Years'.[148] It was the opening gambit.

Four days later the 'Chairs' attended the Board by request. Written proposals were put before them, and as they read them the representatives of the Company must have caught their breath. The first of the propositions contained the essence of the matter.

That all British Ships . . . shall have liberty to go round Cape Horn and through the Streights of Magellan to any part of the Western Coast of the Continent of America not occupied by Spain (according to the Terms of the Convention) or to any part of the Pacific Ocean, for the purpose of Trade and Fishery; and to sail from thence to any of the Ports of China, or to any part of the Coast of Asia, North of China, or to any Islands to the East of the Longitude of Canton, for the purpose of selling there any Articles the produce of such Trade or Fishery.

Then followed certain stipulations. Any such ships returning home by way of South America or South Africa could freight only the commodities of Asia on behalf of the East India Company, which was to act as the banker, receiving bullion from the ships' masters at Canton and providing bills of exchange on London at a fixed rate. Ships sailing as far west as the China coast must be obliged to touch at Canton and not depart thence without receiving a certificate from the Company's Supercargoes to the effect that they were carrying no Asian goods except on the Company's account; and such certificate must be produced on first arrival in the British Isles.[149]

After 'much discussion' the proposals were referred to the Court of Directors. When the latter on 25 February recorded their opposition, they were requested to appoint a special committee of the Court to consider the scheme at a joint conference with the Board of Trade and the Board of Control. On 7 March the conference began. Pitt, Dundas and Grenville, as well as Hawkesbury, were present; and when they were ready the Company's representatives were called in. The latter were thus confronted, in effect, by the 'inner Cabinet' acting on this occasion as the Board of Control and the Board of Trade combined. For once Dundas and Hawkesbury saw eye to eye on a matter of commercial policy. The latter was concerned with the expansion of British 'trade and navigation' on all fronts, while the central object of Dundas at the India Board was to develop Britain's position in the Indian Ocean and Further Asia, the chief obstacle to which in his opinion was the Company's charter.

At this first meeting the Ministers brought forward an additional

---

[148] Minute of 10 Feb., 1791. *B.T.* 5/7, pp. 45-6.
[149] Minute of 14 Feb., 1791. *B.T.* 5/7, pp. 52-5.

proposition to the effect that the ships in question, 'when they come into the Seas of the East Indies', should be considered as Country Ships, subject to the normal restrictions governing that category. If anything this proposition was even more obnoxious. The recognition of a special class of ships plying between America and Asia was in itself fraught with dangers to their monopoly, but they had no intention whatever of admitting the intruders into the seas between India and China. When the Conference resumed three days later Lushington, for the Company, put in counter-proposals.

Ships trading from the west side of America should be confined exclusively to Canton, 'because it was notorious that the Chinese Government prohibits all Intercourse with Europeans in any of their Ports to the Northward of Canton'. This, of course, was true, but it touched Dundas nearly, for he was about to promote the dispatch of an official embassy to Peking for the express purpose of opening northern China as a market for British goods. The special committee of the Court also argued that these ships ought not to be permitted to import European goods into Canton, since the Company itself constantly supplied the Chinese with British manufactures 'to the extent of at least £500,000 per Annum', and in addition goods to a considerable amount were taken to Canton by their ships' captains in private trade. Supporting statistics were produced. Strenuous opposition was made to the additional proposal.

It will be very dangerous to permit the Ships to be considered as Country Ships finally to proceed to Europe, because such Ships will load with the Produce of Bengal and other parts of India, which they may smuggle into England and Ireland or carry to other parts of Europe, to the great injury of the Revenue and the Company.

Furthermore divers persons, unknown to the Company, might find their way in these ships to their settlements in India. This was a form of intrusion to which the Directors and the Presidencies in India were always strongly opposed. In this year, 1791, the Company was also being assailed by the British manufacturing interests who asserted that Indian calicoes were competing unfairly with British piece goods in the home market and only the dead hand of the Company was preventing India from buying great quantities of British manufactures. The tides of commercial penetration were beginning to flow from several quarters and the Company were manning the dykes.

Since total resistance to the Ministers' proposals would in the circumstances be unwise, the Directors offered to freight these trans-Pacific ships at Canton with Company goods to the extent of 1,500 tons each season.[150] But that was not nearly good enough for

---

[150] Select Committee of the Court of Directors to the Board of Trade, 9 March, 1791 (B.T. 5/7, pp. 74-6). The members of this Committee were: Stephen Lushington, William Devaynes, Hugh Inglis, Thomas Fitzhugh, and David Scott.

the Ministers, who prevailed upon the Committee of Directors to assent to the following arrangement. Ships coming to China from America must come to Canton and not to any other Chinese port. While at Canton they would be under the authority of the Company's Supercargoes, but they would be free to sell their own cargoes which could consist of the products of any part of the eastern coasts of Asia outside Chinese jurisdiction or of any of the islands lying eastward of Canton, obtained by them 'in Exchange for the produce of their Trade and Fishery'. But they were not to take Asian goods back to Europe except as agents of the Company. The fishing limits beyond the Cape of Good Hope were to be extended to include Australia and New Zealand, and for this region no licences from the Company would be required.[151]

But this was too much for the Court of Directors, who dug in their toes. Further negotiations followed, and it was not until the last days of March that an agreed compromise was reached. On the 28th Russell of the India Board prepared a summary of a bill for Parliament. At the end of it he wrote: 'The India Company being consenting parties, no Opposition to the Bill can be expected from them.' By way of preamble he produced a clear statement of ministerial policy:

In order that the privileges obtained by the late Convention with Spain may be rendered as beneficial to the Community as possible, it is intended by the new Bill to throw open to all the subjects of the Realm, not only the Southern Whale Fishery within the Limits of the Charter of the South Sea Company, but likewise the *Trade* at large within those Limits, and to permit ships to carry and dispose of the produce of their said Trade and Fishery within the Limits of the India Company's Charter upon certain conditions and under certain restrictions.[152]

The geographical limitations were more strict than the Ministers had intended. The South Sea ships would be free (without licence) to range the east coast of South America, the western coasts of the American Continent, and all islands of the Pacific Ocean not occupied by Spain for the purpose of trade and fishery. But on the Asian side they were to be narrowly confined. In China they must restrict the selling of their produce to the port of Canton: they must not go to Korea, Formosa, or the islands between Formosa and

---

[151] Ships were to be at liberty to carry on the fishery beyond the Cape of Good Hope (without licence) 'to the 10th Degree of North Latitude, and between the 10th Degree of North Latitude and the 10th Degree of South Latitude as far as the 60th Degree of Eastern Longitude . . . and to the Southward of the 10th Degree to fish without Limitation'. For the Ministers' counter-proposals see *ibid.*, pp. 77-80.

[152] 'Heads of the proposed new Bill', signed – 'H. Russell, India Board, 28 March, 1791'. (*B.T. 6/95.*) The word 'Trade' in the passage quoted is underlined in the original.

Japan; and they were to be barred from South-East Asia.[153] They must not sell European goods at Canton nor take Asian commodities home unless hired for that purpose by the India Company. On the other hand, they were to be entitled to use the banking facilities of the Company at Canton, and the Company would be bound to freight 1,500 tons of this shipping each season and so to that extent provide a gainful return voyage.

The Directors had succeeded in imposing considerable restrictions, but they had also been obliged to recognise and assist a new and independent traffic within their preserve. In theory at any rate a swarm of free-lance vessels from Britain could now converge on Canton with mixed cargoes, the origins of which could not be effectively checked, and which could be sold to Chinese merchants independently of the Company's officials. Canton would become the meeting place of two systems of British commerce – as the Ministers hoped and intended.[154]

On 5 April, 1791, the Attorney- and Solicitor-General were instructed to draft a Bill allowing His Majesty's subjects to carry on a trade and Fishery within the limits of the East India and South Sea Companies under the terms and conditions as amended by the Court of Directors.[155] But nothing materialised. Between the desks of the Law Officers and the table of the House of Commons the Bill sank without trace. The fact that Lord Macartney's embassy to Peking was in preparation and was intended to transform the British trading position in China, and that the Company's charter was due for renewal (or termination) in 1793 may well have caused Pitt to decide against the risk of a premature rumpus in Parliament over chartered rights.[156] Something of the original scheme survived, however, in a clause of the Charter Act of 1793 which required the Court of Directors to issue licences (under regulations to be approved by the Board of Control) permitting ships to proceed from the North-West coast of America 'direct to the Isles of Japan and the Coasts of Korea and Canton', there to dispose of their cargoes and then return direct to the North-West Coast.[157] The efforts of Pitt and his colleagues to capitalise the

---

[153] This was secured by an amendment of the Directors: 'provided that such ships do not trade to the southward of Canton unless to the eastward of 135 Degrees Longitude from London or to the Southward of the 10th Degree of south Latitude.'

[154] Cf. the following observation in ' Heads of the . . . new Bill ': ' As the India Company will not consent that the South Sea Ships shall carry on any trade from port to port in India, all ships fitted out in India are to be (reciprocally) prohibited from trading between the ports of Asia and the Western Coast of the Continent of America and the adjacent Islands.'

[155] B.T. 5/7, pp. 121-2.

[156] Pitt summoned Dundas, Grenville and Hawkesbury to discuss the subject with him in private on 5 Feb., 1791, and again on 7 April, 1792. (Pitt to Hawkesbury on these dates. Liverpool Papers, Select Political Corr., vol. III. Addit. MSS., 38,192, ff. 79 and 87.)

[157] 33 Geo. III, cap. 52, Sect. LXXVIII. Cf. Chap. VII above.

gains of the 1790 Convention on the grand scale and the stubborn rearguard action successfully carried out by the Company in spite of growing pressure from new commercial and industrial interests are indicative of the general situation.

After 1793 the penetration of the Pacific by the Southern Whalers steadily increased in volume and range. Hitherto they had been much concerned with the need for a base of their own on some island adjacent to South America for stores and repair facilities,[158] but with the growth of settlement in New South Wales they became increasingly interested in that Colony, both as a whaling depot and as affording opportunities for trade. A fantastic situation developed. Although whaling ships were frequently chartered by the Government to transport convicts to Port Jackson, Australasia was outside their permitted fishery limits, and their exclusion offered opportunities to American whalers and traders which were not ignored.

Samuel Enderby junr. and Benjamin Champion led a fresh attack upon the East India Company, strongly supported by Hawkesbury (now Earl of Liverpool), and in 1798 they at last secured fishing access to this important area. But the Company persisted in their refusal to allow whalers (now rapidly becoming traders as well) to penetrate as far as the Philippines and Formosa. A fresh and sustained offensive took place from 1801 to 1803 which was supported by Governor King of New South Wales as well as the Board of Trade. Substantial concessions were secured. By an Act of 1802 they were released from the old bugbear of Company licences to sail in the Pacific, and in the following year a further extension of limits to the northward was secured which would enable them to make a shorter return voyage by the north coast of Australia and Torres Strait.[159] But the Company's determination to preserve their monopoly of Asian trade by keeping the whalers out of the Indian ocean and the East Indian Archipelago remained undefeated.

The actual profits gained from oil, whale-bone, ambergris and seal furs were large;[160] but the Southern Whalers were also

---

[158] In April, 1792, Pitt, Dundas, Grenville and Hawkesbury (at a meeting of the Board of Trade) considered representations and agreed to recommend that a King's ship be dispatched to survey the south-west coast of South America and the adjacent islands for this purpose (*B.T. 5/8*, pp. 8 and 16).

[159] *42 Geo. III, cap.* 77 and *43 Geo. III, cap. 90*. During the discussions with the Company in 1803 the Board pointed out that the proposed extension could not injure their interests, while the safer and shorter voyage home for the whalers along the north coast of New Holland would enable them to become thoroughly acquainted with the navigation of the Strait of Torres, which in the Board's opinion might prove 'a matter of great national Importance'. (*B.T. 5/14*, pp. 66-7.)

[160] In 1784 the total value of the produce of the Southern Whale Fishery was stated to be £14,350; in 1785 – £23,480; in 1786 – £55,753; in 1787 – £107,321. Until 1792 it seems to have remained at about £100,000 p.a., when it rose to £189,135. (These figures are compiled from various statements in the Board of Trade papers.)

explorers and pioneers of commercial penetration in unknown seas and in this lay their chief importance. The account of this characteristic manifestation of State-aided maritime expansion may be fittingly concluded by two commentaries, one by Lord Liverpool himself, and the other by old Samuel Enderby's great-grandson in an account of the family, written in 1875 for the benefit of his nephews and nieces.

In 1802 Charles Jenkinson, still alert in mind though now a semi-invalid, looked back with justifiable satisfaction on the successful growth of one of his favourite projects. On that subject he sent the following note to his old friend and associate, Sir Joseph Banks:

Lord Liverpool presents his compliments to Sir Joseph Banks, and if he can conveniently call on him, He will shew him a very curious Account of the Merchants, the Ships, and the Capital now employed in the Southern Whale Fishery which amounts to no less a sum than £547,100. He will also shew him some Charts, coloured to mark the original Exclusive Rights of the East India Co. and the South Sea Co., with the several Alterations that have been made by several Acts of Parliament in these exclusive Rights.[161]

When Charles Enderby, in 1875, wrote his account of the family which had led the industry since the time of the American Revolution, he was considering in retrospect an enterprise which had come to an end. Changed circumstances had caused the British whalers to disappear from the southern seas.[162] As Enderby puts it, the Southern fishery performed its function and then died away.

In considering the results of what they had done he did not conceal that whaling crews had very often proved to be a curse to the native inhabitants of the Pacific. Because of the hazards of voyages among unknown islands, under-water coral reefs, and hostile natives, which frequently lasted for three years or more away from any civilised ports, the crews generally consisted of 'a

---

[161] Liverpool to Banks, 24 Feb., 1802. (Banks MSS. – Halliday.)

[162] The payment of premiums (ranging from £100 to £600) on ships returning with the largest supplies, which were increased in number in 1795, enabled the Southern Whalers to make a profit in spite of the long and expensive voyage; but the demand for whale-oil, which was dear, declined with the increasing use of coal gas and paraffin. Moreover the advent of auxiliary steam power operated to the advantage of the Greenland Fishery, which by this means began to recover something of its former position, for coal supplies in the southern oceans were costly and inadequate. The Southern fishery began to decline in the 1830s and had come to an end by about 1860. On the other hand, American whalers, better situated geographically, with cheaper ships and a growing (rural) home consumption, began to flourish. They concentrated for the most part on northern waters in the region of Bering Strait. By the 1820s they were in a leading position and by 1846 their whaling fleet had reached its maximum of 736 vessels out of a total world fleet of about 900 (W. S. Tower, *A History of the American Whale Fishery*, Phila., 1907, pp. 50-3).

wildish class of young men, fond of adventure and of reckless habit, not to say frequently of disreputable character'. Some were run-aways who never intended to return home but settled among the islanders, got possession of land on fraudulent conditions, and tried to monopolise the trade, which in totality had grown so much that vessels were sent out specially to carry on the business. Because of the shameful damage done among the Maoris, wrote Charles Enderby, his grandfather for many years before his death had urged the British Government to colonise New Zealand but in vain.

On the other hand the achievements in exploration are stated with warrantable pride. Enderby ships had been the first of the British whalers to double Cape Horn, and in later years to visit Japan (in 1819), the Seychelles and the Mozambique Channel. The whalers in general had explored the Sandwich and Friendly Islands, the Moluccas, Fiji, and New Zealand. They had been 'to say the least, the proximate cause of removing the exclusiveness' of the people of Japan, and they had opened a trade in South America 'which eventually brought about the independence of such states as Peru and Chili'.

Allowing for exaggeration, it remains true that the history of the Southern Whale Fishery epitomises to a remarkable degree the invasion of a vast ocean with all its consequential repercussions.

CHAPTER VI

THE DOMINION OF THE EASTERN SEAS

1. THE STRAIT OF MALACCA

T H E Malay Peninsula lies like a long wedge between the territories of Hindustan on the one side and China on the other, and its population, akin to the Maoris of New Zealand, constitutes a racial *bloc* between the peoples of India and Further Asia. The Malays appear to have invaded and conquered the Peninsula in the 12th century, probably from Java and Sumatra. Essentially a maritime people, their commercial ramifications extended throughout the Eastern Archipelago and as far afield as Tonquin, Canton and New Guinea. Their port of Malacca was recognised as one of the first cities of the East. The Malays are a curious people, given to bursts of warlike ferocity, and yet for the most part easy-going and indolent, organised on a feudal basis. Deference to a superior authority sat light upon them and their consequent inability to unite was the chief cause of their failure to gain any foothold on the mainland of Asia or to oppose effective resistance to European penetration.

In 1511 Malacca was captured by the great Portuguese commander, Albuquerque, and the Malay princes turned south to found the Kingdom of Johore. During the twenty years that followed, the ships of Portugal established a trading ascendancy throughout the Malayan Seas, and Malacca became the centre of Portuguese commerce and administration. Indeed the author of the ' Commentaries of Albuquerque '[1] declared that the keys of the East and the principal marts for trade were Aden at the entrance to the Red Sea, Ormuz at the gate of the Persian Gulf and Malacca. When therefore the Dutch in their turn captured Malacca in 1640, the event marked the final substitution of Dutch for Portuguese supremacy and the further decline of the waning influence of the English. During the middle decade of the 17th century the maritime and commercial superiority of the Dutch over their English rivals, in the East as in the West Indies, was at its height. With ships better designed and equipped for long ocean voyages than those of the English, and with a more efficient trading system, the Hollanders were able to enforce a monopoly in the Spice Islands and to extend their activities through the Malay Archipelago into the Pacific. The secrets of Dutch navigation and discovery in these

---

[1] ' The Commentaries of the Great Alfonso Dalboquerque,' ed. W. de G. Birch, vol. I, p. 17 (*Hakluyt Soc.*, 1st Series, No. 53, Lond., 1875).

unknown seas were as carefully guarded as those of their Portuguese predecessors.

A variety of factors, however, combined during the latter half of the 18th century to undermine the position of the Dutch East India Company until it approached the stage of insolvency. On the other hand, the English, who had retreated to the mainland of India at a time of weakness and confusion at home, learned to exploit their insular position and the natural resources at their disposal to achieve a naval and industrial superiority which gave them controlling authority in India and also led them on to expansion in the field of Far Eastern trade. Between the Dutch on the defensive in the Spice Islands and the English, intent upon the consolidation of a trade route to Canton and the Pacific, lay as a bone of contention the Strait of Malacca. A glance at the map is sufficient to reveal the strategic value of the long strait that runs between the Malay Peninsula and Sumatra, linking the Indian Ocean with the China Sea. It is the focal point where the sea routes of the East conjoin. From Europe and India in the West, from Siam, Tonquin and China in the North, from Borneo, Java and the Moluccas to the eastward, and from Australasia in the South the lines of oceanic trade coverage at this Strait. At its southern extremity lies Singapore. With the contraction of distance by virtue of modern speed in warship and aircraft, the Strait has become part of the maritime frontier of Australia and New Zealand, of Hong Kong and India. In the old days of sail the harbours in the Strait were of great importance as ports of call for refreshment; and their central situation (then as now) drew to them men and merchandise of every description. As commercial *entrepôts* Penang and Singapore have achieved front rank among the ports of the world. Thus, when British interest in the possibilities of expansion into Further Asia began to take form and direction after 1760, it was to be expected that special efforts would be made to secure a footing in a region of such peculiar importance.

In the year 1605 the English East India Company made an alliance with the Sultan of Acheen (or Achin), a country occupying the northern extremity of Sumatra. For more than a century the port of Acheen flourished as a busy mart, until trade was brought to a standstill with the treacherous seizure of some English vessels by the Achenese. When the Seven Years War was over, a group of Madras merchants formed themselves into a syndicate to reopen the trade with Acheen and other countries adjoining the Malacca Strait. As agent for the Syndicate one Francis Jourdan in 1766 sent a vessel to Acheen with a suitable cargo under the direction of a factor, named Mr. Cowan Harrop. On arrival Harrop found the Sultan engaged in a violent quarrel with some French merchants; and since peaceful trade was temporarily impossible, he proceeded to Rhio at the southern extremity of the Strait near Singapore. On his return to Acheen the Sultan made him an offer: he would give permission for the establishment of a factory and would grant a half-share in all retail trade in return for armed assistance against his enemies. The offer was promptly accepted; a factory was built, and a garrison of 75 sepoys was sent from Madras. In consequence the place rapidly resumed its old position as an *entrepôt* of trade between the Coromandel Coast and the Malay countries. Moreover it now acquired a new importance as a link in the commercial chain between England and China. At Acheen the wares of India were exchanged for such articles as tin, wax, pepper, gold, and ivory, which found a ready sale at Canton.[2]

The fact that a group of private merchants in Madras took it upon themselves to enter into treaty relations with a foreign Power and establish an important trade of their own within the area of the East India Company's monopoly furnishes an interesting commentary on the Company's system of trade. While the Directors strove to exclude all interlopers from their major transactions in India and China, they allowed considerable latitude to their servants for 'private trade' in commodities other than those specifically retained as a Company monopoly. In addition, what was known as the 'country trade' was left open. This comprised the coastal trade of India itself and with neighbouring countries. Thus private ventures were made to the Persian Gulf, to the Spice Islands (despite the Dutch Company's own monopoly) and elsewhere, and the return cargoes were usually bought for the Company. The arrangement was useful in providing a supplementary vent for the products of India and widening the variety of goods available for the China market.

In December, 1770, a new syndicate was formed which took over the Acheen establishment and its trading connexions as a going concern from the merchants who had founded it. The services of the agents and factors, who in practice ran the business, were retained by the new owners. Unfortunately for them they almost immediately fell foul of the Company. It chanced that a vessel named the *Fortune* on arriving at Acheen was refused permission to trade, and the disgruntled owners complained to the Court of Directors. The Madras Syndicate, they asserted, was establishing a monopoly of its own to the detriment of commerce in general. The Directors at once wrote to the Madras Government in high indigna-

---

[2] For the details of this revival of the Acheen trade see Jourdan's letter to the merchants, Sulivan and Des Voeux, 10 Feb., 1772. *Factory Records – Sumatra*, vol. XV. The writer states that the annual exports to Acheen were worth 300,000 pagodas, and that imports from there, which were mostly sold to the Company for the China trade, were almost as much in value. A (Madras) pagoda was worth approximately 9/-. (See H. D. Love, *Vestiges of Old Madras, 1640-1800*, vol. I, p. 196, and vol. III, pp. 421-26.)

tion. 'The information now laid before us is no less, than that a trading factory has been established at Atchin [Acheen] by a set of Gentlemen of your Presidency, who by the intrigues of their Factors, supported by a Naval Force, and some hundreds of Sepoys from Your Coast, have gained such an ascendancy as to restrain the freedom of trade hitherto enjoyed by Europeans in those parts.' The Directors went on to express their deep anger that this freedom should have been infringed, 'which it is our desire should be open to our Servants wheresoever established'. Moreover such treaties and pacts with native rulers were in violation of express commands because of their tendency to embroil the Company with European Powers. The Governor and Council must have known of these proceedings if they had not actually supported them. A full enquiry and report must be made forthwith.[3]

A month later (8 May, 1771) the Secret Committee of the Directors on further consideration decided that penetration into the Malacca Strait involved consequences of too great importance to be left to private enterprise. Instructions were therefore sent to Madras that, as soon as the circumstances had been ascertained, the merchants' factory at Acheen should be superseded by a Company establishment. In February, 1772, the Madras authorities accordingly requested the Agents, Jourdan and Antonio de Souza, to furnish all particulars of their intercourse with those parts, the privileges which they had obtained, and the state of the countries concerned.[4]

Jourdan and De Souza responded to this request by supplying copies of their factors' correspondence. From these it appeared that the Syndicate was not only conducting a flourishing business at Acheen, but was also securing a foothold in Kedah on the other side of the Strait in the Malay Peninsula. Early in 1771 one of the numerous Malayan wars had broken out. Instigated by certain rebellious nobles, who had been exiled by the Rajah of Kedah, the people of Selangor had invaded the Kedah country and sacked the capital. At that juncture Mr. Francis Light, one of the factors at Acheen, had gone over to Kedah with the idea of establishing himself there if circumstances proved favourable. Light was a man of exceptional ability and enterprise, who fourteen years later became the founder of the British settlement at Penang. Aware that Kedah had for many years conducted a considerable trade with the Coromandel Coast, Bengal, and Surat, exchanging tin, ivory, wax, and betel nut for Indian piece goods, he realised that a footing

---

[3] Court of Directors to Governor and Council of Fort St. George, 10 April, 1771 (Copy). *Factory Records – Sumatra*, vol. XV.

[4] See 'Diary and Proceedings of the Select Committee of Fort St. George in consequence of the Orders from the Secret Committee of the Honble. Court of Directors, dated 8 May, 1771 . . . for forming a Settlement at Atcheen, etc.' *Ibid.*

there in concert with the establishment at Acheen would place his employers in a commanding position with respect to Malayan trade.

The Rajah of Kedah, being impoverished and hard pressed by his enemies, gave a warm welcome to the newcomer as a useful ally. A provisional treaty was negotiated by which the seaport of Kedah City would be handed over to the Syndicate together with a neighbouring fort in return for a promise of assistance against the Selangorians. The Rajah further proposed that the cost of maintaining the factory and garrison should be shared equally between himself and the merchants. In reporting the offer Light urged not only the commercial advantages but the strategic importance of the place for the Company in time of war. If the English did not take it, the Dutch would, 'and I refer to your consideration whether the Dutch possessing this Port may not exclude the English entirely from trading in the Streights'.[5] Three months later Light reported that the Rajah was now willing to extend his original offer to include the coast from the seaport of Kedah down to Pulo Penang, 'and only awaits your answer to deliver the whole Country into your hands'. This area, it may be noted, roughly corresponds to the territory purchased by the British in 1800 from the then Rajah for the better security of the Island of Penang and is known as Province Wellesley.[6]

Light was urgent that the opportunity should not be missed. He had taken it upon himself to accept the offer and if the Syndicate agreed, sepoys and stores should be sent immediately. At the time of writing two Danish vessels from Tranquebar were at Kedah, ready to land forty guns with munitions, a garrison for a factory, and a further 300 sepoys for operations against Selangor. The Rajah had informed the Danes that, having handed over his coast-line to the English, he could admit no other Europeans. But, as Light had pointed out, unless the English responded with the expected assistance, he would be compelled to turn to the Danes or the Dutch, who were both exceedingly anxious to keep their English rivals out of the Peninsula. If the Dutch got in, 'they would possess the entire command of the whole Streights, for on the coast of Quedah is a River capable of receiving their largest Ships at half Flood, defended from all Weather by Pulo Penang'. On the other hand, if the English held this coast, they would acquire an excellent harbour for victualling and repairing ships on their way between Europe and China which would serve them as the port of Malacca served the Dutch. Only send a force of sepoys, he pleaded, and a

---

[5] Light to Messrs. Jourdan, De Souza, and Sulivan, 18 Aug., 1771. Kedah (Copy). *Ibid.*

[6] This protection of an island settlement by the acquisition of a strip of the mainland lying opposite was also adopted in the case of Hong Kong by obtaining the cession (in 1860) of the adjacent promontory of Kowloon.

few European officers and give him leave to help the Rajah against Selangor, and ' I will engage not a slab of Tin, a grain of pepper or Beetlenut or Dammer [resin] shall go out of my hands but for your Service. Had I authority to act, neither Danes, Dutch, French or any else should drive me out '.[7]

Thus Francis Light – very characteristically. What he was asking for – the maintenance of a fort and factory, the protecting of the Rajah's territory, and substantial assistance to him in an offensive war – was probably beyond the capacity of a group of private merchants, especially as they were already involved in serious difficulties at Acheen. When therefore the Madras Government instituted its enquiry into their proceedings they may well have viewed with relief the prospect of Company intervention. At any rate their attractive account caused the authorities to offer protecttion to the rulers of Kedah and Acheen without delay, provided that suitable trading privileges could be secured. On 23 February, 1772, the Honourable Edward Monckton received instructions for an embassy to the Rajah of Kedah. He was to be accompanied by Lieutenant David McClintock with a force of some 140 sepoys. The troops were to be landed and an audience sought with the Rajah, who was to be informed that they had seen sent to defend him against the Selangorians, and that he could count on British support in the future. The conditions to which the offer of protection was subject were as follows: the cession of sufficient land for a fort, warehouses and quarters for the Company's Servants, the grant to the Company in full of the customs dues at the port of Kedah as a fund for defraying military expenses, and an agreement by which the Rajah would contract to buy certain quantities of Indian commodities each year at fixed prices, supplying in return ivory, tin, pepper, ' or other staple Articles for the China Market '. If Monckton was unable to secure the whole of the port dues, he must insist that their collection be entirely in the hands of the Company, who would remit the balance to the Rajah after the military charges had been defrayed. Monckton was further instructed that it was not intended to start trading on the Company's account until the Syndicate had been able to dispose of their goods and collect outstanding debts. In the meantime the Rajah should be prevailed upon to confirm the grants made to the merchants by a new grant to the Company with such additional privileges as might be obtainable.

At the same time the Madras Government carefully adhered to the traditional policy of furthering commercial expansion with as little political commitment as possible. In Further Asia an ideal form of imperialism seemed feasible, where lucrative commercial

---

[7] Light to the same, 25 Nov., 1771. *Ibid.*

treaties could be made which left internal feuds and responsibilities severely alone. 'We are not desirous,' the authorities informed Monckton, 'of an extensive territorial Possession. As the great object is Trade and Barter, such a District round the Factory as may be necessary for its safety and convenience might suffice.' But since an offer had been made of the port of Kedah with all the country as far as Pulo Penang, they saw no inconvenience in accepting it if the Rajah was still of the same mind. If at some future time 'it should be found rather an embarrassment than a convenience, it may be relinquished'. It was a characteristic statement of policy. The same attitude was expressed in the parallel Instructions issued to Charles Des Voeux for his embassy to the Sultan of Acheen, in which orders were given to refuse (as at Kedah) any offer of a share in the retail trade, because they 'wished not to interfere or have any Concern in the Affairs of his Country'.[8]

On 9 April Monckton arrived at Kedah with his sepoys. Four days later, accompanied by Light and an interpreter, he journeyed to the Rajah's Court in Perlis whither he had retired on the devastation of his country. At the subsequent interview a clash of view became immediately apparent. Monckton announced that the Government of Madras had sent a force for his protection and asked for trade concessions, while the Rajah responded by enquiring when Monckton would be ready to invade Selangor and whether he thought that the troops which he had brought were adequate for the purpose. The envoy then explained that his Government had sent the force as a protection against hostile incursions and civil disorder and in return the Rajah would be expected to bear the cost of maintenance and to hand over the fort at Kedah with sufficient land to support it. In token of friendship he should furthermore enter into a contract with the Company for as much opium and blue cloth as could be disposed of in exchange for tin, ivory, and pepper. But participation in foreign wars was not his to give.

As the Malay Prince conversed with the Englishman he revealed the general reaction of the Malay world to the eastward march of the European Powers. He confided to Monckton that his nobles were strongly opposed to European settlement and that his overlord, the King of Siam, had expressly forbidden it. But he was hard pressed by his neighbours; Siam was involved in war elsewhere; and the present juncture offered a favourable opportunity for securing the armed assistance of which he stood in need. With European help he could carry the war into the enemies' camp and reduce the Princes of Selangor, Pahang and Rhio to subjection, diverting their trade to the benefit of his European ally. He then

---

[8] Instructions of the President (Josias du Pré) and Council of Fort St. George to Monckton, 23 Feb., 1772. Also to Des Voeux of the same date. *Ibid.*

proceeded to speak significantly and with reverence of the power of the Dutch at Malacca. For his part Monckton talked loftily of the prowess of the English Company and how it was 'courted by most of the powers of the Straits'. It was a reproduction on a smaller scale of the situation in India when rival princelings had bargained for the support of a Clive or a Dupleix.

Between the defensive protection offered by Monckton and the offensive operations envisaged by the Rajah there appeared to be little room for compromise. Deadlock however was avoided through the deft diplomacy of Francis Light, which secured the provisional grant of a fort and a factory and a monopoly of the sale of black pepper and ivory in return for protection by sea and land. Having gained a footing, Monckton lost no time in urging upon his superiors at Madras the desirability of intervening in Malayan affairs. He had indeed become completely converted to Light's idea of establishing British control throughout the Peninsula. Madras had only to say the word, he wrote, and he could without further expense secure the reduction of Selangor and set the legitimate rulers of Rhio and Trengganu upon their thrones again. Kedah would then become the focus of Malayan trade, the port of entry to a vast new market for the opium and cloth of India and a great mart for the China trade.[9] If, on the other hand, help in foreign wars was withheld, the Rajah would root out the English and the Danes would accept his offer.

But Madras would have none of it. In June they wrote to Monckton that they had never intended to offer more than to defend the Rajah in his immediate dominions. On no account must the original Instructions be exceeded. The Rajah should be urged to confirm the grant in the original terms; and failing that, he must abandon Kedah with his sepoys and proceed to Acheen.[10] Two months later Monckton reported that when the Rajah learned that the Company had no intention of engaging in offensive war he had replied with indifference that they might go or stay as they pleased. Shortly afterwards he withdrew the grant, contemptuously designating Monckton 'a stuttering boy'. The latter, for his part, regretted the loss of an opportunity of which he was convinced the Dutch or the Danes would avail themselves. The people of Kedah, he wrote, 'have not the least idea of any Company but the Dutch, and they rule the Malays with a rod of iron'.[11]

Before withdrawing from Kedah, Monckton obtained permission from Madras to extend his embassy to the rulers of Rhio and Trengganu, who being far removed from Malacca would be free

---

[9] Letters of Monckton to the President and Council of Madras, 22 April and 2 May, 1772. *Ibid.*

[10] Madras Government to Monckton, 25 June and 10 July, 1772. *Ibid.*

[11] Monckton to Madras Government, 13 Aug. *Ibid.*

of Dutch influence. The desired approval was given and Monckton set forth. At each place he received a cordial welcome and offers of territorial cessions and exclusive commercial privileges, but in each case the essential condition was the same, the provision of armed assistance in external war. Indeed there seems little doubt that at this time the English Company could with small effort have secured control of the greater part of the Malay Peninsula, but at the price of a collision with Siam and the enmity of the Dutch. Monckton returned to Kedah disappointed, and on 26 December, 1772, he and the British officers with the sepoy garrison touched at Acheen on their way back to Madras.[12]

Meantime the Company's attempt to establish a protectorate at Acheen itself on the Sumatra side of the Strait had also failed. Here the situation was different. The Sumatran peoples were more directly within the orbit of European influence than the countries of the Peninsula and entertained a lively apprehension of being brought into subjection either to the British at Bencoolen or the Dutch at Padang. Moreover they lived in constant dread of the fierce hill tribes who would not fail to fall upon them if they accepted the rule of the foreigner. If the latter course proved inevitable it must be thorough in order to provide security. We have already seen the terror of the tribes about Padang at the prospect of being left undefended by either Dutch or British against their ancient enemies of the hills.

When therefore Charles Des Voeux arrived at Acheen with stores and a detachment of troops on 26 March, 1772, he was met with a very different reception from that accorded to Monckton at Kedah. He learned that in January the British Resident at Tapanuli on the west coast of Sumatra had been sent to Acheen by the Council of Fort Marlborough to establish a factory. The Sultan had refused, having been warned by his advisers that a Company establishment had a very different significance from a factory worked by private traders on sufferance. For the same reason they opposed Des Voeux. Privately the Sultan informed him that he had no great objection to the Company establishing itself in his territory, but many of the notables were in virtual rebellion against him and would resist any concession out of fear that the Company's support would enable him to re-assert his authority. Long interviews, much haggling, and secret talks with Kasim, the Sultan's favourite, did little to improve the situation. Des Voeux discovered that the Sultan was as poverty-stricken as he was unreliable and was deeply in debt to Harrop, the Syndicate's factor, who was not cheerful about the prospect of securing payment for the goods which he had advanced on credit. Indeed the importance of Acheen was as an *entrepôt*, whither the

---

[12] Charles Des Voeux to the Madras Government, 1 Jan., 1773. *Ibid.*

Sumatrans brought their wares to barter with the ships of Europe and Asia. The only important revenue out of which the Sultan might have found the means of maintaining a fort and garrison was derived from port dues, the greater part of which had already been mortgaged to the Syndicate.

Towards the end of May Des Voeux wrote to Madras in disgust: ' I am not of opinion that any advantage can possibly accrue to the Company from having a Factory here which will be adequate to the Expence of Supporting it. If the End proposed be provision of Goods for the China Market, I am sure it will never answer.' In reply the Madras Council agreed that the expected advantages of a Company settlement at Acheen seemed improbable, but in view of the interest of the Court of Directors in the project it would be well if Des Voeux remained there as a Resident until further orders were received from London. The interests of the merchants who had initiated the enterprise should not be injured: Company trade (which should be restricted to barter on the spot) should not begin until 1 February, 1773, and even then the original merchants should be allowed to continue 'upon the footing of all other traders '.

But it was not to be. The Rajah, caught between the devils from the hills and the strangers from the deep sea, constantly prevaricated. Evidently he hoped to continue to receive the commercial advantages previously derived from his association with Messrs. Jourdan, Sulivan and De Souza without entering into formal treaty relations with the dreaded power of the Company. In the meantime wild rumours were abroad among the populace. It was said that the English intended to send an army the following year to conquer the country. One morning while Des Voeux was directing the repair and strengthening of the fort a message was received from the Sultan urging him to desist. If his people saw a strong fortification going up, their worst suspicions would be confirmed and they would rise.

Shortly afterwards matters came to a head when the story of the impending English invasion percolated to the hills. The tribesmen came down in force and were only dispersed by the disciplined musketry-fire of the sepoys. On 15 November the Sultan sent word to Des Voeux that the recent disturbance had been due to the conviction of his subjects that he had sold the country to the Company, and that the only way to avoid a general insurrection was for him to surrender the grant and depart with his whole garrison by the first available ship. On 9 December, 1772, the Madras Council decided to end an impossible situation. The Sultan should be acquainted, they wrote, that they had determined to relinquish for the present the idea of an establishment in his dominions. This resolution had been taken merely in compliance with the necessity of his affairs, 'and must not be understood to invalidate the Grant which was made to the Company by his Predecessor in 1605'. By virtue of that grant they held themselves free to make another settlement there at some future time. The barque *Ann* would be sent immediately to assist the schooner *Cuddalore* in evacuating the garrison.[13]

Thus the first attempt of the Company to establish itself in the Strait of Malacca ended in failure. The significance of the episode would in itself be small, were it not part of a larger pattern. The Court of Directors were acting simultaneously in several directions. They gave orders for the hoisting of the British flag at Kedah on one side of the Malacca Strait and at Acheen on the other at the same time that they were sending the ship *Britannia* to begin the occupation of the Bornean Archipelago. With regard to all three of these places the ultimate objective was China and the China market. Acheen relapsed into its previous obscurity, but it was not forgotten in Leadenhall Street. In due course the name was to become only too familiar to the diplomats of Whitehall and the Hague.

The sudden interest in Acheen which the Directors evinced in 1771 had been due to a realisation of its strategic potentialities on the commercial highway to the Far East. Ten years later they seized the opportunity of enlisting the support of Government in reviving the project. It will be remembered that when the Directors failed in 1781 to induce Lord Hillsborough to sanction a second attempt upon the Cape of Good Hope, they proposed as an alternative a concerted drive in the East Indies. The first step, it was suggested, should be the destruction of the French settlement in Seychelles, which threatened to become a more dangerous base than Mauritius for an attack on India. A force from Bombay, assisted by a ship of the line or even a frigate from Admiral Hughes's squadron, would suffice for the task. 'But a still greater and much more important object,' they informed Hillsborough, 'which we also crave permission to state to your Lordship, is the forming of an Establishment at Acheen on the North West point of the Island of Sumatra. Acheen my Lord, has a good River, and a commodious safe port for shipping. It is the key to the Streights of Malacca, and may be made the occasion of resort by His Majesty's ships when the different Monsoons render it expedient. Commercial intercourse with every part of India, China, and the Eastern Archipelago, is open from Acheen and free from difficulty.' Traders from all those countries resorted thither in great numbers. A treaty with the Sultan providing for a settlement, 'would give us proper influence in, if not full control over, nearly one half of the Island'. The

---

[13] The above account of the attempted settlement at Acheen in 1772 is drawn from the correspondence between Des Voex and the Madras Government in *Factory Records – Sumatra*, vol. XV.

instinct of the wild hill tribes in ousting Monckton and his troops had not been ill-founded.

The Directors proceeded to unfold their plan in detail. A tract of country should be procured from the Sultan, 'which in Situation and extent shall be sufficient to bar all erections towards the sea except our own'. A fort should be erected close by the harbour and constructed upon such a scale 'that should we grow more opulent and populous at Acheen, the magnitude of our Fortifications might be proportionately increased'. The new settlement should be placed under the direct control of the Governor-General and Council in Bengal, who should be instructed to negotiate the necessary treaty with Acheen at once. Finally they proposed that small settlements be placed on the Andaman and Nicobar Islands to serve as links between Acheen and India. The harbours in the Nicobars were safe and capable of receiving ships of any size. In sailing from Acheen by way of those Islands, ships would have the advantage of being able to proceed to any part of India at all seasons. Moreover ships' timber, in which Acheen was deficient, was to be had there in great abundance.[14]

It was an interesting peace-time proposal, but it was put forward in the middle of a war when the fate of the British in India was in the balance. With amazing stupidity Hillsborough adopted it and approved of the required orders to Warren Hastings and Admiral Hughes: and they, it will be recalled, promptly turned it down, saying that it was all they could do to retain what the Company possessed already.

It happened, however, that a few weeks after the Directors' orders had reached Hastings (on 8 July, 1782) by the overland route,[15] an opportunity presented itself of re-establishing contact with Acheen at little cost and without the diversion of ships and troops that were badly needed elsewhere. Henry Botham, the leader of the successful expedition against Padang in the previous year,[16] arrived at Calcutta on a mission to replenish the military stores of Fort Marlborough. It occurred to Hastings that the unexpected arrival of an officer of Botham's capacity and experience in Sumatran affairs provided a fortunate chance to give some effect to the Directors' commands.[17]

On 26 August, 1782, the Governor-General proposed to his

---

[14] The Chairs to Hillsborough, 16 Nov., 1781. *Home Misc. S.*, vol. 155, pp. 361-7. Cf. Same to same, 28 Nov., and Hillsborough to the Chairs, 24 Nov. and 6 Dec. *Ibid.*, pp. 409-10, 418, 441.

[15] The letter from the Court of Directors (dated 8 Dec., 1781) to the Governor-General and Council was an almost verbatim copy of that addressed to Hillsborough on 16 Nov. *Home Misc. S.*, vol. 219, pp. 595-6.

[16] See vol. I.

[17] Secret letter from the Governor-General and Council of Bengal to the Court of Directors, 10 Nov., 1782. *Ibid.*, vol. 172(14), pp. 291-324.

Council that Botham be commissioned to conduct an embassy to the court of Acheen on his return journey to Fort Marlborough. He was accordingly provided with Instructions, suitable presents, and an official letter for the Sultan in which the ancient alliance between himself and the Company was recalled and the desire expressed for a mutual intercourse in trade. For this purpose the grant of a suitable 'spot of ground' near Acheen Town was solicited. By December Botham was back at Bencoolen and able to report the result of his mission.[18]

On arrival at Acheen he had found the political situation unpropitious. The Sultan, who ten years before had been embarrassed by the presence of Des Voeux and his Madras contingent, had been subsequently poisoned by his Shahbunder or Grand Vizier; and that official had set on the throne a boy of nineteen who gladly left affairs of state alone and idled away his time in the palace, 'lost in the Pleasures of his Women and the Influence of his Priests'. At first Botham had hoped to gain access to the young Sultan without the Shahbunder's knowledge, for he perceived that the latter would oppose the intrusion of a Power which by its presence would weaken his own authority. Finding this impossible, Botham then acquainted the Shahbunder with the object of his visit and requested an audience to present the Governor-General's letter. Thereupon the envoy was solemnly informed that the Sultan had been forewarned by his priests of an impending disturbance in the government, and that under their directions he was 'confined to a Room for Forty days, undergoing a course of Medicine to render him invulnerable'. A curious picture of two worlds: a servant of the British East India Company, planning a mart for the commerce of Europe and China, and oriental priests, striving, Thetis-like, to clothe their Prince in an inviolable garment of magic.

Botham was impressed with what he saw of the country. The districts to the north and west of Acheen Town were extremely fertile, well-watered and densely populated. Pepper, betel nut, and the sugar cane grew luxuriantly. But to gain an entry was out of the question so long as the Shahbunder remained in power. All his efforts to gain an audience with the Sultan had been defeated; and in the end he had been given a letter in which the Sultan reciprocated the expression of goodwill but refused permission to establish a factory and fort in his territory. The only effective course, said Botham, would be to send a force of 300 sepoys with European officers, 'accompanied by Proper Persons', to get the ear of the young Sultan and induce him to put down the Shahbunder who was greatly hated. There would then be no difficulty in obtaining the desired concessions. 'Should you wish to pave the way for your

---

[18] Bengal Revenue Consultations, 26 Aug., 1782.

Establishment, the present Shahbunder will have no objection to your sending a Resident to live under the Government of Acheen.'[19]

Having digested this information, Warren Hastings circulated a minute, dated 18 December, 1783. 'I dare say,' he wrote, 'the board will concur with me in the inexpediency of forcing a commercial Establishment by Military means, although it might be attempted under the plausible colouring of relieving a King from usurpation and redressing of wrongs. Arms and Compulsions are a bad Supporter of Commerce, which Springs only in peace and thrives alone in freedom.' Instead he advocated the adoption of Botham's more moderate proposal to appoint a resident Consul, who would watch the interests of British merchants and maintain friendly relations with the Acheen Government. Such an official would soon obtain 'a competent Knowledge of whatever is requisite to be discovered in furtherance and support of our Commercial Views and interests there'. Palace revolutions, observed Hastings, were usually short-lived. Already one attempt, it was understood, had been made to bring the Shahbunder down: 'latent Seeds of another may only be waiting a little aid to burst again.' An active agent on the spot would be able to avail himself of any opportunity that might offer, and he would be able to supply the Government in India with reliable information 'for the ground of any further measures which we may think fit to adopt'.[20] On 26 January, 1784, the Council accepted the Governor-General's nomination of Mr. J. Y. Kinlock for the new post, provided him with a suitable entourage, and ordered Captain Agnew of the *Vansittart* to land the party at Acheen.[21]

Three months later another enterprise, undertaken by the Bengal Government with the same ultimate objective, produced unexpected results. Captain Forrest has already appeared in this narrative in connection with the Borneo venture and the attempt to organise a revolt against the Dutch in Celebes.[22] He was now back again from a voyage of discovery in the Mergui Archipelago, a network of islands lying off the north-west coast of the Malay Peninsula. In submitting a narrative of the voyage and a chart incorporating his discoveries, Forrest reported that in the course of his travels he had received a letter from the Sultan of Rhio, offering the English a territorial grant for a settlement in any part of his dominions. The Government jumped at the chance and ordered Forrest to keep the *Esther* in readiness for an immediate voyage.

Rhio was the 18th-century equivalent of Singapore. Situated at

[19] Botham to the Governor-General and Council, 17 Dec., 1782. Fort Marlborough. *Home Misc. S.*, vol. 172(14), pp. 597-605.
[20] Bengal General Consultations, 19 Jan., 1784.
[21] *Ibid.*, 26 Jan.
[22] See vol. I, Chap. IV, pp. 141-3.

the southern gateway of the Malacca Strait, it had immense strategic importance for Asiatic trade. Moreover it was one of the few key-points in that area which had not yet fallen under the control of the Dutch. About 1756 the reigning Sultan of Johore had been able to compel the Batavian authorities to grant him a licence to trade in all classes of goods, whether included in the Dutch monopoly or not; and, thus armed, he had established himself at the port of Rhio (or Riau) in the Island of Bintang on the south side of the Strait of Singapore. Levying a five per cent duty on all cargoes, the Sultan and his nobles had grown rich, while the advantages of a free port, so conveniently situated, attracted an increasing volume of European and Asiatic trade. By 1780 'it had become an object of anxious uneasiness to the Dutch and of great mercantile convenience to the English'.[23]

The entry, however, of France and Holland into the American War severely restricted the range of English commerce in the Eastern Seas because of the large number of French and Malay privateers and the lack of frigates to cope with them. It was not long before the English for that reason lost access to Rhio. It happened that a certain Captain Geddes, arriving there with a cargo of opium, found himself entrapped by a Dutch and a French privateer which took post outside the harbour. The two captains parleyed with the Sultan and obtained his permission to cut out the English vessel in return for handing over a third of the proceeds. Captain Geddes and his valuable cargo were accordingly taken, but the privateers evinced no alacrity in paying the stipulated third into the Sultan's treasury. In high wrath the latter marched upon the Dutch at Malacca with an army and war broke out.

To the Dutch the opportunity of destroying Rhio and the extension of English commerce which its existence promoted was extremely welcome. Already their receipts had dropped off so alarmingly that letters had been sent to the Sultans of Johore and Selangor forbidding them to allow British ships to trade at Rhio or any other of their ports and commanding that all praus having cargoes of tin and pepper were to proceed to Batavia.[24] The first attempt to put Rhio under blockade was a failure and the Dutch fleet was obliged to retire to Malacca. Finding his enemy gone, the Sultan promptly went to the assistance of his nephew of Selangor, who was besieging Malacca itself and pressing its defenders hard. In June, 1784, the tide turned with the arrival at Batavia of some

---

[23] 'A Historical Sketch of the circumstances which led to the settlement of Penang and of the Trade to the Eastward previous to and since that period (1794).' Enclosed by Thos. Graham to Dundas, 29 May, 1795. *Home Misc. S.*, vol. 437(6), pp. 135-89.

[24] 'Information from Captain Light in respect to the late attack of the Dutch on Rhio and the attempts of the Malays against Malacca' (1784). *Factory Records – Straits Settlements*, vol. I, pp. 49-53.

half a dozen fifty-gun ships from Europe with a large military reinforcement. The Malays were compelled to raise the siege and Rhio was once more subjected to blockade. After a strenuous resistance the port was captured in the following year and destroyed, and its inhabitants dispersed. The Sultan, who seems to have been a man of rare courage and tenacity, wandered for some time as a fugitive among the maze of Malayan Islands and ultimately established himself in the Linga Archipelago. There he organised the Malay pirates to such effect that under his leadership they even attacked and captured Dutch cruisers in the Batavian Roads and bade fair to bring European commerce in those regions to a standstill.[25] In the light of these events it is understandable that the Sultan in his struggle to fend off the Dutch should have endeavoured to secure the protection of the British flag by his offer to Captain Forrest. But when the brig *Esther* sailed from Calcutta in July, 1784, bearing offers of alliance and presents for the Sultan, it was just too late. Rhio was closely invested and its days of independence were clearly numbered.

The failure of the British at Kedah and Acheen and the success of the Dutch at Rhio and Malacca gave the latter the mastery of the Strait; and that, combined with their command of the Sunda Passage between Sumatra and Java, constituted a serious menace to the eastward ambitions of their rivals. Wherever the Dutch achieved an entry they invariably bolted the door behind them. The serious nature of the situation was fully appreciated in London and led to the strenuous diplomatic efforts after 1785 to strike a bargain with the Dutch.[26] That the Government in India was similarly alive to the position is well attested by the documents relating to the dispatch of Captain Forrest.

On 31 May, 1784, the Governor-General and Council followed up their previous design to send a mission to Rhio by arranging for a substantial present to the Sultan (or 'king' as they termed him) of opium, silver, muslins, and scarlet cloth, and by preparing careful Instructions. The grant of a site, commodiously situated for commerce and as near to the Sultan's palace as possible, should be solicited and the English flag erected. 'Your first attention,' Forrest was informed, 'should be to induce the King to place the utmost confidence in you by shewing him that his Interest is materially blended with ours, and holding out to him in return for his Protection to our commerce the assistance of the English name and influence in all parts of India, from which he may derive permanent security to himself and his Dominions.' Forrest in fact was to create a British sphere of influence at the entrance to the Eastern Seas, but without going so far as to embroil the Company in open

---

[25] Historical Sketch (*ut supra*), pp. 139-40, 153-4.
[26] See § 2 of this chapter.

hostilities with their Dutch rivals. The policy to be pursued was defined with a delightful observance of diplomatic propriety. 'You will use your endeavours to promote Reconciliation and preserve a friendly Intercourse between the King and the Dutch, always keeping a watchful Eye on the designs of the latter, supporting the King by all the influence you can establish for that purpose, and taking every Opportunity of shewing him the danger he may have to apprehend from them, [as] opposed to the Advantage of a strict friendship with and confidence in the English.'

The object of the mission was declared to be the establishment and maintenance of a free intercourse both with Rhio itself and with 'all the neighbouring islands'. Forrest must therefore ascertain the temper, manners and customs of the natives in those parts, their products, 'and what goods produced in the Company's territories may be successfully bartered'. Moreover it was important that the line of communication between India and this new area of trade at the south end of the Strait of Malacca should be consolidated by the discovery and occupation of convenient harbours in the Mergui Archipelago lying to the north of that passage. Forrest was accordingly instructed to continue his previous survey.[27]

The advantages of navigation and the opportunities for a further extension of trade which a footing in the Mergui Archipelago appeared to offer were considerable. As Captain Forrest's first report had shown, this long chain of islands constituted an effective screen to the South-West Monsoon, while similar shelter from the North-East Monsoon was offered by the coast of Siam. A harbour there would provide refreshment for European ships and give them freedom of movement at all seasons, thus remedying the serious deficiency in that respect of the Coromandel Coast of India.[28] On the commercial side the establishment of a free port in the Archipelago would draw to it the trade of Burma and Siam (particularly the teak of Rangoon and Pegu) and the northern Malay States without involving the Company in the chaotic politics of the mainland. Forrest's report, moreover, was strongly reinforced by the indefatigable Francis Light, who advocated as the most suitable spot in the Archipelago the Island of Jung Saylang – a name which his countrymen with their inveterate habit of anglicising outlandish placenames have cheerfully designated as Junk Ceylon.[29]

The plan of the Bengal Government in 1784 aimed at finding new markets and new sources of supply in Burma, Siam, the Malay

---

[27] Instructions of the Governor-General and Council for Capt. Forrest, 31 May, 1784. Fort William. *Factory Records – Straits Settlements*, vol. I.

[28] 'Remarks on the Islands of the Coast of Mergui and the Strait between them and the Mainland' by Capt. Forrest. *Ibid.*

[29] 'Description of the Island of Junk Ceylon,' by Francis Light. 30 March, 1784. *Ibid.* Light had lived and traded for many years in Jung Saylang after Monckton's withdrawal from Kedah.

Peninsula and the countries to the eastward by the creation of two great *emporia,* one at the northern and the other at the southern extremity of the Malacca Strait. If it succeeded, the very real danger that the Strait of Malacca might become a closed preserve in the hands of the Dutch would be obviated, the East Indiamen on their voyages between Europe and Canton would have two ports of refuge and refreshment beyond the Indian Ocean, corresponding to St. Helena and the Cape of Good Hope in the Atlantic.

When the Dutch captured Rhio in the last months of 1784 and the Sultan fled as a homeless fugitive, the situation became serious. The news was sent home in a private letter to Dundas by a merchant of Calcutta, named George Smith, who for many years acted as his confidential adviser in Indian affairs. Smith took the opportunity of submitting a memorandum which surveyed the whole field of Anglo-Dutch rivalry in Eastern waters. In his opinion the negotiation of a comprehensive settlement was not only urgent but also feasible. It was a sensible view, for there was no doubt that a dangerous and unnecessary state of tension was developing. Between the Dutch, intent on preserving their spice monopoly, and the English, who were concentrating on building a multilateral system of exchange between India and China, there was no essential conflict of interest. Their activities overlapped in two zones: on the ocean route from Europe and in the Strait of Malacca. But in neither case was a peaceful settlement impracticable. Failing that, the British would be faced with the alternative of submitting to virtual exclusion from the Eastern Archipelago or of resorting to the sword, and that at a time when Dutch friendship in Europe was a primary *desideratum.*

The failure of the British in the Malayan area had been chiefly caused by their consistent refusal to imitate the Dutch practice of intervening in native politics. The Dutch in the East Indies were, in fact, pursuing the same territorial policy that the British had themselves adopted on the Indian mainland. While the Dutch retreated from India, the English Company failed to win a footing at Kedah, Acheen or Rhio. The Dutch, on the other hand, had conquered the country about Malacca, defeated the ruler of Selangor, and by the capture of Rhio had reduced Johore to insignificance. The Strait was in their hands, and it seemed that the Peninsula would in the near future be incorporated in the Dutch Empire. For some time, according to Smith's report, Dutch warships at Malacca had been in the habit of exacting pledges from the commanders of English ships not to go to Rhio; and on one recent occasion two Company ships had been fired on and prevented from sailing until the requisition had been complied with. This flagrant violation of the terms of the Peace Treaty, by which the United Provinces had guaranteed the freedom of navigation in

Eastern waters, seemed to Englishmen on the spot to presage obstruction on a wide scale now that the free port of Rhio no longer existed. The fear that the Dutch would be able to cut the main artery of British trade with the Far East was indeed somewhat exaggerated, for the Netherlands Company was itself in too shaky a condition to contemplate anything of the kind. But the fact remained that they were temporarily dominant in the Malay countries, and friction was arising between two Colonial Powers whose interests were fundamentally complementary and not competitive.

Realising that such was the case, George Smith proposed the negotiation of an Anglo-Dutch colonial pact. Under the Peace Treaty the Dutch to their great mortification had been obliged to surrender Negapatam in India. But provision had been made that its restoration might subsequently be arranged in return for a suitable compensation. Let the place be handed over, Smith suggested. Its importance to the English Company was small, and in Dutch hands it served as a useful depot for the purchase of pepper, arrack, and other commodities in which the Coromandel Coast was deficient. Furthermore the Dutch could be materially assisted in the matter of the Ceylon pearl fishery, which was then at a standstill, although normally yielding a valuable revenue.[30] The Nawab of the Carnatic in his capacity as Rajah of Trichinopoly had insisted on exacting a greater tribute from the Dutch in respect of the fishery than the original *firman* had stipulated and the Dutch had refused to pay. The English Company could prevail upon the Nawab to forgo his additional demand and thus enable the Dutch to reopen the fishery.

In return for these and other advantages the Dutch should be required to cede the port of Trincomali in Ceylon which Admiral Hughes had captured in the previous war and then lost again to De Suffren. 'The loss of it cannot be sufficiently lamented. Consequently its Recovery by Negotiation would be a Superlative Advantage.' Trincomali as a naval base was, as we have already seen, of the utmost importance in relation to India. In the hands of a great Power such as France it constituted a major threat: if held by the British their lack of a safe harbour on the east side of India was remedied.

A further measure under Smith's scheme would be the cession to the Dutch of Fort Marlborough at Bencoolen. They had always looked on it 'with a Jealous Eye' by reason of its vicinity to Java,

---

[30] Smith estimated the Dutch receipts from the pearl fishery before its suspension at 100,000 rix dollars per annum – approximately £20,000. The revenue obtained by the English Company between 1796 and 1798 amounted to a total of £396,000, but the pearl banks were exhausted in consequence. The receipts for 1799 fell to £30,000, and no fishing was therefore allowed on the principal banks until 1804. (L. A. Mills, *Ceylon under British Rule*, p. 30, n. 2.)

and the place had never paid its way. Let the Company move the establishment to Acheen. Here a great naval base and a vast commercial mart could be developed. Cargoes would be brought hither from Arabia, the Persian Gulf, the East Coast of Africa and India to be bartered for the products of China, Cambodia, Siam and Malaya. The soil of the hinterland was fertile and would grow many valuable crops – coffee and indigo, cinnamon and cassia, cloves and nutmegs. Finally, as a naval base its value in time of war would be considerable. A small squadron stationed there would be able to keep the Strait of Malacca and the Bay of Bengal clear of privateers, and frequent communication between Acheen and Trincomali would make it impossible for a hostile force to enter those seas undetected. 'From all which causes and its Centrical situation for a General Asiatic Commerce, I am of opinion . . . Acheen would prove a great and important Acquisition.' The Company's treaty of 1605 gave them the right to establish a factory there, and Hastings himself had shown his appreciation of its potential value by appointing a Resident.

Once the settlement was established the Island of Jung Saylang should be acquired as a naval base subsidiary to Acheen. The King of Siam had previously offered it to Madras and would cede it for a trifle. If the English delayed, others would seize the opportunity. 'There is too much reason to apprehend that, should we neglect to establish ourselves there, the French, Americans, or Imperialists will do so.' The French, in particular, were alive to the situation. De Suffren, he was informed, had been heard to give it as his opinion that the possession of Trincomali and Acheen would be regarded by his royal master as tantamount to receiving the keys of Hindustan.[31]

The reasoning on the whole was sound, and the conception of commercial empire was characteristic of the time; but the writer had overlooked the presence of the warlike tribes of the Achenese hills who had so effectively opposed the plans of Des Voeux fourteen years before. Apart, however, from its interest as evidence of the general trend of contemporary British imperialism, the memorandum is noteworthy for its effect upon the mind of Dundas, to whom it was addressed. When the negotiations between London and the Hague (shortly to be described) were in full swing, Dundas will be found persuading Pitt and Grenville that the cession of Trincomali and Acheen was the minimum that could be accepted from the Dutch in a colonial settlement and using precisely these arguments to support his contention.

While ministers and ambassadors wrangled in Europe, the long story of British failure in the Strait of Malacca was brought to an

[31] Smith to Dundas, 27 Jan., 1785, enclosing, 'Observations relating to Trankamalee.' *Home Misc. S.*, vol. 434, pp. 44-54.

end by the men on the spot. The success that was now achieved was due to the enterprise of Francis Light. Sixteen years before, he had grasped the importance of securing a foothold in the Strait and he had worked for that end ever since. The reasons, strategic and commercial, which he had advanced in 1771 in favour of accepting the port and coastline of Kedah were the expression of a fixed objective to which he devoted with conspicuous success the best years of his life. He was the founder of British Malaya and the forerunner of Stamford Raffles. He worked for the extension of British influence throughout the Peninsula, an influence that should preserve the liberty of the Malays and also maintain the freedom of a lucrative trade for his countrymen.

When Monckton and his contingent in 1773 were forbidden by the Madras Government to assist the Rajah in external wars and the treaty was lost in consequence, Light repaired to Jung Saylang. There he lived for several years, trading up and down the Strait and acquiring in the process an unrivalled knowledge of the adjoining countries and their resources. Experience of his character and integrity in commercial transactions also won for him the confidence of the Malay princes, particularly at Kedah and Selangor.

The obvious knowledge and ability which Light displayed in his advocacy of a British settlement in Jung Saylang in 1784 attracted the attention of (Sir) John Macpherson, who may have known him in earlier days, for Macpherson was a writer at Madras when Monckton's embassy was sent to Kedah. As acting Governor-General after Hastings's departure he requested Light on his next voyage to the Strait to gather all the information that he could concerning the Malay States and their relations with the Dutch. The hint was not lost. When he reappeared at Calcutta in January, 1786, he had done much more than gather information.

The news which he reported was depressing enough. After reducing Rhio the Dutch had built a fortress of their own, manned with a strong garrison; and in Light's opinion nothing would induce them to give it up. All communication other than Dutch between the Strait and Borneo was cut off. The Dutch had suffered a reverse at the hands of Selangor, but a squadron from Malacca was still blockading their chief port and forbidding all trade until the Rajah had delivered himself up to their clemency. Indeed the Dutch were in effective control of both sides of the Strait from Cape Romania in the South to latitude 5° North. Only the rulers of Kedah and Acheen remained as possible Powers with whom the English Company could enter into treaty relations.

Light then proceeded to reveal what he had done. 'As I understood from you that it was the wish of this Government to obtain some useful and convenient Port for the protection of the Merchants who trade to China, and for the service of His Majesty's fleet in time of War in either Monsoon, I made use of the influence and friendship I had with the King of Quedah and his Minister to obtain a grant of the Island of Pinang.' This handsome offer was made by His Highness Jang de Per Tuan not entirely out of affection for the British in general or even from respect for Francis Light. His motive was essentially the same as that of his predecessor in 1771. These Western merchants wanted a port and a counting-house: he himself needed the security which their firearms and trained sepoys could ensure. The British were the rivals of the Dutch, who from his point of view evinced a dangerous propensity to pass from being allies into overlords. These considerations appeared to him to provide the basis for a bargain to mutual advantage. Kedah moreover was in a peculiarly exposed position. Situated on the northern frontier of the Malay world, it faced the formidable power of Siam, while being weakened on the south side by the enmity of the warlike Bugis of Selangor. In 1771 an invasion from the latter had been the inducement to attempt to buy the support of a British sepoy garrison. In August, 1785, when Francis Light turned up with new offers, the pressing danger was coming from Siam. Since the early 17th century the Lord of the White Elephant had exercised a certain feudal suzerainty over Kedah, which had been obliged to furnish the customary tribute of gold and silver flowers and give assistance to the Siamese in their wars. Fearing absorption in their Empire and beset by dangers on all sides, the Rajah was prepared to defy his suzerain's command to prevent European settlement in Kedah territory. He was risking the political existence of his State in expectation of armed support from the conquerors of India. In the event his confidence proved to be misplaced and he lost everything.

Fifteen miles long and nine miles across, Penang is divided from the mainland by a channel which varies in width from two miles to five and forms an excellent harbour. At that time it was unculti-vated and almost uninhabited, producing only timber, damar, and tin; but its climate was healthy and there was an abundant supply of fresh water. On the adjacent mainland rice, cattle, and poultry were produced in sufficient quantities to victual a fleet or supply an infant settlement. 'By taking possession of this Island,' Light declared, 'you acquire a Port at which all vessels bound to China may procure refreshments and those articles of trade, which best suit the China markets.' In Penang the Malays would have a place of safety to come to for the purchase of Indian piece goods and European manufacurers. 'You will likewise in a short time obtain a more exact knowledge of the state and utility of the Eastern Commerce and be enabled to form such alliances as may prove beneficial to the Honourable Company in Peace and War.' In this

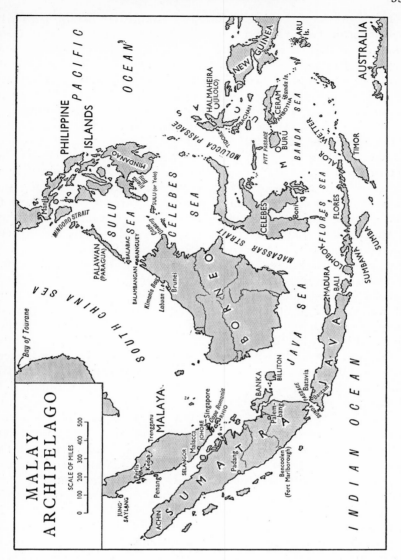

respect the French were rapidly forestalling the English. From his friends in Jung Saylang Light had learned that a French missionary bishop, after visiting the court of Siam, had laid plans for a rebellion by the people of Cochin China against their Siamese overlords. In August, 1785, the war had begun, and 'by the blessed endeavours of the pious bishop' the French had sent two frigates, a number of store ships, and 500 troops to take possession. Similar though less successful efforts had been made in Burma.[32]

---

[32] Light to Macpherson, 25 Jan., 1786. *Factory Records – Straits Settlements*, vol. I.

Three weeks later Light formally submitted his proposals to the Governor-General and Council. Of the three places still available for a British establishment – Jung Saylang, Acheen, and Penang – the first was still mainly a jungle where time and labour would be required to clear the ground for crops, and Acheen was impossible until all the neighbouring tribes had been subdued by armed force. On the other hand Penang was ready for immediate occupation and its ruler was favourably disposed.[33]

On examining the terms of the official agreement with the Rajah, the Government found that they comprised a bargain very similar to that proposed to Madras fifteen years before. A grant of territory was offered in return for effective British protection. Penang was theirs on the following conditions. The Company must agree to pay a compensation of 30,000 Spanish dollars annually for the loss of the Rajah's monopoly in opium, tin, and rattans consequent upon the transfer of trade to the Island: all junks and praus must have unrestricted access to the Kedah rivers; and lastly, the Company must guarantee protection, not only against internal rebellion, but also in the event of invasion by sea or land. The Supreme Council went as far as it could to meet these conditions. As regards monetary compensation they agreed that the Rajah must not suffer financial loss by an English settlement on Penang. They consented to leave native trade with Kedah untouched, to give no countenance to rebels, and to keep an armed vessel stationed to guard the Island and the adjacent coast belonging to the Rajah. But Article II was more difficult: 'If any enemy come to attack us by land, and we require assistance from the Honourable Company, of men, arms or ammunition, the Honourable Company will supply us at our expense.' Here was the rub. Would this stipulation commit the Company to the pursuit of an aggressor into his own territory and so involve them in the internal politics of the Peninsula or (still worse) embroil them with the power of Siam? The Supreme Council did not like it and referred the point to London.[34] But with Rhio gone and Acheen too difficult, Penang was the last chance, and they decided to take it – on their own terms.

On 2 May, Light received Instructions which were as clear in defining *desiderata* as they were guarded in authorising reciprocal pledges. The fall of Rhio and the recent conduct of the Dutch towards the Malay Princes, so the preamble ran, had made it more

---

[33] Light to the Governor-General and Council, 15 Feb., 1786. *Ibid.*, vol. II.

[34] The Agreement is printed by Sir C. Aitchison, *Collection of treaties, engagements . . . relating to India* (Calcutta, 1892), vol. I, pp. 302-3, and by Sir W. G. Maxwell and W. S. Gibson, *Treaties and Engagements affecting the Malay States and Borneo* (Lond., 1924), pp. 95-6. The Agreement was drawn up by Light and the Sultan on 27 Aug., 1785, and was accepted with reservations by the Governor-General and Council on 2 March, 1786. The printed versions give the Bengal Government's amendments attached to each clause.

necessary than ever for the Company to have an established mart, where English ships could meet the Eastern merchants under the protection of their own flag and where praus from Celebes, Borneo and the Philippines could freely barter their wares for the goods of Coromandel and Malabar. The Council had accordingly determined to remedy an evil so detrimental to the Company's commerce by establishing a government at Penang, free of all imposts and restrictions, which, it was confidently hoped, would soon become 'the Emporium of the Eastern Commerce, by which the Trade of Bengal and the Western parts of India will be connected with China'.[35] Light was to proceed to Kedah without delay and to negotiate a treaty for the rendition of Penang, but without exceeding the limits of commitment already described.

Shortly afterwards he sailed from Fort William on board his ship the *Speedwell,* accompanied by two other vessels, the *Eliza* and the *Prince Henry.* Appointed as 'Resident' of Penang at a salary of 12,000 rupees per annum, he took with him Thomas Pigow as assistant officer, and a sepoy garrison with stores and munitions. It must have been a memorable occasion for Light as the ships dropped swiftly down-stream and the sandbanks of the Hooghli slid over the horizon. At last he was the leader of an enterprise which he had been advocating for fifteen years. It must also have been an anxious time. During the discussions at Calcutta he had warned the Council that 'the principal and almost only reason' why the Rajah wished to have an alliance with the Company was his desire for help against his enemies, and that the treaty must be worded with caution so as to distinguish between an enemy aiming at the destruction of the realm and a Power which merely happened to incur the Rajah's displeasure. Yet when he sailed Light had not even received authority to promise assistance against unprovoked attack. How was the Rajah on such terms to be persuaded to part with Penang?

Meanwhile the Court of Directors in London recorded their emphatic approval of the enterprise. On receiving Light's letter to Macpherson (of 25 January) proposing settlements at Penang and Jung Saylang, they sent an express overland empowering the Bengal Government to act in respect of either or both these places as circumstances might dictate. It was much to be regretted, they wrote, that their previous orders to take possession of Rhio had arrived too late. The Directors (supported by Dundas and the Board of Control who had 'revised' the despatch) then proceeded to make a declaration of policy in relation both to Dutch rivalry in the East Indies and to British oriental expansion in general:

---

[35] Instructions of Governor-General and Council for Capt. Francis Light, 2 May, 1786. *Factory Records – Straits Settlements,* vol. I.

We wish, that without embroiling ourselves with the Dutch, or giving them any well founded jealousy of our intending to wrest from them or rival them in the Spice Trade, that every practical method should be tried for extending our commerce amongst the Eastern Islands, and indirectly by their means to China; that every means with the strictest attention to the Faith of Treaties with European powers, should be used to conciliate the esteem and affection of the Natives, and to teach them to look up to the English as their Friends and Protectors. We wish therefore that every proper and judicious method should be taken of counteracting the Policy of the Dutch in enslaving the independent Powers, and that every assistance should privately be given them in resisting any unjust attack upon their liberties. . . . It is unnecessary to dwell on the bad consequences, which may in case of any future war result from the Dutch being suffered to have the sole exclusive possession of such important Passes as the Straits of Malacca and Sunda. Every means short of open and declared hostility on the part of your Government should be used to encourage and support the Natives in resistance to any attempts to enslave them, and to encourage them in trading with us. How far it may be proper to intimate such intentions to the Dutch Government, or only to leave them to take effect by their operation must be left to your judgement.

Looking further eastward, the Directors expressed a desire to gain a footing in the heart of the Dutch zone of influence. A settlement somewhere in the region of the Pitt Passage in the Moluccas would be good policy in 'awing the Dutch'. Moreover by this means a new area could be tapped for commodities urgently required for sale in China. They had high hopes, they said, of the voyage about to be undertaken by Captain Forrest to the Sultanate of Tidore. Perhaps he would be able to bring back information on the feasibility of opening a trade with Mindanao in the Philippines. In short, every step, other than that of war with Holland, must be taken to preserve the integrity of the Malay Peninsula and the freedom of navigation through the Strait of Malacca; and no effort must be spared to find new markets for British and Indian commodities and new supplies for China in the seas beyond.[36]

Light arrived at Kedah at an unfortunate moment. He learned

---

[36] Court of Directors to the Governor-General and Council, 27 June, 1786. The quoted passage is strikingly similar in thought and phrase to the letter which Dundas wrote to Lord Auckland (at the Hague) on 23 Aug., 1791 (see p. 414 below). On 28 July, 1787, Pitt, Dundas and Grenville sent a secret despatch to the Governor-General and Council about the establishment of a settlement at Penang in response to Cornwallis's letters of 30 Nov. and 27 Dec., 1786. 'We certainly wish to avoid every unnecessary expense, at the same time we must confess that we always felt the importance of every Measure which tended to facilitate our Commerce in the Eastern Seas and thereby promote a more certain intercourse of Commerce with China. As it seems the object of other Nations, particularly the Dutch, to impede our success in that pursuit, it may of course be our business by every means to counteract their attempts.' (*Secret Despatches to Bengal*, 1786-8, vol. 28, p. 158.)

that war had broken out between Burma and Siam, that Kedah would probably become involved, and that the British were being counted on to intervene. It was an embarrassing situation. His first step was to deliver the Governor-General's letter explaining the terms which the Supreme Government were prepared to accept. On 8 July he was received in audience. He found Jang de Per Tuan and his chamberlain with a translation of the letter before them. Their disappointment was evident and their manner cool. They noted that the Governor-General had referred the main question to Europe. Since that was the case, it was needless for him to go to Penang and incur an expense that would perhaps prove useless. If the terms of the letter were rejected, would he and his followers repair to Bengal quietly and without enmity?

It was a stiff beginning, pointing to a repetition of the failure of 1772. But Light's sanguine temperament refused to accept defeat. Exactly what pledges he gave is not known, but it seems evident from his subsequent letters that he promised that, so long as the British were established in Penang, they would stand by the Rajah in case of attack. By doing so he gambled with his honour and by implication with the Company's also.

On 17 July, 1768, Light and his contingent landed at Penang and on 11 August to the accompaniment of drums and gunfire the British flag was hoisted, and a new name for the place – Prince of Wales Island – was proclaimed.[37] Light, in fact, had achieved his object and that of the Government which had sent him by sailing very near the wind. He had induced the Rajah to allow him to make a provisional occupation in the expectation that the Governor-General's guarded letter would be supplemented by a defensive treaty of alliance. The Rajah, no doubt unwisely, put his trust in that expectation and so came to his utter undoing. In a series of letters during the following year Light used every argument to persuade the Government of Bengal to accord the desired protection. But in vain. In January, 1788, the answer came. 'With respect to protecting the King of Quedah against the Siamese, the Governor-General in Council has already decided against any measures that may involve the Company in Military operations against any of the Eastern princes.' Light might use the Company's influence for the security of Kedah, but he must strictly guard against any act or declaration involving the honour, credit, or troops of the Company. By promising more than he could fulfil, Light had brought upon himself and his countrymen the odium of bad faith. But the chief onus lay with the Bengal Government, whom Light had warned at the outset that the Rajah's price for Penang was protection against the formidable power of Siam.

[37] Light to the Governor-General and Council, 9 Oct., 1786. Penang. *Factory Records – Straits Settlements*, vol. II.

Disillusioned and now in grave peril from his angered suzerain, the Rajah sought a defensive alliance with the Dutch of Batavia and the French at Pondicherry. At the same time he refused to consider Light's request for the cession of Penang until the Company had given a definite promise of armed support against attacks from Siam. Early in 1790 he gathered his forces and attempted to eject the faithless intruders. Obliged to defend himself, Light crossed to the mainland with 400 men and defeated in battle the man who had trusted him. On 20 April, 1791, a treaty was made by which the Company was to pay 6,000 dollars a year as long as they occupied Penang and each party agreed to respect the rights of the other: but of protection or alliance there was no word.[38] The agreement was ratified by the Bengal Government.

The impending blow from Siam, against which the Rajah had struggled to defend himself, did not fall until 1821, when he was summoned to Bangkok to answer an improbable charge of intriguing with Burma. Siamese anger at his admission of a European Power into Kedah territory was probably the real reason. On his refusing to go a large Siamese fleet appeared off the Kedah coast. The Rajah's forts were stormed and the defenders massacred with revolting cruelty. Most of the Rajah's followers were killed or died from exposure in the jungle and he himself escaped to Penang, where he was housed and given a pension on condition of refraining from all political activity. When in an effort to regain his throne he tried to stir up Burma and Selangor to wage war on Siam, the Penang authorities reported his action to the Siamese conqueror of Kedah. After that it was not surprising that Siam firmly rejected British suggestions for his restoration. At the Treaty of Bangkok (1826) the British plenipotentiary, Burney, abandoned the cause as hopeless and agreed to an article by which the Siamese were to remain in possession of Kedah and the ex-Rajah was to be removed from Penang. He was accordingly deported to Malacca. At last, in 1842, his eldest son made the journey to Bangkok and offered submission in his father's name. In response to the plea of the Governor of the Straits Settlements, the old man was put in charge of Central Kedah, one of the three Governorships into which the original territory had been divided.[39]

It was not a pleasant story. By his death in 1794 Francis Light was spared the humiliation of seeing the devastation of the country and the breaking of the man who had trusted to his rash promises.

---

[38] Printed by Maxwell and Gibson (*ut supra*), pp. 96-8.

[39] In the above account of the destruction of the political power of Kedah I have drawn freely on (Sir) R. O. Winstedt's valuable work, *A History of Malaya* (Lond., 1935, revised edn., 1961). See also *Journal of the Malayan Branch of the Royal Asiatic Soc.*, vol. XIII, pt. I, March, 1935.

Other considerations apart, the fall of Kedah is significant as illustrating the determination of the English Company to put a term to the territorial expansion to which they were committed in India and yet to build a great commercial empire beyond the Indian Ocean, insulated from the shock and cost of native wars and the responsibilities of political administration. Penang became more than a link in a commercial chain. From that Island and later from Singapore British interest in the chronic disorder of the Peninsula inevitably grew. The small beginning at Penang proved to be the first step in the creation of British Malaya.

The swift rise of the new settlement to prosperity justified the prophecies of its founder. At the outset his resources were slight in the extreme – a handful of sepoys, stores and a stock of opium and piece goods for barter. No regular establishment had been constituted, and the Resident was left to create a community, frame regulations, and develop trade entirely at his own discretion. Having satisfied the authorities at home, Cornwallis and the Bengal Government returned to the gigantic task of reconstruction and reform in India which imperatively demanded attention and left the problem of the Strait of Malacca to the man on the spot. Although impatient at neglect and humiliated by the refusal to defend Kedah against Siam, Light thoroughly enjoyed responsibility and the chance that a free hand offered.

His first step was to issue a general declaration, proclaiming in the name of the Bengal Government that settlers coming to Penang would be accorded protection in person and property with liberty to turn their industry to account at pleasure, and all lands which they cleared would be granted to them in perpetuity as soon as the necessary surveys had been made. Toleration would be given to every form of religion compatible with peace and the general good. The response was immediate. A steady stream poured in of Malays, Chinese, people from Tanjore and various parts of India – agriculturalists, middlemen, and merchants. A flourishing port came into being, and plantations of rice, paddy, vegetables, pepper and sugar-cane began to appear. In 1789 Light was able to report that over two hundred Chinese families were established on the Island, among whom were people of property, maintaining from ten to fifty dependants. Many families were coming in from Borneo, Celebes, Java, and Sumatra. Approximately 2,500 acres of land had been cleared and planted; and in January of that year 10,000 maunds of rice had been harvested, while a crop of double that amount was expected next season. Ships on their way to and from China had been refitted and supplied with fresh provisions. Between 1 March and 31 October, 1789, imports from ships and Malay praus had been valued at 423,426 Spanish dollars, and exports to the Archipelago, Canton, and India at 431,046 dollars.[40] A new source of wealth had been established in which British, Chinese and Malay traders participated: at the same time a plural society was being formed, thus adding one more problem to future race relations.

It was a good record for the first three years of a new settlement. As Light had foreseen, he was satisfying a pressing need by providing a free port, unhampered by monopolies or restrictions, where Eastern peoples who had not yet fallen under Dutch control could exchange their goods for the commodities of Europe and India. Chinese and Malay merchants and ships' captains hurried to the new emporium. Moreover traders within the Dutch zone came secretly in increasing numbers, tempted by the greater profits. The establishment of Penang, indeed, acted like the cutting of a canal between two rivers of trade. The Malayan countries sold pearls, pepper, tin, and a variety of other commodities to China, but took little of Chinese products in return while demanding those of India. At the same time Britain was short of saleable commodities with which to balance her vast purchases of tea at Canton. As a merchant of Penang expressed it: 'The Archipelago wants much from Bengal and India and has little [that is] wanted in Bengal and India to give in return. . . . The squaring the deficiency of England by supplying the Archipelago with their wants from Bengal and India and giving the Chinese the return is a national benefit.'[41] More than 20 years before, it will be remembered, the same argument had been advanced by Alexander Dalrymple, who had hoped to do in Borneo what Light and his successors subsequently achieved at Penang.[42] The declared

---

[40] 'Capt. Light's Report of the present state of Prince of Wales Island' enclosed by George Smith to Dundas, 10 Jan., 1790. *Home Misc. S.*, vol. 434, pp. 367-9.

[41] 'A Historical Sketch of . . . the Settlement of Penang and of the Trade to the Eastward . . .' (1794) *ut supra*. This able memorandum seems to have been written by James Scott, Light's trading partner at Penang.

[42] The growth of Penang as an *entrepôt* is illustrated by the following entries of ships arriving:

Years		Ships	Tonnage
	95	English	25,640
1799	37	American, Portuguese and Danes	8,299
	36	Asiatic	5,432
	168		39,371
	100	English	31,097
1800	31	American, Portuguese and Danes	8,025
	51	Asiatic	5,785
	182		44,907
1801	265	(Total)	53,828
1802	241	(Total)	56,820

From a report by Sir George Leith. *Factory Records – Straits Settlements*, vol. II.

objectives throughout the period were to erect a barrier against further Dutch encroachments, to keep open the main ocean route to Canton, and to bring in the Eastern Archipelago to redress the commercial equilibrium between England, India and China.

That the essential condition of success was complete freedom of trade was well understood by the founders of Penang who had probably never heard of Adam Smith. As a resident merchant pointed out, there was a basic difference between an emporium such as this and the position in British India. In the case of an *entrepôt* which existed by providing an easy and expeditious exchange, import and export duties should be the last method adopted for raising revenue. Trade would fly to other and freer marts – 'when Penang would revert to the Jungle it originally was'.[43]

The pioneer who after long and persistent effort brings an enterprise to fruition can be expected to put a high value upon it and perhaps exaggerate its importance in the general plan of national policy. The estimate of Francis Light about Penang must therefore be tested against the views of Ministers in London and Cornwallis in India. The Board of Control and the Directors had approved the scheme, but it remained to be seen what the official view would be of the relative importance of Penang. Within a few months of its inception one, George Smith, a Free Merchant of Calcutta, visited the place on his way to Canton and reported his opinion to Dundas.[44] Further reports from naval officers and others followed. Smith was favourably impressed. Its situation was 'very proper for the Eastern trade': its harbour was good and its safe and spacious road 'wou'd contain the whole Navy of England'. It would be a convenient place for warships during the breaking-up of the North-East Monsoon which was often so dangerous on the Coromandel Coast. The run to and from Madras at all seasons was no more than ten or twelve days' sail.

Dundas agreed about its usefulness, but he did not regard it as ideal either as a mart or as a port of call for the China ships or as a naval base. In a memorandum which he wrote in connexion with the negotiations for an Anglo-Dutch commercial treaty he

---

[43] 'Historical Sketch,' *ut supra*. 'It is this perfect freedom of Exchanges,' the writer added, 'which has given to the place a Trade in eight years equal to fifty to sixty Lacks in the aggregate. It is this perfect freedom in the application of Industry which has in the bosom of Jungles begun an extensive commerce of Agriculture, . . . and a continuance of this perfect freedom . . . will with a rapidity unknown to colonisation carry our Trade and industry to a maximum.'

[44] Smith to Dundas, 26 Nov., 1786. This is one of a large collection of letters written by Smith to Dundas between Jan., 1785, and April, 1791, in which he supplied confidential information about the French, Dutch, and Malays and Eastern trade generally. Dundas made considerable use of his information and suggestions. His letters are collected together in *Home Misc. S.*, vol. 434(1). Copies of a few of them, including that cited above, are in *Factory Records – China*, vol. 19.

pointed out that Penang lay too far to the westward to be a convenient depot for the barter of Indian products for those of the Eastern Islands, 'because the prows and other Vessels coming from the Eastward must pass through every difficulty and Impediment which the Dutch can throw in their way before they can reach the new Settlement'. Moreover it was situated in the Strait of Malacca, whereas the ships which proceeded directly from England to China did not use that passage but sailed through the Straits of Sunda between Java and Sumatra. As a place of refreshment on the China run it would be used only by ships touching at Madras where they were supplied with everything needed. For a naval base affording protection against the North-East Monsoon he favoured a harbour in the Andaman Islands in the Bay of Bengal.

In his memorandum he expressed agreement with the opinion of Cornwallis that Penang's chief value would be as a local depot where the products of Bengal could be exchanged for Malayan tin and pepper for which there was a ready demand in China. But he was thinking in wider terms. If the Dutch were to be given a guarantee of the spice trade, as was proposed, it must be clearly understood that the rigid monopoly which they imposed in that commerce must not extend to the general trade in the vast area beyond the Moluccas. They did business there by selling Bengal textiles and opium. They did not pay for these, however, in cash but took them 'as a medium of remittance through China to England of the private fortunes of our Company's Servants'. There was no reason at all, therefore, why British merchants should not themselves develop a great trade in this area, exchanging Bengal commodities (at much cheaper rates) for tin, gold-dust, pepper, rattan canes, beeswax and other products, which could be used for purchasing tea at Canton, 'instead of the ruinous export of specie'. The area must and could be opened to British trade in spite of the Dutch.

The Princes and Inhabitants of the Spice and other Islands, and also the Chinese who carry on a vast traffick, and which is daily increasing, and other Merchants hold the Dutch universally in detestation, and are exceedingly desirous of forming Alliances with us, and to grant us Harbours and Settlements, which when established and the trade thrown open and rendered free from exactions, would be frequented by the Prows and vessels of all the more Eastern Countries which now from the necessity of the case can carry on their Traffick only with the Dutch.

A precisely similar objective was being pursued by the British Government in relation to the closed doors of Latin America by means of Free Ports in the Caribbean. Accordingly it was considered essential to establish an *entrepôt* near the main streams of traffic and away from such bottlenecks as the Straits of Malacca. Dundas quoted with approval the opinion of one of his correspondents ('an intelligent Naval Officer of the Company') that 'to make such a Traffick successful, a new Settlement contiguous to the Spice Islands he conceives to be absolutely necessary'. Other reports from men on the spot suggested the Island of Jung Saylang, a port in Trengganu on the east side of Malaya, or Rhio. Dundas concluded that this last was the most eligible, both because of its strategic situation and of the very substantial trade which British vessels had enjoyed there between 1779 and 1785 before the Dutch had taken possession. 'A Settlement at Rhio would make that of Penang unnecessary.'[45] Having made up his mind, Dundas did his utmost to make the cession of Rhio an essential condition of a settlement with the Dutch. To achieve that object he urged upon Pitt and Grenville the desirability of surrendering both Negapatam in India and Penang; and when the Dutch pointed out that if Britain were in possession of both Penang and Rhio she would control the Malacca Strait, it is significant that Ministers in London were disposed to meet the objection by abandoning the former.

The possibility that Penang would be abandoned for the sake of acquiring Rhio (which possessed most of the advantages subsequently demonstrated by its neighbour Singapore) was increased by the fact that Dundas revived the idea of creating a great naval base for the Bay of Bengal in the Andaman or in the Nicobar Islands. The need for a safe base in the Bay during the North-East Monsoon had been a serious lack in the previous war – which Francis Light had sought to remedy. But the Government at home clung to the idea of a naval establishment in one or other of these island groups, partly because of their proximity to Bengal, and partly from a fear that the French might seize them as an advance base from Mauritius.

In April, 1785, the Board of Control with Cabinet approval sent secret instructions to the Bengal Government to send 'a prudent and well qualified person' to investigate the situation in the Nicobar Islands. If not occupied by any European nation, he was to take immediate possession and establish a small settlement at the harbour in Nancowery Island, but if the Danes or the subjects of the Austrian Emperor were found to be settled there, another

---

[45] 'Observations on the Dutch Spice Trade.' This long memorandum which seems to have been intended as a brief for Ministers and for Lord Auckland, the Ambassador at the Hague, begins: 'It is not the intention of these observations to argue against the propriety of giving and guaranteeing the Spice Trade to the Dutch; but in negotiating with them, it is right to ascertain the Value of the gift we make to them.' It is undated, but judging from the references to the latest information received about the development of Penang, it seems to have been written in 1790 (*Auckland Papers, Addit. MSS.*, 34,467, ff. 126-32).

island should be chosen. There was every prospect, it was added, that the Danes would be willing to negotiate a transfer to the group.[46]

The acting Governor-General and Council replied with a discouraging report, not only on the Nicobars but on the Andamans as well. The former group was out of the question. There were no good harbours, the coasts were rocky and dangerous, the climate unwholesome. Danes and Imperialists had made intermittent efforts to establish themselves there for several years; but 'we do not find that they have gained the slightest advantage from them'. As to the Andamans it was true that there were rumours of French plans to settle there and that the Islands offered safe harbours to the windward of Bengal and Madras; but they were convinced that these inducements would not be sufficient to persuade the French to take post there, for the Islands were covered with jungle and the inhabitants were wild and savage.[47]

This negative response had been sent off by the Bengal Select Committee only a few days after the arrival of the new Governor-General and did not represent his own view. Cornwallis considered that a good harbour for ships of war in the Bay of Bengal would be 'of inestimable value' for the security of the British territories in India. For that purpose, as he afterwards informed Dundas, he spent two years in collecting from all possible sources an exact knowledge of the adjacent islands and coasts. In December, 1788, he dispatched Lieut. Archibald Blair of the Bombay Marine on board the *Viper* to explore and survey the Andaman group. Five months later he was back again and submitted an admirably thorough and clear description with maps and charts.[48]

Cornwallis was enthusiastic. His brother, Commodore (after-

---

[46] See *Secret Minutes of the Board of Control*, 9 April, 1785, vol. I, No. 3. The instruction, dated 12 April and marked 'most secret and confidential', was sent through the Secret Committee of the Court of Directors. It was noted that the Nicobars had been 'visited and stocked' by Alexander Dalrymple under the orders of Governor Pigot of Madras in 1762 and had been surveyed in 1771 by Capt. Ritchie from Bengal. The Governor-General was not at this stage to make an expensive establishment or fortify the harbour, but, if practicable, 'to make such a Settlement as may establish a right of possession' and to send back information in order that effective measures might be taken in London 'for rendering the Settlement permanent and useful' (*Secret Despatches, 1778-1786*, vol. A, No. 4).

[47] Bengal Select Committee to the Secret Committee of the Court of Directors, 23 Sept., 1785. Endorsed: 'Fort William, Secret Dept., 27 Oct., 1785 – Letter from the Governor-General and Council to the Secret Committee – Answer to the Orders relative to Nicobar Islands – Mr. Dundas – Recd. per *Intelligence* Packet, 27 March, 1786.' *Home Misc. S.*, vol. 555(2), pp. 283-9. A similar view was expressed by Capt. Kidd in 1787, who, having been asked to submit a report, analysed the advantages of the Mergui Archipelago, Jung Saylang, the Andamans, the Nicobars, and Penang as possible naval bases and came down strongly in favour of Penang. 'Memoir of Capt. Kidd Regarding Prince Edward Island [Penang] and the other Objects recommended to his Enquiry. Fort William. 1 September, 1787.' *Factory Records – Straits Settlements*, vol. I.

[48] Arch. Blair to Cornwallis, 9 June, 1789. (*Addit. MSS.*, 34,467, ff. 145-62.)

wards Admiral Sir William) Cornwallis was consulted on his arrival at Calcutta, and Blair was sent back to take formal possession of the Islands and form a preliminary establishment on the best of the three harbours which he had found, which was named 'Port Cornwallis', in Great Andaman or Chatham Island. If, wrote the Governor-General, the Commodore was satisfied that it would meet the requirements of refitting, watering and providing secure anchorage for a fleet of warships, he would probably take it upon himself to abandon Penang, 'which we hold at a considerable expence', and transfer its civil and military establishment to the new settlement in the Andamans.[49]

The Commodore arrived at Port Cornwallis on 19 December, 1789, and – to Blair's great relief – said that he was fully satisfied. Blair wrote in high feather to his brother, Robert, who was professor of astronomy at the University of Edinburgh: 'Commodore Cornwallis . . . seems perfectly satisfied that it is a place of infinite national importance. I have therefore but little doubt but the Government of Bengal will instantly take the necessary steps to establish it as our principal naval port in India.' That letter was forwarded by the professor to his fellow Scot, Dundas, and he in turn passed it on to Grenville. The enclosed letter, he explained, was the latest news available about the Andaman project 'concerning which we entertain such sanguine expectations'.[50] When Blair's report and charts reached London Grenville sent them to the King.[51] Yet in spite of keen Government interest Port Cornwallis in the Andamans never became a great naval base. The construction and maintenance of forts, wharves, careenages, and other necessary installations would have been costly, and before long Cornwallis was involved in the heavy expense of war with Tipu of Mysore; and from 1795 Trincomali – always regarded as the ideal base for the Bay of Bengal – was in British hands.

Penang, however, continued to flourish. The Treaty of 1791 with Kedah was ratified, and the Dutch plenipotentiaries in Europe made it quite clear that they had not the slightest intention of parting with Rhio in return for Penang and Negapatam or anywhere else. Matters hung fire as long as the Dutch negotiations continued, and both Penang and Port Cornwallis were neglected

[49] Cornwallis to the Secret Committee of the Court of Directors, 1 Aug., 1789. 'Secret' (Ibid., f. 168). Cf. Governor-General and Council to the Secret Committee, 10 Aug. Subject to Commodore's formal report possession would be taken of the Andaman group. The conduct of Lieut. Blair was highly commended (Ibid., f. 170).

[50] Dundas to Grenville, 19 Aug., 1790, enclosing (i) Robert Blair to Dundas, 6 Aug., 1790, (ii) Arch. Blair to Robt. Blair, 26 Dec., 1789, at Port Cornwallis (Grenville Corr. (Dropmore), vol. I, pp. 604-5.)

[51] Grenville offered to have copies made for him to retain. 'Mr. Grenville hopes from Captain Blair's statement that the discoveries made by him will prove of the utmost importance to Your Majesty's Interests in that part of the World.' (Grenville to the King, 19 and 22 Dec., 1790. Royal Archives, Windsor.)

impartially. But vigorous propaganda on behalf of Penang by Francis Light and his supporters and criticisms of Port Cornwallis produced their effect.[52] Penang was at last given the recognition and support which Light had begged for, but did not live to see accorded. After receiving an exhaustive report on the place from Captain Kidd, the Bengal Government in 1795 promoted the Resident to the rank of Superintendent with a substantial increase in salary, and gave him three assistants instead of one. Five years later Sir George Leith was appointed Chief Officer with the title of Lieutenant-Governor. He it was who after much difficulty and the expenditure of 2,000 dollars on bribes for the women of the Rajah's seraglio obtained the cession in perpetuity of the tract of land opposite to Penang known as Province Wellesley. By that acquisition the Company secured possession of both sides of the Penang channel and rendered the Island independent of foreign supplies of food. Two years later the provisional (and irregular) government of the settlement, which had been appointed and controlled by the Governor-General in Council, was superseded, and the Company with the assent of the Board of Control established a regular system of administration, consisting of a President, three Councillors, a Secretary, 'and other subordinate officers of the Government thereof'.[53]

Penang suffered during its early years from the fact that its geographical situation did not entirely fulfil requirements either as an *entrepôt* for trade with the Eastern Islands or as a naval base in relation to India. With the capture of Malacca in 1807 at the southern end of the Strait a highway for Eastern trade was cleared and Penang's prosperity increased. But the swift rise of the free port of Singapore after 1819 as a great international mart eclipsed Penang and so justified the judgement of Dundas (and the Dutch) about the strategic importance of Rhio.

Francis Light was the successor of men such as Dalrymple and Forrest who for more than twenty years had explored unfrequented seas and had endured the ceremonial and intrigue of sultans' courts in the steamy heat of Indonesian jungle because they understood the potentialities of commercial expansion in these regions. It had been a long process of trial and error. Borneo had been a

---

[52] Cf. 'A Memoir of Prince of Wales Island considered politically and commercially' (*Factory Records – Straits Settlements,* vol. I), and 'A Concise Account of Port Cornwallis, Andamans, with a Sketch of the Plan of the Harbour, inclosed in Col. (John) Murray's of 15 May, 1794.' (*Home Misc. S.,* vol. 388, pp. 97-101.)

[53] Owing to a doubt whether the Company was competent under its Charter to establish a regular form of government and to provide for the administration of justice in Penang without recourse to Parliament, the creation of a court of judicature was delayed until 1806. See 'Copy of a Warrant for a Bill for a Charter or Letters Patent, establishing a Court of Judicature at Prince of Wales Island . . .' (1806) and other relevant documents. (*Factory Records – Straits Settlements,* vol. II.) It was decided that recourse to Parliament was not necessary.

failure, and the attempts to penetrate into Cochin China, Celebes, Rhio, and northern Sumatra had all been thwarted. But Penang was a beginning; and at home Dundas, with the active support of Pitt and Grenville, put the weight and authority of the Government behind the frontiersmen. The reformation of the administration of Bengal by Cornwallis and the growing vigour of industrial enterprise at home were propitious circumstances. Now was the time, declared George Smith of Calcutta in a letter to Dundas, when the Directors might make Leadenhall Street the emporium of Asiatic trade to the western world. 'As a mercantile Company the Ball is at their feet, and it rests with the Board of Controul to take care that they keep it in motion.'[54]

Having observed the struggle on the ocean frontiers, we must now come back to Europe to watch Ministers and plenipotentiaries in their efforts to reach a working arrangement between Britain and Holland in the Indian Ocean and the China Seas. In the course of these negotiations alien names like Trincomali, Rhio and Acheen came to be familiar counters in the hands of diplomacy.

2. THE EAST INDIES IN ANGLO-DUTCH DIPLOMACY
1784-1792

To the men who sailed and traded in the Malayan Seas the power of the Dutch appeared to be a formidable and growing menace. They saw them spreading eastwards step by step, extinguishing the independence of native princes, and threatening to exclude all traders but themselves from the oceanic zone beyond the Bay of Bengal. Ministers in London, on the other hand, viewed the situation in a rather different perspective. For them it was not so much the rivalry of the Dutch as their declining strength that provided matter for concern. Since the Scheldt might command the Thames, and the Cape and Ceylon could jeopardise the safety of India, it was a vital British interest that these vantage points should not fall from the weakening grasp of the Hollanders into the purposeful hands of the French. While, therefore, the East India Company harped on the outworn theme of driving the Dutch out of the Moluccas, Pitt and his colleagues were more concerned to create an Anglo-Dutch imperial partnership as the best means of defending the approach to India and maintaining an open passage to the Eastern Seas. They were as intent as Francis Light himself on preventing their ancient rivals from closing the Strait of Malacca, but the safety of India was a prerequisite; and they calculated that both these ends could be attained by acquiring certain strategical assets from the Dutch in return for commercial and financial concessions.

---

[54] Geo. Smith to Dundas, 10 Sept., 1787. *Factory Records – China,* vol. 19.

Provided that the terms were sufficiently generous, there was good prospect of reaching agreement, for the Dutch were in a sorry plight. At home their industries were declining. Cheaper articles imported from abroad were driving the native product off the market. Sugar refineries, dyehouses, and weaving works had in consequence been removed to Hamburg, Berlin, St. Petersburg, and elsewhere. Shipbuilding had sunk into insignificance; Delft pottery was being superseded by the porcelain of England and Rouen; the paper-makers of Holland and Gelderland had been ousted by rivals in France and Prussia; and the fine but expensive cloths of Utrecht and Leyden failed to hold their own against the cheaper foreign varieties. The United Provinces, in fact, were lagging behind in the new industrial race. Villages, once busy and flourishing, were in a state of decay. Pauperism, little known until now, was widespread. The situation, indeed, called for a thorough reconstruction of industry, which could be attempted only by a government that had been reformed from top to bottom.

Thoughtful men, imbibing novel ideas of political and commercial freedom from France and England, began to work for a renaissance of the Dutch people. As a Dutch historian has put it, 'renewal and reform became the universal wish'.[55] The weakest spot in the Dutch economy, and yet the one in which a process of rejuvenation offered the greatest promise, was represented by the Netherlands East India Company. Its capital was far too small and its ships too few to cope with the expansion of powerful rivals. Clogged and hampered, as it was, by antiquated restrictions, it fell increasingly into the hands of corrupt officials abroad and unscrupulous speculators at home who enriched themselves at the Company's expense. The population of Batavia, which in 1760 had amounted to 16,000, had fallen twenty years later to 12,000, only a few hundred of whom were Europeans and not half of those Dutch. But these few lived like princes. In 1774 when the Company's charter was due to expire there was an outcry for reform; but in the end the Stadtholder used his influence to secure its continuance on the old terms for a further twenty years. The process of decay accordingly continued at an accelerated rate. As its credit sank, the expedient of raising loans was more and more resorted to and became correspondingly more difficult. 'A sinking ship,' so the Company was described, 'which is kept above water by the pumps.'[56]

The War of the American Revolution in its early years was a

[55] P. J. Block, *History of the People of the Netherlands, Pt. V, Eighteenth and Nineteenth Centuries*. Translated from the Dutch by O. A. Bierstadt (New York and London, 1912), p. 191.

[56] For the decline of Dutch industry and commerce in this period see P. J. Block (*ut supra*), pp. 186-92. While the share capital of the Dutch East India Company was no more than 6 million guilders, its debts in 1787 amounted to 200 million.

godsend to the United Provinces and appeared to be solving all their difficulties. From their depots at St. Eustatius, Curaçao, and elsewhere, the Dutch supplied France and Spain and the Americans with vast quantities of naval and military stores and afforded free access to American privateers for the disposal of their plunder. The profits were enormous and for a time Dutch commerce reached its old level of prosperity. But their success was too detrimental to the British cause to escape reprisals, which were applied with disastrous effect. Hard pressed by their enemies, and aware of Dutch weakness, the British Government responded in a high-handed manner, searching Dutch ships and making numerous seizures of their cargoes. In some cases the goods confiscated were genuine contraband of war, but in others seizure was made merely because the cargoes were French or were being conveyed to enemy ports.

The Dutch protested that this was a violation of the principle of *Free Ships Free Goods,* specifically affirmed in the Treaty of 1674, which had declared all goods, other than contraband, to be free from seizure and stipulated that either party might trade freely with the enemies of the other. This too was the attitude of the Armed Neutrality. On her side England contended that the United Provinces were bound by the Treaties of Alliance of 1678 and 1716, which provided that when either Power was attacked the other should come to its aid. While it was not expected that the Dutch should declare war upon France and Spain, the least that an ally could do was to refrain from unfairly assisting the enemy. Strong diplomatic pressure was applied at the Hague, which only served to play into the hands of the pro-French party and encourage increasingly unfriendly acts. At length on 20 December, 1780, Great Britain peremptorily declared war.

The effect upon the Dutch was devastating. Their mercantile marine was swept from the seas: St. Eustatius was captured and plundered; the factories in Sumatra capitulated without a blow on the appearance of a few armed merchantmen; and only the arrival of De Suffren and his French squadron at the Cape saved the entire Asiatic Empire from falling into British hands. When the Anglo-Dutch peace treaty was signed in 1784, the weakness of the Netherlands had been completely exposed. Industry at home, cut off from markets and raw materials, had sunk into a deeper depression, and important branches of the carrying trade had been diverted elsewhere with little prospect of being recaptured. Moreover the restoration of prosperity by a revival of the Dutch East India Company seemed to be thwarted by the growing ascendancy of the British. The commerce of the Dutch factories in India had become dependent to a large extent upon the goodwill of the English Company, while the Commutation Act of 1784 in reducing the import duties on tea enormously enhanced Britain's competitive capacity in selling that commodity and correspondingly contracted the Dutch trade with China.[57]

Economic distress exacerbated political dissension in Holland. The seven Provinces had long been divided by the existence of two factions representing two traditions. On the one side the *Patriots,* led by the merchants of Amsterdam, stood for provincial republicanism and relied on French support to enable them to seize power and reform the political and economic structure of the country. Their normal dislike and jealousy of Britain, coupled with their republican tradition, drew them to the side of the Americans and their allies and led to the provocation which occasioned the British declaration of war; and the damage which Britain then inflicted deepened their resentment against the Power which stood revealed as the only begetter of their adversity. On the other side were the more conservative Orange Party who supported the Stadtholder as the representative of a limited centralisation. And since by tradition they favoured Britain as against France, the heavy losses of the war swung popular opinion against them and immensely assisted the cause of the *Patriots* and their French patrons.

Accordingly after 1780 France rapidly acquired a controlling influence in the affairs of Holland and the Dutch Empire. A chain of trading depots and naval bases, extending from the Cape of Good Hope to Ceylon, Malacca, and the East Indian Archipelago, had become a French asset. If it remained so, the operation of British sea-power in the Indian Ocean could be crippled and the ocean line of communication with India and China interrupted.

The prospect was so alarming that Shelburne in 1783 had tried to restore the balance by securing the cession of Trincomali and had pressed the demand to the point of jeopardising the entire peace settlement. Vergennes had been adamant in his refusal. Chagrined by his inability to secure the rehabilitation of France in India, he was determined that a naval base which could command the Bay of Bengal should remain under French influence – for use when circumstances might favour renewed French intervention in India.

While therefore British concern about the adverse situation in the Indian Ocean continued, so did the alienation of the Hollanders. The anger of the British over what they regarded as a treacherous betrayal was matched by the Dutch conviction that the attack upon them had been the unwarranted aggression of a jealous rival. The Anglo-Dutch peace treaty of 1784 tended to deepen the con-

---

[57] By reducing the tax on tea in England from 119 per cent *ad valorem* to 12 per cent, this Act within a year increased the Company's sale of tea from 6,500,000 lbs. to 16,300,000 lbs., and the demand for tonnage in the Company's China service was thereby increased from 6,000 to 18,000 tons a year (C. H. Philips, *The East India Company, 1784-1834,* p. 82).

viction. The Dutch had watched the persistent efforts of the English to establish themselves in the Eastern Archipelago and the countries adjacent to the Straits of Malacca with alarm and suspicion. Consequently Article VI of the Treaty which pledged the States General 'not to obstruct the navigation of British subjects in the Eastern Seas' was taken as proof of intention to destroy them in the Spice Islands. Another source of irritation was the retention by Britain under the Treaty of their factory of Negapatam in South India, but subject to the stipulation that it might be restored in exchange for an agreed territorial equivalent, which meant that it was retained as a bargaining counter.[58]

In reality Holland stood to gain far more, both in Europe and Asia, by an amicable arrangement with Britain than by accepting the protection of France. As a competitor for the use of Dutch bases in the East France had little, if anything, to offer in return, whereas Britain's territorial position in India and pre-eminence in the tea trade with Canton put her in a position to offer substantial commercial advantages. But as long as French influence was dominant in Holland the British Government could do little else but wait. When the revolution in Dutch affairs happened and an Anglo-Dutch alliance became possible, British Ministers were ready with a plan for a comprehensive Asian partnership which would guarantee and support Dutch trade in its own sphere and ensure Britain's strategic security in the Indian Ocean and beyond.

In the long negotiations which followed the alliance success was to depend on whether the British Ministry was strong enough to make concessions which, while in the national interest, would involve some departure from traditional ideas, and also on whether the Dutch, thus encouraged, could break away from suspicion and accept the implications of partnership. The arguments between London and the Hague and among the British Ministers themselves provide valuable evidence of the trends in British economic expansion in the Far East.

When that very able courtier-diplomat, Sir James Harris (later Earl of Malmesbury) took up his duties as British Minister at the Hague in December, 1784, he encountered the suspicion which was to be expected on the part of popular opinion against an ex-enemy State. He found too an internal and an external situation which threatened to break up the United Provinces; and although their cohesion and independence was a prime British interest, he could do little about it since Britain was without a friend in Europe. The affairs of the Republic were in the hands of three Patriot leaders, the Pensionaries of Amsterdam, Dort, and Haarlem, who dictated policy to the grand Pensionary, Van Blyswick, and the

---

[58] See vol. I, pp. 384-93.

States General. These three were determined to extinguish the Stadtholderate and secure the autonomy of the individual Provinces, and they were inveterately hostile to Britain. At this juncture disunity among the Dutch was particularly dangerous in face of the territorial ambitions of powerful neighbours. The Emperor Joseph was planning to bring the Scheldt within the borders of his Netherlands dominions, and the French Government in accordance with Marie Antionette's pro-Austrian leanings were disposed to acquiesce – on terms. Moreover the weakling, Frederick William II of Prussia, hankering after a French alliance, was (at this stage) ready to sacrifice the interests of his sister, the Princess of Orange, to join with France in abolishing the Stadtholderate in all but name.[59]

In these circumstances the Prince of Orange, pleasant but inert, contemplated abdication, and his cowed and disunited supporters lost hope. The conclusion of a formal treaty of alliance with France in November, 1785, appeared to place the direction of Dutch affairs in the hands of the Patriot party for a long time ahead. The British Minister, who was under instructions to do no more than gather information and encourage the friends of the Stadtholder in general terms, had few assets and little room for manœuvre.[60] Both George III and Pitt were determined to keep Britain with its heavy burden of war debts clear of European trouble.

Within a few months Harris with his usual facility had established numerous friendly contacts, and from these sources he learned that the financial plight of the central Government, the States General, and the Estates of the seven Provinces was almost as grave as that of the central organ of the East India Company, the Council of Seventeen, and the constituent provincial Chambers. Financial distress tended to make East India Directors susceptible to Patriot assertions that Britain's purpose was to swallow Dutch trade and Dutch territorial possessions in the East. At the same time he discovered that there was a great deal of goodwill towards the British among them, particularly in the Zeeland Chamber, and an awareness that the interests of the English and Dutch Companies were not necessarily antagonistic. Acting on a hint thrown out by a Dutch Director, Harris began to work on a plan by which the two Companies would adjust their commercial regulations to

---

[59] See Harris's despatches to Carmarthen, 7, 10, 21 and 28 Dec., 1784 (printed extracts in *Diaries and Correspondence of the Earl of Malmesbury* (Lond., 1844, vol. II, pp. 75-89). (This collection will be cited hereinafter as – *M.C.*)

[60] Instructions dated 26 Nov., 1784 (*F.O. 37/5*). Under § 6 he was required to obtain information about the French forces in the Cape of Good Hope or in any other Dutch territories in the East or West Indies, and to furnish details of any agreement on the subject between the Republic and France or whether the Republic had asked for the removal of French troops and, if so, what the French response had been. Cf. 'Memorandum for Sir James Harris, October, 1784' (*Ibid.*).

mutual advantage and enter into reciprocal guarantees of their territorial possessions. If this could be achieved, 'there is no doubt but that the two nations might divide the Riches of the East between them'. Moreover the establishment of confidence and co-operation in the commercial field would be the surest basis for a subsequent political friendship.[61]

Carmarthen, the Foreign Secretary, approved the idea. Harris should at once let it be known that Britain was ready to enter into commercial arrangements of mutual benefit. A reciprocal guarantee of territories in the East could be highly advantageous to both. 'We are in truth the only two powers that can materially injure each other in the East Indies, and I am sure if once connected there, and mutually supporting each other's interests in that quarter of the Globe, we should both derive additional weight and consequence among our European Neighbours by the increase of wealth and Commerce.' The success of the plan, added Carmarthen, must largely depend on the extent to which the Dutch Company was competent to act independently of the political government of the Republic; and there of course was the rub. Even so, an understanding with the Dutch Company would be valuable, for it was in the East that Holland stood to lose most in becoming identified with the cause of France.[62]

Thus encouraged, Harris began conversations with some of the Directors and with F. W. Boers, the Company's solicitor; but the political difficulty at once emerged. They readily agreed about the advantage of uniting the interests of the Dutch Company with those of Britain, but they explained that the Company was in debt to the Government to the extent of £2½ million, their dividends were stopped, and they were trying to obtain a further loan of £500,000. In these circumstances it would be very difficult to induce the majority of Directors to run the risk of offending the ruling Party by making any approach to England.[63] The difficulty was obvious enough and indeed appeared insuperable. Yet so serious was the Company's financial situation that Boers returned for more

---

[61] Harris to Carmarthen, 11 March and 9 August, 1785 (*F.O.* 37/6 *and* 7). In order to relieve the footnotes from a constant repetition of the names of the Foreign Secretary and the Minister, subsequent despatches from the one to the other will be cited under the name of the sender only.

[62] Carmarthen, 16 August, 1785 (*F.O.* 37/7).

[63] Harris, 19 August (*Ibid.*). In these conversations Boers repeatedly urged that Britain should pave the way towards a commercial agreement in the East Indies (pending the time when it became politically possible) by guaranteeing the Dutch monopoly of the spice trade and offering concessions, such as a share in the opium and saltpetre trade of Bengal. Harris countered with the argument that, since by their own confession the greater advantage would be on the Dutch side, the first move should come from them. The point of view of Boers, on the one hand, and of Harris and Carmarthen, on the other, during these early tentative discussions are indicative of the positions adopted by each side when serious negotiations began on the conclusion of a political alliance between the two countries.

conversation, spoke of 'a cordial and well digested union' with the Company of England and then proposed that the latter might make them a loan and by a novel method.

The suggestion was that the Dutch should hand over three China ships, loaded with tea, at a certain price and for a specified time. In return the English Company were to advance the value of the cargoes (reckoned at about £50,000 each) immediately as a loan, bearing interest until the loan had been liquidated by the delivery of the tea. The ingenuity of the proposition was further revealed when Boers explained that a measure of this sort could be carried through by the 'Committee of China', consisting of five Directors, without reference to the Council of Seventeen.[64] Carmarthen was disposed to consider the proposal, provided that the loan of £150,000 could be relied on to procure 'a real beneficial connection between the two Companys'.[65] He referred it to the Board of Control; but not for the first time he found that he had spoken out of turn. When Pitt heard of it he informed Grenville that it seemed to him 'to deserve no sort of encouragement'. It was no more than a scheme to give the Dutch 'part of our China trade' while in addition advancing them a loan 'on no stated security and on a very doubtful credit'. If Grenville agreed, the opinion of the Board (as dictated by Pitt) should be sent to Carmarthen for transmission to Harris, who must give no encouragement to such a proposal unless it was accompanied with such collateral advantage as might make it worth while to listen to it. Evidently in Pitt's view this was not a case of casting bread upon the waters but rather of consigning good money to the drain. He was, however, careful to add that Harris should repeat 'our general readiness' to consider any suggestions for bringing the two Companies together under arrangements that would be of mutual benefit.[66] This was now official policy, and the results, if and when a political change occurred in Holland to make it practicable, could be far-reaching.

At this stage, however, the prospects were quite different. In November, 1785, the Dutch alliance with France was formally confirmed. Apart from the European implications, it seemed probable that the alliance would extended to include active co-operation in the Far East. At the French Court there was a bellicose group, led by the Marquis de Castries, Minister for the Marine, who advocated the restoration of French prestige and prosperity by seizing Egypt – with Russian and Austrian support – and at a

---

[64] Harris, 16 and 23 Sept., 1785. *F.O. 37/8.*

[65] Carmarthen, 27 Sept. *Ibid.*

[66] Pitt to Grenville, 4 Oct., 1785. *Grenville Corr. (Dropmore) (Hist. MSS. Comm., 13th Rept., App. Pt. III),* vol. I, p. 257. This episode affords a further illustration of Pitt's close supervision during the early years of his Administration of the executive boards which he created, his reliance on Grenville, and his cavalier treatment of the unfortunate Carmarthen.

favourable juncture restoring France's position in India. Louis XVI and his Foreign Minister, Vergennes, were averse to military exploits which the country was in no condition to undertake, but the forward group seems to have employed some of the numerous French agents in Holland to induce the Patriot party to support an expansionist policy at British expense. The Dutch could be rewarded, and from the French point of view strategic control over the Dutch bases in the Indian Ocean would be of the first importance in an attack on the British position in India itself. For this purpose it was necessary to bring the Dutch East India Company into line.

Encouraged by Brancken and other French agents, the States General began to press the Company to reinforce their garrisons overseas by taking into their service contingents of the ' Free Corps ' which had been recruited by the Patriots. The garrison at the Cape was to be raised to 4,000 men, that at Trincomali to 3,000, and a proportionate increase was to be made in the other settlements. When the Company pleaded, as was expected, their complete inability to meet the expense the States General announced their intention of doing so themselves.

Harris reported these developments with growing concern. They illustrated the absolute sway of France in Dutch affairs : perhaps there was a secret article in the treaty of alliance of a more hostile tendency. ' It calls our utmost attention to the East Indies, and confirms what has been said of the Designs of France, to aim her first blow at us there.'[67] It is unlikely that Harris really believed that France was meditating an immediate onslaught in India, for he constantly argued that France was in such a state of disorder that her bluff could be safely called; but he knew that a Franco-Dutch combination in the East would weigh heavily with Ministers in London as a threat for the future.

The anti-French parties in the Company's directorate were as anxious as Harris himself to avoid subordination and in spite of the unpromising situation they continued to appeal to him for a substantial British loan. Early in January, 1786, an emissary informed him that unless such a loan could be arranged quickly the Company would have no option but to apply for aid to the States General and so ' throw itself entirely into the hands of the ruling faction '. Nor did he fail to stress the point that the consequences for Britain would be serious, particularly in the East Indies. Reluctantly but inevitably Harris replied that neither his Government nor the English East India Company would be justified in advancing a single florin unless positive assurances could be given that ' in return for this essential assistance from England,

---

[67] Harris, 13 Dec., 1785. *F.O.* 37/9.

none of these innovations in the East Indies (so near taking place in favour of France) should ever be adopted here'.

I gave him every possible Encouragement I could on this head, being every day more and more convinced that the principal Object of France, in making an Alliance with this Country, was to acquire Strength in the East Indies – and in some future day to direct her whole force against our Settlements there.[68]

A few days later Boers himself went to see Harris in a final effort to save the situation. The latter repeated the stipulation and Boers readily admitted its reasonableness. The Company, he said, ought to subscribe to it without hesitation since their very existence depended on the continuance of peace in their overseas establishments, but their Charter did not allow them to contract any engagements of a political nature with European Powers. That was a matter for Their High Mightinesses. At the end of the interview Boers made a proposal which, far-fetched as it was in the existing circumstances, was highly significant for the future. The only action, he thought, which would produce a sufficiently powerful effect upon the policy of the Directors and upon opinion in the Republic at large would be a formal declaration by Britain that she had no intention by virtue of the article in the peace treaty granting free navigation in the Indian Seas to establish a spice trade or to interfere 'in any Shape whatever' with the trade in the Moluccas which the Dutch Company had so long operated as an exclusive monopoly'.[69]

In any case the independence of the Company was about to be ended. A plan to take the management (and the patronage) out of the hands of the Council of Seventeen and vest it in a Committee of six deputies miscarried; but the States General then announced that they could no longer guarantee the Company's debts unless six deputies were included in the Direction. A stiff resistance, led by the Chamber of Zeeland, was countered by a threat to leave the Company to go bankrupt 'rather than let the Direction remain totally independent of their inspection and authority'. In the event two, instead of six, deputies were admitted, but the ruling faction won over two more votes and so gained a majority of one in the Council of Seventeen. The government of the Company, wrote Harris, would now be forced into subservience to the interests of France. 'All Plans for Conciliation are now at an end.' Instead of trying to secure the friendship of the Company by acts of kindness and cordiality, 'we must awe them into respect by making them feel our power and weight in the East'. To defend British interests it might prove necessary to get in first, occupy the Dutch

---

[68] Harris, 13 Jan., 1786. *F.O.* 37/10.
[69] Harris, 27 Jan., 1786. *Ibid.*

settlements and seize the spice trade. Harris was a staunch advocate of Anglo-Dutch interdependence, both in Europe and overseas, and this alternative was set down in a mood of passing desperation.[70] Soon a more hopeful method of dealing with the problem came to his hand, and he exploited it with his customary skill.

Meanwhile the danger in the East which he (and the British Ministers) so much feared was real enough, although it was not as imminent as they thought. The acquisition of control over the Company was followed by a series of memoranda sent to Vergennes by the Rhinegrave of Salm, military adviser to the Patriots, and by several of the French agents in Holland. It was proposed that a joint expeditionary force should be sent to the East Indies under the command of the Marquis de Bouille and (later) that Trincomali might be handed over for French use in the event of war as an arsenal and naval base. These plans were supported by de Castries, who himself submitted similar proposals.[71]

The response from Vergennes was equivocal. During the peace negotiations in 1782 he had made strenuous efforts to secure adequate enclaves in India for future use in re-establishing French paramountcy, and his disappointment had been correspondingly intense.[72] The use of Dutch bases could be a valuable asset at some future date, but a renewal of war with Britain at this juncture would have been singularly inopportune. According to the terms of the peace settlement an Anglo-French commercial treaty was to be negotiated and Vergennes was impatiently awaiting the arrival of a British envoy (who was to be William Eden) to start detailed discussions. Moreover co-belligerency with the Dutch would have involved France in their affairs more ostensibly than the hesitant Vergennes really wished, and in any case the financial situation was incapable of sustaining the burden of a major war. Some countenance was given to the idea of co-operation in Indian waters, but the recommendations of de Castries for decisive action were received with scepticism.[73]

During this critical time in Dutch affairs Harris was engaged on two diplomatic fronts. His major object, of course, was to safeguard British security in Europe by rallying the supporters of the Stadtholderate against the Patriots and their patron, France. A complementary aim was to achieve an Anglo-Dutch partnership in Eastern trade and defence by going to the rescue of the Dutch

---

[70] Harris, 3 Feb., 1786 (private). *Addit. MSS.*, 28,061, ff. 21-2; Harris, 3 Feb. (official) and 14 Feb. *F.O. 37/10.*

[71] For the various memoranda submitted to Vergennes and the Foreign Ministry and the reaction thereto see H. T. Colenbrander, *De Patriottentijd*, II, Bijl, pp. 4-6, 8-10, 11-16, 22-7, 30-4, cited in A. Cobban, *Ambassadors and Secret Agents: The Diplomacy of the First Earl of Malmesbury at the Hague* (Lond., 1954), Chap. IV, 2.

[72] See vol. I, Chap. VII, of this work.

[73] Colenbrander (*op. cit.*), III, Bijl, p. 16.

Company; and this, if successful, would have been useful in helping to draw the United Provinces to the British side as well as being
valuable in itself. But when the Company succumbed to Patriot
pressure a potential British asset in the internal contest looked
like becoming a formidable instrument of overseas aggression in
the hands of France. The battle on this front was not, however,
entirely lost. The Dutch Company was a federal and not a unitary
organisation, and control of the central executive did not necessarily extend to the constituent parts. In each Province there was
a ʻChamberʼ of shareholders with a local Board of Directors
(*Bewindhebbers*) which – like its political counterpart – exercised
a considerable degree of autonomy. The Central Council (*Heeren
XVII*) consisted of managers deputed by each of the provincial
Chambers on a basis of proportional representation.

The Zeeland Chamber, which had led the resistance against
attempts to remodel the Companyʼs constitution, was traditionally
anglophile. While not comparable in weight with the Province of
Holland, Zeeland had important strategic advantages.[74] If the
Union was disrupted by civil war (and as dissensions deepened
Harris began to fear that it might be), Zeeland might well become
the nucleus of a group of Provinces prepared to accept British aid
in a fight against Patriot-French influence. In October, 1785, Harris
established contact with the Zeeland leaders through a trusted
emissary, one Baron Kinckel. Three months later he was able to
report to Carmarthen that Zeeland was ready to go even to the
extreme length of separating from the Republic and accepting
British protection. The suggestion was rejected in London for it
would have precipitated open war which George III and Pitt were
determined to avoid.[75]

In May, 1786, the Pensionary of Zeeland, Van de Spiegel, visited
Harris and in several conversations repeated the previous offer in
a modified form. Harris was told that the Zeeland Chamber would
refuse to adopt the reform of the Company, already accepted by
others, in the administration of East Indian affairs. The consequence would be ʻthe immediate disjunction of the Companyʼ,
and Zeelandʼs right to take this step would be contested, even by
force, on the part of the Chamber and Province of Holland, unless
the Zeelanders were known to have some powerful support. For

---

[74] Its port, Flushing, was the only one in the United Provinces capable of taking
large ships of the line and a British naval force there could prevent a junction
between the French and Dutch fleets. ʻIt is of immense importance to preserve
Zeland, since, whilst that is friendly, France, as a maritime power at least, gains
little or nothing by being in possession of the other 6 provinces.ʼ Harris, 19 Sept.,
1786 (*F.O. 37/12*).

[75] Harris, 25 Oct. (*M.C.*, vol. II, p. 162) and 16 Dec. (*F.O. 37/9* and *M.C.*, vol.
II, p. 179). Carmarthen, 23 Dec. (*F.O. 37/9* and *M.C.*, vol. II, p. 180). Cf. Cobban
(*op. cit.*), pp. 81-2.

that reason the Pensionary made a formal offer which Harris reported in the following terms:

Zeland is ready to consent that their share[76] of the Dutch East India Company shall be annexed (*incorporée* was the word) to that of England, to whom they will make over a participation of all the rights they hold by Charter both in Europe and Asia, provided the whole Trade is carried on under the English flag, and that England will consent to afford the same protection to the Zeland ships in India as to its own.

When Harris objected that the inevitable result would be a European war, Van de Spiegel displayed what has come to be termed in modern jargon 'brinkmanship'. A Zeeland threat of secession, backed by Britain, would demoralise the Patriots and bring about a restoration of British influence; and even if France was unwise enough to begin hostilities the strategic position of the Zeeland ports and British sea-power would be decisive.[77] There was no chance that the British Ministry would contemplate any such adventure. Even though Zeeland was 'the last bulwark of British influence in the United Provinces', Pitt was slow to respond to Harris's arguments that the Province should at least be afforded financial assistance of which it stood in great need. Eventually a loan of 2 million florins (£136,000) at 4½ per cent interest was provided, but that was after the political revolution had turned the Republic into a British ally.[78]

Although Harris was unable to follow Van de Spiegel's dramatic

---

[76] Harris stated that the Zeeland Chamber's share in the Company's capital amounted to a quarter of the total. Zeeland also represented almost a half of the capital of the Dutch West India Companies. Harris, 12 June, 1787 (*F.O. 37/14*).

[77] Harris, 26 May, 1786 (official despatch and secret letter of the same date. *F.O. 37/11*). Van de Spiegel's sincerity is attested by a private memorandum of his own which he entitled: 'The last sheet-anchor if the Republic should suffer shipwreck.' In this document he specified the conditions which Zeeland should prescribe. Its liberties, laws and government must be preserved: no foreign troops to enter without permission: British warships to be sent to protect Zeeland waters: the Province to be under no obligation to raise troops apart from its own militia; and if necessary British ships to be lent for service in the East Indies or elsewhere. Cobban (*op. cit.*), pp. 83-4.

[78] Boers went over to England on behalf of the Zeeland Chamber on 11 Sept., 1787, and on the same day Harris commended him to Carmarthen. 'Your Lordship may rely with perfect security on his principles, his Honour, and his Judgement – for which I am very ready to be responsible' (*F.O. 37/18*). When the efforts of Zeeland to raise a loan of 2 million florins on their own account had failed, Boers had a number of conversations with Pitt (see his memo to Pitt of 13 Oct., 1787. P.R.O. 30/8/356, Holland). Eventually – in May, 1788 – the British Government themselves provided a loan of that amount through Coutts and Co. The money was transmitted to the States of Zeeland, who transferred it to the Zeeland Chamber. This was done because – 'the Directors are very apprehensive of having disagreeable discussions with the other Chambers, if the money be lent directly to them, as coming from a Foreign Power'. James Crawford to Harris, Rotterdam, 19 May, 1788 (*F.O. 97/247*). In this volume and also in *F.O. 95/5* there are numerous documents relating to this and other loans to Dutch Provinces and their repayment.

plan, he made good use of Zeeland's wish to co-operate. Pitt was persuaded to build up support in a group of Provinces, centred on Zeeland, by assisting them in their efforts to raise loans. Then if the worst happened and civil war supervened, Britain would be well placed to prevent interference by a French fleet. Harris hoped that it would never come to this: that it would be possible to swing opinion against the Patriots and re-establish the Stadtholder and his supporters in power. But if that failed, an alliance with Zeeland and associated Provinces could be a last line of defence – which would at any rate prevent France from exploiting Dutch maritime resources both at home and overseas. This latter consideration was constantly in his mind. In July, 1786, he wrote: 'My efforts would be of no use if they did not tend, ultimately, towards saving the Dutch East Indies from the clutches of France.'[79] Again in September he reported that if the disorders in the Republic increased he had no doubt that France, without waiting for any representations from the Hague, would 'throw Troops into the Dutch Settlements in the East Indies, and under pretence of defending them appropriate them to herself'.[80] In January, 1787, he described 'a plan of association' which was to be signed by the States of Zeeland, Gelderland and Friesland, and he submitted proposals (which were accepted) for providing them with some financial assistance. 'We shall be able,' he urged, 'not only to discover and trace the design of the French in the East Indies – as far at least as they intend to make this Country subservient to them – but also have it in our power to control them by the influence we shall acquire over the Chamber of Zeeland.'[81]

Moved by Harris's warnings of French intentions in the East Indies and of the imminent possibility of the break-up of the United Provinces, Carmarthen (now Duke of Leeds) put a question to him – 'What would become of the foreign settlements of this Republic in case of a rupture of the Union?' Harris replied that the Company remained absolute masters of their territorial possessions until the expiry of their Charter in 1796. 'It seems to me that the great point is, who shall be the first to occupy them – and to leave the right of possession to be discussed hereafter.' British policy should therefore be to influence Dutch Governors and commanders of ships in the East Indies against admitting the French no matter under what authority they might purport to be acting.[82]

---

[79] Harris, 21 July, 1786 (*F.O.* 37/11).

[80] Harris, 12 Sept., 1786 (*F.O.* 37/12).

[81] Harris proposed that the State of Friesland be assisted to raise a loan by providing an additional 2 per cent interest amounting to 40,000 florins annually and that the Chamber of Zeeland be aided on the same basis, which would come to a further 20,000 florins annually. Harris, 5 Jan., 1787 (*F.O.* 37/13). Carmarthen (now Duke of Leeds) agreed, 23 Feb. (*Ibid.*).

[82] Harris, 12 June, 1787 (*F.O.* 37/14).

That was all very well so far as it went, but the Ministry in London was anxious about the overseas implications now that the crisis in Dutch affairs was coming to a head. Before Harris's reply was received Leeds sent him a long despatch. An official request from the four Provinces and Chambers of the Company which were anti-French and anti-Patriot 'respecting the Foreign Establishment of the Republic being taken under the protection of England' might be very desirable from some points of view, but the inevitable consequences would be so important that the utmost delicacy and caution must be employed. Any impression that such a request had been instigated from the British side must for obvious reasons be avoided. On the other hand, if such a proposal were made, it would be indispensably necessary that the British Government should have been fully informed beforehand of the naval and military forces which the Dutch had in their various settlements; how far they could be relied on to co-operate if England sent them assistance. Moreover the proposal, if it came, would have to be considered in the light of the fact that the Cape of Good Hope and Trincomali were now garrisoned 'to a considerable degree' by French troops, which meant that acceptance of a Dutch invitation would involve Britain at the outset in the strongest measures of actual hostility. Should such a measure be adopted by Britain's friends, the utmost secrecy must be observed in order to prevent the French from having the least suspicion of the plan 'till such time as it may be ready to be carried into effect'. Meanwhile Harris must provide the Ministry with as much information as possible in order that they might be fully prepared to take the necessary measures before any official application was received.[83]

On 13 September Frederick William II of Prussia after long hesitation intervened and led his army across the Dutch frontier in support of the Stadtholder. The outbreak of a European war now depended on whether France would respond by sending troops to support the Patriots. While the issue hung undetermined Leeds sent Harris an urgent despatch. 'It is . . . extremely material to know, immediately, the State of the Foreign Possessions of the Republic, particularly the Cape and Trimcomale. If a War should happen, it will be of the utmost Importance that they should not be occupied by the French.' The Ministry must be informed of the strength of the garrisons, their political dispositions, and all other relevant particulars. According to accounts received in London the troops at the Cape and Trincomali were not very dependable. If the Republic had no troops of its own to send there, levies could probably be raised for the purpose from among the Scottish Dutch in Britain.

[83] Leeds, 12 June, 1787 (*F.O. 37/15*. Draft in *F.O. 97/246*).

It would perhaps not be easy to prevail upon the Provinces to admit any Garrisons of ours, nor is there the least wish that They would do so, if the Safety of those Posts can be otherwise provided for.[84]

Harris replied in confident mood, for France's failure to send military aid to the Patriots had broken their morale. Resistance had collapsed: Prussian troops were closing in on Amsterdam, and the Orange party was triumphant. As far as he could gather the Governor at the Cape was well disposed and as long as he remained in command the garrison could be depended on. This man's brother was Governor at Trincomali and his principles too were thought to be sound, but it was certain that some of the Dutch troops stationed in Ceylon could not be trusted. Harris, however, was already thinking in broader terms. He was hard at work, he told Leeds, getting the East India Company placed under its former Direction. As soon as Amsterdam capitulated French and Patriot influence would henceforth be at an end. It would then be an easy matter to establish an Anglo-Dutch 'Plan of Concert'. In conclusion he took the opportunity to revive his favourite project. 'I submit it to Your Lordship, whether it would not be adviseable to bring the Two Companies to come to some formal Agreement, both as to their Commercial and Political Interests – which agreement may be, afterwards, guaranteed by the two Nations.' F. W. Boers was at present in London (for the purpose of negotiating a large loan), and he would be able to give the fullest information about 'the kind of arguments most likely to operate with success on the minds of the Dutch Directors'.[85]

The British ambassador's unremitting efforts to keep the Dutch bases out of the hands of France and, if and when possible, to arrange an Anglo-Dutch partnership in the Eastern seas have been separated out from his other diplomatic activities at the Hague because they constitute the essential background of the negotiations which followed. We have seen how staunch friends of the Stadtholderate and of Britain warmly appreciated the mutual benefits of a partnership in Eastern waters; and yet, even when their backs were to the wall in politics and their financial plight as East India merchants was desperate, they insisted that general fear and mistrust of British maritime expansion must be laid to rest by formal renunciations in such matters as the spice trade and commercial penetration into the Moluccas.

The course of Anglo-Dutch relations with regard to overseas trade and defence was naturally conditioned by the revolution

---

[84] Leeds, 25 Sept., 1787 (*F.O. 37/18*). Leeds added that, although it was very improbable that France would mount an attack against the British in India, the contingency should be guarded against. Orders should therefore be sent as soon as possible to the Dutch naval and military forces in all parts of India 'to act in concert with the Forces of this Country' if France made any attempt in that quarter.

[85] Harris, 2 Oct., 1787 (secret) (*F.O. 37/18*).

within the Republic and the resulting contest between French and British influence, but that is a different story and has been brilliantly expounded elsewhere.[86] At the risk of over-simplifying a very complex situation it may perhaps be said that the crisis in the United Provinces was caused by a revolt of the bourgeoisie, organised as the Patriot party, against the authority of the hereditary Stadtholderate. On the one hand, they preached democracy (within strict limits), but that heady doctrine drove them into ever more extreme courses which eventually alienated their allies, the urban patriciate. On the other hand, their declared policy of reducing the central authority of the House of Orange to nullity intensified ancient provincialism. Jealousy of the Province of Holland (a Patriot stronghold) widened the rift between pro-Orange and anti-Orange Provinces. Yet there were numerous cross-sections. As a whole the rural aristocracy and peasantry were Orangist; but so were the dock-workers of Amsterdam and some of the leading merchants. Roman Catholics, on the other hand, looked to the Patriots to relieve them of their disabilities under a heretic Prince.

Of the three neighbouring Powers who watched the convulsion – France, Britain and Prussia – none was anxious to become involved to the point of war, but all wished to prevent the domination of the Republic by either of the other two. For France, Vergennes and his successor, Montmorin, were dragged in more deeply by the French Embassy at the Hague and by adventurous French agents than they had intended or could afford; and when the challenge came the French Government suffered the humiliation of having to default on their promises. As in North America they had backed the forces of democracy which were shortly to overwhelm their own régime at home. For Britain, George III and Pitt were extremely averse to running the risk of war with France, but Harris gradually persuaded them to give financial support; and when the crisis came they were resolute. Frederick William of Prussia, who undertook the decisive intervention, did so without enthusiasm and only when he was clear of possible trouble from the Austrian Netherlands and was sure of British support. The salvation of the House of Orange probably owed more to the tireless and brilliant diplomacy of Harris (Lord Malmesbury) than to any other factor. The Triple Alliance which followed gave Britain a new security in Europe and an opportunity to gain the friendship and co-operation of the Dutch – weakened and mistrustful though they were – along the oceanic trade routes.

---

[86] A. Cobban, *Ambassadors and Secret Agents* (Lond., 1954). This work, which is based throughout on the original British, French, Dutch and Prussian diplomatic sources, corrects at many points, and indeed supersedes, the accounts of J. H. Rose, *William Pitt* (Pt. I, Chaps. XV and XVI) and articles in *Am. Hist. Rev.*, vol. XIV, pp. 262-83, and *Eng. Hist. Rev.*, vol. XXIV, pp. 278-95.

The negotiation of an alliance between Britain and the United Provinces as European Powers occasioned no difficulty. Britain guaranteed the constitutional status of the Stadtholderate and the contracting parties pledged themselves to assist in the defence of each other's possessions. But it was a very different matter when they tried to make an agreement as mercantile Powers in Asia. Each side was aware that their essential interests as such were complementary and intended that the Treaty should incorporate the terms of a commercial and strategic partnership. Yet deadlock supervened.

Fortunately for the historian, Pitt, Grenville and Dundas argued the Dutch problem among themselves very fully in the form of private letters. The debate begins with Grenville in August, 1787, soon after his return from a three-weeks' visit to the Hague which he had made at Pitt's request in order to provide a 'second opinion' on the situation.[87] In the course of his stay there Harris had introduced him to Boers, who in several conversations had explained the structure of the Company, its relationship with the State, and the character of its trade particularly in India. The interesting point emerged that the remittance of English profits had for many years furnished the entire funds for Dutch trade in Bengal. They would willingly, said Boers, receive moneys from the English Company in India and repay in Leadenhall Street. This would be an advantage to Britain as well as to the Dutch whose minute revenues in India were quite inadequate to maintain their military establishments there. The French were compelling them to increase their forces in the East and at a time when they were threatened with almost complete bankruptcy. But if England would come to the rescue with a loan, that could pave the way to putting the English and Dutch Companies on 'a footing of strict union and friendship in the East Indies' and to the conclusion of a treaty of mutual guaranty between the two Countries. By this means the Dutch would be relieved of a heavy burden of defence and Britain would gain the advantage, which France had enjoyed during the late war, of using the Dutch arsenals at Batavia and elsewhere.

Grenville listened and took notes, although he might have learned all about it from Harris's numerous despatches in Carmarthen's office. It was arranged that Boers should follow Grenville to London for ministerial consultations about the proposed loan. Financial assistance on a large scale, followed by an arrangement by which the Dutch Company would have become virtually a subsidiary of the English corporation and a pooling of British and Dutch strategic resources in the East, amounted it was hoped to a major issue of national policy. Before the arrival of Boers in

[87] The correspondence between Pitt and himself during his visit to Holland is printed in *Grenville Corr.* (*Dropmore*), vol. III, pp. 408-16.

London Grenville sought the advice of Dundas, the Eastern expert, sending him the notes of his conversation at the Hague.

Since Dundas had followed his usual practice of escaping to Scotland for the entire summer (which annoyed his colleagues) Grenville wrote to him at length. He posed a series of questions. Would it on the whole be an advantage or detrimental to British interests 'that the Dutch East India Company should become bankrupts'? If Britain refrained from taking action to prevent this, could France with her embarrassed finances undertake it, and if so would she derive any adequate advantage? Was there any practicable method by which the British Government could render assistance – 'considering the forms of our Government and the jealousies to be expected on such a subject both in the East India Company and even in Parliament'? Finally, supposing the thing could be done, what benefits would Britain receive and what security could the Dutch provide?[88]

Pondering on these matters Grenville observed: 'One's mind at once runs to Trincomale.' Shelburne's mind had run strongly in the same direction in 1783, and it continued to be a prime preoccupation with British Ministers until the Dutch settlements in Ceylon finally passed to the British Crown after the fall of Napoleon. In this month of August, 1787, Pitt had already written to Cornwallis in India, warning him that Dutch independence was in jeopardy and that a war with France might ensue.

In this Situation the first struggle will naturally be for the foreign dependencies of the Republic; and if at the outset of a war we could get possession of the Cape and Trinquemele, it would go farther than anything else to decide the fate of the Contest. We should certainly be justified in taking Possession of those Posts on behalf of the Majority of the States, and to secure them against France.

It was, therefore, very desirable, continued Pitt, that on the first news of hostilities Cornwallis should find the means of striking a blow at Trincomali: and if anything could be attempted against the Cape, it must, of course, be done from Britain.[89] That was in case the worst should happen; but it was obviously more desirable to exclude the French by peaceful means than allow them to gain control and then attempt to drive them out in a war and alienate the Dutch in the process. Since the Ministers put such a high value

---

[88] Grenville to Dundas, 26 Aug., 1787. (Secret.) *Ibid.*, vol. I, pp. 279-81.

[89] Pitt explained what he meant by acting 'on behalf of the Majority of the States'. France, he stated, would probably be supported by the Provinces of Holland, Gröningen and Overyssel, 'while we shall have on our side the Remaining Provinces'. This was based on Harris's estimate of the situation. Pitt to Cornwallis, 2 Aug., 1787. ('Private.' P.R.O. 30/8/102.) When a British force occupied the Cape in 1795 it was then done with the assent and in the name of the Stadtholder, who had obtained asylum in England.

on these naval establishments in the East, it was to be expected
that they would go a long way to meet the Dutch on other counts.
Grenville was certainly alive to the importance of reaching a
comprehensive agreement, but in consulting Dundas he pointed
out quite correctly that the question of Trincomali in the minds of
the Dutch was tied up with that of the spice trade, which was the
only means by which they could repay a British loan or ever recover
themselves. Yet by demanding freedom of navigation in the Eastern
Seas in 1784 Britain had given 'an almost unsurmountable jealousy
on this subject', and the Dutch were convinced that if the English
Company were given access to Trincomali they would interfere
in the Dutch cinnamon trade in that Island. It was not merely a
question of exchanging Negapatam near Madras for a naval base
in Ceylon.

Dundas replied promptly and with vigour. On a purely commercial view he could see no justification for sinking large sums to
extricate the Dutch Company from its plight. 'I confess I feel
pretty decisively that, if we attend to our own commercial interests
in India, the advantages we possess are of so predominant a nature
as to render us independent of the situation of the East India
Companies of the other European nations.' If the charter of the
English Company were terminated and the territorial revenues in
India were in the hands of the public that would be a different
matter.[90] In that event it might well be that the trade of British
subjects from India would not be adequate for bringing home the
surplus revenue in the form of trade goods and the interest of this
Country would be promoted by the stability of other East India
Companies in so far as they could be made channels of remittance.
In any case it would be a mistake to suppose that Britain, however
successful, could have a monopoly of the trade with India and
China. Other nations, such as France, Holland, Denmark and
Sweden, would certainly have a considerable share, to the extent
at least of their domestic consumption; and it was in Britain's
interest that they should.

This, however, was no more than a theoretical proposition, for
the English Company's Charter was very much in being.

I need not in writing to you enlarge on the ignorance and narrow-
mindedness of that society. It would be in vain to state to them the
happy effects to both nations from a liberal exercise of the trade and

---

[90] Dundas did not conceal his desire to see the end of the Company's monopoly in
the interests of British commercial expansion in the East. On 27 Sept., 1786, he
had written to Grenville: ' Do not be jealous of me when I mention the chance of
the dissolution of the monopoly of the East India Company. But you will agree
with me there are events which may lead to such a dissolution.' It would, therefore,
be wise to take advantage of opportunities as they arose to make arrangements with
foreign nations so as to ensure adequate channels of remittance. (*Grenville Corr.*
(*Dropmore*), vol. I, pp. 268-9.)

industry of both. They would feel every bale of goods that went to Holland, although bought from their own provinces in India, as so many pounds taken out of their pockets, and would of course execrate any idea of interposing, to save the India Company of Holland.

Accordingly it would be a waste of time to start negotiations for a union between the two Companies. On the other hand a 'national' treaty between the two Governments was 'an object of the first magnitude', nor if the political situation in Holland could be altered did he think that any difficulty would arise. Many people were disposed to challenge the Dutch monopoly of the spice trade; he disagreed. 'I cannot feel the importance of the spice trade, nor have I the least disposition to disturb the Dutch in the possession of it.' An explicit surrender of that trade to them would enable Britain to enjoy the advantages of the Cape, Trincomali, and the arsenals of Batavia in time of war.

I do not see how there is any inconsistency between their having the exclusive spice trade, and yet our having Trincomale as a safe asylum for our fleets, or our having a free navigation in the Eastern seas for the purposes of our China trade, and likewise for the purpose of opening new markets both for our Indian and European manufacturers.[91]

Within a fortnight Prussian troops moved into Holland and the revolution in favour of the Stadtholder began. Grenville was sent off to join Eden in Paris in order to estimate French intentions, and Boers, arriving in London, had a number of inconclusive interviews with Pitt about obtaining a loan for the Province of Zeeland.[92] From the British point of view, however, political stabilisation must come first. By October the way was clear for concluding a Treaty of Alliance with the new régime and Instructions were sent to Harris.

Aware of the thorny issues involved in a negotiation about the Far East and of the importance of speed, Pitt drafted a *projet* for a treaty concerned solely with mutual defence, and Harris was instructed to steer clear of the old controversy about *Free Ships Free Goods* by refusing to renew the articles in the Anglo-Dutch Treaties of 1668 and 1674 which had recognised that principle. Such stipulations, it was stated, were contrary to the spirit of the new alliance.[93] But this did not at all satisfy the Dutch, who were extremely anxious to secure a commercial agreement as part of a comprehensive treaty. Such an agreement, it was felt, was essential for their economic recovery. Britain must give them a guaranteed share in the India and China trades and must remove any suspicion of interference in their cherished monopoly of the spice trade in the Moluccas. Dutch leaders, such as the new Grand Pensionary,

---

[91] Dundas to Grenville, 2 Sept., 1787. *Ibid.*, vol. III, pp. 419-22.
[92] See p. 377 above, n. 78.
[93] Instructions to Harris, 12 Oct. (*F.O.* 37/19).

Van de Spiegel, and the Greffier, Baron de Fagel, were aware that Britain would make no difficulty about either of these require- ments and that the concessions which she expected in return in the sphere of defence would be a genuine reinforcement to Dutch security. But they also knew that they had to carry with them a merchant class who had been rendered almost morbidly suspicious by adversity and jealousy of Britain's expanding economic power in Asia.

The prevailing mood was revealed as soon as discussions about the proposed treaty began. Britain, it was argued, ought to wipe out old resentment by restoring Negapatam (without equivalent) and should allay all alarm about the Molucca trade by abandoning her right of free navigation in Eastern waters.[94] At the same time trad- ing concessions in India should be arranged. From the point of view of the British Ministers whose prime concern was to establish a solid front against French maritime power in the East, this was a lopsided proposition and irrelevant to the purpose. In December, when no noticeable progress had been made, Pitt instructed the India Board (in effect Dundas and Grenville) to prepare an *exposé* of British ideas on the subject in the form of a draft agreement with explanatory comment. The very able document which they produced became the basis for all the subsequent negotiations.

The treaty, the authors wrote, should secure the favourite objects of both countries. On their side the Dutch should be granted the cession of Negapatam, a guarantee of their monopoly of the spice trade and a full share of the trade in India and with Canton. These concessions could not be granted without some return, and since the States General were not in a position to provide anything of direct economic benefit, the return should take the form of increas- ing the security of Britain's Asiatic possessions. As a basis for dis- cussion in those terms they prepared a draft treaty on which the Ambassador was to negotiate.[95]

---

[94] The following clause which expresses the Dutch point of view was forwarded to London by Harris: *Sa Majesté Britannique pour donner une marque non- équivoque de son amitié et d'affection envers la République et en consideration de la forme actuelle de son Gouvernement, ainsi que pour effacer entièrement toutes les Traces de la dernière guerre heureusement terminée par la Paix de 1784, consent à restituer, céder et guarantir en toute propriété la ville de Negätam, avec la dépendance d'elle, comme elle avait appartenu à la République avant l'Epoque de la dite Guerre, et pour ces mêmes causes, sa Majesté Britannique consent que, pendant la durée de cette alliance, ses sujets n'exerceront d'autre Navigation dans les Mers Orientales qu'ils n'avaient exercée avant cette même Epoque.* (Enclosed in No. 154 of 9 Nov., 1787. F.O. 37/19.)

[95] It was entitled – *Projet of a Treaty of Defensive Alliance and Mutual Guarantee of Territories and Commerce at the Cape of Good Hope and the East Indies between Great Britain and the States General* – and was incorporated in ' Report from the Commissioners for the Affairs of India '. Dated 21 Dec., 1787, and signed by Dundas, Grenville and Mulgrave (F.O. 37/20). There is another copy in the Auckland Papers (*Addit. MSS.*, 34,467, ff. 110-19).

The first article provided a reciprocal guarantee of protection for each other's possessions at the Cape and in the East Indies. Britain was not to be obliged to send troops to Batavia or any Dutch settlement beyond the west coast of Sumatra. Nor were the Dutch on their side to be committed to any war in Bengal apart from rendering naval assistance. Secondly, Negapatam was to be ceded, and the authors did not fail to emphasise the value of the offer. It would be of the greatest importance for Dutch trade in India, 'and from its situation as the key to the Tanjore Country and as a check upon the very important French possession of Kurrical (Karikal), is a strong proof of our confidence as well as our liberality'. The Dutch must guarantee never to cede it to another Power and to keep it in a proper state of defence.

Turning to the question of Dutch trade in India which was so much exercising the minds of the Dutch because of Britain's new territorial authority, Dundas and Grenville proposed that Holland 'shall enjoy every privilege and advantage of Commerce in Bengal and its dependencies, and in every other part of India subject to the British power, which may have been granted to any other Nation'. This meant, in effect, that the Dutch would be put on the same most-favoured-nation footing as France. It is an interesting fact that, although Britain and France were engaged in a sustained struggle for mastery in Asian waters, they had nevertheless concluded a convention in that year (as stipulated in the Anglo-French Commercial Treaty) by which the factories of the French East India Company were guaranteed their former trading rights in India. The French hoped and intended to extinguish the British position in the sub-continent, but while it remained it was in the interests of both Powers to co-operate commercially. Dutch trade was to be ensured on similar terms; and 'We, being perfectly liberal, are open to further suggestions'. This was a characteristic and quite sincere Dundas touch. The more the Dutch were able to buy Indian textiles the better for the prosperity of Bengal and thus of Britain. There were questions of old firmans granted to the Dutch by local nawabs at Surat and elsewhere. All such matters must be settled now so that no room was left for later disputes.

The proposed fourth article dealt with the touchy question of free navigation in the Eastern Seas. The Dutch had asked that British subjects should be inhibited from increasing the extent of that navigation beyond their customary exercise of it before the late war. 'Were we inclined to grant only what they ask and not what is their real object,' the Board observed, 'there might be no difficulty in closing with this expression which would grant nothing.' Although the right was denied by the Dutch, it had, in fact, been enjoyed and exercised by the British previous to the war. The ambiguity was destructive of Dutch interests, and the British

Ministry, it was indicated, were determined to clarify the situation – as they were soon to do with Spanish claims in the Pacific.

The proposed wording precisely defined that part of the 'navigation' which Britain would formally abjure. British subjects would not carry on any trade with any of the islands to the east of Sumatra, nor for many establishments there without the consent of the States General. But if the Dutch granted any privilege of trade or establishment to another European nation in those seas the concession would become void.

It is intended to give the Dutch the monopoly of the Spice Trade, secured fully from our interference by any means not incompatible with the free exercise of our other Trade. For this purpose it is intended to give up as a condition of this Treaty, the Navigation of the Eastern Islands by British Ships. But we can neither renounce the trade to be carried on by the Inhabitants of those islands in all articles, except Spices, to our own settlements, nor can we give up the Navigation through those seas, which it is necessary to preserve to our men of war and East India ships, that they may avail themselves of the different passages through the Islands to China as the season and other Circumstances may require.[96]

The exclusion of British trade from all the islands eastward of Sumatra, the Report continued, was a very comprehensive term, but if the Dutch suggested some other it could be adopted. 'It must not however be so worded, as to cramp any trade we may choose to carry on upon the coast of Siam or Cochin China, or our free intercourse at all seasons with China.' The large commercial strategy here implied had been developing for some twenty years. It was nothing less than the establishment of a great emporium beyond the Dutch Spice Islands – in Borneo, the Philippines, and the rich countries of South-East Asia – where the goods of Britain and India could be bartered for a wide range of local products which in turn could reinforce and diversify the cargoes sent to China. In their proposals to the Dutch the object of the British Ministers was to safeguard the very exposed ocean flank of this nexus, extending from the Cape of Good Hope to Ceylon and on to Sumatra and Malaya.[97]

That this was the central object of the Asian side of the Treaty was made manifest in the final article, which for the Dutch was the sting in the tail. In return for the commercial advantages, as specified, and the retrocession of Negapatam the States General were to

---

[96] It was further proposed that legislation should be submitted to Parliament prohibiting the importation of spices from the East Indies into British territories in India or into Britain except by the Dutch East India Company.

[97] See vol. I, Chap. III. Warren Hastings had been actively interested in the possibilities of trade with Cochin China, but in 1787 it was already too late, for the French penetration had begun there two years earlier (*Ibid.*, pp. 97-102).

cede all interest and claims to Trincomali and Rhio. The importance of the former as a naval base had been fully demonstrated during the critical contest at sea between Hughes and De Suffren, and the recent near-success of France in obtaining control of it in time of peace made the British regard it as a *sine qua non*. It might be supposed, wrote Dundas and Grenville, that it would suffice if Britain were given exclusive use of this port in time of war, but France was well placed (in Mauritius) to get in first upon the outbreak of hostilities. The purpose of the Treaty was to establish 'an intimate friendship and union' between Britain and Holland, and Trincomali in British hands could safeguard the interests of both nations in the Bay of Bengal and beyond.[98] This argument was repeatedly advanced and as frequently resisted in the long negotiations which followed. The proposal offended Dutch pride which was all the more sensitive because Holland as an imperial Power was passing through a period of weakness and decline.

The strategic importance of Rhio has already been noted. From now on Dundas made its acquisition a prime objective of British policy in the East. Rhio never became a great *entrepôt,* Dutch or British, but the prominence given to it in diplomatic negotiation led to a ready acceptance of Raffles's subsequent alternative of Singapore. The arguments now advanced on account of Rhio supplement the picture of British commercial policy in the Eastern Seas. In enemy hands it could intercept all the traffic between Madras and Canton: in British hands it could secure that trade and check French designs in Cochin China and Siam, which was a Dutch as well as a British interest.

That was Britain's real intention, and if the Dutch should suggest that Britain would in fact use Rhio to develop trade with the Eastern Islands to their injury, then good faith required that there should be 'an open and fair avowal' of British purpose. Although the Dutch would be guaranteed their monopoly of the spice trade, Britain had no intention of refraining from every branch of commerce in the entire Malay Archipelago.

We do not mean to renounce that market, which we must have by this or some other *entrepôt* for the exchange or sale of the produce of Bengal. We cannot suffer so important a branch of our commerce and

---

[98] The demand for Trincomali was limited to the harbour and the outer road, and the report was at pains to rebut the Dutch argument (previously noted by Grenville) that interference with their cinnamon trade in Ceylon would inevitably follow. ' The situation of the Cinnamon Country and the absolute renunciation of all right and even means of trading from Trincomale entitles us to treat such an apprehension as entirely chimerical, whilst on the other hand, the importance of this station in all Naval Operations for the security of our Possessions on the Coromandel Coast and Bengal render this Article highly important in any Treaty. . . .' This, it was emphasised, was the only *quid pro quo* which Holland could furnish in return for the many advantages being offered.

one so intimately and materially connected with the carrying on to advantage our China trade, to be at the mercy of any European Power, or entirely in their hands, altho' we mean by other parts of this Treaty to admit them to a full and fair participation of it.

The British Ministry were thinking in terms of global strategy in which Holland, as a valued subsidiary, was to have an assured place in return for handing over one or two strategic assets. On their side the Dutch East India Company regarded such demands, not as part of a fair compact, but as clear evidence of the predatory propensities of the Anglo-Saxon.

Resistance to the Dundas-Grenville recommendations was immediate and uncompromising. Van de Spiegel did his best for them, but the Regents of Amsterdam and some of the East India Directors informed him that, while they recognised that Britain was offering considerable advantages, nothing could justify the exchange of Rhio and Trincomali for Negapatam. Rhio was the key to the Strait of Malacca, and Trincomali commanded 'in a manner' the Indian seas. If at some future time the two nations should be at variance, Britain's possession of these two ports would put the whole Dutch trade and their possessions in India at their mercy. Spiegel and Harris both urged that Eastern affairs should be left to one side in order to avoid further delay and London agreed.[99]

To separate the treaty of alliance from Anglo-Dutch relations in the East was not as simple as it seemed. Popular opinion in Holland demanded that there be no alliance at all unless Britain would forgo the two exactions imposed in 1784: the cession of Negapatam and access to Eastern navigation. What had been forced from an enemy should be restored to an ally. British policy in Europe urgently required the alliance, and yet acquiescence in the Dutch demand would have destroyed the basis for the kind of Eastern agreement on which Pitt and his colleagues had set their hearts The friends of the alliance in both countries became alarmed.[100] In mid-March a new clause was agreed, which – with a soothing phrase – left these two questions to be settled in a separate convention to be concluded within six months.[101] The treaty of alliance

---

[99] Harris. 1 and 4 Jan., 1788; Carmarthen, 1 Feb. (*F.O.* 37/21). Cf. Carmarthen, 8 Feb. (*F.O.* 37/21).

[100] Harris, 22 Feb. 'If the alliance fails, the influence we have recovered here will very soon drop and the System we have taken such pains to restore be eclipsed in its dawn.' Cf. Harris, 5, 12, and 25 Feb., 11, 14, 18, 20 and 28 March, 1788. (*F.O.* 37/21 and 22.)

[101] *Sa Majesté Britannique n'exigera rien que ne soit favorable aux intérêts et à là Sûreté réciproques des deux parties contractates dans les Indes* (Art. II). In accepting this formula Carmarthen gave warning (to Harris, 27 Feb.) that Britain was not prepared to lose Negapatam without gaining Trincomali. 'We want no increase of Territory, no advantages of Commerce, but solely that port which happens to be the only one in that part of the world, and which we wish to possess for their benefit as well as our own.'

and mutual defence passed the States General on 8 April, 1788, but the negotiations for an Asiatic convention continued for five years.[102]

During the inter-war period, 1782-93, British Ministers were much attracted by the notion that two sovereign states could each secure substantial advantages by a mutual adjustment of commercial interests. The acceleration of European and particularly of British economic expansion on a world scale involved the elaboration of a system of multilateral commodity exchange which obliged the participants to recognise, however reluctantly, their underlying interdependence. It was hard doctrine for nation states with a long tradition of embattled self-sufficiency. The fact that a system of world free-trade proved to be no more than a fleeting vision of the mid-19th century, entertained by a few outside the United Kingdom, indicates how hard such doctrine was, and is. Strenuous efforts were made during these ten years and with varying degrees of elasticity to establish commercial bargains with Ireland, the United States of America, France, Spain and Holland. In the case of the Dutch the negotiations which began on a broad and enlightened basis became so twisted and distorted that in the later stages they were scarcely recognisable. As the student picks his way through one of the most complicated diplomatic transactions of the 18th century the shifts and turns occasioned by conflicting pressures reveal the springs which actuated national policy overseas.

The first phase of these negotiations for an Eastern treaty (in 1788-9) was in the hands of Sir James Harris. Dutch friendship had been so hardly regained and its continuance was so important as the linch-pin of the Triple Alliance that Harris was determined to avoid arousing latent resentments. Accordingly he strove to effect an acceptable compromise on the very sensitive issues raised by Britain's demands with regard to Trincomali and Rhio and commercial penetration into the Malay Archipelago. Although his instructions were to negotiate on the basis of the draft treaty prepared by Dundas and Grenville (a copy of which he had shown to Spiegel and a few others), he suggested important modifications.

When a Commission was appointed by the States General in July, 1788, for the negotiation, Harris produced a *projet* under which Britain would have pledged herself not to engage in any sort of trade in the Moluccas and would have agreed to a joint arrangement for maintaining the defences of Eastern bases. In particular the Dutch were to undertake the fortification of Trin-

---

[102] Professor J. H. Rose (*Life of Pitt*, vol. I, p. 383) made the astonishing statement that 'the negotiation was never even begun'. The error evidently arose from omitting to look at the original despatches in the series, *F.O.* 37, where the greater part of the contents of thirteen volumes relates to the negotiations between 1788 and 1791, and from relying on the printed extracts of despatches in the *Malmesbury Correspondence*, the editor of which omitted documents relating to these negotiations.

comali and garrison it with 2,000 European troops while Britain would annually subsidise the expenditure on condition that all foreign ships, other than British, would be excluded from the port.[103] Being keen business men, the Dutch Commissioners expressed interest in the scheme: they told Harris that a garrison of that strength would cost not less than £50,000 p.a., the transportation charges would amount to about £80,000, and the expense of the fortifications to as much more; and they then asked to be informed what proportion Britain would bear in these outgoings.[104]

By deviation from his Instructions which required the absolute cession of Trincomali as the essential part of a comprehensive commercial 'union' Harris had placed himself in an awkward situation. As long ago as the previous March, when the Treaty of Alliance was being negotiated, he had thrown out a hint in a private letter to Grenville that he had hopes of securing access to Trincomali 'on something like the same terms on which the Dutch held the barrier towns'. There was no hope, he had then added, of getting 'a more positive possession of it'.[105] It was an ingenious idea, but none knew better than the Dutch that such an arrangement amounted to effective occupation and control. When Harris reported that conversation had taken place on the basis of a British subsidy without control so that the Dutch Government could at any time rescind its previous orders and close the port to British ships, Ministers in London not unnaturally took alarm.[106]

During a summer visit to London Harris was firmly told that the place must be defended by a British garrison, and his own previous suggestion was adopted of making an arrangement similar to that which had applied in the case of the Barrier fortresses in the Austrian Netherlands. Nothing less would do; and the stipulation was repeated in a formal despatch on his return to the Hague.

Every other Proposal which has hitherto been suggested in this Subject appears inadequate to any real Object in Question in providing no Security against any Change of System, and, in the meantime,

---

[103] A summary of Harris's plan was subsequently sent to the Foreign Secretary by Lord Auckland. (Enclosure in No. 7 of 21 Jan., 1791. *F.O. 37/33.*)

[104] Harris, 3 Aug., 1788 (*F.O. 37/24*).

[105] Harris to Grenville, 4 March, 1788 (*Grenville Corr., Dropmore*, vol. III, pp. 446-7).

[106] Duke of Richmond to Pitt, 29 Aug., 1788. 'Pray how have you got over with Sir James Harris the very awkward Proposition he chose to make? For I trust you have not been persuaded to give way to it, and I should hope that this business will be finished, now that the Dutch are in a good disposition and other circumstances are favourable for our getting possession of Trincomale' (P.R.O. 30/8/171). Dundas was less rigid and was evidently prepared to accept the Dutch offer of exclusive access to Trincomali by British warships as affording sufficient security if it was faithfully executed. But on that point Grenville (now as later) thought otherwise, and as usual he had his way with Pitt. (See Dundas to Pitt, 13 Aug., 1788. P.R.O. 30/8/247.)

subjecting this Country to the Expense of a Subsidy for keeping up the Defence of a Port which might nevertheless, on the first Appearance of Hostilities, be used against us.[107]

Not the least of the difficulties was the impoverished condition of the Dutch East India Company which rendered it incapable of providing anything approaching adequate defence for its Eastern bases. During the summer of 1788 repeated requests for financial assistance by the Chamber of Zeeland were at last met by a loan of 2 million florins, but it was done with understandable hesitation.[108]

In the London despatch already quoted the emphasis is repeatedly laid on the need for 'security'. 'A full and perfect Union of our Interests in the East Indies is unquestionably desirable to both Countries, and by no means exclusively to us.' Extensive commercial concessions were in contemplation, but they could not be granted 'without some Security on the only Point in which any return is asked'.

Reasonable as all this seemed from the London end, Harris (now Lord Malmesbury) knew his Dutchmen. There was much goodwill towards Britain and a general expectation that the impending commercial treaty would revive their East Indian prosperity, but the Stadtholder and others warned him that a demand for the surrender of Trincomali would, despite all argument, be taken as an unfriendly act and a blow to Dutch prestige in the East. He adopted the doubtful expedient of concentrating upon commercial details and evading 'the particular Point on which the Negotiation was likely to hitch'.[109] The result was doubly unfortunate. The mysterious lack of progress caused ill humour and irritation in Holland which hostile elements exploited,[110] and British Ministers in London, concerned at an unexpected setback, tended to blame Malmesbury for being vague and indecisive.

---

[107] Carmarthen, 3 Oct., 1788. Draft. (*F.O. 97/247.*)

[108] The interest charges and capital repayments were duly met at the stipulated times with characteristic Dutch integrity. The hesitation was due to an apprehension that by granting large loans independently of a comprehensive commercial settlement the British Treasury might be injuring the English Company by subsidising a competitor who was trying to undercut the English in the European tea market. See Grenville to Harris, 27 Feb., 1788 (*Grenville Corr., Dropmore*, vol. III, pp. 444-6).

[109] Malmesbury, 7 Oct., 1788 (*F.O. 37/24*). In this despatch he reported the failure of his efforts with that consistent friend of Britain, the Grand Pensionary. 'I . . . could not by any Arguments in my Power get him to acquiesce that it was either safe for the Republic to put Trincomale into our Hands under Stipulations similar to those under which the Barrier Towns in the Austrian Netherlands were formally garrisoned by the Dutch troops, or that it was reasonable in us to require it.' To attempt to carry it would raise too great a clamour in the Estates of the several Provinces. England's enemies and many of her friends would say that she was grasping at power and endeavouring 'to act towards the Republic as towards a dependent Province '.

[110] See Lindsay (a Dutch emissary in London) to Pitt, 1 and 4 Nov., 1788 (P.R.O. 30/8/336).

The impetuous Richmond went further. In a letter to Pitt he attributed the growing discontent among the Dutch to the fact that Malmesbury had not frankly stated that the restoration of Negapatam would not be contemplated without receiving in return 'the effective though qualified possession of Trincomali'. The Ambassador had brought forward a *projet* of his own which was 'in direct contradiction to his Instructions and what he knew to be the sentiments of the Cabinet'. That, of course, was an exaggeration. After hinting that perhaps Malmesbury and the Foreign Secretary had had a private understanding which did not appear in the official despatches, he concluded: 'Useful as I still think Lord Malmesbury may be in that country, I had rather lose him than lose Holland, and I fear that if the murder must out, he must be recalled and with disgrace.'[111]

He was not recalled; but he did not return as Ambassador to the Hague. Worn out and in ill health he went for a holiday to Switzerland and afterwards to Germany. It was not until 1793 that he received his next diplomatic appointment.[112] With Malmesbury's departure (in November, 1788), followed by the King's first attack of mental disorder and the consequent political crisis, the Dutch negotiations lapsed. In the following July Alleyne Fitzherbert, whom we have already encountered during the peace negotiations in Paris, was appointed Envoy Extraordinary to the Hague. It was a holding operation, for he was instructed to consult Van de Spiegel in order to form a basis for fresh negotiations, pending the re-appointment of Dutch Commissioners. In view of Malmesbury's deviation from his Instructions 'I think,' wrote the Foreign Secretary, 'we had much better proceed as if the former negotiation had never taken place'.[113]

---

[111] Richmond to Pitt, 6 Nov., 1788 (P.R.O. 30/8/171). The suggestion that Carmarthen and Malmesbury had a private understanding contrary to Cabinet policy was without foundation. In August, 1789, the Foreign Secretary wrote to Fitzherbert, Malmesbury's successor: 'It is perfectly true Ld. Malmesbury had given in a projet on the subject to which no official answer has been sent from hence. That projet in fact differed essentially from the one ministerially communicated and of course rendered it difficult to make any answer to . . . without either retracting the former instructions or conveying some degree of censure on the Ambassador himself' (F.O. 97/247). Grenville had been corresponding privately with Malmesbury on Pitt's behalf, and Richmond resented the way in which Grenville was being obviously 'groomed' for the foreign secretaryship. Pitt's concentration of executive authority in the hands of his henchmen, Grenville and Dundas, inevitably aroused jealousy in the Cabinet. (See Richmond to Pitt, 3/4 Nov., 1790. P.R.O. 30/8/171.)

[112] He was a supporter of Fox and when Pitt in 1784 had offered to confirm Fox's appointment of him to the Hague had very honourably stipulated that he should not be expected to abandon his political party affiliation. When he was in Switzerland Fox urged him to come home because of the King's illness. He did so and duly voted against the Government's Regency Bill in the Lords. He was not employed again until he, with the Portland Whigs, joined the Administration in November, 1793. (M.C., vol. II, p. 434.)

[113] Carmarthen, 21 and 25 Aug., 1789 (F.O. 97/247).

Conversations with the Pensionary quickly convinced Fitzherbert that the projected exchange of Negapatam for the use of the port of Trincomali and the right to provide its defence was 'liable to insuperable difficulties'. The only way to bring the negotiation to a successful conclusion, he reported, was to narrow its basis, confining it to commercial points only, and leaving the territorial possessions of the two countries as they had been settled by the peace treaty in 1784.[114] In the circumstances that appeared to be the common-sense thing to do, but Pitt, Dundas and Grenville with their eyes on India and the commercial potentialities of the China seas were not prepared to abandon their design for ensuring the maritime security which the new developments required.

It is a measure of their determination that in making a fresh start at the Hague they refused to limit the scope of their original scheme and that the ambassador selected for the task was William Eden, Lord Auckland, the skilled negotiator of the Anglo-French Commercial Treaty of 1787. Furthermore, in order to ensure direct control of the negotiation, Pitt arranged that his *alter ego* Grenville should be the effective channel of communication and the Duke of Leeds was left with little more than the duty of adding his signature to the formal despatches. It was also decided to enlarge the scope of the intended agreement into a comprehensive treaty of trade and navigation. There was much to be said for taking this unique opportunity of clarifying the economic relations of the two countries in all sectors, so consolidating the alliance. But Holland, as a European Power, was exceptional in that a very important part of her economy was the maritime carrying trade, and from the time of Cromwell Dutch insistence on the claim of a neutral to fetch and carry for belligerents had been a recurring source of issue, involving on each side considerations of national survival, and could therefore be resolved only if both parties were ready to make difficult sacrifices. Otherwise the inclusion of this long-standing controversy could overwhelm the entire negotiation.

After some preliminary work in London Auckland arrived at the Hague in March, 1790, to find that the atmosphere was sour. Almost a year had passed since the signature of the Treaty of Alliance, and the stipulated Commercial Convention appeared to be as far off as ever. At their first interview the Pensionary expressed himself with a soreness which Auckland had not expected in an introductory interview. The new Commissioners were importunate for a conference 'even a few hours after my arrival'; and when he did meet them, 'their Tone . . . was so high and their claims and Pretensions so grossly unreasonable that it was a painful effort to me to listen to them'. In reply Auckland treated

---

[114] Fitzherbert 10 July, 18 and 28 Aug., 1789 (*F.O.* 37/26).

them to some plain speaking. Britain sincerely desired to extend to India and the East the intimate friendship and union with the Republic which existed in Europe; but she was under no obligation to give up any possession, relax any existing monopoly, 'or to desist from any exercise of accustomed Trade in whatever Line of Navigation We may think proper or expedient to conduct it '.[115]

An unpropitious start: but Auckland was efficient and quick and the Dutch Commissioners soon appreciated that he meant business. Within a month a *projet* of fourteen Articles emerged from their conferences. Neither party was committed to any of the propositions, but the *desiderata* of both had been brought together and a large measure of agreement had been reached. With regard to ' Neutral Rights' Auckland succeeded in persuading the Dutch, although with difficulty, to accept a very adequate list of commodities as contraband of war and therefore liable to seizure when found in neutral ships. By way of compensation for this concession the Dutch Commissioners requested the insertion of an Article declaring that in the event of war between one of the contracting parties and some other nation the ships of the neutral Power would be free to trade in the European ports of the belligerent. Auckland expressed doubts about this but was hopeful that it would not be finally urged.[116] In fact this was the stipulation upon which the Dutch insisted throughout the negotiation.

With regard to trade in India the Dutch were to enjoy the same privileges as had been granted in 1788 to the French. Dutch factories within British territory would continue to exercise their own jurisdiction. Additional factories might be established there, but in such cases those residing in them would be liable like British subjects to the ordinary justice of the region. Dutch shipping coming into Indian ports under British jurisdiction would not be liable to an import duty of more than $2\frac{1}{2}$ per cent above that levied upon British subjects. Finally (and in response to a special request) the Dutch Company in Bengal was to receive a specified annual consignment of saltpetre and opium at prime cost for use in the China trade. The original provision for guaranteeing the Dutch monopoly of the spice trade in India, Britain and Ireland was repeated, together with the Article by which Britain abjured all trade with the islands to the east of Sumatra.

On the touchy point of ' equivalents' for these concessions Auckland noted that the Ministry appeared to have dropped the claim for joint possession of Trincomali, but he had included an

---

[115] Auckland, 13 March and 6 April, 1790 (*F.O.* 37/28).

[116] The four propositions laid down by the League of Armed Neutrality in 1780 were: (1) neutral ships may sail freely from port to port of the belligerent nation, (2) goods carried by them, except contraband, to be free from seizure, (3) only certain specified goods to be regarded as contraband, (4) no blockade to be recognised which was not effective.

Article giving British shipping access to the port in peace or war.[117] As to Rhio (now a prime British objective) he gave warning that the Dutch Commissioners had expressed strong doubts about agreeing to its cession.[118] They had pointed out that Britain now had a fortified port at Prince of Wales Island (Penang) which, they claimed, would afford a decisive command of the Malacca Strait at all times and in all circumstances. To that he had replied that he wished this might be the case, 'and that it ought not to give just cause for uneasiness to them if the Friendship of the Republic towards us is what it ought to be' – which is an apt illustration of the difference in point of view between the stronger and the weaker member of an alliance.[119] A few days later the Commissioners came to see Auckland in a body 'to represent the extreme difficulties which they foresee will arise respecting the cession of Rhio'.

In Auckland's opinion it was a good treaty – 'highly eligible'. Within a week of sending the *projet* to London he reported a further development which seemed to him to solve the difficulty over Rhio which was unobtainable. The Dutch had offered to cede Broach Padang or another of their trading depots on the west coast of Sumatra in exchange for Negapatam.[120] This proposition, wrote Auckland (repeating the arguments of the Dutch Commissioners), was equal to a substitute for Rhio which was no longer needed by the British as a port of call between Bengal and Canton because they had now established a port in the Andaman Islands.[121] On a general view, he concluded, he was confident that in the existing mood of the Commissioners and the States General he could bring 'this complicated business' to a conclusion on the basis of the *projet* with such amendments as the Ministers might think admissible – 'if we do not insist on the cession of Rhio'; and he asked for full powers as quickly as possible.[122]

In the view of the man who had successfully negotiated a commercial treaty with France this Anglo-Dutch agreement (in

---

[117] 'Though we seem to have desisted,' he wrote, 'from our original request to have a joint possession with the Dutch of Trincomale, and though the importance of that object is much lessened by other establishments now making in India, I conceive that it may be of consequence to us to have both in Peace and in War, admission into that port for His Majesty's Ships and Fleets, with an exclusion of the vessels of all other Powers.'

[118] On the restoration of Negapatam to the Dutch in return for an 'equivalent' Auckland wrote sound sense: 'If the possession of Rhio should be of any importance to us, I am willing to confess that it is more than an equivalent for Negapatam, which in good policy we should certainly wish to be in the hands of the Dutch, if they can apply it to an extension of fair commerce within our possessions.'

[119] The above is a summary of Auckland's *projet* and of the explanatory comment in his covering despatch of 5 May, 1790. No. 28 (*F.O. 37/28*).

[120] A British force had seized these posts in 1789. (See vol. I, pp. 136-42.)

[121] See p. 363 above.

[122] Auckland to Leeds (private), 7 May, 1790 (*Addit. MSS.*, 28,065, f. 336); Auckland (official), 8 and 11 May, Nos. 30 and 31 (*F.O. 37/29*).

many respects the more important of the two) ought to be clinched before anyone had time to think up more awkwardness. In return for guaranteed status and trading opportunities in India the Dutch had accepted an extensive list of commodities as contraband of war,[123] and treacherous ground on the general issue of Neutral Rights had been circumvented. To jeopardise the whole by insisting on the acquisition of a port in a remote and undeveloped island seemed unreasonable. Auckland, in fact, was assuming that the object was to protect the route between Bengal and Canton, whereas the three Ministers – and especially Dundas – had fastened on Rhio for a different, although related purpose, namely, as a necessary *entrepôt* for British-Indian trade with South-East Asia. The Dutch monopoly of the spice trade could be guaranteed (in spite of the English East India Company's narrow-minded acquisitiveness in that direction), but Rhio became an important component in an expanding Asian system.[124]

An extraordinary situation now developed. When Auckland's *projet* and covering despatch of 5 May arrived in London, Britain and Spain were on the verge of war over the Spanish seizure of British ships in Nootka Sound.[125] On 30 April the Cabinet had decided to advise the King to demand 'immediate and adequate satisfaction' and to give orders for fitting out a squadron of ships of the line. On 9 May Grenville wrote privately to Auckland to say that, if war broke out, the Dutch could be of material assistance in supplying intelligence about the enemy. In 1756-63 the best information in the whole course of the war had come through Holland. In the present instance it was most probable that the Dutch would not be involved, although they would furnish their quota of ships under the treaty of alliance. 'Their Merchants and Trading Vessels will consequently have free access to all the coasts and harbours of Spain.' In these circumstances it should not be difficult to have Dutch agents constantly resident in all the ports of Spain, who could report to Amsterdam and the Hague, whence the intelligence could 'without risk or delay' be sent over to England.[126]

---

[123] The list comprised – *la poudre à canon, mêches, saltpetre, balle et toute genre d'armes et d'instrumens de guerre quelconque servant à l'usage des troupes, et aussi tout fer, plomb, cordages, cables, voiles, toiles propre à faire des voiles, goudron, résine, ancres, mats de navire, et autres bois et choses nécessaires ou servant à construire et radouber des vaisseaux.* The British Ministry added *chauvre* (hemp) to the list 'for further precision'. Subsequently the Dutch accepted a much more detailed list of naval and military stores as contraband.

[124] See Leeds, 12 June, 1790. No. 12 (*F.O. 37/29*). 'The object of this country in wishing for Rhio is the acquisition of a Port which may be made the entrepôt for such articles of our Commerce as might find a market in the Eastern Islands and be exchanged for Commodities which might thence be carried to China.' Bengal, it was added, had always enjoyed this commerce and should not be debarred from it.

[125] See Chap. VII below.

[126] Grenville to Auckland, 10 May, 1790. *Addit. MSS.*, 34,431, f. 101.

Auckland replied at once that he would attend to the matter. 'This country, as you presume, speculates on retaining a mercantile access to the ports of Spain, though the Republic may furnish the stipulated succours to us.' He did not think, however, that Spain would long allow that construction, for the Dutch trade in the Mediterranean and the West Indies would 'give good prizes to Spain'. A few weeks later he reported that the Pensionary had taken every possible step in arranging for Dutch agents to operate as suggested; and in this case, as in naval equipment, 'he refuses our money'. The naval preparations were proceeding with abundant alacrity, and if mere justice was done to the Republic, 'it will appear that we have a very efficient and useful ally in these Provinces'.

Auckland did not fail to point the obvious moral. 'It would be a material circumstance at this moment if we can complete the commercial *projet* which I have sent, and I see no material objections to it.' Such a treaty at that juncture would have a good effect and many resulting conveniences, but it should not be delayed. When three more weeks passed without a response his tone became urgent.

I entreat as a great favour of you, that you will contrive to expedite the return of the commercial *projet*. The Articles of contraband and Trincomale are of such importance to us, and the other Articles, to the best of my belief, of such indifference, that I believe it to be greatly our interest to expedite the business.

The delay, he added, was causing more ill-humour among useful friends than would have arisen from entirely declining the negotiation which had now lasted two and a half years.[127] If some clairvoyant could have revealed to Auckland that he himself would still be struggling with this business for a further two years he might well have decided to throw in his hand there and then.

Under pressure of impending war it might have been expected that Pitt, Grenville and Dundas would have decided to consolidate relations with an ally by authorising the Ambassador to conclude the agreement even without Rhio. But not so. The tenacity of Dundas with regard to Rhio and the policy which its acquisition represented remained unshaken and carried the other two with him.[128] In the summer of 1790 the Triumvirate decided not only to

[127] Auckland to Grenville, 15 May and 8 June, 1790. Private. (*Grenville Corr., Dropmore*, vol. I, pp. 585-6, 588-9.)

[128] Pitt relied a great deal on Grenville's judgement. In the previous September, when Dundas was in Scotland, he wrote: 'I own to you . . . that the more I consider the points, the more I have been puzzled about the detail, especially of the Spice business; and I do not like to trust my own single opinion, *which is nearly all I have to trust to on this subject at present.*' (Italics inserted.) Pitt to Grenville, 22 Sep., 1788 (*Ibid.*, p. 356).

take up the Spanish challenge in order to gain open access to the Pacific but at the same time to risk antagonising their Dutch allies in order to ensure the opening of the Malay Archipelago beyond the Moluccas.

One evening at Wimbledon towards the end of May Dundas harangued his colleagues on this aspect of the Anglo-Dutch *projet* which they had before them. Perhaps Pitt and Grenville hesitated, for Dundas afterwards sought out one Robert Ferguson, whom he described as 'the greatest European merchant I suppose, who ever came from India'.[129] He then wrote to Grenville to say that the conversation had confirmed his opinion on the following points:

1. That the spice trade, except as a monopoly, is of no value worth mentioning.
2. That a place of intercourse in the course of navigation between India and China, where our ships may meet the traders and inhabitants of the Eastern Isles, and barter their commodities, is essentially necessary; and
3. That Rhio is, without exception, the best, or to speak more properly, the only unexceptionable place for that purpose.[130]

Grenville accepted this view, but he was alive to the difficulties. When he mooted the idea to Baron van Nagell, the Dutch Ambassador, the latter bluntly responded that the cession of Rhio was as much out of the question as that of Trincomali, in fact more so. The leading people of Amsterdam had warned him to have nothing to do with the proposal. Britain, he pointed out, had already acquired Penang at the northern end of the Strait of Malacca, and if Rhio at the southern extremity was also secured, the Strait would be under British control. Pondering on this, Grenville wrote off to Dundas, suggesting a modification of the proposal. Since Rhio seemed to offer all the advantages of Penang, 'we might, if pushed to extremities, consent to shove that into the bargain, giving up both Negapatam and Prince of Wales Island [Penang] for Rhio'.[131] Dundas at once agreed. Penang, he answered, would lose much of its strategic value if Commodore Cornwallis's report on the Andaman Islands (which was being eagerly awaited) was sufficiently favourable to warrant their occupation.[132] But even if the Andamans did not come up to expectations, he still thought that both Penang and Negapatam ought to be ceded rather than lose Rhio. A station for the development of trade in the Eastern Seas was essential.

[129] He was the founder of a House of Agency which long remained prominent in Calcutta.

[130] Dundas to Grenville, 30 May, 1790 (*Grenville Corr.* (*Dropmore*), vol. I., p. 588).

[131] Grenville to Dundas, 25 June (*Ibid.*, p. 590). He added that Lord Cornwallis had stated his intention of withdrawing the establishment from Penang if the Andamans came up to expectations.

[132] Cf. p. 363 above.

' The want of a station such as Rhio would be hourly felt in the exercise of our commerce; and there is no substitute for it the moment we, by giving the spice trade exclusively to the Dutch, depart from an unlimited communication directly with the Malays in their respective islands.'[133] Thus the general proposition, as originally set out in the Dundas-Grenville Report, of an open commerce with the islands beyond the Moluccas in return for a guarantee with respect to the spice trade, was now made conditional upon the acquisition of a depot from which the desired commerce could be developed.

On their side the Dutch concluded (wrongly) that the motive behind the British demand was to gain strategic control of the Strait of Malacca and establish a smuggling trade with the Spice Islands; and the more the British pressed their demand the deeper the suspicion became. For the same reasons they afterwards resented the establishment of a free *entrepôt* at Singapore.

Meanwhile Auckland's draft treaty had been returned to him with the Ministers' amendments. The clauses relating to Dutch privileges in India were left untouched, but the arrangements about the Malay Archipelago were remodelled in order to give precision to the requirements of the Dundas policy. The whole question was brought together in one comprehensive clause. In consideration of the cession of Rhio His Majesty would recommend legislation to the Parliaments of Great Britain and Ireland to prohibit the importation of spices except by the Dutch into those Kingdoms from Ceylon, Sumatra, Java, the Moluccas or from any other place to the east of the Cape of Good Hope, and to forbid the formation of British establishments in any of the aforementioned islands. But the previous offer to give the Dutch the exclusive right to import spices into British India was now omitted.

The reason for the change was explained in the covering despatch. The new clause confined the British renunciation to that branch of trade in which the Dutch could reasonably expect their exclusive claims to be recognised; but Britain had every intention of developing a commerce with Eastern Islands (from Rhio) in order to obtain commodities which could be marketed in China. ' The stipulation that we should form no Establishment to the east of Sumatra was too vague, and might be construed to extend to the Coasts of New South Wales, or even to the West Coast of America.'

An explicit declaration of this kind was hard for the Dutch to swallow, even though it related to a sphere of trade which was beyond their own capacity. But there was more. It had not escaped the attention of Ministers that, if war broke out between Britain

---

[133] Dundas to Grenville, 25 June (*Ibid.*, p. 591).

and Spain (and possibly France as well), the Dutch as neutrals
could become important carriers for the enemy. Auckland had
kept to the safe line of specifying the commodities to be recognised
as contraband of war, but now London moved on to debatable
ground. The first Article, which stated the right of either of the
Allies, if neutral, to transport every kind of merchandise except
agreed contraband to enemy ports, had the following clause inserted
into it – *à l'exception cependant des chargemens ou Marchandise
appartenantes aux sujets de la puissance Ennemie.*[134]

Auckland's reaction was sharp. The cession of Rhio was out of
the question and for reasons which he had repeatedly explained.
The British renunciation of the spice trade was no longer to apply
to India. The new stipulation that enemy goods (in addition to
contraband) were to be liable to seizure in neutral ships would not
pass. Indeed, the treaty as now amended fell so far short of the
original propositions that 'I greatly fear the whole negotiation
will be at a stand'.[135]

That was written in a mood of understandable irritation on
22 June. Nevertheless fresh discussions were at once begun and
eight days later a fresh draft, for which he had secured a large
measure of support from the Commissioners, was sent off to London.
In order to secure quick agreement the scope of the treaty was
contracted. Certain tangled issues were dropped altogether and in
other cases difficulties were avoided by not attempting to say too
much. The whole of the original plan for adjusting trade and
navigation in the Eastern seas and in the Spice Islands as between
the two nations was to be abandoned. That, in effect, was to be the
price which the Dutch would pay for the withdrawal of the British
demand for Rhio. The *status quo ante* would still apply and British
commercial expansion would continue as planned but without the
proffered assurances. The provisions granting trading privileges to
the Dutch in India were to remain unchanged. As an 'equivalent'

---

[134] The revised *projet* was enclosed in Leeds to Auckland, 12 June, 1790. No. 12
(*F.O.* 37/29). In the Anglo-Dutch treaty of 1674 the principle of 'Free Ships Free
Goods' had been explicitly accepted, but on this occasion it had been (wisely)
ignored. The near-possibility of war seems to have made the Ministry determined
to take precautions against a repetition of the Anglo-Dutch rupture of 1780 on the
same issue. 'Your Excellency will however observe', ran the official despatch, 'this
to be grounded in the supposition that it is understood by the Dutch Commissioners
with whom you treat, that by the omission of the Stipulation inserted in the former
Treaty [of 1674] declaring that Enemies' goods might be carried in Neutral Vessels,
that question is left to stand on the general footing of the Law of Nations, according
to which such goods are liable to capture.' If this interpretation was wrong, it
must be ascertained at once; and since the matter was so important, it should be
settled 'by precise expressions'. Britain had always contended that the Treaty of
1674 had been superseded by the treaties of 1678 and 1716 which provided that,
when either Power was attacked, the other must come to its aid – and so by implication refrain from giving valuable assistance to the enemy by giving his goods the
protection of a neutral flag.

[135] Auckland to Leeds, 22 June, 1790. No. 54. (*F.O.* 37/29).

for Negapatam the Commissioners had been induced to agree that British warships should have the right, hitherto denied to all foreigners, of free access to the port of Trincomali.

The vexed problem of Neutral Rights was handled with discretion. The central issue was the new British demand for an explicit stipulation about enemy goods in neutral ships. When that had been put to the Commissioners they had made a silencing rejoinder by adopting a clause from the Anglo-French commercial treaty which was the reverse of that proposition. 'I speak from full conviction when I say I see no prospect whatever of my being able to enforce the adoption of the Clause proposed by Your Grace' – and despite the fact that British influence in Holland was much greater at that moment than it had ever been in the course of the past fifty years.

Faced with this impasse, Auckland had perforce rejected the Commissioners' clause but had refrained from putting anything in its place. He was hopeful that the States General and even the Estates of Holland (the most difficult of the Provinces) could be induced to pass the Treaty without a clause on the subject. 'The result would be that the question as to Enemies' goods would remain undecided and subject to the explanation which each party may give to it.' This, he pointed out, had been the method adopted in the treaty with Denmark, and he earnestly hoped that the Dutch treaty could be saved by adopting a similar approach.[136] On the same day he sent a private letter to Grenville urging him to procure a speedy and favourable response to the new plan. 'There is nothing in the *projet*, as it now stands, which may not be decided in half an hour's conversation.' If (in view of the crisis with Spain) the Ministry accepted the agreement at once, they would gain great credit; and what was more material it would be of essential importance to the public interest.[137]

Auckland had handled a complicated and delicate negotiation with skill and judgement. The argument that future Dutch behaviour as a neutral should be left for solution *per ambulando* and in reliance on mutual goodwill was that of a diplomat; and in this case there can be little doubt that it was the more far-sighted course. But statesmen, responsible for the security of the State, rarely feel at liberty to exercise the trust and confidence which they would normally employ as private individuals. The Dutch had been under treaty obligation to render assistance to Britain at the time of the War of American Independence, and yet their very injurious activities in claiming and exercising neutral rights

[136] Auckland to Leeds, 30 June, 1790. His *nouveau projet* was enclosed (*F.O.* 37/29).
[137] Auckland to Grenville, 30 June. Private (*Grenville Corr., Dropmore*, vol. I, p. 591).

had impelled Britain in 1780 to declare war upon them. Auckland's plea that the question should be left undetermined in the interest of Anglo-Dutch friendship was met by the ministerial reaction that national security demanded the removal of a dangerous ambiguity. Even so, it is not surprising that Auckland was completely taken aback by what actually happened in London.

In spite of frequent requests for a quick decision a month passed without response.[138] Then on 3 August there was a meeting of the Cabinet which Lord Hawkesbury (not yet a member) seems to have been invited to attend in his capacity of an acknowledged expert on the technicalities of neutral trade. In 1757 he had first published his well-known *Discourse on the Conduct of the Government of Great Britain in respect to Neutral Nations*.[139] By reference to maritime law and custom he had very ably defended the British 'Rule' that neutrals were not to be allowed to carry on a trade during war in which they had not participated during peace.[140] Hawkesbury was as rigid an exponent of British maritime claims in time of war as he was of the regular laws of trade and navigation. When, therefore, he was consulted about the proposed commercial treaty with the Dutch it was not to be expected that he would consider it from the point of view of a trade-and-defence pact in Asia reinforcing a valuable political alliance in Europe. For him the Dutch were the arch-exploiters of war-time opportunities whose

---

[138] See Auckland to Grenville, 27 July. Private and Secret (*Ibid.*, pp. 595-6). 'I had great hopes that the Commercial *projet* would have been long ago returned to me; there are evidently in England some objections to it, though I must confess that they have not occurred to me here.' The delay was causing much ill humour among the Commissioners. 'I am in daily expectation that they will make a report and resign their appointment.' Cf. Auckland to Leeds, 27 July, No. 69. Secret (*F.O. 37/30*).

[139] Other editions appeared in 1759 and 1781. In 1785 it was prefixed to Hawkesbury's *Collection of all the Treaties of Peace, Alliance and Commerce, between Great Britain and Other Powers from . . . 1648 to . . . 1783* (London, 3 vols.). The pamphlet was re-issued separately in 1794 and 1800 and again in 1837.

[140] The traditional British attitude had been defined in the working formula known as the 'Rule of 1756', which held that a neutral power could not engage in a trade which was opened to them only by 'the pressure of war'. British maritime supremacy during the Seven Years War had rendered the French West Indies largely dependent on the Dutch for supplies and for the transport of their produce to Europe. Acting on this general principle, the British Courts of Admiralty had condemned all Dutch vessels that were found engaged in a trade which had been opened to them not by the voluntary act of France, but by the exercise of British force. By this means the intercourse between the Dutch depots of St. Eustatius and Curaçao and the French Islands had been broken, but at the cost of considerable friction. During the War of the American Revolution the controversy threatened to ruin England by banding all Europe in war against her. The 'Armed Neutrality' comprising Prussia, Russia, the Emperor, Sweden and Denmark, adopted the principle that neutral ships made neutral goods. France and Spain and the Americans (who all stood to gain by it) immediately acquiesced; but England, whose interests as a naval Power would have been damaged by the proposed regulations, rejected them. Only the disinclination of Catherine of Russia to fight saved the British from being crushed by a war with the Baltic Powers upon whom they were dependent for naval stores.

interest lay in thwarting Britain's efforts to prevent the colonial produce of France and Spain from reaching Europe. As Secretary-at-War under North (from 1778) he had had bitter experience of the Dutch in that regard. Consequently the prime consideration in any commercial agreement must be to tie them down as neutral traders with explicit and comprehensive prohibitions.

Once this issue had been stated, no responsible Minister, even if he had wished, could resist the demand. An attack in Parliament on the score that the security of the nation had been betrayed would have been devastating. Pitt and the Cabinet acquiesced and and the character of the proposed treaty was fundamentally altered. There was, of course, much weight in the argument that the Anglo-Dutch alliance should be made as impervious as possible to the strain which a further war with France would impose upon it. But the Ministers cannot be exonerated from the charge that they forfeited the goodwill of an ally in Europe and Asia by refusing to be content with concessions on neutral rights which previous British Administrations would have been thankful to secure.

When the Cabinet broke up, the unfortunate Foreign Secretary wrote in angry impotence to Lord Henry Spencer, Secretary to the Embassy at the Hague.

I am very sorry the Dutch Treaty meets with so many and such serious difficulties on this side of the water, owing to *certain References* being made to *certain Persons*. I protest I am at a loss how to write to Lord Auckland a dispatch (which of course must be an official paper) upon the subject. . . . The Dutch ought, I think, to be treated with friendly attention at least by us, and not merely as an Indifferent Power. This Sentiment, however justly prevalent among the Cabinet Ministers, does not seem to convince some persons of influence beyond the Threshold. . . .

Perhaps some alternative to the *projet* sent over might have been expedient, but he could not but regret the delay, if not the difficulty, attending the completion of this desirable object 'which must result from what has passed to-day'.[141] Cabinet instructions were obeyed and Leeds sent an official despatch in which he put the new situation as best he could. On the principle of the law of nations it was clear that the protection of a neutral flag could never be allowed to any part of the trade of an enemy, but if the Dutch would agree that their ships should not be entitled to carry on trade from the colonies of a Power at war or any other to which

---

[141] Leeds to Lord Henry Spencer, 3 Aug., 1790 (*Addit. MSS.*, 28,066, f. 173). The words printed in italics were underlined in the original. I have inferred that Hawkesbury actually attended the Cabinet in question and was not merely asked to furnish a memorandum. He had attended (as President of the Board of Trade) when questions of much less moment were under discussion.

they were not admitted in time of peace, it might be considered whether His Majesty ought not for the present to agree to desist from the right of capturing enemy goods of any other description when found on board Dutch vessels. In other words, if the Dutch would agree to abstain from transporting the colonial produce of Britain's enemies, the principle of *Free Ships Free Goods* might in other respects be conceded.[142] Thus Hawkesbury's views had only partially prevailed; and in fact he fought this concession with all the reasoned stubbornness of which he was master – and eventually won.

Auckland's protests both to Pitt and Grenville were frank in their indignation. Indeed in this period when 'career' diplomats were the exception an ambassador (provided that he was of the nobility) would on occasion address himself to the head of the Administration or to a Foreign Secretary with a freedom that would have been rash in a later age. To Pitt Auckland wrote that he did not know who had suggested the terms of the long-awaited reply to his *projet*, but it would be treated with the respect due to a communication from the King's Cabinet Council. Nevertheless he would risk a few confidential remarks, 'and without fear of offending you, even if you were concerned in penning it'. He then pointed at the person whom he knew to be responsible for the change of front. He would do justice to a certain pamphlet, recently republished with a collection of treaties, as being well written for the purpose which it had originally in view, 'but the rigid and warm application of it to the Negotiation which has subsisted so long with this Republic never entered into my Mind'.

He then set out the substantial advantages which the Cabinet had declined to accept: a most comprehensive list of commodities to be declared contraband of war and in addition Dutch agreement to leave the controversial question of enemy goods in neutral ships to be governed by the law of nations – 'whatever it may be'. Naturally he had presumed that the Ministry would at least accept this gratuitous acquisition. Yet to his astonishment the Cabinet's answer had conveyed 'an implied rejection of what the Instructions both to me and to my two Predecessors during the last three years had

---

[142] Leeds to Auckland, 6 Aug., 1790 (*F.O.* 37/30). 'It must be understood,' he added, 'that this could only be agreed to as an exception to the general principle of the Law of Nations in favour of a power in alliance with us, and that the principle itself cannot be abandoned.' Leeds also indicated that the Cabinet considered that access to Trincomali was an insufficient return for Negapatam but would be prepared to exchange the latter for Cochin on the west coast of Southern India. But when Auckland put this suggestion to the Dutch Commissioners they answered that Cochin had been purchased at a high price and that they could not accept less than 7 million florins (about £612,500) – which Auckland rejected as 'too ridiculous to be further mentioned'. He had been privately informed that Tipu of Mysore had offered this price for it and had been refused. (Auckland to Leeds, 30 Nov., 1790. *F.O.* 37/32.)

directed us to sollicit and if possible to accomplish: and surely it is of great consequence to be accomplished '. Furthermore this rejection had been justified on the ground that there was no clause to regulate neutral trade with enemy colonies – 'which never before was mentioned in all the volumes that are among my papers on the subject '. 'I fear,' he concluded, 'that the Treaty is gone and that the manner in which it is gone will leave an unpleasant and mischievous impression here.'[143] The debate now centred upon three individuals: an ambassador ardent to cement a friendship with the country to which he was accredited: a rigid and deter- mined defender *contra mundum* of British maritime interests: and a hesitant Prime Minister balancing one interest against the other.

Auckland did not write to Grenville for almost a month; and when he did so it was in similar terms. 'I have not yet had energy enough to return to the Commercial treaty. In truth the objections made to the *projet* were so unexpected, that they have made me doubt my own comprehension on the subject.' He suspected that there was a misapprehension in London about what the Dutch actually claimed as neutral rights. 'But if I am to propose clauses to the rigour of all the doctrines so well argued in Lord Hawkes- bury's printed pamphlet, and so far, far beyond what is practised in respect to all other nations, all negotiation is at an end.'[144]

The diplomatic contest was, however, far from being terminated, for neither side was willing to admit failure. For Britain the friend- ship of Holland was an essential factor in sustaining the indispens- able Triple Alliance; and the impoverished Dutch needed British support in their Asian commerce. After further exchanges with Auckland, Pitt and Grenville themselves took the initiative. Gren- ville prepared a final *projet* and submitted it to Pitt who re-drafted the neutrality clauses himself. Early in January, 1791, a long explanatory despatch and the text of the *projet* were agreed between them, and Pitt then sent both documents to the Duke of Leeds who obediently signed the despatch as his own.[145]

---

[143] Auckland to Pitt, 11 Aug., 1790. P.R.O. 30/8/110.

[144] Auckland to Grenville, 4 Sept. 1790 (*Grenville Corr. Dropmore*, vol. I. pp. 605-6). 'We suppose that the Dutch meant to maintain a claim to carry the produce of the colonies of France and Spain in time of war: this was not the case.' From the British point of view, however, the chief difficulty lay in the fact that, even in peace-time, there was a large trade in French and Spanish colonial produce through the Dutch free port at St. Eustatius, and in time of war the traffic through this neutral channel increased enormously.

[145] See Pitt to Grenville, 11 January, 1791 (*Ibid.*, vol. II, p. 12). 'I now send them [i.e. his comments on the *projet* and the Instructions to Auckland] on a separate paper. You will find very little in them, as, on the whole, I am satisfied that in substance Your proposal is the best that can be made. I have suggested some altera- tion as to the form, which I wish you to consider and to dispose of as soon as you think best. . . . *I see no possibility of conveying this to the Office without its being known that you have been chiefly concerned in the manufacture. I have thought that the best way of avoiding any difficulty on that account was to send a letter to the*

The pith of the matter (as rephrased by Pitt) was set out in the following terms:

The idea adopted in the *projet* now sent is that of settling:
First. That no articles of that description called *contrebande de guerre*
. . . shall be carried to enemies' ports in neutral ships, whether such goods are the property of enemies or of neutrals.
Secondly. That no right shall accrue to the neutral nation, in consequence of the war, to carry on with the enemy any sort of commerce which was not permitted to such neutral nation previous to the commencement of the war; and particularly that neutrals shall neither trade to nor from the enemies' colonies, nor protect the commerce of such colonies in its passage home, either by means of neutral ports in the West Indies or elsewhere, or by what is called transhipping.
Thirdly. That enemies' goods, not falling under either of the two descriptions above mentioned, may be carried in neutral ships to the enemies' European ports.

The second of these principles, added Grenville, was the most material and required particular attention, for it was upon the precision and efficacy of the terms in which it was expressed that the propriety of conceding the third point entirely depended. With Hawkesbury, formidable and resistant in the background, Pitt and Grenville were rigid in their insistence on the second principle in order to justify the concession contained in the third.[146]

The contest now concentrated upon two issues. On the one side, the British demand for 'no trade, direct or indirect, with the colonies of an enemy'; and on the other, the Dutch demand, now vigorously revived, that Britain's open access to the Eastern Seas must at least be defined and limited. All the latent fears and suspicions of the Dutch about British intentions in the East Indies had been aroused by the heavy pressure to acquire Rhio, followed

---

Duke of Leeds, which Smith can seal, and forwarded with the draft.' (Italics inserted.) Leeds resigned three months later (to be succeeded by Grenville) on the ostensible ground of his disagreement with Pitt's change of front with regard to Russia, but at least a contributory cause of his resignation must have been his humiliation in being consistently ignored in the Dutch negotiations. Pitt's 'separate paper', headed *Draft to Lord Auckland,* has been misdated and misplaced by the editor of the Grenville Papers at Dropmore and is to be found (under the assigned date, July-August, 1790) in vol. I, pp. 598-602, and is headed 'W. W. Grenville to Lord Auckland'. The instructions which Leeds signed and sent to Auckland on 14 January, 1791 (No. 2) (*F.O. 37/33*), are copied *verbatim* from Grenville's draft.

[146] Bland Burges, Under-Secretary in the Foreign Department, regarded this compromise as a defeat for Hawkesbury and assumed (unwarrantably) that all would now be plain sailing. 'At length I have the satisfaction to inform you that all our difficulties about the Commercial Treaty are at an end, and that, unless something happens which I cannot at present forsee, it will be sent to you by Thursday's mail [i.e. 14 January] . . . I make no doubt of your being pleased with this termination of the affair tho' I am somewhat apprehensive of its effects upon the President of our Commercial Board, who will probably disapprove of it in every respect whatever.' (Burges to Auckland, 8 Jan., 1791. *Addit. MSS.,* 34,435, f. 91.)

(on rejection) by the withdrawal of the British guarantees about the spice trade and future penetration beyond the Moluccas.

It is a remarkable tribute to Auckland's skill and pertinacity as a negotiator and to the courage of Britain's friends in Holland that the Dutch Commissioners were induced to go so far towards meeting the British requirements about neutral trade – much further than any Dutch Government had gone before. In an amended draft treaty, based on Grenville's Instructions, which Auckland sent to London on 24 January, 1791, the Dutch delegates agreed to renounce the right to engage in any war-time colonial trade which had not been operated in time of peace. On the other hand, the Dutch were extremely resistant to the British right of navigation in the Eastern Seas. Although confirmed, it was to be restricted to such trading rights as had subsisted before the peace treaty of 1784, which was no more than a very limited traffic with Bengal.[147]

Grenville replied in an unofficial letter at once. The proposed wording about the colony trade lacked the precision of the formula which he had sent and would not do. The words used did not satisfy the British requirement. 'They would on the contrary give a complete protection to French sugars to be imported into any neutral port of Europe from Eustatius for the supply of the continent in general, or into the port of Ostend for the supply of France itself.' In fact the Ministry was trying to obtain the complete closure in all future wars with France of the neutral channel for trade through St. Eustatius and other Dutch depots in the Caribbean. The desire to secure the stoppage of this 'leak' is understandable enough, but the demand raised insuperable difficulties.[148]

As to the Dutch demand, continued Grenville, for a delimitation of Eastern navigation the proposed clause was so ambiguous that it could only afford a ground for future cavils. Auckland had referred to the Report of the Board of Control in 1787 (written by Grenville and Dundas), but that Report, even when contemplating a total renunciation of the spice trade, had not suggested an abandonment of all trade between Bengal and the Eastern Islands. The British had an unquestionable right to trade 'with such of those islands as are not in the possession of the Dutch'.[149] Thus two nations which had started discussions five years before with the

---

[147] The new draft consisted of Auckland's *projet* of 30 June, 1790 (in his despatch No. 58) with additions and amendments, shown in red ink, designed to meet Grenville's Instructions. (Enclosed in Auckland, 21 Jan., 1791, No. 7. *F.O. 37/33*.)

[148] The Dutch had a clear right to transport their own sugars, etc., to their own (neutral) ports in time of war. Secondly, St. Eustatius and other Dutch *entrepôts* in the Caribbean normally did a considerable business in French and Spanish sugars and other products so that it could not be maintained that this trade was *created* by war conditions, although it was very greatly increased thereby. Thirdly, a cargo leaving St. Eustatius in time of war would be of mixed origin, and it would be impossible to ascertain what proportion was Dutch and what French or Spanish.

[149] Grenville to Auckland, 24 Jan., 1791 (*Addit. MSS.*, 34,435, f. 226).

intention of cementing their political alliance with a mutually generous and advantageous partnership in the Indian Ocean and the Far East were now locked in diplomatic combat over two questions which both parties regarded as vital to their national security.

Again and again Auckland despaired of reaching agreement and as frequently he strained the goodwill of the pro-British elements in edging the Dutch negotiators closer to the British position. But London asked too much in requiring a clause which would have inhibited the Dutch in time of war from carrying French or Spanish West Indian produce from St. Eustatius to Dutch ports in Europe, notwithstanding that this branch of commerce was ordinarily practised in time of peace.[150] As Auckland rightly pointed out, Britain had never before carried her pretensions on the subject to such a length.[151]

A deadlock agreement on this particular issue was reached to Britain's satisfaction, and then (in April, 1791) the broad underlying difficulty emerged. Grenville had actually prepared Instructions authorising acceptance and was about to submit them to the Cabinet when Pitt evidently intervened. At that moment there was an imminent prospect of war with Russia, and Grenville in a private letter to Auckland explained that it had been decided that the Anglo-Dutch treaty must be held up. If an agreement recognising certain neutral rights were published on the eve of war with a great Power, the effect might be 'very mischievous'. He admitted that Britain would gain substantial advantages under the treaty with regard to naval stores and trade with enemy colonies; but these would be of no help to her in the case of Russia, who neither possessed colonies nor imported naval stores. On the other hand the treaty contained a clause which would authorise the Dutch to do business in Russian ports in (now contraband) commodities. 'The admission by us of the principle, free ships free goods, would appear to operate against us with particular force under the circumstance of the present moment.' It was certainly awkward, he added, to suspend the Dutch negotiations when they were so near to reaching a conclusion, but it would be still more awkward to conclude it at a time when its impression might be so unfavourable to the Government.[152]

---

[150] See Auckland to Leeds, Feb., 1791. *Ibid.*, f. 413.

[151] Auckland to Leeds, 13 Feb. (*Addit. MSS.*, 34,436, f. 1.) He added that in 1759 and on many subsequent occasions Sir Joseph Yorke (at that time British Ambassador at the Hague) had offered arrangements about neutral trade which fell 'far short' of what the Dutch were now ready to concede and Yorke's proposals had all been rejected without hesitation.

[152] Grenville to Auckland, 16 April, 1791. (*Addit. MSS.*, 34,436, f. 401.) Printed in *Gren. Corr., Dropmore*, vol. II, pp. 50-1. More than a month earlier Auckland had 'entreated' Grenville to read the papers which he had sent on the treaty. 'I have brought it to the verge of conclusion, if Mr. Pitt can bestow one hour's consideration of it.' (*Ibid.*, vol. II, pp. 38-9).

The notion that the Dutch as neutral sea-carriers could be of any material significance for the Russians was ludicrous; but the theoretical possibility constituted a precedent.[153] This incident and the negative attitude adopted thereafter by Pitt and his colleagues are indicative of their embarrassment. With all Europe in a state of ferment, Ministers felt bound to heed the warnings of Hawkesbury that the less Britain committed herself to a recognition of neutral rights in the event of war the better.

In July-August Auckland made his most strenuous effort to clinch matters about neutral rights.[154] On 9 August he sent to Grenville three Articles on neutral trade which he had drafted in consultation with his friend and ally, the Pensionary. The first repeated the previously agreed concession that neutral ships might trade freely with enemy ports in Europe in any commodities. 'There are, I know,' he wrote in a private letter on the same day, 'some expressions which, when brought into friction with a famous pamphlet, will electrify Lord Hawkesbury at the first perusal.' He went on, however, to claim and with justice that the other two Articles secured 'far more than we have ever attempted to establish by Treaty in respect to any other power in Europe'.[155] Under the second Article the Dutch would have renounced the right to carry enemy colonial produce directly or indirectly to enemy ports in Europe, and the third Article detailed a greatly extended list of military and naval stores as contraband of war.

Auckland's surmise that the author of a famous pamphlet would be hostile to the concession in the first of these three Articles was, of course, correct.[156] Some months later at the end of an argument,

---

[153] Auckland's reply (on 10 May) to Grenville's suspension of the negotiations because of the Russian crisis was very sensible. He agreed that a commercial treaty with the Dutch would be of no value to Britain in the event of war with Russia, but he was not aware that it could be of any disservice. It was unlikely that important commodities would be sent as Russian property in Dutch vessels. On the other hand, it would be very valuable 'to give so hard a blow, as the treaty would give, to the system of Armed Neutrality', and the political alliance with Holland would be reinforced. (*Ibid.*, pp. 70-2.)

[154] See Auckland, 23 July, Private. *Ibid.*, p. 238.

[155] Auckland, 9 Aug. Private. (*Addit. MSS.*, 34,439, f. 102. Printed in *Gren. Corr.*, vol. II, p. 161.)

[156] Enclosed in Auckland's official despatch of 9 Aug. (*F.O.* 37/35). The three Articles are set out with the corresponding three Articles of the original *projet* in parallel columns. The essential part of Article 2 runs as follows: *Les Vaisseaux appartenans aux sujets de l'une des Hautes Parties Contractantes, ne pourront naviguer aux Ports ou autreslieux des Colonies ou possessions hors d'Europe d'aucune Puissance ennemie de l'autre des Hautes Parties Contractantes: Ils ne pourront, par conséquent, y porter aucun chargement ou Marchandise que se soit: Ils ne pourront non plus porter en Europe aux Ports de la dite Puissance Ennemie aucun hargement ou marchandise que ce soit, venant directement ou indirectement des dites Colonies ou Possessions, ni même porter en d'autres ports de l'Europe aucun chargement ou marchandise que ce soit, étant la proprieté de l'Ennemi et le produit des dites Colonies.* From the British point of view this was ' common form '. Cf. the dictum of 1759 of James Marriott, afterwards a judge in the High Court

probably in Cabinet, during which he had urged that on no account should the Dutch be authorised to be the carriers of enemy property in any way, Pitt – somewhat wearily no doubt – asked him to set out his reasons in writing. He complied to the extent of producing a dissertation of seventy-one quarto pages. Like everything that he wrote it was cogently argued from the point of view of national security and aggrandisement and with a wealth of detail; but it completely ignored the fact that alliances between nations (upon which survival might depend) cannot long subsist without some degree of give and take. Fair copies of the dissertation were prepared and sent to each member of the Cabinet. The arguments were such that, if ventilated in Parliament (by Lord Sheffield for example), they would have aroused an overwhelming opposition to the proposed agreement.[157]

'I really am sorry,' wrote Auckland when he had seen a copy of it, 'under all the circumstances and speculations of the times, that Lord Hawkesbury's manifesto is likely to impede the rivetting of our friendship with the Republic: I think that it will do so. If his reasonings are well founded (which I do not believe they are) they ought to prevail; and if they are ill founded, they necessarily induce a pause and more caution.'[158]

Yet this was only one of two intractable issues. The other related to trade and navigation in the Eastern seas. Auckland in his despatch of 9 August, 1791, had repeated previous warnings that the

---

of Admiralty: 'the Subjects of Holland have no Right to cover the Property of the Enemy of England, going to, or coming from the Colonies of that Enemy, directly or indirectly to do it, thro' the Medium of the Dutch Colonies; nor to carry to the Colonies of France directly, or indirectly, any Commodities, altho' Neutral Property, which have a Tendency to support the Enemy.' (Quoted by G. L. Beer, *British Colonial Policy, 1754-1765* (N.Y., 1922), p. 95). The contention that a neutral Power had no legal right to intrude into a commerce which had been uniformly shut against it in time of peace was expounded by Sir William Scott in connexion with the well-known case of the ship *Immanuel* in 1799.

[157] 'Letter from Lord Hawkesbury on the subject of the Commercial Negotiations with Holland.' Fair copy with Hawkesbury's signature and addressed to Pitt. N.D. The author summarised his conclusions as follows: 'The great southern Kingdoms of Europe will rejoice at these Concessions, because they will afford protection to their Commerce and Resources when they are engaged in War with Great Britain. The smaller Northern States of Europe and the United States of America will rejoice at these Concessions, because they will hope from this Example to obtain equal privileges for the encouragement and increase of their Commerce and Navigation when Great Britain is at war and they are at Peace. Great Britain alone will have cause to lament these Concessions, because her Naval Power will receive a wound from the restraints thereby imposed on it.' Finally Britain would derive no corresponding advantages in return for such concessions (*F.O. 95/5*).

[158] Hawkesbury's dissertation seems to have been written in October (1791). The above-cited letter from Auckland (now in England) to Grenville is dated 12 November. The former had been asked by Grenville to prepare a written reply to Hawkesbury's arguments, but he explained that he had not yet been able to do so, 'because Mr. Pitt has taken away Lord Hawkesbury's dissertation in order to its being exchanged for another which is said to be more correct' (*Grenville Corr.*, vol. II, pp. 227-8).

Dutch were insisting upon a clarification of this question, and he had suggested that their suspicions would be allayed if Britain would explicitly renounce any interest in 'the Molucca Islands'. But Grenville had already expressed doubts about the interpretation which the Dutch might put upon this geographical expression. If they meant to include only those islands of which they were in effective occupation there would be less difficulty; 'but I suspect those words would include many to which we do now trade, and always have, and which the Dutch only *mean* to conquer'.[159] He sent the despatch to Dundas. Did he think that it would be 'safe' to accept this? Dundas replied in the affirmative and supported his opinion with a forthright re-statement of his original design. The spice trade, as he had said before, was of no moment to Britain, and there was no reason why Grenville should not declare to the Dutch Government 'at all times and in every shape' that trade in the Eastern seas 'with a view to the Spice Trade' was not an object that need cause a moment of uneasiness or jealousy between the two nations.

Their apprehension rests on a ground they dare not avow. I mean their consciousness of the radical and internal weakness of the sovereignty they claim in the Eastern Isles, and they are afraid that the communication we may have with the Nations would lay the foundation for their shaking off the miserable dependence in which they are held by the Dutch. It is not for the Spices we can have a desire to trade with them, but they have other articles fit for the China Market, which may be procured by opium and other articles from the continent of India and by Hardware and other articles from Britain.

He had received definite proof, declared Dundas, that 'British liberality' in their commercial dealings would lead the native peoples to throw off the Dutch monopoly. In these terms he applied to the Malay Archipelago the same policy of 'liberation' for commercial purposes which others (including Hawkesbury and Pitt) were pursuing in respect of Latin America. The Dutch were no more disposed to open the door to the economic liberators than were the Spaniards in the Western hemisphere.

Turning to the question of Dutch trade in India and China he propounded the radical policy of amalgamation which he had advocated five years before. A European nation at enmity with Britain, of course, required fortified establishments in India to protect their commerce there, but that the Dutch should continue to do so when their establishments were useless against British power and when they could have the benefit of that power and

---

[159] Grenville to Auckland, 29 July, 1791. Private. *Ibid.*, vol. II, pp. 144-5.

protection at almost no expense was 'truly surprising'. He could demonstrate that if the Dutch would hand over 'something considerably less than the modified possession of Trincomale we formerly asked', they could relieve themselves of the expense of every establishment in India, acquire a larger Investment, and by relieving Britain of the expense of Penang and every other establishment in those seas, enable her to gratify them 'in their utmost wishes' regarding the Eastern Seas.

Nay more, if the same spirit of amity was extended to a proper understanding between us at Canton, we would not only be great gainers in the purchase of the China Investment, but that trade would exclusively belong to our two nations, with a very considerable addition to each of us beyond what we now possess.[160]

Dundas did not delude himself into thinking that his plan was immediately practicable. Five years of fruitless negotiation had demonstrated the difficulty of arranging terms which would satisfy British opinion and at the same time be sufficiently generous to be acceptable to Dutch national pride, which was the more sensitive because their affairs in the East were in a declining state. Not much, said Dundas, could be accomplished at the moment: 'You never can till the Dutch know their own commercial interests in India, which . . . I take upon me to assert they do not.'

When Grenville forwarded this remarkable exposition to the Hague, Auckland received it as a breath of fresh air. His despatches show that he had always hoped to be able to break away from bazaar-bargaining over bases and arrange the terms of a comprehensive Anglo-Dutch partnership in Eastern trade and defence. It was also clear from reported conversations that this had been the consistent aim of the Grand Pensionary and the Greffier. Auckland replied to Dundas at once, saying that he agreed that Dutch jealousy was the major difficulty, but he did not despair of bringing them by degrees to appreciate the advantages of mutual defence in the East. But 'the great point' in Dundas's letter, with which he entirely agreed, was to bring about effective co-operation in conducting the trade from Bengal and the Eastern Island to China, to reach 'a right understanding' on the respective Investments for that trade, and to act conjointly at Canton.[161] With Grenville's assent Auckland arranged with the Dutch negotiators to reserve the whole business of Asian trade and defence 'to some subsequent and separate discussion with the Ministers to get the question of neutral rights settled and out of the way. The Pensionary and the

---

[160] Dundas to Auckland, 23 Aug. 1791. (*Addit. MSS.*, 34,439, f. 237 *et seq.*)
[161] Auckland to Dundas, 30 Aug. (*Ibid.*, f. 339).

Greffier were cordially supporting this plan as the best means of promoting the wider aim, which would 'solidly unite the two Countries if we can accomplish it'.[162]

Auckland returned to England in September and discussions and correspondence with Grenville ensued. Their principal topic was the problem of the Austrian Emperor's activities in the Netherlands; but at the end of a letter written to Auckland on 29 October Grenville added: 'I also send you the famous manifesto [by Hawkesbury] about our treaty on which we will talk when you have read it.' Afterwards at Grenville's request he wrote a memorandum on it, which not only rebutted Hawkesbury's objections *seriatim*, but also surveyed the Anglo-Dutch negotiation in all its aspects. 'I am convinced that we cannot now abandon the negotiation without abandoning every advantage of cordial friendship and concert with the United Provinces in time of peace and without leaving the two Countries in a more dangerous predicament respecting each other in time of war.'[163]

But it was no good. The question of finding an acceptable definition of Holland's exclusive sphere in Indonesia was tied up with the whole business of Anglo-Dutch association in the Far East; and that by mutal consent was in abeyance. And on the matter of mutual rights the Dutch insistence on *free ships free goods* became an insuperable obstacle as soon as Hawkesbury and his supporters raised the general issue; and it remained so in spite of the fact that Auckland had succeeded in securing unprecedented concessions with regard to contraband of war and trade with enemy colonies. Auckland himself appreciated this when Hawkesbury produced his 'manifesto'. Those who first brought this business forward, he wrote, committed an error 'where they supposed themselves to be rendering a service', but he admitted that they shared their mistake 'with men of distinguished Judgment and Experience in almost every Administration of the present Century'.[164]

---

[162] Grenville informed Auckland: 'I am persuaded that we might, tho' reluctantly, conclude upon the article of the Commercial Treaty respecting the Navigation in time of war, if this Business of the 6th Article of Peace [i.e. British rights in the Eastern Seas] was not one of great and increasing difficulty.' He agreed with the policy as set out by Dundas, but just because of that he could not agree with Dundas's assurance that it would be 'safe' to accept the description, 'Molucca Islands', as the region from which all British trade would be barred. 'I am persuaded we never can bring this question to a satisfactory issue till Mr. Pitt Mr. Dundas and myself have had the opportunity of talking it over fully with you.' (These statements are taken from two letters to Auckland, dated 23 and 26 Aug. *Addit. MSS.*, 34,439, ff. 253 and 298. Printed in *Gren. Corr.*, vol. II, pp. 172 and 176-7.) Auckland announced his suspension of talks on Eastern trade and defence and his return to discuss the question of neutral rights in a letter to Grenville, dated 31 Aug. (*Ibid.*, pp. 180-1.)

[163] Auckland to Grenville, 3 Jan., 1792 (*Addit. MSS.*, 34,441, f. 13 *et seq.*).

[164] *Ibid.*

o*

Auckland's riposte to Hawkesbury was delivered on 3 January, 1792. There is no record of any further discussion, and after Auckland had at last returned to the Hague in the following June his despatches were concerned with European affairs of increasing complexity and danger. After more than five years' strenuous negotiation with both sides desiring a settlement, the remains of the Anglo-Dutch treaty *projet* were quietly interred. Twelve months later General Dumouriez of the Army of the Revolution issued a manifesto to the Hollanders, calling upon them to rise against the tyranny of the Anglophile House of Orange and adjuring them not to surrender their vital establishments at the Cape and Ceylon and their entire commerce in the Indies *à la seule nation dont vous avez à craindre l'incessante Rivalité*. The invading armies were accorded a tumultuous welcome. The Stadtholder and his chief supporters fled to England: Amsterdam was entered in triumph: and the Batavian Republic was proclaimed. The Cape, Ceylon, and the highway to the Far East were not only in the hands of a hostile Holland, but were at the service of a re-invigorated French nationalism that sought to eliminate the British from Asia.

An Anglo-Dutch commercial treaty could not have raised an effective barrier against the irruption of French arms and ideology; but the fact remains that the diplomatic *coup* of 1787 presented Britain with a great opportunity to allay past bitterness and establish a cordial co-operation with the Dutch in overseas affairs and that the opportunity was lost through attempting to drive too hard a bargain. International negotiations which fail are sometimes even more indicative of national aims and outlook than those which succeed. In this case the long arguments between London and the Hague reveal as perhaps nothing else the working of ministerial minds and the conflicting pressures to which they were subject in promoting a commercial nexus in regions between the Cape of Good Hope and Canton. The long exposed ocean flank of this commercial system was to be safeguarded by joint action (in one form or another) in the defence of Dutch bases. The original design was impressive in its range and content. In return the tottering edifice of the Dutch East India Company was to be underpinned by protection and assistance in India, by a guarantee of exclusive enjoyment of the spice trade, and with a prospect (if and when the English Company's Charter were to be terminated) of a much wider participation in commercial and financial benefits both in India and China.

In purely commercial terms a powerful combine offered to come to the rescue of a weaker organisation on the basis of converting it into a semi-autonomous subsidiary. The result, as is usual in such cases, would have greatly benefited both parties. But the scheme could not be carried through as an exclusively economic transaction. Politics, national pride, and the turbulent history of Anglo-Dutch relations were the decisive factors.

The demand for the possession or at least the effective occupation of Trincomali was a mistake and aroused latent suspicion. Dundas would have been content with access to the port, but Grenville and Pitt (with eyes on Leadenhall Street and Westminster) objected that permission to use, granted by one Dutch régime, might at a critical moment be withdrawn by another. On the other hand Dundas was too pertinacious about Rhio. This was the most delicate and significant part of the negotiation. Britain's determination to do business in South-East Asia as an adjunct to the China trade was already regarded by the Dutch as a dangerous intrusion. The demand for Rhio at a key point, followed, on refusal, by insistence of precise geographical definition, was intended to preclude future misunderstandings and bickering; but a certain degree of ambiguity would have left room for later adjustment. However that might be, the determination of the Ministers to have no treaty without recognition of the British right to develop trade in the eastern parts of Indonesia is a measure of the importance which they attached to it as part of their general policy of expansion in the Pacific.

The treaty foundered because the British Government decided that a convention with Holland could not be confined to Asia but must also include a settlement in precise terms of the thorny question of Dutch activities as a neutral carrier in the Western hemisphere and Europe. While the Dutch may perhaps be blamed for a dog-in-the-manger attitude in the East, the fault with regard to the latter issue certainly lay with the British. The Dutch agreed to severe restrictions with regard to war contraband and the colonial trade which they had in all previous discussions rejected; and on more than one occasion Grenville had indicated his own readiness to settle 'tho' reluctantly'. But with Europe in a state of ferment Pitt was not prepared to risk a public outcry on the score of 'British maritime power betrayed', even though acceptance of Auckland's proposals would have dealt a heavy blow against the Armed Neutrality and even though recognition of the right to ply between enemy ports in Europe had already been conceded (and without specifying war-contraband) in commercial treaties with France, Spain and Sweden.

In those long negotiations Pitt, Grenville and Dundas attempted an ambitious and enlightened *projet* which was intended to be an important reinforcement of the wider design of an empire of trade in Asia. Complete success would have required considerable modifications in the exclusive system of the English East India

Company on the one side and the Dutch Company on the other;[165] and when the plan became distorted by the different issue of neutral rights the force of long-established precedent prevailed. The argument portrays the emergence of new concepts of expansion and the resulting pressure upon traditional rigidities.

---

[165] In 1788 Dundas repeated his belief that it would do no injury to British interests if the Dutch were allowed to participate as agents in bringing surplus revenue to Europe in the form of Investment. He also supported the view that by concerted action at Canton the British and Dutch could command the market in tea against all competitors. But he knew that such ideas were at that time impracticable. ' I am aware,' he wrote, ' that this is a doctrine not palatable to the East India Company.' (Dundas to Pitt, 13 Aug., 1788. P.R.O. 30/157.)

CHAPTER VII

THE CHINA TRADE AND THE CANADIAN PACIFIC COAST

THE opening of the Pacific Ocean to European penetration took place from two widely separate directions. On the one side, British, Dutch, French and others pushed outward from the Indian Ocean into South-East Asia and on to the China market. On the other side, British whalers began to feel their way round Cape Horn into the southern areas of the Pacific, profiting by the discoveries of James Cook. The possibility that the Asian and American coasts of this huge expanse of sea might be linked together in commercial exchange offered, it seemed, immense opportunities. Moreover the hoped-for discovery of a direct sea-route between Europe and the Pacific through Baffin and Hudson Bay would provide the means of creating a new triangular trade. British goods such as iron tools, cloth, and trinkets would be sold along the North-West American coast for furs and other natural resources, which with British commodities would make up assorted cargoes for China and (it was hoped) Japan. Then home with cargoes of tea: triple profits and shorter, cheaper voyages.

The hope of a navigable North-West Passage, so strenuously pursued in Tudor times, had never been entirely abandoned; and, as we have seen, Cook in his last voyage had been under instructions to make a landfall in the vicinity of Drake's New Albion and to explore the coast northward in search of a channel which might lead on into the Atlantic. The Admiralty had also dispatched a complementary expedition to search for a channel from the eastern end.[1] In the course of carrying out his orders Cook had explored Nootka Sound on the west coast of the island which was afterwards named after Capt. Vancouver.[2] Many of the crew had taken the opportunity of acquiring in exchange for articles of trifling value some 1,500 sea-otter skins, and when they offered these for sale at Kamchatka and later at Canton they found to their surprise and joy that they fetched high prices. One sailor sold his consignment for 800 Spanish dollars (about £170). The crew were all for going back for more.

When Cook's discoveries in the north Pacific became known in Europe the information aroused widespread interest. Political con-

---

[1] See vol. I, pp. 55-61.

[2] Nootka Sound had been previously visited in 1774 by a Spaniard, Juan Perez (*Relacion del Viaje hecho por las Goletas Sutil y Mexicana*, Madrid, 1802, p. xcii *et seq.* Cited by F. W. Howay, 'Early Days of the Maritime Fur-Trade on the North-West Coast'. *Cam. Hist. Rev.*, vol. IV, No. 1, 1923).

fusion at the close of the war of American independence ruled out an immediate follow-up from England, but the Imperial Asiatic Company of Austria became interested and enlisted the services of George Dixon and a number of others who had been with Cook in the *Endeavour*. A special ship for an exploring expedition to the Pacific was built at Marseilles, but the financial state of the Company compelled them to abandon the enterprise. The French Government then became interested and after elaborate preparations two vessels sailed from Brest in August, 1785, under the command of François de la Perouse. His task was to fill in the gaps left by Cook. In addition to extensive exploration in the south Pacific he was to explore the coasts from China to Kamchatka and then to make a thorough examination of the North-West American coast with the view to finding a passage to the Atlantic. At the same time he was to observe the possibilities of trade.

News that such an expedition was being fitted out reached London early in the year and an enterprising group of merchants decided that, if possible, they would be beforehand with the French. In March George Taswell, a merchant of Madras then in London, wrote to Lord Sydney, seeking Government approval for 'an Expedition of Experiment to our new Discoverys on the N. Wt coast of America'. In order to open a new source of trade sanction was sought for an initiatory voyage through the Straits of Magellan to the North-West Coast for the purpose of collecting furs which would be taken only to China for sale. At Canton the proceeds of the sales would be paid into the East India Company's treasury, which would give bills of exchange on London in return. The expedition would be carried out under such restrictions as might be thought necessary 'to prevent Interference with the present Trade of the said Company either to, or from, China, which the traffick in Furs will not in any manner do'. But speed was essential both because of the approach of the season for setting out and also to anticipate the French.[3]

Official encouragement having been given, the group acted quickly. A syndicate was formed with the name of the King George's Sound Company. The principal subscribers were Richard Cadman Etches and three other members of the Etches family, and the membership included George Dixon and Nathaniel Portlock, both of them sea captains of exceptional ability.[4] A scheme

---

[3] Geo. Taswell to Lord Sydney, 23 March, 1785. London. *Home Misc. S.*, vol. 190 (13), p. 617.

[4] The members were listed as follows: Richard Cadman – merchant, London; John Hanning – gentleman, Dawlish, Devon; William Etches – merchant, Asborne, Derbyshire; Mary Camilla Brook – tea dealer, London; William Etches – merchant, Northampton; John Etches – merchant, London; Nathaniel Gilmour – merchant, Gosport, Hants; Nathaniel Portlock – Capt. of the *King George*; George Dixon - Capt. of the *Queen Charlotte*. (*Ibid.*, p. 248.)

was prepared which received (in general terms) 'the Countenance of His Majesty's Ministers' and was considered by the Court of Directors on 29 April. The schemes was not lacking in boldness or publicity appeal.

It was proposed that Government should grant them a Charter of exclusive privileges for a period of years to trade the entire length of the North-West Coast from Cape Blanco in latitude 43° 6' N. up to Bering Strait, with the right to establish a factory at Nootka Sound or at another convenient place as a mart for furs and other products obtainable from the natives. With such cargoes they were to be at liberty – 'to endeavour to open a friendly intercourse with the Island of Japan, Jesso [Yezo], the Kuriles, and the Coast of Asia from Siberia to the Gulf of Siam – ever subject to a prohibition of trading with the Chinese in any Article whatever except the produce of the said North-West Continent of America, nor to return to Europe with any traffic the manufactory or produce of China'. And since they might find it difficult to secure sufficient freight for the return voyage to Europe, they sought permission to import into Britain whale-oil, whalebone and seal skins caught by them in the North-East Pacific duty-free. In this connexion it will be recalled that Hawkesbury and the Board of Trade strongly encouraged the Southern Whalers to take part in the new maritime fur trade. The north Pacific was rich in sperm whales, as the Americans afterwards discovered; but it may be doubted whether that formidable trio, Enderby, Champion and St. Barbe, would have quietly acquiesced in the promotion of a new and competitive fishery.

The King George's Sound Company submitted further ideas. Following Cook, they stated their intention of using the Sandwich Islands with their healthy climate and abundance of foodstuffs as a rendezvous in case of sickness or accident. It seemed probable that these Islands at some future period would become 'the grand emporium of Commerce between the two Continents and the innumerable Islands of that immense Ocean'. Furthermore there was the possibility of discovering a passage from the North-West Coast into the Atlantic.

As there are a number of Inlets in the Prince William's Sound and Cook's River that time would not permit Captain Cook to explore, it is very probable that, in prosecuting a Trade in those parts, some very essential discoveries may be made and perhaps a communication carried on to Hudson's or Baffin's Bay.[5]

Perhaps someone at the Board of Control warned the Syndicate

---

[5] It was stated that these observations were based on the opinion of some of the officers who had been with Capt. Cook (e.g. George Dixon) 'and from the remarks of the natives'.

that their comprehensive scheme was well calculated to freeze the Court of Directors into rigidity unless more care was taken to accommodate their plans to the Charter rights of the East India Company. Attached to the original document there are 'Additional Proposals' which attempted to meet this and other possible objections.[6] 'The Japanese Islands would be our grand object.' Although the Japanese would not admit European traders except the Dutch on a very limited scale, the new Company had learned that sea-otter skins were so highly prized in Japan that there was a very good prospect of effecting sales and so opening a new commerce of great importance to Britain. It was the custom of the East India Company to license numbers of merchant ships to trade in any part of the seas beyond the Cape of Good Hope and to purchase their cargoes for disposal in Canton. 'We cannot see any reason why they should not, on application, license our vessels in the same manner. There cannot be a possibility of any detriment, and it may prove a source of great advantage to them.' The manufactures and natural products of Japan were known to be much superior in value to those of the Eastern Islands which the Company collected in this way, and the only Japanese goods which had been hitherto obtained came by very circuitous routes. It would be for the Japanese to determine whether they would buy the furs with natural products, manufactures or with cash. Whichever they might decide upon, the proceeds would be most useful to the Company's Supercargoes in Canton in supplementing their resources for the purchase of tea – which was true enough.

The Syndicate then set out their situation if the Company refused to license their ships. They would have to make the best market they could in the Japanese Islands for cash – 'return to the Coast of America, collect what furs they can in running down the Coast – make up a freight with whale fins and oil, and return to Europe by the same route they went out'. If, however, the cash sales were sufficiently remunerative, they could afford to come home directly by Cape Horn; and in that event they would not infringe the East India Company's Charter in any respect whatever – which again was true. But the entire enterprise in that case would have been dependent upon the willingness of the feudal lords of Nippon to open their ports to the despised and mistrusted barbarians from the West. They might conceivably prefer to buy their furs (at higher prices) from the Chinese.

Finally, it was explained that the promoters intended that in addition to their own subscriptions the nominal capital would be £200,000, divided into shares of £100 each, to be offered to the public as circumstances might require after the first undertaking

---

[6] The first of these is headed: 'Proposal for doing away any Objection the East India Company may make relative to their Charter.'

had proved a success. Further capital issues might be desirable in due course, for they had been advised by men who were knowledgeable about Japan that, if they could secure access, they might open 'a very extensive and valuable source of commerce to this Country'.[7]

They painted a rosy picture of what was, in fact, an extremely hazardous enterprise. Yet this was not a company prospectus, coloured to attract money out of the pockets of gullible potential shareholders, but a petition to the Government and the East India Company for permission to spend their own money in testing the validity of their scheme. Like the founders of the Southern Whale Fishery they received encouragement from the Government, although no more was heard of a charter; but the East India Company gave no more than a grudging assent. The proposition that their resources at Canton should be reinforced with American furs and goods from Japan offered advantages without risk on their part; but the Court of Directors disliked all these intrusions into the Pacific by independent British ships coming in from a new direction outside their effective control. The next step would be a demand for a free and independent trade at Canton.

The papers were submitted to the Court of Directors on 29 April, 1785, when it was decided to take them into consideration five days later at a meeting to be attended by the Company's Counsel and Solicitor.[8] The proposals were then referred to the Committee of Correspondence who called in Cadman Etches for consultation and reported on 6 May. Since the adventure had been considered by Government and it was thought to be in the national interest to endeavour to open such a trade, the Committee recommended that the Company might 'with safety to themselves' give encouragement thereto as far as to license two ships for one voyage 'by way of experiment'.

The conditions imposed aptly illustrate the Company's policy in relation to the new trade developments in the Pacific. The two ships might proceed from the American Coast to Japan and places to the northward, but they must not, under a penalty of £5,000, go to any country to the south or west of Canton or to the west of New Holland, that is to say, they were barred from South-East Asia and the Indian Ocean. If they were driven into any of these regions by stress of weather they might purchase stores and provisions for cash, but they must not sell or barter there 'any European goods whatsoever'. Nor must any European goods be brought to China. Infractions were to be punished by fines at the rate of

---

[7] Minutes of the Court of Directors, 29 April, 1785 (*Court Book*, No. 94, p. 39. A copy of the papers submitted is in *Home Misc.*, vol. 494(5), pp. 359-67).

[8] Minutes of 3 May (*Court Book*, No. 94, p. 40).

£100 per cent of the value of the goods sold. If the ships failed to dispose of their cargoes in Japan they were to be at liberty to explore and trade along the coast of Korea on their way down to Canton. On arrival there a detailed list of all goods unsold and of ships' stores must be presented to the Company's Supercargoes. The ships must be searched and any unauthorised goods found in them must be confiscated and heavy penalties exacted. Moneys received in Japan or Korea were to be paid into the Company's treasury in return for bills of exchange. Furs and other products from the American Coast, not previously sold, which might be suitable for the European or Indian markets must be offered to the Supercargoes 'at a fair price', and if not wanted for this purpose but considered suitable for China were to be sold by the Company on the customary commission.

On the question of a return freight the Supercargoes might hire them to carry Company goods back to London at the rate of £13 per ton, provided that the ships were seaworthy and 'free from any smell which may be likely to hurt or damage Tea'. If the ships were not so hired, they would be free to return to the American coast and thence to load home with goods for Europe. But in that case they must return by Cape Horn or the Straits of Magellan and must not visit any port in North America.[9]

The restrictions, which were very similar to those imposed upon the Southern Whalers in the following year, indicate the Company's determination to prevent British manfactures being sold in any part of Asia except through their own channels. Their chief concern was to avoid disturbance in the tea trade which they commanded. These thrusts into the Pacific might represent the thin end of a very broad wedge. The English venturers on the North-West Coast benefited from the Company's organisation, but the restrictions imposed a heavy hardship. They had also to bear the cost of a five-year licence from the South Sea Company. When merchants from New England began to compete in the new field, as they soon did, they had the advantage of being able to buy and sell where they pleased, and instead of being hired at a low rate for the return voyage they were able to buy tea and other China goods on their own account and make an additional profit by selling them in their home ports.

The Board of Control considered these recommendations on 27 May, but it was not until August that the 'Chairs' sent copies of the Licence and the Deed of Covenant to Lord Sydney for the approval of His Majesty's Ministers.[10] Shortly afterwards the *King*

---

[9] At a Committee of Correspondence held 6 May, 1785 (*Correspondence Memoranda, 1785*. No. 31. Copy in *Home Misc. S.*, vol. 494(5), pp. 367-82).

[10] *Minutes of the Board of Control*, 27 May, vol. I, p. 81. William Devaynes and Nathaniel Smith to Lord Sydney, 11 Aug. *Home Misc. S.*, vol 190(13), pp. 247-8).

George (Capt. Portlock) and the *Queen Charlotte* (Capt. Dixon) set sail on the long haul for the Straits of Magellan and the Pacific coast of the future Dominion of Canada. They were under instructions to establish factories at convenient places along the North-West Coast, and Portlock was to forward all his despatches to Richard Etches through George Rose, Secretary to the Treasury.[11] Although no more was heard of the request for an exclusive Charter, the Government thus supported the venture and took steps to be kept closely informed of its progress. It was all the more desirable that they should, in view of Hawkesbury's notion that the Southern Whalers might be induced to come northwards to take part in the new trade.[12] In this initial stage the Government acquiesced in the restrictions and penalties imposed upon it by the East India Company, but eventually Dundas and the Board of Control secured less onerous conditions.[13]

When Portlock and Dixon dropped anchor in Nootka Sound they were surprised and angry to find that they had been anticipated by Englishmen from India. It was an odd thing that almost identical projects for developing the fur trade with China and Japan from the North-West Coast and continuing the search for a channel into the Atlantic should have been launched almost simultaneously from London, Bombay and Calcutta. It might have been expected that the two ventures from India had been inspired by news of the London enterprise and a desire to emulate it, but there is no evidence to indicate that the preparations of the Etches

---

[11] John Cadman Etches, *An Authentic Statement of the Facts Relative to Nootka Sound* (Lond., 1790), p. 29.

[12] Alexander Dalrymple was rightly critical of this idea. ' I am confident every one fully conversant with the subject will perceive that it would be ruinous to the Southern Fishery to blend *Fishery* and *Commerce*.' Vessels fitted out for the fishery required a small capital outlay, and the crews, instead of receiving wages, were paid by shares in the profits of the voyage. It was, therefore, in the interests of the owners that the captains and crews should have no other concern but to make the fishing as successful as possible. ' If Merchandize is put on board these ships, the value of this is greatly enhanced, and instead of *all gain*, as the Fishery truly is to Industry, it is converted into an Adventure of *risk* and speculation.' (Dalrymple's Memo., *loc. cit infra*, p. 429, n. 18.)

[13] It was not until Dec., 1793 (when the controversy with Spain had been settled and the new Charter Act of that year had been passed), that the ' Regulations concerning the Trade of private Adventurers from the North-West Coast of America, and Islands adjacent, to the Isles of Japan and the Coasts of Korea and China ' were finally agreed between the Board of Control and the Board of Directors. In a report to Dundas the Solicitor to the Board of Control suggested amendments to clarify the geographical limits and make substantial reductions in the penalties. To exact penalties, he wrote, upon the Adventurers themselves for breaches of the regulations by their employees ' beyond the value of the Ship and Cargo ' was unjust and seemed calculated to discourage men of ability who might otherwise be disposed to speculate in the new trade, ' and if strictly enforced might even operate as a prohibition '. Russell, the Board's Solicitor, and Smith, the Company's Solicitor, reached agreement on revised regulations, and Dundas approved them (*Home Misc. S.*, vol. 494(5), pp. 355, 385-91).

syndicate were known in India at the time. All three expeditions seem to have been inspired independently by the widespread interest aroused by Cook's experiences on that Coast when the narrative of his last voyage was published in 1784.

In the following year James Charles Stewart Strange, a Company Servant on the Madras establishment who afterwards became a son-in-law of Dundas, pondered on the matter during his passage to India. On arrival in Bombay he presented a paper about it to his 'valuable Friend and Patron', David Scott, a Free Merchant of much substance and outstanding ability who afterwards became Chairman of the Court of Directors and a close ally of Dundas and Pitt in promoting a policy of expansion in India and a liberalisation of Eastern trade.[14]

With his two partners, Tate and Adamson, Scott took up the project with an imaginative thoroughness which seems to have left Strange a little breathless. By 1 September, 1785, an outline plan had been submitted to the President and Council of Bombay. The ship *Betsy* (300 tons), 'one of the compleatest vessels ever built', was purchased, sheathed with planks and then with copper, and re-named the *Captain Cook*. Failing to find a suitable vessel of smaller size, they induced the Bombay Government to sell them a 'luggage boat' which was then being built for use with the Royal Navy, and its construction was adapted for exploration in northern waters. The officers and crews (61 for the *Captain Cook* and 37 for the new boat, named the *Experiment*) were all Europeans and hand-picked. Five of the officers had served as lieutenants in the Royal Navy during the previous war and included specialists in astronomical observation and survey work. The services of fifteen artificers in the military service of the Company, who had recently arrived from England, were applied for and obtained. Instruments, charts, stores sufficient for several years, and provisions for fifteen months were supplied. It was an exceptionally well-found expedition.

Scott and his partners had hoped that the Bombay Government would officially sponsor the undertaking, but without authority from Bengal or London they were cautious. Approval and consider-able practical assistance were given, but – 'this Government do not think themselves authorised to grant them any particular Patronage agreeable to their request'. And when they were asked whether they had any specific directions for Mr. Strange, they replied in the negative, but added that if copies of the sea-logs of the two vessels with all nautical observations were delivered on

---

[14] See C. H. Philips (ed.), ' The Correspondence of David Scott, Director and Chairman of the East India Company . . . 1787-1805 ' (*Camden Third Series, vol. XXV, Roy Hist. Soc.,* 1951), vol I, Intro. *passim.*

the return to Bombay, 'they will be acceptable to the Honble. Company'.[15]

By late November the ship *Experiment* had been launched and fitted out and the two vessels were ready to put to sea. On 7 December Strange received his formal Instructions which in their boldness and attention to detail emulated those issued by the Admiralty to Capt. Cook. 'The Principal Purposes for which we mean this Expedition are in the first Instance, Exploring for the benefit of Navigation, and secondly with a view to Establish a new Channel of Commerce with the North-West Coast of America.' Strange, who was put in 'sole controul' of the expedition, was to take with him letters from Scott to the Governors and chief officers at Goa, Mangalore, Tillicherry, Cochin and Macao. At Goa the Portuguese Captain-General would supply him with passes, colours and letters to ensure a good reception at the Portuguese factory at Macao. The ostensible reason given in the Instructions for sailing to China under Portuguese colours was that the ships would probably arrive there at a season of the year 'when the Intercourse with English ships is not admitted at Canton', and they might therefore be distressed for provisions and refitting. But Scott and his partners took the precaution of appointing an agent at Macao who had been instructed to execute any orders that he might receive from Strange 'during the continuance of your voyaging'. The arrival at Canton of ships engaged in a new commerce which had not been formally licensed by the Company might have caused difficulties with the Supercargoes. Other vessels coming from Calcutta on a similar enterprise, as will be seen, took the same precaution.

At Mangalore, Tillicherry and Cochin, Strange was to collect articles suitable for the China market, such as sandal-wood and tin ware, which the agents of Scott and Co. had been instructed to have ready. Leaving the Malabar Coast the expedition was to proceed to Macao by way of the Bali Strait, then between Celebes and Borneo and keeping to the westward of the Philippines. Having landed the trade goods for the China market at Macao, they were to proceed with the utmost speed across the Pacific, making the American coast at about 40° North latitude. The object was to explore the coast northward, 'making every Discovery you can'. Surveys must be made of every place and the positions fixed with precision.

Every precaution must be taken to prevent officers from trans-

---

[15] See the following documents: ' Outlines for an Exploring expedition to be conducted by Mr. Strange ', Bombay, 1 Sept., 1785 (*Home Misc. S.*, 494(4), pp. 419-22); Scott and Co. to President and Council, Bombay, 17 Sept.; Minutes of Consultations, 30 Sept. and 18 Nov.; President etc to Scott and Co., 30 Sept.; Scott and Co. to President etc., 15 and 18 Nov. (*Bombay, Secret and Political Consultations, 1785*, vol. 72, pp. 268-334).

mitting information about the expedition, and Strange was to send
back by every opportunity correct journals and surveys, 'and particularly your Remarks on whatever relate to the possible and
probable advantages to be derived to the East India Company from
a Commercial Intercourse between America and China'. And since
the Bombay Government had given aid and encouragement, 'We
mean to Transmit all such Information thro' this Government to
the East India Company'.

If on making their landfall they found that the Spaniards had
possessions in that latitude, the expedition must proceed northward
and not begin to explore until the most northerly of the Spanish
possessions had been passed. The primary object with the promoters was discovery, but the outfit had proved so very heavy that
every opportunity should be taken to establish contact with the
natives and exchange trade goods for furs and any other useful
commodities.

We would wish You to range along the whole American Coast up
through Berring's Straits, and from thence to proceed on towards the
Pole . . . untill the Ice impedes your nearer approach to it, and
then steering to the westward to keep as far North as the Ice will permit untill you make the Coast of Asia, which you will in like manner
Survey, and afterwards direct your course to Kantskatha (sic).

In case an accident should happen to the expedition before the
return to China, Strange was to write a letter in cypher from that
port to Scott, who by then would be in London, giving him information which would be valuable to the Company. The letter should
be sent under cover to the British Ambassador at the Court of
Russia. On leaving Kamchatka he was to steer along the coast of
Asia for China, surveying, as well as time would permit, all the
islands on the way, 'and particularly those of Japan'. On returning to China Strange was to use his own judgement. If there was
no good prospect of making a profitable second voyage to the
American coast, he should return to Bombay. On the other hand,
if he was satisfied that he could continue to make discoveries and
at the same time defray the cost by trade – 'You will in such Case
continue in Exploring as long as you please', subject, of course, to
the receipt of further orders. Finally it would be of such value for
the future to make contact with the natives and have knowledge
of their language, that generous rewards should be offered to any
who would volunteer to stay on the Coast: and in that event
Strange must adjust his plans so as to make certain of picking them
up again.[16]

---

[16] 'Instructions to James Strange Esqr., Director of the Exploring Expedition to
the No West Coast of America and towards the North Pole. Bombay.' 7 Dec., 1785
(Home Misc. S., vol. 494(5), pp. 422-7).

The resemblance of these Instructions to those issued by the King George's Sound Company to Portlock and Dixon is remarkable, even when allowance is made for the fact that they both derived from the aims and proceeding of Cook. There seems little doubt that Scott hoped and intended, if his expedition produced results, to be able to induce the East India Company to develop this trans-Pacific trade itself, and from India. There was much to be said for the argument. If the trade had been based on India the Company could have encouraged and controlled it as part of their system of supplementing the China Investment. Scott was to find, however, that his expansive and liberal views were not popular. On returning to London he took a prominent part in a campaign for increasing the export trade from Britain to India, but his proposals, submitted in June, 1787, were unanimously rejected by the Court of Directors.[17]

With regard to the North-West American Coast his policy had the support of the veteran explorer and promoter of trade and discovery, Alexander Dalrymple, who was now 'Examiner of Sea Journals' for the Company. Dalrymple was keenly interested in the enterprise and, although a defender of the Company's monopoly as an administrative necessity, he deplored 'that left-handed policy too often visible' by which the Company left this new trade to private merchants (under severe restrictions) instead of undertaking it themselves.[18] But a complex organisation, defending exclusive rights and carrying heavy overhead expenses, is not easily induced to alter established arrangements for uncertain enterprises.

The ships *Captain Cook* and *Experiment* were so well found and manned that there was every reason to expect that valuable exploration work would have been effected. Unfortunately the leadership was deficient. James Strange was not robust either in physique or in temperament. From his own narrative it is evident that he was imaginative and had a gift for observation and literary expression but that he was fearful of responsibility and easily discouraged. Too often he was exerting all his philosophy 'in order to Suppress with becoming fortitude' the painful feelings which

---

[17] Minutes of 21 and 27 June, 1787 (*Court Book*, No. 96, pp. 213 and 223-4). The Directors added that they would at all times be mindful of accomplishing this desirable object by such means as might appear to them eligible for the purpose, ' in effecting which should Mr. Scott from the experience he has gained by his long residence in India be able to afford them any useful information, every due attention will be paid thereto'. Some improvement was made in 1790 as the result of Scott's further suggestions (Scott's *Correspondence*, ed. Philips, vol. I, Intro. p. xii).

[18] Memo on the Fur Trade, by Alex. Dalrymple (1791) (*Home Misc. S.*, 494(5), pp. 429-39). Some of the charts and a drawing in Dalrymple's *Charts of the North West Coast of America* (Lond., 1789-91), Portfolio II, are inscribed to Scott in recognition of his public spirit in patronising the expedition of the *Captain Cook* and the *Experiment*.

some set-back stirred within him. He had a long and respectable career as a civil servant, but to rely on him to display the iron resolution and hardihood of a maritime explorer was to expect too much.

Leaving Bombay in December, 1785, the expedition reached the American Coast on 24 June in latitude 47° 54′ North. After three days they arrived in Nootka Sound and searched for the cove where Cook had anchored.[19] Strange gives a lively account of his impressions: the magnificence of the rugged snow-capped peaks and dense pine forests and the welcoming Indians, their verminous condition and 'beastly habits'. The channel at the north end of Vancouver Island was examined and Strange thought that it led on to 'a very extensive Sea'. He 'displayed the Flag' and took possession of it (for whatever that might be worth) in the name of His Britannic Majesty, naming it Queen Charlotte Sound. The ships then sailed slowly northward, but little survey was done because of the foggy weather. Sea-otter skins were collected, and at the end of August they reached Prince William Sound – their furthest north – which Cook had explored. And there the blow fell.

While engaged in cleaning furs, word was brought to him that a strange vessel was standing in for the bay. This painful event, he sadly recorded, appeared to give 'the *coup de grace* to my future Prospect of Success in this line of Life'. The stranger turned out to be the *Sea Otter* (150 tons), commanded by Capt. Tipping, and came – not from London but from Calcutta. The two men treated each other with wary civility. The *Sea Otter* had left the Hooghli in March of that year with a companion ship the *Nootka* (230 tons), commanded by John Meares, the promoter of the expedition.

Strange departed for Macao nine days later on board the *Experiment*, followed shortly afterwards by the *Captain Cook*. Surgeon Mackay volunteered to stay behind (in accordance with Scott's Instructions) to learn the language of the native Indians and collect information about them for future use. The two vessels took with them 604 sea-otter skins which sold for 24,000 Spanish dollars (about £5,100). It was a good price (for the market was not yet glutted), but the venture must have shown a heavy loss, and its value as exploration was virtually *nil*. A second voyage to the American Coast was not attempted. The expedition returned to

[19] Instead of proceeding to Macao, as instructed, Strange put in at Batavia to obtain his provisions for the trans-Pacific voyage. The Dutch officials there were extremely suspicious of his intentions and refused all information about the navigation of the Strait of Macassar – where both ships subsequently ran aground. Most of them, wrote Strange, were inclined to think 'that the Object of our Voyage was rather to explore their Spice Islands than the North West Coast of America' (*Narrative*, 29 Jan., 1786).

Bombay and Strange to his new post at Tanjore.[20] After he had departed from the scene of action, his speculative bent reasserted itself. He wrote a vivid account of the expedition and urged the Madras Government to put the scheme to the Court of Directors. In January 1788 he addressed the Council on the subject and in February wrote a long letter to the Governor, Sir Archibald Campbell. Therein he emphasised that the haphazard arrival of private traders on the West American Coast would never answer. An expedition might ruin its promoters if it arrived shortly after the market had been denuded of furs by a predecessor. The only effective method was the establishment of a permanent depot by the East India Company, for they alone possessed the requisite personnel and resources.

The most central position for the depot and factory was Nootka Sound. Factors and a small garrison for local security might be spared from Bombay, and not less than three small vessels of 100 or 120 tons should be employed. Two of them should ply regularly between America and China, while the third should be sent along the Coast during the summer season as far north as Cook's River (or Inlet), collecting furs wherever they were to be had.[21] Strange's *Narrative* and proposals were duly forwarded to the Directors and no more was heard of them. They echoed the expansive ideas of

---

[20] *A Narrative of a Voyage to the North West Coast of America. Most respectfully inscribed to the Honourable Major-General Sir Archibald Campbell . . . by James Strange of the Madras Establishment.* Endorsed: Received with Public Letter from Fort St. George, dated 1 March, 1788. (*Home Misc. S.,* 800.) The Narrative was published in 1928 by the Madras Record Office. Strange, who was born in 1753, was the son of the celebrated engraver, Sir Robert Strange, and elder brother of Sir Thomas Strange, the first Chief Justice of the Supreme Court of Madras. He became a Writer in the Madras Presidency in 1772. Owing to ill health he took long leave in 1780, and on his return to India in 1785 he undertook the expedition described above. In 1787 he was appointed Pay-Master and Storekeeper at Tanjore. His first wife died in Madras in 1791. ' Strange's private affairs necessitating his presence in England, he resigned the service in 1795.' He was M.P. for East Grinstead, 1796-1802, and for Okehampton, 1802-4. He married Ann Dundas and became a banker, but was disappointed in his hopes of becoming a Director of the East India Company. He returned to Madras in 1804; became Postmaster-General and senior member of the Board of Trade there: retired from the Service in 1815 and died in 1840 (A. V. V. Ayyar, ' An Adventurous Madras Civilian: James Strange, 1753-1840.' *Proceedings, Indian Historical Records Commission,* vol. XI (1928), pp. 22-24: *Scott Corr.,* ed. Philips, pp. 229 and n., 272. Cf. Furber, *Henry Dundas,* pp. 165-6). It is tempting to assume that it was Dundas who inspired Strange to promote the enterprise and that Dundas encouraged Scott to finance it; but Strange did not become Dundas's son-in-law until some fifteen years later and Scott had no opportunity of becoming acquainted with Dundas until his return to England – after the expedition had taken place.

[21] Madras, *Public Consultations,* vol. 147 (15 Jan., 1788) and vol. 148 (22 Feb.). Strange's letter to Sir Archibald Campbell is printed by A. V. V. Ayyar (*ut supra*), pp. 29-34. Cf. D. H. Love, *Vestiges of Old Madras,* vol. III, pp. 348-9. Strange in this letter added that there was abundance of whales in those waters and excellent timber along the coast. Moreover, the Russians, who had almost annihilated the sea-otters in the Alaskan Islands which they frequented, could be expected to push southward their exploration of the coast.

David Scott, but the development of a profitable trade in the Pacific
by Company-owned Indian-built ships was sure to be regarded as
a dangerous precedent by the group of Directors who comprised
the Shipping Interest. As such they were about to engage in a long
and bitter struggle with Scott himself in defence of their lucrative
and restrictive monopoly. The proposal may, however, have influenced the Government, who a year later decided to take action
on these lines themselves.[22]

Ten days after Strange's departure the *Nootka* with John Meares
in command dropped anchor in Prince William Sound, and its
consort the *Sea Otter* thereupon sailed for China.[23] Thus a third
expedition – this time from Calcutta – followed the track of Cook
to a wild coast on the north Pacific for the purpose of opening a
new trade with Japan and China. The genesis of the Meares adventure is obscure. He seems to have picked up current gossip about
Cook's experiences on the North-West American Coast and to have
persuaded one or more Agency Houses in Calcutta who traded as
Country Merchants with Canton to finance a trial expedition.
Meares was a lieutenant in the Royal Navy who (like many such)
had gone out to India in 1783 from lack of employment. He lacked
the financial substance of the Etches family, the navigational and
exploring experience of Portlock and Dixon, and the semi-official
support given to James Strange; but these handicaps did not deter
him from building up a position which enabled him to speak as
though he had been the only begetter of a new trade between
America and Asia and to stand forth when the crisis with Spain
arose as the *civis Romanus* who had been wronged and the national
representative who must be vindicated. He was a man of great
initiative and enterprise and with considerable ability as an
organiser. He was above all a first-rate propagandist. His pertinacity
in exaggerated lament is reminiscent of his predecessor, Captain
Jenkins of the severed ear. Indeed, it would not be entirely beside
the mark to describe him as a cross between Capt. Jenkins and
Edward Gibbon Wakefield.

It is possible to supplement the meagre description of the expedition of 1786-7 which Tipping vouchsafed to Strange from the
more detailed account which Meares afterwards gave in evidence
before the Privy Council.[24] He then claimed that the enterprise
had been undertaken with the knowledge of the Governor-General,
who had permitted two gentlemen of the Bengal establishment
' to accompany me in order to assist me in surveying the Countries '.

[22] See p. 438 below.
[23] Tipping reached Macao in February, 1787, and sold an assortment of furs for
8,000 dollars. He and his ship were afterwards lost at sea (*Official Papers Relative
to the Dispute between the Courts of Great Britain and Spain on the subject of
the Ships Captured in Nootka Sound* . . . Lond., 1790. Intro., p. iv).
[24] *Privy Council Register*, 8 Feb., 1791 P.C. 2/135, p. 439 *et seq.*

As arranged the *Sea Otter* sailed from Macao along the north coast of China, 'in Order to ascertain the Existence of the Straits of Teso, which separate Corea from Japan'. Tipping had been ordered in the course of his voyage 'to endeavour to open an amicable Intercourse with the Inhabitants of Corea or Japan, or of the Islands to the North or South'.[25] Thereafter he was to rendezvous with the *Nootka* in Prince William Sound.

Meares himself on board the *Nootka* sailed along the American Coast as far north as Cook's Inlet in latitude 61° N. to see what opportunities of trade might offer, to establish contact with the natives, 'and of fixing a Post there if found expedient'. It was not expedient, for on entering the Inlet they came upon a Russian settlement of forty or fifty men who had built some fifteen houses which were defended by a mud redoubt and cannon. The Russians prevented the Indians from bringing furs to the English ship, and so after sending a boat 'to take possession of the Point called Point Possession, which had formerly been taken possession of by Capt. Cook ', Meares departed southward for Prince William Sound, where he arrived on 25 September, 1786. While trading in that region, Meares declared, he formed a treaty of commerce with a chief named Shenawah. 'The terms of this Treaty were that Shenawah should, in consideration of some presents made to him for that purpose and not in return for any Articles of Trade, agree to grant us an exclusive right to Trade with his People, and that they should deal only with us, that is with the Ships under my Command.'[26]

Having decided to winter there, Meares had a house built ashore 'for the reception of the Carpenter, etc'; and by the beginning of November the ship was frozen in. Lack of fresh foodstuffs and anti-scorbutic remedies during the long severe winter exposed them to the ravages of scurvy from which several officers and artificers and all but nine of the crew died. When spring came at last (in May) Capt. Portlock in the *King George* and Capt. Dixon in the *Queen Charlotte* from London anchored at the entrance to

---

[25] 'I had given these Orders,' stated Meares, 'in consequence of some imperfect Knowledge we had obtained of a communication between the Chinese, Japanese and Coreans. Those Empires being at Hostility with each other, the only Communication carried on between them was through the Islands lying in those Seas. The Emperor of China rather winked at this Communication.' (*Ibid.*) Possibly because the *Sea Otter* had failed to open a trade in this region, Meares concealed the fact that Tipping reached the North-West Coast and made a return voyage to China. Immediately after the quoted passage Meares states, 'the *Sea Otter* was lost ', but Strange's account of the arrival of the *Sea Otter* at Prince William Sound and the official entry of his sale of a cargo of furs at Macao on 12 March, 1787, shows that the vessel must have been lost thereafter, possibly while returning to India. Meares was very anxious to convince the Government of the feasibility of a trade with Japan. It is discrepancies such as this which make Meares such an unsatisfactory witness.

[26] *Ibid.*

the Sound. Learning to their great surprise from the Indians that there was another ship some twenty leagues up the Sound, Dixon went in a long-boat to investigate and came upon the *Nootka*. The response of Portlock and Dixon to Meares's requests for help were certainly harsh and ungenerous, and they used his necessitous condition to compel him to sign a bond in the sum of £500 to do no more trade on the Coast but to sail for Hawaii and China without delay.[27]

After the three had made their several ways back to London this episode became the subject of an acrimonious controversy; but, apart from personalities, the cause of the trouble was plain enough.[28] Meares of Calcutta was an interloper, and the more so since he was sailing under Portuguese colours. The Etches syndicate, on the other hand, had been given Government support, their ships were licensed by the East India and the South Sea Companies, and the promoters were determined to establish themselves permanently and exclusively on the Coast. Richard Etches had instructed both Portlock and Dixon to establish such factories as might be necessary 'for the future securing the trade of the continent and islands adjacent'. Nootka Sound was recommended as the most central situation: land was to be purchased from the natives and a long-house erected as a permanent trading depot, to be stocked with provisions, trade goods, and with arms and ammunition for defence. When Surgeon Mackay of Strange's expedition was discovered at Nootka Sound living amicably with the Indians and learning their language and customs, he was forcibly removed to Canton. In fact the King George's Sound Company, hoping to develop into a national chartered corporation, were trying to organise the trade very much as Scott had hoped to induce the East India Company to do.[29]

The acknowledged need to obviate uncontrolled competition in bartering for furs on the Coast and, still more, in selling them at Canton or Macao gave the resilient Meares his chance.[30] Within

---

[27] The letters between Portlock and Meares during this encounter (May-June, 1787) are printed in Meares, *Voyages made in the Years 1788-1789 from China to the North-West Coast of America* (Lond., 1790), p. xxiii *et seq*.

[28] F. W. Howay (ed.), *The Dixon-Meares Controversy* (Toronto, 1929); N. Portlock, *A Voyage round the World, but more particularly to the North-West Coast of America . . .* (Lond., 1789); Geo. Dixon, *A Voyage Round the World . . . in 1785 to 1788* (Lond., 1789). Cf. Howay, 'Early Days of the Maritime Fur-Trade on the North-West Coast' (*Cam. Hist. Rev.*, vol. IV (1923), p. 28).

[29] Instructions from R. C. Etches to Portlock, 3 Sept., 1785. Printed in *The Dixon-Meares Controversy*, p. 61.

[30] Meares himself in the *Nootka* reached Macao on 20 Oct., 1787, with about 350 sea-otter skins which he sold for about 14,000 Spanish dollars, i.e. at an average price per skin of 40 dollars. Portlock and Dixon in the *King George* and *Queen Charlotte* arrived a few weeks later with no less than 2,552 skins which they sold for 50,000 dollars – average price 19 dollars. (Dalrymple's list of ships and sales, *ut supra*.)

a few weeks of his arrival at Macao he enlisted the financial support of a merchant house named John Henry Cox and Daniel Beale and Co. It may be that he thereupon ended his engagement with his original employers of Calcutta, or alternatively the representatives of the latter in Canton may have joined in the new venture. At any rate the ' Merchant Proprietors ', as they called themselves, fitted out two ships for the purpose, the *Felice* and the *Iphigenia*, and on 24 December, 1787, provided Meares with final Instructions.[31]

From the tone of this document, which was probably drafted by Meares himself, the object was to get in quickly and stake a claim as against the monopoly pretensions of Portlock and Dixon and their employers, the King George's Sound Company. By way of preamble it was stated that the trading situation in China (i.e. at Canton and Macao) was such 'as must shortly destroy all competition and give us the exclusive possession of this valuable branch of trade'. The success of the voyage would depend upon an early arrival at Nootka, and the route and later movements of the ships were planned so as to collect cargoes of furs before the arrival of competitors. At the end of the season they were to winter in the Sandwich Islands and then return to the Coast early in the following March.

The final paragraphs of these Instructions are the most significant. If any 'Russian, English or Spanish vessels' were met with, they must be treated with civility. But should they attempt to seize the *Felice* or *Iphigenia*, 'or even carry you out of your way', the attempt must be prevented, if necessary by force. If in any such conflict the Proprietors' ships had the superiority they must take possession of the attacking vessel and its crew and bring them to China, 'that they may be condemned as legal prizes, and their crews punished as pirates'.[32] Since neither Russian nor Spanish vessels had yet been encountered, these bellicose orders seem to have been primarily intended as a directive to defy any attempt by London ships to enforce exclusive rights. The proposed invocation of admiralty law and process on the part of a trading association which had begun operations without the knowledge or approval of any British Administration at home or in India and had no licence from either of the Chartered Corporations concerned was bold to the point of Elizabethan impudence. But the purpose was to stake a claim and to create a bargaining counter.

---

[31] The *Felice* was the *Nootka* under a new name (see evidence of Meares before the Board of Trade, 27 May, 1790. *B.T.* 5/6, p. 225). It may be, therefore, that Cox, Beale and Co. were the employers of Meares on his first voyage from Calcutta. It could be that Meares himself was part owner of this ship, but in the subsequent Agreement between Cox and Beale and the Etches Company the *Felice* and the *Iphigenia* are listed as the property of the former, and the name of Meares does not appear in the document.

[32] 'Instructions . . . to Capt. John Meares, 24 Dec., 1787 ' (Meares, *Voyages* . . . App. I. Printed in *Brit. Col. Dev.*, pp. 30-2).

The plan was pushed forward during the summer of 1788 while Meares was at Nootka with the *Iphigenia* and the *Felice*. Permission to use a plot of land was obtained from the local Indian chief Maquilla, on which a long-house was erected, and a party was left behind to establish a trading depot and to complete the building of a 50-ton vessel which was named the *North-West American*. Back again at Macao in the autumn, Meares, with his associates Cox and Beale, established contact with John Cadman Etches (brother of Richard) who had also returned from the North-West Coast. Discussions began with a view to some form of association. A partnership between the Etches syndicate with its official authorisation and an enterprising firm of Free Merchants, strongly based on the China Coast and connected with India, offered advantages to both parties, and more particularly since each of them had hitherto been trading at a loss.[33] In combination they could expect to keep out any British rivals and avoid periodic scarcities of furs on the Coast and over-supply at Canton and Macao. A further inducement to work together must have been the appearance at Nootka during the summer of new and formidable competition in the form of the first ships to come from the United States – the *Eleanora* from New York, followed by the *Columbia* and the *Washington* from Boston.[34]

By the formal agreement which was signed on 23 January, 1789, the two Companies pledged themselves not to equip or charter any vessel except on joint and mutual accounts. As the owners of the *Iphigenia* and the *North-West American*, Cox and Beale agreed to place these vessels to joint account, while the Etches Company did likewise in respect of the *Princess Royal*. Profits were to be shared; but the arrangement was not a complete 'merger' and the Etches Company retained its separate identity.[35] A major attraction from the point of view of Meares and his patrons was that the arrangement (as they thought or pretended) brought them

---

[33] See statement to this effect in *The Journal of Capt. James Colnett aboard the Argonaut from April 26, 1789, to November 3, 1791*, ed. F. W. Howay (Champlain Soc., Toronto, 1940), p. 3.

[34] Howay, 'Early Days of the Maritime Fur Trade' (*ut supra*), p. 31 *et seq.*

[35] The text of the Agreement is in Colnett's *Journal*, pp. 4-7. In 'Sailing Orders for the Argonaut,' dated 3 April, 1789, the following passage occurs: 'Should you meet with any of the Ships of Messrs. Etches and Co. on the coast, you will of course afford them any Assistance in Your power, but as we shall have no interest in those Ships, if you can induce the Commanders to trade on our Joint accounts it will be most agreeable to us, but no trading connections whatever must be [carried on] except on the Account of the present Company, . . . to the person entrusted with the Charge of those Ships You will make known the nature of our connections with Mr. Etches' (*Ibid.*, p. 23). The *Prince of Wales* (an Etches ship), having arrived at Canton with a cargo of sea-otter skins in Nov., 1788, sailed in the following February for England – and not the North-West Coast. There is some evidence of friction between John Etches and Meares about financial adjustments after the Agreement had been made. (*Ibid.*, pp. 16 and 23.)

under the umbrella of the permits held by the King George's Sound Company. One of the reasons given in the Agreement for the mutual pledge to trade on the Coast only on joint account was that 'the said Licences will expire in the Year 1790 or thereabouts'. And by way of assurance for the future it was added: 'The said Richard Cadman Etches and Co. shall use their endeavours to have the aforesaid Charters renew'd for the Joint Benefit of all the parties herein mentioned or their Heirs and Assigns'. But there were no such 'charters'. Richard Etches and his partners had tried unsuccessfully to secure one from Government. A general permission 'to fit out ships or vessels for the said seas' for the five years, 1785 to 1790, had been obtained from the South Sea Company,[36] but that had not released them from the obligation to obtain (and pay for) a licence for each ship and voyage. Those held by Etches and Co. in 1788-9 were confined to the *Prince of Wales* and the *Princess Royal*. Much more important were the licences issued by the East India Company, and those too were for a given number of ships on a specified voyage. Neither Company would or could give *carte blanche* to a group of private merchants to charter unknown ships, based on a foreign port, and partly financed by unauthorised persons. The situation illustrates once more the severe handicaps under which independent adventurers laboured when they encountered the exclusive claims of chartered rights and their devious methods of circumvention. It also indicates incidentally the dubious status of Meares when he afterwards stood forth as the representative of wronged British merchants.[37]

As soon as the new association was formed, vigorous preparations were made to implement the policy which Richard Etches had planned in London four years before. An effective monopoly of the trade was to be secured by establishing a permanent and fortified factory at Nootka with a number of subsidiary 'trading houses' at other advantageous points, by maintaining a permanent squadron of small craft on the Coast to ply up and down collecting furs throughout the season, and by organising regular sailings of larger vessels between Nootka and China. A fresh ship, the *Argonaut*, was

---

[36] The text is printed in Howay's edition of Colnett's *Journal* as App. II.

[37] As already noted, the Government, although acknowledging that the South Sea Company could legally exact licensing fees, regarded their monopoly claims as derisory, since they had become solely a financial house and had had no connexion whatever with Pacific trade for many years. The Southern Whalers, who were obliged to pay them a fee for each ship, frequently petitioned the Government to be relieved of a meaningless impost. On the other hand, the licences of the East India Company (who controlled British trade at Canton) were issued under strict conditions which were subjected to the approval of the Board of Control. (See, for example, the *ad hoc* applications by R. C. Etches in 1786 – *Court Books*, No. 95, pp. 280, 306-7, 362.) Such licences had no relevance to ships fitted out by Meares and his supporters, who continued to use Portuguese colours even after the association with the Etches Company had been formed.

acquired and fitted out for a three years' expedition under Capt. James Colnett, who (with John Etches) had arrived in November, 1788, from the North-West Coast in command of the *Prince of Wales*. For building a factory and fort twenty-nine Chinese carpenters, blacksmiths and other craftsmen were hired and put on board the *Argonaut*. ' In placing a Factory on the Coast of America we look to a solid establishment, and not to one that is to be abandon'd at pleasure.'[38] Instructions under the new arrangements were sent to Capt. Douglas of the *Iphigenia*, which was wintering in the Hawaiian Islands, and on 26 April, 1789, the *Argonaut* sailed under orders to put the trade on a permanent and exclusive basis. The promoters were certainly right in thinking that this was the only possible method of doing so; but it seems extremely doubtful whether their resources could have stood the strain. The East India Directors groaned at the heavy maintenance costs of places such as Bencoolen and Penang. Moreover the Etches ships (such as the *Princess Royal*) were obliged to submit to the authority of the Supercargoes at Canton under pain of extremely heavy penalties; and even though the ships which Cox, Beale, and Meares had contributed to the pool might sail under Portuguese colours (as they did) and sell furs through a Portuguese agent at Macao, it was a precarious business and liable to vitiate their claim to be an integral part of ' the United Company of Merchants trading under the Sanction of the South Sea and Honble. East India Companies' Charters '.[39] Such then was the ambiguous situation of an undertaking which was intended to span the Pacific with a new trade and in doing so was about to encounter unimpeded competition from the United States and the prescriptive claims of Spain.

In 1789 the British Government decided that these new developments must be given active official support. Public as well as ministerial interest in the Pacific was keen, and requests for governmental intervention may have come from a variety of quarters. David Scott, who had hoped that his pioneer expedition would induce the East India Company itself to sponsor the trans-Pacific trade, had come home and was finding Dundas a natural ally in pressing the Company to serve expanding national interests by widening its own scope and adopting more flexible methods. Projects to that end could expect ready support from Dundas who at this time had been organising an embassy to Peking (despite the Company's reluctance) in the hope of obtaining unrestricted access to the China Market.[40] During the same period Samuel Enderby

---

[38] Sailing orders for the *Argonaut*. Macao, 3 April, 1789. Printed in Colnett's *Journal* (pp. 19-23).

[39] This is the description given in the orders sent to Capt. Douglas of the *Iphigenia*, dated 3 Feb., 1789, at Macao. (*Ibid.*, pp. 17-18.)

[40] Colonel Cathcart, whom Dundas had chosen to lead the embassy, had died in 1788, and the venture had been postponed. (See Chap. VIII below.)

and his associates of the Southern Whale Fishery had been urging upon Hawkesbury and the Board of Trade that a permanent base for refreshment and repairs was needed for their ships on prolonged voyages in the South Pacific and that a naval expedition was required to discover and take possession of a suitable place.

A sloop was accordingly purchased by the Admiralty while it was still building and was specially fitted out for an extended voyage of exploration in the South Seas and along the North-West Coast of America. The vessel was named *Discovery* after Cook's famous ship, and in the autumn (of 1789) Capt. Henry Roberts was appointed to the command with Lieut. George Vancouver as his second officer. Both of them had sailed with Cook on his voyage towards the South Pole and also on his last voyage and were thus experienced in the navigational conditions and the character of the various native peoples in the regions to be explored.[41] The expedition was intended to supplement Cook's surveys in the South Pacific and on the North-West Coast, especially with regard to suitable harbours for bases.

In the following January the first fragmentary news of the arrest of British ships by a Spanish officer in Nootka Sound reached London. As will be seen later, the British Ministry reacted sharply; but they must have assumed that this was a minor clash to be settled with the release of the ships and a suitable expression of regret, for action was planned in March which could not otherwise have been contemplated. It was then decided that the *Discovery* should have an armed escort, consisting of H.M.S. *Gorgon* from England and a frigate which was to be detatched from Commodore Cornwallis's squadron in the East Indies. *Discovery* and *Gorgon* were to proceed to Port Jackson, New South Wales, where supplies were to be provided and the ship's company of *Gorgon* was to be reinforced with as many officers and men as could be spared from H.M.S. *Sirius* which was stationed there. The two ships were then to sail for Hawaii and wait there – but not later than April, 1791 – for the frigate from India, whose captain was to take command of the expedition. Its chief purpose was explained in draft Instructions to Governor Phillip.

> One of the objects of this expedition being to form a settlement on the nor.-west coast of America, it is his Majesty's pleasure that you should select from among the people with you a proper number of persons to compose it, and that you should embark them either on board the *Discovery* or *Gorgon*.

It may have been no more than a matter of administrative expediency, but it is intriguing to find the Pitt Administration

---

[41] See Vancouver, *A Voyage of Discovery to the North Pacific Ocean and round the World* (3 vols., 1798), Intro.

planning to use ' Botany Bay' in Australia as the parent of a trading settlement on what became the Pacific coast of Canada. Governor Phillip was also required to furnish a garrison.

The extent of this establishment, it is imagined, need not at first exceed thirty persons, a moiety of whom at least should consist of drafts from the new corps, under the command of a discreet subaltern officer, who is to be entrusted with the temporary superintendence of the new settlement. The remainder should consist of two or three of the most intelligent of the overseers, who have lately been sent out, a storekeeper, and any other persons who may be desirous of accompanying them, together with a few of the most deserving of the convicts, to whom you may offer a remission of a part of their service as an inducement to go.

Governor Phillip was also to be instructed to put on board *Discovery* and *Gorgon* a sufficient supply of stores, medicines and utensils for building, ' in order to enable them to fulfil the object of forming such a settlement as may be able to resist any attacks from the natives, and lay the foundation of an establishment for the assistance of His Majesty's subjects in the prosecution of the fur trade from the N. W. Coast of America'.[42]

From these draft Instructions certain deductions can be drawn. The fact that Commodore Cornwallis was ordered to detach a frigate from the squadron entrusted with the defence of the sea approaches to India and that the captain of this vessel (if she arrived in time) was to be in command of the expedition is an indication of the Government's determination to provide the new settlement and the fur traders who would use it as their headquarters with effective naval protection against possible Spanish intereference. Secondly, the drawing of civilian personnel and a contingent of the New South Wales Corps from Port Jackson (where they would have been ill-spared) together with some selected convicts, and the order that *Discovery* and *Gorgon* must not wait at Hawaii for the frigate later than April, 1791, indicates the sense of urgency. The initial establishment of about thirty men under the 'temporary superintendence' of the discreet subaltern was evidently to be increased later and a more senior official sent out to take charge. Since the founding of the settlement was described as ' one of the objects', the original plans for the further exploration of the North-West Coast and the South Pacific were presumably still included.

Finally, the preparations for an exploratory voyage in 1789 and the decision to persist in the establishment of a trading settlement under naval and military protection in the following spring, after news of the Spanish seizures had reached London, demonstrates

[42] Draft Instructions from Grenville to Gov. Phillip. Whitehall, March, 1790. Printed in Geo. Godwin, *Vancouver, A Life*, App. pp. 189-91.

the Government's determination to underwrite the enterprise of the Southern Whalers and the new America-China trade, despite obstruction, whether from the English East India Company or from Spain.

Towards the end of April *Discovery* was almost ready for sea, but by then John Meares had burst upon London with his flamboyant account of what had happened at Nootka. The expedition was cancelled,[43] and the Cabinet decided to send an ultimatum to Madrid and to back it up with the mobilisation of a large fleet. Thus instead of asserting British rights of trade and navigation in the Pacific by means of a settlement, officially established and guarded by His Majesty's ships and troops, the Government was now obliged to rely on the exaggerated and imprecise reports and in some respects irregular proceedings of Meares and his trading associates.

On 6 May, 1789, a Spanish warship of 26 guns, the *Princessa*, commanded by Don Estaban Jose Martinez, anchored in Nootka Sound and on the 13th was joined by a snow[44] of 16 guns, the *San Carlos*. What exactly transpired is not easy to determine since the subsequent accounts were written for propaganda purposes in the heat of public excitement. The *Iphigenia*, which had recently arrived (under Portuguese colours) after wintering at the Hawaiian Islands, was examined and then allowed to return to China after Capt. Douglas had signed a bond to pay on demand the value of the ship and cargo if later adjudged to be lawful prize. Her companion ship, the *North-West American* (also using the Portuguese flag) had gone northward along the coast to collect furs; and when she appeared she was seized and her crew taken prisoners. A few days later the *Princess Royal* turned up but was 'permitted instantly to depart' and was allowed to take away the furs which had been seized on board the *North-West American*. The two ships from Boston, *Columbia* and *Washington*, which had wintered at Nootka, were left unmolested and their officers treated with courtesy.

Having placed look-outs on the promontories at the entrance of the Sound, Martinez waited for further arrivals. He had some time to wait, and then on 3 July the *Argonaut* came in with Capt. Colnett in command, and he too was received with civility. Ten days later Capt. Duncan on board the *Princess Royal* was unwise enough to make a second appearance. Evidently he assumed that after the lapse of two months the Spanish warships would have resumed their patrol and the coast would be clear. But this was not a chance encounter with a routine Spanish patrol such as

---

[43] Vancouver, *Voyage*, Intro, p. 6. Cf. Godwin, *Life*, pp. 23-5, 27.

[44] A snow was a small vessel, similar to a brig, carrying a main- and fore-mast and a trysail mast close behind the main-mast.

had earlier occurred at Puerto Deseado when the two Southern whaling ships had been ordered away. Martinez was under orders from the Viceroy of Mexico to put a stop to a systematic intrusion.

Very naturally the Spanish Government was alarmed at the increasing British challenge to their claims of exclusive right in the Western Hemisphere and the Pacific. The dispute over the Falkland Islands was remembered as one of many indications of Britain's determination to force the doors of direct trade with Spanish America; and the systematic exploration of the Pacific by Cook had been followed by the invasion of British whalers who were continually using unfrequented harbours in South America and the Pacific Islands as bases for repair and refreshment and for hunting seals. And now this new menace along the North-West Coast.

Although one vessel was seized as lawful prize, Martinez seems at first to have intended to do no more than assert Spanish rights and warn intruders off the course. But it soon became apparent that the *Argonaut* had other assignments than the collection of furs. Colnett refused to produce his papers: the ship's stores included unusual items, and the presence on board of a party of Chinese artisans called for explanation. When challenged Colnett took a high line, declaring (according to Martinez) that he 'brought orders from his sovereign, the King of England, to take possession of that part of Nootka and its coast, to fortify it and make an establishment'. He had, of course, no warrant for claiming the specific authorisation of his Government; but otherwise he was reciting his employers' instructions.

For Martinez the affair had taken on a much more serious aspect: a permanent British settlement was about to be established in territory claimed by His Catholic Majesty. Instead of taking written evidence and referring the issue to Mexico for reference to Madrid and London, he arrested Colnett and his crew (together with the unlucky Chinese) and sent the *Argonaut, Princess Royal* and *North-West American* under guard to the port of San Blas.[45]

Ashore the British flag was hauled down and replaced by the standard of Spain, and Martinez formally proclaimed that the

---

[45] The above account of the Spanish proceedings at Nootka is based on (i) Colnett's *Journal* (ii) the diary of Martinez (iii) *Official Papers Relative to the Dispute* (Intro.) (iv) Meares's *Memorial* (v) John Etches, *An Authentick Statement of the Facts*. I have discounted the details of indignities and brutalities purveyed by Meares for propaganda purposes, but Colnett does appear to have been harshly treated. Martinez himself describes Colnett's attempt to jump overboard after being taken prisoner. The two men had quarrelled violently. The marked friendliness of Martinez towards the Americans and his participation in their celebrations of American independence roused English ire, and the temper of the Spaniard was not improved by the abusive epithets of the Indians who were alleged to have been incited thereto by their English friends. The relevant portions of the diary of Martinez are printed in translation in Howay's edition of Colnett's *Journal* (App. III).

entire coast from Cape Horn up to the line of 60° North latitude was in the possession of the Spanish Crown. The choice of this northern limit is significant. After the exploration of the Alaskan coast in 1741 by Bering and Chirikov, a Russian Company had been formed which established a number of fur-trading stations along the coast and the adjacent islands; and as the sea-otter became scarce, the traders had pushed slowly southward. Diplomatic exchanges had taken place betwen Spain and Russia and an understanding seems to have been reached that each would respect the coastal claims of the other. For some time the Russians had been intent on developing a large naval and trading base on Cook's Inlet (in latitude 60° to 61°); and soon after the Anglo-Spanish crisis they established an organised settlement there.[46]

According to the information which reached London from Mexico (by way of Madrid) in January, 1790, two vessels under Martinez had been sent by the Viceroy in 1788 'for the purpose of reconnoitering the new establishments of the Russians in the North of this Continent'. The report stated that Martinez had sailed as far north as latitude 61° and had visited the chief Russian establishment on the Island of Kodiak. A second expedition under Martinez in 1789 had been directed to investigate the situation at Nootka or San Lorenzo, as the Spaniards called it.[47] It seems probable therefore that the proclamation which

---

[46] See Charles (afterwards Earl) Whitworth to the Duke of Leeds, 2 July, 1790. After reporting a conversation during which Russian Ministers had claimed Cook's Inlet (or 'River' as it was then called) with the adjacent territory as a Russian possession, Whitworth added: 'It may perhaps be already known to your Grace that previous to the Commencement of the present war [with Turkey], it was determined to send a very considerable Force into those parts under the command of Captain Trevanion, a Lieutenant of the British Navy and one of those who had accompanied Cook in his last voyage. It was meant that he should make an establishment on Cook's River. A Town was to have been built, as well as a Dock for the Vessels, and it was intended to make this the great deposit of Commerce with the West Coast of America. The War however put a stop to this project – but I now find that they have not abandoned it' (F.O. 65 (Russia), vol. 19). On 11 Nov., 1790, he further reported to Leeds: 'I have reason to believe that this Court has admitted the exclusive right claimed by Spain to the whole of the North West Coast of America lying to the South of Cook's River. Ounalonsky, the Fox Island and others already frequented by the Russians are of course not included.' (Ibid.) It will be recalled that Meares in 1786 had found a small Russian trading station in Cook's Inlet.

[47] 'Extract of a Letter from Mexico, dated 20 August, 1789' enclosed in Merry (British Consul-General at Madrid) to the Duke of Leeds, 15 Jan., 1790 (F.O. 72/16). Leeds sent a copy of the despatch and the enclosure to the Home Dept. on 1 Feb. (H.O. 32/2). The report from Mexico gave the unlikely information that Martinez had learned in 1788 that the Russians intended to send a powerful expedition from Kamchatka to make an establishment of their own at Nootka, but it does seem to have been the case that the Viceroy's main purpose in sending Martinez to the North-West Coast in 1789 was to warn off Russians. In his Memorial to the British Government of 13 June, 1790, Count Florida Blanca stated that the Viceroys of Mexico and Peru had been informed 'that several Russian vessels were upon the point of making commercial establishments upon that coast'. The Spanish Minister continued: 'At the time that Spain demonstrated to Russia the inconveniences

Martinez made there was intended to give notice to all comers (especially Russians) that the coastal gap between the Russian settlements in and about 61° latitude and the most northerly of the Spanish posts (at Monterey on the Californian coast) was closed.

News of what had happened naturally reached the Spanish Government first by an official report from the Viceroy of Mexico. On 4 January, 1790, Anthony Merry, the British Consul-General at Madrid, reported to the Foreign Secretary that an English vessel had been seized at Nootka and that according to rumour it had been equipped to establish a settlement. Ten days later he forwarded an extract of a letter received from Mexico which described the movements of the Martinez expedition and the capture of the three vessels at Nootka, one of them 'Portuguese' and the third 'a strange vessel from London' (the *Princess Royal*).[48]

When the news was reported to the Cabinet there was general agreement that the matter must be taken up 'with a high hand', and on 7 February Leeds proceeded to do so with vigour. In a letter to the Spanish Ambassador, the Marquis del Campo, he demanded the instant release of 'the English vessel' and asserted that until this was done there could be do discussion about territorial rights.[49] The Foreign Secretary had, however, used more intemperate language than the Prime Minister relished. By laying down this condition at the outset and before the facts were properly known, Leeds committed the Administration to a tactical position which Pitt later strove to modify in spite of strong opposition in the Cabinet. When he rebuked Leeds, the latter defended himself in the following terms:

I have only written an Answer to what I conceive the most material of del Campo's letters . . . As it seemed the unanimous sense of the Cabinet that this business was to be taken up with a high hand, it occurred to me that it might not be unbecoming the Dignity of this Government to insist upon satisfaction for that insult before we enter upon any discussion whatever with the Court of Madrid upon the subject.[50]

---

attendant upon such encroachments, she entered upon the negociation with Russia, upon the supposition that the Russian navigators of the Pacific Ocean had no orders to make establishments within the limits of Spanish America, of which the Spaniards were the first possessors, (limits situated within Prince William's Streight) purposely to avoid all dissensions . . .' Russia had replied that orders had already been given to make no settlements in places belonging to other Powers, and that if any settlements had been made in Spanish America, Spain should put a stop to them in a friendly manner. (Printed in *Official Papers Relative to the Dispute* (Lond., 1790), p. 52 *et seq*.)

[48] Merry to Leeds, 4 and 15 Jan., 1790 (*F.O. 72/16*).

[49] Leeds to del Campo, 7 Feb. (*Ibid.*)

[50] Leeds to Pitt, 23 Feb. (P.R.O. 30/8/151). In Pitt's letter to Leeds (of the same date) he also rebuked him for not circulating the relevant papers before the Cabinet meeting (*Ibid.*). Pitt seems to have vacillated at this stage, for in March, as already

From now on Pitt himself drafted most despatches for Madrid
– as he was already doing with Grenville's assistance in the case
of Holland.[51] He was as tenacious as his colleagues in resisting
Spanish claims of prescriptive right, but he was not anxious to
disturb existing amicable relations with Madrid.[52] And there was
the Monarch to be considered. As with France over the Dutch
situation in 1787 George III did not conceal his reluctance to go
to war.[53] Moreover strenuous though unavailing efforts had been
made from 1786 to 1789 to negotiate an Anglo-Spanish commercial
treaty in order to promote a flow of British manufactures to
Spanish America through the ports of Spain, and that project was
resumed after the Nootka crisis was over.[54]

Meanwhile del Campo, as instructed from Madrid, assumed the
offensive. In a formal protest, sent to the Foreign Secretary on
11 February, he reported the capture of an English ship, emphasising the point that the Spanish officer concerned had himself explored the Sound fifteen years before. He also widened the issue
by condemning the incursions of whalers and other English ships
in the South Seas and called upon the British Government to
punish those responsible for planning such expeditions in order
to deter others from infringing the rights of Spain. Since the
Cabinet were in the dark about the circumstances, the reply of
February 26 was in the nature of a holding operation. The Ambassador was informed that 'the act of Violence' which he had reported
must necessarily suspend all discussion on the pretensions of right
until the vessel had been restored and proper reparation made.
Thus the principle of reparation as the prerequisite of any discussion about Spanish rights was maintained, although in more
restrained language. Some weeks later it was stated in reply to a
further letter from del Campo that when His Britannic Majesty

---

noted, Grenville drafted Instructions under which Spain would have been presented
(in due course) with a *fait accompli* in the form of an official settlement on the
North-West Coast, established and defended by H.M.S. *Discovery* and *Gorgon* and a
frigate from India with a garrison drawn from Port Jackson.

[51] There are several expressions of thanks from Leeds to Pitt in the Leeds Papers
(*Addit. MSS.*, 28,066) for being shown the drafts before they were prepared for
(his own) signature.

[52] J. Bland Burges (of the Foreign Dept.).

[53] George III to Grenville, 1 May, 1790 (*Royal Archives, Windsor*).

[54] It was hoped to secure a treaty of reciprocity on the lines of the Anglo-French
commercial treaty of 1787, but the idea was anathema to most Spaniards. The
long and tortuous negotiations can be followed in *F.O.* 72, vols. 7-15. The British
Ministry finally abandoned the project in the summer of 1792 when the Board of
Trade reported: 'It may fairly be inferred that Spain has never been sincerely
disposed to conclude a Commercial Treaty on the Basis of Reciprocity and mutual
convenience according to the Engagement taken in the 9th Article of the Treaty of
Peace of 1783 . . .' (*F.O. 72/24*). Florida Blanca, was much less rigidly traditionalist
than his colleagues, especially the Minister of Finance, Pedro de Lerena, in such
matters. (See the appraisal of him in Fitzherbert to Leeds, 5 Oct., 1790. 'Private
and Confidential.' *Royal Archives, Windsor*.)

had obtained the satisfaction demanded, he would be ready and desirous to examine charges against British subjects accused of giving cause for offence to the Governments established in any of the Spanish settlements. Moreover His Majesty would at all times be 'willing to take such measures as may restrain his subjects from interfering with the just Rights of His Catholic Majesty in any part of the World, though His Majesty cannot admit those rights should be made a foundation for claims inconsistent with the Privileges which belong to all other nations'.[55] While maintaining a stiff insistence on satisfaction for the act of violence and refusing to admit Spain's territorial pretensions by implication, Pitt was going some way towards lowering the temperature.

In Madrid the Spanish Foreign Minister was becoming uneasy. Count Florida Blanca tended to be temperamental and was an extremely difficult man to deal with in diplomatic negotiation, as Shelbourne, Fitzherbert (and Vergennes) had discovered in 1782,[56] but he had no wish for a rupture with Britain and knew well enough that Spain was in no shape for war. The stiff replies which del Campo was receiving and passing on to Madrid irritated Florida Blanca, who, having ordered the release of the ship which had been seized, had expected that the episode could be settled by routine methods without raising basic issues. He decided to ignore British denials of Spanish claims to exclusive rights in areas not actually occupied; and to Anthony Merry he expressed the hope that London 'did not really mean to make this matter an object of serious dispute'.[57]

After two months of argument over the seizure of a ship which the Spanish Government had ordered to be released it must have seemed likely that an apology and some compensation to the owners 'without prejudice' to the standpoint of either Government would settle the matter. But London was still uninformed about the details, and great issues were close to the surface. The British were buoyantly and aggressively engaged in a multiple invasion of the Pacific and its markets and were at last breaking through the walls of Spanish-American commercial monopoly. Aware of these external dangers and of a rising spirit of revolution within her western Empire, Spain was anxious to avoid trouble and yet was determined to defend her huge patrimony on the principle that any retreat might involve the loss of the whole.

---

[55] Secretary of State to Spanish Ambassador (March, 1790). Draft. (*F.O. 95/7.*)

[56] See vol. I, p. 342 *et seq.*

[57] See Merry to Leeds, 22 Feb., 22 and 29 March, 5 and 19 April, 1790 (*F.O. 72/16*). On 29 March Merry reported that in an interview Florida Blanca had 'dwelt much on the circumstance of our demanding satisfaction before any discussion had taken place of the matter of right on either side, and said from this, and above all, from the manner of our expressions he could draw no other conclusion than that it must be our Wish to make the affair in question a ground for quarrelling'.

Early in April John Meares arrived in London from China, bringing with him the materials and possibly the completed draft of his *Memorial* with its documentary appendixes. When Capt. Douglas on board the *Iphigenia* had turned up at Macao in the autumn of 1789 Meares had listened to his account of the activities of Martinez at Nootka up to the time when the *Iphigenia* had been released under orders to leave the Coast. At Meares's request Douglas produced a written statement which was sworn before the East India Company's Supercargoes at Macao and Canton. Armed with this and other information collected from the ship's crew, Meares sailed for England.

Contact with Ministers was quickly established – probably through Richard Etches – and by about the middle of April his *Memorial* was in their hands.[58] For the first time the Government learned that not one ship but four had been seized, of which three had been confiscated with their cargoes and their crews taken prisoner. There were also embellishments to the story such as that the brutal treatment received by Capt. Colnett of the *Argonaut* had driven him out of his mind – which, although one-sided, had a certain substratum of truth. More serious was the statement by Meares that he and his associates had actually established a settlement at Nootka (an assertion which will be examined at a later stage) and that Martinez had taken possession of it as a rightful possession of the Spanish Crown.

The reception of this information coincided with an uncompromising response from Spain. On 5 April Merry reported that Spanish Ministers were making soundings with a view to forming a five-Power coalition against Britain and were mobilising a fleet;[59] and then on the 20th del Campo at last delivered the official reply to the British note of 26 February. It was stated that orders had been given for the release of the arrested crews but only as an act of courtesy to the British Crown. It was assumed, del Campo went on, that the individuals concerned could only have resorted to

---

[58] See J. M. Norris, 'The Policy of the British Cabinet in the Nootka Crisis' (*Eng. Hist. Rev.*, vol. LXX, No. 277 (Oct., 1955), p. 569). Mr. Norris states that the *Memorial* was published at the Government's expense and cites a letter from Geo. Chalmers to Lord Hawkesbury (*Addit. MSS.*, 38,225, f. 313). But this letter is dated 15 Nov., 1790, i.e. after the Convention with Spain had been signed and the *Memorial* had ceased to have any political value. The *Memorial* was published on 5 May – the day when the King's message about the Nootka crisis was presented to Parliament. The cited letter from Chalmers states that Lieut. Meares had called at the Board of Trade that morning and that Chalmers had given him a message for Hawkesbury 'in as civil a manner as I could'. He went on to say that Meares had stated that he could not proceed with publication 'without the use of the largest Map, on which is traced the several Voyages, having no other compleat Copy than the one sent Yr Lordship'. This clearly refers to the publication of Meares's volume of *Voyages made in the Years 1788 and 1789*. Hawkesbury was much interested in accounts of voyages of discovery which were of commercial significance.

[59] Merry to Leeds, 5 April, 1790 (*F.O.* 72/16).

P*

those regions to carry on a commerce and make establishments in ignorance of the undoubted rights of Spain. The demand for reparation was ignored.[60] Thus Pitt's efforts to find a *modus vivendi* on the basis of an apology and compensation to the merchants, to be followed by a negotiation on specific territorial claims, were rebuffed – as indeed from the Spanish point of view was almost inevitable.

In the circumstances no British Administration dare refrain from resolute action, even if they were privately disposed to temporise, which they were not. Sixty years earlier Sir Robert Walpole had ignored the excited resentment of merchants against the 'insolence' of Spanish *guarda costas* and had refused to take official action when Capt. Jenkins had inflamed public opinion with his accounts of ill-usage and his exhibition of a severed ear; and in consequence Walpole had been driven into a war which had terminated his long and useful career. On the present occasion Meares had even more formidable propaganda material at hand than his predecessor: he represented more extensive claims; and the crisis came at a time when the British were penetrating the Pacific from all sides.

The Cabinet met on 30 April when it was decided, in view of the information received from Meares and the nature of del Campo's communication, to advise the King that a memorial should be addressed to the Court of Madrid 'demanding an immediate and adequate satisfaction for the outrages committed' and that orders should be given to fit out a squadron of ships of the line 'in order to support that demand and to be prepared for such events as may arise'.[61] A press for the manning of the fleet was ordered two days later.[62]

The majority of the Cabinet (Thurlow, Camden, Richmond and Leeds) believed that war was inevitable and were strongly opposed to long arguments which might give Spain time to collect a powerful coalition. Pitt and Grenville, on the other hand, hoped that a show of force would secure the 'satisfaction' which public opinion demanded and that a comprehensive settlement could then be negotiated in a calmer atmosphere. In forwarding the Cabinet Minute to the King, Grenville expressed the hope that the actions recommended 'may produce their effect without the necessity of Your Majesty's having recourse to those extremities which might otherwise become unavoidable'.[63] To the Lord-Lieutenant of

---

[60] Del Campo to Leeds, 20 April (*ibid*).

[61] Cabinet Minute of 30 April. The original (in Grenville's handwriting) is in the *Royal Archives, Windsor*. A copy is in *F.O. 95/7*, and a copy which Grenville made is printed in *Grenville Corr.* (*Dropmore*), vol. I, p. 579. Also printed in Harlow and Madden, *op. cit.*, p. 33.

[62] Grenville to the King, and the King to Grenville, 2 May. *Grenville Corr.*, pp. 579-80.

[63] Grenville to the King, 11.45 a.m., 1 May. *Royal Archives, Windsor*.

Ireland (the Earl of Westmorland) he wrote that a comparative estimate of the situation and strength of Britain and Spain offered 'a very flattering prospect of our being able to assert our rights without the risk and expence of war'. On the other hand the object was regarded by Spain as being of such importance that 'we must not be too sanguine in our hopes of succeeding without a contest'. 'The prospect of a war,' he added, 'is certainly in many respects a disagreeable one.'[64]

The King's Message to Parliament of 5 May (which would be drafted by Pitt himself) was firmly but carefully worded. Only two of the four vessels were claimed to be owned by British subjects and navigated under the British flag. No reference was made to the alleged establishment of a settlement at Nootka or of the territorial eviction. The circumstances were narrated and it was noted that no satisfaction had been offered and that Spain had made a direct claim 'to the exclusive rights of sovereignty, navigation, and commerce, in the territories, coasts, and seas in that part of the world'. But Pitt's previous approach to the issue was retained. It was the King's earnest wish that the wisdom and equity of the Crown of Spain would ensure the satisfaction which was due and that an arrangement might be made which would 'prevent any grounds of misunderstanding in future'. Reparation first, and then a negotiation about territorial claims. In his supporting speech Pitt again avoided any reference to a British settlement. An established British trade had been forcibly interrupted 'in places to which no country could claim an exclusive right of commerce and navigation'. Exactly the same line of argument was at that very time being maintained in the Dutch negotiations with reference to navigation and trade in the East Indies.

Pitt condemned the Spanish claim of exclusive right in the Pacific as 'absurd' and 'indefinite in its extent'. If the claim were admitted, 'it must deprive this country of the means of extending its navigation and fishery in the southern ocean' (the major consideration), and it would tend to exclude British subjects from 'an infant trade', the future extension of which could not fail to be

---

[64] Grenville to Westmorland, 3 May. 'Private and Secret.' *Grenville Corr.*, vol. I, p. 580. In this letter Grenville raised an interesting constitutional question. With regard to the situation of Ireland a war would be most inconvenient both from the point of view of the internal security of that country and of its contribution to the war effort. It would be very desirable if a militia could be established on a proper footing. On the question of Irish participation Grenville was aware that, although Ireland would be committed to belligerency by a British declaration of war, the autonomous Parliament in Dublin was at liberty to refrain from taking positive action. 'Some assistance,' wrote Grenville, 'we must naturally expect from thence in return for unlimited concessions, and I hope we shall not be entirely disappointed.' (See Westmorland's discouraging replies of 10 and 14 May. *Ibid.*, pp. 538-5.) For a study of the problem of Irish autonomy in relation to Imperial defence see vol. I, Chap. XI, of this work.

highly beneficial to British commercial interests.[65] The omission of
any reference to a British territorial claim at Nootka was immediately pounced on by Charles Fox, who had not failed to read his
copy of the Meares *Memorial*. He wished that the royal Message
had told them more than it did. Parliament ought to have been
informed what the ships in question were doing or intended to
do: 'whether they were about to make an establishment, or whether
Spain knew that we were about to make an establishment.' It was
open to question whether what had happened could not have been
foreseen or prevented.[66] He hastened to add, of course, that British
honour must be vindicated. The Opposition were equally ready to
attack on the ground that the Ministry had blundered into an
unnecessary war or (if adequate satisfaction were not secured) by
asserting they were unfit to be in charge of the nation's interests.
With the Opposition waiting to exploit a false move, with public
opinion excited by the prospect of war, and an impulsive Cabinet
in which Grenville was the only member whose judgement he
would trust, Pitt had an exceptionally difficult course to steer.

He made his dispositions quickly. Two days before the debate
on the King's Message Anthony Merry was informed that Alleyne
Fitzherbert was on his way to Madrid to take over as Ambassador.
One of the ablest of the professional diplomats had been put in
charge.[67] At the same time Merry was sent the text of a formal
representation to be given to Florida Blanca, together with a
Spanish translation of the Meares *Memorial* which had been laid
before the British Monarch. Three demands were made: immediate and adequate satisfaction for 'these repeated outrages'; compensation to the merchants for losses sustained; and that proper
measures must be taken for the future to secure British subjects in
'the unmolested enjoyment of their Commerce and Navigation in
that part of the World'. On 5 May a note in similar terms was

---

[65] *Parl. Hist.*, vol. XXVII, 76 *et seq.* Leeds's speech in the Lords, though more
fiery than Pitt's, was similarly confined to the question of reparation for the seizure
of the ships.

[66] *Ibid.*, 772-3. Burke (with his head full of the Hastings impeachment) followed
this up by declaring that ' Extent of dominion would do us no good; on the contrary if all the territories of Spain abroad were thrown into the scale of England,
he did not think it an object for a wise man to desire . . . we should be the weaker
for our accumulation of distant dominion '. (*Ibid.*, 781.) Fox repeated his anti-war
line of attack on 10 May when he demanded papers in order that the House might
learn ' whether they were likely to be plunged into a war by accident not to be
guarded against by human foresight, or through the supineness of His Majesty's
Council '. (*Ibid.*, 784-5.)

[67] Leeds to Merry, with enclosures, 4 May (*F.O.* 72/17). The original draft of the
representation to the Spanish Government is in *F.O.* 95/7. This document also
shows that Pitt and his colleagues had accepted Meares's account in full, although
they became more dubious about the details at a later stage. It was now stated that
the (attached) narrative of ' the Agent of the British Merchants trading to that
part of the Continent of America ' afforded the strongest ground for believing that
the traders had ' purchased grants of land from the natives at a time when the
said Harbour was unoccupied by any other European Nation '.

presented to del Campo,[68] and five days later the Commons voted an additional credit of £1 million towards the cost of the naval armament.[69]

Pitt's policy was fully set out in a despatch to Fitzherbert, dated 16 May, which followed him out to Madrid. Once satisfaction and reparation had been made, the Ambassador was to start negotiating a permanent and comprehensive settlement with Spain in the Pacific in order to 'do justice to the fair rights and interests of both countries and remove occasions of misunderstanding and uneasiness in future'. Spain must not again be able to claim exclusive rights in indeterminate areas. The basis of the negotiation should be: recognition and definition of the British Southern Whale and Sea fishery; the return of the factory or depot at Nootka Sound to British possession; the opening of the North-West Coast to settlement by all European nations; mutual freedom for British and Spanish subjects to trade in each other's settlements; and lastly an agreement between the two Powers that neither would permit their subjects to establish settlements in the southern extremities of South America unless a third Power intervened to do so.[70]

The concept was characteristic of Pitt, and, as already indicated, bore a striking resemblance to the plan which he, with Grenville and Dundas, was trying to effect with regard to Holland. In both cases the British tried to secure a precisely defined working arrangement which they regarded as just and reasonable: their rivals, being obstinate in retreat, thought otherwise. The Dutch were resistent because, as Leeds put it, they were determined to maintain a monopoly both in the areas which they had actually conquered and also in those 'which they mean to conquer'.

Pitt wanted a similar deal with Spain and for like reasons. His previous efforts to secure a commercial treaty had been evaded because the Spaniards feared and disliked the political and other consequences of an influx of British industrialism into their Empire. The proposals which Pitt now brought forward, that British and Spanish Colonies should be allowed to trade freely with each other, would have opened the vast Spanish-American market and removed the irritant of the British Free Port system. Similarly his demand for recognition under precise conditions of the whale fishery in the South Pacific and for 'freedom of trade and navigation' on the North-West Coast represented a determination to effect an adjustment in specific terms as between the facts of British commercial expansion and the ambiguous but extensive prescriptive rights claimed by Spain. British public opinion would insist upon satisfaction for the 'outrage' at Nootka in any case, but Pitt went

[68] Leeds to del Campo, 5 May (F.O. 72/17).
[69] Parl. Hist., vol. XXVIII, 784-5.
[70] Leeds to Fitzherbert, 16 May (F.O. 72/17).

further and demanded a settlement of the general issue as an essential step in developing an Indian-Pacific empire of trade. On their side the Spaniards, apprehensive that their ancient dominance in the New World was disintegrating, fought a rearguard action against an aggressive intrusion which in different ways was being pressed by the Anglo-Saxons on both sides of the Atlantic.

Pitt's tactic of securing an immediate apology to the Crown and compensation to the traders and then settling down to negotiate a comprehensive settlement had the advantage that the dispute about territorial right in Nootka Sound itself would be postponed and become part of the wider negotiation. But it was just this which caused angry dissension in the Cabinet. The majority contended that Spain ought to be challenged on all counts simultaneously. If the basic questions in dispute were postponed for subsequent discussion, it was argued, the terms of the initial satisfaction would have little significance, and Spain would be able to drag out the subsequent negotiations and so postpone hostilities until a time of her own choosing.

On 2 June Leeds wrote to Pitt regretting that he would not be present at Cabinet, but adding that he could not see that his presence could be of much use since he could not possibly approve of the intended method of negotiation. His letter was almost incoherent with anger and frustration and certainly inconsistent in argument; but the general ground of his opposition was clear enough. Nothing short of 'a direct unqualified satisfaction for the insult' would do, and none of the objects in dispute ought to be prejudiced by any promise on the British side with reference to later discussions 'by way of purchasing the compliance of Spain with the satisfaction demanded'. Postponement might well weaken Britain's position with regard to the Southern Whale Fishery – 'perhaps an object of full as much importance in point of national advantage as any stipulation respecting Nootka Sound itself'. After all that had been asserted on both sides war in his opinion could not be avoided without disgrace to one or other of the parties. 'I trust we are all determined not to participate in the smallest degree to that Disgrace.'[71] A Prime Minister' s lot is rarely a happy one.

[71] Leeds to Pitt, 2 June (P.R.O. 38/8/151). Leeds was doubly inconsistent. While arguing that everything should be demanded from Spain at sword point, he maintained that even if Spain gave the satisfaction demanded, 'I do not think the question of Nootka Sound determined'. But he admitted that 'Great Legal Authority' (Lord Chancellor Thurlow) thought otherwise. In other words the more logical Chancellor held that if Spain admitted in the terms of the satisfaction that her officers had been in the wrong at Nootka, she thereby acknowledged that she possessed no jurisdiction there. Florida Blanca afterwards made the same point. Leeds was also inconsistent in opposing Pitt's instructions to Fitzherbert that he must follow up the granting of the required satisfaction with further demands, 'cramming down Florida Blanca's throat, either a formal cession of Nootka Sound, or the admission of our Fishing vessels to the southward', instead of giving the Spanish Ministers 'time to breathe'. Leeds's real concern, of course, was that in

In the minds of those Ministers who opposed Pitt the operative factor was probably reflected in an outburst some weeks later by Bland Burges, the Under-Secretary in the Foreign Department: 'Before we know where we are, we shall have the Americans, and possibly the Russians, on our backs, if we lose a week in commencing the war with Spain by some vigorous and decisive stroke.'[72] He was wrong; but it does not seem to have occurred to the fire-eaters that some such stroke might well have lit the general conflagration which they wished to avoid. Pitt was obliged to modify his plan in some degree in response to pressure from his ministerial colleagues and resistance on the part of Florida Blanca, but he eventually secured the substance of what was desired in the furtherance of national policy overseas without a war, although it must be added that even his careful and temperate approach to the problem would have certainly failed if Spain could have secured the traditional support of France and the French navy.

Alleyne Fitzherbert did not reach Madrid until 9 June but on his way through Paris he had sought an interview with the French Minister, M. de Montmorin, who, while not prepared to agree that Spain had been entirely at fault over the Nootka episode, assured him that he would use all his influence with the Court of Spain to procure the redress which Britain demanded. He thereupon wrote a letter to Florida Blanca which (as Fitzherbert afterwards learned) greatly annoyed the recipient, who observed that in so clear a case he stood in no need of advice.[73] Since neither France, Russia, Austria nor the United States of America was showing much sign of responding to his overtures for active support, Florida Blanca had sent a temporising reply to the British representation of 5 May which Merry had presented (with a copy of the Meares *Memorial*) ten days later. When Fitzherbert arrived and was shown a copy of this reply (dated 4 June), he at once urged upon the Spanish Minister that it must necessarily be considered in London as falling short in every particular with regard to the 'preliminary Demand' for redress and satisfaction and that he should with-

---

these circumstances the Spanish Ministers might refuse to negotiate on the basic issues – and get away with it. As a reasoned protest by a Foreign Secretary it was not, however, an impressive document and goes far to explain why Pitt insisted on running the Foreign Department himself.

[72] Burges to Leeds, 27 June (*Leeds Papers, Addit. MSS.*, 28,066, f. 55).

[73] Fitzherbert to Leeds, 14 May. Paris (*Addit. MSS.*, 28,065, f. 364). See Bland Burges, *Continuation of a Narrative of what has passed relative to the present dispute* . . . (Lond., 1790). This and the first part of the *Narrative* are based on accurate summaries of the relevant despatches. A manuscript copy of the *Continuation* is in the Windsor Archives and both parts may have been originally compiled for George III's use as a convenient *résumé*. They were published (separately) as part of the Government's publicity campaign. Fitzherbert reported that the American envoy, Mr. Carmichael, was being 'greatly caressed at Court', but that the latter had indicated to him that there was little prospect of Washington proving responsive.

out loss of time send some more satisfactory communication.

Florida Blanca retorted that Spanish compliance with the pre-liminary demand would of necessity invalidate her claims of terri-torial right. He must therefore insist that the two discussions must proceed simultaneously and *pari passu*.[74] He also presented Fitz-herbert with a lengthy memorandum which, after reciting the events at Nootka, set out the historic claims in their fullest extent – 'the Spanish territories, navigation, and dominion on the Con-tinent of America, isles and seas contiguous to the South Sea'. On the west side of America Spain had retained her rights entire as far north as 'the borders of the Russian establishments'. With regard to the assertion in the British representation of 5 May that the King considered it as incumbent upon him to protect his subjects in the continued enjoyment of their fishery in the Pacific Ocean, Spain believed that this pretension involved trespass into ancient limits and therefore would have 'good reasons for disputing and opposing this claim'. As to satisfaction and reparation Spain would willingly afford them if it was proved that justice was not on her side, provided that England did as much if she was found to be in the wrong.[75]

This document, which had been circulated to all the Courts of Europe as a manifest of the Spanish case, amounted to a flat rejection of Pitt's plan of procedure and a denial of any British right of access along the North-West Coast or to engage in a fishery in the South Seas. Fitzherbert at once set about the uphill task of persuading Florida Blanca to give the kind of satisfaction which was customary in such cases and a *promise* of future indemnification, leaving all the larger issues for later discussion. But at his first interview he sensed that the real obstacle was a deep suspicion that Britain's real purpose was to destroy the Spanish Empire. In reporting to London he likened the Spanish Minister to Don Quixote.

He gave me to understand that he considered our sending ships to purchase skins at Nootka as a shallow artifice calculated to cover a real design of making ourselves Masters of the Trade of Mexico, that our Southern Whale Fishery covered a like design against Peru and Chili, and as to our Colony at Botany Bay that it must necessarily have been founded with a view of seconding these designs and adding to our other conquests that of the Philippines.[76]

---

[74] Fitzherbert to Leeds, 16 June (*Addit. MSS.*, 28,066, f. 29).

[75] Memorial presented by Florida Blanca to Fitzherbert, 13 June. Printed in *Official Papers Relative to the Dispute* . . . pp. 52-65.

[76] Fitzherbert to Leeds, 16 June (*Addit. MSS.*, 28,066, f. 27). ' I cannot better describe to your Grace the general turn of Count Florida Blanca's political system and ideas than by suffering him to have borrowed them from the Life and Adven-tures of his renowned countryman Don Quixote, the dreams and visions of both being precisely of the same cast and description. . . .'

It was true enough that nothing would have better pleased the merchants of London, Bristol and Liverpool and the industrialists of the Midlands and the Clyde than to become 'Masters of the Trade' of Mexico, Chile and Peru; but it was beyond the credibility of Spanish officials that the merchants and manufacturers who swayed their Government – men such as Jos. Wedgwood and Sam Enderby – preferred dividends to dominion.

After some three days of argument both by interview and correspondence Florida Blanca made an offer on behalf of his Government that the question whether Britain or Spain had been in the wrong and the form and substance of the satisfaction and reparation to be provided (by whichever Power should be adjudged the offending party) should be submitted to the arbitration of a ruling monarch in Europe to be selected by Britain.[77] In forwarding this proposal to London Fitzherbert stated that he had the strongest reason for believing that the Spanish Government were 'entirely bent upon a war with Great Britain' but were refraining from hostilities while continuing to refuse satisfaction in the expectation that Britain would resort to reprisals and so enable Spain to demand the assistance of France against an aggressor.[78] On the other hand, he went on, there were certain expressions in Florida Blanca's letter which might be taken as supporting a rumour that the Spanish Government would not now be averse to an accommodation provided that it could be done on terms not incompatible with what they considered as their point of honour; but Fitzherbert considered that this conjecture carried little weight.[79]

In London the Ministry had decided not to answer the Spanish note of 4 June in the hope that Fitzherbert's arrival in Madrid might produce something less negative. There is, of course, no record of the 'full consideration' in Cabinet which took place when his despatches arrived towards the end of the month; but it is evident that Pitt encountered opposition from those who wanted a comprehensive ultimatum and was obliged to make a concession in that direction. Following up Fitzherbert's hint, he himself (possibly assisted by Grenville) drafted a Declaration and Counter-Declaration, a Memorial for the Spanish Government, and instructions to Fitzherbert. The terms of the Memorial were forthright. The Spanish reply was unsatisfactory: Spain could have no possible

---

[77] Fitzherbert to Florida Blanca, 13 June, and the latter's reply of 15 June (printed in *Official papers Relative to the Dispute* . . . pp. 61-5). In his letter containing the offer of arbitration the Spanish Minister insisted that the Nootka episode could not be dealt with under the customary procedure because the vessels detained had been trying to form a settlement and to become masters of a port already in the possession of Spain.

[78] Fitzherbert to Leeds, 16 June (*Addit. MSS.*, 28,066, f. 31).

[79] Fitzherbert to Leeds, 16 and 19 June (*Addit. MSS.*, 28,066, ff. 31-4).

pretension to the possession of Nootka: British and other nationals had traded there for some years: an act of violence had therefore been committed which 'must be done away' before any discussion could take place. The British claim for satisfaction could no longer be delayed without producing those consequences which His Majesty sincerely wished to avoid.

The covering despatch rejected the proposed arbitration as inadmissible, and repeated Pitt's suggested method of proceeding. Then came the substantial point on which Pitt had surrendered to the Cabinet majority.

His Majesty considers that the giving the satisfaction must amount to an admission that the Court of Spain was not in possession of an actual, known and acknowledged Sovereignty and Dominion at Nootka, which could justify detaining the Ships of other nations . . . No subsequent discussion can therefore take place on this Point after the Satisfaction has been given. . . .[80]

Any other ground of claim, the despatch continued, would still be open to discussion and would in no degree be precluded by the satisfaction, but it must not be founded on the argument of possession by abstract right. The position thus taken up was a logical impossibility which Pitt had hitherto avoided. If Spain explicitly renounced at the outset her claim of sovereignty at Nootka, her case for exclusive rights along the North-West Coast up to the Russian trading depots would automatically go by the board. But Pitt had used the words 'amount to an admission', and he went on in the despatch to express the hope that Fitzherbert might be able to induce the Spanish Government to give the satisfaction demanded without inserting in the Declaration 'any words of Reference to the Claims to be afterward brought forward'. In short, he relied on the Ambassador's skill to reach agreement on a formula which the two Governments could interpret according to their respective standpoints.

The draft despatch was shown to Leeds on the night of 4 July, and he gave it a grudging and partial assent. The earlier part, he wrote, was free from the objection which he had stated in a previous letter. He had been apprehensive that this would be the ground on which the despatch 'was meant to have been drawn'. For once Leeds had his way, for his opinion represented the attitude, not only of most of the Cabinet, but of the Opposition and the generality of public opinion.[81]

---

[80] Leeds to Fitzherbert with enclosures, 5 July (*F.O.* 72/18).

[81] Leeds to Pitt, 5 July. Copy (*Addit. MSS.*, 28,066, ff. 67-8). It may be that Leeds's letter caused the despatch to be amended at the last moment, for he added: ' I cannot [believe], much less can I venture [to assert as some], I believe, are ready to do, that the giving the satisfaction demanded precludes Spain from any [claims] to Nootka Sound. . . . It seems at present we confine our claim to satisfaction for

While the British Ministry anxiously awaited the outcome of this final *démarche* which would decide the issue of peace or war, Fitzherbert in Madrid was reporting conflicting trends. On the one hand, Spanish naval preparations both in Europe and America were proceeding vigorously and public opinion in Spain expected that a rupture was imminent. On the other hand Fitzherbert began to think that Florida Blanca was showing signs of moving towards an accommodation. On 9 July he informed the Ambassador that reliable news had been received that the British fleet had sailed from Portsmouth and that the Spanish fleet had therefore been ordered to sea but with orders not to fight unless attacked.[82] On the following day the Minister invited Fitzherbert to an interview and produced in the form of some loose notes in his own hand-writing an outline plan for a comprehensive settlement. He proposed, first, that Spain should retain the exclusive possession of the North-West Coast up to and including the port of Nootka: secondly, that from Nootka up to the beginning of the Russian sphere at 61° N. Britain should share with Spain the right to trade and form establishments along a coastal strip to be defined; and thirdly, that British subjects should enjoy fishing rights in the South Sea and the Straits of Magellan and should be permitted to land and erect temporary buildings on such islands and parts of the mainland coast as should be agreed upon, but the whalers must not approach within a certain distance of any Spanish settlement. By such an arrangement, it was added, the two Powers would avoid all discussion of rights and Britain should therefore waive her demand for satisfaction, and in that event Spain would pay the full amount of the loss incurred by the owners of the captured vessels.[83]

The offer met Britain's demand for practical recognition of her commercial expansion in the North and South Pacific, but for the British Ministry to abandon the demand for satisfaction after all that had passed and to accept by implication the general principle of Spanish exclusive rights was a political impossibility; and apart from that Pitt and his colleagues were determined to get

Injury. I thought at first we had talked of Insult. In this, however, my memory may deceive me . . .' (the words in square brackets are conjectural insertions to fill gaps where the manuscript is torn). By way of indicating Spanish intransigence (and so justifying a rupture if it came) the Government had inspired a pamphlet by Alexander Dalrymple, *The Spanish Memorial of 4th June Considered* (Lond., 1790). And in August or September they published Florida Blanca's Memorial of 13 June with correspondence between him and Fitzherbert and some other documents under the title, *Official Papers Relative to the Dispute* (*ut supra*). There is a useful list of Government and Opposition pamphlets published during the crisis in J. M. Norris (*loc. cit.*), p. 574, n. 4 and 5.

[82] Grenville had sent a recommendation to the King that Admiral Barrington with twenty ships of the line which were assembled at Spithead should proceed forthwith to Torbay. (Grenville to Geo. III, 23 June. *Roy. Arch., Windsor.*)

[83] Fitzherbert to Leeds, 12 July (*F.O. 72/18*). Cf. *Continuation of a Narrative* . . .

this ancient obstacle out of the way once and for all. Fitzherbert knew this and had no option but to reject the plan as inadmissible, but he appreciated that here at last was a basis for negotiation and that since there was no longer any prospect of a supporting alliance Spain was eager for an accommodation. After much further argument Florida Blanca on 23 July agreed the wording of a Spanish Declaration and a British Counter-Declaration.[84]

Spain gave way to the extent of promising to give satisfaction to the British Sovereign 'for the injury of which he has complained', to restore the captured vessels, and to indemnify the owners. But the Spanish Minister defeated Pitt (or rather his colleagues) by insisting on putting a sting in the tail of the document: 'this declaration is not to preclude or prejudice the ulterior discussion of any right which his Majesty may claim to form an exclusive establishment at the port of Nootka'.[85] The British Counter-Declaration accepted the promise of satisfaction and reparation but without prejudice to the right of the British Crown to any establishment which his subjects 'may have formed, or shall be desirous of forming in future, at the said bay of Nootka'.

All in all it may be justly said that Florida Blanca had won on points and in spite of his lack of diplomatic or military support. The principle of prescriptive right had not been surrendered – nor was it to be in the 'ulterior discussion'. He had no reason to be apprehensive about the second stage of the argument. Nootka itself would be an awkwardness, but he had already offered to recognise the activities of the Southern Whalers (under specific limitations and safeguards) and the British right of access to the West Coast, northward of the Spanish settlements. Spain was not particularly interested either in whale-oil or sea-otter skins: it was not her métier.[86] The British tended to mock Spanish pertinacity in asserting ancient claims as an exhibition of antique pride and a blind refusal to recognise changing conditions. In fact the Court of Madrid was acutely aware of impending change. The contagion of revolution in British North America (which Spain had assisted) was spreading into Latin America and into the feudal society of France, her traditional prop and stay. Florida Blanca

---

[84] Fitzherbert, 23 July (*ibid*).

[85] The original draft Declaration which Fitzherbert forwarded to London on 25 July concludes with the following addition: *ni servir d'exempter pour les autres Domaines des Indes Espagnoles, selon la Possession, les limites et les Droits reconnus dans les Traités avec toutes les Nations et nominiser avec la Grande Bretagne.* The official English text is printed in *Parl. Hist.*, vol. XXVIII, 914-15.

[86] In 1789 the Spanish Government made an ambitious but unsuccessful attempt to establish a whaling and general fishery throughout the oceans adjoining the Spanish dominions. (See Précis of a Spanish Edict, dated 19 Sept., 1789, granting special privileges to 'The Royal Maritime Company for the Establishment of a Fishery' for twenty years from 1 January, 1790. Forwarded by Merry from Madrid. *F.O.* 95/7.)

and some of his colleagues were beginning to think that the Spanish and British monarchies had a common interest in preserving the established order; and, as will be seen, Pitt's mind was moving in the same direction. But the latter, with strong support from Grenville and Dundas, pressed for a commercial partnership, in other words, free access to Spanish colonial markets as an essential condition of political alliance. Failing that, the alternative was to promote the independence of the Latin American territories. On their side the Spanish Government understandably, though on a long view unwisely, resisted a proposal which would draw their cherished patrimony overseas into the commercial nexus of a foreign State. Britain was calling upon Spain to introduce the sort of economic revolution into the Spanish Empire which she herself had refused to contemplate with respect to her own; and Britain had the less excuse, because as the pre-eminent industrial Power she would have continued to command her colonial markets – as Spain could not hope to do.

For some reason the courier carrying Fitzherbert's important despatches of 23 and 25 July made slow going and did not reach London until 5 August. On the same day Grenville (and not the Foreign Secretary) wrote to the King congratulating him upon the signature of the two Declarations which appeared to offer 'the most favourable prospect' of a satisfactory final settlement, and stating that he proposed to publish the news at once, 'without waiting for Your Majesty's express Commands'.[87] The Bank, the Exchange and Lloyd's were at once informed, a letter was sent to the Lord Mayor of London, and the text of the Declarations was published that day in a special edition of the *Gazette*.

The Ministry naturally made the most of the fact that war had been averted and that Spain had given way to the extent of promising reparation; but the news does not appear to have evoked any great excitement and there was little speculation in the Funds.[88] Obviously the central issue in the dispute was still unresolved. The Government had in fact forced and won a general election without the advantage of having gained the diplomatic victory for which some pamphleteers were clamouring. Parliament had been prorogued on 10 June and then dissolved, and by the time that the Declarations had been signed and published the election was over.

---

[87] Grenville worked at speed. His letter to the King (*Roy. Arch., Windsor*) is dated, '5 August, 1790, 10 p.m.' His letter to the Lord Mayor was sent off at 1.30 p.m. (*Official Papers Relative to the Dispute . . . p.* 66).

[88] Cf. Horace Walpole to H. S. Conway, 9 Aug., 1790. 'So the peace is made, and the stocks drank its health in a bumper; but when they waked the next morning, they found that they had reckoned without their host, and that their majesties the King of big Britain and the King of little Spain have agreed to make peace some time or other, if they can agree upon it; and so the stocks drew in their horns: but, having great trust in some time or other, they only fell two pegs lower.' *Letters of Horace Walpole* (Lond., 1840, edn., 6 vols.), vol. VI, p. 364.

No doubt the impending dissolution of Parliament and the need to satisfy public clamour had influenced the Government's handling of the situation, particularly in the swift mobilisation of a large fleet and strong land forces. On the other hand, it says much for Pitt's supreme confidence in his personal ascendancy (reinforced by a phenomenal rise in national prosperity) that he resisted the pressure of Leeds and other Ministers to present an ultimatum in terms which would have compelled Spain to surrender her claims forthwith or go to war. If Pitt had felt insecure and at all doubtful about the result of the coming election, nothing would have been easier than to ensure that he went to the country either with a resounding diplomatic triumph or alternatively as a leader calling for support in prosecuting a war for the vindication of the national honour. At an early stage in the election returns he wrote to his mother with quiet confidence: 'upon the whole I have no doubt of our being considerably stronger than in the last Parliament'. As to the Spanish business – 'I hardly know what to conjecture of the probability of peace or war'.[89]

As Fitzherbert was well aware, the signing of the British and Spanish Declarations on 24 July represented no more than clearing the first hurdle: the toughest part of the exercise was still to do, for questions of abstract rights could no longer be evaded. The Spanish tactic for obvious reasons was to make such concessions as could not be avoided in as generalised a form as possible, while the British tried to insist on precision at all points. Florida Blanca had already indicated his willingness to concede some degree of trading access to the North-West Coast and to recognise the right of British whalers to fish in the South Seas, but he balked at a

---

[89] Pitt to Lady Chatham, 24 June, 1790. Stanhope, *Life of Pitt*, vol. II, p. 53. Mr. J. M. Norris in his article, 'The Policy of the British Cabinet in the Nootka Crisis' (*loc. cit.*) makes (for the first time) the useful point that the British Administration handled the Spanish crisis under the pressure of an impending general election; but it is going much further than the evidence warrants, in my view, to state that the Government was far more concerned in the spring of 1790 with the forthcoming dissolution and the danger of a resurgence of the Opposition than with overseas affairs (p. 566) and that Pitt realised that he must negotiate an agreement acceptable to the new Parliament 'or face political annihilation' (p. 574). There is no reference, so far as I am aware, in any of the personal correspondence between Ministers which links the conduct of the Spanish negotiations with the impending elections. Pitt himself had no doubts about the electoral verdict. As Lord Stanhope states: 'There was little of popular excitement in the new elections. It was felt by the nation at large that when Pitt had declared earlier in the Session that "we are adding daily to our strength, wealth and prosperity", he had uttered no vain or empty boast. . . . Under the impression of these feelings the triumphant Ministerial majority which the old elections had given was more than confirmed by the new.' (*Life*, pp. 51-2.) And that verdict was given before the Spanish Government had made any concessions to British demands. There were occasional differences among the divers groups which supported Pitt, but there was no sign of a resurgence on the part of the Opposition whose treatment of the King during his first mental illness in 1788 and of his chosen Minister had caused widespread resentment.

formal rendition of Nootka Sound as a British 'possession', and he was determined to keep the whalers right away from the South American coasts where he believed that the pursuit of whales was an excuse for engaging in illicit trade with the Spanish settlements. On the other side the British Ministers could not afford to give way on either issue. The former not only comprised the 'satisfaction' originally demanded, for which, if refused, they were committed to go to war, but also involved the principle of freedom to form establishments in areas not already occupied by other European Powers. Similarly the Southern Whale Fishery was regarded as an important national enterprise. Its right to exist had been challenged (unwisely) by del Campo in his original counter-protest, and Enderby and his associates had long been pressing Hawkesbury and the Board of Trade for the formal occupation of an island base and for permission to enter South American ports for fresh water, provisions and repairs. The need for such facilities in the case of whaling voyages which often lasted for three years was urged by Enderby in letters to Pitt in the course of the negotiations; but Pitt had no need to be reminded of the importance of the Southern Whale Fishery in the development of British oceanic commerce and the powerful support which it enjoyed. When the Anglo-Spanish Convention came to be debated in the Commons, Charles Fox criticised its inadequacy but quoted with approval the statistics which the Government had laid on the table showing that the produce of the Fishery had risen in five years from £12,000 to £97,000. ' This estate we had, and were daily improving; it was not to be disgraced by the name of an acquisition.'[90]

In September Florida Blanca presented a Counter-Project consisting of four Articles which made concessions in vague terms, evaded the retention of Nootka, recognised the whale fishery but prohibited any landing, and provided that any alleged infractions of these arrangements (which were bound to be numerous) should be settled by discussion. The British Cabinet rejected these propositions as inadmissible on the ground that they settled nothing definitively and referred questions to subsequent negotiation, whereas His Majesty was determined to leave nothing open to discussion.

The great object which His Majesty has had in view . . . is that of effectually securing the rights and interests of his subjects from being questioned hereafter, and of removing all causes of Misunderstanding between the two Courts.[91]

The fleet was ordered to put to sea, and Fitzherbert was in-

---

[90] *Parl. Hist.*, vol. XXVIII, 990 (14 Dec., 1790).
[91] Leeds to Fitzherbert, 2 Oct., 1790 (*F.O. 72/19*). Cf. Burges to Auckland, 30 Sept. (*Addit. MSS.*, 34,433, f. 198).

structed to present an ultimatum. The European situation, he was told, could not allow of 'any further delay'. Yet the rupture did not happen, and the Minister and the Ambassador in Madrid continued their game of diplomatic chess for almost another month. Although the prospect of war was obviously very close, there was a curious undertone of confidence on both sides, not only that a peaceful settlement would be reached, but that it would be followed by a political alliance and a commercial partnership – on lines not dissimilar from Pitt's plan for an overseas partnership between Britain and Holland.

On the same day that Fitzherbert was sent instructions to deliver an ultimatum Leeds wrote him a personal letter: 'I sincerely hope that, however threatening appearances may be at present, the conclusion may be as agreeable as surprising, and the Drama, which is already historical, [may] keep clear of a Tragic Denouement and, like the Beggars Opera, end . . . with a wedding.'[92] On 5 October Fitzherbert reported a conversation with the Spanish Minister in which the latter had dilated upon the infinite difficulties with which he had to contend in trying to induce his colleague, Pedro de Lerena, the Minister for Finance, to modify any part of his commercial system; but after much argument he had 'finally obtained his Consent to certain fundamental points of a commercial connection with England'.[93]

At last on 28 October the two plenipotentiaries signed an Anglo-Spanish Convention. The concession which now made agreement possible and had stuck so long in Spanish throats was the restoration of 'the buildings and tracts of land' on the North-West Coast of which British subjects had been dispossessed' in April, 1789. The validity of the British claim in that regard will be considered shortly. The previous promise to pay compensation for losses incurred by the British traders at Nootka was confirmed, but in the event Spain fended the business off for three years until it became lost in the exigencies of war when Spain joined the coalition against Jacobin France. Richard Etches, Meares and their associates did not receive a dollar.[94]

---

[92] To Fitzherbert, 2 Oct. (*Addit. MSS.*, 28,066, f. 285).

[93] Fitzherbert to Leeds, 5 Oct. (*F.O. 73/19*).

[94] During the summer of 1790 Meares bombarded Grenville and Under-Secretary Nepean with letters and memorials purveying news items about later events on the North-West Coast and pressing the claims of himself and his associates for compensation for losses. The friction between the Etches and the Meares groups which had begun in China flared into open dispute in London on the question of the proportion of the compensation money which each group was to receive (Meares to Grenville, 29 June. *F.O. 95/7*). On 7 Sept. Meares presented to Grenville 'A Recapitulation and General Account of the Losses and Damages sworn to have been sustained by the United Company of British Merchants Trading to the North West Coast of America by the Capture of their Vessels and the being dispossessed of their Settlements . . .' (*ibid.*). The actual loss from the capture of the ships was put at £106,322 and the probable loss arising from the interruption of the

The arrangement about the North-West Coast followed the lines previously suggested. British as well as Spanish subjects were to be free to trade without molestation and to form establishments anywhere along the coast to the north of the parts already occupied by Spain. As already noted, the Southern whalers were accorded the facilities which had been demanded, but the Spanish Minister secured a proviso which he and his colleagues rated highly. Britain engaged to take effective measures to prevent the Fishery in the South Seas from 'being made a pretext for illicit trade with the Spanish settlements', and for that purpose the whalers were barred from fishing within ten leagues of any parts of the coasts already occupied by Spain. Pitt (unlike Hawkesbury) did not regard that as important, for he was bent on securing free access to the Spanish-American markets by a treaty of commercial reciprocity, or failing that by encouraging a war of Spanish-American independence.

Florida Blanca also had his way on another point to which he and his Government attached great importance, that is to say, the omission from the Convention of any geographical demarcation of the limits of Spanish sovereignty. Britain had objected strongly, for example, that the term 'Coast of California' was 'a very vague expression and not easily definable'. And what exactly was the extent of the territories 'already occupied by Spain' along the east and west coasts of South America and the islands adjacent? The British Government had no desire to found colonies of settlement in those regions, but one of their prime objects was to secure for British whalers and traders the right of free access to coastal regions and islands where the writ of Spanish jurisdiction did not run. Shortly after the text of the Convention reached London Pitt was so dissatisfied with Florida Blanca's rejection of his demand for precise demarcation that he was inclined to open a fresh negotiation to secure it, but Leeds dissuaded him.[95] When (in December)

---

trade in 1790 and 1791 was estimated at about £258,000. No progress was made and in August, 1792, Meares wrote bitterly of 'the subtility of Spain' in evading the commitment. By then the sum hoped for had dwindled to £50,000 (Meares to Sir Ralph Woodward, 31 Aug., 1792. *Ibid.* Cf. J. Jackson (at Madrid) to Grenville, 5 Nov. (*F.O.* 72/25). On 4 Dec. Jackson reported to Grenville that there was no likelihood of the proposed £50,000 being obtained. (*Ibid.*)

[95] Leeds to Pitt, 21 Nov., 1790 (*Addit. MSS.*, 28,066, f. 347). 'Florida Blanca, having thought proper to prefer the Mode adopted in that Instrument to that of settling the Limits by Demarcation, will probably be induced by the same motives to object to any specific boundary to the Spanish Dominions in America being established.' Leeds added that in the probable event of British subjects navigating within the stipulated distance of a Spanish settlement, the Spaniards would of course complain of an infraction of the Convention: the *onus probandi* would lie with them and the discussion would go forward in a regular manner. 'We may then lament their not having adopted the Plan of Demarcation in the first instance.' But to reopen the question so soon after the signing of the Convention would amount to an admission by Britain that the agreement was 'not completely adequate to its professed purpose'. Leeds, of course, was right; but Pitt had been intent on avoiding such wrangles for the future.

the Convention was debated in the Commons the Opposition fastened on this lack of territorial definition, and Fox declared that the Convention for that reason had achieved nothing, since the British right to trade and navigate in the South Seas was already an established fact. To that Dundas retorted that previous boundaries were impracticable.

We are not contending for a few miles, but a large world. . . . We did not insist on any right to invade the colonial rights of other nations in order to extend our Commerce; but the spirit of commercial adventure in this Country was unbounded.[96]

If the Spanish Minister could have been present, he would have nodded a bitter assent. By omitting any territorial demarcation the Convention became a compromise between the doctrine of ' effective occupation ' and the Spanish claims of prescriptive right. The question of how far and with what degree of validity the British claims were based on effective occupation has been the subject of controversy. The broad issue is clear enough. Britain was engaged in a commercial invasion of the Pacific from every quarter, and when the seizure of British ships and crews at Nootka was followed by a claim that the Southern Whalers were guilty of trespass, the Administration had no option but to take up the challenge in order to compel Spain to accept a more realistic interpretation of her ancient pretensions in view of rapidly changing circumstances.

The only effectual way of countering the Spanish claim to the exclusive possession of the North-West Coast (up to 61° N.) was to demonstrate that British subjects had actually formed an establishment there and to insist upon the traditional British argument that this constituted a valid title, transcending claims of prescriptive right which were not so supported by occupation. The argument was fortified by the fact that Spain had recognised the legality of the Russian trading stations which had been established along the Alaskan Coast. If, therefore, Nootka Sound was to be a successful test case, there must be clear evidence that Meares and his trading associates had actually established a permanent depot there (and possibly at other places too) before the Spaniards evicted them. The evidence available to Pitt and his colleagues consisted of information provided by John Meares and the sworn depositions of Capt. Colnett; but the latter were confined to the course of events after the arrival of Martinez and the Spanish ships. All, therefore, turned on the witness, Meares, and he was given to adorning a tale when the occasion seemed to require it. Apart from his published *Memorial* it is not known what he may have said to Ministers at the outset of the crisis. Fortunately, however, there is a full

---

[96] *Parl. Hist.*, vol. XXVIII, 979.

record of what he did say to the Cabinet under oath after the Convention had been signed, and there is no reason to suppose that he took the gratuitous risk on this later occasion of deviating from his original account.

On the 8, 11 and 13 February, 1791, the full Cabinet (as Privy Councillors) assembled and spent three lengthy sessions in listening to Meares's account of activities on the North-West Coast and in questioning him.[97] The reason for this exceptional procedure was that the Instructions for Commander George Vancouver's voyage to the Coast were being prepared and there was uncertainty as to what exactly were 'the buildings and tracts of land' at Nootka which he was to receive back on behalf of the British Crown from the Spanish representative. On the first day Meares described his original voyage from Calcutta to the Coast in 1786. He had, he said, entered Cook's River (or Inlet) in latitude 61° to examine the possibilities of trade 'and of fixing a post there if found expedient'. But on discovering a Russian trading station he had departed. He described his wintering in a part of Prince William's Sound which he named Sutherland's Cove, how he had built a house ashore for the carpenter and other artificers and had made an agreement with a local chief for an exclusive trade with his people. But he played down the importance of this first voyage. 'I made no settlement', he stated, 'except the House in Sutherland's Cove is to be called one.'

Had Meares established one or more trading posts in 1788, which was the operative occasion? He maintained that he had and gave details. In Nootka Sound he had given the local Indian chief 'considerable Presents for leave to build a House, which was erected by the joint labour of my People and the Natives, who were paid for their Services'. About an acre of land about the house had been enclosed with a fence and ditch. The house could accommodate about thirty-five people and was situated some 400 yards from the Indian village. The house was built of wood, some of which had been brought on board the ships and the rest obtained on the spot. In the village itself a vegetable garden had been planted. While the *Iphigenia* and the *Felice* explored the coast to the north and south a party was left behind to build a 50-ton vessel (the *North-West American*) for which frames and moulds had been previously made on board. The working party had been put under the protection of the two local chiefs, Maquilla and Callicum 'who accepted of the trust'. Meares made no reference on this occasion to hoisting the British flag, but he insisted as before that he had

---

[97] *Privy Council Register (P.C. 2/135).* Meeting on 8 Feb., pp. 439-44; on 11 Feb., pp. 447-50; on 13 Feb., pp. 450-53. Those present (on all three occasions) were – Pitt, Lord Chancellor Thurlow, Earl Camden (Lord President), the Marquis of Stafford (Lord Privy Seal), the Duke of Leeds, and Lord Grenville.

taken formal possession at Nootka. The practical difficulty was to ascertain the exact area involved.[98]

Continuing his discourse Meares recounted how at several places along the coast he had 'purchased' long-houses from the local chiefs to be used as trading posts if he returned. On this Ministers questioned him closely. He was asked for exact details about these purchases. Had he occupied them on more than one occasion? 'Did you leave any Person in possession of the Houses you purchased or any Flag flying or other sign of possession?' To which he replied: 'I did not.' Apart from Friendly Cove in Nootka Sound the only place where he claimed to have formed a permanent factory in agreement with the local chief was at a spot which he had named Fort Cox, fifty miles to the southward. These two territorial claims were duly forwarded to Madrid and were entered in Florida Blanca's instructions to the officer who was to carry out the formal rendition.

Upon what grounds did Pitt and his colleagues base their case against the Spanish claim of exclusive and prescriptive right? The answer appears to be clear enough if their attitude on this occasion is compared with their policy during the same period in the South Pacific, the Indian Ocean and the Indonesian Archipelago. Their insistence throughout was on the natural right to 'freedom of trade and navigation' in all oceans and in all places where no European Power had established effective jurisdiction. That was the traditional attitude of a small sea-faring people; but in the late 18th century the 'unbounded spirit of commercial adventure', as Dundas called

---

[98] In describing the arrival of the American sloop, *Washington*, he told how he had gone on board the vessel and acquainted the commander, Capt. Gray, that he had made an establishment there. Gray had thereupon formally asked leave to enter the harbour to refit, 'thus acknowledging us as Proprietors of the soil' (*P.C.* 2/135, p. 450). When in Sept., 1792, Capt. Vancouver found that the Spanish representative was not prepared to hand over anything except the rocks which fringed Friendly Cove, he questioned one Robert Duffin who had been an eyewitness of Meares's proceedings in 1788 and Duffin made a sworn statement. Therein he declared: 'Mr. Meares accompanied by myself and Mr. Robert Funter our 2d officer, went on shore and treated with the said Chiefs for the whole of the land that forms Friendly Cove in his Britannick Majesty's name. He accordingly bought it of them for 8 or 10 sheets of copper and several other trifling articles. The Natives were fully satisfied with their agreement. . . . The British flag was displayed on shore at the same time, and those formalities were used as is customary on such occasions – and not the Portuguese Flag, as has been insinuated by several people who were not present at the time. . . . The Chiefs, with their subjects, offered to quit the Cove intirely and reside at a place called Tashees and leave the place to our selves, as entire masters and Owners of the whole Cove and lands adjacent. Consequently we were not confined merely to that spot, but had full liberty to erect a House in any other part of the Cove. . . . On Mr. Meares's departure, the House was left in good condition, and he enjoined Maquilla to take care of it untill his return or any of his associates on the coast again. It has been reported that on the arrival of Don Jose Esteven Martinez in the Cove, there was not the least vestige of the House remaining. However that might be I cannot say, as I was not at Nootka at the time.' (Printed in Godwin, *Life*, App., pp. 213-15.) The punctuation has been modernised.

it, caused special attention to be paid to the establishment of oceanic trading posts and naval bases at strategic points. The principles followed in such cases are well illustrated in the case of the Andaman Islands. On that occasion Commodore Cornwallis was instructed to establish a naval station in one of the excellent harbours there: he was to secure the free assent of the native people (a necessary precaution if the expense of a strong garrison was to be avoided); and if the Austrians were found to be still there, he must respect their rights and find some other good harbour in the vicinity. Free access with territorial rights limited to the area actually occupied.[99] Similarly the long negotiations with the Dutch had centred on the struggle between the Dutch determination to keep the British entirely out of Indonesia and the British insistence that they had every right to sail, to trade, and in order to trade to establish factories among the island groups eastward of the Moluccas. The Dutch feared (as Dundas pointed out) that a commercial connexion of that sort would fortify the native peoples to resist the advance of Dutch conquest, just as the Spanish Government feared that the opening of the Spanish-American markets would undermine metropolitan control. Both fears were well justified.

When the Nootka storm suddenly blew up, the Pitt Administration perforce sprang to the defence of the national honour. But that apart, Pitt's tactics conformed to the general pattern of British overseas policy at the time. The major concern was to compel Spain to recognise the navigational rights of the Southern Whalers. The maritime fur-trade along the North-West Coast was, as Pitt said, ' an infant trade'. It needed, first of all, guaranteed access to the coast, and it also required a number of *pieds-à-terre* for the bartering and collecting process, just as it needed marketing facilities in China. As already noted, the Ministry had themselves intended to establish a garrison post to protect the trade at a strategic point. Neither the merchants of London, Bombay and Calcutta who planned their several and parallel enterprises, nor the British Government, were thinking in terms of establishing the sovereignty of George III over long stretches of the American coast. The factory at Bencoolen was not thought of as conveying sovereignty over the coastlands of Sumatra, nor had Dalrymple's unfortunate settlement at Balambangan been considered as a title to exclusive rights along the northern coast of Borneo.

British ships had been detained or ordered away from forbidden coasts before. But in this instance the general issue of access to a closed coast was identified with the claim that a particular place had been rightfully occupied. From the British point of view a specific act of occupation had been proved, although the circum-

---

[99] See Chap VI, p. 363 above.

stances were not as full and precise as could have been wished.[100] The arrangements which Meares had made with local chiefs in 1788 were clearly *ad hoc* and not officially authorised. On the other hand the original plans of the Etches Company, which had been examined and approved by the Board of Control and the Directors of the East India Company, had explicitly stated that permanent trading posts were to be established, and the expedition under Capt. Colnett in 1789 had been organised under the aegis of that Company and had been specially equipped for that purpose. Martinez had felt impelled to take drastic measures, as his Diary indicates, just because the visitors from China were (on their own admission) engaged in constructing a permanent trading station.

The British case was not complete, for a frustrated attempt could not of itself constitute 'effective occupation' unless it was followed up,[101] but enough had been done to assert the *right* to occupy, and the forcible denial of that right by Spain constituted the issue. When by the terms of the Convention Spain agreed to 'restore' a tract of land of which British subjects had been 'dispossessed', the whole stretch of coast between the most northerly Spanish post (at Monterey) and the most southerly of the Russian trading stations (at Cook's Inlet) was automatically thrown open to all nations. The right to trade and establish supporting factories – at Nootka or anywhere else within those limits – had been conceded. Hence the Spanish Government's prolonged resistance to the demand, for it involved an abandonment of the cherished principle of prescriptive right. On their side Pitt and his colleagues opposed this claim with the traditional British argument that sovereignty, conveying exclusive right, was not established until there had been effective occupation. It was not an argument which the British were entirely consistent in applying to themselves (as, for example, the seasonal use of the Newfoundland shore in earlier times or the wide territorial claims of the Hudson's Bay Company); but the counter-claim in 1790 that the North-West Coast was open to all comers was not an *ad hoc* expedient, thought up for the occasion. In the process of establishing networks of maritime commerce under the impulsion of a growing industrialisation, the Pitt Administration were contending for the principle of 'freedom of trade and navigation' in every ocean.[102]

As soon as the Convention was signed Britain and Spain both

---

[100] See the Note at the end of this Chapter.

[101] See W. R. Manning, *The Nootka Sound Controversy* (Annual Rept. of the Am. Hist. Assocn. for 1904. Washington, 1905).

[102] J. M. Norris (*loc. cit.*, pp. 579-80) contends that the British purpose in demanding free access for all nations was 'to give a gloss of respectability to a ruthless act of expropriation', and that 'the decision to commit that act was not occasioned primarily by a desire to correct injustice, still less by a coherent theory of imperial ambition'.

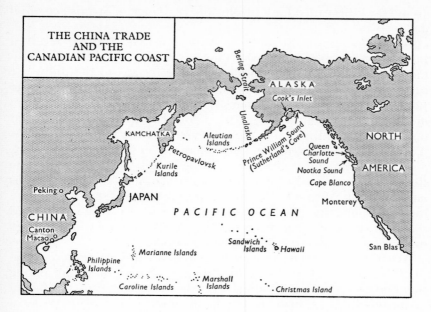

began to think in terms of an alliance, and in spite of the fact that they had so recently been on the edge of war. Florida Blanca, with his eyes on the ominous developments beyond the Pyrenees, was looking to a political and military compact. Pitt, on the other hand, was much more interested in reviving his plan for an Anglo-Spanish treaty of commercial reciprocity on similar lines to that negotiated in 1787 with France. For Pitt the Nootka crisis had been a dangerous episode which had to be handled with firmness and caution in order to clarify the status of British commercial expansion in the Pacific. When that was out of the way, he sought to resume the trade negotiations which Sir Robert Liston had been conducting in Madrid between 1786 and 1788.[103] His object was to secure a mutual lowering of tariffs which would enable British manufactures to flow into Spain and thence (through lawful channels) into Spanish-America. London merchants trading to Spain naturally pressed for it, but Spanish merchants would also have greatly benefited and the Spanish Government would have been relieved to a large extent of the vexations arising from the British use of Free Ports and 'hovering' ships. But the proposition (which would have been greeted with enthusiasm by Elizabethan

---

[103] As already noted, Florida Blanca had informed Fitzherbert that he was doing his best to further the idea of a commercial treaty even before the Convention was signed (p. 457 above.) A month after the Convention definite moves towards a treaty of alliance were made. The Spanish Government wanted it, but were hesitant in case the royal authority in France was re-established, and in that event Spain would not wish to break the Family Compact (Fitzherbert to Leeds, 28 Nov., 1790. F.O. 72/20).

John Hawkins) called for a revolutionary change in Spanish colonial policy.

In August, 1791, Fitzherbert (now Lord St. Helens) received instructions to start negotiations for a combined political and commercial alliance. On the commercial side he was to re-submit the previous proposals in order that the Ministry might be able to judge 'how far it is in any manner practicable to conclude a commercial arrangement with Spain'.[104] But the Spanish Minister did not like this linking of a trade agreement with a political alliance. The former would require a considerable length of time to work out, and meanwhile 'the two Courts would be deprived of the Benefits to be expected from the political union'.[105] Five months later a Counter-Project for a commercial treaty was sent to London, but St. Helens thought that much of it was inadmissible and added that Florida Blanca had been replaced by D'Aranda, who was even more reluctant about it than his predecessor.[106]

Alarm and indignation over developments in France were drawing the European Powers together, divided though they were among themselves. In February, 1793, St. Helens was sent back to Madrid to negotiate 'a permanent system of alliance', or failing that a preliminary understanding. Yet so important in British estimation was the gaining of access to the markets of the Spanish Empire that even at this stage of European affairs Pitt strove to make an alliance conditional upon a trade agreement. 'His Majesty's Servants continue in the opinion that no permanent alliance with Spain can be entered into without including the commercial points on which Your Excellency is already fully instructed.'[107] St. Helens reported that he was given repeated assurances that it was the earnest wish of the Spanish Government 'to form the proposed commercial System on the most comprehensive basis' and thereby remove all the grievances of which British merchants complained; but he noted that discussion of practical details was avoided.[108] War supervened and the project died. The support of British sea-power was important in the struggle with French Jacobinism, but Spain was not, and never had been, prepared to take the suicidal step, as she regarded it, of opening her Empire to British industry.

Between the peace treaties of 1783 and the outbreak of Europe's war with the revolution bred by France the exuberant expansion of Britain's empire of trade pressed hard on the territorial Empire of Spain. The outcome of the episode in Nootka Sound represented a diplomatic acknowledgement of British penetration into the

---

[104] Grenville to St. Helens, 26 Aug., 1791. A set of the Leeds/Liston correspondence covering the previous negotiation was sent for information (F.O. 72/22).

[105] St. Helens to Grenville, 15 Sept. Ibid.

[106] To Grenville, 28 Feb., 1792 (F.O. 72/23).

[107] To St. Helens, 8 and 15 Feb., 1793 (F.O. 72/26).

[108] To Grenville, 25 March, 1793 (ibid.).

North and South Pacific, and the abortive negotiations for an Anglo-Spanish commercial compact represented a phase in a sustained and eventually successful effort to gain commercial entry into South America. In the same years that Lord St. Helens was pressing Spanish Ministers in Madrid to open their doors to British goods, another ambassador of Britain, Lord Macartney, was seeking out the Manchu Emperor in the hope of inducing him to grant direct access to the still wider market of the Celestial Empire for the ingenious manufactures of the Western barbarians.

The new maritime fur trade on the North-West American Coast became the meeting place of two distinct spheres of trade expansion – one concerned with the Pacific Ocean and the other with the North American Continent. As originally planned in London, Bombay and Calcutta the trade in sea-otter skins was to be a trans-Pacific affair, an American adjunct to the China.trade. As it turned out, however, this sea approach to the west side of North America became absorbed by the territorial fur trade which was spreading westward from the St. Lawrence and Hudson Bay. Thus the oceanic enterprise which occasioned the Nootka episode contributed to the creation of British Columbia and to the emergence of Canada as a Pacific as well as an Atlantic Power. This chapter may fitly conclude, therefore, with a summary of later events in connection with the North-West Coast from these two aspects, both of which are of essential significance in the evolution of the Second Empire.

The need to send out a British officer to receive the formal surrender of the site at Nootka was the occasion for resuming the project of sending *Discovery* to explore the Coast, which had been interrupted by the crisis. The close similarity of the objects of the voyage as stated in 1789 and now in 1791 is a further indication of the continuity of British policy in that region before and after the dispute with Spain. On 11 February, 1791, Grenville sent directions to the Admiralty Commissioners who cast them in the form of Instructions, which were issued to Capt. Vancouver on 8 March.

The sloop *Discovery*, accompanied by the brig *Chatham*, were to proceed forthwith to the Hawaiian Islands where they were to winter and carry out a further survey of the group. It was hoped that it would be possible within a few months to send out more precise details about the tract of land to be restored by Spain at Nootka; but if the vessel carrying these later instructions had not arrived by the end of January, 1792, Vancouver was to proceed without further delay to survey the coast of North-West America between latitudes 60° and 30° North. Two 'principal objects' were to be kept in view. The first of these was to acquire accurate information with regard to the nature and extent of any water communication 'which may tend in any considerable degree to facilitate an intercourse for the purposes of Commerce between the North-West Coast and the Countries upon the opposite side of the Continent which are inhabited or occupied by His Majesty's Subjects'.

It will be noted that the Tudor objective of an open sea passage between the Pacific and the Atlantic had been reduced to the more realistic aim of finding a connected system of inlets and rivers linking the two oceans. This was partly due to the negative results of Cook's third voyage and partly to the increasing knowledge of rivers and lakes in the North-West which enterprising Canadian fur traders were collecting and passing on to London. 'It would be of great importance if it should be found that by means of any considerable inlets of Sea or even of large Rivers communicating with the Lakes in the interior of the Continent, such an intercourse . . . could be established.' Since this was the principal purpose of the coastal survey Capt. Vancouver was given a considerable degree of discretion, but in general he was not to pursue an inlet or river beyond the point where it appeared to be navigable by vessels of such burthen as might safely navigate the Pacific Ocean. Particular attention should be given to 'the supposed Straits of Juan de Fuca' between 48° and 49° North latitude which the American sloop *Washington* was said to have entered in 1789.[109] 'The discovery of a near communication between any such Sea or Strait and any River running into or from the Lake of the Woods, which is commonly laid down nearby in the same latitude would be particularly useful.'

If such an inlet or river was not discovered, Vancouver was to follow up an alternative, though less attractive, possibility further north on the Alaskan coast, that is to say, Cook's 'River'. 'There appears the greatest probability that it will be found that this River rises in some of the Lakes already known to our Canadian Traders and to the Servants of the Hudson's Bay Company.' But, it was added, the discovery of any similar communication more to the southward (and avoiding the Arctic regions) 'would be much more advantageous for the purposes of Commerce' and should therefore be given a preferable attention.

Two summers were to be devoted to the coastal survey and during the intermediate winter the ships were to complete their examination of the Hawaiian Islands. If time permitted, Vancouver was to undertake a further survey for the benefit of the Southern Whalers: he was to examine the west coast of South America from the southern end of Chiloe Island in 44° South

---

[109] This instruction seems to have been inserted as the result of repeated assertions of Meares about the importance in this connexion of the Strait and of the activities there (which he greatly exaggerated) of the American sloop *Washington*. (See Memorials of Meares to Grenville, 4 and 20 July, 1790, *F.O. 95/7*.)

latitude towards Cape Horn in order to ascertain the most southerly of the Spanish settlements on that coast 'and what Harbours there are south of any such Settlement'. If any Spanish vessel engaged in exploration was encountered, Vancouver was to offer 'a free and unreserved' exchange of all plans and charts of discoveries made.[110]

After a voyage lasting more than four and a half years the *Discovery* and *Chatham* came safely home in 1795. Vancouver had completed a magnificent undertaking. The vast stretch of the North-West Coast had been surveyed and charted – in his own phrase – with scrupulous exactness, and in addition a survey had been made of parts of the coast of south-west Australia and New Zealand. By the time of his return England had been immersed in war for some two years and there was no sign of an end to it. The plan of March, 1790, under which a survey of the coast was to have been followed up by establishing a garrisoned base for the protection and promotion of the maritime fur trade was not pursued. The search for a waterway, or a series of waterways, connecting the Atlantic with the Pacific continued with unremitting vigour, but it was a land and not a sea enterprise, undertaken by Canadian fur-traders travelling by canoe and on foot from the St. Lawrence into the North-West. It was this territorial movement which eventually absorbed the fur trade of the Pacific coast, drawing consignments of pelts by way of Montreal and Hudson Bay to London, and extinguishing the ocean trade between the Coast and Canton. Nootka Sound (or some similar location) did not become a permanent outpost of the China trade nor a half-way house between Canton and London.

Richard Etches and his partners had hoped that a successful beginning would enable them to launch a chartered Company which, with adequate capital, would have established a regular system of trans-Pacific trade, underpinned by an intermediate base for re-fitting and refreshment in the Hawaiian Islands and a number of permanent collecting depots along the Coast similar

---

[110] Draft Instructions from Grenville to the Admiralty, 11 Feb., 1791 (*H.O. 28/8*, pp. 17-24. Extracts printed in *Brit. Col. Dev.*, pp. 40-43). The formal instructions were issued by the Admiralty to Vancouver on 8 March. (Printed in Vancouver, *A Voyage of Discovery . . .*, vol. I, Intro., p. xv *et seq*.) They follow Grenville's draft almost *verbatim*, although occasionally the phrasing is condensed. Quotations in the text are taken from the Grenville draft. It seems probable that the original composer of the document was Alexander Dalrymple, for the directions correspond with the plans which he had been advocating in official memoranda and published pamphlets and he was at this time completing the publication of his great collection of charts of the North-West Coast. No one in Grenville's office could have possessed the specialised knowledge of the maritime and territorial exploration of North America upon which the instructions are based. Sir Joseph Banks was also actively concerned and was evidently consulted in the planning of it, for another version of the draft instructions is among his papers. (Printed in *Hist. Recs. of N.S.W.*, vol. I, Pt. ii, pp. 451-4.)

in function to those of the Hudson's Bay Company inland. David Scott had hoped to induce the East India Company to undertake the enterprise itself. After the Anglo-Spanish crisis private traders entered the field with vigour and success, but British traders were obliged to operate under the Company's restrictive control which imposed heavy handicaps in relation to American competition. Traders from Boston enjoyed the further advantages of a shorter haul, cheaper ships, and more economical outfits. Had it been practicable, the British traders would have been in a stronger competitive position, as later developments showed, if they could have functioned in the China market as subsidiaries of the Hudson's Bay Company.

The American ships which had been present in Nootka Sound when the seizures took place were quickly followed by others, and the fur trade of the North-West Coast soon became and continued for forty years to be 'Boston's high school of commerce'.[111] The following figures indicate the changing situation:[112]

Years	British Vessels	American Vessels
1785-1794	35	15
1795-1804	9	50
1805-1814	3	40

The maritime trade as a whole reached its zenith about the turn of the century, but the Americans had also to come and go by way of Cape Horn; and they in their turn were ousted in consequence of a new development. When fur traders of the North-West Company, based on Montreal through a network of overland communication, appeared on the Pacific coast, they created 'an intensive and aggressive all-the-year-round competition which slowly brought the end'. By about 1837 the maritime fur trade had disappeared.[113] The ocean fur traders made no settlements and contributed nothing to the evolution of modern North America.[114] That was not to be expected, for they stood, so to speak, with their backs to the Rocky Mountains and looked out across the sea to China and (with expectant eyes) to the closed markets of Korea and Japan.

---

[111] S. E. Morrison's phrase (*Maritime History of Massachusetts*), quoted by F. W. Howay, 'An Outline Sketch of the Maritime Fur Trade' (*Canadian Hist. Assocn. Rept.*, 1932, pp. 1-14). Cf. H. A. Innis, *The Fur Trade in Canada* (Toronto, 1956 edn.), pp. 204-6.

[112] Howay, p. 7. The pressures of war were, of course, a contributory factor in the decline of the British share in the trade.

[113] *Ibid.*, p. 14.

[114] Their activities (like those of the Russians further north who sold their furs at the northern Chinese port of Kiahkta) had the effect of wiping out the unfortunate sea-otter. Their cargoes became progressively supplemented with seal skins and other furs.

According to its Charter in 1670 the Hudson's Bay Company was to develop the fur trade and also to promote exploration for a passage into the South Sea. Complaints were made at home that the Company clung to its fur trade round the Bay and neglected its other commission, but from 1742 onwards a number of attempts were made to find a western passage leading from the Bay into the Pacific. With the rapid expansion of British oceanic commerce in the later decades of the century men such as Alexander Dalrymple and Sir Joseph Banks became increasingly interested in North-West America as an area of trade which might be linked with Canton as well as London.

By no other way [wrote Dalrymple], than Hudson's Bay, can the communication be made with so much facility, nor with so little expense as by a ship from China: and having thus the option of the Chinese, as well as the European markets, no other traders can stand in competition.[115]

The man who rightly claimed to have disproved the existence of a passage between Hudson Bay and the Pacific was Samuel Hearne, a Servant of the Company. After two unsuccessful attempts he set out again in 1770, striking further west than before. He came upon the Coppermine River and followed it to the Arctic Sea. On the return journey he discovered a lake which he named Athapuscow. Some have identified his discovery with Lake Athabaska, but the direction of his route seems to show that he had found the Great Slave Lake.[116]

Hearne's reports and charts were sent to London where they were later studied by Dalrymple. The discovery of a lake some 400 miles long raised hopes that this might be the source of 'the great river of the west', flowing into the Pacific Ocean, which haunted the minds of theoretical geographers and explorers for so long.[117] But it was not the Hudson's Bay Company which carried out the major task of exploring the regions to the west and north of the Great Lakes. The Canadian fur traders of Montreal,

---

[115] A. Dalrymple, *Plan for promoting the Fur Trade* (Lond., 1789), p. 31. (Extract printed in *Brit. Col. Dev.*, pp. 35-6.) For this purpose Dalrymple advocated combined action by the East India and Hudson's Bay Companies. Cf. the same author's *Memorandum on Trade to the South Seas and the North West Coast of America*, 23 February, 1791 (*Home Misc. S.*, 494/5, p. 441 *et seq.* Extracts in *Brit. Col. Dev.*, pp. 36-40).

[116] See J. N. L. Baker, *A History of Geographical Discovery* . . . (Lond., 1931), p. 221.

[117] S. Hearne, *A Journey from Prince of Wales's Fort in Hudson's Bay to the Northern Ocean . . . in the Years 1769, 1770, 1771 and 1772* (Lond., 1795. Edited by J. B. Tyrell for the Champlain Soc., Toronto, 1911). Cf. Vancouver's reference in one of his reports to the Admiralty. 'The northern part (of Cross Sound) brought us within about three hundred and fifty geographical miles of the South-West borders of the Arathepescow Lake, as delineated in Captain Cook's General Chart.' (Vancouver to Stephens, 8 Sept., 1794. Printed in Godwin, *Life*, App., pp. 259-61.)

using the more flexible and enterprising methods of the old French *voyageurs*, began to spread out into the North-West, thus turning the flank, so to speak, of the Hudson's Bay Company.

In 1783-4 various competing Canadian groups amalgamated as the North-West Company. One of the moving spirits was Peter Pond, a trader who during the previous ten years had himself been pushing steadily westward. At the time of the formation of the new Company Pond saw accounts in Montreal of Cook's survey of the Pacific coast during his last voyage, and he conceived the idea that the Athabaska River flowed into Cook's 'River' on the Alaska coast which Cook had visited. Thus the profound and diverse influence of Cook's exploration upon British overseas commercial expansion also contributed a stimulus to a territorial penetration which led to the creation of western Canada. The Athabaska-Cook River waterway, if it existed, would be a good deal further north than geographers hoped. Vancouver, it will be recalled, was instructed to investigate this possibility, but only if he failed to find a route in more southerly latitudes.

The North-West Company applied to the British Government for a grant of exclusive trading privilege for ten years in the areas which they were opening up, and they offered to explore and supply maps of the western country from 55° to 65° north latitude. The application was rejected as involving an infringement of the Charter rights of the Hudson's Bay Company: but the exploration proceeded, and London followed the new developments with active interest. Peter Pond himself journeyed through Clear Lake and Buffalo Lake, over the Mathye Portage, and so down the Clearwater River to Lake Athabaska, where a fortified trading station, named Chipewyan, was established. In 1788 he sent a party still further to the north-west which found a waterway to the Great Slave Lake and established a post on its shores. Full reports of these discoveries were sent to Evan Nepean of the Home and Colonial Office: Dalrymple was consulted, and plans were made for sending a ship (the *Discovery*) to search the Pacific Coast, while at the same time another vessel was to be sent in one more effort to find a water communication to the west from Hudson Bay.[118]

Meanwhile Alexander Mackenzie, the greatest inland explorer of the century, was building on the work already done by his colleague, Peter Pond. Leaving Fort Chipewyan on Lake Athabaska on 3 June, 1789, he made his way down the Slave River (in spite of its rapids) to the Great Slave Lake. No one knew whether the large river which drained that lake flowed into the Pacific or the Arctic, and Mackenzie's purpose was to find out. That river (which now bears his name) flows westward for a considerable

---

[118] See H. A. Innis, 'Peter Pond and the Influence of Capt. Cook . . ' (trans., *Roy. Soc. of Canada*, 1928, vol. XXII, Sect. II).

distance in the early part of its course but then turns to the north. Mackenzie himself seems to have realised the truth before his followers, who, he writes, 'were animated by the expectation that another day would bring them to the Mer d'Ouest'. When on 10 July they approached the delta it had become obvious that the Mackenzie River flowed into the Arctic Ocean. On returning to Fort Chipewyan in September he had covered almost 3,000 miles and had accomplished what has been justifiably described as 'one of the most remarkable exploits in the history of inland discovery'.[119]

Having eliminated one possibility, Mackenzie returned to England in order to perfect his knowledge of surveying and to study the history of exploration on the west coast in preparation for a further expedition across the Continent in search of a water communication with the Pacific. In London he would be able to study the reports and publish narratives of Meares, Dixon, Portlock and others, and he would almost certainly be informed of the Government's decision to resume the plan of sending *Discovery* under Vancouver's command to tackle the problem from the coastal end.

Leaving England early in 1792 Mackenzie proceeded without delay to Fort Chipewyan. His plan on this occasion was to follow the Peace River westward to its source, to cross the Rocky Mountains, and then explore possible routes to the coast. Having reached the junction of the Peace and Smoky Rivers on 1 November, he built winter quarters and there remained until the following May. The expedition continued up the Peace River until they reached the canyon of that name which necessitated a twelve-mile portage. The Parsnip River was followed to its source, and thence by a short portage they came to one of the headstreams of the Fraser and so into the main river. To their joy and relief they had come upon a navigable waterway on the west side of the first great range of the Rockies. When, however, they had gone a little beyond the site of the modern town of Quesnel, the Indians told them that it was impracticable to follow the river further. Mackenzie returned upstream and then struck westward, probably along the Blackwater. Crossing over to the Bellacoola, he finally reached Dean Channel and salt water on 22 July, 1793. From Indian reports he learned that great ships of the white men had recently passed that way. He had, in fact, missed Vancouver with *Discovery* and *Chatham*, searching the coast northward from Nootka, by only a few weeks.[120]

That near-meeting on the Pacific coast between a sea captain who

---

[119] See Baker (*op. cit.*), pp. 224-5 and the footnote references.
[120] A. Mackenzie, *Voyages from Montreal . . . through the Continent of North America to the Frozen and Pacific Oceans* (Lond., 1801).

had sailed from the Thames by Cape Horn and a fur trader who had come from Montreal by canoe and on foot may be taken as a symbol. Mackenzie had not, of course, discovered a navigable waterway between the oceans; but he had achieved his great object of proving that, by organising lines of communication, the fur trade could be extended to include the resources of the Pacific coast, and that, if developed with British capital, it could participate in the growing commerce between Europe and Asia.

By opening this intercourse [he wrote] between the Atlantic and Pacific Oceans, and forming regular establishments through the interior, and at both extremes, as well as along the coasts and islands, the entire command of the fur trade of North America might be obtained . . . To this might be added the fishing in both seas and the markets of the four quarters of the globe.[121]

As Dundas observed in the House of Commons 'the spirit of commercial adventure' among the British was 'unbounded'. As Mackenzie had intended, trading activities were effectively extended to the Pacific coast (and after 1821 by the North-West and the Hudson's Bay Companies as one organisation); but the eventual outcome was far different from what the Scottish fur trader could have anticipated. As the late Professor H. A. Innis has observed: 'By 1821 the Northwest Company had built up an organisation which extended from the Atlantic to the Pacific. The foundations of the present Dominion of Canada had been securely laid. . . . The Northwest Company was the forerunner of Confederation.'[122]

The technique of the continental fur traders was not so very different from that of the ocean traders. The former roamed vast areas of wasteland in North-West America and (like their maritime counterparts) provided a framework for their fluid operations by establishing fortified trading stations at strategic points. Fort Churchill on Hudson Bay and Chipewyan on Lake Athabaska were not dissimilar in purpose and function from Penang in the Strait of Malacca.

But there the analogy ends. The continental traders had no more use for colonies of settlement than those who were developing an oceanic network of commerce; but the former were penetrating great areas of thinly populated fertile land, below the surface of which were gold and other rich mineral resources. Lord Selkirk's founding of the Red River Settlement was a portent of an invasion which gradually replaced nomadic fur traders with farms, cities, mine shafts and oil derricks. The process furnishes an apt illustration of the alternation between the methods of 'informal' and 'formal' empire.

---

[121] *Ibid.*, p. 407.
[122] H. A. Innis, *The Fur Trade in Canada*, p. 262.

NOTE ON THE SPANISH 'RESTORATION' OF NOOTKA
TO BRITAIN

By Article I of the Anglo-Spanish Convention, signed on 28 October, 1790, it was agreed 'that the buildings and tracts of land, situated on the north-west coast of the continent of North America, or on islands adjacent to that continent' were to be restored to the British subjects who had been dispossessed of them. The purpose of the three lengthy examinations of John Meares by the Cabinet in February, 1791, was to ascertain precise details of these buildings and tracts of land. As we have seen, Meares claimed possession on behalf of the 'United Company' of a house inside a stockaded enclosure of one acre, situated about 400 yards from the Indian village, a vegetable garden closer to the village, and Friendly Cove itself where the British flag had been hoisted. Further construction which Colnett had been ordered to carry out by means of the ships' artificers and the party of thirty-five Chinese artisans had been prevented by Martinez. This was evidently less than the Ministers had expected. (Dundas in the Commons had spoken of 'a few miles'.) The Instructions issued to Vancouver on 8 March, 1791, accordingly stated that further details would follow him out to the Sandwich Islands, 'as the particular specification of the parts to be restored may still require some further time'. Probably they hoped to obtain these details from Colnett, who had been released by the Spanish authorities in New Mexico and had already sent letters to the Admiralty (see Meares to Nepean, 7 Aug., 1790. *F.O. 95/7*).

When, however, the transport *Daedalus* reached him at the rendezvous, precise instructions were still lacking. A copy, with an English translation, of Florida Blanca's orders to the Spanish officer commanding at Nootka had been sent which directed that the British officer must be immediately put in possession of 'the Buildings and Districts or parcels of Land' which were occupied by British subjects in April, 1789, at the port of Nootka and at Port Cox – the place fifty miles to the south where Meares had said he had purchased a long-house to be used as a factory. When Vancouver met Don Quadra at Nootka in August, 1792, the latter refused to hand over (in Vancouver's words) anything more than 'a small chasm . . . not a hundred yards in extent in any one direction, being the exact space which the house and brest work of Mr. Meares occupied'.

According to Lieut. Menzies, one of Vancouver's officers, Quadra had at first been willing to hand over 'all the houses, gardens, &c as they stood' but had been persuaded by an American, Capt. Ingram, not to do so. (Menzies to Sir Joseph Banks, 26 Sept., 1792. *Hist. Records of N.S.W.*, vol. I, Pt. 2, p. 641.) This may be true, for American traders from Boston were beginning to use the Sound and they would not have welcomed an extensive British establishment which might be used to interrupt their own trade. Friendly Cove was, of course, only a tiny spot in a very 'spacious' inlet.

Vancouver refused to accept the rendition of such terms and departed to continue his coastal exploration. He also wrote a very angry and frustrated private letter to Under-Secretary Nepean. 'Can this chasm possibly be considered as the districts or parcels of Land, etc intended to be ceded to me on the part of His Britannic Majesty? Now there is little doubt I should either have proved myself a consummate fool or a traitor to have acceded to any such cession without positive directions to that effect.' He also complained that he had been left in the dark about what he was to do with the ceded territories thereafter. (Vancouver to Nepean, 7 Jan., 1793. Printed, Geo. Godwin, *Vancouver, A Life*, Lond., 1931, pp. 219-23.) Representatives of the Etches Company ought, of course, to have been present to enter into possession, but although their ships had been released, the British Ambassador in Madrid was making no progress in securing the promised reparation for their losses. Their original capital had been small: the Etches and the Meares groups were at odds with each other; and they can have been in no financial shape to man and maintain an establishment.

When the matter was referred to Lord St. Helens in Madrid he made repeated efforts to settle it. In November, 1793, he wrote: 'I am still without any answer from the Spanish Minister upon the proposed Nootka arrangements', and he went on to point out that he could not press beyond a certain point for Britain and Spain were now allies engaged together in a war. A month later he reported: 'I have at last received the Answer of this Court upon the Nootka business, which I am sorry to say is highly unsatisfactory.' (St. Helens to Grenville, 20 Nov. and 25 Dec., 1793. *F.O. 72/28.*) At last in the following January it was settled that both Governments would issue fresh instructions to their commissioners who were to meet at Nootka. The Spanish representative was to sign an approved declaration formally restoring 'the Buildings and Districts of Land' of which British subjects had been dispossessed. That done – 'the British officer shall then cause the British flag to be hoisted on the Land thus restored in token of Possession, and . . . after these Formalities the Officers of the two Crowns shall respectively withdraw their People from the said Port of Nootka'. (Draft Instruction from the Duke of Portland, 31 March, 1794. *F.O. 95/7.*) At last in February, 1795, the ceremony was duly carried out on the spot by Brigadier-General Alava and Lieut. Thomas Pearce of the British Navy. Thus by employing the gentle art of procrastination the Spanish Government avoided paying compensation to the traders and making any more than a token cession of territory. The British Government, after spending more than £1 million on naval and military preparations, secured the theoretical title to a number of unspecified buildings and small parcels of land. The ceremony, nevertheless, established the right of Britain (and therefore of any other Power) to trade and acquire land at places along the Coast by occupation.

CHAPTER VIII

AN EMPIRE OF TRADE IN FURTHER ASIA

1. INDIA'S PLACE IN ORIENTAL COMMERCE

THE ancient trade routes of Asia by land and sea were extensive and complex, but the traffic which moved along them was not of prime importance in the economy of the states which engaged in it. The many millions who inhabited the great sub-continents of China and India and the countries between them grew their own rice and other food-stuffs and clothed themselves with their own silk and cotton fabrics. With some exceptions they were grouped in territorial empires, constituting vast internal markets, and were therefore highly self-sufficient. China and the principalities of India and South-East Asia had little need of each other's basic products and still less for those of peoples beyond the Asian orbit. The principal items in external trade were luxury goods. Chinese junks, hugging the coasts and following the monsoons, did business in Indo-China, Siam and the Malay Archipelago, selling silks, lacquer work, sandalwood, chinaware, sugar-candy, zinc (tutenhage) and camphor, and purchasing in return such commodities as sharks' fins, pearls, gold, spices and Malayan tin. The external trade of India under successive empires was likewise diverse but marginal. Native products such as gems, pepper, opium and piece-goods found markets in Burma, Malaya, the Persian Gulf, the Red Sea, and the east coast of Africa.

Commercial contacts between Asia and the Western World were of a like nature, and it was the latter which took the initiative as buyers. Following upon the Greek penetration of India the Romans in their heyday developed a taste for the exotic articles of the East. Chinese silks were purchased (with Spanish silver) from middlemen at Tashkurghan and Yarkand and brought to the eastern Mediterranean by caravan routes which avoided the hostile Parthians; and Indian jewels and pepper were shipped to Aden under Roman direction and thence transported overland to the great commercial centres of Petra, Antioch and Alexandria. But these were subsidiary transactions: the bulk of the trade of the Roman Empire, which became highly organised and increasingly important, was conducted inside its expanding frontiers. If the empires of China and India had permanently sealed their ports and caravan routes, the disturbance to their economies would have been inconsiderable. The comparative insignificance of foreign commerce in the estimation of oriental rulers indicated a situation and an attitude which Europeans of a later age often failed to appreciate.

When the peoples of Christendom, headed by the Portuguese, circumvented Islam and opened the Atlantic route to the Orient they initiated an economic and social revolution which is still in progress. For the first time in history Asian products were drawn in great quantities to non-Asian markets. Willy-nilly the races involved became mass exporters. Unlike previous invaders, the Europeans were voracious for trade goods and their equipment for that pursuit became increasingly formidable. In the course of the 17th and 18th centuries they evolved a highly developed financial system which was European in scope despite the economic nationalism which divided the competing units. Secondly the resources of the European homelands were powerfully reinforced, directly and indirectly, by new European productivity in North, Central and South America. Furthermore East-West exchange on a massive scale became possible when the limited carrying capacity of (hazardous) overland transport by camel was superseded by large ocean-going ships delivering in bulk. The transit of Mexican silver through Madrid to Amsterdam, London, Paris, Lisbon and Copenhagen and thence to India to buy cotton fabrics and to China to buy tea was symptomatic. Thus equipped the Europeans gradually effected a deep penetration into the economic structure of Asia and eventually transformed it.

When the Dutch made it clear – by methods which could not be ignored – that they regarded the English in the East Indies as unwelcome competitors, the latter began increasingly to concentrate their trading efforts on the Coromandel and Malabar coasts of India. In spite of political and other hazards and dissensions at home during the second half of the 17th century the English merchants trading to India prospered. 'Fenceless factories' were developed into Presidencies, fortified and garrisoned, and partly sustained by revenues derived from adjoining enclaves. Rivalry with the Dutch and other European companies brought them into diplomatic relations with Country Powers and into close association with the home Government. The amalgamation of the 'Old' and the 'New' companies in 1709 enabled the united corporation to take full advantage of the twenty years of national prosperity (1719-1739) under Sir Robert Walpole. It became by far the largest and most complicated trading organisation of the country and (with the Bank of England and the South Sea Company) the centre of the rising financial market in London.[1]

Had the imperial power of the Moghuls achieved and maintained a control over India as comprehensive and effective as that of the Manchus in China, instead of contracting in decay, Dupleix would not have been able to make his bid to establish a French sphere

---

[1] L. S. Sutherland, *The East India Company in Eighteenth-Century Politics*, p. 17.

of influence in the south and so destroy English trade with the weapon of political power. The capture of Madras by a French force in 1746 and its restoration to Britain in exchange for Cape Breton Island in North America signalised the involvement of a disintegrating India in the global rivalry of two European Powers. The English Company, supported by the British Crown, fought back, imitating Dupleix's technique. When Clive acquired the *diwani* of Bengal, Bihar and Orissa for his employers, the Company became in effect an Indian Government which used 'surplus' revenue to finance a form of state trading. In the early years of the new dispensation the Court of Directors were led to expect that after all charges, civil and military, had been met, an annual credit balance of not less than £1 million would be available which could be remitted in the form of trade goods. The proceeds of the sales would offset the interest payable on the bonded debt and other Home Charges. In practice this hoped-for balance obtained only when Bengal was prosperous and the Company was not involved in war. The Bengal revenues (two-thirds of which derived from land dues) were expected to carry a four-fold load: the costs of the administration and defence of Bengal itself, the regular deficits of Madras and Bombay, military assistance for the other Presidencies at need, and remittances to help finance the China trade. When the surplus diminished or became a deficit, the Investment in Indian cotton manufactures was purchased – in part or in whole – by means of loans raised in India at high interest rates. The onset of the third Mysore war in May, 1790, so aggravated the shortage of specie that a financial crisis ensued. Recovery took place in response to vigorous action by Cornwallis, but when a long period of almost continuous war began in 1793 the Bengal Government was obliged to burden the revenues, in spite of territorial acquisitions, with a mounting load of debt.

The Company – as an Indian Government – was virtually bankrupt. Yet as a commercial organisation before 1765 it had conducted a profitable business on sound lines. In those days silver had been purchased in London (with funds raised by long-term loans and short-term credits), shipped to India and invested in the cotton goods which sold to such advantage in Europe. The export of bullion for this purpose represented the investment of purchasing power accumulated through other transactions by British merchants in Europe and across the Atlantic. By 1732 the annual receipts from these sales of Indian goods in London had reached the level of £1,940,000, and they remained at that level until a sharp rise occurred in 1763-4, followed by a further rise after the acquisition of the *diwani*.[2]

---

[2] 3rd Report of the Committee of Secrecy, 1773. Cited by L. S. Sutherland (*op. cit.*), p. 32.

The 'good' years after 1765 and again after 1783 could have become the norm only if the sub-continent had been in a state of political stability; and in that event power in Bengal and the neighbouring territories could not have been acquired by a foreign commercial corporation. A portent of what could happen was afforded by the Company's statement of Indian accounts for the war year, May, 1781 – April, 1782. The returns of the auditor at East India House put the total net revenues of Bengal at £2,528,768 and the total charges at £2,594,646, thus showing a deficit of £65,878. For the same years the charges of the Bombay Presidency exceeded the revenues by £357,639, while the deficit at Madras amounted (very approximately) to £680,000.[3] In such a year the Investment in cotton goods for sale in London – costing about £1 million – was purchased with borrowed money, the lenders being Company Servants, ex-Servants and to some extent Indian financiers. In a narrow money market the rate of interest was frequently as high as 12 per cent. By 1785 the combined debts of the Presidencies were stated to be £9,364,496.[4] Apart from the capital stock of £5 million (market value – £7,780,000) the bonded debt at home totalled £9,247,019.[5]

It has been aptly said that Cornwallis in India 'inherited bankruptcy', but improving conditions in Bengal during a period of peace, aided by the penal clauses against abuses in the India Act of 1784 and Cornwallis's reforming vigilance, led observers in the

---

[3] ' An Account of the Gross Amount of all the Territorial and other Revenues received by the East India Company with the Charges of Management, Civil, Military and other Expenses and Accounts of the Nett Proceeds at each of their Settlements . . . and also accounts of the Debts due . . . according to the latest Advices.' East India House, 22 June, 1785 (Home Misc. Series, 338(7), pp. 65-78). There is a similar return covering the period 1782/4 and dated East India House, 4 Aug., 1786 (ibid., 340(4), pp. 69-79). Statistics of the financial transactions of the Company's Governments in India are notoriously defective, and the transactions themselves were so intricate and elusive and subject to such rapid changes that anything approaching an accurate assessment of the true situation at a given date is impossible. For example, at the foot of the statement of ' total charges ' incurred by Bombay and its subordinate depots for 1782-3 the Auditor adds this note: ' The above cannot be considered as the whole of the charges incurred in the year, considerable arrears being due [for payment] at the end of April, the exact amount of which cannot be ascertained.' In a similar note relating to Bengal's own charges he computed that the arrears ' owing in the several departments ' at the end of April, 1785, amounted to £1,230,000. Each Presidency too had to meet the interest on a fluctuating mass of short-term debt. A complete picture is not ascertainable, but broad trends under changing conditions can be observed. The best statistical analysis is in A. Tripathi, Trade and Finance in the Bengal Presidency, 1793-1833 (Longmans, Bombay, 1956), Chap. I.

[4] The list is as follows: ' Bengal, at 31 Dec., 1785 – £4,036,721; Madras, at 31 Oct., 1785 – £1,878,198; Bombay, at 30 April, 1785 – £3,376,010; Bencoolen (in Sumatra), at 17 Oct., 1785 – £74,577 (Home Misc. S., 338(7), p. 78). By 31 Jan., 1792, the third Mysore War had raised the Bengal debt to £6,643,622. (In calculating the sterling equivalent of Indian currency the accountants at East India House stated: ' The current rupee is valued at 2s. 3d.' Ibid., 340(4), p. 69.)

[5] Tripathi (op. cit.), pp. 2-3.

years 1790-2 to take an optimistic view of the future. A number of these, including Francis Russell (Solicitor to the Board of Control), George Anderson (Accountant-General to the Board), David Scott, Francis Baring, and Nathaniel Smith, were asked by Dundas to make individual assessments of the Company's financial situation and prospects. One of the first tasks to which Dundas had applied himself at the India Board had been to relieve the Governments in India of their dangerous load of debt by securing its transference to London, where it was to be paid off gradually by a substantial increase in the sale of Asian goods. Although the scheme was a comparative failure,[6] it was only an initial step in a comprehensive policy, promoted by Dundas, which had for its object the development of a British empire of trade in Asia with London as its world emporium. By the early 1790s Britain's commercial connexions with India, China and the Malay countries had expanded and become increasingly inter-dependent. The situation in India itself was changing as the Company's highly vulnerable financial arrangements became interlocked with an extensive system of ' private ' and clandestine trade. At the same time the entire nexus of British-Indian commerce, official and non-official, was being drawn into a stimulating relationship with China as the Company became the dominant supplier of tea to Europe. As the great commercial triangle linking Britain with India and China developed, Dundas sought to divert the export of Indian goods away from centres in Europe to London, to promote the sale of British manufactures in India with the aid of private enterprise, and to persuade the Chinese Government to open the doors of northern China, which was believed to be a vast potential market for woollens and other British products. An expansive national policy of such dimensions called – in the opinion of Dundas – for a closer governmental control over the Company, a reform of its financial structure, and a modification of its trading monopoly. The approach of the year 1794 when the Charter would be due for renewal and possible revision afforded an opportunity which self-confident manufacturers and merchants were not slow to take.

It was against this background of improved conditions in Bengal and widening opportunities in Eastern trade that the computations which Dundas had called for were made. One of the most careful of these, which seems to have been compiled by George Anderson, presented the following estimate of the situation.[7] Based on recent returns, the total annual revenues of the three Presidencies were

---

[6] See pp. 169-75 above.

[7] The several computations are collected together, with a comparative analysis of them all (apparently prepared by George Anderson) in *Home Misc. S.,* 399. Cf. a previous estimate of Francis Russell, dated 14 April, 1790. ' A Concentrated View of the Affairs of the East India Company, regarding their Commerce and Finance ' (*ibid.,* 208(13), pp. 195-211).

put at £7,134,110 and the total charges (on a peace establishment) at £5,107,110, leaving a surplus of £2,027,000. Taking the round figure of £2 millions he deducted £560,000 for interest payments on the debts in India on the assumption that they could be funded at 8 per cent – an expectation which proved to be unwarranted. A balance remained of £1,440,000 available for investment and the payment of commercial charges. To this was added the sum of £280,000 accruing from the sale of British goods in India,[8] making a grand total of £1,720,000. Out of this he allotted £1,320,000 for the Investment, that is to say £1,200,000 for the purchase of India goods at prime cost and £120,000 for the consequential charges. There would thus remain a balance of £400,000 which could be used to pay off debts in India, 'or to answer contingencies, if any should arise which are not allowed for, or if any defalcation should take place in the Revenues'. The very hypothetical nature of this credit balance of £400,000 emerges when it is realised that £280,000 of it was supposed to represent the proceeds from the sale of British goods in India – which (apart from military stores) usually sold at a loss.[9]

Anderson then followed an actual Investment to London and from the Company's accounts for the year 1790 did the following sum:

To sale of India goods	£2,403,684
Their prime cost	£1,111,552
'Charges of Customs, Freight & Merchandize'	£ 968,102
	£2,079,654
Profit on goods sold in 1790	£ 324,030

A similar calculation for 1791 showed a profit of £411,626, making an average on the two years of £367,828. Later in the analysis the dividend and interest charges payable in London were put at the (low) figure of £530,000.[10] Thus if the Company's activities had been confined to buying Indian goods for the London

---

[8] On this figure Anderson comments: 'The Sales on Imports in India have not hitherto amounted to £300,000 per annum, except in the last year, 1790-91, and then a considerable quantity of stores expended for the use of the Army is included. The general average for some years past is about £250,000.' No deduction is made for prime cost.

[9] See p. 489 below.

[10] This total comprised £400,000 for the 8 per cent dividend on the capital stock of £5 million, £60,000 for bond interest – 'if £2,000,000 of Bonds could be kept in the Market at 3 per cent', and £70,000 for £2 million of 'other debts' funded at 3¼ per cent. To these items Baring added a disbursement of £90,000 on annuities, making a total of £611,000 p.a. The total indebtedness of the Company at home, including short-term loans, amounted to £10,601,069 – having risen from £9,247,019 as the result of debt transference from India. In 1793 the Company's debts in India were put at £9,084,550.

market with the net surplus revenue of Bengal and with borrowed money, East India House would have barely balanced their accounts, even when they were not involved in Indian wars. The situation was saved by the profits earned in supplying Britain and most of Europe with tea from China. The profits from the sale of China goods amounted on an average for the same two years to £563,729, and a further (estimated) profit of £100,000 arose from the Company's sales of goods and bullion in Canton.[11]

If an appraisal of British trade in Asia were limited to the Chartered Company's purchase and sale of Indian piece-goods and Chinese tea and silks, the resulting picture would be distorted and inadequate. As a trading organisation it was far from being self-contained. At home it had become the principal nerve centre of an elaborate European credit system. A threat of drastic action in London – as, for example, in Fox's India Bills – or the prospect of a collapse of the Company's credit in India could induce a major financial crisis in Europe. Again, the Company's financial operations in India were interlocked with an intricate commercial network which was increasingly dominated and developed by British subjects (Company Servants and ex-Servants) acting in a private capacity. When the Company became involved from 1790 onwards in costly and expansive wars this unofficial network, which included foreign European and American interests as well as Indian traders and financiers, eagerly took advantage of the opportunities for profit that wars afforded. The official Company with its monopoly and political power and the unofficial system of trade with its developing resources became increasingly inter-dependent. In turn each found itself obliged to come to the rescue of the other. In combination they comprised an intricate exchange of goods and specie, based on the three Presidencies in India, and extending eastward through the Malay Archipelago to Canton and westward to Europe. A working association between a monopoly corporation and various forms of free enterprise was a makeshift compromise which from the national point of view exhibited serious anomalies and weaknesses. Whereas the Company readily licensed individuals and merchant houses to undertake certain types of regional trade which

---

[11] Francis Baring stated that in his opinion Anderson's figures, which he had seen at Wimbledon, were too low. While Anderson's estimate of the net annual gain on the sale of India and China goods was £414,557, Baring was confident that after deducting all charges a credit balance of at least £1 million would accrue for debt liquidation. In his India budget speech of 25 Feb., 1793, Dundas stated that the average net profit during the years 1786-89 had been low (£434,581), but that since then the Company's situation had greatly improved. For the years 1790 to 1793 it had amounted to £916,497. It had dropped to £743,602 in the year 1793 because of the war with Mysore (*Parl. Hist.*, vol. XXX, 496-513). The returns of Indian revenue with the charges thereon for the years 1782-3 to 1787-8 are in *Parl. Papers* (*Gen. Coll.*), vol. 80, Nos. 525 and 539.

it was not equipped to operate itself, the restrictions imposed caused these peaceful privateers to use devious and illicit channels to get their profits home which violated the terms of the Charter and allegedly injured the national economy.

The contention of private traders that British-Indian commerce could be immensely strengthened and developed by relaxing the Company's restrictions and broadening the legitimate channels of remittance was reinforced by the clamour of the industrialists who argued that the Company had conspicuously failed to sell British manufactures in India while preventing private enterprise from doing so. They also complained that the Company for its own reasons (as an Indian Government) supplied Britain and most of Europe with Indian piece-goods and so created unfair competition with British products. The compelling reason for the meagreness of British exports to India was that the native inhabitants did not want them. They preferred to wear *dhotis* and *saris* made of cottons and silks woven by skilled Indian craftsmen, and they had no use for British woollens. Although British expertise in cotton industry was rapidly improving, the time had not yet come when Manchester goods could undersell the native product in the Indian bazaars.[12]

While British products (such as woollens, cutlery and hardware) were penetrating the Western hemisphere on a widening front it irked ambitious manufacturers to see India and China goods being imported into London on a massive scale without a corresponding export, and the blame was laid exclusively at the door of East India House. The Directors could and did produce cogent explanations, but the arguments of the private traders that moderate and sensible adjustments would enable them to transform a defective system to national advantage were more difficult to refute. This dual pressure naturally increased as the terminal date of the Charter Act approached, and the form which the pressure took was indicative of the revolutionary changes taking place in Far Eastern trade and of a growing sense that the British system was in need of reform. During the same period (1785-93) Dundas and Pitt were engaged, as earlier chapters have described, in restoring the Company's shattered credit, tightening up the administrative control through the India Board, and in trying to extend by diplomacy British commercial and strategic power in the Indian Ocean and the

---

[12] Crompton's mule was invented in 1779 and Cartwright's power loom in 1785. Cylinder printing and an improved method of bleaching were also introduced. The manufacturers stated (in 1787-8) that they already excelled the Indians in the middle and lower grades, including common calicoes, but could not yet produce comparable quality in fine muslins, being unable to spin such fine yarn. They accordingly pressed for a prohibition against the importation of fine yarn and for restrictions upon fine India piece-goods, while trying to encourage the importation of raw cotton from India. (Tripathi *op. cit.*, p. 24. Cf. pp. 505 *et seq.* below.)

Pacific. When, therefore, the manufacturers and the private traders, led by David Scott, mounted their respective campaigns, the Ministers naturally took account of their claims and proposals as part of the general overhaul of the Company's organisation which changing circumstances demanded and for which the termination of the existing Charter provided the opportunity. Alongside the question of future State control in Indian affairs Dundas and Pitt were thus called upon to decide whether a more flexible instrument of national commercial policy ought to be devised by modifying the Company's trading structure in favour of private enterprise, and if so to what extent. Before considering the arguments adduced and the decisions taken, which constitute an important stage in the development of Britain's empire of trade in Asia, it will be convenient to summarise the unofficial and illicit system which had grown up around that of the Chartered Company and had become interwoven with it.

When Europeans penetrated the Indian Ocean they superimposed their own oceanic lines of commercial communication upon a long-established pattern of native coastal trade. Bengal was linked with the Coromandel coast and Madras, and Madras with Ceylon, the Malabar coast, Cochin, Surat and Bombay. Westward across the Indian Ocean Arab *dhows* and Indian *bombaras*, financed by Parsee, Armenian and Muslim merchant princes, conducted a lucrative trade with Arabia and the ports of East Africa. To a lesser extent there was an eastward traffic with Malaya and the Archipelago. It was the ambition of all incoming Europeans – Portuguese, Dutch, English, French and Danes – to participate in what they described as the 'Country' trade.

It was not a field which the several East India Companies, as such, could profitably enter. Individual initiative was required which could not be provided by the remote control of a corporation from a European metropolis. On the other hand its Servants on the spot, receiving meagre salaries, could and did. Although, as private traders, they put their own profit before that of their masters whenever there was a conflict of interest, the Company concerned was aware that its trading resources were being indirectly supplemented and diversified. Moreover official 'masters' were often themselves interested in unofficial enterprises.

By the time of the American War the English had out-distanced their European rivals and were dominating the Country trade. The capital invested in it by Company Servants derived initially from their usual sources of profit – commissions, collusive contracts, the sale of military equipment to Indian rulers, and so forth. Retired military officers sometimes stayed on in India and employed their savings in the trade, and in certain branches native Indian merchants and financiers continued to participate in a considerable proportion.[13] As it expanded 'free mariners' came out from England and established themselves as Country Captains, men of skill and enterprise, who in some cases became independent traders owning their own ship. In Bombay and Bengal and then in Burma copper-bottomed vessels were built to serve the growing volume of traffic. The coastal voyages in which such vessels engaged, manned by a Lascar crew under an English commander, revolutionised the commerce of the Indian Ocean: a great stimulus was given to the exchange of products between the three Presidencies and the inter-vening ports. The system proliferated as it exploited the expand-ing authority and the consequential growing needs of the English Company. When, for example, the Bengal Government was obliged to send remittances to meet the perennial deficits at Madras and Bombay, it avoided exporting specie, which was always scarce, by arranging with Country merchants to ship cargoes of rice, opium (for eventual sale in the Malay Archipelago), piece-goods and other Bengal produce in return for bills of exchange.

In the latter half of the 18th century and more particularly after Pitt's Commutation Act of 1784 there was a phenomenal and con-tinuing rise in the English Company's imports of China tea from Canton. A new field of enterprise was thus opened to the Country merchants, for the Company was paying for its teas and silks with Spanish dollars, obtained in Europe, and was making little head-way in inducing the Chinese to buy either British or Indian pro-ducts. On the other hand the Country merchants were well equipped to take advantage of the situation and did so with alacrity. The magnet of the China market drew them into Malaya and the Archipelago – Dutch preserves – where they bought Banka tin, spices, sharks' fins, and other commodities for which there was a Chinese demand: the principal products which found a vent were raw cotton from Bombay and at a later stage Bengal opium. The Company's Supercargoes at Canton gladly filled their ware-houses with these assorted shipments, paying for them with bills on London. To such an extent did the attraction of the Chinese market draw the lines of trade from Indian ports to Canton that the coastal traffic between the Indian Presidencies was for a time seriously diminished. By the early 1790s, however, the efforts of Cornwallis (and Charles Grant) had lowered duties so substantially that virtual free trade was established between the British settle-

---

[13] This was particularly the case in the trade with the Persian Gulf and East Africa. Owing to epidemics and political disturbances the European trade with Persia declined, but the old indigenous traffic across the Indian Ocean continued and indeed seems to have increased as the British commercial houses of Bombay became absorbed in the China trade. Warren Hastings was interested in the possibility of developing a British Country trade between India and the Red Sea, but European ignorance of its navigation and Arab hostility at Jeddah rendered the project abortive. (See papers on this subject in *Addit. MSS.*, 29,139 and 29,140.)

ments, and the gross value of exports from Bengal to other Indian ports rose again to be almost equal to the value of exports by Country traders to the eastward. The growth of the Country trade is indicated by the increase in British-owned tonnage which was employed in it. For 1773 the total was put at 25,080 tons; ten years later at 44,865 tons and for 1791 at 175,407 tons.[14]

If the Country trade had remained in the hands of individual venturers it could not have developed into the vast commercial and financial complex which it became. The Agency houses, as they were called, entered the field and eventually monopolised it. Their initial capital came from the Nabobs, whose fortune-making was at its height during the 1760s and 1770s; and the managing partners were mostly retired Company Servants who had useful contacts in official quarters. These Agency houses afforded convenient investment facilities for men of substance who did not wish to run the risks involved in sending too much of their gains to Europe by illicit and precarious channels and also for the small man whose savings were not on a scale to enable him to engage in major transactions on his own account. The intermediate group, who did engage in independent private trading and had been pioneers in developing the Country trade, found the trend of events turning against them.

Fear of the statutory pains and penalties, the suppression of abuses by Cornwallis, and the regulations of 1788 which drastically restricted the opportunities of private trade by Company Servants – all reduced the capacity of individuals to compete with the Agency houses. By 1790 the latter dominated all branches of non-official European business and had become indispensable to the Presidency Governments and to the Company's Supercargoes in China. 'They controlled the Country trade, financed indigo and sugar manufacture, cornered the Government contracts, ran the three banks and the four insurance companies at Calcutta and speculated in public securities.'[15] Firms such as Fergusson, Fairlie and Co. of Calcutta and Scott, Tate and Adamson of Bombay worked in close alliance with houses in London, such as John and Francis Baring and Co., who collected their remittances and provided finance, and, on the other hand, with houses established at Canton (Jardine, Matheson and Co. was the most prominent) who supplied the China market. Thus the chain of commodity-exchange, linking England, India, South-East Asia and China, was developed and diversified through a strange marriage of convenience between a monopoly

---

[14] For a detailed account of the Country trade (in which these figures are cited) see H. Furber, *John Company at Work: A Study of European Expansion in India in the late Eighteenth Century* (Harvard Hist. Studies, vol. LV, Harvard, 1951), Chap. V.

[15] Tripathi (*op. cit.*), p. 11.

corporation and an elaborate (and exclusive) form of private enterprise.

While the system supplemented the operations of the Company it also presented the monopoly with a growing challenge. The authorised avenues of trade between Britain and the East were in the exclusive control of the Company, and they were constricted and clogged. Alternative – and illicit – channels were utilised, notably the media offered by the French and Dutch East India Companies and a clandestine trade with European ports, run by Englishmen under foreign flags. These methods will be summarised in turn in order to round out the picture of the British system of trade in the East. We shall then be in a position to consider the significance of the campaign which began in 1786 for the reform of the Company's trading structure to meet the expanding needs of the nation.

The new French East India Company, formed in 1783, worked in close and cordial co-operation with British Agency houses both in London and India. Of the London houses the French chiefly relied on Charles Harris and Co., who arranged most of their purchases of ships and consignments of heavy metals for export to India as well as their insurance. In 1787-9 the French insured their ventures for a total sum of 19·75 million *livres*: of this 8·75 million was underwritten in London through Harris and Co., together with a further 500,000 *livres* through an allied house, George Keith and Co., at Ostend.[16] There was, however, another form of Anglo-French co-operation which touched the English Company more nearly. This was the French use of British capital in India. Agency houses and individual Englishmen resident in Bengal and Madras had funds available which they wished to remit to London: the French who operated in these two Presidencies needed cash to supplement their supplies of silver bullion for purchasing an Investment. Accordingly they offered bills of exchange payable in London at six or twelve months' call, and payment was made there by French agents through British colleagues.

The attraction of this method of remittance lay in the fact that it was secret and also more lucrative than the English Company's own bills, the supply of which was in any case restricted. Between 1785 and 1790 French bills of exchange amounting to £757,177 were presented for payment in London.[17] From the point of view of the English Court of Directors the practice was doubly obnoxious: the accumulation of private wealth by their Servants was injuring the interests of the Company as well as the economy of Bengal, and these gains were being used to finance the trade of a foreign rival. When, therefore, the French Company in 1784-5

---

[16] Furber (*op. cit.*), pp. 39-40.

[17] It is thought that the lists which produce this total are incomplete (*ibid.*, p. 50).

opened negotiations with the English Directors, the latter agreed (by a majority vote) to provide the French under a three-year contract with a quota of Bengal silk and saltpetre and other trade goods to the annual value of 4 million rupees. Francis Baring, actively supported by Pitt and Dundas, carried the day with the argument that the contract would prevent the French Company from trading 'on the capitals of our servants'.[18] Although this agreement did not materialise, Dundas followed the same reasoning during the subsequent negotiations with the Dutch when he proposed that they should be provided as part of the bargain with a guaranteed quota of trade goods in India.[19]

Before the American War the old French Company had been able to secure large quantities of silver from the English Company's Servants, but after 1784 the pressure of the new régime in Bengal diminished the supply and rendered its transference precarious. Agency houses which had funds to remit, became scared, and when they did use this channel were careful to keep their names off the bills of exchange. For those who remained domiciled in India the high-interest loans which the Bengal Government was obliged to raise offered a more attractive field of investment. Madras, on the other hand, still provided considerable funds for the use of foreign companies, for Cornwallis's reforms had not yet become effective there.

The Dutch and Danish East India Companies, like the French, needed British-held capital to help finance their purchases of Indian products for the European market. Before the war with Britain the Dutch had collected large supplies of specie in the British settlements by selling bills of exchange, and with the connivance of British officials they had used the proceeds to secure consignments of Bengal opium, piece-goods and saltpetre. After the war the situation changed, and like the French they experienced increasing difficulty. The competition for a diminishing supply of

---

[18] *Ibid.*, pp. 32-7. It should be remembered that foreign remittances by Servants of the Company had been made illegal by the Act of 1780. Clearly this measure had failed to prevent them.

[19] See Chap. VI above. The more intelligent among the observers of the Indian situation were aware that it was to Britain's interest that the manufactures of Bengal should be extended by sales to European foreigners. See, for example, Sir John Macpherson's comment in 1785: 'The weaver who works for your [Dutch] Company contributes equally to pay the revenue with the weaver who works for our own Board of Trade, and perhaps more so, and an extension of the sale of Bengal manufactures is more profitable to Great Britain than a monopoly in the purchase of such goods as would restrain the manufacture.' (Quoted, Furber, p. 87.) The implications of the argument were far-reaching. For a very useful collection of documents on the French negotiations see 'Papers relative to a proposed Treaty between the English and French East India Companies'. These include: *Bases des Arrangements de Commerce que la Compagnie des Indes de France désiroit prendre avec la Compagnie des Indes Angloises*, 11 Aoust, 1785. Aug. Périer. (*Addit. MSS.*, 34,466, ff. 78-254.)

trade goods through prohibited channels dwindled.[20] The Danes, on the other hand, enjoyed the substantial advantage of being a neutral Power. When Britain was at war with the French from 1777 and with Holland from 1780 until 1783 and again from 1793, the Danes drove a flourishing contraband trade in military stores. In the ten years of peace they were well situated at Tranquebar to take advantage of the venality of the English Servants at Madras. Gold *pagodas* collected there were sent overland to Tranquebar, whence they were sent to the Tanjore country to buy cloth. North of Madras the Danes could not operate directly and depended on the favours of the English Company's officials – who exacted their price.[21]

The comparative success of the Bengal Government's measures against this unofficial traffic between European foreigners and resident Englishmen (whether Servants, retired Servants or organised as commercial houses) was an indication of its increasing political power; but an even more elusive method of violating the Company's Charter had been invented and was being actively pursued. Private venturers engaged secretly in a direct trade between Europe and India which was organised on an international basis. The first Englishman to take part in it was said to have been that enterprising rogue, William Bolts, who had previously been in the Company's Bengal service. 'Conceiving himself oppressed by the Company's monopoly', he loaded a vessel of 700 tons with European commodities and in 1777 dispatched it to India under the flag of the Imperial East India Company of Trieste.[22] By the 1780s Copenhagen, Ostend and Lisbon had become the centres of an Indian trade 'which was for the most part British in all but name'.[23]

In Copenhagen the private trade with India was managed by three or four great commercial houses. They had connexions all over Europe, but a large part of the capital employed was of British

---

[20] Owing to their grave financial difficulties and political dissensions the Dutch were unable to emulate the French and Danes in easing the situation by exporting silver from Europe. Between 1787 and 1793 the Danish Company exported bullion to India valued at 2 million rix dollars – approximately £350,000 (Furber, *op. cit.*, p. 128). The English Company should have done likewise instead of increasing their indebtedness in India.

[21] Between 1783 and 1793 the Dutch Company's bills of exchange, sold in Madras and payable in London, represented a total of £480,550. During the same period £377,666 was paid in London to the account of British holders of the Dutch Company's Bengal bills. A considerable proportion of the latter represented funds collected in Madras and transferred by the Danes to Bengal (*ibid.*, pp. 115 and 121).

[22] A statistical survey of Eastern trade (1792). *Home Misc. S.*, vol. 399, p. 2. Before the Trieste Company went bankrupt Bolts seems to have had extensive dealings with them. On 5 Feb., 1781, Laurence Sulivan wrote to Lord Macartney: 'We are now mortified in knowing that a Mr. Bolts has made a settlement for the Austrians on one of the Nicobar Islands, and it's my anxious wish to secure the others . . .' (*Addit. MSS.*, 29,147, f. 310).

[23] For an analysis of this clandestine trade see Furber (*op. cit.*), Chap. IV.

origin, and they worked in close alliance with London houses, particularly Edmund Boehm and Co., the head of which was a Director of the English Company. According to reports from British agents in Copenhagen approximately fifty-five private voyages to India took place under the Danish flag between 1783 and 1793, and it seems that a further ten voyages should be added to that total. The total value of European goods exported to India by this means has been estimated at more than two million rix dollars (£350,000) and the value of India goods brought back to Europe at 19½ million. During the years of peace such ventures usually did little better than break even, and there were frequent losses since the India (and China) goods were sold in markets already over-stocked by the English Company's Investment. Nevertheless there was a profit in the business for Agency and finance houses in Copenhagen and London: otherwise the trade would not have continued to increase. Probably higher profits were gained when the goods were smuggled directly into an English port. The individuals most likely to suffer loss were the British residents in India who invested in *respondentia* bonds, the redemption of which depended upon the success of the sales in Europe. Yet, precarious as this method was, it provided a channel of remittance for some £2 million over the ten-year period.

After 1786 Ostend began to outrival Copenhagen. Any ship engaged in the Eastern trade, however mysterious its origin and whatever flag it might (for the nonce) be flying, was given facilities with no questions asked. Dr. Furber cites as a characteristic example the ship *Concordia*, said to be owned by Tod and Atkinson of London. She cleared from Ostend for Bombay with a cargo which had been shipped from London in three small vessels. On the return voyage in 1788-9 her invoices included every kind of India and China goods, including a consignment of raw cotton from Surat. Off the Isle of Wight part of her cargo was smuggled ashore under cover of darkness: the rest was sold at Bruges by George Keith and Co. of Ostend for the account of her nominal owner, the Vicomte de Walkiers.[24] In 1792 an observer in London stated that in the previous season twenty-two ships, engaged in the clandestine trade, had sailed from European ports carrying – 'besides Treasure' – a total of 10,255 tons of European goods valued at £615,300. By way of comparison he added that the annual average of the English Company's exports to India for the years 1784-90 amounted to no more than 4,893 tons valued at £346,070.[25]

---

[24] *Ibid.*, p. 138.
[25] *Home Misc. S.*, vol. 399, p. 2. Before the war the annual average had been considerably less. Estimates of an illicit trade, which British participants had good reasons for keeping under cover, are bound in the nature of the case to be imprecise.

The overall situation of British trade in Asia was plain to see. The official East India Corporation was confiding itself almost entirely to the business of importing China teas and silks and India goods representing a 'surplus' revenue which was becoming increasingly unreal. Outside this import business, though closely connected with it, an intricate and expanding pattern of trade between Europe and Asia had developed which was dominated by the private enterprise of British subjects – established in Calcutta, Madras, Bombay, Canton, London, and in European centres such as Copenhagen, Ostend and Lisbon. Organised through a network of commercial and financial houses, it was they who managed the Country trade of India and supplied the China market. It was they who became the indispensable creditors of the Presidency Governments while surreptitiously providing foreign companies in India with ready money. At the same time they had become the predominant element in an international free-lance traffic between Europe and India. Critics of the English Company did not fail to point out that the 'Ostenders' and their like were disposing of European products to twice the value of those exported by East India House.

Specialists in British-Asian trade did not, however, press for the abolition of the monopoly: they were aware that the Company's system, financial and administrative, was the base upon which the credit structure as a whole depended. But they also knew from their own experience that the narrowness of the Company's practice was impeding private trade at many points and driving it into illicit (and precarious) courses. The remedy, therefore, was to establish a co-ordinated system. By this means private trade would enjoy increased facilities provided by the Company: leakages of goods and capital through foreign channels would dwindle to insignificance, and the export of British manufactures to Asia would be promoted. The plan represented an adaptation of mercantilist method to meet the demands of an industrial and commercial offensive. It was the oriental counterpart to the methods that were being simultaneously applied in the Western hemisphere. The object was not, of course, Free Trade, but rationalisation within the national orbit and a more realistic policy towards foreigners in the interests of Britain. Europe's trade with Asia was to be centralised in London – the metropolis of a commercial empire.

The attitude of Francis Baring was indicative of the changing climate of commercial opinion. As a Director of the East India Company representing the City interest and the founder of Baring Brothers and Co., which was involved in many branches of the private trade and closely associated with the French, Baring – like Edmund Boehm – had a foot in each camp and worked for the co-ordination of the two. Accordingly he is to be found urging that private trade should be attracted into the Company's channels by offering freight in East Indiamen at reasonable rates.[26] He also gave consistent support to Pitt and Dundas in their efforts to strike a bargain with the Dutch Company and with the French. Many of his fellow Directors were shrewd enough to appreciate that changing national circumstances required a less rigid and more co-operative policy in Leadenhall Street: hence Baring's success in securing a majority vote in favour of the French proposals.[27] But the Shipping and other entrenched interests clung to a dog-in-the-manger attitude towards foreign rivals as well as private British venturers. Their response to the proposals of the Spanish Philippine Company affords a good illustration of the reluctance to deviate from tradition.

After preliminary negotiations the Spaniards approached the Agency houses of Calcutta and the Court of Directors in London with a view to reaching an agreement whereby they would purchase India goods for sale in Manila, Spain and Spanish America. The British stood to gain a double advantage. Production in India would be stimulated with a consequential increase in the revenue, and the Calcutta treasury would receive a much-needed supply of hard currency in the form of Spanish dollars. In December, 1788, a three-year agreement was initialled by Pitt, Dundas and Grenville, who were strongly in favour of the project; but a majority of the Directors, avid though they were for dollars, imposed such severe restrictions upon the sale of Spanish products in India that the agreement never had a fair trial.[28] It will be recalled that Hawkesbury at the Board of Trade encountered similar resistance

---

[26] ' Mr. Baring's Statement '. *Home Misc. S.,* vol. 399, p. 167.

[27] In a letter to Pitt, dated 9 Oct., 1785, he stated the case for ' establishing ' and for ' crushing ' the French and other foreign East India Companies. On balance he favoured the former course and therefore supported the French proposals: it was in Britain's interest to encourage the consumption of Indian manufactures abroad. ' Upon this principle we should encourage a general trade to India.' An agreement with the French should be followed by similar arrangements with the Swedes, Danes, Dutch and Germans. (*Pitt Papers,* P.R.O. 30/8/111.) Twenty-two years later he castigated the Court of Directors for their plan to exclude (neutral) American trade from the French settlements in India. ' It appears to me to be a great mistake in some political economists to rest on the opinion that one Country must be injured because another prospers. The Americans are flourishing – ergo – it must be at our expence. . . . If America increases in wealth, how is it disposed of? In the consumption of British manufactures! ' It was essential to promote the sale of Indian manufactures in foreign countries, and especially through the Americans, who had no manufactures of their own to dispose of in India and who (unlike the French) had no political ambitions there. ' We are highly interested in the increased Commerce and general prosperity of the Indian Empire, which makes us returns in other and numerous ways, so that it will be folly to adopt the narrow principles of a Haberdasher's Shop.' (' Sir Francis Baring to the Honble. Directors of the East India Company. East India House. 15 Sept. 1807.' *Home Misc. S.,* vol. 337, pp. 937-53.)

[28] Cf. *Minutes of the Secret Committee of the Court of Directors,* vol. IV (1782-1806). Minutes of 26 Dec., 1785, 25 and 30 Jan., 20 Feb., 1786, 1 Feb., 1788.

when he supported British trading pioneers in their penetration of the North and South Pacific.

Between 1783 and 1793 the East India Company fought a rearguard action against demands for revolutionary change. On the political side Pitt and Dundas imposed an indirect but effective form of State control: the Company survived, but as an administrative instrument of the Crown. In the economic sphere rapid national expansion gave rise to a mounting pressure against the Company's traditional methods. Industrial inventions improved commodity-production which in turn stimulated a widening search for oceanic markets. Self-confident manufacturers and merchants (who sometimes over-reached themselves) were increasingly disposed to challenge restrictions and monopolies, whether domestic or foreign. Ministers, however, were not disposed to be more iconoclastic in handling the commercial problem than the political. Dundas in particular was impatient with the narrow and rigid views upheld by the less intelligent (and less disinterested) Directors and was consistently supported by Pitt in his efforts to extend the sale of British manufactures in Eastern markets; but the Ministry refused to countenance attacks on the chartered system as such: the time for abrogating the Charter had not yet come. As the several campaigns developed, they steered a middle course, the object of which was to incorporate private trade and free initiative in a more flexible system and so establish a more efficient means of promoting commercial expansion on a national basis.

In the summer of 1786 David Scott, of Scott, Tate, Adamson and Co., the leading commercial house in Bombay, returned to London after twenty-three years' residence in India.[29] Unlike most men in that situation he had come home not to buy an estate and set up as a country gentleman, but with the fixed purpose of bringing about a revolution in the British system of Eastern trade. His independent cast of mind and wide experience as an expert in the Country trade quickly attracted the attention of Dundas. The two became firm allies. In many respects Dundas found him a kindred spirit – well informed, self-reliant, keeping a weather eye on the main chance, sometimes lacking in judgement, but also warm-hearted and single-minded. When Scott was elected Chairman of the Court of Directors in 1796 and Dundas became overburdened with war responsibilities, the Minister left the conduct of India affairs very largely in the hands of the Chairman.[30]

Scott's first step was to establish a new commercial house in

---

[29] Shortly before leaving Bombay Scott had financed one of the pioneer expeditions sent out to establish a fur trade between the North-West American Coast and China (see Chap. VII, p. 426 above).

[30] See C. H. Philips, *The East India Company*, p. 91.

London under his own name, thus creating a finance and trading organisation which could mobilise the resources of similar houses in London and India. His next move was to prepare an elaborate memorandum which he submitted to the Court of Directors in April, 1787. The weaknesses in the Company's existing system were analysed and a comprehensive plan of reform and rehabilitation was proposed.[31] He began by describing the gravity of the Company's situation in India as the result of the long strain of the war. Creditors in India, British and native, held more than £1,300,000 of the Company's bonds, the negotiable value of which had dropped 50 per cent below par. The Company's credit in India was almost annihilated: specie was extremely scarce; and if another war or other emergency arose the Presidency Governments would be unable to raise any further loans for defence. Before he left India the unfortunate creditors had requested him to represent their plight to the Directors and to suggest remedial measures.

The first essential was to raise the level of British exports to India, which was lamentably low. Having acquired a territorial revenue, the Company had lost interest in making a profit on its exports. Most of the East Indiamen went out in ballast instead of being loaded, as they ought to have been, with home manufactures. For many years past not more than a quarter of the tonnage on the outward voyage had been in goods. Even the private 'privilege' trade allowed to the commander and ship's officers (usually about eighty-seven tons) was restricted in kind: important commodities, such as copper, tin and cloths, were reserved to the Company. Furthermore the methods of sale in India had remained unaltered for a century: adequate perhaps for a company in its infancy, but quite unsuited to contemporary conditions. The Indian Investment was sold at home wholesale and at fixed times because London was the European market for piece-goods, but it was futile to employ the same method when attempting to sell European goods in India.

The Company's Exports to India, on the contrary, after being landed there, must be either by them or others, at second hand, retailed over countries more extensive than all Europe. The greater the Company, the more unequal it is to such a detail.

Private venturers, expert in the business, would make up assortments in England that were calculated to meet known demands: they would sell a wide variety of goods which it would not suit a

---

[31] For more effective publicity the memorandum was printed in pamphlet form: *Remarks and Ideas upon the Export Trade from Great Britain to India, with a Plan and Proposals for the Increase thereof. Submitted to the Consideration of the Directors of the East India Company, By a Letter from David Scott Esq., dated 3 April 1787.* Copy in *B.T. 6 (Misc.) bundle 42.*

great Company to deal in; and as they would dispose of two-thirds of their goods in barter for those of other countries they would make a higher profit. As a merchant with long experience of a Country trade which extended from the Red Sea to Canton, Scott was insisting that British goods must not be dumped but could be infiltrated into the ramifications of the system.

It might be objected, continued Scott, that if the Company gave up the export trade (in its own ships) to the private merchants, that trade would in effect be thrown open to the nation at large and the monopoly would be destroyed. Such an objection would be difficult to disprove without trying the experiment, but as a means of keeping private enterprise within the Company's super-vision he proposed that the Directors should negotiate an agree-ment with 'a set of merchants' who would guarantee to send out a specified quantity and quality of goods over a five-year period. In the first year they would send 6,000 tons, value £550,000, in the second year 8,000 tons, value £650,000, and so rising in the fifth year to 14,000 tons, value £1,050,000. By means of such a plan a thorough knowledge could be gained of the extent to which exports could in future bear being increased. If the Company charged only £5 per ton on the outward voyage, it would be an encouragement to the merchants while affording the Company an additional and increasing revenue. Should it be deemed improper for the Company to give up the export trade, then they should increase it themselves by adopting business-like methods. But if private merchants had the handling of it, there was no reason at all, he asserted, why the annual value of exports should not be raised from £350,000, as it then stood, to at least £700,000.[32] To extend the sale of British products through the India channel, accepting payment in Company's bonds, was the soundest method of retrieving the financial position in India. The Company's credit, upon which the entire trading structure depended, would be re-established: the interest rate on the bonded debt in India could then be reduced to five per cent and the debt itself be gradually redeemed: and at home the production of manufactures would be stimulated.

Such a policy of expansion and financial rehabilitation offered the further advantage that it would enable the Company to regain ground lost to the foreigner. As a private merchant Scott was critical of the Company's refusal to allow British subjects in India to send their fortunes home by buying Company bills of exchange. The gentlemen in question had been obliged to choose between the alternatives of 'giving up all hopes of seeing again their native country' or remitting through foreign channels. With the aid of

---

[32] At the end of his memorandum Scott submitted a detailed scheme for which he himself would accept responsibility.

these funds foreign corporations had not only been enabled to get possession of the export trade from Europe but also to compete in the return trade from India. As an investment *respondentia* bonds were very risky and the British subject had no means of judicial redress if he lost his money. 'Millions', asserted Scott (with some exaggeration), 'have remained unpaid for several years and will be finally liquidated with a spunge.' The nation and the English Company were injured thereby, and many individuals suffered ruin. This capital should be drawn into the national pool by permitting remittances through the Company's channel at a reasonable rate of exchange; but the final and decisive method was to recapture the European export trade. At the same time Scott was opposed to the narrow attitude of the Company towards the foreigner in India who was operating his own Country trade. He was useful and should be drawn into the British orbit. Attempts to exclude him by high import duties only served to turn him into other channels and to promote smuggling on the part of his British associates.[33] Because foreign ships were obliged to pay nine per cent more than British ships they avoided the Company's ports. High duties at Bombay had produced the inevitable result: the fair trader had traded less and the less rigid trader had 'defrauded more'. Import duties at all the Company's ports should be reduced to a uniform rate of four per cent for all comers. Scott was thus anticipating the fiscal reforms in India which Cornwallis was about to effect.

Finally he turned to the China trade. This, he anticipated, could become the focus of the entire system of British commerce in Asia. Such a development was possible, and indeed essential because of the steep rise in the Company's tea imports. If the British purchase of tea rose to 18 million lbs. annually, as seemed probable, there would be a corresponding increase in the shipping used to transport it.[34] Fifteen large vessels, or twenty-three of the smaller type as then used, would be required. Was this increased tonnage to go out to Canton in ballast?

The cost of purchasing the teas, together with raw silk and china-ware, would amount to at least £1,300,000. At present it appeared

---

[33] As an illustration Scott mentioned that at one time the Governor and Council of Bombay had imposed a duty of twenty per cent on imported copper. In consequence copper had ceased to come to Bombay and was sent instead to the Maratha Dominions 'not twenty miles away', where it was bought by the same merchants who would otherwise have bought it at Bombay. Protests by the Bombay merchants (presumably led by Scott himself) had caused the removal of the tax.

[34] In fact the Company's importation of tea soon greatly exceeded this figure. Already in 1786 the Supercargoes at Canton had been instructed to buy consignments totalling 18,900,000 lbs. ('Quantity and Assortment of Tea expected from China in 1787, according to the Orders last sent out.' *Parl. Papers* (*Gen. Coll.*), vol. 68 (1786), No. 162). Between Sept., 1784, and 22 May, 1785, there had been thirteen sales in London, at which a total of 27,236,424 lbs. was sold. (*Ibid.*, No. 159.)

that the Company was realising less than £150,000 p.a. on the sale of goods at Canton: the rest of the bill was being paid in specie. The Company's credit needs in China had already increased three-fold. Clearly such an immense and increasing liability could not continue to be met with cash.

The Company have as yet found out no other mode of supplying those wants, but by draining the mother country, or, what in my opinion is by far more ruinous, Bengal, of its specie . . . to continue such exports of specie any longer would be destroying the Trunk on which all the other branches have hitherto depended, and must in future depend.[35]

Expanding imports from China must be paid for in goods, thus imparting an immense stimulus to every branch of British trade in Asia. Two methods were available: a substantial increase in direct exports from Britain to China, and secondly the develop-ment of Bombay as a great depot through which a wide variety of Indian, Arabian and Malay products could be channelled to the Chinese market. With regard to the direct trade Scott was confident that it would surpass British sales in India – 'provided we had any settlement on the coast of China for a magazine'. If such a base were acquired, goods could be unloaded and stored in ware-houses until a convenient season. Under the existing conditions ships must dispose of their cargoes on arrival and 'at whatever price a company of [Chinese] monopolisers at Canton pleases to give' or carry the same goods back. If British exports were increased in proportion to the tonnage their annual value (in China) could be raised to £300,000.

Scott proposed that the trade between Britain and China should continue to be managed by the Company itself, but he urged that the India-China trade should be thrown open to private merchants; and as an incentive they should be permitted to transport their consignments in the Company's ships freight free on condition that the Company had the refusal of the proceeds at Canton for their bills on London. The Company would be supplied with funds

---

[35] The extent to which Bengal was 'drained' of silver to pay for tea at Canton has been greatly exaggerated. During the American war shipments of silver from India were valued at Canton as follows: in 1776-7 – 394,016 taels; in 1777-8 – 70,252 taels; in 1778-9 – 21,600 taels. No further shipments took place until 1783-4 when the figure was 8,640 taels. Thereafter the export of bullion ceased except for the season 1788-9 when shipments valued at 102,240 taels were made. (See E. H. Pritchard, *The Crucial Years of Early Anglo-Chinese Relations, 1750-1800.* Research Studies of the State College of Washington, vol. IV, Nos. 3-4. Pullman, Washington, 1936. App. IX.) Cornwallis was frequently pestered by the Directors to provide specie for Canton, but – except in 1788 – he successfully resisted the pressure for the good reason that specie was not available. The requests ceased when the flow of goods to Canton became greater in value than the products purchased for export. (The tael was a hypothetical coin of pure silver valued at 6s. 8d.)

and would lose nothing by giving up the tonnage to individuals, for the ships carried little or no cargo from India to China on Company's account and to his own knowledge always made a loss when they did so.[36] The Company, as such, was not equipped for the business, whereas the private merchants were specialists in all the ramifications of the Country trade.

It was impossible to say what the increase in this trade would amount to in private hands, but the potentialities were greater than was understood in England because of the wide range of products which could be supplied. From Bengal Bombay purchased rice, sugar, saltpetre and opium: from the Malabar coast such products as pepper, sandal-wood, ivory, sharks' fins, putchock (a form of incense) and pearls; and through the Malay traders tin, gold dust, pepper and wax. From the trade with Arabia Bombay realised more than £450,000 a year in German crowns, Venetian sequins and two-lire pieces and other currency. All these commodities commanded a ready sale in China. Furthermore gentlemen in India who did not trade themselves would soon begin to remit their fortunes home by way of China in preference to the clandestine trade with foreign centres in Europe.

Scott's thesis, that a partnership between the Company and private enterprise had become a national necessity and could effect a vast expansion, was prophetic. Developments took place broadly – though not precisely – along the lines which he indicated. His ideas received cautious support from the Government and a divided response from the Directors. Among the latter the Shipping interest recognised a threat to their freight monopoly and fought Scott à l'outrance; but the City interest, which included merchant-financiers such as Baring and Boehm, favoured a broader policy. Twelve months before Scott's memorandum appeared, the inability of the Bengal Government to contribute to the China Investment had caused the Secret Committee of the Directors to investigate the possibility of promoting the export of raw cotton to China from Bombay on the Company's account. They found that the annual delivery of cotton by British and foreign shippers averaged 1,864 tons and that in spite of the high profit obtainable not more than 673 tons was carried in the Company's ships, and of this only 82 tons was on the Company's account. It was resolved to take vigorous action to remedy the situation.[37] In

---

[36] Cf. Dundas in 1793: 'The exports to China of goods, stores, and bullion, are not supposed to yield any profit; so that, on the whole, the export trade is estimated to produce a loss of £50,000 per annum' (Parl. Hist., vol. XXX, 508-9).

[37] The Secret Committee resolved (i) that shipments on the Company's account could be increased to 500 tons weight, or 2,965 bales, annually, (ii) that five ships should be directed to proceed to Bombay in the ensuing season in order that each might take in 100 tons of cotton, (iii) that £15,700 in bullion should be remitted to Bombay 'for the sole and express purpose of purchasing the said Quantity of Cotton'. (Secret Mins., Ct. of Drs., vol. IV. Minute of 1 June, 1786.)

practice, however, the Company found it more convenient to leave the export trade from India to China to be developed by the private trader. Scott's proposals in 1787 did not secure immediate results, but they heralded a revolution which gradually co-ordinated the British system of trade in the East, rendering it more flexible and enormously more extensive.[38]

Before Scott returned to the charge the Directors were subjected to pressure from a different, though closely related, quarter. On 27 March, 1788, the Board of Trade had before them a memorial from the manufacturers of calicoes and muslins in Great Britain complaining that the East India Company was dumping very large quantities of piece-goods on the home market which were underselling the British product. It was impossible, they declared, to carry on in the face of such competition. This proved to be a sighting shot for an organised barrage. A week later petitions were received from Manchester and Ashton-under-Lyme inveighing against this 'foreign' competition which would beggar them.[39] These were followed up by further petitions from Manchester, Bolton, Preston, Stockport, Chorley, Blackburn and towns in the west of Scotland, representing 'the very distressed state of their Trade'.

The occasion of the attack was a sharp recession in the cotton industry.[40] When one of these periodic crises occurred John Company was usually the first object of blame. In 1788 the Directors' efforts to increase the importation of Indian textiles (i.e. the Investment) probably exacerbated the situation. The attack was delivered at a time when the Company was already fighting a rearguard action against the Government. Early in March the violent quarrel between Dundas and the Directors over the powers of the Board of Control had culminated in the passage of a declaratory Act – after a storm in the Commons;[41] and on 26 March the 'Chairs' had been summoned to the Board of Trade and informed by Hawkesbury that their lordships desired to have the Company's consent to an extension of the whale fishery in the Southern Oceans 'with all convenient speed' – a demand which the Company regarded as a dangerous encroachment upon their preserves.[42] In fact Hawkesbury's steady promotion of British maritime trade was

---

[38] Scott's proposals were referred by the Court of Directors to a special committee. In their report the latter did not take up his ambitious scheme, but they did recommend that the Company should raise its annual exports to 10,000 tons in order to reduce debts and re-establish its credit in India. As Scott afterwards observed, however, virtually nothing was done to implement this recommendation. (See *Home Misc. S.*, vol. 399, pp. 34-5.) *B.T.* 5 (*Minutes*), vol. III, p. 69.

[39] *Ibid.*, pp. 72-3.

[40] See 'An important Crisis in the cotton manufactures of Great Britain explained.' 1788. MS. and printed copies, *B.T. 6/140.*

[41] See Chap. III, pp. 200-2.

[42] See Chap. V, above, p. 319.

bringing him into increasing contact with the commercial concerns of the Company,[43] and on general grounds he was predisposed to favour the demands of the home manufacturer.

When the mill owners of Lancashire loudly asserted that it was the Company's duty to bring home cargoes of raw cotton, they were addressing their protests, as they well knew, to a President of the Board of Trade who was employing every means in his power to increase their supplies, notably by multiplying cotton production in the West Indies. Dundas, on the other hand, though contemptuous of the Company's narrow commercial views, was primarily concerned with their viability as an Indian Government and was therefore disposed to encourage them to sell more piece-goods in Europe and so acquire the wherewithal to reduce their debts.[44] The Government as a whole were not prepared to identify themselves with manufacturers and others whose aim was to eliminate the Company's exclusive rights, but they were impressed by the need to increase the exports of British products through the Company channels and by the claim of the private commercial houses that they were the fittest instrument to effect it. The Company was thus under simultaneous pressure from two flanks with the Government giving weighty, though qualified, support to each.

In response to the spate of petitions the Board of Trade requested the Chairman of the Court of Directors to furnish an account of all goods imported by the Company from India since 1765. Two days later (21 April) he was summoned to the Board and advised to arrange a meeting between the Directors and the delegates representing the cotton manufacturers 'for the purpose of discussing the points in agitation and of settling some method for carrying on in future the Trade in Callicoes and Muslins as well by the said

---

[43] When Jenkinson was raised to the peerage in 1786 as Baron Hawkesbury and became a Government spokesman in the House of Lords, Dundas began to re-educate him in Indian affairs. In September he told Hawkesbury that he would spare him as much as possible, ' but you will comfort yourself by recollecting that what of your time you now give will be so much gained hereafter, as you will be under the necessity of making Yourself Master of India business, even in its minute detail to a certain extent, as a great part of the Load of maintaining the ground of Government in the House of Lords on India, as well as other Matters, must of course rest on your shoulders.' (Dundas to Hawkesbury, 8 Sept., 1786. *Liverpool Papers, Select Political Correspondence*, vol. III. *Addit. MSS.*, 38,192, ff. 40-1.) Three days later Dundas sent him two secret despatches on India and warned him that he was having a complete set of all letters of the Board of Control from its inception prepared for him. ' I will not frighten you at this moment with them . . .' (*ibid.*, f. 42). Some fourteen years earlier Jenkinson had been the expert on India affairs and Dundas the apprentice.

[44] It would appear that some difference of opinion arose between Dundas and Hawkesbury on this issue, judging by an unusually curt note sent by Dundas. ' I send you the Information I promised on the subject of the Cotton Trade of the East India Company. My mind is made up on the Subject, and We may resume the Consideration of it when your Conveniency suits. Yours faithfully, H.D.' (Dundas to Hawkesbury, 28 Feb., 1787. *Ibid.*, f. 45).

Company as by the said Manufacturers on such equitable plan as may best correspond with their respective Interests'. Not surprisingly the discussions were abortive and each side presented the Board with a written case.

The proposals put forward by the manufacturers' delegates were revolutionary. In future the quantity of calicoes, muslins and nankins offered for sale by the Company in any one year was not to exceed the quantity sold in 1787. It was further proposed that the Company should gradually increase the importation of fine cotton and other raw materials and that their investment in piece-goods should be proportionately diminished. The plan was received by the angry Directors as a blatant attempt to dictate the conduct of their business: they would decide on their answer, the Board was informed, as soon as the relevant information had been collected and considered. Their Lordships' reaction to the conflict was significant. A soothing letter was sent to the Directors, but there was a sting in its tail. Some of the manufacturers' suggestions, it was intimated, would require further investigation before it could be decided whether they were practicable, but in the Board's opinion most of them were reasonable. About a month later the Directors submitted their report. Guarded promises were made to promote the production of raw materials in India and to encourage the sale of British manufactures, but the proposed restrictions would only serve to drive the trade into foreign channels, would lead to a reduction in the Company's Indian revenues and so to a diminution in British exports. Furthermore the high-grade piece-goods imported from India did not compete with the coarser grades produced at home and were mostly re-exported to Europe.[45]

It was the stock answer which was to be repeated again and again in subsequent battles. In fact it was more profitable to export raw cotton to China, and the implication of a gradual withdrawal from the European market in piece-goods (which the Company dominated) was regarded by the Directors as a compound of stupidity and impudence. In this period the cotton manufacturers were still apprentices in the business, but they were learning fast; and their demands were a presage of the revolution to come. The Board declared themselves 'satisfied' with the Directors' report and ordered a copy of it to be sent to the delegates. The Company had won the first round; but it was to be followed by others in quick succession, and later events showed that Minister-members of the Board were not, in fact, 'satisfied'.[46]

---

[45] B.T. 5/5, pp. 82, 84-6, 90, 91, 97, 98, 103, 108, 117, 120. (Minutes of 19 and 21 April, 3, 9 and 29 May, 2, 5 and 7 June, 3 and 23 July, 1788.) The proposals of the manufacturers' delegates and the objections of the Directors are in B.T. 6/140.

[46] At the two decisive meetings during this contest the Board consisted of Pitt, Hawkesbury, Dundas, Grenville and Lord Frederick Campbell. Twelve months

Some six months later (March, 1789) David Scott resumed his efforts to induce the Company to adopt a more liberal and realistic policy. As the spokesman of the commercial houses his approach was that of an ally offering mutually advantageous co-operation. The proposals now put forward on behalf of the private trader were less ambitious than the previous scheme but were based on the same principles. A new feature was the marked support given to the claims of the manufacturers. It was most important that their exports to the East should be promoted and that the Company should avoid competing with them in the home market. The close connexion between the interests of the latter and those of the commercial houses was clearly implied as Scott urged the Company to remedy the twin evils of their indebtedness in India and their failure to scotch the foreign and clandestine trade. The Company's restrictions were enabling foreigners to sell British manufactures in India; but this competition restricted the Company's own sales there, raised the purchase price of Indian goods in India, and reduced the Company's sales in Europe. The only sound remedy was to send out the East Indiamen fully loaded with British goods. This could be done on the Company's own account, if that method was preferred, or on that of private merchants who should not be charged more than £10 per ton or £5 freight and £4 duty, payable in India. The proceeds would accrue to the Presidency Governments in exchange for Company bonds.[47] At the same time the flow of capital into foreign channels must be diverted. 'The Gentlemen of India' should be allowed to send a reasonable remittance home in goods up to an annual maximum value of £400,000.[48] The effect of this indulgence would be 'to leave none of them spare cash to lend to Foreigners'. In fact he confidently predicted that the combined effect of these arrangements would be the elimination of the clandestine trade in two years.

In this new memorandum Scott was at pains to reconcile the interests of the manufacturers with those of the Company, and in doing so he reflected the views of the Government. It was most

---

earlier Sir Joseph Banks had written to Dundas pointing out the enormous potential of India as a producer of raw materials. 'The greatest part of the merchandises imported from India have hitherto been manufactured goods of a nature which interfere with our own manufactories at home . . . our cotton manufactories are increasing with a rapidity which renders it politic to give them effectual encouragement. . . .' (Banks to Dundas, 15 June, 1787. Copy. *Royal Archives, Windsor*).

[47] Scott calculated that in a given season twenty-seven ships, each carrying 200 tons at £10 per ton, would produce a revenue of £54,000 for freight, that the prime cost of the goods shipped out would be £270,000 and that they would sell in India for £324,000.

[48] The suggested allotments were – for Bengal 450 tons (value £220,000), for Madras 225 tons (value £112,500), for Bombay 330 tons (value £67,500).

important that the goods sent home on private remittance should be those 'which would least interfere with our Company's sales or with those of the British Manufacturers'. As a safeguard he suggested that only a specified proportion of the remittance should be allowed in the form of piece-goods and that the remainder must consist of indigo, coffee, drugs and other primary products. Similarly the Company should endeavour to make up its own Investment in commodities which did not injure home manufactures. The only articles which threatened to do this were Bengal coarse muslins. It would be a happy event indeed, wrote Scott, if a tariff could be agreed with the manufacturers which 'would enable our Company to undersell Foreigners and at the same time leave our British Manufacturers a reasonable return for their industry'. Looking to the future he came near to adopting the position recently taken up by the Lancashire mill-owners, that the Company should gradually change over from being an importer of fabrics to a supplier of raw materials.

Under the idea of assisting the British Manufacturers, the greatest encouragement should be given to bring home the revenue in other articles than piece-goods, and from the freight being so low, I should hope, in a few years, for some hundred thousand sterling per annum coming home in indigo alone, besides what industry [in India] might produce from other articles.[49]

This plan of adjustment and reform received special attention from the Court of Directors, for it obviously represented views which carried formidable support from the manufacturers, the commercial houses, and the Government.[50] A special committee of Directors was appointed which submitted a detailed report five months later. Scott's contention that the illicit and foreign trade could be countered only by increasing British exports was accepted, but the practical difficulties were pointed out. It was useless to attempt to increase the sale of woollen goods: metals, however, were a different matter and the committee recommended that the export of copper should be raised from 1,170 tons (in 1788-9) to

---

[49] *Regulations proposed for remedying the difficulties which at present press hardest on the Company, and for giving them such an Increase of Commerce at Home and Abroad as they are entitled to, from their influence in the East.* Submitted to the Consideration of the Directors by David Scott, Esq., 4 March, 1789. (*B.T. 6/42.*) The growing demand in Britain for indigo as a dye caused a large development of indigo plantations in Bengal. As a Bombay merchant, interested in the China trade, Scott ignored the question of supplying British manufacturers with Indian cotton. Later a struggle developed between the producers of Indian and West Indian sugar which had repercussions on the movement to abolish the slave trade and afterwards West Indian slavery.

[50] These three sources of pressure differed widely in their views about the Company's future role, but Scott's proposals represented common ground.

3,130 tons.[51] On the other hand they rejected the proposition that the export business should be thrown open to private traders: the 'privilege' should continue to be confined to the ship's officers, but in future *all* surplus tonnage should be made available to them and free of all charges.[52]

It was agreed that steps should be taken to equalise the duties in Bombay and Bengal, and that Bombay was the most suitable centre for extending and diversifying the trade to China. To this end they recommended that 2,500 tons of additional shipping should be sent to Bombay, making 6,500 tons in all, of which 1,369 tons would be surplus. This should be offered, first to the ship's officers, and then to private merchants at reasonable rates. A similar approach was made to Scott's proposals for increasing the importation of India goods into Britain. Additional shipping should be sent out to Bengal and Madras, and if the Presidencies were unable to fill the ships with goods on the Company's account, individuals should be permitted to use the spare tonnage and on reasonable terms – 'as those which have been exacted hitherto are in general too high and amount to a total prohibition against some of the articles of the growth and Manufacture of India'. The revenues in India did not at present furnish a sufficient surplus for the Investment. 'Your Committee cannot flatter the Court with an expectation of supplying the whole of that deficiency in consequence of any regulations whatsoever.'[53] There was no intention of admitting private enterprise on any substantial scale as a competitor in Europe.

The concerted pressure that was building up against the East India Company at this time is well illustrated by a memorial submitted to Pitt by a London merchant. His arguments for using private trade to liquidate the Company's debts in India and to eliminate the clandestine trade are the same as those of David Scott, but this writer went much further in the direction of a free trading system. Was it better, he asked, for Britain to allow a free trade between Bengal and all Europe, so extending the consumption

---

[51] To illustrate the situation the Committee quoted the following figures of goods remaining in India unsold: Bengal – 8,538 pieces of woollens (no value given) and 730 tons of metals: Madras – £40,206 of woollens and 8,573 tons of metals: Bombay – £74,686 of woollens.

[52] In 1791 Hawkesbury asked the Directors why it was that, while 245 tons had been employed in consequence of this concession in the season 1789-90, only ten tons had been made available in the following season. The Directors replied that the number of army recruits and the quantity of military stores then sent out (owing to the threat of war with Spain) had occupied more than the chartered tonnage.

[53] The Committee's report is reproduced in full in the *Minutes of the Court of Directors* for 19 August, 1789. The Government's interest in Scott's proposals and the Company's response is indicated by the fact that a verbatim copy of his Minute is in the papers of the Board of Trade (*B.T. 6/42*).

of Indian goods and thus enriching the value of our territorial possessions, or to monopolise this trade for our immediate benefit but to the injury of the country? Foreign Europeans, he maintained, should be given free entry in Bengal and British subjects should be allowed to do business with them. British traders should also be given liberty to distribute the products of India to all parts of Europe, and 'without subjecting them to that odious and impolitick *Colonial* Restriction of first importing them into the Mother Country'. They should, however, be required by law to use only British ships and to touch at a British port, paying duty there, before proceeding to their European destination. The monopoly of the East India Company should be confined to the China trade, 'which it is conceived will afford ample Profits for a Commercial Dividend'. Under this system the prosperity of Bengal would be promoted, the price of Indian goods would be reduced, their sale in Europe would be extended, and Britain's mercantile profit and navigation would be greatly increased.

By an adoption of this Plan the Government of India would be rendered more simple, the Trade more productive, and the unnatural Junction of State Concerns with commercial Adventures be dissolved. . . . The Company cannot stand its present situation long. The most powerful support on the part of Government must be given to maintain the present system. It is therefore to be considered whether it is [not] most adviseable to form a new Arrangement, instead of supporting an Establishment too unwieldy for Management, and borne down by the Weight of Evils naturally growing out of a Constitution so heterogeneous.[54]

In 1790 joint action by the Government and the Company was being planned against the Spanish Empire in case of war and the domestic conflict was left to simmer; but in the following year public agitation revived with the approaching expiry of the Charter Act. The time for ministerial decision was drawing near. On the commercial side it was Hawkesbury who took the initiative. In April, 1791, he remarked in a letter to Cornwallis: 'our Manufacturers complain bitterly that the markets of the East are not sufficiently open to them and in my opinion they never will be

---

[54] *Important Alterations in the System of British Government in India.* Endorsed: ' A Plan for altering the system of British Government in India. Signed P.L., 15 July, 1789.' (*Pitt Papers*, P.R.O. 30/8/355.) On the political side the author advocated that ' the Sovereignty and territorial Possessions of India should be assumed for the Benefit of the State'. ' The East India Company,' he declared, ' is not fit to govern the Empire of India, nor is it fit they should be allowed to do it. From this state of things a System has been generated which confounds Responsibility and creates a Competition of political and commercial Systems that must have injurious Effects, both to the Nation and the East India Company.'

R*

satisfied till they have carried this point'.[55] Parliament rose for the summer recess on 10 June: on the following day Hawkesbury took the unusual course (for him) of writing a letter to the Prime Minister. He enclosed a draft statement of policy to be communicated by the Board of Trade to the East India Company. A copy was also sent to a trusted adviser, Samuel Garbett, for comment. To the latter he wrote that, if Mr. Pitt did not object to the document, he would arrange a conference with the Company to secure their assent. 'If I am supported by Government, I shall be able to speak with authority to the Chairman and Deputy Chairman of the East India Company, and tho' they may raise Objections, I think that in the end I shall succeed.' It was also his intention, Garbett was informed, to send a circular letter to all the appropriate manufacturing towns, informing them of the Board's proposals and inviting their co-operation.[56]

The policy statement began by observing that in consequence of the near approach of the termination of the Company's exclusive trade it would be necessary, among other points, to consider what measures could be adopted to extend the export trade to India, 'in order to meet as far as possible in this respect the reasonable expectation of the Manufacturers and others concerned therein'. Their Lordships were of the opinion that possibly no plan might be thought sufficient for the purpose which did not give to individual traders the liberty of exporting on their own account; but in that case it would be a question whether they ought not to be required to export only in the Company's ships, provided that a sufficient number of ships was made available and at reasonable freight rates.

So far this was familiar stuff and closely resembled David Scott's proposals; but there was more to come. It appeared to their Lordships that, since adequate information was lacking, no final arrangement ought to be made until the Company and the manufacturers had worked out together an experimental plan in order to ascertain the nature and extent of any trade that might be established. What

---

[55] In the same letter he made the following observation: 'This Country was never in so perfect a State of Prosperity. . . . In this moment of British Greatness all the Nations around us are in a State of anarchy or in dread of it, owing to Distress in their Finances or to a sort of Political Phrenzy . . . so that We have no reason to apprehend a War, at least of any Duration, for many years.' (*Hawkesbury's Letter-Books, 1780-1794. Addit. MSS.*, 38,310, f. 51.) As Earl of Liverpool he lived to see Napoleon attempt to strangle Britain's economic life by the Berlin and Milan Decrees.

[56] Hawkesbury to Garbett, 11 June, 1791. Hawkesbury added: 'I am pleased always to hear Objections, before I commence a business; they afford Matter of Reflection, and I am more likely in the end to be in the right. . . . These are subjects which you understand better than I can, and you are best acquainted with those topics which are most likely to recommend a Measure of this nature to the Manufacturers whom it may be proper to consult upon it.' (*Ibid.*, f. 65.)

was meant by this was more explicitly stated in the draft circular
letter to the manufacturing towns. It was suggested that each of
these should send delegates to confer with a committee of the Court
of Directors on the whole subject, 'and particularly on the Terms
and Conditions on which each of the said manufacturing Towns
should be allowed to send one or more discreet and intelligent . . .
Agents to the different Parts of the East Indies with proper Assortments of their respective Manufactures'. By this means the market
could be tested and information collected about varying the types
of each commodity so as to meet the taste and fashions prevailing
in the individual countries. When the agents returned they should
make a report to the Board of Trade in order that it might be laid
before Parliament, 'to assist their Judgement in forming a permanent Plan for extending the Sale of British Manufactures in the
East Indies under proper Regulations'.[57] When the Court of
Directors eventually learned of this proposition they were horrified.
An invasion of India by brisk and brash salesmen from Birmingham and Manchester would introduce all the troubles of *colonisation*: relations with the inhabitants would be disturbed, and the
Company might well be dragged into wars with native princes.

The more general statement, intended for the Directors, concluded with an intimation that they should turn their thoughts
towards the best means of increasing the exports and ascertaining
the most suitable products for the purpose. Pitt approved the document, adding in his own hand the two words – 'without delay'.[58]
Dundas also agreed in principle, but as the chief architect of commercial empire in the East he was better acquainted with the
system and was opposed to the idea of a direct assault upon oriental
markets on the part of the manufacturers. 'I am satisfied,' he wrote
a little later, 'that the Merchants or rather the Manufacturers of
this Country are under a delusion, which will vanish on a nearer
approach to the Subject.' It was very probable that the export
trade could be improved very considerably, but he was convinced
that the trade to India could never be developed to an extent that
would induce an intelligent trader to embark his individual capital
in it. Moreover any attempt to divert it from the channel of the
East India Company would be hurtful and not beneficial to the

---

[57] *Draft of Letter to the Mayor or Chief Magistrate of Manchester, Birmingham,
Wolverhampton, Leeds, Devizes, Norwich, Stroud, Sheffield, Halifax, Exeter,
Colchester, Glasgow and Paisley. Mr. Wedgewood for the Potters. Qu[ery] Ireland?*
(*B.T.* 6/42.)

[58] *Memo. Mr. Pitt.* Endorsed: 'Increase of the Company's Trade to India.' In
addition to Pitt's amendment two others were added in the margin. The fact that
this document is in the *Home Miscellaneous Series* (vol. 404(2), pp. 41-5) seems to
indicate that Pitt referred it to Dundas at the Board of Control. A fair copy, which
includes all three amendments, is in *B.T.* 6/42. It is entitled: 'Heads of Conversation between the Committee of the Lords of Trade and the Deputy-Chairman.
24 June, 1791.'

manufacturing interests of this country. Indeed, with regard to the export trade with China it would be 'rashness in the extreme' to make any change until a new arrangement had been agreed with the Chinese Government. For that reason he had promoted the embassy to Peking which had been frustrated by Colonel Cathcart's death.[59] Instead of giving way to the clamour of the manufacturers for direct access to Eastern markets Dundas intended to achieve the desired expansion by cajoling the Company into a working partnership with the commercial houses who operated the great complex of the Country trade. The most effective way, he added, of improving the European export trade would be for the Company to open its outward tonnage to those who were prepared to adventure in those exports. 'I likewise think the Import Trade of the Company from India may be rendered more instrumental than it hitherto has been to the manufacturers of this Country by the importation of Raw Materials.'[60] These were the ideas of David Scott.

On 22 June, 1791, the Board of Trade considered Hawkesbury's two documents – the proposed communication to the Court of Directors and his draft circular letter to the manufacturers. It was formally decided that the 'Chairs' should be summoned to attend in two days' time to be informed of the plan.[61] On the 24th Francis Baring, as Deputy-Chairman, duly presented himself.[62] As he faced Pitt and his ministerial colleagues across the table and listened to Hawkesbury's reading of the prepared statement, his reaction must have been one of concern not unmixed with dry amusement. Pitt and Dundas he knew well, being a supporter of the Ministry and an ally of Dundas, who frequently called him to Wimbledon for consultation.[63] The presence of the Prime Minister and 'the Secretary of State for India' was a clear indication that the Government was about to make a determined effort to induce the Com-

---

[59] See § 3 of this chapter.

[60] *Memorandum of Instructions: Mr. [Francis] Russell.* Endorsed: 'Dundas: Private Instructions re the New Arrangements for India. 1 Oct., 1791' (*Home Misc. S.,* vol. 413(6), pp. 241-99). Dundas could not be expected to support Hawkesbury's idea that the manufacturers should be allowed to send their own representatives to explore the markets of Asia, but he and Pitt were on common ground with Hawkesbury in wishing to compel the Company to increase the volume of trade between Britain and India. In his instructions to Russell Dundas proposed that there should be a clause in the new Charter Act, empowering the Treasury, the Board of Control, or the Board of Trade to grant licences to private shipping to take part in the India trade if it were proved to the satisfaction of the Board in question that the Company's imports or exports were not commensurate with the demand in India or Britain. By the Charter Act of 1793 this discretionary power was vested in the Board of Control.

[61] The Board on this occasion consisted of Hawkesbury, Pitt and Dundas (*B.T.* 5/7, p. 205).

[62] Smith Burgess, the Chairman, did not attend.

[63] Baring was M.P. for Grampound from 1784 to 1790 and for Chipping Wycombe and Calne between 1794 and 1806.

pany to come to terms with the industrialists. It would be equally clear from his knowledge of their policy that Pitt and Dundas had no intention of allowing the Ministry to become identified with unrealistic demands from the manufacturers; and Dundas, immersed as he was in devising a new Charter Act under Pitt's guidance, could hardly fail to regard Hawkesbury's *démarche* as an unwelcome intrusion. The Company were coming under heavy official pressure to broaden their trading practice; but beyond that point they could expect protection from the ministerial quarter that mattered. They could, therefore, afford to resist the proposition that they should engage in combat with vociferous delegates from all the principal industrial towns in the country.

'After some conversation' their Lordships were pleased to adjourn the further consideration of the subject.[64] Three weeks later Hawkesbury (sitting alone) wrote in the name of the Board to the Chairman: it had been understood that the Directors intended to appoint a committee to confer with the Board. Had such a committee been selected? A speedy reply was requested.[65] A few days later (19 July) the answer came that four Directors had been chosen for the purpose; but their meeting with the Board did not take place until 31 August. The directorate then undertook to prepare a full report on the export trade to India 'in order to enable their Lordships to judge whether the same can be further extended for the benefit of the Manufacturers of this Country'.[66] They had been unable to avoid an investigation; but they had refused to be stampeded, and there was to be no nonsense about a conference with the industrialists. Hawkesbury's plans in that regard sank quietly without trace.[67]

At the same time the Court of Directors were aware of the power of the national tide that was setting against them. During the following months their committee produced three major reports which constituted an elaborate exposition and defence of the Company's commercial system. The first report, submitted in November, 1791, dealt with the export trade of India. The Company, it was explained, exercised an exclusive right to export cloth, woollens, copper, naval and military stores, clocks, toys and other articles ornamented with jewels, and bullion; but any other goods could be sent out privately through the commanders and ship's officers

---

[64] *B.T.* 5/7, p. 211. The conversation is not recorded in the Minutes. The document in *B.T.* 6/42, 'Heads of Conversation . . . 24 June, 1791', consists solely of the statement which Hawkesbury had submitted to Pitt beforehand.

[65] *B.T.* 5/7, p. 218.

[66] *Ibid.*, pp. 219, 242.

[67] While Hawkesbury was trying to push Pitt and Dundas into compelling the East India Company to broaden their methods for the benefit of British exports, he was at the same time (in the summer and autumn of 1791) stubbornly and successfully resisting their plan to broaden the basis of British trade in the Far East by striking a bargain with the Dutch. (See Chap. VI, § 2, above.)

who were allowed eighty-seven tons in the larger ships. It was true
that in practice this private trade in the Company's ships often
included prohibited commodities, and ships were fitted out for
India in British ports without the Company's licence. It was also
admitted that illicit trade, largely financed with British capital,
was carried on from certain European ports, although 'no certain
information' was obtainable. The committee then used the admission to produce a telling counter-argument. If it was true that a
great potential demand for British goods existed in India, why
was it that private enterprise did not exploit the situation through
the medium of these illicit channels? At the ports where such
vessels were loaded for India, British manufactures could be had
in abundance and at not more than $3\frac{1}{2}$ per cent above the prime
cost in England; and there was no prohibition in India against
the importation of British manufactures by foreigners. 'Should
the Company have been negligent, or the Commanders and Officers
of their Ships inattentive to their own Interests by failing to Supply
Eastern Markets with the full extent of their demand, it is evident
that a Channel has ever been open for transmitting British Manufactures to India.'

In fact, the Report went on, the acquisition of the *diwani* of
Bengal had brought about a total change in the foreign trade with
India. Before that time the English Company had been obliged
to send out £500,000 in silver each year for the purchase of Indian
textiles: now the foreign companies, experiencing similar conditions, were all in a declining state for they made little or no
profit on the outward voyage and depended for their homeward
cargoes on the cash provided by Agency houses. 'What has happened to foreign Companies must be the fate of individuals at
home, should they be admitted to a participation in the Commerce
with India.'

The committee were at pains to demonstrate that the Court of
Directors had done their utmost to increase the sale of British goods
and how limited the opportunities were. Cottons and silks were
out of the question: the Indian products were better and cheaper.
The same applied to earthenware, which in any case could not be
transported, and metal manufactures. It was true that naval and
military stores were in demand and that they constituted a large
proportion of the illicit exports; but the Company had adopted
David Scott's plan for attracting the commerce of India to Bombay,
and they hoped by sending a wide range of these commodities
thither to draw the entire sale of them into the Company's hands.
This, however, was an exceptional case. British woollens presented
a constant problem: no one in India used them except the troops,
and even a slightly increased export was sufficient to glut the
market. During the preceding six years the Company had sustained

a total net loss on woollens of £37,790.[68] On the other hand there was an increasing demand for metals, for these were raw materials and the Company were extending their sales very greatly, especially in copper. They had relieved distress in Cornwall by exporting tin to China and the experiment had succeeded so well that it would be repeated. If desired, large quantities could also be exported to India; but in that event it would be necessary to exclude Malayan tin by laying an import duty, and the Malays might retaliate by restricting the sale of Bengal opium in the Eastern Seas. There was a general misapprehension at home. However reasonable it might be to look for an increased export to other parts of the world, trans-Atlantic countries did not possess, as India did, 'raw Materials in the highest perfection and Millions of ingenious and industrious Manufacturers, who work for one fifth part of the Wages given in England'.

In the twentieth century European trade relations with the Far East have come full circle: in the period under review the East India Company represented an Asian manufacturing interest which was coming into collision with the rising industrialism of Britain. 'The Ideas suggested by their Lordships,' the Report concluded, 'of suffering Individuals to participate in the Export Trade would not Answer those liberal purposes nor produce those beneficial consequences which their Lordships had in contemplation.' In the present political state of India it would be very dangerous for private persons to 'explore' the country on the pretext of promoting the sale of British manufactures: this might well embroil the Company with native princes and also lead to colonisation – 'an Event highly injurious to our Country and to India'. The committee, therefore, had no specific propositions to offer: they would merely repeat that they were willing to try any experiment that their Lordships might suggest.[69] The ball was thus neatly returned into the opposite court.

---

[68] David Scott afterwards derided this computation, asserting that a misleading impression had been given by debiting the receipts with heavy freight and other charges. In reality, he contended, there was a profit margin, for such goods ought to be accounted as exported freight free. The ships in which they were transported would have made the outward voyage in any case, and if necessary in ballast, in order to bring home the Indian Investment and cargoes of tea from China.

[69] This and two subsequent reports (on the trade with China and with Japan and Persia respectively) are in *B.T. 6/42*. Another set is in *Home Misc. S.*, vol. 401. In the first report emphasis was laid on the difficulties encountered in trying to develop trade between the Presidencies and neighbouring countries. Bengal had tried in Assam, but it seemed that the only saleable article was salt. Even less fortunate had been their efforts, spread over many years, to promote trade with Tibet. A commercial treaty had been concluded with Oudh but had proved ineffective because the Nawab's government was weak and unable to restrain lawless subjects. The trade of Madras with Mysore had fallen steeply since the last war, and Bombay had reported that an attempt to extend trade with the Maratha country 'would rather tend to awaken jealousy and suspicion of our intentions,

Hawkesbury was not slow to respond. When the Report came before the Board of Trade (in September) discussion was postponed,[70] and Hawkesbury prepared a detailed criticism of it which he sent to the Directors. It contained, he wrote, a great deal of useful information well put together, but in certain respects it was defective. 'I wish to receive an answer to the following Questions.' After putting a number of factual queries he raised the central issue. 'If these Papers should be published and read by the Merchants and Manufacturers of Great Britain, will they not infer from the foregoing Facts that the Company and their Servants do not carry on this trade with proper Mercantile Judgement and Discretion?' He observed that the committee had urged as an argument for not extending the export trade that their outward-bound ships were usually loaded almost to capacity, especially when there was a war in India, but he apprehended that this argument would make no impression on the manufacturers. They would not agree that the exclusive right of the Company to navigate the seas beyond the Cape of Good Hope should be allowed to limit and restrain the export trade to the East Indies if no other sufficient reason could be assigned to convince them that the sale of British manufactures in those countries could not be increased: they would insist that the Company must provide an adequate quantity of tonnage for that purpose or alternatively that his Majesty's subjects in general should be allowed to navigate those seas in order to extend the export trade in British products by their own efforts.

In this Report the Committee of Directors offer many Arguments to prove that the Company have used their utmost Endeavours to extend the Sale of British Manufactures in India, and that they have been charged unjustly with Neglect in this Respect; but the Complaint of Want of Zeal in the Company is not the only one which will be urged by the Manufacturers. They will complain that an exclusive Company is not qualified to carry on a Trade of this Nature in its full Extent, and they will refer to most of the eminent Writers on Commerce in Support of the Opinion.

The only way to remove their complaint, he added, was to prove that private venturers could not carry on this branch of trade 'to a greater extent and in a better Manner' than the Company had

---

than to answer the liberal end proposed'. It was impossible, stated the Report, to establish a free intercourse with neighbouring Powers except 'on the Faith of Treaties or under the protection of a military Force'. The latter was impossible, and the case of Oudh showed that treaties would not make any material difference to the sale of European manufactures.

[70] B.T. 5/7, p. 250.

done.[71] The reply of the Directors was acidulated. As to the reference about neglect and want of zeal, no specific charges had been brought forward: still less had any proof been adduced. The Company was eager for a proper investigation (presumably by a select committee of the House of Commons), but they did not think it necessary to reply to 'mere rumour and surmise'. It was entirely for His Majesty's Ministers to decide whether or not it would be prudent to promote the sort of enquiry which would rouse 'the ignorant, the prejudiced, and the self-interested, into a general mass or body of clamour'. The eminent writers on commerce whose opinions had been cited had never properly understood the circumstances of the East India Company.[72] Indeed the fact that Charles Jenkinson had on this occasion cited the views of Adam Smith and his disciples was not without its irony, but it was indicative of a neo-mercantilism which marked the beginning of a movement away from traditional rigidity towards the more empirical policy which the development of a global strategy in trade required.

On 21 November the Directors' report was read at the Board once more together with Hawkesbury's 'Observations' on it and the reply. There is no record in the Minutes of a discussion, and no action was taken. Since the Court of Directors had refused blankly to join with the manufacturers in an investigation, there was nothing to be done until the Charter Act came up for review. Instead the Directors were asked to furnish a further report on the export trade to China, Japan and Persia, 'so that their Lordships may be enabled to judge what prospect there may be of extending or opening such Trade with any of those Countries'.[73] The report on the China trade was signed on 29 December and was transmitted on 4 January, 1792, and this was followed a fortnight later by a report on the trade with Japan and Persia.[74] In the former, statistics were produced to show that the sale of British products was increasing considerably, but the point was stressed that if Canton was thrown open to private competition the trade would be ruined and the Company with it. British trade with Japan had ceased since the

---

[71] This riposte immediately follows the Report in *B.T.* *6/42*. It is unsigned and undated. I have ascribed the authorship to Hawkesbury from internal evidence. No other person could have written to the Court of Directors in such terms – except Dundas – and he regarded the manufacturers' hopes concerning the Indian market as delusive.

[72] 'Answer to the Observations on the Report of the Select Committee of East India Directors on the Export Trade to India, etc. Read, 24 Nov., 1791.' *Ibid*.

[73] *B.T.* *5/7*, pp. 307-8, 342. In his observations Hawkesbury had criticised the first report for its failure to deal with these countries. This was unfair, since the Directors had been requested to report on trade with 'the East Indies'.

[74] These reports were signed by the four Directors constituting the committee – John Manship, John Hunter, the Honble. W. F. Elphinstone, and Hugh Inglis – together with the Chairman of the Court, J. Smith Burgess, and the Deputy-Chairman, Francis Baring.

17th century and there was no prospect of selling European manufactures there. In the Persian Gulf the Company maintained trading factories at Bushire and Bussora at a heavy loss: the demand was for Indian goods, which were largely supplied (although the report did not say so) by the native merchants of Bombay and the west coast.

These reports were read and laid aside. In fact the focus of official action was shifting from Hawkesbury at the Board of Trade to Dundas at the Board of Control. During the year 1792 Dundas was supervising the preparations for sending an embassy to the Emperor of China, which, it was hoped, would revolutionise the conditions of British trade with that vast country. At the same time the manufacturing interests began to bombard Dundas with petitions. Frustrated in their previous efforts and faced by another recession, they turned to the man who, with the Prime Minister, would decide the terms on which the East India Company's charter was to be renewed. Deputations and memorials came from Manchester, Glasgow, Exeter, Liverpool and elsewhere. In some cases the demands were contradictory, but the general trends were familiar: a prohibition, or at the least drastic restrictions, on the importation of Indian cotton goods, increased supplies of Indian raw materials, especially cotton and indigo, greater opportunities for private trade, and substantial reductions in the Company's freight charges.[75]

This onslaught was reinforced by a joint attack from a committee representing the Agency houses in London, led by David Scott, and the New Shipping Interest. The demand was for cheaper freight. The existing charges were exorbitant and were kept so by the Old Shipping Interest – an entrenched and very formidable monopoly within the monopoly.[76] In some of the pamphlets the point was made that increased supplies of raw materials from India could be secured only if private trade were enabled to carry them more cheaply. Indeed all Scott's previous advocacy of a comprehensive partnership between the Company and private trade implied a breaking down of the restrictive practices employed by the Shipping Interest. After his election as a Director in 1793 he became involved in an embittered conflict with this group which continued until his death and darkened his last years.[77] On this issue Dundas was in sympathy with the would-be reformers but cautious. Freight rates, he declared, ought to be settled once and for all on a reason-

---

[75] The petitions and related correspondence are in *India Office Charters*, vols. 10 and 11. Cf. Tripathi (*op. cit.*), pp. 25-6.

[76] For an account of the long contest against it, led by Dundas and Scott, see Philips (*op. cit.*), Chap. IV.

[77] See *The Correspondence of David Scott, Director and Chairman of the East India Company, Relating to Indian Affairs, 1787-1805*, ed. C. H. Philips (Roy. Hist. Soc., Camden, Third Series, vols. LXXV and LXXVI, Lond., 1951).

able basis: it was not right that those who had taken shares in the
East Indiamen which were hired to the Company should be kept
in constant agitation.[78]

A middle course was also steered by Pitt and Dundas in dealing
with the manufacturers. Their demands for the exclusion of Indian
cotton goods and for the opening of the trade from India to private
shipping were refused. On the other hand they were promised
that a certain proportion of tonnage would be allotted for the conveyance of raw materials by free merchants – but under licence
from the Company. It was impracticable to open the China trade
to private enterprise: all transactions with the Chinese must be
controlled by the Company's supercargoes, but Country traders
would be free to send their own consignments of British manufactures to Canton from India. The Company's monopoly, wrote
Dundas, must be regulated so as to ensure that the manufacturers
were enabled to export their products to the full extent of the
demand and that Indian raw materials needed for British and
Irish industries should be brought home at as reasonable rates as
circumstances would permit.[79]

It was on this basis that the Board of Control on 14 January,
1793, began negotiations with the Directors for the revision of the
commercial provisions of the Charter. The various pressure groups
were, however, far from satisfied with the Ministers' compromise.
As the spokesman for the Agency houses of London and Bombay
David Scott was determined to convince them that more far-reaching reforms were needed if the Company was to function adequately
as the vehicle for an expanding trade with Asia. Having been shown
the reports of the Directors' committee to the Board of Trade, he
contended that they had concealed the Company's inefficiency as
exporters by playing down the potential demand. They had evaded
the question of foreign and clandestine trade and Ministers were
therefore unaware of the extent of the damage that was being done
to Britain's interests.

Towards the end of March Scott presented Pitt and Dundas
with a comprehensive analysis of every branch of the commerce
between Europe and Asia. On the export trade to India he had
scathing things to say about the Company's neglect and mismanagement at the London end and also in India. Private merchants
were prohibited from sending out a wide range of goods, and yet
every other European nation was free to supply India with these
articles. 'The absurdity of these restrictions by our Company seems
too gross to be accounted for.' The 'undue influence' of the Shipping Interest was exerting a stranglehold: private consignments

---

[78] Dundas to Baring, 23 March, 1793. *I.O. Charters*, vol. 11.
[79] Dundas: Personal Observations . . . , 16 Feb., 1793 (*Home Misc. S.*, vol. 401,
p. 248).

from India were frequently diverted into foreign channels because tonnage in the Company's ships was not available. In the China trade, improved organisation had increased the sale of British goods, but the enormous increase in the purchase of teas had thrown the markets into the hands of the consumers and the advantage was not being exploited. More than 18,000 tons of shipping was sent each year to Canton, but not a quarter as yet was taken up with goods of European origin.

Scott's most damaging criticism was contained in his revelations about the extent of the foreign and clandestine trade of which he had first-hand knowledge. According to his estimate the annual average of European exports to India for the previous ten years had been approximately 37,000 tons costing about £2,400,000. Of this some 32,000 tons at a prime cost of £2,047,000 represented foreign, clandestine and private trade. The English Company's own exports had amounted (on an average for the years 1786-90) to no more than 4,800 tons, valued at £346,000. American ships were loading in the Thames for India with British manufactures, many items of which were prohibited to the British merchant; but if the latter chose to operate from Ostend or Lisbon he could buy an unlimited range of British goods and ship them to India for an outlay of not more than two per cent above that of Americans in London.[80] Everyone could export to India without let or hindrance – except the British merchant in London who chose to obey the rules.

Individual Directors should not, in Scott's opinion, be blamed for this lamentable situation. The system was at fault. The establishment of a standing committee of the Court for each department had brought considerable improvements, but most of the Directors had too much business of their own to be able to give sufficient attention to that of the Company and far too small a stake in East India stock to make it an object of consequence. A few were men of enlightened and liberal mind who did their best to drag the others along with them; but it was mere chance whether a person of ability was allocated to the committee for which he was best fitted. 'They rise to the different Committees by Seniority, so that an officer of the Army may be in the Shipping Committee and a Linen draper, Clothier, or some such profession in the Secret and Political department.' The constitution of the Court of Directors was out of date and by no means suited to the present state of the

---

[80] Scott also asserted that most of the (British-financed) traffic from India to Europe would have been brought to London and not to foreign ports if the charges on importing by the Company's ships had been as moderate as the charges at foreign ports. He stated that the Company's charges exceeded those at Ostend by the following percentages – on piece-goods, £16⅔ per cent; on raw silk £13⅔ per cent; and on indigo £9½ per cent. Comparable differences were quoted for Dutch ports and Lisbon.

Company's commerce, and the less so from their being possessed of such extensive territory.[81]

Scott's weighty document was masterly as an analysis and skilful as propaganda. It portrayed the East India Company as an indispensable national institution in great need of reform and the Agency houses of London, Bombay, Calcutta and Madras as the necessary instrument of private enterprise, which, if allowed to operate freely within the Company's framework, could enable Britain to extend her commercial empire throughout the Eastern Seas. It urged the export and import needs of the industrial interests while avoiding their free-trade inconoclasm; and lastly it demonstrated that British capital was being used to sustain and develop foreign competition. With most of these contentions Dundas was already in agreement, but Scott's exposure of the damaging extent of illicit trade convinced him that immediate action was required to safeguard London's future as the world centre for Asian trade (a cardinal object with him) and that a proper recognition and encouragement of the Agency organisation was the way to do it. In this regard the attitude of Pitt and Dundas towards the Directors stiffened;[82] but when the hard bargaining was 'at last' concluded on 17 April, the hopes of Scott and his associates were only partially realised.

In the circumstances that was almost inevitable. As a trading corporation the Company was covering up its indebtedness in India with profits made from dealing in China teas; but as an Indian territorial power (a *legatus* of the British Crown) the Directorate contended that it was imperative that the Company should pay its way by supplying Europe with Indian manufactures. Only so could financial stability in India be attained. Scott and his associates retorted that it was they who could redeem the situation, both in India and Europe, if the Company would afford them adequate facilities; and the manufacturers, as we have seen, clamoured for the exclusion of Indian competition, the transformation (in effect) of Indian territories into 'plantations', producing usable raw materials, and for a trade invasion of Asia with all barriers removed.

Faced by this conflict of interests (all of them important for an expanding national economy), Pitt and Dundas leaned heavily on the Company's monopoly and 'regulated' it within comparatively narrow limits. The private trader was given a statutory increase of

---

[81] Statistical Survey of the East India Company's Trade (*Home Misc. S.*, vol. 404, pp. 99-255). Another copy is in vol. 399, pp. 1-152, of the same series. The latter volume ends with a comparison of the computations of David Scott, Francis Baring, Nathaniel Smith and 'self' – George Anderson. In quoting Scott's statistics I have reduced them to round figures, since they were in the nature of the case only approximate estimates.

[82] See Tripathi (*op. cit.*), pp. 28-31.

export tonnage – in the Company's ships – at a cheap rate, but the homeward rate remained high. Import charges, however, were cut to three per cent in order to lower the price of raw materials. The Agency houses were released from a number of restrictions in India and in the years ahead they were to extend their business very considerably;[83] but they were not allowed to operate in India further afield than ten miles from Calcutta, Bombay or Madras without special permission, and they were not enabled, as they had hoped, to eliminate the illicit trade in European ports. The Company's Shipping interest stood in the way. The demands of the manufacturers with respect to India were treated as being unrealistic, as indeed they were at this stage, but Dundas was determined that the Company should serve them adequately as their need for export tonnage increased, and he intended that the doors of northern China should be opened wide for them (under Company control) as the result of Lord Macartney's diplomatic mission which at this time was nearing the China coast. The Company itself was fortified by having its Investment stabilised at £1 million (i.e. a crore of current rupees at 2s.) with the provision that it could be increased as and when the debt in India was redeemed. This sum did not greatly differ from the existing Investment, revenue surplus and the proceeds of the Company's exports. In short, the Government defended the Company's exclusive trading structure as a necessary vehicle of national expansion in the Far East while providing for a gradual adjustment of its methods to fit a changing and developing situation.[84]

---

[83] Between 1785 and 1802 the Company carried 31,669 tons of private trade, worth £741,254: during the following seven years the private trade tonnage amounted to 60,518 tons with a value of £1,281,740. (*Select Committee Rept. IV (1812)*, 445. Quoted by Philips, *The East India Company, 1784-1884*, p. 117.)

[84] The principal changes relating to trade in the new Charter Act (*33 Geo. III, cap. 52*) other than those mentioned above were as follows: (i) the list of exports exclusively reserved to the Company was now confined to naval and military stores and copper, but the prohibition against the importation of piece-goods by private or privilege trade was continued, (ii) if the Company had not purchased by 31 August in any given year 1,500 tons of copper for export, the proprietors of copper might make up the difference in the Company's ships on their own account, (iii) if the Company failed to import sufficient calicoes and other piece-goods to meet the home demand, the Board of Control might make regulations to admit private trade to make good the deficiency, (iv) the Company was to provide not less than 3,000 tons of shipping each season for the use of individual traders and the Board might from time to time increase this total upon representations being made, but in that event the Court of Directors could appeal to the Privy Council, (v) private traders were to pay at the rate of £5 per ton out and £15 per ton on the homeward voyage, (vi) in the event of altered circumstances (i.e. war) these rates might be increased, but subject to the prior approval of the Board of Control, (vii) every three years the Court was to confer with the Board on the possibility of making further reductions in freight charges, and the decision of the Board was to be final, (viii) at the request of private traders the Board would require the Court to license additional agents resident in India, (ix) all goods imported by private traders were to be lodged in the Company's warehouses and sold by auction under the Com-

On 23 April, 1793, Dundas rose in the Commons to move the
first of thirty-three resolutions which were to be the basis of a bill
for the renewal of the Company's Charter. After dealing with the
political relationship of State and Company he turned to the questions of trade. It was true that the best contemporary writers on
commerce took the view that all monopolies were baneful and
destructive but the circumstances attending the East India trade
were peculiar. The case against an 'open' trade was then set out,
and Dundas went out of his way to quote the arguments which
the Committee of Directors had advanced in 1791 and in their
retort to Hawkesbury. It had lately been the fashion in the manufacturing towns, said Dundas, to hold meetings and pass resolutions in favour of abolishing the Company's exclusive privileges,
but had they considered how limited was the Indian market for
British goods? An open trade would involve free emigration, and
colonisation would necessarily follow. European vagrants with
their contemptible behaviour had long been a curse in India. Was
this pernicious influence to be multiplied? 'An unrestrained
liberty to the Europeans to emigrate to, and to settle among, the
Indians, would in a short time annihilate the respect paid to the
British character and ruin our Indian empire.'[85] Disappointed
adventurers might seek, and would certainly find, service in the
armies of the Marathas and Tipu of Mysore; and could it be supposed that private traders would refrain from supplying these rivals
with military stores and so equip their armies to oust the British?

It had been asserted, continued Dundas, that the Company's
neglect had been responsible for the employment of British capital
in an injurious clandestine trade; but the measures which he was
about to propose for encouraging the export of manufactures and
the import of raw materials would remove the incentive to engage
in that trade and would, he did not doubt, annihilate it.

My plan is, to engraft an open trade upon the exclusive privilege of

---

pany's authority, (x) licensed free merchants, resident in any territory within the
Company's limits, could trade in India with any foreign nation or state and could
act as import and export agents for any foreign company or foreign individual.
The onset of war with revolutionary France probably reinforced the Ministers'
caution, but they are not reported as having mentioned the war as a conditioning
factor in the parliamentary debates on the Charter Bill.

[85] In the ensuing debate Philip Francis pointed out that the climate of India ruled
out the possibility of emigration thither for the purpose of establishing settlements.
The real colonist could only subsist by cultivating the soil. 'Be assured that these
labours will never be performed in India by British hands.' The migration of
undesirable adventurers could be prevented by a vigorous administration on the
spot – under the direct and overt authority of the Crown. The high value which
Dundas placed on 'our Indian Empire' was fallacious. The Company had been
better off and more secure before they intervened in Indian politics. They had
become involved in debt and perpetual wars as the result of being burdened with
territorial possessions, 'which it was impossible for them to manage and govern
either for the benefit of the people or for their own advantage'.

the Company, and to prove by experiment, first, how far the complaints, to which I have referred, are well founded; and next, how far it is practicable to cure the evil without injury to the public.[86]

In declaring that his plan was to engraft an open trade Dundas was indicating the initiation of a process rather than the immediate attainment of an objective. The concessions gained for the private trader and the manufacturer, though limited, were sufficient to establish a starting position from which to proceed and 'prove by experiment'. To achieve a progressive adjustment between exclusive privilege and private enterprise Dundas relied on the new discretionary powers vested in the Board of Control, that is to say, in himself, acting under Pitt's supervision. But in using this weapon for commercial reform he found himself on weaker ground than in the political sphere. All his efforts, in a fighting alliance with Scott, to secure more and cheaper shipping facilities produced but meagre results; and when the Governor-General, Wellesley, decided to license India-built ships to bring home the surplus India trade which the Company could not cope with, his action deepened the Company's bitterness against him which, in 1805, culminated in his recall. A large illicit trade continued: it was estimated that the British-Indian Agency houses in 1799 had invested £200,000 in American ships sailing from India.[87]

This long and complicated struggle between monopoly, 'regulated' monopoly, and free trade provides in many respects a case-study in the general evolution of British commercial policy which so deeply influenced the character of the British Empire in the 19th century, both in its formal and informal aspects. The assault upon the Company as a restrictive monopoly-exporter was the last chapter in an old story; but it was also assailed as an overseas dependency which was producing and selling manufactures when it ought (like all well-conducted dependencies) to have been supplying the metropolis with raw materials. Later the offensive was pressed home and the Indian cotton industry was defeated (for a period) on its own ground by British techniques, furnished with the raw material by an ex-dependency – the United States of America.

The two major components of Britain's Asian empire of trade were the markets of China and Europe. British India linked the two together. The silk and cotton goods of India flowed into Europe in large part through the London metropolis. On the eastern side of the network China made these goods herself and was not inter-

---

[86] *Parl. Hist.*, vol. XXX, 660-701. The Bill itself was considered in Committee on 13 May, was reported on 17 and passed the third reading – with little debate – on 24. (*Ibid.*, 935-48.)

[87] Philips, p. xvii, *Scott's Correspondence*, Intro. (*ut supra*).

ested in the Indian product, but there was a ready demand at Canton for raw cotton and opium which British Agency houses in India supplied together with assorted commodities collected from South-East Asia. These in turn paid for the huge quantities of tea which the East India Company brought and dispensed at home, in Europe, and (to a diminishing extent) across the Atlantic. During the period under review China was the focal point of the system, and it is to this aspect that we must now turn.

2. THE CHINA TRADE

From ancient times the peoples of China had evolved a culture which owed nothing to the distant civilisations of the Euphrates, the Aegean or the Nile, and possessed a quality which enabled it to absorb one wave of conquest after another. Situated in the huge land-mass of further Asia, the 'Middle Kingdom' established a pre-eminence over its neighbours and regarded itself – not uniquely – as of celestial origin and the ordained centre of the universe. In spite of periodic famines, floods and epidemics its fecund population multiplied enormously through the centuries, as it still continues to do. The millions of peasants afforded leisure to the few, and this in the past has been the pre-condition of a cultural flowering. A predominantly agricultural economy, supplemented by limited industrialisation, fed and clothed the multitude and provided the cultured minority with luxury goods of the finest craftsmanship.

Such a society was almost entirely self-contained. External trade, which increased the amenities of Chinese living, had always been marginal. The Chinese grew their own food, drank their own tea, and clothed themselves in their own silks and cottons. Their wares, such as silks, porcelain and lacquer work, percolated westward along the caravan routes (when wars permitted), while trading junks did business with South-East Asia, sailing as far afield as Malaya and Ceylon, where they linked with the Indian and Arab trade to East Africa, the Red Sea and the Persian Gulf. Chinese exports were exchanged for the gold and silver of western Europe and for Russian furs. By the southern sea-routes returns were made in a diversity of goods – sandal-wood, sharks' fins, ivory, pepper, tin, pearls and precious stones, gold and incense. This was a luxury trade and the national economy was independent of it.

The ancient network of Eastern commerce was disrupted by the maritime penetration of the Europeans and superimposed a new pattern which centred first in Lisbon, then in Amsterdam, and later in London. By establishing fortified posts at strategic points the Portuguese forced the bulk of the trade, which they monopolised, into the ocean-route round the Cape of Good Hope. They were then ousted almost completely by the Dutch who in the course of the 17th century dominated the trade of the Spice Islands and Ceylon and established lucrative depots in India, the Strait of Malacca and Japan. A century later political weakness at home caused the Dutch commercial system, as we have seen, to fall into decline, while the growing power of the English Company in India, based on the resources of Bengal, resulted in a great flow of Indian piece-goods along the ocean highway to London and so into the markets of Europe.

Invasion and economic extraction drew the Indian peninsula and the Spice Islands increasingly into the European orbit, but for more than two centuries the land-mass of China, huge, almost entirely self-sufficient, and not easily accessible, remained on the fringe of the Western trade system. The efforts of European merchants to penetrate the China coast were rebuffed as an unnecessary nuisance: they might come and buy and provide a useful source of revenue, but they must be held at the tradesmen's entrance. It was only when the Chinese began to sell to foreigners on a massive scale (for the first time in their history) that the pressure upon their insulating barriers began to rise until it eventually overcame them. China then received a flood of manufactured articles, machines and ideas with consequences for the world at large which are not yet predictable.

The vicissitudes of European traders in their early efforts to establish a direct trade with China have been frequently narrated.[88] Between 1545 and 1549 the piratical proceedings of the Portuguese caused the Chinese to retaliate, expelling them from the coast with heavy losses and destroying their factories. Eight years later they were permitted to form an establishment at Macao, on the estuary below Canton, where they strove to exclude all European competitors and where they still remain. The Dutch and English Companies were kept out of the Canton trade during the 17th century, and their attempts to do business at Amoy and Tongking were given a rough reception. European turbulence and aggressiveness were matched by Chinese contempt and rapacity.

The alternative for this *avant garde* of the European invasion of Asia was an indirect trade with the Chinese junks at the ports which they visited, such as Hirado in Japan, Taiwan (Formosa), and Bantam in Java. British efforts to develop such indirect contacts with China continued into the late 18th century. To that end Alexander Dalrymple led a sustained campaign for the establishment of trading posts in Borneo and the Sulu Archipelago: Warren Hastings sought to form trade connexions with Tibet through

[88] See, for example, H. B. Morse, *The Chronicles of the East India Company trading to China 1635-1834* (Oxford, 1926), vol. I, and Sir William Foster, *England's Quest for Eastern Trade* (London, 1933).

Bhutan and with Cochin China: Francis Light acquired the Island of Penang; and Dundas strove persistently to induce the Dutch to cede the Island of Rhio near Singapore.

The circumstance which brought the Chinese Empire into direct and important economic association with the West was the growth of an English thirst for tea, of which China was then the sole producer. In the 1660s small consignments were obtained through indirect contacts and shipped to England where it was still a novelty.[89] During the first half of the 18th century the Chinese Government gradually regulated the direct European trade and confined it to Canton, which, as it happened, was situated comparatively close to the main tea-growing area. With an assured supply the consumption in Britain increased steadily: the Company's tea sales in London rose from 91,183 lbs. in 1700 to 2,710,819 in 1751, and by 1770 they had reached the eight million mark.[90] Moreover the imposition of high duties and to some extent the Company's heavy overhead costs raised the price of tea at the auctions to a level which caused the growth of an enormous smuggling trade. It has been estimated that between 1771 and 1780 a further eight million lbs. was smuggled into England each year by European competitors.[91]

The indifference of the Chinese to European staples obliged the English Company to follow the general practice of purchasing its cargoes of tea (and other 'China' goods in small quantities) with coin and bullion. The export of English silver coins was prohibited, and the Company, like other European traders to Canton, furnished themselves with Spanish silver dollars minted in Mexico or Seville.[92] Britain's trade with the Americas and Europe provided the credit which enabled her to buy Chinese luxuries through the medium of Mexican silver. The arrangement was unpopular at home. Although the influence of 'bullionist' doctrine was declining in the later 18th century, this dependence on a foreign currency raised some practical difficulties. Whenever there was a war with Spain the supply of dollars tended to dry up and after 1778

---

[89] Under the date 25 Sept., 1661, Pepys made the following entry in his Diary: 'I sent for a cup of tea (a China drink), of which I had never drunk before.'

[90] After deducting the quantity of tea which was re-exported, the amount remaining at the Company's sales for home consumption was 141,995 lbs. in 1711, 2,738,136 lbs. in 1755, and 7,723,538 lbs. in 1770. (William Milburn, *Oriental Commerce* (Lond., 1813), vol. II, pp. 531-4.)

[91] J. R. McCulloch, *A Dictionary . . . of Commerce and Commercial Navigation* (Lond., 1844 edn.), p. 1233. See also pp. 531-3 below.

[92] The dollar or 'real of eight' became the standard medium of international exchange in China and remained so until 1857. Its intrinsic value was 4s. 2d. and after 1619 the Company invoiced it at 5s., the difference being the cost of laying down the coin. It was packed in chests, each containing about 4,000 coins. The Chinese accepted it by weight and not by count. Occasionally consignments were made up with Venetian duccatoons, French crowns and rix dollars. (Morse, *Chronicles*, vol. I, pp. 47 and 68.)

the remission of specie from India virtually ceased.[93] Moreover the expectation that the Chinese could be induced to buy British goods in return for their teas and silks developed with advancing industrialisation into an insistent demand by the manufacturers for a broad and deep penetration of the China market.

In the early period the persistent efforts of the Company's super-cargoes or factors to 'flog' British woollens (broadcloth, long ells and camletts) met with a very limited response from the Chinese merchants of Canton who were reluctant to saddle themselves with an unprofitable and difficult commodity. In 1699, for example, the galley *Macclesfield,* under charter by the Company, left London with a stock consisting of £26,611 in silver and only £5,475 in goods, of which one quarter remained unsold. In 1701 the super-cargoes reported to the Directors: 'We cannot tell what to advise Your Honours to send to these Parts, the Natives being fond of nothing but Silver and Lead; and probably if the rest of your Goods were thrown over board at Sea, your Cargoes home would not be much the less.' Twenty-one years later the four ships sent to China carried a stock of £141,828 of which at least nine-tenths was in silver. Throughout the first half of the 18th century this ratio of goods and silver remained constant. During this period the pattern of the Chinese trade was similar to that with India: in both cases Britain was a substantial buyer and a negligible seller. Between 1710 and 1759 the English Company exported to the East almost £27 million in treasure and slightly less than £9¼ million in merchandise.[94]

As the British people became a nation of tea-drinkers, Chancellors of the Exchequer took advantage of the insatiable demand and found an easy means of raising revenue by loading the imported commodity with duties – as their modern successors have done in the case of tobacco. The duties were pushed up until they accounted for one-tenth of the Government's income. Between 1768 and 1772 they amounted to 64 per cent: during the years 1773-7 they were raised to an average of 106 per cent; and by 1784 they amounted to 119 per cent.[95] A fiscal burden of such proportions naturally enhanced the price at the Company's sales[96]

---

[93] See Pritchard, *The Crucial Years of Early Anglo-Chinese Relations*, App. IX, p. 399. 'Silver imported into China from England and India by the East India Company, 1760-1800.'

[94] Morse, *Chronicles*, vol. I, pp. 8, 74-5, 76, 114.

[95] Pritchard (*op. cit.*), pp. 146-7.

[96] As early as 1745 Parliament (under the Pelham Ministry) had given statutory permission to the East India Company to supplement its own supply by importing from Europe in order 'to keep this Market supplied with a sufficient Quantity of Tea at reasonable Prices'. If at any time the Company neglected to do this when necessary, the Treasury was authorised to issue licences to private traders to import teas from Europe, paying, of course, all duties. It was explained that the Company might not always be able to satisfy the home demand and that the purpose of the

and afforded a splendid opportunity for European (and English) rivals to dodge the imposts by a clandestine importation from Ostend, Amsterdam and other continental ports which were already engaged in a similar traffic with Indian textiles. The steep rise in duties from 1773 onwards caused the smuggling trade in tea to advance by leaps and bounds until it greatly exceeded the importation of the Company itself. Two results followed. The Company's sales (and in proportion the Government's revenue) dropped from 8 million lbs. per year to about 5 millions.[97] The Company was faced with bankruptcy while the smugglers reaped the benefit of the growing demand among the less wealthy. Secondly the loss of the greater part of the tea trade threatened to exclude the British from the sector of oriental commerce which appeared to offer by far the greatest opportunities for development.

The challenge of the smuggler had to be met and defeated if the East India Company was to be saved from ruin and the national revenue from increasing loss; but the action eventually taken developed into much more than a safeguarding operation. It became a counter-offensive, designed to oust European rivals from Canton and to secure the dominance of the China trade. Its success revolutionised the structure of Britain's commercial empire in Asia.

The individual responsible for initiating the new policy was William Richardson, the East India Company's deputy accountant. Between 1778 and 1781 he organised a publicity campaign for a moderate reduction of the duties, but in this his efforts were unsuccessful. The proposed reduction (of 16 per cent) would have caused a further decline in the revenue receipts without appreciably affecting the business of the smuggler. When Shelburne became First Minister in July, 1782, Richardson submitted a drastic plan, that all duties on tea should be abolished and be replaced by a tax on windows which would be paid by the wealthy. The plan was very much in accord with Shelburne's views on commercial and fiscal matters in general and also with those of his young Chancellor of the Exchequer, William Pitt. It was referred to the Customs and Excise Commissioners for their opinion. In elaborating the plan for their benefit Richardson pointed out that with the elimination of smuggling the Company would be able to increase its own importation of tea three-fold, and that as the principal

---

measure was ' to keep the Price of Tea in this Kingdom upon an Equality with the Price thereof in other the neighbouring Countries of Europe'. (*18 Geo. III, cap 26, sect. X and XI.*) In the unquiet time of the Jacobite rebellion and the Austrian Succession War these provisions were forgotten and were never implemented.

[97] During the three years, 1776-8, the annual average of tea sold by the Company amounted to 4,977,068 lbs., whereas the yearly average of tea exported from Canton by other European traders was estimated at 14,085,400 lbs. In the season of 1783-4 this latter figure reached a peak of 19 million libs. (Milburn, *op. cit.*, vol. II, p. 534. Cf. Pritchard, p. 193.)

buyer it would acquire a commanding position at Canton and so
be able to defeat European competitors by offering superior exchange facilities on London; and this in turn would stimulate the
Company's trade between India and China.[98] The whole would
constitute a triangular system organised and managed from England.

In November, 1783, the Fox-North Ministry moved for a Select
Committee to investigate the smuggling menace and to recommend
remedial measures. Lord John Cavendish, then Chancellor of the
Exchequer, was elected chairman and was later succeeded by
William Eden.[99] In its third report the Committee adopted Richardson's suggestions with some modification. Two days later Parliament was dissolved and Pitt won his general election. Within a
month of the meeting of the new Parliament Pitt moved (in June)
a series of resolutions based on the recommendations of the now
defunct committee. The tea duties were to be very substantially
reduced but graduated at the lower level according to the quality
of the various types of tea, and there was to be a compensating tax
on windows. As soon as the controversial India Act had been passed
Pitt introduced (in July) his Prevention of Smuggling or 'Commutation' Bill. After the first reading it underwent considerable
modifications. All existing duties, subsidies and surtaxes were
repealed and replaced by a simple duty of $12\frac{1}{2}$ per cent on the gross
amount realised at the Company's sales, and there was a drawback
of the whole on re-exportation to Ireland or the British Colonies
in America.[100]

The importance of the Commutation Act as a turning point in
British fiscal history is, of course, fully recognised, but the general
historian, as a rule, pays little attention to its spectacular consequences with regard to British commerce in the Far East, and
yet the transformation which occurred in this field of national
enterprise profoundly influenced British foreign and imperial
policy throughout Asia and indirectly in eastern Africa. The quantity of tea imported by the East India Company rose from just
under 10 million lbs. in 1784 to more than 23 million lbs. in
1795, and its annual profit on this trade, which had stood at an

---

[98] Richardson estimated that between 1772 and 1780 the average annual exportation
of tea from China amounted (in round figures) to 18,800,000 lbs. was consumed
was shipped to England by the East India Company, 5,500,000 lbs. was consumed
on the Continent, and 7,700,000 lbs. was smuggled into England. If the whole of
the tea consumed in Britain was provided by the Company, the number of large
ships so employed each season would increase from eighteen to thirty-eight.

[99] On 17 December the Company's Court of Directors requested the Chairs to wait
on North and Cavendish in order to seek their support for Richardson's plan. The
Ministry was dismissed on the following day.

[100] The amount of the duties paid on tea dropped from £836,201 in 1783 to
£324,730 in 1785. It remained at about that total until 1794. The estimated annual
yield of the new window tax in 1784 was £600,000. (D. Macpherson, *Annals of
Commerce . . . and Navigation*, Lond., 1805, vol. IV, p. 338; Morse, *Chronicles*,
vol. II, p. 117.)

approximate average of £250,000 before 1784, rose to £500,000 in 1790-1 and thereafter steadily climbed (with seasonal fluctuations) to a little over £1 million in 1805-6, where it remained until 1815-16.[101] 'The Commutation Act,' an official observed in 1792, 'has thrown the Trade with China into the hands of the consumers,'[102] The fact that the English Company became the sole suppliers of the largest tea market in Europe imparted an expanding stimulus to the general exchange of goods and credit between England, India, South-East Asia and China. The closure of the smuggling trade into England deprived the other European companies trading at Canton of a growing outlet for their teas. Gradually their decline became catastrophic as the Chinese became large buyers of raw products from British India and of woollen goods from Britain. Britain's rising imports of China tea became the basis upon which the entire nexus of Anglo-Asian commerce subsisted. The early stages of this process which continued during the 19th century, are indicated by the following quantities of tea imported from China into Europe: [103]

Year	The English Company	Other European Companies
1783	4,138,295 (lbs).	14,630,300 (lbs.)
1784	9,912,760	19,072,300
1785	10,583,628	16,654,000
1786	13,480,691	15,715,900
1787	20,610,919	10,165,160
1788	22,096,703	13,578,000
1789	20,141,745	9,875,900
1790	17,991,032	7,174,200
1791	22,369,620	3,034,660
1792	13,185,467	4,431,730
1793	16,005,414	7,864,800
1794	20,728,705	3,462,800
1795	23,733,810	4,138,930

[101] See Pritchard (op. cit.), App. VII, p. 397.

[102] This is a marginal comment (possibly by an official at the Board of Control) inserted in David Scott's 'Survey of the East Company's Trade' (Home Misc. S., vol. 399, p. 44).

[103] Extracted from a statistical table in Macpherson, Annals, vol. IV, p. 337. The foreign companies included in Macpherson's compilation are – Swedish, Danish, Dutch, French, Imperial, Tuscan, Prussian, Spanish, Genoese, and American. The first American return (under 1785) is given at 880,100 lbs., that for 1794 at 1,974,130 lbs., and that for 1795 at 1,438,270 lbs. It must be emphasised that, in spite of their appearance of meticulous detail, the totals of foreign importation are no more than broad approximations, based on indirect and piece-meal information. There are numerous gaps in the entries for individual countries. The statistics of the annual quantities of tea sold at the English Company's sales as given by Pritchard (App. V) are somewhat lower than those given by Macpherson. The latter included tea imported by private traders in the Company's ships, while the former

There is little, if any, evidence to support the view that Pitt foresaw and planned this vast commercial revolution at the time of the Commutation Act. Throughout the debates on the preliminary Resolutions and on the Bill itself his speeches dealt exclusively with three themes: the need to protect the revenue by destroying the smuggling traffic, the efficiency of the window tax, and the East India Company's need of assistance.[104] Two years later Fox in the House declared that the principle of the Act had been to ensure that the East India Company enjoyed a monopoly of the tea trade to England, but also to avoid an increasing consumption of tea. In reply Pitt accepted the first part of the statement but denied that a rising demand for silver to pay for the tea at Canton was necessarily an evil, provided that the sale of British manufactures elsewhere continued to increase in proportion.[105] He held out no expectation that his Act would so stimulate the flow of primary products and capital from India to China that the transmission of bullion from London would become unnecessary, and yet this was what actually happened. William Richardson, the initiator of the commutation plan, had foreseen this consequence and had stressed the magnitude of its importance. When the Company began to acquire a predominant position in the Canton market under the operation of the Act, a few specialists directed the attention of Pitt and Dundas to the wider potentialities and official action was taken.[106]

The campaign which David Scott conducted on his return to England in 1786 for the purpose of inducing the Company to broaden the basis of trade between Britain and India has already been considered. His parallel efforts in connexion with the China trade were accorded a better reception. In the memorandum which he addressed to the Directors in 1787 he pointed out that the Company's annual tea purchases at Canton were now of the order of 18 million lbs. 'owing to the wise Commutation Act', and this

---

subtracted an (estimated) amount on that account. A parallel aspect of the situation was illustrated by David Scott in 1792 when he estimated that the annual average tonnage employed in importations from China by other European companies during the six years preceding the Commutation Act had amounted to 16,150 tons (including 2,625 tons used by English adventurers under foreign flags) as against 7,837 tons by the English Company, whereas during the five years following the Act (1785-90) the average of foreign tonnage, including 'irregular' ships, had dropped to 8,490, while that of the English Company had risen to 19,189. (Scott's 'Survey', loc. cit., pp. 43-4.)

[104] Parl. Hist., vol. XV, 1008-11, 1218-19, 1228-9, 1348-54.

[105] Ibid., vol. XVI, 168-9.

[106] Pritchard (op. cit., p. 146) tends, I think, to anticipate events when he writes: 'A secondary and equally important, although less talked of, object [of the Act] was the encouragement of British trade with China at the expense of Continental competitors. . . .' The original purpose of the Act, both with regard to protecting the national revenue and affording assistance to a near-bankrupt Company, was defensive. As the British China trade was transformed, Pitt and Dundas realised that they had built better than they knew and took full advantage of the fact.

meant that they needed three times their former resources with which to pay. Yet the Company had hitherto found no method of meeting this need except that of shipping bullion, the annual cost of which Scott estimated at £1,300,000. Less than £150,000 was realised on the sale of British goods. He inveighed against the Company's obsessive idea of drawing specie from Bengal (which had been their practice during the American War and which Cornwallis rightly vetoed), particularly at a time when the Company's credit in India was verging towards annihilation.

To remedy the extreme unbalance in Britain's trade with China Scott made a number of recommendations. First, the direct exports from England to China ought to be greatly increased. This was a not unfamiliar idea to the Company's Supercargoes at Canton who were frequently pressed from London to dispose of British woollens to reluctant customers, but Scott added the proposal that a settlement ought to be acquired on the coast of China 'for a magazine'. Goods could then be warehoused and kept until a convenient opportunity for sale arose. Under existing conditions ships reaching Canton 'must sell on their arrival at whatever price a company of monopolizers at Canton (the Co-Hong) please to give, or carry the same goods back'. 'I conceive,' he added, 'some island or place might be had (by proper application) on the coast of China where these Exports would most probably exceed the Exports of India.'[107] Secondly he took note of the fact that the enormous increase in the Company's tea imports involved the employment each season of twenty-three of the smaller ships then in use or fifteen of the large 'foreign-sized' vessels.[108] Why was most of this tonnage left unused on the outward run to Canton when it could be filled up in India with products which the Chinese would willingly buy?

The Company, to my knowledge, have dealt at times in opium, cotton, and other articles; but . . . they have never gained by it, on the contrary they have lost, nor did they ever by such means effect a capital remittance. Indeed, in general, their ships have carried little or no cargo on the Company's account from India to China.

Yet the Country traders of Bombay and the Malabar coast had proved by experience that there was a demand in China for cotton and opium as well as a wide variety of other commodities, such as

---

[107] Anticipating British notions about the Portuguese possessions in Africa in more modern times, Scott observed: 'The Portuguese gain nothing by Macao; if it could be purchased by our Company, it would be a most consequential acquisition.' Portuguese Macao, like British Hong Kong, still survives (in 1961) and for the same basic reason as in the 18th century – as a bridge between Chinese exclusiveness and the internationalism of Western commerce.

[108] In this same year (1787) the first of the large East Indiamen, the *Nottingham*, designed by Mr. Snodgrass, was launched. Scott described them in 1792 as 'the finest in the world'.

sandal-wood, pepper, ivory, pearls and incense. For reasons not entirely altruistic Scott emphasised that Bombay was the ideal entrepôt for an extensive trade from India to China. The latter needed raw cotton to supplement her own supplies: Bombay was adjacent to the Gujarati cotton-growing region. Saltpetre and opium were imported into Bombay from Bengal and the trade of Bombay with the Persian Gulf and the Red Sea was worth £450,000 a year, 'a pretty large part of the proceeds of which goes annually to China'.

Scott insisted that the East India Company was no more capable of selling Asian goods in China than of retailing British manufactures in India. The acquisition of wares acceptable to the Chinese called for a minute attention to the business which only individuals could give who had been trained to it and possessed wide local knowledge. The Company should organise a working association with the Country merchants. Sixteen of the tea ships should be required to touch at Bombay on the outward run, and all their ships proceeding from India and China should offer available tonnage to the merchants, freight free and at the Company's risk, provided that the Company had the first refusal of the proceeds of the merchants' sales. The Company would thus acquire credits in China which would take the place of bullion in purchasing cargoes of tea, and the merchants' profits should be remitted to London by bills of exchange on liberal terms. Moreover this new channel of indirect remittance from India, once established, would be used by individuals other than the Country merchants – to the additional advantage of the Company. 'Gentlemen, both British and foreigners, who did not trade, would endeavour to remit their fortunes in gold and silver by the way of China.'[109]

Scott's proposals were ambitious and far-reaching, but they materialised. Twenty years of practical experience as a Bombay merchant had shown him the possibilities in developing an export trade to China from an Indian entrepôt, and he was quick to appreciate the immense importance of the Commutation Act in that connexion. As the Company became the principal buyer at Canton, the Chinese merchants would find it increasingly convenient to purchase goods from their best customer, provided that acceptable commodities at acceptable prices were supplied. In arguing that this could be done by gearing the private enterprise of the Country trade to the Company's organisation, Scott was elaborating an arrangement which on a small scale had been in operation for many years. While the Court of Directors were sceptical about the possibility of increasing the sale of British manu-

---

[109] Scott's memorandum to the Directors, 3 April, 1787, ' Remarks and Ideas upon the Export Trade from Great Britain to India . . .' (Printed as a pamphlet). *B.T. 6/42.*

factures, they were very much alive to the advantages to be derived from promoting an export trade in primary products from India. In 1792 Scott noted with satisfaction that most of the Company's ships outward-bound for China were being ordered to touch at Indian ports. Out of a total of about 18,000 tons of shipping so employed some 14,000 tons was thus being made available to Country merchants who were glad to fill it up with their consignments for China, paying only the demurrage charges.[110] This 'Freight Free Privilege', as it came to be known, almost doubled the shipping space available to the Country trade during this period. Under the impetus of the Company's rising tea purchases the Country merchants began to build more of their own ships which they sent to Canton under licence from the Company. In 1785-6 they sent ten ships (about 5,000 tons) whereas they employed eighteen large ships (about 14,850 tons) in 1795-6.

It had long been the practice of private traders in India, British and Parsee, to send assorted cargoes to Canton, made up from a wide variety of products collected from the Malay Archipelago and countries bordering the Indian Ocean. But this miscellaneous trade had always been on a modest scale: it had to face the competition of the Chinese junks, and none of the commodities was in sufficiently large demand to constitute a staple. The merchants of Bombay found the required article in raw cotton. China itself grew cotton in large quantities, but the requirements of its spinners and weavers normally exceeded the supply of the Nanking crop. For some forty years Indian cotton filled the gap. The value of cotton exports from Bombay and Surat (supplemented at a later stage by supplies from Bengal) jumped from 206,160 taels (£68,720) in 1784-5 to 1,927,932 taels (£642,644) in 1787-8, and it remained at approximately that level until the end of the century.[111] Cotton thus became 'a grand staple' of the Country trade and a principal source from which the Company's supercargoes at Canton financed their purchases of tea.[112]

---

[110] Scott's 'Statistical Survey of the East India Company's Trade' (1792). *Home Misc. S.*, vol. 399, p. 14. This estimate appears to be on the high side. According to the Company's own shipping returns the total tonnage employed on the China run for the season 1785-6 amounted to 15,413 tons and for 1795-6 to 14,766 tons (Pritchard, *op. cit.*, p. 142). There was also the Private or Privilege trade. The Company allowed its commanders and ship's officers 103 tons among them free of charge. This space was frequently bought up by merchants in India for £20-£40 per ton.

[111] The sale value of cotton exports reached its peak in 1797-8, amounting to 2,330,444 taels out of a total of 3,375,207 taels for the Country trade as a whole. (Pritchard, *op. cit.*, App. XII.) The principal commodities making up the residue were – tin, opium, pepper, camphor and sandal-wood.

[112] The market price of Indian cotton tended to fluctuate with the seasonal rise or fall in the value of the Nanking crop, but even so the profits were usually high, particularly on Gujarati cotton from Bengal. (M. Greenberg, *British Trade and the Opening of China, 1800-42*, Cambridge, 1951, p. 79.) In 1786 Philip Francis attacked

From about 1819 the Canton market for India cotton encountered a prolonged and acute depression from which it never fully recovered. The price dropped catastrophically and in certain seasons consignments were unsaleable. Confined as they were to Canton and lacking any contact with the interior of China, the Agency houses (the 'private English') could only guess at the causes. They warned their clients of a general economic stagnation, accentuated by China's periodic affliction – terrible mortality and high food prices occasioned by floods; but the most significant comment came from James Matheson (afterwards a founder of Jardine, Matheson and Co.) in 1824. 'Cotton seems under an irretrievable depression, which I suspect is connected with large importations of British manufactures interfering with the native manufacture.'[113] After the termination in 1813 of the Company's trade monopoly in India, Lancashire textiles began to inundate the Indian market and overwhelm the indigenous industry. The Company retained its exclusive rights in the China trade until 1834, but already in the 1820s British piece-goods were beginning to make an independent entry into the China market by way of the newly-established Free Port of Singapore.

In spite of the declining state of the market for raw cotton the Country trade between India and China continued to flourish and expand. Cotton was replaced by opium as the staple. From the early years of the 18th century British and Armenian traders had shipped small quantities of the drug to China as well as to Sumatra, Java and Borneo.[114] Shipments were also made by the Portuguese from Goa and Damaun to Macao. Once more the operative factor was the huge and continued increase in the English purchase of tea. From the point of view of the East India Company the sale

---

Dundas in the Commons for boasting about the rising export of Indian cotton to China. 'Was it possible,' he asked, 'that the right hon. gentleman could seemingly contend that it was right to export cotton, a raw material of our Bengal manufacture, a material which we ourselves imported into Bengal at considerable expense and trouble? Far better would it be to export silver wherever it could be had!' (*Parl. Hist.*, vol. XXVI, 159.) As already noted, the British manufacturers of calicoes and other cotton goods began to press the Government to impose protective tariffs against Bengal piece-goods, imported by the East India Company as its Investment, and to oblige the latter to supply the home market with the raw material.

[113] Quoted, Greenberg (*op. cit.*), p. 92.

[114] In 1733 the supercargoes warned the commanders of two of the Company's ships which were *en route* from Madras to Canton that any consignments of opium found on board must be got rid of before they left Malacca, because it had been learned that an Imperial decree (of 1729) had prohibited the importation of opium on pain of confiscation of ship and cargo and of death to any Chinaman who offered to buy the drug. (This was the first of a long series of such decrees.) The supercargoes stated that it had been 'a usual thing heretofore for shipps bound from Fort St. George to carry opium with them for sale to China'. (Morse, *Chronicles*, vol. I, p. 215.)

of Indian opium offered an even better means than cotton of improving the balance of commodity exchange at Canton. The Company were the *de facto* rulers of Bengal where the 'Patna' and 'Benares' varieties of opium were grown. As rulers they had acquired the monopoly of its sale in 1773, and in 1797 they assumed control of its production. Within a few years the manufacturing process had been so perfected that the Company's hallmark on an opium chest was accepted in China with the same readiness as when affixed to bales and cases of legal imports. But the Company could not itself sell a product which had been repeatedly prohibited by decree of the Emperor, nor could the Hong merchants, who alone held official licences to trade with foreigners, have direct dealings in it. While, therefore, the Company organised the production, they left the sales business to the Country merchants in Calcutta and Bombay.[115]

The export to China of cotton, tin, pepper and the rest had been left to the private traders because the arrangement was convenient and profitable. They were directly controlled by the supercargoes at Canton, and their takings were banked with the Company's treasury. The same financial advantage was obtained from the sale of opium, but in this case there was a significant difference which eventually became a prime factor in the destruction of the Company's monopoly in China. Since this was a contraband traffic, it operated of necessity outside the official commercial system of Canton. During the early 1800s opium was either shipped to Macao under Portuguese colours or smuggled by the Country merchants (in their own ships licensed by the Company) up the Canton River to Whampoa, where sales were effected through a devious system of Chinese commission agents and dealers who organised the bribing of Chinese officials.[116]

By 1823 the annual value of imported opium passed that of cotton and thereafter rose rapidly until seven years later it had

---

[115] 'Malwa' opium, an inferior variety grown in some of the native states in India and purchased by the Portuguese at Goa and Damaun, was attracted to Bombay as an entrepôt by a system of transit passes.

[116] The periodic drives of the Imperial Government against the traffic caused temporary, and sometimes serious, dislocation; but they were always defeated in the end by the venality of the local officials, of which the Europeans had had long and painful experience in the conduct of legal commerce. In 1817, for example, the Committee of Supercargoes was informed that two years before a Portuguese merchant, named Arriaga, had arranged a regular levy of 40 dollars per chest from the purchasers, 'which was to form a fund for stated distribution among the local Officers of Government'. On an importation of 2,500 chests this would provide a sum of 100,000 dollars a year, and it was pointed out that so large a corruption fund, collected in so public a manner, encouraged discontented persons to bring constant denunciations to the higher authorities. (Morse, *Chronicles*, vol. III, p. 323. Other details of official connivance are scattered about in vols. III and IV of this work.)

reached £3,222,000.[117] This enormous growth of the trade had important consequences in addition to the purely financial. A fleet of Country ships, clipper built, ignored Whampoa and used Lintin and other 'outer anchorages', where their cargoes of opium were discharged into Chinese boats – some of which were officially engaged in suppressing the traffic. At a later stage they spread out establishing their own contacts at ports along the east coast. All this was beyond the purview of the Company's supercargoes at Canton. Hitherto the Committee (sarcastically known as 'the Select') had governed the small confined community of British traders, handling disputes with the Chinese officials as well as the Company's business. Indeed according to the Company's regulations 'free' merchants had no right to become resident in Canton, being required to depart in their ships at the close of the season when the supercargoes retired for relaxation to Macao.[118] This had been increasingly evaded as the Country trade expanded after 1784: merchants established themselves with their own factories by taking out foreign papers or acquiring the improbable status of a Prussian, Imperial or some other vice-consulship – a subterfuge which sometimes proved embarrassing after Europe went to war in 1793. Even so, the Committee was held responsible for the community by the mandarins.

Opium altered the situation. Agency houses and individual traders flocked from Bombay and Calcutta, attracted by an expanding trade with high profits. In dealing with a contraband article they made their own independent arrangements for bribing and selling, as did their Portuguese and Amercian competitors. With commercial power behind them they could afford to flout the authority of the supercargoes. The Company's monopoly was being undermined and invaded: more and more it took on the appearance of a needless obstruction. As opium smugglers the Country merchants were breaking through the traditional Chinese barriers, and the opening of a breach invited legitimate trade to follow.

Behind the network of 'free' merchant houses at Canton, Bombay and Calcutta stood the home merchants and manufacturers. Triumphant in the Indian market (after 1813), they campaigned with increasing power against restrictions in China, whether English or Chinese. Their hostility against the Company's remaining monopoly was accentuated when enterprising Americans began to

---

[117] Opium shipments during the first two decades of the 19th century averaged about 4,000 chests. In 1822-3 the number rose to 7,773, and by 1838-9 it had reached 40,200 chests. (Greenberg, *op. cit.* Opium Tables, App. I, D. The author points out that these statistics are – in the nature of the case – imprecise.)

[118] Pritchard (*op. cit.*, pp. 177-80) mentions some thirty-five commercial houses in Bombay, Calcutta or London who carried on an extensive business at Canton during the late 18th century. Those who had no established agent there sent a supercargo of their own (often a Parsee) on board each ship.

export British manufactures thither while private British subjects were debarred.[119] The abolition in 1833 of the Company's chartered rights in respect of China removed a barrier but destroyed a buffer between the Chinese authorities and the Country traders. These two forces came into direct contact – and conflict – when the Company's Committee of Supercargoes ceased to function. Thereafter a dispute no longer involved the servants of a Court of Directors but the representatives of the British Sovereign, whom the Manchu Emperor regarded as a tributary, though dangerous, barbarian. When the Imperial Commissioner, Lin Tse-hsu, began an unusually drastic campaign against the opium traffic in 1838 a crisis between Governments was almost inevitable. The opium question sparked off an armed conflict because of its economic importance for both sides.[120] But the underlying issue, which had been latent for more than a century and long before opium became important, was the difference between an expansionist West which sought to absorb China into a system of international commerce and an exclusionist East which was willing to acquire marginal profit from external trade, provided that it was kept at arm's length and not allowed to interfere with a self-sufficient economy. The Chinese, after enduring an economic invasion, have changed their methods, but not their attitude: the difference between then and now, viewed externally, is one of power.

The Anglo-Chinese war of 1839-42 was ended by the Treaty of Nanking by which the Imperial Government agreed to open five 'Treaty Ports' – Canton, Amoy, Foochow, Ningpo and Shanghai – to British and other foreign trade under reasonable imposts, to cede the Island of Hong Kong for an entrepôt, and to pay the debts due to British merchants, including their claims for confiscated opium.[121] The gates of China had been (temporarily) forced open. From the British standpoint the Chinese had been compelled to do business for the future under normal and reasonable conditions.

---

[119] See Morse, *Chronicles*, vol. IV, p. 330. 'Included in the American imports [in 1832] were cotton and woollen goods valued at 1,084,906 dollars, all of British manufacture, shipped from England to Canton in contravention of the East India Company's monopoly – at least the English manufacturers sold the goods to the Americans, who then transported them to Canton, as they were entitled to do, while the English were not.'

[120] The Chinese Government emphasised the economic aspect. The demand for opium was causing an increasing outflow of silver to India in payment, with the result that the internal market for all kinds of goods was 'daily diminishing'. (Greenberg, *op. cit.*, p. 143.) From the British standpoint receipts from the opium industry had come to constitute one-seventh of the total revenue of the Company's territories in India. Contemporary writers stated that the flourishing condition of the industry in Bengal had raised the value of land fourfold between 1825 and 1835 and that the increased purchasing capacity of the population had made possible a steep rise in the consumption of British manufactures (*Ibid.*, pp. 105-7).

[121] The best account of Anglo-Chinese relations in this period is W. C. Costin, *Great Britain and China, 1833-1860* (Lond., 1937).

The Government in London had been induced to include recognition of the opium traffic in the wider settlement because the material advantages were large and obvious while the moral implications of selling a noxious drug were indirect and remote. Yet the same generation had put an end to the British slave trade and had abolished British slavery. The conscience of a nation is rarely, if ever, uniform in the range of its sensitivity.

These considerations have taken us far beyond the chronological limits of the present volume, but an excursion into the later period makes it possible to put the formative phase, that is to say, the years between 1784 and 1793, into perspective. The economic triangle which developed between Britain, India and China profoundly affected Britain's connexion with the Far East in general and with India in particular. The great expansion of the Country trade after 1784 not only enabled this triangular system to function, but its success convinced the Ministers at home (and the manufacturers) of the immense possibilities if the Chinese Government could be induced by official intervention to remove restrictions, discipline its rapacious officials, and open the gates.

The policy which Dundas pursued with Pitt's support in relation to the China question reflected the ambitions of an industrialism which was becoming confident (sometimes overweeningly so) in the capacity of its wings. The objects which Dundas sought to attain and the way he set about it portray a cardinal feature of his general plan for commercial expansion throughout the East, based on London, which included the penetration of the South Pacific and the opening of the North-West American coast. His efforts also represented the first attempt of a British Government to establish normal diplomatic and commercial relations with the Government of China. Before examining this significant episode we must take note of the Country trade as an indispensable link in the triangular system and how it worked, for the situation which developed in this connexion inspired Governmental intervention.

The normal proportion of the East India Company's exports to China was 90 per cent silver and 10 per cent goods. When the prime cost of the Company's purchases of tea jumped from approximately $1\frac{1}{2}$ million taels in 1784-5 to almost $4\frac{1}{2}$ million in 1787-8 the amount of silver required to settle the account, in default of selling goods to the Chinese, would have been enormous. In this situation the Company's supercargoes possessed one advantage: as the largest buyers they could require a Hong merchant to invest in a certain amount of British woollen goods as a condition of his securing a tea contract. The latter responded reluctantly and on a limited scale. He would buy only at a cut price, and if a higher figure was demanded, he and his fellow Hongists put up the price of tea. None the less the sales value of British cloth which (in round figures) had been no more than £36,000 in 1760-1 had risen to £530,000 by 1792-3, and seven years later amounted to £690,000.[122]

Even so the trade gap was large. In the season 1787-8 when, as already noted, the cost of the tea purchases amounted to almost T.4,500,000, the Company's own resources for paying the bills totalled T.2,746,000, consisting of T.1,912,000, the realised value of the imported silver, and T.834,000, the sales value of Company goods imported from England and India. The gap was filled by the earnings at Canton of Country traders. In this same season their imported goods realised T.2,412,000. As the Country trade increased the Company were able to make a progressive reduction in their supply of Spanish dollars.[123]

In the ordinary way of business the Country ships would have loaded up with a cargo for the return voyage, but except for raw silk and sugar candy in limited quantities there was almost no demand for Chinese products in India. In these circumstances Country merchants had every inducement to bank the proceeds of their sales at Canton with the Supercargoes who in return issued bills of exchange on the Court of Directors. When the bills were redeemed – usually at 365 days' sight – the money was available for re-investment in the numerous enterprises, commercial and financial, which the metropolis afforded.[124] Thus developed a circuitous flow of profit from India to Britain which grew steadily

---

[122] See Pritchard, App. I. The Europeans in Canton and Macao were prevented from acquiring any knowledge of internal conditions in China, but this large increase in sales seems to afford a clear indication that there was a considerable potential demand for woollen goods in the colder regions of northern China and that the Hong merchants succeeded in establishing a vent there. One of their reasons for insisting on buying at low prices seems to have been (as later evidence showed) that inland transport costs were extremely high. This situation reinforced the argument that permitted access to northern ports would enable more cloth to be sold at better prices.

[123] In 1792-3 (the last season in the period of peace) the cost of imported silver dropped to T.537,900 (realised value – T.518,400). The figures given in this paragraph are abstracted from tables compiled by Pritchard (op. cit.), Apps. I, IV, IX, and XII. It must again be emphasised that owing to the variety of possible interpretations of costs and other imponderable factors, such statistics can only be approximate.

[124] A supplementary source of credit obtained by the Company at Canton derived from the 'Privilege' or 'Private' trade permitted to the commanders and ship's officers of Company ships. These individuals received 'certificates' on the Court of Directors against the sums deposited. Receipts at the Canton treasury arising from this subsidiary trade accounted for approximately 3 per cent of the total. When specie was scarce at Canton a method known as 'Transfers in Treasury' was frequently adopted. For example, a Hong merchant who had sent large sums of money inland to buy tea to sell to the Supercargoes would seek permission to make an order against the treasury in payment of goods bought by him from the Country merchants. (See Morse, Chronicles, vol. II, Chap. XLII.) The most authoritative exposition of the Company's financial system in the Chinese trade is the same author's article, 'The Provision of Funds for the East India Company's Trade at Canton during the 18th century'. (Journal of the Royal Asiatic Society, April, 1922.)

in volume. It was further augmented as clients of the Agency houses in Bombay and Calcutta began to invest their accumulated capital in the China trade.

The Company's needs in financing their tea trade so stimulated the export of primary products from India and of British woollen materials that the balance of trade began to turn. In 1795-6 (for the first time) the sales value of goods imported into China exceeded the actual cost value of goods exported. In that season part of the residue, valued at T.23,882, was remitted to Bengal in the form of Chinese bullion. This was a climacteric for which China's purchases of Indian cotton were chiefly responsible. At a later period when the export of Indian opium superseded and vastly exceeded that of cotton, the reversal of the old position was accentuated. Instead of receiving a stream of Mexican dollars from London, China became a heavy exporter of bullion in various forms to British India. Long before this position had been reached the success attained in exporting British and Indian goods to China had demonstrated how great were the further possibilities if the Imperial Government could be induced to break the closed circuit of the Canton system, restrain the tyranny of the local mandarins, and open the northern ports to Western industrialism. This was the situation which Pitt and Dundas were urged from various quarters to remedy and the opportunity which they were urged to grasp.

3. THE EMBASSY TO PEKING

The decision to send an official mission to Peking for the purpose of establishing regular diplomatic relations with the Manchu Emperor arose from the revolutionary changes in the China trade which began after 1784. The resulting strains upon the established commercial system at Canton exacerbated old grievances and intensified the desire of British interests, both at home and in India, for a new deal with the Chinese authorities. Formal intervention by the Government of the day marked the beginning of a new epoch.

The history of British discontent which contributed to the intervention promoted by Pitt and Dundas has been fully narrated by previous writers and need only be summarised here as necessary background to ministerial policy.[125] The chief grievance was the plethora of dues, levies and 'presents' exacted by the various grades of port officials, headed by the chief customs officer, the

---

[125] A mass of illustrative detail is furnished in – Alexander Dalrymple, *Oriental Repertory* (Lond., 1791-7), vol. II; Morse, *Chronicles*, *passim* and particularly vol. V; Morse, *International Relations of the Chinese Empire* (Lond., 1910-18), vol. I; and Pritchard, *Anglo-Chinese Relations during the 17th and 18th centuries* (Univ. of Illinois Press, 1929); J. L. Cranmer-Byng, ed. *An Embassy to China: Being the journal kept by Lord Macartney during his embassy to the Emperor Ch'ien-lung, 1793-1794* (Lond., 1962).

Hoppo, who functioned under the supervision of the Viceroy of the Province. The sum of these exactions was onerous enough and multiplied with the expansion of the trade, but irritation was chiefly caused by their capricious fluctuation. No one was able to ascertain what were the legal duties, sanctioned by the Emperor, and what was unauthorised plunder. During his term of office the Hoppo normally made a large fortune out of the Canton trade and by methods not dissimilar from those employed by the English Company's Servants in India before the advent of Cornwallis The Hoppo 'squeezed' the Hong merchants, who in turn applied a corresponding pressure to the Europeans; and on their side the Viceroy and the Hoppo were subjected to squeeze by senior mandarins of the central government in the Emperor's name.

Some of the restraints and restrictions were in the nature of pin-pricks and others were more serious. Chinese subjects were forbidden to teach the language (Cantonese or Mandarin) to any foreigner or to enter his personal service: direct access to the officials was normally prohibited and on the rare occasions when audience was granted European representatives were treated with contumely. Complaints were frequently made that the official display of anti-foreign placards tended to inflame the populace and promote disturbances. More serious protests were directed against the commercial system itself. The requirement that every foreign ship must be placed under the control of one of the Chinese 'security' merchants, through whom the duties must be paid, was regarded as an irksome impediment, and the Country traders in particular became increasingly impatient with the obstructions placed in the way of attempts to extend their business to northern ports.

Vigorous representations were made by the Supercargoes in 1753, but unfortunately they coincided with a number of affrays between British and French seamen and made the situation worse. By way of response a series of edicts, issued by the Viceroy and the Hoppo, tightened up the security merchant system, established a strict monopoly of the Hong merchants, and generally confirmed existing regulations. When further protests proved unavailing the Supercargoes in 1759 adopted a suggestion of the Court of Directors and dispatched a ship to Ningpo under the direction of a colleague, James Flint, with a memorial for the Emperor, Ch'ien Lung. Failing at Ningpo, Flint succeeded by bribery at Tientsin, where senior mandarins accepted a Chinese translation of the memorial and forwarded it to the capital. A special commission from Peking and a Manchu general from Fukien were thereupon ordered to Canton and carry out a thorough investigation. The Hoppo of the day was recalled in disgrace and many of the complaints were found to be true. A number of minor abuses were temporarily removed and the commissioner's report resulted in an Imperial decree (in 1760)[126] which required that justice must be accorded to the foreigners. By the same decree, however, the existing system was codified and confirmed. A Co-Hong, or association of licensed merchants limited to a maximum of thirteen, was formed.[127] They were ordered to act together in order to be able to dictate prices: all charges for which foreigners were liable were to be paid through a member of the Co-Hong: they were constituted the sole channel for petitions to the officials and were to be held responsible for the behaviour of their foreign clients. In practice this organisation did not exercise the rigid and all-powerful control which was intended, but in the early years the English Company feared the worst, particularly as foreign trade was now strictly confined to Canton. As a defensive measure the Directors abandoned the system of sending a Supercargo on board each of their ships to conduct its business, and replaced it by a permanent resident committee at Canton which was given authority over all British subjects there.[128]

The fact that the Co-Hong was not without value for the foreign traders was demonstrated in 1771 when the Committee secured its dissolution by giving a large bribe to the senior Hong merchant. This action proved to be a disastrous blunder. Exposed individually instead of collectively to the demands of the officials, the weaker members of the association found themselves unable to meet their financial commitments; and the Country traders, seeking to collect their debts, took up residence in defiance of the Company's orders. By 1778-9 the debt situation had reached the point where all the Hong merchants were either insolvent or were on the verge of becoming so, and the Peking Government was obliged to intervene. As part of the settlement the Co-Hong was re-constituted in 1780 under more direct official control and a Consoo or guild fund was established by means of a three per cent levy on foreign trade. In future cases of bankruptcy the debts due to foreign creditors were to be met out of this fund.[129] Thereafter

---

[126] The Chinese individual who had dared to translate the memorial was routed out and beheaded, and Flint was imprisoned at Macao for three years.

[127] The most balanced account of the Co-Hong in action is provided by Greenberg (op. cit., Chap. III), for he was able to supplement and modify Morse's account (drawn from the Factory Records and therefore devoted exclusively to the dealings of the Committee of Supercargoes with the organisation) with evidence from the papers of Jardine, Matheson and Co.

[128] They exercised a certain degree of control over the commercial transactions of Country merchants, whose licence from the Company could in the last resort be revoked, but they lacked judicial authority to deal with criminal offences (see pp. 549-53 below).

[129] Foreign merchants were thus protected by an insurance scheme to which they (or rather the European and Chinese consumers) paid the premiums. It was frequently complained, however, that the officials formed the habit of raiding the fund when additional State revenue was required.

the Co-Hong remained the central feature of China's trade with Europeans until its dissolution under the Treaty of Nanking in 1842. Its methods and relative importance, however, were progressively modified as the trade extended and carved out new channels. The Imperial policy of relying on it as an organ of control and concentration became less and less realistic.

The Co-Hong was a loose association which cannot accurately be likened either to a mediaeval guild merchant or to a regulated company. Each member traded independently with the Europeans on behalf of his own Hong or firm. Their corporate bargaining power proved to be slight, partly because they did not sufficiently trust each other, and also because the capacity of the English Company to buy immense quantities of tea gave them command of the market. The rule that every foreign ship must pay its dues and transact its business exclusively with a member of the Co-Hong gave the association an apparent monopoly, but it began to develop substantial leaks. The 'Private English' and the Americans found that they could get better terms from Chinese 'shopmen' who were outside the privileged – and burdened – circle. The shopmen had always been permitted (under licence) to sell small quantities of personal articles to the foreigners, but with the expansion of free-lance trade they became interlopers, trading even in the staples; and junior Hong merchants, being short of capital, were glad to provide them with the necessary cover.[130]

Shortage of capital was endemic and bankruptcies frequent. The basic reason seems to have been that liquid capital in China, as in mediaeval Europe, was limited and scattered. By far the greatest part of China's resources were represented by a huge subsistence economy: the country was not geared to cope with a large international trade. Although the estimated profits of the Chinese merchants from their English business amounted to over 700,000 Spanish dollars annually, their reserves were evidently inadequate. While being exposed to extortionate demands from the Hoppo and others at short notice, the Hongist had to lay out large sums with the tea growers and also pay 'on the nail' for raw cotton and other commodities purchased from the Country trade. Only one or two members of the Co-Hong were really wealthy men who could support the outlay, the weaker brethren met their necessities and indulged their extravagances by borrowing from British-Indian lenders at rates of interest which were frequently as high as 20 per cent. British Agency houses not only organised an extensive triangular traffic but also provided the Chinese participants with an increasing portion of the requisite finance.

---

[130] Intermittent efforts were made to suppress this illegal trade. In 1817 over two hundred ' outside ' shops were closed down and their goods confiscated. (Greenberg, *op. cit.*, p. 55.)

The question of Chinese indebtedness to 'free' merchants provoked a crisis in the 1770s which had some bearing on later British policy. An unusual combination of circumstances brought it about. The action of the Supercargoes in procuring the dissolution of the Co-Hong in 1771 was followed by a period of great weakness and disorder in the English Company's affairs. In 1773 and 1774 Country traders found that they could not obtain the usual bills of exchange for the remission of their profits to London and consequently took the opportunity of lending large sums to the Hong merchants, who in their difficulties offered extragavant rates of interest. The demand also attracted loans from non-traders in India, particularly in Madras, who had likewise been using the Company's treasury at Canton as a channel for sending home their capital gains. When one Hong merchant after another drifted into insolvency, the creditors, unable to collect, took fright and refused to lend more.

By the end of the year 1777 the situation was becoming desperate: only four of the Hong merchants could be relied on to meet their trading obligations, and the trade as a whole was being crippled. In the following summer Charles Gordon, one of the principal creditors, arrived in London where he organised meetings and made representations to the Ministry and the Court of Directors. It was alleged that the Canton officials had persistently evaded the issue, and a proposal was made that they should be bypassed by sending someone with a royal commission and in a King's ship to Tientsin, and thence overland to Peking. The commissioner should offer a reasonable settlement of the debts and negotiate a general reform of the Canton commercial system. Neither the North Ministry nor the Directors responded to the suggestion, but the latter instructed the Supercargoes to do everything in their power to assist the private creditors.

Meanwhile the situation was not improved by the aggressive action of the creditors in Madras. In defiance of the Presidency Government they enlisted the support of Admiral Vernon who at their instance dispatched a frigate, H.M.S. *Sea Horse* under the command of Capt. J. A. Panton, to Canton with a memorial for the Viceroy. Panton arrived there in October, 1779, and presented Vernon's letter which was forwarded to Peking. Thus encouraged, the Madras creditors decided to follow up with a repeat performance, again ignoring their Government's opposition. In June, 1780, Admiral Hughes ordered Capt. Panton, who was due to sail again for Canton on convoy duty, to present a further demand that justice be done.[131]

---

[131] See Morse, *Chronicles*, vol. II, Chaps. XXXIV and XXXV.

This unauthorised intervention angered the Directors[132] and prejudiced the protracted negotiations between the Supercargoes and the officials at Canton. An investigation by the Peking Government produced a decision which scaled down the total claims of the creditors from $4,400,222 to approximately $1,200,000 to be repaid in ten annual instalments.[133] This figure was only slightly more than the original principal: the remainder was accumulated compound interest.[134] It seems that more than twice this amount might have been realised if the negotiations at Canton had not been interrupted by an appeal to Caesar. For an admiral (and so presumably a mandarin of high rank) to have had the effrontery to approach the celestial throne on a matter of mercantile debts only went to show how lost to decency the Western barbarians were. By the same decree the Co-Hong was reconstituted and the old system confirmed. The episode, which exhaled something of the odour of the Arcot Debts, was significant to the extent that it illustrated the inadequacy of the organisation at Canton in serving a rapidly expanding commerce and the need for a special effort at the highest level if the Chinese Government was to be persuaded to alter its attitude.

There was also the problem of criminal jurisdiction. Each year in October, when the trading season began, the English Supercargoes and other European chiefs ended their four-months' sojourn at Macao and opened up their factories at Canton. Soon English, French, Danish, Swedish and American ships began to

---

[132] Arising from this situation they prepared (in Jan., 1782) special instructions for the Committee of Supercargoes. These loan transactions, it was stated, had been carried on 'to too great an extent': most of the debts claimed appeared to be interest. The creditors had requited the Company's lenience and support by ordering Sir Edmund Vernon and then Sir Edward Hughes to intervene on their behalf. 'The appearance of sending a Man of War to a Chinese Port on such an Occasion is too plain an intimation of Threat to admit of a double Construction; and the consequences flowing from it are apparent. The Chinese is an absolute Government, the Company are situated there merely in the Capacity of Traders, without force and without Authority.' The conduct of Vernon, Hughes and Panton had been 'most blameable': the Company's representatives must assert their authority. 'Our positive determination and Order is that no British subject whatsoever (except the Supercargoes and those employed by them) shall from henceforth be suffered to reside in China.' Free merchants who refused to go back to India at the end of the season must be compelled to do so and their licences must be revoked. (*Factory Records, China*, vol. 19.)

[133] The Supercargoes stated that the claims of the creditors at the end of the year 1779 amounted at compound interest to $3,808,075, and that the Chinese debtors had never received more than $1,078,976 in money and goods (Supercargoes to Court, 15 Jan., 1780. *Ibid.*).

[134] The claims on Coqua, one of the senior Hongists, amounting to $1,156,162, were not included in this settlement, nor were those of non-Hong merchants. In Nov., 1783, George Vansittart and Ewan Law, acting as attorneys for Coqua's creditors, requested the Company's assistance in obtaining a settlement, but the Directors informed these creditors (in 1785) that any further action would be detrimental to the Company's interests. They then pressed Dundas to include their claims among the objects of the embassy to Peking. (See p. 562 below.)

come in and an international mart started its complicated business. Ship's crews were confined to the immediate environs of their quarters at Whampoa (twelve miles below Canton) and to a couple of small islands in the river.[135] Habits of turbulence, boredom and animosity between nations led to frequent brawls among themselves and sometimes with the Chinese. Nor were Country merchants slow to take reprisals in Canton itself.

The central government and the local authorities accepted this annual invasion philosophically as a source of revenue and individual profit, but they remained determined to keep it concentrated and segregated at the one port. Foreigners must be kept in complete subjection, and as their numbers multiplied the Chinese attitude became more ruthless. Fear was blended with disdain. The expanding power of the British in India and to the north of Bengal, of the Dutch in the Malay Archipelago, of the Russians in Siberia and the Alaskan coast, and now the French in Cochin China were known in Peking: the circling tide must not penetrate. In 1780 for the first time in China a European was executed – by public strangulation – for killing another European. (A French sailor had stabbed a Portuguese sailor in a quarrel at night.) In their report on the affair the Committee of Supercargoes described it as 'a very dangerous precedent' which could involve Europeans in inextricable difficulties.

The man executed to-day could have no trial of Common Justice . . . we do not understand that the Chinese Government took any means in their Courts to find out the truth. Foreigners are not here allowed the benefit of the Chinese Laws, though in this instance one of them suffers by the rigor of them; nor have they any privileges in common with the Natives.[136]

Four years later an incident occurred which in its implications dismayed all Europeans at Canton and caused the British Government to intervene. In the course of firing a salute at Whampoa one of the guns of the Lady Hughes, a Country ship from Bombay, hit and badly damaged a Chinese lighter. Three of its occupants were wounded, two of whom died. The unfortunate gunner (an old man, it was said) promptly went into hiding, fearing 'the undiscriminating Severity of the Chinese Government'. Two officials, together with the Hong merchants, visited the chief of the Super-

---

[135] English crews were permitted to land on Danes Island and French crews on French Island – so that they might stretch their legs without kicking each other. English requests to the Viceroy in 1793 and again in 1825 for permission to build a hospital on Danes Island were promptly refused (Morse, Chronicles, vol. IV, p. 114).

[136] Hitherto, they added, the mandarins had usually exacted monetary compensation for offences from the Hong Security Merchants instead of employing rigorous methods. 'Their Corruption, therefore, in part is the foreigners' security.' (Ibid., vol. II, p. 59.)

cargoes and demanded that the individual concerned be sent up to Canton for examination. He would be taken under armed guard from the English factory to appear before a judicial tribunal. The Supercargoes promised co-operation but pointed out that they had no authority over Country ships (which in 1784 was still true) and that armed men could not be admitted into any of the factories. 'We should not think our persons in safety if such a precedent was once established.' The latter point was waived, but drastic action followed.

The Supercargo of the *Lady Hughes*, George Smith, had agreed to remain in Canton for a few days while the enquiry took place. On the same evening he was decoyed from his factory by 'a pretended message' from a Hong merchant, seized and marched into the City under a guard with drawn swords. The English Committee were deeply alarmed for Smith's safety, since under Chinese law a subordinate was held personally responsible for his own subordinates. The Chinese officials were evidently determined to make this a test case and to teach the Europeans an enduring lesson. Barricades were set up across all roads leading to the quays and manned with troops, communication between Canton and Whampoa was prohibited, and all trade was brought to a standstill. The European quarter was put in a state of siege.

In face of a common danger the French, Dutch and American merchants joined the English in a united front, offering to send up armed parties from their several ships to help in defending the English factories; and a joint protest was addressed to the Viceroy. After five days the gunner was found and handed over. A week later two representatives of each of the nations concerned were summoned to the presence of the *Anchasze*, the Provincial Judge. After dilating upon the graciousness of the Emperor in allowing them to trade in China at all and his displeasure over the delay in surrendering the offending gunner, he emphasised the extreme moderation of the Government in demanding only one life for the two which had been lost by the accident and called upon them to receive the Emperor's decision in the matter with all proper respect, whatever it might be. They were then dismissed. Afterwards they were informed that at about the time when they were listening to this admonition the gunner had been strangled.

The difference between the European and the Chinese conceptions of justice had been plainly demonstrated. As the Europeans saw it, a judicial murder had been committed: a man had been executed for causing a fatal accident. From the Chinese point of view true justice had been done and with restraint. In the course of a conversation while the affair was still in progress certain Chinese officials explained to the English Committee that in the case of death a man must be given up. They agreed that the gunner had been innocent of any ill intention. If the culprit escaped arrest, a substitute must suffer: if none was provided, the Supercargo of the ship would be apprehended, or failing him the chief representative of the nation involved. Since the English appeared to be much interested in the fate of Mr. Smith, the Supercargo of the *Lady Hughes*, they suggested that a servant 'or some person of less consequence' be put in his place. In their report to London the Supercargoes set out the dilemma in forthright terms. Future resistance in like cases might put an end to the Company's trade, yet compliance would entail the abandonment of what Europeans deemed humanity and justice. The implication was plain: London should intervene to secure a different arrangement respecting criminal jurisdiction before the dilemma was encountered.

The indignities we personally suffer, the vexations and impediments in our business, we have been taught by gradual encroachment to bear: but if the Trade be once lost, and the necessities of England oblige her to regain it, we apprehend it can be done only by a submission that must be disgraceful, or by the use of force, which however successful, must be productive of very serious calamities. We think that no application to the Chinese Government for any, the most reasonable, privilege would be successful unless made in a manner that would awe them.[137]

The Court of Directors thought otherwise. The Supercargoes were rebuked. The power of the Chinese Government, they were reminded, was absolute and attempted resistance to it was folly. In cases of murder they must co-operate with the local authorities in apprehending the culprit, and when there was an accidental killing they should arrange for monetary compensation through the Hong merchants. They then reverted to the question which they regarded as fundamental: the contumacy of the private traders. Evidently they were annoyed that Capt. Williams of the *Lady Hughes* had failed to produce the gunner at once and had thus precipitated a crisis. The Supercargoes were informed that they possessed complete power over Country ships.[138] This communication (of February, 1786) was followed up in April by regulations which supplemented those of 1782 and attempted to tighten control over the Country trade. Their declared object was to prevent 'the mischiefs arising at China from private traders'. All ships belong-

---

[137] *Canton Consultations*, vol. LXXIX, pp. 169-74 (India Library, C.R.O.). For more detailed accounts of the *Lady Hughes* episode see Morse, *Chronicles*, vol. II, pp. 99-107, and Pritchard, *op cit.*, pp. 226-30. The Supercargoes proposed a modified form of extra-territoriality. When a British subject was charged with murder, he should be tried by them in the presence of a Chinese magistrate. If found guilty he would be handed over, but if found innocent their right to protect him should be recognised. For cases of manslaughter a scale of adequate punishments should be agreed between the Supercargoes and the Chinese authorities.

[138] Court to Supercargoes, 24 Feb., 1786. (*Factory Records, China*, vol. 19.)

ing to Europeans resident in one of the Presidencies must be registered and the owner or agent must enter into a deed of covenant with the Company by which no ship could be sold to foreign Europeans or Americans except at the place of registration and by special licence from the Governor: no foreign goods might be carried except by special licence: only British subjects could be employed as captains or Supercargoes: there must be no trading in China, except at Canton where the certificate of registration was to be produced. Finally, when a Country ship arrived there it must pay all dues and debts and conform to the laws of the Chinese Government, and if any dispute arose the ship must be bound by the decision of the 'China Council'.[139] In other words the Directors were preoccupied with the importance of maintaining the *status quo* at Canton, even if that involved putting up with oppressive and extortionate behaviour on the part of the local officials. Otherwise the rapidly expanding Country trade might cease to be the Company's useful servant and become instead its destructive master – as it eventually did.

At the Board of Control Dundas was meditating on the bolder course which the Supercargoes had in mind, but with wider objects. Since the autumn of 1784 he had been devoting himself with immense energy and zest to the administrative and financial rehabilitation of the Company. As he became familiar with the great possibilities that lay open to British initiative in India itself, he became the protagonist of the proposition that territorial power in Bengal and its outliers could constitute the core of an expanding sphere of influence and profit throughout the Eastern Seas. Warren Hastings and many others had been animated by a similar conception, but the stabilising leadership of Pitt and growing industrial power gave such ambitions new range and depth.

In 1785 Dundas's Eastern policy began to take shape, notably with regard to Britain's relations with France and Holland as Asian Powers. In the autumn of '85 the Board of Control strongly commended the proposed commercial agreement between the French and English East India Companies;[140] and in a later letter to Grenville Dundas stressed the point that, if and when the English Company's monopoly came to be dissolved, such foreign connexions

---

[139] 'Certain regulations to prevent our Supercargoes from experiencing the inconvenience they have often felt by Captains of Country Ships not being under their control. . . .' Court to Supercargoes, 5 April, 1786. (*Factory Records, China,* vol. 20.) Further regulations were issued on 19 Jan., 1787, on action to be taken against unlicensed ships (*ibid.*). In order to arm the 'China Council' with judicial authority a phrase was inserted in Pitt's Act of 1786 ('for the further regulation of the trial of persons accused of certain offences committed in the East Indies') which gave them the same powers over persons, ships and goods as the Indian Presidencies. (*26 Geo. III, cap. 57, sect. XXXV.*)

[140] See Board of Control to Court of Directors, 10 Sept., 1785 (*Board-Court Correspondence,* vol. I, p. 125).

would assume a national importance.[141] More ambitious and precise, though following the same line of policy, were his later efforts to strike a strategic-commercial bargain with the Dutch in the East Indian Ocean and beyond. During the same period he kept a vigilant eye on the Eastern implications of the Anglo-French commercial treaty while it was being negotiated; and when a provisional convention for regulating French trade in British India, which had been agreed in Mauritius in April, 1786, was referred to the Board of Control, he opposed some of the concessions to the French and expressed regret that the Bengal Government had taken the initiative.[142]

During these two years the outstanding importance of the China trade in relation to general expansion in the East was borne in upon him. In the summer of 1786 David Scott returned to England full of plans for modifying the Company's monopoly in order to stimulate an increasing flow of goods and credit between Britain, India and China. As we have seen, he quickly established himself as Dundas's principal adviser in this field. In June of that year the same doctrine was urged by the Honble. John Cochrane in an elaborate memorandum to the Board of Control. The revolution in the Company's affairs occasioned by the Commutation Act was opening 'a new field for Speculation and Trade, not only to the Company, but to the nation at large'. A pamphlet of Francis Baring was cited to show how paltry was the existing export of British goods to China. The Company should surrender its export trade to the merchants of Britain who would pay for freightage in the Company's ships and desposit their profits in the Company's treasury at Canton. 'It requires but this regulation to make the Commutation Act complete and give the Coup de Grace to all the other India Companies of Europe.' Surplus revenue in India should be used to stimulate the exports from Bengal and the Coromandel coast to the Red Sea and the Persian Gulf, whence cargoes fetching high prices in China could be obtained. Similarly British manu-

---

[141] Dundas to Grenville, 27 Sept., 1786. *Grenville Papers, Dropmore*, vol. I, pp. 268-9.

[142] The negotiations had been conducted by the Honble. Charles Cathcart, representing the Bengal Government, and the Vicomte de Souillac. Cathcart returned to England and submitted the draft Convention with related despatches to the Secret Committee of the Court of Directors on 12 Aug., 1786. They were considered by the Secret Committee of the Board of Control (consisting of Pitt, Dundas and Mulgrave) on 26 Aug., when a copy of the Convention was transmitted to Carmarthen, the Foreign Secretary. The matter was taken into further consideration on 19 Oct. and on 29 Jan., 1787. Finally Cornwallis was informed that he might make the provisional Convention 'the rule of your intermediate conduct' at discretion until the negotiations for an Anglo-French commercial treaty had been completed. (Mins. of the Secret Committee of the Board, Nos. 14, 16, and 17, and Secret Committee of the Court to the Gov.-Gen. and Council, 27 March, 1787, *Cornwallis Corr.*, vol. I, p. 294. Cf. H. Furber, *Henry Dundas*, Oxford, 1931, pp. 66-7.)

factures should be introduced into Cochin China, Cambodia and the Malay Archipelago so that the valuable trade between these countries and China would pass into British hands. Everything possible should be done to enable Britain to oust her European rivals from the Country trade in the Indian Ocean.[143]

As early as July, 1783, while the Fox-North coalition was still in office, one George Smith, a Country merchant of Bombay, submitted a memorandum to Dundas in which he stressed the precarious state of the China trade owing to the oppressive behaviour of the mandarins at Canton and the injury done to the Country merchants by the 'unjust' debt settlement of 1780. Yet the possibilities were enormous if the trade were put on a regular footing. To this end an ambassador should be sent to the Imperial Court at Peking to negotiate a treaty of friendship and commerce and an alliance against France and Russia. He should try to secure the opening of the ports of Amoy and Ningpo as a means of extending the sale of British manufactures in northern China: Imperial dues should be clearly stated and the price of imports and exports stabilised.[144]

Two years later George Smith sailed for the East, evidently in the hope of repairing his broken fortunes. In the course of his voyaging he wrote a series of letters to Dundas which are of some interest as illustrating the kind of information about Eastern trade which he was receiving. In a report on the Dutch situation in Ceylon and Java he pointed out that cinnamon paid all the expenses in Ceylon and yielded an annual profit of about £300,000. He also suggested that Britain would do well to help the Dutch to avoid French domination by lending them money.[145] From Madras he sailed to Canton and on his way touched at Capt. Francis Light's recently established settlement at Penang. Its situation, he wrote, was 'very proper' for the Eastern trade, but he urged upon Dundas the still greater importance of Junk Ceylon (Puket Island) to the northward. 'I will not hesitate to declare that if we do not take immediate possession of it some foreign Nation will, when . . . it would become an Asiatic St. Eustatia.' Arrived at Canton, which

---

[143] 'Plan concerning the Export Trade of Great Britain to the East Indies . . . with a Sketch of the Trade with India, Madagascar, China and the Malay Archipelago, by the Honble. John Cochrane, June, 1786.' (*Home Misc. Series*, vol. 404, pp. 1-39.)

[144] 'Some Propositions tending to the Establishment of the East India Company's trade to China on a firm and advantagious Basis . . . humbly submitted to the Consideration of the Right Honble. the Lord Advocate, enclosed in a Letter from Mr. George Smith, dated Kingston, July, 1783' (*Ibid.*, vol. 434, pp. 15-32). The author added the delightful suggestion that a hundred light horsemen should be sent out as the ambassador's bodyguard and should be left in China to introduce European discipline among the Emperor's troops – 'which would occasion an immense demand for Fire arms and Woollens'.

[145] Smith to Dundas, 12 Mar., 1786. Cited, Furber (*op. cit.*), p. 64.

he had last visited in 1765, he was appalled at the greatly increased obstructions placed upon the trade. The impositions of the mandarins had become intolerable as had the extortions which they inflicted upon the Hong merchants. After describing them in detail, he added: 'it appears to me, Sir, that nothing less than an Embassy would remove them'.[146] The Canton situation was the one impediment to unprecedented prosperity. Back in Calcutta in September, 1787, he assured Dundas that the Company's affairs in India were now in such good train that European competition had become negligible and there was every prospect that they would be able to 'make Leaden Hall Street the Emporium of the Asiatic Trade to the western world'. 'The Ball is at their foot, and it rests with the Board of Controul to take care that they keep it in motion.'[147]

The decision to send an embassy to the Chinese Emperor was evidently taken by Dundas, after consultation with Pitt, some time in March, 1787.[148] Pitt himself strongly supported the project and took an active part in its planning.. The Court of Directors, on the other hand, looked at it askance. The restriction of the trade to Canton was a safeguard which alone made it possible to exercise control over the increasing numbers of Country merchants. If northern ports were opened to Indian produce and British manufactures the Company's monopoly would crumble. Concentration suited the Company as well as the Chinese Government. Hence the rebuke to the Canton Committee when they urged a formal intervention to secure redress: Chinese law must be obeyed and extortions endured. When the Ministers announced their inten-

---

[146] Smith to Dundas, Canton, 26 Nov., 1786. (*Factory Records, China*, vol. 19.) Smith added the sensible observation that the ambassador should refrain from stating specific grievances (e.g. old debts), since the result would be 'certain ruin to the present Merchants'. He should confine himself to complaints against the public acts of the mandarins which were officially recorded. In a later letter from Canton, dated 12 Dec., 1786, he suggested that the President of the Committee of Supercargoes should be appointed His Majesty's Consul in order that he might have judicial powers to apprehend British offenders (against other British subjects) and send them home for trial. (*Ibid.*)

[147] Smith to Dundas, Calcutta, 10 Sept., 1787. (*Ibid.*) In this letter he asked Dundas to recommend him to Cornwallis. He was old and had been unfortunate. He also renewed his application for a writership for his son.

[148] In a letter to Dundas of 23 March, 1787, George Smith (of Guildford) referred to 'the intended embassy' and to a conference on the subject which Dundas had arranged for the following day with the Chairman and Deputy-Chairman of the Court of Directors (*Melville Papers, National Libr. of Scotland*, MS. 1069, f. 15). This George Smith (of Guildford, Surrey and Madras) is not to be confused with the George Smith (of Kingston, Surrey and Bombay) who corresponded with Dundas from Calcutta and Canton in 1786-7. 'Smith of Guildford' was one of the Madras traders who had lent large sums to Hong merchants and had incurred the particular wrath of the Court of Directors, who in 1782 ordered the Supercargoes to send him home. His financial transactions at Canton evidently reduced him to insolvency. In 1786-7 he led the creditors in a campaign to induce the Ministry to intervene for the purpose of securing a revision of the Chinese debt settlement in their favour (see below p. 562).

tion of negotiating a commercial agreement with Peking in the national interest (as though Peking were Paris or Madrid), the Directors co-operated, having no option in the matter; but on some counts they were sceptical and on others apprehensive.[149]

The person chosen to undertake the mission was Lt.-Colonel the Honble. Charles Cathcart, who had recently returned from his negotiations with the French in Mauritius. A protégé of Dundas, he had been elected M.P. for Clackmannan in 1784 and had then gone out to Bengal to be quartermaster-general. He had been selected, wrote Dundas, as a man of noble birth, good understanding, a member of the British legislature, and having no connexion with commerce.[150] As such he should prove acceptable at the Imperial Court. Cathcart prepared for his task by a round of interviews with men who had served on the Canton Committee and by reading the China records at East India House. On 20 June he submitted a report to Dundas in which he considered two questions: the method of appointing the Mission, and secondly 'the Place which would best suit the Commerce of Great Britain as a Depot in China'. On the first he declared that the Mission would have no chance of success at Peking unless it was in the King's name: any attempt through the Servants of the Company only would be ineffectual. In support of this view he cited the recommendation of the Canton Committee after the *Lady Hughes* episode – which the Directors had angrily rejected. No one, he added, who had read the diaries of the Supercargoes between 1781 and 1786 could fail to be sympathetic with their situation. 'After all this personal Risque and Humiliation they repeatedly warn their Employers of the Probability of a sudden Loss of this important Commerce.' To mark and distinguish a Mission from the King 'the only proper Conveyance' would be a large frigate of the Royal Navy.

Turning to the question of a British 'depot' in China, he suggested that it might be left to the Chinese Government to choose the site, only stipulating that it should be healthy, safe for shipping, and convenient for the dispersion of British manufactures and the collection of tea, china-ware and other products of the eastern provinces. He had been advised that the most eligible

---

[149] Pritchard (*op. cit.*, pp. 236-7) makes the assumption that the Directors 'warmly' seconded the enterprise, but the evidence contradicts it. In a letter to Cornwallis Dundas wrote: 'I have discovered that the Court of Directors are rather hostile to the expedition, and give out that it may be highly prejudicial to their interests, if, by creating jealousies among the Mandarins and other Chinese at Canton, it should suspend in any degree the intercourse with them, by which only, under present circumstances, their trade can be carried on.' (Dundas to Cornwallis, 1 Aug., 1789. *Cornwallis Corr.*, vol. II, p. 1.) This was exactly the view which the Directors had expressed to the Canton Committee in 1785.

[150] He was the younger son of Charles, ninth Baron Cathcart, a lieut.-general (1760) and envoy to Russia, 1768-71.

place for the purpose would be Amoy which possessed a good harbour.

But if the Jealousy of the Chinese shall bear against our getting a Footing in their Empire, and not against the Introduction of our Manufactures into their Country, the Security of our Commerce might be attained, and our great Depot might be placed without the Empire, in a situation accessible to the Junks of the whole Coast, so that our Commerce would have the double chance of our Supercargoes in China, and of Chinese Traders.

If the Chinese refused to grant 'a convenient privileged Depot', the only alternative was to remedy the defects of the situation at Canton as much as possible; but the Chinese could not be expected to reciprocate unless and until British authority exerted a better control over its own people. How could the Chinese be expected to have confidence in us when they annually witnessed the arrival of fifty or sixty of our ships whose sailors were subject to no law? Finally Cathcart drew attention to the fact that the British were entirely ignorant of the navigation of the northern coasts of China.[151] As will be seen, this was a point which Dundas took up with vigour.

Soon after receiving this report Dundas sent a memorandum to Pitt which was in effect the agenda for a special meeting of the Board of Control. Among the items listed were the following: 'To consider and finally adjust the instructions . . . for exploring the real state of Indian navigation with a view to Mr. Pitt's taking the measures for putting the Plan in execution: To consider and prepare instructions for Colonel Cathcart's Mission to China for the purpose of obtaining a Commercial Establishment, and providing a Depot for British Manufactures exported there.'[152] The draft Instructions which Dundas prepared epitomise the policy which the Ministry had adopted. The China trade, it was stated, had become a matter of great national importance owing to the effect of the Commutation Act in drawing the tea trade out of the hands of other European nations. In consequence the opportunity had arisen of promoting the prosperity of the territorial possessions in

---

[151] 'Preliminary Proposals by Lt.-Col. Cathcart, 20 June, 1787' (*Factory Records, China*, vol. 90). This document is printed in Morse, *Chronicles*, vol. II, pp. 157-9, but, as Pritchard points out, it is there mis-dated as 18 August, 1787. There is a letter from Cathcart to Dundas of this latter date (in *Melville Papers*, MS. 1069, f. 23), but it deals with other matters connected with the embassy. The suggestion that a depot might be established outside the Chinese Empire which would have the additional advantage of attracting the junks may have derived from Alexander Dalrymple (now Hydrographer to the Admiralty), who had consistently advocated the plan for many years, and who was being consulted about the embassy (see Cathcart to Dundas, 25 July, 1787. *Factory Records, China*, vol. 18).

[152] Memorandum for the Members of the India Board.' N.D. (*Pitt Papers*, P.R.O. 30/8/355.)

India by selling their products in the extensive Empire of China. The hazardous and discouraging circumstances under which this trade was conducted were then recited. It would be Cathcart's prime duty to discover whether this was due to a settled policy of the Chinese Government or to jealousy of Britain's national influence or merely to the misbehaviour of distant provincial administrators. If political jealousy was the cause he was to declare that our only object was commerce, to be protected by the Chinese Government, subject to its laws, and on a permanent principle mutually beneficial. There was no wish for territory nor the right of fortification or defence, and he must obviate any prejudice which might have arisen from 'our present Dominion in India' by stating that it had arisen 'almost without our seeking it'. Britain wished to obtain 'a Grant of a small tract of Ground or detached Island' in some more convenient situation than Canton where goods could be warehoused and trade would not be confined to the short season that was allowed for European ships to arrive and depart. Any such grant must be received in the name of the King and should, if possible, include authority to make police regulations. If the Emperor wished to exclude his own subjects from the operation of British justice, that could be accepted provided that British subjects were exempt from the criminal jurisdiction of China. If, however, a new establishment was refused, he should turn his whole attention to the relief of the existing embarrassments at Canton by an extension of privileges.

The Instructions then referred to the touchy question of the opium trade. This must be handled with the greatest circumspection. There was no doubt that a considerable proportion of the opium grown in Bengal found its way to China, 'where the vicious manners of the People call for an increasing use of that pernicious Drug'. If the Chinese Government insisted on a commercial treaty being made conditional upon the inclusion of an article prohibiting the import of opium, Cathcart must accede to it rather than risk losing an essential benefit. In that event Bengal opium must take its chance in an open market or find a vent through the circuitous traffic of the Eastern Seas. If all went well, he should propose that the Emperor might receive an occasional or a perpetual British Minister at Peking and send one of his own to London.[153] In such terms Western minds conceived of a reciprocal business arrangement between the Son of Heaven and King George III of Great Britain.

On 21 July, 1787, Dundas sent a copy of these draft Instructions

[153] 'Proposed Instructions to the Honble. Lt.-Colonel Cathcart on the Intended Embassy to China.' N.D. (*Factory Records, China*, vol. 20). They were adopted as they stood (with one deletion) and a fair copy was signed by Lord Sydney, as Secretary of State, on 30 Nov., 1787. (Printed in Morse, *Chronicles*, vol. II, pp. 160-7.)

with other related documents to Cornwallis in India. In his cover-ing letter he wrote that he had learned from various quarters that a Mission sent directly from the King to the Emperor would prob-ably have the desired effect of securing a commercial establishment, which would answer very valuable purposes in extending the sale of British and Indian produce and manufactures throughout the Chinese Empire and its dependencies. 'I know not whether it will succeed or not, but I am sure it is worth the attempt.'[154] Ten days later the Board of Control received a formal communication from Lord Sydney that Cathcart had been appointed Ambassador to the Emperor of China.[155]

The Ministers and Cathcart soon found themselves involved in argument, on the one side with the Court of Directors and on the other with the Canton creditors. When the Chairs were given a copy of the draft Instructions they at once took exception to a clause which stipulated that, if a new establishment in China were conceded, Cathcart was to try to obtain 'free permission of Ingress and Regress for ships of all Nations' upon the payment of fixed duties to the Chinese Government. On 16 August Cathcart was interviewed by the Chairs who expressed their apprehension. Apart from admitting foreign competitors to the depot, this arrangement would open the door to British private traders operat-ing under foreign flags. Cathcart was cautious. Although he had been given a copy of the Instructions for his perusal he had no authority to offer an official interpretation; but he pointed out that the proposed stipulation would not preclude the Company from limiting the British Country ships to whatever number they might be pleased to license. As to the policy of giving access to the ships of other European nations they should apply for information to the Government. Cathcart at once reported the interview in a letter which he showed to Pitt and then addressed to Dundas, warning them that a representation from the Directors was to be expected within a few days.

He was not sure, he wrote, what alteration in the Instructions the Chairs would request, but he imagined that they would ask for the exclusion of foreign ships or at any rate that only those would be admitted which had been given a permit by the Com-pany. He recalled that in conversation Dundas had told him that the line to be observed, if he was fortunate enough to obtain an

---

[154] Dundas to Cornwallis, 21 July, 1787. (*Cornwallis Corr.*, vol. I, pp. 327-8.) He added: 'There is every reason to believe that the French are at this moment very anxious to acquire such a situation in that part of the world.' This idea probably derived from reports received about French interest at this time in Egypt, the Persian Gulf and Cochin China.

[155] *Minutes of the Board of Control*, vol. I, No. 24 (31 July, 1787). Secret. The Board was instructed to submit Instructions and a letter to the Emperor for the King's approval and signature.

establishment, was 'to take Possession in the name of the King of Great Britain and for the use of the East India Company during the Currency of their Charter'.[156] The Chairs duly presented a memorandum to Pitt which was on the lines which Cathcart had anticipated. Pitt then discussed the question with Cathcart, and Cathcart with Dundas. The Prime Minister agreed with Dundas that the grant must be in the name of the King but evidently wished to avoid a collision with the Directors.

Before the Instructions are finally delivered to me [wrote Cathcart], Mr. Pitt inclines to some little alteration in the wording of the Paragraph relative to the New Establishment, so as to direct me, while I stipulate for the general admission of all Ships, to preserve in our Hands a discretional latitude of Exclusion. So this Point appears to be settled.[157]

The words 'in our hands' could be taken to refer to the Company or to the Government. When the Instructions were finally issued under Sydney's signature the reference to this question had been cut down to one sentence: 'Should a new Establishment be conceded, you will take it in the name of the King of Great Britain.' Dundas had in substance won his point. Secure the grant of a depot under the authority of the Crown and argue with the Company afterwards – from strength. The attitude of the Directors was, of course, preposterous. All European nations had access to Canton, and the establishment of a British 'closed shop' at another Chinese port would have incurred the particular hostility of France, with whom a commercial treaty had recently been concluded, and of the Dutch, whose co-operation in Eastern waters as in Europe was a prime objective. In the autumn of 1787 the quarrel between the Board and the Court was coming to a head and culminated in an Act of Parliament declaratory of the Crown's authority over the Company. At this stage too the confident expectation of Dundas that the Company's chartered privilege would be drastically curtailed, if not terminated in 1793, had not yet felt the restraining hand of the Prime Minister. The projection of British commerce into China was to be pursued as a national policy, and it was exactly that which stirred the Directors' suspicions. A new base under the direct control of the Crown might

---

[156] Cathcart to Dundas, 18 Aug., 1787. (*Melville Papers*, MS. 1069, f. 23.) 'The consideration of this subject,' he added, ' is put off to the 24th instant. . . . I have requested the favor of Mr. Pitt to glance over this Letter before it is dispatched, because application on some of these Points will probably be made in a few days.'

[157] Cathcart to Dundas, 31 Aug., 1787 (*ibid.*, f. 27). Cathcart added that the Chairman and Deputy now appeared to be well satisfied with the Instructions. ' The Line which you state of asking the Grant in the name of the King, coincides with Mr. Pitt's opinion, and suffices for my guidance.'

well reduce Canton to a commercial backwater and overwhelm the Company's position in China.

Less serious but more irritating was the pressure of the Canton creditors. Those resident in England had been finally told by the Court of the Directors in February, 1785, that any further support for their case would be detrimental to the Company's interests; but one of them, George Smith (of Guildford and Madras) was a very pertinacious gentleman and received powerful backing from George Vansittart and Ewan Law (brother-in-law of Sir Thomas Rumbold), who became his assigns.[158] Undeterred by the rebuff, Smith began to bombard Dundas with memoranda and requests for an interview. A 'narrative' of the debt question was submitted and a friend of Dundas, General Sir Archibald Campbell, Governor-designate of Madras, was induced to give his 'warm' commendation. In the spring of 1786 the campaign was extended to Lord Walsingham as a member of the Board of Control. The particular issue of the debts was identified with the general question of national interests in China. The export of bullion, Walsingham was informed, could never be replaced by British goods until 'a permanent Establishment in China' had been secured. To effect these purposes, it would be absolutely necessary 'to destroy the Co-Hong by its total dissolution', for as long as European trade was confined to ten Chinese houses, the sale of British manufactures could never be extended. The voice of Private Trade was being heard again.

Walsingham was a cipher at the Board of Control and Dundas was unresponsive; but when it became known in March, 1787, that an embassy to Peking was intended, Smith and Vansittart redoubled their applications. On the day before Dundas was due to confer with the Chairs on the project they secured an interview and proffered much advice. Only one or two of the Directors had any knowledge of the Company's situation in China: Macao should, if possible, be purchased from the Portuguese with Chinese consent, or failing that, Danes Island near Whampoa might be obtained, and so on. Within a few hours of the interview Smith followed up with a letter to Dundas (28 March) in which he asserted that the debt question would be 'extremely instrumental' in forwarding a permanent regulation of the trade to China, 'and will strongly aid the Ambassador in obtaining from the Court of Peking redress of the Company's Grievances and putting their trade on a respectable Footing'. Nothing could have been less true. A royal ambassador who gave the impression in Peking that one of the objects of his long journey was to upset an Imperial decree

---

[158] Smith was one of the principal creditors of the Hong merchant, Coqua, whose debts had not been included in the settlement ordered by the Chinese Government. Smith seems to have become bankrupt in consequence.

and obtain more money for a group of foreign tradesmen and money-lenders, would have brought his mission to an immediate and unfortunate termination. When in July the preparations for an embassy reached an advanced stage George Smith sent Dundas a memorandum of forty-three closely written foolscap pages, together with an up-to-date statement of the debt claims. In a covering letter he had the effrontery to suggest that he himself might be included in Cathcart's entourage – as the debts expert.[159]

On the whole the Ministers were disposed to give this pressure group a certain measure of assistance, perhaps because Madras creditors were awkward customers to thwart. 'After full consideration of the subject,' Dundas replied, 'it is thought improper to load the Intended Mission with any official Instructions relative to the Debts in which you are interested, far less to take any of you as Coadjutors in the Mission.' If, however, some of them would care to wait upon Colonel Cathcart the latter would be glad to receive information and to be of any service to them which was not inconsistent with the important task which had been entrusted to him.[160] In consequence the unfortunate ambassador became involved in complicated discussions with the creditors and frequent references to Pitt and Dundas for guidance. After much difficulty and delay the creditors agreed to vest Vansittart and Law with full powers to act on their behalf.[161] Papers were prepared which Cathcart was to take with him, but they were not ready at the time of his departure. In the end nothing materialised from this sustained campaign, but it is a useful illustration of Pitt's reaction to a pressure group which attempted to exploit a line of national policy in its own interests.

On Friday, 21 December, 1787, Cathcart and his staff of five sailed from Spithead on board the frigate, *Vestal*, Capt. Sir Richard Strachan, Bt., commanding. Cathcart was suffering from a lung

---

[159] ' Memorandum and Hints offered with the greatest Deference and Submission for Instructions to be drawn out for his Excellency the British Ambassador to Tien Lung, Emperor of China, in so far as regards the Debts Oweing from the Chinese to British Subjects, by George Smith, Guildford, 12 July, 1787.' (*Factory Records, China*, vol. 18.) The covering letter of the same date is in *Melville Papers*, f. 21. The above summary of the debt negotiations is based on letters to Dundas from Smith, Vansittart, Cathcart, etc., extending from 5 Jan., 1786, to 21 Feb., 1788, in MS. 1069, ff. 3-41.

[160] Dundas to G. Smith, 3 Aug., 1787. Private. Quoted in Cathcart to Dundas, 18 Aug., 1787. (MS. 1069, *ut supra*, f. 23.)

[161] ' With Mr. Pitt's permission I have written to Mr. George Smith to this effect: " That Government have no objection to his offering his Services, in conjunction with Mr. Vansittart, Mr. Hunter and Mr. Law, to the Creditors of the Chinese, upon the ground of having had Conference with Government on the subject, and having found a disposition on the part of Government to aid them." ' For that reason they were requesting the creditors to delegate to them full powers to treat with Government and to send secret instructions to their agents in China. (Cathcart to Dundas, 31 Aug., 1787. *Ibid.*, f. 27.)

infection and was a very sick man.[162] On 10 June, 1788, he died in the Straits of Banka near Malaya. The *Vestal* thereupon returned to England. A project to which much thought and labour had been devoted was thus brought abruptly to a standstill.

A few weeks after Strachan had reported to the Admiralty with his sad news the King's mental illness developed and the Administration was soon engulfed in the Regency Crisis. When that storm had passed (in February, 1789), Ministers were able to turn their attention again to external affairs. The problem presented by the China enterprise was to find a man who combined diplomatic experience with some knowledge of India but without being involved in Company politics. 'The difficulty,' wrote Dundas, 'of finding such a successor to Colonel Cathcart as was altogether satisfactory has occasioned a frequent change of resolutions on that subject.' Despairing of finding a suitably qualified person at home, the Triumvirate decided to obtain a commission under the Great Seal and send it out to India, where Cornwallis was to choose the man and fill in his name. In July a draft despatch from Grenville, as Secretary of State, was prepared in which the situation was explained and the main points to be incorporated in Cornwallis's instructions to the new ambassador were indicated.[163] Grenville, however, bethought himself that this mode of proceeding might be open to legal objection and applied to Lord Chancellor Thurlow for an opinion. The object, he explained, was too important to be abandoned without further trial, and success largely depended on sending someone to Peking authorised by the King and not merely by a trading company. Did Thurlow see any objection to the proposed procedure?[164] As might be expected, Thurlow did. The appointment of the person of the ambassador and his Instructions must flow from the King himself. Under modern conditions of communication the difficulty could not have arisen. After a cabled

---

[162] 'I am concerned to inform you that Col. Cathcart left this country with an exceeding bad cold which seemed much to affect his Lungs and breast by the violence of a Cough, and was looking extremely ill. He was in good spirits and said when he got into warm weather he would soon be well.' (Smith to Dundas, 21 Feb., 1788.) Never willing to miss a trick, Smith enclosed some papers on the debts which Dundas might care to forward to Cathcart's successor – 'in case of accidents'.

[163] Headed – 'Whitehall, July, 1789 [unsigned] to Cornwallis': endorsed – 'Proposed letter from Mr. Grenville . . . to Lord Cornwallis on the subject of an Embassy to China' (*Factory Records, China*, vol. 20). A copy of Cathcart's Instructions was to be enclosed for the Governor-General's guidance, but it was pointed out that these dealt only in general terms with the important object of extending the sale of British manufactures in China, because Cathcart had been fully briefed on the subject by persons in England who were fully acquainted with it. Details were given about specific commodities which should be included in the new Instructions. It was stated that, while the Company found difficulty in selling even small quantities of British goods in Canton, the northern province of China had been supplied with them by a long and expensive land route through Russia.

[164] Grenville to Thurlow, 15 July, 1789. (*Grenville Papers, Dropmore*, vol. I, p. 484.)

enquiry and a cabled reply, the recommended name would have been adopted at the instance of a responsible Minister.[165]

A further obstacle made its appearance. Somewhat belatedly Dundas discovered that the Court of Directors were opposed to the Mission on the ground that it might excite the jealousy of the mandarins and merchants at Canton and thus jeopardise the Company's trade. 'I feel so much,' observed Dundas, 'the importance of establishing a commercial connexion with the great empire of China, that I am not disposed to be discouraged from the plan by any trivial obstructions.' At the same time he felt obliged to pause. 'Considering,' he continued, 'the near approach of the period when a total new arrangement with the East India Company must take place, and considering how much the prosperity of their affairs depends on the resources of the China trade, it occurred to me as imprudent to give them a handle for saying that any measure suggested or promoted by Government had proved prejudicial to them.' In this letter (to Cornwallis) he stated that Pitt and Grenville agreed with him on this point,[166] but since all three were anxious to push the business forward and their previous plan had been vetoed by Thurlow, it was now suggested that Cornwallis should himself send an emissary to China. He might go either as a secret agent without avowed authority or with the Governor-General's commission to settle such points as fell within the sphere of his Government. Such a person could collect information about the disposition of the Chinese Government and their commercial needs, 'as may enable you and us to judge how far we are justified in the notion we entertain of the importance of a more extended commercial connexion with China, and how far there is a reasonable prospect of our being able to accomplish it'.[167] It was at best a lame proposal, and Dundas was probably not sorry when the imminence of another war with Tipu of Mysore prevented Cornwallis from pursuing it.

During the interval action was taken to gather further information about the navigation of Eastern waters. The ignorance of the British concerning the China coast beyond Canton had been noted during the planning of Cathcart's mission. At this time too, the Ministry was intent on taking advantage of the Dutch recognition of the right of free navigation through the Malay Archipelago. In 1790 Captain (later Rear-Admiral) John Blankett was dispatched to the East with His Majesty's frigates, *Leopard* and *Panther*, both of 50 guns. This officer's far-ranging views on commercial-naval

---

[165] Thurlow's opinion is cited in Dundas to Cornwallis, 1 Aug., 1789. Private. *Cornwallis Corr.*, vol. II, p. 1.

[166] Dundas said that he had put the difficulty to his two colleagues who had concurred. On the whole it seems more probable that it was they who restrained Dundas.

[167] Letter to Cornwallis, 1 Aug., 1789, *ut supra*.

strategy were attracting increasing attention, and on this expedition he was given absolute discretion. In the course of the voyage he sent three confidential reports to Hawkesbury at the Board of Trade in addition to his official despatches to the Admiralty. In the first of these he gave an appraisal of the commercial possibilities of the Cape of Good Hope, 'as it may give Your Lordship some hints relative to the state of the Dutch Settlements in India'. These and the Cape were interdependent. The Cape settlers were so discontented with the restrictions of the Dutch East India Company that any accidental aggravation would blow the embers to a blaze which the form of government there would be insufficient to resist. If the settlers established a free entrepôt, the situation of the Colony would enable them to develop an extensive commerce. 'America and Africa might be furnished from thence with all the produce of India and China, and many parts of Europe and Asia would find a vent and return for many of their productions without being subject to the risque and expense of a longer Navigation.'[168]

In the second report he described his passage to China which he decided to make by way of Timor and the Moluccas, 'as not only the clearest passage, but as it might tend to establish the right of the King's subjects to the free navigation of those Seas conformable to the late treaty with Holland'. No English ships, he added, had taken that route, to his knowledge, since the days of Dampier. The Dutch officials in Timor received him with civility but without enthusiasm. A detailed account was given of the Dutch trade with these islands, for his Lordship would appreciate its importance in relation to their trade with China. Sandal-wood, spices, ambergris and wax were thus acquired which were much sought after by the Chinese. It would not be difficult for English traders to obtain these commodities in return for their own manufactures.[169]

From the Archipelago Blankett made his way to the China coast steering for the 'Island of Sandalwood', situated three days' sail from Macao. Here (at the end of December, 1790) he found a good harbour with wood and water – a possible 'depot' outside the frontiers of the Chinese Empire. The natives were well disposed: the 'King' was interviewed and gifts presented. An interpreter waved the Dutch flag, 'of which I did not take the least notice'. From Macao the *Leopard* surveyed the coast to the northward, while the *Panther* surveyed the Pellew Islands (to the east of the Philippines) which Drake had visited in 1579. 'I ever have been of

---

[168] Cf. vol. I, pp. 133-5.
[169] The innumerable inhabitants of these seas, he added, would readily buy such articles as 'Knives, Razors, Saws, Hatchets, Iron Pots, Arms, Powder, shot, etc.' 'The Black and White Portuguese who are numerous in Timor . . . and several other Islands, would assist in the first introduction.'

opinion,' wrote Blankett, 'that much is to be done in the North East Seas of China, and I am now more fully convinced than ever.' At Macao he encountered the American trader, Capt. Douglass, and was deeply interested in his account of the fur trade on the North-West American coast and of his confident belief that he had discovered the opening of a strait which led into the North Atlantic. Douglass told him that he was about to sail again to collect a cargo of furs and then explore the supposed strait. If he failed to find a passage, he intended to take his furs to Japan in hope of obtaining copper for the China market, as the Dutch did. It was a pity, remarked Blankett, that this maritime fur trade had been left in hands likely to make a bad impression – which was an interesting commentary, coming from a naval officer, on John Meares and his associates. Blankett's reports were thus immediately relevant to the Ministry's Eastern policy at numerous points.[170]

Meanwhile the relationship between the Ministry and the East India Company had changed. The long battle with the Court of Directors had culminated in a Declaratory Act of 1788 which asserted the Crown's authority. Thereafter Dundas accepted the view that it was more expedient to use the Company as a political and economic instrument rather than attempt to get rid of it. From 1789 his ascendancy over the Directors was usually unquestioned.[171] It was no longer necessary to hold off from the China enterprise for fear of stirring up opposition on the part of the Company and its political supporters, and in the light of the development of British commercial policy in the Far East and the Pacific since 1787 Dundas was determined to resume the project and on a much more imposing scale. Yet the Company's fear and dislike of having the *status quo* at Canton disturbed had not abated.[172] It was indicative of the situation that Francis Baring (who became Deputy-Chairman in April, 1791, and Chairman in the following year), while a supporter of Dundas in Company affairs and of the Administration in Parliament, conducted a pertinacious and extremely skilful campaign to divert Dundas from taking action in China

---

[170] The three reports are dated respectively – Macao, 25 Feb., Macao, 1 March, and H.M.S. *Leopard* (at sea), 8 April, 1791 (*Addit. MSS.*, 38,226, ff. 105-17).

[171] C. H. Philips (*op. cit.*, p. 63) points out that from this date most of the business was disposed of in conversation with the Chairman. The subservience of the Directors should not, however, be exaggerated. On issues in commercial policy they offered a tenacious defence of their position which on the whole proved successful.

[172] In their second Report (4 Jan., 1792) the special committee of Directors observed that when complaints had been made in the past about conditions at Canton, justice had been done, but the Company had found themselves 'burdened with pecuniary Impositions on their Commerce fully equal to the restitution made'. It was almost impossible to persuade the Chinese of the benefits to themselves of importing European goods, and the Committee therefore considered that 'the only mode of encreasing and extending the consumption of British Articles in China is by means of the usual and accustomed Channels of Trade now open'. (*B.T. 6/42*.)

which might damage the Company's interests. The tussle, amicably waged, affords a useful insight into the policy of Dundas, Pitt and Grenville and the difficult situation of the Company in relation to Far Eastern expansion.

Towards the end of December, 1791, George Macartney, a baron in the Irish peerage, was formally invited to undertake the embassy to Peking. His wide administrative experience in Ireland, the West Indies and India, together with a diplomatic mission to Russia, well fitted him for the task.[173] He was essentially an autocrat, winning respect rather than affection, and meeting presumption with hauteur and insubordination with uncompromising severity. These traits were evident while he was Governer of Madras and afterwards as Governor of Cape Colony. At Madras his attempts to dictate to the Army and the Navy caused him to fall foul of Sir Eyre Coote (which was all too easy to do) and Admiral Sir Edward Hughes, and for a similar cause he quarrelled with Warren Hastings. In January, 1786, the reluctance of Cornwallis to undertake the governor-generalship in India led to an approach being made to Macartney, but he insisted that the prevalent insubordination required that he be given direct control over the troops and be empowered to act, when necessary, independently of his Council.[174] In his undeviating pursuit of the main chance he was blatantly (and disarmingly) frank and at each stage of his career he proved adept at establishing the right contacts for the next move. The charm which he could exercise with women extended – in varying degrees – to such diverse characters as the Czarina Catherine of Russia, the society wit and beauty Mrs. Crewe, and Lady Anne Barnard.[175]

At a conference with Macartney on 22 December Dundas arranged for him to be supplied with all the papers which had been previously prepared and collected for Cathcart and requested him to submit his ideas on the best means whereby a ' well conducted ' embassy to China might achieve the desired results. His reply on 4 January listed the commercial objectives as they had been set out in the Instructions to Cathcart, but he emphasised the point that these should be kept in the background. An embassy which

---

[173] He was Chief Secretary for Ireland 1769-72, Governor of Grenada from 1775 until its capture by the French in 1779, Governor of Madras 1780-5, and Governor of Cape Colony 1796-8. From 1764 to 1767 he had been envoy extraordinary at St. Petersburg for the negotiation of a commercial treaty.

[174] ' Heads of Minutes of a Conversation between Lord Macartney, and the Chairman and Deputy-Chairman of the East India Company – 13 January, 1786.' (Pitt Papers, P.R.O. 30/8/355.) Eventually Cornwallis secured the powers which Macartney had postulated. See above, p. 209.

[175] For Macartney's Indian career see The Private Correspondence of Lord Macartney, Governor of Madras 1781-85 (Roy. Hist. Soc., Camden Third Series, vol. LXXVII, 1950, ed. C. C. Davies). For Macartney's governorship at the Cape see C.H.B.E., vol. VIII, p. 178 et seq.

only sought redress of grievances would arouse disgust and suspicion. It should take the higher ground that the British Sovereign, well known for his promotion of maritime discovery, wished to observe the celebrated institutions of 'the most civilised and most ancient race on the Globe'. It should not be difficult to impress the Chinese with the King's wisdom and justice and the wealth and power of his dominions, and this might lead naturally to a treaty of friendship and alliance. British sea-power was the only form of assistance which they would value. It should be stipulated that resident Ministers be permanently located at Peking and London.

Since Dundas had made it clear that the embassy was to be on a much more ambitious scale than that projected in 1787, Macartney took the cue with zest. The great pomp of former Dutch, Portuguese and Russian embassies to Peking had established a kind of precedent. Gentlemen of science should be included in his entourage who should be provided with instruments and materials for making 'the most curious and striking experiments', and models of the latest inventions, such as the new cotton machines, should be included. The Chinese might thus be induced to reciprocate with a free inspection of their own arts and improvements. A military guard of infantrymen and gunners with field pieces should also be sent to perform evolutions in the presence of the Emperor. On the commercial side he put forward a number of ideas suggested to him by individuals or culled from the documents. A British Consul should be established at Canton, and new representatives of the Company should be dispatched thither to remedy abuses of which, it was understood, the supercargoes had been guilty.[176] To ensure that this new Committee would co-operate it ought to be placed under the control of the Ambassador. Finally (and this reflects the comprehensive views of Dundas himself) it was suggested that he should be furnished with letters of credence from the King to the Emperor of Japan. That country, asserted Macartney, produced teas as good as those of China: the old barriers against foreign trade had almost ceased to exist, and if Japan became a competitive tea-exporter, the purchaser would benefit from lower prices.[177]

At an interview on 6 January Dundas gave his general approval and requested Macartney to furnish a detailed list of the personnel

---

[176] Both of these suggestions had been put to Macartney by William Richardson, Secretary at the East India House – and the man who first proposed the policy of the Commutation Act. A resident Consul, he had written, who was a man of good sense and firmness, would be able to keep the supercargoes and the free merchants and their crews 'in some order' (Pritchard, op. cit., p. 275). Richardson was an eager advocate of the embassy and seems to have backed the Government's views rather than those of his own employers.

[177] Macartney to Dundas, 4 Jan., 1792 (Factory Records, China, vol. 91, p. 37).

to be included, and this he did on the following day.[178] Dundas
also intimated that the preparations should be hurried forward
in order that the mission might sail at the beginning of April.
Within the next three days Sir George Staunton (who was to be
Secretary to the embassy) was sent off to Paris to search for an
interpreter;[179] Macartney was permitted to choose Capt. Erasmus
Gower to command the King's ship which would convey the mission
to China; and Dundas with Macartney worked out a detailed
plan. At the same time the two letters and the 'tableau' of the
Ambassador-designate were sent to the Company's Chairman and
Deputy, John Smith Burges and Francis Baring. On the 12th these
two were called to an interview with Pitt and Dundas when they
were officially informed of the intended embassy and requested to
pay for it.

This was an obvious attempt to rush an awkward hurdle, but
the Chairs could not tamely submit on an issue which touched the
nerve centre of the Company's trading system. During the previous
summer and autumn they had successfully resisted Hawkesbury's
pressure campaign for widening the entry of British manufactures
into India, and on the same day (4 January) that Dundas had
formally approached Macartney about the China enterprise a
special committee of the Directors (consisting of Burges, Baring
and four others) had presented a report which insisted that the only
reliable method of increasing the sale of British commodities in
China was to develop the existing channels of trade, 'now open'.[180]
With a rapidly expanding national economy the Company's exclusive system was in a state of siege. During preliminary discussions
in November and December Baring and Burges had expressed
their disquiet about the proposed approach to Peking, and now as
they faced Pitt and Dundas they repeated their 'grave doubts'.
Four days later at another interview with Dundas they accepted
the inevitable and agreed to support the enterprise with their fellow
Directors.[181] On the following day Dundas wrote to the Chairmen
pointing out the importance of speed and secrecy and suggesting

---

[178] Letter of 6 Jan., enclosing 'Tableau or Sketch of an Embassy . . .' The list
included a scientist, a 'machinist', 'a person from Birmingham in the hardware
branch well acquainted with Metallurgy', a specialist in the cotton and stuff
industries from Manchester, and another 'from Mr. Wedgwood in the Pottery
Branch'. In addition to the civil personnel of 30, there were listed 35 infantrymen
and 15 gunners with 3 commissioned officers. (Ibid., pp. 37-62.)

[179] George Leonard Staunton had long been Macartney's right-hand man. M.D. of
Montpellier, he had practised in Grenada while Macartney was Governor and for a
short time in 1779 acted as Attorney-General. As Macartney's secretary at Madras he
had negotiated a peace settlement with Tipu in 1784. In the following year he was
pensioned by the East India Company and created an Irish baronet. He was a
friend of Dr. Johnson and later of Burke. F.R.S. in 1787, Hon. D.C.L. Oxford in
1790.

[180] See p. 567, n. 172 above.

[181] See Pritchard (op. cit.), p. 278.

that the Court should give the Chairs full discretion to act in concert with the Ministers.[182]

Francis Baring, the effective leader of the Directors at this time, was by no means a blind exponent of monopoly. A merchant-financier himself, he appreciated the need for adjustment and adaptation, but was determined to protect the Company's China trade, which was now a great national interest, from injury. The policy which he followed with regard to the Macartney embassy was to head it off as much as possible from laying complaints at Peking, which would only serve to exasperate the Chinese officials at Canton, who in routine administration were virtually a law to themselves. He appreciated the importance of securing entry to other Chinese ports and the acquisition of a British depot further north. The latter could introduce a healthy competition with the Hong merchants at Canton, thus checking the rising price of tea while improving the balance of trade by affording wider opportunities for disposing of British goods. But like his colleagues he was determined that the Company and not the Government should administer any new depots and remain in control of the Country trade at Canton. Otherwise a renewed influx of foreigners and Englishmen masquerading under foreign colours could wreck the system.[183] In general Dundas accepted the proposition that the Company's organisation was indispensable in China as in Japan; but he hoped and intended, as will be seen, that Macartney's mission would initiate a drive for the opening of the whole of Further Asia to British commerce. When that happened the Company's control over free merchants would inevitably dissolve.

On 20 January Baring and Burges sent Dundas their considered opinion on Macartney's suggestions. The proposed manner of the embassy, they wrote, appeared to be 'highly proper'. Having said that, they continued with criticism and concluded – on certain

---

[182] Dundas to the Chairmen, 17 Jan., 1792 (*Factory Records, China*, vol. 20). Dundas was anxious for speed and secrecy in order to hinder foreign ambassadors in London from learning about the embassy and sending despatches warning their Government to take action to frustrate it. On 19 January the Court of Directors agreed that the Chairs should act as a secret committee to negotiate with the Government about the China embassy and authorised them to spend £20,000 on the enterprise. The Directors were not to know that the total outlay would eventually exceed four times that amount.

[183] Later the special commission sent out by the Company wrote to Macartney (at Canton): 'If we feel the competition and injury that may arise to the Company's Commerce by the participation of other Nations . . . in the benefits of the Embassy, we are still more sensible to the prejudice and inconvenience that such an encouragement to individuals, not under the Company's protection, may occasion.' They urged Macartney to make a particular disavowal of the interests 'of such Nations who have British subjects, consuls at Canton, to manage the nominal interests of their respective flags'. These British subjects by bartering their honour for money were encouraging and protecting an illicit commerce to the manifest injury of the Company. (Secret and Superintending Committee to Macartney, 28 Sept., 1793. *Ibid.*, vol. 93, pp. 298-301.)

specific points – with downright resistance. 'We think that the slightest suspicion of an Embassy whose ostensible object shall be the correction of abuses, must ensure its miscarriage.' They felt very doubtful about the relative importance of the various griev- ances which Macartney had listed: retired supercargoes with expert knowledge should be consulted. They agreed that the embassy must be conducted 'with dignity and with considerable eclat', but they trusted that a reasonable attention to economy was not incompatible with these objects. Macartney's idea of a military escort was strongly criticised, and particularly his pro- posed inclusion of light artillery. The Chinese were a cautious people, and a display of this sort might well confirm them in their policy of confining foreigners to a remote corner of the Empire – which was by far the most important impediment to be overcome. They then proceeded to resistance. The accuracy of Macartney's statements about frequent disputes between the Committee of Supercargoes and Chinese officials was denied: the only serious incident in recent years had been that of the *Lady Hughes*. It was, of course, essential, as Macartney had stated, that the Supercargoes should co-operate with the embassy, and the most explicit instruc- tion to that effect would be sent out; but the suggestion that the Ambassador should be put in authority over them was inadmiss- ible. Furthermore they objected to the proposed appointment of a British Consul at Canton: he would be an encumbrance. What they meant was that a Consul, as the representative of the Crown, would take the place of the supercargoes in dealing with Chinese officials and so become, as it were, a one-man Board of Control. 'We trust that on this occasion we may be permitted to express our fullest confidence and firm reliance, that the measure in contemplation will not affect in any shape the rights and privileges of the East India Company.'[184] Three weeks later Baring informed Dundas that a plan had been submitted to the Court of Directors 'Wherein it is proposed to correct such abuses as are known to exist [at the Canton factory], to establish an efficient superior Council, and more particularly to send out Commissioners with the most ample powers by the ships of the present Season'. The chief motive for sending out a special Commission at that time, it was

---

[184] The Chairs to Dundas, 20 Jan., 1792 (*Ibid.*, vol. 91, p. 63). When Macartney was shown this letter he observed that the Company must be the best judges of the commercial benefits which they hoped to derive from the embassy, but it was for the King's Ministers 'to contemplate how far they may be extended and rendered productive of, and subservient to, political advantages'. The embassy might inaugurate 'a new era in the diplomatic annals of Great Britain', and therefore called for some degree of splendour. Since the export of British manufactures to Canton had multiplied five times since the Commutation Act, what might not be expected if access could be obtained to the northern ports in the vicinity of Peking, thus introducing almost at first hand 'the produce of our daily improving ingenuity and industry?' (Macartney to Dundas, 23 Jan. Private, *ibid.*, pp. 75-8.)

added, was to assist Macartney's efforts at the Court of Peking: it also ensured that the Company's authority at Canton would be reinforced before Macartney arrived.[185]

The Instructions for the three Commissioners (Henry Browne, Eyles Irwin and William Jackson) were the subject of prolonged discussions between Dundas, Baring and Macartney. They consisted of two parts, commercial and political. On the commercial side they formulated Baring's policy of reforming the Company's system at Canton on more efficient lines so as to render it capable of dealing with any expansion which the embassy might be able to secure. The Committee of Supercargoes was to be reduced from six to three, with Commissioner Browne as Chairman. In future the supercargoes were to be prohibited from acting as agents for Country merchants, a practice which had enabled them to amass large private fortunes while neglecting the Company's business. Instead a House of Trade was to be established and managed by two or three of the Company's Servants who were not members of the Committee. This clearing house for the Country trade was to do business at fixed commission rates. Every power at the Company's disposal was to be employed (yet again) to prevent the private English from residing permanently at Canton.

The Commissioners were then directed how to proceed if the Ambassador were successful in obtaining a new establishment to the northward. The resulting competition from the new port would compel Canton to reform abuses and break the monopoly of the Co-Hong, so that it would not be necessary for the Ambassador to submit direct complaints. If the Chinese Government granted a depot the Commissioners were to arrange for its administration by a group of Company servants, headed by two mature and experienced men, under suitable regulations. In this way Baring strove to preserve and adapt the Company's position in China under changing conditions. A new depot might be received in the name of the King, but it was to be administered by the Company as effectively as their Bankulen factory in Sumatra. On the political side the Commissioners were directed to inform the Viceroy at Canton about the impending embassy and to do everything in their power to ensure its gracious reception.[186] On 5 May the Commissioners sailed for China on board the *Thetis*.

Meanwhile Macartney himself was working extremely hard.

---

[185] Baring to Dundas, 10 Feb., 1792. (*Ibid.*, p. 103.)

[186] See Baring to Dundas – April 1792, with enclosures (*Factory Records, China*, vol. 91, pp. 197-215). Pritchard (pp. 284-90) gives a detailed account of these Instructions and their compilation, incorporating additional information from the Macartney papers in the library of Cornell University and in his own possession. Like the great Melville collection, the Macartney papers (forming part of the collected manuscripts of Sir Thomas Phillipps) have been broken up and sold by auction.

Putting first things first, he battled with Francis Baring to secure a large ambassadorial salary and eventually secured almost but not quite all that he had demanded.[187] In reporting the contest to Dundas the Chairman (as he now was) paid Macartney a handsome tribute. He had taken 'incredible pains' to acquire all the information about China that Europe afforded, 'so that if the Embassy doth not succeed, it will not be his fault'. Baring's hopes of economy in the matter of presents for the Emperor were, however, dashed. The collection of scientific instruments and curious mechanical devices which were acquired cost the Company upwards of £15,000. From the Government Macartney requested – with the nonchalance of the period – that he be created an earl: his prestige at the Imperial Court required it. Pitt settled for an (Irish) viscountcy, while holding out hopes of an earldom in due course.[188]

Since the prime object of the mission was to obtain the opening of a port within easy reach of Peking and the grant of a permanent trading station, it seemed obvious sense to Macartney that manufacturers in Britain should be given the opportunity of sending out selected specimens of their products so that Chinese merchants of the northern regions might be interested in what the British would have to offer. On 28 June he wrote to Hawkesbury at the Board of Trade to this effect, pointing out that cargo space would be available in the East Indiaman, *Hindustan*, which was to accompany the King's ship to China. Hawkesbury promptly offered assistance and suggested that representatives of the Court of Directors and Macartney should confer with the Board on the most suitable articles to be sent. In taking this initiative Macartney unwittingly provoked the kind of reaction which results when an unwary stranger jogs a hive of bees. The failure of the campaign in the previous year to obtain direct access to the Indian market was fresh in Hawkesbury's mind – as in those of the manufacturers themselves. The Board took the question into consideration on the 27th, and on the following day Thomas Fitzhugh, a Director, attended with Macartney.[189] Difficulties appear to have arisen at once. Although the Board then agreed that a circular letter should be sent in their name to 'some proper person' in each of the

---

[187] Macartney tried to hold out for a salary of £16,000 p.a., or alternatively £12,000 p.a. with a present of £10,000. If, Baring drily observed, the embassy terminated in two years the first option would be the cheaper. Finally the Chairs settled for £10,000 p.a. and a present of £5,000. (Baring to Dundas, 30 May, 1792. Private. The Chairs to Dundas of the same date. *Factory Records, China*, vol. 91, pp. 237 and 241.)

[188] Pitt to the King, 25 June, 1792 (*Royal Archives, Windsor*). On 28 June he was gazetted Viscount Macartney of Derrock in the County of Antrim.

[189] Dundas had used his influence to secure the election of Fitzhugh to the Direction, but he developed into 'the most violent and formidable of his opponents at the India House'. (Philips, *op. cit.*, p. 60 n.)

principal manufacturing towns in Britain and in Dublin,[190] requesting that samples be forwarded to India House, the circular was not dispatched until 19 July.[191] The dispatch of a large and varied assortment of British products to Peking was just the kind of initiative which the Directors had resisted with regard to India. If accepted, it would inevitably be followed by pressure from the manufacturers to push their wares themselves and turn the new depot – under nominal Company control – into a free-for-all.

The response from the manufacturers was vigorous, especially on the part of Samuel Garbett and Matthew Boulton of Birmingham. According to the latter an adequate collection of Birmingham patterns would cost at least £1,000, but the Directors indicated that they would pay no more than £150. Garbett went further and insisted that unless samples to the value of £3,000 were accepted he would have no part in the business. He and his colleagues did not expect the Company to pay a penny but wished to send the consignment on their own account. To that the Directors refused consent: they recognised the thin end of a dangerous wedge. Macartney did his best to arrange a compromise and finally persuaded the Company to accept – at their own charge – Birmingham hardware, sword-blades and firearms to the value of £646. As a parting shot Boulton wished the embassy success in preparing the way for an extension of the national commerce to the East which in his opinion could only be done by establishing depots free from the Company's control and open to all British traders. The industrialists of Manchester and Paisley were even more recalcitrant, refusing to send out patterns and specimens 'from a disinclination to send them through the East India Company'.[192] Eventually a reasonably representative selection of manufactured articles was brought together, but in one respect the manufacturers betrayed an attitude as obstructionist as that of the Company itself. They resolutely refused in spite of all arguments to allow any of

---

[190] On this, as on all similar occasions, Ministers were always careful to secure that autonomous Ireland should not be excluded from any advantages in foreign commerce that might be available. On 31 July Hawkesbury wrote to Baring to point out that when the latter had last attended the Board of Trade nothing had been recorded in the Minute about sending patterns of Irish poplins with Macartney. From its elegance and lightness this material was likely to make a special appeal to the Chinese. 'Lord H. thinks also that it is of Importance that the Interests of the Manufacturers of Ireland, in an Article peculiar to that Kingdom, should not appear on this occasion to be neglected.' (*Addit. MSS.*, 38,310 (Letter-Book 1787-92), § 17.) Although the independence of the Irish Parliament was unreal and the attempt to establish an Anglo-Irish *zollverein* had failed, the Pitt Administration took care that Ireland should not be induced by British neglect to try to enter into separate commercial arrangements with other Powers.

[191] *Minutes of the Board of Trade*, 27 and 28 June, 19 July, 1792 (*B.T. 5/8*, pp. 91-6, 109). The list of manufacturing towns to which the circular letter was sent (addressed to the Mayor) included – Sheffield, Leeds, Halifax, Exeter, Glasgow, Paisley, Manchester, Birmingham and Dublin.

[192] Minute of 13 August, 1792 (*ibid.*, p. 129). Cf. Pritchard, pp. 295-7.

T*

their trained artisans to go out with the embassy: they might remain in China and betray trade secrets.[193] The attitude was characteristic of the early stages of industrialisation and contributed to the general opposition during this period to the founding of colonies.

These and other complications inevitably delayed the departure of the mission. The sailing date had been postponed from April to August and in the event Macartney was not able to embark until 21 September. During these months Auckland at the Hague was struggling manfully to effect an Anglo-Dutch treaty of co-operation in the Far East, and Grenville, as Foreign Secretary, was anxious that the elaborate preparations for sending a British diplomatic mission to China – now widely known in Europe – should not excite the jealousy of the Dutch. In May Auckland wrote to reassure him. The Grand Pensionary had spoken to him about the Macartney mission 'with great liberality of sentiment', and Auckland expected that he would write on behalf of the Dutch Company, asking that the ambassador should favour their interests so far as they did not affect those of his own country.[194] In June Grenville again expressed his anxiety that everything possible should be done to promote the success of the embassy. Auckland thereupon sought the co-operation of the Dutch Ministers who arranged a meeting for him with the representatives of the Company's China Committee. The latter indicated that they had no requests to make but added that they would send immediate orders to their several factories to show Lord Macartney all proper attention.[195] At Auckland's suggestion the thanks of the British Government were conveyed to the Council of Seventeen.[196] Then on 31 August the Dutch Commissioners responded to Auckland's

---

[193] See Macartney to the Chairs, 23 Dec., 1793. Canton. 'Notwithstanding my own and the repeated applications of others to Manchester and to the porcelane manufactures in Staffordshire and Shropshire, I was disappointed in my expectations; and I at last found that the failure arose in some degree from a Jealousy which arose in some men's minds of any tradesmen sent with me remaining in China and communicating some of the most valuable processes of their art, instead of returning home fraught with new lights from hence. I do not pretend to judge of the propriety of this cautious procedure, but it certainly deprived me of the assistance you were aware was necessary to enable me to collect very accurate or important information relative to those branches of manufacture in this Country.' (*Factory Records, China*, vol. 92, pp. 369-92.) A century later Japanese armament and textile specialists visited British factories and returned home loaded with information which was put to excellent use. For details of the samples and manufactured articles collected through the Board of Trade see *B.T.I.* (*In-Letters*), pp. 19-20.

[194] Auckland to Grenville, 15 May, 1792 (*Grenville Papers, Dropmore*, vol. II, pp. 268-9).

[195] Auckland to Grenville, 3 July, 1792. Private. (*Ibid.*, vol. II, p. 268. Copy in *Addit. MSS.*, 34,444 (*Auckland Papers*), f. 169.) Judging from Macartney's initial reception at Batavia, they do not appear to have done so (see p. 580 below).

[196] Auckland to Grenville, 20 July. Private. (*Ibid.*, vol. II, p. 294.)

offers of Macartney's services with a memorial, stating the well-known grievances of European traders at Canton, and expressing the hope that any advantages obtained would be shared.

When the document reached London Dundas sent a copy of it to Macartney with the observation that he would be well aware of the close connexion between Britain and the States General and would of course pay every attention in his power to the Dutch representations – 'always keeping in view, however, that the object of your Embassy is rather to obtain future accommodation and facilities to Commerce than to enlarge on past grievances'.[197] The chief purpose of the memorial, he wrote in reply, appeared to be to elicit information about the real objects of the embassy. Certainly any redress of grievances which Macartney might secure ought to apply to Europeans in general, otherwise there would be a race of envoys to Peking which would be 'destructive to all'. He concluded with a strong *caveat* which illustrates the distrust felt in Leadenhall Street regarding the ministerial policy of attaching the Dutch East India Company as a junior partner in a comprehensive development of Eastern trade.

The object of obtaining a Depot or Establishment is very different from a redress of grievances, and it is presumed that if that object can be accomplished, it will be desirable to exclude all Foreigners whatsoever in the first instance, leaving the question open for discussion hereafter, whether they shall be admitted to a participation under any circumstances whatsoever.[198]

On 8 September, 1792, Dundas signed the official Instructions. Macartney's own draft had been accepted with minor amendments. In substance they were very similar to those prepared by and for Colonel Cathcart. The stipulation that the grant of 'a small tract of ground or detached Island' must be received in the name of the Sovereign was retained. Pitt and Dundas were determined that the place should be under the political control of a servant of the Crown in spite of Baring's pressure to the contrary.[199] A new feature was the reference to a possible Anglo-Chinese treaty of friendship and alliance under which British naval support would be available. Also new and indicative of the more ambitious plan which Dundas was promoting was the wide discretion given to Macartney in attempting to establish diplomatic and commercial

---

[197] Dundas to Macartney, 8 Sept., 1792 (*Addit. MSS.*, 34,444, f. 233. Another copy in *F.R. China*, vol. 91, pp. 377-8).

[198] Endorsed: 'Mr. Baring's Observations on the Memorial transmitted by the Dutch Government. Copy East India House. 7 Sept., 1792' (*Addit. MSS.*, 34,444, f. 234. Another copy in *F.R., China*, vol. 91, p. 395).

[199] There had been a final tussle on this point when the Instructions of the Chairs to Macartney were being scrutinised (see Pritchard, p. 302).

relations with Japan, Cochin China and other Eastern states.[200] To further that purpose he was furnished with Letters of Credence to the Emperor of Japan, and Sir George Staunton, Macartney's secretary, was given dormant credentials as a minister plenipotentiary. As Macartney afterwards wrote in his orders to Capt. Gower – 'the great object of my Mission is to spread the use of British Manufactures throughout every part of Asia from whence any valuable Returns may be made to Europe '.[201]

At Portsmouth on 21 September, 1792, Macartney and his suite went on board H.M.S. *Lion* (64 guns), commanded by Capt. (now Sir) Erasmus Gower. Five days later the *Lion* sailed with a fair wind, accompanied by the *Hindustan* and the tender *Jackall*. The cargo on board the *Hindustan* included a planetarium (valued at £1,438), mathematical, optical and electrical instruments, numerous samples of cloth and Irish poplins, Birmingham and Sheffield goods, copper and tin ware, and Wedgwood pottery. Some of these were presents, intended to delight and impress the Son of Heaven, and the rest to whet the appetite of Chinese merchants. What was probably the most costly embassy ever to leave the shores of Britain was combined with a carefully organised trade exhibition. To the Western (and particularly the British) mind the conjunction seemed eminently sensible and practical, based on the assumption that every nation must regard commercial inter-change as a paramount advantage: in Chinese estimation the blending of high diplomacy with commercial travelling was incongruous and crude, the product of an uncultivated mind. The tangible advantages gained by this enterprise, which cost a reluctant East India Com-

---

[200] Strenuous efforts had been made to find an interpreter for the Japanese language. Grenville had written to the British Ambassador at Moscow about a Japanese subject who was reported to be in Russian hands. He had also asked Auckland about a manuscript account of the interior of Japan which was supposed to be in the possession of the Stadtholder. (Letter to Auckland, 15 May, 1792, *ut supra*.)

[201] See p. 582 below. Macartney's Instructions are printed in Morse, *Chronicles*, vol. II, pp. 232-42. One subject was ignored to the great disappointment of an interested group, the Canton creditors. As soon as the resumption of the China embassy was known, our old acquaintances, Vansittart, Law and George Smith, resumed their siege of Dundas, urging him to instruct Macartney to include the repayment of the debts among the requests which he was to lay before the Emperor. As before, Dundas was half inclined to give them some support, if it could be done without militating against the objects of the embassy, but the Directors were even more hostile than they had been in 1787. They regarded it as a characteristic piece of impudence on the part of the ' Private English ' whom they were determined to discipline. From long experience, they informed Dundas, they had learned that when complaints in such cases were made, relief was granted, but the European trade was then burdened with fresh impositions. In a separate directive to Macartney of the same date Dundas declared that it was totally incompatible with his duty to give instructions in the matter. At the same time he could not remain indifferent to the claims of British subjects for so large an amount. Macartney was to investigate the claims and then consider whether any interposition could be made without injury to the interests of the Company (*ibid.*, p. 243). The question was not pursued.

pany rather more than £80,000, were few and transitory; but Macartney's progress from Tientsin to Jehol and Peking marked the beginning of a new era in which resistant China was drawn into a shattering economic and political association with the West.

On the outward voyage Macartney and his staff were afforded glimpses of British overseas commerce in action.[202] At Madeira and Teneriffe they found the trade engrossed by a few British firms who exchanged manufactured goods from London for local products. At the Cape de Verde Islands they encountered ships from Dunkirk, manned chiefly by English sailors and 'full of English goods', destined to be imported under French colours into Chili and Peru. At Rio de Janeiro an English whaler lay at anchor with a cargo of oil and whalebone valued at about £14,000. The shops were full of Manchester and other British manufactures, and Brazil in general was in a flourishing state. In spite of Government prohibitions a number of articles were being manufactured there for local consumption. Indeed so prosperous was the country that the balance of trade had turned in its favour so that bullion was being exported thither from Europe. There was talk, wrote Staunton, of the King of Portugal transferring himself to Brazil or of leaving it to go its own way as an independent state. It was also noted with interest that there had recently been an attempted revolt against Portugal. The opportunities of extending Britain's empire of trade were not confined to Asia.

Sailing from Rio on 17 December, the *Lion* and *Hindustan* passed within sight of Tristan d'Acunha. It was an island, wrote Gower in his Journal, well worth a more particular investigation as a watering place for vessels on the outward voyage to the Coromandel coast and China and as an excellent rendezvous in time of war. Staunton noted that a settlement there had been twice contemplated, once as a whaling station and on another occasion as an entrepôt for the sale of Indian textiles in South America. On 6 March, 1793, the ships anchored in Batavia roads. In spite of being ill with gout Macartney went ashore and was received with great respect; but he discovered that the Dutch authorities, alarmed

---

[202] Except where otherwise stated, this account of the outward voyage and of Macartney's experiences in China is drawn from the following sources: Macartney's despatch to Dundas, dated 9 Nov., 1793 (*F.R., China*, vol. 92, pp. 31-111); Macartney's 'Journal', printed in John Barrow, *Some Account of the Public Life, and a Selection from the Unpublished Writings of the Earl of Macartney* . . . (Lond., 1807, vol. II, pp. 163-531), also in Helen M. Robbins, *Our First Ambassador to China* (Lond., 1908); Capt. Sir E. Gower, *A Journal of H.M.S. Lion, Beginning the 1st of October, 1792, and Ending the 7th September, 1794* (*Addit. MSS.*, 21,106); Aeneas Anderson, *A Narrative of the British Embassy to China* . . . (Lond., 1795); and Sir G. L. Staunton, *An Authentic Account of an Embassy . . . to the Emperor of China* (Lond., 2 vols., 1797). A detailed modern account is in Pritchard, *op. cit.*, Chap. VIII.

at the rumoured intentions of the embassy, had instructed their factors at Canton to unite with other Europeans there in opposition to it. Macartney explained that the Dutch Company had agreed to co-operate and that there was 'room enough' for the commerce of both nations. Counter-instructions were thereupon dispatched to Canton.

Here also Macartney received good news from Canton in a long despatch from the English Company's Commissioners who were carrying out a thorough investigation of the trading arrangements. They had also been active in preparing the way for the embassy. Macartney's letter of introduction and explanation had been presented to the Governor of Canton in the absence of the provincial Viceroy, who was commanding Chinese troops in a war with Tibet. The Chinese officials had been dismayed and suspicious to learn that the vessels carrying the embassy intended to proceed to the port of Tientsin instead of Canton. Although this arrangement would avoid an overland journey of 1,400 miles to the capital, it was contrary to normal procedure and would moreover enable the Ambassador to lay direct complaints against them at the Imperial Court. However the letter had been forwarded to Peking and an Imperial edict had been issued assuring the embassy of a favourable reception and giving orders to the mandarins for the safety of the English ships and the conveyance of the Ambassador and his suite to Peking.[203]

Sailing from Batavia on 17 March, the expedition made its way to the Bay of Tourane on the north-east coast of Laos – then included in Cochin China. This was a region which had long attracted the attention of enterprising Englishmen. In 1778 Warren Hastings had sent Charles Chapman and four other Company Servants thither for the purpose of concluding a commercial treaty and had given instructions that, if he succeeded, Chapman was to take up residence there as the official representative of the Bengal Government. In a Minute Hastings had emphasised the commercial importance of Cochin China – as a market for the products of Britain and Bengal and as a central depot from which trade could be extended to all the countries of South-East Asia and where an indirect trade with China could be established. He had been informed,

---

[203] Brown, Irwin and Jackson (now styled the Secret and Superintending Committee) to Macartney, 6 Jan., 1793 (*F.R., China*, vol. 93, pp. 118-44). With the despatch were a number of enclosures providing information about the China trade. It was reported that the steep rise in the price of tea was partly due to the fact that cheap transport by sea from the tea-growing regions of the north had been discontinued because the coasts were infested with pirates. 'To so humiliating a situation is the formidable Empire of China reduced by the want of a Navy to protect her Trade.' Dundas hoped that an offer of naval assistance might induce the Chinese Government to conclude a treaty of alliance. In the early 17th century the Portuguese had performed a like service and had been rewarded by being allowed to occupy Macao.

Hastings added, that some seventy or eighty Chinese junks regularly visited the port of Tourane alone.[204]

Dundas had inherited the ideas of Dalrymple, Hastings, David Scott and many others about the potentialities of the Malay Archipelago and Indo-China as units in a British commercial network, but fresh circumstances had given the plan larger dimensions. Trade in the intermediate zone of South-East Asia could now be developed within the triangular system established by the export of China teas to London and of Bombay cotton to Canton. Cochin China had been particularly mentioned in Macartney's Instructions. A chart of Tourane Bay was prepared, a site for a fort provisionally selected, and 'many other useful particulars' recorded. This was done, wrote Macartney, in order to furnish the East India Company with all the information procurable, 'in case they should ever think proper to make a settlement at this place'. But since the country was still plagued with the civil wars which had frustrated Chapman's effort in 1778, Macartney directed John Barrow and Capt. Parish of the tender, *Jackall*, to survey a small island to the south named 'Callao' (Kulao Bay), which the French at one time had thought of purchasing. Barrow reported that Kulao was fertile, only the south-west corner was inhabited, and a bay had been found with a sufficient depth of water for the largest ships.[205] 'If from these circumstances,' wrote Staunton, 'a solid settlement in Cochin China were to be productive of advantage to any European nation, it must particularly be so to Great Britain.'

The three vessels sailed from Tourane Bay on 15 June and arrived in Chinese waters on 2 July at the roadstead of Chusan. Earlier in the century English ships had frequently visited this port before the Chinese Government confined foreign trade to Canton. It represented the farthest limit of recorded European navigation. Difficulty in procuring pilots delayed the expedition for several days during which the *Lion* received a swarm of visitors. After the ships had entered the Gulf of Pe-Chih-Li Macartney issued a special Order of the Day, impressing upon all personnel, civilian, naval and military, the absolute necessity of strict dis-

---

[204] See vol. I of this work, pp. 97-102. Manuscript copies of Chapman's *Narrative of the Occurrences in a Voyage to the Kingdom of Cochin China, 1778*, are in F.R., China, vol. 18, and in *Addit. MSS.*, 29,214. Printed in the *Asiatic Annual Register* for 1801, p. 62 *et seq*.

[205] John Barrow, 'Memoir of a Plan of Turon Harbour on the coast of Cochin-china . . .' and 'Remarks on an Expedition of the Jackall tender to the Island Callao . . .' (F.R., China, vol. 93, pp 127-33). In a despatch to Dundas, dated 25 March, 1793, 'North Island off the Sumatra Coast', Macartney wrote that he hoped to reach Tourane in Cochin China by April, when he would report upon its condition and 'whether any useful intercourse may hereafter be formed with it' (C.O. 77/29. Original Correspondence Secy. of State). In addition to letters and enclosures from Macartney this bundle also includes letters from Capt. Gower to Under-Secretary Nepean.

cipline and good behaviour in China, avoiding any conduct which
might give offence. In order to maintain the dignity of the embassy
it was particularly important to refrain from buying and selling
even trifling articles.[206]

On reaching the mouth of the Pai-Ho River below Tientsin (on
25 July) the embassy was greeted by three mandarins 'of high distinction'. Two of them, named Wan and Chou, were Imperial
Commissioners, appointed to receive and escort the Ambassador
and his suite. They seemed to be, wrote Macartney, 'intelligent
men, frank and easy in their address, and communicative in discourse'. They remained in attendance throughout the stay in China
and very friendly relations were established. Senior to them was
a Tartar legate, Cheng Jui, Imperial Salt Commissioner, who was
in charge of all the arrangements. A liberal supply of fresh meat,
rice and vegetables was sent to the ships: the Europeans were now
the Emperor's guests. These supplies were badly needed for the
long voyage had exacted its usual toll. Ninety-three men of the
Lion were reported sick on 27 July, and during subsequent weeks
the number rose to one hundred and twenty-eight. Macartney
therefore obtained permission for the *Lion* and the *Hindustan* to
return to Chusan and disembark their crews.

Before the ships sailed Macartney gave Sir Erasmus Gower
written instructions for a reconnoitring voyage, to be undertaken
after the sick had recovered. They indicate the extensive plans
which had been worked out with Dundas before leaving London.
The *Lion* was to proceed to Jedo on the southern coast of Japan
where Gower was to request delivery of a letter to the 'temporal
Sovereign of that Country'. Nautical observations were to be made
and the opportunity taken of judging how far Japanese needs might
lead them to purchase any British manufactures and whether in
that case the Country afforded any primary products (apart from
copper) which might profitably be imported into England. Gower
would soon be able to ascertain whether the Japanese entertained
that marked aversion to all foreigners which had been attributed
to them – perhaps from interested motives – by former European
visitors. The failure to find in Europe an interpreter for the Japanese language would make it difficult for Gower to conduct specific
negotiations with that Court, but for the purpose of this preliminary
reconnaissance three individuals were being sent who spoke
Chinese and Malay. One of them, Macartney's personal servant,
Lorenzo, also spoke Latin and Portuguese.

As soon as a reply was received from the Japanese Sovereign, or
if no reply had come after a fortnight, Gower was to sail for Manila,
where he was to present a letter of introduction to the Spanish

[206] Macartney's 'Declaration and Instructions to his Train'. (*F. R., China,* vol.
92, pp. 127-33.)

Governor of the Philippines and obtain fresh provisions. Useful information concerning the state of the country, its trade, and the disposition of the people should be collected from non-Spanish Europeans who were permitted to settle there, among whom, he understood, were a few Roman Catholic Irish. At Manila Gower might well find some individuals who had been to Japan and had learned the language. If the services of such a person could be secured Macartney was ready to pay him handsomely: he would be a vast acquisition 'in the event of my going to execute my Commission of Ambassador to the Emperor of Japan'.[207]

About November the *Lion* was to proceed southward into the Malay Archipelago, taking advantage of the monsoon. Trade routes were to be explored, good harbours sought, and commercial treaties made with local rulers. It was to be a voyage expressly based on 'the experience of Mr. Dalrymple', gained twenty years earlier.[208] The Island of Salutaya, near Palawan, should be visited: it was said to have a good harbour. A letter from Macartney was to be delivered to the Sultan of Mindanao, who was at variance with the Spaniards and had on former occasions professed himself a friend of the English to whom he had granted a small island opposite his principal port as a trading depot. If possible the voyage should be extended to Jilolo, one of the Molucca Islands which was not subject to the Dutch. There the attitude of the natives to Europeans in general was uncertain, but if Gower discovered an inclination on their part to favour the British, he was to convey Macartney's intention, if his stay in Asia allowed, to visit Jilolo and negotiate 'a useful compact between the two nations'. Either from Jilolo or directly from Mindanao Gower was to explore 'that part of Celebes which is supposed not subject to the Dutch'; and then the great island of Borneo should be similarly investigated. 'I have,' wrote Macartney, 'besides the special commissions with which the King was pleased to entrust me for particular Princes, general Credentials to treat in His Majesty's name with all or any of the Asiatic Powers.' But in this fringe area of Dutch influence Gower was to be careful not to excite jealousy: he must appear to be employed

---

[207] The idea of sending a diplomatic mission to Japan as well as China had been suggested by a Company Servant (or possibly a free merchant) of Bengal in a long memorandum written while the Cathcart embassy was being planned. The writer had learned that the Japanese Government had abandoned their former isolationism, being satisfied that the entry of European merchants would not give rise to renewed attempts to introduce the Christian religion. The establishment of a tea trade with Japan would oblige the Hong merchants of Canton to lower their prices. The writer also made the point that an offer of British naval support would be the best way to induce the Chinese Emperor to enter into treaty relations. Both of these arguments were adopted by Macartney and appeared in his original memorandum to Dundas. The Bengal document was almost completed when a copy of Cathcart's Instructions arrived – i.e. in 1788. It is unsigned and without title (*F.R., China*, vol. 20).

[208] See vol. I, pp. 70-97.

only in discovery and marine observation, 'and not in preparing for any future Enterprise or Negociation of Policy or Commerce'. Macartney's instructions to Captain Gower of the *Lion* followed up the previous reconnaissance in those waters of Captain Blankett with *Leopard* and *Panther* and were in exact accord with the policy of Dundas, Pitt and Grenville in their stubborn negotiations for an Eastern compact with the Dutch.[209]

On 5 August the members of the embassy went ashore at the town of Ta-Ku near the mouth of the Pai-Ho, where on the following day Macartney and Staunton were received with great ceremony by the aged Viceroy of Chih-Li, Liang K'eng-t'ang, 'a man of the most polished manners . . . who behaved with refined and attentive politeness'. Here Macartney was informed that the embassy, together with some Tartar princes and tribute-bearing envoys from Burma, was to be received by the Emperor at Jehol, whither he was going to celebrate his eighty-third birthday. At Ta-Ku a fleet of richly furnished barges was waiting to convey the company up-river, and as soon as the five hundred 'unwieldly' packages of presents for the Emperor had been brought up in junks, the journey began with much beating of gongs.

At Tientsin, which was reached two days later, a throng of officers, civil and military, came to visit and inspect the strangers. The Ambassador and his suite were entertained by the Viceroy and the Legate who now took charge. In contrast to the Viceroy's urbanity the Legate, according to Macartney, betrayed 'a perverse and unfriendly disposition', regarding all foreigners with a mixture of jealousy and utter contempt. The two Chinese Commissioners of escort, Wan and Chou, already on very friendly terms with the Europeans, did not conceal their dislike of the Tartar; but he had been named first in the commission and they could not oppose him. In general it was noticed that most of the senior posts were held by Tartars while Chinese officials of equal ability were relegated to subordinate offices. The journey up-stream to Tung-Chow was a luxurious and leisurely affair. Crowds of villagers flocked to watch the procession of barges which carried banners bearing the device in large Chinese characters—'The Ambassador bearing tribute from the Kingdom of England'.

From Tung-Chow a short journey overland brought them to Peking on 21 August. The city itself did not greatly impress the

---

[209] Macartney to Gower, 27 July, 1793. 'Tien Sing Road' (*F.R., China*, vol. 92, pp. 137-50). In acknowledging these orders (on the same day) Gower wrote that he anticipated no difficulty in visiting the places specified, provided that the native peoples were co-operative, but he wished to keep his orders secret because the officers and crew were very tired and had looked forward to a period of rest after Macartney had landed in China. (*Ibid.*, pp. 151-3.) After completing the projected voyage the *Lion* was to return to Macao to pick up the embassy on or about 1 May, 1794.

visitors, but they viewed the Emperor's Summer Palace with delight. The artificial lakes, dotted about with little islands which were adorned with 'a variety of fanciful edifices', and the hills of different heights crowned with palaces and summer houses contrived for retreat and pleasure, produced an ensemble which 'had somewhat the appearance of enchantment'. Europe of the 18th century appreciated Chinese art and artifice. A different view, however, was taken of the ancient Chinese concept of the Son of Heaven, to whom all mankind owed obeisance and vassalage. Previous hints about the *kotow* – the nine full prostrations on entering the Imperial presence – now became a sustained pressure. Every European embassy to China had been faced with this question and Macartney had been given instructions about it. The argument continued until very shortly before the actual audience, but the Chinese finally agreed that he might kneel on one knee as he would on being presented to his own sovereign.

The embassy left Peking on 2 September, escorted by a hundred mandarins on horseback, and Jehol was reached four days later. Here, so Macartney hoped, the real business of the embassy would begin. At an interview with Ho Shen, the First Minister (on the 12th), he took the opportunity of emphasising the value of Anglo-Chinese trade, Russia's territorial ambitions and the non-aggression policy of the British in India. Ho Shen was very affable and agreed to discuss these matters at a later date – which he never did. The Emperor himself proved to be extremely gracious but no less elusive. Macartney and Staunton were received in audience on the 14th in a scene of great splendour, when the letter from George III to Ch'ieng Lung was presented in a gold casket. A formal statement from the British sovereign, explaining the objects of the embassy, was now before the Chinese Government. When, however, Macartney was given the opportunity four days later of conversing with the Emperor at a Court entertainment and made repeated efforts to discuss the business in hand, the aged Ch'ieng Lung, benign and alert, adroitly turned the conversation at each attempt into other channels.

Meanwhile the King's letter was being considered by the Emperor's Ministers, who called into consultation the former Viceroy of Canton, Fu K'ang-an, and even sought the views of a former Hoppo of Canton who had been dismissed and imprisoned for malpractices. Their decision was a foregone conclusion. An edict was prepared on 22 September which refused the request for a resident Minister at Peking on the ground that he would be of no use to traders at Canton, who were adequately protected by the Emperor's officials. The Ambassador should return home forthwith, bearing the valuable gifts which the Emperor had provided for his King.

Unaware of this edict, but sensing the official hostility to the embassy, Macartney and his entourage returned to Peking in advance of the Emperor. There it was clearly indicated that his ill health (he was suffering from gout again) made his immediate departure for home eminently desirable. Protesting that the hope and intention had been that he should reside for a considerable period in Peking in order to have numerous discussions with the Emperor and his Ministers and so cement the friendship 'so happily begun', he insisted on submitting to Ho Shen a list of the desired concessions.[210] But it was all one. An immediate reply was drafted in the Emperor's name, translated into Latin and delivered to Macartney on 7 October, the date assigned for his departure. All the requests were peremptorily rejected.[211] The King's letter had been answered, but his Ambassador had not been allowed to negotiate.

Even before the disheartened embassy had begun the homeward journey the Chinese Government took further action which had future significance. On the same day that the letter of rejection was written a secret edict was sent to all provinces, giving warning that the English might retaliate because their requests had been refused. Troops were to be mobilised in the provinces as the embassy passed through, and coast defences were to be strengthened so that if the English attempted to trade at additional ports contrary to the Imperial order they might be driven off. These orders were to be kept secret to avoid alarm among the people.[212]

At the same time the English were to be conciliated. The official chosen to conduct the embassy back to the ships was a young member of the Council of State, a Tartar named Sung Yün. He was one of those who had shown a very friendly disposition at

---

[210] In view of the unpromising attitude of the Chinese Ministers it was not very diplomatic of Macartney to have put the requests at their maximum. Possibly he did so 'for the record' in London. He asked that the English be permitted to trade at Chusan, Ningpo and Tientsin, to establish an unfortified trade depot near Chusan, to be allowed to reside all the year round at Canton and to enjoy some freedom of movement there, and to establish a warehouse at Peking. To these he added a request for the regularisation of duties and fees at Canton. (*F.R., China*, vol. 92, pp. 259-61.) It will be recalled that Baring had urged that grievances relating to Canton should not be raised in Peking: he had also argued that it would be unwise to have a factory in the capital because of the probability of friction arising with the populace.

[211] The English version of this letter, which addressed itself in alternate passages to the King and to the Ambassador, is printed in Morse, *Chronicles*, vol. II, pp. 247-52. The edict of 23 September appears to have been taken as a general directive when composing the rejection of Macartney's specific requests.

[212] Cited by Pritchard (p. 349) from Chinese works. The appearance of the *Lion*, a warship of 64 guns, may well have reminded Chinese officials of the aggressive actions of Admirals Vernon and Hughes at Canton. Nor had Macartney's idea of taking a military escort, which included a party of gunners with field pieces, been a good one. They had not been allowed to go to Jehol, and when Macartney proposed that they might carry out 'evolutions' for the Emperor's entertainment at Peking, the suggestion had been coldly declined.

Jehol, where he had conversed at length with Macartney on Russian affairs. During the river journey back to Tientsin his desire to allay resentment and re-establish friendly relations was made very evident. At Tientsin it was learned that Gower had left Chusan and sailed southward for Macao by way of the Ladrone Islands in search of a better climate and medicines for his crew, sixty of whom were still ill with fever. The embassy and its escort were thus obliged to undertake a journey of more than a thousand miles overland to Canton, and during the ensuing weeks Sung Yün engaged in the discussions which Macartney had expected in Peking.

The Chinese Minister explained that the Ambassador's requests constituted innovations which were unacceptable but assured him that abuses at Canton would be reformed. Macartney thereupon turned to that subject and set out in detail the nature of the grievances. Sung Yün sent a series of reports to Peking emphasising the pacific intentions of the English and the need for reform at Canton. In response a number of Imperial letters were received which expressed appreciation of the friendly (and deferential) purpose of the embassy and gave assurances in increasingly gracious terms that foreign trade would be protected. Action followed. The hostile Viceroy of Canton, Fu K'ang-an, was replaced by the Viceroy of Chekiang Province, Ch'ang Lin. At Hangchow Macartney was introduced to him and detailed discussions about reforms took place. Both then and later Ch'ang Lin evinced a determination to master the intricacies of the Canton trading system and to remedy legitimate grievances. When, therefore, the embassy entered Canton in state on 19 December Macartney was in high expectation that he would have benefits of some substance to show on returning to London. Unfortunately these hopes did not materialise. The new Viceroy did his best, but reforming efforts were resisted by the Hoppo and his colleagues who saw their fortune-making facilities in jeopardy. Officials in Peking also stood to lose their *douceurs*. Vested interests proved too strong. Before long the new Viceroy abandoned the thankless task and obtained a transfer to another post. The corrupt *status quo ante* was resumed.

At Canton Macartney learned that the French Jacobins had declared war on Britain in the previous February. The world war which was to last, with two short intervals, until July, 1815, had begun. A voyage of commercial diplomacy to Japan and the countries of South-East Asia was now out of the question. It was decided that H.M.S. *Lion* on the homeward voyage would convoy the seasonal merchant fleet of fifteen ships, which was carrying cargoes to the value of about £3 million.[213] On 10 January, 1794, the *Lion*

---

[213] Five East Indiamen, being fast and well-armed, sailed home independently.

with the embassy on board dropped down the Canton River and made for Macao. On 4 September she anchored in Portsmouth harbour.

An embassy upon which so much effort and expense had been lavished came home a total failure. The principal reason, according to Macartney, was a suspicion on the part of the Chinese Government that the English in Bengal had given support to the Rajah of Nepal in 1791. The latter had been defeated by a Chinese army which had marched into Tibet to prevent that country from falling under Nepalese control.[214] The open hostility of the Viceroy of Canton (Fu K'ang-an), who had commanded the Chinese forces in that campaign, and the questioning of Macartney on the subject by other senior officials certainly suggests that the Chinese Government had accepted rumours of hostile intent as further evidence of English aggressiveness; but Macartney made too much of it. At most it was a straw in the wind.

The Manchu régime was on the defensive. Internally there was unrest and incipient revolt in a number of provinces. On the land and sea frontiers of the Empire a strange new world was creeping up, powerful, repulsively clever, and obviously uncultivated. From the testimony of both Macartney and Staunton it appears that there was a minority of senior mandarins (men such as the commissioners, Wan and Chou, and the Tartar prince, Sung Yün) who were interested in European inventions and thought it wise to establish friendly relations. On the other hand, the majority held the view that the security of the Empire and the dynasty necessitated a rigid resistance to the penetration of alien ideas and power. The occasional appearance of Western warships, such as the *Lion*, capable of sailing about the world and carrying an armament which made Chinese shore defences look silly, must have been intimidating to the more wide-awake officials who saw them and were aware that their own Government lacked even the means to suppress the swarm of pirate junks which infested the coasts.

The embassy, which had been so carefully equipped to impress, evoked an unexpected reaction. Most of the mandarins disliked and feared what they saw – and looked quickly away. When Macart-

---

[214] War had broken out as the result of the efforts of the Rajah of Nepal to impose his authority upon the Dalai Lama of Tibet. The latter, being hard pressed, had called in the Chinese who intervened with a large army which advanced to within a short distance of Khatmandu. Hard pressed in turn, the Rajah appealed to Bengal for help, which Cornwallis declined to give. But before the latter's reply was received the Rajah had sued for peace and had obtained it at the price of accepting Chinese overlordship. The Dalai Lama had written to Cornwallis expressing alarm at the possibility of British assistance being given to Nepal. Cornwallis replied that he was sending an envoy (Capt. Kirkpatrick) to Nepal at the Rajah's request, who would be willing to act as a friendly intermediary. (See Ross's summary of these events in his edition of the *Cornwallis Correspondence*, vol. II, pp. 190-1). No doubt the Dalai Lama would report his (unfounded) fears to Peking.

ney proposed that experts should demonstrate 'modern' methods of Western surgery, the latest improvements in spinning and weaving cotton, and even to arrange for the ascent of a balloon, his offers were declined. Afterwards when he mentioned this to the new Viceroy of Canton, the latter could not conceal his regret for 'the Court's coldness and indifference to our discoveries'. There seems to be no good ground for doubting Macartney's veracity or the Viceroy's sincerity. The embassy was received with celestial politeness and condescension: it was got rid of as speedily as decorum permitted and with a brusqueness which seems to have caused the Ministers in Peking, or some of them, to veer round towards panic. The notion that fifty-three British soldiers with a few light field pieces would attempt to stir up trouble in the Provinces as they passed through was fantastic. Then careful measures were taken to allay resentment: the foreigners must be made more easy at Canton, otherwise they might use their naval power to force an entry into the northern ports in defiance of Imperial orders.

There was also an economic factor which further stiffened an attitude which one may perhaps be permitted to describe as a form of *apartheid*. In his narrative Staunton states that the influx of silver from Europe had caused a great increase in the price of all articles of consumption and had 'altered the proportion between the fixed salaries of the several officers of government and the usual expences of their respective stations'. In another passage he writes that many officials, and particularly Tartars, regarded the increasing dependence of China upon European imports as an evil to be kept under as close restriction as possible. To speak of China being 'dependent' upon imports from Europe at this stage was, of course, a great exaggeration, but when the balance of trade began to turn against China and in favour of British India so that Chinese silver began to flow out to Calcutta to pay for cotton and opium, the profits derived from selling tea to Europeans and Americans took on a different look, and the desire to insulate the economy of China behind the ancient wall of self-sufficiency became identified with nationalist fervour against foreign devils in general.

The Macartney embassy is significant on several counts. It affords a further illustration of the determination of the Pitt Ministry, representing merchants, financiers and industrialists, to build a commercial empire in Asian waters, based on London and India. It also marked the emergence of a new kind of 'imperial' problem. In the western hemisphere it was being found that the economic barriers enclosing the Portuguese and Spanish Empires could be penetrated by the device of Free Ports and – it was hoped – eventually demolished by encouraging political independence. But how could the barriers around the Chinese Empire be removed? China

was a vast independent state. 'Liberation' from the Tartar régime
was not a practicable proposition. Could then persuasion be relied
on?

The fair promises made to Macartney during the last stage of his
sojourn in China convinced him that this was so, and the Government at home accepted his diagnosis. He was convinced that with
'great skill, caution, temper and perseverance' trade with China
could be extended along the lines that Britain desired. Patience
and persistent friendliness would in a few years convince the
Chinese that commercial association was of mutual benefit and so
induce them to enter into a treaty relationship. 'I dare say,' he
added, 'there are many hasty spirits disposed to go a shorter way
to work; but no shorter way will do it.' It was true enough that if
China were to lay an embargo on British trade ample means of
retaliation lay to hand. A few British frigates could in a few weeks
destroy all their coastal navigation, demolish the forts in the Canton
River, and cut off communication between Formosa and the mainland. In any case the thread of connexion between Formosa and
the Chinese Empire was extremely slender, 'but a breath of foreign
interference would instantly snap it asunder'. It would not be
difficult to stir up trouble for the Chinese in Tibet, where the
people appeared to require only a little encouragement and assistance to start a revolt. Similarly if the people of Korea saw ships in
the Yellow Sea operating against China they might well be induced
to attempt the recovery of their independence.

All this was well enough in theory, but it was not to be supposed
that in such a situation the Czarina Catherine, whose ambition was
already extending beyond Alaska to the east, would refrain from
seizing territory at her door. Moreover an interruption of the China
trade would inflict immense damage in India and deal a heavy
blow against the woollen industry of England. Indeed – so Macartney thought – the danger lay in the probability that China would
break up through internal weakness and so occasion a complete
subversion of the commerce of Asia. 'The empire of China,' he
opined, 'is an old crazy first-rate man of war, which a fortunate
succession of able and vigilant officers has contrived to keep afloat
for these hundred and fifty years past.' But the Manchu dynasty
was uneasily poised. If an insufficient man happened to take command, then good-bye to the discipline and safety of the ship. 'She
may perhaps not sink outright . . . but she can never be rebuilt on
the old bottom.' Prophetic; but he was antedating the wreck and
the reconstruction.

The moral then was clear. By selling enormous quantities of tea to
the West, China had committed herself to a trade connexion which
must in the order of nature become increasingly reciprocal. British
sea-power could without difficulty force the gates, but that would

be a most injurious course for all concerned and should be avoided except as a last resort.

Our present interests, our reason, and our humanity equally forbid the thought of any offensive measures with regard to the Chinese whilst a ray of hope remains for succeeding by gentle ones. Nothing could be urged in favour of an hostile conduct but an irresistible conviction of failure by forbearance. The project of a territory on the Continent of China (which I have heard imputed to the late Lord Clive) is too wild to be seriously mentioned, and especially if all can be quietly got without it that was expected to be got with it.[215]

The policy of patient persistence, advocated by Macartney, was adopted and pursued throughout the wars with the French revolutionaries and Napoleon. As a follow-up to the embassy, presents were sent in 1795 to the Emperor, the Viceroy of Canton and the Hoppo, consisting of superfine cloth and ' fleecy hosiery ', together with a letter to the Viceroy from the Chairman of the East India Company.[216] In May, 1804, while General Arthur Wellesley and General Lake were conducting campaigns against the Marathas, who had been incited to attack by Napoleon, Castlereagh agreed that it would be useful to send congratulatory letters to the new Emperor of China, taking the opportunity to warn him against any ' invidious attempts ' that Napoleon might make to loosen the ties of friendship between China and Britain. Letters from George III to the Emperor and from Castlereagh to the ' Prime Minister ' of China and the Viceroy of Canton were dispatched with substantial and varied gifts.[217]

The old familiar problems at Canton remained, and the old familiar remedies continued to be sought. In 1807 a memorandum was submitted to the Board of Control which pointed out that China was in a deplorable condition. Powerful and daring gangs of rebels were at large in the southern and western provinces and piratical rebels were dominating the coast from Hai Nan to the Gulf of Pe-chih-li. If Britain were to offer the assistance of a few warships, ' invaluable advantages might be obtained for the concerns of the East India Company at Canton '. If, on the other hand, no action was taken Napoleon might exploit his commanding influence in Portugal to incite that nation against the English in China. A familiar argument was then advanced. In grateful acknowledgement of naval assistance the Chinese Government could probably be persuaded to grant an establishment at Chusan,

---

[215] Macartney's Journal (ut supra), pp. 395-402.

[216] James Cobb to Matthew Meheux, with enclosures, 25 April, 1804 (F.R., China, vol. 20). The value of these presents was put at about £1,000.

[217] Copies of these letters and relevant ' office ' correspondence are in Ibid., vol. 20.

situated close to the tea-growing region and conveniently placed for the sale of British woollens in the north.[218]

Six years later (in 1813) an episode occurred at Canton which indicated the true situation. Fresh exactions and threats by a new Hoppo culminated in a major row between the Committee of Supercargoes and the Viceroy. The latter issued an edict ordering the expulsion from Canton of J. W. Roberts, one of the three members of the Committee. The President, J. F. Elphinstone, took such a serious view of this new threat that he refused to allow the Company's ships to unload and declared that, if necessary, all trade would be suspended pending an appeal to Peking. 'When engaged in any discussion with the Chinese Government,' he minuted, 'we may be prepared to expect just as much delay, insult and oppression as they may conceive we will submit to.' After several months of deadlock (during which Mr. Roberts died at Macao), the Viceroy issued a fresh edict which conceded almost all the demands against interference and oppression that the Committee had made.[219]

The news of the clash created such concern in London for the future of the China trade that Castlereagh, as President of the Board of Control, very unwisely agreed to the dispatch of another embassy, to be led this time by Lord Amherst. His Instructions, dated 1 January, 1816, were similar to those of Macartney, although drawn in somewhat sharper terms. He was to request the termination of abuses at Canton, an exchange of resident ministers between London and Peking, and the opening of a northern port. The unfortunate Amherst was dismissed with contumely almost as soon as he had reached the Imperial Court. In his written reply the Emperor intimated that 'the curious and ingenious productions' of Britain were not esteemed in the Celestial Empire, nor was there occasion for sending any more ambassadors. It would be sufficient if the Prince Regent would pour out the heart in dutiful obedience.[220] In the atmosphere of the Brighton Pavilion perhaps.

---

[218] 'Memorandum respecting the present disturbed state of China, and the advantages to be drawn from it by Great Britain.' Signed, 'J.B.' (*Ibid.*) 'One of the main objects of the late Embassy . . . was to gain permanent settlement on some of the numerous islands in the Yellow Sea.' Such an acquisition, the writer added, would follow almost as a matter of course if there was a flying squadron of small armed vessels cruising in those seas for the protection of the Chinese sea-ports. 'J.B.' may possibly have been Sir John Barrow, Second Secretary at the Admiralty, who had been a protégé of Sir G. T. Staunton and had been a member of the Macartney embassy.

[219] *Canton Secret Consultations*, 15 Nov., 1813. The details of the episode are described in Morse, *Chronicles*, vol. III, Chap. LXIX.

[220] Documents relating to the Amherst embassy are printed in Morse, *op. cit.*, vol. III, App. V. See Sir George Thomas Staunton, *Notes of Proceedings and Occurrences during the British Embassy to Peking in 1816* (Lond., 1824) and the same author's *Miscellaneous Notices Relating to China* (2 vols., Lond., 1822-50). As in 1787 and again in 1793 the East India Company disliked the sending of an

The policy of patient persistence had foundered as it was bound to do. The anomaly remained. While China continued to live in a cultural and political world of her own, she was allowing herself to become interlocked with an economic system dominated by the West. The logical course would have been to close the port of Canton to foreigners and forbid the export of tea. But that draconian measure would have inflicted hardship upon an important Chinese industry and deprived the Imperial treasury of a growing source of revenue and in a period when the country was impoverished by internal disturbance. The Chinese Government very understandably intended to continue to make profit out of the foreigners on its own terms, which in the 19th century became increasingly impracticable as the interchange of manufactured articles and primary products became world-wide.

It was unfortunate that the great increase in the illicit sale to China of Bengal opium, which introduced a moral factor, exacerbated a difficult situation until it developed into a *casus belli*. The moral issue has tended to obscure the underlying continuity of British commercial policy in the Far East. After the armed intervention in 1839, which Macartney had foreseen in 1794 and had hoped could be avoided, China was required in the Treaty of Nanking to make the concessions which Dundas had tried to secure by diplomacy half a century earlier. Hong Kong was the type of 'depot' on the coastal fringe of China which Cathcart, Macartney and Amherst in turn had been instructed to seek.

During the struggle with Napoleon, who inherited French ambitions in the East, the development of a British empire of trade, based on London and India, was accelerated. The interest which Warren Hastings and then Dundas had shown in the possibilities of trade with Cochin China, for example, was reflected in Castlereagh's initiative in arranging for the dispatch of an envoy to the ruler of that country in 1803.[221] When Hong Kong became a British entrepôt, it completed a chain of strategic-commercial

---

embassy which would not obtain the desired concessions and would only exasperate the Chinese officials at Canton and make conditions worse. The only effective method was local negotiation *ad hoc* by the Company's representatives (Staunton, *Miscellaneous Notices*, vol. I, pp. v-viii).

[221] Castlereagh to the Chairman of the East India Company (Jacob Bosanquet), 3 April, 1803. Private. 'I cannot avoid,' wrote Castlereagh, 'expressing to you the importance which appears to me to attach to the relations which Europeans may form with so growing a Native Power . . . placed as it is so immediately in the Track of our Trade to China. We cannot watch the conduct of our Government [in relation to the French] too narrowly.' It was his earnest wish that steps should be taken to open a communication with the King of Cochin China with a view to acquiring information which might enable the Company to judge to what extent it might be advisable 'to follow it up by arrangements of a more permanent nature'. (*F.R., China*, vol. 20.) See also Castlereagh to the Chairs, 11 April, 1803. Secret. (*Ibid.*)

bases which included Singapore, Penang, Ceylon, Mauritius and the Cape of Good Hope. In the 20th century a new (and industrialising) dispensation in China has closed and locked the gates again. The situation of Hong Kong in our own day is not entirely dissimilar from that of the little enclave on the Canton River in the time of George III.

CHAPTER IX

AN EMPIRE OF TRADE IN THE WESTERN HEMISPHERE

1. CANADA AND THE MISSISSIPPI BASIN

In British eyes the Western Hemisphere after 1783 consisted of two great regions under foreign jurisdiction, the United States and the Spanish Empire. On the northern flank of the United States were the British Provinces of Quebec and the Maritimes, and fringing the Spanish Gulf of Mexico were the British islands of the Caribbean. Westward of Montreal was a vast no-man's-land, the fur-trading country, extending to the Rockies, the Pacific coast and Alaska. Behind the thirteen American States and across the Allegheny Mountains lay the Mississippi Basin and the wide plains beyond. In the Caribbean the British islands were strategically situated outside the Spanish and Portuguese tariff walls which extended (in theory) from New Orleans to Patagonia and thence up the Pacific coast to the Bering Strait. From the point of view of Britain as a naval and industrial Power which had recently lost all but a few remnants of a territorial empire the United States and Latin America were regions of enormous commercial opportunity.

English efforts to do business in South America, either by force or consent, dated back to the elder William Hawkins in the time of Henry VIII and had continued in one form or another ever since, but the sudden demise of British jurisdiction in the greater part of the northern Continent created a novel situation. In negotiating a settlement with the former Colonies Shelburne had worked for a reconciling peace, to be quickly cemented by full commercial reciprocity, and so leading in due time to some kind of political partnership. On that basis the drawing of political frontiers had seemed to be of secondary importance, since they were not to constitute economic barriers. Americans would trade freely with Britain and her West Indian and North American dependencies, while British manufactures would follow the American flag (or flags) into the West.[1]

Although this enlightened plan foundered on the rocks of prejudice and tradition, certain parts of it corresponded with the national outlook regarding overseas commerce in general and were pursued. Deep-rooted tradition occasioned the exclusion of Ameri-

---

[1] See vol. I, Chap. VI.

can shipping from the West Indian carrying trade. On the other hand a lively appreciation of the Americans as some of Britain's best customers caused them to be given special privileges in British ports. 'So great an Indulgence,' wrote the British Consul in Philadelphia, ' has been granted by Great Britain to the United States as to put their Trade upon a Footing of the most favour'd Nations in Europe – our best and oldest Allies.'[2] Similarly, Shelburne's view that in future the United States would be the ' imperial ' Power in North America, colonising, administering and defending the Middle West, while British industrialists reaped the advantage of an ever-expanding market, was shared by his successors. Altered circumstances, however, gave rise to a difference in method. The failure of the American Congress and the individual State Governments to honour the pledge to provide compensation for dispossessed Loyalists was one of the reasons why a resentful Britain continued to retain the Western Posts in defiance of the peace treaty, until angry Americans threatened to take them by force. Again British discrimination against American shipping in the Atlantic traffic, which hit New England hard, engendered bitterness and inspired retaliatory legislation.

In an atmosphere of growing tension British policy veered towards the idea of making separate commercial treaties with the new settlements in the Ohio country and Kentucky. Reports from British Consuls in the United States and proposals from enterprising merchants in Montreal and Quebec pointed out that Congress, still weak in authority and financial resources, was observing westward expansion without enthusiasm. Meanwhile independent-minded pioneers (like frontier-folk the world over) resented interference from a central government which presumed to interfere without affording adequate assistance or protection. To outside observers it seemed probable that the great region between the Allegheny Mountains and the Mississippi would develop as a congeries of autonomous states. Overland communication with the Atlantic seaboard would be difficult and increasingly expensive as the settlements extended, whereas the St. Lawrence, the Great Lakes and the upper reaches of the Mississippi could become a convenient ' corridor ' through which British manufacturers could be distributed in a market whose ultimate limits could scarcely be discerned. In the same period efforts were being made to establish commercial alliances with territories in South-East Asia which had not been brought within the jurisdiction of the Dutch. If the North American plan materialised, Montreal-Quebec would become a central clearing-house, doing business to the south while operating the fur trade to the west.

---

[2] Phineas Bond to Carmarthen, 29 April, 1789. Philadelphia (*F.O. 4/7*, p. 187).

The persistent efforts of General Etham Allen and his two brothers, Ira and Levi, to steer the Colony of Vermont into an independent course, possibly in alliance with Britain, achieved no practical result, except perhaps to assert the separate identity of the Green Mountain Boys; but the proposals submitted caused Ministers in London to consider the implications in a wider context. The Vermonters had been engaged in territorial disputes with New Hampshire, New York and Massachusetts, and the attitude of Congress (according to Colonel Ira Allen) was so unsympathetic to their cause that they expected to see their country divided up among 'the claimant States' as soon as the revolutionary war was over. A strong faction, headed by the Allens, decided that Vermont should withdraw from the war and stand neutral, while holding their frontiers against all comers.

Garbled reports reaching London led the Ministry to entertain high hopes that Vermont was about to return to the King's obedience. In a despatch to Governor Haldimand of Quebec in March, 1780, Lord George Germain emphasised the 'vast' strategic importance of Vermont and instructed him to ascertain the real sentiments of the inhabitants and to assure them that their country would be erected into a separate province.[3] A year later Germain wrote in still more optimistic terms;[4] but he was soon to be disillusioned. When Haldimand sent an emissary to open discussions with Ira Allen, the latter made it very clear that the people of Vermont in general were strong supporters of the American cause, and that he himself was of the same mind. The oppressive behaviour of Congress was causing a swing in the Assembly in favour of neutrality, but that was as far as even 'the initiated' were prepared to go until the outcome of the war was known. With a full report of the conversations before him Haldimand rightly concluded that the Allen party would much prefer to see Vermont admitted to the American Union as a State in its own right, freed from the jurisdictional claims of its neighbours, and were using the threat of withdrawal from the war as a weapon with which to attain it. Meanwhile the possibility of an eventual 're-union' with Britain was being kept alive in case Congress refused the required status.[5]

---

[3] Germain to Haldimand, 17 March, 1780. No. 23. *C.O.* 43/8 (1768-87).

[4] 'All late accounts from New York give the strongest reason to expect Etham Allen and the people of Vermont are taking their Measures very judiciously for a general Declaration in our favour as soon as the Season will permit you to send a body of Troops among them. . . .' (Despatch of 12 April, 1781. No. 31. *Ibid.*)

[5] Haldimand to Germain, 8 July, 1781. 'Most Private.' The numerous documents enclosed with this despatch include: (i) Haldimand's instructions to his emissary, dated 20 Dec., 1780, (ii) a day-to-day journal of the conversations with Col. Allen between 8 and 25 May, 1781, (iii) 'information of the State of Vermont' by Col. Allen. Haldimand's envoy was instructed to offer that Vermont would be constituted a separate province independent of any Government in America and would be

After the terms of the provisional peace treaty had reached America in the Spring of 1783 Haldimand in Quebec received a number of visits from 'several Persons of influence in the State of Vermont'. All these people, he reported, agreed that Vermont was very opposed to Congress, were confident that none of the New England States would obey a Congress order to reduce them by force, and for that reason made no scruple to set the State of New York and its claims of jurisdiction over them at defiance. They further asserted that, if they were admitted as the Fourteenth State, they would refuse to be bound by debts contracted by Congress previous to their admission.

They made no Scruple of telling me that Vermont must either be annexed to Canada, or become Mistress of it, as it is the only channel by which the Produce of their Country can be conveyed to a Market, but they assured me that they rather Wished the former.

This was taking a high line, especially with a soldier like Haldimand, who had suspected the merchants of Quebec and Montreal of entertaining pro-American sentiments during the war and was now determined to preserve the *ancien régime* of the Quebec Act against republican subversion.[6] The incorporation of Vermont with a population of 70,000, which was rapidly increasing, would indeed represent a damnable inheritance. (In our own day the Union of South Africa would presumably hold a similar view about a possible inclusion of Southern Rhodesia.) Moreover the situation had been completely changed by the peace treaty. The United States was now an international personality; and although Vermont was not yet a constituent member-state, Congress would of course regard the question of its future status as an internal matter in which Britain, as a foreign Power, had no right to interfere. Haldimand informed Lord North that he had listened to the Vermont spokesmen 'with patience' but had told them that he could not interfere in these matters since he had the most positive orders from the King to do everything in his power to effect a reconciliation between the subjects of the United States and those of Britain.[7] When Pitt took office he naturally agreed, and Haldi-

---

'entitled to every Prerogative and Immunity which is promised to the other Provinces in the Proclamation of the King's Commissioners'. (*C.O. 42/41.*) In response to further pressure from London Haldimand repeated (in a despatch dated 17 July, 1782) his previous conviction that the Vermont spokesmen were merely temporising (*C.O. 42/15*).

[6] See Chapter XI below.

[7] Haldimand to North, 24 October, 1783 (*C.O. 42/22.* Printed in Short and Doughty, *Documents Relating to the Constitutional History of Canada, 1759-1791*, Ottawa, 1918 edn., pp. 735-7). Documents illustrating these later negotiations have been printed in S. F. Bemis under the title 'Relations between the Vermont Separatists and Great Britain, 1789-1791' (*Am. Hist. Rev.*, vol. XXI, No, 3, April, 1916, pp. 547-60).

mand was ordered in a despatch from Sydney to keep clear of political entanglement. It was also necessary to proceed warily in the regulation of trade. Sea-borne traffic between the United States and British territories was on a provisional *ad hoc* basis. In 1785 Ira Allen arrived in Quebec to negotiate a free-trade agreement between Vermont and the British Provinces, but the proposition was evaded. The Vermonters were in a critical situation. On the one hand they were at odds with the rest of New England and with Congress; and on the other they were faced with the probability of being virtually cut off from Montreal, their natural outlet. Since the end of the war they had begun to colonise the region on the east side of Lake Champlain right up to the Canadian border.

'If,' wrote Hugh Finlay of the Quebec Council, 'the Governor would permit the Vermontese to come in and purchase British Manufactures, the Stores in Montreal and Quebec would soon be emptied, but he seems very averse from having any kind of connexion with them. The merchants grumble confoundedly, and cannot conceive his reasons for refusing to accept of American gold for English goods.' And again: 'If for reasons which I must own I cannot comprehend, we are to have no sort of intercourse with Vermont, we shall lose a good trade . . . in short, if we please, Britain will reap every advantage a trading Nation can wish to reap from a Colony without a farthing of expence for supporting its internal Government.'[8]

In March, 1785, soon after his return to England, Haldimand was summoned to give evidence before the Board of Trade in the course of their examination of future trade relations between the British provinces in North America and the United States. He was particularly questioned about inland communication with Vermont. He replied that while he was in Canada he had not in general permitted any such intercourse, except that Vermont traders had been encouraged to buy British manufactures, but always under permit. He proposed that the export of furs across the American border and the import of foreign European goods by that route should be prohibited: otherwise the existing arrangements should be allowed to continue.[9] The Board resolved accordingly, and an Additional Instruction, dated 26 May, was issued to the Governor

---

[8] Finlay to Colonel Skene, 6 March, 1784. Montreal. (*C.O. 42/16.*) On 6 Nov., 1784, Finlay wrote in similar vein to Under-Secretary Nepean. The geographical position of Vermont made it dependent upon Canada for European manufactures and West Indian sugar and rum, while their surplus produce must pass down the St. Lawrence in *British* ships. 'Their lumber, salted beef and pork, flour, etc. for the West Indian market – Pig iron, flax seed, oak staves for the London market . . . must come to us at a cheap rate in Exchange for British Manufactures.' Vermont, he added, could be as advantageous to Britain as if the inhabitants were subjects of the Crown. (*Ibid.*)

[9] Minutes of the Board of Trade, 7 March, 1785. *B.T.* 5/2, pp. 207-9.

to that effect.[10] This was a negative attitude which Sir Guy Carleton, now Lord Dorchester, reversed when he returned to Quebec as Governor in the following year. In the internal government of the Province he opposed all efforts to modify the system enshrined in the Quebec Act,[11] but in promoting the economic development of British North America he showed himself to be a statesman of considerable vision. Soon after his arrival in Quebec in 1786 Levi Allen waited upon him to state that the Government of Vermont had appointed three commissioners, of whom he was one, to negotiate a treaty of commerce. Dorchester replied that he had no authority to make treaties but wished to live in friendship with all the neighbouring states, and Allen was asked to state the wishes of Vermont in writing, which he did in November. In the following April a proclamation, followed by an ordinance, authorised the free importation by the Lake Champlain route of all kinds of timber, naval stores, cereals, hemp, flax and livestock, together with a free export of all articles (except furs) produced or grown in British territories. In July of that year the Board of Trade considered the question and decided that the regulation of inland trade between Canada and the neighbouring American States should be left to Dorchester and his Council at their discretion.[12] Accordingly in 1788 further ordinances were passed which elaborated this inland commerce into a comprehensive system. Levi Allen had got most, although not all, of what he wanted, and the Canadian merchants were well satisfied. His Lordship might be haughty and disdainful respecting their political demands, but he appeared to have the right ideas about trade.

Dorchester's policy in this regard extended far beyond Vermont. In a number of despatches to Grenville at this time he described the formation of new settlements beyond the Allegheny and Appalachian Mountains, especially in Kentucky, their inclination to be independent of Congress, and the great opportunities which Canada presented as a corridor for British commerce. Similar ideas were being put forward from various quarters. In 1788 a group of London merchants, closely associated with firms in Montreal and Quebec, submitted a long memorandum on the subject.[13]

---

[10] Additional Instructions, 26 May, 1785 (printed in Short and Doughty, pp. 783-4).

[11] See Chap. XI below.

[12] Minutes of the Board, 13 July, 1787 (*B.T. 5/4*, pp. 323-5). The usual prohibition against exporting furs or importing foreign manufactures and spirits by the inland route was reaffirmed.

[13] The memorandum is unsigned, but its provenance is inferred from the following points of internal evidence. Reference is made to news arriving of political discontent in Canada: the writers state that they have little knowledge of the country beyond the districts of Montreal and Quebec: and the fact that they brush aside the claims of the Hudson's Bay Company, reflects the attitude of individuals associated with its rival, the North-West Company.

Hitherto, they declared, Britain had shown herself indifferent to Canadian interests. The government of the Province seemed to be 'a chaos made up of French despotism and English Liberty, jumbled together so as to produce confusion and Anarchy'. It might not be advisable to promote settlement to the westward, but the policy of 'thus far and no farther' had proved fatal in the case of the American colonists, and it could not be expected that people in Canada (that is to say, the immigrant Loyalists) could be held, except on fair and liberal terms. These people lived within sight of a great American invasion of the Ohio country and at a great distance from Quebec, their source of protection. The policy which had been adopted with regard to Vermont offered a double advantage. It secured the custom of that State for British goods as well as a vent for them in the adjacent States. It also encouraged the people of Vermont 'to continue stedfast in maintaining views and Interests separate from Congress'. The same principle of policy should be given wider application. 'We may, it is apprehended, look for the same advantage in many parts of America, particularly in all the numerous states now forming behind the Allegheny, along the Waters of Ohio, Mississippi, and the Lakes.'

That this was no gratuitous prediction, the memorial continued, was shown by the various declarations published by the new settlements, stating that their situation beyond the mountains required that they be independent and upon the same principle which had justified separation from Britain. It would be vain for Congress to deny such claims, since they would have to combat the views, not only of the new settlements, but of all those on the east side of the mountains, 'who regard the Country on the Western Waters, as they call it, in the Light of a Land of Promise'. These people had in any event a long land carriage to and from the ocean. One route crossed the mountains; another went along the Mississippi through Spanish territory; and the other two crossed the Lakes through Canada, either by the St. Lawrence or Hudson Bay.[14] Hitherto the Spaniards had refused passage through the Mississippi, contrary to the terms of the peace settlement, and Congress (it was suggested) had given little support to the settlers' complaints because it was intended to compel them to use the Atlantic ports for the sake of the resultant revenue. 'From this conflict the Western settlers must be glad to turn aside towards Canada, where we can at once make them free of the Ocean.' A substantial and lasting basis would thus be established for 'a league of amity' with them.

If, however, Britain was to profit from these settlements, as she

---

[14] Ignoring the climatic facts of life, the memorialists maintained that the southern shore of Hudson Bay and the rivers flowing into it afforded the best access from the Atlantic into the central regions of the Continent.

already did from the people of Vermont, she must study to be useful to them. A 'fit station' was needed for ready communication, and in order to serve as 'a commercial thoroughfare' it must not be too far inland. For situation, soil and climate the region best adapted to the purpose was that adjoining Lakes Ontario and Erie. If steps of this kind were taken, Britain could expect full and lasting possession of this trade – 'a Trade superior, not only to what Vermont may ever be fit to furnish, but far beyond all that we lost by the thirteen states of America'.[15] Such were the views of a merchant group which soon found reflection in official policy.

At this time British anger at the failure of Congress or of individual state governments to enable Loyalists to claim debts owing to them, and American exasperation at Britain's continued refusal to hand over the Western Posts or to allow their ships to participate in the carrying trade between British territories, were bringing a renewal of hostilities uncomfortably close. In October, 1789, Grenville wrote a secret letter to Dorchester in which he acknowledged the latter's despatches about the new settlements in Kentucky. They contained information highly important to the future interests of the British Provinces in North America, and the King's Ministers had therefore seen with great satisfaction the attention which Dorchester had given to the subject.

It appears extremely desirable that the turn of Affairs in those Settlements should lead to the establishment of a Government distinct from that of the Atlantic States, and if that should be the case, every means should be taken to improve and cultivate a Connection with the former, as being likely to prove highly advantageous to the Interests of this Country.

It did not appear, continued Grenville, that direct interference by Britain in this business would be either proper or prudent; but the retention of the Western Posts ('a just indemnification') had made relations with the United States uncertain. In the event of a dispute 'a connection with the Kentucky Settlers' might be very advantageous. It was also most desirable to prevent any close association being formed between these new settlements and the Government of Spain. Dorchester should, therefore, cultivate a friendly intercourse with their leading men in order to be able to exercise some influence upon their conduct, but he must give no promises of eventual, and still less of immediate, assistance against the Atlantic States. The British Government must be at liberty to decide on the degree of support which it might be proper to give, if the occasion arose. Nor must he use any expressions (to the Ken-

---

[15] 'Considerations, Political and Commercial, relating to Canada' (1788). *C.O. 47/112.*

tucky people) which might in the slightest degree make Britain a party to an attack on Spanish Louisiana.[16]

The state of flux throughout European North America at this time confronted Ministers in London with novel and complicated problems. In the Province of Quebec a new Constitution which would take account of a large French-speaking majority and small groups of English-speaking merchants and Loyalist settlers, had become an urgent necessity. Along the Atlantic seaboard thirteen American states, after drifting close to anarchy, had in 1787 hammered out a federal constitution which in the following year was submitted for ratification to each of the state conventions. On 30 April, 1789, George Washington was inaugurated as President of the United States. The belief, widely held in Europe, that republican institutions were intrinsically incapable of maintaining the cohesion of such a large group of widely divergent units, was being disproved. But to a European observer it seemed probable that the western frontier of the United States would remain at the Allegheny and Appalachian Mountains. It did not seem practicable that a federal government near the Atlantic coast could extend its authority over a vast ultramontane wilderness. Ministers in London and Madrid thought it desirable as well as probable that the new communities stretching out towards the Mississippi would develop as separate and independent states: otherwise the United States would become a colossus, capable of overwhelming the British Provinces in the north and Spanish territories to the south. When in 1790 war appeared to be imminent Grenville ordered Dorchester to remain at his post ' to protect the whole of the remaining British Empire in America '.[17]

In 1789 Ministers were very conscious that they needed more information. The Board of Trade accordingly prepared a questionnaire which the Foreign Secretary (the Duke of Leeds) was requested to circulate to all British Consuls in the United States. They were asked to furnish information about any discriminatory legislation against British ships and goods, the agricultural production of each state, whether local manufactures were being encouraged by bounties or premiums, the number of European vessels entering American ports since 1783, the flow of indentured servants with an account of their treatment and conditions of service, and about the rise and fall of population in each of the states. Finally, they were particularly asked to report on – ' the proceedings of those who have migrated from the Countries belonging to the

---

[16] Grenville to Dorchester, 20 Oct., 1789. No. 15. ' Secret.' (*C.O. 43/10*.) A public despatch to Dorchester, and another marked, ' Private and Secret ', both dated 20 Oct., are printed in Short and Doughty; but this one was omitted – on the ground, no doubt, that it was not relevant to Canadian constitutional affairs.

[17] Grenville to Dorchester, 6 May, 1790. No. 22. ' Secret.' *C.O. 43/10.*

United States into other parts of America not under their Government, such as the Banks of the Great Lakes, the Ohio, the Missouri and Mississippi, with a view to establish themselves in those parts, to provide subsistence, to form Governments, or to carry on any branch of Commerce, with any Observations they may have to offer on this Subject'.[18]

The consular reports sent in reply were prompt and full, particularly from Phineas Bond in Philadelphia and Sir John Temple in New York. The production of grain, rice and tobacco, wrote Temple, was rapidly approaching the pre-war level, and the manufacture of linen, cotton materials, silk, iron goods and glass was springing up in many States. Shipping returns were enclosed which showed that much of the greatest part of external trade was still with Britain. As to immigration it was estimated that some 45,000 indentured servants had arrived in Philadelphia during the first few years after the peace and considerable numbers in New York and Baltimore, coming chiefly from Ireland, Scotland and Germany; but the flow had greatly diminished of late owing to the disappointment of extravagant expectations. The number who emigrated from the Atlantic States to Kentucky and the Ohio region was not less than 50,000 during the past five years, but the population of the original States was rising so rapidly that this outflow was scarcely noticed. The new settlements lived 'under a sort of Government of their own', the land produced plenty of subsistence, but as yet no branch of commerce had developed.[19]

Similar appraisals came from Bond in Philadephia. On migration from Britain and to the United States he proposed measures that would, he claimed, restrain and eventually annihilate 'a Traffic which annually strips the Nation of many of its valuable inhabitants'. For a long time the American States would be obliged to import vast quantities of British and other European manufactures. As in the past the preference would be given to British goods, both because they were of the best quality and would come cheapest to the consumer in the end, and also because the merchants of England allowed their American customers far more liberal credit than any other nation on earth could afford – so much so, indeed, that many articles of foreign European manufacture, calculated for the American market, were brought in circuitously through England in order to secure the advantage of deferred payments. On the other hand, in branches of manufacture which required only a small capital outlay and where the raw materials (such as

---

[18] Wm. Fawkener, joint secretary to the Board of Trade, to the Duke of Leeds, 18 June, 1789 (*F.O. 4/7*, p. 225).

[19] Temple to the Duke of Leeds, 23 Sept., 1789. New York (*F.O. 4/7*, p. 409). These consular reports, and especially those of Phineas Bond, in the series *F.O. 4*, are a valuable source of information on Anglo-American commercial relations during this period.

iron ore) were at hand, 'the Americans do, and will, succeed'. And this, wrote Bond, was no bad thing. He had never held the view that such developments were injurious to Britain. It was true that the restraints upon New England in the fisheries (the St. Lawrence estuary and the Newfoundland Banks) had caused the people to turn to manufactures, but Manchester cotton goods sold 25 per cent cheaper than those made in Philadelphia, and the southern States, growing affluent by producing tobacco and cotton, preferred the British article. The production of local manufactures 'brings the means of Payment nearer to the Ability of the People'.

On the question of western settlements Bond reported that 'a considerable Jealousy' existed between them and the Government of the United States. The latter felt the inconvenience of expanding frontiers and were trying to discourage it, while the leading men among the settlers were complaining that they were not being given adequate aid and security.

Nature . . . seems to have pointed out a plain line of Division between the Eastern and Western Parts of this Continent. That wonderful Range of Mountains, which runs between the Atlantic Ocean, the River Mississippi and the Lakes, will probably one day . . . be the line of Partition, when the Western Country shall either have attained a Degree of Strength and Population competent to separate Establishment, or be driven to the Expedient of seeking support from some other Empire, more capable of contributing to its Progress and Protection.[20]

A few days before the Board of Trade had asked for their list of queries to be circulated, Grenville sent the Board a memorial by Levi Allen.[21] Tenacious and self-confident as ever, Allen had come to London to press the case for a commercial treaty with Vermont in person. Grenville had held several conversations with him and was evidently puzzled to know what more he required beyond the very comprehensive trade arrangements already in operation between Vermont and Quebec and whether in fact Vermont possessed the constitutional status to enter into a formal treaty. Evan Nepean was given the task of finding out.[22]

---

[20] Bond to the Duke of Leeds, 10 Nov., 1789. Philadelphia (*F.O. 4/7*, pp. 481-509). See also Bond's preliminary report in response to the Board of Trade's questionnaire of 22 Sept. (*Ibid.*, pp. 399-408.)

[21] Grenville to the Board of Trade, 10 June, 1789 (*ibid.*, p. 221).

[22] Later Nepean wrote to Hawkesbury to say that he had failed to discover whether the Americans had admitted that Vermont was a separate and independent State. He had searched the proceedings of Congress but had found no trace of any such acknowledgement. 'Mr. Grenville, from the information he has been able to collect, thinks that Vermont is allowed to be independent; but, in order to establish that point, he desired me yesterday to write to a person upon the subject who is now in Town.' Later on the same day Nepean sent Hawkesbury a letter which he had just received from J. G. Simcoe (the future Lieut.-Governor of Upper Canada),

The report of the Board of Trade (which was not submitted until ten months later) did not confine itself to the issue of Vermont but reviewed the whole question of British policy in relation to frontier settlements in North America. In addition to Levi Allen's memorial they had considered several papers from Lord Dorchester 'concerning the Policy of opening and facilitating a Passage into Canada' for all commodities produced by adjacent American territories, whether they were part of the United States, or belonged to the State of Vermont, 'or to other People of various Descriptions who are now forming new Settlements in that Part of the World'. It was recalled that the question had been considered by the Board in 1787, but they had then been in doubt whether goods so brought into Canada could be legally exported to other British dominions. The Law Officers had been consulted, and their report (only 'lately' received) stated that no law existed which made any distinction in this respect between the products of territories in America under foreign jurisdiction and of those belonging to the Crown of Great Britain, provided that they were carried from a British Colony in British ships, navigated according to law.

Further consideration, the report continued, had confirmed the Board in their previous opinion that it would be advisable 'in a commercial, and, They may add, a political View also' to encourage the importation into Canada of all the produce of the neighbouring territories in exchange for British manufactures, such products to be conveyed down the St. Lawrence in British ships to Europe or other parts of America on the same footing as commodities of Canadian origin. 'There can be no doubt that the various Settlements which are now forming in the interior Parts of America afford the prospect of a more extensive and valuable Commerce to those Nations who can secure to themselves the best Means of availing themselves of it.' On the particular question of Vermont it was observed that Mr. Levi Allen must be well aware that the Province of Quebec had been opened to their trade as widely as they had wished. It was reasonable to infer, therefore, that his continued pressure for a treaty had some other object in view about which he had probably received secret instructions. For political reasons the northern States would want Vermont to become a member of the Federal Government as a frontier for their security, 'and there is Ground to suppose that they are on that account apprehensive of its becoming connected and forming an alliance with the British Government'. There was, moreover,

---

saying that he was not absolutely certain on the point, but the people of Vermont had declared their independence of Britain long before the other Colonies. He added that he had before him a letter from the late General Etham Allen, dated 1785, in which the latter had stated that he had mustered 15,000 Vermont troops to maintain it. (Nepean to Hawkesbury, 1 April, 1790. *Addit. MSS.*, 38,225, ff. 130 and 132.)

another reason why the newly constituted Congress would probably decide to settle the territorial controversy and invite Vermont to join the Union, and that was the position of Kentucky. This territory had applied to Virginia and to Congress to be acknowledged as a separate State. Virginia was disposed to agree on the ground of the expense and inconvenience which the territory was causing, and many members of Congress took the same view; but the northern States were not prepared to accept this addition to the voting strength of the South unless it was counter-balanced by the admission of Vermont. These facts, the Board observed, sufficiently explained the impatience of the agent for Vermont to ascertain the views of the British Government about an alliance.

It was not for the Committee of Privy Council for Trade to say whether such an engagement might be proper or politically prudent, involving, as it would, the risk of giving offence to the United States. 'But', the report continued, 'the Lords are of Opinion that in a commercial view it will be for the benefit of this Country to prevent Vermont and Kentucke and all the other settlements now forming in the Interior parts of the great Continent of North America from becoming dependent on the Government of the United States, or on that of any other Foreign Country, and to preserve them on the contrary in a state of Independence and to induce them to form Treaties of Commerce and Friendship with Great Britain.'

Then followed the geographical argument. The area of settlement was separated from the United States by a long range of mountains. The cost of transporting goods from the Atlantic ports would be expensive and increase prices, while the conveyance by that route of settlers' produce, being bulky, would be still less practicable; and yet the settlers must export in order to pay for the manufactured articles they needed. It was certain, therefore, that the western settlements would wish to open communication with foreign nations, either by the Great Lakes and the St. Lawrence or by following the tributaries of the Mississippi and thence to the ocean. Of the two the passage through the Lakes and the St. Lawrence would probably prove to be much the more convenient – and for Britain specially advantageous, since the ships employed in it 'must belong wholly to the Subjects of the British Empire'.

At the same time Britain had a substantial interest in the Mississippi route. The Spaniards were very jealous of any communication that the Americans might make by that river with the inhabitants of the interior. 'To prevent such Communication they now employed English Agents, Subjects of His Majesty and attached to the British Interests, to manage the Indians in the Southern Parts of this Continent, and to supply them with British Manufactures, which are sent out annually from Great Britain by

vessels under the Protection of Passes given by the Spanish Ambassador residing in London.' These goods were paid for with great
quantities of deer skins and other peltry, which were permitted
to be exported from Spanish ports directly to Britain in British
ships. There was also every reason to believe that a very lucrative
commerce was now being carried on from Providence in the
Bahamas and from the Free Ports in Jamaica to the Spanish ports
of East and West Florida with the connivance of the Spanish
Government, 'in order to prevent the people of the United States
from obtaining any Influence over the Indians or having any share
in this Trade'. For these reasons it seemed to the Board that the
navigation of the Mississippi was bound to cause trouble between
Spain and the United States, and the latter could be expected to
support the new settlements in the interior to secure their friendship and gain entry into the Mississippi for American vessels. The
issue of the contest between the two Powers was very uncertain,
and it would be imprudent as yet to pronounce what line of policy
in this regard Britain ought to take; but, the Board opined, American ships were more serious rivals in those waters than were the
Spanish.

In conclusion the report emphasised that the question of Vermont could not be treated in isolation. In a commercial light the
same considerations ought to govern British policy in relation to
the western settlements. Some of these were being sponsored by
the United States, some by Spain, and some had no connexion
with any foreign Power. Britain should establish bonds of friendship and commercial intercourse with them all. There were two
major factors to be considered. On the one hand, there was 'reason
to suppose' that a commercial treaty with the United States would
soon be negotiated. On the other hand, this was a time when
British manufactures were improving and increasing 'in so great
a Degree that it is necessary to seek for new Markets in every part
of the World in order to afford sufficient scope and further
Encouragement to the Industry of His Majesty's Subjects'.[23] Such
was the combined effect of expanding industrialisation and American independence upon British 'imperial' policy.

Less than a fortnight after Grenville had received this report
the Cabinet decided to demand immediate and adequate satisfaction from the Court of Madrid for the 'outrages' committed against
British ships in Nootka Sound and that orders be given for fitting
out a squadron of ships of the line.[24] 'We must not be too sanguine',

---

[23] Stephen Cottrell, joint secretary to the Board of Trade, to Grenville, 17 April,
1790. (*Addit. MSS.*, 38,255, ff. 162-80.) Cf. *B.T. 5/6*, p. 179. Minute of the same
date. Another copy of the Report is in *Pitt Papers* (P.R.O. 30/8/343). It has been
printed (by F. J. Turner) in *Am. Hist. Rev.*, vol. VII, No. 1 (Oct., 1902), pp. 78-86.
[24] Cabinet Minute of 30 April, 1790 (*Grenville Papers, Dropmore*, vol. I, p. 579).

wrote Grenville, 'in our hopes of succeeding without a contest': the exclusion of other European nations from the west coast of North America was for the Spaniards an object of great and almost exaggerated importance.[25] Three days later (6 May) he sent three secret despatches to Dorchester in Quebec. In the first he wrote that it was extremely improbable that Spain would attack the British North American Provinces, but it was to be expected that a war with Spain, and perhaps with France, would encourage the United States to demand the cession of the forts on the Canadian frontier, 'and it is possible that, by holding out to them a prospect of obtaining this favourite Object, the Court of Spain may be able to induce them to take an active part in the War'.[26] The second despatch related to Vermont. Levi Allen was still in London trying without success to obtain a treaty, but war with the United States would obviously alter the situation. One of Allen's requests, wrote Grenville, had been that flour might be added to the list of commodities which could be exported from Vermont into Canada. 'I am strongly inclined to think that, if this concession could be the means of attaching the people of Vermont sincerely to the British Interest, it would under the present circumstances be expedient to make it.' Dorchester, as he well knew, would neglect no proper steps for ensuring 'so considerable an accession of strength as that which we should derive from the friendship of Vermont'.[27]

Grenville's notion of a commercial empire in North America, stretching out towards fur-trading depots on the North-West Coast and down the Mississippi, was as comprehensive in its own way as that of Dundas in the Far East. But it had yet to be recognised that the success of the southern part of the plan would depend upon the maintenance of amicable relations with the United States and that these were unlikely to be promoted by encouraging the western settlements to turn their backs on the American Union. After 1787 it began to be evident that the 'Middle' West would be integrated, territory by territory, with the federal Union: it also came to be realised that the insistent demand for British manufactures in the western zone – as in the eastern States – would not

[25] Grenville to Westmorland, 3 May, 1790. 'Private and Secret.' (*Ibid.*, p. 580.)

[26] Grenville to Dorchester, 6 May, 1790. No. 22. 'Secret' (*C.O. 43/10*).

[27] Grenville to Dorcester, 6 May. No. 23. 'Secret' (*ibid.*). As late as March, 1796, Levi Allen's brother, Ira, wrote to the Duke of Portland, pointing out that his memorial, submitted in January, had received no reply, and he was anxious to return soon to the United States. After repeating the arguments about the convenience of the Lake Champlain route he concluded: ' In case a Canal be opened so that Vessels of one hundred Tuns or more can pass from the Lake Champlain to the River St. Laurence and the Privileges of Navigation granted, as stated in the former Memorial, it would be materially advantageous to both Countries, especially when Great Britain is at war with Foreign Powers.' (Memorial of Ira Allen to the Duke of Portland, 4 March, 1796. *C.O. 42/22*.) In this same year Vermont was at last admitted as a State in its own right into the American Union.

thereby be diminished. That the realisation was not immediate and that British statesmen and merchant groups continued for a while to hanker after free-trade arrangements with independent territories, was not at all surprising in view of the unique character of the political and imperial experiment in which the American people were engaged.

The necessary adjustment in Grenville's mind seems to have begun during the crisis of 1790 when the possibility of renewed war with the thirteen American States underlined the importance of allaying the tension which was becoming dangerous. Fortunately the Americans, who were faced with Indian hostility in the Ohio region and wished to secure shipping concessions from Britain, felt the same need and took the initiative. In his third despatch to Dorchester of 6 May Grenville told him about a tentative approach which had been made by the American Government. President Washington had requested 'Gouverneur' Morris to use the opportunity of a forthcoming visit to London to converse informally with the British Ministers. He was to enquire what objections there might be to handing over the frontier posts in accordance with the terms of the peace settlement and whether they inclined to a trade treaty and, if so, on what conditions.[28] Although, wrote Grenville, Washington's letter had been 'vague and inexplicit', it seemed to indicate a disposition to cultivate a closer connexion with Britain than had subsisted since the separation. It had been necessary in the first instance to use firm language in replying to Morris, but it would certainly be the Ministry's object to establish a greater degree of interest than Britain had hitherto possessed in that Country. Dorchester should send a personal representative (without a formal commission) to the United States for the furtherance of this object and also to give early intimation of any hostile designs against the Western Posts or against Canada itself.[29] Grenville thought that it was by no means impossible to turn the tide of American opinion in Britain's favour if the dispute with Spain resulted in war. The Spanish claim was exclusive against all the world, including the United States. The fur trade of the North-West Coast might become a valuable accessory to the China trade, in which the Americans had already embarked on an extensive scale.[30]

[28] Washington to Morris, 13 Oct., 1789. New York. Morris to the Duke of Leeds, 30 April, 1790. Covent Garden. (Copies in *F.O.* 4/8, pp. 479 and 483.) The conversations of Morris with Pitt and the Duke of Leeds (as reported by Morris to President Washington) are described in S. F. Bemis, *Jay's Treaty: A Study in Commerce and Diplomacy* (New York, 1924), pp. 55-6.

[29] Dorchester complied by sending one of his aides de camp, Lt.-Col. George Beckwith. The latter's reports on his discussions with Alexander Hamilton and other American leaders were forwarded by Dorchester to London. (See Bemis, *op. cit.*, p. 44 *et seq.*)

[30] Bond's reports to the Foreign Secretary contain frequent references to the American trade with Canton for tea and silk.

The object which we might hold out to them, particularly to the Kentucke and other Settlers at the back of the old Colonies, of opening the Navigation of the Mississippi to them, is one at least as important as the possession of the Forts, and perhaps it would not be difficult to shew that the former is much more easily attainable with the assistance of Great Britain against Spain, than the latter is by their joining Spain in offensive operations against this Country.[31]

Others had the same idea. A secret agent reported to the Foreign Secretary that the United States was not yet 'a settled Nation' and in the event of a war between European Powers would observe 'an exact Neutrality', but the people in general would be in Britain's favour. It was to their own interest that they should. 'Take the Floridas', he advised. 'Open a free Navigation of the Mississippi for the Western Inhabitants, and you bind that Country and its inhabitants for Ever in spite of Congress or all the World.'[32] The advice of the British Consuls was more sober. Bond at Philadelphia thought that it would be expedient to attack the Spanish settlements on the Mississippi and that the western (American) settlers would probably co-operate, but he doubted whether the United States Government would concur except 'upon stipulations mutually beneficial'.[33] Miller at Charleston was still more cautious. It was true that the Spaniards had made themselves 'very obnoxious' to the Americans, both as neighbours in the Floridas and in obstructing the passage of the Mississippi, and on some future occasion the United States could be expected to take appropriate action. With regard to East and West Florida he gave a reasoned statement to show why in his judgement their acquisition would not serve the permanent interests of Great Britain.[34]

From Washington's letter it was evident that any negotiations with the United States would centre upon two questions – the cession of the frontier posts in accordance with the peace treaty and the re-admission of American ships into the carrying trade from which they had been excluded since independence. The British Ministers badly wanted to retain the posts. The initial argument that they must be retained until the United States honoured their pledge about Loyalist debts had been valid enough.

---

[31] Grenville to Dorchester, 6 May, 1790. No. 24. 'Secret' (C.O. 43/10).

[32] The agent in question was an American who sent his reports under the name of 'P. Allaire'. His services were terminated in Nov., 1790, as being 'no longer necessary', but Pitt had taken a keen interest in his proposals about East and West Florida, the code name for which was 'southern farms'. 'Mr. Pitt lately expressed himself satisfied with the Correspondence (of Allaire) and directed encouragement to be given for Information relative to what he calls *Southern Farms*, the meaning of which is understood.' (George Aust, of the Foreign Dept., to Sir George Yonge, 20 Nov., 1790, and 16 Feb., 1791. F.O. 4/8, p. 843, and F.O. 4/9, p. 329.)

[33] Bond to Leeds, 3 Jan., 1791 (F.O. 4/9, p. 7).

[34] G. Miller to Leeds, 3 Sept., 1790. Charleston (F.O. 4/8, p. 673).

British insistence on this point in 1782 had angered and embarrassed the American envoys and had come near to bringing the peace negotiations to a deadlock. But since then additional motives had arisen. Shelburne's generosity (or, according to his critics, his criminal carelessness) in demarcating the frontier with Canada led his successors to contemplate the creation of a broad neutral zone south of the Lakes to be an Indian 'reserve'. This arrangement would protect Canada against American encroachment, preserve hunting grounds for Indian tribes who had been under British protection, and incidentally enable Canadian fur-traders to continue to operate in a region from which they might otherwise be excluded. From the American point of view this was completely unacceptable. In the words of Professor Bemis, 'This ambitious stratagem would have cut the very heart out of the future American Middle West. Nowhere would the territory of the United States have reached north of the Ohio River.'[35]

In addition to safeguarding Canadian security and maintaining good relations with the Indian tribes, there was a further inducement to retain the frontier Posts. In July, 1791, Instructions were prepared for George Hammond who was to go as British Minister to the United States to start negotiations. With these Instructions Grenville sent him a covering letter in which he stressed the importance of the Posts as 'the means of commanding the Navigation of the Great Lakes and the communications of the said Lakes with the River St. Laurence'. In order that Hammond should understand Government policy in the matter Grenville provided him with extracts from the Board of Trade's report of 17 April, 1790, which would explain the nature and purpose of Dorchester's regulations 'and the Advantages likely to be derived from the Navigation of these Lakes in the Intercourse between His Majesty's Subjects in Canada and the Settlements which are now forming in the interior parts of the Continent of North America '.[36]

By the time that John Jay, as the United States Minister, was due to arrive in London to resume the negotiations (in 1794), Grenville had made up his mind that the Posts must be surrendered, subject to the two conditions already stated. There were,

---

[35] Bemis, *op. cit.*, p. 109. In referring to the Treaty of Greenville of 1795 between the United States and the western tribes, by which the former acquired most of the present State of Ohio, the same author (p. 263) observes that General Wayne's compaign against the tribes and his ' inexorable ' diplomacy broke the back of the Indian confederacy and opened up the Ohio country for colonisation. From the Indian point of view Wayne's diplomacy might be thought to deserve a harsher appellation.

[36] Endorsed, ' Draft of a Letter to Mr. Hammond.' N.D. (*F.O. 4/10*, p. 319.) At Grenville's request Hawkesbury at the Board of Trade had prepared the preliminary draft of Hammond's Instructions (*ibid.*, pp. 299-314). As the architect of the revised Navigation law, Hawkesbury was determined to concede as little as possible to the Americans, particularly with regard to their shipping. On certain points Grenville modified his draft.

however, significant modifications. In a document entitled, 'Project of Heads of Proposals to be made to Mr. Jay', he stipulated that there should be no interruption of communication and trade between Upper and Lower Canada and the Indian tribes to the south and east of the Lakes, and that British subjects should be free to pass and repass with their merchandise and to hire or possess warehouses 'in all parts of the territory now possessed, or which may here after be possessed by the United States'. The extension of American sovereignty was to be accepted. Similarly, the passage of the waters and the use of the portages and adjoining roads was to be without impediment, and no duties were to be levied. This was amplified in a marginal note: 'and unlimited freedom of inland trade and communication shall be established between the two Canadas and the United States.'[37]

Dorchester's plan, which Grenville had adopted, was still regarded as a *desideratum*. The Canadas were to be a perpetual free-trade corridor through which British manufactures would flow into the regions about the Ohio and the Mississippi in exchange for primary products, but now with the assent and co-operation of the United States Government. The conception was remarkably reminiscent of that entertained by Shelburne twelve years before; but, more logically than Grenville, he had coupled it with some form of 'federal union' between Britain and the American States. In 1794 the idea was clearly impracticable and does not appear to have been pressed.[38] In the 18th century the notion of a 'Common Market' was a very long way over the horizon, and in any case the United States Government was too dependent for its revenue upon import duties to be prepared to contemplate such a self-denying ordinance.

An empire of trade in North America materialised even beyond expectation, although not quite as originally planned. In the south the idea of sending a sea-borne expedition to free the navigation of the Mississippi and expel the Spaniards from East and West Florida was followed by an unexpected turn of events in which British sea-power was indirectly the determining factor. When Louisiana and the Floridas were ceded by Spain to France, Jefferson made his famous declaration (in April, 1802) to the American Minister in Paris that French possession of New Orleans would compel the United States to 'marry' themselves to the British fleet and nation. Such a conjunction, undesirable though it might be,

---

[37] This document, which is among the *Grenville Papers* (*Dropmore*), has been printed by Bemis, *op. cit.*, App. II. It is printed, as in the manuscript, in two columns, the left-hand column consisting of queries and annotations.

[38] The marginal note containing the sentence, 'an unlimited freedom of inland trade . . .', continues: 'See Lord Dorchester's Suggestion to this Effect; but Q(ery) whether this is an object which ought to be brought forward?' This latter part was crossed out.

would enable the two nations to maintain exclusive control over the adjoining ocean. The threat of an Anglo-American alliance which would cut France's sea communication with these new acquisitions was sufficient to induce Napoleon to agree to the sale of a territory which more than doubled the area of the original Union and converted the Mississippi into an American waterway.[39]

In the north the St. Lawrence-Lakes route did not become a great conduit for the flow of British merchandise into the Middle West, although the trading connexion between the Maritime Provinces and New England was close and Montreal imported timber and provisions by way of Lake Champlain. The efforts of the United States Government in 1808 and 1809 to impose an embargo on all trade with the belligerents, Britain and France, gave rise to a flourishing smuggling traffic through Montreal and Quebec and by sea from Halifax in Nova Scotia, and similar activities were renewed in 1812-13.[40] But these were due to temporary and abnormal conditions. According to the Customs returns the value of British manufactures exported to the British North American Provinces amounted (in round figures) to £638,000 in 1783-4. The stated total for the year 1785-6 was £510,000, for 1790-1 – £623,000, for 1792-3 – £908,000, and for 1794-5 – £735,000. Even if the whole of these manufactured articles had been re-exported to the United States, they would have borne a small proportion to the direct export from Britain to Atlantic ports, such as Boston, New York, Philadelphia, Norfolk, and Charleston. British goods so exported were valued at £1,347,000 for the year 1783-4. By 1790-1 the figure had risen to £3,178,000. For 1794-5 it stood at £3,588,000, and in 1801-2 it rose to over £7 million.[41]

The River-Lakes route required large capital investment for the construction of canals, whereas the direct export of British goods (and capital) to the Atlantic seaboard followed long-established channels, maintained by British and American commercial houses which were closely connected and had wide ramifications. British manufactured articles supplied the needs of the rapidly

---

[39] G. S. Graham, *Empire of the North Atlantic: The Maritime Struggle for North America* (Toronto and London, 2nd edn., 1958), pp. 230-1.

[40] *Ibid.*, pp. 242, 252-3.

[41] These figures are extracted from the annual statements made up in the Inspector-General's office and entitled, 'The State of the Navigation, Revenues and Commerce of the British Empire' (*Customs*, 17, ledgers 8, 10, 12 and 22). As previously indicated, these statistics were calculated on the basis of an arbitrary valuation made a century earlier. They are, therefore, useful only for purposes of comparison. The total figure of British exports to B.N.A. in 1783-4 includes £231,000 to Canada and £197,367 to Nova Scotia: that for 1794-5 includes £256,000 to Canada and £95,000 to Nova Scotia. Direct British exports to the U.S.A. dropped in 1808-9 to £3,892,000 in consequence of the embargo measures (*Customs*, 17/30). Calculated on a different basis, the 'declared' value of British exports on an annual average for the years, 1837-42, to the U.S.A. amounted to £6,171,000 and to B.N.A. – £2,551,000 (J. R. McCulloch, *Dictionary of Commerce*, Lond., 1844 edn., p. 691).

increasing population of the eastern States and from that broad base followed the waggon trails over the mountains into Kentucky and the plains of Ohio. Montreal and Quebec found their trading opportunities to the west and north-west of the Lakes. The purchase of British goods in the United States was met, partly by earnings in other branches of overseas trade (particularly in the Caribbean), but increasingly by selling raw cotton to Lancashire. American production rose from about half a million bales in 1824-5 to over two million bales in 1842-3, and Britain bought three-quarters of the crop.[42] The unbalance of Anglo-American trade, which had been chronic in colonial days, disappeared.

In the mid-19th century the trading connexion between Britain and the United States represented what had long been regarded as the ideal form of 'empire'. The former furnished the manufactures, and the latter reciprocated with needed primary products, while British sea-power in the course of its normal routine provided the necessary security. The territorial empire of the British Provinces naturally followed a similar economic pattern. In our own age the wheel has come full circle. The United Kingdom and Canada, as equal members of the Commonwealth, and the United States, are political associates. In the field of commerce British products still hold considerable markets across the Atlantic, but against fierce internal and international competition, while the economy of a highly industrialised United States has grown to such dimensions that its fluctuations exert an influence upon every country in the world which is not subjected to the control of a Marxist empire.

2. THE 'LIBERATION' OF SPANISH-AMERICAN MARKETS

Having considered the sober and effective method developed by Hawkesbury to breach the walls of Spanish monopoly in South America, it remains to trace in that connexion the history of a fantasy, which is as it should be, for there is an element of the fantastical in every generation of men. A more spectacular means of opening the central and southern regions of the Western Hemisphere to English commerce was to promote an American revolution within the borders of the Spanish Empire. Independence, gained with English assistance, would be accompanied by commercial reciprocity on favourable terms, reinforced perhaps by political alliance. A project, pursued for almost two centuries through the realm of fantasy, eventually became a reality; and, although its fulfilment was not due to the intervention of British arms, many of the Spanish-American Republics associated themselves with Britain – for a period – in a close economic entente.

---

[42] McCulloch, p. 433.

The enormous extent of Spain's territorial claims in the New World disturbed the balance of power in Europe itself and excited the jealousy and fear of other European tribes who were following the Iberians across the oceans and staking out claims of their own. At the same time it committed the Spaniards to tasks of government and defence which were always beyond their resources, and these commitments had been rendered the more onerous by the ruthless destruction of indigenous cultures and the hatred of the uncivilised conquered. While Spain was hard put to it to maintain minimal garrisons and a thinly-spread administration, she was continually on the defensive against possible external attack. Sea communication with the metropolis had to be maintained and many thousands of miles of coast defended against the depredations of European rivals. That this was done with a substantial measure of success and for so long was a very considerable achievement.

Perhaps the most important economic feature of the Spanish Empire in America was the existence of rich silver mines in Mexico. This new supply of a precious metal profoundly affected the economy of Europe and to some extent of Asia, but on a long view the least of the beneficiaries was Spain herself. Mexican silver flowed through Madrid to industrial centres in other parts of Europe.[43] Nevertheless Spain had become a giant, and most Elizabethan Englishmen concluded, with Walsingham and Drake, that the only way to avoid subjugation was to isolate Spain as much as possible from the trans-Atlantic source of her wealth and power. Piratical attacks along the sea-routes and destructive raids against key points on the Main offered the additional advantage, when fortune smiled, of being financially profitable.

The more ambitious plan of reducing, and if possible eliminating, Spanish power in America by internal revolution could in theory, take one of two forms. Either the discontent of Spanish settlers against the rigid economic restraints imposed by Madrid could be used to encourage revolts and the establishment of independent Spanish-American states, or, alternatively, the oppressed Indian tribes could be assisted to regain their freedom in return for political alliance and an open door for British trade. The two methods were, of course, mutually incompatible. In general the earlier protagonists relied on a native risorgimento, while the growth of British industrialisation in the later 18th century con-

---

[43] Englishmen thought that Spain's supply of the precious metals was the cause of her neglect of industry, but that was not necessarily true. Very high taxation was certainly an impediment, and the influx of bullion would exert an ' inflationary ' effect. Later in the 18th century China was similarly affected by the inflow of Mexican dollars. Possibly the social structure of Spain and the national temperament were the chief reasons for the lack of interest in mechanical invention which is the *sine qua non* of industrial success. Natural resources at home and from overseas were not lacking.

centrated attention upon the advantages of unrestricted commerce with Spanish colonists. The Englishman who was primarily responsible for the adoption of the former method as an object of national policy was Sir Walter Ralegh. From a perusal of Spanish narratives describing the conquest and exploration of South America he learned that from 1535 onwards a long series of expeditions had been undertaken to discover a lost empire of the Incas which was believed to exist somewhere to the east of the Andes in the vast regions between the Amazon and the Orinoco. Piecing together a number of Indian legends, Spaniards came to believe that Inca princes, fleeing from the conquistadores of Peru, had succeeded in establishing a new empire, protected from Spanish intrusion by mountain ranges and trackless forests. Inevitably its capital, Manoa, was as richly furnished with gold as its Peruvian predecessors. To this legend was added another which was historically true and referred to a religious rite practised at the sacred lake of Guatavita in the uplands of Bogotá, but which had ceased about the year 1480, when that kingdom had been conquered by Peru. At a great annual festival the Prince of Guatavita, having covered himself in gold dust, embarked with his nobles and proceeded to the centre of the lake where precious gifts were dropped into the water as offerings to the god. Then, amid the rejoicings of his people assembled along the lake shore, the Prince himself plunged in to perform a solemn expiatory ablution. Thus the authentic ritual of *el hombre dorado*, the Gilded Man, became attached to the legend of a mythical empire.

The prospect of emulating the feats of Cortéz and Pizarro incited Spanish adventurers to undertake astonishing journeys and to face great hazards and hardships with reckless courage. Gradually the location of Manoa or El Dorado was shifted eastward until it was placed on the shore of 'Lake Parima', which was believed to exist in the interior of Guiana.[44] The last expedition in search of El Dorado took place in 1772. In the course of more than two centuries many thousands had lost their lives in pursuit of a myth.[45]

The Spanish certitude that another Inca Empire had yet to be discovered communicated itself to the imagination of Ralegh. In April, 1595, he arrived at Port of Spain, Trinidad, with four ships and a number of launches for river navigation. The town of S. José was attacked and captured and with it the Spanish explorer, Antonio de Berrio, who had just completed his third and greatest journey from the Pacific coast to the Atlantic in search of Manoa.

---

[44] This 'lake' was eventually proved to be an area of seasonal inundation in the course of the Rupununi, a tributary of the River Essequibo.

[45] An account of the successive Spanish expeditions is given in my edition of Sir Walter Ralegh's *Discoverie of the Empire of Guiana* (Lond., 1928), Intro., pp. xlv-xcv.

Berrio's accounts confirmed Ralegh in his belief that the Orinoco was the gateway to the Empire which the Spaniards were seeking so assiduously. He and his men proceeded in their launches for some distance along the lower reaches of the River, making friends with the local tribes and assuring them that they would soon enjoy the protection of the English Queen against the Spaniards. Having carried out this preliminary reconnaissance, Ralegh sailed home and wrote at speed his famous *Discoverie of Guiana* which was published in 1596. After describing Spanish efforts to discover Manoa and his own experiences, he propounded his plan. It was in the nature of a manifesto to the Queen and the nation. He had gained the friendship of the tribes of the lower Orinoco, whom he termed ' the borderers '. They were joyfully awaiting the coming of the English and would fight as their allies against a powerful kingdom far to the west beyond the mountains which some time ago had overcome them and carried off their women. This kingdom, Ralegh concluded, was undoubtedly Manoa, and its ruler would not fail to appreciate the advantage of accepting English protection as a guarantee against sharing the fate of Mexico and Peru. A garrison of three or four thousand Englishmen would provide security, and the Inca would naturally be willing to pay all the expenses – an argument nicely designed to appeal to Elizabeth and her Lord Treasurer. The Manoan Empire had never been ravished by a European Power, and it was rich in gold and other natural products, and its only means of entry from the ocean was by the Orinoco which could be sealed by two forts at a point where the River became very narrow. With little effort and cost the Queen of England could establish a ' protectorate ' over a country as important as Peru, and with the great advantage that the population would be friends and allies instead of helots. ' After the first or second year I doubt not but to see in London a Contratation house of more receipt for Guiana then there is nowe in Seville for the West Indies.' Thus was born an idea which in varying forms possessed or obsessed the minds of Englishmen until the time of Simón Bolívar and his fellow liberators in the 19th century.[46]

An aggressive edge was given to the scheme by a supporter of Ralegh who was evidently an ardent Puritan. The new emphasis could not be to the taste of the Queen or of Sir Robert Cecil, but it represents the form in which the scheme was afterwards adopted by Oliver Cromwell. All Ralegh's arguments were set forth, and

---

[46] At least four editions of the *Discoverie* were issued in 1596. It was reprinted by Hakluyt and afterwards in 1751 by Birch and by Cayley in 1805. It also attracted wide attention on the Continent. An abridged Latin translation was published in Nuremberg in 1599 and another in the same year at Frankfurt in De Bry's collection of voyages. By 1602 three editions in German had appeared. It was translated into Dutch in 1598 and reprinted in 1605, 1617, 1707, 1727, and 1747. A French translation was included in Coreal's voyages in 1722.

the proposition was then advanced a long stage further. Manoa and all the adjoining countries must be informed of the barbarities practised by the Spaniards and that they held their religion of the Pope, 'the great inchantor or cousner, and troubler of the world, who sent them first to invade those countreys'. These nations must be brought together in a great confederacy against the Spaniards and at the same time be attached to the English cause by certain 'allurements' – 'By presents sente from her Majestie to the Emperor and principall cassiques, by shewing them the commoditicytes of our countryes, by due commending of her Majestie, as that She is a most gratious, mercifull and juste Princess.' Two hundred years later the English sought to commend themselves for comparable purposes to the Emperor of China. But what was entirely characteristic of the earlier period was the condition that the peoples of Guiana must first renounce their idolatry and embrace the Gospel, otherwise it would be doubtful whether the English, being Christians, would be justified from Scripture in joining them in arms against the Spaniard.

The writer was realist enough to state that England lacked the numbers either to conquer or to hold the Manoan Empire. Such a course was neither possible nor needful. In making a compact England must engage to do certain things, which he listed.

1. First that we will defend them, their wives, children and countryes against the Spaniards and all other intruders. 2. Then that we will helpe them to recover their country of Peru. 3. That wee will instructe them in liberall arts of civillity behoosfull for them that thei may be comparable to any christian people. 4. And lastly that we will teach them the use of weapons, how to pitch theyr battells, how to make armor and ordnance. . . .[47]

Elizabeth still ruled when these words were written, but they anticipated the later attitude of the Puritan merchant class towards trade expansion overseas. While a combination of religious and economic motives led to the founding of colonies in North America, other English venturers jostled with the Dutch for the East Indian spice trade and continued the persistent efforts of the Elizabethans to discover an independent route to China. At the same time a series of attempts was made to follow up Ralegh's plan for opening the gates of Guiana. These took the form of establishing settlements along the great stretch of coast between Pará, the western outpost of Portuguese Brazil, and the eastern outposts of the

---

[47] 'Of the Voyage for Guiana' (*Sloane MSS.*, 1133, f. 45 *et seq.*). Printed in Schomburgk's edition of Ralegh's *Guiana* (Hakluyt Soc., Lond., 1848) and in my edition as App. C.

Spanish Main. 'The vast basin of the Amazon, in many respects the most accessible area of the continent, remained unsubdued and virtually unexplored, although its waters would float a sea-going ship from the Atlantic to Peru.'[48] A number of these enterprises disappeared without record, but something is known of colonies on the River Wiapoco or Oyapok – those of Charles Leigh (1604-13) and of Robert Harcourt between 1609 and 1613. The aim was to establish self-supporting settlements to serve as bases from which contact could be made with rich countries in the interior.

The most promising channel of entry appeared to be the Amazon itself, although its estuary was uncomfortably close to the Portuguese outposts. In 1610 Sir Thomas Roe (who afterwards conducted embassies to the court of the Moghul in Delhi, the Sublime Porte, and King Gustavus Adolphus) sailed up the Amazon for three hundred miles and spent over a year in exploring the coast between the Amazon and the Orinoco. From a cautiously worded report which he sent to Robert Cecil, Earl of Salisbury, it seems evident that his intention was, if possible, to give direct effect to Ralegh's design.[49] His reconnaissance was followed by the formation of the Amazon Company and the establishment of settlements near the mouth of the River which survived until 1625, when they were wiped out by the Portuguese.

The renewal of war with Spain after the death of James I and the growing discontent with the policies of his successor revived the latent interest in Spanish America. Like the Puritan who wrote the commentary on Ralegh's project, his successors blended commercial and political ambition in the New World with the desire to extend the Protestant faith. In 1630 a Company was formed which included the Earl of Warwick as chairman, John Pym (Treasurer), John Hampden, Oliver Cromwell, Oliver St. John, Lord Saye and Sele and other Puritan leaders. A patent was obtained for the settlement of Santa Catalina, an island off the coast of Nicaragua, which they renamed Providence. The purpose was two-fold: to found a Puritan theocracy, insulated against Arminianism, and to establish a strategic base for trade, licit and illicit, with the Spanish dominions. Five years later a Spanish expedition suddenly fell upon the English pirate colony on the Island of Tortuga and carried out a wholesale massacre of the inhabitants. The expedition then delivered an assault

---

[48] J. A. Williamson, *English Colonies in Guiana and on the Amazon, 1604-1668* (Oxford, 1923), p. 10.

[49] Printed in Williamson, *op. cit.*, pp. 55-7. In this letter Roe reported that Ferdinand de Berrio (Antonio's son) had been given royal support and was at work in founding a new city up the Orinoco, 'and in pursuing the Conquest of Guiana, which hath long slept, and is now by new and more direct intelligence opened to him'.

against Providence which was beaten off with great courage.[50]

It has been well said that both Warwick and Cromwell looked back to the Elizabethans as godly heroes whose crusade against the Spaniards ought to be revived, and they certainly gave effect to their conviction. In retaliation for the attack on Providence letters of marque were obtained from the King which empowered the Company to undertake reprisals against Spanish goods and shipping. Warwick and his partners thus obtained a privilege of considerable commercial value. Various private merchants made agreements which enabled them to fit out privateering expeditions under Warwick's legal commission, and in return for that privilege the Company received a fifth share in the profits.

Under this arrangement raids were carried out in 1638-40 by Captain William Jackson; and in 1642 the Company itself invested in a larger enterprise, under the same commander, which, as it happened, afterwards exerted an important influence over national policy. In September, 1642, Jackson arrived in Barbados with 'an ample commission' from the Earl of Warwick for warlike operations against the Spaniards. After obtaining additional recruits from Barbados and St. Kitts, he set out to attack the ports and shipping of the Main with six well-armed vessels, a transport ship, and a land force of about 800 men. For more than two years he terrorised the region, capturing the towns of Maracaibo and Truxillo, and by storming the forts of Santiago de la Vega made himself temporarily master of Jamaica. The amount of plunder taken was not great, for as soon as warning was given of the squadron's approach the wretched inhabitants stripped their houses of valuables and fled inland. The Spanish authorities put up as effective a defence as they could with widely dispersed forces. The significance of the expedition lay in the demonstration which it afforded of the military weakness of the Spanish Empire. Jackson concluded his Narrative on that note. The strength of the Spaniards in the West, he wrote, was far inferior to what they themselves pretended. 'The Vaile is now drawne aside and their weakness detected.' Consideration of what a handful of men had been able to accomplish would, he hoped, encourage the English nation to undertake 'some noble designe against ye professed Enemys of our Religion, which will prove not only acceptable to God, but beneficiall to the Commonwealth'.[51]

---

[50] Soon afterwards the rigid theocracy which had been established in the Colony collapsed, and it became a pirate stronghold which the Spaniards eliminated in 1641. From 1637 the Council of the Providence Company became a nucleus round which parliamentary opposition to the King formed and grew. (See A. P. Newton, *The Colonising Activities of the English Puritans.* Yale Historical Publns., Misc. I, 1914.)

[51] 'The Voyages of Captain William Jackson, 1642-45,' ed. Harlow (*Roy. Hist. Soc., Camden Misc.,* vol. XIII, 1923).

In December, 1654, Colonel (later Sir) Thomas Modyford, a leading Barbadian planter, wrote to Protector Cromwell, reminding him of the ease with which Jackson's small force had dominated the Caribbean and how thinly spread he had found the Spanish forces. Cromwell was urged to undertake a full-scale invasion. Using Barbados as a base, the invading force should first secure Trinidad and Cuba as spring-boards for the conquest of the Main. After securing control of the estuary of the Orinoco, the army should proceed westward, with naval coverage, along the coast of what is now Venezuela, conquering and consolidating as it went. The culminating objective of the campaign was to be the capture of Cartagena in order to cut off Peru from all trans-Atlantic communication with Spain.[52] At about the same time an almost identical scheme was submitted to the Protector by Thomas Gage, author of *A New Survey of the West Indies* (1648), who, before coming to England and turning Protestant, had lived for some years as a Dominican priest among the Indians of Nicaragua.[53]

As Lord Protector, Cromwell had no doubts about the line of his foreign policy. When both France and Spain approached the new ruler of England with a view to alliance, the Protector and his Council debated the issue. ' Oliver himself,' wrote Mr. Secretary Thurloe, ' was for a war with Spayne, if satisfaction were not given for the past damages, and things well settled for the future.' Negotiations with the Spanish Ambassador on this basis broke down, and it was thereupon resolved to maintain a good understanding with France on the ground of the former alliance, ' and to send a fleet and land forces into the West Indies '.[54] Modyford's plan was adopted in detail and incorporated in instructions to General Venables.

Such was the origin of Cromwell's ' Western Design ', which was intended to make England a great (and wealthy) territorial Power in South America. To commit his country to an aggressive and expensive foreign policy so soon after an exhausting civil war has sometimes been accounted to Cromwell for personal ambition, but such a judgement misconceives the man and many of his generation. In their view the combined power of Spain and the Papacy in Europe was dangerously enlarged by their exclusive control over South America. If that Continent (or the more important parts

---

[52] *Ibid.*, Intro, pp. xx-xxii. Modyford was a cousin of General Monk, but he had fought for the King in the west of England. He emigrated to Barbados in 1647 where he played an equivocal part as between the Royalist and Parliamentary factions. After the Restoration he proved to be a very able Governor of Jamaica.

[53] Like Jackson and Modyford, Gage asserted that Spanish power in America was so rotten that it would collapse at a touch, ' a Colossus stuffed with clouts '.

[54] ' Mr. (Secretary) Thurloe's account of the negotiations between England, France and Spain from the time of Oliver Cromwell's assuming the government to the restoration, delivered to the lord chancellor, Hyde.' (*Thurloe State Papers,* vol. I, pp. 759-63.)

of it) could be released and its riches thrown open, the prosperity of England and the survival of religious and political Protestantism could be simultaneously assured.

After protracted preparations the armament that was to conquer the Spanish Main and isolate Peru set forth at Christmas-tide, 1654. The fleet was commanded by Admiral Penn and the land forces, which with recruits collected in the West Indies numbered about 9,000 men, by General Venables. An attack on S. Domingo was a disgraceful failure: Jamaica was conquered and retained: but beyond that nothing was achieved. Quarrels between Venables and Penn, the poor quality and indiscipline of the troops, and the ravages of fever were the principal causes of failure. Cromwell signified his angry disappointment by sending the two commanders – for a short while – to the Tower.[55] The myth that the Spanish Empire in America could be broken up by a frontal assault had been exploded. In a later period the same object was pursued with assiduity, but by other methods.

Circumstances after the Restoration were not conducive to grandiose schemes of overseas conquest. Moreover the growth of English colonies and sugar plantations in North America and the Caribbean called for some sort of *modus vivendi* with Spain. By a commercial treaty in 1667 it was provided that Spain was not to interrupt the trade between England and her colonies and vice versa. This concession (for so it was regarded in Madrid) was subject to the condition that England would prevent her subjects from trading with the territories of Spanish America. In 1670 a further treaty was negotiated. The prohibition against trade with each other's colonies was re-affirmed, but the fundamental clash between Spanish and English claims in the New World was evaded by a judicious ambiguity. The treaty was silent about the legitimacy of the methods employed by Spain to repress the English trade with her American possessions. Furthermore, the pretensions of both Powers were set down – in vague terms – and the dichotomy between the two principles was left for future resolution. On the Spanish side it was stipulated that the treaty should in no way derogate from any pre-eminence which either Power possessed in the seas and fresh waters of America, but should retain the same in as ample a manner 'as of right they ought to belong to them'. The English position was likewise reserved: 'it is always to be understood that the freedom of navigation ought by no manner of means to be interrupted, when there is nothing committed contrary to the true sense and meaning of these articles.' But there was

---

[55] For a fully documented account of the expedition see Sir Chas. H. Firth, *The Narrative of General Venables* (Lond., 1900). An account of the assault on Jamaica by a Spanish eye-witness has been translated and edited by Irene A. Wright, 'The English Conquest of Jamaica' (*Camden Misc.*, vol. xiii, 1924).

nothing in the treaty to show that either party recognised the validity of the claims of the other. As the thrust and weight of British commercial penetration into America grew, an ambiguity that had been judicious for the time became the subject of exasperated dispute and bloodshed until the younger Pitt finally forced acceptance of the British position in 1790.[56]

When Louis XIV allowed his grandson, Philip of Anjou, to accept the inheritance of Carlos II and become ruler of Spain, the Netherlands, half Italy and the Spanish-American Empire, he made a bid for the mastery of Europe. Such a concentration of power appeared to the British to threaten their security at home and to jeopardise their position overseas. The possible conjunction of Spanish territorial resources in the New World with French sea-power became a recurrent nightmare until the 'liberation' of Spain herself in the Peninsular War.[57] By way of compensation for recognising Philip as King of Spain and the Indies, Britain received strategic and commercial acquisitions by the Utrecht treaties (1713), which included a limited entry into the markets of Spanish America. This last concession was made in a roundabout way which was productive of a load of trouble for the future. Britain was granted an Asiento or contract for supplying slaves to Spanish America, and under conditions which enabled this traffic to become a channel for the smuggling of British manufactures. The contractors were permitted to send small vessels from time to time to supply the needs of their factors and negroes in Spanish ports. They were also given the right to hold land on the River Plate to accommodate the slaves. 'Since Buenos Aires was in itself an unimportant market for slaves, this provision was meant to enable them to smuggle goods overland into Chile and Peru.'[58] In addition Britain was granted the privilege of sending a ship of 500 tons every year to the fair at Portobello; but since this Annual Ship could be filled up again and again from tenders with fresh cargo under the name of 'refreshments', it operated as a kind of floating Free Port. Foreign goods could be supplied to the Spanish colonies in the regular way through the ports of Spain, where they were transshipped under the names of Spanish merchants, but the direct smuggling trade avoided imposts and restrictions and became increasingly an object of British national policy.

After 1721 the economy of Britain for almost twenty peaceful years was in the capable hands of Sir Robert Walpole. Overseas

---

[56] For an analysis of the treaties of 1667 and 1670 in relation to the subsequent conflicts see R. Pares, *War and Trade in the West Indies, 1739-1763* (Oxford, 1936), pp. 29-38, 42-3.

[57] Until 1733 forebodings about this conjunction were falsified. As Professor Pares has observed, 'Spain was ruled by an Italian Queen, not a French King' (*op. cit.*, p. 13).

[58] *Ibid.*, p. 11.

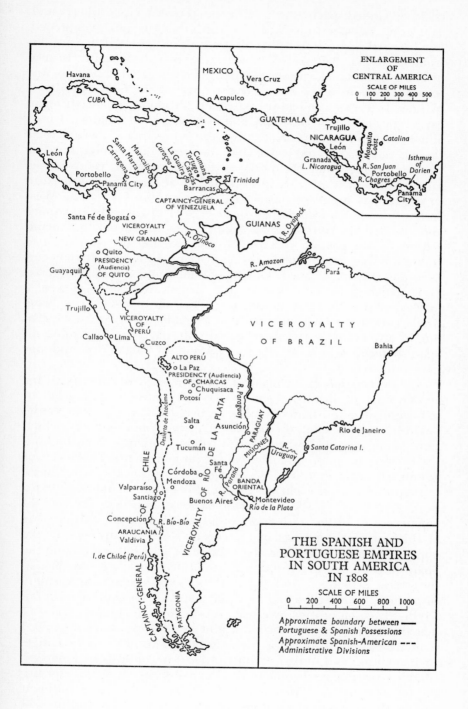

MEXICO
Vera Cruz
Acapulco

GUATEMALA
Trujillo
NICARAGUA
León
Granada
L. Nicaragua
Mosquito Coast
Catalina
R. San Juan
Portobello
R. Chagres
Isthmus of Darien
Panamá City

Havana
CUBA
León
Portobello
Panamá City
Santa Marta
Maracaibo
Cartagena
Curaçoa
La Guaira
Tocuyo
Caracas
Cumaná
Barrancas
Trinidad

Santa Fé de Bogatá
CAPTAINCY-GENERAL OF VENEZUELA
VICEROYALTY OF NEW GRANADA
R. Orinoco
GUIANAS
R. Oyapock

Quito
PRESIDENCY (Audiencia) OF QUITO
R. Amazon
Pará

Guayaquil

Trujillo
VICEROYALTY OF PERÚ

Callao
Lima
Cuzco

V I C E R O Y A L T Y
O F   B R A Z I L
Bahia

ALTO PERÚ
La Paz
PRESIDENCY (Audiencia) OF CHARCAS
Chuquisaca
Potosí

Salta

Desierto de Atacama

Tucumán

R. Paraguay
PARAGUAY
Asunción
MISIONES
R. Uruguay
Rio de Janeiro
Santa Catarina I.

CHILE

Córdoba
Mendoza
Santa Fé
VICEROYALTY OF RÍO DE LA PLATA
R. Paraná
BANDA ORIENTAL

Valparaíso
Santiago
Buenos Aires
Montevideo
Río de la Plata

Concepción
R. Bío-Bío
ARAUCANIA
Valdivia

I. de Chiloé (Perú)

CAPTAINCY-GENERAL

PATAGONIA

THE SPANISH AND PORTUGUESE EMPIRES IN SOUTH AMERICA IN 1808

SCALE OF MILES
0   200   400   600   800   1000

Approximate boundary between ———
Portuguese & Spanish Possessions
Approximate Spanish-American ---
Administrative Divisions

trade expanded, particularly with the Western Hemisphere; and, as it grew, exasperation against Spanish exclusiveness heightened. For her part Spain found that the concessions granted in 1713, far from satisfying, had served to whet the British appetite. Instead of being eliminated, the smuggling traffic increased. The only way to stop it was to make more extensive use of the *Guarda-Costas* – manned by crews who had inherited a tradition of violence from an earlier period when they had fought a plague of English, Dutch and French buccaneers. Not only were smuggling ships and their cargoes seized and confiscated and the crews imprisoned, but fair traders, sailing from the ports of British colonies, received the same treatment if any article suspected of being Spanish-American in origin was found on board. In the autumn of 1737 the West Indian merchants complained to George II of these depredations, and the British Ambassador at Madrid was instructed to demand redress on the ground that the treaties existing between the two countries were being violated. The price of ambiguity in 1667 and 1670 had now to be paid. During the long and involved negotiations which followed, most of the British Ministers showed a marked desire to avoid a rupture. Their failure to do so arose partly from their own ineptitude in the game of diplomatic chess; but in any event a settlement could only have been obtained on Spanish terms which mercantile opinion in England would not have tolerated.

The declaration of war against Spain in 1739 was the signal for an outburst of jingoism, which derived from a combination of self-confidence and frustration. It occurred because a rising trade-potential was pressing against the Spanish colonial barriers, which were being defended by methods involving violent retaliation; and the barriers in question encircled a great continent and the oceans adjoining. From 1739 until Canning's recognition of Latin-American republics in 1824 schemes for the 'liberation' of South America were part of the stock-in-trade of national policy, to be revived whenever a collision with Spain occurred. During the earlier years of this period the project of fomenting a general uprising of the oppressed Indian tribes and the alternative plan of encouraging the Spanish colonists to revolt were muddled together. As British industries developed and external markets became increasingly important, interest was concentrated on a 'colonial' revolution. Civilised communities overseas represented a higher scale of demand than primitive peoples, and as the owners of organised plantations they had more useful products to offer in exchange, such as cotton and indigo. Spanish-American colonists in a mercantile view became analogous to the English-speaking settlers spreading out towards the Mississippi. Early reports of their resentment against the *chapetones* (Spaniards born in Spain, who held most of the official posts) and against the restraints of imperial authority were probably wishful exaggerations; but when the rise of Spanish-American nationalism became unmistakable in the late 18th century, its encouragement was seen as a more promising and profitable enterprise than attempts to establish backward native states.

Walpole and his colleagues were supplied with a variety of paper schemes to disrupt the Spanish Empire.[59] They are of interest because most of the ideas were adopted and attempted by the Ministry. We cannot conquer the Spanish West Indies ourselves, argued one writer, since there are not people enough to hold and colonise them. Plundering and laying waste would not the sooner induce Philip V to grant freedom of navigation in the American seas. Nor was territorial conquest a feasible policy. Many a hearty Briton, he declared, was proclaiming that the capture of Cartagena, if properly followed up, would make us masters of all Spanish America and bring the nation much glory and riches. 'But I believe we shall have more of both if we limit our desires.' The prime object was to secure a 'dominion of trade'. But if we were to force the King of Spain to give us exclusive rights, we would rouse the just envy of our neighbours. Alternatively he might be compelled to open the ports of the Spanish Empire to all nations. If that happened, British manufacturers would have nothing to fear from competitors: we could 'out trade all the world in Spanish America'. But if the King of Spain remained sovereign of the Indies, high imposts would continue, as in old Spain, in order to support the viceroys and all the paraphernalia of the imperial system. The wisest course was to conclude treaties of commerce and alliance with liberated states. 'It well becomes a free people to place others in the same condition with themselves', and by doing so they would gain truer glory than Alexander with all his victories.[60]

Specific plans along these lines included a proposal for an attack

---

[59] The more important of these projects have been summarised by the late Richard Pares, *op. cit.*, chap. III, § i. Prof. Pares, whose premature death was a severe loss to historical scholarship, very kindly allowed me some years ago to work over his selection of photostats from the *Vernon-Wager MSS.* (Library of Congress) in which these papers are included. Most of them are unsigned, and some appear to be departmental memoranda.

[60] Memo. entitled, ' Some thoughts relating to our Conquests in America, 6 June, 1741 '. It is endorsed in Vernon's hand: ' Mr. Step. de Veros ' (possibly Devereux). On commercial policy this writer was ahead of contemporary thought and reflected a robust confidence which became more general some forty years later. ' I am far from thinking ', he added, ' that opening a free trade for all nations to the Spanish dominions would be of any injury to us. For whoever considers the Situation [of Britain] . . . and of our Colonies in America, can never think that we shall be out traded to Spanish America by any nation whatsoever, if we can have but the common discernment not to obstruct our own trade.' (*Vernon-Wager MSS.*, Library of Congress, vol. 14, ff. 46,604-5. Printed in *Am. Hist. Rev.*, vol. IV, No. 3, Jan., 1899, pp. 325-8.)

on Vera Cruz and Mexico. It would not be difficult, this writer maintained, to set up an independent government by playing on the settlers' grievances; and Mexico had the great advantage that Vera Cruz was its only gateway, whereas Spanish colonies on the Main had many such, all of which would have to be secured.[61] The alternative method of establishing independent native states was consistently advocated by Edward Trelawney, the Governor of Jamaica. Influenced by his knowledge of Indian tribes in Nicaragua (along the Mosquito Coast) and in the Panama region, who were on friendly terms with the English and bitterly hostile to the Spaniards, he urged that the discontent of the Creole Spaniards and of the Indians should both be exploited to secure the break-up of the Empire into a congeries of separate states; but in Central America military aid should be given to friendly tribes in order that Britain should gain command of the overland trade routes, particularly in the Isthmus of Panama.[62]

Ministers were impressed by these possibilities, especially Sir Charles Wager, First Lord of the Admiralty. At an early planning stage he prepared a paper in which he listed the expeditions that were being planned and the forces required for each. The expedition against Manila (the focal point for the Spanish shipment of bullion and goods across the Pacific) was to consist of five warships, two or three transports and a thousand soldiers.[63] It was also proposed to send the same number of ships to the South Seas to distress the Spaniards along the Pacific coast, which was scantily defended. 'There is also a probability of persuading the Vice Roy and people of Peru to Revolt from the Spanish Government, and making themselves independent of it, especially if a number of troops can be conveyed thither by way of Panama.' A thousand men (from the Pacific side) was thought to be sufficient, if they were joined by a further thousand who were to do the two days' march across the

---

[61] 'Proposal for an attack on Vera Cruz and Mexico' (1739 or early 1740). Another writer, commenting on this proposal, 'already delivered', stressed the importance of conciliating the settlers by remedying their grievances. It would be to their advantage as well as of Britain if their purchasing power was increased by the encouragement of local industries, as, for example, the production of local wines, which (the writer understood) was forbidden by the Government of Spain (*Ibid.*, vol. 10, ff. 45,962-7).

[62] Trelawney to the Duke of Newcastle, 15 Jan., 1740-1 (*C.O. 137/57*. Quoted by Pares, pp. 74-5). It had been the received opinion, wrote Trelawney, that because of her indolence Spain was the most suitable of all the European Powers to hold the Indies, but the situation had altered now that the influence of France over the Spanish Government (as he mistakenly thought) had become dominant. No European Prince should have the exclusive government of so rich a trading area of the world – it should be in the hands of the natives, who would naturally break into so many independent governments, no one of which could arrogate to itself the commerce of the whole. See also Trelawny to Wager, 29 Aug. and 12 Sept., 1740 (*Vernon-Wager MSS.*, vol. 12, ff. 46,252-5 and 46,236-7).

[63] The expedition against Manila was called off at the instance of Newcastle in order to effect a greater concentration in the West Indies.

Isthmus from Porto Bello or the River Chagres. It was believed that a combined force of that strength could 'easily' take and hold Panama City.[64] With the Isthmus in British hands and communication with Spain across the Atlantic severed, Peru was to be induced to declare itself a separate state.

Popular opinion demanded spectacular victories in the traditional style – the capture of Havana or Cartagena for example; and the fatuous Newcastle, eager for approbation, was only too willing to oblige. The conquest of Cuba and other Spanish sugar islands would also attract the active support of the North American Colonies who needed wider markets in the Caribbean for their growing output of timber and provisions.[65] Accordingly the main weight of the attack in 1740 and again in 1741 was delivered in the West Indies. In the case of Spanish islands and territories on the Main conquest and liberation were curiously combined. Lord Cathcart, who commanded the armament sent in 1740, was given a proclamation to be distributed in all Spanish colonies which were willing to place themselves peaceably under His Majesty's protection. They would be maintained in their lands and other possessions: they would enjoy the full and free exercise of their religion; and they would be freed from the increased imposts and prohibitions of the existing régime. In particular Indians would be exempt from the royal tribute and services to which they had been subjected. The settlers would have the right to trade directly with Britain and the North American Colonies and would in all respects be treated as the natural-born subjects of Britain. In fact, voluntary incorporation in the British Empire.

The design to detach Chile and Peru by operations from a naval base to be established on the Pacific coast and from Panama was set out in the Instructions to Commodore Anson. Both methods of establishing independent states were to be attempted, if the circumstances were favourable. In general terms it was indicated that Chile might become a native state while Peru would be ruled by a Spanish Creole government.[66] It was understood that the Indians of the Chilean coast greatly outnumbered the Spaniards there and might not be averse to co-operate with the expedition against their oppressors. In that event Anson was to cultivate a good understanding with all the tribes who might be willing to join in an attempt against the Spaniards. On the other hand, there was reason to believe from private intelligence that the Spanish settlers in Peru, and particularly those in the region of Lima, were inclined

---

[64] Paper in Sir Charles Wager's hand, 6 Nov., 1739 (*Ibid.*, vol. 9, ff. 45,925-6).

[65] The British West Indian planters, however, feared that increased supplies of sugar and rum in the home market would lower prices and profits. After 1713 their prosperity had declined with the loss of the European market to their more efficient French rivals.

[66] A Creole was not a half-caste, but a pure-blooded Spaniard born overseas.

to revolt against the King of Spain 'in favour of some considerable person among themselves'. If there was any foundation for these reports, Anson should encourage and assist such a design by every possible means. Commercial agreements should be made with any new governments on the most advantageous conditions. They were to be offered (as in the Guiana project of 1596) an alliance, freedom of worship, a naval force and a garrison for their defence, to the cost of which they should make a reasonable contribution. If, on the other hand, they refused to respond, they were to be warned that they would be treated as enemies and that Spain would not be in a position to support them.[67]

The disgraceful failure of Vernon and Wentworth before Cartagena, the delay at Porto Bello which ruined the Panama enterprise, and Anson's capture of the Acapulco galleon and his voyage round the world are well known. In 1742 Britain became involved in the European war over the Austrian succession and was faced three years later by a Jacobite rebellion. Spanish-American ambitions were temporarily laid aside. Anson's conviction that they would be revived when opportunity served and could be brought to fulfilment was emphasised by Richard Walter, who accompanied the expedition as naval chaplain and was given the use of the Commodore's papers in preparing his narrative for publication. The enterprise, he asserted, had failed, not because the plan itself was unsound, but as the result of grossly inefficient preparation. The men drafted as sailors and mariners had been either elderly and infirm, unfit for foreign service, or untrained youths. Repeated delays by the Admiralty in fitting out the expedition had prevented Anson from sailing until eight months after receiving his Instructions. In consequence the squadron had been obliged to make the passage round Cape Horn in the most tempestuous season of the year: the ships had been scattered, and the flagship, *Centurion,* had sailed into the Pacific alone. None the less, Walter insisted, their experiences had proved that a better timed and better organised expedition could certainly achieve what had been intended. A good harbour had been found on the Chilean coast (at Valdivia), which could be held as a naval base without difficulty. The fortifications of Panama were in a decayed condition, and letters between the Viceroy of Peru and other governors, captured in the prizes, had fully confirmed previous reports about unrest and the weakness of the provincial governments. 'Whilst the Creolian Spaniards were thus dissatisfied, it appears by the letters we intercepted, that the Indians, on almost every frontier, were ripe for a revolt, and would have taken up arms upon the slightest encourage-

---

[67] The Instructions for Cathcart and Anson and the proclamations with which they were supplied are quoted in Pares, pp. 75-7. Similar Instructions were issued to (Sir) Charles Knowles for his expedition to La Guaira in 1743.

ment.' If an intact squadron had established itself at Valdivia, it could, by a prudent use of other advantages, have given a violent shock to the authority of Spain, 'and might have rendered some at least of her provinces independent'. This disquisition, he added, might be serviceable to those who would hereafter form a like project or be entrusted with its execution.[68] Premature and unrealistic though it was at that period, the idea retained its hold on the English imagination.

The dissolution of the Spanish Empire, as seen from London, was primarily a commercial objective, to be attempted as and when a war with Spain occurred. In practice, however, Britain found that the prosecution of this enterprise was increasingly governed by her great contest with France, for after 1743 Madrid and Paris remained closely associated. In that partnership Spain gradually sank to a subordinate position, while France sought to establish an overall supremacy both in the home Continent and overseas. A sustained and extended struggle of this sort usually exacerbates other latent disputes, which then merge with the central conflict. Having been challenged in North America, the Caribbean, and the Indian Ocean, Britain launched a counter-offensive which, while it destroyed the power of France in North America, removed a sanction from the British colonists and hastened their collision with metropolitan control. France and Spain sought revenge and recovery from their previous defeat by supporting the American cause. In its turn the independence of the Thirteen Colonies stirred the Protestant minority in Ireland to claim and obtain a form of independence for themselves. The internecine strife of the European peoples on both sides of the Atlantic was then extended and deepened by the shattering of French feudalism and the emergence of a new ideology. In the ensuing conflict between the old and the new the Jacobins became the champions of universal revolution under French hegemony. From the British point of view Jacobin imperialism was a greater menace than that of the Bourbons, and more especially when the former was re-moulded by the masterful hands of Napoleon.

In the midst of this complicated surge and resurge of international rivalry and social revolution the future status of Latin America, political and economic, continued to be an important consideration in British policy; but this particular question had become entangled with the general issue. The ideas of Ralegh, Cromwell and Anson retained their attraction, but the possibility that revolution in the Spanish Empire might open the gates to French Jacobinism and the massacre of Europeans as in the

---

[68] R. Walter, *A Voyage Round the World . . . by George Anson* (Lond., 1748), Chap. XVI. Walter had accompanied the expedition as a naval chaplain. By 1769 this work had run to fourteen editions.

French Islands gave rise to second thoughts and a more cautious attitude. The theory of a nice tidy revolt which would provide moderate and reliable government by a balanced elective system scarcely appeared to fit the Spanish-American facts. From time to time the alternative method of conquest and occupation, followed by a form of British protectorate to guarantee moderation and reliability, was seriously contemplated, but Ministers in general recognised its impracticability.

When Spain revolted against the Napoleonic dictatorship in 1808 and became Britain's ally, the 'liberation' of the Spanish Colonies was perforce set aside. The prime consideration was a united front against Napoleon, and Spanish-American revolutionaries who came to London found that their stock was no longer marketable. British manufactures were finding their way into Latin America in considerable volume through clandestine channels: the achievement of a free flow of British goods and capital into that region with the assent and encouragement of indigenous governments, could not receive forthright British support until the long contest with France had concluded at Waterloo.

Half a century earlier the pursuit of British aims in Latin America had become subordinated to her world-wide contest with France. In the autumn of 1761 the elder Pitt became aware that Spain intended to intervene on the French side. His reaction was to strike first and hard, before the Spanish Government could assemble and deploy its land and sea forces. Her war potential should be weakened by cutting the lines of communication with her overseas territories and more particularly by capturing the fleet which gathered each year at Cartagena and Vera Cruz and then sailed together from Havana, transporting goods and bullion. But the British in general had had enough of heavy war taxation, even though the tide of victory overseas was running strongly in their favour. Apart from Earl Temple none of Pitt's colleagues were ready to support his heroic and expensive proposals. He resigned in disgust and a new Ministry took office under Lord Bute. Spanish hostility left Bute no option but to declare war (4 January, 1762), as Pitt had predicted, but with the difference that Spain had been given several valuable months to prepare. Bute was determined to end the war, but not without regard to the substantial gains already won and the need to establish a strong negotiating position in relation to the new belligerent.[69]

Preparations were at once begun for an expedition against Havana, which commanded the Gulf of Mexico and the direct sea-route linking Tierra Firme and Peru with Seville and Cadiz.

---

[69] Cf. J. Steven Watson, *The Reign of George III, 1760-1815* (Oxford, 1960), pp. 73-5.

Within about a fortnight Bute sought the advice of an expert on
Spanish America. What, he enquired, would be the 'most probable' measures for distressing the Spaniards overseas? The person
in question was one Alexander Wright who had retired to Bath
after residing for many years in Havana and Panama City. During
that time, as he informed Bute, he had made it his business to
collect and record information from Spanish acquaintances who
were intimately acquainted with the various Provinces. Using
these papers of his, he produced a series of very precise and detailed
memoranda, describing the administrative and military organisation, the fortifications of the chief towns and ports, and Spanish
relations with native tribes. Wright was, in fact, a convinced
believer in the feasibility of eliminating Spanish power in South
America. In 1740 he had been in contact with Admiral Vernon at
Porto Bello and had supplied him with information and a chart
of Havana harbour. The methods which he advocated were not,
however, those of Vernon, who had favoured a purely naval war,
but those of Wager and Anson.

In his first communication he advised against direct assault
against Havana, which would be strongly defended, and suggested
as an alternative that a fortified naval base should be established
in an unused harbour to the north of Vera Cruz. From this place
a British fleet could command the Gulf of Mexico, and Spain would
be cut off (on the Atlantic side) from her supply of Mexican silver.
But Wright, not being a politician, had hopes of persuading the
Bute Ministry to undertake a much more ambitious project. In an
elaborate memorandum he analysed the population of Chile and
gave a detailed account of its military defences. The gist of the
argument was that a thinly spread Spanish occupation was opposed
by warlike Indian tribes, occupying extensive areas on both sides
of the Andes, who had never been conquered. A strong military
and naval expedition should be sent to capture the port of Valdivia,
which had the best harbour on the Chilean coast.[70] From this base,
which should be heavily fortified, British naval power would be
able to maintain open access to the South Seas. Like Richard
Walter, the narrator of Anson's voyage, he advocated the establishment of an intermediate naval station and settlement in the Falkland Islands.[71]

---

[70] The recommended naval force was to be considerable – about fourteen ships of
the line, six or eight of which ought to be of sixty to seventy guns, and four man-of-
war sloops. All must have a full complement of seasoned sailors and mariners.

[71] Four years later Commodore John Byron was sent to take formal possession of
the Islands, and in 1766 a settlement was founded at Port Egmont. This enterprise
provoked the Anglo-Spanish crisis of 1770. Then (as in 1790) Spain would have
declared war if her ally, France, had been prepared to support her (see vol. I,
p. 26 et seq.). It was characteristic of the general attitude towards colonisation in
this period that Wright should have recommended that the Islands should be

The interior behind Valdivia was inhabited by free Indian nations with whom the British Commander-in-Chief should at once establish 'a Friendly Correspondence'. Thirty thousand young warriors, most of them expert horsemen, would be available and eager for an opportunity to fight the Spaniards; but it would be sufficient to train and arm three thousand of them as regular troops, led by their own officers. A further five thousand of their best horsemen could be employed as irregular cavalry. With this support a British force of three thousand foot, six hundred dragoons, and a train of siege artillery should march against Concepcion, the second city of Chile and unfortified. The overland army should then attack Santiago, the capital, while a supporting force with cannon and mortars should be shipped from Valdivia to the Bay of Valparaiso on board the transports and some of the men-of-war. 'After the reduction of the Capital the whole Kingdom of Chili must of necessity submit.'[72] When the Spaniards had been disarmed, the government of the Country should be 'adapted to the genius and disposition of the inhabitant'. The principal gain for Britain would be the trade of the Pacific Coast as far north as Acapulco.

Some two months later the same author sent Bute a detailed plan for the reduction of Peru. Using Chile as the base of operations, this further enterprise could easily be accomplished. All would turn on the capture of Lima. In this case less emphasis was laid on an Indian revolt and more upon the hatred of the Creole Spaniards for the Madrid Government and its local officers, who were alleged to treat the colonists like slaves. Whereas in Chile the establishment of some form of British rule was envisaged, it was recognised that the much larger proportion of Spaniards in Peru and its proximity to the Spanish Main would make any attempt to retain possession of it 'very imprudent'.

Peru should immediately be declar'd a Free and independent Kingdom. A man of Spirit and Capacity, of the Ampuero or of some other of the most Ancient and powerful families, chosen King, with the general approbation of the inhabitants: Proper care being taken at the same time that the poor oppress'd Indians may for ever enjoy the same Lawfull Liberty equally in every respect with the Creolian white people.

By this means the Indians would soon recover 'their former

'settled with People that are of no use to Society, such as Debtors, who are at present Confin'd for small Sums . . . with their Wives and Children; all sorts of Strolling Gypsies of both Sexes; condemned Malefactors, and those Abandon'd women who infest the Streets of London and Bristol, etc.' A pretty prospect.

[72] Alex. Wright to Lord Bute, 20 Feb., 1762, enclosing a memorandum entitled, 'A Method proposed for the Entire reduction of the Kingdom of Chili and of obtaining the Dominion of the South Seas' (*North MSS.*, Bodleian Libr., Oxford, b. 6. ff. 59-78ᵛ).

Spirit' and become the strongest safeguard against a reimposition of Spanish sovereignty. The Creole Spaniards would also welcome the change of régime, for they would be relieved of extortionate taxes and would enjoy all the offices, civil, military and ecclesiastical, previously filled by (insolent) nominees from Spain. The King of Peru (who would be of mixed Spanish and Inca descent) would ensure the continued independence of the Country by maintaining a standing army of some 30,000 Indian troops, 'with a well disciplin'd Militia of all the Creolians'. To enable the newly raised army of Indians to be trained, His Britannic Majesty should leave in the Peruvian service a few hundred regular troops, with supernumerary officers, N.C.O.s, and engineers.[73] A biracial partnership on such terms was scarcely in accord with the traditional outlook of the Iberians, who usually rely on retaining their cultural and political dominance by a penetrative process which includes (and indeed postulates) the mingling of their blood with that of the indigenous mass.

These two related projects of 1762 represent a nice exercise in 18th-century imperialism. They afford a fair sample of the strategic planning which periodically attracted Ministers in London when the circumstances appeared to be propitious.[74] They made no appeal, of course, to Bute, who was the last person to contemplate prolonging the war by opening a territorial campaign of continental dimensions. The object of the Ministry with regard to Spain was to deliver the kind of blow that would induce her Government to negotiate a peace settlement quickly. On 6 June Lord Albemarle arrived off Havana with an expeditionary force consisting of twelve ships of the line and twelve thousand troops: the Spanish forts were gradually reduced, and after a resolute defence the Spaniards capitulated on 10 August. The British casualties were slightly less than a thousand men, killed and wounded; but by October more than five thousand had died from sickness. This crippling loss prevented Albemarle from proceeding with an intended attack on Louisiana. On the other side of the world a smaller expedition under Admiral Cornish and General Draper sailed from Madras on 1 August and reached the bay of Manila seven weeks later. Caught unprepared, the Spanish garrison offered only a feeble resistance and surrendered within ten days.

---

[73] The Peruvian project is set out in two letters to Bute, dated 10 and 30 April, 1762 (*ibid.*, ff. 84-90, 94-104). Detailed information about the fortifications of the city and harbour of Havana was supplied in letters, dated 12 May, 2 and 12 June (*ibid.*, ff. 124-145). See also Wright's 'Observations on the Inability of Spain to carry on the war, with Remarks on the several Conquests in America'. 12 June. 1762 (*ibid.*, ff. 150-161ᵛ).

[74] It is curious that the letters and memoranda of Alex. Wright about Spanish America appear among North's papers. Possibly Bute handed them over to the latter in 1780 when North had become involved in Spanish-American schemes which were then thick in the air.

These were notable achievements which effectively isolated Spain from the most valuable parts of her American Empire. Havana commanded the channels between the Gulf of Mexico and the Atlantic, and the capture of Manila (and with it the Philippines) could prevent Spain from receiving silver and other Mexican products by the trans-Pacific route. Two ships of the British fleet lost no time in capturing a treasure ship from Acapulco with a cargo valued at about £700,000. The preliminaries of peace had, however, been signed before the news of the capture of Manila had reached Europe.[75] Spain ceded East and West Florida and received back Havana and all other conquests. Spain had been allowed to extricate herself from the war at far less cost than France, but the successses of Havana and Manila were remembered in Britain as a demonstration of the vulnerability of the Spanish Empire when superior sea-power was used against it.

The belief that the inhabitants of the Spanish Empire were discontented and in favour of revolt was not without warrant, although the picture was not as clear-cut as outside observers tended to assume. From the middle of the 16th century onwards there had been sporadic risings, some of them serious, on the part of warlike Indian tribes who had never been brought under effective control. As late as 1781 Tupac Amaru, one of the last descendants of the Incas, led a formidable revolt in Peru, declaring that the tyranny of the Spaniards had become intolerable. It was ruthlessly suppressed and its leader condemned to a horrible death.[76] The consternation of the authorities arose from their appreciation of the danger that a rising of this kind could spread to the 'civilised' Indians (who lived in villages under the supervision of a Corregidor) and also to the large slave population. This appears to have been the last major effort of the unsubdued Indians, but in the same period the Spanish colonists began to resort to armed insurrection to express their own grievances. The wealthy Creoles – planters and merchants – had long resented the European Spaniards as well as the imperial taxes and monopolies, which (as in Old Spain) were very onerous. In April, 1781, a rebellion took place in certain parts

---

[75] The inhabitants of Manila were allowed by Cornish and Draper to ransom their property for 4 million Spanish dollars. Half of this sum was paid in the form of bills on Madrid, but the Spanish Government refused to honour them. Negotiations about 'the Manila Ransom' dragged on for several years, but Madrid – not unnaturally perhaps – never paid. The operations against Havana and Manila are described in J. W. Fortescue, *A History of the British Army* (Lond., 1910), vol. II, pp. 550-4.

[76] A detailed narrative of this rising, written at Cuzco in the form of a diary and including copies of Tupac Amaru's proclamations, was acquired by Francisco de Miranda, who prepared a condensed version of it for Pitt in 1790. It is unsigned and is endorsed: 'Relative to Tupac Amaro, Inca. Translated and abridged from the Spanish. Intelligence from Cuzco and Lima. 6 April, 1781' (*Pitt Papers*, P.R.O. 30/8/345).

of the vice-royalty of New Granada. The insurgents were well-armed and led. The aim was not a break-away from the Spanish Crown but reform of the fiscal system. The local authorities eventually accepted the rebels' demands; but when the promises were not fully honoured, there was fresh trouble which led to the execution of the ringleaders. In the late 1790s conspiracies and revolts became widespread, but these were of a different character. The imperial State and the Church took fright at the spread of French revolutionary ideas and strove to insulate the mainland territories from them. The discontent of the colonists, encountering rigid resistance, deepened, while events in North America and then in Europe enhanced their self-confidence and ambition. The object now was to eliminate the authority of the Spanish Crown and establish independent republics – to be ruled by the Creoles.

These changing circumstances naturally affected British policy. The beginning of serious unrest in the Spanish territories coincided with the opening of a new phase in the contest between Britain and the Bourbon Powers. Encouraged by Burgoyne's surrender at Saratoga, France and then Spain recognised the independence of the Thirteen Colonies and declared war. This intervention in pursuit of revenge and a reversal of the British triumph of 1763 exacerbated public anger in England, already roused over the colonial issue, and caused an immediate revival of plans for a counter-blow against the Empire of Spain. There was, however, an important practical difference between the accepted policy (in any Anglo-Spanish war) of isolating Spain from the resources of South America and the more far-reaching plan of initiating revolution. As insurrections multiplied and Spanish-American conspirators began to appear, pleading for British aid, Ministers in London became increasingly drawn towards them. The general attitude on the question was expressed by Governor Thomas Pownall, who had foretold the course of events in North America.[77] In 1780 he published a memorial in which he stated the opinion that South America was becoming too much for Spain to manage. As soon as a suitable opportunity was afforded there would be a revolution, but unlike the revolt in the British Colonies it would be led by some enterprising genius who would capture the prevailing sense of alienation and establish a great trans-Atlantic monarchy.[78] The right kind of revolution, in fact.

As soon as Spain entered the war in 1779 Germain and North gave orders for attacks on the Spanish dominions. The Governor

---

[77] In his famous work, *The Administration of the Colonies* (Lond., Pt. I, 1764, Pt. II, 1774).

[78] T. Pownall, *A Memorial, Most Humbly Addressed to the Sovereigns of Europe, on the Present State of Affairs, between the Old and New World* (Lond., 1780).

of Jamaica, General Dalling, was instructed to assist General (Sir) Archibald Campbell, if he could, in an attack from West Florida on New Orleans: he was also to supply the Mosquito Indians with arms and ammunition and encourage them to harass the Spanish settlements in Nicaragua. It was not Britain's policy, Germain explained, to make conquests or establish colonies in Spanish America, but to deprive Spain of the most profitable branches of her commerce.[79] Dalling eagerly interpreted this latter instruction in grandiose terms. An expedition was to sail to the Mosquito coast, capture the fort of S. Juan on the river of that name, and then cross Lake Nicaragua to seize Granada and Leon, thus cutting off Mexico and the other northern territories from communication with the Spanish dominions to the south.

The military contingent which Dalling could spare was fantastically inadequate for the purpose; but, as it happened, the naval convoy which Admiral Sir Peter Parker provided (H.M.S. *Hinchingbroke*) was commanded by Capt. Horatio Nelson. His instructions were confined to escorting the transports to the mouth of the river, but when Nelson found that the troops were entirely ignorant of the terrain, he manned the river-craft with his own sailors and personally led the attack on the fort of S. Juan. The garrison promptly fled, but the expedition then fell into the hands of climate and disease. In fever-stricken swamps, infested by mosquitoes and other pests the men were destroyed like flies: Nelson himself very nearly died of dysentery and after a long illness in Jamaica was invalided home (September, 1780).

Undeterred, Dalling sought Germain's approval for a still more ambitious project for intervention in Mexico. A detailed scheme was forwarded to London which had been submitted to Dalling by a Swiss officer, named Cardinaux. It was said to be the outcome of many conferences held (in Europe) by a group of Mexican leaders. A general rising in Mexico was to be organised to coincide with the arrival of a British expeditionary force. When independence had been won, Mexico was to become a republic under British protection, enjoying its own constitution and the free exercise of the Roman Catholic faith. In return Britain would be granted the exclusive monopoly of the import trade.[80]

Even before Dalling's proposals reached London, North and Germain had been playing with the idea of large-scale intervention in Spanish America. In 1779 (Sir) John Coxe Hippisley, an agent of the British Government in Italy, put forward a plan for a Mexican revolt which had been suggested to him by exiled Jesuit

---

[79] Germain to Dalling, 17 June, 1779 (*C.O. 136/16*).

[80] Dalling to Germain, 26 March, 1780, enclosing a letter from F. L. Cardinaux, dated 26 Feb., 1780, and a memorandum by the latter, entitled ' Observations on the Facilitating a General Revolt in the Empire of Mexico ' (*C.O. 136/19*).

fathers, and on his return North had held several discussions with him.[81] In the same year one Robert White of Hampstead sent Germain a comprehensive plan for promoting revolution in the Spanish dominions, which, he was informed, had been 'well received' by His Majesty's Ministers.[82] That Germain should have adopted Dalling's project, as he seems to have done, is some measure of his unfitness to be Secretary of State for the American Department and of the general disorderliness of the North Administration. William Knox, the Under-Secretary in that Department, afterwards asserted that Germain had promoted the enterprise with vigour and hinted that it had been prevented by the intrigues of guilty men.[83] There is some evidence to support the view that the Cabinet approved plans for an assault on the Pacific coast of Spanish America, based on India, and some preliminary preparations appear to have been made there by Colonel William Fullarton; but the resources available to Warren Hastings and Admiral Hughes were too fully extended in dealing with the French for such extraneous adventures to be practicable. Nothing further had been done when North thankfully resigned and Shelburne began his peace negotiations.[84]

The new Minister worked for the kind of settlement which would lead on to a commercial partnership between Britain and the United States and a reciprocity treaty with France. Had he

[81] Hippisley served in Italy 1778-80 and 1792-6, created baronet 1796, employed by the East India Company 1786-9. M.P. for Sodbury 1790-6 and 1802-19.

[82] Even Germain, however, pointed out that the objects were 'vast' and that it was not practicable to employ so large a force in that part of the world. In October, 1790, the persistent White sent a copy of his plan to Sir Archibald Campbell, who forwarded it to Pitt with the comment that it was a general outline of 'extensive operations', but that hints could be drawn from it 'of Publick use', especially with regard to the methods to be employed 'to inspire the Natives against their present Masters and of freeing them from the Oppressions of the Spanish Monarchy'. (Campbell to Pitt, 26 Oct., 1790, enclosing White to Campbell, 25 Oct. *Pitt Papers*, P.R.O. 30/8/120.)

[83] Just before sending his own book to press (in 1789) Knox read the second volume of Sir John Dalrymple's *Memoirs of Great Britain and Ireland*, in which the author had reproduced a plan for an attack on the Pacific coast of South America which had been presented to Germain. In a postscript Knox hastened to the defence of his late chief. 'Lest it might be supposed from that publication that it was not properly attended to, I will take upon me to assure Sir John and the public, that whoever can obtain leave to read over his Lordship's secret correspondence with Governor Dalling at Jamaica, and Governor Robertson at New York, will find sufficient information to satisfy him, that the object of that plan was so far from being treated with neglect, that it was comprehended in one of *much greater extent*' (Knox's italics). Dalling, he added, had thought so highly of the scheme and had been so confident of its success that he had applied to be appointed the King of England's first Viceroy of Peru and Mexico. 'How it happened to fail will, I hope, become one day the object of Parliamentary enquiry' (Knox. *Extra Official State Papers*, Lond., 1789, Pt. II, pp. 62-3).

[84] W. S. Robertson (*ut infra*, pp. 199-200), citing documents in *Memoirs and Correspondence of Visct. Castlereagh* (Lond., 1848-53), vol. VII, pp. 261, 263-5, 268, 269.

x*

remained in office a similar agreement with Spain – and other European Powers – would have been attempted. The encouragement of revolution in the Spanish Empire was not a preoccupation of British Ministers in time of peace and would have been particularly inappropriate if Shelburne's ideas on international trade had been accepted. Yet when the peace negotiations were imperilled by the sweeping demands of Spain, Shelburne himself for a passing moment was prepared to use the traditional weapon against her, being well aware of her weakness in South America.[85]

Richard Oswald, the envoy whom Shelburne sent to Paris in April, 1782, was an unsophisticated soul, who viewed Britain's prospects with excessive gloom. In the previous year he had put forward a plan to destroy the Bourbon Compact and permanently reduce the power of Spain by means of an Anglo-Russian alliance. The inducement to be held out to the Court of St. Petersburg was the offer of a free hand in the Pacific (at Spain's expense) while Britain established a strategic hold over the Gulf of Mexico. The British Ambassador should explain that Britain intended to establish a barrier on the shores of Lake Nicaragua by way of the River S. Juan – despite the previous failure there – and should persuade the Czarina Catherine to send a force of some 5,000 men from Kamchatka to occupy California and from that base to conquer Mexico and Peru. Thenceforward Britain and Russia would share a common interest against Spain.

The proposition was not quite so fanciful as it seemed. Britain had already made efforts to secure a Russian alliance: for some time Russian explorers had been active in the northern Pacific and Russian fur-traders were beginning to arouse Spanish alarm by pushing southward along the Alaska coast. In his despair over Britain's situation Oswald had evolved a novel variant of a traditional plan. It had become traditional, in one form or another, because there was a continuing fear that the combined weight of France and Spain might prove too much for the more limited resources of Britain and also a confident belief that the menacing association could and must be broken – at the weakest link.

On arrival in Paris Oswald turned at once to his favourite notion. Spain, he informed Benjamin Franklin, was likely to prove the chief obstruction to a settlement, but if she was unreasonable, there were means to hand of bringing her to reason, and he proceeded to outline his Russian plan.[86] Towards the end of June, when the extent of French and Spanish claims were known, he produced for Shelburne's benefit a revised (and dreadfully prolix)

---

[85] See vol. I, pp. 338-9.
[86] See R. A. Humphreys, 'Richard Oswald's Plan for an English and Russian Attack on Spanish America, 1781-82.' (*Hispanic Am. Hist. Rev.*, vol. XVIII, No. 1, Feb., 1938, pp. 95-101.)

version of it. As before, the British Ambassador was to point out the prevailing discontent in the Spanish dominions and the weakness of their defences, and that a Russian expedition from Kamchatka would have no difficulty in starting a movement by which Russia would acquire the mastery of a vast and rich country. As a further inducement it was now suggested that the transport ships could be escorted by a British naval squadron and be financed by a British loan. Even if the two Powers were not prepared, argued Oswald, to undertake the enterprise at that particular juncture, the mere news that they were preparing to co-operate in this way would cause such alarm that Spain would be forced to abate her demands. Once the principle of co-operation in this sphere had been established, the long-term advantage would accrue when the next crisis in European affairs arose. Russia in the Pacific would emerge as a great maritime Power; Spain would be correspondingly reduced; and France would find the naval balance of power tilted against her. The Anglo-Russian alliance would become a permanent factor, for the Russians would need the aid of British sea-power to maintain their trade routes between the Mexican Gulf and the Baltic.[87]

The probability that Spanish intransigence would wreck the entire peace settlement unless special pressure was brought to bear, weighed so heavily with Shelburne that – as a forlorn hope, no doubt – he instructed the Foreign Secretary, Grantham, to put Oswald's proposal to Sir James Harris at St. Petersburg.[88] Harris's response was a polite but decisive negative.

> The Hint Your Lordship suggests to me of tempting Her Imperial Majesty with a prospect of Possessions in Spanish America is a very important one. I shall not lose sight of it . . . At this moment nothing can find a way to the Empress's Ear that does not bear an immediate reference to the Troubles in the Crimea.[89]

---

[87] Oswald set out his plan in three documents (comprising sixty closely written pages): 'Minutes relative to the Situation of England in the present War' (written 26 June-1 July), 'Summary of Objections and Queries regarding the Contents of these Papers' (3 July), and 'Supplement to the Preceding Papers' (5 July). (*Shelburne MSS.* (W. L. Clements Library, Ann Arbor, Michigan) 72/27, ff. 121-89 and 72/28, ff. 181-203. Copies, which I have used, are in the Stevens transcript from the Shelburne papers, British Museum.) The three documents were sent to London on 12 July.

[88] Grantham wrote as follows: 'As I am persuaded that nothing would be more agreeable to the Empress, than an Extension of Her Empire, it had occurred to me to suggest to You a Hint which You may perhaps be able to employ with Advantage. Several Plans have been offered for Expeditions to Spanish South America. Might not her Impl. Majesty be tempted to acquire Possessions of this Kind, which we know are a favourite object of her Ambition? The Assistance she might give on this Occasion would be liberally rewarded in a Participation of the Advantages to be obtained.' (Grantham to Harris, 27 July, 1782. *F.O.* 65/7.)

[89] Harris to Grantham, 16-27 Aug., 1782 (*ibid.*). In a previous despatch he had warned Grantham that there was no hope of forming 'anything like a Connection' with the Czarina (Harris to Grantham, 9-10 Aug., 1782. *Ibid.*). When Professor

When the war was ended and Pitt, with the King's support, had ousted Fox and North, schemes concerning Spanish America were naturally laid aside. George III and the nation looked to the young Prime Minister to provide political stability and economic recovery in the course of a long period of profound peace. The ten years of uneasy non-belligerency which followed 1783 did indeed witness a spectacular recovery and a commercial expansion of impressive extent. Had it been less, the strain of the long conflict with French revolutionary nationalism would probably have proved insupportable. Yet this expansion was of its very nature provocative. The development of manufacturing techniques, reinforced by an efficient credit system and sea skills, accelerated the growth of an empire of oceanic commerce, which, being basically non-territorial, observed no formal limits. Such a challenge could scarcely have failed to cause a new resort to arms on the part of France (and Spain), even if Louis XVI had died quietly in his bed.

Meanwhile a succession of Spanish-American conspirators began to turn up in London, seeking support for revolution. Many of them appear to have been men of straw, mere self-seeking adventurers, and they could scarcely have chosen a more inappropriate time for 'selling' their proposals. Direct representations from Spanish colonists were, however, a new development. Requests for assistance from people who asserted that their own native provinces were ripe for revolt were not without effect at a later stage. One of these was a mysterious character known as Don Juan Antonio de Prado, who according to the Spanish authorities was actually a Frenchman resident in Peru. In 1782 he and a group of malcontents had worked out a plan by which a British force of 6,000 troops and a naval squadron were first to attack Buenos Aires and then proceed to effect the overthrow of the Spanish Government in Peru in conjunction with a local rising. When 'Don Juan' arrived in England the war was over. He and his English supporter, Edmund Bott, thereupon reduced the project to an unofficial filibustering expedition which the British Government could disavow if unsuccessful. One spark, however, would suffice to start a general conflagration. For Britain the inducement was to be a treaty guaranteeing an exclusive trade with South America for ten years. The plan was pressed upon the Pitt

Humphreys wrote his short article on Oswald's scheme (*loc. cit.*), he was not aware that the proposal had been referred to St. Petersburg. Oswald himself thought that it was an outside chance that the Czarina would rise to the bait. In response to a query whether it was likely, he wrote: 'Perhaps not in the present female Reign and considering all the circumstances relative to that Empire.' But the mere rumour that Russia was thinking of joining Britain in an attack on the Spanish dominions would suffice for the present purpose. A firm Anglo-Russian alliance with its numerous advantages could develop later.

Administration during the autumn and spring of 1783-4, but of course without result.[90]

In May, 1784, a further project was presented to the Ministry by Don Luis Vidal, representing two Creole generals of the Spanish army in New Granada. Their requests were more modest, although the objective was equally ambitious. They asked that supplies of arms and ammunition should be shipped under Dutch colours through the Island of Curaçao. They would be paid for on delivery in gold. A group of English officers and engineers should be taught the Spanish language and then sent out to New Granada, where an Indian rising would have ensured that the fire was well lit. The example of New Granada would be quickly followed in the provinces of Maracaibo, Sta. Marta, Cartagena and Lima.[91]

In the summer of 1786 Francisco de Mendiola arrived in England with a letter addressed to George III and signed by three notables, who claimed to represent the city and kingdom of Mexico. The oppressions of the Court of Madrid, it was stated, had reduced the people of Mexico to the condition of slaves so that they were now constrained to throw off the yoke by armed rebellion. These writers declared that they possessed sufficient treasure to equip a force of 40,000 men and requested that military stores should be supplied to them in Jamaica, for which they pledged themselves to pay two million piastres. Mendiola was empowered to conclude a treaty of amity and commerce with England: trade with liberated Mexico would prove immensely lucrative.[92] According to the Spanish Ambassador in London, Don Bernardo del Campo, Mendiola was interviewed by Pitt and 'various persons of character'. Indeed, this procession to London of potential revolutionaries was watched with a vigilant eye by Campo, who faithfully reported their movements to Florida Blanca in Madrid.[93]

The Spanish authorities were even more concerned about an able young man, named Francisco de Miranda, who made his first appearance in London in February, 1785. He was to become a thorn in their side for many years and for a time exerted a considerable influence in British South American policy. He was the

---

[90] The project was set out by Bott in three memoranda, dated 6 and 21 Dec., 1783, and 7 April, 1784 (*Pitt Papers*, P.R.O. 30/8/345). Cf. W. S. Robertson, *Francisco de Miranda and the Revolutionizing of Spanish America* (Annual Rept. of the Am. Hist. Assocn. for 1907, Washington, 1908, vol. I, Pt. XII, pp. 203-6).

[91] A proposal for a revolution in New Granada, presented to the British Government by Luis Vidal (or Vidalle). London, 12 May, 1784. 'Authentic Copy' (*Pitt Papers,* 345). Printed in Robertson (*loc. cit.*), pp. 513-14.

[92] A proposal for a revolution in Mexico, presented to the British Government in 1786 by Francisco de Mendiola, Mexico, 10 Nov., 1785. (*Pitt Papers*, 345. Printed in Robertson, p. 512.)

[93] Numerous letters between Campo and Florida Blanca concerning the various Spanish-American conspirators who visited London are cited from the Spanish archives by Robertson, Chap. I.

son of a wealthy Creole merchant of Caracas, and as a subaltern in the army he seems to have developed an early resentment against metropolitan Spaniards, which was not allayed when his Government indicted him for illegal practices while arranging an exchange of prisoners in Jamaica.[94] Thereafter he became entirely possessed by the idea of creating a United States of South America, extending from the upper Mississippi to Cape Horn, and enjoying a status not less than that of the United States of the north. He became the dedicated revolutionary for whom life had no other meaning, and perhaps for that reason his inclination towards intrigue became habitual. Shrewd statesmen, such as Jefferson and Hamilton in the United States, received him with interest and reserve. He was the founder of the first Republic of Venezuela, an enterprise in which he was assisted by the youthful Simon Bolivar. In a desperate effort to save the Republic from being overthrown by the royalist opposition he made himself a dictator, was betrayed by some of his supporters and died in misery in a Spanish prison.

The appearance in London of a young Creole, fresh from talks with leaders in the United States, who spoke with passionate eloquence about colonial liberty and supported his arguments with charts and documents, seems to have intrigued polite society. According to the watchful Campo he made contact with a number of prominent personalities, but there is no indication that he attempted to approach the Government.[95] After a stay of six months he undertook an extensive tour of the Continent, which included parts of the Turkish Empire. In each capital city he was pursued by alerted ambassadors of Spain who tried to get possession of his person and papers; but the Czarina Catherine took him under her

---

[94] During his stay in Jamaica in 1781 he supplied Governor Dalling with valuable information about the fortifications of Havana, furnished his own Government with even more valuable information about the fortifications of Jamaica and the disposition of British ships and troops, and engaged in lucrative contraband trade. (The most detailed and reliable study of Miranda's career is by W. S. Robertson, loc. cit.)

[95] In response to an enquiry from Hawkesbury in Dec., 1787, Mr. Thos. Hood replied that Miranda had not yet returned to England, but that he would let Hawkesbury know as soon as he did. Hood was an enthusiast for South American independence and praised Miranda in glowing terms. He hoped that the Ministry would always keep the project in mind, for in a war with Spain it could be accomplished with a small force. 'All this would effect a Great Revolution and open the Ports of Mexico and Peru to the Commerce of Great Britain, which would be attended with more real advantage than that of Conquest or Collonising.' Hood claimed that it was he who had persuaded North to withdraw troops from North America when failure was becoming obvious and to order Governor Dalling to send them on an expedition against Leon on Lake Nicaragua in co-operation with the Mosquito Indians. That attempt had failed, he added, because Dalling and the troops employed knew nothing of the locality or its inhabitants. Afterwards Dalling's secretary, Barry, had collected some very interesting material and had worked out a plan for the invasion of Mexico, a copy of which Hood had sent to Shelburne. (Hood to Hawkesbury, 11 Dec., 1787. Liverpool Papers, Addit. MSS., 38,222, ff. 176-7.)

protection, and thereafter he was secure from arrest. When he finally returned to London in June, 1789, the cause of Spanish-American independence had not been appreciably advanced, but its protagonist had equipped himself with a wide knowledge of European affairs. On 21 January, 1790, news reached Whitehall of the seizure of English ships in Nootka Sound. Three weeks later, when the Spanish Ambassador presented a note demanding the punishment of the interlopers and claiming the region as part of the Spanish domain of California, it became evident that Pitt had decided to take up the challenge. Unrestricted access to the South Pacific and freedom to develop a trade between North America and China had become objects of national policy. It seemed to Miranda that the opportunity for which he had been waiting had come at last.

The first approach to the Prime Minister was made on his behalf by Thomas Pownall, a friend and supporter, who obtained an interview and explained the 'Grand Plan', as it was called.[96] On 14 February Miranda met Pitt by appointment at Hollwood, when 'a very long conference' took place. As then requested, he prepared a full account of the Spanish territories in America, their products, population, military resources, and so forth, which was delivered three weeks later. Nothing further seems to have transpired until 6 May, that is to say, two days after the note had been sent to Madrid declaring that the Spanish reply of 20 April was totally inadmissible. On that evening Pitt summoned him to a meeting in Whitehall, where he was introduced to Grenville, and another lengthy discussion took place. Miranda was questioned about the readiness of the inhabitants of Spanish America to co-operate with the British, and the Ministers were assured that the general mass of the people could be relied on if they were satisfied on the delicate points of their religion and future independence. Thereafter (according to Miranda) 'various interviews' took place at Pitt's house in Downing Street. Meanwhile Alleyne Fitzherbert was negotiating in Madrid and preparations were going forward for a large naval and military armament.

In the course of these discussions Miranda presented a draft constitution for a federation of all Spanish America. It was elaborate and in some important respects artificial.[97] The northern

---

[96] Pownall had published a pamphlet, advocating Spanish-American independence, ten years earlier (see p. 637 above).

[97] The Head of State was to be hereditary and styled Emperor of Inca. The central legislature was to be bicameral, the upper chamber to be a fixed number of life-members, chosen by the Inca from among those who had held high office, and the 'chamber of communes' to be elected by all the citizens voting as one electorate and to hold office for five years. Federal judges were to be chosen by the Inca and to hold office for life unless deprived for misbehaviour. Provisions for amending the constitution were similar to those of the U.S.A. The relationship between the federal and provincial governments and the structure of local government were

boundary of this vast state was to be a straight line, the parallel of 45° North latitude, drawn from the source of the Mississippi to the Pacific coast. The islands situated within 10° of the western coast were to be included, as well as Cuba on the Atlantic side. The inclusion of the latter was justified on the ground that Havana was the 'key to the Gulf of Mexico'. But the other Spanish islands of the Caribbean and South Atlantic were excluded and were apparently to be retained by Britain for strategic purposes. The vast continent, it was declared, ought to be sufficient for a purely territorial and agricultural power.

Pitt's actions during the summer of 1790 show that he was sufficiently impressed by the proposition to be ready to commit large forces for its attainment. Evidence of serious unrest in the Spanish Colonies was being received from various quarters, and even if British landings did not prove to be the signal for a general rebellion, the threatened damage to Spain's economy could be decisive.[98] As for Miranda he was evidently to be employed but kept in leading-strings. Pitt refused his repeated requests for funds (until after the crisis was over), and the planning of the military operations was carried on without reference to him.[99]

The officer entrusted with this task was General Sir Archibald Campbell, who had recently come home from India, where he had

---

ignored. (*Project de Constitution pour les Colonies hispano-américaines. Pitt Papers,* P.R.O. 30/8/345.) In the same bundle (345) there is a draft proclamation, dated 3 Aug., 1790, to be issued to the inhabitants on the landing of an expeditionary force. The outline of an interim government was provided, which was to consist of a Governor (who must be a native nobleman) and a supreme Council, and was authorised to make a treaty of 'federal' alliance and commerce with Britain as well as treaties with all powers recognising Spanish-American independence. In preparing the constitution and the proclamation Miranda may have been assisted by Pownall, who had outlined similar ideas in his own pamphlet.

[98] See for example, Auckland to Pitt, 29 June, 1790. The Hague. 'It is believed that there are serious troubles in South America; but that circumstance seems to afford the strongest reason for avoiding a quarrel with England' (*Auckland Papers, Addit. MSS.,* 35,542).

[99] In a letter to Pitt, written in Sept., 1791, Miranda recounted his successive interviews with him during the summer of 1790, acknowledged that he had received £500 from Pitt's secretary in July, 1791, with a promise of further provision, and pressed for a pension (which he quite sincerely described as a loan) of £1,200 p.a. (Miranda to Pitt, 8 Sept., 1791. *Pitt Papers,* P.R.O. 30/8/345. Printed in *Am. Hist. Rev.,* vol. VII, No. 4 (July, 1902), pp. 711-15). Pitt replied, refusing the pension, and stating that the £500 must suffice for expenses during his visit to England (Pitt to Miranda, 12 Sept., 1791. *Ibid.,* bdle. 102). A year later Pitt wrote to Grenville: 'The 500 l. about which you enquire was for Miranda, and Smith (Pitt's secretary) has his receipt, which I have mentioned this morning to Burges.' (Pitt to Grenville, 7 Sept., 1792. *Grenville Corr. (Dropmore),* vol. II, p. 310.) For later financial arrangements with Miranda see p. 656 n. 115 below. In 1799 Miranda stated that a solemn undertaking had been given to him in 1790 that the project would be carried out if there was war with Spain, *et uniquement pour leur indépendance absolue, comme l'avoient obtenu les Etats Unis de L'Amérique; ce qui fut ponctuellement exécuté, et réunir à Mr. Pitt par le Soussigné le 5 Mars, 1790.* (Miranda to Pitt, 19 March, 1799 (Copy). *Pickering MSS., Mass. Hist. Soc. Libr.,* vol. XXIV, f. 150. Quoted in Robertson (*loc. cit.*), p. 272, note C.)

been Governor of Madras for three years. During the two previous wars he had seen much service in North America and Jamaica. Advice and information were sought by Pitt, Grenville and Campbell from many quarters. One of their consultants, Colonel William Dalrymple, who had served under Campbell in Jamaica as adjutant-general, was a strong advocate of an attack on Louisiana; but Campbell very sensibly turned down a further proposal of his for an overland invasion of Mexico from New Orleans. The march of an army through twelve hundred miles of unknown savannah and forest and among hostile tribes, he wrote to Pitt, might be attended with 'the most fatal consequences'. Another consultant was a naval officer, named Home Riggs Popham, who achieved notoriety sixteen years later at Buenos Aires. He was asked to recommend the most appropriate places along the Pacific coast for the establishment of naval and military bases.

Out of such consultations emerged a plan for a multiple assault on the Spanish Empire. From the Atlantic side Campbell, it seems, was to lead the major attack against Mexico, which was to be cut off from the south by a holding operation in Guatemala. A subsidiary expedition against Louisiana was contemplated which (it was hoped) would attract support from the new American settlements and free the navigation of the Mississippi.[100] On the Pacific side the intention was to mount the assault from India, using British and Indian troops seasoned to a hot climate, to be reinforced later by warships and troops proceeding from England by way of Cape Horn. After the capture of Manila (the first and necessary objective) bases were to be established on the coast of Mexico, and perhaps of Chile and Peru, as springboards for advances inland.[101] A very similar and equally ambitious pattern was adopted in 1804 and again in 1807.

If Spain in 1790 had refused to give way, in spite of the absence of French support, she would have exposed her overseas trade and a discontented Empire to Britain's undivided attention. That

---

[100] In fact the projected expedition against Louisiana would almost certainly have been abandoned. As already noted, Grenville at this time was anxious to resolve, if possible, Anglo-American differences, and he had been informed by Col. Beckwith, Dorchester's agent in the United States, that Alexander Hamilton and his colleagues were showing a lively concern over Spanish obstructiveness on the lower Mississippi, but had expressed their aversion to the reappearance of Britain as an 'imperial factor' in that region (see documents in *Report on Canadian Archives, 1890*, ed. Brymner (Ottawa, 1891), pp. xxvii-xxviii, 160-61).

[101] See letters of Dalrymple to Pitt, dated 10, 12, and 16 May, 1790 (*Pitt Papers*, P.R.O. 30/8/128): Campbell to Pitt 26 and 28 Oct. and his memo. of 28 Oct. giving reasons against the proposed invasion of Mexico from New Orleans (*ibid.*, bdle. 120): 'Note sur la Chili', endorsed: 'From Mr. de la Rochette, 23 Aug., 1790' (*F.O. 95/1*). In his letter to Pitt of 26 Oct. Campbell wrote: 'I have perused the papers sent me by Mr. Grenville regarding the Bay of Honduras, as well as the Plan of Major Despard for an attack upon Guatimala. Whenever it may be most convenient for you, I shall have the honour of waiting upon you.'

would have been a novel situation, for Britain's main concern in these oceanic wars had been with France. Operations against Spain had been subsidiary, usually designed to reduce her contribution to France's war potential. The special circumstances in 1790 gave Pitt good grounds for expecting that the Spanish Government would feel obliged to abate its claims of commercial monopoly, and he hoped (as the Instructions to Fitzherbert showed) that thereafter an Anglo-Spanish *rapprochement* might be effected. If not, the preponderance of the Franco-Spanish *bloc* could be eliminated by detaching the Spanish Colonies and diverting the flow of their trade (by virtue of industrial superiority) to London. Either way the object was to rectify an adverse situation in the Old World by making fresh arrangements in the New.

Whether the appearance of British armies of liberation in the Gulf of Mexico, at Acapulco and Valparaiso would have been the signal for a general rising of the inhabitants, or whether they would have resisted alien intruders, as at Buenos Aires in 1806, it is, of course, impossible to estimate. On the whole it seems likely that the invading heretics would have become beleaguered garrisons, calling on the Navy to evacuate them, instead of victorious columns, welcomed – and fed – by Spanish settlers and Indian tribes. Yet Home Popham at his trial in 1807 was able to declare (and call Dundas to witness) that Spanish-American independence had been 'a favourite object' with Pitt throughout his career as a war minister. His appreciation of the potential power of colonial nationalism was sound enough, but the method was premature. The Colonies in North America had organised a representative Congress, raised an army of their own, and won the battle of Saratoga before France and Spain ventured to intervene.

During the long war with France British policy towards South America was determined by the fluctuating relations between Paris and Madrid. At the outset Britain and Spain were nominal allies, members of a European coalition against the French Jacobins. In 1795 Spain withdrew from the war and in August, 1796, made a defensive and offensive alliance with the Directory. In the following October she declared war on Britain. The Court of Madrid had concluded that imperial interests and claims, economic and strategic, would be best served by swinging back to the side of the French, militantly democratic as their old associates had become. Once more Britain was faced by the combined sea-power of France, Spain and Holland. In the perilous days that followed one might have expected adventures in Spanish America to be struck off the agenda. Ambitious plans, as contemplated in 1790, were certainly set aside and all proposals for their revival were for the time being firmly rejected. But the proposition itself was not discarded.

There were two good reasons for this, or at any rate reasons which seemed good at the time. There was, of course, the strategic incentive. As the scene in Europe darkened almost to desperation, the encouragement of revolution in the Spanish Empire held obvious attractions as a diversionary blow. France for a while entertained a similar calculation with regard to discontented Ireland. The complementary incentive was commercial. When Napoleon struck at the British position in India, he was attacking the nexus of all the British trade routes in the Indian Ocean and the China Seas. The loss of these trades would have entailed economic collapse. His tightening grip upon Europe, culminating in the formal exclusion of British trade by the Berlin Decrees, came closer to success. In spite of the breaches that were driven into the Continental System, British warehouses were filled with unsold goods. A generation of industrialists and merchants who had experienced a phenomenal expansion of markets in the Far East and in Europe became increasingly alarmed. The old desire for unrestricted access to the markets of South America, for which the Free Port system had afforded an appetiser, assumed a fresh urgency, and the government of the day was expected to show energy and initiative in either forcing the doors from without or employing suasion within.[102]

How ingrained this expectation had become was exemplified when Spain in 1786 again aligned herself with France. In that year Nicholas Vansittart (a younger son of Henry Vansittart), who became Secretary of the Treasury under Addington and afterwards Chancellor of the Exchequer, drafted a plan for the invasion of Spanish America from the Pacific side. Previous expeditions had failed because they had been based on the West Indies and directed against Tierra Firme, which were unhealthy regions, whereas the Spanish territories bordering the Pacific Ocean enjoyed a healthy temperate climate and could be invaded with 'greater ease'. A naval squadron should sail from England (in 1797) with a few regiments of infantry and a detachment of artillery on board to occupy Buenos Aires, and then, after rounding Cape Horn, to seize Valdivia, Valparaiso and Concepcion on the coast of Chile. Meanwhile a force of 13,000 Indian troops was to be drafted from the battalions at Madras and Bombay and assembled at Trincomali – now in British hands. When the army had joined up with the British expedition, Peru was to be invaded and afterwards Mexico.[103]

---

[102] See Grenville's remark some years later on this pressure from commercial interests (p. 654 below).

[103] Robertson (*loc. cit.*), pp. 310-11, citing *Bexley MSS., Misc. Papers, 1796-1844,* f. 1 *et seq.* Nicholas Vansittart became a strong supporter of Miranda. He was Secretary of the Treasury, 1801-4 and 1806-7, Chief Secretary for Ireland, 1805, Chancellor of the Exchequer, 1812-23. Created Baron Bexley, 1823.

The year of the naval mutiny at the Nore, of an attempted French invasion of Ireland and an incipient Irish rebellion, was scarcely an opportune time for invading a continent across the Pacific; and yet the very gravity of the British situation led a colonial governor to press for a similar, though more limited, attack on the Atlantic side. The occupation of the Cape of Good Hope in 1795 had anticipated the French and safeguarded the sea-route to India and China: it also afforded a naval and military base within easy sail of Buenos Aires, the thriving commercial centre of the region which was to become the Republic of Argentina. Between 1796 and 1798 Governor Robert Brooke of St. Helena addressed a series of letters to Lord Macartney at the Cape, urging him to organise a joint expedition against the Spanish settlements on the Rio de la Plata. A naval squadron could be sent from the Cape during the 'blowing season' of the north-east monsoon with eight or nine hundred men from the garrisons there, while he himself could furnish some three hundred, including artificers and a train of light artillery, from St. Helena.

If Monte Video could be taken and retained, the consequences, I humbly suppose, would inevitably be, that all communication from Spain to this great division of South America would be cut off and an immediate opening for all our Manufactures into the interior of the Country, and would naturally have every effect that could be wished in the present critical situation in which Great Britain is placed.[104]

Such a stroke, urged Brooke, would weaken the resources of the enemy and help divert Napoleon from invading Britain, and it would raise morale at home. A purely defensive war would never bring the enemy to terms.[105] If the attack failed or did not produce the important results that were anticipated, the expedition could quickly return to its bases. Macartney expressed approval in general terms, but, of course, took no action: his duty was to hold the Gibraltar of the Indian Ocean. In September, 1797, Brooke sent his

---

[104] Brooke to Macartney, May, 1797, enclosing 'Ideas respecting the eligibility of making an immediate attack on the Spanish Settlements on the River Plate, with Plan, etc., annexed'. Letters in similar vein were sent to Macartney, dated 25 Oct., 1796, 2 April, 1797, 19 Sept., 1797, and 4 April, 1798. (*Macartney MSS.* in the possession of Messrs. Francis Edwards, Ltd., of Marylebone High St., London, who very courteously allowed me to make copies.)

[105] 'Considering that it is impossible to crush the Enemy, or reduce them to the Necessity of making Peace meerly by carrying on a defensive War, something surely should be attempted abroad, if possible as Brilliant as unlooked for, opening new hopes to the Speculative turn of our monied People, Manufacturers, &c. And certainly the obtaining Possession of Monte Video, the Key to so many Rich and extensive Provinces, might not only Effect all these purposes . . . but cast a Material Damp upon the Exertions of the Allies of France or at least effectually divert their attention from England' (Brooke to Macartney, 2 April, 1797. *Ibid.*).

papers on the project to Dundas, but (as he observed to Macartney) affairs at home were 'in such a shocking situation' that he was afraid that little could be attended to for the time being beyond 'the immediate salvation of the state'.[106]

In fact Dundas himself had already moved in the matter of Spanish America. One of his principal objects as Secretary of State for War was to reduce the war potential of France and Spain by mastering their possessions in the Caribbean: a costly line of policy for which he has been much criticised. The capture of the Island of Trinidad in February, 1797, represented the acquisition of an important strategic base on the door-step of Venezuela. In April Dundas instructed the military Governor, Colonel (Sir) Thomas Picton, to encourage the inhabitants to continue their previous contacts with the Spanish Main and to announce that Trinidad had been declared a Free Port and would thus become an emporium with direct trade to Britain. Picton was to conduct himself in a manner best adapted to effect the liberation of the adjacent regions from an oppressive and tyrannical system which so rigorously imposed a 'monopoly of commerce under the title of exclusive registers'; and he was to assure the Spanish colonists that whenever they were disposed to resist their Government, they could rely on assistance from Trinidad, either in the form of troops or arms and ammunition. They were to be further assured that the intentions of His Britannic Majesty did not extend beyond securing their independence, 'without pretending to any sovereignty over their Country'. There would be no interference with the rights of the people, either political, civil or religious. Picton set out these promises in a proclamation which was widely distributed along the Main. In supplementary Instructions of 5 July he was required to collect information about the civil, military and commercial conditions in the neighbouring Spanish colonies and the disposition of the inhabitants.[107]

Picton responded with enthusiasm and in particular urged upon Dundas the commercial importance of the Spanish settlements along the Orinoco. S. Tomé de Guayana or Barrancas was eminently suitable for an *entrepôt*, and the river was navigable for 150 miles. His presentation of commercial strategy resembled that of Sir Walter Ralegh in 1595. But he warned Dundas that any idea of conquest would be 'Chimerical and Ruinous'. There was

---

[106] Letter of 19 Sept., 1797 (*Ibid.*).

[107] Draft Instructions to Picton of April and July, 1797. *C.O. 295/1.* Cf. Robertson (*loc. cit.*), pp. 313-15. In 1802 Picton became involved in a fierce dispute with William Fullarton, a fellow Commissioner in Trinidad, who accused him of cruel practices under Spanish law which authorised the use of torture. He resigned, faced an indeterminate trial at home, and rendered distinguished service on numerous occasions during the Peninsular War. Promoted Lieut.-General in 1813, killed at Waterloo.

general discontent but the inhabitants were looking forward to independence. It would not be difficult to subvert the Spanish Government in the Provinces of Cumaná and Caracas, and this example 'would shake their Empire over the whole Continent and would open immediate as well as immense Commercial Advantages to Great Britain'.[108]

It is evident that Pitt and his colleagues were now convinced that the Spanish Empire was moving quickly towards a revolution which Spain would be unable to suppress. All reports reaching London confirmed that view – which was natural enough since they emanated, directly or indirectly, from a discontented minority. The movement did not become dynamic until after 1815, but the belief in London that the eruption was imminent made it necessary for Ministers to handle the South American question as an urgent war problem. It perplexed them greatly. To intervene, or to await the event, were alike dangerous. Under constrictive pressure from France the traditional aim of turning South America into a huge British market and source of supply was seen, not so much as an expansionist ambition, but rather as a means of salvation. Furthermore there was a lively fear that, unless Britain seized the initiative, Buonaparte would convert the southern continent into a French dependency in all but name. On the other hand, if Britain intervened, the Latin Americans might respond by sending nobility and bourgeoisie to the guillotine. The bringing of a New World into existence could easily become a disaster. On many counts a revolution was a consummation to be wished, but somehow it must be guided and controlled. These considerations may account for the Ministry's persistence in retaining the services of Miranda, even though Pitt and Grenville distrusted his plausible tongue. Here was a conspirator to hand who was very much a monarchical republican, more enthusiastic for liberty than equality.

Miranda returned to London in January, 1798, after a seven years' sojourn in France. He came, apparently with the British Government's knowledge and approval, and complete with cloak and dagger. On the day of his arrival he submitted a document to Pitt which was supposed to emanate from a junta of deputies in Paris representing revolutionary organisations in most of the Spanish-American Provinces. Miranda proposed a defensive alliance between Britain, the United States and Spanish America. In return for intervention on a massive scale an independent Spanish America would accord special commercial privileges to the two English-speaking Powers. Liberty would thus be vindicated against 'the detestable maxims' avowed by the French Republic. The

---

[108] Picton to Dundas, 18 Sept. and 17 Dec., 1797 (*C.O. 295/1*).

draft treaty left certain matters, such as boundaries and the future possession of the Spanish-American islands, open for negotiation – first with Britain and then with the Government of the United States. All arrangements, military and political, were to be entrusted to Miranda.[109]

The Ministry considered the proposition, turned it down for the time being, but decided to keep Miranda in England. Their hesitation and the reasons for it are clearly indicated in Grenville's communications with the U.S. Minister in London, Rufus King. He informed King (on 1 February) that he distrusted Miranda and doubted the wisdom of taking immediate action. A revolution could not be long delayed, but the terrible scenes in France had instilled a fear in his mind that they might be repeated on the American Continent if Miranda's plan were put into operation at that moment. A fortnight later the U.S. Minister was told that the Cabinet had decided not to intervene, provided that Spain proved her ability to maintain her own independence and prevent a revolution in her government; but if there was a real danger of Spain falling under French control, they would endeavour to prevent France from acquiring the resources of Spanish America. In that event they would immediately open conversations on the subject with the United States. 'At present they deemed it impolitic to engage in the plan of Miranda.'

In the following year (1799) Dundas caused the question to be reconsidered. On 30 September he received a letter from Miranda suggesting a conference and enclosing a number of documents which had come to him from Caracas through Governor Picton of Trinidad. Dundas, as always, believed in a forward policy. Having (very wisely) prevailed upon his colleagues to strike at Napoleon in Egypt, he now argued that they should not lose the initiative in South America. In a memorandum of 3 October he asked the Cabinet to consider Miranda's letter and its enclosures, which stressed the danger of the Spanish Empire becoming a Colony of France. No one, he wrote, would wish to see any part of the world set adrift at the present time in a revolution, but there was a danger that the desire of the United States for new markets might induce that Government to promote insurrection in Spanish America. The Cabinet ought to consider whether to allow the movement there to take its course or to what extent Britain should participate in order to prevent the mischief of an 'immense empire' plunging into revolution 'without guidance or control'.

William Windham, Secretary for War, gave qualified support. He agreed that Britain ought not to remain inactive, but dreaded the outcome of a revolution, whether engineered by Miranda, whom

---

[109] Miranda to Pitt with enclosure, 16 Jan., 1798. P.R.O. 30/8/345.

he greatly distrusted, or by the United States, in whose alleged intentions he placed no confidence. Since Spain was in great danger of losing her Empire, might she not be prepared to accept Britain as a mediator? A form of self-government might be worked out which would satisfy colonial aspirations, while preserving some degree of authority in Madrid, and the new constitution for Spanish America could be safeguarded by a British Guarantee. The dangers of revolution would be avoided, and Spain would be drawn into association with Britain and away from France. In proposing mediation of this sort, Windham was, in fact, anticipating an approach to the problem which Canning attempted some twenty years later.

The Foreign Secretary, Grenville, took a similar line. As before, he stressed the danger of encouraging revolutionary sentiment in another continent and now strongly opposed any participation in the projects either of Miranda or of the United States. Britain should intervene only if there was a clear and certain 'propect of good'. Pitt's own views on this occasion are not recorded, but he evidently leaned towards the caution of Grenville rather than the more venturesome ideas of Dundas. Miranda – glib and tortuous in method but violently sincere in his object – had to possess himself with such patience as he could muster.[110]

During the next five years or so the Government of the day would neither commit themselves to the enterprise nor let it alone. Again and again they were drawn to it as a means of delivering a diversionary blow against the imperialism of Napoleon, while meeting the fears and ambitions of British manufacturers. They as frequently retreated from it because they had no means of knowing whether an initiatory intervention would, in fact, spark off a revolution from Mexico to Patagonia (as Miranda confidently asserted), whether such a movement could be relied on to observe moderation and produce stability, or whether Britain in attempting to control it would become entangled in the internal affairs of a country three times as large as India. Would a British victory in Mexico or Peru be attended by consequences comparable with those which had flowed from the battle of Plassey? While he was Prime Minister, Lord Grenville wrote: 'I always felt great reluctance to the embarking in South American projects, because I knew it was much easier to get into them than out again.'[111] And yet a month later he committed the Government to a multiple invasion of that Continent and was himself actively engaged in planning it. Risky as the operation might be, the Spanish-American Vice-royalties must be rescued from French (or Spanish)

---

[110] See his letter to General Bourdon, quoted Robertson, p. 344.

[111] Grenville to the Earl of Lauderdale. Private. 22 Sept., 1806 (*Grenville Papers, Dropmore*, vol. VIII, p. 352).

monopoly and opened by a treaty relationship to British trade.[112]

When Pitt resigned office in March, 1801, over Catholic Emancipation, the Addington Ministry faithfully followed the war policy of their predecessors – including the South American project. In May they considered a plan for the liberation of Tierra Firme, submitted by Miranda, which was to be started in his native province of Caracas. In June instructions were sent to Governor Picton of Trinidad to take every opportunity of gathering information about 'the real state' of the adjacent Spanish Colonies, so that if England decided to intervene at some future time, she would be able to do so with 'a reasonable chance of success'.[113] As on previous occasions Picton's report was encouraging: the inhabitants were ready to throw off the rule of Spain, and the defences were weak. In September the Cabinet took the whole matter into consideration. The ensuing debate revealed the familar division of opinion. The Home Secretary, Lord Pelham, wanted to know more about the principles of those with whom Britain would be associated: the enterprise would require a force of 12,000 men and, if successful, might well reduce Spain to still greater dependence upon France. Was it not better policy to support the independence of *Old* Spain, securing participation in the trade of New Spain in recompense?[114] Spain rightly suspected and feared the expansionist aims of Britain, as their continuous vigilance about Miranda and his fellow conspirators and the frequent warnings to the South American Governments showed; and even if she could have been drawn (at that stage) to the British side, the prospect of a grateful Court of Madrid throwing open the doors of their Empire was so remote as to be invisible. In the mind of Pelham, and of many others, fear of revolution outmatched commercial gain. Yet eventually it was the latter consideration which prevailed.

Instead of fitting out an armament, the Ministry commissioned a single ship which was to transport Miranda to Caracas; and a London contractor, Alexander Davison, was instructed to purchase a supply of 'necessary articles' (presumably uniforms and arms) on Government account, and this he duly did. Miranda's sanguine expectations were to be put to the test, but without the support of a British expedition. Shortly afterwards Napoleon offered to treat: peace negotiations began in October; and preliminaries were

---

[112] Two years earlier Home Popham had quoted Grenville as having observed to Rufus King, the U.S. Minister in London, that the independence of South America was 'essential' to the future of Great Britain (Memo. of Capt. Home Popham, 14 Oct., 1804. *Pitt Papers*, P.R.O. 30/8/345. Printed in *Am. Hist. Rev.*, vol. VI, No. 3 (April, 1901), pp. 509-17).

[113] Draft of Instructions to Picton, 29 June, 1801 (*C.O.* 295/2).

[114] *Castlereagh Correspondence*, vol. VII, pp. 287-8. Cf. Robertson (*loc cit.*, pp. 350-2).

signed in the following March. Miranda's ship was countermanded: the supplies were warehoused, and Miranda himself was consoled with a pension, or – as Popham put it – 'a fair and honourable means of subsistence'.[115] The revolutionary leader from Venezuela was being kept warm.[116]

In May, 1803, Napoleonic aggression and Britain's retaliatory retention of Malta brought a renewal of the war. Faced by a massive concentration of French troops and landing craft along the Brittany coast, the British people responded by organising a 'Home Guard' of 347,000 volunteers to reinforce the regular army of 120,000 and the militia, which numbered 78,000. In the autumn of that year Pitt was recalled by popular acclaim to reassume the national leadership. The threat of invasion became more imminent in 1804 when Napoleon decided to strengthen his arm with the resources of Spain. Under pressure Carlos IV opted to supply Spanish-American treasure rather than an auxiliary fleet. On his side Pitt warned Madrid that hostilities might be opened at any moment unless Spain ceased to give underhand assistance to France. On 5 October a squadron under Capt. (Sir) Graham Moore[117] attacked and captured the annual *flota*, including three treasure ships, on its way to Cadiz. This was done without a declaration of war, and Spain became Napoleon's open ally.

This swift (and illegal) blow was an indication of the importance that was attached to preventing Napoleon from exploiting Spanish-American resources. It was naturally followed up by renewed consideration of plans for attaining this end as a permanency.[118] Capt.

---

[115] In 1804, when Pitt's second Ministry was again considering the Spanish-American question, Davison informed Dundas (Lord Melville) that during the late Administration 'I had secret Orders to provide a variety of Articles for South America, and at one period, so bent was Government on sending out General Miranda without loss of time, that I received an Order to purchase a Store Ship, which however was countermanded before I concluded the bargain; and so secret has this transaction been kept, that not a syllable has transpired'. Dundas ought to know that the articles in question were still in store, 'in case there should be any sudden call for these things'. (Davison to Melville, 21 Sept., 1804. *Pitt Papers*, P.R.O. 30/8/128.) It is possible that a naval vessel with Miranda and a small contingent of troops on board would have accompanied the store ship, but the rumour which both Rufus King, the U.S. Minister in London, and the Spanish Government believed, that a powerful expedition was ready to sail when the preliminaries of peace were signed in Oct., 1801, seems to have been unfounded. Davison's statement is supported by Popham, who afterwards stated that a ship had been named to carry Miranda to Spanish America, that a supply of necessary articles had been obtained, but that 'at that moment' the peace settlement had brought the enterprise to a halt (Popham's Memo. of 14 Oct., 1804).

[116] In spite of war conditions the Addington Administration responded to merchant pressure by passing legislation in 1802 which freed British ships from the obligation to obtain a permit from the East India Company before proceeding to the South Seas and thus to the Pacific coasts of America (*42 Geo. III, cap. 77*).

[117] Brother of General Sir John Moore.

[118] On 27 July, 1804, Thos. Picton, who had resigned his post in Trinidad and was now in England, had reminded the Government of his numerous reports on

Home Popham, an enthusiast for intervention, had already been consulted on the subject by the Addington Administration. At that time he had proposed that Miranda's favourite plan of a descent upon the Spanish Main should be combined with a separate assaut on the Río de la Plata.[119] By obtaining control of the Isthmus of Darien the former would go a long way towards depriving Spain and France of their supply of Mexican silver, while Buenos Aires and Monte Video were becoming the most important South American market for the products of British industry. When Addington resigned, Popham sent all the relevant papers to Dundas (now Lord Melville), who, as before, was deeply interested. The two discussed the matter by correspondence, and then early in October (1804) when open war with Spain seemed probable, Popham was invited to attend a conference at Melville's house in Wimbledon. Probably because of Pitt's mistrust of Miranda, Popham was requested to make a thorough enquiry into his antecedents. He was also to consult him and then submit a comprehensive scheme.

On 4 October Popham reported strongly in favour of Miranda's reliability and submitted a plan of campaign which incorporated Miranda's ideas with his own. It is of interest because it resembles the plan which was worked out in detail in 1807 by Sir Arthur Wellesley and which the Grenville Ministry adopted and was prepared to implement. The idea of conquering South America, wrote Popham, was totally out of the question, but the possibility of securing all the strategic points so as to detach it from its present European connexions, of retaining possession of certain military positions, and of 'enjoying all its commercial advantages', could be reduced to a fair calculation, if not a certain operation. There should be three co-ordinated assaults. First, Trinidad should be the rendezvous for operations on Tierra Firme. A preliminary attack on Caracas (where Miranda was sure he could raise 20,000 recruits) was to be followed by an advance through Santa Fé and Quito to the Isthmus of Darien, which would be held with the support of a naval force from Jamaica. Secondly, an expedition of 3,000 men should be sent out from England to capture Buenos Aires. That done, the danger of warnings being sent overland to the Pacific coast would be eliminated and warships could then be sent without detection round the Horn to dominate the coast of Chile from Valparaiso. But this would be ancillary to the third operation which

the situation in the Colonies of the Spanish Main. If hostilities were to break out with Spain, 'a fair opportunity' would be presented of starting a movement in that region which might 'eventually deprive her of all her Continental Colonies' (quoted, Robertson, p. 355).

[119] See *Minutes of Capt. Sir Home Popham's Court Martial, 6th to 11th March, 1807* (2nd edn., Lond., 1807), p. 77 (cited hereinafter as Popham's *Trial*). Printed in *American Historical Review*, VI, p. 512.

should be mounted in India, comprising 4,000 sepoys and a small contingent of Europeans. The first objective of the Indian expedition was to be Panama, which would become the base for further operations southward towards Lima. The new sources, wrote Popham, which would thus be opened for British manufactures and navigation from Europe to Tierra Firme and from Asia to the Pacific coast were 'equally incalculable'.[120] Shortly afterwards he was sent for by Pitt who wished to go through the memorandum with him.[121]

More important in the long run than the ideas of Spanish revolutionaries, adventurous naval officers, and West Indian governors were the needs and aims of the industrialists. These were put before Pitt at this time in the form of an elaborate dissertation by William Jacob, F.R.S., an economist and a London merchant who had traded for some years to South America.[122] After an introductory survey of the topography, population and trade of the several provinces, he expounded the commercial point of view. 'The intention of Great Britain in establishing a connexion with South America would be rather with view to the Solid Benefits of Commercial Intercourse, than the mere Achievement of unproductive Conquest.' If she professed to conquer and reduce the inhabitants to the conditions of British Colonists, 'promising, as in Canada, to preserve their Civil and Religious Customs', only a small number would respond. Were it, on the other hand, the policy of the Cabinet to erect them into independent Governments, 'as similar as their different views and circumstances would admit to those of the Anglo-Americans', every class would give support, except the officials imported from Spain, who were few in number and generally hated. The result would be a cordial union on principles of reciprocal benefit, which no change in European politics would affect. It was not his intention, he continued, to consider the political aspect beyond noting that independence would wrest from Spain one of the most powerful means of annoyance she possessed and would cut off 'that channel which at present provides France with the ability to disturb the Peace of the World'.

Behind this immediate benefit lay the prospect of enormous advantage for British industry. The needs of the two countries were complementary. Only a fraction of the fertile land in South America was yet cultivated; and however rapidly the population might increase, some centuries must elapse before the state of society would cause them to become manufacturers. With an

---

[120] Popham's Memo. of 14 October (*ut supra*).

[121] Popham's *Trial*, p. 78.

[122] He was M.P. for Rye in the Tory interest from 1808 until 1812; Comptroller of Corn Returns, 1822-42: wrote extensively on the corn trade, the corn laws, and precious metals. He was one of Wellesley's consultants during the planning of the invasion of South America in 1807.

exaggeration characteristic of contemporary commercial ideas he asserted that even in their present condition, 'to say nothing of what Improvements may be produced by infusing a British Spirit amongst them', the inhabitants would consume commodities equal in value to Britain's total exports to the rest of the world. No one could contemplate the future of this extensive Country without appreciating the importance of opening an intercourse, 'on which the Subsistence of our Labourers, the Payment of our Taxes, and even the very existence of our Country depends'.

Britain must not, however, imitate the errors of Spain in shackling the trade with monopolies. Jacob noted with satisfaction that a 'judicious' Act had been passed in 1802 which 'annilated' the exclusive right of the East India and South Sea Companies to the trade, so that no impediment remained to hinder any British subject from a full participation.[123]

In War as well as in Peace, we shall derive from Spanish America, the solid Advantage of productive Commerce: and advantage, not arising from Restrictions or Monopolies, but from the Mutual Wants and Abilities of the two Countries.[124]

This was the authentic voice of the commercial imperialism of the time, which we have already seen in action in North America, the Indian Ocean, and the Empire of China.

To a Government faced with renewed threats of Napoleonic aggression and even of invasion, there were, however, other urgent considerations; and while they might recognise the desirability of detaching these territories from Spain and removing them from the grasp of France, ministers were in doubt how best to exploit the alleged discontents of Spanish Americans and the opportunities they might provide. Further delays in mounting a war of liberation on Caracas and Buenos Aires caused Miranda, that tireless architect of revolution, to lose confidence in British assistance and to turn for active sympathy to the North Americans. Despite the tragic fiasco of the filibuster at Porto Cavello, Miranda persisted in his projected invasion: his capture of Coro in the summer of 1806 coincided with Popham's initiative in seizing Buenos Aires. But Miranda had cautiously to withdraw and Popham was hurriedly

---

[123] The Act in question (*42 Geo. III, cap. 77*) was entitled, ' An Act to permit British-built Ships to carry on the Fisheries in the Pacific Ocean without Licence from the East India Company or the South Sea Company '. This piece of legislation represented the final release of the Southern Whale Fishery from the limitation which the East India Company had so long insisted upon. It was symptomatic that William Jacob should have assumed that the Act covered every branch of trade in the Pacific, potential as well as actual.

[124] ' Plans for occupying Spanish America, with Observations on the Character and Views of its Inhabitants, 26 October, 1804 ' (Endorsement) (*Pitt Papers*, P.R.O. 30/8/345).

recalled.[125] For in Britain a new Administration, wary of any tacit approval which Pitt or Melville might have given to Miranda or Popham[126] were not prepared to commit themselves in any undue haste. When there seemed – temporarily at least – some possible hope of a general peace by agreement, they did not wish to precipitate a revolution in the *status quo*. So by a change of ministers Popham was left exposed to court martial for his action in removing his ships from the Cape of Good Hope to Buenos Aires. It is true that at his trial he gave Melville an uncomfortable quarter of an hour in a cross-examination which testified to the active interest of their predecessors in earlier plans of attack upon the Spanish Main;[127] but the new ministers required time to consider the position and felt the need to be educated and advised on the objects and methods involved in liberating the Spanish Colonies. When French victories on land squeezed Britain relentlessly from her continental markets and a British victory at Trafalgar secured that naval supremacy which made possible a counter-attack in the Western Hemisphere, William Jacob reiterated his plea for a drive to secure 'the rich resources' of the Spanish empire for Britain.

Castlereagh, who became Secretary of State for War and the Colonies again in March, 1807, was not unsympathetic to plans for an attack upon New Spain. Ralegh or Cromwell would have recognised as familiar some of his reasoning; but he doubted whether an occupancy by conquest would be worth the drain it would impose upon British resources.[128] He questioned whether some principle of 'acting more consonant to the sentiments of the people of South America' could not be adopted. It was his belief that the British should present themselves not as conquerors but auxiliaries and protectors: they should work through the colonists themselves and make clear that their sole object was to deprive the enemy of one of his chief resources and to open the continent to their manufactures. While ready in the context of the Napoleonic menace to justify such subversion, *The Times* in January, 1808, argued similarly that the fostering of Spanish-American independence was greatly to be preferred to conquest, for

they would in that case have been laid open to our mercantile speculation without the burdensome expence of forming establishments for them: we should have no Governors, Vice-Governors, Comptrollers of Customs, Tidewaters and Searchers to maintain, grievous, but perhaps necessary evils.[129]

Arthur Wellesley, to whom Castlereagh had earlier referred plans

---

[125] Windham to Baird, 26 July, 1806 (*W.O.* 1/161.)
[126] See Popham's explanation to Castlereagh, 30 April, 1806 (*W.O.* 1/161).
[127] 9 March, 1807: *Annual Register . . .* for 1807. Lond., 1809, pp. 402-3.
[128] Memo., 1 May, 1807. Correspondence of Castlereagh, VII, pp. 314 ff.
[129] *The Times*, 9 January, 1808.

for such a conquest for comment, reported in similar vein a month later. He asserted that, though the Spanish territories were 'the most fertile in the world' and might be the most valuable colony Britain ever possessed, their annexation would bring her 'little positive advantage' and even in commerce no great additional returns, for large quantities of British goods already found their way into the continent, presumably by way of the free ports. The establishment of an independent government following a revolution supported by Britain would create opportunities most favourable for her. The government of such a free state should, he believed, be monarchical and aristocratic, based on their ancient institutions and tempered by an elected body representative of men of influence.[130] This was the form of constitution advocated later by Miranda, probably under British influence and advice, for the Spanish-American federation of 1808, but it was rejected in favour of a more ostensibly democratic form by Bolivar and the founding fathers of the South American states on the morrow of their independence.

It seemed that at last the British Government was ready to intervene in South America, but once again Miranda was doomed to be disappointed, for Napoleon was not able to restrain himself from flouting Iberian patriotism and Britain was prepared to respond to appeals for help from Spain itself. So in June 1808 it was Wellesley who had to break the news to Miranda that the forces collected in Ireland were to be employed, not in a campaign against the outposts of Spanish empire in America, but in a daring assault upon a bastion of the Napoleonic empire in Europe: a foothold on the continent which would in the long run lead to a reversal of Britain's fortunes and the downfall of Napoleon.

This narrative has already pursued that fitful dream in which Pitt and Dundas may have been tempted to indulge, well beyond the limited period of study and into the next decade. But something of the grand design to liberate the Spanish colonies in America and to win their goodwill, their emulation and their markets persisted into the nineteenth century. When Canning called in the New World to redress the balance of the Old, he was renewing this earlier aspiration. When the liberators made their own constitutions, some doctrinaire 'infusion of the British spirit', however inappropriate, was present in their deliberations. Above all, in the 'informal empire' of South America, which British merchants and investors established in the mid-century,[131] there was some substantial and significant realisation of the earlier vision.

---

[130] Memo., 8 February, 1808: quoted W. S. Robertson, *op. cit.*, pp. 406-7.
[131] H. S. Ferns, *Britain and Argentina in the Nineteenth Century*. Oxford, 1960.

CHAPTER X

THE GOVERNMENT OF DEPENDENCIES

T H E first part of this volume has been concerned with the dilemma which was forced upon the attention of a reluctant Government when Clive's intervention in Bengal elevated traders into *de facto* rulers. Two things happened: the hesitant imposition of State control over the *imperium* of a powerful commercial corporation in London and the assertion of the authority of the King in Parliament over defiant Company Servants in India. This in itself involved something of a revolution in the traditional view of the role of the State in relation to the *libertas* of its citizens. In this way Britain became involved in a completely novel field of administrative experience which in later years exerted a profound influence over British methods of rule in Africa and elsewhere. Moreover the power and prestige of the British position in India and the Indian Ocean became an important and sometimes overriding consideration in foreign policy. Alongside this unlooked-for involvement in territorial commitment British merchants and industrialists pursued with relentless zeal the search for spheres of commercial influence in the North and South Pacific, in China and Japan, along the moving frontier in North America, and in the vast regions of the American Empires of Spain and Portugal.

These were the dominant features of British overseas expansion for rather more than half a century. They represented the initial stages in the projection of an industrial revolution by a State which was also a strong maritime Power. But the second Empire, as it developed in the 19th century, did not consist only of a global trading system, underpinned by strategic and commercial bases. After the defeat of Napoleon changing conditions compelled the British people in general to turn once more to emigration. The process of industrialisation which produced influential manufacturers also gave rise to a phenomenal increase in the population and various forms of social and economic dislocation. Under these pressures the more enterprising began to look overseas, as previous generations had done; and their primary interest was in land, good cheap land, as the means of wider opportunity. Unless they went to the United States, as many did, they looked to the British Crown to assume the status and burdens of territorial sovereignty, always subject, of course, to the inalienable rights of migratory Englishmen. A fresh outcrop of colonies of settlement began to appear – in British North America and the Antipodes.

This development, which lies beyond the chronological span of the present work, was viewed with disfavour by politicians and industrialists until they came round to the view that the employment of 'surplus' labour overseas was a good thing. In the late 18th century merchants and manufacturers disliked emigration as a dangerous loss of man-power which was needed at home to man the machines and grow food. Ministers adopted a similar attitude because the fluidity of trade penetration was more profitable than the maintenance of struggling (and probably fractious) colonies and less liable to provoke collisions over questions of sovereignty with European rivals.

The second Empire thus became a much more diverse affair than its predecessor. So diverse, in fact, that spheres of commercial influence (as in China), bureaucratic control (as in India), and the growth of colonies to political and economic maturity appeared to be self-contained compartments. Yet these different forms of overseas expansion frequently influenced each other and sometimes overlapped – as in Southern Africa and Kenya. Unforeseeably the outcome has been the linking of colonies, grown to nationhood, with independent Asian and African territories in the same political association.

The late 18th century witnessed the emergence of all the major developments which contributed to the establishment of this new and diversified Empire save that of large-scale emigration. Yet even in the 'colonial' sphere problems of government arose during the period under review, and the official response which they evoked in terms of constitutional ideas and instruments exercised a formative influence. There were two such problems. One of them arose from the conquest and retention – for strategic and commercial reasons – of territories where non-British Europeans were solidly entrenched. British institutions, political, judicial, and social, did not fit. How then were they to be governed? The question presented itself, first in French Canada and the French Island of Grenada, and later in other French, Dutch and Spanish dependencies in the Caribbean and the Indian Ocean. The second problem had to do with the government of English-speaking colonists. The dilemma involved in trying to reconcile metropolitan authority with the claims of colonial self-management, which had defeated Britain in the case of the Thirteen Colonies, reappeared when American Loyalists moved into Upper Canada and Nova Scotia. Grenville's attempt to resolve it by providing a genuine replica of the parent constitution, although inevitably a failure, was of great significance in relation to subsequent constitutional development. These two issues are the theme of the present chapter.

1. THE QUEBEC ACT, 1774

The decision in 1763 to retain possession of conquered French Canada was taken for the sake of the future security of the Thirteen American Colonies and without enthusiasm, but the inclusion in the Empire of a large community of Frenchmen, alien in their institutions, laws, religion, and language, confronted Ministers with a novel situation. Was it possible to anglicise them to the extent of imposing the constitutional and judicial pattern which was common form throughout the British settlements in North America and the Caribbean? And if institutional homogeneity was impracticable, what was the alternative? Soon a further complication was introduced with the establishment in Montreal and Quebec of a small but flourishing body of British merchants. This enclave, set in the midst of a feudal (and Roman Catholic) society, began to clamour for the British model of laws and government, the control of which must be vested in themselves.[1]

In May, 1763, Charles Wyndham, Earl of Egremont, as the appropriate Secretary of State in the George Grenville Ministry, called upon the Board of Trade to prepare a report on questions arising from the acquisition under the Treaty of Paris of new territories in North America, the Caribbean and the West African coast.[2] The Board was to consider how far it might be expedient to retain or depart from the forms of government established in Canada by the Crown of France, having regard to the privileges which had been guaranteed to the French Canadians under the terms of the Capitulation. Recommendations for the ceded regions to the west of the American Colonies were to conform to certain principles of policy which the Administration had decided upon. The Indian tribes must be conciliated by providing effective protection of their hunting grounds, and to that end there must be a definite boundary beyond which further settlement by the Thirteen Colonies must 'for the present' be forbidden. The outward flow of surplus population would thus be diverted laterally into Nova Scotia to the north and southward to Florida, and the region between the Appalachians and the Mississippi would be kept as a great Indian reserve and as a protected trading area.

The report submitted by Shelburne as President of the Board on 8 June adopted almost all of Egremont's ideas and elaborated

---

[1] The present chapter, which attempts to trace and analyse the reactions of successive Ministers in London to the problems of government in Canada, should be read in conjunction with the excellent and comprehensive history of the Province during this period by A. L. Burt (*The Old Province of Quebec,* Toronto, 1933).

[2] The efforts of successive Ministers to devise a workable system of administration and defence for the American 'Middle West' have already been traced in the present work (vol. I, Chap. V, § 2). For the reader's convenience they are briefly recapitulated.

them. On an attached map a fixed boundary was drawn between the old Colonies and the Reserve, but apparently room was left for a limited amount of settlement at certain points. Useful settlements, it was stated, could be established in Nova Scotia and Canada for furnishing lumber and fish, and at the southern end additional supplies of sub-tropical products could be obtained by developing Georgia and Florida; but this should be done by means of surplus population from the old Colonies and by emigrants from Europe and not by colonisation from Britain. The Report also supported Egremont's proposals with regard to the form of government for newly acquired territories. As a provisional arrangement Canada, an enlarged Nova Scotia, and the Floridas should be administered by a Governor and a nominated Council; but as soon as these Colonies had reached a sufficient stage in development they should be granted elective Assemblies. The existence of representative institutions would be a strong attraction for potential settlers.

This evolutionary process was in accord with ancient precedent, but it was recognised that the circumstances of French Canada were exceptional and required particular treatment. It was obvious, the Report declared, that the new Government of Canada would have within its jurisdiction a very great number of French inhabitants who must greatly exceed 'for a very long period of time' the American and European immigrants who might attempt to settle there.

From which Circumstances, it appears to Us that the Chief Objects of any new Form of Government to be erected in that Country ought to be to secure the ancient Inhabitants in all the Titles, Rights and Privileges granted to them by Treaty, and to increase as much as possible the Number of British and other new Protestant Settlers, which Objects We apprehend will be best obtain'd by the Appointment of a Governor and Council under Your Majesty's immediate Commission and Instructions.

At the same time the Board wisely declined to lay down any fixed or uniform procedure: specific provisions would have to be adapted 'to the different Circumstances and Situation'. Instructions to individual Governors could maintain the required flexibility. Each of the newly acquired territories should graduate from conciliar to representative government as soon as its growth and viability permitted; but in the case of French Canada the introduction of elective institutions must await a sufficient inflow of 'Protestant' settlers. Meanwhile the Territory, with French-Canadian privileges guaranteed, would continue to be governed paternally, and this arrangement, it was implied, must in the nature of the case subsist for a long time.

Unfortunately the implementation of this well-considered plan was adversely affected by the prevailing confusion in British domestic politics. The sudden death of Egremont in August, 1763, was followed by the replacement of George Grenville's Ministry with the Bedford-Grenville coalition. Halifax succeeded Egremont and Hillsborough took Shelburne's place at the Board of Trade. The new Ministers adopted the policy of their predecessors with regard to the Indian Reserve and the encouragement of colonisation in the new territories to the north and south; but their sense of urgency (which was well justified) caused them to rush the business and apply a rule of thumb which involved a crude oversimplification of the complex and disparate situation. The American frontier was in a state of anarchy. The lack of a civil administration and of an organised frontier force had given free rein to land speculators and lawless fur-traders: the Indian tribes had joined together, as never before, in a formidable war against the white man. Egremont and Shelburne had left behind them a draft Proclamation which would have announced that henceforth the security of the Indian hunting grounds would be guaranteed and that European penetration would be prevented beyond certain fixed limits. It had been intended that this gesture of conciliation to the Indians would be followed up by a detailed survey and demarcation of the frontier which, while preserving the principle of a fixed frontier, would have allowed for limited European settlement (subject to imperial control of all land-sales) in certain areas on the east side of it.

But Shelburne had failed to produce a 'palatable' plan by which the American Colonies would contribute to the cost of frontier administration and defence, and the demarcation of a boundary, extending from the Great Lakes to the mouth of the Mississippi, could not be accomplished quickly. Impressed by the urgency of a dangerous situation, Halifax and Hillsborough decided to declare the Appalachian Divide as the frontier without qualification or compromise: and since this would involve opposing a rigid barrier to a human flood, they were concerned to ease the pressure and therefore to accelerate the policy of their predecessors. In order to attract settlers quickly to the new Territories the draft Proclamation was re-cast as a simplified overall plan.[3]

---

[3] Cf. the speech of Thurlow (then Attorney-General) in the Commons on 26 May, 1774: 'I have heard a great deal of the history of the famous proclamation of 1763 . . . I think it meets with nobody to avow it. . . . It certainly, likewise, was not the finished composition of a very considerable and respectable person, whom I will not name [Egremont], but went unfinished from his hands, and remained a good while unfinished in the hands of those to whom it was consigned afterwards. It professed to take no care of the constitution of Canada . . .' (Sir Henry Cavendish, *Debates of the House of Commons in . . . 1774*. Ed. J. Wright, Lond., 1839, pp. 28-9. Cited hereafter as *Cavendish Debates*).

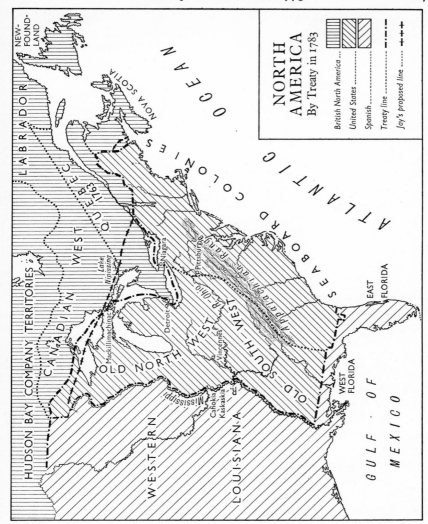

As issued on 7 October, 1763, it offered the inducements which
were customary in establishing all new settlements: free grants
of land would be available to British retired soldiers and sailors
actually resident in North America; the Letters Patent constituting the four new Governments would authorise the Governor and
Council in each case to summon an elected assembly as soon as
local circumstances permitted; and in the meantime all residents
in the said Colonies would be assured of the enjoyment of the laws
of England by the establishment of courts of judicature which
would determine all causes, criminal and civil, in accordance with
British law and equity. In offering a 'package deal' of this sort
(and in extreme haste) there was no room for qualifications or

refinements, taking into account the widely differing conditions obtaining in Canada, East and West Florida, and the Island of Grenada.[4] Shelburne's *caveat* that it would be a long time before there would be a sufficient proportion of British settlers in Canada to warrant the introduction of representative government was left to the future, but inevitably the undifferentiated terms of the Proclamation conveyed the impression that the four new Colonies would broadly conform to a common time-table of settlement and constitutional advance. British traders who established themselves in Montreal and Quebec regarded themselves – very understandably – as the designated beneficiaries in a new Protestant Ascendancy.

Ministers in London had thus stumbled almost unawares into a problem of race relations which was to recur again and again in varying forms during the evolution of an Empire which under the impulsion of industrial development became increasingly multi-racial. The fact that a British Administration was required to produce almost simultaneously a system of government for some 20 million Bengalis and about 80,000 French Canadians was symptomatic. These two issues, so different and yet strangely inter-related, caught Britain at a time when her own political system was at the nadir of confusion. Furthermore the problem of how to incorporate within the imperial system a large 'foreign body' in North America was interlocked with incipient revolution in the Thirteen Colonies and the need to rescue a vast continental frontier from anarchy. In this tangled scene, where disunited Ministries were groping in search of a policy, are to be found the first tentative experiments in a new form of colonial government which provided an alternative to the standard pattern and by degrees a probationary stage leading on to it. Our present purpose, therefore, is not to narrate the well-known history of French Canada under British rule but to select examples of ministerial reactions to the situation in the light of subsequent developments elsewhere.

There was general acceptance of the idea that French Canadianism must be 'assimilated' into the British system. The objective in the words of Francis Masères was 'that coalition of the two nations, or the melting down the French nation into the English in point of language, affections, religion and laws, which is so much to be wished for'. It might, he thought, be effected in a generation or two, 'if proper measures are taken for that purpose'. Lord Durham and his colleagues in 1839 still relied, like their predecessors, on the melting-down process. Anglo-Saxons, it seems, have always been prone to overestimate their absorptive capacity, whether in the British Isles or overseas. In the era of the American Revolu-

---

[4] It was drafted, revised and approved by the Privy Council within a week (vol. I of this work, p. 175).

tion, however, this form of self-confidence was temporarily shaken, and British Ministers became more cautious about anglicisation, fearing that the end-product might be that subversive thing, American radicalism. Tenderness towards French Canadianism established an important precedent.

The carelessness of the Proclamation of 1763 had the effect of putting British action in French Canada on a basis of anglicisation in its crudest form. In accordance with its terms the Commission and Instructions issued to General James Murray as the first civil Governor of the Province authorised the establishment of courts of judicature. In applying himself to 'these great and important Objects' he was to have regard to the system obtaining in other American Colonies and 'more particularly in Our Colony of Nova Scotia'. In these new courts, extending from the centre down to local Justices of the Peace, all causes, criminal and civil, were to be determined 'according to Law and Equity' – which could be taken to mean anything. The general notion seems to have been that the judiciary should be modelled on the standard British colonial pattern and that the law to be administered was to be British, but adapted – somehow and in unspecified directions and extent – to local custom.[5] The issue was soon to become of cardinal importance in 'British' India. In French Canada ambiguity in the matter created chronic confusion.

On the constitutional side Murray's Commission followed the usual form for new colonies, giving directions for convening an assembly of 'freeholders and planters' and regulating the scrutiny of legislation. In the Instructions, however, tardy recognition was given to the exceptional situation. While the Governor was required to give this matter all possible attention as soon as the more pressing affairs of government would allow, it was accepted that the establishment of an elected assembly 'may be impracticable for the present'. As an interim measure a nominated Council was constituted, consisting of four senior officials and eight (Protestant) inhabitants to be selected by the Governor. Five were to be a quorum, and any of them could be suspended or removed, provided that a majority of the Council assented, and this provisio might be ignored if the Governor decided that his reasons were

---

[5] The prevailing ambiguity is illustrated in Hillsborough's lame defence of the Proclamation of 1763 which he made five years later: 'I can take upon me to avow, that it never entered into Our Idea to overturn the Laws and Customs of Canada, with regard to Property, but that Justice should be administered agreeably to them, according to the Modes of administering Justice in the Courts of Judicature in this Kingdom, as is the Case in the County of Kent, and many other parts of England, where Gavel-kind, Borough-English, and several other particular customs prevail, altho' Justice is administered therein according to the laws of England.' Hillsborough to Carleton – March, 1768. *Documents relating to the Constitutional History of Canada, 1759-1791*, ed. Shortt and Doughty (Ottawa, 1918 edn.), p. 297. Hereinafter cited as *S. and D.*

not fit to be communicated to the Council. In that event he was to submit a full report to the Board of Trade.[6] Ten years later Warren Hastings pleaded in vain for any comparable degree of authority over his Council in Bengal.

A Governor and a nominated Council, acting both as an executive and a legislature, were traditionally regarded as a temporary expedient, and here again the precedent of Nova Scotia was intended to apply. In that Colony conciliar government had been instituted but with the promise of an assembly; and in 1758 an elected Chamber had been duly established in spite of the Governor's objection that the step was premature.[7] Tradition was broken when the temporary expedient became (by an Act of Parliament) the established constitution in Quebec Province for almost thirty years.

From the conquest until 1764 the Province had been directly administered by British Army officers who treated the conquered population with courtesy and humanity. Justice had been dispensed by a system of military courts, and with the co-operation of local militia officers disputes were settled according to French law and custom. As military Governor of Quebec James Murray had become warmly attached to the French Canadians and they on their side regarded him as their benign protector. When appointed as head of a civil Government he was faced with the formidable task of establishing a British judiciary which was to administer the laws of England to the greatest practicable extent. With the aid of two conscientious but very inadequate Law Officers he did his best to devise a workable compromise. By an Ordinance which passed the Council on 17 September, 1764, a Court of King's Bench was to be established to determine all criminal and civil causes, with appeal to the Governor and Council and thence to the Privy Council. By way of easing the situation as between the two systems of law there was to be an inferior Court of Common Pleas to determine disputes about property above the value of £10 and with the right of appeal to the superior court in cases involving £20 and upwards. In the Court of Common Pleas the judges

---

[6] For Murray's Commission (dated 28 Nov., 1763) and his Instructions (dated 7 Dec., 1763) see S. and D., pp. 173-181, 181-205 respectively. The expectation that there would be a large flow of settlers into the Province from the Thirteen Colonies is indicated by the inclusion in the Instructions of detailed directions, usual for new colonies, for the allotment of plots of land and the planning of townships. In order that the French Canadians might ' by degrees be induced to embrace the Protestant religion ' and their children be brought up in its principles, land was to be set aside for the support of Protestant clergymen and schoolmasters, and Murray was to report ' by what other means the Protestant religion may be promoted '.

[7] The Law Officers of the Crown had expressed doubts whether legislation without the participation of a representative chamber was legal. Prince Edward Island, on being separated from Nova Scotia in 1769, started with a Governor and Council, but was given an assembly (for the same reason) in 1773. (See W. P. M. Kennedy, The Constitution of Canada (Lond. and Toronto, 1922) p. 80.)

were to determine 'agreeable to Equity', but having regard to the laws of England as far as the existing situation would admit and until proper ordinances 'for the information of the People' could be enacted. In all cases coming before this Court where the cause of action had arisen before 1 October, 1764, French laws and customs were to be admitted and Canadian advocates were to be admitted to practice.

In both the Courts of King's Bench and Common Pleas Canadians were to be eligible to sit on juries. This provision Murray defended on the ground that their exclusion would be unjust since it would place the lives and property of 80,000 new Roman Catholic subjects in the hands of 200 Protestant subjects, most of whom were disbanded soldiers 'of little property and mean capacity'. This arrangement, he explained, was no more than a temporary expedient, 'to keep Things as they are until His Majesty's Pleasure is known on this critical and difficult Point'.[8]

The reaction of the British minority in the Province was swift and violent. They disliked Murray, who seemed to them to be the friend of the King's recent enemies to the detriment of rights and interests of loyal subjects, and their suspicions were not allayed by Murray's unconcealed contempt for an inferior order of persons many of whom were truculent Dissenters. A month later some of the leading spirits seized the initiative when they were summoned to serve on a Grand Jury in Quebec. They drew up a list of Presentments which were not lacking in impudence. The Grand Jury, they declared, must be considered at present as 'the only Body representative of the Colony', and therefore they as British subjects had the right to be consulted before any Ordinance affecting those whom they represented was passed into law. They proposed that the public accounts be laid before the Grand Jury at least twice a year to be examined and checked by them. They then went on to denounce the Ordinance establishing courts of judicature as 'grievous' and 'unconstitutional', particularly in admitting Roman Catholic Canadians to serve on juries and to practise the Common Law.[9]

When the seven French jurors had obtained a translation of the Presentments which their fifteen British colleagues had induced them to sign, they at once issued a lengthy disclaimer, and this was followed up (in January, 1765) by a petition to the King, signed by ninety-three leading *Canadiens*. The injuries suffered in cases of debt and property at the hands of British lawyers, ignorant of French law and custom, 'to whom it is only possible to speak with guineas in one's hand', and the wisdom of

---

[8] 'An Ordinance for regulating and establishing the Courts of Judicature, Justices of the Peace . . . in this Province'. *S. and D.*, pp. 205-10.
[9] Presentments of the Grand Jury of Quebec, 16 Oct., 1764. *S. and D.*, pp. 212-15.

the concession provided in Murray's Ordinance, were set out with Gallic fervour and eloquence.[10] The conflict between the two races within the bosom of a single state had begun.

When one of the contesting parties in an overseas dependency consists of a tiny minority of metropolitan subjects, it is natural that they should try to achieve supremacy by impelling the home Government to put effective political power in their hands. Such minorities always have; but this was the first important manifestation of the phenomenon. The French address to the Crown was followed by a petition from British resident traders. In time-honoured fashion they asked for redress of grievances. Some – such as the territorial limitation upon the fur trade and Murray's rudeness to them – were of substance; but they also protested that the latter was fomenting race dissension by encouraging the French to apply for judges who spoke their language and that 'the Pro-testant Cause' was being neglected. The Governor must, therefore, go: otherwise they themselves would be obliged to leave the Province. They also demanded representative government: 'there being a number more than Sufficient of Loyal and well affected Protestants . . . to form a competent and respectable House of Assembly.' To gain this crucial point they offered to agree to what must have seemed to many of them an extreme concession, that Roman Catholic French Canadians should be eligible to vote for British Protestant representatives.[11] In order to reinforce the pressure on the home Government twenty-five commercial firms in London who were concerned with Canadian trade signed a supporting petition.[12]

We must now return to London to observe official reactions. In the first place the Law Officers of the Crown on reference stated their opinion that Roman Catholics resident in territories ceded to Britain by the Treaty of Paris were 'not subject to the Incapa-cities, disabilities and Penalties to which Roman Catholicks in this Kingdom are subject by the Laws thereof' – a formula capable of far-reaching interpretation. Secondly, Murray's Ordinance with supporting and opposing petitions was referred by the Privy Council to the Board of Trade, and in September (1765) the latter submitted a detailed report. It is of particular interest since the President of the Board was Lord Dartmouth who was afterwards responsible for the framing of the Quebec Act. Some of the mer-chants' complaints against Murray were denounced: they were 'as unjust as they were uncandid and indecent'. The protests

---

[10] Statement by the French Jurors, 26 Oct., 1764. *Ibid.* (pp. 219-23) and the Address of French Citizens to the King regarding the Legal System, 7 Jan., 1765 (pp. 227-9).

[11] Petition of the Quebec Traders, *ibid.*, pp. 232-5.

[12] Petition of the London Merchants, *ibid.*, pp. 235-6.

against his action in establishing new courts was rejected. In these courts the judicial procedure best suited to Canadian law relating to property would gradually emerge: a necessary development since good policy required that in this sphere due regard ought to be paid to local law wherever it was not inconsistent with the fundamental principles of the laws of England.

At this point the Board's approbation of Murray's ordinance ceased. He had not gone far enough. In an attempt to devise a working compromise he had provided an inferior court where French law and custom relating to property and debt would be recognised and Canadian advocates could plead in their native tongue; but this was condemned as his principal mistake. The Board could see no good reason why native Canadians should not be admitted to the superior court either as suitors or as advocates, for they could not be excluded on the score of personal incapacity, nor were their usages regarding property 'so entirely done away' that they could not be pleaded in that court. 'This Distinction and Exclusion seem to us to be as inconsistent with true Policy as it is unwarrantable upon the Principles of Law and Equity.' At the same time the Board upheld the objection of the British settlers to the absence of provisions for bail and the issue of writs of Habeas Corpus: these should form part of the fundamental constitution of the Colony.

On the constitutional issue the Board decided to adopt the suggestion of the Quebec traders. The Province should be divided into three counties – Quebec, Montreal and Trois Rivières. In each of these, it was thought, there would be a sufficient number of British residents qualified to serve as representatives in the election of whom all the Roman Catholic inhabitants could join. This, the Board opined, would give great satisfaction to all concerned. The difficulty of operating through a Governor and Council with only limited powers would be removed, and all the objects of civil government could be fulfilled – 'and above all, that essential and important one, of establishing by an equal Taxation a permanent and Constitutional Revenue, answering to all the exigencies of the State'.[13]

As an intermediate measure Murray was instructed (in November, 1765) to remove all discrimination against French Canadians

---

[13] Report of the Board of Trade, 2 Sept., 1765. *Ibid.*, pp. 237-48. In a separate representation to the King of the same date the Board recommended that the Governor be summoned home to answer the numerous charges against him and he was formally recalled in April, 1766. On his return he was warmly received by the King, and when the Privy Council called upon the representatives of the Quebec merchants to substantiate their charges, they admitted their inability to do so. The complaints were accordingly dismissed (by an Order in Council of 13 April, 1767) as groundless and scandalous, but they had served their intended purpose. Although publicly exonerated, Murray had had enough and decided against a return to Canada. (See Burt, *op. cit.*, pp. 126-7.)

as advocates and jurors. The major issues raised in the Report touching laws and the constitution of courts were referred to the Law Officers who submitted their recommendations in the following May. They agreed that the courts should be reorganised on a basis of complete equality between New and Old Subjects and added the suggestion that one or two *Canadiens* might be appointed as magistrates in each district. With regard to law they went further than the Board had done in recognising French usage. In all suits relating to land and real property local custom should prevail, otherwise confusion and injustice would result. Judges sent out from England could soon learn from Canadian lawyers and so be able to adjudicate according to the custom of Canada, just as the Privy Council followed the custom of Normandy in reviewing cases from Jersey. With regard to other branches of civil law (which were of particular concern to the British minority) the Law Officers endeavoured to establish common ground by laying down a general rule. In all personal actions relating to debts and contracts and in *torts* requiring compensation in damages judges should follow the 'substantial maxims' which were accepted in all civilised countries. In this way they would not deviate materially either from the laws of England or the customs of Canada.[14] In criminal cases the laws of England should be followed. These were benefits which ought to be secured to His Majesty's Canadian subjects in accordance with his royal word in 1763.[15]

Momentarily firm ground appeared to be in sight, and then the mists of domestic politics supervened. These very practical recommendations were accepted and the Board of Trade was directed to incorporate them in Additional Instructions. This was done; but they were never sent. When they came before the Cabinet in June the Lord Chancellor, Northington, made an unexpected appearance and forced a quarrel with his colleagues by attacking the plan.[16] A few weeks later he used the situation which he had himself created to inform the King that the Administration was too weak to go on and that he must resign. Rockingham wished to struggle on and proposed that Northington should be replaced by Charles Yorke; but the disunited crew was beginning to desert the ship. In the hope of at last securing a stable Administration the King decided to dismiss Rockingham and called in the elder Pitt who took office, not as the head of a party, but as the leader

---

[14] In the 1760s the application of these general principles would have gone a long way towards meeting the British merchants' demands, but the issue was subsequently complicated by the differentiation between English commercial law and that of Europe which was initiated in a series of judgements by Lord Mansfield.

[15] Report of the Attorney- and the Solicitor-General (C. Yorke and W. De Grey), 14 April, 1766. (*S. and D.*, pp. 251-7.)

[16] See R. A. Humphreys and S. M. Scott, 'Lord Northington and the Laws of Canada' (*Can. Hist. Rev.*, vol. XIV, pp. 42-61).

of a group of selected individuals. In the event this combination proved to be 'inherently diseased'.[17]

The new Secretary of State for the Southern Department, which included colonial affairs, was Shelburne. On taking office he immersed himself in the task, which he had begun three years before, of planning a frontier policy for the Middle West.[18] The problems of Quebec were set aside. But members of the Rockingham Ministry, now in opposition, had not forgotten the plan for Canada which had been used to bring about their dismissal. Warned (in May, 1767) that the Government was about to be attacked for neglecting this question, Shelburne read the recent papers relating to Canada and was at once convinced of the value of his predecessors' plan.[19] In a lengthy memorandum to the Board of Trade he deplored the failure to send out the intended Instructions and supported the proposition of a representative legislature. But government by a Protestant Council and Assembly in a territory where the population was overwhelmingly French and Catholic did not appeal to him as a hopeful method of promoting harmony. The Rockingham Administration had applied the same device in Grenada only the year before where the planters had been enfranchised without being admitted to the legislature; and the Island was in an uproar. Perhaps he recalled Governor Melville's despatches on the situation. At all events he now proposed that French Canadians be admitted to the Council and to an elected Assembly in the proportion of one quarter of the total number in each chamber.[20]

Unfortunately Chatham's withdrawal into seclusion and melancholia had left a heterogeneous Cabinet leaderless. Each Minister was running his department with a minimum of reference to the others. That 'brilliant trifler', Charles Townsend, Chancellor of the Exchequer, persuaded his colleagues that a short-fall in the revenue could be met (in part) by imposing external taxes upon the Americans without causing any trouble. Such a policy, which touched his own department nearly, was anathema to Shelburne, but he was isolated by the mistrust which he inspired and eventually ceased to attend Cabinet meetings. His plan to provide for considerable westward expansion in order to accommodate American ambition was over-ruled and his Canadian proposals were modified. Presumably his colleagues were unwilling to out-Rockingham their predecessors. Their response to the suggested

---

[17] The phrase is Sir Keith Feiling's (*The Second Tory Party*, Lond., 1938, p. 91).

[18] See vol. I of this work, pp. 183-95.

[19] On 2 June, 1767, the Duke of Richmond in the Lords successfully called for papers on Canada and carried a resolution that the Province of Quebec had lacked for a considerable time and now stood in urgent need of further regulations concerning its civil government and religious establishment. *Parl. Hist.*, vol. XVI, 361.

[20] Burt (*op. cit.*), pp. 151-2.

introduction of representative government with a quota of elected French Canadians does not appear explicitly, but the emphasis of the ministerial directive was concentrated upon legal and judicial adjustments, and even these were to await further investigation.

In June Shelburne informed Murray's successor, Sir Guy Carleton,[21] that Ministers were giving serious consideration to the question of improving the civil constitution of the Province. They wished to be apprised of everything that might throw light on the subject and help them to elucidate 'how far it is practicable and Expedient to blend the English with the French Laws in order to form such a System as shall at once be Equitable and Convenient both for His Majesty's Old and New Subjects'. It was intended that the whole should be confirmed and 'finally established' by the authority of Parliament.[22] Thus for the first time it was proposed to regulate the affairs of this conquered Province by parliamentary legislation[23]: a purpose which became legally necessary in accordance with the judgement in *Campbell* v. *Hall* later if the Crown were to be freed from the deadweight of its hasty promise of an Assembly in 1763.

The determination to be fully briefed by officials on the spot before taking decisions was re-affirmed by the Privy Council two months later. The Instructions about the judiciary, prepared the year before, were set aside on the ground that they were not supported by adequate evidence. It would be, their Lordships declared, 'unwise and Dangerous to the Province to frame or reform Laws in the Dark and upon speculation only'. It was, therefore, agreed that Shelburne should give directions for a comprehensive enquiry to be undertaken in Quebec by the Governor with the assistance of his Council, the Chief Justice, and the Attorney-General. Their conclusions were to be embodied in a report which was to be signed by the Governor and the two Law Officers. If they failed to agree, the dissenting opinions must also be recorded in full and with supporting arguments. A qualified person was to be appointed to go out to Quebec and bring back the Report. Such a person, it was stated, would be able to explain to Ministers on his return any difficulties that might arise from the Report.[24] Shelburne's

---

[21] Carleton administered the government with the rank of Lieutenant-Governor until Murray's commission terminated in 1768.

[22] Shelburne to Carleton, 20 June, 1767. *S. and D.*, p. 281.

[23] One of the arguments advanced by the Board of Trade in 1767 in favour of establishing an elected Assembly had been that a fully-fledged legislature would possess the necessary authority to erect an Anglo-French system of law and judicial procedure. The declared intention in 1767 to do this by a detailed imperial statute would seem to imply that the establishment of representative government in Quebec was not then contemplated.

[24] Minute of the Privy Council, 28 Aug., 1767. *Ibid.*, pp. 285-7.

confidential secretary, Maurice Morgann, was selected and in December, 1767, set off on his mission.[25] Thus, in effect, a commission of enquiry was set up and a 'civil servant' from London was dispatched to act as liaison officer and *rapporteur*.

The hope that clear and agreed guidance would be forthcoming from the men on the spot proved illusory. When Morgann at last returned to England early in January, 1770, he brought with him, not one report, but three. In response to Shelburne's orders Carleton had instructed the Attorney-General, Francis Masères, to prepare a draft. The result some twelve months later (27 February, 1769) was a massive document in which Masères recited with a lawyer's clarity the history of the successive stages since the Proclamation of 1763; but with a lawyer's caution he refrained from making any definite recommendation. Four possible variants or proportions as between British and French law were set out with the advantages and drawbacks attaching to each, and His Majesty's Ministers were left to take their choice. Carleton, who was first and foremost a soldier and already imbued with a fixed notion of the proper solution for the Province, would have none of it. The Report was rejected and 'other hands' were set on to prepare one 'agreeable to the Governor's sentiments'. These were simple. The complications which had arisen from attempts to introduce certain branches of English law were ignored and this second draft strongly recommended that, while the laws of England should apply in criminal matters, 'the whole body' of French law in use before the conquest should be revived. This, it was declared, was 'the only way of doing justice and giving satisfaction to the Canadians'.[26]

Masères and Hey, the Chief Justice, dissented and (in September) put in two lesser reports. About a week later Morgann received the reports from Carleton and departed in haste for London. Masères had opposed the Governor's judicial plan on the ground that it was a deviation from official policy which ever since the conquest had sought to introduce the law of England and the English manner of government, 'and thereby to assimilate and associate this province to Your Majesty's other colonies in North America and not to keep it distinct and separate from them in religion, laws and manners, to all future generations'. The issue between assimilation (of which much was to be heard for many years to come) and the contrary doctrine of preserving

---

[25] In 1782 Shelburne again sent Morgann on a confidential mission. On the second occasion he was sent to join Carleton in New York in an effort to effect an Anglo-American reconciliation (vol. I, p. 265).

[26] The text of the second draft which Carleton approved and signed is missing: the above description is based on Masères's summary of it (*S. and D.*, pp. 369-70). For the first draft report and Masères's dissenting opinion on the second draft see *ibid.*, pp. 327-76.

indigenous custom as a means of ensuring loyalty was fairly joined.[27]

French law, argued Masères, should certainly be recognised in all matters concerning the holding and inheritance of land and property, but a total revival of the Custom of Paris in civil causes would occasion grave inconveniences. British subjects would find it extremely difficult to administer justice under an unknown code in a foreign language: the French Canadians would be continually encouraged to regard the French system as the best and to seize the first opportunity to return to it, if and when France sought to recover the Province by force of arms: and lastly, British subjects would be discouraged from settling in a country governed by a set of laws against which they were prejudiced. Let an Anglo-French code of laws be compiled, suggested Masères, and so end the prevailing confusion; or alternatively English law could continue as 'the general law of the Province' while French laws relating to property and intestacy could be revived by specific ordinances. From now on the Governor and his Law Officers contended for their respective policies until Carleton at last had his way in 1774 under the terms of the Quebec Act. A discreet silence was observed about the second term of reference – the civil constitution. But shortly before Morgann's arrival in Quebec Carleton had clearly indicated in a letter to Shelburne the lines along which his mind was working. His prime care (then as afterwards) was the military security of the Province. In a previous letter he had urged the necessity of building an adequate citadel for protection against French assault, and now (in January, 1768) he made the point that a disaffected Canadian population could not be expected to stand with the British 'in case of a French War'. Unless practical measures were taken to conciliate them, sentiment and self-interest alike would lead them to rally to the standard of 'their natural Sovereign'. Sources of discontent ought to be removed. They should be maintained in the quiet possession of their property according to their own immemorial customs. How could they be expected to remain loyal in the event of a French invasion when they were excluded from all affairs of trust and profit? Four or five of their 'principal Gentlemen' should be admitted to the Council and to a few 'trifling' appointments in the civil department. There should also be a few companies of Canadian Foot, 'judiciously officered'. Such gestures would have a considerable

---

[27] During the first months after their arrival in Quebec (Sept., 1767) Carleton and his legal advisers had been in agreement on the question. Carleton's despatch of 24 December, denouncing Murray's ordinance of 17 Sept., 1764, as having overturned the legal system of the country, closely resembled the writings of Masères at that time (see Burt, op. cit., p. 159). But the latter, with Hey, subsequently diverged from the extreme 'Canadian' position adopted by Carleton. They agreed with him, however, about the inappropriateness of representative government at that stage.

effect on the minds of the people: the sons of gentlemen would have some prospect of a career outside the French Services; and if there was a war with France at least part of the population could be relied on.

Clearly such a policy of conciliation was not compatible with putting the Country into the hands of a British Assembly which would exercise all the customary powers of making laws and levying taxes. The leaders of the British community, he informed Shelburne, had been urging that this must be done and soon.

I told them . . . I had no Objection to Assemblies in General, yet such was the peculiar Situation of Canada, tho' I had turned that Matter often in my Thoughts, I could hit off no Plan that was not liable to many Inconveniencies and some Danger.

He then went as far as he properly could in seeking to prevent his masters from falling into error. The British constitution, he said in effect, suffered a sea-change in the course of exportation. Governor, Council and Assembly did not in practice reproduce the balance of King, Lords and Commons, and the reasons were clear. The King's representative, possessing no patronage could exercise no influence, 'nor could the dignity of peerage be reproduced in the American forests'. Moreover, office holders were men who had made the highest bid to the patentee and lived on their fees: if checked by the Governor in their views of profit they became hostile.

It therefore follows, where the executive Power is lodged with a Person of no Influence . . . but coldly assisted by the rest in Office, and where the two first Branches of the Legislature have neither Influence nor Dignity . . . that a popular Assembly, which preserves its full Vigor, and in a Country where all Men appear nearly upon a Level, must give a strong Bias to Republican Principles.

Whether the independent spirit of a democracy was well adapted to a subordinate government, or whether their 'uncontrolable Notions' ought to be encouraged in a province so lately conquered and circumstanced as Quebec was, Carleton with great humility submitted to the superior wisdom of His Majesty's advisers.[28] Carleton's analysis was old and familiar; but his deduction was revolutionary. He was suggesting that for security reasons the Province of Quebec should become the first Crown Colony, although the term had not yet been invented. Some twenty years later William Grenville made a very similar appraisal but concluded that the right answer was to give Canada (British and French) a

---

[28] Carleton to Shelburne, 20 Jan. 1768, *S. and D.*, pp. 294-6. Cf. his previous letter to Shelburne of 24 Dec., 1767, enclosing a draft Ordinance for continuing and confirming French law and custom relating to the tenure, inheritance and alienation of land. (*Ibid.*, pp. 288-94.)

more faithful reproduction of the constitution of the parent state. Eventually as a result of a profound social revolution Britain brought her own constitution into closer accord with the 'democratic' system of representation in her own colonies; but that time lay far ahead.

Carleton wrote his self-revealing letter in Quebec only a few days before Shelburne in London had handed over his colonial responsibilities to Hillsborough. The tottering Ministry, now headed by Grafton after the final withdrawal of the stricken Chatham, was being shored up by the inclusion of the Bedford group who were bent upon enforcing the constitutional right to tax the Colonies. Primarily in order to find room in the Cabinet for Hillsborough a separate Secretaryship of State for American affairs was created.[29] On taking over from Shelburne he wrote to assure Carleton that the Ministry shared his tender concern for the welfare of the Canadians and approved his proposal to revive the French law of property. He should, however, hold up his draft Ordinance on the subject, since the Ministry were about to take the whole state of the Province into immediate consideration in order to devise a 'permanent settlement'. It might seem that such assurances were becoming a stock formula unrelated to practical action, but there is no reason to doubt that successive Ministers were genuinely anxious in spite of the anarchy in domestic politics and growing friction in North America to find a solution for the Canadian problem; but they were in the dark and perplexed by conflicting opinions. Three different policies were being advocated: quick anglicisation by imposing English legislative and judicial institutions; gradual anglicisation by combining conciliatory measures with the encouragement of immigration from the American Colonies and the weaning of French Canadians from the Roman Catholic faith (the dream of the Huguenot Masères); and thirdly Carleton's argument that for the sake of the overriding claims of security French-Canadian privilege and custom must be entrenched.

In September, 1768, a determined effort was begun to work out a comprehensive settlement. Under reference from the Privy Council Hillsborough and the Board of Trade were required to consider all the available data relating to the administration of justice, religious establishments and revenue and to advise whether an elected Assembly should be convened, and if so under what limitations. Their report was not presented until July, 1769. The Board, it was then explained, had been aware of the need for 'some speedy reform', but they had been determined to proceed 'with the greatest circumspection' and not to reach conclusions

---

[29] Hillsborough combined this post with that of President of the Board of Trade and Plantations which he had held since Sept., 1763.

until they had marshalled all available evidence. The relevant documents from 1763 onwards had been examined, including the correspondence from officials in Quebec, and they had interviewed persons in London with first-hand knowledge of the country. The Report began with a statement of the dilemma. On the one hand, the French Canadians, consisting of more than 80,000 'brave and loyal Subjects', were apprehensive and resentful, for they stood 'proscribed from every privilege, and denied every right, the possession of which can alone ensure their affection and fix their attachment to the British Government'. On the other side stood the British traders of Quebec and Montreal. Consideration of their proposals had demonstrated that it was not possible to give 'full satisfaction' to the French population 'without violating those principles upon which the British Government is fundamentally established'.

In their recommendations the Board went to what they considered to be the farthest practicable limits in giving the French Canadians a square deal. Representative government was to be introduced in a form which went further in bringing them in than either the Dartmouth plan of 1765 or Shelburne's amended version of it. Nothing less than a 'complete' legislature would do. The Council was to become an upper chamber and be enlarged from twelve to fifteen in order that 'a reasonable number' of His Majesty's New subjects (a maximum of five) might be included; and these were to be exempt from making the declaration against transubstantiation which was normally required. There should also be a House of Representatives, as originally intended; but the proposal now was to make it biracial. It should consist of 27 members, of whom 14 were to be British (Protestants) and 13 French (Catholics). The proportion was to be secured by an ingenious arrangement. The members of the towns of Quebec (7), Montreal (4), and Trois Rivières (3) would be required to subscribe to the doctrinal declaration which automatically excluded Roman Catholics, while the thirteen representatives of the rural districts could be French, being exempted from that test. Although the New subjects would thus be given almost equal representation with the Old, the Board expressed the hope that the Privy Council, when it took into account 'the very great Superiority in number and property of the new Subjects', would not think that the suggested proportion was more favourable to them than justice and equity required. Only seigneurs were to be eligible to represent the 'French' constituencies.[30]

---

[30] In 1791 the British Cabinet urged that the Protestant Parliament in Dublin should admit the Catholic gentry to a limited political participation and so establish an indispensable alliance with them against republicanism. (Cf. vol. I, pp. 631-9.)

The prime consideration was that justice should be done. To secure the loyal co-operation of the French Canadians was essential, not only for the security of the Province, 'but with it that of all His Majesty's other Dominions in America'. Furthermore there was the standing financial argument for establishing a form of representative government: it was 'neither just nor reasonable' that the expense of administering the Province should continue any longer to be a burden carried by Britain.

With regard to ecclesiastical affairs the Board accepted and confirmed the recommendations of their predecessors in May, 1765, but the proposed settlement was set out in more precise detail. Worship in accordance with the Roman Catholic faith was to be freely tolerated in accordance with the Treaty of Paris, but careful precautions were to be taken to prevent the exercise of any foreign ecclesiastical jurisdiction; and the Superintendent (to be appointed by the Crown) must not take upon him 'any outward Pomp or Parade incident to the dignity of Episcopacy', nor must he exercise any authority beyond what the Governor and Council might think absolutely necessary to the exercise of the Roman Catholic religion. Certain religious houses were to be abolished and others reduced as being 'institutions of such a nature and tendency as ought not to be allowed in a British Colony'. The property of these communities was to be vested in the Crown and devoted, partly to the support of the Catholic priesthood, and partly 'to establish a Fund out of which the Crown will be enabled to make a better provision for the support of a Protestant Ministry'. In religion as in politics – conciliation combined with long-term anglicisation.

On the vexed question of British and French law and judicial procedure the Board pointed out that they were still without specific recommendations from Quebec. The Commission of enquiry, consisting of Carleton and his Law Officers, which had been instituted by Shelburne in August, 1767, had not yet reported; and when Shelburne's emissary at last came home (in January, 1770) he brought with him, as we have seen, conflicting opinions. The Board had before them a letter from Carleton, written in March, 1769, which held out hopes that the report would be finished 'ere long' and added that in the meantime he would not trouble the Secretary of State with his ideas. Might he come home on leave for a few months? Personal discussions could clear up many points and remove many difficulties. But Hillsborough and his colleagues did not see why their entire scheme for the Province should be held up. However satisfactory it might be, they reported, to receive Governor Carleton's sentiments, the danger of delay was too obvious to justify waiting any longer. Nor was it necessary. Even in the complex field of judicial arrangements the policy to be adopted seemed clear enough. They endorsed, with a few modifications, the Board's recommendations of September, 1765, and the Law Officers' opinion thereon. The error of excluding French Canadians from serving on juries and practising in the courts as advocates had been rectified. One major ambiguity remained, namely, the validity of French law and custom in all cases relating to property; and on this question Carleton's own letters to Shelburne (which they reproduced in an appendix to their Report) made it abundantly clear that satisfaction ought to be afforded to the New subjects without delay. If, therefore, the plan was approved, fresh Instructions should be drawn to bring it into operation in all its aspects, constitutional, ecclesiastical and judicial. Prompt action would thus be secured in giving effect to a comprehensive settlement of the Canadian problem. At the same time the Board evidently wished to avoid going too far in dictating to the responsible officers on the spot; they recommended that the Governor should be given a discretionary authority to stay the execution of any part of the new Instructions if he and his official colleagues asked for such deferment pending further consultation.[31]

In the light of the troubled race relations which plagued the subsequent evolution of a Canadian nation it is tempting to look back to the proposition of a united Anglo-French legislature as a great might-have-been; but the practical interest of the plan lies in the reasoning and calculation which gave rise to it. A number of projects had been considered and eliminated. In the first place the existing arrangement of a Governor and Council with inadequate legislative authority could continue no longer: it had reduced the Colony to a state of 'the greatest disorder and confusion'. Secondly, the claim of the tiny British minority to monopolise an elected Assembly was rejected, even on the basis of allowing Roman Catholics to vote for Protestant candidates. On the positive side Hillsborough and his associates decided that the establishment of a 'complete' legislature was essential both to enable the Colony to settle its own internal problems (within a framework devised in London) and also on financial grounds. Furthermore they endorsed the conclusion, which had been steadily gaining acceptance since 1763, that humanity and security in North America alike demanded that a population of 80,000 French Canadians must be given adequate satisfaction in the realms of religion and social custom.

Taken together, these conclusions seemed to the Board to point inescapably to one solution, that is to say, the establishment of the traditional system of representative government, combined with the admission of the New subjects to the highest degree of

---

[31] Report of the Board of Trade and Plantations Relative to the State of the Province of Quebec, 10 July, 1769. S. and D., pp. 377-93.

participation compatible with security. While the French, with
13 seats out of 27 in the lower House, would be taken into partnership on reasonable terms, the British minority would exercise a
decisive influence in a political system for which they were clamouring. Their bare majority of one in the lower House would be
balanced by a representation of approximately 10 against 5 in
the nominated Council. At the same time the Board stressed the
point that their plan was experimental: the number and character of the constituencies and the franchise would have to be
adjusted as circumstances changed.

There can be little doubt that if the plan had been adopted the
course of later Canadian history would have been (unpredictably)
different, but whether an Anglo-French legislature could have
survived the stresses of the American Revolution and the subsequent influx of Loyalists seems much more dubious. The habitans
were not apparently enamoured of the *ancien régime* under which
they had lived, and yet the seigneurs whom they were to elect
could hardly have been expected to support legislation for its
reform. The French as a whole would scarcely have relished British
notions of taxation and the purposes for which voted supplies
should be appropriated. Nor could they be expected to acquiesce
in measures to alter the law in respect of contracts and commercial
usage in general, which the British merchants would certainly
have promoted. The elements conducive to deadlock in the legislature would have been numerous and formidable. Nonetheless
the plan was an imaginative attempt to conciliate and incorporate
an alien community by adapting the constitutional pattern to meet
a novel situation and appears in retrospect to have been well
worthy of trial.

When Hillsborough (who was Secretary of State for the American Department as well as President of the Board) submitted the
project to his ministerial colleagues they evidently hesitated. His
proposals were not rejected, but action was to be suspended until
Carleton had been able to consider the Report and give his opinion.
The anxiety of Ministers to secure the prior concurrence of the
man on the spot was very understandable. To impose the scheme
by formal Instructions, as Hillsborough had proposed, while leaving the Governor with the responsibility of suspending such of
the provisions as he might wish to contest, was not a very hopeful
mode of procedure. Accordingly in the following December (1769)
the Secretary of State sent a copy of the Report to Carleton. Its
importance in ministerial estimation was indicated by the strict
secrecy that was imposed. Carleton was enjoined to communicate
no part of it to anyone: any difficulties or doubts that he might
wish to test against opinion in the Province must be represented as
arising from his own ideas; and when he came home on leave, he

must bring his copy back with him. If details of the projected Anglo-French legislature had 'leaked', there would have been uproar in Quebec and Montreal, and the plan would have been fatally prejudiced. Hillsborough's policy had been to do what had to be done – quickly. Shelburne had made a similar attempt.

The decision to wait for Carleton's opinion, although correct and indeed necessary, gave the scheme its quietus.

Carleton entirely agreed with the ministerial view that the New Subjects must be conciliated by giving their religious and social traditions the widest possible recognition, but he disagreed with the political aspect of the Hillsborough plan. The proposal to associate the two races in an elective Assembly where they were to work out agreed adjustments and raise a necessary revenue was in his view impracticable and dangerous. The standard pattern of colonial government did not fit the exceptional circumstances. An Assembly in Canada would follow the American example and frustrate the executive; and since there must be for security reasons a British majority, however narrow, that power would be used to promote subversive republicanism – in the heart of a conveniently feudal society. This was not Carleton's notion of what was good for the stability and happiness of the Province.

Even a stable government in time of profound peace might well have hesitated to take the responsibility of imposing its policy in the face of divided counsels from the local experts and a resident Governor. As it was, the Administration of the day was in a state of helpless confusion. In 1769, while the Board of Trade was excogitating a settlement of the Canadian problem, London was in ferment over Wilkes and his thrice repeated election for Middlesex, and a leaderless Ministry was faced by mob violence which came near to a revolt. Early in January, 1770, Chatham emerged from seclusion to denounce in passionate and calculated oratory the Ministry which had betrayed his name at home and in America. Chathamites, such as Camden, began shamefacedly to resign, and before the month was out the hapless Grafton threw in his hand. North came in as the King's lieutenant and after a shaky start gathered the support of many moderate men, dismayed by the sudden menace of sweaty nightcaps. The Townsend duties, except on tea, were annulled, and first blood was shed in the Boston 'massacre'. Although Hillsborough stayed on for two more years as American Secretary, the problems of Quebec remained – under consideration.[32]

---

[32] On Carleton's departure for England Hector Cramahé was sworn in as Lieut.-Governor on 14 Aug., 1770. Hillsborough periodically assured Cramahé that a decision on the affairs of Quebec would soon be reached, but that delay was unavoidable in view of the difficulties of the situation. (See Hillsborough to Cramahé, 11 Dec., 1770, 4 May, 3 July, and 4 Dec., 1771. *Rept. on Canadian Archives* (1890), ed. Brymner, Calendar of State Papers, pp. 44-7.)

In September, 1772, Hillsborough was replaced by North's half-brother, William Legge, second Earl of Dartmouth. A humane and upright man and a strong supporter of the Methodists, his attitude towards the Americans was much more conciliatory than that of his predecessor. Having previously prepared a report on Quebec, he took office with a considerable knowledge of the subject.[33] He at once informed Cramahé that everything relating to the civil and ecclesiastical constitution of the Province was under review. The old familiar formula; but on this occasion it meant what it said. Quebec was also informed that the vacant seats in the Council would not be filled until a new constitution had been promulgated. In the circumstances of the time more speedy action could hardly have been expected. As we have seen, Jenkinson and Robinson had almost despaired in their efforts to induce North to apply his mind to the urgent problems of Bengal. The Regulating Act passed in June, 1773, at the tail end of the session, and as soon as Parliament was in recess action on the Canadian question began.

Early in August Lord Chancellor Apsley[34] sent Dartmouth a collection of reports and other documents relating to Quebec, 'to enable his Lordship to form a plan of government for that province fit to be laid before Parliament'; and he went on to express his appreciation of Dartmouth's 'assurances . . . that he means to undertake it'. Hillsborough's proposal to take summary action through the instrument of Governor's Instructions under the royal prerogative was thus discarded in favour of proceeding (as Shelburne had intended in 1767) by means of parliamentary legislation. It seems that preliminary discussions had already taken place. Carleton and Masères had both been in England on leave for a considerable time and had presumably not failed to press their respective views in ministerial circles and upon North in person – as and when they had been able to gain his fleeting attention. They were now called into consultation. Three weeks after Dartmouth had begun work on the problem he received a letter from Masères telling him of a conversation which he had had with North. The First Minister had assured Masères that he was fully deter-

---

[33] The view expressed by Chester Martin (*Empire and Commonwealth: Studies in Governance and Self-Government in Canada*, Oxford, 1929, pp. 119-24) that Hillsborough's intentions with regard to Quebec were 'generous' while Dartmouth, 'whose well known piety and benevolence . . . covered vicariously a multitude of sins', aligned himself with the forces of reaction and coercion, is in odd contrast with their respective personalities and colonial outlook. Moreover the 'sinister' influence of William Knox can easily be exaggerated. He was much given (in 1774, in 1783, and afterwards in his efforts to regain office under Pitt) to representing himself as a policy-maker. The decision to await Carleton's opinion on the Hillsborough plan was taken some time before 1 Dec., 1769: Knox was not appointed Under-Secretary in the American Department until July, 1770.
[34] Lord Apsley succeeded to the title of Earl Bathurst in 1775.

mined 'to do something towards the settlement of that province in the next session of parliament and particularly with respect to the establishment of a revenue and a legislature. His Lordship was clearly of the opinion that this ought to be by a legislative Council and not an Assembly.'[35] The critical decision had been taken.

It had been reached by a process of elimination. The series of investigations and reports prepared by officials in Quebec and Ministers and Law Officers in London from 1764 onwards had indicated the emergence of a general consensus that the original guarantee of religious tolerance for an alien society within the Empire was not in itself a sufficient means of conciliation. French-Canadianism, as expressed in its own social customs, civil law and language, must be respected and adequately recognised. It had then remained to choose the type of constitution which seemed best suited to promote that object in the prevailing circumstances. The experiment of an elective Anglo-French legislature in the Island of Grenada was evoking racial friction and unrest, and when the Quebec officials (in conflict on details) agreed in advising against its application in Canada, the North Ministry chose the only remaining option – direct paternal rule.[36] Conciliar government, they concluded, armed with adequate powers but operating under direct imperial control, would be the most effective guarantee of the intended charter of French-Canadian privilege; and that in turn would best serve the interests of British security in a restive North America. The proportionate weight to be attached to these considerations of principle and expediency is less important than the precedent which was established.[37]

---

[35] Lord Chancellor to Dartmouth, 4 (or 7) Aug., 1773. *Dartmouth MSS.* (Public Can. Arch., VI, 2319). I am indebted to Dr. B. D. Bargar for making this and other references in the Dartmouth Papers available to me.

[36] Francis Masères proposed that during an interim period of seven or eight years there should be a (large) nominated Legislative Council, consisting entirely of Protestants. This legislature should be made 'perfectly independent' of the Governor by providing that no member could be removed or suspended except by the King in Council. This was greatly to be preferred to an elected Assembly 'into which any Catholicks should be admitted'. The institution of an Assembly should be postponed 'until the protestant religion, and English manners, laws and affections should have made a little more progress there'. (Masères to Dartmouth, 4 Jan., 1774. *S. and D.*, pp. 486-7.) In his evidence before the House of Commons he modified his proposal to the extent of suggesting that the seven-year nominated Council might include a prescribed minority of Roman Catholics, but he repeated his insistence that it must be independent of the Governor. (*Cavendish Debates*, pp. 124, 132, 247. Cf. his pamphlet, *Draught of an Act . . . for investing the Governor and Council . . . without an Assembly . . . with the Power of making Laws*. Lond., 1772-3.) Experience of the Governor's power under the Quebec Act caused this latter point to be strongly urged by the minority group in the Council.

[37] The motives behind the Quebec Act have long been a subject of controversy. Broadly there have been three types of interpretation: that its chief purpose was to provide means of coercing the Thirteen Colonies; that it was not necessarily of sinister intent but was motivated by a misguided expediency which among other

The compilation of the Quebec Bill – like the Regulating Act which preceded it and the succession of India Bills which followed it – was a composite affair in which numerous persons had a hand. From early August, 1773, the type of constitution to be adopted and the need to give extensive recognition to French law and custom were not in doubt: Governor Carleton's arguments had at last been accepted – in principle. But the recommendations, written and oral, which converged upon Dartmouth revealed how much room there was within that framework for differences of emphasis and method. The report submitted by Attorney-General Thurlow had been unhelpful: that of Solicitor-General Wedderburn had taken a clear line in rejecting the idea of an elected Assembly, but he was now at variance with Dartmouth on judicial issues; and the reports of the Quebec officials – Carleton, Masères, Hey and Marriott – conflicted in important particulars. Many other persons, including Lord Mansfield, were consulted, and some (like General Gage) intervened of their own accord to press their views.

In this welter of divergent advice Dartmouth had the ungrateful task of finding the highest common factor in questions of great technical difficulty. On what lines should an amalgam of British and French law and court procedure be devised? How to adjust two very different systems of land tenure and inheritance? To what extent was it right and wise to perpetuate Roman Catholic institutions and ecclesiastical jurisdiction? These were fundamental questions, and they indicated the intricacies involved in working out a *modus vivendi* for French-Canadianism within a colonial system which had been designed by and for people of British origin. The retention of Canada for strategic reasons after the victory of Wolfe precipitated the British into a realm of governmental experience which in its own way was as novel and complex as that other incursion into the unknown occasioned by the battle of Plassey.

Since the law experts were speaking with discordant voices, Dartmouth had to pick his way as best he could. 'Thus it fell out,' recorded William Knox, the Under-Secretary, 'that after all the pains which had been taken to procure the best and ablest advice, the Ministers were in a great measure left to act upon their

---

consequences hardened French-Canadian feudalism when it was beginning to dissolve; and that it was basically an enlightened and realistic measure of lasting value because it recognised the indefeasible claims of nationalism. These interpretations and variants of them can be studied (among other works) in the following: J. C. Miller, *Origins of the American Revolution* (Boston, 1943), A. L. Burt, *The Old Province of Quebec* (Toronto, 1933), Chester Martin, *Empire and Commonwealth: Studies in Governance and self-Government in Canada* (Oxford, 1929), and (Sir) R. Coupland, *The Quebec Act: A Study in Statesmanship* (Oxford, 1925).

own judgement.'[38] In fact, most of the decisions seem to have been taken by Dartmouth acting in consultation with North.[39] In these circumstances it is not surprising that the scope of the Bill was restricted to the establishment of a constitution and to broad outlines in the fields of law and religion. Complicated questions relating to judicial structure and process and future arrangements for the religious houses (which the Report of 1769 had dealt with in precise detail) were left to be determined by the new legislature in Quebec. As Carleton afterwards observed, 'the Act is no more than the Foundation of future Establishments'.[40] Wedderburn, the Solicitor-General, made the same point during the debates: 'I confess, upon a perusal of the bill, that none of the leading views embraced in it appear to me in any degree complete.' Although he had deprecated this deficiency while the measure was being prepared, he now went on to affirm that it was necessarily 'a bill of experiment'.[41] That was North's view, and it was characteristic of his belief in the maxim, *solvitur per ambulando*. As with the India Regulating Act he preferred to be imprecise and tentative at the initial stage. Unhappily the technique of leaving it to the men on the spot to work out the practical details of Anglo-French adjustment occasioned ceaseless confusion in everyday life and continual conflict in the local legislature.

Even so, the compilation of the Bill was a protracted process. Most of the drafting was done by Wedderburn under Dartmouth's instructions and with substantial assistance from Hey, the Chief Justice of Quebec. Four successive drafts have survived, and there must have been at least one other intermediate version. The timetable is not easy to discern, since the drafts and commentaries on them are undated; but there were evidently two stages with an intervening hiatus: the first from August until early December, 1773, and the second in March and April, 1774. On 1 December Dartmouth wrote to Cramahé, the acting Governor, to tell him that the future government of the Province was under the immediate consideration of the Cabinet 'and will probably be settled in a very short time'. He then proceeded to give a broad

---

[38] Knox, *The Justice and Policy of the late Act . . . for the Government of the Province of Quebec* (Lond., 1774), p. 9.

[39] See Mansfield to Dartmouth, 28 April, 1774. 'I mean it [a suggested amendment] to avoid, what Ld. North and Yr Lop. seemed very desirous of avoiding, the necessity of the Canadian Gentlemen taking the Oath of Supremacy . . .' (*S. and D.*, p. 551, n. i). When challenged about the origin of the Bill, North stated during the opening debate in the Commons: 'Every person who could give information has been consulted. I do not know that this Bill agrees precisely with the opinion of any one of them; but, Sir, this bill . . . was the result of the opinion of the noble Lord [Dartmouth] who offered what he conceived to be the best plan for Canada, the best plan for Great Britain, after considering and weighing every information . . .' (*Cavendish Debates*, p. 8.)

[40] Carleton to Gage, 4 Feb., 1775. *S. and D.*, pp. 660-2.

[41] *Cavendish Debates*, pp. 54 and 56.

hint about the nature of the ecclesiastical settlement and the Government's intention to extend the boundaries of the Province.[42]

Fifteen days later (on the night of 16 December) the 'Tea Party' took place in Boston harbour; and when the news of that outrage reached London, the attention of Ministers was diverted from Quebec to preparing punitive measures against Massachusetts. The Boston Port Bill and the Massachusetts Government Bill were introduced in the Commons in March, 1774:[43] the preparation of the Quebec Bill was then hastily resumed and was not ready for Parliament until 1 May. Indeed such was the scramble to get it through before the end of the session that objections raised by Hillsborough were only considered in Cabinet twenty-four hours before the Colonial Secretary introduced it in the Lords, and a very important amendment, suggested by Lord Mansfield, did not catch up with the Bill until it had reached the Committee stage in the Commons.[44] Thus the interruption caused by these two 'Intolerable Acts' held up the Canadian measure, already long delayed, and gave it a legislative juxtaposition which in the existing atmosphere of American suspicion and resentment could not have been more unfortunate. No one was more bitterly aware of this fact than Governor Carleton.[45]

In analysing the lines of policy in the Bill as they gradually emerged it will be convenient to trace the course of each in turn, that is to say, the constitution, the inclusion of new territory in the Province, and the provisions concerning law and religion. The constitution was the primary consideration. The first formal step in this new effort to reach a decision had been taken in December, 1772, when Wedderburn, as instructed by the Privy Council, examined the accumulated reports and produced a comprehensive plan of his own. Having considered the idea of an elected Assembly, he rejected it and firmly recommended a conciliar government. An Anglo-French Assembly would be 'an inexhaustible source of dissension' between the two races: an exclusively British Assembly would be no more representative than a council of state: and to admit French representatives not of the *noblesse* would be injurious to the social order.

It seems, therefore, totally inexpedient at present to form an Assembly

---

[42] Dartmouth to Cramahé, 1 Dec., 1774. *S. and D.*, pp. 485-6.

[43] *Parl. Hist.*, vol. XVII, 1189 and 1192.

[44] See Dartmouth to Hillsborough, 1 May, 1774, *S. and D.*, p. 554; Mansfield to Dartmouth, 28 April and Dartmouth's reply, 1 May, *ibid.*, p. 551, n. 1; *Cavendish Debates*, pp. 250-1.

[45] 'Had the present Settlement taken place, when first recommended, it would not have aroused the Jealousy of the other Colonies, and [would have] had the appearance of more disinterested Favor to the Canadians.' (Carleton to Gage, 4 Feb., 1775, *ut supra*.)

in Canada. The power to make laws could not with safety be entrusted to the Governor alone; it must, therefore, be vested in a Council consisting of a certain number of persons, not totally dependent upon the Governor.[46]

Wedderburn's reasoning against an elected Assembly was in line with that of Carleton, but thereafter the Solicitor-General's views diverged considerably and came close to those of Masères. The new Council must be a genuine legislature: it must not, therefore, be subservient (like its predecessor) to the Governor. Accordingly its members should be nominated by the Crown and only removable by a royal order. It must be armed with adequate powers of legislation if the prevailing confusion in the Province was to be ended. On the other hand too much authority vested in a nominated legislature might cause trouble. 'As power lodged in a few hands is sometimes liable to be abused, and [is] always subject to suspicion, some controul to this authority is necessary.' As a safeguard he recommended that all ordinances affecting the life or limb of the subject, or by which any taxes would be imposed, or by which any law of England or custom of Canada declared by the forthcoming Act to be of force in the Province would be altered, must be submitted within a specified number of months to the Board of Trade and both Houses of Parliament, and their operation must be suspended until approved by the King in Council. As a further restriction Wedderburn proposed that the new Council of Quebec should be allowed to act in a legislative capacity only for a limited period in each year, that is to say, during the six weeks preceding the opening of the St. Lawrence to navigation. Under these restraints it seemed reasonable, he thought, to entrust them with the power of making laws 'for a limited number of years'. Their local knowledge would furnish them with the necessary detail for implementing the new system of British and French law and for regulating the administration of justice, the collection of revenue, and the improvement of trade and agriculture.

Being bound down by certain rules upon the great objects of legislation, and subject to the constant inspection of government, they will be sufficiently restrained from abusing the power committed to them.

A legislature in embryo, operating under direct imperial tutel-

---

[46] The original text of Wedderburn's report is missing. Extracts, published in Robt. Christie, *A History of the late Province of Lower Canada* . . . (Lond., 1791) are printed in *S. and D.*, pp. 424-32. See also ' Abstract of such of the Regulations proposed in Mr. Solicitor Genl^s Report as it may be expedient to establish by Act of Parliament – Inclosed in Mr. Sol. Genls Report of 6th Decr. 1772 '. (*Ibid.*, pp. 432-4.)

age for an interim period, and leading on to the establishment of normal representative government when the situation in the Province should warrant it. Nevertheless a legislature – which would be able to relieve Britain of a financial burden by levying taxes under prescribed safeguards and also implement in detail the judicial and ecclesiastical settlement to be set out in the imperial statute. Interesting as the plan was as an attempt to provide a transitional stage on a 'municipal' basis, such close control would have proved impossibly irksome. Every important ordinance would have been held up for at least six months, and the result would have been accumulating frustration. Nevertheless Wedderburn's proposals seem to have commended themselves to Dartmouth and North, for they were incorporated in the initial draft of the Quebec Bill which Wedderburn prepared. All legislation was to be carried by a majority and when not less than thirteen (out of a maximum membership of twenty-one) were present.[47] The Act was to continue in force for fourteen years unless the Crown 'shall think fit before the expiration of that Term to direct a Lower House of Assembly or House of Representatives to be convened within the said Province of Quebec'.[48] If the constitution had been presented to the Commons in this form, most of the arguments used against it would have been anticipated.

When the drafting process was resumed in February, 1774, Wedderburn's device for controlling the legislative activities of the Council remained unaltered; that is to say, no ordinance touching religion or which imposed a tax or a punishment greater than three months' imprisonment could take effect until the approval of the Crown had been received. But there were some changes. The nomination of the original members of the Council was now to be made by royal prerogative in Letters Patent under the Great Seal and not by the Act itself. The purpose of both methods was

---

[47] The permissible maximum was subsequently increased to twenty-three.

[48] It seems a reasonable deduction that Dartmouth instructed Wedderburn to prepare this draft sometime in the autumn of 1773. The latter's Report, dated December, 1772, was the latest in the collection of recommendations which the Lord Chancellor handed over to the Colonial Secretary in the following August. It represented a considered appraisal of previous proposals, including those of the Board of Trade in 1769 and those received in 1770 from Carleton, Masères and Hey. It is improbable that Wedderburn would have been instructed to draft a Bill for Parliament before Dartmouth had taken charge of the business. As already noted, North informed Masères towards the end of August, 1773, that he was clearly of the opinion that Quebec should be given a legislative Council and not an Assembly. The initial draft, however, stops short after setting out the form of government and does not deal with judicial and ecclesiastical affairs nor with the intended extension of the Province to include the Ohio country. The drafting process seems to have come to an abrupt halt in December, 1773, when news of the Boston Tea Party caused Ministers to turn their attention to punitive measures against Massachusetts. Work on the Quebec Bill was not resumed until the following February. (See Wedderburn to Dartmouth, 2 March, 1774. *S. and D.*, p. 536, n. 1.)

to render the Council more 'independent' of the Governor: an idea which was eventually discarded. There was also a significant omission. It was no longer provided that the Act was to remain in force for a specified term of years. The new draft merely stated that it was 'at present inexpedient to call an Assembly' and left future developments as an open question.[49] In the subsequent debates the Opposition fastened on this as evidence of intention to perpetuate despotism; but, as modern experience has shown, the stability of a colonial constitution tends to be undermined from the outset when its duration is specifically limited.

By April the time available for getting the Bill through Parliament before the end of the session was becoming very short and there was a flurry of amendments. The principal features of the Bill remained, but the character of the legislature was changed. Enactments imposing taxation were now removed from the category of legislation which was to be automatically suspended. Although not elective, the legislature was thus vested by implication with power to raise revenue, subject only to the discretionary authority of the Governor. The method of nominating members of Council was also altered: they were now to be appointed under the Sign Manual. This was the normal procedure, and it could give the Governor substantial influence since the selection, dismissal and replacement of Councillors was usually done on his recommendation. In their determination to shift the financial burden from London to Quebec the Ministry had decided to grant to a legislature, consisting of a Governor and nominated Council, the taxative authority normally wielded by Governor, Council and Assembly.

Then almost at the last moment they changed their minds. In contrast to the 'third' draft the text of the Bill, as introduced by Dartmouth on 1 May, expressly prohibited the Council from levying any tax or duty other than local rates.[50] The desired revenue was to be raised by means of an imperial statute, replacing the old customs duties by new import duties on spirits, rum and molasses, and continuing the feudal dues payable to the Crown.[51] In practice the moneys so obtained proved quite inadequate to sustain the expenses of government, and the British Treasury was obliged to

---

[49] See Wedderburn's comment on this alteration. 'In either way the Nomination of the Members must be vested in the King and no greater Power in effect is acquired by the first mode (by Letters Patent) than by the latter, tho' in appearance the Power of erecting a Legislative Council seems to import more than the power of naming the Members and will from the appearance excite more opposition.' (*Ibid.*, p. 540, n. 2.)

[50] For the text of the 'third' draft of the Bill see *S. and D.*, pp. 543-7.

[51] This was done by a separate statutory instrument, the Quebec Revenue Act (*14 Geo. III, cap. 88*).

meet an annual deficit which by 1790 had risen to £100,000.[52]

Few constitutions, even in modern times, have been preceded by such prolonged and detailed investigations. When the proposition of an exclusively British and then of an Anglo-French Assembly had been considered and discarded in turn, Dartmouth and his advisers were faced with the question of what powers should be entrusted to a nominated legislature. Wedderburn (like Masères) proposed that its status in relation to the Governor should approximate in some degree to that of an elected chamber, but that any major enactment must stand suspended until it had passed the scrutiny of the Privy Council. The suggestion of greater 'independence' was at first adopted and then abandoned – Carleton would have disliked it intensely: the control of legislation by a wide use of the suspending power was adopted and retained. The decision to withhold fiscal powers must have been taken with great reluctance, but trans-Atlantic control of money bills would have been scarcely feasible;[53] and in any case the imposition of taxes by a non-elective body would have been a touchy business.

When the Constitution of 1774 at last emerged, patched in many places with compromise, Dartmouth and North acknowledged that it was no more than a temporary *modus vivendi*, but they could reasonably claim that every practicable precaution had been taken to make it just and workable. The new Council was carefully balanced, resembling in its composition the proposed Anglo-French Assembly of 1769. It was to consist of three officials (the Lieut.-Governor, the Chief Justice and the Provincial Secretary), nine French-speaking and eight English-speaking residents.[54] Since no legislation could pass unless a majority of the total membership was present, it was reasonable to assume (in London) that this almost-equal balance between the two race groups would make it virtually impossible for either of them to carry a measure against the united opposition of the other.[55] Behind that, as a further safeguard, was the close supervision of Canadian Bills by the Privy Council. Furthermore, in order to ensure that the new system would be launched on an even keel, Dartmouth provided a detailed directive in the form of a draft ordinance to be submitted to the Quebec legislature which would have met most of the legal and judicial

---

[52] See p. 756 below.

[53] In his Report of Dec., 1772, Wedderburn had recognised that the delays which would have been involved in suspending money bills necessitated the provision of a regular revenue under the authority of an Act of Parliament.

[54] As set out in the new Instructions to Carleton, dated 3 Jan., 1775 (*S. and D.,* pp. 594-614).

[55] It was further provided that any five of the Council were to constitute a Board or executive committee 'for transacting all Business in which their Advice and consent may be requisite'. It could not be anticipated that Carleton would distort this Instruction so as to establish an executive *junta* of his own choosing (cf. p. 706 ff. below).

complaints of the English-speaking merchants. Taken together, these precautions appeared to offer the best available means of securing inter-racial harmony and co-operation.

Unfortunately the constitution in operation produced different and less happy results. The previous system by which power was concentrated in a Governor's or King's party continued. With a few exceptions the British officials sided with the nine seigneurs to resist innovation, and so provided the Governor with a majority which was frequently narrow but usually reliable. The *noblesse* naturally used their position as the spokesmen of French-Canadianism to preserve the traditional social order and saw no reasons for making concessions either to peasants or to foreign merchants. On their side British officials, dependent upon the Governor's goodwill, were not disposed to encourage their English-speaking brethren, many of whom were in sympathy with rebellious friends and kinsmen in New England. Under the stress of a losing war against colonial radicalism the division in the Quebec legislature followed the line of ideology instead of race. In consequence the merchants had a hard time, being denied most of the benefits which the home Government had intended that they should receive, and their clamour for a predominantly British Assembly, which had been rightly rejected, was renewed as the way of deliverance.

The Canadian Government under the constitution of 1774 was thus an oligarchy, out of sympathy with the mass of the people, on the one hand, and on the other with the merchant minority who represented the import-export economy of the country. Yet in the circumstances it is difficult to see how the unhappy situation could have been avoided. No Governor would have recommended, and no Administration at home would have approved, the appointment to the legislature of illiterate habitans. The rancour of the merchants could certainly have been allayed if a more conciliatory policy had been initiated by the governor of the day. But if Carleton or his successor Haldimand had been disposed to favour alleged friends of republicanism, the legislature would then have divided – dangerously – under the banners of race.

In addition to framing a constitution for the Province the authors of the Quebec Act were faced with the necessity of coming to a decision about the regulation of westward expansion. In the autumn of 1773 General Thomas Gage was in England, having recently returned from North America where he had been Commander-in-Chief. He sought out North and Dartmouth to discuss the government of the scattered settlements to the west of the Quebec boundary as laid down in the Proclamation of 1763.[56] This revived a

---

[56] J. R. Alden, *General Gage in America* (Baton Rouge, 1948), p. 195.

very wide issue. Although the immense area lying to the north of the Ohio and east of the Mississippi had been explored and claimed by the French, the boundaries of Quebec Province had been narrowly restricted in order to discourage settlers from spreading into that region until a plan could be formulated for the protection of the Indian tribes and the regulation of the fur trade.[57] For reasons already noted, Shelburne's scheme for administering the interior as a great Indian reserve and controlling the westward expansion of the American Colonies had never materialised; but he had successfully opposed a suggestion that the region should be annexed to Canada.[58] For ten years, therefore, the Ohio country had been a vast Tom Tiddler's Ground. Near the trading depots of Detroit and Michilimakinac there were small French settlements, and elsewhere fur traders and other less reputable adventurers roamed at will, exploiting and making trouble among the Indians.

Once the issue had been raised, the original plan of putting the region under the administrative control of Quebec was seen to be easiest way out of a long-standing dilemma. Moreover the failure to reach a working arrangement with the American Colonies for the control of westward settlement and for meeting the cost of administering and defending an Indian reserve rendered an alternative solution increasingly urgent. By the end of November, 1773, the decision had been taken in principle and Dartmouth took it upon himself to inform Cramahé, the acting Governor:

There is no longer any Hope of perfecting that Plan of Policy in respect to the interior Country, which was in Contemplation when the Proclamation of 1763 was issued; many Circumstances with regard to the Inhabitancy of parts of that Country were then unknown, and there was a Variety of other Considerations that do, at least in my Judgement, induce a doubt both of the Justice and Propriety of restraining the Colony to the narrow Limits prescribed in that Proclamation. His Majesty's Subjects therefore may with confidence expect that an Attention will be shewn to their wishes in this respect.[59]

If the Ohio country was brought under administrative control from Quebec, the development of the fur trade in that region by the British merchants of Montreal would be greatly facilitated. Ministers hoped that this commercial *quid pro quo* would help

---

[57] Report of the Board of Trade, 8 June, 1763. ' The Advantage resulting from this restriction of the Colony of Canada will be that of preventing by proper and natural Boundaries, as well as the Ancient French Inhabitants as others from removing and settling in remote Places . . .' (*S. and D.*, p. 141).

[58] Report of the Board of Trade, 5 Aug., 1763. *Ibid.*, pp. 151-3. Cf. Fitzmaurice, *Life of Shelburne* (Lond., 1876), vol. I, pp. 189-91.

[59] Dartmouth to Cramahé, 1 Dec., 1773 (*ut supra*).

to allay the disappointment of the British element in not being granted an elective Assembly. After the Act had passed and Carleton had returned to Canada, Dartmouth instructed him to remind the 'natural born subjects . . . of the attention that has been shown to their Interests . . . in the opening to the British Merchant, by an Extension of the Province, so many new Channels of important Commerce '.[60]

There were, however, other and more important reasons. One of these was anxiety lest the outrages committed by settlers and land speculators might stir up serious trouble with the Indian tribes, and coupled with that the well-justified fear that lawless frontier settlements were springing up which colonial governments were unable to control. In a letter to General Haldimand, then commanding in Florida, Dartmouth expressed the hope that 'the general tranquillity will be secured and the ill-effects of the licentious conduct of the Frontier Inhabitants prevented; at the same time I see with great concern the little attention that is paid in the different Colonies to the danger to which they are exposed by the disorderly conduct of [these] people '.[61]

The determination of Ministers to hinder the settlement of the interior was well illustrated by an exchange between Carleton and Hillsborough which took place a few days before the Bill was introduced. When the text was then submitted to Hillsborough (apparently for the first time), he jumped to the conclusion that the extension of the Quebec boundaries implied the recognition of a right to form settlements in the annexed territory and he protested violently. Dartmouth hastened to assure him that he was mistaken. It was the unanimous opinion of the Cabinet that the extension of the Province to the Ohio and the Mississippi was 'an essential and very useful part of the Bill '. By this means civil government would be established over numerous French settlements but there was no intention whatever of permitting further colonisation in the interior. On the contrary – 'nothing can more effectually tend to discourage such attempts, which in the present state of that Country, Your Lordship knows very well, it is impossible to prevent '.[62]

---

[60] Dartmouth to Carleton, 10 Dec., 1774. (*P.C. Arch., Q. 12A, 138,* Ottawa.) Printed in *S. and D.,* pp. 585-6.

[61] Dartmouth to Haldimand, 14 Oct., 1773. (*P.C. Arch., 35-42,* Ottawa.) Haldimand further reported that there was a 'constant emigration of families going to settle on the banks of the Ohio'. Such settlements, he added, were remote from the operation of the law and would soon become the resort of licentious characters from all the American Colonies. Haldimand to Dartmouth, 3 Nov., 1773 (*ibid.,* 35-46). The same apprehension had been expressed by the Board of Trade in 1763.

[62] 'Lord Hillsborough's Objections to the Quebec Bill in its Present Form' and Carleton's reply to Hillsborough, 1 May, 1774. (*S. and D.,* pp. 551-4.) In order to avoid all ambiguity about settlement, Hillsborough proposed that the draft Bill be amended so as not to include the Ohio country in the Province but was overruled.

The fear of a disorderly frontier was not new; but it had been deepened by the failure to achieve a system of controlled expansion. No less strong was the fear that Britain's resources in manpower might be drained by wholesale migration to North America. In May, 1774, the Governor of Nova Scotia considered it his duty to report the arrival of 200 Highland Scots and 100 Yorkshiremen because he knew that migration from the British Isles 'is by its increase become a matter of great concern'; and Dartmouth replied that, although he appreciated that such an influx of settlers would be of advantage to Nova Scotia, 'emigration from this Kingdom . . . is a circumstance of very alarming consequence'.[63] How much more so if this overflow had been multiplied by opening the vast fertile region which now constitutes the American States of Ohio, Indiana and Michigan.

The point of view of the Government and the ruling classes generally was forcefully expressed by Wedderburn in the Commons debates on the Bill.

I do not wish to see Canada draw from this Country any considerable number of her inhabitants. I think there ought to be no temptation held out to the subjects of England to quit their native soil, to increase colonies at the expence of this Country.

If British merchants chose to establish themselves in Canada to push their commercial views they should not regard it as a hardship to be required to accept 'the law of the land'. Their trading colleagues who went to Holland, the Baltic ports, and elsewhere, continued to look upon England as their home: and so should they. 'It is one object of this measure, that these persons should not settle in Canada.' Likewise the Americans:

I would not say, 'cross the Ohio, you will find the Utopia of some

---

[63] Legge to Dartmouth, 10 May, and Dartmouth to Legge, 6 July, 1774 (*P.C. Arch., A. 90 and A. 162-3*). Some twenty years later changing conditions began to cause occasional advocacy of the contrary view. In 1795 the anonymous author of a pamphlet entitled *A Description of the Island of St. John in the Gulf of St. Laurence, North America* . . . pointed out that the incidence of the war and the growing use of machinery were causing widespread dislocation and unemployment with the result that a heavy burden was falling on the parish rates. He suggested 'that these industrious but unemployed people' should be sent to the British Colonies in North America and be supported for the first few years as the American Loyalists had been. This would ease the burden on the rates; 'and these new Colonies, formed by the emigrations from different parts of England, Scotland, and Ireland, might rapidly increase the consumption of our manufactures, which would form a plan of reciprocal benefit, and preserve a mutual and lasting attachment'. (Bodleian Libr., *Godwyn Pamphlets*, 172(1).) But it was not until the teaching of Malthus had been reinforced by the great depression after 1815 that Ministers became frightened by the idea of over-population and began to encourage and attempt to regulate the rising tide of emigration. (Cf. L. C. A. Knowles, *The Economic Development of the British Overseas Empire*, Lond., 1928, 2nd edn., vol. 1, pp. 90-1.)

great and mighty empire'. I would say, 'this is the border, beyond which, for the advantage of your whole empire, You shall not extend Yourselves'.[64]

When the Imperial Factor, whether for reasons of security, economy or humanity (or all three), collides with a colonial sense of Continental Destiny, the connotation of the term, imperialism, tends to become confused.

The enlargement of the Province was decided on for two distinct purposes. The first was to bring isolated French-Canadian settlements situated to the west of the Proclamation Line and a group of French seal-fishing hamlets along the Labrador coast (which was transferred from the jurisdiction of Newfoundland) under the authority of the same civil government as the rest of the 'New' subjects. The second was to establish an Indian protectorate in the Ohio country to be attached for administrative convenience to the Government of Quebec.[65] The latter did not represent a new departure but was intended to implement the policy which had been declared in the Proclamation of 1763.[66] In the Instructions issued to Carleton in January, 1775, the provision in the Proclamation that the fur trade of the interior was to be free and open to the inhabitants of all the American Colonies was cited and confirmed. Regulations must be prepared by the Quebec Government and published throughout British North America. 'They must have for their object the giving every possible facility to that Trade, which the nature of it will admit, and as may consist with fair and just dealing towards the Savages with whom it is carried on.' Attached to the Instructions was a copy of the plan which had

---

[64] *Cavendish Debates* (debate on 26 May, 1774), pp. 57-8. In the same debate Thurlow said that he was persuaded to think the extension of the boundaries southward was a proper measure, 'in order to prevent the inconvenience of uncontrolled settlement'. (*Ibid.*, p. 25.)

[65] In 1763 Egremont had proposed that this should be done, but the Board of Trade (under Shelburne) had successfully opposed it, on the grounds that it would give Quebec an advantage in the fur trade, that the Governor of Canada would become involved in matters of defence which were the responsibility of the Commander-in-Chief, and thirdly that annexation of Quebec might seem to rest the British claim to the Ohio region on France's cession under the Treaty of Paris, whereas British sovereignty derived from a succession of treaties with the Six Nations and other Indian tribes – 'a more solid and even a more equitable Foundation'. (See Egremont to Board of Trade, 14 July, and Board of Trade to the King, 5 Aug., 1763. *S. and D.*, pp. 147-53.)

[66] The Proclamation stated that it was 'just and reasonable, and essential to our Interest, and the Security of our Colonies, that the several Nations or Tribes of Indians with whom we are connected, and who live under our Protection, should not be molested or disturbed in the Possession of such Parts of our Dominions and Territories as . . . are reserved to them . . . as their Hunting Grounds'. All Governors in North America were forbidden, until further directions were given, to grant warrants of survey or to pass patents 'for any Lands beyond the Heads or Sources of any of the Rivers which fall into the Atlantic Ocean from the West and North West, or upon any Lands whatsoever, which . . . are reserved to the said Indians. . . .'

been proposed by the Board of Trade in 1764. This was to be used by Carleton 'as a Guide' in framing the regulations. As a system of 'native policy' it derived from the principles and practice of that great Superintendent of Indian Affairs, Sir William Johnson. It would assuredly have received the warm approval of humanitarians of the later 19th century.[67]

As an administrative arrangement it all seemed tidy and ship-shape. The 'lost' French settlers would be brought again within the orbit of regular government: the disgruntled British minority would be compensated by a great extension of the fur trade; and a dangerous frontier would be stabilised by providing security and justice for the tribes. None of this was new or novel. The toleration of the Roman Catholic religion in Quebec and the continuance of a non-representative form of government had been in operation for thirteen years: the restraint upon American expansion to the west and the maintenance of an Indian reserve were a reaffirmation of the policy proclaimed in 1763. Yet these elements, when brought together and exposed to the heat of the Anglo-American dispute, coalesced into a compound which had the characteristics of political dynamite.

While the enlargement of the Province infuriated the Americans and so became a major factor in precipitating the Revolution, the internal adjustment concerning religion, law and custom determined the future status of French-Canadianism and set a precedent for subsequent occasions when other non-British communities were brought within the framework of the Empire. Freedom of worship in accordance with the Roman Catholic faith was from the outset unquestioned: a pledge had been given under the capitulation and confirmed in the Treaty of Paris – subject to the royal supremacy. North and Dartmouth were not, however, minded to grant more than 'a bare Toleration', and it was not until two days before the Bill was brought into Parliament that more generous treatment

---

[67] *Plan for the future management of Indian affairs* . . . (*ibid.*, pp. 614-20). The territory was to be divided into a Northern and Southern District with a Superintendent, appointed by the Crown, in charge of each. In every tribal area in the Southern District and at every fortified post in the Northern there was to be a Commissary, an interpreter, and a smith. Traders (who must operate under licence) were to be strictly controlled by the administrative service, and they were forbidden to sell spirituous liquor or rifles to Indians or to allow them credit above 50s.; and no debt beyond that sum was to be recoverable at law. Magisterial powers were vested in the Commissaries with a right of appeal to the Superintendent in disputes between an Indian and a trader or between one trader and another. By a process of indirect election each tribe was to elect a chief who was to function in close association with the local Commissary and with the Superintendent, acting 'as Guardian for the Indians and Protector of their Rights'. The evidence of Indians was to be accepted in all criminal and civil causes, whether tried by a Superintendent or a Commissary or in any of the colonial courts. This Plan for the protection of the Indians involved severe restrictions upon the activities of the traders. It had been abandoned when it became apparent that its implementation would become prohibitively expensive.

was conceded. The question was raised by Lord Mansfield to whom at this very late stage a copy of the Bill was sent for scrutiny.

'Will your Lordship (upon reflection),' he enquired of Dartmouth, 'think it sufficient barely to tolerate a large and powerful Body of Men, the R.C. Clergy in Canada, in the exercise of their Religion, without any other means of support than what is to arise from the Voluntary Contributions of their Parishioners?' Would Dartmouth, he went on, apprehend that any mischief would arise from acknowledging their right to 'a decent and moderate maintenance' under the sanction of a British Act of Parliament? The point was taken, and the Bill was altered to authorise the continued payment of tithes by Roman Catholics for the support of their priests.[68] In Parliament this act of justice was bitterly and discreditably denounced (by Chatham among others) as virtually establishing the Roman in place of the Anglican Church.

The ecclesiastical settlement was clearly related to the arrangements made concerning law and custom. As we have seen, there had been a steady movement in London away from the draconian anglicisation of 1763 and a groping after some form of compromise which would provide an acceptable *modus vivendi* for the French Canadians while leaving the way open for their gradual assimilation.[69] On his return to England in 1770 Carleton had sent Dartmouth a forthright memorandum. The first necessity, he declared, was 'to get rid of' the Proclamation of 1763 and the local ordinances deriving from it and 'to restore the old Law and Constitution'. Proper courts must be established and the nearer they were in form to 'the Old Ones' the more agreeable they would be to the inhabitants and therefore the more effective in operation. Even with certain reservations, which he added,[70] this wholesale adoption

---

[68] A copy of the Bill was sent to Mansfield at 10 p.m. on 27 April. He read it at once and returned it to Dartmouth on the following day with his suggested amendments. As already noted, he complied with the wishes of North and Dartmouth by drafting a substitute oath to be taken by Roman Catholics in place of the oath of supremacy, but this did not catch up with the Bill until it had reached the Committee stage in the Commons (see p. 709 below). The delicate question of the future of the various religious houses and seminaries in the Province was left (at Carleton's request) to be dealt with locally. (See Mansfield's paper, 'The Clause concerning Religion in the Third Draught' and the exchange of letters between him and Dartmouth, *S. and D.*, pp. 549-51.)

[69] Even with regard to religion. In his letter to Dartmouth of 28 April, 1774, advocating the payment of tithes by Roman Catholics for the support of their priests, Mansfield wrote: 'They should pay to the Priest till the time is ripe for their paying to the Minister of some other Religion' (*ut supra*, p. 551, n. 1).

[70] Carleton proposed that (i) defendants charged with capital offences should be allowed the benefit of being tried by a jury according to the laws of England, (ii) the use of torture should be abolished, (iii) the inhabitants should be given the privilege of the Common Law writ of *habeas corpus*. (*A Memorandum of things necessary for establishing Laws and Government . . . S. and D.*, pp. 533-4. The document is unsigned but it is in Carleton's handwriting. See Martin, *Empire and Commonwealth*, p. 116, n. 1.)

of the Custom of Paris and its attendant procedure was contrary to all previous proposals and evidently encountered opposition. A tentative compromise was gradually evolved.

The shift in official opinion can be clearly seen. According to the second draft of the Bill, prepared by Wedderburn under instructions from Dartmouth, French criminal law was to be restored but with strange injections of British law and practice. This was Carleton's idea, dictated by his desire to win the support of the seigneurs who desired the restoration of French law in full, criminal as well as civil; but it was not the view of Masères and Chief Justice Hey. Appreciating the impracticability of the arrangement, Wedderburn consulted Hey and took his advice. In the third and in the final drafts British criminal law and procedure were adopted.[71]

Civil law and custom were at the heart of French-Canadianism for in large measure they governed the everyday lives of the people. From the early stages of the Bill the intention to recognise and preserve this social system in as ample a manner as possible was evident. But there was ambiguity, and again it was Hey who, on being consulted, successfully urged the necessity of converting vague generalisations into precise terms. His revision of this part of the Bill, which was adopted, made the restoration of these rights not only explicit but extensive.[72] His Majesty's Canadian subjects were to enjoy 'all Customs and Usages' relating to property – which covered the feudal relationship between seigneur and habitan – and all other civil rights as fully as if the Proclamation of 1763 had not been made. And in order to avoid any doubt he inserted a new clause to the effect that in all matters of controversy within this sphere, involving either British or Canadian subjects, resort must be had to the laws of Canada and not the laws of England for decision.

Hey, however, proposed certain exceptions. These provisions were not to extend to lands already or subsequently granted by the Crown under English tenure: any subject might in future change the tenure of his land by a prescribed process into free and

---

[71] Wedderburn to Dartmouth, 2 March, 1774. 'It seems very strange to have a Criminal Code in which for Treason the Law of England is followed; for other capital offences the Law of France (which avoids all definition) is to define the Crime, and the Law of England to prescribe the punishment and mode of Trial; in offences not Capital, the Crime, its Trial and punishment are all referred to the Law of France which lets in all their arbitrary punishments of cutting out Tongues, slitting noses, etc. I have had much conversation with Mr. Hey who says that the idea of reviving any part of the French criminal law . . . would be as little agreeable to the Canadians as it would be to the English Inhabitants.' (*S. and D.,* p. 537, n. 1.) It was not, however, intended that the British code should be applied *in toto.* Archaic or barbarous provisions could be removed or amended by local legislation. As with Canadian civil law it was to be a framework amenable to adaptation.

[72] See 'Notes on third Draught of Quebec Bill' (by Wedderburn). *S. and D.,* pp. 538-9.

common soccage; and property and other possessions could be bequeathed by will under either British or French procedure. Much the most important of these was the second. Liberty to get rid of feudal tenure at will would have accelerated a social revolution among the French population and could have been a potent factor in the desired process of 'assimilation'; but when Hillsborough and Carleton heard of this proposal – a few days before the Bill went to Parliament – they protested strongly on the ground that the authority of the seigneur would be undermined. The Cabinet agreed to drop it.[73] The episode furnishes a good illustration of the conflict between the policy of entrenching French-Canadian usage and that of a gradual assimilation.

To remodel the law and constitution of an overseas territory by an Act of Parliament instead of employing instruments under the royal prerogative was unusual and the Government intended that the statute should do no more than establish a nominated legislature with defined powers and provide the outline of a judicial system. There was to be 'a general basis' of British criminal and French civil law, but neither was to be rigid or definitive. Law and judicial process could be 'varied and altered' by ordinances of the Governor-in-Council. Difficult adjustments could thus be left to be sorted out on the spot. The method was explained in the Commons by North himself: 'There must be a general basis . . . ready to be amended and altered as occasions shall arise, and as the circumstances of the colony shall require.' And again: 'In a general plan of government, it is not possible to enter into a detail what is proper, or what is improper, in Canada: it must be left to the legislature on the spot to consider all their wants and difficulties.'[74] In short the Ministry had retained its policy of a gradual blending but was now relying on a nominated instead of an elective legislature to give it effect.

On the face of it this was a flexible and sensible method of dealing with a complex situation. In fact it involved an abrogation of responsibility and imposed an impossible task upon a local legislature representing opposed traditions and conflicting interests. Modifications by mutual agreement did not happen: grievances remained and festered. When the Opposition attacked the conciliar form of government as despotic and argued that the New Subjects must be brought within the normal type of British constitution, North again exemplified the idea of gradual adjustment and adaptation.

It is not at present expedient to call an assembly. That is what the

---

[73] See ' Lord Hillsborough's Objections to the Quebec Bill in its Present Form ' and Dartmouth to Hillsborough, 1 May, 1774. *Ibid.*, pp. 551-4.
[74] *Cavendish Debates*, pp. 11-12.

Act says, though it would be convenient that the Canadian laws should be assimilated to those of this Country as far as the laws of Great Britain admit, and that British subjects should have something or other in their constitution preserved for them, which they will probably lose when they cease to be governed by British laws. That it is desirable to give Canadians a constitution in every respect like the constitution of Great Britain, I will not say; but I earnestly hope that they will, in the course of time, enjoy as much of our laws, and as much of our constitution, as may be beneficial for that country and safe for this. But that time is not yet come.[75]

William Hey, Chief Justice of Quebec, stated in evidence at the bar of the House that French Canadians regarded an Assembly as 'a house of riot'. In the case of Quebec that would have been a particularly apt description. Suspicious and conservative seigneurs would have been locked in constant combat with aggressive British merchants. The nominated Council, established by the Act, was similarly composed and there were incessant quarrels; but it did not possess the power of the purse and could not bring government to a standstill. In common with Dartmouth's other consultants Hey rejected an elected assembly at that stage: but he was a consistent advocate of the proposition that a blending of the two systems of law in such proportions as to satisfy both French and British, combined with a wide religious toleration, could provide a basis for racial harmony and gradual acceptance of assimilation which in due course could be given constitutional expression. This was not the view of Guy Carleton who from 1768 had urged that the only possible way of winning and retaining the loyalty of an ex-enemy community was to guarantee the continuance of its personality. In his view assimilation, if encouraged, would not be with the British system but with American republicanism.[76] Yet it was Hey whose advice, as we have seen, was increasingly taken by Wedderburn and Dartmouth during the protracted drafting process. When asked in the Commons for his views about the system of law to be adopted, he replied:

I myself have been unfortunate enough to differ with General Carleton in that respect: . . . the remedy proposed to be applied was the restoration of their own laws and customs *in toto*. I own, myself, I thought that went too far. I thought that such a mixture might be made, as would be agreeable both to the Canadians and British subjects, at least the reasonable part of both, and answer every purpose

---

[75] *Ibid.*, p. 248.
[76] Cf. Thurlow's forthright attack on the constitutional implications of the doctrine of assimilation. ' Do you mean to vest the sovereignty of the province, either by repartition or otherwise, in any other place than in the House of Lords and Commons of Great Britain? Yet, if you follow your assimilating idea, you must do that and I only know that none of the charters intended it.' (*Ibid.*, pp. 35-6.)

of state policy here at home. My idea was, that a country conquered from France . . . was, if possible, to be made a British province. I was, and still am, very sensible, that must be a work of time and diffi-culty; but, however, I thought it an object worth attending to.[77]

In further evidence he summarised the detailed recommenda-tions which he had prepared in Quebec in 1769.[78] These, it will be recalled, had been rejected by Carleton, who had called on others to prepare a report 'more agreable' to his own views. If Hey's original proposals are compared with the relevant sections in the Act and with his draft ordinance for establishing Courts of Justice' which Dartmouth subsequently accepted and sent out to Carleton, it will be seen how closely ministerial policy came into line with Hey's ideas. Yet Hey was not alone in his advocacy: he represented a considerable body of expert opinion. As early as 1766 the Law Officers had emphasised the vitality of Canadian custom and usage and the necessity of proceeding gradually and gently with the process of anglicisation;[79] and in the same year Francis Masères (before setting out for Quebec) had argued on similar lines.[80]

Carleton, on the other hand, was not interested in anglicisation however gradual. As a soldier he was concerned with security. From 1767 onwards he had insisted that the preservation of French-Canadianism was of prime importance in maintaining British

---

[77] *Ibid.*, p. 156.

[78] He had been willing, he stated, to allow the French 'the whole law' with respect to land tenure, real estate, and rights of dower and marriage. 'This I thought was a very large field for them, quieting and securing their possessions according to their own notions of property. . . . The rest of the law, as the law respecting contracts, debts, disputes of a commercial nature, the law of evidence, and many other matters of that kind, I thought might safely stand upon English bottom. These, with the whole criminal law of England, with trial by jury . . . together with the establishment, or at least, toleration of their religion with some reformation in the proceedings of the courts of justice . . . would, I had hoped, have made up a system that should not reasonably have been objected to by either British or Canadians.' He added that he was doubtful whether the latter would now be satisfied with such a compromise, and when asked why he thought so, he answered: 'I apprehend they have risen in their demands of late, and hope to be gratified to the utmost extent of their desires.' Part of the responsibility for the raising of the French-Canadian bid was undoubtedly due – directly or indirectly – to Carleton. (*Ibid.*, p. 157.)

[79] Report of the Attorney- and Solicitor-General Regarding the Civil Govern-ment of Quebec, 14 Aug., 1766. *S. and D.*, pp. 251-7.

[80] In the same passage he expressed the opinion that an elected assembly would be inexpedient for some years to come and he supported his contention in terms almost identical with those of North eight years later. An assembly manned by the British minority would be oppressive and would stimulate hostility between the two races. On the other hand, it would be dangerous to grant the Canadians a substantial degree of power. For some years to come they would be likely to resist all such measures 'as should gradually introduce the Protestant religion, the use of the English language, and the spirit of the British laws'. (Masères, *Considerations on the Expediency of Procuring an Act of Parliament for the Settlement of the Province of Quebec*. Lond., 1766, reprinted, *S. and D.*, pp. 257-69.)

control over North America. The extent of his influence with
Dartmouth and North is not easy to estimate, for direct evidence
is lacking. It seems to have been considerable but not always
decisive.[81] When he argued that the *ancien régime* in Quebec was
a providential bulwark and that grateful Canadians could be a
valuable source of military aid in case of need, he was putting a
case which no prudent statesman, faced with rising Anglo-American
tension, would be likely to neglect. Nor did they. When the crisis
broke, Dartmouth wrote to Carleton (July, 1775) confidently requesting that a force of 3,000 Canadians be raised to assist in suppressing rebellion.[82] But the sequence of ministerial action does
not permit these expected advantages to be elevated to the status
of primary motives. All the major decisions had been taken several
months before the trouble in Boston harbour: the coercive legislation against Massachusetts did not precipitate but seriously delayed
the passage of the Quebec Bill and did not alter its previous
character.

The divergence between the attitude of Dartmouth and North
towards the Canadian problem and that of Carleton became
apparent soon after the Act had passed. Carleton's behaviour on
his return to Quebec was odd. He did not at once publish the text
of the Act in the *Gazette* but merely inserted a summary of it which
gave a misleading impression of rigidity; and when the text was
eventually made public he did nothing to explain that a considerable field had been left open for local adjustment.[83] It is not easy
to understand this proud frustrated man who afterwards ordered
the destruction of all his private papers. In some respects he was
an eighteenth-century Curzon. His conception of British destiny
in North America and of his own rightful place in guiding it was
on the grand scale. To portray him as no more than an arrogant
autocrat would be an over-simplification. When the American
quarrel became a war he was one of those who by generosity to
prisoners and in other ways strove to mitigate its rigours in the
hope that misguided subjects might eventually return to their
allegiance. After American independence he was quick to recognise the new pattern of North American affairs and saw the problems and opportunities in Canada in a continental setting. On the
other hand he was totally lacking in the art of political management, being too imperious; and this deficiency, when combined
with a capacity for planning in the grand manner, made him the

---

[81] His ' Memorandum of things necessary ' corresponds with the basic provisions
in the Act, but there are important differences. Moreover, all Dartmouth's other
known consultants agreed in rejecting an elected assembly as impracticable at that
time.

[82] Dartmouth to Carleton, 1 July, 1775. When the news became worse he wrote
again (24 July) asking for 6,000 Canadians. (*S. and D.*, p. 667, n. 1.)

[83] See W. P. M. Kennedy, *The Constitution of Canada* (Lond., etc., 1922), p. 56.

prescient advocate of a British North American federation – with himself as proconsul – which was so constitutionally inept that none of the local legislatures would have tolerated it. Opposition from subordinates he could not endure, and when his superiors at home disagreed with him and sought his co-operation in devising an alternative he silently resisted in morose disdain. As with all egoists his insensitivity towards the opinion of others was matched by an ultra-sensitivity in relation to his own.

It is evident that he had returned to his post (in the autumn of 1774) disappointed and apprehensive. The rehabilitation of French-Canadianism was not as definitive as he had hoped, and there was no knowing what concessions to the English-speaking minority the Secretary of State might recommend in the new Instructions which were being prepared. In a letter to General Gage he explained that when the Act came into force on 1 May, 1774, all civil regulations would lapse and be replaced by a new system. The Quebec Government would not be in a position to start on this difficult task 'untill the final Determination of the Ministry upon all these Matters is known'.[84] As will be seen, his fears on this score were exceeded by the event.

In Carleton's judgement the danger of compromise at the London end was made infinitely more serious by what was happening in North America. When the terms of the Quebec Act became known in the Thirteen Colonies the reaction was violent, particularly in New England. Britain had fashioned an engine of despotism and Popery, a threat as 'intolerable' as the punitive measures against Massachusetts. The argument could be employed with formidable effect among the merchants of Quebec many of whom were closely associated with New England; and the habitans might well respond to appeals to join the cause and rid themselves of feudal burdens. Carleton found himself at a double disadvantage. Concessions to the English-speaking minority (favoured by Dartmouth for the sake of inter-racial co-operation) had become a security risk and must be resisted even to the point of defiance. Secondly the imminence of war put him in the humiliating position of having to admit that his promises of substantial assistance from Canada had been illusory. The long delay in granting a charter for French-Canadianism had left him no time to recover lost ground and reinspire loyalty. That was his defence; but he had been unwise to raise such hopes in London, for on his own showing he had known better.

The challenge came immediately. Within twenty-four hours of his arrival in Quebec (in September, 1774) Carleton received an express letter from General Gage in Boston enquiring whether Canadian support would be forthcoming if matters came to extremities. He replied at once that the seigneurs had expressed their

---

[84] Carleton to Gage, 4 Feb., 1775. (*S. and D.*, pp. 660-2.)

gratitude for the Quebec Act and he was sure that they would promote the raising of a regular Canadian Regiment. This, he reminded Gage, was a measure which he had advocated long ago as a useful means of gratifying the seigneurs.[85] In December Gage repeated his enquiry and Carleton answered (in the following February) in a different tone. The mobilisation of a militia force force was not practicable: the seigneurs were unused to that form of service and did not relish it. The proper method, as he had said before, was to raise a regular corps; but now difficulties were stated. The seigneurs were aggrieved because the Canadian Regiment, raised in 1764, had been suddenly disbanded without provision for gratuities or the half-pay for officers which had been expected. This was not likely to encourage them to engage a second time in the same way. Nevertheless the Canadian Regiment ought to be re-formed: it would attach the gentry to the British interest, give them employment, and help to restore them 'to a significance they have nearly lost'. With this unpromising assessment of the officer class he presented a picture of the peasants which offered small prospect of recruiting 'other ranks' whether as regulars or as militia-men.

As to the Habitans or Peasantry, ever since the Civil Authority has been introduced into the Province, the Government of it has hung so loose, and retained so little Power, they have in a Manner emancipated themselves, and it will require Time, and discreet Management like-wise, to recall them to their Ancient Habits of Obedience and Discipline.

For ten years these people had been imbibing 'the new Ideas'. If they were now suddenly called up and marched off to face the rigours of war in remote provinces, it would give an appearance of truth to the language of 'our Sons of Sedition' who were busily insinuating that the Quebec Act had been passed merely to enable the Government to rule the habitans 'with all the Despotism of their ancient Masters'.[86]

The argument underlying this letter and his later despatches to the Secretary of State provides a pointer to Carleton's subsequent behaviour. From his own point of view he had supplied all the right answers in 1767. Precious years had been lost through in-decision and neglect and the cohesion of the Canadian community, essential for maintaining the British connexion, had consequently deteriorated. The long delay had caused a remedial measure for Canada to coincide in time with an ideological revolution which was spreading (across an open frontier) into the Province itself;

---

[85] Gage to Carleton, 4 Sept., 1774, and Carleton's reply of 20 Sept. (Extracts in S. and D., pp. 583-4.)

[86] Carleton to Gage, 6 Feb., 1775. Ibid., pp. 660-2.

and no sooner was the belated statute promulgated than he was called upon to make good his word and produce an army of grateful Canadians before the process of using the Act to recover lost ground had even begun.

There was, of course, a deal of special pleading in all this. The delays had not been due to the blindness to Carleton's views of successive Ministers, but rather to their better appreciation of the complexities involved. His egoism led him to claim a degree of responsibility for the Quebec Act which was unwarranted and also inhibited him, while in London, from warning Dartmouth and North that immediate results in terms of military support were not to be counted on. The same trait in his character engendered an almost fanatical determination to retrieve the situation in spite of the evidence that Canadian feudalism was crumbling. He and his original policy would be vindicated by the future. With time and discreet management the seigneurs could be restored to their lost significance and the peasantry to their ancient habits of obedience. Accordingly the Province must remain essentially French in structure: concessions had become dangerous.

Dartmouth, in London, was tilting the balance the other way. There is some evidence to support the view that certain elements within the Administration had exerted pressure upon North and Dartmouth. Wedderburn, it will be recalled, had stated in the Commons that British merchants who went to Canada ought to accept the legal system of the country just as they did when they settled in the ports and capitals of Europe: Thurlow had poured scorn on the policy of assimilation; and Hillsborough, supporting Carleton, had secured the deletion of Hey's provision enabling the habitan to change over from feudal to British tenure. It may be that concessions to the English-speaking minority were omitted from the Act in order to avoid ministerial wrangles: the balance could be rectified later – within the broad framework of the Act through the local legislature and away from the floor of the House of Commons. Certainly Dartmouth took exceptionally strong action to ensure that this should happen. Immediately after the Quebec Act had received the royal assent he requested William Hey and Under-Secretary John Pownall to prepare a Plan of Judicature for transmission to Quebec in the form of a draft ordinance.[87] Hey's draft, which was adopted, set out a new system of courts and procedure in great detail and included a provision that in civil cases

---

[87] The Act received the royal assent on 22 June, 1774: on 17 July Pownall reported to Dartmouth that he and Hey had each prepared a plan and had then compared notes. Hey had said that Pownall's plan would do as well as his, but Pownall had declared, ' I am convinced that his ought to be preferred '. (S. and D., p. 585, n. 2.) Hey then went ahead and elaborated his ' epitome ' into a complete ordinance – ' Draught of an Ordinance for Establishing Courts of Justice in the Province of Quebec.' (Ibid., pp. 637-60.)

the facts could be decided by a jury instead of the judges if either the plaintiff or the defendant so required. As a Canadian historian has observed, this would have satisfied the merchants and would have aroused no popular disapproval.[88]

This was not the procedure which Carleton was expecting. He had left London in the knowledge that new Instructions would follow him incorporating a ministerial directive, but he naturally assumed that the Governor-in-Council would be left to prepare and enact the necessary legislation. As he explained to General Gage, the Quebec Government would have to recast the entire system of civil regulation – an undertaking full of difficulty and requiring time and careful consideration.[89] Instead the Secretary of State was having the job done in London under his own supervision, and the man employed to do it was the Chief Justice who had opposed the rigidity of Carleton's policy in 1769, who had afterwards repeated the grounds of his disagreement before the House of Commons, and whom Dartmouth had relied on to an increasing extent in drafting the Quebec Bill. In view of Carleton's imperious temperament and the subversive activities of certain elements among the merchants, it is not perhaps surprising that he took the extreme course of concealing the draft ordinance from the Council when it eventually reached him.

Meanwhile the business of preparing the Governor-General's Instructions was going forward. These, as Carleton had been informed, were to convey 'His Majesty's gracious Intentions' with regard to the future system of judicature in the Province. They were therefore exceptionally important. In Dartmouth's hands they became a gloss upon the Act itself.[90] Under the authority of the royal prerogative the Secretary of State took it upon himself to include directives the purpose of which was to conciliate the mercants and win their co-operation, but they did not stem from the terms of the Act. When Carleton received these Instructions he found the new legislature was required 'to consider well' the desirability of accepting the laws of England as the rule in all cases of personal action covering debts and contracts; and this was followed by a forthright recommendation in favour of adopting the writ of Habeas Corpus: a fundamental principle of justice in all free governments and an object which the Quebec legislature 'ought never to lose sight of it'.[91] The former was in exact con-

---

[88] W. P. M. Kennedy (op. cit.), p. 56.

[89] Carleton to Gage, 4 Feb., 1775 (ut supra).

[90] Notes and memoranda among Dartmouth's private papers indicate the personal attention which he gave to the drafting of the Instructions. (See S. and D., p. 594, n. 1.)

[91] On 5 Dec., 1774, the Board of Trade (of which Dartmouth was President) submitted Carleton's new Commission for the royal approval. On 22 Dec. the new Instructions were similarly submitted and were issued on 8 Jan., 1775. The latter are printed in S. and D., pp. 594-614.

formity with the terms of Hey's original scheme which, in opposition to Carleton, he had repeated in evidence before the Commons; and the privilege of Habeas Corpus, now so strongly urged,
had been stubbornly withheld by North and his colleagues in the
Commons in spite of sustained pressure from the Opposition. It
is possible that the Ministry had changed their minds after the
Act had passed, but there is some evidence to show that Dartmouth
had consistently held to the view that it was neither just nor politic
to carry the recognition of French-Canadianism so far as to cause
legitimate discontent among the English-speaking minority, and it
seems more likely that he was now using the weapon of executive
authority – after a successful general election and with the assent
of North and the King – to restore a balance which had been sacrificed in Parliament for party reasons.[92]

Carleton's response was to disobey orders. He had been required
to communicate to the Legislative Council all those parts of his
Instructions which needed their concurrence. Not a line of them
was communicated; nor, as we have seen, were the Council told
about the draft ordinance when it arrived with the Secretary of
State's blessing. Its author, who had been elected M.P. for Sandwich at the general election in 1774, had only agreed to resume
his post as Chief Justice under strong ministerial persuasion;[93] and
when he returned to Quebec (in April, 1775) he found that his
handiwork had been quietly suppressed. It was a piquant situation.
During the summer months while the Council was in session Hey
did not fail to fight in support of his views, but the odds were
against him. By the end of August he had had enough and wrote
to the Lord Chancellor asking that means might be provided to
enable him to make 'an honourable and decent retreat'. The
attitude of the French Canadians had greatly disappointed him. The
habitans had been frightened by wild rumours, but it was the
seigneurs whom he chiefly criticised. 'Inflexible to any arguments
either of expediency or Justice, they will admit no alteration in
their ancient Laws, particularly in the article of commerce which
I insist upon and believe shall carry in favour of the English mer-

---

[92] On 10 Dec., 1774, Dartmouth wrote to Carleton expressing his disquiet over the
silence in his reports about the merchants' reception of the Act. His Majesty trusted
that when his 'gracious Intentions' concerning the judicial arrangements became
known prejudices which popular clamour had excited would cease and that his
subjects 'of every description' would then be convinced of the equity and good
policy of the Act. (*Ibid.*, pp. 585-6.) This was written at a time when the Instructions
were in an advanced stage of preparation. As already noted, the outline of Hey's
judicial plan, which was followed in the Instructions, was in Dartmouth's hands
within three weeks of the passing of the Act. The petition of the Quebec and
Montreal merchants is endorsed – Recd. 22d January, 1775', i.e. nineteen days
after the Instructions had been issued. (*Ibid.*, pp. 589-91.)

[93] See Dartmouth to Carleton, 10 Dec. (*ut supra*.)

chants, with whom almost the whole trade of the country lyes.'[94]
He went home shortly afterwards.

War supervened and the Council did not meet again until 1777.
The business of judicial reconstruction was then dealt with in
three separate ordinances which were drafted by the Attorney-
General, William Grant, in close consultation with Carleton.[95]
In spite of pressure the latter continued to refuse to divulge his
Instructions, and it was not until 1781, when Governor Haldimand was reprimanded for imitating his predecessor's obduracy,
that they were at last communicated to the Council. From the
point of view of repairing and defending the citadel of French-
Canadianism Carleton's defiance is understandable enough, but
his obstruction foiled Dartmouth's efforts to conciliate the merchants and left a lasting legacy of bitterness and dissension.

The conquest and incorporation of French Canada into the
British Empire was a momentous event: it accelerated the secession of the Americans and impelled Britain to adapt her system
of colonial government to meet the special requirements of a
colony of non-British Europeans. The ten years of enquiry and
hesitation between conflicting claims and contrary proposals which
culminated in the Quebec Act deeply marked the character of
Canadian nationalism as it emerged: they also have a significance
for the Empire at large extending far beyond the Canadian context. At the outset it was assumed that the region of the lower St.
Lawrence would soon be anglicised by an influx of settlers from
the American Colonies so that the standard model of colonial
representative government could be applied. When it became
evident (by 1766) that the population of the Province was likely
to remain overwhelmingly French in origin a compromise was
sought which would associate the *Canadiens* with normal elective
institutions while retaining control in the hands of the English-
speaking minority. As first suggested the New subjects were to be
allowed to vote but for British candidates only: then they were to
be given a small quota of elected members; and lastly Shelburne
proposed almost equal representation of the two races in the
lower house.

These were attempts to adapt the normal political structure to
abnormal circumstances. The desire to do so was strong and for
two reasons. The standard type of legislature would have the
authority to raise a revenue and so relieve the imperial exchequer:

---

[94] Hey to Lord Chancellor Apsley (later Earl Bathurst), 28 Aug., 1775 (*ibid.*,
pp. 668-71). He resigned his commission of Chief Justice in 1776 and in the same
year was appointed Customs Commissioner in London, an appointment which he
held until his death twenty years later.

[95] Grant seems to have used Hey's omnibus draft as a general basis. English rules
of evidence were adopted for commercial cases, but the optional use of juries was
rejected in Council by seven votes to five.

it would also provide the necessary mould for a gradual 'melting down' of French distinctiveness. But the argument of officials on the spot (and not only Sir Guy Carleton) that the French peasant was ignorant and illiterate and incapable of working the machine and that the political dominance of a British oligarchy (however important in the economy) would be oppressive was echoed in London and settled the matter. The decision in 1773 to break with tradition and establish a nominated biracial legislature with limited powers had been reached by a process of elimination. There was also the security factor. In a nominated legislature the Governor would be able to recommend persons of known loyalty who, if they wavered in their allegiance, could be removed by the King-in-Council. While making this point in the Commons North emphasised that when a sufficient degree of anglicisation had been achieved the Province would be brought into conformity with the rest of the Colonial Empire.[96] A predominantly alien unit was, so to say, to be diverted to a loop line which would eventually join the main constitutional track. The same interpretation of the purpose of 'Crown Colony' government was given by Lord Hobart, as Secretary of State, in 1804.[97]

Below the crust of constitutional reforms was the enduring ethos of the French Canadians as expressed in language, religion and social usage. The Act of 1774, amplified in the Governor's Instructions, gave very substantial recognition to the organisation and jurisdiction of the Roman Catholic Church in Canada. Provided that priests were not recruited from foreign countries (especially France), British Ministers showed that they were not disposed to enforce too strictly the prescribed limitations upon the exercise of 'Episcopal and Vicarial Powers'. At the same time the object of gradual anglicisation in religion was not abandoned. Protestant clergy and schoolmasters were to be given – so the Governor was instructed – 'every Countenance and Protection in your Power'. After religion, civil law and social custom affected the day-by-day affairs of the people most closely, and here again the indigenous system was accepted – with intended modifications. Carleton's resistance (which stiffened the intransigence of the seigneurs) defeated Dartmouth's attempt to mollify the English-speaking merchants by establishing a reasonable *modus vivendi*.

The acquisition of French Canada thrust Britain into a new field of experience, and not only in North America. The problem of how to incorporate foreign bodies (that is to say, elements that

---

[96] 'That this establishment,' he declared, ' is not to be considered perpetual, is admitted in the Bill itself. . . . As soon as the Canadians shall be in a Condition to receive an Assembly, it will be right they should have one.' (*Cavendish Debates*, p. 290. For further observations by North on the constitutional question see *ibid.*, pp. 10, 13, 235-6, 247-8.)

[97] See *C.H.B.E.*, vol. II, p. 158, and Marlow and Madden (*op. cit.*), pp. 90-1.

were European but non-British) into the imperial texture was to re-appear twenty years later in many different territories along the ocean-routes which were occupied during a world war for purely strategic reasons. Revolution, war, and political distractions at home bedevilled the experiment of 1774, and further complications arose when Loyalists and other English-speaking immigrants began to settle in the upper parts of the Province. William Grenville devised the Canada Act of 1791 in the hope that the penetrating quality of British institutions would gradually bring about political integration. In that respect he resembled Dartmouth before him and Durham afterwards. Each was working in a different political climate and their methods differed accordingly; but they were alike in their confident reliance on the inherent superiority and power of the British political mould. A century later a similar conviction possessed Milner and Chamberlain. The delusion died hard.

2. THE CANADA ACT, 1791

Circumstances prevented the Quebec Act from operating as Dartmouth had intended. Eleven days before the Act came into force first blood had been shed in the American Revolution at Lexington (19 April, 1775), and the fight at Bunker's Hill took place in June. In the same month the Continental Congress decided on the invasion of Canada. Convinced that an attack upon them was being organised by Sir Guy Carleton with a Canadian army and Indian auxiliaries, they planned to anticipate it in the expectation that the appearance of American forces would swing the Canadians to their side. Unable to secure reinforcements Carleton defended Canada as best he could with puny resources. After the surrender of Montreal on 13 November the American columns under Benedict Arnold and Richard Montgomery began the siege of Quebec, and Carleton's situation within the fortress appeared to be desperate. On the American side, however, equipment, ammunition, provisions and winter clothing were all in short supply and the siege was never made effective. With the arrival of reinforcements from England in May, 1776, the Americans retreated and by 18 June the invasion of Canada was over.

The Canadian habitans had disappointed both the American Congress and the British Government. It appears that they had been considerably influenced by propaganda from the south urging them to support the cause of liberty and rid themselves of feudal authority and burdens such as the *corvée*, but the performance of the American levies, when they arrived, and their frequent inability to pay cash for provisions, induced second thoughts and a withdrawal into cautious neutrality. The 'Fourteenth Colony' was more interested in its racial and religious identity than in political protestantism. On the other hand the expectation of Lord George Germain and other Ministers in London that the habitans would be inspired by their seigneurs to flock to the royal standard was also wide of the mark. Some of them did volunteer and others obeyed orders to follow the army under *corvée*, but there was no mass movement to aid an alien (and heretical) monarchy which supported feudal obligation. The peasant farmer of Quebec Province was neither pro-British, pro-French, nor pro-American: he was French Canadian.

Involved during the war years in 'a world turned upside down', Carleton stiffened in the defiant attitude which he had adopted immediately after his return from London. He did not conceal his resentment against a Ministry which apparently expected him to produce Canadian loyalty as out of a hat and at the same time to appease a merchant minority infected with republicanism.[98] When General Burgoyne reported that some of the Canadians had deserted and that the population as a whole were giving him little assistance, Carleton replied that he was not surprised: he was himself having a similar experience which in the circumstances was what he had expected. Dartmouth's successor, Lord George Germain, who was by nature a bully, infuriated him by implying that the blame lay with Carleton himself. Compulsory service, he retorted, was distasteful to the people, and it was small wonder that the restoration of the ancient obligations was encountering difficulties – 'without either Laws, Strength in Government, or even Your Lordship's Countenance as Minister to assist me'.[99]

The pressures of a revolutionary war strengthened Carleton's determination to prevent any dilution of the Quebec Act as 'a sacred Charter'. Limitation of privileges might undermine the

---

[98] Carleton's statement that if Ministers had led Burgoyne to anticipate substantial support from the Canadians their misapprehension was not due to information supplied by himself is difficult to accept. (Carleton to Burgoyne, 29 May, 1777. *S. and D.*, p. 677, n. i.) Apart from Germain's later pressure Dartmouth himself had sent a prompt and confident request for Canadian reinforcements: he would scarcely have done so had not Carleton during his prolonged visit to London held out the expectation that such aid would be readily forthcoming. On the other hand Carleton's contention that the merchants were turbulent and untrustworthy was not without some warrant. Even in Quebec where they were mostly of British origin he had found it necessary to issue a proclamation (22 Nov., 1775) ordering all who refused to take up arms in defence of the place to leave it within four days. Three years later his successor, Haldimand, exactly echoed this point of view. Although the Quebec Act, he wrote, had come ten years too late, it had prevented the pro-American element among the Old Subjects from turning the Province into one of the United States. Its existence had baulked the efforts of agents from France and the rebellious Colonies. The Government should, therefore, lose no opportunity of declaring that the Act was an inviolable charter. 'For this reason, among many others, this is not the time for Innovations.' (Haldimand to Germain, 25 Oct., 1780. *Ibid.*, p. 720.)

[99] Carleton to Germain, 10 July, 1777. *Ibid.*, p. 677, n. 2.

allegiance of the *noblesse* and the Canadian clergy, which in any case would be under strain if France were to join the conflict. His refusal to conciliate the merchant class at the expense of French law and practice in civil cases was accordingly paralleled by a persistent disregard (which had a better justification) of those parts of his Instructions which required him to enforce the Royal Supremacy in relation to the Roman Catholic Church. His orders were to forbid under severe penalties all appeals to 'any foreign ecclesiastical jurisdiction' or correspondence therewith. No episcopal or vicarial powers were to be exercised within the Province except those which were indispensably necessary for the exercise of the Roman faith; and no one was to be ordained into that Church or be inducted into a benefice until a licence had been obtained from the Governor. These requirements represented an attempt on the part of the lawyers to reconcile freedom of worship for Roman Catholics with the supervision of their ecclesiastical administration by the King's representative. But Carleton would have none of it. When Bishop Briand of Quebec read the Act itself he was troubled by the fact that freedom of worship and the declared right of the clergy to collect tithes were made 'subject to the Royal Supremacy', which could have little, if any, meaning unless they renounced their allegiance to Rome. The Bishop had previously rejected the Elizabethan oath of supremacy and had proposed a form of words for insertion in the Act which 'every Catholic can subscribe to'. But the offending reference had re-appeared in another clause and he made his way to the Castle to protest. Presumably he would have been even more agitated had he been aware of the Governor's very specific instructions in the matter. At the interview Carleton waved all this aside: the Bishop was not to trouble himself any further about the Act. It would not have been passed without the proviso about the royal supremacy, but the King had no intention of exercising that power. Until Carleton's final departure in 1796 the elaborate compromise worked out in London was ignored.[100]

In general he pursued his own policy and imposed it upon the

---

[100] In a letter, dated 10 March, 1775, and addressed presumably to the Papal Nuncio in Paris, Bishop Briand described the interview and quoted Carleton's response in the following terms: *Qu'avez vous à faire au bill? Le roi n'usera point de ce pouvoir, et il consent bien et il prétend même que le Pape soit votre supérieur dans la foi, mais le bill n'aurait pas passé sans ce mot. On n'aurait point dessein de gérer votre religion et notre Roi ne s'en mêlera pas autant que celui de France; on ne demande pas, comme vous le voyez, par le serment, que vous reconnaissez cette suprématie. Laissez dire et croyez ce que vous voudriez.* (Quebec Archives, Rept. for 1929-30, p. 109. I am indebted to Mrs. Helen Taft Manning for providing me with this reference.) Later the Anglican Bishop of Quebec, Jacob Mountain, brought pressure to bear with the result that in 1801 the Secretary of State, the Duke of Portland, sent a despatch ordering the Instructions of 1775 to be made operative, but the Roman Catholic hierarchy put up a successful resistance. The subject continued to be a perennial source of dispute.

nominated legislature. This was not difficult, for a combination of seigneurs and British officials provided him with a working majority. There was, however, a substantial group who consistently opposed him. They stood for moderate concessions to the British merchants. Their opposition was not directed against 'the Government' as such or against imperial policy, but against a Governor who was refusing to implement an important part of it.[101]

After an initial meeting in September, 1775, the Council was not convened again until January, 1777. By that time four members had been taken prisoner by the Americans, several others had died, and out of the original twenty-one only twelve were available. At long last the important business of establishing regular courts of justice in accordance with the terms of the Quebec Act was undertaken. Three ordinances, based on the comprehensive draft previously prepared by William Hey, were compiled by the Attorney-General, William Grant, in close consultation with Carleton. On the civil side it was provided that English rules of evidence were to be followed in commercial cases; but when Edward Harrison moved an amendment that the judges should determine upon the evidence in accordance with English law and custom and that juries should be allowed at the request of either party, Carleton intervened and succeeded in getting the amendment defeated by seven votes to five. Juries, he declared, would spoil his regulations. In criminal procedure the recommendation in his Instructions for instituting the writ of Habeas Corpus and Hey's proposed modification of some of the severities of English criminal law were ignored.

Faced with the prospect that French and not English civil law would henceforth be the basis of decision in commercial matters, the minority group on the Council prepared a plan for a Chamber of Commerce for the city and district of Quebec. Subscribers were to elect annually a board of twenty-five directors, any five of whom could decide commercial disputes brought before them by mutual consent of the parties. In cases exceeding £50 there was to be right of appeal to a majority of the full board.[102] Copies of the plan were sent to the Governor and members of Council: on the same day Carleton peremptorily terminated the session. His behaviour, reminiscent of Stuart kings, was not dictated by an obsession with

---

[101] The high-handedness of Carleton and his successor went far to justify the criticism of the Opposition in Parliament that a legislature, the members of which were selected and removable on the Governor's recommendation, would lead to a personal dictatorship. Much had been said about making the Legislative Council more 'independent' of the Governor, and it had been suggested that its members should be named in the Act itself and so rendered immune from local dismissal. Other measures for circumscribing the powers of the Governor and enlarging those of the Council were repeatedly urged by the merchants and their supporters after 1783.

[102] The Plan is printed in S. and D.. pp. 692-4.

the French system as such (his attitude towards American Loyalists when they began to migrate into the Province is witness of that) but by reliance on an impartial application of Strafford's 'Thorough'. When forwarding copies of the ordinances to Germain he stated that they had been framed on the principle of securing the dependence of the Province upon Britain by suppressing the spirit of licence and independence, pervading all the North American Colonies, which had been making 'a most amazing Progress in this Country' through the efforts of a turbulent faction. As for the Canadians there was no doubt that they could be reduced to their ancient state of 'Deference and Obedience', but it would necessarily be a work of some time. He concluded with a blunt (and rude) warning that all regulations would be in vain and all his efforts must come to nothing unless they were steadily supported by the Cabinet in general and by Germain's office in particular.[103]

That was no way to address a Secretary of State, but Carleton had just been informed that the expedition which was to march from Canada by Lake Champlain and the Hudson River to attack the American Colonies in the rear had been entrusted to Burgoyne and not to himself. He had indeed escaped command of an ill-conceived and ill-fated expedition which met disaster at Saratoga; but he was furious at the slight and began to write despatches to Germain which became progressively insulting. Evidently he had decided that the divergence in policy between the North Administration and himself had made his position as Governor intolerable and proceeded to force his recall in order to use his influence at Court to secure a senior military command. In June he expressed the hope that he might be allowed to come home during the autumn. Meanwhile the King, who had a high regard for him, had regretfully agreed that his behaviour towards Germain had made recall inevitable.

The year which elapsed before the arrival of Carleton's successor (in June, 1778) was marked by a personal quarrel which revealed the extent to which the Constitution of 1774 was being distorted. Whereas the architects of the Quebec Act had designed a legislature in which the two races were to work out mutually acceptable adjustments, with the Governor as umpire, Carleton had established a 'French' government. A combination of seigneurs and officials could usually command a Governor's majority to defeat unpalatable motions; but not always, for the officials were divided. As a complete safeguard against dangerous innovation Carleton had devised an executive instrument of his own. Under the Act the Governor was authorised to transact non-legislative business when any five

---

[103] Carleton to Germain, 9 May, 1777. *Ibid.*, pp. 676-8.

members of Council were present. Taking advantage of this provision, Carleton had constituted a standing executive or 'Privy' Council of five named councillors selected by himself. Among other duties this body had been entrusted with the examination of the public accounts, the regulation of the police, and the establishment of criminal jurisdiction in the districts. Much of the administration of the Province was thus withdrawn from the cognisance of the Council as a whole and confided to a permanent *junta*. The reforming element in the Council strove to thwart this device by moving that given items of business be referred to *ad hoc* committees – of their own choosing.[104]

The opposition acquired a forthright leader in the person of Peter Livius. Formerly a member of Council in New Hampshire, he had been appointed by Dartmouth in 1775 to a judgeship in Quebec. Carleton's annoyance over this unpalatable appointment had been much increased when Germain nominated Livius (in August, 1776) to succeed William Hey as Chief Justice. In that capacity he took his seat at the Council Board at the opening of the session in March, 1778, and battle was quickly joined between him and the Governor. When Carleton requested the House to consider the regulation of fees Livius was appointed chairman of a committee to go into the matter. Thereupon he moved a resolution to direct the judges in Common Pleas to report on the rules and practice of their respective courts. Carleton was very anxious to remedy the evil of exorbitant fees which had become a public scandal, particularly those pertaining to certain offices, but he was evidently not prepared to allow the Chief Justice to use the occasion for initiating a judicial inquisition which might become far-reaching. The resolution was voted down, and 'the Committee proceeded on their Business'.

The next skirmish took place when Hugh Finlay and William Grant – both men of moderate views and very capable officials – proposed certain improvements in managing the revenue in their departments.[105] The Chief Justice voted in favour of having both sets of proposals referred to a committee, but the Governor's majority defeated the motion. This refusal, declared Livius, was 'a breach of decency in the proceedings'. Recommendations put forward by the relevant experts should have been given 'the common attention' of being considered in committee. Thoroughly roused, Livius followed this up with an attack on the inner citadel of Carleton's system. On 8 April (1778) he moved that His Excellency be humbly requested to communicate such of his Instructions as the legislature needed to know in order to comply with

---

[104] Cf. A. L. Burt (*op. cit.*), p. 251 *et seq.*

[105] Hugh Finlay was joint Postmaster for the British Provinces in North America and Grant was at that time acting Receiver-General.

His Majesty's intentions. By rejecting the motion, as he did, Carleton underlined his continued defiance of Government policy. A fortnight later the Chief Justice pressed the attack home with a further motion which drew attention to the Governor's unconstitutional action in establishing a standing executive committee. The proceedings of this body, the motion declared, were irregular and illegal, 'and if not timely remedied, will give Opportunity and Means of Collusion, and Impunity to future speculation and perversion of public Money under any future Governor'.

Carleton was under recall, and Livius was determined to force the issue and if possible break the system (and the policy behind it) before the new Governor established himself. Even though Carleton was at the extremity of exasperation his response to the challenge was the worst possible way of defending the continuance of his policy and method. The Council was at once prorogued – after a session of only one month – and the Chief Justice was summarily dismissed. This latter action was taken, as Livius did not fail to point out to Germain, in disregard of the Governor's Instructions which forbade him to displace a judge or any government officer without submitting a detailed report to the home authorities. When the issue was referred by the Privy Council in February, 1779, to the Plantations Board, Carleton, then in London, declined to attend to support his written accusations. The Board decided that the conduct of the Chief Justice in Council had been entirely regular, although his motions should have been couched in less offensive terms, that an additional Instruction should be issued ordering the discontinuance of the practice of appointing a so-called Privy Council, and that there had not been good and sufficient cause for displacing the Chief Justice especially as no complaint had been made against him in his judicial capacity.[106] The additional Instruction was duly issued and a *mandamus* was sent to the new Governor to reinstate Livius as Chief Justice of the Province.[107]

The choice of a successor to Carleton was not easy. In the midst of a North American revolution the security of the Province needed a governor who combined military experience with some knowledge of its peoples and problems. Various names were considered and eventually Sir Frederick Haldimand was selected. Of Swiss birth,

---

[106] Report of the Board of Trade and Plantations, 2 March, 1779. Printed in *S. and D.*, pp. 698-704.

[107] As late as 14 Jan., 1785, Livius (in London) submitted a petition to the Treasury stating that, although he had been reinstated, no reparation had been made for his financial losses and complaining that it was now proposed to reduce his salary as Chief Justice by half during his prolonged absence (*C.O. 42/16*). Cf. 'Mem° for Mr. Pitt' (1786). Unsigned, but probably written by Lord Sydney. In this memorandum the author stated that he had decided to prevent the return of Livius because of his declared opposition to Haldimand, Carleton's successor (*C.O. 42/18*). For a further reference to this memorandum see p. 731 below.

he had been in the Dutch service for some years before transferring
to the British army in which he had served with distinction during
the conquest of Canada.[108] A kindly upright man whose loyalty to
the sovereign and country of his adoption was undeviating: an
administrator with no taste for political manipulation, but a soldier
with whom concern for security was paramount. After some two
years of office he informed the Secretary of State that he had steered
clear of all parties, taking great care not to enter into 'the resentments of my Predecessor or his Friends'; but in his policy he was
entirely a disciple of Carleton and so the wrangles with Hugh
Finlay and the moderate reformers on the Council continued. 'This
is not the time,' he declared, 'for Innovations. . . . The Province
is surrounded by Enemies from without and as happens in all Civil
Wars is infested with Spies and Secret Enemies from within.' In
these circumstances he begged the home authorities to give him
their fullest support.

The Quebec Act, he maintained, had saved the Province from
joining the rebels, and it must continue to be implemented in its
entirety if the *noblesse* and the clergy were to be enabled to hold
the Canadian population to their allegiance. As for the English-
speaking community they only numbered about 2,000; three-
quarters of them were traders and could not properly be regarded
as residents. He had been under the unhappy necessity, he reported,
of imprisoning several of them for corresponding with rebels
or helping them to escape, and he suspected many more of the
same practices. He also suspected them (without justification
as it proved) of deliberately creating a scarcity of provisions
by making a corner in wheat and took drastic but unavailing
action.[109] To concede the right of Habeas Corpus to such people
would be an unwarrantable risk. Optional juries in civil cases
were also undesirable: juries of disaffected 'traders' were not to
be trusted. Following Carleton's example, he steadily declined to
communicate his Instructions on these matters although he had
been specifically ordered to do so. A further special Instruction,
forbidding him to continue his predecessor's practice of nominating a standing executive committee, was also disobeyed.[110] In a
secret despatch to Germain he expressed the view that it would
be unwise in the existing state of the Province to expose all the

---

[108] At Ticonderoga (1758), Oswego (1759) and with Amherst's expedition against
Montreal in 1760. At the time of his appointment as Governor he was Inspector-
General of the forces in the West Indies. Cf. *S. and D.*, p. 696, n. 1. His Instructions
(*ibid.*, pp. 696-704) were issued on 15 April, 1778, and on the same day Germain
consulted him about the appointments of the judges in the Provinces (Germain to
the King. *Corr. of G. III*, vol. IV, p. 112). He arrived in Quebec on 30 June, when
he took over from Carleton.

[109] The real cause of the scarcity was a bad harvest.

[110] Additional Instructions of 29 March, 1779. *S. and D.*, pp. 704-5.

measures of Government 'to that mixture of People which compose our Council'.[111]

The inevitable consequence was a severe reprimand from London. In April, 1781, the Plantations Board reviewed his conduct in forthright terms. The Instructions in question had been founded upon the 'the most convincing necessity' and His Majesty's pleasure had been conveyed so peremptorily that they were at a loss to conceive how it had been possible for him 'to hesitate upon an instant obedience to them'. They acknowledged (with warmth) that he had been solely actuated by loyalty to the King's service, but in these instances his policy had been mistaken. He must at once comply with his Instructions: 'we forbear to add what we must upon a contrary Conduct of necessity do.'[112] In forwarding this missive Germain wrote that he had nothing to add to it except his concurrence and the observation that Haldimand's conduct had furnished 'such an Instance of disobedience to the Royal Authority as ought not to be passed over, if longer persisted in'.[113]

Yet Haldimand did persist. His compliance was partial and delayed, while the general line of his policy towards the English-speaking minority remained unaltered. Indeed the home Government was in no shape to enforce discipline. In October of that year Cornwallis suffered disaster at Yorktown: Germain was dismissed from office; and in the following March North and his colleagues threw in their hand. Within a month the Rockingham Administration was obliged to recognise the independence of the Irish Parliament, and Shelburne was faced with the task of negotiating a peace settlement with a ring of enemies. The Governor of Quebec might be narrow and prejudiced in the conception of his duty, but at any rate Canada was quiet. Nonetheless on taking office Shelburne was concerned to find a collection of petitions on his table demanding redress against Haldimand for arbitrary imprisonment. Some of these, he informed Haldimand, carried 'the appearance of hardship', but he would suspend judgement until he had received the Governor's explanation. Meanwhile he must show the tenderest

---

[111] Haldimand to Germain, 14 Sept., 1779. 'Secret and Confidential.' *Ibid.*, p. 705, n. 2. A small executive council, nominated on the Governor's recommendation, subsequently became a standard feature of colonial constitutions and was obviously a convenient arrangement. The insistence of the metropolitan Government at this time that *any* member of the Council had the right to participate in executive business was in accordance with previous practice; but hitherto a nominated council had normally formed part of a bicameral system with an elected assembly. Since the Governor-in-Council under the Quebec Act was the entire government, and since all (non *ex-officio*) members of it had been selected for their reliability, the home authorities regarded the creation of an inner or Privy Council as unnecessary and undesirable. Carleton and then Haldimand clung to the device because they had created an opposition in the Council at large by refusing concessions which were known to have been authorised.

[112] Board of Trade and Plantations to Haldimand, 10 April, 1781. *Ibid.*, pp. 722-4.

[113] Germain to Haldimand, 12 April, 1781. *C.O. 43/8.* Another copy in *C.O. 42/15.*

regard for the rights, liberties and property of those living under his administration so that they would recognise that they enjoyed a greater security in these matters than those who in other parts of America had withdrawn their allegiance.[114]

The American Revolution altered the destiny of Canada. While Loyalists sought a new life within its borders, American settlement began to flow into the region between the Ohio and the Great Lakes which was no longer British territory. Loyalists were welcomed and assisted in recompense for their sufferings and also because they could constitute a barrier against the northward flow of republicanism. In May, 1783, North observed in a despatch to Haldimand that the changed situation of public affairs in the Province 'will naturally call for some alteration in the Measures of Civil Government': [115] in July and August a land-settlement scheme for refugee loyalists and disbanded troops was sent out;[116] and at the end of September His Majesty's 'ancient' subjects petitioned for an elective House of Assembly.[117]

The wind of change was blowing in the Province, but Haldimand saw no reason at all for altering course. In a private letter to North he wrote that it was a matter of indifference to him what form of government was adopted, but his duty to the King and the British nation impelled him to state that the continued dependence of the Country required that no change be made in the Quebec Act. The Minister was reminded – somewhat unnecessarily perhaps – that the local legislature had power under the Act to alter such parts of the French law as might be found inadequate for commercial purposes and also adapt the criminal law of England to local circumstances.

These Alterations ought to be Made with prudence and discretion, and no doubt the Legislative Council will do it at a proper time. It is an easy Matter to repeal the Quebec Act, but it will be a difficult Task to substitute another in its Place.[118]

---

[114] Shelburne to Haldimand, 22 April, 1782. *C.O. 43/8.*

[115] North to Haldimand, 12 May, 1783. *C.O. 43/8.* Another copy in *C.O. 42/15.*

[116] Additional Instructions for this purpose were issued on 16 July, 1783 (printed in *S. and D.,* pp. 730-2), and again on 7 August (*C.O. 42/15*). The latter provided for an allotment of 1,000 acres for a field officer, 700 for a captain, 500 for a subaltern or warrant officer and an additional 50 for each member of their families. (The July Instructions had provided 200 acres for every N.C.O., 100 for a private.) Officer allotments were to be interspersed among those of N.C.O.s and Men, 'that the several settlements may be thereby strengthened and united and in case of attack be defended by those who have been accustomed to bear Arms and Serve together'. A similar plan was afterwards adopted in the case of the '1820 settlers' in South Africa.

[117] Petition of 30 Sept., 1783 (*C.O. 42/15*). An amended petition, dated 24 Nov., 1784, was signed by some Loyalists (in the districts of Quebec and Montreal) as well as 'ancient' subjects. The text of the latter is printed in *S. and D.,* pp. 742-52, and differences between the two petitions are summarised on p. 742, n. 2.

[118] Haldimand to North, 24 Oct., 1783. *Ibid.,* pp. 735-7.

Carleton and Haldimand had put up a determined and successful resistance to such concessions because they regarded the English-
speaking minority as a bad security risk. Ministers at home appreciated the motive but tried to insist on obedience to official policy
for the opposite reason – that if the merchant interest were not
reconciled to the system they might become dangerously alienated.
When American independence became an established fact the need
to provide a balance of privilege in Canada became compelling.
As Shelburne had indicated, it was essential that the liberties and
property rights of residents within the Province should be seen to
be more secure than those of persons outside it who had renounced
their allegiance. The absorption of Canada into the United States
would follow unless the Colony could offer superior attractions
alike to French-Canadianism and to the enterprise of British traders
and settlers. Whether this dual requirement would necessitate the
introduction of British representative government was one of the
numerous post-revolution conundrums which confronted William
Pitt.

The formal recognition of the United States as a sovereign and
alien Power profoundly changed the position of Canada both in
relation to the North American Continent and as part of the
Empire. Separated from the United States, the 'Fourteenth Colony'
developed a Continental Destiny of its own; and as a colony its
importance was immensely enhanced in British estimation as the
intended substitute for the United States in the imperial economy.
The outlines of this greater Canada of the future have been partly
indicated in previous chapters of the present work. As fur traders
from Montreal and Quebec pushed westward to the Rockies and
the Pacific coast and north-westward into the Arctic in vigorous
competition with the Hudson's Bay Company, their remarkable
achievements in exploration attracted keen attention at home because of their relevance to the search for a short sea-passage between
Britain and the North Pacific.

The determined efforts to open that ocean and the countries
bordering it to British trade brought the North-West American
Coast within the purview of official policy. The episode at Nootka
Sound was treated by the Pitt Ministry as of such significance that
the British claim was maintained to the brink of war, and the
Anglo-Spanish Convention which followed guaranteed freedom of
access to the ocean and the untenanted parts of the American coast.
Vancouver's Instructions of 1791 – drafted by Grenville, the architect of the Government of Canada Act of that year – required the
navigator to examine the nature and extent of any water communication 'which may tend in any considerable degree to facilitate an
intercourse for the purpose of commerce' between the North-West
Coast and the British Colonies on the Atlantic side of the Continent.

The Minister who had just devised a new Canadian constitution was also thinking in terms of trans-continental commerce based on Montreal.[119]

As an Atlantic territory it was hoped and intended that Canada would, on the one hand, gradually replace the United States as the chief supplier of provisions and timber for the British sugar plantations in the West Indies and the Newfoundland fishery and, on the other, would become a corridor through which British manufactures could be directed to the rapidly expanding settlements in the basin of the Mississippi. The concept of a great commercial nexus extending across the Continent to the Pacific and southward into the Middle West naturally involved a change in perspective with regard to the small British Province bordering the St. Lawrence. As a forward base for the distribution of British manufactures, trading centres of Quebec and Montreal would in any case have assumed an enhanced significance in the estimation of Ministers in London, and the merchants' demands for political and judicial emancipation would presumably have been met by proportionately greater concessions; but the pressure for such changes became irresistible with the influx of American Loyalists. The initial settlement on the seigneurie of Sorel – bought for the purpose by the British Government – was followed by planned and assisted settlement in the western parts of the Province. While a similar migration was taking place into Nova Scotia and the Islands of Cape Breton and Prince Edward, Canada received approximately 20,000 Loyalist refugees.[120]

---

[119] Grenville's draft of Instructions to be issued to Vancouver by the Admiralty, 11 Feb., 1791. Printed in Harlow and Madden (*op. cit.*), pp. 40-3. Cf. *Observations relatg. to the proposed Settlement on the N.W. Coast of Am*ª. Secret (1788-9). The principal object of the settlement, it is stated, was the preservation and extension of the fur trade, which would otherwise be exposed to constant interruptions by Spain and Russia. ' An additional inducement to this step arises from the great probability that the late discoveries hold out of finding a considerable and extensive water communication with the interior parts of the Continent, which may in all probability afford the means of establishing a communication with our Posts in the possession of the Hudson's Bay Company, or with the Lakes of Canada, and thereby of acquiring the compleat command of the Fur Trade, by the greater facility of intercourse with the interior Country which we should then possess, and by the means which such a circumstance would afford for exporting the Furs, either by the Atlantic or by the Pacific Ocean, as occasion might require.' If a British post was not established, other nations would gain a footing on that coast ' for the purpose of rivalling our present Fur Trade, and perhaps for that of materially distressing our back settlements on the lakes of Canada by incursions of the Indians '. (*C.O. 42/21.*)

[120] Of these it was estimated that about 15,000 came from the Colony of New York and most of them from the western frontier districts. (See *C.H.B.E.*, vol. VI, p. 191.) Giving evidence before the Board of Trade in 1789, Thos. Ainslie, Collector of Customs for Canada, stated that the population of the Province had risen from 76,000 in 1760 to rather more than 113,000 (including both ' New ' and ' Old ' subjects) in 1784. (*B.T. 5/5*, p. 226.) When the main flow of Loyalist immigration came to an end in 1786 the population of the Province can be estimated (very

The original promise to establish representative government had been given in the expectation that there would be a flow of American settlers into Canada, diverted thither by the halting of westward expansion. That had not happened, but a revolution had brought it to pass twenty years later. The result was the creation of a plural society and a political dilemma. An enclave of some 2,000 merchants had been supplemented by a large influx of like-minded people of their own stock from the south. How was it possible to satisfy the political demands of this enlarged English-speaking community without undermining the French-Canadian system which in 1774 had been entrenched and guaranteed? Involved with that dilemma was another arising from the transformation of the Thirteen Colonies into a foreign power which was spreading out towards the (retracted) Canadian frontier.[121] If the last remnants of British North America were to be saved from absorption by the United States and consolidated as a continental commercial base, the Canadian Province must be fashioned into a bulwark against republicanism. But how? The political and social system of the Quebec Act was no longer adequate for the purpose: on the other hand, to revert to the standard pattern of colonial institutions appeared to be an extremely dubious proposition. In the case of the Thirteen Colonies it had proved disastrously vulnerrable to the very forces which were now to be resisted.

Pitt's reaction to this dilemma during the early years of his Administration was resolutely negative. The existing system, which apparently satisfied four-fifths of the population, was to be preserved, at any rate for the time being. Meanwhile more urgent matters were demanding attention: India, Ireland, financial rehabilitation at home and the adjustment of external commerce to changing circumstances. Other issues also crowded in. The diplomatic crisis over Holland in 1786-7 and the negotiation of a commercial treaty with France were followed by the Regency crisis and then in 1790 by the dispute with Spain over access to the Pacific. Pitt had his own ideas about finance and foreign diplomacy: in Indian affairs he relied on Dundas; and Jenkinson was expert in overseas trade and navigation. But the conflicting demands emanating from Canada presented a baffling problem in a field of policy where authoritative advice, based on local knowledge, was particularly required and notably lacking. Moreover Pitt's

---

roughly) at 88,000 French-speaking and 25,000 English-speaking inhabitants. The Loyalist migration to Nova Scotia amounted to 35,000 which doubled the population of that Colony.

[121] In 1783 the Home Government was urged to take immediate steps to form a settlement in the peninsula between Lakes Ontario and Huron in order to check American expansion. ' The number of Inhabitants who have passed the Appalachian Mountains during the Civil War in America is scarcely credible.' Lt.-Col. J. Connolly to Evan Nepean, 13 June, 1783 (*C.O. 42/15*).

inclination to avoid change was reinforced by the attitude of the King and his Cabinet henchmen, Thurlow and Sydney, who regarded the preservation of the Quebec Act as the essential safe-guard against the forces of subversion.

As Home and Colonial Secretary, Sydney was accordingly left with the congenial task of marking time and resisting innovation. When Haldimand's deputy, Lieut.-Governor Hamilton, began to initiate measures for removing some of the grievances of the English merchants he was promptly recalled (in August, 1785) and replaced by Colonel Henry Hope, a strong supporter of the Haldimand policy.[122] He had been appointed, Sydney informed him, 'with a view towards the suppression of that Party Spirit which has recently shewn itself upon many Occasions within the Province of Quebec, even among those whose immediate Duty it becomes to discourage such a destructive Enemy to good Government'.[123] In short, the King's representative had backed the Opposition.

Eight months later, however, Hope was specially commended in a despatch from the Secretary of State. His sentiments, he was told, on the general affairs of the Province were 'directly correspondent' with the opinion of His Majesty's Ministers, who were well aware of the efforts that had been made by a certain description of people to raise discontents in the Province by organising petitions to the throne against the existing constitution. But in spite of these pro-ceedings, there was no intention of taking any measures whatever for a change in the system of government until opinion in the Province had been consulted and it had been clearly ascertained that such a change would be of material benefit to its general interests and happiness. Meantime favourable consideration was being given to a proposal from Hope which would have stiffened the existing system.

His Majesty feels the strongest disposition to give His [French] Canadian Subjects every proof of his Confidence and will forthwith take under His Royal Consideration the Measure you recommend for increasing their Numbers in the Legislative Council, which indeed had been in contemplation previous to the receipt of your Letter upon that head.[124]

If that had been done the group in the Council (led by Hugh Finlay) which had frequently opposed the Governor and sometimes secured a majority of one or two would have been reduced to

---

[122] Sydney to Hamilton, 13 Aug., 1785. *C.O. 43/8.* It was also stated that Hamil-ton had made appointments to posts which formed part of the patronage of the home Government.

[123] Sydney to Hope, 16 Aug., 1785. *Ibid.*

[124] Sydney to Hope, 6 April, 1786. *Ibid.* Cf. Hope to Sydney, 2 Nov., 1785. (*S. and D.*, pp. 783-6.)

permanent subordination.[125] Pitt's idea seems to have been to broaden the basis of the nominated Council in order to make it more adequately representative of the overwhelming French-Canadian majority and at the same time to allay the discontent of the merchant group. The intention of Dartmouth and North that the English-speaking enclave should be reconciled to a predominantly French system had been frustrated by external events and the obduracy of Carleton and Haldimand. Since the Governor-in-Council had not made the anticipated adjustments by local legislation, Pitt apparently intended to do so at Westminster, when more pressing matters had been concluded, as part of a comprehensive revision of the existing régime. The policy embodied in the Quebec Act was to be developed and reinforced.

That this was thought to be his intention as late as the autumn of 1788 is indicated in a private letter from Lieut.-Governor Hope. While on leave in England his views had been sought by the Prime Minister, and on returning to Canada he wrote in some desperation to Under-Secretary Nepean, expressing the hope that Pitt would not change his mind.

I wish much that Mr. Pitt's honourable intentions towards the Canadian part of the Province, of which I had such striking proof in the conversations he honour'd me with, may not be led away by erroneous statements to give up these poor people's Cause by consenting to a House of Assembly, which . . . will make them the most miserable distracted people under the Sun . . . I shudder for the consequences of what will be likely to pass this Winter in the House of Commons, not without some hopes, however, that the superior Sagacity and penetration of the Minister may prove their Salvation.[126]

Four years earlier the Montreal-Quebec merchants and their supporters in London had also concluded from their own, very different stand-point that in Pitt's 'superior sagacity' lay their best hope. On 25 April, 1785, the London Committee of Canadian merchants with Francis Masères, the agent for the Montreal committee, waited on the Prime Minister. They presented a petition

---

[125] Hope reported that he had been given a very cordial reception by the seigneurs on taking up his appointment and 'that on their support of the present Government as it stands I will venture to assure Your Lordship there is little doubt; and which Sentiments too will be extended to all their Countrymen of every denomination I may also hazard a promise, if it shall be thought adviseable to place so much confidence in them as by adoption of those Measures which I have thought it my Duty to point out in my public letter to Your Lordship, such being my real Sentiments on the most effectual mode to render this Country at the same time satisfied and secure'. (Hope to Sydney, 4 Nov., 1785. *C.O. 42/17*.) This plan would also have put an end to the practice of referring a Governor's recommendation to an *ad hoc* Committee of the Council – as a counter to the Governor's inner or 'Privy' Council.

[126] Hope to Nepean, 2 Jan., 1789. Endorsed: 'recd. 14 April.' *C.O. 42/21*.

from Canada which demanded a greatly enlarged legislative council (nominated for life), an elected assembly, and a redress of judicial grievances.[127] Pitt replied that he could not express an opinion until he had consulted his fellow Ministers, which he promised to do without delay; but he did apparently give a general approbation to the proposition that the Quebec Act should be amended to provide a less autocratic form of government and give better satisfaction to both races in Canada.

The deputation regarded Pitt's response as evasive and Masères complained that he had been kept 'at a bay' by similar general statements from the Prime Minister for the past nine months; but the London merchants refused to antagonise the Ministry by organising an agitation in the City as the Montreal committee had urged Masères thereupon turned to an ally of his, Thomas Powys (later Lord Lilford), a Member of Parliament on the Opposition side.[128] In 1783 he had been active in the negotiations to bring about an all-Whig coalition and was clearly connected with the merchants in Canada. Like Masères he favoured a reform of the existing régime and both seem to have been confident that Pitt was of their way of thinking. Powys accordingly agreed to bring pressure to bear on the Government by presenting the merchants' petition in the Commons. He did so on 3 May (1785) and Pitt

---

[127] Printed in *S. and D.*, pp. 742-52. This petition which was dated 24 Nov., 1784, was an amended version of the petition of 30 Sept., 1783, and reached London in April, 1785. The merchants also produced a plan for a House of Assembly to consist of not more than 70 representatives, of whom 15 were to be elected by the cities of Quebec, Montreal and Trois Rivières and the remainder by rural constituencies. (*Ibid.*, pp. 753-4.) At that time the settlement of Loyalists had just begun.

[128] The proceedings of the London Committee, the interview with Pitt, and the subsequent consultations between Masères and Powys are described in letters of 15, 20 and 26 April, 1785, from Pierre Roubaud to Evan Nepean. (*C.O. 42/20.*) Roubaud had been a Jesuit missionary to the Indians in Canada and had been sent to England in 1764 by General Murray to provide the Government with information about Canadian affairs. While in London he had turned Protestant and his pension had been stopped by his Jesuit colleagues. Thereafter he eked out a precarious existence by trying to make himslf useful to successive Ministers. Hugh Finlay described him as 'a merry companion, an agreeable fellow who made tollerable french verses', but he earned Finlay's scorn by his efforts to undermine the cause of the reformers. During the year 1785 he kept in close touch with Masères and other Canadian figures in London and reported their proceedings (almost daily) to Nepean. Sydney and his Under-Secretary regarded him as 'a very dubious' character but found him useful. In June of that year Roubaud appealed to Sydney's son to approach his father for him as he was entirely without money to buy food. (Roubaud to J. T. Townshend, 1 June, 1785. *C.O. 42/16.*) He was disreputable and unscrupulous, but his letters are interesting and useful – if only for the statements which could not have been inserted had he not thought that they would please his patron. He frequently stated, for example, that Haldimand was the intimate friend of the King and Sydney, who strongly approved his policy and desired to see him sent back to Canada to continue it; and by way of traducing Masères he reported him as having said: 'Let them send back to Quebec their Haldimand . . . we shall take care to have previously informed Mr. Pitt, who will not repent of the concessions in favour of the Canadians for which he has already promised his Ministerial and parliamentary influence and protection.' (To Nepean, 20 April, 1785 *C.O. 42/20.*)

responded with an assurance of the Ministry's intention to remedy
the complaints which had been made.[129] But no action was taken:
Pitt was fighting a rearguard action against the storm of opposition
which had been aroused by his scheme for adjusting relations with
Ireland.

Important action was, however, taken late in July when the
parliamentary session was drawing to a close. A new factor had
been introduced into the situation by a petition from a group of
Loyalist officers in London who intended to settle in Canada.
They had prayed that the new settlements in the western districts
should be detached and given a lieutenant-governor and council
of their own, though subordinate to the Governor in Quebec, and
that land in these districts should be held under the English
system of tenure and not the French.[130] To this the Ministry had
made no response. Yet it was evident that English merchants and
English settlers would soon join forces and Loyalist pressure would
become increasingly formidable.[131]

In Sydney's opinion the Canadian régime was in jeopardy. The
strong arm of Haldimand, whom Sydney supported, was absent,
and it was rumoured that some of the Ministers were opposed to his
return.[132] When further delay in reaching a policy decision became
probable Sydney addressed an agitated memorandum to Pitt.
The British hold on the Province, he wrote, was very precarious.
Two parties were 'raging against each other' (an exaggerated
picture which reflected Pierre Roubaud's reports), and the Americans and the French were busy fomenting these divisions 'with the
assistance of some Persons in Great Britain'. Long ago a précis of
the correspondence with the original petitions for and against the
repeal of the Quebec Act and the establishment of an elective
assembly had been circulated. Since then no other documents
had been called for by any member of the Cabinet; but now it
was declared that the circulation of further correspondence was
necessary. Considerable delay was bound to result, and if more

---

[129] Cf. Roubaud to Nepean, 3 May. *C.O. 42/16.* 'Mr. Powis is this day . . . to
bring into the house of commons Mr. Masères' plan on the Canadian affairs, as
approved by Mr. Pitt who is (as it is pretended) to countenance it with all his
Ministerial influence.' This, of course, was inaccurate, but the draft bill for amending the Quebec Act which Powys introduced in the following April was in line
with what was thought to be Pitt's own views at that time. (See p. 733 below.)

[130] 'The Petition of Sir John Johnson, Bar^t^, and others in Behalf of the Loyalists
settled in Canada' – Dated London, 11 April, 1785. (*S. and D.*, pp. 773-7.)

[131] They were already preparing to do so. See letter from the committee of
Montreal merchants to the London committee of 2 Nov., 1785, quoting a letter
received from a Loyalist in London, dated 15 June. (*Ibid.*, pp. 801-3.)

[132] 'The return of General Haldimand begins to be contradicted from every
quarter. Saturday last Mr. Cramahé informed his friend, Mr. Frémond, that the
king, Lord Sydney and you countenanced that Governor, but that the other Ministers
were very far from befriending him . . .' (Roubaud to Nepean, 3 May, 1785,
ut supra).

than a month was lost it would be too late in the season to write to Canada to any effect.

I can not help dreading . . . that the Cabinet will separate without a decision upon that Point, upon which in my humble Opinion depends whether Canada shall remain ours a twelvemonth longer or not.

Sydney then proceeded to suggest certain measures to retrieve the situation. He was sorry to say that Lt.-Governor Hamilton, in spite of his character and extremely good service in the army, appeared to have led a party in the Legislative Council against Haldimand and after the latter had left the Province 'to have officiously affected to counteract every measure of the Governor'. An excellent substitute would be Colonel Hope: 'the King has not a more valuable Servant in that Country.' The proposal was adopted. In mid-August Hamilton was recalled and Hope was appointed in his place. Sydney also recommended a more important appointment. 'If a Governor-General of all that remains of British Possessions in N. America can be now appointed, Sir Guy Carleton is in my opinion for many reasons infinitely preferable to any other Person . . . and particularly so as the other Governments have in general been *officered* pretty generally by his recommendation.'[133] Again Pitt assented. On 3 September Nepean informed Hope that Carleton had accepted the post and that his powers were to be very extensive, 'so as to give him a full Controul over all other Possessions in America, excluding only the West Indian Islands'. Sir Guy, he added, had just come to Town to be consulted upon the extensive business he was to undertake.[134] Although the purpose of associating all the remaining North American colonies under the authority of a Governor-General seems to have been confined in the first instance to internal security and defence (as in India), the arrangement might have done much to promote a corporate sense; but the natural inclination of the individual governments to correspond directly with London was encouraged rather than otherwise by Ministers and the idea developed little content.

Pitt's reasons for accepting Carleton as Governor-General are not difficult to discern. The inherited dilemma in Canada was

---

[133] 'Memo for Mr. Pitt.' Endorsed – 'Canada Business'. (1785.) The memorandum is unsigned and my identification of Sydney as the author is therefore conjectural; but no one except the Home and Colonial Secretary possessed the knowledge or the status to write in such terms. Apart from his recommendations regarding Hamilton, Hope and Carleton, he refers to the action which he had taken in the case of Chief Justice Livius. 'The Chief Justice, when he was in Quebec, was in constant opposition to Sir Guy Carleton. He made no secret to me, that he should do the same by Gen. Haldimand, if he returned, which made me resolve to prevent his return.' (*C.O. 42/18.*) Livius, though formally reinstated as Chief Justice, never did return to Canada.

[134] Nepean to Hope, 3 Sept., 1785. 'Draught – private.' (*C.O. 42/17.*)

developing fresh complications arising from the incidence of American independence, and the Prime Minister needed responsible advice based on first-hand knowledge. In contrast to the parallel problem of government in India Pitt in this case had neither a Dundas nor a Cornwallis. As Secretary of State in charge of colonial affairs Sydney was useless: his only positive notion was to find a strong man to hold a position which was patently becoming untenable. Instead of being able to rely on a Governor to provide a balanced assessment the Ministry was exposed to direct pressure from two race groups demanding contrary systems of law and government within the bosom of a single state. Carleton was a soldier who had successfully defended Quebec against the Americans: he had already governed the Province for some years and knew its peoples and problems; and there was no one else available of comparable status and experience.[135] Pitt was extremely short of capable administrators to man the Cabinet; and persons of comparable endowment who were prepared to exchange the diversions of London, Bath and their estates for the rigours of distant exile were rare indeed.

Nevertheless Pitt blundered in bringing Carleton back again. A fresh, if uninformed, mind in Canada would have served him better. Carleton was vain and arrogant and the captive of a fixed idea. He was the last person to turn to for new ones, and as the reputed architect of the Quebec Act he was something of a political liability.[136] The choice was probably made without much enthusiasm. Five months earlier the King and Pitt had been astonished to learn from the Duke of Richmond that Carleton had requested a pension of £1,000 p.a. for three lives (his wife and two sons), the colonelship of a regiment of dragoons, and the creation of a new office for himself entitled, Inspector of the Troops. It was also intimated that, unless these favours were conceded, he would decline to serve on the Board of Generals who were to examine the proposed new fortifications.

George III's response was tart. He remembered that Carleton had been promised a pension in 1775 (when Burgoyne was given command of the overland expedition against New York), but North had procrastinated. As to the regiment of dragoons Carleton was

---

[135] Sydney suggested that after Carleton – and a long way after – Lord Adam Gordon might be considered as a possible Governor-General. His rank and family, he said, would impress the French Canadians and he knew and would get on well with Sir John Johnson, Superintendent-General of the Dept. of Indian Affairs and a spokesman for the Loyalists. (Memo., *ut supra*.) Gordon was the second son of the Duke of Gordon, M.P. for Kincardineshire, had served in Jamaica as Colonel of the 66th, 1762-6, and was Commander-in-Chief in Scotland, 1782-98.

[136] When Masères heard a rumour that Carleton was to return to Quebec he was reported as having 'inveighed bitterly against the appointment . . . as the means of compleating the despotism in Quebec'. Roubaud to Nepean, 22 April, 1785 (*C.O. 42/20*).

'little used to get on horseback'; the Inspectorship of Troops was an office unheard of in the British military list and quite uncalled for in view of the smallness of the army in Britain. He should be satisfied with a pension and the promise of 'a good Military Government' when vacant, but to demand a 'heap of favours' as a condition of undertaking a piece of service was a proposition 'not calculated to do him credit'.[137]

Between the uncompromising interpretation of the Quebec Act as maintained by Carleton and Haldimand and the demands for a democratic constitution there was a possible middle course, and this was chalked out by Thomas Powys in a draft Bill which he introduced in the Commons on 28 April, 1786. The exercise was evidently intended as a demonstration against Carleton's appointment and, if possible, to jockey the Government into broadening the terms of the Quebec Act before he could reimpose his authoritarian rule. Powys concluded his introductory speech with the observation that Carleton was an unsuitable person to act as legislator and that the necessary reforms should be effected by Parliament itself before he went out. The Bill avoided the controversial issue of an elected assembly and followed the line of moderate reform which Powys and Masères (who probably drafted it) had understood to be Pitt's own views.

In effect the Powys-Masères plan would have replaced a purely 'Crown Colony' system, in which the Governor was supreme, by a form of constitution which could be termed nominated-representative government. The powers of the Governor were to be curtailed by endowing the Legislative Council with powerful executive checks, and the latter was to be enlarged so that, as a legislature, it would reflect public opinion more accurately and be in a stronger position to reconcile the demands of the two races by agreed legislative adjustments. The Governor would thus operate within defined constitutional limits, and his duty would be to act as arbiter and conciliator as between New and Old subjects.

In future no person for any cause was to be imprisoned by the Governor's own warrant or order, but only by a judicial officer

---

[137] The King to Pitt, 28 March, 1785. *Royal Arch., Windsor.* Draft, original in *Pitt Papers,* P.R.O. 30/8/. Pitt replied (on the same day) that it was cersaintly 'a great object to prevent any disgust being taken by so accredited an Officer', but it would not be easy 'to find a proper Fund'. In consequence of the restrictions placed upon the use of the Civil List by Burke's Act (22 *Geo. III, cap. 82*) it became necessary to submit this proposed pension for the approval of Parliament and Pitt did so – after more than a year's delay. The Resolution was carried *nem. con.,* but not before John Courtenay had taken the opportunity to state that the proposed pension was not in fact a reward for military prowess, but for services of a different character, 'and principally for contriving the law [the Quebec Act] by which British subjects were deprived of the privileges of the British constitution'. (*Parl. Hist.,* vol. XXVI, 190-5. 28 June, 1786.) In the following August he was created Baron Dorchester.

having competent jurisdiction, and such warrants were to be retained by the keepers of the prisons and produced when required under a writ of Habeas Corpus. No member of the Legislative Council was to be removed or suspended for however short a time by the Governor, but only by an order of the King-in-Council or under the Sign Manual, counter-signed by a Secretary of State. The judges were to be similarly protected, but with the proviso that any of them might be suspended for one year for alleged misconduct or neglect of duty on an address being presented by a majority of the Legislative Council and pending final decision from London. Likewise no advocate could be suspended by any authority but that of the judges of the courts in which he practised, and any such order by a judge was to be subject to appeal to the Legislative Council and to a further appeal to the King in Privy Council. As from 1 September, 1785, trial by jury in civil actions was to be introduced whenever either of the litigants desired it, and after the same date all the laws of England relating to the writ of Habeas Corpus and the protection of personal liberty were to have effect in civil, as well as in criminal, cases. Finally, in order that the proceedings of the Legislative Council might be made 'more agreeable to the general sense and Inclinations of the People', the minimum membership was to be raised from seventeen to thirty-one.[138]

In expounding the Bill, Powys declared that a Council dependent on 'the breath of the Governor' was an absurd farce: rather than that it would be better to have no Council at all and make the Governor solely and directly responsible for his actions. His only intention was to afford the inhabitants some degree of personal and political liberty without endangering government in any way. But Pitt was now in a position to justify delay. It was not his intention, he said, to declare against the introduction of a new constitution for Quebec, but the very contrary petitions which had been received were an indication of the great differences of opinion which existed. The appointment of Sir Guy Carleton would afford an early opportunity for an investigation and report by him on the real disposition of the country upon which a solid and permanent establishment could be based. Meanwhile it would be improper to adopt half-concerted and immature measures.

Fox, Sheridan and the rest of the Opposition supported Powys,

---

[138] 'Draught of a Proposed Act of Parliament for the better Securing the Liberties of His Majesty's Subjects in the Province of Quebeck in North America.' (Printed in S. and D., pp. 767-73.) Under the existing quorum of nine the Governor had frequently been able to carry motions with the aid of only five supporters. These clauses providing for the independence of the judiciary and forbidding arbitrary imprisonment derived from Carleton's dismissal of Chief Justice Livius and Haldimand's committing to prison certain persons whom he had reason to suspect of sedition.

criticising Carleton as an unsuitable appointment and the least likely person to report in favour of diminishing his own authority. Fox declared that he was willing and ready to go much further than the Bill proposed. He would give the people of Canada a House of Assembly, for British subjects in every colony ought to have 'a share in their own legislation'. Such a House should consist of men chosen by the people without restriction, regardless of whether they were Roman Catholic or Protestant or indeed of any religion whatever. 'If distinctions of that kind were to be taken, it would not be a free House of Assembly, the true representatives of the people, but one of the vilest oligarchies that had ever existed.' There, of course, was the rub; and had Charles Fox been in office he would, no doubt, have rushed in with his 'solution', consigning both merchants and Loyalists to the care of a predominantly French Assembly. By way of contrast William Young on the Government side opined that Britain had lost the Thirteen Colonies by 'an improvident and inattentive extension of our own government to each of them' and warned the House against repeating the error.[139] Mr. Young did not subscribe to the doctrine of assimilation.

Having taken the potentially important step of creating the post of Governor-General, Pitt was determined to proceed no further until Carleton had furnished him with positive recommendations. Meantime, however, a different aspect of imperial policy was being developed which deeply influenced the character of the system embodied in the Canada Act of 1791. Since the days of the early Stuarts the conjunction of political radicalism and religious dissent had been widely regarded with suspicion and distrust. That sentiment had been sharpened when dissenting New England, the spearhead of revolution, had found natural allies among reforming dissenters at home. For those who held that the interdependence of Church and State was the essential basis of order and good government the American revolt came as a warning that the export of political institutions without their ecclesiastical counterpart could be a disastrous enterprise, depriving the monarchical system in the colonies of its principal sanction.

The policy of planting the Anglican Church overseas by sending clergy (under the jurisdiction of the Bishop of London) and endowing incumbencies by allocating land as glebe had been pursued since the early days of American settlement; but it had been done sporadically and with obvious territorial exceptions. With the rise of colonial discontent and defiance one of the remedial measures

---

[139] For accounts of this debate see *London Chronicle*, vol. 59, pp. 308 and 407. This and subsequent debates on the Canadian question are fully summarised in E. A. Cruikshank, ' Genesis of the Canada Act' (*Procs. of the Ontario Historical Soc.*, vol. 28). Powys's motion was defeated by 61 to 28.

which was contemplated was to strengthen and extend the influence
of Anglican clergy. William Knox, while Under-Secretary for the
Colonies, had prepared (according to his own account) 'a general
plan for the introduction and establishment of the Church of
England and thro' it combating and repressing the prevailing disposition of the Colonies to republicanism, and exciting in them
an esteem for Monarchy'. As part of the plan he proposed the
appointment of a bishop, dean and archdeacon for Nova Scotia and
recommended that their salaries and those of all parochial clergy
should be paid out of the quit rents: a precarious source of revenue.
The presentation of all benefices should be vested in the Governor.
The scheme was considered and approved by the North Administration; but there were more urgent matters to attend to in North
America, and when North resigned nothing had been done.

When his under-secretaryship was abolished Knox remained out
of employment, but during the Fox-North coalition he was used
as an unofficial consultant on colonial affairs, and he took the opportunity of submitting an amended version of his ecclesiastical plan.
In addition to a bishop and endowed benefices for Nova Scotia he
now proposed that there should be an Anglican bishop – with a
larger salary – in Canada; and in Nova Scotia the bishop should
also be head of a seminary in Halifax 'for the instruction of youth
and qualifying them for Orders'. This was essential, as he afterwards wrote to Pitt, otherwise episcopal seminaries in the United
States would become the source of supply, and students from these
colleges would be inculcated with republican principles. 'The
supplying the Churches in the British Colonies with such Pastors
would be like Garrisoning our strongest Fortresses with Troops of
the Enemy.'[140] North agreed that a bishop for Nova Scotia should
be appointed forthwith, but before this could be done the Coalition
had been driven into the wilderness.

One feature of Knox's scheme was, however, put into operation
before Fox and North left office. The question arose of providing
land in Canada for the settlement of Loyalist ex-servicemen and
Knox probably assisted in drafting the Instructions. The land

---

[140] Knox described his previous activities in this connexion in a letter to Pitt,
dated 7 August, 1787. (*Royal Arch., Windsor.*) When Pitt ignored the letter Knox
sent a copy of it to the King. In his covering letter (dated 5 October, 1787) he
declared that his zeal for the royal service was not abated by the continued neglect
which he was meeting from Ministers. The only attention which they had shown
him was the offer of a knighthood which he had declined because he had previously
asked (through Shelburne) for a baronetcy when his under-secretaryship had been
abolished. Although he put forward several schemes, Pitt refused to employ one
whose views on colonial affairs were so notoriously authoritarian. Some two years
later Knox wrote again to the King, reciting his grievances, and stating that in spite
of ministerial opposition he hoped to secure a seat in Parliament, 'with a view to
restore the Royal Influence and to oppose that democratic System which threatens
the depression of the Monarchy'. (Knox to the King, N.D., *ibid.*)

offered for settlement was to be divided into seigneuries or fiefs held of the Crown under feudal tenure: each N.C.O. was made eligible for a grant of 200 acres and each private 100 acres with a further 50 acres for each member of their families; 'and in each Seigneurie a Glebe be reserved and laid out in the most convenient spot, to contain not less than 300 nor more than 500 acres'.[141]

Knox delighted in devising 'systems' as instruments for promoting order and efficiency in a disorderly Empire. His ecclesiastical scheme was not original: it rationalised ideas that were widely held in governmental circles. As early as 1768 the Governor and Council of Nova Scotia had applied to the Board of Trade for financial assistance in establishing an educational institution on Anglican lines in the Colony, and the Board had promised 'liberal aid' as and when a beginning was made under local initiative. A year later a similar application was put to the Society for the Propagation of the Gospel. Again the response was sympathetic, but a decision was postponed because of lack of funds. There the matter rested until after the American Revolution. After the loss of the Thirteen Colonies the increased importance of strengthening Church and State in Nova Scotia was recognised. In March, 1783, a conference of eighteen Loyalist clergy met in New York. They formulated proposals for establishing an American and colonial episcopate and worked out 'A Plan of Religious and Literary Instruction for the Province of Nova Scotia'. The scheme outlined comprehensive proposals for the support of the Church of England in the Colony, including grants of land for the maintenance of clergy and parish churches. It was also recommended that a public seminary or college should be instituted without delay 'at the most centrical part of the province (suppose at Windsor), consisting at first of a public grammar school' and conducted by a teacher of approved abilities and principles who should be a communicant member of the Anglican Church. Carleton, then commanding in New York, was consulted and he forwarded the plan to Lord North.[142]

At home these proposals received a ready welcome. In 1786 Shute Barrington, then Bishop of Salisbury and later of Durham, produced a monograph recommending the establishment of grammar schools in Nova Scotia and a college for the purpose of educating candidates for the ministry of the Church. The monograph was

---

[141] Additional Instructions to Governor Haldimand, 16 July, 1783. (Printed in *S. and D.*, pp. 730-2.) A fortnight earlier the Order in Council of 2 July, regulating commercial intercourse between the United States and British Colonies, had been issued. It incorporated detailed recommendations which Knox had prepared at North's invitation. (See vol. I, pp. 478-81.)

[142] See R. V. Harris, *Charles Inglis, Missionary, Loyalist, Bishop, 1734-1816* (Toronto, 1937), pp. 108-10. Cf. J. W. Lydekker, *The Life and Letters of Charles Inglis* (S.P.C.K., Lond., 1936), Chap VII.

submitted to the Ministry and appears to have been influential.[143]
In this year when ecclesiastical arrangements for Nova Scotia were
under official consideration, Jenkinson at the Board of Trade gave
his old colleague, Knox, an opportunity to re-submit his views
on religious and educational policy in British North America. He
did so promptly and in detail.

> In each of those Provinces immense Tracts of Land remain ungranted.
> Two or three thousand Acres set apart for a Glebe and the Use of a
> School in every new Township or District, would lay the foundation
> of a future Maintenance for Clergymen and Schoolmasters . . . the
> Prevalence of the Church of England in those Colonies is the best
> Security that Great Britain can have for their Fidelity and attachment
> to her Constitution and Interests.

Each colony must have its full complement of Anglican clergy
from the bishop down to the minister in the parish. Parallel with
this there should be an educational system with local schoolmasters
and a college with a professorial staff following a curriculum which
gave special attention to agriculture. The revenue required for
these purposes was to be provided by appropriating 400 to 500
acres of land in each parish or township. In poor or thinly populated
areas the British Government would probably have to provide the
schoolmaster's salary for some time, and the scheme as a whole
might cost the imperial exchequer £4,000 p.a. until the settlement
had developed: but surely, he urged, it was worth it. Lack of such
arrangements had been responsible for the gradual weakening and
final destruction of 'the Bond of Union' between the Thirteen
Colonies and the Mother Country. The continuance of 'doing
things by halves' in the case of the remaining colonies could only
hasten the approach of another revolution.[144]

It does not appear that either Pitt or Grenville was shown this
memorandum,[145] but the similarity between Knox's proposals and
the policy eventually pursued by Government is indicative of a
prevailing sentiment that the established Church, 'sound' educational methods, and the laws of trade were indispensable for preserving imperial cohesion. The real division of opinion arose on
the question whether the reproduction of 'the British Constitution'
was, or was not, a similar bond of union.

In August, 1786, the Board of Trade was at last able to take up
the question of establishing a bishopric in Nova Scotia. They had
before them a supporting representation from the Archbishop

---

[143] Harris (*op. cit.*), p. 110.

[144] 'Proposals for Promoting Religion and Literature in Canada, Nova Scotia
and New Brunswick, left for the Perusal of the Rt. Honble. Mr. Jenkinson.'
3 April, 1786 (*Liverpool Papers, Addit. MSS. 38,219*, f. 58 *et seq.*)

[145] It seems to have remained with Jenkinson. I have found no copy or reference
to it either in the Pitt or the Grenville papers or in the official *C.O.* series.

of Canterbury and the Bishop of London and copies of correspondence on the subject between Carleton and North in 1783. Carleton, now Lord Dorchester, was called in to give evidence and was asked whether he still favoured the project and whether it would be agreeable to the inhabitants. He answered both questions affirmatively, adding that he did not think that the Dissenters in Nova Scotia and New Brunswick would have any objection.[146] Further discussion took place at a meeting on 21 November, and a few days later it was decided to request the Law Officers of the Crown to prepare a legal instrument for the erection of an episcopate within the Province of Canterbury and under specified conditions.[147] In the following March it was decided to extend the bishop's jurisdiction to cover the Province of Quebec, New Brunswick and Newfoundland, and the draft commission was finally approved for submission to the King on 26 April, 1787.[148] In August the Governor-General was given special Instructions to support the Bishop and to promote the establishment of Anglican clergy and schools in all the Provinces.[149]

The first Bishop of Nova Scotia, Charles Inglis, was a Loyalist from New York who had taken a prominent part in formulating the recommendations put forward in 1783 by the clerical conference in that city; and on returning to England he had kept up a correspondence with Carleton on the subject.[150] As soon as he reached Nova Scotia he went to work with a will. At his instance the special Instructions issued to Lieut.-Governor Parr were laid before the Assembly, which responded by passing a series of resolutions. It was recommended that a public school should be established as soon as possible and that an 'exemplary clergyman of the established Church', well versed in classical learning, divinity, and *belles lettres*, should be placed at the head of it with an annual salary of not less than £200. A sum not exceeding £400 was voted for hiring a proper house in the neighbourhood of Windsor and

---

[146] Minutes of the Board of Trade, 23 Aug., 1786 (*B.T.* 5/3, pp. 454-5).

[147] Minutes of 21 Nov. and 5 Dec., 1786. The latter meeting was attended, among others, by Pitt, Sydney, Grenville and the Archbishop of Canterbury (*B.T.* 5/4, pp. 83 and 101).

[148] Minutes of 19 March and 26 April (*ibid.*, pp. 213-5 and 256).

[149] Instructions to Dorchester, 25 Aug., 1787. He was to take care that Churches now built or to be built were kept in good order, 'and that besides a competent Maintenance to be assigned to the Minister of each Parish Church, a Convenient House to be built at the Common Charge for each Minister'. He was also to recommend to every legislature within his government 'to make due Provision for the erecting and Maintaining of Schools where Youth may be educated in Competent Learning and in Knowledge of the Principles of the Christian Religion'. No person in any of the Provinces was to be allowed to keep a school without first obtaining a licence from the Governor-General. (*S. and D.*, pp. 888-90.)

[150] He had engaged in missionary work among the Mohawk Indians and had been the incumbent of Holy Trinity Church, New York, from 1777 to 1783. In 1779 he had been attainted as a Loyalist.

paying the salary of the President of the Academy for one year. The Academy was formally opened on 1 November, 1778, with 20 pupils and in the presence of a numerous and respectable company. Thus was founded King's Collegiate School, Windsor, the oldest residential school in the overseas Empire.

For the Bishop this was only the first instalment: it must be followed up by establishing a college or seminary to provide adequate training for potential ordinands. 'In fact,' he wrote, 'the want of a Seminary will totally defeat in this respect one principal object Government had in view by appointing a Bishop.'[151] Early in 1789 his efforts were rewarded by the passage of an Act through the Nova Scotia legislature, constituting a college and appropriating £500 for the erection of buildings at Windsor to house both the college and the school. It was an ambitious project which would need substantial support from Britain to survive. Without delay Bishop Inglis elicited the aid of his good friend, John Moore, Archbishop of Canterbury, and sought financial assistance from the home Government through Richard Cumberland, the Agent for Nova Scotia.

At this juncture Pitt intervened and in spite of foreign and domestic pre-occupations worked out a scheme of his own. He had evidently been told about the Act passed by the Nova Scotia legislature but does not appear to have been aware that a school had already been started. In April, 1790, he sought the advice of the Bishop of Chester with whom he had previously discussed his plan. Originally, wrote Pitt, he had contemplated a training college in Nova Scotia but now thought that a senior school would be preferable. Each year all the students on this foundation should be sent to London where they would be examined by a board of trustees which would include 'persons of station' from Oxford and Cambridge. The most promising candidates were to be awarded exhibitions to enable them to proceed to Oxford or Cambridge for further study prior to ordination. 'One of the most material points to be settled is the number of Exhibitions necessary to keep up a supply for the Churches in America.' Would the Bishop of Chester please go into this very carefully with the assistance of three or four selected persons, including the Dean of Christ Church, 'as you will of course see the importance of its being accurately arranged?' 'You will observe,' added Pitt, 'how much I dwell on the point of certificates of application and good conduct. I am most strongly impressed with the necessity of carrying this part of the plan into actual and efficient execution.'[152] Apparently the

---

[151] In a pamphlet entitled, *A brief Sketch of the plan on which it is proposed to conduct the Academy of Nova Scotia* . . . Quoted in Harris (*op. cit.*), pp. 111-12.

[152] Pitt to the Bishop of Chester, 11 April, 1790. Copy. (*Royal Arch., Windsor.*) With the original Pitt had enclosed a copy of a letter of his to the Archbishop of

cost of the scheme was to be borne by the British Exchequer.

On 5 June, 1790, Grenville, as Secretary of State, wrote to tell Bishop Inglis that the Act of the Nova Scotia legislature, establishing a college at Windsor, had received the royal assent. He was also informed of the King's intention 'to grant a Royal Charter to that Seminary' and to make further provision for the students. Grenville acknowledged that the Bishop had complied with his previous request for particulars 'concerning the number of Clergymen in the three Provinces and of the sources from which they derive their support', but he now put further questions concerning the state of religion and education 'and the means of promoting them'. In a similar letter of the same date, addressed to Lieut.-Governor Parr, Grenville stated that Parliament had responded to an application from the Agent for Nova Scotia by granting £1,000 on that year's estimates towards the cost of erecting the buildings and that the Crown intended to allocate sufficient land in the Colony to constitute a permanent and growing endowment for the College. Parr was therefore requested to furnish a report on lands still ungranted. His Majesty was of the opinion, continued Grenville, that it would be of the utmost benefit for the education of youth and the maintenance of religion in the British Provinces of North America that the benefices there should be filled by persons properly instructed in the principles of the Church of England. Pitt's plan for the furtherance of that object was then propounded.[153]

Parr and Inglis both supported the project, the latter with enthusiasm. 'I cannot sufficiently applaud the intended foundation for Youth, elected from this Seminary, to compleat their education in the English Universities.' It was a measure founded in wisdom and sound policy. It would stimulate the young men to apply themselves to study, 'attach them to the Constitution both Civil and Ecclesiastical, and become a firm bond of union between the parent State and the Colonies in future'.[154] A general election in Britain

Canterbury on the same subject. In that letter he had considered in some detail the steps which might be taken 'for ascertaining the proportion which the Exhibitioners ought to bear to the Churches, it being of great consequence that the former should not be too numerous'.

[153] Grenville to Lt.-Gov. Parr, 5 June, 1790. Copy in *H.O. 48/1*, ff. 527-33 (Law Officers' papers). Grenville added that he understood that Nova Scotia and New Brunswick had not yet been divided into parishes and Parr was therefore requested to prepare a plan for such a division, 'specifying the Glebe Land and other Emoluments, if any . . . which would in such case be allotted to the clergymen officiating in each Parish in order that proper steps may be taken for placing the Ecclesiastical Establishment of those Colonies on a fixed and permanent footing, liable only to such alterations as their increasing Wealth and Population may hereafter be found to require'.

[154] Bishop of Nova Scotia to Grenville, 19 July, 1790, Halifax. (*Royal Arch., Windsor.*) He implied that the funds provided were somewhat exiguous – not knowing of the Government's plan for an endowment out of Crown lands. He stated that he would probably move to Windsor in the following summer, 'to assist in

and the threat of war with Spain during the summer and autumn of 1790 thrust all such projects aside, but in the following January (when the Canada Bill with its system of Clergy Reserves was almost ready for Parliament) Grenville took up the Windsor College plan again. A letter was sent to the Attorney- and Solicitor-General informing them of the King's intention to grant the College a royal charter and an endowment from the Crown lands. They were also informed of the King's wish that provision should be made at Oxford and Cambridge for a certain number of scholars, 'natives of His American Dominions and elected by the Nova Scotia college', who were to be entitled to the benefit of such foundation for a certain number of years, at the end of which, if qualified, they would be admitted into Holy Orders to fill vacancies in those Provinces. Copies of the Nova Scotia Act and Grenville's correspondence with Parr and Inglis were enclosed, and the Law Officers were instructed to submit a draft of an Instrument 'proper for carrying the above purpose into execution'.[155]

Pitt's idea of providing 'state scholarships' from the college at Windsor, N.S., to Oxford and Cambridge did not materialise; perhaps the university authorities were not co-operative; and the grant of a royal charter was held up until 1802. But in that year John Inglis, the Bishop's son, paid a visit to England and secured a charter which declared that the College was to be 'the Mother of an University' and was to enjoy 'like privileges as are enjoyed by our universities in our United Kingdom'. In all the home Government had made contributions amounting to £4,500.[156] 'Old King's' continued to function at Windsor until 1920 when the main building was destroyed by fire: some years later it was moved to Halifax where it continues in association with Dalhousie University. The early history of this notable enterprise indicates the climate of opinion in which Grenville framed the ecclesiastical provisions of the Act of 1791, and Pitt's personal intervention illustrates the value that was placed on 'anglicanisation' as a means of assimilating colonies to the metropolitan pattern.

Assimilation to the metropolitan constitution was a different proposition and opinion at home was as deeply divided about it as

applying, as far as it will go, the sum granted for building a College, faithfully and frugally'. Thirty students had enrolled, and there would no doubt soon be double that number, 'if the College was once built, and the Institution had more Tutors, and was brought to a proper state of maturity'.

[155] Secy. of State to Attorney- and Solicitor-General, 7 Jan., 1791 (*H.O. 48/1*, ff. 523-5.)

[156] The Bishop laid the corner stone of the new building in August, 1791, but its construction was then held up by lack of funds and 'apprehension of an invasion by France'. Students of the College and of the Academy moved into the completed building in October, 1795. It has been stated that between 1809 and 1866 the Society for the Propagation of the Gospel contributed over £28,000 in grants and scholarships to the College and exhibitions to the School — 'without which both would have failed entirely'. (Harris, *op. cit.*, p. 117.)

in the Province itself although for different reasons. Pitt himself was in favour of a moderate reform of the existing system, but it was evident that the introduction of an amending bill of that sort would have raised the major issue, and the Ministry had no answer to it. To replace 'Crown Colony' Government with the standard model of Governor, nominated Council, and elected Assembly would resolve certain difficulties while creating others. On the credit side the clamour of the Montreal-Quebec merchants would be stilled and the expectancy of the incoming Loyalists satisfied, and it was recognised that the continued allegiance of the new settlers required that their political institutions should not compare unfavourably with those of the up-and-coming American States. On the debit side of the account was the awkward fact that a House of Representatives, elected on any reasonable franchise, would put political power in the hands of an illiterate French peasantry whose loyalty in 1775 had been dubious. Reliance on the local aristocracy in alliance with British officialdom would become impossible and the interminable battle between executive and legislature which had fomented the American revolution would start all over again on Canadian soil – with the added exacerbation of race. On the other hand the merchants' demand that the urban centres of Montreal, Quebec and Trois Rivières should be given a dispro-portionate weightage in the Assembly would produce 'the vilest oligarchies'. Moreover there was the wider issue of Canada's function as a continental commercial base. From the defensive point of view there was apprehension lest the Province should become the recipient of foreign (and particularly French) manu-factures from the United States across an extended and ambiguous frontier, while it was confidently hoped that Canada would develop as a great corridor of British trade into the Mississippi Basin. Both the defensive and offensive aspects of commercial policy called for an effective imperial control of government which had been notably lacking in the case of the American Colonies.[157]

---

[157] Cf. the following comment: With a House of Assembly power might fall into the hands of the disaffected and then no effectual means would be taken to prevent smuggling. It might be argued that the best way of putting Canada on a better footing than the American States and securing that Province to the Mother Country would be to allow the inhabitants to do as they pleased in point of trade. But what use would it be to the Crown? 'The Fur Trade, the only object, would be at an end and the British Goods find very little Vent . . . Very little Rum, which is the principle Article of Commerce, would be entered [from the British West Indies] at the Custom House of Quebec, and the Beaver of the North West would be manu-factured in New York and Philadelphia. In short, Great Britain would lavish Thousands in protecting a Province for the benefit of France and America.' (*Memorandums of the Present Political sentiments of the United States of America, with some remarks on the Navigation of the St. Laurence and Hudson Rivers to the Upper Lakes, and General Observations on the Petition for a House of Assembly for the Province of Quebec.* Endorsed: 'Canada Affairs, from Major Ross, Rd. 2 May, 1785.' *C.O. 42/17.*)

Lord Dorchester's departure for Canada in the autumn of 1786 enabled Pitt to resist all demands for constitutional change with the firm statement that the Ministry had no intention of taking any action until the Governor-General had investigated and made recommendations. Sydney with no constructive ideas of his own relied on Dorchester to hold the fort and to recommend as few changes as possible. In that he probably represented the attitude of the King (who had supported Haldimand) and certainly that of his Cabinet ally, Thurlow. There was, however, a possible compromise which was tentatively put to Dorchester as soon as he had agreed to accept the appointment. The Province, it was suggested, might be partitioned. 'French' Canada and the new Loyalist settlements to the west would be given separate administrations, each with a Lieut.-Governor acting under Dorchester as Governor of the whole. It was assumed that the original province would continue under the conciliar system of 1774 with perhaps certain modifications, but with regard to the new Loyalist province Dorchester was asked to consider whether the Quebec type of constitution should apply or whether it should be given the normal colonial model of council and elected assembly.[158]

Eventually the Government decided to proceed with partition in spite of Dorchester's dislike of it, but that did not advance them very far towards a solution. The situation would be eased if the Loyalists in the west were given an elected Assembly of their own, but in the old Province the merchants of Quebec and Montreal would still be a frustrated minority. Moreover the existing régime was beginning to founder: the British officials, who were expected to do their duty by supporting 'Government' in the Legislative Council, were violently at odds with each other, some supporting the reforming opposition. Perturbed at the prospect of a breakdown, the Ministry decided to resist any change until the officials

---

[158] See 'Plan of General Directions for Sir Guy Carleton' (1786). He was to report as soon as possible on 'the real state of the opinion of the people in general' on the demands for constitutional change: 'to give an Opinion whether there should be any Division of the province . . . what the Constitution of the proposed province should be and whether, if it is expedient to put it upon a different footing from that of Quebec and more analogous to that of the other British possessions, the Loyalists . . . should not be settled there preferably to Quebec. . . .' A caution was added: he was to consider whether a division of the Province 'may not be the means of promoting a Connection with United States, as they may more easily get supplies thro those States than from Quebec'. (Endorsed: 'this for Sir G. C.' C.O. 42/18. Printed in S. and D., pp. 812-13.) These and other directives were incorporated in 'Draught of Particular Instructions to Carleton'. In this later document there are some interesting additions. The words 'for the present' were inserted with reference to the proposed creation of a new province and the alternative forms of its constitution were stated to be either 'similar' to those of Nova Scotia, etc., or 'similar to what is at present, or may hereafter be established' in Quebec Province. (Ibid., pp. 813-15.) As already noted, the Ministry were thinking in terms of a more numerous and more broadly based nominated Council for the latter.

had been brought to heel and pending the receipt of constructive recommendations from the Governor-General.

His Majesty's Servants [wrote Sydney] very much lament that Opinions of so contrary a Nature prevail in the Province upon its Laws and Form of Government. . . . Whatever may be the Event hereafter, it is highly necessary to prevent as far as possible such violent Proceedings among the Servants of the Crown, which cannot fail of weakening His Majesty's Government. At present I am authorised to mention to your Lordship, that it is not the Intention of His Majesty's Servants to recommend at least an immediate change of the Constitution of the Province, and Your Lordship, being in possession of this Information, will be enabled to guide the Servants of the Crown in their future Proceedings.[159]

In a private letter which followed this despatch Sydney still further revealed the ambiguity of his attitude – and evidently that of the Cabinet in general at this time – towards the Canadian problem. The disputes in the Legislative Council, he wrote, were 'extremely disgusting, not to say disgraceful, to the Government'. Some means must be found of preventing this kind of animosity between the King's servants in the Province for no government could subsist in such circumstances. With regard to the British merchants he echoed the views of Haldimand. They ought to be content with the laws of the people with whom they dealt, as they were in foreign countries. In other words they ought to accept a status similar to that of their opposite numbers resident in Amsterdam or Canton. The French Canadians had a right to the laws which had been guaranteed to them and no constitutional change could be made without attending to their rights and opinions. 'Otherwise under the shew of giving a free Constitution, We are really practicing Tyranny.' No one had yet produced a definite plan for an Assembly and in the existing circumstances it would be difficult to form one which was not open to very great objections. 'But I foresee, as well as Your Lordship, that in proportion as the number of British and Loyalists increases in the Province, the applications for one will grow more frequent and pressing.'

This plea for a rearguard action against the introduction of representative government was coupled with support for the idea of dividing the Province. All the disputes in the Council, he wrote, seemed to tend to such a division. 'I wish Your Lordship had given me your thoughts upon that Subject, as well as upon any other plan of adjusting the differences subsisting in the Province.' Dorchester was in a better position to form 'a decisive opinion' on the spot than were Ministers in London. In short, the Govern-

---

[159] Sydney to Dorchester, 14 Sept., 1787. (*C.O. 43/10.*)

ment was at a stand and was relying on him to suggest a way out
of the dilemma, and Sydney personally hoped that he would recommend no fundamental change in the constitution unless and until
he considered that the demand had become irresistible.[160]

Unhappily Dorchester was even more negative than the Secretary of State. His behaviour was not to his credit, for Ministers
had made it abundantly clear to him during the preliminary discussions that he was being sent out to assess the opinion of the
various groups in the Province, to consider against that background
the constitutional alternatives (which were put to him), and to
guide the Cabinet in making its choice. Yet from first to last he
did nothing of value to carry out the mandate which had in effect
been the condition of his appointment. The situation defeated him.
Perhaps for that reason and because of his pro-consular cast of
mind he was mainly preoccupied with the role which he hoped
to play as Governor-General of British North America. As such
his aim was to consolidate Britain's position in the St. Lawrence
basin by stabilising relations with the American States and by
drawing the British Provinces together in some form of federal
association.[161]

When he returned to Canada the new situation evoked a conflict
in his mind. While still convinced that the mass of illiterate French
Canadians required an authoritarian régime, he was very much
alive to the claims of American Loyalists who had suffered for King
and Country. As Commander-in-Chief he had held up the evacua-
tion of New York until a passage had been provided for every
loyalist refugee in that city who asked for it, and in a private

---

[160] Sydney to Dorchester, 20 Sept. Private. (*S. and D.*, pp. 863-5.) The division of
the Province into two parts, each with its own government, would not of itself have
made any difference in the wrangles between the Governor (or Lt.-Governor) and
and those officials in Quebec who advocated legal and judicial reforms. As far as
one can deduce, Sydney's notion seems to have been to retain the Quebec Act
unaltered in ' lower ' Canada while increasing the number of French Canadians in
the Legislative Council and to concede an Assembly to ' upper' Canada if and
when the concession became inevitable. Taken together, his support for partition
and his resistance to an elected Assembly for the Province as a whole only make
sense on that basis.

[161] By the terms of his commission he was empowered to intervene at discretion
and impose his views upon any of the Governments within his jurisdiction. Before
going out to Canada he suggested that one ' intelligent' member of each Council
and one from each Assembly should meet him in May, 1787, ' to arrange and prepare all such measures as they shall judge most likely to promote the security and
happiness and prosperity of the King's American Subjects '. The result of their
joint deliberations were to be submitted to London for approval. Centralisation of
this sort bore no relation to local realities. (See Dorchester's *Memoranda for
Instructions*, 28 July, 1786. *S. and D.*, pp. 811-13.) It is significant that in this
document he ignored the constitutional issues in Quebec Province and asked such
questions as the following: What policy should he follow with the United States?
With each separate State? With Vermont? With the Indians? For his views on
commercial policy see his evidence before the Board of Trade, 16 March, 1784
(*B.T.* 5/1, pp. 26-31).

memorandum of 1786 he had urged the importance of retaining the remaining Colonies in their allegiance by removing sources of discontent. Benefits, he wrote, would fail of their proper effect unless they were granted 'unasked, as soon as may be, and as flowing spontaneously from the benevolence of Government'.[162] An impeccable sentiment; but in trying to translate it into practical terms he dodged the issue. How were incoming Loyalists with their American background to be satisfied and to be made to feel 'at home' without establishing a political system which would draw the French habitans, bewildered and angry, into an inter-racial competition for power?

Dorchester's response was to avoid political decisions by granting administrative benefits. This involved a slight shift in his position. Instead of maintaining the French system *in toto* as before, he now urged concessions to the British minority which he had previously resisted. Changes in commercial law and judicial process were now favoured, provided that they were made gradually; and whereas he himself had been responsible for imposing French feudal tenure in the new settlements, he now advocated the adoption of free and common soccage and that all other burdens on land, such as quit rents, should be taken off. He also proposed that a power should be lodged 'on that Continent' (perhaps in himself?) to protect the people from all vexations, particularly those suffered at the hands of officials.

He was realist enough to recognise that the influx of settlers of British origin would eventually compel the introduction of repre-sentative government, but the consequences so appalled him that he determined to fend it off as long as ever possible. When, there-fore, the Ministry at home repeatedly asked him for a sign, no sign was vouchsafed to them. In June, 1787, he sent home a bundle of petitions, some demanding and others resisting changes in the laws and constitution, which had been submitted to one of his com-mittees of enquiry. The opportunity was taken in the covering despatch to warn Sydney and his colleagues against precipitate action. 'The English party' was steadily increasing in numbers so that the desire for an Assembly would probably grow year by year.

Yet common prudence seems to require, before an alteration of that magnitude should be attempted in a country composed of different languages, manners, and religions (where nine tenths of the people are ignorant of the nature and importance of an Assembly) that the whole plan should be minutely unfolded and its effects upon the Legislature and the provincial economy clearly discerned.[163]

---

[162] Memorandum of 20 Feb., 1786 (S. and D., p. 811, n. 2).
[163] Dorchester to Sydney, 13 June, 1787 (S. and D., pp. 946-8).

An exposition of this kind, he added, ought to be published and time given for all men to read and digest it: otherwise disappointment and disorders might arise even at the outset. 'For my own part, I confess myself as yet at a loss for any plan likely to give satisfaction to a people so circumstanced as we are at present.' Meanwhile let removal of grievances and the dispensation of benefits continue. Once more he urged that the Loyalists be allowed to hold their lands by British tenure.[164] And then came a proposal which gives some indication of how Dorchester envisaged the future if only the Ministry could be deterred from taking premature decisions. In every township of 30,000 acres let 5,000 be retained by the Crown.

These reserved parcels will enable His Majesty to reward such of His provincial Servants as merit the Royal favour, and will also enable the Crown to create and strengthen an Aristocracy, of which the best use may be made of this Continent, where all Governments are feeble and the general condition of things tends to a wild Democracy.[165]

The aim presumably was a united Canada secured against disorders by a colonial gentry working in alliance with French seigneurs. The common interests of aristocracy were to be the guarantee of political stability. Four years later Dundas pressed for a similar conjunction of aristocratic interests, Protestant and Catholic, in the case of Ireland.[166] A policy on these lines (had it been practicable) required constitutional integration, and we find Dorchester strongly opposed to the Cabinet's idea of partition, even though it would have enabled him to recommend the continuance of the *ancien régime* in one part of the Province, while permitting the Loyalists to indulge in political warfare, so beloved of their race, in the other.

In May, 1788, the Government came under violent attack from the Opposition in the Commons for their continued inaction. The new and formidable agent for the reform party in the Province, Adam Lymburner, was introduced by Thomas Powys and was heard in committee. In a paper, which he read, he elaborated the petition before the House, demanding the reforms which Powys had incorporated in his Bill two years before and the establishment of

---

[164] 'It is not on account of these [Loyalist] petitions,' he added, 'that I propose the alteration, but because I judge it highly expedient to remove the Smallest Cause of discord between the King's Government and His people, or between Great Britain and these Provinces, on any score whatever.' (*Ibid.*)

[165] In an additional note Shortt and Doughty comment: 'This paragraph indicates the central policy of much of the Constitutional Act of 1791, and the basis of the Crown Reserves, in addition to the Clergy Reserves.' (*Ibid.*, p. 948, n. 1.)

[166] See vol. I, pp. 631-3.

an elected Assembly. In his reply to the debate Pitt insisted, despite dissent, that the Ministry could not and would not make a decision until fuller information had been received from Lord Dorchester. That information was expected at any time, and he accepted a resolution that the matter would be taken into consideration by the House early in the next session.[167]

During the recess the Cabinet decided to force an opinion out of the Governor-General. In a despatch, dated 3 September, Sydney referred to the debate and to the necessity of the King's servants being in a position to bring forward definite arrangements for the Province when Parliament re-assembled. Once more he was requested to furnish an analysis of the numbers and property of the various groups, district by district, who were for or against a change in the constitution. His letters and enclosures had supplied some information, but Ministers did not think they were 'sufficiently explicit to enable them to form a decided opinion'. An outline plan was set out and a definite Yes or No was requested to each part of it. The Ministry were contemplating a division of the Province: did he agree? If this plan were adopted, did he think that the numbers and situation of the inhabitants in the western district 'are such as do, or do not, make the immediate Establishment of an Assembly . . . practicable and adviseable'? With regard to the remaining part of the Province the Ministry intended to be guided very largely by the information which they expected to receive from him, but it was broadly hinted that they were disposed to 'resist' any change in its constitution.[168]

Reticence and evasion were no longer possible.[169] Dorchester's response was definite enough but singularly unhelpful. For the Province as a whole he saw no immediate need for any alterations except in the sphere of law. 'A division of the province, I am of opinion, is by no means adviseable at present, either for the interests of the new or the ancient districts.' The western settlements were not yet in a condition for a form of government above the level of a county, which had lately been given to them. Although he was against a division, he considered that no time should be lost in appointing a person with the title of Lieut.-Governor, who possessed the confidence of the Loyalists, 'to superintend, and lead them, and to bring their concerns with dispatch to the knowledge of Government'. If, however, His Majesty's Ministers decided that the Province must be divided, he saw no reason why the western

---

[167] This debate (of 18 May) is reported in *Parl. Hist.*, vol. XXVII, 506-33. The petition which was then re-read had been previously submitted on 11 March.

[168] Sydney to Dorchester, 3 Sept., 1788. (*S. and D.*, pp. 954-8.)

[169] Cf. Hugh Finlay's observation: 'I am ignorant of Lord Dorchester's way of thinking relative to a house of the representatives of the people; I do not believe that he has confided his opinion to any person on this side of the Atlantic.' (To Nepean, 9 Feb., 1789. *Ibid.*, p. 961.)

settlements should not have an Assembly and an English system of law.[170]

As an adviser Dorchester had failed in his duty. He had not provided the detailed assessment of local opinion and conditions which had been repeatedly requested. Nor when the Ministry put a definite plan before him did he explain his reasons for opposing it. Yet his attitude was not merely that of petulant obstruction as is sometimes assumed. Aware, as he was, that the consequences of American independence had transformed the situation in Canada and the maritime Provinces, he championed the thesis that the old mistakes could and must be avoided and a balanced society evolved, buttressed against the subversion of 'wild democracy'. That could best be done by a paternal supervision of the entire area from Quebec. The western settlements should remain – 'at present' – as a sub-division of the Province to enable the moulding process to be effected. For French Canada he envisaged a lengthy period of continued paternalism while the merchant minority was placated with gradual adjustments in commercial law and kept in political subordination. His desire was to buy time for a gradual evolution on the 'right' lines.[171] A similar desire, defeated by the political facts of life, has been a common experience in our own age in Asia and Africa. Dorchester's reactions at this critical juncture in the history of British colonial government represent an important element in contemporary thinking.

We must now turn our attention to the action of Ministers on this issue when a decision could no longer be postponed. After the

---

[170] Dorchester to Sydney, 8 Nov., 1788 (*ibid.*, pp. 958-60). Instead of producing a full-scale report, as ordered, he prefaced this despatch with a laconic summary (comprising three paragraphs) of the population ratio of the French Canadians and the British and of the general attitude of the merchants, the seigneurs and the habitans. It added little or nothing to what the Government already knew from the various petitions.

[171] This is, I think, a valid interpretation of his brief official statements, but he never expounded them with supporting arguments. In a private letter to Sydney, dated 14 Oct., 1788, he reported that he had visited the Loyalist settlements in upper Canada and had found them happy and grateful. In a few years' time they would make a very considerable portion of the Province, 'and under proper management will afford no small support to the interests of Great Britain'. With reference to Sydney's remark that the disgraceful wrangles on the Legislative Council pointed strongly to a partition he commented: 'a division of the Province would not . . . afford a remedy to that evil, though the measure might otherwise be attended with good consequences and may indeed become necessary in a little time.' He also indicated his attitude towards legal and judicial alterations. 'One party will not admit of any change in the Ancient Laws . . . ; The other would change too much, and in these Extremes has lain the Error.' The sudden introduction of volumes of unknown Laws for the disposal of private property would be neither wise nor just. 'On the other hand, it was never the intention of the Quebec Act to shut the door against every alteration.' He concluded this letter with a remark which must have surprised and annoyed the waiting Ministers: 'An early decision upon the affairs of Canada at home is much to be wished; people's minds are now in constant agitation.' (Précis of Dispatches received from Lord Dorchester – from No. 80 of 28 July, 1788 to No. 97 of 8 Dec., 1788. *C.O. 42/20.*)

jolt administered by the Opposition in May, 1788 (when Pitt was having a difficult passage over the slave trade), the Administration was virtually committed to bringing in a Canadian Constitutional Bill 'early in the next session'. The Cabinet's provisional plan was sent off to Dorchester late in the sailing season by a special packet boat; but even if a speedy reply had been possible, the normal work of the Administration was suddenly interrupted early in November by the King's first attack of insanity. When the Regency crisis had passed, a recovered but weakened monarch resigned himself to taking a less active part in the direction of state affairs and Pitt was able to begin the process of reinforcing his own leadership in the Cabinet. In June, 1789, Sydney was superseded by Grenville as Home and Colonial Secretary. Another session had been lost: a decision before Parliament reassembled was imperative.

Grenville set to work at once and within a few weeks produced an outline plan which he embodied in a long explanatory memorandum. This was discussed and agreed with Pitt and then – as a necessary gesture – submitted to the Lord Chancellor. Early in October he sent a copy of it to the King. In a covering letter he wrote:

The business of Quebec [was] the most important and extensive of any of the subjects which Mr. Grenville found in the office when Your Majesty did him the honour to intrust him with the Seals. Mr. Grenville has bestowed as much attention as was in his power upon this interesting Subject, and he now presumes to lay the inclosed paper before Your Majesty as the result of the best opinion which he can form upon it.[172]

When Grenville applied himself to the Canadian problem with his customary thoroughness and clarity he found most of the evidence which he needed already available in the Department, and this was organised for him by Under-Secretary Nepean and his clerks. Annotated summaries were made and a large collection of reports from 1765 onwards was referred to the Law Officers for

---

[172] Grenville to the King, 12 Oct., 1789. 11 p.m. (*Royal Arch., Windsor.*) He went on to say that he had availed himself of the assistance of the King's other Ministers and in particular had communicated it 'some time since' to the Lord Chancellor and Pitt who had appeared to agree with him 'upon the leading points'. If in these circumstances the King would approve, he proposed to write to Dorchester in order to receive from him before Parliament met 'an opinion upon several points of detail which are necessary to the execution of the Plan stated in the inclosed Paper'. The memorandum is not among the King's papers at Windsor and was evidently returned to Grenville, but this letter confirms the previous identification of Grenville as the author. Cf. H. T. Manning, *British Colonial Government after the American Revolution, 1782-1820* (Yale and Oxford, 1933), p. 328, n. 37. For George III's comments on the memorandum (sent to Grenville on the following day) see p. 765 below.

their opinion.[173] Grenville did not take long to make up his mind about the underlying principles and the main features of his constitutional plan, but he lacked the precise statistical information which Dorchester had failed to provide. On applying to Sir Frederick Haldimand he learned that the latter had sent just such a document to Hawkesbury for the use of the Board of Trade, and Nepean secured a copy of it.[174]

Among the facts and opinions available to Grenville were those provided by Hugh Finlay, the leader of the moderate reform party in the Canadian Council, in a long series of letters to his friend Nepean. A number of the points which Finlay made in his temperate way are reflected in Grenville's memorandum. When first asked his opinion on the demand for an Assembly, he had replied (in November, 1784) that no one could say with certainty that a majority of the people desired it. The habitans had not been consulted, probably because they were thought to be too ignorant and would be 'revolted' when it was explained to them that representation would involve the voting of taxes. 'I am aware that the word, tax, will startle a Canadian, yet a little pains may bring them to acquiesce.' But he was troubled about the British element. 'The Loyalists who have sat down among us will keep us in constant hot water until they obtain a house.' Being landowners and segregated in the western settlements they would be able to elect their own members; but would French Canadians be adequate representatives of British-merchant interests in the eastern districts?[175]

Two months later he presented the French-Canadian problem in more forceful terms. The habitans, he repeated, might be brought to agree 'by dint of reasoning', but to instil constitutional prin-

---

[173] See for example, 'Notes relative to Quebec' (1785-88) (*C.O. 42/20*); précis of Dorchester's despatches (*ut supra*); précis of papers relating to ecclesiastical affairs; and lists of papers relating to the laws and government of the Province sent to the Law Officers in successive batches (*C.O. 42/21*). Adam Lymburner, the Canadian Agent, also supplied a number of useful documents, including extracts from a book by a French official, Petit, *Sur Le Gouvernement Des Colonies Françoises* (Paris, 1771).

[174] Nepean to Hawkesbury, 29 Aug., 1789. 'Mr. Grenville has been endeavouring by every means to find out a tollerably accurate Account of the State of the Population in the Province of Quebec, distinguished under the different heads of British Settlers before the War – Loyalists settled in the Upper Country – Canadians – Number of Noblesse among the Canadians – the number among them who are Heads of Families, etc. . . . .' Mr. Grenville, he added, was now looking into the Affairs of that Province and was in need of Haldimand's report. It would be returned as soon as a copy had been made. (*Addit. MSS.*, 38,224, f. 268.)

[175] Finlay to Nepean, Quebec, 6 Nov., 1784. (*C.O. 42/16*.) Cf. George Pownall, Secy. of Quebec Province, to J[ohn] P[ownall], 11 Nov., 1784. 'The Freeholders here being almost all french, would they not return french men, and at least twenty to one? I know they would. The Seigneurs have ever been so unpopular among the habitants [*sic*] that I am persuaded few of them would ever be returned and that consequently the Assembly would consist of the lowest of the people.' (*Ibid.*)

ciples into the minds of twenty or thirty thousand peasants who could not read would be a work of time: it would have to be done from the pulpit. 'Exempt a Canadian peasant from taxes, *corvées*, and from billeting soldiers, let him go to Mass, and little will he care who governs, or what form of Government he lives under.' Careful explanation would always be necessary, otherwise the imposition of every tax, even though imposed by their own elected representatives, would be regarded as an act of oppression. Twice before the conquest the French Government had ordered taxes to be imposed and on each occasion the Intendant had deemed it inadvisable to obey.[176]

The real answer in Finlay's opinion was education – on English lines. The first step was to have a free school in every parish. 'Let the schoolmasters be English if it would make Englishmen of the Canadians'; and let the schoolmasters be Roman Catholics if that was necessary to overcome the opposition of the priests. When the people became more enlightened they would probably wish for an alteration of the present system: in the meantime let it be known that an elective house would be granted as soon as a majority of the people asked for it.[177] From the same point of view he strongly criticised (in 1787) the attitude of those of his British colleagues on the Council who maintained that the French Canadians ought to be left as a distinct and separate community, 'a strong barrier between our Settlements and the United States'. That was not, he opined, the most likely means to turn them into Englishmen.[178]

Finlay's prescription was to educate the French-Canadian peasant in order to achieve political integration. A general understanding and acceptance of British political institutions would enable the minority groups of British origin to work harmoniously with French-speaking colleagues in a united elective legislature. All would be 'English in their hearts'. The doctrine of assimilation, so much discussed in 1774, naturally reappeared after 1783; but its advocates recognised that a lengthy period of preparation, perhaps ten or fifteen years, was required; and that time was no longer

---

[176] Finlay to Nepean, 10 Jan., 1785. (*Ibid.*)

[177] Finlay to Nepean, 22 Oct., 1784. (Printed in *S. and D.*, pp. 739-42.)

[178] Finlay to Nepean, 13 Feb., 1787 (*Ibid.*, pp. 843-5). On 12 April, 1787, he sent Nepean the text of a speech which he had intended to deliver in the Legislative Council. It included the following passages: 'the Laws we make relative to commercial matters ought to be assimilated to the Mercantilist Laws of the Country which supports our trade, and let us ever remember that England holds her Colonies but in a commercial view . . . I may safely assert . . . that there is not two thousand of the King's new subjects that have any particular attachment to the ancient form of Government . . . I have ever been of opinion that the Peasants of this Country would be just what it may please us to make them in temporal matters, by means of good and wholesome laws properly promulgated. A little pains will make them Englishmen, and the sooner they get rid of unnecessary predilections (if any remain) the better it will be for this as a British Colony where we ought all to be English in our hearts.' (*C.O. 42/19.*)

a purchasable commodity. A possible alternative was to grant an Assembly at once while safeguarding the position by giving the English-speaking districts additional representation; but Sydney had already stated the Cabinet's resolute opposition to this device as a form of tyranny.

During the Commons debate in May, 1788, Pitt had expressed his general agreement with the reforms which Powys had again brought forward, but he resisted his new advocacy for an elected Assembly. Powys was reminded that in 1786 he had said that the proposition was too delicate to be supported. Now, said Pitt, a decision was infinitely more delicate and difficult. Opinion in the Province was deeply divided. 'To give Canada an House of Assembly, therefore, under the present circumstances, would be to change a solid blessing into a substantial curse.' Powys had referred to the fact that Nova Scotia and New Brunswick enjoyed representative government, but those colonies bore 'not the most distant analogy' to that of Canada. And in response to an onslaught from Fox he pointed out that the proposed legislature would be such as had scarcely ever existed: 'An Assembly in which Catholics were to sit equally with Protestants, and to enjoy the same powers.' Would the right honourable gentleman be prepared to say that this was a system universally desired?[179]

In fact, the Ministry had virtually decided, as we have seen, to divide the Province and to grant an Assembly to the upper or western division, while being disposed to retain the conciliar system for the remainder. When Grenville succeeded Sydney this was the provisional framework within which he worked; but a nominated legislature which lacked the power to impose taxation had proved an expensive luxury. The revenue raised from indirect taxation had been disappointing, partly because of evasion by the merchants, and the British Exchequer had been obliged to carry an increasing burden in meeting the Province's deficits. In 1788 the cost to the Treasury had amounted to £152,583.[180] This was the price of paternalism, and the arrangement ran counter to the general policy of inducing the outlying parts of the Empire as far as possible to pay their own way. To establish a taxative house of representatives in western Canada, where pioneer farmers were struggling to

---

[179] *Parl. Hist.*, vol. XXVII, 516-21.

[180] See 'An Account of the Expences paid, or payable by the Rt. Honble the the Paymaster-General or his Deputies on Account of the Provinces of Canada, Nova Scotia, New Brunswick and the West India Islands for the Years 1784 . . . 1791.' (*C.O. 42/21.*) In the (abnormal) year, 1784, the amount for Canada was £289,535; in 1791 it was £165,785. The wage bill for the staff of the Dept. of Indian Affairs (under Sir John Johnson) had been reduced from £17,420 in 1782 to £3,344 for 1787. (Returns of appointments in the Dept., *C.O. 42/18.*) On the other hand the sums paid in presents to the Indian tribes between 1784 and 1788 amounted on an annual average to about £22,000. ('Amount of Presents sent to the Indians in Canada . . .' *Pitt Papers*, P.R.O. 30/8/346.)

make ends meet, while leaving the prosperous merchants of Quebec and Montreal and the self-sufficient habitans to rely on the British taxpayer was not an attractive proposition. Moreover Britain's renunciation in 1778 of the right to impose internal taxation in the colonies ruled out the possibility of increasing local revenue by action from Westminster; and the merchants in lower Canada who were clamouring for an Assembly pointed out with justification that the restrictions of Treasury control (to use a modern phrase) were causing roads to fall into decay and the general development of the Province to be retarded. The financial case for running the political risk of establishing a predominantly French Assembly in Quebec was strong – almost to the point of compulsion.

Grenville also inherited two basic ideas concerning future British policy in Canada which coincided with his own outlook. They figure prominently in the texture of the Constitutional Act of 1791. One of these was to extend and endow the Church of England in the Province as a natural means of promoting a genuinely 'British' political and social order. The other idea, proposed by Dorchester, was complementary to the first. One-sixth of the land in each new area should be reserved to the Crown and granted as occasion served to persons in Canada who had merited the royal favour. Thus endowed, such persons would constitute a local aristocracy.

These were the raw materials which lay to Grenville's hand. He began his memorandum with an analysis of the arguments for and against a change in the constitution.[181] From these he adduced a reasoned case for granting representative institutions throughout the Province. The attitude of each group was considered in turn. The merchants had repeatedly urged it. As for the Loyalists their silence on the subject could not be construed as indifference: indeed every circumstance appeared to indicate that they wished 'to partake of the forms of the British Government'. Turning then to the mass of habitans, he noted their hostility to paying taxes; but they were going to be taxed in any case, and they would be much more reluctant to see a taxative power vested, not in a body of persons chosen by themselves and actuated by the same interests, but 'in some other body whatever it might be' over which they had no control. It did not appear, wrote Grenville, that this point

---

[181] For this purpose he used the petition of Nov., 1784, and the objections to it, together with the arguments advanced by Adam Lymburner in 1788. At this stage Lymburner seems to have exercised considerable influence with Ministers. In January, 1788, he had several interviews with Pitt and supplied him with documents, including an able memorandum of his own, setting out the position of the Quebec-Montreal merchants in the Canadian economy. (Lymburner to Pitt, 24 Jan., 1788. London. *Pitt Papers*, P.R.O. 30/8/346.) Later, however, his efforts to secure a disproportionate representation in the Assembly for his clients were rejected.

had ever been put to them. As for the seigneurs they were afraid
that a predominantly English-speaking legislature would be hostile
to their seigneurial privileges and to French law and custom. 'But
no sufficient objection will arise from hence against the establishment of an Assembly, if it can be accompanied with such measures
as will guard against the danger of the preponderance apprehended.'

The essential factor was the need to raise an adequate revenue
in Canada. At the time of the Quebec Act it was clearly intended
that the Parliament of Great Britain should authorise additional
imposts as occasion might require; but no such power resided any
longer at Westminster, and in any case it had never been understood with respect to the ancient Colonies that the right of the
British Parliament should be so used as to take the place of contributions raised by provincial legislatures for domestic purposes.
The absence of any power of taxation in Canada itself could continue no longer. 'In our present circumstances the establishment of
such a power is the only mode by which Great Britain can hope
to be delivered from the heavy expences which she now supports on
account of that province' – a burden which was bound to increase
as the population expanded.[182] If a taxing power must be established on the spot, the question arose as to the character of the
legislature in which it was to be vested; and Grenville answered
that such authority could not be supposed to reside 'without the
greatest difficulties' in the hands of any man or body of men other
than a legislature 'formed nearly on the model of the Constitution
of Great Britain'.

To combine French Canadians and Loyalists in one (elective)
legislative body would, however, provoke dissension and animosity;
and since their interests differed the victory of either party might
well be injurious to the other. The Province was already divided,
'in fact, tho' not by law', and the 'natural remedy' was to accept
the fact and establish two distinct legislatures in which the separate
interests of the Old and the New subjects would respectively pre-
ponderate. If this were done, the wishes of all parties might be
gratified and the establishment of a Council and House of Assembly
in each part would secure 'the essential object of taxation'. Grenville thus endorsed the previous opinion of the Cabinet about the

---

[182] The policy of inducing overseas dependencies to carry their own costs of
administration and defence as much as possible was vigorously pursued by Dundas
when he succeeded Grenville as Home and Colonial Secretary in 1791. In a despatch
to Dorchester about the intended establishment of a locally recruited corps in
Upper Canada he wrote: 'It is in every Point of View highly essential to adopt any
Plan which has for its Object the gradual Increase of the internal Strength of the
remote Dependencies of the Empire.' It was right that in their infant state they
should be maintained and protected by the Mother Country, but it was also the
duty of the home Government to promote their development by every means, 'with
the View of gradually relieving this Country from the Expences of its Colonial
Establishments'. (Dundas to Dorchester, 16 Sept., 1791. *C.O. 43/10*.)

desirability of partition but took new ground in insisting that for financial reasons representative government must be introduced into Lower as well as Upper Canada.

Two awkward problems remained. In the first place the aversion of French Canadians to paying taxes might not be overcome even by vesting fiscal authority in the hands of their own elected representatives. The latter, Grenville implied, might refuse to vote supplies. That argument he brushed aside. 'Such an Objection cannot be allowed to operate, unless Great Britain were content to take permanently upon herself the whole present and future expence of the province.' Secondly, in this House the British merchants would be in a decided and permanent minority: partition would separate them from their natural allies, the Loyalists, and they would be subordinated to the will of a race group which had always opposed their efforts to secure the introduction of English commercial law and practice.

This was a difficulty which could not be ignored. Small in number, they represented almost the entire trade of Canada, which, it was hoped, would rapidly extend into the Mississippi basin and across the Pacific. Adam Lymburner and his London Committee saw to it that Ministers did not overlook the importance of this merchant minority. Grenville tried to meet the difficulty with the suggestion that Parliament should intervene before the creation of the new Canadian legislatures and amend the commercial code of the Province in so far as might on examination be found ' to be really necessary for the security and protection of the British Merchant '. The whole subject, he added, had been referred to the Law Officers for consideration and report. Similar action, it will be recalled, had been proposed at the time of the Quebec Act, but the decision of Dartmouth and North to leave adjustments to be made by local legislation had been almost inevitable. There was, in fact, no self-contained code or 'law merchant' which could be applied to Canada: the regulation of matters pertaining to commercial transactions was widely diffused in the common law. A review of all the relevant British statutes, conventions and legal processes and their adaptation to local conditions in the light of French law and custom would have been a vast and intricate undertaking, involving an impracticable degree of metropolitan interference. When the lawyers convinced Grenville of this, he abandoned the idea; but he informed Dorchester that he had done so with considerable reluctance and with apprehension of the possible consequences for British trade.[183]

---

[183] Grenville to Dorchester, 5 June, 1790. (*S. and D.*, pp. 1024-7.) Having decided not to include major changes in commercial law in the Constitutional Act, he also informed Dorchester that ' the insertion of those of smaller importance would not be desireable '. On the eve of granting representative government this was a very

Having stated a reasoned case for a complete break from the political system of 1774, Grenville proceeded to the next stage of his argument: that a Canadian constitution on the British parliamentary model need not result in another American revolution. The fatal mistake in the case of the Thirteen Colonies, he contended, was not that they had been given the British Constitution but that they had been allowed to distort it into caricature. At home the House of Lords, representing the aristocracy, was a support to the Crown and a check on the 'democratical' element in the Commons. But in the old colonial governments this 'intermediate power' had been lacking: the weakness of the second chamber 'was, of all others, the point in which they were the most defective'. To this more than to any other general cause the defection of the American Provinces was to be ascribed.

The influence of the old colonial councils as the upper house of the legislature had been undermined by the fact that they were also part of the executive government and that, as such, members were liable to be removed from their legislative function at the pleasure of the Crown. They could thus acquire no permanent status above the rest of the community. It followed, therefore, that there ought to be two distinct councils, one legislative and the other executive; and in order to assimilate the former more closely to the House of Lords its members should be appointed for life and if possible given some mark of inheritable distinction, such as a baronetcy or perhaps later on a peerage. Members of the Executive Council should continue to be removable at pleasure and might be composed in part of members of either branch of the legislature.

Carrying the principle of assimilation a stage further, he urged that the power and influence of the representative of the Crown must also be reinforced. This had been a weakness in the old system scarcely less glaring than the lack of a strong aristocratic upper chamber. Here, however, he was on more difficult ground and his proposals were tentative. Could not the royal power of veto be made more efficient both on the spot and as exercised at home by the King-in-Council? The subject was worthy of 'attentive consideration'. In cases of urgent and temporary pressure the Governor might be invested with 'the full legislative power of the Crown' so that in such cases he could issue decrees on his own authority. With regard to normal legislation the usual powers of reservation and disallowance might continue, or alternatively (and

understandable decision. On the other hand, the establishment by imperial legislation of one or two principles, such as the optional use of juries in civil causes, would have done much to allay the discontent of the merchants which continued to be a major source of inter-racial rancour. In this despatch Grenville evinced considerable uneasiness about the future in this respect – 'but the difficulty appears to me unavoidable'.

here he revived an idea which had been mooted and then discarded in 1774) all provincial bills might be suspended until the
King's assent had been expressly given.

The suggestion was impracticable on a number of grounds, but
Grenville was concerned to show that the powers of the executive
government in all its aspects needed to be reviewed and strengthened wherever possible. At home this branch of the constitution
operated through the immediate presence of the Sovereign 'and
the influence of his Court', but not in a distant dependency. An
adequate substitute could not be provided unless the viceroy overseas was vested with proper influence and dignity. Unhappily the
Governors in the American Colonies had enjoyed neither. Limited
in authority, often dependent for their maintenance on the local
Assembly and with little consequence attached to their station,
they had sometimes been men whose character and rank were ill
adapted to remedy the defect arising from the absence of the
Sovereign.

It was noted with satisfaction that much had been done since
the revolution to enhance the dignity of the office by creating a
Governor-General for British North America and uniting in his
person supreme civil and military power. At this point, however,
Grenville ran on to thin ice and he was obliged to skate delicately.
If the analogy of the parent constitution was to hold good, the
King's representative ought to be in a position to underpin his
Government by a discreet use of patronage. But a colonial Governor
possessed no such resource, for colonial patronage was a closely
guarded perquisite of the Government at home and was employed
for domestic purposes. Grenville was obliged to cast about for
alternative means. He noted that the situation had been improved
by the Act of 1782 preventing persons appointed to colonial offices
from holding them in absence.[184] In consequence a number of
officials were now constantly resident within the Provinces who by
virtue of their employment were attached to the existing form of
government and to the connexion with the Mother Country. But
many more were needed, not only as supporters of the régime, but
also to provide an adequate administrative service. Moreover the
need would grow as Canada developed. No additional expense to
Great Britain for this purpose could or ought to be proposed. On
the other hand, colonists in Canada, like those in the American
Provinces, would naturally be very slow to tax themselves 'for
the purpose of maintaining establishments in which they were
hardly allowed to share'.

It was difficult, wrote Grenville, to find a remedy. In Britain
the Crown possessed a large hereditary revenue which was

---

[184] 22 Geo. III, cap. 75.

exchanged for a Civil List; but nothing of the sort had been established in America. Perhaps it was not too late, even now, for the adoption of such a system. Even in Lower Canada there were large tracts of land still ungranted which would rise in value with the increase of population, and in Upper Canada cultivation was still in its infancy. If a proportion of the land were reserved to the Crown in all future grants a permanent and growing revenue would be secured. The colonial Government would thus gain in strength and status by being enabled to provide an efficient, loyal and expanding administrative service without having recourse to the British taxpayer or to a resistant Assembly.[185] In the event it was to be the Protestant clergy and not administrative officials who were endowed by this method, and with unhappy consequences.

It is significant that Grenville felt it necessary to conclude with an apologia which sought to prove that the constitution of 1774 was no longer workable and that his own version of representative government could be introduced with safety. The tone is defensive. 'A doubt may naturally suggest itself, both from an opinion which seems to be pretty generally received, and from an observation of the late events in America, whether the degree of freedom which the measure, now proposed, would give to the Canadians, is not inconsistent with the existence of a dependent Government.' That had been Sydney's point of view: it was certainly Thurlow's; and Grenville's remark that the doubt seemed to be pretty generally received would seem to indicate that it was shared by some other Ministers and certain elements among the Government's supporters.

In countering the anticipated opposition Grenville began by admitting that it was open to question whether any form of administration which could now be established would prevent such a large and distant dominion as Canada from eventually leaving the Empire, but the real issue facing the Ministry was to decide on the system that was best calculated to postpone that event to a distant period and in the interval to render the connexion 'advantageous to the Mother Country without oppression or injury to the Colony'. The notion that the independence of the American Provinces had come about because they had been given the British Constitution was not in accord with the facts: their form of government had differed in essential respects from the constitution of the Mother Country, and it was precisely these differences which had most operated to produce separation. Full

---

[185] Grenville referred to Dorchester's proposal in this connexion: 'this measure of a reservation to be made in all future Grants is recommended by Lord Dorchester in one of his Letters, tho' as it appears, rather with a view of retaining the power of rewarding individuals, than with that of securing a revenue to the Crown for the purposes of the Provincial Government.'

scope and vigour had been given to the principles of democracy by establishing popular representation in their Houses of Assembly, but no care had been taken 'to preserve a due mixture of the Monarchical and Aristocratical parts of the British Constitution'.

In a trenchant summary he drew together the arguments against the possibility of clinging any longer to the paternalism of the Quebec Act. His own plan, which had been designed to obviate past errors, might be thought to afford a more just and effectual security against the growth of a republican and independent spirit than any which could be derived from a government more arbitrary in its form or principles.

But even if the advantages which appear to result from these measures were visionary and chimerical, and if it were agreed that the danger of separation would be increased by giving to Canada a Constitution, assimilated, as is here proposed, to that of Great Britain, it may still be asked whether this Plan is not become a point of almost inevitable necessity.

The proximity of the American States and even of the British maritime Colonies seemed to rule out the possibility that the people of Canada would acquiesce much longer in a system at all resembling that under which they were now governed. If the Ministry really intended to support the continuance of the existing régime in Canada when they faced Parliament in the ensuing session, then they must speak out and fairly avow that their object was to retain the dependence of the Province by a system of government 'less free' than that of the ancient Colonies or than that already established in Nova Scotia and New Brunswick.[186]

Grenville spoke in the authentic accents of late eighteenth-century aristocracy. The revolt of the American colonists had brought into the open the wide divergencies which had developed between the parent state and these societies of the New World; and when the rupture came the great majority of the landed and commercial classes in Britain had been shocked by the revealed affinity linking colonial ideas of liberty with the recurrent manifestations of innovating radicalism at home. The ruling groups with some individual exceptions reacted to the situation in one of two ways. On the domestic front the negative response was to clamp down on any movement which might undermine the existing order, whereas Pitt and some of his colleagues sought to preserve and re-vitalise the heritage of a balanced society by a cautious reform of economic

---

[186] The memorandum is headed: 'View of the several Points, prayed for by the Petitions, in favour of a change of Government in Canada; together with the objections stated to them by the Counter-Petitions, And the Remarks which occur upon them.' (C.O. 42/21. Printed in S. and D., pp. 970-87 and in Harlow and Madden (op. cit.), pp. 197-210.)

and political anomalies. With regard to the remnants of the colonial Empire there was a similar difference of opinion. No one wished to revive old controversies, and there was a general consensus that colonies of settlement would eventually follow the American example and slough off their allegiance; but continued control of the St. Lawrence basin as a source of supply and as a springboard for a commercial offensive was recognised as important and desirable. The difference arose about the best method of postponing the advent of republicanism and secession. A 'proper' subordination for as long as possible or assimilation to the parent constitution? Probably many Members of Parliament, on both sides of the House, could be classed under the heading, 'Don't know', wishing to avoid any further trouble with colonists, vaguely aware that their demands for a measure of self-management should not be resisted, yet seeing no way out of the ancient dilemma. For these Grenville supplied an apparently convincing answer: by applying his system the imperial connexion could be sustained until a distant future. His immediate task was to overcome the opposition of those elements in the Administration, represented by the Lord Chancellor, who disliked the idea of introducing 'American' Assemblies into Canada on the same sort of grounds that they resisted a reform of Parliament or the abolition of the slave trade.

Having discussed his ideas with Pitt and obtained his approval, Grenville sent the memorandum to Thurlow on 26 August – with an apology for not having consulted him at an earlier stage. After what had passed in Parliament it was essential, he wrote, that the Cabinet should come to a decision about Canada before the opening of the next session. Immediately after the prorogation (on 11 August) he had examined all the relevant information which could be procured, and in order to save time he had set out his conclusions in a paper. Would Lord Thurlow return it with his comments? He hoped to be able to transmit to Lord Dorchester in the course of the autumn 'the decision of the King's servants upon the whole question'.[187]

It was a delicate situation, for Thurlow had been a defender of the Quebec Act, and his relations with Pitt were not far from breaking point. In his reply he regretted that Grenville wanted his paper back so quickly: it would be rash to hazard an opinion on many of the points raised without more mature consideration. He then went into the attack. He disagreed with Grenville's contention that the cause of the American revolt was the lack of resemblance between the colonial constitutions and that of Great Britain. The real trouble was that their form of government had

---

[187] Grenville to Thurlow, 26 August, 1789. *Grenville Papers* (*Dropmore*), vol. I, pp. 496-7.

not provided a sufficient degree of dependence upon the Mother
Country. The British system had been based too much on that of
colonies in the ancient world, 'which never were meant to have a
political connection with their metropolis'. He then assailed the
whole concept of constitutional assimilation as he had done in
1774. The notion that the reproduction of the British constitution
in a colony would prolong its association with the parent state as
a dependency was founded on a false premiss.

If political liberty, which is the governing principle of our Constitution, be established in a colony, the sovereignty which, following
that principle, must be distributed in certain proportions among the
people, will also be established there; and the immediate effect of that
will be an habitual independent attention to a separate interest. . . .
Perhaps a mean might have been found; to have given them more
civil liberty, without political liberty, which, if I don't mistake, must
necessarily include sovereignty, and consequently independence;
because the share of the Crown in the sovereignty is certainly not
enough by itself to create dependence.

Half a century later Lord John Russell argued against the
reproduction of the British system of ministerial responsibility
from the same standpoint. If, he maintained, a colonial Governor
obeyed the 'advice' of an Executive Council, operating as a
Cabinet, he would cease to be a viceroy and become an independent sovereign.[188] Thurlow acknowledged that great changes had
taken place since 1774 and implied that adjustments had become
necessary which would not be in accord with the general principle
of maintaining colonial dependence; but although institutions
might now be required to satisfy the 'prejudices' which had taken
root, he still wished to shape them 'so as to preserve the greatest
degree of habitual influence possible in the executive branch of
government . . . the only point of contact between this mother
and her Colonies'.

Grenville had stressed that point in his paper and had tried to
meet the difficulty of the Governor's lack of patronage by suggesting the creation of an hereditary revenue derived from Crown
Reserves. On the other hand Thurlow exposed the fallacy of Grenville's reliance on a colonial hereditary aristocracy. If placed in the
hands of persons unequal to it, the status would only be despised,
and if lodged with families of permanent consideration, it would
grow into 'an independent interest'. Although the Family Compact
which developed in Upper Canada was not quite Grenville's idea of
aristocracy, Thurlow's judgement in the light of its subsequent

---

[188] Russell to Poulett Thomson (afterwards Lord Sydenham), 14 Oct., 1839.
(*Documents of the Canadian Constitution, 1759-1915*, ed. W. P. M. Kennedy.
Toronto, 1918 edn., pp. 522-4.)

behaviour was not unprophetic. In general the Chancellor's response amounted to a reluctant admission that the establishment of some form of elective institutions had become inevitable with changed conditions: Grenville's plan was perhaps worth testing by trying it out, although he denied the validity of its basic assumption. Canada's continued connexion and dependence would not thereby be promoted; but no constructive alternative was suggested. He ended on a negative note. Continued dependence was certainly an object, but it was no use pressing for it to the point of producing 'still more considerable inconveniences'. The most important factor favouring its continuance was the position of Canada 'as a seat of commerce'. He concluded with a hint that conversation would be more effective than an exchange of dissertations.[189]

Grenville hastened to placate. The paper was returned to the Chancellor to give him more time and a paragraph was added which sought to make the point that the only alternative to his plan would be to concentrate all legislative authority at Westminster; and it was too late in the day for that. Thurlow's criticism of a Colonial aristocracy was countered with the argument that a powerful interest would be created which would be a natural support to Government since nomination to the upper House from its ranks would be at the discretion of the Crown.[190] Thurlow was assured that conversations on the subject would be very welcome and they may have taken place; but the plan remained unaltered.

At a period of the year when Ministers were usually disporting

---

[189] Thurlow to Grenville, (early) Sept., 1789. *Grenville Papers (Dropmore)*, vol. I, pp. 503-5.

[190] In the additional passage Grenville acknowledged that the establishment of a separate legislature in a distant province naturally tended to prepare the way for an entire separation. 'If therefore the Subject were entirely new, and if the preservation of the dependence of a colony on its Mother Country were the only object to be considered, it should seem that this would best be attained by reserving at home the whole right and exercise of the power of Legislation.' This system, though less adapted to promote the prosperity of the Province, would probably be effective in maintaining the union of the Empire for a very considerable time, but a different principle had been adopted 'either from accident or necessity' in the formation of all the British Colonies. In defending his plan for an aristocracy he explained that a group of families with hereditary titles would be gradually formed from whom the Crown would select the members of the upper House. These would have an interest in the established régime, 'while, at the same time, the power reserved to the Crown of calling to seats in that House such only of those persons as might individually be judged proper for it, would retain to the British Government a great degree of weight and influence among this discription of persons'. (Grenville to Thurlow, 12 Sept., 1789. *Grenville Papers (Dropmore)*, vol. I, pp. 506-10). The unsigned copy of the memorandum in the departmental file (now *C.O.* 42/20) includes the additional passage cited above. From this and from Grenville's phrase in his letter of 12 Sept. – 'my paper as it before stood' – it appears that this office copy represents the version, as amended after the first draft had been seen by Thurlow, which was circulated to the rest of the Cabinet and afterwards submitted to the King.

themselves in the country or by the sea the circulation of a Cabinet memorandum with related documents took time. It was not until a month later that Grenville was able to submit his paper to the King. He did so not perhaps without apprehension. The King was assured that the other Ministers had been consulted and in particular that both the Lord Chancellor and Mr. Pitt appeared to agree 'upon the leading points'. Grenville's letter was dated 11 p.m., 12 October: the enclosure was returned on the following day with a short brusque note. The King had read Mr. Grenville's paper: he assumed that the general approval given to it by the Lord Chancellor and Mr. Pitt meant that as much attention had been paid to the interests of 'the old inhabitants' as the involvement of Parliament in the business from the start would permit. By the Articles of Capitulation these people had every degree of right to be first attended to.

I owne I am sorry any change is necessary, for I am aware to please all concerned is impossible, and that if things could have gone on in its present state for some years, it would have been very desirable.[191]

That was exactly the view of Thurlow, Sydney and Dorchester. Having cleared the royal hurdle, Grenville had his proposals incorporated in a draft bill which he sent off to Dorchester a week later. The days when the latter was urged and cajoled to produce a policy were over: he was now presented with one. The request for his opinion was confined to 'the several points of detail'. But they were details requiring local knowledge – the location of boundaries, the size of the two Houses in each legislature, the franchise, and so on; and the Bill could not go forward in Parliament without them. In his letter of 20 October Grenville wrote that there would be 'full time' to receive Dorchester's reply since Parliament was not expected to reassemble until towards the end of January, but he seems to have been unaware of the character of Atlantic gales or a Canadian winter. His despatch did not reach Dorchester in Quebec until 20 January; the latter sent off his reply on 8 February, and it arrived belatedly in London on 10 April. By that time it was considered that the session of Parliament was too far advanced to bring the Bill forward: another year was to be lost.[192] The parliamentary calendar in London and the meteorological cycle

---

[191] George III to Grenville, 13 October, 1789. Windsor. (*Ibid.*, vol. I, p. 530.)

[192] An additional reason for postponement was the difficulty of defining the boundary between Upper Canada and the United States until negotiations had taken place with the American Government about the handing-over of the frontier Posts in accordance with the terms of the peace settlement. Grenville wrote in June: 'what your Lordship states of the general weakness of those Posts, and of the nature of the force collected by the Americans, affords but too much ground to apprehend that, in the event of a Spanish War, we should not hereafter be secure in that Quarter.' (Grenville to Dorchester, 5 June, 1790. Secret. *C.O.* 43/10.)

across the North Atlantic did not fit very well. In any case Dorchester's despatch was quickly followed by news from Nootka Sound which precipitated an international crisis.

Before the Canada Bill was put temporarily into cold storage Grenville accepted and adopted most of the details which Dorchester had supplied. Both the Governor and his Chief Justice, William Smith, must have worked very hard between 20 January and 8 February. Taking Grenville's outline draft as the framework, they produced a fuller version which included the specific recommendations regarding boundaries, the minimum size of the legislatures and electoral qualifications, which the Secretary of State had requested. Only on one policy issue was it open to Dorchester to offer comment, and that was Grenville's pet scheme of hereditary upper chambers. He oppposed it. Many advantages might result, but the fluctuating state of property in Canada would cause hereditary honours to fall into disregard. For the present, therefore, it would be more advisable to appoint members of the Legislative Councils for life, subject to good behaviour and continued residence in the country. Grenville was induced to compromise. In the final form of the Canada Bill it was provided that the Crown should nominate life members, but it was also enacted that whenever His Majesty thought fit to confer any hereditary title he might annex thereto a descendible right to be summoned to the Legislative Council. The intention, Pitt explained in the Commons, was to convert that body into an hereditary House 'gradually'; but Fox was derisive and the project was still-born.

Having failed to preserve the unity of the Province, Dorchester made a last effort to give effect to his wider policy of consolidation. At his request the Chief Justice drafted an additional section to the Canada Bill which would have established a 'general' Government for all the British Provinces in North America. One of its purposes, as the Chief Justice explained, was to give a 'real and useful significancy' to 'the nominal command' at present exercised by the Governor-General.[193] The central legislature was to consist of the Governor-General, a Legislative Council and a General Assembly. The Council would be composed of a certain number of life members from each Province selected by the Crown, and each provincial Assembly would elect representatives to the lower House. Every Act must be passed by a majority of the total

---

[193] Chief Justice Smith to Dorchester, 5 Feb., 1790. (Printed *S. and D.*, pp. 1018-20.) ' Mr. Grenville's plan will most assuredly lay a foundation for two spacious, populous, and flourishing Provinces . . . I miss in it, however, the expected Establishment to put what remains to Great Britain of her Ancient Dominions in North America, under one general direction, for the united interest and safety of every Branch of the Empire.' (William Smith had been a member of the New York Council and was an ardent Loyalist.)

membership of the Council and in the General Assembly 'by such and so many Voices as will make it the Act of the majority of the Provinces'. The Crown might also at its discretion establish a General Executive Council.[194] No attempt was made to demarcate the respective fields of the central and the territorial legislatures. Presumably any provincial Act would have been void to the extent of its repugnancy to any Act of the central legislature. Since it was also provided that all provincial Acts must be submitted without delay to the Governor-General, who could exercise the power of suspension, the Law Officers in London would have had a sorry time in sorting things out. The plan was imaginative and evidently influenced by the American example; and it could have been given a more practicable shape. But even if isolated pioneer communities had accepted it, the French Canadians would scarcely have tolerated the interference of a central legislature which would have been predominantly British. Grenville replied that the proposal had been under consideration, 'but I think it liable to considerable objection'. The principle of uniting the executive government under a Governor-General was important and had already been adopted. That was his only comment.

The Canada Bill appears to have been laid to one side until the end of the year. A general election took place during the summer months, and a few days before the new Parliament assembled (25 November) Grenville was raised to the peerage in order to reinforce the Ministry in the Lords. At that time he was involved *inter alia* in the final stages of the Anglo-Spanish negotiations, with British policy in relation to the Czarina's war with Turkey, and with the complicated proposals for a commercial agreement with the Dutch in the Far East. During the January recess it became necessary to work on the Bill at speed. On 11 January he sent an urgent note to Pitt who had gone into the country taking with him Dorchester's despatch and his draft of the Bill. 'My own draft I have here, but cannot work upon it without his, and I begin to be afraid of being pressed in point of time.' Pitt replied that night to say that Grenville could make so much more use of the Quebec papers than he himself could find any chance of doing that he was returning the whole contents of the despatch box including Dorchester's draft.[195] He was, in fact,

---

[194] 'Proposed Additions to the New Canada Bill for a General Government.' Enclosed in Dorchester's to Grenville of 8 Feb. (*Ibid.*, p. 1024.)

[195] Grenville to Pitt, and Pitt to Grenville, 11 Jan., 1791. (*Grenville Papers (Dropmore)*, vol. II, p. 13.) Dorchester had asked for leave to come home during the summer, but Grenville had replied that, while he would have welcomed the opportunity of personal consultation on the draft Bill, the crisis with Spain rendered it necessary that he should remain in Quebec. William Grant, however, was in London and his local knowledge proved very useful. He was exceptionally able; had been Attorney-General for Quebec Province (1775-7) and had co-operated with Hugh Finlay on the Council in pressing for moderate reforms on behalf of the

leaving the business almost entirely to the Secretary of State.

On 25 February, 1791, action began in the Commons when Pitt presented a royal message. It consisted of two parts. The first recommended the division of Quebec into two separate Provinces: the second sought parliamentary approval for a plan to enable the Crown to make a permanent appropriation of lands in the Provinces for the maintenance of a Protestant clergy. This was new: no reference had been made to it in Grenville's first draft of the Bill. His tentative suggestion for a system of Crown Reserves for the support of the Canadian administration had been abandoned and for understandable reasons. A proposal to equip the Crown with a new and substantial source of patronage would have played into the hands of the Opposition. The idea of applying the same principle for ecclesiastical purposes had been mooted, as we have seen, by a variety of persons.[196] On 4 March the King's message was considered and leave given to bring in the Bill.[197]

The ensuing debates in April and May were distorted on several occasions by the famous quarrel between Burke and Fox over the French Revolution, a quarrel which ended a friendship of half a century. An unguarded jibe by Fox to the effect that nobility was apparently to be established in Canada while it was being destroyed in France ignited embers which had been smouldering since Fox's eulogies on Liberty had been countered in the previous November by Burke's *Reflections*. The impassioned outbursts of the latter against the Revolution and its inevitable consequences were not, however, quite so irrelevant in debates on Canada as might appear at first sight, for Fox in the name of Liberty was advocating a colonial system well to the 'left' of that of Grenville and Pitt.

The love of liberty, he declared, was gaining ground with the diffusion of literature and knowledge through the world. A constitution for Canada ought, therefore, to be as consistent as possible with the principles of freedom. A colony such as this, capable of freedom and of great development, could only be preserved to Britain 'by the choice of its inhabitants'. It followed that they ought to find nothing to excite their envy when they observed their neighbours. Of all the forms of government in the ancient or the modern world the constitutions of the American States, as amended since independence, were in his opinion the best adapted to the

---

merchants. At the general election of 1790 he entered Parliament with Pitt's support as M.P. for Shaftesbury. He rose to be Solicitor-General under Pitt (1799) and Master of the Rolls (1801-17).

[196] The plan may have been pressed by the Society for the Propagation of the Gospel, of which William Knox, a protagonist of the scheme, was a prominent member. I have not been able to search the archives of the Society to test this possibility. The King's Message is printed in *Parl. Hist.*, vol. XXVIII, 1271.

[197] Pitt gave a brief explanation of the reasons for the two recommendations. (*Ibid.*, 1376-9.)

situation of the people living there, and yet it was now proposed that the adjacent Canadians should be given 'something like the shadow of the British Constitution' while denying them the substance.

Fox's main attack in support of this contention was delivered against the Legislative Councils – the keystone of Grenville's arch. Whether they were composed partly of life members or were entirely hereditary, he would equally object. 'A council so constituted would only be the tool of the Governor as the Governor himself would only be the tool and engine of the King.' To attempt to establish a servile imitation of the British aristocracy was peculiarly absurd: we might give them lords, but it was not possible to give them a genuine House of Lords which by reason of its weight and dignity acted as a counterpoise in relation to the monarchical and popular elements in the Constitution. Legislative Councils ought to be 'totally free', frequently chosen, and 'in a considerable degree independent of the Governor and the people'.

This was not a new proposal. For the past six years the reformers in Quebec and their spokesmen in London had been urging that the Governor's powers were excessive and ought to be reduced by enlarging those of the Council; but Fox's intention went further. In a curious passage he argued that the new Legislative Councils should be given an 'independent' character because the House of Commons could not itself control so distant a Province by calling Ministers to account 'for any abuse of the prerogative' of which they might be guilty through mis-directing the Governor. This, he said, was a clear argument why the Council ought not to be appointed by the Crown. According to his India Bill the Commons would have exercised direct control by a commission of their own members: in Canada the curb was to be applied to the royal executive, that is to say, the King, the Ministers, and the Governor, by a powerful upper House on the spot.

Having ruled out nomination by the Crown and having dismissed the idea of hereditary second chambers in North America as derisory, Fox advanced the proposition that they should be elected. Property, he asserted, was the true foundation of aristocracy. 'Infinitely higher' qualifications should be required for councillors and their electors than in the case of the Assembly. Men of real substance would thus hold the intermediate position in the constitution, giving 'stability and firmness' to the whole – as at Westminster. Every part of the British Dominion ought to possess a government in which the three elements were blended and united.

The establishment of an elected upper chamber while the Governor-in-Executive-Council remained obedient to the Crown and an imperial Cabinet would have brought the constitution to a standstill. At that stage the idea of a Cabinet of Colonial Ministers, responsible to the local legislature, was neither practicable nor conceivable. The only way out of the impasse, therefore, would have been an elective governorship – which would have turned Upper and Lower Canada into independent republics. To some extent Fox seems to have recognised and accepted the implication.

It was impossible to foresee what would be the fate of distant colonies at a distant period of time; but in giving them a constitution, his idea was, that it was our interest as well as our duty, to give them as much liberty as we could, to render them happy, flourishing, and as little dependent as possible. We should make the free spirit of our Constitution applicable wherever we could render it so.[198]

In his mordant way Thurlow would no doubt have observed that Fox had unwittingly provided an admirable demonstration of the truth that assimilation to the metropolitan constitution was a logical absurdity leading inexorably to separate sovereignty.

With Grenville's departure to the Lords, Pitt was left to pilot the measure through the Commons almost unaided. Except on details he followed Grenville's brief. He objected to Fox's idea of an elected upper House, comprised of men of property, because 'it would render the poise nearer to the people than it was to the Crown in the British constitution'. It was better to imitate the latter than to infuse republican principles; and when Fox denounced as absurd the system of Clergy Reserves, by which no less than one-seventh of all land grants were to be devoted to the maintenance of a Protestant clergy, Pitt defended it as a measure to encourage the established Church and added that it might be proposed to send an Anglican bishop to sit in the Legislative Council.[199] Fox, however, did secure a number of amendments which gave the Canadian legislatures a more democratic character. The electoral qualification in land was reduced from a yearly value of £5 to one of forty shillings. Fox admitted that this would probably make little practical difference, but it established the principle that the Canadian franchise was not higher than that of Britain.[200] The life of the Assemblies, originally fixed at seven

---

[198] The above account of Fox's argument is a conflation of a series of speeches and interventions by him during the passage of the Bill through the Commons. These debates are reported in *Parl. Hist.*, vol. XXIX, 104-13, 359-430, and (in the Lords), 655-60.

[199] Fox's attack in this respect rather mis-fired because he assumed that the words 'Protestant Clergy' were meant to include Dissenters. This question, as is well known, proved a fruitful source of dissension for the future.

[200] In Grenville's original draft Bill the electoral qualification for town-dwellers was fixed at the possession of 'any house' or of personal property to the value of £100. In the Act the town-dweller must either own a house of the yearly value of £5 or be paying an annual rental of £10. Under Canadian conditions these qualifications enfranchised all but the artisans and the landless farm-workers, who at this period were not numerous.

years, was reduced as a compromise to four: Fox had advocated annual or triennial parliaments. Thirdly, the latter had insisted that the proposed minimum of thirty members for the Lower Canadian Assembly was totally inadequate to represent a population of 100,000. He demanded that it be a hundred and Pitt compromised at fifty. The effect was to broaden the basis of that Assembly and to increase the predominance of the French Canadians.

It is not difficult to criticise the constitution established by the Canada Act of 1791. As an instrument of government in the changed conditions of the 1820s and 1830s it was a dismal failure. A more relevant consideration is whether a different and better system could have been evolved at the time, having regard to the available stock of political experience and the existing climate of opinion. The decision to divide the Province into two units was not taken without awareness of the disadvantages. The alternative was a united legislature in which either the Loyalists would have been dominated by the superior numbers of the French Canadians or the two races by an artificial arrangement would have been given approximate parity – as suggested in 1769. It is hard to resist the conclusion, maintained by Grenville and Pitt, that the one would have evoked fierce antagonism and the other confusion.[201] Although re-union took place in 1840 (without resolving the problem), it was a reasonable expectation in 1791 that French Canadians and Loyalists would each live more contentedly in a political domicile of their own. Pitt's expressed hope that Lower Canada would become politically anglicised by the force of their neighbours' example has been derided, and it was certainly too optimistic, but it was less unreal than Durham's fixed idea that French-Canadian nationalism could be crushed and absorbed.

In practice the Legislative Council did not fill the role which Grenville had cast for it. In Lower Canada it came to be denounced as 'the servile tool' of a British executive. Accordingly the clamour of Papineau and his supporters in the Assembly for an elective Council was motivated as much by racial animosity as by republicanism. In Upper Canada it became an entrenched oligarchy which held the King's representative to ransom and provoked an increasingly violent struggle with a frustrated Assembly. The theory that the metropolitan balance of monarchy, aristocracy and democracy

---

[201] Fox was against partition and in the Commons rightly pointed out that if the lower Province had a legislature of its own, it might 'enact laws that would very much disturb our commerce with the upper province'. But he appreciated the arguments on the other side and admitted that, 'if there was any middle mode that could be pursued, he, for one, should be much inclined to adopt it'. (*Parl. Hist.*, vol. XXIX, 406-7.) Theoretically the way out of the dilemma was a British North American federation.

could be reproduced in an overseas dependency was finally disproved when the constitution ground to a standstill in 1837 and
both Provinces were the scene of a rebellion. Lord Durham and
his fellow reformers were then able to proclaim a new version of
the doctrine of assimilation because the parent constitution was
itself responding to social and economic change so that it became
possible to conceive of a colonial governor functioning – in internal
affairs – as a limited monarch and an executive council being converted into a responsible ministry after the pattern of the metropolitan Cabinet.

The long debate on the problem of government in Canada which
continued intermittently from 1763 to 1791 constitutes the main
constitutional link between the first Empire and the second. The
decision in 1774 to break with tradition and govern an alien people
through a paternal system afforded a precedent which was followed
some twenty years later in the case of other alien and conquered
territories. Meanwhile American independence changed the
Canadian problem and the outlook of the British statesmen and
officials who were concerned with it. If the 'Fourteenth Colony'
had gone with the rest and Britain had been obliged to evacuate
the Continent, the problem of governing settler dependencies
would not have arisen again until the cry of colonial rights was
heard in Cape Colony and New South Wales; but the existence of
a British Province along the northern frontier of the United States,
exposed to the infiltration of ideas and persons from that ex-colonial
Power, presented London with an inescapable challenge. Since the
Americans had fought their way out of the British colonial system,
how was the allegiance of French-Canadian habitans and ex-
American Loyalists to be retained?

The response to the challenge reflected the varying reactions in
Britain to the rise of *demos* across the Atlantic and the English
Channel. Grenville's proposed restoration of the constitutional
balance was characteristic of the current middle-of-the-road attitude
towards the expression and regulation of political liberty. To the
'left' stood Fox and his small minority who had applauded the
American revolt as they were now praising events in Paris. For
Canada they advocated a more 'republican' variant of the parent
constitution and thus a more tenuous link with metropolitan
authority. To the 'right' stood the King with men such as Thurlow, Sydney, and Dorchester who continued to favour the authoritarian system of the Quebec Act long after it had ceased to be
relevant to the situation. To them it seemed to be the only reliable
barrier against the flood. Under the stress of war with revolutionary
forces and answering discontent at home all movement towards
reform was frozen, and it is perhaps an open question whether Pitt
and Grenville would have been prepared to trust to a form of

'guided democracy' in Canada if the review of its constitution had been postponed until after 1793.

Apart from Acadia, which became Nova Scotia, the Province of Quebec was the first large European Colony to be incorporated in the British Empire.[202] The policy of anglicisation and, on the other hand, that of recognising alien institutions were both intended, in their different ways, to secure the loyalty of newcomers, and efforts were made to combine the two in proportions which varied with changing circumstances. Even when French-Canadianism was entrenched in 1774 North had expressed the hope that the Province would conform – gradually but eventually – to the British institutional pattern; and there is no good reason for doubting that he meant what he said. Seventeen years later when a growing English-speaking population was settling alongside the French, Pitt and Grenville confidently expected to see the process accelerated.

Since the object was to imitate the image of the parent state it was logical that special efforts were made to reproduce that of the established Church. Pitt's active promotion of his scheme for ensuring a regular supply of native-born clergy throughout British North America by means of a seminary in Nova Scotia, linked with Oxford and Cambridge, was symptomatic; and the endowment of a benefice in every new district by the system of Clergy Reserves was a logical application of the general principle. The attempt to reproduce the English social structure of 'Squire and Parson' in a New World was as doctrinaire as the complementary policy of creating replicas of King-Lords-Commons; but the underlying idea of 'assimilation' eventually reappeared and was applied in different ways and under different criteria in a new age.

3. OCEAN TERRITORIES

The inclusion of French Canada in the Empire was followed during the Napoleonic wars by the conquest and incorporation of other European dependencies, French, Spanish and Dutch. These presented similar constitutional issues and the pattern of government which was adopted to meet the situation derived in part from previous experience in Canada and became an essential feature of the political structure of the second Empire. Accordingly a brief account must be given even though these developments are beyond the chronological limit of the present work.[203]

The French Island of Grenada in the West Indies, ceded to Britain in 1763, was given the standard form of colonial constitution

---

[202] When New Amsterdam (which became New York, New Jersey and Delaware) was conquered in 1664 most of the Dutch residents departed.

[203] They have been described in some detail in my chapter, 'The New Imperial System, 1783-1815', C.H.B.E., vol. II, pp. 129-87.

and an Assembly had been convened.[204] Because of the requirement that members must take the oath against transubstantiation the French planters were excluded: French candidates were elected but were refused admission. While the British resented the fact that the numerical preponderance of the French gave them control over elections, the French refused to acknowledge the authority of a legislature solely composed of representatives of the British minority. The Island was in a tumult. In 1768 an Order in Council authorised the participation of the French in the legislature and public office and – after stormy scenes – they were admitted to both Council and Assembly. Their treatment of the British after the capture of the Island by France in 1779 caused such bitterness, however, that when the sufferers came into their own again after 1784 they announced their determination to exclude the French from the legislature for ever.

Petitions and counter-petitions followed each other to London until in 1789 the Privy Council referred the issue to the Law Officers who decided – inevitably – that the Order in Council of 1768 in favour of the French was *ultra vires*. They followed and amplified the famous judgment of Lord Mansfield in the case of *Campbell* v. *Hall*, ruling that when the Crown established a form of representative government in Grenada it automatically lost the prerogative power of amendment. Any alteration in the constitution now required an Act of Parliament and that would have involved the Ministry in a very considerable controversial issue in both Houses. Thus a large French Roman Catholic electorate was left to be represented and taxed by the members of a (British) Protestant minority. The French planters decided that the situation was intolerable, sold their plantations, and departed. These events were taking place while Grenville was in charge of the Canada Bill and must have reinforced the Ministry's rejection of a united Anglo-French Assembly for the Province of Quebec, while they gave point to Pitt's observations about 'antagonism' and 'confusion'.

The next phase in the story of British policy in relation to conquered European colonies begins with the capture of Martinique, Guadeloupe, S. Lucia and parts of French S. Dominique. In the summer of 1794 Dundas, as Secretary for War, wrote to the Duke of Portland that Sir Charles Grey, Commander-in-Chief in the West Indies, had requested that a Governor he sent out at once to each captured island with instructions for establishing some form of constitution. The task of preparing a preliminary draft of Instructions (for Portland's consideration) was undertaken by Hawkesbury. Although constitution-making was not his usual sphere he held characteristically strong views about the proper form

---

[204] The Proclamation of 7 Oct., 1763, had promised representative government for Quebec, East and West Florida and Grenada.

of government for non-British peoples. Some twenty years earlier he and John Robinson had done their best to centralise administrative authority in British India under a supreme Governor-General, and it was Hawkesbury who had moved the insertion in the Quebec Bill of the special oath of allegiance which had enabled French-Canadian Catholics to sit in the Legislative Council.[205]

In the copy of the draft Instructions which is in his collected papers he inserted marginal notes to explain his approach to the subject. In the first of these he remarked that he was strongly impressed with the recollection of what had occurred when Grenada first came into British possession and with the consequences resulting from the measures then taken.

By not establishing in that Island a Government agreable to the Inhabitants they were all of them gradually driven out of the Island. . . . The conduct of the British Government at that time was absurd in policy, and cruel in its consequences to the original Possessors of the Island. The mistake then committed sprung from the idea that the Government and Laws of Great Britain, which are the best in the world for the people of that Kingdom and conformable to their opinions and habits, must be equally good, and equally agreable to foreigners. . . . These Instructions are drawn with a view of obviating these evils as much as possible, and yet with due attention to the political prejudices of the People of this Country.

Until a new form of government could be established, these Islands were, therefore, to be governed according to the constitution and laws subsisting in each island immediately preceding the year 1789.[206] The right of making laws was for the present vested in the Crown, but it was His Majesty's intention to exercise this right in as few cases as possible. Each Governor must therefore refrain from making any alteration, except in great emergency, until approval had been obtained from London. The executive government, civil and military, must be 'reserved wholly' to the King's representative. In the case of those parts of S. Dominique which had already surrendered it had been stipulated in the capitulation

---

[205] See *Cavendish Debates*, pp. 250-1. Hawkesbury (at that time a commoner) stated in the House: 'I have drawn up a new oath, which I beg leave to bring up.' Actually the clause in question had been drafted by Lord Mansfield (see p. 701, above), but Hawkesbury introduced it on behalf of the Ministry.

[206] Characteristically Hawkesbury stressed the essential importance of deviating from French law in one respect: 'The first and principal exception is, that all the British Laws of Trade and Navigation, as far as they relate to any commercial Intercourse between the said Islands and His Majesty's Dominions, and other Countries in any part of the world, immediately attach upon these Islands, and care must be taken that they be *punctually executed*.' He had ordered Reeves of the Board of Trade and the Solicitor of the Customs to prepare an abstract of these laws and to have a French translation made in order that the inhabitants might be fully apprised of their nature.

that the Governor was to be assisted in the administration by six commissaries to be chosen by him from among the planters. He was therefore instructed to act in conformity with their advice except when the interest of the Crown was in the Governor's opinion essentially concerned. On such occasions he might act contrary to their opinions, but in that event written explanations of his and their views must be prepared and transmitted to the Secretary of State. As in the Government of India Act of 1784 the supremacy of the chief executive officer was to be ensured.

No fresh taxes were to be imposed and expenditure out of existing sources of revenue was to be controlled by the Treasury. The Roman Catholic faith would be recognised and maintained in all the conquered islands, but no form of Protestant worship was to be excluded and British officials must be particularly careful that the priests did not attempt under cover of their religious duties to alienate the inhabitants from their new allegiance. In a marginal note Hawkesbury glanced sideways at the Canada Act of 1791. 'Nothing is said in these Instructions respecting Protestant Ministers or the mode of defraying the expence of them. It may perhaps be prudent in no way to encourage the residence of these, at least in any number, in these islands.' He went further: 'these colonies were more likely to remain in a state of tranquillity and subjection if His Majesty's ancient subjects did not intermix with the inhabitants or settle there, except in the sea ports for the sole purpose of carrying on a commerce with the Mother Country.' No repetition of the troubles in Grenada – and no nonsense about 'assimilation'.

Hawkesbury then considered the possible alternatives for a permanent form of government which the commander-in-chief and the respective governors were to recommend after consulting the inhabitants. He cited three possibilities: the ancient French system before the beginning of the Revolution; that established by the decrees of the French National Assembly of March, 1790, and September, 1791; and the representative form of government as administered in the British Islands. In another marginal note Hawkesbury indicated his confident expectation of the direction which the majority planter opinion would take.

The wise and discreet Inhabitants of these Islands will prefer their ancient government. The turbulent and factious will prefer a popular government in which there is an Assembly. The inhabitants of moderate principles will for the present at least agree in opinion with those of the first of the above Descriptions, having fatally experienced the Evils arising from the late Innovations.

Like most of his countrymen he underestimated the terrible explosive force of European revolutionary propaganda when brought into contact with the race hatred of a slave population.[207]

It was a simple matter to provide that the *ancien régime* should be restored in the French islands in its entirety; but when considering permanent constitutional arrangements Hawkesbury was faced with a problem which had plagued British Ministers in French Canada, that is to say, the extent to which the French law and judicial procedure ought to be allowed to subsist; and like his predecessors he hesitated. It might be expedient, he wrote, that the French system of judicature, criminal as well as civil, should continue in respect of the French inhabitants; but to make British subjects resorting to these Islands punishable by laws with which they were wholly unacquainted and amenable to a foreign system of justice might be thought contrary to the principles of the British constitution. On the other hand a general introduction of trial by jury might be dangerous, particularly at that juncture and contrary to the habits and wishes of the French inhabitants. In a marginal comment he re-stated the old dilemma in terms which were all too familiar.

The great difficulty of establishing a form of government in these newly acquired Islands arises from the necessity of forming a system of Criminal Judicature equally adapted to the new and ancient Subjects of His Majesty. The just predilection of Englishmen for the Trial by Jury makes it improper to deprive them of this mode of Trial in any part of His Majesty's dominions where it can be established with propriety; and yet it will be found the worst mode of Trial for persons not accustomed to it, and not qualified to exercise the functions of Jurymen.[208]

Finally he left the issue undetermined. There could not be two separate judicial systems, he indicated in the Instructions, for the different classes of persons 'who may inhabit these Islands'. 'It will be for you to consider upon the spot and report to me what measure

---

[207] At the same time Hawkesbury appreciated the importance of gaining the goodwill of the free people of colour, who, as he noted, were more numerous in the French Islands than in the British, and were 'frequently persons of considerable Influence and importance'. They were to have the same privileges as in the British Islands, and the Government were very ready to give serious consideration to proposals for granting them greater privileges 'with the consent and good will of the White Inhabitants' if such a measure would 'induce these different classes of Inhabitants to live on better terms with each other'. When French republican forces arrived in Guadeloupe, they were welcomed and assisted by a large part of the Creole population.

[208] Hawkesbury went on to quote an observation which the late Lord Camden had made to him some years previously to the effect that trial by jury was the best possible system for Englishmen, but if established among a people who were not fitted to discharge the duties, it might become one of the worst by being perverted to injustice and oppression. 'What has lately passed,' added Hawkesbury, 'in the French Colonies, as well as in Old France, is a full confirmation of the truth of this observation.'

in your judgment can best be adopted for removing this difficulty.'[209] It had been Hawkesbury's idea that Sir Charles Grey should visit each conquered island to discuss the future constitution with the Governor and the leading planters and then return to England towards the end of February, 1795, with recommendations for ministerial consideration. But the situation in the occupied islands was precarious and the establishment of a regular administration was urgent. Already (in June, 1794) troops of the French Republic had landed in Guadeloupe: the royalists had proved unreliable, and a large part of the creole population had welcomed the revolutionary forces led by Victor Hugues, a former innkeeper on the Island. By 10 December the outnumbered British were obliged to evacuate their last stronghold. The number of royalists executed at the order of Hugues has been variously estimated at 300 and 1,200.[210]

There was no time for an enquiry on the spot followed by reference back to London. Detailed constitutional Instructions were prepared forthwith for the Governors of Martinique and S. Dominique and Hawkesbury's draft was closely followed. All executive powers, civil and military, were vested solely in the Governor, who was directed to select a small advisory Council whom he was to consult in major executive matters and in framing regulations; but he might over-ride them, provided that their objections in such cases were stated in writing and forwarded to the Secretary of State. Members of the Council, as in Lower Canada, might be Roman Catholics, taking the oath prescribed in the Quebec Act. The Roman Catholic faith was to be maintained, but all other forms of Christian worship were to be tolerated. As under the Quebec Act no taxes could be imposed, but the traditional French revenues were to be collected and appropriated under the control of the British Treasury. Hawkesbury's doubts on the judicial side were resolved by the provision that the French system of courts and French law were to be retained *in toto* – with the right of appeal to the Privy Council in all cases involving more than £500. Any adjustments in the laws or administration were to await detailed reports on the political, economic and social situation. Hawkesbury's proposals for incorporating the French Islands in the British commercial system were also followed.[211]

The close resemblance between these arrangements and the

---

[209] Draft Instructions for Sir Charles Grey by Lord Hawkesbury with marginal notes. (1794.) *Liverpool Papers, Addit. MSS.* 38,351, ff. 202-32a.

[210] For a detailed account of the military operations in the Caribbean at this time see Sir J. B. Fortescue, *History of the British Army* (Lond., 1899-1930), vol. IV, p. 370 *et seq.*

[211] The Martinique Instructions are in *C.O. 319/4* and those for General Adam Williamson, Governor of S. Dominique, are in *C.O. 319/5*. The latter are printed in Harlow and Madden (*op. cit.*), pp. 83-8.

principles of the Quebec Act is natural enough in view of the parallel circumstances and of Hawkesbury's active interest in the Canadian measure. The deviation from that model in continuing French criminal law and procedure was a matter of common sense: it would be time enough to introduce modifications when it was seen to what extent British merchants and planters were establishing themselves in the Islands. The resolute refusal to establish elective assemblies was dictated by the revolutionary situation; and the previous imbroglio in Grenada was sufficient reason for avoiding the establishment of constitutions by parliamentary legislation. The Crown's prerogative of amendment was preserved.[212]

In one other important respect the Quebec precedent was not followed. The Canadian Council, as established in 1774, was a legislature. Ordinances were made by the Governor with the advice and consent of a majority of the whole Council and executive business required the approval of at least three Councillors out of a quorum of five. In the case of the French Islands the Governor was supreme and his Council was purely advisory. The procedure to be followed when he decided to act contrary to advice was the same as that provided for the Governor-General in Bengal. The device of concentrating power in the hands of the chief executive officer had been adopted in India, after long hesitation, because the need to enforce order and discipline had become paramount. It was applied in tumultuous French territories by Hawkesbury and Dundas for similar reasons.[213]

The chief interest in these constitutional arrangements lies in the fact that they were afterwards used as the model for other conquered territories such as Cape Colony, Ceylon, and Mauritius. 'They were destined,' as an American historian has put it, 'to serve as a nucleus for the main instruments of government in half a dozen British colonies for more than a quarter of a century.'[214] It had always been the habit of the law clerks to copy from a standard format when preparing the Commission and Instructions for a colonial Governor, and the instruments for Martinique and

---

[212] Hawkesbury seems to have assumed that the authority of Parliament would be invoked. In his draft for Instructions he wrote: 'It is impossible to foresee what time may be required for the execution of this commission; but if you [Sir Charles Grey] should find it possible to return to England about the end of February next [1795] – His Majesty's Ministers will then have it in their power to take your Report into consideration, and to submit to Parliament any measures proper for their consideration, before the conclusion of the ensuing Session.'

[213] The Duke of Portland, having brought his followers over to the side of Government, had been appointed Home and Colonial Secretary, but Dundas, as Secretary for War, was the driving force behind the costly efforts to expel the French Republic from the Caribbean.

[214] H. T. Manning, *British Colonial Government after the American Revolution, 1782-1820* (Yale and Oxford, 1933), p. 342.

S. Dominique provided them with a ready-made pattern which was in accord with the ideas of their political masters who were primarily concerned with security and the conciliation of alien communities.

If Quebec Province had joined the United States and if Clive had not conquered Bengal, it is likely enough that a form of paternal despotism would have been independently devised for the foreign territories acquired in the Caribbean, the Mediterranean, and the Indian Ocean. As it happened, however, the experience of dealing with French Canadians and with the problem of ruling the Indian Presidencies afforded useful precedents. Masterful Governors-General in Calcutta were matched on a smaller scale by such redoubtable Crown Colony Governors as General Sir Thomas Maitland ('King Tom'), who ruled successively in Ceylon, Malta, and the Ionian Islands. Such men were benevolent despots, forthright defenders of the interests of the populace and with no patience at all for local notables who might think – as Lord Bathurst put it – they could make a constitution 'as they would make a pudding according to a British or French receipt'.[215]

In the middle decades of the 19th century governmental paternalism was extended to the original British islands in the West Indies (Barbados excepted) because analogous conditions had supervened. Small planter oligarchies, frightened and incapable of representing the interests of the restive coloured masses, agreed to exchange their ancient representative institutions for direct rule by the metropolitan Power. A system and experience in working it were to hand.[216] Yet Crown Colony government could not be kept in an insulated compartment. When British settlers encountered the system (as in Cape Colony and New South Wales) they fought against it as the British merchants in Canada had done. Nominated Councils were broadened to include non-officials and then an increasing quota of elected members. In many dependencies the conciliar system gradually approximated to the standard pattern of representative government – which under the new device of

---

[215] Bathurst to Maitland, 2 Dec., 1815. (Quoted in *C.H.B.E.*, vol. II, p. 184.)

[216] The purpose of the Home Government was well expressed in a circular despatch in 1868: 'The population at large, consisting of uneducated negroes, neither had, nor could have, any political powers; . . . and the consequence was that the Assemblies performed their office of legislation under no real or effective responsibility. . . . For these ends [the welfare of all classes in the Islands] Her Majesty's Government were willing to accept the trust which the Assemblies were desirous to place mainly in their hands. But Her Majesty's Government were not willing to accept this trust unless accompanied by such a measure of power and authority as would enable them to perform effectively the duties which it was expected of them to undertake.' (Quoted in H. Wrong, *Government of the West Indies*, Oxford, 1923, p. 79.) Too often, however, in other territories the 'trust' was surrendered to 'Assemblies' whose conception of responsibility for non-European peoples was circumscribed.

local ministerial responsibility led on to independence. The process was unplanned and empirical, but as the successive stages became established by accumulated precedent a route was chalked out by means of which the demands for political advance, Asian, coloured West Indian and African, could be conceded – slowly and hesitantly at first and then at a rapidly accelerating pace under the pressure of racial assertiveness. Thus the constitutional experience of an Empire of English-speaking colonists unexpectedly permeated and transformed a totally different system of government which had been designed for other races and other conditions; and by the same token paternal authoritarianism ceased to be available for the protection of the many or the few.

CHAPTER XI

THE QUESTION AND THE NATURE
OF RESPONSIBILITY

IN 1763 the Peace of Paris would appear to have seen the final triumph of Britain over France both in the Old World of India and in the New World of the Americas: in 1793 Britain found herself locked in renewed combat with her ancient enemy, now indeed in revolutionary guise but still formidable and lacking nothing in imperial instinct and ambition. The intervening period of thirty years straddles that momentous crisis of the British Empire which had seen the birth of the first independent ex-colonies of Britain. In the travail and bloodshed of a civil war between British subjects who had grown apart by living apart, the American Declaration of Independence asserted, not perhaps yet a new sense of nationality, but certainly a new identity which might appear to demolish the assumptions of the existing colonial system. This revolution and schism in Anglo-American relations has been regarded as the great divide of imperial history: moreover, between the failure of one empire and the creation of a successor legend has interpolated a pause, a decade or more of shock, convalescence and recovery, when Britain contemplated in numb apathy the ruin of her imperial hopes before her interest was gradually reawakened to new possibilities and new forms in a new empire acquired 'in a fit of absence of mind'. The present study has shown the line drawn across the ledger between the First and the Second British Empires to be unreal, a division of convenience rather than of substance. The mainsprings of an empire based not on settled colonies but on a line of trading posts can be found in a period much earlier than the secession of the Americas: the foundations of a Second British Empire antedate the schism in the First. The 'new' orthodoxy of an empire of world-wide commerce was no makeshift or dispirited alternative born in defeat and despair, but, in a measure, a rediscovery of pristine design and vigour. It was, indeed, a return to the normal concept of a maritime nation which the vicissitudes of seventeenth-century English history with its emigrations of persecuted or discontented communities overseas had distorted and temporarily overwhelmed. In that process the New World had been sown with its own sturdy particularism and a latent antipathy towards the Old. This was the harvest which was reaped in 1776. But in the meantime, it has been argued, something of the old Tudor faith had been rediscovered and its soundness was being proved. The improvisation and the experiment it stimulated had already begun in what was a fertile and formative generation of overseas adventure; and these were to continue to flourish, to be tested and to be adapted to the new circumstances in the period that followed.

The American Revolution, therefore, made no revolution in British thinking on empire because that revolution, or maybe that return to first principles, was already in train. That amputation of the body politic of Greater Britain which rocked the North Administration, rekindled the ambitions of Britain's colonial rivals and prompted the King to draft his own notice of abdication, did not have those immediate and catastrophic effects which some in the realm and many in the dominions had anticipated. George III had believed that 'the die is not cast whether this shall be a great empire or the least significant of European states'. John Adams had expected that the Declaration of Independence would spark off a revolution in Britain. Indeed, there were many Americans who felt that they were fighting in the cause of British liberty against a tyrannous Crown or a corrupt Parliament. But they miscalculated. The exposure of an inefficient imperial administration may have provoked in time a realisation of the need for some separate colonial department, as it also gave additional point to the campaign for economical reform, and to the discussion of the unrepresentative nature of the House of Commons; but George III was too loyal a Parliamentarian, and liberty was, at least temporarily, a cause no longer fashionable, rather a foolish humour indulged by a lunatic fringe of Wilkes's followers or an excess dangerous in the hands of a rioting mob. It is true of course that there had been some hostility to the American war but it was opposition to the King rather than sympathy with the Americans: on the central matter of the legality of parliamentary sovereignty there was in effect but one voice and that was anti-American. Opinion in Britain remained loyal to old ideas: mercantilist instincts remained. Dean Tucker and Adam Smith had made few converts; the concepts of a quasi-commonwealth under the Crown, which had stirred within the minds of Franklin, Jefferson and Madison, had struck sympathetic chords in the writings of Cartwright, Price and Priestley and, belatedly but still under conditions, was indeed offered in one form to the American colonists in 1778 and later to the Anglo-Irish in 1783-5. But the majority of people in Britain, recognising the fact that America had seceded and that the Americans were now aliens, were reconciled to the loss of America, not (as Tucker would have them believe) as desirable, but as inevitable. The rallying of the old guard against concession, first, to the Americans in 1783, and then, two years later, to the Irish in the colonial trade, is proof of the automatic response to old stimuli. Security was preferable to opulence, as Adam Smith himself had concluded, and security in trade as in defence lay in the orthodox paths. So Shelburne's somewhat vague scheme for a continuing federal relationship with the Americans proved abortive. Only after a generation of fearful anxiety and final victory over France did the conviction grow that Britain was secure and could be more opulent, and the policy of reciprocity he had urged so prematurely became an acceptable experiment. In the years immediately after the recognition of American independence in 1783 and the defeat of the principles of reciprocity the public relapsed into a general indifference which took for granted its traditional principles. If the old colonial system was receiving its mortal blows, it was an 'unconscionable time a-dying'. In changed and changing conditions, its presumptions were salvaged from the episode of attempted reciprocity and were enforced by the exigencies of a war emergency; and, even if modified in practice, they remained generally accepted for another generation.

The prevailing mood was one of tenacity: to hold on (even a little more securely) to what remained, largely by the old forms and for the old purposes. The authority of the realm must be asserted over dependencies for the benefit both of the empire as a whole and of British commerce as a necessary guarantor of that general interest. Imperial self-sufficiency, many comforted themselves, was still not impossible. The empire which had been lost was a haphazard agglomeration. The new empire could be fashioned on a rational analysis of imperial needs, commercial and political alike; and, balanced and stable itself, could break into other empires and find vent for surplus goods in the trading preserves of rival powers or in hitherto untapped corners of the world. In such ventures merchants might find profitable returns for the nation without the countervailing deterrent of formal dominion and administration. Some in Britain might, indeed, adjust themselves to the loss of the American empire by showing that Britain had been relieved thereby of an intolerable defence burden, that a potential commercial rival from within the ring of the imperial monopoly had been removed, or that they had been emancipated from buying inferior American products, such as timber, to satisfy the principles of imperial self-sufficiency at the expense of British shipbuilders and carpenters. Again, many of the problems which had exercised British administrations in the pre-revolutionary period were now placed by the American revolt beyond the responsibility of British ministers, as they had proved to be beyond their ability. There was some comfort that American independence meant that the nature of inter-colonial co-operation down the American tidewater, the problem of restraining the restless frontiersmen, and the inveterate suspicions of any central executive were now American, and not imperial, concerns.

It is true that the central imperial issue still faced British governments; for American secession had not solved the question of the nature of imperial authority. All it had shown was that earlier methods had led to the loss of half the old Empire: an assertion of a separate identity by the colonies and the abdication of all responsibility by the metropolis. It had given a warning indeed: a warning that it might prove impossible to lay down a prescribed and uniform pattern of empire where fellow subjects at a distance retained an unshakeable awareness of their liberties as 'true born Englishmen' or their rights as freemen; but it was a warning which it was difficult for a generation of still convinced mercantilists to grasp immediately.

So the imperial dilemma, the problem of combining colonial autonomy with imperial unity, remained for the future. To the generation who had lived through the crisis of empire in America, separation might seem inevitable. Was the fall of the ripe fruit a law of empire as of nature? It seemed certain that without due care it must be so. If any immediate lesson were to be learned, it was that the mother country had been too liberal to her colonies, too tolerant of disobedience, too neglectful of the means she had already at hand to discipline wayward progeny and to mould their proper development. Too little interference, not too much, had facilitated the disruption of the empire; it might indeed have caused it. If so, a similar fate elsewhere might be avoided by accepting the need to exercise a more direct control and responsibility in the remaining colonies. So, while experience counselled against any repetition of those disastrous efforts towards a more uniform imperial system which had precipitated crisis in America, an impulse towards greater central control persisted. If prudence prompted the acceptance of the existing diversities, it also emphasised the need for painstaking supervision and the guidance of growth: a solicitude enforced at the same time by a dawning consciousness of trusteeship. In practice, of course, the momentum of events, the preoccupation with the French wars, and the need to content both old and new subjects of the Crown and retain their loyalties, permitted temporary adjustments which were the germs of a new system; but in theory those most concerned with imperial governance still hoped ultimately, like William Knox, for an 'orthodox' disciplined empire: and, where settlement or conquered colonies might still exist, to secure their 'necessary subservience' to the central authority and interest of the metropolis. Events in America had re-emphasised the inconvenience of having such colonies, but where they had remained within allegiance they should not be wantonly given up. Instinct for empire continued. Britain refused to surrender Quebec to the Americans in 1782-3. New South Wales was founded as a colony as well as a prison;

Sierra Leone as a plantation as well as an asylum. United Empire Loyalists colonised Canada and made it more English. The British Government stood firm against Spanish claims to Nootka Sound. The post-1783 generation was not anti-imperialist. If they were disappointed imperialists, it was that one particular pattern of empire – that of settlement – had proved inconvenient. The denouement of a colonial empire at Yorktown might indeed be inevitable; but, whether it were so or not, it liberated them to pursue, with relief perhaps and certainly with more single-minded enthusiasm, that alternate pattern which had been developing, with such rich variety of expedient, and opportunity, during the previous decades: the empire of commerce in Indian and Pacific Oceans. The swing to the East had begun before the losses in the West took place. The Second British Empire was a development, not a departure, from the First.

During the period between 1763 and 1793 the character of the Second British Empire was being formed. In characteristic fashion there was no blueprint, and for long there was no new character stamped on it; but there were ideas and experiments in plenty, some of which came to nothing and others often tentative which made a permanent contribution to the shape of things to come. In the process Britain itself was being subjected to strange experiences and was being forced to undertake new responsibilities.

The struggle with France in the Seven Years War had results therefore which ranged far afield in the thirty years that followed. In India the British counter-offensive drew the government of the realm itself on the morrow of Plassey into the chaos of a disintegrating Moghul Empire. For reasons of national self-interest, honour and humanity the State became gradually, but increasingly, involved in the novel and complex problems of the native polity, of controlling its hitherto masterless agent, the Company, and of building an administrative structure capable at once of contributing to the national revenue and security and of rescuing Hindu and Muslim inhabitants from the corruption and oppression practised under the hallowed name of chartered liberties. Equally the British counter-offensive in America, by freeing the American colonists from their dependence upon British protection against the French and from any vestigial need for loyalty, hastened the first great schism in the empire. At the same time, by establishing British rule in the St. Lawrence valley both for the strategic convenience of America settlers and for the springboard of commercial assault by British merchants into the Mississippi valley and westwards, it thrust into inexperienced hands the problem of a non-British, European people whose integration into the empire was a searching challenge. Both in India and in Canada new responsibilities demanded new thinking: how could the British Government combine its considerations for security and for justice? Was it the wisest, the safest and the most just policy to preserve the old traditions and usages or to press forward for assimilation to British laws and institutions which were deemed superior?

In Canada the *threat* of American revolt was itself instrumental not so much in moulding the particular form of the Quebec Act as in making the arguments of Carleton against an unconsidered, doctrinaire anglicisation of a French province seem prudent and his concern for the security of one part of British North America appear attractive: the absence of any large-scale British emigration into Quebec in the decade since 1763 and the possibility of keeping the Canadian French out of the American revolt endorsed Carleton's assessment of the situation and made second thoughts on the specific problem of government in a plural society urgent. The *fact* of American protest against British rule and the unprecedented solicitude shown for 'new' subjects in Quebec by their conqueror prompted a prolonged struggle by the fractional British community in Canada to secure as 'old' subjects their prior claim to exclusive rights in representative institutions and English law; and later the *fact* of American independence, by driving Loyalists over the border into Canada, made the identity of this new Canada a protest against American republicanism. Furthermore, while securing the belated fulfilment of the rule-of-thumb promise of representative government in the proclamation of 1763, it conceded to a non-British population in 1791 those rights of representation previously considered as rights of blood and it promoted the possibility of an evolutionary assimilation, in the context and faith of continuing Canadian allegiance, to the greater unity of empire. Even in the British Isles themselves, that same American revolt sparked off a constitutional revolution in Ireland where it emboldened the settler minority of Anglo-Irish to assert their own authority to govern, replacing the British as rulers of the native Irish. Grattan was seeking, not freedom by a Declaration of Independence, but freedom within the empire, and, perhaps due to American success, the Anglo-Irish were (temporarily) able to achieve that freedom in Ireland's name without fighting and without foreign aid. In the circumstances of the American war the British Government was ready to make concessions, to conciliate Ireland (as in 1778 it had attempted too late with the Americans), to surrender to claims for autonomy and even to renounce parliamentary authority over Ireland. In some haste and without formal conditions Ireland was recognised in a status of legislative independence not matched until 1931; but the partnership experiment of 1783-5, the establishment of commercial reciprocity and quasi-dominion status, was abortive because the Anglo-Irish were not prepared to make the defence contribution demanded in return.

The same need for security which had driven Grenville to the disastrous Stamp Act still was an obsession. This worried Pitt (as it worried Chamberlain a century later). When the British government showed how unsatisfied and distrustful it was of merely voluntary and implicit conditions which were not 'secured by permanent provisions', and when the revised resolutions of 1785 virtually demanded a surrender of Irish autonomy in external affairs and seemed to demote Ireland to a tributary nation once more, the deal in effect lapsed. The principle of making concessions gracefully rather than having them forced from British hands had been accepted as 'a point of true policy' by Grenville in 1789;[1] even the attempted appeasement of the American colonists in 1778 left its mark in the renunciation of statutory taxation and the application of customs revenues to local colonial needs. But where imperial defence was concerned and where British merchants feared radical change in their monopolies, there was a limit to concession. The need to secure stable control was a paramount consideration. The unreliability of the Anglo-Irish oligarchy as an instrument of imperial control was as repeatedly proved to British eyes as was that of the Company in India. The Irish Parliament was resistant to reform which would have made it representative, and the Irish Executive was incapable of becoming in some way answerable to that Parliament. So when revolutionary ambitions took shape under Wolfe Tone it served to enforce a growing conviction that the Irish Parliament must be absorbed into the central prototype at Westminster where (it was magnificently miscalculated) a minority of Irishmen would be unimportant and impotent. The Union of 1800 was frankly acknowledged by Pitt as the end of his experiment. Alarmed at the display of Irish nationalism, the British Government sought to secure Irish loyalty and dependence by union. The failure of 'equal association' postponed experiment in colonial self-government for half a century and deepened conviction in Britain that empire could tolerate no rival sovereign legislature independent of Westminster. Perhaps there was then no solution possible that was intermediate between revolutionary independence and strictly subordinated control. Certainly in a dominion so closely bound up with Britain's own security, concession had proved risky. Such centralisation as that in the Act of Union was one extreme expression of the instinct for vigorous

---

[1] Lord Grenville to Lord Dorchester, 20 October, 1789: private and secret, quoted in W. P. M. Kennedy, *Statutes, treaties etc.*, 2nd edition, p. 184.

with a need to escape from war debts and heavy taxation prompted
her to raise the subscription to the imperial association: to require
from her colonies not only the accustomed contribution through
acceptance of the British commercial monopoly but also an
additional levy in the form of direct or guaranteed revenues. If
her methods were clumsy, even disastrous, her doubts were proved
sound. For France did intervene in the American cause and threaten
not only British expansion but her very existence in twenty years
of war. Adam Smith had got his priorities right; if a choice had to
be made, security was preferable to opulence and security remained
an over-riding concern until the Napoleonic bogy had been laid.
Only then could Britain bend efforts more single-mindedly to creating wealth and could Huskisson's policy succeed where Shelburne's
had failed.

Nevertheless it is also true that the generation of Adam Smith
did not see security and commerce necessarily as alternatives. A
profitable trade, soundly based, would promote the defence of the
realm: the riches of Britain must benefit the strength of empire
as a whole and the security of the colonies. So even in the period
before 1793 the growing industrial self-confidence of British merchants and manufacturers can be seen in a new adventuring spirit
that was abroad. These were the men who would supply the goods
upon which the empire or trading posts would be built. Colonies
had proved to be potential industrial rivals and complex administrative burdens. They were not necessary to the expansion or
security of an informal empire of trade. An empire of ships, of
ocean routes, of naval bases and entrepôts was preferable to one
of dominion: it reduced expenses and increased profits; it was
more economical to defend.

Thus urged by this remarkable spirit of commercial adventure
the drive gathered momentum. Efforts were made to secure bases
in the Far East, in the Pacific, in the unknown Southern Continent
and in North-West America; to penetrate the closed system of rival
mercantile powers, the Spanish or the Dutch, to liberate their
colonies and to detach and attract their trade; or, again, where
co-operation could secure advantage, to attempt some reciprocal
partnership with the Americans, the Spanish, the Dutch or even
the French. The incipient industrial revolution in Britain stimulated this boundless self-confidence and provided the opportunities
which could be seized in the wake of Cook or Vancouver,
Mackenzie or Enderby, Forrest or Light. Further opportunities
were sought in the Malacca Straits or in China itself where
the States' agent, the East India Company, apathetic in its entrenched monopoly, was, by the narrow focus of its interest and
the bluntness of its initiative, failing to press the national advantage.
When the Company assumed the *diwani* in Bengal, it seemed to

offer a hard-pressed metropolitan government that opportunity –
'a gift from heaven' – to achieve that financial contribution from
the Company which it had failed to obtain from the Americas.
But here again it was elusive. A subscription to the defence of the
imperial association which would be entirely under the control of
the British government was as unthinkable to the interests of the
proprietors of the Company as it was to the Americans, or later the
Anglo-Irish. But in search of a stable Indian government which
would prove a profitable basis for expanding trade and security
to the realm the State was drawn deeply into the affairs of its
agent.

The revival of Tudor ambitions, the return to an ideal of trade
not dominion, did not therefore prevent the Government from
becoming involved or finding itself saddled with new colonies.
The factories, the entrepôts, and the forts which had not been
regarded as implying British annexation or sovereignty led Britain
into the interior: from Bengal or Madras into neighbouring principalities; from Cape Town into Central Africa; from Trincomali
into Kandy; from Penang into Malaya. The search for a new Cathay
led unexpectedly perhaps not to Nootka Sound as a halfway house
to Canton or to a business deal between George III and the Emperor
of China, but to settlements in Australasia. The loss of the Americas
did of course make more possible such colonial developments elsewhere. One result of American secession was that such imperial
instincts as there were could be diverted to other areas. The need
for new receptacles for transported felons meant that the plea of
Joseph Banks for some settlement in Australia had immediate point.
Furthermore the customary arguments of the commercial advantage from a South Pacific entrepôt and even more particularly of
a producer of flax were ventilated and it was further urged that
such a plantation would provide an asylum for dispossessed Loyalists. Some of these had trekked in force into Canada; others were
seeking absorption into the somewhat exclusive plantocracy of the
Caribbean, trying (without much success) to produce there the
increased quantities of cotton needed by the new machines of Hargreaves, Arkwright and Crompton. Still others, liberated Negroes,
settled first in Nova Scotia and then helped to found the philan-
thropists' own colony on the West African Coast, Sierra Leone:
like New South Wales, this was to be a new plantation for the
encouragement of the 'spirited cultivation' of exportable African
produce, and unlike Botany Bay to be a benevolent recompense
for injuries done to Africa and a beacon light of Christianity,
civilisation and 'legitimate trade' in a dark and barbaric continent.
This plantation was not merely to be a mercantile speculation for
the prosperity of all concerned but a grand design calculated to sap
the roots of the slave trade by 'diverting the stream that waters it

and destroying the principles from which it derives its nutriment'.
The American secession certainly made the task of ameliorating and
finally of abolishing slavery more complex by the warning it gave
against use of parliamentary sovereignty, but it may well have
accelerated the date of emancipation; for with that Act imposing
a revolution upon the internal social structure of the colonies, 1833
would surely have meant American secession if that had not taken
place half a century earlier. As for the trade in slaves it is clear, if
we state it no higher, the American Revolution did remove one
strong argument, one clamant interest, from those making for its
continuance. Moreover, in this new colony of Sierra Leone blacks
and whites were recognised as having 'equal rights to the privileges
of British subjects' and enjoyed civil and political rights under a
colour-blind law and a representative constitution.

The thirty years which spanned the events preceding and following the American secession are further instructive in presenting a
case study of an imperial government in the painful process of
appreciating the complexity of many of its nominal overseas responsibilities and of realising the necessity for shouldering some larger
share of them itself. By virtue of the crisis in America, India and
Ireland it was being compelled to consider afresh the nature of
imperial responsibility and, with hesitation and distaste, to devise
some system of management which implied the resumption of
responsibility hitherto delegated or neglected. Moreover, this period
demonstrates plainly the difficulties of determining the degree of
responsibility a metropolitan government could, or should, undertake and the kind of machinery required to acquit itself of that
'trust'.

One solution, which might commend itself and which was
theoretically possible, was the renunciation of territorial empire:
the immediate emancipation of all colonies, the abolition of all ties
of allegiance, and the abdication of all imperial responsibility. This
had in effect been the result of British policy towards the Americas;
but the end of that empire had been involuntary. Neither consistent tyranny nor timely concession, but niggling vacillation had
produced an independent United States. A spontaneous surrender
of the remaining fragments was a counsel of despair: it might seem
foolishly improvident where, on a plantation basis, those possessions
might still provide strength, security and wealth to the metropolitan
power. Strategic bases and trading posts were still needed: those
colonies which were potentially the industrial rivals of Britain
had departed; those which remained could perchance be developed
to provide the raw materials required – sugar and cotton from the
Caribbean, whether direct or through free ports; grain from Quebec
or the Maritime Colonies; fish and seamen from Newfoundland,
which was indeed less a colony than a factory moored off the Grand

Banks. The fact of empire persisted. In practice, total disengagement from dominion was impossible.

So too was the bold stroke of policy: the acceptance by the government of the realm of full responsibility for rule in all the dominions of the Crown and the assertion of direct control over all subordinate instruments of government. The strict enforcement of policy from the metropolis was ruled out by geographical, historical and political facts. The territories were strange and far distant; on the morrow of the Peace of 1763 the attempt of Crown and Parliament to impose uniform and centralised reforms had already failed disastrously; and the King's Ministers were thwarted in their purpose by the want of a reliable civil service overseas and were weakened at Westminster by manœuvres of dissident groups among sympathisers in the opposition clans. In dealing with expatriate rebels, whether Sons of Liberty, Anglo-Irish squires or parvenu 'nabobs', the government had to expect opposition denunciation of the invasion of chartered or natural rights of Englishmen overseas and the cry of 'liberties in danger'; and any move to centralise and assert authority by establishing a body of officials responsible only to the King's Ministers would be attacked as a device to increase Crown patronage overseas and as a setback for the cause of 'economical reform'. Moreover the new tasks were hazardous and burdensome; complex and detailed beyond the knowledge of cabinet ministers and confused and remote beyond the comprehension of their departmental clerks. To rule an empire from London required a feat of constitutional and administrative engineering beyond the skill of that (or any) generation. Because it was unsure both of its ends and its means the imperial government had to proceed, not with boldness but with circumspection.

In recognising its responsibility the home government had still to determine both the degree and the methods of superintendence. Even when it had realised the need to do something about overseas possessions rather than to let national assets lie idle, dwindle away or slide into chaos, it was racked by uncertainty. It feared to do too little; it feared to do too much. The prolonged crisis in East Indian affairs well illustrates this dilemma. Withdrawal from Bengal was impracticable, so also was direct rule. The failure of *laissez-faire* was only too evident. The Company had once been a convenient *locum tenens*; it had become an embarrassing and dangerous wastrel. Autonomous as the Massachusetts Bay Company had been before it lost its first charter at the English Revolution, its proprietors could not be permitted any longer to mismanage an interest of the nation as a whole or to bring shame upon the good name of Britain. Its control of its own servants had been proved precarious, even nominal; its authority had been undermined by systematic corruption and had been flouted with impunity. The gold of the nabobs seemed to threaten the stability of the Company, the balance of the constitution, and the honour of the realm. The affairs of the agent of the State could no longer continue virtually unsupervised in private and irresponsible hands. This *imperium in imperio* must be first rendered amenable to influence, then painstakingly managed, and finally subordinated and made accountable to the control of the imperial government. But the moves towards a more direct rule were gradual and tentative. In the process of trial and error the State had to make do with what it had. It was hardly politic to abrogate chartered liberties or sensible to destroy an administrative machine, when the Company had an experience and knowledge which the State lacked and which it might find valuable. The means and forms of superintendence would naturally be experimental, even pragmatic: for generations the variants attempted would remain within the context of indirect rule; nevertheless, the realm itself had been committed to an extension of its responsibility over private enterprises which was revolutionary.

The search for financial aid from its dependencies, as in America and Ireland, had drawn the imperial government deeply into difficulties. Seeing in the Company's revenues a likely milch cow for the eagerly pursued defence contribution, the State acquired an immediate interest in the health and prospects of the Company. Such returns as it sought in increased trade or regular revenues demanded a stability which, it appeared, only the realm could supply. The necessary prerequisite of a non-territorial empire was a dependable native rule – a basis signally lacking in the days of the break-up of the Moghul empire. As an instrument of government the nawabship had proved itself wholly unreliable. Resting on a web of confused or fictitious feudatories, the first experiment in indirect rule, Clive's 'dual system', had been a pretence. The Company's Servants had collected revenues without obligation to the taxpayers; they had enjoyed and abused power without responsibility. Another method of securing better and more certain government was urgent. The jealous and frustrating vendetta of Hastings and Francis sprang in part from alternative forms of indirect rule: Hastings's empiricism favouring a remodelling of native institutions under strong expatriate supervision, and Francis's formalism preferring a recognition of a royal protectorate with minimum intervention in the administration of the zemindari whom he saw as country gentry (or seigneurs) protecting the peasants against British depredation. That quarrel led the State into further experiment to penetrate deeper and to assume responsibilities greater than either protagonist contemplated. The need to secure honest and profitable returns drew the Company and its imperial overseer relentlessly into the anarchy of Indian politics, the complex of Koran and Hindu law, and ultimately the exacting task of formal 'raj'. Meanwhile in the metropolis the 'double government' device of Company and State moved a stage further. Control of the Company by influence alone was proving a brittle system: whether the painstaking management of Jenkinson for Indian, or that of Atkinson for Irish, affairs. If the liquidation of the Company as a political agent was contemplated as an end, there were many suggestions as to time and means – Jenkinson shying away from radical intervention, Robinson contemplating bold assimilation of the Company's constitution to that of a colony, and Dundas pursuing a middle way but demanding both a strong governor-generalship and full responsibility to Parliament. In the end the desultory regulation of the Company provided by the Act of 1773 was replaced eleven years later by Pitt's Act which bid to establish centralised direction under a standing watch committee of the Cabinet, a Board of Control, operating (it was hoped) 'under the very eye of parliament', and when Cornwallis claimed, and was granted, over-riding, quasi-ministerial powers which Hastings had failed to obtain, the main structure of the new system of control was complete. It was symptomatic of the current mood in imperial governance, that of vigorous paternalism: the balance of the strong local instrument and the firm central superintendence which had characterised the new deal in Quebec. Pitt had temporarily created an inner triumvirate who had cognisance and direction of all aspects of overseas policy: a co-ordination of colonial business which was not again achieved – and then only gradually and without premeditation – for another quarter of a century. But it was not only a concentration of power which Pitt had asserted. The dawning sense of imperial trusteeship had been reflected in the report of Burke's Select Committee, and it was on that basis that Pitt justified the increase of control. The greater the power exercised, he declared, the greater was the responsibility. Though there were setbacks as a result of the Directors' tactics of masterly inactivity, Cornwallis began to inculcate a sense of service and to build a corps of disciplined Servants who would learn, and seek to fulfil, the implications of that imperial trust.

This period of defeat and schism was, then, one also of new horizons: a generation which had lost one empire was being forced reluctantly and sometimes even bitterly to understand more of the opportunities and the burdens of empire elsewhere. It was furthermore a period of fertile experimentation in devising methods for exercising those responsibilities. Some of these lay within the context of indirect rule: the uses of those means locally at hand within a plural society to solve the problems under disciplined guidance; hence the remodelled institutions and the improved bureaucracy in India and their counterpart in ministerial control of the administrators of the Company at Westminster. Elsewhere in British North America, in Ireland or the West Indies there were bold attempts to come to terms with the facts of empire: to refashion, rationalise, and revitalise mercantilist principles; to buttress the British commercial system in changed conditions by developments like that of the free ports, or to venture into new spheres of influence, new markets, and a new commercial empire in the Middle West, the South Pacific, China or the Malayan archipelago; to prevent possible separation not only by a last-minute bid of unprecedented concession to the Americans in 1778 but by a timely offer of some agreed partnership to the Anglo-Irish in the 1780s; to minimise the expected frictions of secession by the recognition of reciprocal need and interdependence and by the forging of a new amicable relationship of mother country and ex-colonies such as Shelbourne tried in 1783; or to direct colonial evolution away from republicanism or schism by strong and responsible governorship or by careful and regulated assimilation to a balanced English constitution and society. The assertion of authority was urgent; in newly conquered or ceded colonies it could temporarily be exercised, but in the interests of tranquillity and economy it would be impermanent. Authoritarianism was limited by the facts of empire: distance and diversity. To secure the dependencies, to control democratic instincts, to build up the prosperity of the empire as a whole, it was imperative to create confidence among the local men of influence. So alien law and institutions, indigenous custom and practices, and religions of all kinds were tolerated: the gentry, the princes, zemindari or seigneurs must be won over to accept the imperial rule of which they now became privileged instruments.

To acquit itself of its responsibilities, therefore, the British government might in Quebec, India or the new 'Crown' colonies seek to work through strong governors in alliance with local élites as guardians of native ways, but the recognition accorded to such alien forms was justified only as temporary and makeshift. Their object was 'the laying the foundation of the gradual advancement . . . to such a state as will enable His Majesty in due time to extend . . . further benefits of the constitution of the other British colonies':[3] in other words (and now more explicitly than ever before), 'to assimilate their constitution to that of Great Britain as nearly as the differences arising would admit'.[4] Assimilation, this new nostrum of the King's servants for his empire, was thought of in no liberal context: it was conceived as a means of improving

---

[3] Lord Hobart to Hislop, 2 February, 1804: *C.O. 295/8*. Quoted in Harlow and Madden, *op. cit.*, p. 90.

[4] Lord Grenville to Lord Dorchester, 20 October, 1789. Quoted in W. P. M. Kennedy, *Statutes, treaties, etc.*, 2nd ed., p. 185.

2c*

control – a device to assert authority and to guide democracy. The more careful the replica of British eighteenth-century society in the colonies the more secure would be the imperial structure. Even those who groped (like Mornington) towards some transplantation overseas of the elements of responsible government, yet undefined, were concerned with greater stability – the need of 'apparent responsibility' of Ministers as 'one of the great securities' of the Crown.[5] The colonists might come to see the principle of 'assimilation' in a different, a liberating light, and a further half-century of development would give coherence to the concept of responsible government in Britain and enable Lord Durham to formulate a new orthodoxy for the relations of executive and legislature in government which became accepted both at home and overseas. But in the 1790s that progressive dimension had no part in the usage of the word: the identity was formally conditioned, its purpose cautiously restrictive in the interest of the Crown.

Nevertheless, in the process of moving towards the designated goal of a colonial society exactly assimilated to Britain, the mother country, whether for reasons of generosity or expediency, had shown herself ready to accept differences. Even in Grenville's declaration of intention quoted above, that was admitted. When it became clear that hopes of raising a brood of eighteenth-century 'little Englands' overseas were proving vain, Britain had the resilience and wisdom (and maybe too the want of enthusiasm) to appreciate that the toleration of diversity was a necessary condition for an enduring imperial association. Then the principle of assimilation could be liberated from its static eighteenth-century mould, the superficial shell-like identity to a parent model which was, indeed, already in 1793, about to undergo fundamental changes and to release new ideas. The principle of assimilation to the stature of Britain could be progressively applied and the identity between realm and dominions become more real as responsible government, competence in international affairs and equality of status were evolved in the context of the embryonic nations within the Commonwealth. The first steps in that education which alone made such a multinational association possible were taken by Britain in this period.

---

[5] See Paper on the *Government of Ireland*, probably by the Earl of Mornington, in *Dropmore Papers* (*H.M.C.*, 1899), vol. III, p. 552 *et seq*.

INDEX